SIXTH EDITION

MANAGEMENT AND COST ACCOUNTING

COLIN DRURY

THOMSON

Australia • Canada • Mexico • Singapore • Spain • United Kingdom • United States

Management and Cost Accounting, 6th edition

For more information, contact Thomson Learning, High Holborn House, 50–51 Bedford Row, London WC1R 4LR or visit us on the World Wide Web at:
http://www.thomsonlearning.co.uk

British Library Cataloguing-in-Publication Data
A catalogue record for this book is available from the British Library

---

ISBN 1-84480-028-8

First edition published by Chapman & Hall 1983
Second edition published by Chapman & Hall 1988
Third edition published by Chapman & Hall 1992
Fourth edition published by International Thomson Business Press 1996
Fifth edition published by Thomson Learning 2000
Sixth edition published by Thomson Learning 2004
Reprinted 2005

Typeset by Saxon Graphics Ltd, Derby

Text design by Design Deluxe, Bath

Printed in Singapore by Seng Lee Press

ABBREVIATED CONTENTS

CONTENTS

PART 3
Information for Decision-making 261

PART 4
Information for Planning, Control and Performance Measurement 587

PREFACE AND WALK THROUGH TOUR

The aim of the sixth edition of this book is to explain the principles involved in designing and evaluating management and cost accounting information systems. Management accounting systems accumulate, classify, summarize and report information that will assist employees within an organization in their decision-making, planning, control and performance measurement activities. A cost accounting system is concerned with accumulating costs for inventory valuation to meet external financial accounting and internal monthly or quarterly profit measurement requirements. As the title suggests, this book is concerned with both management and cost accounting but emphasis is placed on the former.

After many years of teaching management and cost accounting to various professional, undergraduate, postgraduate and post-experience courses I became convinced there was a need for a book with a more 'accessible' text. A large number of cost and management accounting text books have been published. Many of these books contain a detailed description of accounting techniques without any discussion of the principles involved in evaluating management and cost accounting systems. Such books often lack a conceptual framework, and ignore the considerable amount of research conducted in management accounting in the past three decades. At the other extreme some books focus entirely on a conceptual framework of management accounting with an emphasis on developing normative models of what ought to be. These books pay little attention to accounting techniques. My objective has been to produce a book which falls within these two extremes.

This book is intended primarily for undergraduate students who are pursuing a one or two year management accounting course, and for students who are preparing for the cost and management accounting examinations of the professional accountancy bodies at an intermediate or advanced professional level. It should also be of use to postgraduate and higher national diploma students who are studying cost and management accounting for the first time. An introductory course in financial accounting is not a prerequisite, although many students will have undertaken such a course.

Structure and plan of the book

A major theme of this book is that different financial information is required for different purposes, but my experience indicates that this approach can confuse students. In one chapter of a typical book students are told that costs should be allocated to products including a fair share of overhead costs; in another chapter they are told that some of the allocated costs are irrelevant and should be disregarded. In yet another chapter they are told that costs should be related to people (responsibility centres) and not products, whereas elsewhere no mention is made of responsibility centres.

In writing this book I have devised a framework that is intended to overcome these difficulties. The framework is based on the principle that there are three ways of constructing accounting information. The first is cost accounting, with its emphasis on producing product costs for allocating costs between cost of goods sold and inventories to meet external and internal financial accounting inventory valuation and profit measurement requirements. The second is the notion of decision relevant costs, with the emphasis on providing information to help managers to make good decisions. The third is responsibility accounting and performance measurement, which focuses on both financial and non-financial information, in particular the assignment of costs and revenues to responsibility centres.

This book is divided into seven parts. The first part (Part 1) consists of two chapters and provides an introduction to management and cost accounting and a framework for studying the remaining chapters. The following three parts reflect the three different ways of constructing accounting information. Part 2 consists of five chapters and is entitled 'Cost accumulation for inventory valuation and profit measurement'. This section focuses mainly on assigning costs to products to separate the costs incurred during a period between costs of goods sold and the closing inventory valuation for internal and external profit measurement. The extent to which product costs accumulated for inventory valuation and profit measurement should be adjusted for meeting decision-making, cost control and performance measurement requirements is also briefly considered. Part 3 consists of seven chapters and is entitled 'Information for decision-making'. Here the focus is on measuring and identifying those costs which are relevant for different types of decisions.

The title of Part 4 is 'Information for planning, control and performance measurement'. It consists of seven chapters and concentrates on the process of translating goals and objectives into specific activities and the resources that are required, via the short-term (budgeting) and long-term planning processes, to achieve the goals and objectives. In addition, the management control systems that organizations use are described and the role that management accounting control systems play within the overall control process is examined. The emphasis here is on the accounting process as a means of providing information to help managers control the activities for which they are responsible. The organizational, social and political aspects of management accounting are included as separate chapters in this section. Performance measurement and evaluation within different segments of the organization is also examined.

Part 5 consists of two chapters and is entitled 'Cost management and strategic management accounting.' The first chapter focuses on cost management and the second on strategic management accounting. Part 6 consists of three chapters and is entitled 'The application of quantitative methods to management accounting'. The final part contains a list of the case studies that are available in the text and from the website accompanying this book.

In devising a framework around the three methods of constructing financial information there is a risk that the student will not appreciate that the three categories use many common elements, that they overlap, and constitute a single overall management accounting system, rather than three independent systems. I have taken steps to minimize this risk in each section by emphasizing why financial information for one purpose should or should not be adjusted for another purpose. In short, each section of the book is not presented in isolation and an integrative approach has been taken.

When I wrote this book an important consideration was the extent to which the application of quantitative techniques should be integrated with the appropriate topics or if they should be considered separately. I have chosen to integrate quantitative techniques whenever they are an essential part of a chapter. For example, the use of probability statistics are essential to Chapter 12 (Decision-making under conditions of risk and uncertainty) but my objective has been to confine them, where possible, to Part 6.

This approach allows for maximum flexibility. Lecturers wishing to integrate quantitative techniques with earlier chapters may do so, but those who wish to concentrate on other matters will not be hampered by having to exclude the relevant quantitative portions of chapters.

Major changes in the content of the sixth edition

To accommodate the enormous changes that occurred in the theory and practice of management accounting during the 1990s the previous edition incorporated the most extensive rewrite of the text since the book was first published. Although significant changes in the content have been made to the sixth edition, the major focus has been on pedagogical changes. The most notable alterations are:

1. Rewriting of material relating to the mathematical model of cost functions in Chapter 7 (Income effects of alternative cost accumulation systems).
2. The appendix to Chapter 8 (Cost–volume–profit analysis) relating to the application of cost–volume–profit analysis to absorption costing has been rewritten.
3. In Chapter 10 (Activity-based costing) new material has been added relating to volume-based and non-volume-based cost drivers.
4. In the two chapters relating to capital investment decisions (Chapters 13 and 14) the introductory sections to Chapter 13 have been rewritten. The material relating to authorization of capital investment decisions in Chapter 14 has been replaced by a new section entitled 'The capital investment process' and transferred to Chapter 13.
5. New text providing an overview of contingency theory has been added to Chapter 17 (Contingency theory and organizational and social aspects of management accounting) and the content relating to 'The impact of contingent factors on management accounting information systems' has been rewritten.
6. New material relating to basing transfer prices on marginal cost plus opportunity cost has been added to Chapter 21 (Transfer pricing in divisionalized companies).
7. In Chapter 22 (Cost management) a new section has been added entitled 'Environmental cost management'.
8. The content relating to strategic management accounting and the balanced scorecard in Chapter 23 (Strategic management accounting) has been rewritten and new material has been added.
9. The introduction of illustrative boxed examples (entitled 'Real World Views') throughout the text highlights the practical application of management accounting concepts and techniques by real companies operating in a range of industry sectors in various countries throughout the world.
10. The end-of-chapter summaries for all the chapters have been rewritten and replaced with a comprehensive summary of the learning objectives listed at the beginning of each chapter. This will enable readers to test their knowledge of key concepts and evaluate their ability to achieve chapter learning objectives.
11. Revision of end-of-chapter assessment material. The assessment material consists of Review questions and Review problems. The Review questions are short introductory questions that enable readers to assess their understanding of the main topics included in the text. Each question is followed by page numbers within parentheses that indicate where in the text the answers to specific questions can be found. The Review problems are more complex and require readers to relate and apply the chapter content to various business problems. The problems are graded by their level of difficulty. The Review problems normally begin with multiple-choice questions that generally take about 10 minutes to complete. The multiple-choice questions are followed by questions that generally progress according to their level of difficulty. Fully worked solutions to the Review problems that are not contained within the white boxes are provided in a separate section at the end of the book. For those questions within the white boxes the worked solutions are provided in the

Student's Manual accompanying this book. A major feature of the sixth edition is that the number of solutions to the Review problems provided in the separate section at the end of the book has been substantially increased.

12 Previous editions of the book contained end-of-chapter questions where the answers were only available to lecturers in the *Instructor's Manual* accompanying this book. Case studies were also included in a separate section at the end of the book. These questions and case studies have now been removed from the text and are available for students and lecturers to access on the accompanying website www.drury-online.com. Solutions to the questions and case study teaching notes are only available to lecturers on the lecturer's password protected section of the website. The questions and answers are also contained in the *Instructor's Manual* that is available in print format, free to adopting lecturers.

Case Studies

The final section of this book includes a list of over 30 case studies that are available on the dedicated website for this book. Both lecturers and students can download these case studies from the open access section of the website. Teaching notes for the case studies can be downloaded only by lecturers from the password protected lecturer's section of the website. The cases generally cover the content of several chapters and contain questions to which there is no ideal answer. They are intended to encourage independent thought and initiative and to relate and apply your understanding of the content of this book in more uncertain situations. They are also intended to develop your critical thinking and analytical skills.

Highlighting of advanced reading sections

Feedback relating to previous editions has indicated that one of the major advantages of this book has been the comprehensive treatment of management accounting. Some readers, however, will not require a comprehensive treatment of all of the topics that are contained in the book. To meet the different requirements of the readers, the more advanced material that is not essential for those readers not requiring an in-depth knowledge of a particular topic has been highlighted. As shown here, the start of each advanced reading section is marked with a symbol and a blue line is used to highlight the full section. If you do require an in-depth knowledge of a topic you may find it helpful to initially omit the advanced reading sections, or skim them, on your first reading. You should read them in detail only when you fully understand the content of the remaining parts of the chapter. The advanced reading sections are more appropriate for an advanced course and may normally be omitted if you are pursuing an introductory course. For some chapters all of the content represents advanced reading. Where this situation occurs readers are informed at the beginning of the relevant chapters.

International focus

The book has now become an established text in many different countries throughout the world. Because of this a more international focus has been adopted. A major feature is the presentation of boxed exhibits of surveys and practical applications of management accounting in companies in many different countries, particularly the European mainland. To simplify the presentation, however, the UK pound monetary unit has been the main system used throughout the book, although in a few cases dollars and euros have been used instead. Most of the assessment material has incorporated questions set by the UK professional accountancy bodies. These questions are appropriate for worldwide use and users who are not familiar with the requirements of the UK professional accountancy bodies should note that many of the advanced level questions also contain the beneficial features described above for case study assignments.

Recommended reading

A separate section is included at the end of most chapters providing advice on key articles or books which you are recommended to read if you wish to pursue topics and issues in more depth. Many of the references are the original work of writers who have played a major role in the development of management accounting. The contribution of such writers is often reflected in this book but there is frequently no substitute for original work of the authors. The detailed references are presented in the Bibliography towards the end of the book.

Assessment material

Throughout this book I have kept the illustrations simple. You can check your understanding of each chapter by answering the Review questions. Each question is followed by page numbers within parentheses that indicate where in the text the answers to specific questions can be found. More complex Review problems are also set at the end of each chapter to enable students to pursue certain topics in more depth. Each question is graded according to the level of difficulty. Questions graded 'Intermediate' are normally appropriate for a first year course whereas questions graded 'Advanced' are normally appropriate for a second year course or the final stages of the professional accountancy examinations. Fully worked solutions to the Review problems not contained within the white boxes are provided in a separate section at the end of the book.

This book is part of an integrated educational package. A *Student's Manual* provides suggested answers to the questions that are contained within the white boxes at the end of each chapter. Students are strongly recommended to purchase the *Student's Manual,* which complements this book. Additional questions and case studies are available for students and lecturers to access on the accompanying website www.drury-online.com. Solutions to the questions and case study teaching notes are only available to lecturers on the lecturer's password protected section of the website. The questions and answers are also contained in the *Instructor's Manual* that is available in print format, free to adopting lecturers.

In recognition of the increasing need for the integration of IT teaching into the curriculum, this book is accompanied by an on-line Spreadsheet Applications Manual, which has been written by Dr Alicia Gazely of Nottingham Trent University. This explains basic spreadsheet techniques and then builds up ten spreadsheet models which illustrate, and allow students to explore, examples in the main text. The spreadsheets, guidance notes and on-line access are available to teachers on adoption. Further details of this package are given in the section covering the dedicated website below.

Supplementary material

Dedicated website

The dedicated website can be found at www.drury-online.com. The lecturer section is password protected and the password is available free to lecturers who confirm their adoption of the sixth edition – lecturers should complete the registration form on the website to apply for their password, which will then be sent to them by e-mail.

The following range of material is available:

For students and lecturers (open access):

Case studies

Internationally focused case studies. (NB Teaching notes to accompany the cases are available in the password protected lecturer area of the site).

Additional questions

Solutions are available on the password protected lecturer area of the site.

Testbank *(compiled by Wayne Fiddler of Huddersfield University)*

Interactive multiple choice questions to accompany each chapter. The student takes the test online to check their grasp of the key points in each chapter. Detailed feedback is provided for each question if the student chooses the wrong answer.

Links to accounting and finance sites on the web

Including links to the main accounting firms, accounting magazines and journals and careers and job search pages.

For lecturers only (password protected)

Instructor's manual

Available to download free from the site in PDF (Portable Document Format), the manual includes answers to the additional questions on the open access website. (Please note: the *Instructor's Manual* incorporating both the additional questions and their solutions is also available in print format, free to adopting lecturers, ISBN 184480030X.)

Teaching notes to the case studies

To accompany the case studies available in the student area of the website.

Spreadsheet exercises *(compiled and designed by Alicia Gazely of Nottingham Trent University)*

Created in Excel to accompany the self-assessment exercises in the book, the exercises can be saved by the lecturer to their own directories and distributed to students as each topic is

80 CHAPTER 3 COST ASSIGNMENT

specific products. On what basis should we allocate non-manufacturing overheads? The answer is that we should select an allocation base/cost driver that corresponds most closely to non-manufacturing overheads. The problem is that allocation bases that are widely used by traditional costing systems, such as direct labour hours, machine hours and direct labour cost are not necessarily those that are closely related to non-manufacturing overheads. Therefore traditional systems tend to use arbitrary, rather than cause-and-effect allocation bases, to allocate non-manufacturing overheads to products. The most widely used approach (see Exhibit 3.4) is to allocate non-manufacturing overheads on the ability of the products to bear such costs. This approach can be implemented by allocating non-manufacturing costs to products on the basis of their manufacturing costs. This procedure is illustrated in Example 3.3.

Because of the arbitrary nature of the cost allocations, some organizations that use traditional costing systems as a basis for setting selling prices do not to allocate non-manufacturing overheads to products. Instead, they add a percentage profit margin to each product so that it provides a profit contribution and a contribution to non-manufacturing overheads. We shall consider in more detail how cost information can be used in determining selling prices in Chapter 11. Recent developments in ABC have provided a mechanism for more accurately assigning non-manufacturing overheads to products. These developments will be explained in Chapter 10 when ABC is examined in more depth.

Summary

The following items relate to the learning objectives listed at the beginning of the chapter.

- **Distinguish between cause-and-effect and arbitrary allocations.**
  Direct costs can be directly traced to cost objects whereas indirect costs cannot. Therefore, indirect costs must be assigned using cost allocation bases. Allocation bases which are significant determinants of costs that are being allocated are described as cause-and-effect allocations whereas arbitrary allocations refer to allocation bases that are not the significant determinants of the costs. To accurately measure the cost of resources used by cost objects cause-and-effect allocations should be used.
- **Explain why different cost information is required for different purposes.**
  Manufacturing organizations assign costs to products for two purposes: first for external (financial accounting) profit measurement and inventory valuation purposes in order to allocate manufacturing costs incurred during a period to cost of goods sold and inventories; secondly to provide useful information for managerial decision-making requirements. Financial accounting regulations specify that only manufacturing costs should be assigned to products for meeting inventory and profit measurement requirements. Both manufacturing and non-manufacturing costs, however, may be relevant for decision-making. In addition, not all costs that are assigned to products for inventory valuation and profit measurement are relevant for decision-making. For example, costs that will not be affected by a decision (e.g. depreciation) are normally not relevant for decision-making.
- **Describe how cost systems differ in terms of their level of sophistication.**
  Cost systems range from simplistic to sophisticated. Simplistic systems are inexpensive to operate, involve extensive use of arbitrary allocations, have a high likelihood of reporting inaccurate product costs and generally result in a high cost of errors. Sophisticated costing systems are more expensive to operate, rely more extensively on cause-and-effect allocations, generally report more accurate product costs and have a low cost of errors. Further distinguishing features are that simplistic costing systems have a small number of first-stage cost centres/pools and use a single second-stage cost

NON-MANUFACTURING OVERHEADS 81

	(%)
Allocation as a percentage of total manufacturing cost	32
Direct labour hours/cost methods	25
Percentage of total selling price	12
Non-manufacturing overheads not traced to products	23
Other method	8
	100

SOURCE: Drury *et al.* (1993).

EXHIBIT 3.4
Methods used by UK organizations to allocate non-manufacturing overheads to products

EXAMPLE 3.3

The estimated non-manufacturing and manufacturing costs of a company for the year ending 31 December are £500 000 and £1 million respectively. The non-manufacturing overhead absorption rate is calculated as follows:

$$\frac{\text{estimated non-manufacturing overhead}}{\text{estimated manufacturing cost}}$$

In percentage terms each product will be allocated with non-manufacturing overheads at a rate of 50% of its total manufacturing cost.

driver. In contrast, sophisticated costing systems use many first-stage cost centres/pools and many different types of second-stage drivers.

- **Understand the factors influencing the choice of an optimal costing system.**
  The optimal costing system is different for different organizations and should be determined on a costs versus benefits basis. Simplistic costing systems are appropriate in organizations whose indirect costs are a low percentage of total costs and which also have a fairly standardized product range, all consuming organizational resources in similar proportions. Under these circumstances simplistic costing systems may report costs that are sufficiently accurate for decision-making purposes. Conversely, organizations with a high proportion of indirect costs, whose products consume organizational resources in different proportions are likely to require sophisticated costing systems. Relying on sophisticated costing systems under these circumstances is likely to result in the additional benefits from reporting more accurate costs exceeding the costs of operating more sophisticated systems.
- **Explain why departmental overhead rates should be used in preference to a single blanket overhead rate.**
  A blanket (also known as plant-wide) overhead rate establishes a single overhead rate for the organization as a whole whereas departmental rates involve indirect costs being accumulated by different departments and a separate overhead rate being established for each department. A blanket overhead rate can only be justified when all products or services consume departmental overheads in approximately the same proportions. Such circumstances are unlikely to be applicable to most organizations resulting in blanket overheads generally reporting inaccurate product/service costs.

Summary
Bulleted list at the end of each chapter reviewing briefly the main concepts and key points covered in each chapter, linked back to the Learning objectives.

188 CHAPTER 5 PROCESS COSTING

36 000 units were transferred to finished stock and 3200 units remained in work-in-progress at the end of October which were complete as to material and half-complete as to labour and production overhead. A loss of 1200 units, being normal, occurred during the process.

The average method of pricing is used.

You are required to

(a) prepare for the month of October, a statement (or statements) showing
   (i) production cost per unit in total and by element of cost;
   (ii) the total cost of production transferred to finished stock;
   (iii) the valuation of closing work-in-progress in total and by element of cost;
   (15 marks)

(b) describe five of the characteristics which distinguish process costing from job costing.
   (10 marks)
   (Total 25 marks)
   CIMA Stage 2 Cost Accounting

5.26 **Intermediate: Equivalent production with no losses (FIFO Method)**

A company operates a manufacturing process where six people work as a team and are paid a weekly group bonus based upon the actual output of the team compared with output expected.

A basic 37 hour week is worked during which the expected output from the process is 4000 equivalent units of product. Basic pay is £5.00 per hour and the bonus for the group, shared equally, is £0.80 per unit in excess of expected output.

In the week just ended, basic hours were worked on the process. The following additional information is provided for the week:

Opening work in process (1000 units):
  Materials £540 (100% complete)
  Labour and overheads £355 (50% complete).
During the week:
  Materials used £2255
  Overheads incurred £1748
  Completed production 3800 units
Closing work in process (1300 units)
  Materials (100% complete)
  Labour and overheads (75% complete).
There are no process losses.
The FIFO method is used to apportion costs.

Required:

(a) Prepare the process account for the week just ended.
   (10 marks)

(b) Explain the purpose of the following documents which are used in the control of, and accounting for, the materials used in the process described in part (a)
   (i) purchase requisition
   (ii) materials (stores) requisition.
   (4 marks)
   (14 marks)
   ACCA Foundation Stage Paper 3

ASSESSMENT MATERIAL 189

5.27 **Intermediate: Equivalent production and losses in process**

A concentrated liquid fertilizer is manufactured by passing chemicals through two consecutive processes. Stores record cards for the chemical ingredients used exclusively by the first process show the following data for May 2000:

Opening stock	4 000 litres	£10 800
Closing stock	8 000 litres	£24 200
Receipts into store	20 000 litres	£61 000

Other process data for May is tabulated below:

	Process 1	Process 2
Direct labour	£4880	£6000
Direct expenses	£4270	—
Overhead absorption rates	250% of direct labour	100% of direct labour
Output	8000 litres	7500 litres
Opening stock of work in process	—	—
Closing stock of work in process	5600 litres	—
Normal yield	85% of input	90% of input
Scrap value of loss	—	—

In process 1 the closing stock of work in process has just passed through inspection, which is at the stage where materials and conversion costs are 100% and 75% completed respectively.

In process 2 inspection is the final operation.

Required:

(a) Prepare the relevant accounts to show the results of the processes for May 2000 and present a detailed working paper showing your calculations and any assumptions in arriving at the data shown in those accounts.
   (18 marks)

(b) If supplies of the required chemicals are severely restricted and all production can be sold immediately, briefly explain how you would calculate the total loss to the company if, at the beginning of June, 100 litres of the correct mix of chemicals were spilt on issue to process 1.
   (4 marks)
   (Total 22 marks)
   ACCA Foundation Costing

Review problems (with answers in the Student's Manual)

5.28 **Intermediate: Preparation of process accounts with all output fully completed**

A chemical compound is made by raw material being processed through two processes. The output of Process A is passed to Process B where further material is added to the mix. The details of the process costs for the financial period number 10 were as shown below:

Process A	
Direct material	2000 kilograms at 5 per kg
Direct labour	£7200
Process plant time	140 hours at £60 per hour

Review problems
Graded by their level of difficulty, the Review problems allow you to relate and apply the chapter content to various business problems. The multiple-choice questions are the least demanding. Fully worked solutions are found in the back of the text. Worked solutions for the questions in the white box can be found in the Student's Manual that accompanies this text.

A companion website accompanies
MANAGEMENT & COST ACCOUNTING, 6TH EDITION
by Colin Drury

Visit the *Management & Cost Accounting* website at www.drury-online.com to find further teaching and learning material, including:

For Students

- Multiple Choice Questions for each chapter
- Case studies with accompanying questions
- Related weblinks
- Instructor Questions

For Lecturers

- Instructor's Manual – including model answers to Instructor Questions found on the students' side of the site
- Downloadable PowerPoint™ slides and overhead transparencies
- Case Study Teaching Notes to accompany the case studies on the website and within the text
- Spreadsheet Models to accompany exercises within the text. The models incorporate a range of spreadsheet techniques which are explained in text notes adjacent to the calculations

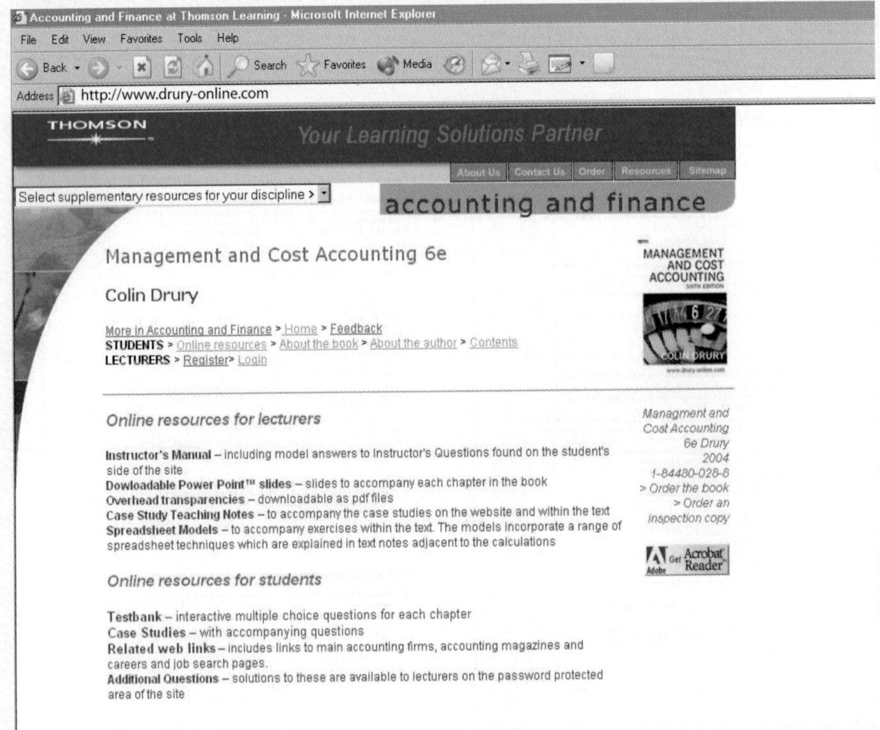

Accounting and Finance at Thomson Learning - Microsoft Internet Explorer
File Edit View Favorites Tools Help
Back Search Favorites Media
Address http://www.drury-online.com
THOMSON
Your Learning Solutions Partner
About Us Contact Us Order Resources Sitemap
Select supplementary resources for your discipline >
accounting and finance
Management and Cost Accounting 6e
Colin Drury
More in Accounting and Finance > Home > Feedback
STUDENTS > Online resources > About the book > About the author > Contents
LECTURERS > Register> Login
MANAGEMENT AND COST ACCOUNTING
COLIN DRURY
Online resources for lecturers
Instructor's Manual – including model answers to Instructor's Questions found on the student's side of the site
Dowloadable Power Point™ slides – slides to accompany each chapter in the book
Overhead transparencies – downloadable as pdf files
Case Study Teaching Notes – to accompany the case studies on the website and within the text
Spreadsheet Models – to accompany exercises within the text. The models incorporate a range of spreadsheet techniques which are explained in text notes adjacent to the calculations
Managment and Cost Accounting 6e Drury 2004 1-84480-028-8
> Order the book
> Order an inspection copy
Get Acrobat Reader
Online resources for students
Testbank – interactive multiple choice questions for each chapter
Case Studies – with accompanying questions
Related web links – includes links to main accounting firms, accounting magazines and careers and job search pages.
Additional Questions – solutions to these are available to lecturers on the password protected area of the site

MANAGEMENT AND COST ACCOUNTING

PART 1

Introduction to Management and Cost Accounting

The objective of this section is to provide an introduction to management and cost accounting. In Chapter 1 we define accounting and distinguish between financial, management and cost accounting. This is followed by an examination of the role of management accounting in providing information to managers for decision-making, planning, control and performance measurement. In addition, the important changes that are taking place in the business environment are considered. Progression through the book will reveal how these changes are influencing management accounting systems. In Chapter 2 the basic cost terms and concepts that are used in the management accounting literature are described.

Introduction to management accounting

1

There are many definitions of accounting, but the one that captures the theme of this book is the definition formulated by the American Accounting Association. It describes accounting as

the process of identifying, measuring and communicating economic information to permit informed judgements and decisions by users of the information.

In other words, accounting is concerned with providing both financial and non-financial information that will help decision-makers to make good decisions. An understanding of accounting therefore requires an understanding of the decision-making process and an awareness of the users of accounting information.

During the past two decades many organizations in both the manufacturing and service sectors have faced dramatic changes in their business environment. Deregulation combined with extensive competition from overseas companies in domestic markets has resulted in a situation where most companies are now competing in a highly competitive global market. At the same time there has been a significant reduction in product life cycles arising from technological innovations and the need to meet increasingly

LEARNING OBJECTIVES

After studying this chapter, you should be able to:

- distinguish between management accounting and financial accounting;
- identify and describe the elements involved in the decision-making, planning and control process;
- justify the view that a major objective of commercial organizations is to broadly seek to maximize the present value of future cash flows;
- explain the factors that have influenced the changes in the competitive environment;
- outline and describe the key success factors that directly affect customer satisfaction;
- identify and describe the functions of a management accounting system;
- provide a brief historical description of managment accounting.

discriminating customer demands. To compete successfully in today's highly competitive global environment companies have made customer satisfaction an overriding priority. They have also adopted new management approaches, changed their manufacturing systems and invested in new technologies. These changes have had a significant influence on management accounting systems. Progression through the book will reveal how these changes have influenced management accounting systems, but first of all it is important that you have a good background knowledge of some of the important changes that have occurred in the business environment. This chapter aims to provide such knowledge.

The objective of this first chapter is to provide the background knowledge that will enable you to achieve a more meaningful insight into the issues and problems of management accounting that are discussed in the book. We begin by looking at the users of accounting information and identifying their requirements. This is followed by a description of the decision-making process and the changing business and manufacturing environment. Finally, the different functions of management accounting are described.

The users of accounting information

Accounting is a language that communicates economic information to people who have an interest in an organization managers, shareholders and potential investors, employees, creditors and the government. Managers require information that will assist them in their decision-making and control activities; for example, information is needed on the estimated selling prices, costs, demand, competitive position and profitability of various products that are made by the organization. Shareholders require information on the value of their investment and the income that is derived from their shareholding. Employees require information on the ability of the firm to meet wage demands and avoid redundancies. Creditors and the providers of loan capital require information on a firm's ability to meet its financial obligations. Government agencies like the Central Statistical Office collect accounting information and require such information as the details of sales activity, profits, investments, stocks, dividends paid, the proportion of profits absorbed by taxation and so on. In addition the Inland Revenue needs information on the amount of profits that are subject to taxation. All this information is important for determining policies to manage the economy.

Accounting information is not confined to business organizations. Accounting information about individuals is also important and is used by other individuals; for example, credit may only be extended to an individual after the prospective borrower has furnished a reasonable accounting of his private financial affairs. Non-profit-making organizations such as churches, charitable organizations, clubs and government units such as local authorities, also require accounting information for decision-making, and for reporting the results of their activities. For example, a cricket club will require information on the cost of undertaking its various activities so that a decision can be made as to the amount of the annual subscription that it will charge to its members. Similarly, local authorities need information on the costs of undertaking specific activities so that decisions can be made as to which activities will be undertaken and the resources that must be raised to finance them.

The foregoing discussion has indicated that there are many users of accounting information who require information for decision-making. The objective of accounting is to provide sufficient information to meet the needs of the various users at the lowest possible cost. Obviously, the benefit derived from using an information system for decision-making must be greater than the cost of operating the system.

An examination of the various users of accounting information indicates that they can be divided into two categories:

1. internal parties within the organization;
2. external parties such as shareholders, creditors and regulatory agencies, outside the organization.

It is possible to distinguish between two branches of accounting, that reflect the internal and external users of accounting information. **Management accounting** is concerned with the provision of information to people within the organization to help them make better decisions and improve the efficiency and effectiveness of existing operations, whereas **financial accounting** is concerned with the provision of information to external parties outside the organization. Thus, management accounting could be called internal accounting and financial accounting could be called external accounting. This book concentrates on management accounting.

Differences between management accounting and financial accounting

The major differences between these two branches of accounting are:

- *Legal requirements.* There is a statutory requirement for public limited companies to produce annual financial accounts regardless of whether or not management regards this information as useful. Management accounting, by contrast, is entirely optional and information should be produced only if it is considered that the benefits from the use of the information by management exceed the cost of collecting it.
- *Focus on individual parts or segments of the business.* Financial accounting reports describe the whole of the business whereas management accounting focuses on small parts of the organization, for example the cost and profitability of products, services, customers and activities. In addition, management accounting information measures the economic performance of decentralized operating units, such as divisions and departments.
- *Generally accepted accounting principles.* Financial accounting statements must be prepared to conform with the legal requirements and the generally accepted accounting principles established by the regulatory bodies such as the Financial Accounting Standards Board (FASB) in the USA and the Accounting Standards Board (ASB) in the UK. These requirements are essential to ensure the uniformity and consistency that is needed for external financial statements. Outside users need assurance that external statements are prepared in accordance with generally accepted accounting principles so that the inter-company and historical comparisons are possible. In contrast, management accountants are not required to adhere to generally accepted accounting principles when providing managerial information for internal purposes. Instead, the focus is on the serving management's needs and providing information that is useful to managers relating to their decision-making, planning and control functions.
- *Time dimension.* Financial accounting reports what has happened in the past in an organization, whereas management accounting is concerned with *future* information as well as past information. Decisions are concerned with *future* events and management therefore requires details of expected *future* costs and revenues.
- *Report frequency.* A detailed set of financial accounts is published annually and less detailed accounts are published semi-annually. Management requires information

quickly if it is to act on it. Consequently management accounting reports on various activities may be prepared at daily, weekly or monthly intervals.

The decision-making process

Because information produced by management accountants must be judged in the light of its ultimate effect on the outcome of decisions, a necessary precedent to an understanding of management accounting is an understanding of the *decision-making process*.

Figure 1.1 presents a diagram of a decision-making model. The first five stages represent the decision-making or the planning process. **Planning** involves making choices between alternatives and is primarily a decision-making activity. The final two stages represent the *control process*, which is the process of measuring and correcting actual performance to ensure that the alternatives that are chosen and the plans for implementing them are carried out. You should note that the decision-making model specified in Figure 1.1 is a theoretical model based on the assumption of rational economic behaviour. This assumption has been challenged on the grounds that such behaviour does not always reflect actual real world behaviour. Alternative views to those assumed in the traditional model outlined in Figure 1.1 will be described in Chapter 17. Let us now examine each of the items listed in Figure 1.1.

Identifying objectives

Before good decisions can be made there must be some guiding aim or direction that will enable the decision-makers to assess the desirability of favouring one course of action over another. Hence, the first stage in the decision-making process should be to specify the **goals** or **objectives of the organization**.

Considerable controversy exists as to what the objectives of firms are or should be. Economic theory normally assumes that firms seek to maximize profits for the owners of the firm (the ordinary shareholders in a limited company) or, more precisely, the maximization of shareholders' wealth. Various arguments have been used to support the profit maximization objective. There is the legal argument that the ordinary shareholders are the owners of the firm, which therefore should be run for their benefit by trustee managers. Another argument supporting the profit objective is that profit maximization leads to the maximization of overall economic welfare. That is, by doing the best for yourself, you are unconsciously doing the best for society. Moreover, it seems a reasonable belief that the interests of firms will be better served by a larger profit than by a smaller profit, so that maximization is at least a useful approximation.

Some writers (e.g. Simon, 1959) believe that businessmen are content to find a plan that provides satisfactory profits rather than to maximize profits. Because people have limited powers of understanding and can deal with only a limited amount of information at a time (Simon uses the term **bounded rationality** to describe these constraints), they tend to search for solutions only until the first acceptable solution is found. No further attempt is made to find an even better solution or to continue the search until the best solution is discovered. Such behaviour, where the search is terminated on finding a satisfactory, rather than optimal solution, is known as **satisficing**.

Cyert and March (1969) have argued that the firm is a coalition of various different groups – shareholders, employees, customers, suppliers and the government – each of whom must be paid a minimum to participate in the coalition. Any excess benefits after meeting these minimum constraints are seen as being the object of bargaining between the various groups. In addition, a firm is subject to constraints of a societal nature. Maintaining

FIGURE 1.1 *The decision-making, planning and control process*

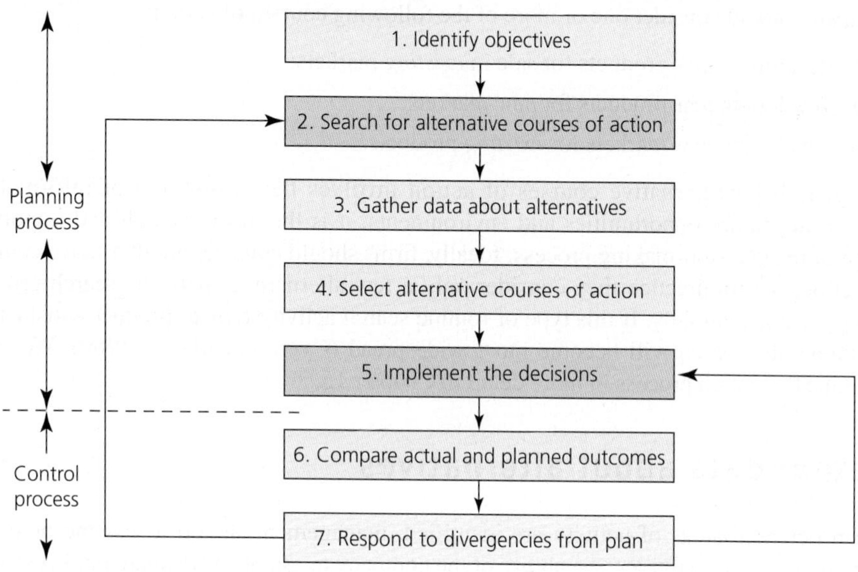

a clean environment, employing disabled workers and providing social and recreation facilities are all examples of social goals that a firm may pursue.

Clearly it is too simplistic to say that the only objective of a business firm is to maximize profits. Some managers seek to establish a power base and build an empire; another goal is security; the removal of uncertainty regarding the future may override the pure profit motive. Nevertheless, the view adopted in this book is that, broadly, firms seek to maximize the value of future net cash inflows (that is, future cash receipts less cash payments) or to be more precise the present value of future net cash inflows.[1] This is equivalent to maximizing shareholder value. (The concept of present value is explained in Chapter 13.) The reasons for choosing this objective are as follows:

1 It is unlikely that any other objective is as widely applicable in measuring the ability of the organization to survive in the future.
2 It is unlikely that maximizing the present value of future cash flows can be realized in practice, but by establishing the principles necessary to achieve this objective you will learn how to increase the present value of future cash flows.
3 It enables shareholders as a group in the bargaining coalition to know how much the pursuit of other goals is costing them by indicating the amount of cash distributed among the members of the coalition.

The search for alternative courses of action

The second stage in the decision-making model is a search for a range of possible courses of action (or **strategies**) that might enable the objectives to be achieved. If the management of a company concentrates entirely on its present product range and markets, and market shares and cash flows are allowed to decline, there is a danger that the company will be unable to generate sufficient cash flows to survive in the future. To maximize future cash flows, it is essential that management identifies potential opportunities and threats in its current environment and takes specific steps immediately so that the organization will not be taken by surprise by any developments which may occur in the future. In particular, the company should consider one or more of the following courses of action:

1 developing *new* products for sale in *existing* markets;
2 developing *new* products for *new* markets;
3 developing *new* markets for *existing* products.

The search for alternative courses of action involves the acquisition of information concerning future opportunities and environments; it is the most difficult and important stage of the decision-making process. Ideally, firms should consider all alternative courses of action, but, in practice they consider only a few alternatives, with the search process being localized initially. If this type of routine search activity fails to produce satisfactory solutions, the search will become more widespread (Cyert and March, 1969). We shall examine the search process in more detail in Chapter 15.

Gather data about alternatives

When potential areas of activity are identified, management should assess the potential growth rate of the activities, the ability of the company to establish adequate market shares, and the cash flows for each alternative activity for various **states of nature**. Because decision problems exist in an uncertain environment, it is necessary to consider certain factors that are outside the decision-maker's control, which may occur for each alternative course of action. These uncontrollable factors are called states of nature. Some examples of possible states of nature are economic boom, high inflation, recession, the strength of competition and so on.

The course of action selected by a firm using the information presented above will commit its resources for a lengthy period of time, and how the overall place of the firm will be affected within its environment that is, the products it makes, the markets it operates in and its ability to meet future changes. Such decisions dictate the firm's long-run possibilities and hence the type of decisions it can make in the future. These decisions are normally referred to as **long-run** or **strategic decisions**. Strategic decisions have a profound effect on the firm's future position, and it is therefore essential that adequate data are gathered about the firm's capabilities and the environment in which it operates. We shall discuss this topic in Chapters 13–15. Because of their importance, strategic decisions should be the concern of top management.

Besides strategic or long-term decisions, management must also make decisions that do not commit the firm's resources for a lengthy period of time. Such decisions are known as **short-term** or **operating decisions** and are normally the concern of lower-level managers. Short-term decisions are based on the environment of today, and the physical, human and financial resources presently available to the firm. These are, to a considerable extent, determined by the quality of the firm's long-term decisions. Examples of short-term decisions include the following.

1 What selling prices should be set for the firm's products?
2 How many units should be produced of each product?
3 What media shall we use for advertising the firm's products?
4 What level of service shall we offer customers in terms of the number of days required to deliver an order and the after-sales service?

Data must also be gathered for short-term decisions; for example, data on the selling prices of competitors' products, estimated demand at alternative selling prices, and predicted costs for different activity levels must be assembled for pricing and output decisions. When the data have been gathered, management must decide which courses of action to take.

Select appropriate alternative courses of action

In practice, decision-making involves choosing between competing alternative courses of action and selecting the alternative that best satisfies the objectives of an organization. Assuming that our objective is to maximize future net cash inflows, the alternative selected should be based on a comparison of the differences between the cash flows. Consequently, an incremental analysis of the net cash benefits for each alternative should be applied. The alternatives are ranked in terms of net cash benefits, and those showing the greatest benefits are chosen subject to taking into account any qualitative factors. We shall discuss how incremental cash flows are measured for short-term and long-term decisions and the impact of qualitative factors in Chapters 8–14.

Implementation of the decisions

Once alternative courses of action have been selected, they should be implemented as part of the budgeting process. The **budget** is a financial plan for implementing the various decisions that management has made. The budgets for all of the various decisions are expressed in terms of cash inflows and outflows, and sales revenues and expenses. These budgets are merged together into a single unifying statement of the organization's expectations for future periods. This statement is known as a **master budget**. The master budget consists of a budgeted profit and loss account, cash flow statement and balance sheet. The budgeting process communicates to everyone in the organization the part that they are expected to play in implementing management's decisions. Chapter 15 focuses on the budgeting process.

Comparing actual and planned outcomes and responding to divergencies from plan

The final stages in the process outlined in Figure 1.1 of comparing actual and planned outcomes and responses to divergencies from plan represent the firm's control process. The managerial function of **control** consists of the measurement, reporting and subsequent correction of performance in an attempt to ensure that the firm's objectives and plans are achieved. In other words, the objective of the control process is to ensure that the work is done so as to fulfil the original intentions.

To monitor performance, the accountant produces **performance reports** and presents them to the appropriate managers who are responsible for implementing the various decisions. Performance reports consisting of a comparison of actual outcomes (actual costs and revenues) and planned outcomes (budgeted costs and revenues) should be issued at regular intervals. Performance reports provide **feedback** information by comparing planned and actual outcomes. Such reports should highlight those activities that do not conform to plans, so that managers can devote their scarce time to focusing on these items. This process represents the application of **management by exception**. Effective control requires that corrective action is taken so that actual outcomes conform to planned outcomes. Alternatively, the plans may require modification if the comparisons indicate that the plans are no longer attainable.

The process of taking corrective action so that actual outcomes conform to planned outcomes, or the modification of the plans if the comparisons indicate that actual outcomes do not conform to planned outcomes, is indicated by the arrowed lines in Figure 1.1 linking stages 7 and 5 and 7 and 2. These arrowed lines represent **'feedback loops'**. They signify that the process is dynamic and stress the interdependencies between the various stages in the process. The feedback loop between stages 7 and 2 indicates that the plans should be regularly reviewed, and if they are no longer attainable then alternative courses of action must be considered for achieving the organization's objectives. The second loop stresses the corrective action taken so that actual outcomes conform to planned outcomes. Chapters 15–19 focus on the planning and control process.

Changing competitive environment

Prior to the 1980s many organizations in Western countries operated in a protected competitive environment. Barriers of communication and geographical distance, and sometimes protected markets, limited the ability of overseas companies to compete in domestic markets. There was little incentive for firms to maximize efficiency and improve management practices, or to minimize costs, as cost increases could often be passed on to customers. During the 1980s, however, manufacturing organizations began to encounter severe competition from overseas competitors that offered high-quality products at low prices. By establishing global networks for acquiring raw materials and distributing goods overseas, competitors were able to gain access to domestic markets throughout the world. To be successful companies now have to compete not only against domestic competitors but also against the best companies in the world.

Excellence in manufacturing can provide a competitive weapon to compete in sophisticated world-wide markets. In order to compete effectively companies must be capable of manufacturing innovative products of high quality at a low cost, and also provide a first-class customer service. At the same time, they must have the flexibility to cope with short product life cycles, demands for greater product variety from more discriminating customers and increasing international competition. World-class manufacturing companies have responded to these competitive demands by replacing traditional production systems with new just-in-time production systems and investing in advanced manufacturing technologies (AMTs). The major features of these new systems and their implications for management accounting will be described throughout the book.

Virtually all types of service organization have also faced major changes in their competitive environment. Before the 1980s many service organizations, such as those operating in the airlines, utilities and financial service industries, were either government-owned monopolies or operated in a highly regulated, protected and non-competitive environment. These organizations were not subject to any great pressure to improve the quality and efficiency of their operations or to improve profitability by eliminating services or products that were making losses. Furthermore, more efficient competitors were often prevented from entering the markets in which the regulated companies operated. Prices were set to cover operating costs and provide a predetermined return on capital. Hence cost increases could often be absorbed by increasing the prices of the services. Little attention was therefore given to developing cost systems that accurately measured the costs and profitability of individual services.

Privatization of government-controlled companies and deregulation in the 1980s completely changed the competitive environment in which service companies operated. Pricing and competitive restrictions were virtually eliminated. Deregulation, intensive competition and an expanding product range created the need for service organizations to focus on cost management and develop management accounting information systems that enabled them to understand their cost base and determine the sources of profitability for their products, customers and markets. Many service organizations have only recently turned their attention to management accounting.

Changing product life cycles

A product's life cycle is the period of time from initial expenditure on research and development to the time at which support to customers is withdrawn. Intensive global competition and technological innovation combined with increasingly discrimating and sophisticated customer demands have resulted in a dramatic decline in product life cycles. To be successful companies must now speed up the rate at which they introduce new products to the market. Being later to the market than the competitors can have a dramatic effect on product profitability.

In many industries a large fraction of a product's life-cycle costs are determined by decisions made early in its life cycle. This has created a need for management accounting to place greater emphasis on providing information at the design stage because many of the costs are committed or locked in at this time. Therefore to compete successfully companies must be able to manage their costs effectively at the design stage, have the capability to adapt to new, different and changing customer requirements and reduce the time to market of new and modified products.

Focus on customer satisfaction and new management approaches

In order to compete in today's competitive environment companies have had to become more customer-driven' and make customer satisfaction an overriding priority. Customers are demanding ever-improving levels of service in cost, quality, reliability, delivery, and the choice of innovative new products. Figure 1.2 illustrates this focus on customer satisfaction as the overriding priority. In order to provide customer satisfaction organizations must concentrate on those key success factors that directly affect it. Figure 1.2 identifies cost efficiency, quality, time and innovation as the key success factors. In addition to concentrating on these factors organizations are adopting new management approaches in their quest to achieve customer satisfaction. These new approaches are illustrated in Figure 1.2. They are continuous improvement, employee empowerment and total value-chain analysis. Let us now examine each of the items shown in Figure 1.2 in more detail.

Since customers will buy the product with the lowest price, all other things being equal, keeping costs low and being cost efficient provides an organization with a strong competitive advantage. Increased competition has also made decision errors due to poor cost information more probable and more costly. If the cost system results in distorted product costs being reported, then overcosted products will lead to higher bid prices and business lost to those competitors who are able to quote lower prices purely because their cost systems produce more accurate cost information. Alternatively, there is a danger that undercosted profits will result in the acceptance of unprofitable business.

These developments have made many companies aware of the need to improve their cost systems so that they can produce more accurate cost information to determine the cost of their products, pinpoint loss-making activities and analyse profits by products, sales outlets, customers and markets.

In addition to demanding low cost products customers are demanding high quality products and services. Most companies are responding to this by focusing on total quality management (TQM). The goal of TQM is customer satisfaction. TQM is a term used to describe a situation where *all* business functions are involved in a process of continuous quality improvement. TQM has broadened from its early concentration on the statistical monitoring of manufacturing processes, to a customer-oriented process of

FIGURE 1.2 *Focus on customer satisfaction*

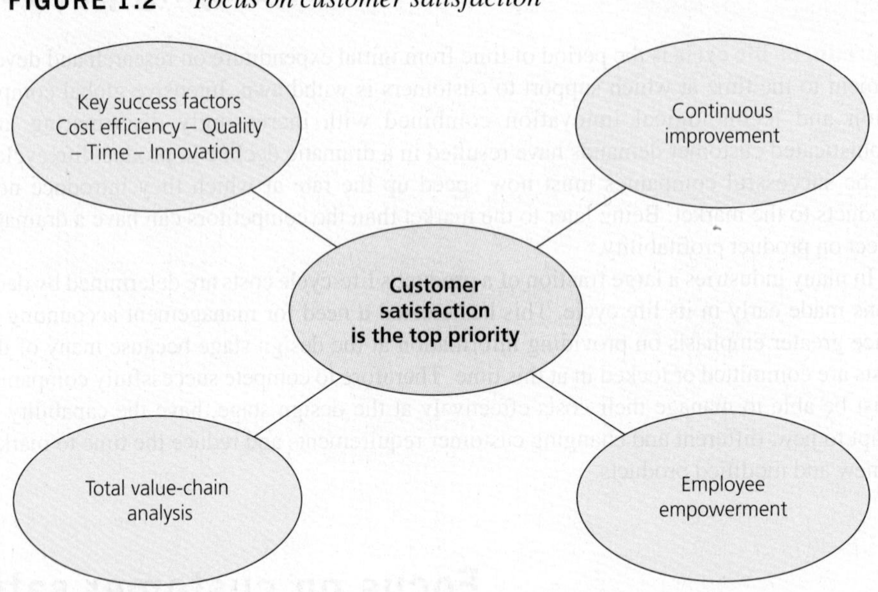

continuous improvement that focuses on delivering products or services of consistently high quality in a timely fashion.

Most European and American companies had always considered quality an additional cost of manufacturing, but by the end of the 1980s they began to realize that quality saved money. The philosophy had been to emphasize production volume over quality; but this resulted in high levels of stocks at each production stage in order to protect against shortages caused by inferior quality at previous stages and excessive expenditure on inspection, rework, scrap and warranty repairs. Companies discovered that it was cheaper to produce the items correctly the first time rather than to waste resources making substandard items that had to be detected, reworked, scrapped or returned by customers. In other words, the emphasis in TQM is to design and build quality in rather than trying to inspect and repair it in. The emphasis on TQM has created fresh demands on the management accounting function to expand its role by becoming involved in measuring and evaluating the quality of products and services and the activities that produce them.

Organizations are also seeking to increase customer satisfaction by providing a speedier response to customer requests, ensuring 100% on-time delivery and reducing the time taken to develop and bring new products to market. For these reasons management accounting systems now place more emphasis on **time-based measures**, which have beome an important competitive variable. **Cycle time** is one measure that management accounting systems have begun to focus on. It is the length of time from start to completion of a product or service. It consists of the sum of processing time, move time, wait time and inspection time. Move time is the amount of time it takes to transfer the product during the production process from one location to another. Wait time is the amount of time that the product sits around waiting for processing, moving, inspecting, reworking or the amount of time it spends in finished goods stock waiting to be sold and despatched. Inspection time is the amount of time making sure that the product is defect free or the amount of time actually spent reworking the product to remedy identified defects in quality. Only processing time adds value to the product, and the remaining activities are **non-value added activities** in the sense that they can be reduced or eliminated without altering the product's service potential to the customer. Organizations are therefore focusing on minimizing cycle time by reducing the time spent on such activities. The management accounting system has an important role to play in this process by identifying and reporting on the time devoted to value added and non-value added activities.

The final key success factor shown in Figure 1.2 relates to **innovation**. To be successful companies must develop a steady stream of innovative new products and services and have the capability to adapt to changing customer requirements. It has already been stressed earlier in this chapter that being later to the market than competitors can have a dramatic effect on product profitability. Companies have therefore begun to incorporate performance measures that focus on flexibility and innovation into their management accounting systems. Flexibility relates to the responsiveness in meeting customer requirements. Flexibility measures include the total launch time for new products, the length of development cycles and the ability to change the production mix quickly. Innovation measures include an assessment of the key characteristics of new products relative to those of competitors, feedback on customer satisfaction with the new features and characteristics of newly introduced products, and the number of new products launched and their launch time.

You can see by referring to Figure 1.2 that organizations are attempting to achieve customer satisfaction by adopting a philosophy of **continuous improvement**. Traditionally, organizations have sought to study activities and establish standard operating procedures and materials requirements based on observing and establishing optimum input/output relationships. Operators were expected to follow the standard procedures and management accountants developed systems and measurements that compared actual results with predetermined standards. This process created a climate whereby the predetermined standards represented a target to be achieved and maintained rather than a policy of continuous improvement. In today's competitive environment performance against static historical standards is no longer appropriate. To compete successfully companies must adopt a philosophy of continuous improvement, an ongoing process that involves a continuous search to reduce costs, eliminate waste, and improve the quality and performance of activities that increase customer value or satisfaction.

Benchmarking is a technique that is increasingly being adopted as a mechanism for achieving continuous improvement. It is a continuous process of measuring a firm's products, services or activities against the other best performing organizations, either internal or external to the firm. The objective is to ascertain how the processes and activities can be improved. Ideally, benchmarking should involve an external focus on the latest developments, best practice and model examples that can be incorporated within various operations of business organizations. It therefore represents the ideal way of moving forward and achieving high competitive standards.

In their quest for the continuous improvement of organizational activities managers have found that they have had to rely more on the people closest to the operating processes and customers to develop new approaches to performing activities. This has led to employees being provided with relevant information to enable them to make continuous improvements to the output of processes. Allowing employees to take such actions without the authorization by superiors has come to be known as **employee empowerment**. It is argued that by empowering employees and giving them relevant information they will be able to respond faster to customers, increase process flexibility, reduce cycle time and improve morale. Management accounting is therefore moving from its traditional emphasis on providing information to managers to monitor the activities of employees to providing information to employees to empower them to focus on the continuous improvement of activities.

Increasing attention is now being given to **value-chain analysis** as a means of increasing customer satisfaction and managing costs more effectively. The value chain is illustrated in Figure 1.3. It is the linked set of value-creating activities all the way from basic raw material sources for component suppliers through to the ultimate end-use product or service

FIGURE 1.3 *The value chain*

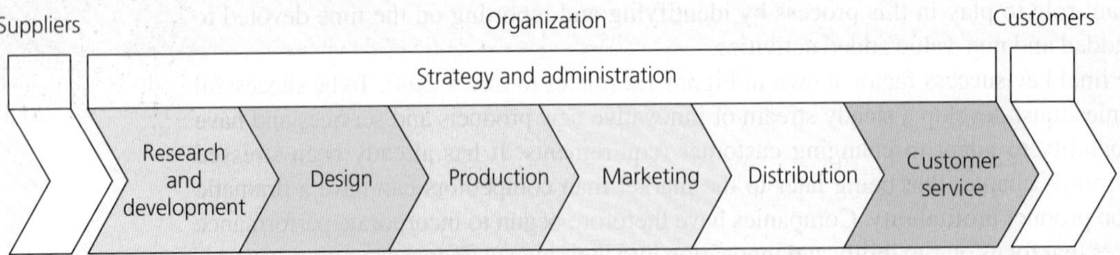

delivered to the customer. Coordinating the individual parts of the value chain together to work as a team creates the conditions to improve customer satisfaction, particularly in terms of cost efficiency, quality and delivery. It is also appropriate to view the value chain from the customer's perspective, with each link being seen as the customer of the previous link. If each link in the value chain is designed to meet the needs of its customers, then end-customer satisfaction should ensue. Furthermore, by viewing each link in the value chain as a supplier–customer relationship, the opinions of the customers can be used to provide useful feedback information on assessing the quality of service provided by the supplier. Opportunities are thus identified for improving activities throughout the entire value chain. The aim is to manage the linkages in the value chain better than competitors and thus create a competitive advantage.

Finally, there are other aspects of customer satisfaction that are not specified in Figure 1.2 – namely, **social responsibility** and **corporate ethics**. Customers are no longer satisfied if companies simply comply with the legal requirements of undertaking their activities. They expect company managers to be more proactive in terms of their social responsibility. Company stakeholders are now giving high priority to social responsibility, safety and environmental issues, besides corporate ethics. In response to these pressures many companies are now introducing mechanisms for measuring, reporting and monitoring their environmental costs and activities. A code of ethics has also become an essential part of corporate culture. In addition, professional accounting organizations play an important role in promoting a high standard of ethical behaviour by their members. Both of the professional bodies representing management accountants in the UK (Chartered Institute of Management Accountants) and the USA (Institute of Management Accountants) have issued a code of ethical guidelines for their members and established mechanisms for monitoring and enforcing professional ethics. The guidelines are concerned with ensuring that accountants follow fundamental principles relating to integrity (not being a party to any falsification), objectivity (not being biased or prejudiced), confidentiality and professional competence and due care (maintaining the skills required to ensure a competent professional service).

The impact of information technology

During the past decade the use of information technology (IT) to support business activities has increased dramatically with the development of electronic business communication technologies known as **e-business**, **e-commerce** or **internet commerce**. These developments are having a big impact on businesses. For example, consumers are becoming more discerning when purchasing products or services because they are able to derive more information from the internet on the relative merits of the different product offerings. E-commerce has provided

A look at a key feature of easyJet's business

As one of the pioneers in the low cost airline market, easyJet bases its business on a number of principles:

- Minimize distribution costs by using the internet to take bookings. About 90% of all easyJet tickets are sold via the Web. This makes the company one of Europe's largest internet retailers.
- Maximize efficient use of assets, by increasing turn-around time at airports.
- A 'simple-service model' means the end of free on-board catering.
- Ticketless travel, where passengers receive an e-mail confirming their booking, cuts the cost of issuing, distributing and processing tickets.
- Intensive use of IT in administration and management, aiming to run a paperless office.

Source: easyJet website (www.easyjet.com)

the potential to develop new ways of doing things that have enabled considerable cost savings to be made from streamlining business processes and generating extra revenues from the adept use of on-line sales facilities (e.g. ticketless airline bookings and internet banking). The ability to use e-commerce more proficiently than competitors provides the potential for companies to establish a competitive advantage.

One advanced IT application that has had a considerable impact on business information systems is **enterprise resource planning systems** (ERPS). The number of adopters of ERPS has increased rapidly throughout the world since they were first introduced in the mid-1990s. An ERPS comprises a set of integrated software applications modules that aim to control all information flows within a company. They cover most business functions (including accounting). Standard ERPS accounting modules incorporate many menus including bookkeeping, product profitability analysis and budgeting. All the modules are fully integrated in a common database and users can access real-time information on all aspects of the business. A major feature of ERPS systems is that all data are entered only once, typically where the data originate. There are a number of ERPS packages on the market provided by companies such as SAP, Baan, Oracle and J.D. Edwards. SAP is the market leader with more than 7500 users in 90 countries (Scapens *et al.*, 1998).

The introduction of ERPS has the potential to have a significant impact on the work of management accountants. In particular, ERPS substantially reduce routine information gathering and the processing of information by management accountants. Instead of managers asking management accountants for information, they can access the system to derive the information they require directly by PC. Because ERPS integrate separate business functions in one system for the whole company co-ordination is usually undertaken centrally by information specialists who are responsible for both the implementation and operation of the system. In multinational companies this has standardized the global flow of information, but it has also limited the ability to generate locally relevant information.

Because ERPS perform the routine tasks that were once part of the accountants' daily routines, accountants must expand their roles or risk possible redundancy. ERPS provide the potential for accountants to use the time freed up from routine information gathering to adopt the role of advisers and internal consultants to the business. This role will require management accountants to be involved in interpreting the information generated from the ERPS and to provide business support for managers.

International convergence of management accounting practices

This book has become an established text in many different countries throughout the world. It is therefore assumed that the content is appropriate for use in different countries. This assumption is based on the premise that management accounting practices generally do not differ across countries. Granlund and Lukka (1998) provide support for this assumption. They argue that there is a strong current tendency towards global homogenization of management accounting practices within the industrialized parts of the world.

Granlund and Lukka distinguish between management accounting practices at the macro and micro levels. The macro level relates to concepts and techniques; in other words, it relates mainly to the content of this book. In contrast, the micro level is concerned with the behavioural patterns relating to how management accounting information is actually used. Granlund and Lukka argue that, at the macro level, the forces of convergence have started to dominate those of divergence. They identify various drivers of convergence but the most important relate to the intensified global competition, developments in information technology, the increasing tendency of transnational companies to standardize their practices, the global consultancy industry and the use of globally applied textbooks and teaching.

Firms throughout the world are adopting similar integrated enterprise resource planning systems or standardized software packages that have resulted in the standardization of data collection formats and reporting patterns of accounting information. In multinational companies this process has resulted in the standardization of the global flow of information, but it has also limited the ability to generate locally relevant information. Besides the impact of integrated IT systems, it is common for the headquarters/parent company of a transnational enterprise to force foreign divisions to adopt similar accounting practices to those of the headquarters/parent company. A large global consultancy industry has recently emerged that tends to promote the same standard solutions globally. The consultancy industry also enthusiastically supports mimetic processes. Granlund and Lukka describe mimetic processes as processes by which companies, under conditions of uncertainty, copy publicly known and appreciated models of operation from each other, especially from successful companies that have a good reputation. Finally, the same textbooks are used globally and university and professional accounting syllabuses tend to be similar in different countries.

At the micro level Granlund and Lukka acknowledge that differences in national and corporate culture can result in management accounting practices differing across countries. For example, national cultures have been categorized as the extent to which: (1) the inequality between people is considered to be normal and acceptable; (2) the culture is assertive and competitive as opposed to being modest and caring; (3) the culture feels comfortable with uncertainty and ambiguity; and (4) the culture focuses on long-term or short-term outcomes. There is evidence to suggest that accounting information is used in different ways in different national cultures, such as being used in a rigorous/rigid manner for managerial performance evaluation in cultures exhibiting certain national traits and in a more flexible way in cultures exhibiting different national traits. At the macro level Granlund and Lukka argue that the impact of national culture is diminishing because of the increasing emerging pressures to follow national trends to secure national competitiveness.

Functions of management accounting

A cost and management accounting system should generate information to meet the following requirements. It should:

accounting purposes. They conclude that managers did not have to yield the design of management accounting systems to financial accountants and auditors. Separate systems could have been maintained for managerial and financial accounting purposes, but the high cost of information collection meant that the costs of maintaining two systems exceeded the additional benefits. Thus, companies relied primarily on the same information as that used for external financial reporting to manage their internal operations.

Johnson and Kaplan claim that, over the years, organizations had become fixated on the cost systems of the 1920s. Furthermore, when the information systems were automated in the 1960s, the system designers merely automated the manual systems that were developed in the 1920s. Johnson and Kaplan conclude that the lack of management accounting innovation over the decades and the failure to respond to its changing environment resulted in a situation in the mid-1980s where firms were using management accounting systems that were obsolete and no longer relevant to the changing competitive and manufacturing environment.

During the late 1980s, criticisms of current management accounting practices were widely publicized in the professional and academic accounting literature. In 1987 Johnson and Kaplan's book entitled *Relevance Lost: The Rise and Fall of Management Accounting*, was published. An enormous amount of publicity was generated by this book as a result of the authors' criticisms of management accounting. Many other commentators also concluded that management accounting was in a crisis and that fundamental changes in practice were required.

Since the mid-1980s management accounting practitioners and academics have sought to modify and implement new techniques that are relevant to today's environment and that will ensure that management accounting regains its relevance. By the mid-1990s Kaplan (1994) stated that:

> *The past 10 years have seen a revolution in management accounting theory and practice. The seeds of the revolution can be seen in publications in the early to mid 1980s that identified the failings and obsolescence of existing cost and performance measurement systems. Since that time we have seen remarkable innovations in management accounting; even more remarkable has been the speed with which the new concepts have become widely known, accepted and implemented in practice and integrated into a large number of educational programmes.*

Summary of the contents of this book

This book is divided into six parts. The first part (Part One) consists of two chapters and provides an introduction to management and cost accounting and a framework for studying the remaining chapters. Part Two consists of five chapters and is entitled 'Cost Accumulation for Inventory Valuation and Profit Measurement'. This section focuses mainly on cost accounting. It is concerned with assigning costs to products to separate costs incurred during a period between costs of goods sold and the closing inventory valuation. The extent to which product costs accumulated for inventory valuation and profit measurement should be adjusted for meeting decision-making, cost control and performance measurement requirements is also briefly considered. Part Three consists of seven chapters and is entitled 'Information for Decision-making'. Here the focus is on measuring and identifying those costs which are relevant for different types of decisions.

The title of Part Four is 'Information for Planning, Control and Performance Measurement'. It consists of seven chapters and concentrates on the process of translating goals and objectives into specific activities and the resources that are required, via the short-term (budgeting) and long-term planning processes, to achieve the goals and objectives. In addition, the management control systems that organizations use are described and the role that management accounting control systems play within the overall control process is examined. The emphasis here is on the accounting process as a means of providing information to help managers control the activities for which they are responsible. The organizational, social and political aspects of management accounting are included as a separate chapter in this section. Performance measurement and evaluation within different segments of the organization is also examined.

Part Five consists of two chapters and is entitled 'Cost Management and Strategic Management Accounting.' The first chapter focuses on cost management and the second on strategic management accounting. The sixth part consists of three chapters and is entitled 'The Application of Quantitative Methods to Management Accounting'. The final part includes case study assessment material.

Guidelines for using this book

If you are pursuing a course of management accounting, without cost accumulation for inventory valuation and profit measurement, Chapters 4–7 in Part Two can be omitted, since the rest of this book does not rely heavily on these chapters. Alternatively, you could delay your reading of Chapters 4–7 in Part Two until you have studied Parts Three and Four. Chapter 19 in Part Four is only appropriate if your curriculum requires a detailed knowledge of the technical aspects of variance analysis. If you wish to gain an insight into cost accumulation for inventory valuation and profit measurement but do not wish to study it in depth, you may prefer to read only Chapters 3 and 7 of Part Two. It is important that you read Chapter 3, which focuses on traditional methods of tracing overheads to cost objects prior to reading Chapter 10 on activity-based costing.

The chapters on the application of quantitative techniques to management accounting have been delayed until Part Six. An alternative approach would be to read Chapter 24 immediately after reading Chapter 8 on cost–volume–profit analysis. Chapter 25 is self-contained and may be assigned to follow any of the chapters in Part Four. Chapter 26 should be read only after you have studied Chapter 9.

A comprehensive treatment of all of the topics that are contained in this book will not be essential for all readers. To meet the different requirements of the readers, the more advanced material that is not essential for those readers not requiring an in-depth knowledge of a particular topic has been highlighted. The start of each advanced reading section has a clearly identifiable heading and a vertical blue line is used to highlight the full section. If you do require an in-depth knowledge of a topic you may find it helpful initially to omit the advanced reading sections, or skim them, on your first reading. You should read them in detail only when you fully understand the content of the remaining parts of the chapter. The advanced reading sections are more appropriate for an advanced course and may normally be omitted if you are pursuing an introductory course.

Summary

The following items relate to the learning objectives listed at the beginning of the chapter.

- **Distinguish between management accounting and financial accounting.**

  Management accounting differs from financial accounting in several different ways. Management accounting is concerned with the provision of information to internal users to help them make better decisions and improve the efficiency and effectiveness of operations. Financial accounting is concerned with the provision of information to external parties outside the organization. Unlike financial accounting there is no statutory requirement for management accounting to produce financial statements or follow externally imposed rules. Furthermore, management accounting provides information relating to different parts of the business whereas financial accounting reports focus on the whole business. Management accounting also tends to be more future oriented and reports are often published on a daily basis whereas financial accounting reports are published semi-annually.

- **Identify and describe the elements involved in the decision-making, planning and control process.**

  The following elements are involved in the decision-making, planning and control process: (a) identify the objectives that will guide the business; (b) search for a range of possible courses of action that might enable the objectives to be achieved; (c) gather data about the alternatives; (d) select appropriate alternative courses of action that will enable the objectives to be achieved; (e) implement the decisions as part of the planning and budgeting process; (f) compare actual and planned outcomes; and (g) respond to divergencies from plan by taking corrective action so that actual outcomes conform to planned outcomes or modify the plans if the comparisons indicate that the plans are no longer attainable.

- **Justify the view that a major objective of commercial organizations is to broadly seek to maximize the present value of future cash flows.**

  The reasons for identifying maximizing the present value of future cash flows as a major objective are: (a) it is equivalent to maximizing shareholder value; (b) it is unlikely that any other objective is as widely applicable in measuring the ability of the organization to survive in the future; (c) although it is unlikely that maximizing the present value of future cash flows can be realized in practice it is still important to establish the principles necessary to achieve this objective; and (d) it enables shareholders as a group in the bargaining coalition to know how much the pursuit of other goals is costing them by indicating the amount of cash distributed among the members of the coalition.

- **Explain the factors that have influenced the changes in the competitive environment.**

  The factors influencing the change in the competitive environment are (a) globalization of world trade; (b) privatization of government-controlled companies and deregulation in various industries; (c) changing product life cycles; (d) changing customer tastes that demand ever-improving levels of service in cost, quality, reliability, delivery and the choice of new products; and (e) the emergence of e-business.

- **Outline and describe the key success factors that directly affect customer satisfaction.**

  The key success factors are cost efficiency, quality, time and innovation. Since customers will generally prefer to buy the product or service at the lowest price, all other things being equal, keeping costs low and being cost efficient provides an organization with a strong competitive advantage. Customers also demand high quality products and services and this has resulted in companies making quality a key competitive variable. Organizations are also seeking to increase customer satisfaction by providing a speedier response to customer requests, ensuring 100 per cent on-time delivery and reducing the time taken to bring new products to the market. To be successful companies must be innovative and develop a steady stream of new products and services and have the capability to rapidly adapt to changing customer requirements.

- **Identify and describe the functions of a management accounting system.**

  A cost and management accounting system should generate information to meet the following requirements: (a) allocate costs between cost of goods sold and inventories for internal and external profit reporting and inventory valuation; (b) provide relevant information to help managers make better decisions; and (c) provide information for planning, control and performance measurement.

- **Provide a brief historical description of management accounting.**

  Most of the management accounting practices that were in use in the mid-1980s had been developed by 1925, and for the next 60 years there was virtually a halt in management accounting innovation. By the mid-1980s firms were using management accounting systems that were obsolete and no longer relevant to the changing competitive and manufacturing environment. During the late 1980s, criticisms of current management accounting practices were widely publicized in the professional and academic accounting literature. In response to the criticisms considerable progress has been made in modifying and implementing new techniques that are relevant to today's environment and that will ensure that management accounting regains its relevance.

Note

1 The total profits over the life of a business are identical with total net cash inflows. However, the profits calculated for a particular accounting period will be different from the net cash flows for that period. The difference arises because of the accruals concept in financial accounting. For most situations in this book, decisions that will lead to changes in profits are also assumed to lead to identical changes in net cash flows.

Key terms and concepts

Each chapter includes a section like this. You should make sure that you understand each of the terms listed below before you proceed to the next chapter. Their meanings are explained on the page numbers indicated.

Key examination points

Chapter 1 has provided an introduction to the scope of management accounting. It is unlikely that examination questions will be set that refer to the content of an introductory chapter. However, questions are sometimes set requiring you to outline how a costing system can assist the management of an organization. Note that the examiner may not distinguish between cost accounting and management accounting. Cost accounting is often used to also embrace management accounting. Your discussion of a cost accounting system should therefore include a description (with illustrations) of how the system provides information for decision-making, planning and control. Make sure that you draw off your experience from the whole of a first-year course and not just this introductory chapter.

Assessment material

Review questions

The review questions are short questions that enable you to assess your understanding of the main topics included in the chapter. The numbers in parentheses provide you with the page numbers to refer to if you cannot answer a specific question.

Review problems

The remaining chapters also contain review problems. These are more complex and require you to relate and apply the chapter content to various business problems. Fully worked solutions to many of the review problems are provided in a separate section at the end of the book.

Case studies

The website also includes over 30 case study problems. A list of these cases is provided in Part Seven of this book. The Electronic Boards case is a case study that is relevant to the introductory stages of a management accounting course.

Review questions

1.1 Identify and describe the different users of accounting information. *(pp. 6–7)*

1.2 Describe the differences between management accounting and financial accounting. *(pp. 7–8)*

1.3 Explain each of the elements of the decision-making, planning and control process. *(pp. 8–12)*

1.4 Describe what is meant by management by exception. *(p. 11)*

1.5 What is a product's life cycle? *(p. 13)*

1.6 Describe what is meant by continuous improvement, benchmarking and employee empowerment. *(p. 15)*

1.7 Describe the different activities in the value chain. *(pp. 15–16)*

1.8 Explain why firms are beginning to concentrate on social responsibility and corporate ethics. *(p. 16)*

1.9 Describe the different functions of management accounting. *(pp. 18–20)*

1.10 Describe enterprise resource planning systems and their impact on management accountants. *(p. 17)*

1.11 Provide a brief historical description of management accounting. *(pp. 20–21)*

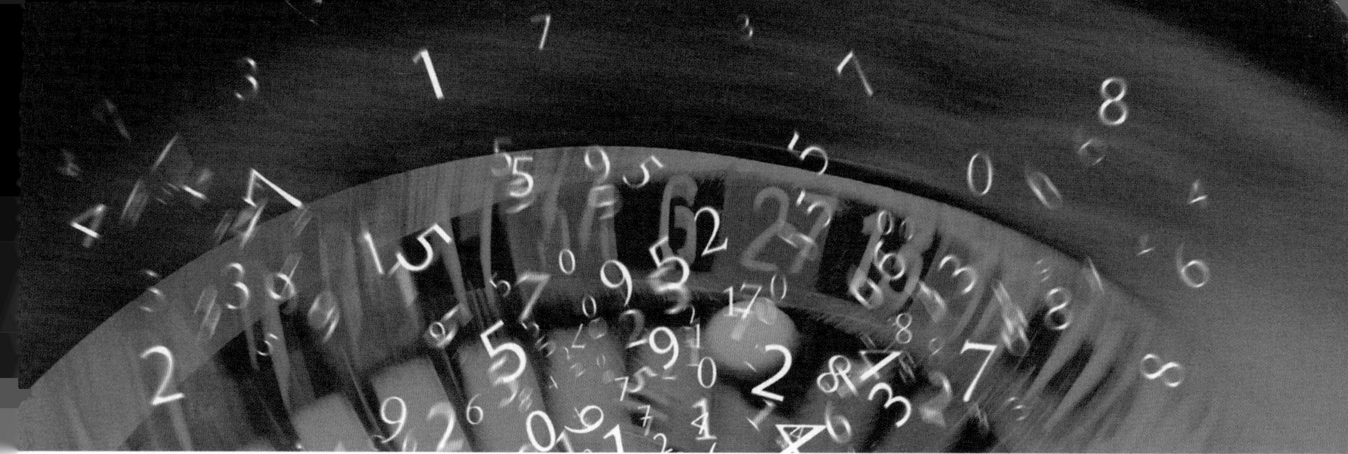

An introduction to cost terms and concepts

2

In Chapter 1 it was pointed out that accounting systems measure costs which are used for profit measurement and inventory valuation, decision-making, performance measurement and controlling the behaviour of people. The term cost is a frequently used word that reflects a monetary measure of the resources sacrificed or forgone to achieve a specific objective, such as acquiring a good or service. However, the term must be defined more precisely before the 'cost' can be determined. You will find that the word *cost* is rarely used without a preceding adjective to specify the type of cost being considered.

To understand how accounting systems calculate costs and to communicate accounting information effectively to others requires a thorough understanding of what cost means. Unfortunately, the term has multiple meanings and different types of costs are used in different situations. Therefore a preceding term must be added to clarify the assumptions that underlie a cost measurement. A large terminology has emerged to indicate more clearly which cost meaning is being conveyed. Examples include variable cost, fixed cost, opportunity cost and sunk cost. The aim of this chapter is to provide you with an understanding of the basic cost terms and concepts that are used in the management accounting literature.

LEARNING OBJECTIVES

After studying this chapter, you should be able to:

- explain why it is necessary to understand the meaning of different cost terms;
- define and illustrate a cost object;
- explain the meaning of each of the key terms listed at the end of this chapter;
- explain why in the short term some costs and revenues are not relevant for decision-making;
- distinguish between job costing and process costing;
- describe the three purposes for which cost information is required.

Cost objects

A **cost object** is any activity for which a separate measurement of costs is desired. In other words, if the users of accounting information want to know the cost of something, this something is called a cost object. Examples of cost objects include the cost of a product, the cost of rendering a service to a bank customer or hospital patient, the cost of operating a particular department or sales territory, or indeed anything for which one wants to measure the cost of resources used.

We shall see that the cost collection system typically accounts for costs in two broad stages:

1. It accumulates costs by classifying them into certain categories such as labour, materials and overhead costs (or by cost behaviour such as fixed and variable).
2. It then assigns these costs to cost objects.

In this chapter we shall focus on the following cost terms and concepts:

- direct and indirect costs;
- period and product costs;
- cost behaviour in relation to volume of activity;
- relevant and irrelevant costs;
- avoidable and unavoidable costs;
- sunk costs;
- opportunity costs;
- incremental and marginal costs.

Direct and indirect costs

Costs that are assigned to cost objects can be divided into two categories: direct costs and indirect costs. **Direct costs** are those costs that can be specifically and exclusively identified with a particular cost object. In contrast, **indirect costs** cannot be identified specifically and exclusively with a given cost object. Let us assume that our cost object is a product, or to be more specific a particular type of desk that is manufactured by an organization. In this situation the wood that is used to manufacture the desk can be specifically and exclusively identified with a particular desk and can thus be classified as a direct cost. Similarly, the wages of operatives whose time can be traced to the specific desk are a direct cost. In contrast, the salaries of factory supervisors or the rent of the factory cannot be specifically and exclusively traced to a particular desk and these costs are therefore classified as indirect.

Sometimes, however, direct costs are treated as indirect because tracing costs directly to the cost object is not cost effective. For example, the nails used to manufacture a particular desk can be identified specifically with the desk, but, because the cost is likely to be insignificant, the expense of tracing such items does not justify the possible benefits from calculating more accurate product costs.

Direct costs can be accurately traced because they can be physically identified with a particular object whereas indirect costs cannot. An estimate must be made of resources consumed by cost objects for indirect costs. Therefore, the more direct costs that can be traced to a cost object, the more accurate is the cost assignment.

The distinction between direct and indirect costs also depends on the cost object. A cost can be treated as direct for one cost object but indirect in respect of another. If the cost object is the cost of using different distribution channels, then the rental of warehouses and the salaries of storekeepers will be regarded as direct for each distribution channel. Also consider a supervisor's salary in a maintenance department of a manufacturing company. If the cost object is the maintenance department, then the salary is a direct cost. However, if the cost object is the product, both the warehouse rental and the salaries of the storekeepers and the supervisor will be an indirect cost because these costs cannot be specifically identified with the product.

Categories of manufacturing costs

In manufacturing organizations products are frequently the cost object. Traditionally, cost accounting systems in manufacturing organizations have reflected the need to assign costs to products to value stocks and measure profits based on imposed external financial accounting requirements. Traditional cost accounting systems accumulate product costs as follows:

Direct materials	xxx
Direct labour	xxx
Prime cost	xxx
Manufacturing overhead	xxx
Total manufacturing cost	xxx

Direct materials consist of all those materials that can be identified with a specific product. For example, wood that is used to manufacture a desk can easily be identified as part of the product, and can thus be classified as direct materials. Alternatively, materials used for the repair of a machine that is used for the manufacture of many different desks are classified as **indirect materials**. These items of materials cannot be identified with any one product, because they are used for the benefit of all products rather than for any one specific product. Note that indirect materials form part of the manufacturing overhead cost.

Direct labour consists of those labour costs that can be specifically traced to or identified with a particular product. Examples of direct labour costs include the wages of operatives who assemble parts into the finished product, or machine operatives engaged in the production process. By contrast, the salaries of factory supervisors or the wages paid to the staff in the stores department cannot be specifically identified with the product, and thus form part of the **indirect labour costs**. The wages of all employees who do not work on the product itself but who assist in the manufacturing operation are thus classified as part of the indirect labour costs. As with indirect materials, indirect labour is classified as part of the manufacturing overhead cost.

Prime cost refers to the direct costs of the product and consists of direct labour costs plus direct material costs plus any direct expenses. The cost of hiring a machine for producing a specific product is an example of a direct expense.

Manufacturing overhead consists of all manufacturing costs other than direct labour, direct materials and direct expenses. It therefore includes all indirect manufacturing labour and materials costs plus indirect manufacturing expenses. Examples of indirect manufacturing expenses in a multi-product company include rent of the factory and depreciation of machinery.

To ascertain the total manufacturing cost of a product, all that is required for the direct cost items is to record the amount of resources used on the appropriate documents. The specific product or order (i.e. the cost object) to which the costs should be assigned should be entered on the document. For example, the units of materials used in making a particular product are recorded on a stores requisition, and the hours of direct labour used are recorded on job cards. Having obtained the quantity of resources used for the direct items, it is necessary to ascertain the price paid for these resources. The total of the resources used multiplied by the price paid per unit of resources used provides us with the total of the direct costs or the prime cost for a product.

Manufacturing overheads cannot be directly traced to products. Instead they are assigned to products using **cost allocations**. A cost allocation is the process of estimating the cost of resources consumed by products that involves the use of surrogate, rather than direct measures. The process of assigning indirect costs (overheads) to cost objects will be explained in the next chapter.

Period and product costs

External financial accounting rules in most countries require that for inventory valuation, only manufacturing costs should be included in the calculation of product costs (see United Kingdom Statement of Standard Accounting Practice (SSAP 9), published by the Accounting Standards Committee). Accountants therefore classify costs as product costs and period costs. **Product costs** are those costs that are identified with goods purchased or produced for resale. In a manufacturing organization they are costs that the accountant attaches to the product and that are included in the inventory valuation for finished goods, or for partly completed goods (work in progress), until they are sold; they are then recorded as expenses and matched against sales for calculating profit. **Period costs** are those costs that are not included in the inventory valuation and as a result are treated as expenses in the period in which they are incurred. *Hence no attempt is made to attach period costs to products for inventory valuation purposes.*

In a manufacturing organization all manufacturing costs are regarded as product costs and non-manufacturing costs are regarded as period costs. Companies operating in the merchandising sector, such as retailing or wholesaling organizations, purchase goods for resale without changing their basic form. The cost of the goods purchased is regarded as a product cost and all other costs such as administration and selling and distribution expenses are considered to be period costs. The treatment of period and product costs for a manufacturing organization is illustrated in Figure 2.1. You will see that both product and period costs are eventually classified as expenses. The major difference is the point in time at which they are so classified.

Why are non-manufacturing costs treated as period costs and not included in the inventory valuation? There are two reasons. First, inventories are assets (unsold production) and assets represent resources that have been acquired that are expected to contribute to future revenue. Manufacturing costs incurred in making a product can be expected to generate future revenues to cover the cost of production. There is no guarantee, however, that non-manufacturing costs will generate future revenue, because they do not represent value added to any specific product. Therefore, they are not included in the inventory valuation. Second, many non-manufacturing costs (e.g. distribution costs) are not incurred when the product is being stored. Hence it is inappropriate to include such costs within the inventory valuation.

An illustration of the accounting treatment of period and product costs for income (profit) measurement purposes is presented in Example 2.1.

Cost behaviour

A knowledge of how costs and revenues will vary with different levels of activity (or volume) is essential for decision-making. Activity or volume may be measured in terms of

EXAMPLE 2.1

The Flanders company produces 100 000 identical units of a product during period 1. The costs for the period are as follows:

	(£)	(£)
Manufacturing costs:		
Direct labour	400 000	
Direct materials	200 000	
Manufacturing overheads	200 000	800 000
Non-manufacturing costs		300 000

During period 1, the company sold 50 000 units for £750 000, and the remaining 50 000 units were unsold at the end of the period. There was no opening stock at the start of the period. The profit and loss account for period 1 will be as follows:

	(£)	(£)
Sales (50 000)		750 000
Manufacturing costs (*product costs*):		
Direct labour	400 000	
Direct materials	200 000	
Manufacturing overheads	200 000	
	800 000	
Less closing stock (50% or 50 000 units)	400 000	
Cost of goods sold (50% or 50 000 units)		400 000
Gross profit		350 000
Less non-manufacturing costs (*period costs*)		300 000
Net profit		50 000

Fifty per cent of the production was sold during the period and the remaining 50% was produced for inventories. Half of the product costs are therefore identified as an expense for the period and the remainder are included in the closing inventory valuation. If we assume that the closing inventory is sold in the next accounting period, the remaining 50% of the product costs will become expenses in the next accounting period. However, all the period costs became an expense in this accounting period, because this is the period to which they relate. Note that only product costs form the basis for the calculation of cost of goods sold, and that period costs do not form part of this calculation.

units of production or sales, hours worked, miles travelled, patients seen, students enrolled or any other appropriate measure of the activity of an organization. Examples of decisions that require information on how costs and revenues vary with different levels of activity include the following:

1. What should the planned level of activity be for the next year?
2. Should we reduce the selling price to sell more units?

FIGURE 2.1 *Treatment of period and product costs*

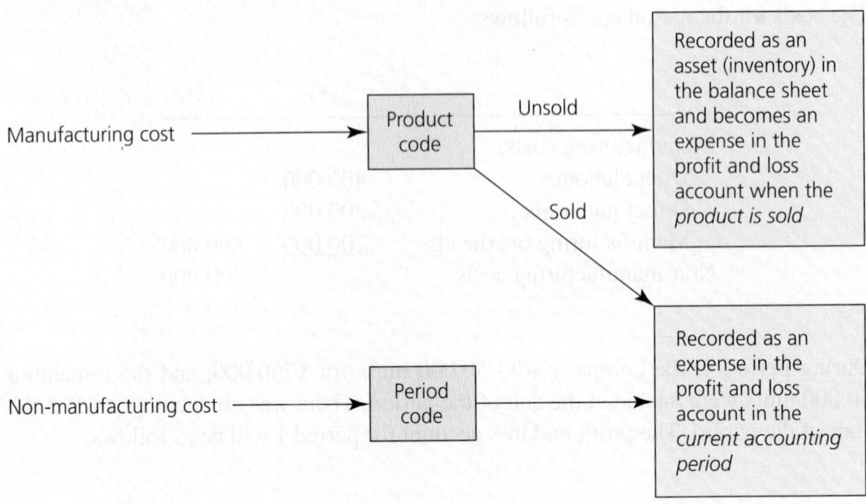

3 Would it be wiser to pay our sales staff by a straight commission, a straight salary, or by some combination of the two?

4 How do the costs and revenues of a hospital change if one more patient is admitted for a seven-day stay?

5 How do the costs and revenues of a hotel change if a room and meals are provided for two guests for a seven-day stay?

For each of the above decisions management requires estimates of costs and revenues at different levels of activity for the alternative courses of action.

The terms 'variable', 'fixed', 'semi-variable' and 'semi-fixed' have been traditionally used in the management accounting literature to describe how a cost reacts to changes in activity. Short-term **variable costs** vary in direct proportion to the volume of activity; that is, doubling the level of activity will double the total variable cost. Consequently, *total* variable costs are linear and *unit* variable cost is constant. Figure 2.2 illustrates a variable cost where the variable cost per unit of activity is £10. It is unlikely that variable cost per unit will be constant for all levels of activity. We shall discuss the reasons why accountants normally assume that variable costs are constant per unit of activity in Chapter 8. Examples of short-term variable manufacturing costs include piecework labour, direct materials and energy to operate the machines. These costs are assumed to fluctuate directly in proportion to operating activity within a certain range of activity. Examples of non-manufacturing variable costs include sales commissions, which fluctuate with sales value, and petrol, which fluctuates with the number of miles travelled.

Fixed costs remain constant over wide ranges of activity for a specified time period. Examples of fixed costs include depreciation of the factory building, supervisors' salaries and leasing charges for cars used by the salesforce. Figure 2.3 illustrates fixed costs.

You will see that the *total* fixed costs are constant for all levels of activity whereas *unit* fixed costs decrease proportionally with the level of activity. For example, if the total of the fixed costs is £5000 for a month the fixed costs per unit will be as follows:

FIGURE 2.2 *Variable costs: (a) total; (b) unit*

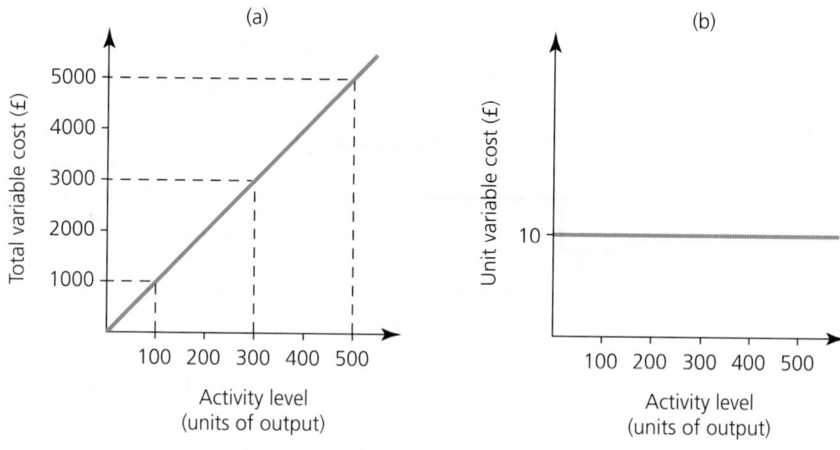

FIGURE 2.3 *Fixed costs: (a) total; (b) unit*

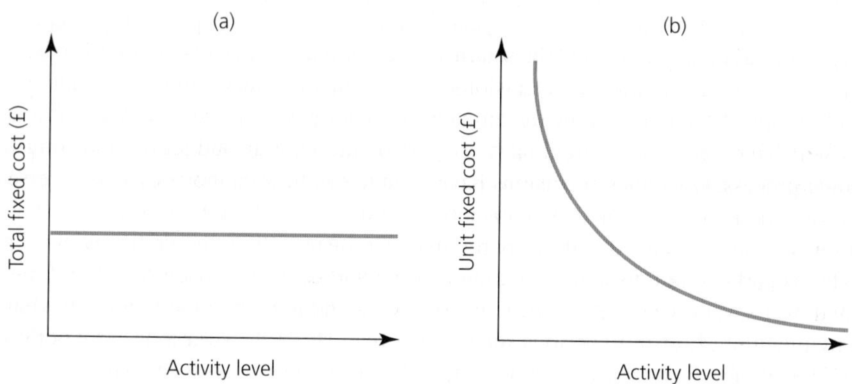

Units produced	Fixed cost per unit (£)
1	5000
10	500
100	50
1000	5

Because unit fixed costs are not constant per unit they must be interpreted with caution. For decision-making, it is better to work with total fixed costs rather than unit costs.

In practice it is unlikely that fixed costs will be constant over the full range of activity. They may increase in steps in the manner depicted in Figure 2.4. We shall discuss the justification for assuming that fixed costs are constant over a wide range of activity in Chapter 8.

The distinction between fixed and variable costs must be made relative to the time period under consideration. Over a sufficiently long time period of several years, virtually all costs are variable. During such a long period of time, contraction in demand will be accompanied

FIGURE 2.4 *Step fixed costs*

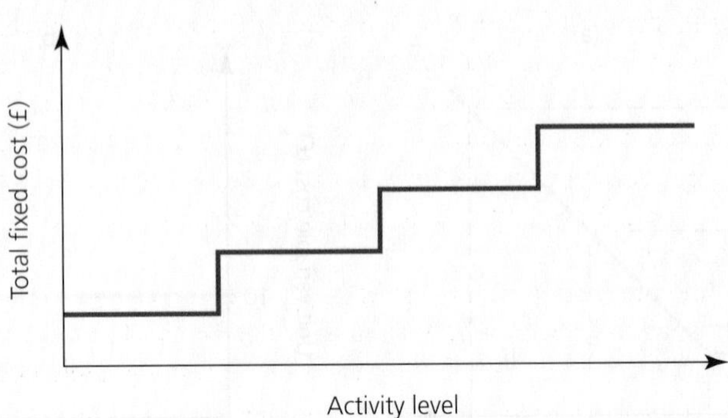

by reductions in virtually all categories of costs. For example, senior managers can be released, machinery need not be replaced and even buildings and land can be sold. Similarly, large expansions in activity will eventually cause all categories of costs to increase.

Within shorter time periods, costs will be fixed or variable in relation to changes in activity. The shorter the time period, the greater the probability that a particular cost will be fixed. Consider a time period of one year. The costs of providing the firm's operating capacity such as depreciation and the salaries of senior plant managers are likely to be fixed in relation to changes in activity. Decisions on the firm's intended future potential level of operating capacity will determine the amount of capacity costs to be incurred. These decisions will have been made previously as part of the capital budgeting and long-term planning process. Once these decisions have been made, they cannot easily be reversed in the short term. Plant investment and abandonment decisions should not be based on short-term fluctuations in demand within a particular year. Instead, they should be reviewed periodically as part of the long-term planning process and decisions made based on long-run demand over several years. Thus capacity costs will tend to be fixed in relation to changes of activity within short-term periods such as one year. However, over long-term periods of several years, significant changes in demand will cause capacity costs to change.

Spending on some fixed costs, such as direct labour and supervisory salaries, can be adjusted in the short term to reflect changes in activity. For example, if production activity declines significantly then direct workers and supervisors might continue to be employed in the hope that the decline in demand will be temporary; but if there is no upsurge in demand then staff might eventually be made redundant. If, on the other hand, production capacity expands to some critical level, additional workers might be employed, but the process of recruiting such workers may take several months. Thus within a short-term period, such as one year, labour costs can change in response to changes in demand in a manner similar to that depicted in Figure 2.4. Costs that behave in this manner are described as **semi-fixed** or **step fixed costs**. The distinguishing feature of step fixed costs is that within a given time period they are fixed within specified activity levels, but they eventually increase or decrease by a constant amount at various critical activity levels as illustrated in Figure 2.4.

Our discussion so far has assumed a one-year time period. Consider a shorter time period such as one month and the circumstances outlined in the previous paragraph where it takes several months to respond to changes in activity and alter spending levels. Over very short-term periods such as one month, spending on direct labour and supervisory salaries will be fixed in relation to changes in activity.

You should now understand that over a given short-term period, such as one year, costs will be variable, fixed or semi-fixed. Over longer-term time periods of several years, all costs will tend to change in response to large changes in activity (or to changes in the range and variety of products or services marketed), and fixed costs will become semi-fixed and change in the manner depicted in Figure 2.4. Because fixed costs do not remain fixed in the long-term, some writers prefer to describe them as **long-term variable costs**, but we shall continue to use the term fixed costs' since this is the term most widely used in the literature.

Note, however, that in the short term, even though fixed costs are normally assumed to remain unchanged in response to changes in the level of activity, they may change in response to other factors. For example, if price levels increase then some fixed costs such as management salaries will increase.

Before concluding our discussion of cost behaviour in relation to volume of activity, we must consider **semi-variable costs** (also known as **mixed** costs). These include both a fixed and a variable component. The cost of maintenance is a semi-variable cost consisting of planned maintenance that is undertaken whatever the level of activity, and a variable element that is directly related to the level of activity. A further example of a semi-variable cost is where sales representatives are paid a fixed salary plus a commission on sales.

Relevant and irrelevant costs and revenues

For decision-making, costs and revenues can be classified according to whether they are relevant to a particular decision. **Relevant costs and revenues** are those *future* costs and revenues that will be changed by a decision, whereas **irrelevant costs and revenues** are those that will not be affected by the decision. For example, if you are faced with a choice of making a journey using your own car or by public transport, the car tax and insurance costs are irrelevant, since they will remain the same whatever alternative is chosen. However, petrol costs for the car will differ depending on which alternative is chosen, and this cost will be relevant for decision-making.

Let us now consider a further illustration of the classification of relevant and irrelevant costs. Assume a company purchased raw materials a few years ago for £100 and that there appears to be no possibility of selling these materials or using them in future production apart from in connection with an enquiry from a former customer. This customer is prepared to purchase a product that will require the use of all these materials, but he is not prepared to pay more than £250 per unit. The additional costs of converting these materials into the required product are £200. Should the company accept the order for £250? It appears that the cost of the order is £300, consisting of £100 material cost and £200 conversion cost, but this is incorrect because the £100 material cost will remain the same whether the order is accepted or rejected. The material cost is therefore irrelevant for the decision, but if the order is accepted the conversion costs will change by £200, and this conversion cost is a relevant cost. If we compare the revenue of £250 with the relevant cost for the order of £200, it means that the order should be accepted, assuming of course that no higher-priced orders can be obtained elsewhere. The following calculation shows that this is the correct decision.

	Do not accept order (£)	Accept order (£)
Materials	100	100
Conversion costs	—	200
Revenue	—	(250)
Net costs	100	50

The net costs of the company are £50 less, or alternatively the company is £50 better off as a result of accepting the order. This agrees with the £50 advantage which was suggested by the relevant cost method.

In this illustration the sales revenue was relevant to the decision because future revenue changed depending on which alternative was selected; but sales revenue may also be irrelevant for decision-making. Consider a situation where a company can meet its sales demand by purchasing either machine A or machine B. The output of both machines is identical, but the operating costs and purchase costs of the machines are different. In this situation the sales revenue will remain unchanged irrespective of which machine is purchased (assuming of course that the quality of output is identical for both machines). Consequently, sales revenue is irrelevant for this decision; the relevant items are the operating costs and the cost of the machines. We have now established an important principle regarding the classification of cost and revenues for decision-making; namely, that in the short term not all costs and revenues are relevant for decision-making.

Avoidable and unavoidable costs

Sometimes the terms **avoidable** and **unavoidable costs** are used instead of relevant and irrelevant cost. Avoidable costs are those costs that may be saved by not adopting a given alternative, whereas unavoidable costs cannot be saved. Therefore, only avoidable costs are relevant for decision-making purposes. Consider the example that we used to illustrate relevant and irrelevant costs. The material costs of £100 are unavoidable and irrelevant, but the conversion costs of £200 are avoidable and hence relevant. The decision rule is to accept those alternatives that generate revenues in excess of the avoidable costs.

Sunk costs

These costs are the cost of resources already acquired where the total will be unaffected by the choice between various alternatives. They are costs that have been created by a decision made in the past and that cannot be changed by any decision that will be made in the future. The expenditure of £100 on materials that were no longer required, referred to in the preceding section, is an example of a **sunk cost**. Similarly, the written down values of assets previously purchased are sunk costs. For example, if a machine was purchased four years ago for £100 000 with an expected life of five years and nil scrap value then the written down value will be £20 000 if straight line depreciation is used. This written down value will have to be written off, no matter what possible alternative future action might be chosen. If the machine was scrapped, the £20 000 would be written off; if the machine was used for productive purposes, the £20 000 would still have to be written off. This cost cannot be changed by any future decision and is therefore classified as a sunk cost.

Sunk costs are irrelevant for decision-making, but they are distinguished from irrelevant costs because not all irrelevant costs are sunk costs. For example, a comparison of two alternative production methods may result in identical direct material expenditure for both alternatives, so the direct material cost is irrelevant because it will remain the same whichever alternative is chosen, but the material cost is not sunk cost since it will be incurred in the future.

Opportunity costs

Some costs for decision-making cannot normally be collected within the accounting system. Costs that are collected within the accounting system are based on past payments or commitments to pay at some time in the future. Sometimes it is necessary for decision-making to impute costs that will not require cash outlays, and these imputed costs are called opportunity costs. An **opportunity cost** is a cost that measures the opportunity that is lost or sacrificed when the choice of one course of action requires that an alternative course of action be given up. Consider the information presented in Example 2.2.

It is important to note that opportunity costs only apply to the use of scarce resources. Where resources are not scarce, no sacrifice exists from using these resources. In Example 2.2 if machine X was operating at 80% of its potential capacity then the decision to accept the contract would not have resulted in reduced production of product A. Consequently, there would have been no loss of revenue, and the opportunity cost would be zero.

You should now be aware that opportunity costs are of vital importance for decision-making. If no alternative use of resources exist then the opportunity cost is zero, but if resources have an alternative use, and are scarce, then an opportunity cost does exist.

EXAMPLE 2.2

A company has an opportunity to obtain a contract for the production of a special component. This component will require 100 hours of processing on machine X. Machine X is working at full capacity on the production of product A, and the only way in which the contract can be fulfilled is by reducing the output of product A. This will result in a lost profit contribution of £200. The contract will also result in *additional* variable costs of £1000.

If the company takes on the contract, it will sacrifice a profit contribution of £200 from the lost output of product A. This represents an opportunity cost, and should be included as part of the cost when negotiating for the contract. The contract price should at least cover the additional costs of £1000 plus the £200 opportunity cost to ensure that the company will be better off in the short term by accepting the contract.

Incremental and marginal costs

Incremental (also called **differential**) **costs** and revenues are the difference between costs and revenues for the corresponding items under each alternative being considered. For example, the incremental costs of increasing output from 1000 to 1100 units per week are the additional costs of producing an extra 100 units per week. Incremental costs may or may not include fixed costs. If fixed costs change as a result of a decision, the increase in costs represents an incremental cost. If fixed costs do not change as a result of a decision, the incremental costs will be zero.

Incremental costs and revenues are similar in principle to the economist's concept of **marginal cost** and **marginal revenue**. The main difference is that marginal cost/revenue represents the additional cost/revenue of one extra unit of output whereas incremental cost/revenue represents the additional cost/revenue resulting from a group of additional units of output. The economist normally represents the theoretical relationship between cost/revenue and output in terms of the marginal cost/revenue of single additional units of output. We shall see that the accountant is normally more interested in the incremental cost/revenue of increasing production and sales to whatever extent is contemplated, and this is most unlikely to be a single unit of output.

Job costing and process costing systems

There are two basic types of systems that companies can adopt – job costing and process costing systems. **Job costing** relates to a costing system that is required in organizations where each unit or batch of output of a product or service is unique. This creates the need for the cost of each unit to be calculated separately. The term 'job' thus relates to each unique unit or batch of output. Job costing systems are used in industries that provide customized products or services. For example, accounting firms provide customized services to clients with each client requiring services that consume different quantities of resources. Engineering companies often make machines to meet individual customer specifications. The contracts undertaken by construction and civil engineering companies differ greatly for each customer. In all of these organizations costs must be traced to each individual customer's order.

In contrast, **process costing** relates to those situations where masses of identical units are produced and it is unnecessary to assign costs to individual units of output. Products are produced in the same manner and consume the same amount of direct costs and overheads. It is therefore unnecessary to assign costs to individual units of output. Instead, the average cost per unit of output is calculated by dividing the total costs assigned to a product or service for a period by the number of units of output for that period. Industries where process costing is widely used include chemical processing, oil refining, food processing and brewing.

In practice these two costing systems represent extreme ends of a continuum. The output of many organizations requires a combination of the elements of both job costing and process costing.

Maintaining a cost database

In the previous chapter we noted that a cost and management accounting system should generate information to meet the following requirements:

1. to allocate costs between cost of goods sold and inventories for internal and external profit measurement and inventory valuation;
2. to provide relevant information to help managers make better decisions;
3. to provide information for planning, control and performance measurement.

A database should be maintained, with costs appropriately coded and classified, so that relevant cost information can be extracted to meet each of the above requirements.

A suitable coding system enables costs to be accumulated by the required cost objects (such as products or services, departments, responsibility centres, distribution channels, etc.) and also to be classified by appropriate categories. Typical cost classifications, within the database are by categories of expense (direct materials, direct labour and overheads) and by cost behaviour (fixed and variable). In practice, direct materials will be accumulated by each individual type of material, direct labour by different grades of labour and overhead costs by different categories of indirect expenses (e.g. rent, depreciation, supervision, etc.).

For *inventory valuation* the costs of all partly completed products (work in progress) and unsold finished products can be extracted from the database to ascertain the total cost assigned to inventories. The cost of goods sold that is deducted from sales revenues to compute the profit for the period can also be extracted by summing the manufacturing costs of all those products that have been sold during the period.

The allocation of costs to products is inappropriate for *cost control and performance measurement*, as the manufacture of the product may consist of several different operations, all of which are the responsibility of different individuals. To overcome this problem, costs and revenues must be traced to the individuals who are responsible for incurring them. This system is known as **responsibility accounting**.

Responsibility accounting involves the creation of responsibility centres. A **responsibility centre** may be defined as an organization unit for whose performance a manager is held accountable. Responsibility accounting enables accountability for financial results and outcomes to be allocated to individuals throughout the organization. The objective of responsibility accounting is to measure the results of each responsibility centre. It involves accumulating costs and revenues for each responsibility centre so that deviations from a performance target (typically the budget) can be attributed to the individual who is accountable for the responsibility centre.

For *cost control and performance measurement* the accountant produces performance reports at regular intervals for each responsibility centre. The reports are generated by extracting from the database costs analysed by responsibility centres and categories of expenses. Actual costs for each item of expense listed on the performance report should be compared with budgeted costs so that those costs that do not conform to plan can be pinpointed and investigated.

Future costs, rather than past costs, are required for *decision-making*. Therefore costs extracted from the database should be adjusted for anticipated price changes. We have noted that classification of costs by cost behaviour is important for evaluating the financial impact of expansion or contraction decisions. Costs, however, are not classified as relevant or irrelevant within the database because relevance depends on the circumstances. Consider a situation where a company is negotiating a contract for the sale of one of its products with a customer in an overseas country which is not part of its normal market. If the company has temporary excess capacity and the contract is for 100 units for one month only, then the direct labour cost will remain the same irrespective of whether or not the contract is undertaken. The direct labour cost will therefore be irrelevant. Let us now assume that the contract is for 100 units per month for three years and the company has excess capacity. For long-term decisions direct labour will be a relevant cost because if the contract is not undertaken direct labour can be redeployed or made redundant. Undertaking the contract will result in additional direct labour costs.

The above example shows that the classification of costs as relevant or irrelevant depends on the circumstances. In one situation a cost may be relevant, but in another the same cost may not be relevant. Costs can only be classified as relevant or irrelevant when the circumstances have been identified relating to a particular decision.

Where a company sells many products or services their profitability should be monitored at regular intervals so that potentially unprofitable products can be highlighted for a more detailed study of their future viability. This information is extracted from the database with costs reported by categories of expenses and divided into their fixed and variable elements. In Chapter 9 we shall focus in more detail on product/segmented profitability analysis. Finally, you should note that when the activities of an organization consist of a series of common or repetitive operations, targets or standard product costs, rather than actual costs, may be recorded in the database. Standard costs are predetermined costs; they are target costs that should be incurred under efficient operating conditions. They should be reviewed and updated at periodic intervals. If product standard costs are recorded in the database there is no need continuously to trace costs to products and therefore a considerable amount of data processing time can be saved. Actual costs, however, will still be traced to responsibility centres for cost control and performance evaluation.

Summary

The following items relate to the learning objectives listed at the beginning of the chapter.

- **Explain why it is necessary to understand the meaning of different cost terms.**

  The term 'cost' has multiple meanings and different types of costs are used in different situations. Therefore, a preceding term must be added to clarify the assumptions that underlie a measurement.

- **Define and illustrate a cost object.**

  A cost object is any activity for which a separate measurement of cost is required. In other words managers often want to know the cost of something and the 'thing' that they want to know the cost of is a cost object. Examples of cost objects include the cost of a new product, the cost of operating a sales outlet and the cost of operating a specific machine.

- **Explain the meaning of each of the key terms listed at the end of this chapter.**

  You should check your understanding of each of the terms listed in the key terms and concepts section below by referring to the page numbers that are shown in the parentheses following each key term.

- **Explain why in the short term some costs and revenues are not relevant for decision-making.**

  In the short term some costs and revenues may remain unchanged for all alternatives under consideration. For example, if you wish to determine the costs of driving to work in your own car or using public transport, the cost of the road fund taxation licence and insurance will remain the same for both alternatives, assuming that you intend to keep your car for leisure purposes. Therefore the costs of these items are not relevant for assisting you in your decision to travel to work by public transport or using your own car. Costs that remain unchanged for all alternatives under consideration are not relevant for decision-making.

- **Distinguish between job costing and process costing.**

  A job costing system relates to a costing system where each unit or batch of output of product(s) or service(s) is unique. This creates the need for the cost of each unit or batch to be calculated separately. In contrast a process costing system relates to situations where masses of identical units or batches are produced thus making it unnecessary to assign costs to individual units or batches of output. Instead, the average cost per unit or batch of output is calculated by dividing the total costs assigned to a product or service for the period by the number of units or batches of output for that period.

- **Describe the three purposes for which cost information is required.**

  A cost and management accounting system should generate information to meet the following requirements:

  (a) to allocate costs between cost of goods sold and inventories for internal and external profit reporting and inventory valuation;
  (b) to provide relevant information to help managers make better decisions;
  (c) to provide information for planning, control and performance measurement.

  A database should be maintained with costs appropriately coded or classified, so that relevant information can be extracted for meeting each of the above requirements.

Key terms and concepts

avoidable costs (p. 38)
cost allocations (p. 32)
cost object (p. 30)
differential costs (p. 39)
direct costs (p. 30)
direct labour (p. 31)
direct materials (p. 31)
fixed costs (p. 34)
incremental costs (p. 39)
indirect cost (p. 30)
indirect labour costs (p. 31)
indirect materials (p. 31)
irrelevant costs and revenues (p. 37)
job costing (p. 40)
long-term variable costs (p. 37)
manufacturing overhead (p. 31)
marginal cost/revenue (p. 39)
mixed costs (p. 37)
opportunity cost (p. 39)
period costs (p. 32)
prime cost (p. 31)
process costing (p. 40)
product costs (p. 32)
relevant costs and revenues (p. 37)
responsibility accounting (p. 41)
responsibility centre (p. 41)
semi-fixed costs (p. 36)
semi-variable costs (p. 37)
step fixed costs (p. 36)
sunk cost (p. 38)
unavoidable costs (p. 38)
variable costs (p. 34)

Recommended reading

This chapter has explained the meaning of the important terms that you will encounter when reading this book. For a more comprehensive description and detailed explanation of various cost terms you should refer to the Chartered Institute of Management Accountants' Official Terminology (2000).

Key examination points

First year management accounting course examinations frequently involve short essay questions requiring you to describe various cost terms or to discuss the concept that different costs are required for different purposes (see Review problems 2.23–2.30 for examples). It is therefore important that you understand all of the cost terms that have been described in this chapter. In particular, you should be able to explain the context within which a cost term is normally used. For example, a cost such as wages paid to casual labourers will be classified as indirect for inventory valuation purposes but as a direct charge to a responsibility centre or department for cost control purposes. A common error is for students to produce a very short answer, but you must be prepared to expand your answer and to include various situations within which the use of a cost term is appropriate. Always make sure your answer includes illustrations of cost terms. Multiple choice questions are also often set on topics included in this chapter. Review problems 2.17–2.22 are typical examples of such questions. You should now attempt these and compare your answers with the solutions.

Assessment material

Review questions

The review questions are short questions that enable you to assess your understanding of the main topics included in the chapter. The numbers in parentheses provide you with the page numbers to refer to if you cannot answer a specific question.

Review problems

The review problems are more complex and require you to relate and apply the chapter content to various business problems. The problems are graded by their level of difficulty. The multiple-choice questions are the least demanding and normally take less than 10 minutes to complete. Fully worked solutions to the review problems are provided in a separate section at the end of the book. For those questions in the white box the worked solutions are provided in the *Student's Manual* accompanying this book. Further review problems for this chapter are available on the accompanying website www.drury-online.com. The answers to these problems are available for lecturers on the lecturer's password protected section of the website.

Case studies

The website also includes over 30 case study problems. A list of these cases is provided in Part Seven of this book. The Electronic Boards case is a case study that is relevant to the introductory stages of a management accounting course.

Review questions

2.1 Define the meaning of the term 'cost object' and provide three examples of cost objects. *(p. 30)*

2.2 Distinguish between a direct and indirect cost. *(p. 30)*

2.3 Describe how a given direct cost item can be both a direct and indirect cost. *(pp. 30–31)*

2.4 Provide examples of each of the following: (a) direct labour, (b) indirect labour, (c) direct materials, (d) indirect materials, and (e) indirect expenses. *(p. 31)*

2.5 Explain the meaning of the terms: (a) prime cost, (b) overheads, and (c) cost allocations. *(pp. 31–32)*

2.6 Distinguish between product costs and period costs. *(p. 32)*

2.7 Provide examples of decisions that require knowledge of how costs and revenues vary with different levels of activity. *(pp. 34–36)*

2.8 Explain the meaning of each of the following terms: (a) variable costs, (b) fixed costs, (c) semi-fixed costs, and (d) semi-variable costs. Provide examples of costs for each of the four categories. *(pp. 34–37)*

2.9 Distinguish between relevant (avoidable) and irrelevant (unavoidable) costs and provide examples of each type of cost. *(pp. 37–38)*

2.10 Explain the meaning of the term 'sunk cost'. *(p. 38)*

2.11 Distinguish between incremental and marginal costs. *(pp. 39–40)*

2.12 What is an opportunity cost? Give some examples. *(p. 39)*

2.13 Distinguish between job costing and process costing. *(p. 40)*

2.14 Explain responsibility accounting. *(p. 41)*

Review problems

2.15 Intermediate

Classify each of the following as being usually fixed (F), variable (V), semi-fixed (SF) or semi-variable (SV):

(a) direct labour;
(b) depreciation of machinery;
(c) factory rental;
(d) supplies and other indirect materials;
(e) advertising;
(f) maintenance of machinery;
(g) factory manager's salary;
(h) supervisory personnel;
(i) royalty payments.

2.16 Intermediate

Which of the following costs are likely to be controllable by the head of the production department?

(a) price paid for materials;
(b) charge for floor space;
(c) raw materials used;
(d) electricity used for machinery;
(e) machinery depreciation;
(f) direct labour;
(g) insurance on machinery;
(h) share of cost of industrial relations department.

2.17 Intermediate

If actual output is lower than budgeted output, which of the following costs would you expect to be lower than the original budget?

A Total variable costs
B Total fixed costs
C Variable costs per unit
D Fixed costs per unit

ACCA Foundation Paper 3

2.18 Intermediate

The following data relate to two output levels of a department:

Machine hours	17 000	18 500
Overheads	£246 500	£251 750

The variable overhead rate per hour is £3.50. The amount of fixed overheads is:

A £5250
B £59 500
C £187 000
D £246 500

CIMA Stage 1

2.19 Intermediate

Prime cost is:

A all costs incurred in manufacturing a product;
B the total of direct costs;
C the material cost of a product;
D the cost of operating a department.

CIMA Stage 1

2.20 Intermediate

A direct cost is a cost which:

A is incurred as a direct consequence of a decision;
B can be economically identified with the item being costed;
C cannot be economically identified with the item being costed;
D is immediately controllable;
E is the responsibility of the board of directors

CIMA Stage 2

2.21 Intermediate

Which of the following would be classed as indirect labour?

A assembly workers in a company manufacturing televisions;
B a stores assistant in a factory store;
C plasterers in a construction company;
D an audit clerk in a firm of auditors.

CIMA Stage 1 Cost Accounting

2.22 Intermediate

Fixed costs are conventionally deemed to be:

A constant per unit of output;
B constant in total when production volume changes;
C outside the control of management;
D those unaffected by inflation.

CIMA Stage 1 Cost Accounting

2.23 Intermediate

Prepare a report for the Managing Director of your company explaining how costs may be classified by their behaviour, with particular reference to the effects both on total and on unit costs. Your report should

(i) say why it is necessary to classify costs by their behaviour, and
(ii) be illustrated by sketch graphs within the body of the report.

(15 marks)
CIMA Stage 1 Accounting

2.24 Intermediate

Describe three different methods of cost classification and explain the utility of each method.

(11 marks)
ACCA Level 1 Costing

2.25 Intermediate

Cost classifications used in costing include:

(i) period costs
(ii) product costs
(iii) variable costs
(iv) opportunity costs

Required:
Explain each of these classifications, with examples of the types of costs that may be included.

(17 marks)
ACCA Level 1 Costing

2.26 Intermediate

(a) Describe the role of the cost accountant in a manufacturing organization.

(8 marks)

(b) Explain whether you agree with each of the following statements:
(i) 'All direct costs are variable.'
(ii) 'Variable costs are controllable and fixed costs are not.'
(iii) 'Sunk costs are irrelevant when providing decision making information.'

(9 marks)
(Total 17 marks)
ACCA Level 1 Costing

2.27 Intermediate

'Cost may be classified in a variety of ways according to their nature and the information needs of management.' Explain and discuss this statement, illustrating with examples of the classifications required for different purposes.

(22 marks)
ICSA Management Accounting

2.28 Intermediate

It is commonly suggested that a management accounting system should be capable of supplying different measures of cost for different purposes. You are required to set out the main types of purpose for which cost information may be required in a business organization, and to discuss the alternative measures of cost which might be appropriate for each purpose.

ICAEW Management Accounting

2.29 Intermediate

Opportunity cost and *sunk cost* are among the concepts of cost commonly discussed.

You are required:

(i) to define these terms precisely;

(4 marks)

(ii) to suggest for each of them situations in which the concept might be applied;

(4 marks)

(iii) to assess briefly the significance of each of the concepts.

(4 marks)

ICAEW P2 Management Accounting

2.30 Intermediate

Distinguish between, and provide an illustration of:

(i) 'avoidable' and 'unavoidable' costs;

(ii) 'cost centres' and 'cost units'.

(8 marks)

ACCA Foundation Paper 3

2.31 Advanced

'The diverse uses of routinely recorded cost data give rise to a fundamental danger: information prepared for one purpose can be grossly misleading in another context' (from *Management Accounting: A Conceptual Approach*, by L.R. Amey and D.A. Egginton).

Required:

Discuss to what extent the above statement is valid and explain your conclusions.

(12 marks)

ACCA P2 Management Accounting

2.32 Intermediate: Cost behaviour

Data	(£)	
Cost of motor car	5500	
Trade-in price after 2 years or 60 000 miles is expected to be	1500	
Maintenance – 6-monthly service costing	60	
Spares/replacement parts, per 1000 miles	20	
Vehicle licence, per annum	80	
Insurance, per annum	150	
Tyre replacements after 25 000 miles, four at £37.50 each		
Petrol, per gallon		1.90
Average mileage from one gallon is 25 miles.		

(a) From the above data you are required:

(i) to prepare a schedule to be presented to management showing for the mileages of 5000, 10 000, 15 000 and 30 000 miles per annum:

(1) total variable cost

(2) total fixed cost

(3) total cost

(4) variable cost per mile (in pence to nearest penny)

(5) fixed cost per mile (in pence to nearest penny)

(6) total cost per mile (in pence to nearest penny)

If, in classifying the costs, you consider that some can be treated as either variable or fixed, state the assumption(s) on which your answer is based together with brief supporting reason(s).

(ii) on graph paper plot the information given in your answer to (i) above for the costs listed against (1), (2), (3) and (6).

(iii) to read off from your graph(s) in (ii) and state the approximate total costs applicable to 18 000 miles and 25 000 miles and the total cost per mile at these two mileages.

(b) 'The more miles you travel, the cheaper it becomes.' Comment briefly on this statement.

(25 marks)

CIMA Cost Accounting 1

2.33 Intermediate: Sunk and opportunity costs for decision-making

Mrs Johnston has taken out a lease on a shop for a down payment of £5000. Additionally, the rent under the lease amounts to £5000 per annum. If the lease is cancelled, the initial payment of £5000 is forfeit. Mrs Johnston plans to use the shop for the sale of clothing, and has estimated operations for the next twelve months as follows:

	(£)	(£)
Sales	115 000	
Less Value-added tax (VAT)	15 000	
Sales Less VAT		100 000
Cost of goods sold	50 000	
Wages and wage related costs	12 000	
Rent including the down payment	10 000	
Rates, heating, lighting and insurance	13 000	
Audit, legal and general expenses	2 000	
		87 000
Net profit before tax		13 000

In the figures no provision has been made for the cost of Mrs Johnston but it is estimated that one half of her time will be devoted to the business. She is undecided whether to continue with her plans, because she knows that she can sublet the shop to a friend for a monthly rent of £550 if she does not use the shop herself.

You are required to:

(a) (i) explain and identify the 'sunk' and 'opportunity' costs in the situation depicted above;

(ii) state what decision Mrs Johnston should make according to the information given, supporting your conclusion with a financial statement;

(11 marks)

(b) explain the meaning and use of 'notional' (or 'imputed') costs and quote *two* supporting examples.

(4 marks)

(Total 15 marks)

CIMA Foundation Cost Accounting 1

Review problems (with answers in the Student's Manual)

2.34 **Advanced**

(i) Costs may be classified in a number of ways including classification by behaviour, by function, by expense type, by controllability and by relevance.

(ii) Management accounting should assist in EACH of the planning, control and decision making processes in an organisation.

Discuss the ways in which relationships between statements (i) and (ii) are relevant in the design of an effective management accounting system.

(15 marks)

ACCA Paper 9 Information for Control and Decision Making

2.35 **Intermediate**

(a) 'Discretionary costs are troublesome because managers usually find it difficult to separate and quantify the results of their use in the business, as compared with variable and other fixed costs.'

You are required to discuss the above statement and include in your answer the meaning of discretionary costs, variable costs and fixed costs; give two illustrations of each of these three named costs.

(12 marks)

(b) A drug company has initiated a research project which is intended to develop a new product. Expenditures to date on this particular research total £500 000 but it is now estimated that a further £200 000 will need to be spent before the product can be marketed. Over the estimated life of the product the profit potential has a net present value of £350 000.

You are required to advise management whether they should continue or abandon the project. Support your conclusion with a numerate statement and state what kind of cost is the £500 000.

(5 marks)

(c) Opportunity costs and notional costs are not recognized by financial accounting systems but need to be considered in many decisions taken by management.

You are required to explain briefly the meanings of opportunity costs and notional costs; give two examples of each to illustrate the meanings you have attached to them.

(8 marks)

(Total 25 marks)

CIMA Stage 2 Cost Accounting

2.36 **Intermediate: Relevant costs and cost behaviour**

(a) Distinguish between 'opportunity cost' and 'out of pocket cost' giving a numerical example of each using your own figures to support your answer.

(6 marks)

(b) Jason travels to work by train to his 5-day week job. Instead of buying daily tickets he finds it cheaper to buy a quarterly season ticket which costs £188 for 13 weeks.

Debbie, an acquaintance, who also makes the same journey, suggests that they both travel in Jason's car and offers to give him £120 each quarter towards his car expenses. Except for weekend travelling and using it for local college attendance near his home on three evenings each week to study for his CIMA Stage 2, the car remains in Jason's garage.

Jason estimates that using his car for work would involve him, each quarter, in the following expenses:

	(£)
Depreciation (proportion of annual figure)	200
Petrol and oil	128
Tyres and miscellaneous	52

You are required to state whether Jason should accept Debbie's offer and to draft a statement to show clearly the monetary effect of your conclusion.

(5 marks)

(c) A company with a financial year 1 September to 31 August prepared a sales budget which resulted in the following cost structure:

		% of sales
Direct materials		32
Direct wages		18
Production overhead:	variable	6
	fixed	24
Administrative and selling costs:	variable	3
	fixed	7
Profit		10

After ten weeks, however, it became obvious that the sales budget was too optimistic and it has now been estimated that because of a reduction in sales volume, for the full year, sales will total £2 560 000 which is only 80% of the previously budgeted figure.

You are required to present a statement for management showing the amended sales and cost structure in £s and percentages, in a marginal costing format.

(4 marks)
(Total 15 marks)
CIMA Stage 2 Cost Accounting

PART 2

Cost Accumulation for Inventory Valuation and Profit Measurement

This section focuses mainly on assigning costs to products to separate costs incurred during a period between costs of goods sold and the closing inventory valuation. The extent to which product costs accumulated for inventory valuation and profit measurement should be adjusted for meeting decision-making, cost control and performance measurement requirements is also briefly considered.

Chapter 3 aims to provide you with an understanding of how costs are assigned to cost objects. In particular the chapter focuses on the assignment of indirect costs using traditional and activity-based systems. In Chapter 4 the emphasis is on the accounting entries necessary to record transactions within a job costing system. The issues relating to a cost accumulation procedure for a process costing system are described in Chapter 5. This is a system that is applicable to industries that produce many units of the same product during a particular period. In Chapter 6 the problems associated with calculating product costs in those industries that produce joint and by-products are discussed. The final chapter in this section is concerned with the alternative accounting methods of assigning fixed manufacturing overheads to products and their implications for profit measurement and inventory valuation.

Cost assignment

3

In the previous chapter it was pointed out that companies need cost and management accounting systems to perform a number of different functions. In this chapter we are going to concentrate on two of these functions – they are (i) allocating costs between cost of goods sold and inventories for internal and external profit reporting and (ii) providing relevant decision-making information for distinguishing between profitable and unprofitable activities.

In order to perform the above functions a cost accumulation system is required that assigns costs to cost objects. The aim of this chapter is to provide you with an understanding of how costs are accumulated and assigned to cost objects. You should have remembered from the previous chapter that a cost object is anything for which a separate measurement of cost is desired. Typical cost objects include products, services, customers and locations. In this chapter we shall either use the term cost object as a generic term or assume that products are the cost object. However, the same cost assignment principles can be applied to all cost objects.

We begin by explaining how the cost assignment process differs for direct and indirect costs.

LEARNING OBJECTIVES

After studying this chapter, you should be able to:

- distinguish between cause-and-effect and arbitrary cost allocations;
- explain why different cost information is required for different purposes;
- describe how cost systems differ in terms of their level of sophistication;
- understand the factors influencing the choice of an optimal cost system;
- explain why departmental overhead rates should be used in preference to a single blanket overhead rate;
- construct an overhead analysis sheet and calculate cost centre allocation rates;
- distinguish between traditional and activity-based costing systems;
- justify why budgeted overhead rates should be used in preference to actual overhead rates;
- calculate and explain the accounting treatment of the under/over recovery of overheads;

Assignment of direct and indirect costs

Costs that are assigned to cost objects can be divided into two categories – direct costs and indirect costs. Sometimes the term **overheads** is used instead of indirect costs. Direct costs can be accurately traced to cost objects because they can be specifically and exclusively traced to a particular cost object whereas indirect costs cannot. Where a cost can be directly assigned to a cost object the term **cost tracing** is used. In contrast, indirect costs cannot be traced directly to a cost object because they are usually common to several cost objects. Indirect costs are therefore assigned to cost objects using cost allocations.

A **cost allocation** is the process of assigning costs when a direct measure does not exist for the quantity of resources consumed by a particular cost object. Cost allocations involve the use of surrogate rather than direct measures. For example, consider an activity such as receiving incoming materials. Assuming that the cost of receiving materials is strongly influenced by the number of receipts then costs can be allocated to products (i.e. the cost object) based on the number of material receipts each product requires. The basis that is used to allocate costs to cost objects (i.e. the number of material receipts in our example) is called an **allocation base** or **cost driver**. If 20% of the total number of receipts for a period were required for a particular product then 20% of the total costs of receiving incoming materials would be allocated to that product. Assuming that the product was discontinued, and not replaced, we would expect action to be taken to reduce the resources required for receiving materials by 20%.

In the above illustration the allocation base is assumed to be a significant determinant of the cost of receiving incoming materials. Where allocation bases are significant determinants of the costs we shall describe them as **cause-and-effect allocations**. Where a cost allocation base is used that is not a significant determinant of its cost the term **arbitrary allocation** will be used. An example of an arbitrary allocation would be if direct labour hours were used as the allocation base to allocate the costs of materials receiving. If a labour intensive product required a large proportion of direct labour hours (say 30%) but few material receipts it would be allocated with a large proportion of the costs of material receiving. The allocation would be an inaccurate assignment of the resources consumed by the product. Furthermore, if the product were discontinued, and not replaced, the cost of the material receiving activity would not decline by 30% because the allocation base is not a significant determinant of the costs of the materials receiving activity. Arbitrary allocations are therefore likely to result in inaccurate allocations of indirect costs to cost objects.

Figure 3.1 provides a summary of the assignment process. You can see that direct costs are assigned to cost objects using cost tracing whereas indirect cost are assigned using cost allocations. For accurate assignment of indirect costs to cost objects cause-and-effect allocations should be used. Two types of systems can be used to assign indirect costs to cost objects. They are **traditional costing systems** and **activity-based-costing (ABC)** systems. Traditional costing systems were developed in the early 1900s and are still widely used today. They rely extensively on arbitrary cost allocations. ABC systems only emerged in the late 1980s. One of the major aims of ABC systems is to use only cause-and-effect cost allocations. Both cost systems adopt identical approaches to assigning direct costs to cost objects. We shall look at traditional and ABC systems in more detail later in the chapter.

Different costs for different purposes

Manufacturing organizations assign costs to products for two purposes: first, for internal profit measurement and external financial accounting requirements in order to allocate the manufacturing costs incurred during a period between cost of goods sold and inventories;

FIGURE 3.1 *Cost allocations and cost tracing*

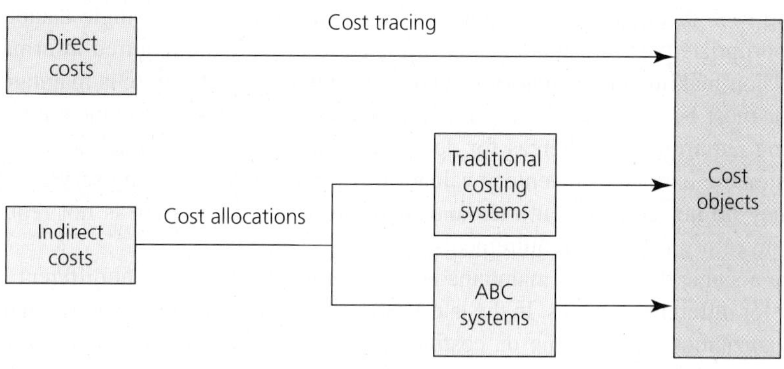

secondly, to provide useful information for managerial decision-making requirements. In order to meet financial accounting requirements, it may not be necessary to accurately trace costs to *individual* products. Consider a situation where a firm produces 1000 different products and the costs incurred during a period are £10 million. A well-designed product costing system should accurately analyse the £10 million costs incurred between cost of sales and inventories. Let us assume the true figures are £7 million and £3 million. Approximate but inaccurate *individual* product costs may provide a reasonable approximation of how much of the £10 million should be attributed to cost of sales and inventories. Some product costs may be overstated and others may be understated, but this would not matter for financial accounting purposes as long as the *total* of the individual product costs assigned to cost of sales and inventories was approximately £7 million and £3 million.

For decision-making purposes, however, more accurate product costs are required so that we can distinguish between profitable and unprofitable products. By more accurately measuring the resources consumed by products, or other cost objects, a firm can identify its sources of profits and losses. If the cost system does not capture sufficiently accurately the consumption of resources by products, the reported product costs will be distorted, and there is a danger that managers may drop profitable products or continue production of unprofitable products.

Besides different levels of accuracy, different cost information is required for different purposes. For meeting external financial accounting requirements, financial accounting regulations and legal requirements in most countries require that inventories should be valued at manufacturing cost. Therefore only manufacturing costs are assigned to products for meeting external financial accounting requirements. For decision-making non-manufacturing costs must be taken into account and assigned to products. Not all costs, however may be relevant for decision-making. For example, depreciation of plant and machinery will not be affected by a decision to discontinue a product. Such costs were described in the previous chapter as irrelevant and sunk for decision-making. Thus depreciation of plant must be assigned to products for inventory valuation but it should not be assigned for discontinuation decisions.

Maintaining a single or separate databases

Because different costs and different levels of accuracy are required for different purposes some organizations maintain two separate costing systems, one for decision-making and the other for inventory valuation and profit measurement. In a survey of 187 UK companies

Drury and Tayles (2000) reported that 9% of the companies maintained two cost accumulation systems, one for decision-making and the other for inventory valuation. The remaining 91% of organizations maintained a costing system on a single database from which appropriate cost information was extracted to provide the required information for both decision-making and inventory valuation. When a single database is maintained only costs that must be assigned for inventory valuation are extracted for meeting financial accounting requirements, whereas for decision-making only costs which are relevant for the decision are extracted. Inventory valuation is not an issue for many service organizations. They do not carry inventories and therefore a costing system is not required for meeting inventory valuation requirements.

Where a single database is maintained cost assignments cannot be at different levels of accuracy for different purposes. In the late 1980s, according to Johnson and Kaplan (1987), most organizations were relying on costing systems that had been designed primarily for meeting external financial accounting requirements. These systems were designed decades ago when information processing costs were high and precluded the use of more sophisticated methods of assigning indirect costs to products. Such systems are still widely used today. They rely extensively on arbitrary cost allocations which may be sufficiently accurate for meeting external financial accounting requirements but not for meeting decision-making requirements. Johnson and Kaplan concluded that management accounting practices have followed and become subservient to meeting financial accounting requirements.

Cost–benefit issues and cost systems design

These criticisms resulted in the emergence of ABC in the late 1980s. Surveys in many countries suggest that between 20 and 30% of the surveyed organizations have implemented ABC systems. The majority of organizations therefore continue to operate traditional systems. Both traditional and ABC systems vary in their level of sophistication but, as a general rule, traditional systems tend to be simplistic whereas ABC systems tend to be sophisticated. What determines the chosen level of sophistication of a costing system? The answer is that the choice should be made on costs versus benefits criteria. Simplistic systems are inexpensive to operate, but they are likely to result in inaccurate cost assignments and the reporting of inaccurate costs. Managers using cost information extracted from simplistic systems are more likely to make important mistakes arising from using inaccurate cost information. The end result may be a high cost of errors. Conversely, sophisticated systems are more expensive to operate but they minimize the cost of errors. However, the aim should not be to have the most accurate cost system. Improvements should be made in the level of sophistication of the costing system up to the point where the marginal cost of improvement equals the marginal benefit from the improvement.

Figure 3.2 illustrates the above points with costing systems ranging from simplistic to sophisticated. Highly simplistic costing systems are located on the extreme left. Common features of such systems are that they are inexpensive to operate, make extensive use of arbitrary allocations of indirect costs and normally result in low levels of accuracy and a high cost of errors. On the extreme right are highly sophisticated systems. These systems use only cause-and-effect allocations, are more expensive to operate, have high levels of accuracy and minimize the cost of errors. Cost systems in most organizations are not located at either of these extreme points. Instead, they are located at different points within the range shown in Figure 3.2.

The optimal cost system is different for different organizations. For example, the optimal costing system will be located towards the extreme left for an organization whose indirect costs are a low percentage of total costs and which also has a fairly standardized

FIGURE 3.2 *Cost systems – varying levels of sophistication for cost assignment*

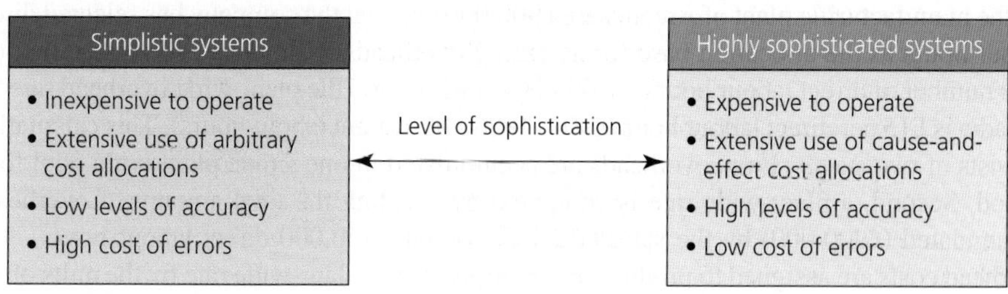

product range, all consuming organizational resources in similar proportions. In these circumstances simplistic systems may not result in the reporting of inaccurate costs. In contrast, the optimal costing system for organizations with a high proportion of indirect costs, whose products consume organizational resources in different proportions, will be located towards the extreme right. More sophisticated costing systems are required to capture the diversity of consumption of organizational resources and accurately assign the high level of indirect costs to different cost objects.

Assigning direct costs to cost objects

Both simplistic and sophisticated systems accurately assign direct costs to cost objects. Cost assignment merely involves the implementation of suitable clerical procedures to identify and record the resources consumed by cost objects. Consider direct labour. The time spent on providing a service to a specific customer, or manufacturing a specific product, is recorded on source documents, such as **time sheets** or **job cards**. Details of the customer's account number, job number or the product's code are also entered on these documents. The employee's hourly rate of pay is then entered so that the direct labour cost for the employee can be assigned to the appropriate cost object.

For direct materials the source document is a **materials requisition**. Details of the materials issued for manufacturing a product, or providing a specific service, are recorded on the materials requisition. The customer's account number, job number or product code is also entered and the items listed on the requisition are priced at their cost of acquisition. The details on the material requisition thus represent the source information for assigning the cost of the materials to the appropriate cost object. A more detailed explanation of this procedure is provided in the next chapter.

In many organizations the recording procedure for direct costs is computerized using bar coding and other forms of on-line information recording. The source documents only exist in the form of computer records. Because direct costs can be accurately assigned to cost objects whereas many indirect costs cannot, the remainder of this chapter will focus on indirect cost assignment.

Plant-wide (blanket) overhead rates

The most simplistic traditional costing system assigns indirect costs to cost objects using a single overhead rate for the organization as a whole. You will recall at the start of this chapter that it was pointed out that indirect costs are also called overheads. The terms **blanket overhead rate** or **plant-wide rate** are used to describe a single overhead rate that is established for the organization as a whole. Let us assume that the total manufacturing overheads for the manufacturing plant of Arcadia are £900 000 and that the company has selected direct labour hours as the allocation base for assigning overheads to products. Assuming that the total number of direct labour hours are 60 000 for the period the plant-wide overhead rate for Arcadia is £15 per direct labour hour (£900 000/60 000 direct labour hours). This calculation consists of two stages. First, overheads are accumulated in one single plant-wide pool for a period. Second, a plant-wide rate is computed by dividing the total amount of overheads accumulated (£900 000) by the selected allocation base (60 000 direct labour hours). The overhead costs are assigned to products by multiplying the plant-wide rate by the units of the selected allocation base (direct labour hours) used by each product.

Assume now that Arcadia is considering establishing separate overheads for each of its three production departments. Further investigations reveal that the products made by the company require different operations and some products do not pass through all three departments. These investigations also indicate that the £900 000 total manufacturing overheads and 60 000 direct labour hours can be analysed as follows:

	Department A	Department B	Department C	Total
Overheads	£200 000	£600 000	£100 000	£900 000
Direct labour hours	20 000	20 000	20 000	60 000
Overhead rate per direct labour hour	£10	£30	£5	£15

Consider now a situation where product Z requires 20 direct labour hours in department C but does not pass through departments A and B. If a plant-wide overhead rate is used then overheads of £300 (20 hours at £15 per hour) will be allocated to product Z. On the other hand, if a departmental overhead rate is used, only £100 (20 hours at £5 per hour) would be allocated to product Z. Which method should be used? The logical answer must be to establish separate departmental overhead rates, since product Z only consumes overheads in department C. If the plant-wide overhead rate were applied, all the factory overhead rates would be averaged out and product Z would be indirectly allocated with some of the overheads of department B. This would not be satisfactory, since product Z does not consume any of the resources and this department incurs a large amount of the overhead expenditure.

Where some departments are more 'overhead-intensive' than others, products spending more time in the overhead-intensive departments should be assigned more overhead costs than those spending less time. Departmental rates capture these possible effects but plant-wide rates do not, because of the averaging process. We can conclude that a plant-wide rate will generally result in the reporting of inaccurate product costs. A plant-wide rate can only be justified when all products consume departmental overheads in approximately the same proportions. In the above illustration each department accounts for one-third of the total direct labour hours. If all products spend approximately one-third of their time in each department, a plant-wide overhead rate can be used. Consider a situation where product X spends one hour in each department and product Y spends five hours in each department. Overheads of £45 and £225 respectively would be allocated to products X and Y using either a plant-wide rate (3 hours at £15 and 15 hours at £15) or separate departmental overhead rates. If a diverse product range is produced with products spending different proportions of time in each department, separate departmental overhead rates should be established.

However, significant usage of plant-wide overhead rates have been reported in surveys undertaken in many different countries. For example, the percentage usages vary from

20–30% in UK (Drury and Tayles, 1994), USA (Emore and Ness, 1991), Australian (Joye and Blayney, 1990; 1991) and Indian (Joshi, 1998) surveys. In contrast, in Scandinavia only 5% of the Finnish companies (Lukka and Granlund, 1996), one Norwegian company (Bjornenak, 1997b) and none of the Swedish companies sampled (Ask *et al.*, 1996) used a single plant-wide rate. Zero usage of plant-wide rates was also reported from a survey of Greek companies (Ballas and Venieris, 1996). In a more recent study of UK organizations Drury and Tayles (2000) reported that a plant-wide rate was used by 3% of surveyed organizations possibly suggesting a move towards more sophisticated costing systems.

Cost centre overhead rates

In the previous example relating to Arcadia the advantages of using departmental overhead rates rather than a single blanket rate were illustrated. In some situations it is possible to go a stage further and establish separate overhead rates for smaller segments within an organization, such as groups of similar machines within the same department.

Consider our previous example relating to Arcadia. The overhead rate for Department B was £30 per direct labour hour derived from dividing £600 000 overheads assigned to department B by 20 000 direct labour hours. Let us assume that the overheads and direct labour hours for department B can be further analysed by production centres as follows:

	Production centre B1	Production centre B2	Production centre B3	Total
Overheads	£80 000	£400 000	£120 000	£600 000
Direct labour hours	2 000	8 000	10 000	20 000
Overhead rate per direct labour hour	£40	£50	£12	£30

A single overhead rate for the whole department will result in the inaccurate assignment of overheads when a department consists of a number of different production centres with products passing through the departments consume overheads of each production centre in different proportions. Consider a situation where a product requires 15 direct labour hours in production centre B3 and does not pass through any of the other two production centres within the department. If a departmental rate is used, overheads of £450 (15 direct labour hours at £30 per hour) will be allocated to the product whereas if a separate rate for the production centre is used, only £180 (15 hours at £12 per hour) will be allocated. In this illustration Arcadia should establish separate overhead rates for each production centre within department B. If a single rate for the whole department were applied, all of the overheads within the department would be averaged out and the product would be indirectly allocated with some of the overheads of the remaining production centres. We can therefore conclude that if a department consists of a number of different production centres, each with significant overhead costs, and products consume production centre overheads in different proportions, separate overhead rates should be established for each production centre within the department.

The terms **cost centres** or **cost pools** are used to describe a location to which overhead costs are initially assigned. The total costs accumulated in each cost centre are then assigned to cost objects using a separate allocation base for each cost centre. This process is illustrated in the next section. However, at this point you should note that frequently cost centres will consist of departments but they can also consist of smaller segments within departments.

The two-stage allocation process

A framework, known as the two-stage allocation process, can be used to summarize the different approaches we have looked at for Arcadia to assign overhead costs to products. The process applies to assigning costs to other cost objects, besides products, and is applicable to all organizations that assign indirect costs to cost objects. The framework applies to both traditional and ABC systems.

The framework is illustrated in Figure 3.3. You can see that in the first stage overheads are assigned to cost centres. In the second stage the costs accumulated in the cost centres are allocated to cost objects using selected allocation bases (you should remember from our discussion earlier that allocation bases are also called cost drivers). Traditional costing systems tend to use a small number of second stage allocation bases, typically direct labour hours or machine hours. In other words, traditional systems assume that direct labour or machine hours have a significant influence in the long term on the level of overhead expenditure. Other allocation bases used to a lesser extent by traditional systems are direct labour cost, direct materials cost and units of output. These methods are described and illustrated in Appendix 3.2 at the end of this chapter. Exhibit 3.1 (Section C) shows details of the extent to which different second stage allocation bases are used in different countries. You will see that direct labour and machine hours are the dominant methods.

Within the two-stage allocation process ABC systems differ from traditional systems by having a greater number of cost centres in the first stage and a greater number, and variety, of cost drivers or allocation bases in the second stage. Both systems will be described in more detail later in the chapter.

You will have noted from our discussion in the previous sections relating to Arcadia that increasing the number of cost centres resulted in a more accurate assignment of overheads to products. We started with a blanket overhead rate and omitted the first stage of the two-stage allocation process and noted that this process resulted in an inaccurate assignment of costs. Next we adopted the two-stage allocation process by establishing separate cost centre overhead rates (based on departments). This change resulted in a more accurate assignment of overheads to products. Finally, we noted that further improvements in the accuracy of cost assignments could be obtained by increasing the number of cost centres by establishing separate cost centres within a department.

How many cost centres should a firm establish? If only a small number of cost centres are established it is likely that activities within a cost centre will not be homogeneous and, if the consumption of the activities by products/services within the cost centres varies, activity resource consumption will not be accurately measured. Therefore, in most situations, increasing the number of cost centres increases the accuracy of measuring the indirect costs consumed by cost objects. The choice of the number of cost centres should be based on cost–benefit criteria using the principles described on pages 60–61. Exhibit 3.1 (Section A) shows the number of cost centres and second stage cost allocation bases reported by Drury *et al.* in a survey of 187 UK organizations. It can be seen that 35% of the organizations used less than 11 cost centres whereas 23% used more than 30 cost centres. In terms of the number of different types of second stage cost drivers/allocation bases 69% of the responding organizations used less than four.

An illustration of the two-stage process for a traditional costing system

We shall now use Example 3.1 to provide a more detailed illustration of the two-stage allocation process for a traditional costing system. To keep the illustration manageable it is

FIGURE 3.3 *An illustration of the two-stage allocation process for traditional and activity-based costing systems*

(a) Traditional costing systems

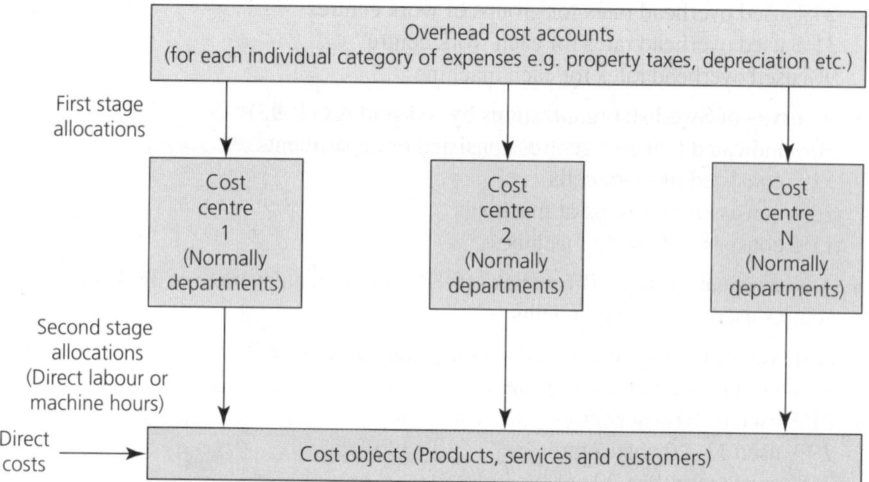

(b) Activity-based costing systems

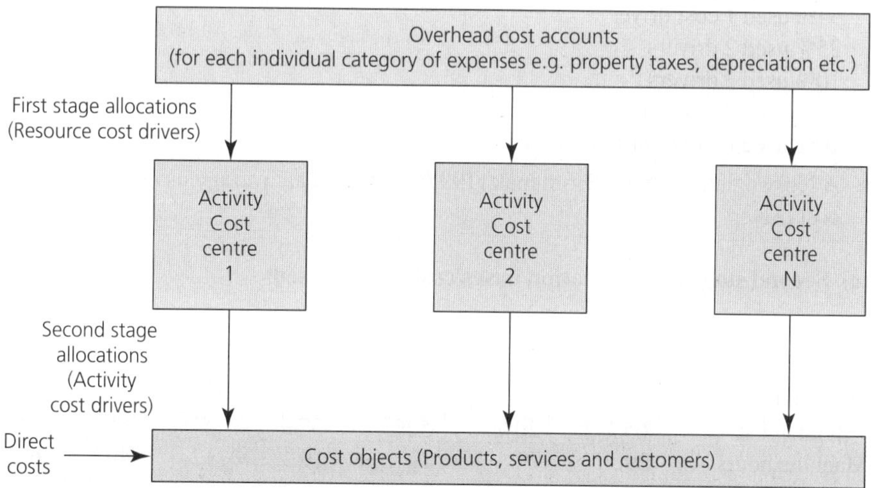

assumed that the company has only five cost centres – machine departments X and Y, an assembly department, and materials handling and general factory support cost centres. The illustration focuses on manufacturing costs but we shall look at non-manufacturing costs later in the chapter. Applying the two-stage allocation process requires the following four steps:

1. assigning all manufacturing overheads to production and service cost centres;
2. reallocating the costs assigned to service cost centres to production cost centres;
3. computing separate overhead rates for each production cost centre;
4. assigning cost centre overheads to products or other chosen cost objects.

EXHIBIT 3.1
Surveys of practice

(a) Cost centres used in the first stage of the two-stage allocation process

- A survey of Australian organizations by Joye and Blayney (1990):
  36% of the responding organizations used a single plant-wide rate
  24% used overhead rates for groups of work centres
  31% used overhead rates for each work centre
  9% used overhead rates for each machine
- A survey of Swedish organizations by Ask and Ax (1992)[a]:
  70% indicated that cost centres consisted of departments
  32% consisted of work cells
  22% consisted of groups of machines
  15% consisted of single machines
- A Norwegian study by Bjornenak (1997b) reported an average of 38.3 cost centres used by the respondents
- A survey of UK organizations by Drury and Tayles (2000):
  14% used less than 6 cost centres
  21% used 6–10 cost centres
  29% used 11–20 cost centres
  36% used more than 20 cost centres

(b) Number of different second stage allocation bases/cost drivers used

- A survey of UK organizations by Drury and Tayles (2000):
  34% used 1 cost driver
  25% used 2 drivers
  10% used 3 drivers
  21% used 3–10 drivers
  10% used more than 10 drivers
- A Norwegian study by Bjornenak (1997a) reported an average usage of 1.79 cost drivers

(c) Second stage cost allocation bases/cost drivers used[a]

	Norway[b]	Holland[c]	Ireland[d]	Australia[e]	Japan[e]	UK[f]	UK[f]
Direct labour hours/cost	65%	20%	52%	57%	57%	68%	73%
Machine hours	29	9	19	19	12	49	26
Direct materials costs	26	6	10	12	11	30	19
Units of output	40	30	28	20	16	42	31
Prime cost				1	21		
Other	23	35	9				
ABC cost drivers						9	7

A survey of Finnish companies by Lukka and Granlund (1996) reported that direct labour costs, direct labour hours, machine hours, materials use and production quantity were the most widely used allocation bases. Usage rates were not reported.

Notes
[a] The reported percentages exceed 100% because many companies used more than one type of cost centre or allocation base.
[b] Bjornenak (1997b).
[c] Boons *et al.* (1994).
[d] Clarke (1995).
[e] Blayney and Yokoyama (1991).
[f] Drury *et al.* (1993) – The first column relates to the responses for automated and the second to non-automated production centres.

EXAMPLE 3.1

The annual overhead costs for the Enterprise Company which has three production centres (two machine centres and one assembly centre) and two service centres (materials procurement and general factory support) are as follows:

	(£)	(£)
Indirect wages and supervision		
Machine centres: X	1 000 000	
Y	1 000 000	
Assembly	1 500 000	
Materials procurement	1 100 000	
General factory support	1 480 000	6 080 000
Indirect materials		
Machine centres: X	500 000	
Y	805 000	
Assembly	105 000	
Materials procurement	0	
General factory support	10 000	1 420 000
Lighting and heating	500 000	
Property taxes	1 000 000	
Insurance of machinery	150 000	
Depreciation of machinery	1 500 000	
Insurance of buildings	250 000	
Salaries of works management	800 000	4 200 000
		11 700 000

The following information is also available:

	Book value of machinery (£)	Area occupied (sq. metres)	Number of employees	Direct labour hours	Machine hours
Machine shop: X	8 000 000	10 000	300	1 000 000	2 000 000
Y	5 000 000	5 000	200	1 000 000	1 000 000
Assembly	1 000 000	15 000	300	2 000 000	
Stores	500 000	15 000	100		
Maintenance	500 000	5 000	100		
	15 000 000	50 000	1000		

Details of total materials issues (i.e. direct and indirect materials) to the production centres are as follows:

	£
Machine shop X	4 000 000
Machine shop Y	3 000 000
Assembly	1 000 000
	8 000 000

To allocate the overheads listed above to the production and service centres we must prepare an overhead analysis sheet, as shown in Exhibit 3.2.

Steps 1 and 2 comprise stage one and steps 3 and 4 relate to the second stage of the two-stage allocation process. Let us now consider each of these steps in detail.

Step 1 – Assigning all manufacturing overheads to production and service cost centres

Using the information given in Example 3.1 our initial objective is to assign all manufacturing overheads to production and service cost centres. To do this requires the preparation of an **overhead analysis sheet**. This document is shown in Exhibit 3.2. In many organizations it will consist only in computer form.

If you look at Example 3.1 you will see that the indirect labour and indirect material costs have been directly traced to cost centres. Although these items cannot be directly assigned to products they can be directly assigned to the cost centres. In other words, they are indirect costs when products are the cost objects and direct costs when cost centres are the cost object. Therefore they are traced directly to the cost centres shown in the overhead analysis sheet in Exhibit 3.2. The remaining costs shown in Example 3.1 cannot be traced directly to the cost centres and must be allocated to the cost centre using appropriate allocation bases. The term **first stage allocation bases** is used to describe allocations at this point. The following list summarizes commonly used first stage allocation bases:

Cost	Basis of allocation
Property taxes, lighting and heating	Area
Employee-related expenditure: works management, works canteen, payroll office	Number of employees
Depreciation and insurance of plant and machinery	Value of items of plant and machinery

Applying the allocation bases to the data given in respect of the Enterprise Company in Example 3.1 it is assumed that property taxes, lighting and heating, and insurance of buildings are related to the total floor area of the buildings, and the benefit obtained by each cost centre can therefore be ascertained according to the proportion of floor area which it occupies. The total floor area of the factory shown in Example 3.1 is 50 000 square metres; machine centre X occupies 20% of this and machine centre Y a further 10%. Therefore, if

EXHIBIT 3.2
Overhead analysis sheet

Item of expenditure	Basis of allocation	Total (£)	Production centres: Machine centre X (£)	Machine centre Y (£)	Assembly (£)	Service centres: Materials procurement (£)	General factory support (£)
Indirect wage and supervision	Direct	6 080 000	1 000 000	1 000 000	1 500 000	1 100 000	1 480 000
Indirect materials	Direct	1 420 000	500 000	805 000	105 000		10 000
Lighting and heating	Area	500 000	100 000	50 000	150 000	150 000	50 000
Property taxes	Area	1 000 000	200 000	100 000	300 000	300 000	100 000
Insurance of machinery	Book value of machinery	150 000	80 000	50 000	10 000	5 000	5 000
Depreciation of machinery	Book value of machinery	1 500 000	800 000	500 000	100 000	50 000	50 000
Insurance of buildings	Area	250 000	50 000	25 000	75 000	75 000	25 000
Salaries of works management	Number of employees	800 000	240 000	160 000	240 000	80 000	80 000
	(1)	11 700 000	2 970 000	2 690 000	2 480 000	1 760 000	1 800 000
Reallocation of service centre costs							
Materials procurement	Value of materials issued	—	880 000	660 000	220 000	1 760 000	
General factory support	Direct labour hours	—	450 000	450 000	900 000		1 800 000
	(2)	11 700 000	4 300 000	3 800 000	3 600 000	—	—
Machine hours and direct labour hours		2 000 000	1 000 000	2 000 000			
Machine hour overhead rate			£2.15	£3.80			
Direct labour hour overhead rate					£1.80		

you refer to the overhead analysis sheet in Exhibit 3.2 you will see that 20% of property taxes, lighting and heating and insurance of buildings are allocated to machine centre X, and 10% are allocated to machine centre Y.

The insurance premium paid and depreciation of machinery are generally regarded as being related to the book value of the machinery. Because the book value of machinery for machine centre X is 8/15 of the total book value and machine centre Y is 5/15 of the total book value then 8/15 and 5/15 of the insurance and depreciation of machinery is allocated to machine centres X and Y.

It is assumed that the amount of time that works management devotes to each cost centre is related to the number of employees in each centre; since 30% of the total employees are employed in machine centre X, 30% of the salaries of works management will be allocated to this centre.

If you now look at the overhead analysis sheet shown in Exhibit 3.2, you will see in the row labelled '(1)' that all manufacturing overheads for the Enterprise Company have been assigned to the three production and two service cost centres.

Step 2 – Reallocating the costs assigned to service cost centres to production cost centres

The next step is to reallocate the costs that have been assigned to service cost centres to production cost centres. **Service departments** (i.e. service cost centres) are those departments that exist to provide services of various kinds to other units within the organization. They are sometimes called **support departments**. The Enterprise Company has two service centres. They are materials procurement and general factory support which includes activities such as production scheduling and machine maintenance. These service centres render essential services that support the production process, but they do not deal directly with the products. Therefore it is not possible to allocate service centre costs to products passing through these centres. To assign costs to products traditional costing systems reallocate service centre costs to production centres that actually work on the product. The method that is chosen to allocate service centre costs to production centre should be related to the benefits that the production centres derive from the service rendered.

We shall assume that the value of materials issued (shown in Example 3.1) provides a suitable approximation of the benefit that each of the production centres receives from materials procurement. Therefore 50% of the value of materials is issued to machine centre X, resulting in 50% of the total costs of materials procurement being allocated to this centre. If you refer to Exhibit 3.2 you will see that £880 000 (50% of material procurement costs of £1 760 000) has been reallocated to machine centre X. It is also assumed that direct labour hours provides an approximation of the benefits received by the production centres from general factory support resulting in the total costs for this centre being reallocated to the production centres proportionate to direct labour hours. Therefore since machine centre X consumes 25% of the direct labour hours £450 000 (25% of the total costs of £1 800 000 assigned to general factory support) has been reallocated to machine centre X. You will see in the row labelled '(2)' in Exhibit 3.2 that all manufacturing costs have now been assigned to the three production centres. This completes the first stage of the two-stage allocation process.

Step 3 – Computing separate overhead rates for each production cost centre

The second stage of the two-stage process is to allocate overheads of each production centre to overheads passing through that centre. The most frequently used allocation bases used by traditional costing systems are based on the amount of time products spend in each production centre – for example direct labour hours, machine hours and direct wages. In respect of non-machine centres, direct labour hours is the most frequently used allocation base. This implies that the overheads incurred by a production centre are closely related to direct labour hours worked. In the case of machine centres a machine hour overhead rate is preferable since most of the overheads (e.g. depreciation) are likely to be more closely related to machine hours. We shall assume that the Enterprise Company uses a **machine hour rate** for the machine production centres and a **direct labour hour rate** for the assembly centre. The overhead rates are calculated by applying the following formula:

$$\frac{\text{cost centre overheads}}{\text{cost centre direct labour hours or machine hours}}$$

The calculations using the information given in Example 3.1 are as follows:

$$\text{Machine centre X} = \frac{\text{£4 300 000}}{\text{2 000 000 machine hours}} = \text{£2.15 per machine hour}$$

$$\text{Machine centre Y} = \frac{\text{£3 800 000}}{\text{1 000 000 machine hours}} = \text{£3.80 per machine hour}$$

$$\text{Assembly department} = \frac{\text{£3 600 000}}{\text{2 000 000 direct labour hours}} = \text{£1.80 per direct labour hour}$$

Step 4 – Assigning cost centre overheads to products or other chosen cost objects

The final step is to allocate the overheads to products passing through the production centres. Therefore if a product spends 10 hours in machine cost centre A overheads of £21.50 (10 × £2.15) will be allocated to the product. We shall compute the manufacturing costs of two products. Product A is a low sales volume product with direct costs of £100. It is manufactured in batches of 100 units and each unit requires 5 hours in machine centre A, 10 hours in machine centre B and 10 hours in the assembly centre. Product B is a high sales volume product thus enabling it to be manufactured in larger batches. It is manufactured in batches of 200 units and each unit requires 10 hours in machine centre A, 20 hours in machine centre B and 20 hours in the assembly centre. Direct costs of £200 have been assigned to product B. The calculations of the manufacturing costs assigned to the products are as follows:

Product A	£
Direct costs (100 units × £100)	10 000
Overhead allocations	
Machine centre A (100 units × 5 machine hours × £2.15)	1 075
Machine centre B (100 units × 10 machine hours × £3.80)	3 800
Assembly (100 units × 10 direct labour hours × £1.80)	1 800
Total cost	16 675
Cost per unit (£16 675/100 units) = £166.75	

Product B	£
Direct costs (200 units × £200)	40 000
Overhead allocations	
Machine centre A (200 units × 10 machine hours × £2.15)	4 300
Machine centre B (200 units × 20 machine hours × £3.80)	15 200
Assembly (200 units × 20 direct labour hours × £1.80)	7 200
Total cost	66 700
Cost per unit (£66 700/200 units) = £333.50	

The overhead allocation procedure is more complicated where service cost centres serve each other. In Example 3.1 it was assumed that materials procurement does not provide any services for general factory support and that general factory support does not provide any services for materials procurement. An understanding of situations where service cost centres do serve each other is not, however, necessary for a general understanding of the overhead procedure, and the problem of service centre reciprocal cost allocations is therefore dealt with in Appendix 3.1.

An illustration of the two-stage process for an ABC system

Earlier in this chapter Figure 3.3 was used to contrast the general features of ABC systems with traditional costing systems. It was pointed out that ABC systems differ from traditional systems by having a greater number of cost centres in the first stage, and a greater number, and variety, of cost drivers/allocation bases in the second stage of the two-stage allocation process. We shall now look at ABC systems in more detail.

You will see from Figure 3.3 that another major distinguishing feature of ABC is that overheads are assigned to each major activity, rather than departments, which normally represent cost centres with traditional systems. **Activities** consist of the aggregation of many different tasks and are described by verbs associated with objects. Typical support activities include schedule production, set-up machines, move materials, purchase materials, inspect items, and process supplier records. When costs are accumulated by activities they are known as **activity cost centres**. Production process activities include machine products and assemble products. Thus within the production process, activity cost centres are often identical to the cost centres used by traditional cost systems.

A further distinguishing feature is that traditional systems normally assign service/support costs by reallocating their costs to production cost centres so that they are assigned to products within the production centre cost driver rates. In contrast, ABC systems tend to establish separate cost driver rates for support centres, and assign the cost of support activities directly to cost objects without any reallocation to production centres.

We shall now use Example 3.1 for the Enterprise Company to illustrate ABC in more detail. It is assumed that the activity cost centres for machining and assembling products are identical to the production cost centres used by the traditional costing system. We shall also assume that three activity cost centres have been established for each of the support functions. They are purchasing components, receiving components and disbursing materials for materials procurement and production scheduling, setting-up machines and a quality inspection of the completed products for general factory support. Both ABC and traditional systems use the same approach to assign costs to cost centres in the first stage of the two-stage allocation process. If you refer to column 2 in the upper section of Exhibit 3.3 you will see that the costs assigned to the production activities have been extracted from row 1 in the overhead analysis sheet shown in Exhibit 3.2, which was used for the traditional costing system. In the overhead analysis sheet we only assigned costs with the traditional costing system to materials procurement and general factory support, and not to the activities within these support functions. However, the costs for the activities within these functions would be derived adopting the same approach as that used in Exhibit 3.2, but to simplify the presentation the cost assignments to the materials procurement and general factory support activity cost centres are not shown.

EXHIBIT 3.3

An illustration of cost assignment with an ABC system

(1) Activity	(2) Activity cost £	(3) Activity cost driver	(4) Quantity of activity cost driver	(5) Activity cost driver rate (Col. 2/Col.4)
Production activities:				
Machining: activity centre A	2 970 000	Number of machine hours	2 000 000 machine hours	£1.485 per hour
Machining: activity centre B	2 690 000	Number of machine hours	1 000 000 machine hours	£2.69 per hour
Assembly	2 480 000	Number of direct labour hours	2 000 000 direct lab. hours	£1.24 per hour
	8 140 000			
Materials procurement activities:				
Purchasing components	960 000	Number of purchase orders	10 000 purchase orders	£96 per order
Receiving components	600 000	Number of material receipts	5 000 receipts	£120 per receipt
Disburse materials	200 000	Number of production runs	2 000 production runs	£100 per production run
	1 760 000			
General factory support activities:				
Production scheduling	1 000 000	Number of production runs	2 000 production runs	£500 per production run
Set-up machines	600 000	Number of set-up hours	12 000 set-up hours	£50 per set-up hour
Quality inspection	200 000	Number of first item inspections	1 000 inspections	£200 per inspection
	1 800 000			
Total cost of all manufacturing activities	11 700 000			

Computation of product costs

(1) Activity	(2) Activity cost driver rate	(3) Quantity of cost driver used by 100 units of product A	(4) Quantity of cost driver used by 200 units of product B	(5) Activity cost assigned to product A (Col. 2 × Col. 3)	(6) Activity cost assigned to product B (Col. 2 × Col. 4)
Machining: activity centre A	£1.485 per hour	500 hours	2 000 hours	742.50	2 970.00
Machining: activity centre B	£2.69 per hour	1 000 hours	4 000 hours	2 690.00	10 760.00
Assembly	£1.24 per hour	1 000 hours	4 000 hours	1 240.00	4 960.00
Purchasing components	£96 per order	1 component	1 component	96.00	96.00
Receiving components	£120 per receipt	1 component	1 component	120.00	120.00
Disburse materials	£100 per production run	5 production runs[a]	1 production run	500.00	100.00
Production scheduling	£500 per production run	5 production runs[a]	1 production run	2 500.00	500.00
Set-up machines	£50 per set-up hour	50 set-up hours	10 set-up hours	2 500.00	500.00
Quality inspection	£200 per inspection	1 inspection	1 inspection	200.00	200.00
Total overhead cost				10 588.50	20 206.00
Units produced				100 units	200 units
Overhead cost *per unit*				£105.88	£101.03
Direct costs *per unit*				100.00	200.00
Total cost *per unit* of output				205.88	301.03

Note

[a] Five production runs are required to machine several unique components before they can be assembled into a final product.

Exhibit 3.3 shows the product cost calculations for an ABC system. By referring to the second column in the upper section of this exhibit you will see that the costs assigned to the purchasing, receiving and disbursement of materials activities total £1 760 000, the same as the total allocated to the materials procurement function by the traditional system shown in Exhibit 3.2. Similarly, the total costs assigned to the production scheduling, set-up and quality inspection activities in column 2 of the upper section of Exhibit 3.3 total £1 800 000, the same as the total costs allocated to the general factory support function in Exhibit 3.2.

Now look at columns 1 and 3 in the upper section of Exhibit 3.3. You will see that with the ABC system The Enterprise Company has established nine activity cost centres and seven different second-stage cost drivers. Note also that the cost drivers for the production activities are the same of those used for the traditional costing system. Based on their observations of ABC systems Kaplan and Cooper (1998) suggest that relatively simple ABC systems having 30–50 activity cost centres and many cost drivers ought to report reasonably accurate costs.

To emphasize the point that ABC systems use cause-and-effect second stage allocations the term cost driver tends to be used instead of allocation base. Cost drivers should be significant determinants of the cost of activities. For example, if the cost of processing purchase orders is determined by the number of purchase orders that each product generates, then the number of purchase orders would represent the cost driver for the cost of processing purchase orders. Other cost drivers used by the Enterprise Company are shown in column 3 of Exhibit 3.3. They are the number of receipts for receiving components, number of production runs for disbursing materials and scheduling production, number of set-up hours for setting up the machines and the number of first item inspections for quality inspection of a batch of completed products. You will see from column 5 in the first section of Exhibit 3.3 that cost driver rates are computed by dividing the activity centre cost by the quantity of the cost driver used.

Activity centre costs are assigned to products by multiplying the cost driver rate by the quantity of the cost driver used by products. These calculations are shown in the second section of Exhibit 3.3. You will see from the first section in Exhibit 3.3 that the costs assigned to the purchasing activity are £960 000 for processing 10 000 purchasing orders resulting in a cost driver rate of £96 per purchasing order. The second section shows that a batch of 100 units of product A, and 200 units of product B, each require one purchased component and thus one purchase order. Therefore purchase order costs of £96 are allocated to each batch. The same approach is used to allocate the costs of the remaining activities shown in Exhibit 3.3. You should now work through Exhibit 3.3 and study the product cost calculations.

The costs assigned to products using each costing system are as follows:

	Traditional costing system £	ABC system £
Product A	166.75	205.88
Product B	333.50	301.03

Compared with the ABC system the traditional system undercosts product A and overcosts product B. By reallocating the service centre costs to the production centres and allocating the costs to products on the basis of either machine hours or direct labour hours the traditional system incorrectly assumes that these allocation bases are the cause of the costs of the support activities. Compared with product A, product B consumes twice as many machine and direct labour hours per unit of output. Therefore, relative to Product A, the traditional costing system allocates twice the amount of support costs to product B.

In contrast, ABC systems create separate cost centres for each major support activity and allocates costs to products using cost drivers that are the significant determinants of the cost of the activities. The ABC system recognizes that a batch of both products consume the same quantity of purchasing, receiving and inspection activities and, for these activities, allocates the same costs to both products. Because product B is manufactured in batches of 200 units, and product A in batches of 100 units, the cost per unit of output for product B is half the amount of Product A for these activities. Product A also has five unique machined components, whereas product B has only one, resulting in a batch of Product A requiring five production runs whereas a batch of Product B only requires one. Therefore, relative to product B, the ABC system assigns five times more costs to product A for the production scheduling and disbursement of materials activities (see columns 5 and 6 in the lower part of Exhibit 3.3). Because product A is a more complex product it requires relatively more support activity resources and the cost of this complexity is captured by the ABC system.

The unit costs derived from traditional and ABC systems must be used with care. For example, if a customer requested a batch of 400 units of product B the cost would not be twice the amount of a batch of 200 units. Assuming that for a batch of 400 units the number of purchase orders, material receipts, production runs, set-up hours and inspections remained the same as that required for a batch of 200 units the cost of the support activities would remain unchanged, but the direct costs would increase by a factor of two to reflect the fact that twice the amount of resources would be required.

Extracting relevant costs for decision-making

The cost computations relating to the Enterprise Company for products A and B represent the costs that should be generated for meeting stock valuation and profit measurement requirements. For decision-making non-manufacturing costs should also be taken into account. In addition, some of the costs that have been assigned to the products may not be relevant for certain decisions. For example, if you look at the overhead analysis sheet in Exhibit 3.2 you will see that property taxes, depreciation of machinery and insurance of buildings and machinery have been assigned to cost centres, and thus included in the costs assigned to products, for both traditional and ABC systems. If these cost are unaffected by a decision to discontinue a product they should not be assigned to products when undertaking product discontinuation reviews. However, if cost information is used to determine selling prices such costs may need to be assigned to products to ensure that the selling price of a customer's order covers a fair share of all organizational costs. It is therefore necessary to ensure that the costs incorporated in the overhead analysis are suitably coded so that different overhead rates can be extracted for different combinations of costs. This will enable relevant cost information to be extracted from the database for meeting different requirements. For an illustration of this approach you should refer to the answer to Review problem 3.27.

Our objective in this chapter has not been to focus on the cost information that should be extracted from the costing system for meeting decision-making requirements. Instead, it is to provide you with an understanding of how cost systems assign costs to cost objects. In Chapter 9 we shall concentrate on the cost information that should be extracted for decision-making. Also, only the basic principles of ABC have been introduced. A more theoretical approach to ABC will be presented in Chapter 10 with an emphasis being given to how cost information generated from an ABC system can be used for decision-making.

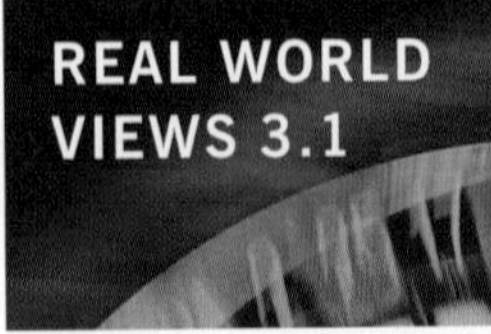

Product diversity and costing system design choice

Two Australian firms, one with three divisions, and the second with two divisions were studied. One of the firms was a leader in the manufacture of products associated with wound management, orthopedics and consumer healthcare ('health care firm'). Each of the three divisions was dedicated to a separate stage of the production of fabric-based first-aid dressings. Division HC1 wove the cloth for the bandages, HC2 applied adhesive gauze to the woven cloth and then slit the cloth into manageable widths for further processing and HC3 was involved in converting the strips into bandages and packaging. The divisions were located in different plants. The second firm is a leading fabric and textile producer. One division manufactures knitted fabrics (FT1) and the other manufactures woven fabrics (FT2).

HC1 and FT1 have the simplest costing systems with all of the overheads accumulated into a single cost pool with overheads allocated to products solely based on a single cost driver, namely direct labour hours (DLHs). In other words, a blanket overhead rate was used. HC2 and HC3 have almost identical costing systems. They have 'work centre cost pools' that reflect manufacturing processes (e.g. in the case of HC2 this includes three cost pools – adhesive mixing, spreading and slitting; in HC3 there were two cost pools). Overheads such as power are directly traced to the work centres. The remaining overheads are allocated to the work centres based on the respective levels of DLHs associated with each of the processes. The work centre overhead rate is then determined by dividing the work centre cost pool by the number of DLHs and allocating the costs to the product according to the consumption of DLHs in each of the work centres.

FT2 was the only research site that had a highly sophisticated costing system. Overheads are allocated to products via a multi-stage allocation process. First, the total budgeted manufacturing overheads are traced directly to nine 'mill' cost pools. Those costs that could not be traced directly are allocated to mills using reasonable allocation bases. For example, personnel department expenses are allocated to mills according to number of personnel and property expenses such as taxes, rates and gardening are allocated according to space occupancy. Each of the nine mill cost pools is divided into 30 'process' cost pools. These represent the major manufacturing stages that products pass through during the manufacturing process. The vast majority of overheads are traced directly to individual processes. For example, each machine is fitted with a meter that enables power, electricity and water to be traced directly to process cost pools.

Once all of the overheads are accumulated in the 'process' cost pools they are allocated to products on the basis of one of two 'unit' level cost drivers, namely direct labour hours and machine hours. The overheads allocated based on DLHs include indirect labour associated with materials handling, packers and factory foremen. Overheads allocated on the basis of machine hours include costs that vary with machine time (e.g. power and electricity) as well as fixed costs such factory management and depreciation.

HC1, HC2 and FT1 all had low product diversity (i.e. products consumed organizational resources in similar proportions) and there was reasonable to high satisfaction with the information provided by the costing system. Both HC3 and FT2 had high levels of product diversity. FT2 had a relatively sophisticated costing system while HC3 maintained a simplistic system. The users of the costing system at FT2 were very satisfied with the system. The level of satisfaction at FT2 is in stark contrast to that found in HC3. Costing information at HC3 is particularly important for determining product costs. However, management believe that the costs are highly inaccurate and are inadequate for setting prices. Overheads were large and product diversity was high, creating the need for a relatively sophisticated costing system. However, a simplistic costing system was implemented. This absence of 'fit' was a major dissatisfaction with the existing costing system. In contrast, there was a 'fit' between the costing systems and the level of product diversity in the four other business units and a general satisfaction with the costing systems.

Source: Adapted from Abernathy, M.A. *et al.*, Product diversity and costing system design choice: field study evidence, *Management Accounting Research*, 2001, 12, pp 261–79.

Budgeted overhead rates

Our discussion in this chapter has assumed that the *actual* overheads for an accounting period have been allocated to the products. However, the calculation of overhead rates based on the *actual* overheads incurred during an accounting period causes a number of problems. First, the product cost calculations have to be delayed until the end of the accounting period, since the overhead rate calculations cannot be obtained before this date, but information on product costs is required quickly if it is to be used for monthly profit calculations and inventory valuations or as a basis for setting selling prices. Secondly, one may argue that the timing problem can be resolved by calculating actual overhead rates at more frequent intervals, say on a monthly basis, but the objection to this proposal is that a large amount of overhead expenditure is fixed in the short term whereas activity will vary from month to month, giving large fluctuations in the overhead rates. Consider Example 3.2.

Such fluctuating overhead rates are not representative of typical, normal production conditions. Management has committed itself to a specific level of fixed costs in the light of foreseeable needs for beyond one month. Thus, where production fluctuates, monthly overhead rates may be volatile. Furthermore, some costs such as repairs, maintenance and heating are not incurred evenly throughout the year. Therefore, if monthly overhead rates are used, these costs will not be allocated fairly to units of output. For example, heating costs would be charged only to winter production so that products produced in winter would be more expensive than those produced in summer.

An average, annualized rate based on the relationship of total annual overhead to total annual activity is more representative of typical relationships between total costs and volume than a monthly rate. What is required is a normal product cost based on average long-term production rather than an actual product cost, which is affected by month-to-month fluctuations in production volume. Taking these factors into consideration, it is preferable to establish a **budgeted overhead rate** based on annual *estimated* overhead expenditure and activity. Consequently the procedure outlined in the previous sections for calculating cost centre overhead rates for traditional and ABC systems should be based on *standard* activity levels and not *actual* activity levels. We shall consider how we might determine standard activity in Chapter 7. However, at this point you should note that surveys of product costing practices indicate that most organizations use annual budgeted activity as a measure of standard activity.

Under- and over-recovery of overheads

The effect of calculating overhead rates based on budgeted annual overhead expenditure and activity is that it will be most unlikely that the overhead allocated to products manufactured during the period will be the same as the actual overhead incurred. Consider a situation where

EXAMPLE 3.2

The fixed overheads for Euro are £24 000 000 per annum, and monthly production varies from 400 000 to 1 000 000 hours. The monthly overhead rate for fixed overhead will therefore fluctuate as follows:

Monthly overhead	£2 000 000	£2 000 000
Monthly production	400 000 hours	1 000 000 hours
Monthly overhead rate	£5 per hour	£2 per hour

Overhead expenditure that is fixed in the short term remains constant each month, but monthly production fluctuates because of holiday periods and seasonal variations in demand. Consequently the overhead rate varies from £2 to £5 per hour. It would be unreasonable for a product worked on in one month to be allocated overheads at a rate of £5 per hour and an identical product worked on in another month allocated at a rate of only £2 per hour.

the estimated annual fixed overheads are £2 000 000 and the estimated annual activity is 1 000 000 direct labour hours. The estimated fixed overhead rate will be £2 per hour. Assume that actual overheads are £2 000 000 and are therefore identical with the estimate, but that actual activity is 900 000 direct labour hours instead of the estimated 1 000 000 hours. In this situation only £1 800 000 will be charged to production. This calculation is based on 900 000 direct labour hours at £2 per hour, giving an under-recovery of overheads of £200 000.

Consider an alternative situation where the actual overheads are £1 950 000 instead of the estimated £2 000 000, and actual activity is 1 000 000 direct labour hours, which is identical to the original estimate. In this situation 1 000 000 direct labour hours at £2 per hour will be charged to production giving an over-recovery of £50 000. This example illustrates that there will be an **under- or over-recovery of overheads** whenever actual activity or overhead expenditure is different from the budgeted overheads and activity used to estimate the budgeted overhead rate. This under- or over-recovery of fixed overheads is also called a **volume variance**.

Accounting regulations in most countries recommend that the under- or over-recovery of overheads should be regarded as a period cost adjustment. For example, the UK Statement of Standard Accounting Practice on Stocks and Work in Progress (SSAP 9) recommends the allocation of overheads in the valuation of inventories and work in progress needs to be based on the company's normal level of activity and that any under- or over-recovery should be written off in the current year. This procedure is illustrated in Figure 3.4. Note that any under- or over-recovery of overhead is not allocated to products. Also note that the under-recovery is recorded as an expense in the current accounting period whereas an over-recovery is recorded as a reduction in the expenses for the period. Finally you should note that our discussion here is concerned with how to treat any under- or over-recovery for the purpose of financial accounting and its impact on inventory valuation and profit measurement.

Maintaining the database at standard costs

Most organizations whose activities consist of a series of common or repetitive operations maintain their database at standard, rather than actual cost, for both traditional and ABC

FIGURE 3.4 *Illustration of under-recovery of factory overheads*

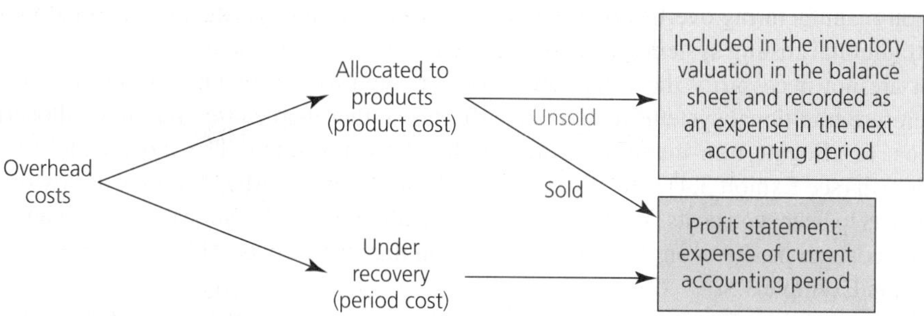

systems. **Standard costs** are pre-determined target costs that should be incurred under efficient operating conditions. For example, assume that the standard direct labour cost for performing a particular operation is £40 (consisting of 5 hours at £8 per hour) and the standard cost of a purchased component (say component Z) is £50. The direct costs for a product requiring only this operation and the purchased component Z would be recorded in the database at a standard cost of £90. Assuming that the product only passed through a single cost centre with a budgeted overhead rate of £20 per direct labour hour the overhead cost for the product would be recorded in the database at £100 standard cost (5 standard direct labour hours at £20 per hour). Instead of a product being recorded in the database at its standard *unit* cost the database may consist of the standard costs of a batch of output, such as normal batch sizes of say 100 or 200 units output of the product.

When a standard costing system is used the database is maintained at standard cost and actual output is costed at the standard cost. Actual costs are recorded, but not at the individual product level, and an adjustment is made at the end of the accounting period by recording as a period cost the difference between standard cost and actual cost for the actual output. This adjustment ensures that the standard costs are converted to actual costs in the profit statement for meeting external financial accounting reporting requirements.

It is not important at this point that you have a detailed understanding of a standard costing system. However, it is important that you are aware that a database may consist of standard (estimated) costs rather than actual costs. We shall look at standard costing in detail in Chapters 18 and 19.

Non-manufacturing overheads

In respect of financial accounting, only manufacturing costs are allocated to products. Non-manufacturing overheads are regarded as period costs and are disposed of in exactly the same way as the under- or over-recovery of manufacturing overheads outlined in Figure 3.4. For external reporting it is therefore unnecessary to allocate non-manufacturing overheads to products. However, for decision-making non-manufacturing costs should be assigned to products. For example, in many organizations it is not uncommon for selling prices to be based on estimates of total cost or even actual cost. Housing contractors and garages often charge for their services by adding a percentage profit margin to actual cost.

Some non-manufacturing costs may be a direct cost of the product. Delivery costs, salesmen's salaries and travelling expenses may be directly identifiable with the product, but it is likely that many non-manufacturing overheads cannot be allocated directly to specific products. On what basis should we allocate non-manufacturing overheads? The answer is that we should select an allocation base/cost driver that corresponds most closely to non-manufacturing overheads. The problem is that allocation bases that are widely used by traditional costing systems, such as direct labour hours, machine hours and direct labour cost are not necessarily those that are closely related to non-manufacturing overheads. Therefore traditional systems tend to use arbitrary, rather than cause-and-effect allocation bases, to allocate non-manufacturing overheads to products. The most widely used approach (see Exhibit 3.4) is to allocate non-manufacturing overheads on the ability of the products to bear such costs. This approach can be implemented by allocating non-manufacturing costs to products on the basis of their manufacturing costs. This procedure is illustrated in Example 3.3.

Because of the arbitrary nature of the cost allocations, some organizations that use traditional costing systems as a basis for setting selling prices do not to allocate non-manufacturing overheads to products. Instead, they add a percentage profit margin to each product so that it provides a profit contribution and a contribution to non-manufacturing overheads. We shall consider in more detail how cost information can be used in determining selling prices in Chapter 11. Recent developments in ABC have provided a mechanism for more accurately assigning non-manufacturing overheads to products. These developments will be explained in Chapter 10 when ABC is examined in more depth.

Summary

The following items relate to the learning objectives listed at the beginning of the chapter.

- **Distinguish between cause-and-effect and arbitrary allocations.**

  Direct costs can be directly traced to cost objects whereas indirect costs cannot. Therefore, indirect costs must be assigned using cost allocation bases. Allocation bases which are significant determinants of costs that are being allocated are described as cause-and-effect allocations whereas arbitrary allocations refer to allocation bases that are not the significant determinants of the costs. To accurately measure the cost of resources used by cost objects cause-and-effect allocations should be used.

- **Explain why different cost information is required for different purposes.**

  Manufacturing organizations assign costs to products for two purposes: first for external (financial accounting) profit measurement and inventory valuation purposes in order to allocate manufacturing costs incurred during a period to cost of goods sold and inventories; secondly to provide useful information for managerial decision-making requirements. Financial accounting regulations specify that only manufacturing costs should be assigned to products for meeting inventory and profit measurement requirements. Both manufacturing and non-manufacturing costs, however, may be relevant for decision-making. In addition, not all costs that are assigned to products for inventory valuation and profit measurement are relevant for decision-making. For example, costs that will not be affected by a decision (e.g. depreciation) are normally not relevant for decision-making.

- **Describe how cost systems differ in terms of their level of sophistication.**

  Cost systems range from simplistic to sophisticated. Simplistic systems are inexpensive to operate, involve extensive use of arbitrary allocations, have a high likelihood of reporting inaccurate product costs and generally result in a high cost of errors. Sophisticated costing systems are more expensive to operate, rely more extensively on cause-and-effect allocations, generally report more accurate product costs and have a low cost of errors. Further distinguishing features are that simplistic costing systems have a small number of first-stage cost centres/pools and use a single second-stage cost

EXHIBIT 3.4
Methods used by UK organizations to allocate non-manufacturing overheads to products

	(%)
Allocation as a percentage of total manufacturing cost	32
Direct labour hours/cost methods	25
Percentage of total selling price	12
Non-manufacturing overheads not traced to products	23
Other method	8
	100

SOURCE: Drury *et al.* (1993).

EXAMPLE 3.3

The estimated non-manufacturing and manufacturing costs of a company for the year ending 31 December are £500 000 and £1 million respectively. The non-manufacturing overhead absorption rate is calculated as follows:

$$\frac{\text{estimated non-manufacturing overhead}}{\text{estimated manufacturing cost}}$$

In percentage terms each product will be allocated with non-manufacturing overheads at a rate of 50% of its total manufacturing cost.

driver. In contrast, sophisticated costing systems use many first-stage cost centres/pools and many different types of second-stage drivers.

- **Understand the factors influencing the choice of an optimal costing system.**

  The optimal costing system is different for different organizations and should be determined on a costs versus benefits basis. Simplistic costing systems are appropriate in organizations whose indirect costs are a low percentage of total costs and which also have a fairly standardized product range, all consuming organizational resources in similar proportions. Under these circumstances simplistic costing systems may report costs that are sufficiently accurate for decision-making purposes. Conversely, organizations with a high proportion of indirect costs, whose products consume organizational resources in different proportions are likely to require sophisticated costing systems. Relying on sophisticated costing systems under these circumstances is likely to result in the additional benefits from reporting more accurate costs exceeding the costs of operating more sophisticated systems.

- **Explain why departmental overhead rates should be used in preference to a single blanket overhead rate.**

  A blanket (also known as plant-wide) overhead rate establishes a single overhead rate for the organization as a whole whereas departmental rates involve indirect costs being accumulated by different departments and a separate overhead rate being established for each department. A blanket overhead rate can only be justified when all products or services consume departmental overheads in approximately the same proportions. Such circumstances are unlikely to be applicable to most organizations resulting in blanket overheads generally reporting inaccurate product/service costs.

- **Construct an overhead analysis sheet and calculate cost centre allocation rates.**

  Cost centre overhead allocation rates are established and assigned to cost objects using the two-stage allocation overhead procedure. In the first stage, an overhead analysis sheet is used to (a) allocate overheads to production and service centres or departments and (b) to reallocate the total service department overheads to production departments. The second stage involves (a) the calculation of appropriate departmental overhead rates and (b) the allocation of overheads to products passing through each department. These steps were illustrated using data presented in Example 3.1.

- **Distinguish between traditional and activity-based costing systems.**

  The major distinguishing features of ABC compared with traditional costing systems are that ABC systems assign costs to activity cost centres rather than departments. ABC systems thus tend to use a greater number of cost centres in the first-stage of the allocation process. In the second-stage they also use a greater number, and variety, of second-stage allocation bases that mostly rely on cause-and-effect allocation bases. In contrast, traditional systems use second-stage allocation bases that rely on arbitrary allocations. To emphasize the point that ABC systems mostly use second-stage cause-and-effect allocation bases the term cost driver tends to be used instead of allocation base.

- **Justify why budgeted overhead rates should be used in preference to actual overhead rates.**

  Because the uses of actual overhead rates causes a delay in the calculation of product or service costs, and the use of monthly rates causes fluctuations in the overhead rates throughout the year, it is recommended that annual budgeted overhead rates should be used.

- **Calculate and explain the treatment of the under/over recovery of overheads.**

  The use of annual budgeted overhead rates gives an under- or over-recovery of overheads whenever actual overhead expenditure or activity is different from budget. Any under- or over-recovery is generally regarded as a period cost adjustment and written off to the profit and loss statement and thus not allocated to products.

- **Additional learning objectives presented in Appendices 3.1 and 3.2.**

  The appendices to this chapter include the following two additional learning objectives: (1) to be able to reallocate service department costs to production departments when service departments provide services for other service departments as well as production departments, and (2) to compute overhead allocation rates for other less widely used second-stage methods used by traditional costing systems. These topics tend to be included in the syllabus requirements of the examinations set by professional accountancy bodies but may not be part of the course curriculum for other courses. You can omit Appendices 3.1 and 3.2 if these topics are not part of your course curriculum.

Appendix 3.1: Inter-service department reallocations

Service departments provide services for other service departments as well as for production departments. For example, a personnel department provides services for other service departments such as the power generating plant, maintenance department and stores. The power generating department also provides heat and light for other service departments, including the personnel department, and so on. When such interactions occur, the allocation process can become complicated. Difficulties arise because each service department begins to accumulate charges from other service departments from which it receives services, and these must be reallocated back to the user department. Once it has begun, this allocation and reallocation process can continue for a long time before a solution is found. The problem is illustrated in Example 3A.1. We shall use the example to illustrate four different methods of allocating the service department costs:

1. **repeated distribution method**;
2. **simultaneous equation method**;
3. **specified order of closing method**;
4. **direct allocation method**.

1. Repeated distribution method

Where this method is adopted, the service department costs are repeatedly allocated in the specified percentages until the figures become too small to be significant. You can see from line 2 of Exhibit 3A.1 that the overheads of service department 1 are allocated according to the prescribed percentages. As a result, some of the overheads of service department 1 are transferred to service department 2. In line 3 the overheads of service department 2 are allocated, which means that service department 1 receives some further costs. The costs of service department 1 are again allocated, and service department 2 receives some further costs. This process continues until line 7, by which time the costs have become so small that any further detailed apportionments are unnecessary. As a result, the total overheads in line 8 of £152 040 are allocated to production departments only.

2. Simultaneous equation method

When this method is used simultaneous equations are initially established as follows: Let

$$x = \text{total overhead of service department 1}$$
$$y = \text{total overhead of service department 2}$$

The total overhead transferred into service departments 1 and 2 can be expressed as

$$x = 14\,040 + 0.2y$$
$$y = 18\,000 + 0.1x$$

Rearranging the above equations:

$$x - 0.2y = 14\,040 \qquad (1)$$
$$-0.1x + y = 18\,000 \qquad (2)$$

We can now multiply equation (1) by 5 and equation (2) by 1, giving

$$5x - y = 70\,200$$
$$-0.1x + y = 18\,000$$

Adding the above equations together we have

$$4.9x = 88\,200$$

Therefore $$x = 18\,000\ (= 88\,200/4.9)$$

EXAMPLE 3A.1

A company has three production departments and two service departments. The overhead analysis sheet provides the following totals of the overheads analysed to production and service departments:

		(£)
Production department	X	48 000
	Y	42 000
	Z	30 000
Service department	1	14 040
	2	18 000
		152 040

The expenses of the service departments are apportioned as follows:

	Production departments			Service departments	
	X	Y	Z	1	2
Service department 1	20%	40%	30%	—	10%
Service department 2	40%	20%	20%	20%	—

EXHIBIT 3A.1

Repeated distribution method

	Production departments			Service departments		
Line	X	Y	Z	1	2	Total
1 Allocation as per overhead analysis	48 000	42 000	30 000	14 040	18 000	152 040
2 Allocation of service department 1	2 808 (20%)	5 616 (40%)	4 212 (30%)	(14 040)	1 404 (10%)	
					19 404	
3 Allocation of service department 2	7 762 (40%)	3 881 (20%)	3 880 (20%)	3 881 (20%)	(19 404)	
4 Allocation of service department 1	776 (20%)	1 552 (40%)	1 165 (30%)	(3 881)	388 (10%)	
5 Allocation of service department 2	154 (40%)	78 (20%)	78 (20%)	78 (20%)	(388)	
6 Allocation of service department 1	16 (20%)	31 (40%)	23 (30%)	(78)	8 (10%)	
7 Allocation of service department 2	4 (40%)	2 (20%)	2 (20%)	—	(8)	
8 Total overheads	59 520	53 160	39 360	—	—	152 040

Substituting this value for x in equation (1), we have

$$18\,000 - 0.2y = 14\,040$$

Therefore $-0.2y = -3\,960$

Therefore $y = 19\,800$

We now apportion the values for x and y to the production departments in the agreed percentages.

Line	X	Y	Z	Total
1 Allocation as per overhead analysis	48 000	42 000	30 000	120 000
2 Allocation of service department 1	3 600 (20%)	7 200 (40%)	5 400 (30%)	16 200
3 Allocation of service department 2	7 920 (40%)	3 960 (20%)	3 960 (20%)	15 840
4	59 520	53 160	39 360	152 040

You will see from line 2 that the value for X (service department 1) of £18 000 is allocated in the specified percentages. Similarly, in line 3 the value for Y (service department 2) of £19 800 is apportioned in the specified percentages. As a result the totals in line 4 are in agreement with the totals in line 8 of the repeated distribution method (Exhibit 3A.1).

3. Specified order of closing

If this method is used the service departments' overheads are allocated to the production departments in a certain order. The service department that does the largest proportion of work for other service departments is closed first; the service department that does the second largest proportion of work for other service departments is closed second; and so on. Return charges are not made to service departments whose costs have previously been allocated. Let us now apply this method to the information contained in Example 3A.1. The results are given in Exhibit 3A.2.

The costs of service department 2 are allocated first (line 2) because 20% of its work is related to service department 1, whereas only 10% of the work of service department 1 is related to service department 2. In line 3 we allocate the costs of service department 1, but the return charges are not made to department 2. This means that the proportions allocated have changed as 10% of the costs of service department 1 have not been allocated to service department 2. Therefore 20% out of a 90% total or 2/9 of the costs of service department 1 are allocated to department X.

You will see that the totals allocated in line 4 do not agree with the totals allocated under the repeated distribution or simultaneous equation methods. This is because the specified order of closing method sacrifices accuracy for clerical convenience. However, if this method provides a close approximation to an alternative accurate calculation then there are strong arguments for its use.

4. Direct allocation method

This method is illustrated in Exhibit 3A.3. It ignores inter-service department service reallocations. Therefore service department costs are reallocated only to production

EXHIBIT 3A.2

Specified order of closing method

Line	Production departments			Service departments		Total
	X	Y	Z	1	2	
1 Allocation as per overhead analysis	48 000	42 000	30 000	14 040	18 000	152 040
2 Allocate service department 2	7 200 (40%)	3 600 (20%)	3 600 (20%)	3 600 (20%)	(18 000)	
3 Allocate service department 1	3 920 (2/9)	7 840 (4/9)	5 880 (3/9)	(17 640)		
4	59 120	53 440	39 480	—	—	152 040

EXHIBIT 3A.3

Direct allocation method

Line	Production departments			Service departments		Total
	X	Y	Z	1	2	
1 Allocation as per overhead analysis	48 000	42 000	30 000	14 040	18 000	152 040
2 Allocate service department 1	3 120 (2/9)	6 240 (4/9)	4 680 (3/9)	(14 040)		
3 Allocate service department 2	9 000 (4/8)	4 500 (2/8)	4 500 (2/8)	—	(18 000)	
4	60 120	52 740	39 180	—	—	152 040

departments. This means that the proportions allocated have changed as 10% of the costs of service department 1 have not been allocated to service department 2. Therefore 20% out of a 90% total, or 2/9 of the costs of service department 1, are allocated to department X, 4/9 are allocated to department Y and 3/9 are allocated to department Z. Similarly the proportions allocated for service department 2 have changed with 4/8 (40% out of 80%) of the costs of service department 2 being allocated department X, 2/8 to department Y and 2/8 to department Z. The only justification for using the direct allocation method is its simplicity. The method is recommended when inter-service reallocations are relatively insignificant.

Use of mathematical models

In practice, the problems of service department allocations are likely to be far more complex than is apparent from the simple example illustrated here. For example, it is likely that more than two service departments will exist. However, it is possible to solve the allocation problem by using computer facilities based on mathematical models. For example, with the aid of computer facilities, matrix algebra can be easily applied to situations where many service departments exist. For a discussion of the application of the matrix method to the reciprocal allocation of service department costs see Kaplan and Atkinson (1998). See also Elphick (1983) for a description of an approach that has been adopted by the ICI group.

Appendix 3.2: Other allocation bases used by traditional systems

In the main body of this chapter it was pointed out that traditional costing systems tend to rely on using two second stage allocation bases – namely, direct labour hours and machine hours. Example 3.1 was used to illustrate the application of these allocation bases. With traditional systems it is generally assumed that overhead expenditure is related to output measured by either direct labour hours or machine hours required for a given volume. Products with a high direct labour or machine hour content are therefore assumed to consume a greater proportion of overheads. In addition, to direct labour and machine hours, the following allocation bases are also sometimes used by traditional costing systems:

1. **direct wages percentage method**;
2. **units of output method**;
3. **direct materials percentage method**;
4. **prime cost percentage method**.

Each of these methods is illustrated using the information given in Example 3A.2.

1. Direct wages percentage method

The direct wages percentage overhead rate is calculated as follows:

$$\frac{\text{estimated departmental overheads} \times 100}{\text{estimated direct wages}}$$

Using information given in Example 3A.2,

$$\frac{£200\,000}{£250\,000} \times 100 = 80\% \text{ of direct wages}$$

If we assume that the direct wages cost for a product is £20 then overheads of £16 (80% × £20) will be allocated to the product.

The direct wages percentage method is suitable only where uniform wage rates apply within a cost centre or department. In such a situation this method will yield exactly the same results as the direct labour hour method. However, consider a situation where wage rates are not uniform. Products X and Y spend 20 hours in the same production department,

EXAMPLE 3A.2

The budgeted overheads for a department for the next accounting period are £200 000. In addition, the following information is available for the period:

Estimated direct wages	£250 000
Estimated direct materials	£100 000
Estimated output	10 000 units

but product X requires skilled labour and product Y requires unskilled labour, with direct wages costs respectively of £200 and £100. If we apply the direct wages percentage overhead rate of 80% we should allocate overheads of £160 to product X and £80 to product Y. If both products spend the same amount of time in the department, are such apportioned amounts fair? The answer would appear to be negative, and the direct wages percentage method should therefore only be recommended when similar wage rates are paid to direct employees in a production department.

2. Units of output method

If this method is used, the overhead rate is calculated as follows:

$$\frac{\text{estimated departmental overhead}}{\text{estimated output}}$$

Using the information given in Example 3A.2, this would give an overhead rate of £20 per unit produced. The units of output method is only suitable where all units produced within a department are identical. In other works, it is best suited to a process costing system, and it is not recommended for a job costing system where all jobs or products spend a different amount of time in each production department. If, for example, two of the units produced in Example 3A.2 required 100 hours and 2 hours respectively then they would both be allocated £20. Such an allocation would not be logical.

3. Direct materials percentage method

The direct materials percentage overhead rate is calculated as follows:

$$\frac{\text{estimated departmental overhead}}{\text{estimated direct materials}}$$

Using the information given in Example 3A.2,

$$\frac{\pounds 200\ 000}{\pounds 100\ 000} = 200\% \text{ of direct materials}$$

If we assume that the direct material cost incurred by a product in the department is £50 then the product will be allocated with £100 for a share of the overheads of the department.

If the direct materials percentage overhead rate is used, the overheads allocated to products will bear little relationship to the amount of time that products spend in each department. Consequently, this method of recovery cannot normally be recommended, unless the majority of overheads incurred in a department are related to materials rather than time. In particular, the method is appropriate for allocating materials handling expenses to products. With this approach, a cost centre is created for material handling expenses and the expenses are allocated to products using a materials handling overhead rate (normally the direct materials percentage allocation method). Companies that use a materials handling overhead rate allocate the remaining factory overheads to products using one or more of the allocation bases described in this chapter.

4. Prime cost percentage method

The prime cost percentage overhead rate is calculated as follows:

$$\frac{\text{estimated departmental overheads}}{\text{estimated prime cost}} \times 100$$

Using the information given in Example 3A.2, you will see that the estimated prime cost is £350 000, which consists of direct wages of £250 000 plus direct materials of £100 000. The calculation of the overhead rate is

$$\frac{\pounds 200\,000}{\pounds 350\,000} \times 100 = 57.14\%$$

A product that incurs £100 prime cost in the department will be allocated £57.14 for the departmental overheads.

As prime cost consists of direct wages and direct materials, the disadvantages that apply to the direct materials and direct wages percentage methods also apply to the prime cost percentage method of overhead recovery. Consequently, the prime cost method is not recommended.

Key terms and concepts

activities (p. 72)
activity-based-costing (ABC) (p. 58)
activity cost centre (p. 72)
allocation base (p. 58)
arbitrary allocation (p. 58)
blanket overhead rate (p. 62)
budgeted overhead rates (p. 77)
cause-and-effect allocations (p. 58)
cost allocation (p. 58)
cost centre (p. 63)
cost driver (p. 58)
cost pool (p. 63)
cost tracing (p. 58)
direct allocation method (p. 83)
direct labour hour rate (p. 71)
direct materials percentage method (p. 87)
direct wages percentage method (p. 87)
first stage allocation bases (p. 68)
job cards (p. 61)
machine hour rate (p. 71)
materials requisition (p. 61)
overhead analysis sheet (p. 68)
overheads (p. 58)
plant-wide rate (p. 62)
prime cost percentage method (p. 87)
repeated distribution method (p. 83)
service departments (p. 70)
simultaneous equation method (p. 83)
specified order of closing method (p. 83)
standard costs (p. 79)
support departments (p. 70)
time sheets (p. 61)
traditional costing systems (p. 58)
under- or over-recovery of overheads (p. 78)
units of output method (p. 87)
volume variance (p. 78)

Recommended reading

If your course requires a detailed understanding of accounting for direct labour and materials you should refer to Chapter 3 of Drury (2003). Alternatively, you can look at this chapter on the website supporting this book. For an explanation of how you can access the website you should refer to the preface. For a more detailed review of cost allocations for different purposes see Ahmed and Scapens (1991, 2000). You should refer to Dhavale (1989) for a review of overhead allocations in an advanced automated environment. Detailed references for these readings are provided in the bibliography at the end of the book.

Key examination points

A typical question (e.g. Review problem 3.24) will require you to analyse overheads by departments and calculate appropriate overhead allocation rates. These questions may require a large number of calculations, and it is possible that you will make calculation errors. Do make sure that your answer is clearly presented, since marks tend to be allocated according to whether you have adopted the correct method. You are recommended to present your answer in a format similar to Exhibit 3.2. For a traditional costing system you should normally recommend a direct labour hour rate if a department is non-mechanized and a machine hour rate if machine hours are the dominant activity. You should only recommend the direct wages percentage method when the rates within a non-mechanized department are uniform.

Where a question requires you to present information for decision-making, do not include apportioned fixed overheads in the calculations. Remember the total manufacturing costs should be calculated for stock valuation, but incremental costs should be calculated for decision-making purposes (see answer to Review problem 3.27).

Finally, ensure that you can calculate under- or over-recoveries of overheads. To check your understanding of this topic you should refer to the solution to Review problem 3.26.

Assessment material

Review questions

The review questions are short questions that enable you to assess your understanding of the main topics included in the chapter. The numbers in parentheses provide you with the page numbers to refer to if you cannot answer a specific question.

Review problems

The review problems are more complex and require you to relate and apply the chapter content to various business problems. The problems are graded by their level of difficulty. The multiple-choice questions are the least demanding and normally take less than 10 minutes to complete. Fully worked solutions to the review problems are provided in a separate section at the end of the book. For those questions in the white box the worked solutions are provided in the *Student's Manual* accompanying this book. Further review problems for this chapter are available on the accompanying website www.drury-online.com. The answers to these problems are available for lecturers on the lecturer's password protected section of the website.

Case studies

The website also includes over 30 case study problems. A list of these cases is provided in Part Seven of this book. Cases that are relevant to the content of this chapter include Oak City and Gustavsson, AB.

Review questions

3.1 Why are indirect costs not directly traced to cost objects in the same way as direct costs? *(p. 58)*

3.2 Define cost tracing, cost allocation, allocation base and cost driver. *(p. 58)*

3.3 Distinguish between arbitrary and cause-and-effect allocations. *(p. 58)*

3.4 Explain how cost information differs for profit measurement/inventory valuation requirements compared with decision-making requirements. *(pp. 58–59)*

3.5 Explain why cost systems should differ in terms of their level of sophistication. *(pp. 60–61)*

3.6 Describe the process of assigning direct labour and direct materials to cost objects. *(p. 61)*

3.7 Why are separate departmental or cost centre overhead rates preferred to a plant-wide (blanket) overhead rate? *(pp. 61–63)*

3.8 Describe the two-stage overhead allocation procedure. *(p. 64)*

3.9 Define the term 'activities'. *(p. 72)*

3.10 Describe two important features that distinguish between activity-based costing and traditional costing systems. *(p. 72)*

3.11 Why are some overhead costs sometimes not relevant for decision-making purposes? *(p. 75)*

3.12 Why are budgeted overhead rates preferred to actual overhead rates? *(p. 77)*

3.13 Give two reasons for the under or over-recovery of overheads at the end of the accounting period. *(pp. 77–78)*

Review problems

3.14 **Intermediate**

A company uses a predetermined overhead recovery rate based on machine hours. Budgeted factory overhead for a year amounted to £720 000, but actual factory overhead incurred was £738 000. During the year, the company absorbed £714 000 of factory overhead on 119 000 actual machine hours.

What was the company's budgeted level of machine hours for the year?

A 116 098
B 119 000
C 120 000
D 123 000

ACCA Foundation Paper 3

3.15 **Intermediate**

A company absorbs overheads on machine hours which were budgeted at 11 250 with overheads of £258 750. Actual results were 10 980 hours with overheads of £254 692.

Overheads were:

A under-absorbed by £2152
B over-absorbed by £4058
C under-absorbed by £4058
D over-absorbed by £2152

CIMA Stage 1

3.16 **Intermediate**

The following data are to be used for sub-questions (i) and (ii) below:

Budgeted labour hours	8500
Budgeted overheads	£148 750
Actual labour hours	7928
Actual overheads	£146 200

(i) Based on the data given above, what is the labour hour overhead absorption rate?

A £17.50 per hour
B £17.20 per hour
C £18.44 per hour
D £18.76 per hour

(ii) Based on the data given above, what is the amount of overhead under/over-absorbed?

A £2550 under-absorbed
B £2529 over-absorbed
C £2550 over-absorbed
D £7460 under-absorbed

CIMA Stage 1

3.17 **Intermediate**

A firm makes special assemblies to customers' orders and uses job costing. The data for a period are:

	Job no. AA10 (£)	Job no. BB15 (£)	Job no. CC20 (£)
Opening WIP	26 800	42 790	—
Material added in period	17 275	—	18 500
Labour for period	14 500	3 500	24 600

The budgeted overheads for the period were £126 000.

(i) What overhead should be added to job number CC20 for the period?

A £24 600
B £65 157
C £72 761
D £126 000

(ii) Job no. BB15 was completed and delivered during the period and the firm wishes to earn $33^1/_3$% profit on sales.

What is the selling price of job number BB15?

A £69 435
B £75 521
C £84 963
D £138 870

(iii) What was the approximate value of closing work in progress at the end of the period?

A £58 575
B £101 675
C £147 965
D £217 323

CIMA Stage 1

3.18 Intermediate

A company absorbs overheads on machine hours. In a period, actual machine hours were 17 285, actual overheads were £496 500 and there was under-absorption of £12 520.

What was the budgeted level of overheads?

A £483 980
B £496 500
C £509 020
D It cannot be calculated from the information provided.

CIMA Stage 1 Cost Accounting

3.19 Intermediate

Canberra has established the following information regarding fixed overheads for the coming month:

Budgeted information:

Fixed overheads	£180 000
Labour hours	3 000
Machine hours	10 000
Units of production	5 000

Actual fixed costs for the last month were £160 000.

Canberra produces many different products using highly automated manufacturing processes and absorbs overheads on the most appropriate basis.

What will be the pre-determined overhead absorption rate?

A £16
B £18
C £36
D £60

ACCA Paper 1.2 – Financial information for Management

3.20 Intermediate

The management accountant's report shows that fixed production overheads were over-absorbed in the last accounting period. The combination that is certain to lead to this situation is

	Production activity	and	Fixed overhead expenditure
A	lower than budget	and	higher than budget
B	higher than budget	and	higher than budget
C	as budgeted	and	as budgeted
D	higher than budget	and	lower than budget

CIMA – Management Accounting Fundamentals

3.21 Intermediate

An engineering firm operates a job costing system. Production overhead is absorbed at the rate of $8.50 per machine hour. In order to allow for non-production overhead costs and profit, a mark up of 60% of prime cost is added to the production cost when preparing price estimates.

The estimated requirements of job number 808 are as follows:

Direct materials	\$10 650
Direct labour	\$3 260
Machine hours	140

The estimated price notified to the customer for job number 808 will be

A \$22 256 B \$22 851 C \$23 446 D \$24 160

CIMA – Management Accounting Fundamentals

3.22 **Intermediate**

A company uses the repeated distribution method to reapportion service department costs. The use of this method suggests

A the company's overhead rates are based on estimates of cost and activity levels, rather than actual amounts.
B there are more service departments than production cost centres.
C the company wishes to avoid under- or over-absorption of overheads in its production cost centres.
D the service departments carry out work for each other.

CIMA – Management Accounting Fundamentals

3.23 **Intermediate**

The management accountant of Gympie Limited has already allocated and apportioned the fixed overheads for the period although she has yet to reapportion the service centre costs. Information for the period is as follows:

	Production departments		**Service departments**		**Total**
	1	**2**	**Stores**	**Maintenance**	
Allocated and apportioned	£17 500	£32 750	£6300	£8450	£65 000
Work done by:					
Stores	60%	30%	—	10%	
Maintenance	75%	20%	5%	—	

What are the total overheads included in production department 1 if the reciprocal method is used to reapportion service centre costs?

A £27 618
B £28 171
C £28 398
D £28 453

ACCA Paper 1.2 – Financial information for Management

3.24 Intermediate: Overhead analysis and calculation of product costs

A furniture-making business manufactures quality furniture to customers' orders. It has three production departments and two service departments. Budgeted overhead costs for the coming year are as follows:

	Total (£)
Rent and Rates	12 800
Machine insurance	6 000
Telephone charges	3 200
Depreciation	18 000
Production Supervisor's salaries	24 000
Heating Lighting	6 400
	70 400

The three production departments – A, B and C, and the two service departments – X and Y, are housed in the new premises, the details of which, together with other statistics and information, are given below.

	Departments				
	A	B	C	X	Y
Floor area occupied (sq.metres)	3000	1800	600	600	400
Machine value (£000)	24	10	8	4	2
Direct labour hrs budgeted	3200	1800	1000		
Labour rates per hour	£3.80	£3.50	£3.40	£3.00	£3.00
Allocated Overheads:					
Specific to each department (£000)	2.8	1.7	1.2	0.8	0.6
Service Department X's costs apportioned	50%	25%	25%		
Service Department Y's costs apportioned	20%	30%	50%		

Required:

(a) Prepare a statement showing the overhead cost budgeted for each department, showing the basis of apportionment used. Also calculate suitable overhead absorption rates.

(9 marks)

(b) Two pieces of furniture are to be manufactured for customers. Direct costs are as follows:

	Job 123	Job 124
Direct Material	£154	£108
Direct Labour	20 hours Dept A	16 hours Dept A
	12 hours Dept B	10 hours Dept B
	10 hours Dept C	14 hours Dept C

Calculate the total costs of each job.

(5 marks)

(c) If the firm quotes prices to customers that reflect a required profit of 25% on selling price, calculate the quoted selling price for each job.

(2 marks)

(d) If material costs are a significant part of total costs in a manufacturing company, describe a system of material control that might be used in order to effectively control costs, paying particular attention to the stock control aspect.

(9 marks)

(Total 25 marks)

AAT Stage 3 Cost Accounting and Budgeting

3.25 **Intermediate: Calculation of product overhead costs**

Bookdon Public Limited Company manufactures three products in two production departments, a machine shop and a fitting section; it also has two service departments, a canteen and a machine maintenance section. Shown below are next year's budgeted production data and manufacturing costs for the company.

	Product X	Product Y	Product Z
Production	4200 units	6900 units	1700 units
Prime cost:			
Direct materials	£11 per unit	£14 per unit	£17 per unit
Direct labour:			
Machine shop	£6 per unit	£4 per unit	£2 per unit
Fitting section	£12 per unit	£3 per unit	£21 per unit
Machine hours per unit	6 hours per unit	3 hours per unit	4 hours per unit

	Machine shop	Fitting section	Canteen	Machine maintenance section	Total
Budgeted overheads (£):					
Allocated overheads	27 660	19 470	16 600	26 650	90 380
Rent, rates, heat and light					17 000
Depreciation and insurance of equipment					25 000
Additional data:					
Gross book value of equipment (£)	150 000	75 000	30 000	45 000	
Number of employees	18	14	4	4	
Floor space occupied (square metres)	3 600	1 400	1 000	800	

It has been estimated that approximately 70% of the machine maintenance section's costs are incurred servicing the machine shop and the remainder incurred servicing the fitting section.

Required:

(a) (i) Calculate the following budgeted overhead absorption rates:

A machine hour rate for the machine shop.

A rate expressed as a percentage of direct wages for the fitting section.

All workings and assumptions should be clearly shown.

(12 marks)

(ii) Calculate the budgeted manufacturing overhead cost per unit of product X.

(2 marks)

(b) The production director of Bookdon PLC has suggested that 'as the actual overheads incurred and units produced are usually different from the budgeted and as a consequence profits of each month end are distorted by over/under absorbed overheads, it would be more accurate to calculate the actual overhead cost per unit each month end by dividing the total number of all units actually produced during the month into the actual overheads incurred.'
Critically examine the production director's suggestion.

(8 marks)
(Total 22 marks)
ACCA Level 1 Costing

3.26 Intermediate: Calculation of overhead rates and under/over-recovery

A factory with three departments uses a single production overhead absorption rate, expressed as a percentage of direct wages cost. It has been suggested that departmental overhead absorption rates would result in more accurate job costs. Set out below are budgeted and actual data for the previous period, together with information relating to job no. 657.

		Direct wages (000s)	Direct labour hours	Machine hours	Production overheads (000s)
Budget:					
Department:	A	25	10 000	40 000	120
	B	100	50 000	10 000	30
	C	25	25 000	—	75
Total:		150	85 000	50 000	225
Actual:					
Department:	A	30	12 000	45 000	130
	B	80	45 000	14 000	28
	C	30	30 000	—	80
Total:		140	87 000	59 000	238

During this period job no. 657 incurred the actual costs and actual times in the departments as shown below:

		Direct material (£)	Direct wages (£)	Direct labour hours	Machine hours
Department:	A	120	100	20 000	40 000
	B	60	60	40 000	10 000
	C	10	10	10 000	—

After adding production overhead to prime cost, one-third is added to production cost for gross profit. This assumes that a reasonable profit is earned after deducting administration, selling and distribution costs. You are required to:

(a) calculate the current overhead absorption rate;

(b) using the rate obtained in (a) above, calculate the production overhead charged to job no. 657, and state the production cost and expected gross profit on this job;

(c) (i) comment on the suggestion that departmental overhead absorption rates would result in more accurate job costs; and

(ii) compute such rates, briefly explaining your reason for each rate;

(d) using the rates calculated in (c) (ii) above, show the overhead, by department and in total, that would apply to job no. 657;

(e) show the over-/under-absorption, by department and in total, for the period, using:
   (i) the current rate in your answer to (a) above; and
   (ii) your suggested rates in your answers to (c) (ii) above.

(20 marks)
CIMA Cost Accounting 1

3.27 **Intermediate: Make or buy decision**

Shown below is next year's budget for the forming and finishing departments of Tooton Ltd. The departments manufacture three different types of component, which are incorporated into the output of the firm's finished products.

	Component		
	A	**B**	**C**
Production (units)	14 000	10 000	6 000
Prime cost (£ per unit):			
Direct materials			
Forming dept	8	7	9
Direct labour			
Forming dept	6	9	12
Finishing dept	10	15	8
	24	31	29
Manufacturing times (hours per unit):			
Machining			
Forming dept	4	3	2
Direct labour			
Forming dept	2	3	4
Finishing dept	3	10	2

	Forming department (£)	Finishing department (£)
Variable overheads	200 900	115 500
Fixed overheads	401 800	231 000
	£602 700	£346 500
Machine time required and available	98 000 hours	—
Labour hours required and available	82 000 hours	154 000 hours

The forming department is mechanized and employs only one grade of labour, the finishing department employs several grades of labour with differing hourly rates of pay.

Required:

(a) Calculate suitable overhead absorption rates for the forming and finishing departments for next year and include a brief explanation for your choice of rates.

(6 marks)

(b) Another firm has offered to supply next years budgeted quantities of the above components at the following prices:

Component A £30 Component B £65
Component C £60

Advise management whether it would be more economical to purchase any of the above components from the outside supplier. You must show your workings and, considering cost criteria only, clearly state any assumptions made or any aspects that may require further investigation.

(8 marks)

(c) Critically consider the purpose of calculating production overheads absorption rates.

(8 marks)
(Total 22 marks)
ACCA Foundation Costing

3.28 Intermediate: Various overhead absorption rates and under/over-recovery

The following data relate to a manufacturing department for a period:

	Budget data (£)	Actual data (£)
Direct material cost	100 000	150 000
Direct labour cost	250 000	275 000
Production overhead	250 000	350 000
Direct labour hours	50 000 hours	55 000 hours

Job ZX was one of the jobs worked on during the period. Direct material costing £7000 and direct labour (800 hours) costing £4000 were incurred.

Required:

(i) Calculate the production overhead absorption rate predetermined for the period based on:
(a) percentage of direct material cost;
(b) direct labour hours.

(3 marks)

(ii) Calculate the production overhead cost to be charged to Job ZX based on the rates calculated in answer to (i) above.

(2 marks)

(iii) Assume that the direct labour hour rate of absorption is used. Calculate the under or over absorption of production overheads for the period and state an appropriate treatment in the accounts.

(4 marks)

(iv) Comment briefly on the relative merits of the two methods of overhead absorption used in (i) above.

(6 marks)
(Total 15 marks)
AAT Cost Accounting and Budgeting

3.29 Intermediate: Reapportionment of service department costs

A company reapportions the costs incurred by two service cost centres, materials handling and inspection, to the three production cost centres of machining, finishing and assembly.

The following are the overhead costs which have been allocated and apportioned to the five cost centres:

	(£000)
Machining	400
Finishing	200
Assembly	100
Materials handling	100
Inspection	50

Estimates of the benefits received by each cost centre are as follows:

	Machining	Finishing	Assembly	Materials handling	Inspection
	%	%	%	%	%
Materials handling	30	25	35	—	10
Inspection	20	30	45	5	—

You are required to:

(a) calculate the charge for overhead to *each* of the *three* production cost centres, including the amounts reapportioned from the two service centres, using:
   (i) the continuous allotment (or repeated distribution) method;
   (ii) an algebraic method;

(15 marks)

(b) comment on whether reapportioning service cost centre costs is generally worthwhile and suggest an alternative treatment for such costs;

(4 marks)

(c) discuss the following statement: 'Some writers advocate that an under- or over-absorption of overhead should be apportioned between the cost of goods sold in the period to which it relates and to closing stocks. However, the United Kingdom practice is to treat under- or over-absorption of overhead as a period cost.

(6 marks)
(Total 25 marks)
CIMA Stage 2 Cost Accounting 3

Review problems (with answers in the Student's Manual)

3.30 Intermediate: Overhead analysis, calculation of overhead rates and a product cost

Knowing that you are studying for the CIMA qualification, a friend who manages a small business has sought your advice about how to produce quotations in response to the enquiries which her business receives. Her business is sheet metal fabrication – supplying ducting for dust extraction and air conditioning installations. She believes that she has lost orders recently through the use of a job cost estimating system which was introduced, on the advice of her auditors, seven years ago. You are invited to review this system.

Upon investigation, you find that a plant-wide percentage of 125% is added to prime costs in order to arrive at a selling price. The percentage added is intended to cover all overheads for the three production departments (Departments P, Q and R), all the selling, distribution and administration costs, and the profit.

You also discover that the selling, distribution and administration costs equate to roughly 20% of total production costs, and that to achieve the desired return on capital employed, a margin of 20% of sales value is necessary.

You recommend an analysis of overhead cost items be undertaken with the objective of determining a direct labour hour rate of overhead absorption for each of the three departments work passes through. (You think about activity-based costing but feel this would be too sophisticated and difficult to introduce at the present time.)

There are 50 direct workers in the business plus 5 indirect production people.

From the books, records and some measuring, you ascertain the following information which will enable you to compile an overhead analysis spreadsheet, and to determine overhead absorption rates per direct labour hour for departmental overhead purposes:

Cost/expense	**Annual amount**	**Basis for apportionment where allocation not given**
	£	
Repairs and maintenance	62 000	Technical assessment: P £42 000, Q £10 000, R £10 000
Depreciation	40 000	Cost of plant and equipment
Consumable supplies	9 000	Direct labour hours
Wage-related costs	87 000	12½% of direct wages costs
Indirect labour	90 000	Direct labour hours
Canteen/rest/smoke room	30 000	Number of direct workers
Business rates and insurance	26 000	Floor area

Other estimates/information

	Department P	**Department Q**	**Department R**
Estimated direct labour hours	50 000	30 000	20 000
Direct wages costs	£386 000	£210 000	£100 000
Number of direct workers	25	15	10
Floor area in square metres	5 000	4 000	1 000
Plant and equipment, at cost	£170 000	£140 000	£90 000

Required:

(a) Calculate the overhead absorption rates for each department, based on direct labour hours.

(9 marks)

(b) Prepare a sample quotation for Job 976, utilizing information given in the question, your answer to (a) above, and the following additional information:

Estimated direct material cost:	£800
Estimated direct labour hours:	30 in Department P
	10 in Department Q
	5 in Department R

(3 marks)

(c) Calculate what would have been quoted for Job 976 under the 'auditors' system' and comment on whether your friend's suspicions about lost business could be correct.

(3 marks)
(Total 15 marks)
CIMA Stage 2 Cost Accounting

3.31 **Intermediate: Calculation of overhead rates and a product cost**

DC Limited is an engineering company which uses job costing to attribute costs to individual products and services provided to its customers. It has commenced the preparation of its fixed production overhead cost budget for 2001 and has identified the following costs:

	(£000)
Machining	600
Assembly	250
Finishing	150
Stores	100
Maintenance	80
	1 180

The stores and maintenance departments are production service departments. An analysis of the services they provide indicates that their costs should be apportioned accordingly:

	Machining	Assembly	Finishing	Stores	Maintenance
Stores	40%	30%	20%	—	10%
Maintenance	55%	20%	20%	5%	—

The number of machine and labour hours budgeted for 2001 is:

	Machining	Assembly	Finishing
Machine hours	50 000	4 000	5 000
Labour hours	10 000	30 000	20 000

Requirements:

(a) Calculate appropriate overhead absorption rates for each production department for 2001.

(9 marks)

(b) Prepare a quotation for job number XX34, which is to be commenced early in 2001, assuming that it has:

Direct materials costing £2400
Direct labour costing £1500
and requires:

	machine hours	labour hours
Machining department	45	10
Assembly department	5	15
Finishing department	4	12

and that profit is 20% of selling price.

(5 marks)

(c) Assume that in 2001 the actual fixed overhead cost of the assembly department totals £300 000 and that the actual machine hours were 4200 and actual labour hours were 30 700.

Prepare the fixed production overhead control account for the assembly department, showing clearly the causes of any over-/under-absorption.

(5 marks)

(d) Explain how activity based costing would be used in organisations like DC Limited.

(6 marks)
(Total marks 25)
CIMA Stage 2 Operational Cost Accounting

3.32 **Intermediate: Calculation of overhead absorption rates and under/over recovery of overheads**

A manufacturing company has two production cost centres (Departments A and B) and one service cost centre (Department C) in its factory.

A predetermined overhead absorption rate (to two decimal places of £) is established for each of the production cost centres on the basis of budgeted overheads and budgeted machine hours.

The overheads of each production cost centre comprise directly allocated costs and a share of the costs of the service cost centre.

Budgeted production overhead data for a period is as follows:

	Department A	Department B	Department C
Allocated costs	£217 860	£374 450	£103 970
Apportioned costs	£45 150	£58 820	(£103 970)
Machine hours	13 730	16 110	
Direct labour hours	16 360	27 390	

Actual production overhead costs and activity for the same period are:

	Department A	Department B	Department C
Allocated costs	£219 917	£387 181	£103 254
Machine hours	13 672	16 953	
Direct labour hours	16 402	27 568	

70% of the actual costs of Department C are to be apportioned to production cost centres on the basis of actual machine hours worked and the remainder on the basis of actual direct labour hours.

Required:

(a) Establish the production overhead absorption rates for the period.

(3 marks)

(b) Determine the under- or over-absorption of production overhead for the period in each production cost centre. (Show workings clearly.)

(12 marks)

(c) Explain when, and how, the repeated distribution method may be applied in the overhead apportionment process.

(5 marks)

(Total 20 marks)

ACCA Management Information – Paper 3

3.33 Intermediate: Analysis of under/over recovery of overheads and a discussion of blanket versus department overheads

(a) One of the factories in the XYZ Group of companies absorbs fixed production overheads into product cost using a pre-determined machine hour rate.

In Year 1, machine hours budgeted were 132 500 and the absorption rate for fixed production overheads was £18.20 per machine hour. Overheads absorbed and incurred were £2 442 440 and £2 317 461 respectively.

In Year 2, machine hours were budgeted to be 5% higher than those actually worked in Year 1. Budgeted and actual fixed production overhead expenditure were £2 620 926 and £2 695 721 respectively, and actual machine hours were 139 260.

Required:

Analyse, in as much detail as possible, the under-/over-absorption of fixed production overhead occurring in Years 1 and 2, and the change in absorption rate between the two years.

(15 marks)

(b) Contrast the use of
   (i) blanket as opposed to departmental overhead absorption rates;
   (ii) predetermined overhead absorption rates as opposed to rates calculated from actual activity and expenditure.

(10 marks)

(Total 25 marks)

ACCA Cost and Management Accounting 1

3.34 Intermediate: Calculation of fixed and variable overhead rates, normal activity level and under/over recovery of overheads

(a) C Ltd is a manufacturing company. In one of the production departments in its main factory a machine hour rate is used for absorbing production overhead. This is established as a predetermined rate, based on normal activity. The rate that will be used for the period which is just commencing is £15.00 per machine hour. Overhead expenditure anticipated, at a range of activity levels, is as follows:

Activity level (machine hours)	(£)
1500	25 650
1650	26 325
2000	27 900

Required:

Calculate:

(i) the variable overhead rate per machine hour;

(ii) the total budgeted fixed overhead;

(iii) the normal activity level of the department; and

(iv) the extent of over-/under-absorption if actual machine hours are 1700 and expenditure is as budgeted.

(10 marks)

(b) In another of its factories, C Ltd carries out jobs to customers' specifications. A particular job requires the following machine hours and direct labour hours in the two production departments:

	Machining Department	Finishing Department
Direct labour hours	25	28
Machine hours	46	8

Direct labour in both departments is paid at a basic rate of £4.00 per hour. 10% of the direct labour hours in the finishing department are overtime hours, paid at 125% of basic rate. Overtime premiums are charged to production overhead.

The job requires the manufacture of 189 components. Each component requires 1.1 kilos of prepared material. Loss on preparation is 10% of unprepared material, which costs £2.35 per kilo.

Overhead absorption rates are to be established from the following data:

	Machining Department	Finishing Department
Production overhead	£35 280	£12 480
Direct labour hours	3 500	7 800
Machine hours	11 200	2 100

Required:

(i) Calculate the overhead absorption rate for each department and justify the absorption method used.

(ii) Calculate the cost of the job.

(15 marks)

(Total 25 marks)

ACCA Level 1

3.35 Intermediate: Reapportionment of service department costs and a product cost calculation

Shown below is an extract from next year's budget for a company manufacturing three different products in three production departments:

	Product A	Product B	Product C
Production (units)	4000	3000	6000
Direct material cost (£ per unit)	7	4	9
Direct labour requirements (hours per unit):			
Cutting department:			
Skilled operatives	3	5	2
Unskilled operatives	6	1	3
Machining department	$^1/_2$	$^1/_4$	$^1/_3$
Pressing department	2	3	4
Machine hour requirements (hours per unit):			
Machining department	2	$1^1/_2$	$2^1/_2$

The skilled operatives employed in the cutting department are paid £4 per hour and the unskilled operatives are paid £2.50 per hour. All the operatives in the machining and pressing departments are paid £3 per hour.

	Production departments			Service departments	
	Cutting	Machining	Pressing	Engineering	Personnel
Budgeted total overheads (£)	154 482	64 316	58 452	56 000	34 000
Service department costs are incurred for the benefit of other departments as follows:					
Engineering services	20%	45%	25%	—	10%
Personnel services	55%	10%	20%	15%	—

The company operates a full absorption costing system.

Required:

(a) Calculate, as equitably as possible, the total budgeted manufacturing cost of:

(i) one completed unit of Product A, and

(ii) one incomplete unit of Product B which has been processed by the cutting and machining departments but which has not yet been passed into the pressing department.

(15 marks)

(b) At the end of the first month of the year for which the above budget was prepared the production overhead control account for the machining department showed a credit balance. Explain the possible reasons for that credit balance.

(7 marks)
(Total 22 marks)
ACCA Level 1 Costing

3.36 Advanced: Reapportionment of service department costs and a discussion of how fully allocated costs can be useful

Megalith Manufacturing divides its plant into two main production departments, Processing and Assembly. It also has three main service-providing departments, Heat, Maintenance and Steam, which provide services to the production departments and to each other. The costs of providing these services are allocated to departments on the bases indicated below:

	Total cost	Basis of allocation
Heat	£90 000	Floor area
Maintenance	£300 000	Hours worked
Steam	£240 000	Units consumed

During the last year, the services provided were:

To	Heat	Maintenance	Steam	Processing	Assembly
From Heat (m^2)		5 000	5 000	40 000	50 000
Maintenance (hrs)	3 000		4 500	7 500	15 000
Steam (units)	192 000	48 000		480 000	240 000

Requirements:

(a) Allocate the costs of service departments to production departments, using each of the following methods:
(i) direct

(3 marks)

(ii) step-down

(4 marks)

(iii) reciprocal

(6 marks)

(b) What is the main problem likely to be encountered in using the information generated by any of the above systems of allocation, given that a substantial proportion of the costs incurred in each service department are fixed for the year? How would you attempt to overcome this problem?

(5 marks)

(c) Given that cost allocation is an essentially arbitrary process, explain how total costs which include substantial amounts of allocated costs can be useful.

(7 marks)
(Total 25 marks)
ICAEW P2 Management Accounting

3.37 Intermediate: Explanation of a product cost calculation

In order to identify the costs incurred in carrying out a range of work to customer specification in its factory, a company has a job costing system. This system identifies costs directly with a job where this is possible and reasonable. In addition, production overhead costs are absorbed into the cost of jobs at the end of each month, at an actual rate per direct labour hour for each of the two production departments.

One of the jobs carried out in the factory during the month just ended was Job No. 123. The following information has been collected relating specifically to this job:

400 kilos of Material Y were issued from stores to Department A. 76 direct labour hours were worked in Department A at a basic wage of £4.50 per hour. 6 of these hours were classified as overtime at a premium of 50%.

300 kilos of Material Z were issued from stores to Department B. Department B returned 30 kilos of Material Z to the storeroom being excess to requirements for the job.

110 direct labour hours were worked in Department B at a basic wage of £4.00 per hour. 30 of these hours were classified as overtime at a premium of 40%. *All* overtime worked in Department B in the month is a result of the request of a customer for early completion of another job, which had been originally scheduled for completion in the month following.

Department B discovered defects in some of the work, which was returned to Department A for rectification. 3 labour hours were worked in Department A on rectification (these are additional to the 76 direct labour hours in Department A noted above). Such rectification is regarded as a normal part of the work carried out generally in the department.

Department B damaged 5 kilos of Material Z which then had to be disposed of. Such losses of material are not expected to occur.

	Department A (£)	Department B (£)
Direct materials issued from stores*	6 500	13 730
Direct materials returned to stores	135	275
Direct labour, at basic wage rate†	9 090	11 200
Indirect labour, at basic wage rate	2 420	2 960
Overtime premium	450	120
Lubricants and cleaning compounds	520	680
Maintenance	720	510
Other	1 200	2 150

Materials are priced at the end of each month on a weighted average basis. Relevant information of material stock movements during the month, for materials Y and Z, is as follows:

	Material Y	Material Z
Opening stock	1050 kilos (value £529.75)	6970 kilos (value £9946.50)
Purchases	600 kilos at £0.50 per kilo 500 kilos at £0.50 per kilo 400 kilos at £0.52 per kilo	16 000 kilos at £1.46 per kilo
Issues from stores	1430 kilos	8100 kilos
Returns to stores	—	30 kilos

*This includes, in Department B, the scrapped Material Z. This was the only material scrapped in the month.

†All direct labour in Department A is paid a basic wage of £4.50 per hour, and in Department B £4.00 per hour. Department A direct labour includes a total of 20 hours spent on rectification work.

Required:

(a) Prepare a list of the costs that should be assigned to Job No. 123. Provide an explanation of your treatment of each item.

(17 marks)

(b) Discuss briefly how information concerning the cost of individual jobs can be used.

(5 marks)

(Total 22 marks)

ACCA Level 1 Costing

Accounting entries for a job costing system

4

This chapter is concerned with the accounting entries necessary to record transactions within a job costing system. In Chapter 2 it was pointed out that job costing relates to a costing system that is required in organizations where each unit or batch of output of a product or service is unique. This creates the need for the cost of each unit to be calculated separately. The term 'job' thus relates to each unique unit or batch of output. In contrast, process costing relates to those situations where masses of identical units are produced and it is unnecessary to assign costs to individual units of output. Instead, the cost of a single unit of output can be obtained by merely dividing the total costs assigned to the cost object for a period by the units of output for that period. In practice these two costing systems represent extreme ends of a continuum. The output of many organizations requires a combination of the elements of both job costing and process costing. However, the accounting methods described in this chapter can be applied to all types of costing systems ranging from purely job to process, or a combination of both. In the next chapter we shall look at process costing in detail.

The accounting system on which we shall concentrate our attention is one in which the cost and financial accounts are combined in one set of accounts; this is known as an

LEARNING OBJECTIVES

After studying this chapter, you should be able to:

- describe the materials recording procedure;
- distinguish between first in, first out (FIFO), last in, first out (LIFO) and average cost methods of stores pricing;
- record the accounting entries for an integrated and interlocking accounting system;
- distinguish between an integrated and an interlocking accounting system;
- describe backflush costing;
- explain the distinguishing features of contract costing;
- prepare contract accounts and calculate the profit attributable to each contract.

integrated cost accounting system. An alternative system, where the cost and financial accounts are maintained independently, is known as an **interlocking cost accounting system**. The integrated cost accounting system is generally considered to be preferable to the interlocking system, since the latter involves a duplication of accounting entries.

A knowledge of the materials recording procedure will enable you to have a better understanding of the accounting entries. Therefore we shall begin by looking at this procedure.

Materials recording procedure

When goods are received they are inspected and details of the quantity of each type of goods received are listed on a **goods received note**. The goods received note is the source document for entering details of the items received in the receipts column of the appropriate **stores ledger account**. An illustration of a stores ledger account is provided in Exhibit 4.1. This document is merely a record of the quantity and value of each individual item of material stored by the organization. In most organizations this document will only consist in the form of a computer record.

The formal authorization for the issue of materials is a **stores requisition**. The type and quantity of materials issued are listed on the requisition. This document also contains details of the job number, product code or overhead account for which the materials are required. Exhibit 4.2 provides an illustration of a typical stores requisition. Each of the items listed on the materials requisition are priced from the information recorded in the receipts column of the appropriate stores ledger account. The information on the stores requisition is then recorded in the issues column of the appropriate stores ledger account and a balance of the quantity and value for each of the specific items of materials is calculated. The cost of each item of material listed on the stores requisition is assigned to the appropriate job number or overhead account. In practice this clerical process is likely to be computerized.

Pricing the issues of materials

A difficulty that arises with material issues is the cost to associate with each issue. This is because the same type of material may have been purchased at several different prices. Actual cost can take on several different values, and some method of pricing material issues must be selected. Consider the situation presented in Example 4.1.

There are three alternative methods that you might consider for calculating the cost of materials issued to job Z which will impact on both the cost of sales and the inventory valuation that is incorporated in the April monthly profit statement and balance sheet. First, you can assume that the first item received was the first item to be issued, that is **first in, first out (FIFO)**. In the example the 5000 units issued to job Z would be priced at £1 and the closing inventory would be valued at £6000 (5000 units at £1.20 per unit).

Secondly, you could assume that the last item to be received was the first item to be issued, that is, **last in, first out (LIFO)**. Here a material cost of £6000 (5000 units at £1.20 per unit) would be recorded against the cost of job Z and the closing inventory would be valued at £5000 (5000 units at £1 per unit).

Thirdly there may be a strong case for issuing the items at the **average cost** of the materials in stock (i.e. £1.10 per unit). With an average cost system the job cost would be recorded at £5500 and the closing inventory would also be valued at £5500. The following is a summary of the three different materials pricing methods relating to Example 4.1:

EXHIBIT 4.1
A stores ledger account

Stores ledger account											
Material: .... Code:							Maximum quantity: .... Minimum quantity:				
Receipts					Issues				Stock		
Date	GRN no.	Quantity	Unit price (£)	Amount (£)	Stores req. no.	Quantity	Unit price (£)	Amount (£)	Quantity	Unit price (£)	Amount (£)

EXHIBIT 4.2
A stores requisition

Stores requisition No.						
Material required for: (job or overhead account) Department: Date:						
[Quantity]	Description	Code no.	Weight	Rate	£	[Notes]
Foreman						

	Cost of sales (i.e. charge to job Z) (£)	Closing inventory (£)	Total costs (£)
First in first out (FIFO)	5000 (5000 × £1)	6000 (5000 × £1.20)	11 000
Last in, first out (LIFO)	6000 (5000 × £1.20)	5000 (5000 × £1)	11 000
Average cost	5500 (5000 × £1.10)	5500 (5000 × £1.10)	11 000

FIFO appears to be the most logical method in the sense that it makes the same assumption as the physical flow of materials through an organization; that is, it is assumed that items received first will be issued first. During periods of inflation, the earliest materials that have the lowest purchase price will be issued first. This assumption leads to a lower cost of sales calculation, and therefore a higher profit than would be obtained by using either of the other

EXAMPLE 4.1

On 5 March Nordic purchased 5000 units of materials at £1 each. A further 5000 units were purchased on 30 March at £1.20 each. During April 5000 units were issued to job Z. No further issues were made during April and you are now preparing the monthly accounts for April.

methods. Note also that the closing inventory will be at the latest and therefore higher prices. With the LIFO method the latest and higher prices are assigned to the cost of sales and therefore lower profits will be reported compared with using either FIFO or average cost. The value of the closing inventory will be at the earliest and therefore lower prices. Under the average cost method, the cost of sales and the closing inventory will fall somewhere between the values recorded for the FIFO and LIFO methods.

LIFO is not an acceptable method of pricing for taxation purposes in the UK, although this does not preclude its use provided that the accounts are adjusted for taxation purposes. The UK Statement of Standard Accounting Practice on Stocks and Work in Progress (SSAP 9), however, states that LIFO does not bear a reasonable relationship to actual costs obtained during the period, and implies that this method is inappropriate for external reporting. In view of these comments, the FIFO or the average cost method should be used for external financial accounting purposes. Instead of using FIFO or average cost for inventory valuation and profit measurement many organizations maintain their inventories at standard prices using a standard costing system. With a standard costing system the process of pricing material issues is considerably simplified. We shall look at standard costing in detail in Chapters 18 and 19.

The above discussion relates to pricing the issue of materials for internal and external profit measurement and inventory valuation. For decision-making the focus is on future costs, rather than the allocation of past costs, and therefore using different methods of pricing materials is not an issue.

Control accounts

The recording system is based on a system of control accounts. A **control account** is a summary account, where entries are made from totals of transactions for a period. For example, the balance in the stores ledger control account will be supported by a voluminous file of stores ledger accounts, which will add up to agree with the total in the stores ledger control account. Assuming 1000 items of materials were received for a period that totalled £200 000, an entry of the total of £200 000 would be recorded on the debit (receipts side) of the stores ledger *control* account. This will be supported by 1000 separate entries in each of the individual stores ledger accounts. The total of all these *individual* entries will add up to £200 000. A system of control accounts enables one to check the accuracy of the various accounting entries, since the total of all the *individual* entries in the various stores ledger accounts should agree with the control account, which will have received the *totals* of the various transactions. The file of all the individual accounts (for example the individual stores ledger accounts) supporting the total control account is called the subsidiary ledger.

We shall now examine the accounting entries necessary to record the transaction outlined in Example 4.2. A manual system is described so that the accounting entries can be followed, but the normal practice is now for these accounts to be maintained on a computer. You will find a summary of the accounting entries set out in Exhibit 4.3, where

EXAMPLE 4.2

The following are the transactions of AB Ltd for the month of April.

1 Raw materials of £182 000 were purchases on credit.
2 Raw materials of £2000 were returned to the supplier because of defects.
3 The total of stores requisitions for direct materials issued for the period was £165 000.
4 The total issues for indirect materials for the period was £10 000.
5 Gross wages of £185 000 were incurred during the period consisting of wages paid to employees £105 000
Tax deductions payable to the Government (i.e. Inland Revenue) £60 000
National Insurance contributions due £20 000
6 All the amounts due in transaction 5 were settled by cash during the period.
7 The allocation of the gross wages for the period was as follows:
Direct wages £145 000
Indirect wages £40 000
8 The employer's contribution for National Insurance deductions was £25 000.
9 Indirect factory expenses of £41 000 were incurred during the period.
10 Depreciation of factory machinery was £30 000.
11 Overhead expenses allocated to jobs by means of overhead allocation rates was £140 000 for the period.
12 Non-manufacturing overhead incurred during the period was £40 000.
13 The cost of jobs completed and transferred to finished goods stock was £300 000.
14 The sales value of goods withdrawn from stock and delivered to customers was £400 000 for the period.
15 The cost of goods withdrawn from stock and delivered to customers was £240 000 for the period.

each transaction is prefixed by the appropriate number to give a clearer understanding of the necessary entries relating to each transaction. In addition, the appropriate journal entry is shown for each transaction together with a supporting explanation.

Recording the purchase of raw materials

The entry to record the purchase of materials in transaction 1 is

Dr Stores ledger control account	182 000	
Cr Creditors control account		182 000

This accounting entry reflects the fact that the company has incurred a short-term liability to acquire a current asset consisting of raw material stock. Each purchase is also entered in the receipts column of an individual stores ledger account (a separate record is used for each item of materials purchases) for the quantity received, a unit price and amount. In addition,

EXHIBIT 4.3

Summary of accounting transactions for AB Ltd

Stores ledger control account

1. Creditors a/c	182 000	2. Creditors a/c	2 000
		3. Work in progress a/c	165 000
		4. Factory overhead a/c	10 000
		Balance c/d	5 000
	182 000		182 000
Balance b/d	5 000		

Factory overhead control account

4. Stores ledger a/c	10 000	11. Work in progress a/c	140 000
7. Wages control a/c	40 000	Balance – under recovery transferred to costing P&L a/c	6 000
8. National Insurance contributions a/c	25 000		
9. Expense creditors a/c	41 000		
10. Provision for depreciation a/c	30 000		
	146 000		146 000

Non-manufacturing overhead control account

12. Expense creditor a/c	40 000	Transferred to costing P&L a/c	40 000

Creditors account

2. Stores ledger a/c	2 000	1. Stores ledger a/c	182 000

Wages accrued account

6. Cash/bank	105 000	5. Wages control a/c	105 000

Tax payable account

6. Cash/bank	60 000	5. Wages control a/c	60 000

National Insurance contributions account

6. Cash/bank	20 000	5. Wage control a/c	20 000
8. Cash/bank	25 000	8. Factory overhead a/c	25 000
	45 000		45 000

Expense creditors account

		9. Factory overhead a/c	41 000
		12. Non-manufacturing overhead	40 000

Work in progress control account

3. Stores ledger a/c	165 000	13. Finished goods stock a/c	300 000
7. Wages control a/c	145 000	Balance c/d	150 000
11. Factory overhead a/c	140 000		
	450 000		450 000
Balanced b/d	150 000		

Finished goods stock account

13. Work in progress a/c	300 000	15. Cost of sales a/c	240 000
		Balance c/d	60 000
	300 000		300 000
Balance b/d	60 000		

Cost of sales account

15. Finished goods stock a/c	240 000	Transferred to costing P&L a/c	240 000

Provision for depreciation account

		10. Factory overhead	30 000

Wages control account

5. Wages accrued a/c	105 000	7. Work in progress a/c	145 000
5. Tax payable a/c	60 000	7. Factory overhead a/c	40 000
5. National Insurance a/c	20 000		
	185 000		185 000

Sales account

Transferred to costing P&L	400 000	14. Debtors	400 000

Debtors account

14. Sales a/c	400 000		

Costing profit and loss account

Sales a/c		400 000
Less cost of sales a/c		240 000
Gross profit		160 000
Less under recovery of factory overhead	6 000	
Non-manufacturing overhead	40 000	46 000
Net profit		114 000

a separate credit entry is made in each individual creditor's account. Note that the entries in the control accounts form part of the system of double entry, whereas the separate entries in the individual accounts are detailed subsidiary records, which do not form part of the double entry system.

The entry for transaction 2 for materials returned to suppliers is

Dr Creditors control account	2000	
Cr Stores ledger control account		2000

An entry for the returned materials is also made in the appropriate stores ledger records and in the individual creditors' accounts.

Recording the issue of materials

The storekeeper issues materials from store in exchange for a duly authorized stores requisition. For direct materials the job number will be recorded on the stores requisition, while for indirect materials the overhead account number will be entered on the requisition. The issue of direct materials involves a transfer of the materials from stores to production. For transaction 3, material requisitions will have been summarized and the resulting totals will be recorded as follows:

Dr Work in progress account	165 000	
Cr Stores ledger control account		165 000

This accounting entry reflects the fact that raw material stock is being converted into work in progress (WIP) stock. In addition to the above entries in the control accounts, the individual jobs will be charged with the cost of the material issued so that job costs can be calculated. Each issue is also entered in the issues column on the appropriate stores ledger record.

The entry for transaction 4 for the issue of indirect materials is

Dr Factory overhead control account	10 000	
Cr Stores ledger control account		10 000

In addition to the entry in the factory overhead account, the cost of material issued will be entered in the individual overhead accounts. These separate overhead accounts will normally consist of individual indirect material accounts for each responsibility centre. Periodically, the totals of each responsibility centre account for indirect materials will be entered in performance reports for comparison with the budgeted indirect material cost.

After transactions 1–4 have been recorded, the stores ledger control account would look like this:

Stores ledger control account

1. Creditors a/c	182 000	2. Creditors a/c	2 000
		3. Work in progress a/c	165 000
		4. Factory overhead a/c	10 000
		Balance c/d	5 000
	182 000		182 000
Balance b/d	5 000		

Accounting procedure for labour costs

Accounting for labour costs can be divided into the following two distinct phases:

1 Computations of the gross pay for each employee and calculation of payments to be made to employees, government, pension funds, etc. (**payroll accounting**).
2 Allocation of labour costs to jobs, overhead account and capital accounts (**labour cost accounting**).

An employee's gross pay is computed from information on the employee's personal record, and attendance or production records. For each employee a separate record is kept, showing the employee's employment history with the company, current rate of pay and authorized deductions such as National Insurance, pension plans, savings plans, union dues, and so on. The clock card contains details of attendance time; job cards provide details of bonuses due to employees; and if a piecework system is in operation, the piecework tickets will be analysed by employees and totalled to determine the gross wage. The gross wages are calculated from these documents, and an entry is then made in the payroll for each employee, showing the gross pay, tax deductions and other authorized deductions. The gross pay less the deductions gives the net pay, and this is the amount of cash paid to each employee.

The payroll gives details of the total amount of cash due to employees and the amounts due to the Government (i.e. Inland Revenue), Pension Funds and Savings Funds, etc. To keep the illustration simple at this stage, transaction 5 includes only deductions in respect of taxes and National Insurance. The accounting entries for transaction 5 are

Dr Wages control account	185 000	
Cr Tax payable account		60 000
Cr National Insurance contributions account		20 000
Cr Wages accrued account		105 000

The credit entries in transaction 5 will be cleared by a payment of cash. The payment of wages will involve an immediate cash payment, but some slight delay may occur with the payment of tax and National Insurance since the final date for payment of these items is normally a few weeks after the payment of wages. The entries for the cash payments for these items (transaction 6) are

Dr Tax payable account	60 000	
Dr National Insurance contributions account	20 000	
Dr Wages accrued account	105 000	
Cr Cash/bank		185 000

Note that the credit entries for transaction 5 merely represent the recording of amounts due for future payments. The wages control account, however, represents the gross wages for the period, and it is the amount in this account that must be allocated to the job, overhead and capital accounts. Transaction 7 gives details of the allocation of the gross wages. The accounting entries are

Dr Work in progress control account	145 000	
Dr Factory overhead control account	40 000	
Cr Wages control account		185 000

In addition to the total entry in the work in progress control account, the labour cost will be charged to the individual job accounts. Similarly, the total entry in the factory overhead control account will be supported by an entry in each individual overhead account for the indirect labour cost incurred.

Transaction 8 represents the employer's contribution for National Insurance payments. The National Insurance deductions in transaction 5 represent the employees' contributions where the company acts merely as an agent, paying these contributions on behalf of the employee. The employer is also responsible for making a contribution in respect of each employee. To keep the accounting entries simple here, the employer's contributions will be charged to the factory overhead account. The accounting entry for transaction 8 is therefore:

Dr Factory overhead control account	25 000	
Cr National Insurance contributions account		25 000

The National Insurance contributions account will be closed with the following entry when the cash payment is made:

Dr National Insurance contributions account	25 000	
Cr Cash/bank		25 000

After recording these transactions, the wages control account would look like this:

Wages control account

5. Wages accrued a/c	105 000	7. Work in progress a/c	145 000
5. Tax payable a/c	60 000	7. Factory overhead a/c	40 000
5. National Insurance a/c	20 000		
	185 000		185 000

Accounting procedure for manufacturing overheads

Accounting for manufacturing overheads involves entering details of the actual amount of manufacturing overhead incurred on the debit side of the factory overhead control account. The total amount of overheads charged to production is recorded on the credit side of the factory overhead account. In the previous chapter we established that manufacturing overheads are charged to production using budgeted overhead rates. It is most unlikely, however, that the actual amount of overhead incurred, which is recorded on the debit side of the account, will be in agreement with the amount of overhead allocated to jobs, which is recorded on the credit side of the account. The difference represents the under- or over-recovery of factory overheads, which is transferred to the profit and loss account, in accordance with the requirements of the UK Statement of Standard Accounting Practice on Stocks and Work in Progress (SSAP 9).

Transaction 9 represents various indirect expenses that have been incurred and that will eventually have to be paid in cash, for example property taxes and lighting and heating. Transaction 10 includes other indirect expenses that do not involve a cash commitment. For simplicity it is assumed that depreciation of factory machinery is the only item that falls into this category. The accounting entries for transactions 9 and 10 are

Dr Factory overhead control account	71 000	
Cr Expense creditors control account		41 000
Cr Provision of depreciation account		30 000

In addition, subsidiary entries, not forming part of the double entry system, will be made in individual overhead accounts. These accounts will be headed by the title of the cost centre followed by the object of expenditure. For example, it may be possible to assign indirect materials directly to specific cost centres, and separate records can then be kept of the indirect materials charge for each centre. It will not, however, be possible to allocate property taxes, lighting and heating directly to cost centres, and entries should be made in individual overhead accounts for these items. Such expenses could, if so requested by management, be apportioned to responsibility cost centres according to, say, floor area, but note that they should be regarded as non-controllable by the cost centre managers.

Transaction 11 refers to the total overheads that have been charged to jobs using the estimated overhead absorption rates. The accounting entry in the control accounts for allocating overheads to jobs is

Dr Work in progress control account	140 000	
Cr Factory overhead control account		140 000

In addition to this entry, the individual jobs are charged so that job costs can be calculated. When these entries have been made the factory overhead control account would look like this:

Factory overhead control account

4. Stores ledger control a/c	10 000	11. Work in progress control a/c	140 000
7. Wages control a/c	40 000	Balance – Under-recovery of overhead transferred to costing profit and loss a/c	6 000
8. Employer's National Insurance contributions a/c	25 000		
9. Expense creditors a/c	41 000		
10. Provision for depreciation a/c	30 000		
	146 000		146 000

The debit side of this account indicates that £146 000 overhead has been incurred, but examination of the credit side indicates that only £140 000 has been allocated to jobs via overhead allocation rates. The balance of £6000 represents an under-recovery of factory overhead, which is regarded as a period cost to be charged to the costing profit and loss account in the current accounting period. The reasons for this were explained in the previous chapter.

Non-manufacturing overheads

You will have noted in the previous chapter that non-manufacturing overhead costs are regarded as period costs and not product costs, and non-manufacturing overheads are not therefore charged to the work in progress control account. The accounting entry for transaction 12 is

Dr Non-manufacturing overheads account	40 000	
Cr Expense creditors account		40 000

At the end of the period the non-manufacturing overheads will be transferred to the profit and loss account as a period cost by means of the following accounting entry:

Dr Profit and loss account	40 000	
Cr Non-manufacturing overheads account		40 000

In practice, separate control accounts are maintained for administrative, marketing and financial overheads, but, to simplify this example, all the non-manufacturing overheads are included in one control account. In addition, subsidiary records will be kept that analyse the total non-manufacturing overheads by individual accounts, for example office stationery account, sales person's travelling expenses account, etc.

Note that these accounts do not form part of the double entry system, but represent a detailed breakdown of the total entries included in the non-manufacturing overhead control account.

Accounting procedures for jobs completed and products sold

When jobs have been completed, they are transferred from the factory floor to the finished goods store. The total of the job accounts for the completed jobs for the period is recorded as a transfer from the work in progress control account to the finished goods stock account. The accounting entry for transaction 13 is

Dr Finished goods stock account	300 000	
Cr Work in progress control account		300 000

When the goods are removed from the finished goods stock and delivered to the customers, the revenue is recognized. It is a fundamental principle of financial accounting that only costs associated with earning the revenue are included as expenses. The cost of those goods that have been delivered to customers must therefore be matched against the revenue due from delivery of the goods so that the gross profit can be calculated. Any goods that have not been delivered to customers will be included as part of the finished stock valuation. The accounting entries to reflect these transactions are:

Transaction 14		
Dr Debtors control account	400 000	
Cr Sales account		400 000

Transaction 15		
Dr Cost of sales account	240 000	
Cr Finished goods stock account		240 000

Costing profit and loss account

At frequent intervals management may wish to ascertain the profit to date for the particular period. The accounting procedure outlined in this chapter provides a data base from which a costing profit and loss account may easily be prepared. The costing profit and loss account for AB Ltd based on the information given in Example 4.2 is set out in Exhibit 4.3 shown on page 117. As cost control procedures should exist at cost (responsibility) centre levels, management may find the final profit calculation sufficient when it is combined with a summary of the various performance reports. Alternatively, management may prefer the profit statement to be presented in a format similar to that which is necessary for external reporting. Such information can easily be extracted from the subsidiary records. For example, the factory and non-manufacturing overhead control accounts are supported by detailed individual accounts such as factory depreciation, factory lighting and heating, office salaries and so on. The items in the costing profit and loss account can therefore be easily replaced with those items normally presented in the financial accounts by extracting from the subsidiary records the appropriate information. The accounting procedure outlined in Exhibit 4.3, however, provides the data base for ascertaining the job costs and stock valuations that are essential to external reporting. In addition, information in the subsidiary records provides the data from which the accountant can extract relevant decision-making and control information to suit the needs of the various users of accounting information.

Interlocking accounting

Interlocking accounting is a system where the cost and financial accounts are maintained independently of each other, and in the cost accounts no attempt is made to keep a separate record of the financial accounting transactions. Examples of financial accounting transactions include entries in the various creditors, debtors and capital accounts. To maintain the double entry records, an account must be maintained in the cost accounts to record the corresponding entry that, in an integrated accounting system, would normally be made in one of the financial accounts (creditors, debtors accounts, etc.). This account is called a cost control or general ledger adjustment account.

Using an interlocking accounting system to record the transactions listed in Example 4.2, the entries in the creditors, wages accrued, taxation payable, National Insurance contributions, expense creditors, provision for depreciation and debtors accounts would be replaced by the following entries in the cost control account:

Cost control account

2. Stores ledger control a/c	2 000	1. Stores ledger control a/c	182 000
14. Sales a/c	400 000	5. Wages control a/c	185 000
Balance c/d	215 000	8. Factory overhead control a/c	25 000
		9. Expense creditors a/c	41 000
		12. Non-manufacturing overhead a/c	40 000
		10. Factory overhead a/c	30 000
		Profit and loss a/c (profit for period)	114 000
	617 000		617 000
		Balance b/d	215 000

The entries in the remaining accounts will be unchanged.

For a detailed answer to an interlocking accounts question you should refer to the solution to Review problem 4.23. Sometimes examination questions are set that require you to reconcile the profit that has been calculated in the cost accounts with the profits calculated in the financial accounts. Most firms use an integrated accounting system, and hence there is no need to reconcile a separate set of cost and financial accounts. The reconciliation of cost and financial accounts is not therefore dealt with in this book. For an explanation of the reconciliation procedure you should refer to the solution to Review problem 4.25.

Accounting entries for a JIT manufacturing system

During the late 1980s and early 1990s many organizations adopted a just-in-time (JIT) manufacturing philosophy. The major features of a JIT philosophy will be explained in Chapter 22 but at this point it is appropriate to note that implementing a JIT philosophy is normally accompanied by a cellular production layout whereby each cell produces similar products. Consequently, a form of process costing environment emerges. There is also a high velocity of WIP movement throughout the cell, and so it is extremely difficult to trace actual costs to individual products. Adopting a JIT philosophy also results in a substantial reduction in inventories so that inventory valuation becomes less relevant. Therefore simplified accounting procedures can be adopted for allocating costs between cost of sales and inventories. This simplified procedure is known as **backflush costing**.

Both process costing and JIT techniques are covered in later chapters but you will find it easier at this point, if we compare the backflush costing system that has been advocated for a JIT production environment with the conventional job costing system that has been described in this chapter. Therefore in this section we shall move away from a job costing environment towards a process costing environment but we shall return to a special form of job costing in the next section.

Backflush costing aims to eliminate detailed accounting transactions. Rather than tracking the movement of materials through the production process, a backflush costing system focuses first on the output of the organization and then works backwards when allocating cost between costs of goods sold and inventories, with no separate accounting for WIP. In contrast, conventional product costing systems track costs in synchronization with the movement of the products from direct materials, through WIP to finished goods. We shall now use Example 4.3 to illustrate two variants of backflush costing. Trigger points determine when the entries are made in the accounting system.

Actual conversion costs are recorded as incurred, just the same as conventional recording systems. Conversion costs are then applied to products at various trigger points. It is assumed that any conversion costs not applied to products are carried forward and disposed of at the year end. The accounting entries are as follows:

Method 1

Trigger point 1 – The purchase of raw materials and components
2 – The manufacture of finished goods

	(£)	(£)
1. Dr Raw material inventory account	1 515 000	
Cr Creditors		1 515 000
2. Dr Conversion costs	1 010 000	
Cr Expense creditors		1 010 000
3. Dr Finished goods inventory (100 000 × £25)	2 500 000	
Cr Raw material inventory (100 000 × £15)		1 500 000
Cr Conversion costs (100 000 × £10)		1 000 000
4. Dr Cost of goods sold (98 000 × £25)	2 450 000	
Cr Finished goods inventory		2 450 000

The ledger accounts in respect of the above transactions are shown in Exhibit 4.4.

Method 2

This is the simplest variant of backflush costing. There is only one trigger point. We shall assume that the trigger point is the manufacture of a finished unit. Conversion costs are debited as the actual costs are incurred. The accounting entries are

	(£)	(£)
1. Dr Finished goods inventory (100 000 × £25)	2 500 000	
Cr Creditors		1 500 000
Cr Conversion costs		1 000 000
2. Dr Cost of goods sold (98 000 × £25)	2 450 000	
Cr Finished goods inventory		2 450 000

The end of month inventory balance is £50 000 finished goods. At the end of the period the £15 000 of raw materials purchased but not yet manufactured into finished goods will not have been recorded in the internal product costing system. It is therefore not included in the closing stock valuation.

You will see that the WIP account is eliminated with both the variants that are illustrated. If inventories are low, the vast majority of manufacturing costs will form part of cost of goods sold and will not be deferred in inventory. In this situation the volume of work involved in tracking costs through WIP, cost of goods sold and finished goods is unlikely to be justified. This considerably reduces the volume of transactions recorded in the internal accounting system. Note, however, that it may be necessary to track the progress of units on the production line, but there will be no attempt to trace costs to units progressing through the system.

The second variant is suitable only for JIT systems with minimum raw materials and WIP inventories. Note that both methods allocate identical amounts to the cost of goods sold for the period. The second method may yield significantly different inventory valuations from conventional product costing systems. It is therefore claimed that this method of backflush costing may not be acceptable for external financial reporting. However, if inventories are low or not subject to significant change from one accounting period to the next, operating income and inventory valuations derived from backflush costing will not be materially different from the results reported by the conventional system. In these circumstances backflush costing is acceptable for external financial reporting.

EXAMPLE 4.3

The transactions for the month of May for JIT plc are as follows:

Purchase of raw materials	£1 515 000
Conversion costs incurred during the period	£1 010 000
Finished goods manufactured during the period	100 000 units
Sales for the period	98 000 units

There are no opening stocks of raw materials, WIP or finished goods. The standard and actual cost per unit of output is £25 (£15 materials and £10 conversion cost). The company uses an integrated cost accounting system.

EXHIBIT 4.4

Ledger accounts for a backflush costing system (Method 1)

Raw materials inventory

1. Creditors £1 515 000	3. Finished goods £1 500 000

Finished goods inventory

3. Raw materials £1 500 000	4. COGS £2 450 000
3. Conversion costs £1 000 000	

Conversion costs

2. Creditors £1 010 000	3. Finished goods £1 000 000

Cost of goods sold (COGS)

4. £2 450 000	

The end of month inventory balances are

	(£)
Raw materials	15 000
Finished goods	50 000
	65 000

Contract costing

Contract costing is a system of job costing that is applied to relatively large cost units, which normally take a considerable length of time to complete. Building and construction work, civil engineering and shipbuilding are some examples of industries where large contract work is undertaken, and where contract costing is appropriate.

A contract account is maintained for each contract. All the direct costs of the contract are debited to the specific contract and overheads are apportioned in the manner prescribed in Chapter 3. The contract price is credited to the contract account, and each contract account therefore becomes a small profit and loss account.

Because of the considerable length of time that is taken to complete a contract, it is necessary to determine the profit to be attributed to each accounting period. Financial accounting normally recognizes revenue when the goods are delivered, but such an approach is inappropriate for long-term contracts, since profits on large contracts would not be reported until they were completed. The profit and loss account would not reflect a fair view of the profitability of the company during the year but would show only the results of contracts that had been completed before the year end. To overcome this problem, it is preferable to take credit for profit while contracts are in progress.

The UK Statement of Standard Accounting Practice on Stocks and Work in Progress (SSAP 9) provides the following guidance on the attributable profit to be taken up for a particular period:

> *Where the business carries out long-term contracts and it is considered that their outcome can be assessed with reasonable certainty before their conclusion, the attributable profit should be calculated on a prudent basis and included in the accounts for the period under review. The profit taken up needs to reflect the proportion of the work carried out at the accounting date and to take into account any known inequalities of profitability in the various stages of a contract. The procedure to recognize profit is to include an appropriate proportion of total contract value as turnover in the profit and loss account as the contract activity progresses. The costs incurred in reaching that stage of completion are matched with this turnover, resulting in the reporting of results that can be attributed to the proportion of work completed.*
>
> *Where the outcome of long-term contracts cannot be assessed with reasonable certainty before the conclusion of the contract, no profit should be reflected in the profit and loss account in respect of those contracts although, in such circumstances, if no loss is expected it may be appropriate to show as turnover a proportion of the total contract value using a zero estimate of profit.*
>
> *If it is expected that there will be a loss on a contract as a whole, all of the loss should be recognized as soon as it is foreseen (in accordance with the prudence concept).*

Let us now prepare some contract accounts and determine the attributable profit to be taken up for an accounting period. Consider Example 4.4.

Before we compile the accounts, some of the terms used in Example 4.4 require an explanation. A customer is likely to be required under the terms of the contract to make **progress payments** to the contractor throughout the course of the work. The amount of the payments will be based on the sales value of the work carried out, as assessed by the architect or surveyor in the **architect's certificate**. A certificate provides confirmation that work to a certain sales value has been completed, and that some payment to the contractor is now due. The amount of the progress payment will consist of:

1 the sales value of work carried out and certified by the architect; less
2 a retention; less
3 the payments made to date.

So if the architect's certificates assess the value of work carried out to be £300 000 and if the retention is 10%, and if £230 000 has already been paid in progress payments, the current payment will be

£300 000 – £30 000 retention – £230 000 previous payment = £40 000

There is frequently a contract clause which entitles the customer to withhold payment of **retention money** for a proportion of the value of work certified for a specified period after

EXAMPLE 4.4

A construction company is currently undertaking three separate contracts and information relating to these contracts for the previous year, together with other relevant data, are shown below:

	Contract A (£000)	Contract B (£000)	Contract C (£000)
Contract price	1760	1485	2420
Balances b/fwd at beginning of year:			
Material on site	—	20	30
Written-down value of plant and machinery	—	77	374
Wages accrued	—	5	10
Transactions during previous year:			
Profit previously transferred to profit and loss a/c	—	—	35
Cost of work certified (cost of sales)	—	418	814
Transactions during current year:			
Materials delivered to sites	88	220	396
Wages paid	45	100	220
Salaries and other costs	15	40	50
Written-down value of plant issued to sites	190	35	—
Head office expenses apportioned during the year	10	20	50
Balances c/fwd at the end of year:			
Material on site	20	—	—
Written-down value of plant and machinery	150	20	230
Wages accrued	5	10	15
Value of work certified at end of year	200	860	2100
Cost of work not certified at end of year	—	—	55

The agreed retention rate is 10% of the value of work certified by the contractee's architects. Contract C is scheduled for handing over to the contractee in the near future, and the site engineer estimates that the extra costs required to complete the contract, in addition to those tabulated above, will total £305 000. This amount includes an allowance for plant depreciation, construction services and for contingencies.

You are required to prepare a cost account for each of the three contracts and recommend how much profit or loss should be taken up for the year.

the end of the contract. During this period, the contractor must make good all contractual defects. When the defects have been satisfactorily completed the customer will release the retention money.

Let us now prepare the cost accounts from the information contained in Example 4.4 for contracts A, B and C:

Contract accounts

	A (£000)	B (£000)	C (£000)		A (£000)	B (£000)	C (£000)
				Wages accrued b/fwd		5	10
Materials on site b/fwd		20	30	Materials on site c/fwd	20		
Plant on site b/fwd		77	374	Plant on site c/fwd	150	20	230
Materials control a/c	88	220	396	Cost of work not certified c/fwd			55
Wages control a/c	45	100	220				
Salaries	15	40	50	Cost of sales – current period (balance) c/fwd	183	497	840
Plant control a/c	190	35					
Apportionment of head office expenses	10	20	50				
Wages accrued c/fwd	5	10	15				
	353	522	1135		353	522	1135
Cost of sales b/fwd	183	497	840	Attributable sales revenue (current period)[a]	183	442	1122
Profit taken this period			282	Loss taken		55	
	183	497	1122		183	497	1122
Cost of work not certified b/fwd			55	Wages accrued b/fwd	5	10	15
Materials on site b/fwd	20						
Plant on site b/fwd	150	20	230				

[a]Profit taken plus cost of sales for the current period or cost of sales less loss to date.

You will see that the contract accounts are divided into three sections. The objective of the first section is to determine the costs that should be included in the cost of sales for the purposes of calculating the profit taken up for the period. The balance shown in the first section of the contract accounts represents the cost of sales (also known as cost of work certified) attributable to each of the contracts.

You should note that unexpired costs such as the cost of work not certified and the written-down balance of the plant at the end of the period are carried forward to the third section of the contract accounts. This section represents the unexpired costs of the current period which will become an expired cost in future periods. The third section of the account should therefore be regarded as a future cost section.

In the second section of the contract accounts the period cost of sales is compared with the sales revenue that is estimated to be attributable to the contracts. The sales revenues attributable to the contracts for each period are estimated by adding the attributable profit taken up for the current period to the cost of sales for the current period (or cost of sales less the loss where a contract is currently running at a loss). The profits/losses on the three contracts to date are calculated by deducting the cost of sales (consisting of the sum of the cost of sales for the current and previous periods) from the value of work certified:

	(£000)	
Contract A	17	(£200–£183)
Contract B	(55)	(£860–£915)
Contract C	446	(£2100–£1654)

However, these profits/(losses) do not necessarily represent the profits/(losses) taken up on the contracts. According to SSAP 9, the concept of prudence should be applied when determining the profits/(losses) taken up on contracts. You are recommended to adopt the following guidelines:

1 If the contract is in its early stages, no profit should be taken. Profit should only be taken when the outcome of the contract can be assessed with reasonable certainty. You will see from Example 4.4 that the contract price for Contract A is £1 760 000, but the value of work certified is only £200 000. The contract is therefore approximately one-eighth complete, and it is unlikely that the outcome of the contract can be foreseen with reasonable certainty. Despite the fact that the profit to date is £17 000, it is recommended that no profit be taken.

2 If a loss is incurred, the prudence concept should be applied, and the total loss should be recognized in the period in which it is incurred. Consequently, the loss of £55 000 on Contract B is recognized in the current accounting period. Where further additional future losses are anticipated, all of the loss should be recognized as soon as it is foreseen and added to the cost of sales. In addition, the foreseeable loss should be shown in the balance sheet under the heading 'Provision/accrual for foreseeable losses'.

3 If the contract is nearing completion, the size of the eventual profit should be foreseen with reasonable certainty, and there is less need to be excessively prudent in determining the amount of profit to be recorded in the profit and loss account. With regard to Contract C, the value of work certified is approximately 87% of the contract price, and the **anticipated profit** is calculated as follows:

	(£000)
Cost of work certified (cost of sales to date = 814 + 840)	1654
Cost of work not certified	55
Estimated costs to complete	305
Estimated cost of contract	2014
Contract price	2420
Anticipated profit	406

The profit taken is calculated using the following formula:

$$\text{cash received to date } \frac{(0.90 \times £2100)}{\text{contract price } (£2420)}$$
$$\times \text{ estimated profit from the contract } (£406) \simeq £317\,000$$

You should note that other more prudent approaches are sometimes used to determine the profit earned to date. The profit for the current period consists of the profit to date (£317 000) less the profit of £35 000 previously transferred to the profit and loss account. The profit taken to the profit and loss account for the current period is therefore £282 000.

4 Where substantial costs have been incurred on a contract, and it is not nearing completion (say it is in the region of 35–85% complete), the following formula is often used to determine the attributable profit to date:

$$\text{profit taken} = 2/3 \times \text{notional profit} \times \frac{\text{cash received}}{\text{value of work certified}}$$

This formula is one of several approaches that can be used to apply the prudence concept. Estimates of anticipated profit are likely to be inaccurate when contracts are not near to completion. To overcome this problem, notional profit should be used instead of anticipated profit. Notional profit is the value of work certified to date less the cost of work certified (that is, cost of sales) to date less a provision for any anticipated unforeseen eventualities.

Note than for Contract C £35 000 profit was recognized in the previous period and cost of sales of £814 000 was recorded. Therefore attributable sales revenue of £849 000 (£814 000 + £35 000) would have been recorded in the contract account for the *previous* period. For Contract B, no profits were recognized in the *previous period* and attributable sales for the period will thus be identical to the cost of sales (£418 000). Contract A commenced in the current period and so no transactions will have been recorded in the previous period. The debit side of the debtors accounts will be as follows:

	Contract A (£000)	Contract B (000)	Contract C (£000)
Previous period – attributable sales	—	418	849
Current period – attributable sales	183	442	1122
Total to date	183	860	1971

Work in progress valuation and amounts recoverable on contracts

The UK Statement of Standard Accounting Practice on Stocks on Work in Progress (SSAP 9) requires that the proportion of the total contract value appropriate to the stage of completion reached at balance sheet date be recognized as sales revenue. The costs relating to that completed work are included in the cost of sales. Any further costs that are attributable to the contract but that have not been included in the cost of sales are included at cost in the balance sheet and separately disclosed as 'Long-term contract balances' under the balance sheet heading 'Stocks'.

The associated balance sheet item for the contract value that is recorded as sales is debtors. The debtors balance is calculated by deducting progress payments received on account from the amount recognized as sales. This balance is included as a separate item within debtors and described as 'Amounts recoverable on contracts'. The balance sheet entries for Example 4.4 are as follows:

	Contract A (£000)	Contract B (£000)	Contract C (£000)	
Stocks:				
Total costs incurred to date	183	860	1709	(814 + 840 + 55)
Included in cost of sales	183	860	1654	
Included in long-term contract balances	0	0	55	
Debtors				
Cumulative sales turnover	183	860	1971	
Less cumulative progress payments	180	774	1890	
Amounts recoverable on contracts	3	86	81	

For Contract B, the total costs incurred to date are £915 000 (£418 000 + £497 000) but £55 000 of these costs have been recognized as a loss in the current period, so that cumulative cost of sales to be matched against cumulative sales is £860 000 (£915 000 – £55 000). Note also that the cumulative progress payments are 90% of the value of work certified and that the loss on Contract B has been charged to the current period. Other balance sheet entries will include the following:

	(£000)
Materials on site	20
Plant on site	400
Accruals	30

Summary

The following items relate to the learning objectives listed at the beginning of the chapter.

- **Describe the materials recording procedure.**

  When the materials are received the quantities and values are recorded in a separate stores ledger account for each item of material. The issues of materials are recorded on a stores requisition, which contains details of the job number product code or overhead account for which the materials are required. The information on the stores requisition is then recorded in the issues column of the appropriate stores ledger account and after each issue a balance of the quantity and value for each of the specific items of materials is calculated. The cost of each item of material listed on the stores requisition is assigned to the appropriate job number, product or overhead account. In practice this clerical process is likely to be computerized.

- **Distinguish between first in, first out (FIFO), last in, first out (LIFO) and average cost methods of stores pricing.**

  Because the same type of materials may have been purchased at several different prices actual cost can take on several different values. Therefore an assumption must be made when pricing the materials used. FIFO assumes that the first item that was received in stock was the first item issued so the earlier purchase prices are used. LIFO assumes that the last item to be received is the first item to be issued resulting in the later purchase prices being used. The average cost method assumes that materials are issued at the average cost of materials in stock.

- **Record the accounting entries for an integrated and interlocking accounting system.**

  A summary of the accounting entries for an integrated accounting system, where all purchases and expenses are settled in cash, is shown diagrammatically in Figure 4.1.

- **Distinguish between an integrated and an interlocking cost accounting system.**

  With an integrated costing accounting system, the cost and financial accounts are combined in one set of accounts whereas the cost and financial accounts are maintained independently with an interlocking accounting system. An integrated accounting system is recommended since it avoids the duplication of accounting entries.

- **Describe backflush costing.**

  Backflush costing is a simplified costing system that aims to eliminate detailed accounting transactions. It is applied when a just-in-time production philosophy is adopted. Instead of tracking the movement of materials through the production process,

FIGURE 4.1 *Flow of accounting entries in an integrated accounting system*

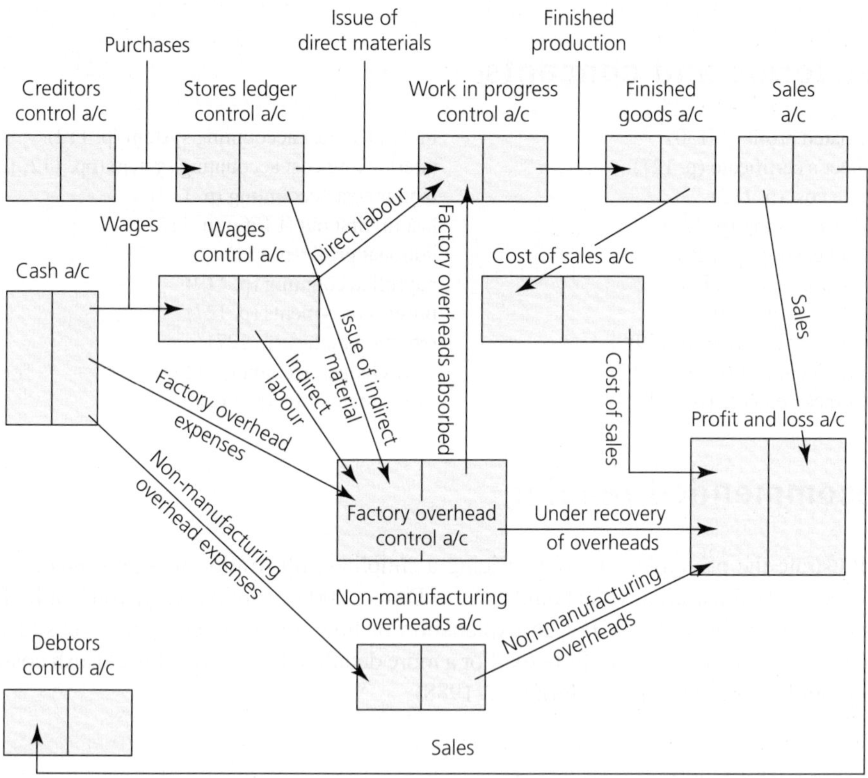

a backflush costing system focuses first on the output of the organization and then works backwards when allocating cost between cost of goods sold and inventories, with no separate accounting for work-in-progress. In contrast, a conventional integrated accounting system tracks costs in synchronization with the movement of the products from direct materials, through work-in-progress to finished goods.

- **Explain the distinguishing features of contract costing.**

  Contract costing is a system of job costing that is applied to relatively large cost units, which normally take a considerable time to complete (normally in excess of one year). It is applied in the building and construction, civil engineering and shipbuilding industries. Where contract costing is not applied, sales revenues are normally recognized for determining profits when the goods are received or the service has been completed. With a contract costing system sales revenues are attributed to the contract based on the proportion of work carried out to date.

- **Prepare contract accounts and calculate the profit attributable to each contract.**

  A contract account is maintained for each contract. Each contract account represents a separate profit and loss account. Typically contract accounts consist of three sections. The objective of the first section is to determine the costs that should be included in the cost of sales attributable to the contract. In the second section the period cost of sales is compared with the sales revenue that is estimated to be attributable to the contracts so that the profit can be derived. The third section represents the unexpired costs of the current period that will become expenses in future periods. The preparation of contract accounts and the calculation of attributable profit were illustrated using the data presented in Example 4.4.

Key terms and concepts

anticipated profit (p. 130)
architect's certificate (p. 127)
average cost (p. 112)
backflush costing (p. 124)
contract costing (p. 126)
control account (p. 114)
cost of sales (p. 129)
cost of work certified (p. 129)
first in, first out (FIFO) (p. 112)
goods received note (p. 112)
integrated cost accounting system (p. 112)
interlocking cost accounting system (pp. 112, 123)
labour cost accounting (p. 119)
last in, first out (LIFO) (p. 112)
notional profit (p. 131)
payroll accounting (p. 119)
progress payments (p. 127)
retention money (p. 127)
stores ledger account (p. 112)
stores requisition (p. 112)

Recommended reading

To illustrate the principles of stores pricing a simplistic illustration was presented. For a more complex illustration you should refer to Drury (2003). Alternatively, you can look at this chapter on the website. For an explanation of how you can access the website you should refer to the Preface of this book. For a more detailed illustration of backflush costing you should refer to Foster and Horngren (1988).

Key examination points

Examination questions set by the professional accountancy examination bodies require the preparation of accounts for both integrated and interlocking accounting systems (see answers to Review problems 4.23 and 4.24 for examples). You may also be required to reconcile the cost and financial accounts. For an illustration of a reconciliation see the answer to Review problem 4.25). However, the reconciliation of cost and financial accounts is a topic that tends to be examined only on rare occasions.

Students often experience difficulty in recommending the amount of profit to be taken during a period for long-term contracts. Make sure you are familiar with the four recommendations listed on pages 130–131 and that you can apply these recommendations to Review problems 4.26 and 4.32–4.33.

Assessment material

Review questions

The review questions are short questions that enable you to assess your understanding of the main topics included in the chapter. The numbers in parentheses provide you with the page numbers to refer to if you cannot answer a specific question.

Review problems

The review problems are more complex and require you to relate and apply the chapter content to various business problems. The problems are graded by their level of difficulty. The multiple-choice questions are the least demanding and normally take less than 10 minutes to complete. Fully worked solutions to the review problems are provided in a separate section at the end of the book. For those questions in the white box the worked solutions are provided in the *Student's Manual* accompanying this book. Further review problems for this chapter are available on the accompanying website www.drury-online.com. The answers to these problems are available for lecturers on the lecturer's password protected section of the website.

Case studies

The website also includes over 30 case study problems. A list of these cases is provided in Part Seven of this book.

Review questions

4.1 Distinguish between an integrated and interlocking accounting system. (*pp. 111–12*)

4.2 Describe the first in, first out (FIFO), last in, first out and average cost methods of stores pricing. (*pp. 112–14*)

4.3 Explain the purpose of a stores ledger account. (*p. 112*)

4.4 Explain the purpose of control accounts. (*p. 114*)

4.5 List the accounting entries for the purchase of issues of direct and indirect materials. (*p. 115, p. 118*)

4.6 List the accounting entries for the payment and the allocation of gross wages. (*pp. 118–19*)

4.7 List the accounting entries for the payment and allocation of overheads. (*pp. 120–22*)

4.8 Explain the circumstances when backflush costing is used. (*p. 124*)

4.9 Describe the major aims of backflush costing. (*p. 124*)

4.10 Explain the major features of contract costing. (*pp. 126–27*)

4.11 Define progress payments, architects certificates, retention money, cost of work certified and notional profit. (*pp. 127–31*)

4.12 Describe the four guidelines that should be used to determine the amount of profit that should be taken for a contract during a specific period. (*p. 130*)

Review problems

4.13 Intermediate

A company operates an integrated cost and financial accounting system.

The accounting entries for the return of unused direct materials from production would be:

A	DR Work-in-progress account;	CR Stores control account.
B	DR Stores control account;	CR Work-in-progress account.
C	DR Stores control account;	CR Finished goods account.
D	DR Cost of sales account;	CR Work-in-progress account.

CIMA Stage 1 – Cost Accounting and Quantitative Methods

4.14 Intermediate

At the end of a period, in an integrated cost and financial accounting system, the accounting entries for overhead over-absorbed would be:

A	DR Profit and loss account	CR Work-in-progress control account
B	DR Profit and loss account	CR Overhead control account
C	DR Work-in-progress control account	CR Overhead control account
D	DR Overhead control account	CR Profit and loss account

CIMA Stage 1 – Cost Accounting and Quantitative Methods

4.15 Intermediate

In an interlocking accounting system, the profit shown in the financial accounts was £79 252 but the cost accounts showed £74 294 profit.

The following stock valuations were the only differences between the two sets of accounts:

Stock valuations	Cost accounts	Financial accounts
Opening stock	£10 116	£9 217
Closing stock	£24 053	X

What was the value of X?

A £18 196 B £23 154 C £24 952 D £28 112

CIMA Stage 1 – Cost Accounting and Quantitative Methods

4.16 Intermediate

The following data have been taken from the books of CB plc, which uses a non-integrated accounting system:

	Financial accounts £	Cost accounts £
Opening stock of materials	5000	6400
Closing stock of materials	4000	5200
Opening stock of finished goods	9800	9600
Closing stock of finished goods	7900	7600

The effect of these stock valuation differences on the profit reported by the financial and cost accounting ledgers is that

A the financial accounting profit is £300 greater than the cost accounting profit.
B the financial accounting profit is £2100 greater than the cost accounting profit.
C the cost accounting profit is £300 greater than the financial accounting profit.
D the cost accounting profit is £900 greater than the financial accounting profit.
E the cost accounting profit is £2100 greater than the financial accounting profit.

CIMA Stage 2 – Operational Cost Accounting

4.17 Intermediate

The profits shown in the financial accounts was £158 500 but the cost accounts showed a different figure. The following stock valuations were used:

Stock valuations	Cost accounts	Financial accounts
	(£)	(£)
Opening stock	35 260	41 735
Closing stock	68 490	57 336

What was the profit in the cost accounts?

A £163 179
B £140 871
C £176 129
D £153 821

CIMA Stage 1

4.18 Intermediate

A construction company has the following data concerning one of its contracts:

Contract price	£2 000 000
Value certified	£1 300 000
Cash received	£1 200 000
Costs incurred	£1 050 000
Cost of work certified	£1 000 000

The profit (to the nearest £1000) to be attributed to the contract is

A £250 000
B £277 000
C £300 000
D £950 000
E £1 000 000

CIMA Stage 2

4.19 Intermediate

The effect of using the last in, first out (LIFO) method of stock valuation rather than the first in, first out (FIFO) method in a period of rising prices is

A to report lower profits and a lower value of closing stock.
B to report higher profits and a higher value of closing stock.
C to report lower profits and a higher value of closing stock.
D to report higher profits and a lower value of closing stock.

CIMA Management Accounting Fundamentals

4.20 Intermediate

MN plc uses a JIT system and backflush accounting. It does not use a raw material stock control account. During April, 1000 units were produced and sold. The standard cost per unit is £100: this includes materials of £45. During April, £60 000 of conversion costs were incurred.

The debit balance on the cost of goods sold account for April was

A £90 000
B £95 000
C £105 000
D £110 000
E £115 000

(2 marks)

CIMA Management Accounting – Decision Making

4.21 Intermediate: Stores pricing

Z Ltd had the following transactions in one of its raw materials during April

Opening stock		40 units	@£10 each
April 4	Bought	140 units	@£11 each
10	Used	90 units	
12	Bought	60 units	@£12 each
13	Used	100 units	
16	Bought	200 units	@£10 each
21	Used	70 units	
23	Used	80 units	
26	Bought	50 units	@£12 each
29	Used	60 units	

You are required to:

(a) write up the stores ledger card using
(i) FIFO and
(ii) LIFO
methods of stock valuation;

(8 marks)

(b) state the cost of material used for each system during April;

(2 marks)

(c) describe the weighted-average method of valuing stocks and explain how the use of this method would affect the cost of materials used and the balance sheet of Z Ltd compared to FIFO and LIFO in times of consistently rising prices. (Do NOT restate the stores ledger card for the above transactions using this method.)

(5 marks)

(Total 15 marks)

CIMA Stage 1 Accounting

4.22 Intermediate: Stores pricing and preparation of the stores control account

A company operates an historic batch costing system, which is not integrated with the financial accounts, and uses the weighted average method of pricing raw material issues. A weighted average price (to three decimal places of a pound £) is calculated after each purchase of material.

Receipts and issues of Material X for a week were as follows:

Receipts into stock			Issues to production	
Day	kg	£	Day	kg
1	1400	1092.00	2	1700
4	1630	1268.14	5	1250

At the beginning of the week, stock of material X was 3040 kg at a cost of £0.765 per kg. Of the issues of material on day 2, 60 kg were returned to stock on day 3. Of the receipts of material on day 1, 220 kg were returned to the supplier on day 4. Invoices for the material receipts during the week remained unpaid at the end of the week.

Required:

(a) Prepare a tabulation of the movement of stock during the week, showing the changes in the level of stock, its valuation per kilogram, and the total value of stock held.

(b) Record the week's transactions in the material X stock account in the cost ledger, indicating clearly in each case the account in which the corresponding entry should be posted.

(9 marks)
ACCA Foundation Paper 3

4.23 Intermediate: Interlocking accounts

CD Ltd, a company engaged in the manufacture of specialist marine engines, operates a historic job cost accounting system that is not integrated with the financial accounts.

At the beginning of May 2000 the opening balances in the cost ledger were as follows:

	(£)
Stores ledger control account	85 400
Work in progress control account	167 350
Finished goods control account	49 250
Cost ledger control account	302 000

During the month, the following transactions took place:

	(£)
Materials:	
Purchases	42 700
Issues to production	63 400
to general maintenance	1 450
to construction of manufacturing equipment	7 650
Factory wages:	
Total gross wages paid	124 000

£12 500 of the above gross wages were incurred on the construction of manufacturing equipment, £35 750 were indirect wages and the balance was direct.

Production overheads: the actual amount incurred, excluding items shown above, was £152 350; £30 000 was absorbed by the manufacturing equipment under construction and under absorbed overhead written off at the end of the month amounted to £7550.

Royalty payments: one of the engines produced is manufactured under licence. £2150 is the amount that will be paid to the inventor for the month's production of that particular engine.

Selling overheads: £22 000.

Sales: £410 000.

The company's gross profit margin is 25% on factory cost.

At the end of May stocks of work in progress had increased by £12 000. The manufacturing equipment under construction was completed within the month, and transferred out of the cost ledger at the end of the month.

Required:

Prepare the relevant control accounts, costing profit and loss account, and any other accounts you consider necessary to record the above transactions in the cost ledger for May 2000.

(22 marks)

ACCA Foundation Costing

4.24 Intermediate: Integrated accounts

In the absence of the accountant you have been asked to prepare a months cost accounts for a company which operates a batch costing system fully integrated with the financial accounts. The cost clerk has provided you with the following information, which he thinks is relevant:

	(£)
Balances at beginning of month:	
Stores ledger control account	24 175
Work in progress control account	19 210
Finished Goods control account	34 164
Prepayments of production overheads brought forward from previous month	2 100

	(£)
Transactions during the month:	
Materials purchased	76 150
Materials issued: to production	26 350
for factory maintenance	3 280
Materials transferred between batches	1 450

	Direct workers (£)	Indirect workers (£)
Total wages paid:		
Net	17 646	3 342
Employees deductions	4 364	890
Direct wages charged to batches from work tickets	15 236	
Recorded non-productive time of direct workers	5 230	
Direct wages incurred on production of capital equipment, for use in the factory	2 670	
Selling and distribution overheads incurred	5 240	
Other production overheads incurred	12 200	
Sales	75 400	
Cost of finished goods sold	59 830	
Cost of goods completed and transferred into finished goods store during the month	62 130	
Physical stock value of work in progress at end of month	24 360	

The production overhead absorption rate is 150% of direct wages, and it is the policy of the company to include a share of production overheads in the cost of capital equipment constructed in the factory.

Required:

(a) Prepare the following accounts for the month:
stores ledger control account
wages control account
work in progress control account
finished goods control account
production overhead control account
profit/loss account.

(12 marks)

(b) Identify any aspects of the accounts which you consider should be investigated.

(4 marks)

(c) Explain why it is necessary to value a company's stocks at the end of each period and also why, in a manufacturing company, expense items such as factory rent, wages of direct operatives, power costs, etc. are included in the value of work in progress and finished goods stocks.

(6 marks)

(Total 22 marks)

ACCA Level 1 Costing

4.25 Intermediate: Reconciliation of cost and financial accounts

K Limited operates separate cost accounting and financial accounting systems. The following manufacturing and trading statement has been prepared from the financial accounts for the *quarter* ended 31 March:

	(£)	(£)
Raw materials:		
Opening stock	48 800	
Purchases	108 000	
	156 800	
Closing stock	52 000	
Raw materials consumed		104 800
Direct wages		40 200
Production overhead		60 900
Production cost incurred		205 900
Work in progress:		
Opening stock	64 000	
Closing stock	58 000	6 000
Cost of goods produced		211 900
Sales		440 000
Finishing goods:		
Opening stock	120 000	
Cost of goods produced	211 900	
	331 900	
Closing stock	121 900	
Cost of goods sold		210 000
Gross profit		230 000

From the cost accounts, the following information has been extracted:

Control account balances at 1 January	(£)
Raw material stores	49 500
Work in progress	60 100
Finished goods	115 400

Transactions for the quarter:	(£)
Raw materials issued	104 800
Cost of goods produced	222 500
Cost of goods sold	212 100
Loss of materials damaged by flood (insurance claim pending)	2 400

A notional rent of £4000 *per month* has been charged in the cost accounts. Production overhead was absorbed at the rate of 185% of direct wages.

You are required to:

(a) prepare the following control accounts in the cost ledger:
raw materials stores;
work in process;
finished goods;
production overhead;

(10 marks)

(b) prepare a statement reconciling the gross profits as per the cost accounts and the financial accounts;

(11 marks)

(c) comment on the possible accounting treatment(s) of the under or over absorption of production overhead, assuming that the financial year of the company is 1 January to 31 December.

(4 marks)
(Total 25 marks)
CIMA Cost Accounting 1

4.26 Intermediate: Contract costing

HR Construction plc makes up its accounts to 31 March each year. The following details have been extracted in relation to two of its contracts:

	Contract A	Contract B
Commencement date	1 April 1999	1 December 1999
Target completion date	31 May 2000	30 June 2000
Retention %	4	3
	£000	**£000**
Contract price	2000	550
Materials sent to site	700	150
Materials returned to stores	80	30
Plant sent to site	1000	150
Materials transferred	(40)	40
Materials on site 31 March 2000	75	15
Plant hire charges	200	30
Labour cost incurred	300	270
Central overhead cost	75	18
Direct expenses incurred	25	4
Value certified	1500	500
Cost of work not certified	160	20
Cash received from client	1440	460
Estimated cost of completion	135	110

Depreciation is charged on plant using the straight line method at the rate of 12% per annum.

Required:

(a) Prepare contract accounts, in columnar format, for EACH of the contracts A and B, showing clearly the amounts to be transferred to profit and loss in respect of each contract.

(20 marks)

(b) Show balance sheet extracts in respect of EACH contract for fixed assets, debtors and work in progress.

(4 marks)

(c) Distinguish between job, batch and contract costing. Explain clearly the reasons why these methods are different.

(6 marks)
(Total 30 marks)
CIMA Stage 2 Operational Cost Accounting

Review problems (with answers in the Student's Manual)

4.27 Integrated accounts and computation of the net profit

Set out below are incomplete cost accounts for a period for a manufacturing business:

Stores Ledger Control Account

Opening Balance	£60 140		
Cost Ledger Control A/c	£93 106		
	£153 246		£153 246

Production Wages Control Account

Cost Ledger Control A/c		Finished Goods A/c	£87 480
		Production O'hd Control A/c	

Production Overhead Control Account

Cost Ledger Control A/c	£116 202		
Prod. Wages Control A/c			

Finished Goods Control Account

Opening Balance	£147 890	Prod. Cost of Sales (variable)	
		Closing Balance	£150 187

Notes:

1. *Raw materials:*

   Issues of materials from stores for the period:

   Material Y: 1164 kg (issued at a periodic weighted average price, calculated to two decimal places of £). Other materials: £78 520.

   No indirect materials are held on the Stores ledger.

   Transactions for Material Y in the period:

   Opening stock: 540 kg, £7663
   Purchases: 1100 kg purchased at £14.40 per kg

2. *Payroll:*

	Direct workers	Indirect workers
Hours worked:		
Basic time	11 140	4 250
Overtime	1 075	405
Productive time – direct workers	11 664	
Basic hourly rate (£)	7.50	5.70

   Overtime, which is paid at basic rate plus one third, is regularly worked to meet production targets.

3. *Production overheads:*

   The business uses a marginal costing system. 60% of production overheads are fixed costs. Variable production overhead costs are absorbed at a rate of 70% of actual direct labour.

4. *Finished goods:*

   There is no work in progress at the beginning or end of the period, and a Work in Progress Account is not kept. Direct materials issued, direct labour and production overheads absorbed are transferred to the Finished Goods Control Account.

   Required:

   (a) Complete the above four accounts for the period, by listing the missing amounts and descriptions.

   (13 marks)

   (b) Provide an analysis of the indirect labour for the period.

   (3 marks)

   (c) Calculate the contribution and the net profit for the period, based on the cost accounts prepared in (a) and using the following additional information:

   Sales £479 462

   Selling and administration overheads:

   variable £38 575

   fixed £74 360

   (4 marks)

   (Total 20 marks)

   ACCA Management Information – Paper 3

4.28 Intermediate: Stores pricing and preparation of relevant ledger accounts

V Ltd operates interlocking financial and cost accounts. The following balances were in the cost ledger at the beginning of a month, the last month (Month 12) of the financial year:

	Dr	Cr
Raw material stock control a/c	£28 944	
Finished goods stock control a/c	£77 168	
Financial ledger control a/c		£106 112

There is no work in progress at the end of each month.

21 600 kilos of the single raw material were in stock at the beginning of Month 12. Purchases and issues during the month were as follows:

Purchases:

7th, 17 400 kilos at £1.35 per kilo
29th, 19 800 kilos at £1.35 per kilo

Issues:

1st, 7270 kilos
8th, 8120 kilos
15th, 8080 kilos
22nd, 9115 kilos

A weighted average price per kilo (to four decimal places of a £) is used to value issues of raw material to production. A new average price is determined after each material purchase, and issues are charged out in total to the nearest £.

Costs of labour and overhead incurred during Month 12 were £35 407. Production of the company's single product was 17 150 units.

Stocks of finished goods were:

Beginning of Month 12, 16 960 units.
End of Month 12, 17 080 units.

Transfers from finished goods stocks on sale of the product are made on a FIFO basis.

Required:

(a) Prepare the raw material stock control account, and the finished goods stock control account, for Month 12. (Show detailed workings to justify the summary entries made in the accounts.)

(12 marks)

(b) Explain the purpose of the financial ledger control account.

(4 marks)

(c) Prepare the raw material usage and the raw material purchases budgets for the year ahead (in kilos) using the following information where relevant:

Sales budget, 206 000 units.

Closing stock of finished goods at the end of the budget year should be sufficient to meet 20 days sales demand in the year following that, when sales are expected to be 10% higher in volume than in the budget year.

Closing stock of raw materials should be sufficient to produce 11 700 units.

(NB You should assume that production efficiency will be maintained at the same level, and that there are 250 working days in each year.)

(9 marks)

(Total 25 marks)

ACCA Level 1 Costing

4.29 Integrated accounts, profits computation and reconciliation relating to absorption and marginal costing

A company manufactures two products (A and B). In the period just ended production and sales of the two products were:

	Product A (000 units)	Product B (000 units)
Production	41	27
Sales	38	28

The selling prices of the products were £35 and £39 per unit for A and B respectively.

Opening stocks were:

Raw materials £72 460

Finished goods:

Product A £80 640 (3200 units)
Product B £102 920 (3100 units)

Raw material purchases (on credit) during the period totalled £631 220. Raw material costs per unit are £7.20 for Product A and £11.60 for Product B.

Direct labour hours worked during the period totalled 73 400 (1 hour per unit of Product A and 1.2 hours per unit of Product B), paid at a basic rate of £8.00 per hour.

3250 overtime hours were worked by direct workers, paid at a premium of 25% over the basic rate. Overtime premiums are treated as indirect production costs. Other indirect labour costs during the period totalled £186 470 and production overhead costs (other than indirect labour) were £549 630. Production overheads are absorbed at a rate of £10.00 per direct labour hour (including £6.80 per hour for fixed production overheads). Any over-/under-absorbed balances are transferred to the Profit and Loss Account in the period in which they arise. Non-production overheads totalled £394 700 in the period.

Required:

(a) Prepare the following accounts for the period in the company's integrated accounting system:
   (i) Raw material stock control;
   (ii) Production overhead control;
   (iii) Finished goods stock control (showing the details of the valuation of closing stocks as a note).

(12 marks)

(b) Prepare the Profit and Loss Account for the period, clearly showing sales, production cost of sales and gross profit for each product.

(4 marks)

(c) Calculate, and explain, the difference in the net profit (loss) for the period if the marginal costing method is employed.

(4 marks)
(Total 20 marks)
ACCA Management Information – Paper 3

4.30 Intermediate: Labour cost accounting

(a) Describe briefly the purpose of the 'wages control account'.

(3 marks)

(b) A manufacturing company has approximately 600 weekly paid direct and indirect production workers. It incurred the following costs and deductions relating to the payroll for the week ended 2 May:

	(£)	(£)
Gross wages		180 460
Deductions:		
Employees' National Insurance	14 120	
Employees' pension fund contributions	7 200	
Income tax (PAYE)	27 800	
Court order retentions	1 840	
Trade union subscriptions	1 200	
Private health care contributions	6 000	
Total deductions		58 160
Net wages paid		122 300

The employer's National Insurance contribution for the week was £18 770.

From the wages analysis the following information was extracted:

	Direct workers £	Indirect workers £
Paid for ordinary time	77 460	38 400
Overtime wages at normal hourly rates	16 800	10 200
Overtime premium (treat as overhead)	5 600	3 400
Shift premiums/allowances	8 500	4 500
Capital work in progress expenditure*	—	2 300*
Statutory sick pay	5 700	3 300
Paid for idle time	4 300	—
	118 360	62 100

*Work done by building maintenance workers concreting floor area for a warehouse extension.

You are required to show journal entries to indicate clearly how each item should be posted into the accounts

(i) from the payroll, and

(ii) from the Wages Control Account to other accounts, based on the wages analysis.

Note: Narrations for the journal entries are not required.

(12 marks)

(Total 15 marks)

CIMA Stage 2 Cost Accounting

4.31 **Intermediate: Calculation as analysis of gross wages and preparation of wages and overhead control accounts**

The finishing department in a factory has the following payroll data for the month just ended:

	Direct workers	Indirect workers
Total attendance time (including overtime)	2640 hours	940 hours
Productive time	2515 hours	—
Non-productive time:		
Machine breakdown	85 hours	—
Waiting for work	40 hours	—
Overtime	180 hours	75 hours
Basic hourly rate	£5.00	£4.00
Group bonuses	£2840	£710
Employers' National Insurance contributions	£1460	£405

Overtime, which is paid at 140% of basic rate, is usually worked in order to meet the factory's general requirements. However, 40% of the overtime hours of both direct and indirect workers in the month were worked to meet the urgent request of a particular customer.

Required:

(a) Calculate the gross wages paid to direct workers and to indirect workers in the month.

(4 marks)

(b) Using the above information, record the relevant entries for the month in the finishing department's wages control account and production overhead control account. (You should clearly indicate the account in which the corresponding entry would be made in the company's separate cost accounting system. Workings must be shown.)

(10 marks)
(Total 14 marks)
ACCA Foundation Paper 3

4.32 Intermediate: Computation of contract profit

A company has been carrying out work on a number of building contracts (including Contract ABC) over the six-month period ended 31 May 2002. The following information is available:

	All Contracts (including ABC)	Contract ABC
Number of contracts worked on in the six months to 31.5.02	10	—
Value	£76.2 m	£6.4 m
Duration	8–22 months (average 13 months)	11 months
Contract months	53[1]	6
Direct labour costs in the period	£9.762 m	£1.017 m
Raw material costs in the period	£10.817 m	£1.456 m
Distance from base	16 kilometres (average)	23 kilometres
Value of work certified at 31.5.02	—	£5.180 m

Note:
[1]Contract months for 'All Contracts' are the sum of the number of months' work on each individual contact during the six-month period.

Contract ABC commenced on 1 September 2001. As at 30 November 2001 cumulative costs on the contract, held in work-in-progress, totalled £1.063 m (including overheads).

The company confidently predicts that further cost after 31 May 2002 to complete Contract ABC on time (including overheads) will not exceed £0.937 m. Overheads incurred over the six-month period to 31 May 2002, which are to be apportioned to individual contracts are:

	£m
Stores operations	1.56
Contract general management	1.22
Transport	1.37
General administration	4.25

The bases of apportionment are:

Stores operations
– contract value × contract months
Contract general management
– direct labour costs
Transport
– distance from base × contract months
General administration
– contract months

Required:

(a) (i) Apportion overheads to Contract ABC for the six-month period to 31 May 2002 (to the nearest £000 for each overhead item).

(6 marks)

(ii) Determine the expected profit/loss on Contract ABC, and the amount of profit/loss on the contract that you recommend be included in the accounts of the company for the six-month period to 31 May 2002.

(7 marks)

(b) The company is introducing a service costing system into its stores operations department.

Outline the key factors to consider when introducing the service costing system.

(7 marks)

(Total 20 marks)

ACCA Management Information – Paper 3

4.33 **Intermediate: Contract costing**

A construction company is currently undertaking three separate contracts and information relating to these contracts for the previous year, together with other relevant data, is shown below.

	Contract MNO (000)	**Contract PQR (000)**	**Contract STU (000)**	**Construction services dept overhead (000s)**
Contract price	800	675	1100	
Balances brought forward at beginning of year:				
Cost of work completed	—	190	370	—
Material on site	—	—	25	—
Written-down value of plant and machinery	—	35	170	12
Wages accrued	—	2	—	—
Profit previously transferred to profit/loss a/c	—	—	15	—
Transactions during year:				
Material delivered to site	40	99	180	—
Wages paid	20	47	110	8

Payments to subcontractors	—	—	35	—
Salaries and other costs	6	20	25	21
Written down value of plant:				
issued to sites	90	15	—	—
transferred from sites	—	8	—	—
Balances carried forward at the end of year:				
Material on site	8	—	—	—
Written-down value of plant and machinery	70	—	110	5
Wages accrued	—	5	—	—
Pre-payments to subcontractors	—	—	15	—
Value of work certified at end of year	90	390	950	—
Cost of work not certified at end of year	—	—	26	—

The cost of operating the construction services department, which provides technical advice to each of the contracts, is apportioned over the contracts in proportion to wages incurred. Contract STU is scheduled for handing over to the contractee in the near future and the site engineer estimates that the extra costs required to complete the contract in addition to those tabulated above, will total £138 000. This amount includes an allowance for plant depreciation, construction services and for contingencies.

Required:

(a) Construct a cost account for each of the three contracts for the previous year and show the cost of the work completed at the year end.

(9 marks)

(b) (i) Recommend how much profit or loss should be taken, for each contract, for the previous year.

(7 marks)

(ii) Explain the reasons for each of your recommendations in (b) (i) above.

(6 marks)

(Total 22 marks)

ACCA Level 1 Costing

Process costing

5

A process costing system is used in those industries where masses of similar products or services are produced. Products are produced in the same manner and consume the same amount of direct costs and overheads. It is therefore unnecessary to assign costs to individual units of output. Instead, the average cost per unit of output is calculated by dividing the total costs assigned to a product or service for a period by the number of units of output for that period. Industries where process costing is widely used include chemical processing, oil refining, food processing and brewing. In contrast, job costing relates to a costing system where each unit or batch of output is unique. This creates the need for the cost of each unit to be calculated separately.

Our objective in this chapter is to examine the cost accumulation procedure that is required for inventory valuation and profit measurement for a process costing system. We shall also discuss briefly at the end of the chapter how cost information should be accumulated and extracted for decision-making and cost control. We begin with a description of the flow of production and costs in a process costing environment. We shall then focus on the cost accumulation system. To provide a structured presentation three different scenarios

LEARNING OBJECTIVES

After studying this chapter you should be able to:

- explain when process costing systems are appropriate;
- explain the accounting treatment of normal and abnormal losses;
- prepare process, normal loss, abnormal loss and abnormal gain accounts when there is no ending work in progress;
- explain and calculate equivalent units;
- compute the value of closing work in progress and completed production using the weighted average and first in, first out methods of valuing work in progress;
- distinguish between the different cost per unit calculations that are necessary for inventory valuation, decision-making and performance reporting for cost control.

will be presented. First, all output is fully complete. Second, ending work in progress exists, but no beginning work in progress, and some of the units started during the period are incomplete at the end of the period. Our third scenario is the existence of both beginning and ending work in progress of uncompleted units. Finally, we shall turn our attention to decision-making and cost control. One of the most complex areas in process costing is accounting for losses when units within the process are both fully and partially complete. Because some courses omit this topic it will be discussed in Appendix 5.1.

Flow of production and costs in a process costing system

The flow of production and costs in a process costing system is illustrated in Exhibit 5.1. The major differences between process and job costing are also highlighted. You will see that production moves from one process (or department) to the next until final completion occurs. Each production department performs some part of the total operation and transfers its completed production to the next department, where it becomes the input for further processing. The completed production of the last department is transferred to the finished goods inventory.

The cost accumulation procedure follows this production flow. Control accounts are established for each process (or department) and direct and indirect costs are assigned to each process. A process costing system is easier to operate than a job costing system because the detailed work of allocating costs to many individual cost units is unnecessary. Also, many of the costs that are indirect in a job costing system may be regarded as direct in a process costing system. For example, supervision and depreciation that is confined to one department would be treated as part of the direct costs of that department in a process costing system, since these costs are directly attributable to the cost object (i.e. the department or process). However, such costs are normally regarded as indirect in a job costing system because they are not directly attributable to a specific job.

As production moves from process to process costs are transferred with it. For example, in Exhibit 5.1 the costs of process A would be transferred to process B; process B costs would then be added to this cost and the resulting total cost transferred to process C; process C costs would then added to this cost. Therefore the cost becomes cumulative as production proceeds and the addition of the costs from the last department's cost determines the total cost. The cost per unit of the completed product thus consists of the total cost accumulated in process C for the period divided by the output for that period.

Process costing when all output is fully complete

Throughout this section it is assumed that all output within each process is fully complete. We shall examine the following situations:

1 no losses within a process;
2 normal losses with no scrap value;
3 abnormal losses with no scrap value;
4 normal losses with a scrap value;
5 abnormal losses with a scrap value;
6 abnormal gains with no scrap value;
7 abnormal gains with a scrap value.

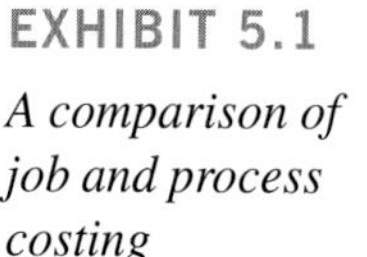

EXHIBIT 5.1
A comparison of job and process costing

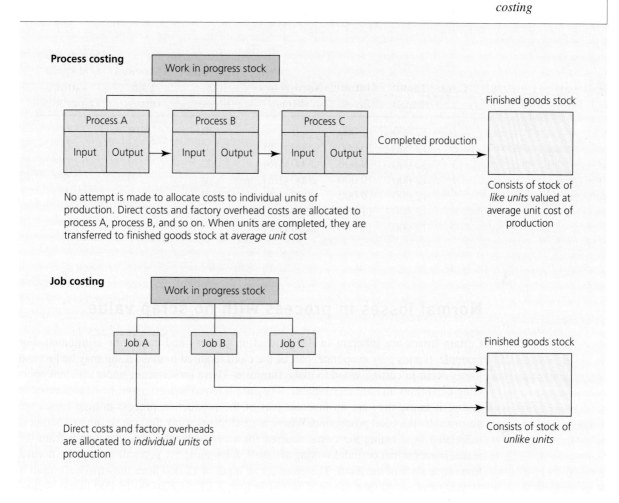

Process costing

Work in progress stock

Process A: Input | Output → Process B: Input | Output → Process C: Input | Output → Completed production → Finished goods stock

Consists of stock of *like units* valued at average unit cost of production

No attempt is made to allocate costs to individual units of production. Direct costs and factory overhead costs are allocated to process A, process B, and so on. When units are completed, they are transferred to finished goods stock at *average unit* cost

Job costing

Work in progress stock

Job A, Job B, Job C → Finished goods stock

Consists of stock of *unlike units*

Direct costs and factory overheads are allocated to *individual units* of production

You should now look at Example 5.1. The information shown in this example will be used to illustrate the accounting entries. To simplify the presentation it is assumed that the product is produced within a single process.

No losses within the process

To calculate the cost per unit (i.e. litre) of output for case 1 in Example 5.1 we merely divide the total cost incurred for the period of £120 000 by the output for the period (12 000 litres). The cost per unit of output is £10. In practice the cost per unit is analysed by the different cost categories such as direct materials and conversion cost which consists of the sum of direct labour and overhead costs.

EXAMPLE 5.1

Dartmouth Company produces a liquid fertilizer within a single production process. During the month of May the input into the process was 12 000 litres at a cost of £120 000. There were no opening or closing inventories and all output was fully complete. We shall prepare the process account and calculate the cost per litre of output for the single process for each of the following seven cases:

Case	Input (litres)	Output (litres)	Normal loss (litres)	Abnormal loss (litres)	Abnormal gain (litres)	Scrap value of spoilt output (£ per litre)
1	12 000	12 000	0	0	0	0
2	12 000	10 000	2000 (1/6)	0	0	0
3	12 000	9 000	2000 (1/6)	1 000	0	0
4	12 000	10 000	2000 (1/6)	0	0	5
5	12 000	9 000	2000 (1/6)	1 000	0	5
6	12 000	11 000	2000 (1/6)	0	1 000	0
7	12 000	11 000	2000 (1/6)	0	1 000	5

Normal losses in process with no scrap value

Certain losses are inherent in the production process and cannot be eliminated. For example, liquids may evaporate, part of the cloth required to make a suit may be lost and losses occur in cutting wood to make furniture. These losses occur under efficient operating conditions and are unavoidable. They are referred to as **normal or uncontrollable losses**. Because they are an inherent part of the production process normal losses are absorbed by the good production. Where normal losses apply the cost per unit of output is calculated by dividing the costs incurred for a period by the *expected* output from the actual input for that period. Looking at case 2 in Example 5.1 you will see that the normal loss is one sixth of the input. Therefore for an input of 12 000 litres the *expected* output is 10 000 litres so that the cost per unit of output is £12 (£120 000/10 000 litres). Actual output is equal to expected output so there is neither an abnormal loss nor gain. Compared with case 1 the unit cost has increased by £2 per unit because the cost of the normal loss has been absorbed by the good production. Our objective is to calculate the cost of normal production under normal efficient operating conditions.

Abnormal losses in process with no scrap value

In addition to losses that cannot be avoided, there are some losses that are not expected to occur under efficient operating conditions, for example the improper mixing of ingredients, the use of inferior materials and the incorrect cutting of cloth. These losses are not an inherent part of the production process, and are referred to as **abnormal or controllable losses**. Because they are not an inherent part of the production process and arise from inefficiencies they are not included in the process costs. Instead, they are removed from the appropriate process account and reported separately as an abnormal loss. The abnormal loss is treated as a period cost and written off in the profit statement at the end of the accounting period. This ensures that abnormal losses are not incorporated in any inventory valuations.

For case 3 in Example 5.1 the expected output is 10 000 litres but the actual output was 9000 litres, resulting in an abnormal loss of 1000 litres. Our objective is the same as that for normal losses. That is to calculate the cost per litre of the *expected* output (i.e. normal production), which is:

$$\frac{\text{input cost (£120 000)}}{\text{expected output (10 000 litres)}} = £12$$

Note that the unit cost is the same for an output of 10 000 or 9000 litres since our objective is to calculate the cost per unit of normal output. The distribution of the input costs is as follows:

	(£)
Completed production transferred to the next process (or finished goods inventory) 9000 litres at £12	108 000
Abnormal loss: 1000 litres at £12	12 000
	120 000

The abnormal loss is valued at the cost per unit of normal production. Abnormal losses can only be controlled in the future by establishing the cause of the abnormal loss and taking appropriate remedial action to ensure that it does not reoccur. The entries in the process account will look like this:

Process account

	Litres	Unit cost (£)	(£)		Litres	Unit cost (£)	(£)
Input cost	12 000	10	120 000	Normal loss	2 000	—	—
				Output to finished goods inventory	9 000	12	108 000
				Abnormal loss	1 000	12	12 000
			120 000				120 000

Process accounts represent work in progress (WIP) accounts. For example, if a second process were required and the 9000 litres had remained from the first process at the end of the accounting period the £108 000 would have represented the work in progress valuation in the process. In our example all of the work in progress has been completed and transferred to the finished goods inventory. Input costs are debited to the process account and the output from the process is entered on the credit side.

You will see from the process account that no entry is made in the account for the normal loss (except for an entry made in the units column). The transfer to the finished goods inventory (or the next process) is at the cost of normal production. The abnormal loss is removed from the process costs and reported separately as a loss in the abnormal loss account. This draws the attention of management to those losses that may be controllable. At the end of the accounting period the abnormal loss account is written off in the profit statement as a period cost. The inventory valuation will not therefore include any abnormal expenses. The overall effect is that the abnormal losses are correctly allocated

How process and activity-based cost analysis meets the needs of a small manufacturer

Kunde Estate Winery is a small wine producer in California's Sonoma Valley. Cost accounting for wine making differs in several ways from the system used by other manufacturers. The system is a hybrid between process costing and job costing. As each lot of wine in a given vintage may be processed differently, each *process* can incur varying costs. Process department costs are clearly identified. The key to costing wine inventory is to follow the wine's movements. Equipment and depredation are identified by department where possible. Otherwise, depredation is allocated based on estimated usage by *process* departments, including Crush and Ferment, Tank Aging, Barrel Aging, Bottling and General Production. Each department incurs costs that are periodically allocated. Allocations of process costs need only be applied to individual lots at bottling and at year end. Between applications of process costs to lots, the lot costs will change with blending activity and losses from it.

Labour and benefits are charged to the general production department. Each month, the wine maker and the cellar master review the work performed and report to accounting the percentage of each employee's time spent in each department. These estimates provide the basis of allocation for labour. The general production department is the overhead department for wine making operations. The wine maker's salary and benefits, and insurance, laboratory and administrative expenses, are collected here for allocation to the process departments, based on estimates of activity by the wine maker.

Source: Kunde Estate Winery and Vineyards

Source: Adapted from Lee, J.Y. and Jacobs, B.G., How process and activity-based cost analysis meets the needs of a small manufacturer, *CMA Magazine* (Canada), April 93, Vol. 67 Issue 3, pp. 15–19.

to the period in which they arise and are not carried forward as a future expense in the closing inventory valuation.

Normal losses in process with a scrap value

In case 4 actual output is equal to the expected output of 10 000 litres so there is neither an abnormal gain nor loss. All of the units lost represent a normal loss in process. However, the units lost now have a scrap value of £5 per litre. The sales value of the spoiled units should be offset against the costs of the appropriate process where the loss occurred. Therefore the sales value of the normal loss is credited to the process account and a corresponding debit entry will be made in the cash or accounts receivable (debtors) account. The calculation of the cost per unit of output is as follows:

$$\frac{\text{Input cost less scrap value of normal loss}}{\text{Expected output}} = \frac{\pounds 120\,000 - (2000 \times \pounds 5)}{10\,000 \text{ litres}} = \pounds 11$$

Compared with cases 2 and 3 the cost per unit has declined from £12 per litre to £11 per litre to reflect the fact that the normal spoilage has a scrap value which has been offset against the process costs.

The entries in the process account will look like this:

Process account

	Litres	Unit cost (£)	(£)		Litres	Unit cost (£)	(£)
Input cost	12 000	10	120 000	Normal loss	2 000	—	10 000
				Output to finished goods inventory	10 000	11	110 000
			120 000				120 000

Note that the scrap value of the normal loss is credited against the normal loss entry in the process account.

Abnormal losses in process with a scrap value

In case 5 expected output is 10 000 litres for an input of 12 000 litres and actual output is 9000 litres resulting in a normal loss of 2000 litres and an abnormal loss of 1000 litres. The lost units have a scrap value of £5 per litre. Since our objective is to calculate the cost per unit for the expected (normal) output only the scrap value of the normal loss of 2000 litres should be deducted in ascertaining the cost per unit. Therefore the cost per unit calculation is the same as that for case 4 (i.e. £11). The sales value of the additional 1000 litres lost represents revenue of an abnormal nature and should not be used to reduce the process unit cost. This revenue is offset against the cost of the abnormal loss which is of interest to management. The net cost incurred in the process is £105 000 (£120 000 input cost less 3000 litres lost with a scrap value of £5 per litre), and the distribution of this cost is:

	(£)	(£)
Completed production transferred to the next process (or finished goods inventory) (9000 litres at £11 per litre)		99 000
Abnormal loss:		
1000 litres at £11 per litre	11 000	
Less scrap value (1000 litres at £5)	5 000	6 000
		105 000

The entries in the process account will be as follows:

Process account

	Litres	Unit cost (£)	(£)		Litres	Unit cost (£)	(£)
Input cost	12 000	10	120 000	Normal loss	2 000	—	10 000
				Output to finished goods inventory	9 000	11	99 000
				Abnormal loss	1 000	11	11 000
			120 000				120 000

Abnormal loss account

	(£)		(£)
Process account	11 000	Cash sale for units scrapped	5 000
		Balance transferred to profit statement	6 000
	11 000		11 000

Abnormal gains with no scrap value

On occasions the actual loss in process may be less than expected, in which case an abnormal gain results. In case 6 the expected output is 10 000 litres for an input of 12 000 litres but the actual output is 11 000 litres resulting in an abnormal gain of 1000 litres. We are assuming for this case that the normal loss does not have a scrap value. As in the previous cases our objective is to calculate the cost per unit of expected (normal) output. The calculation of the cost per unit of normal output is the same as that for cases 2 and 3, which is:

$$\frac{\text{input cost (£120 000)}}{\text{expected output (10 000 litres)}} = \text{£}12$$

and the distribution of the input cost is as follows:

	(£)
Completed production transferred to the next process (or finished goods inventory) 11 000 litres at £12	132 000
Less: Abnormal gain: 1000 litres at £12	12 000
	120 000

The value of the gain is calculated in the same way as the abnormal loss and removed from the process account by debiting the account and crediting the abnormal gain account. The entries in the process account will be as follows:

Process account

	Litres	Unit cost (£)	(£)		Litres	Unit cost (£)	(£)
Input cost	12 000	10	120 000	Normal loss	2 000	—	—
Abnormal gain	1 000	12	12 000	Output to finished goods inventory	11 000	12	132 000
			132 000				132 000

You will see in the process account that 11 000 litres are passed to the next process at the cost per unit of *normal* output. The gain is credited to the abnormal gain account and transferred to the credit of the profit and loss statement at the end of the period. This procedure ensures that the inventory valuation is not understated by gains of an abnormal nature.

Abnormal gains with a scrap value

The only difference between cases 7 and 6 is that any losses have a scrap value of £5 per litre. As in the previous cases we start by calculating the cost per unit of normal output. For normal output our assumptions are the same as those for cases 4 and 5 (i.e. a normal loss of one sixth and a scrap value of £5 per litre) so the cost per unit of output is the same (i.e. £11 per litre). The calculation is as follows:

$$\frac{\text{Input cost less scrap value of normal loss}}{\text{Expected output}} = \frac{£120\,000 - (2000 \times £5)}{10\,000 \text{ litres}} = £11$$

The net cost incurred in the process is £115 000 (£120 000 input cost less 1000 litres spoilt with a sales value of £5 per litre), and the distribution of this cost is as follows:

		(£)
Transferred to finished goods inventory		
(11 000 litres at £11 per litre)		121 000
Less abnormal gain (1000 litres at £11 per litre)	11 000	
lost sales of spoiled units (1000 litres at £5 per litre)	5 000	6 000
		115 000

Note that the cost per unit is based on the normal production cost per unit and is not affected by the fact that an abnormal gain occurred or that sales of the spoiled units with a sales value of £5000 did not materialize. Our objective is to produce a cost per unit based on normal operating efficiency.

The accounting entries are as follows:

Process account

	Litres	Unit cost (£)	(£)		Litres	Unit cost (£)	(£)
Input cost	12 000	10	120 000	Normal loss	2 000	—	10 000
Abnormal gain	1 000	11	11 000	Output to finished goods inventory	11 000	11	121 000
			131 000				131 000

Abnormal gain account

	(£)		(£)
Normal loss account	5 000	Process account	11 000
Profit and loss statement (Balance)	6 000		
	11 000		11 000

Income due from normal losses

	(£)		(£)
Process account	10 000	Abnormal gain account	5 000
		Cash from spoiled units (1000 litres at £5)	5 000
	10 000		10 000

You will see that the abnormal gain has been removed from the process account and that it is valued at the cost per unit of normal production. However, as 1000 litres were gained, there was a loss of sales revenue of £5000, and this lost revenue is offset against the abnormal gain. The net gain is therefore £6000, and this is the amount that should be credited to the profit statement.

The process account is credited with the expected sales revenue from the normal loss (2000 litres at £5), since the objective is to record in the process account normal net costs of production. Because the normal loss of 2000 litres does not occur, the company will not obtain the sales value of £10 000 from the expected lost output. This problem is resolved by making a corresponding debit entry in a normal loss account, which represents the amount due from the sale proceeds from the expected normal loss. The amount due (£10 000) is then reduced by £5000 to reflect the fact that only 1000 litres were lost. This is achieved by crediting the normal loss account (income due) and debiting the abnormal gain account with £5000, so that the balance of the normal loss account shows the actual amount of cash received for the income due from the spoiled units (i.e. £5000, which consists of 1000 litres at £5 per litre).

Process costing with ending work in progress partially complete

So far we have assumed that all output within a process is fully complete. We shall now consider situations where output started during a period is partially complete at the end of the period. In other words, ending work in progress exists within a process. When some of the output started during a period is partially complete at the end of the period, unit costs cannot be computed by simply dividing the total costs for a period by the output for that period. For example, if 8000 units were started and completed during a period and another 2000 units were partly completed then these two items cannot be added together to ascertain their unit cost. We must convert the work in progress into finished equivalents (also referred to as **equivalent production**) so that the unit cost can be obtained.

To do this we must estimate the percentage degree of completion of the work in progress and multiply this by the number of units in progress at the end of the accounting period. If the 2000 partly completed units were 50% complete, we could express this as an equivalent production of 1000 fully completed units. This would then be added to the completed production of 8000 units to give a total equivalent production of 9000 units. The cost per unit would then be calculated in the normal way. For example, if the costs for the period were £180 000 then the cost per unit completed would be £20 (£180 000/9000 units) and the distribution of this cost would be as follows:

	(£)
Completed units transferred to the next process (8000 units at £20)	160 000
Work in progress (1000 equivalent units at £20)	20 000
	180 000

Elements of costs with different degrees of completion

A complication that may arise concerning equivalent units is that in any given stock of work in progress not all of the elements that make up the total cost may have reached the same degree of completion. For example, materials may be added at the start of the process, and are thus fully complete, whereas labour and manufacturing overhead (i.e. the conversion costs) may be added uniformly throughout the process. Hence, the ending work in progress

Process B account

Previous process cost	270 000	Completed production	
Materials	108 000	transferred to finished stock	513 000
Conversions cost	171 000	Closing work in progress c/fwd	36 000
	549 000		549 000
Opening WIP b/fwd	36 000		

You will see that the previous process cost is treated as a separate process cost, and, since this element of cost will not be added to in process B, the closing work in progress must be fully complete as far as previous process cost is concerned. Note that, after the first process, materials may be issued at different stages of production. In process B materials are not issued until the end of the process, and the closing work in progress will not have reached this point; the equivalent production for the closing work in progress will therefore be zero for materials.

Normally, material costs are introduced at one stage in the process and not uniformly throughout the process. If the work in progress has passed the point at which the materials are added then the materials will be 100% complete. If this point has not been reached then the equivalent production for materials will be zero.

Beginning and ending work in progress of uncompleted units

When opening stocks of work in progress exist, an assumption must be made regarding the allocation of this opening stock to the current accounting period to determine the unit cost for the period. Two alternative assumptions are possible. First, one may assume that opening work in progress is inextricably merged with the units introduced in the current period and can no longer be identified separately – the **weighted average method**. Secondly, one may assume that the opening work in progress is the first group of units to be processed and completed during the current month – the **first in, first out method**. Let us now compare these methods using the information contained in Example 5.3.

For more complex problems it is always a good idea to start by calculating the number of units completed during the period. The calculations are as follows:

	Process X	Process Y
Opening work in progress	6 000	2 000
Units introduced during period	16 000	18 000
Total input for period	22 000	20 000
Less closing work in progress	4 000	8 000
Balance – completed production	18 000	12 000

Weighted average method

The calculation of the unit cost for process X using the weighted average method is as follows:

EXAMPLE 5.3

The Baltic Company has two processes, X and Y. Material is introduced at the start of process X, and additional material is added to process Y when the process is 70% complete. Conversion costs are applied uniformly throughout both processes. The completed units of process X are immediately transferred to process Y, and the completed production of process Y is transferred to finished goods stock. Data for the period include the following:

	Process X	Process Y
Opening work in progress	6000 units 60% converted, consisting of materials £72 000 and conversion cost £45 900	2000 units 80% converted, consisting of previous process cost of £91 800, materials £12 000 and conversion costs £38 400
Units started during the period	16 000 units	18 000 units
Closing work in progress	4000 units 3/4 complete	8000 units 1/2 complete
Material costs added during the period	£192 000	£60 000
Conversion costs added during the period	£225 000	£259 200

Process X – weighted average method

Cost element	Opening WIP (£)	Current cost (£)	Total cost (£)	Completed units	WIP equiv. units	Total equiv. units	Cost per [unit] (£)
Materials	72 000	192 000	264 000	18 000	4000	22 000	12.00
Conversion cost	45 900	225 000	270 900	18 000	3000	21 000	12.90
	117 900		534 900				24.90

	(£)	(£)
Work in progress:		
Materials (4000 units at £12)	48 000	
Conversion (3000 units at £12.90)	38 700	86 700
Completed units (18 000 units at £24.90)		448 200
		534 900

Process X account

Opening work in progress b/fwd	117 900	Completed production transferred to process Y	448 200
Materials	192 000	Closing work in progress c/fwd	86 700
Conversion cost	225 000		
	534 900		534 900
Opening work in progress b/fwd	86 700		

You can see from the statement of unit cost calculations that the opening work in progress is assumed to be completed in the current period. The current period's costs will include the cost of finishing off the opening work in progress, and the cost of the work in progress will be included in the total cost figure. The completed units will include the 6000 units in progress that will have been completed during the period. The statement therefore includes all the costs of the opening work in progress and the resulting units, fully completed. In other words, we have assumed that the opening work in progress is intermingled with the production of the current period to form one homogeneous batch of production. The equivalent number of units for this batch of production is divided into the costs of the current period, plus the value of the opening work in progress, to calculate the cost per unit.

Let us now calculate the unit cost for process Y using the weighted average method. From the calculation of the unit costs you can see the previous process cost is fully complete as far as the closing work in progress is concerned. Note that materials are added when the process is 70% complete, but the closing work in progress is only 50% complete. At the stage in question no materials will have been added to the closing work in progress, and the equivalent production will be zero. As with process X, it is necessary to add the opening work in progress cost to the current cost. The equivalent production of opening work in progress is ignored since this is included as being fully complete in the completed units column. Note also that the completed production cost of process X is included in the current cost column for 'the previous process cost' in the unit cost calculation for process Y.

Process Y – Weighted average method

Cost element	Opening WIP value (£)	Current period cost (£)	Total cost (£)	Completed units	WIP equiv. units	Total equiv. units	Cost per unit (£)
Previous process cost	91 800	448 200	540 000	12 000	8000	20 000	27.00
Materials	12 000	60 000	72 000	12 000	—	12 000	6.00
Conversion cost	38 400	259 200	297 600	12 000	4000	16 000	18.60
	142 200		909 600				51.60

	(£)	(£)
Value of work in progress:		
Previous process cost (8000 units at £27)	216 000	
Materials	—	
Conversion cost (4000 units at £18.60)	74 400	290 400
Completed units (12 000 units at £51.60)		619 200
		909 600

Process Y account

Opening work in progress	142 200	Completed production	
Transferred from process X	448 200	transferred to finished stock	619 200

Materials	60 000	Closing work in progress c/fwd	290 400
Conversion cost	259 200		
	909 600		909 600
Opening work in progress b/fwd	290 400		

First in first out (FIFO) method

The FIFO method of process costing assumes that the opening work in progress is the first group of units to be processed and completed during the current period. The opening work in progress is charged separately to completed production, and the cost per unit is based only on the *current period* costs and production for the current period. The closing work in progress is assumed to come from the new units started during the period. Let us now use Example 5.3 to illustrate the FIFO method for process X and Y.

Process X – FIFO method

Cost element	Current period costs (£)	Completed units less opening WIP equiv. units	Closing WIP equiv. units	Current total equiv. units	Cost per unit (£)
Materials	192 000	12 000 (18 000 – 6000)	4000	16 000	12.00
Conversion cost	225 000	14 400 (18 000 – 3600)	3000	17 400	12.93
	417 000				24.93

	(£)	(£)
Completed production:		
Opening WIP	117 900	
Materials (12 000 units at £12)	144 000	
Conversion cost (14 400 units at £12.93)	186 207	448 107
Closing WIP:		
Materials (4000 units at £12)	48 000	
Conversion cost (3000 units at £12.93)	38 793	86 793
		534 900

From this calculation you can see that the average cost per unit is based on current period costs divided by the current total equivalent units for the period. The latter figure excludes the equivalent production for opening work in progress since this was performed in the previous period. Note that the closing work in progress is multiplied by the current period average cost per unit. The closing work in progress includes only the current costs and does not include any of the opening work in progress, which is carried forward from the previous period. The objective is to ensure that the opening work in progress is kept separate and is identified as part of the cost of the completed production. The opening work in progress of £117 900 is not therefore included in the unit cost calculations, but is added directly to the completed production.

Let us now calculate the units costs for process Y:

Process Y – FIFO method

Cost element	Current costs (£)	Completed units less opening WIP equiv. units	Closing WIP equiv. units	Current total equiv. units	Cost per unit (£)
Previous process cost	448 107	10 000 (12 000 – 2000)	8000	18 000	24.8948
Materials	60 000	10 000 (12 000 – 2000)	—	10 000	6.0
Conversion cost	259 200	10 400 (12 000 – 1600)	4000	14 400	18.0
	767 307				48.8948

	(£)	(£)
Cost of completed production:		
Opening WIP	142 200	
Previous process cost (10 000 units at £24.8948)	248 948	
Materials (10 000 units at £6)	60 000	
Conversion cost (10 400 units at £18)	187 200	638 348
Cost of closing work in progress:		
Previous process cost (8000 units at £24.8948)	199 159	
Materials	—	
Conversion cost (4000 units at £18)	72 000	271 159
		909 507

Note that in this calculation the *opening* work in progress is 80% completed, and that the materials are added when the process is 70% complete. Hence, they will be fully complete. Remember also that previous process cost is always 100% complete. Therefore in the third column of the above statement 2000 units opening work in progress is deducted for these two elements of cost from the 12 000 units of completed production. Conversion cost will be 80% complete so 1600 equivalent units are deducted from the completed production. Our objective in the third column is to extract the equivalent completed units that were derived from the units started during the current period. You should also note that the previous process cost of £448 107 represents the cost of completed production of process X, which has been transferred to process Y.

The closing work in progress valuations and the charges to completed production are fairly similar for both methods. The difference in the calculations between FIFO and the weighted average method is likely to be insignificant where the quantity of inventories and the input prices do not fluctuate significantly from month to month. Both methods are acceptable for product costing, but it appears that the FIFO method is not widely used in practice (Horngren, 1967).

Partially completed output and losses in process

Earlier in this chapter we looked at how to deal with losses in process when all of the output in a process was fully complete. We also need to look at the treatment of losses when all of the output is not fully complete. When this situation occurs the computations can become complex. Accounting for losses when all of the output is not fully complete does not form part of the curriculum for many courses. However, most professional management accounting courses do require you to have a knowledge of this topic. Because of these different requirements this topic is dealt with in Appendix 5.1. You should therefore check the requirements of your curriculum to ascertain whether you can omit Appendix 5.1.

Process costing for decision-making and control

The detailed calculations that we have made in this chapter are necessary for calculating profit and valuing stocks. For example, the process work in progress forms part of the balance sheet inventory valuations, and the transfers to succeeding processes become part of the work in progress of these processes or form part of the finished goods inventory. If the inventory is sold, these costs become part of the cost of goods sold for profit calculations. The calculations of unit costs, process work in progress valuations and the completed units valuation transferred to the next process are therefore necessary to determine the balance sheet inventory valuation and the cost of goods sold figure.

It is most unlikely that this same information will be appropriate for decision-making and cost control. In particular, process total unit costs will not be relevant for decision-making. What is required is an analysis of costs into their incremental and non-incremental elements for each process. A detailed discussion of those costs that are relevant for decision-making will be deferred to Chapter 9, but it is important that you should note at this point that the costs for decision-making purposes should be assembled in a different way.

Cost control

In respect of cost control, we must ensure that the actual costs that are included on a performance report are the costs incurred for the *current period only* and do not include any costs that have been carried forward from previous periods. This principle can be illustrated using the information given in Example 5.3 for process X.

The unit cost statement for product X, using the weighted average method, shown on page 166 was as follows:

Cost element	Opening WIP value (£)	Current cost (£)	Total cost (£)	Completed units	WIP equiv. units	Total equiv. units	Cost per unit (£)
Materials	72 000	192 000	264 000	18 000	4000	22 000	12.00
Conversion cost	45 900	225 000	270 900	18 000	3000	21 000	12.90

This statement is not appropriate for cost control, since it includes the value of work in progress brought forward from the previous period. Also, the total equivalent units includes the opening work in progress equivalent units partly processed in the previous period. The inclusion of previous period costs and production is appropriate for inventory valuation and profit measurement, since the objective is to match costs (irrespective of when they were incurred) with revenues, but it is not appropriate to include previous costs for cost control. The objective of cost control is to compare the actual costs of the *current* period with the budgeted cost for the equivalent units produced during the *current* period. We wish to measure a manager's performance for the current period and to avoid this measure being distorted by carrying forward costs that were incurred in the previous period. We must therefore calculate the equivalent units produced during the current period by deducting the equivalent units produced during the previous period from the total number of equivalent units. The calculation is as follows:

	Total equivalent units	Opening WIP equiv. units	Equiv. units produced during period
Materials	22 000	6000	16 000
Conversion cost	21 000	3600 (60% × 6000)	17 400

Note that materials are introduced at the start of the process, and the 6000 units opening work in progress will have been fully completed in the previous period as far as materials are concerned. Assuming that the budgeted costs for the period are £11.40 for materials and £12 for conversion costs we can now present the following cost control performance report:

Performance report

	Budgeted cost (£)	Current period actual cost (£)	Difference (£)
Materials	182 400 (16 000 units at £11.40)	192 000	9 600 adverse
Conversion cost	208 800 (17 400 units at £12)	225 000	16 200 adverse

From this report you will see that we are comparing like with like; that is, both the budgeted costs and the actual costs refer to the equivalent units produced during the *current* period.

Note that information required for cost control must be analysed in far more detail than that presented in the performance report here. For example, the different types of materials and conversion costs must be listed and presented under separate headings for controllable and non-controllable expenses. The essential point to note, however, is that current period actual costs must be compared with the budgeted cost for the current period's production.

Batch/operating costing

It is not always possible to classify cost accumulation systems into job costing and process costing systems. Where manufactured goods have some common characteristics and also some individual characteristics, the cost accumulation system may be a combination of both the job costing and process costing systems. For example, the production of footwear, clothing and furniture often involves the production of batches, which are variations of a single design and require a sequence of standardized operations. Let us consider a company that makes kitchen units. Each unit may have the same basic frame, and require the same operation, but the remaining operations may differ: some frames may require sinks, others may require to be fitted with work tops; different types of doors may be fitted to each unit, some may be low-quality doors while others may be of a higher quality. The cost of a kitchen unit will therefore consist of the basic frame plus the conversion costs of the appropriate operations. The principles of the cost accumulation system are illustrated in Exhibit 5.2.

EXHIBIT 5.2
A batch costing system

Product	Operations 1	2	3	4	5	Product cost
A	✓	✓	✓			A = cost of operations 1, 2, 3
B	✓			✓	✓	B = cost of operations 1, 4, 5
C	✓	✓		✓		C = cost of operations 1, 2, 4
D	✓		✓		✓	D = cost of operations 1, 3, 5
E	✓	✓			✓	E = cost of operations 1, 2, 5

The cost of each product consists of the cost of operation 1 plus a combination of the conversion costs for operations 2–5. The cost per unit produced for a particular operation consists of the average unit cost of each batch produced for each operation. It may well be that some products may be subject to a final operation that is unique to the product. The production cost will then consist of the average cost of a combination of operations 1–5 plus the specific cost of the final unique operation. The cost of the final operation will be traced specifically to the product using a job costing system. The final product cost therefore consists of a combination of process costing techniques and job costing techniques. This system of costing is referred to as **operation costing** or **batch costing**.

Surveys of practice

Little information is available on the extent to which process or job costing systems are used in practice. However, surveys of USA (Schwarzbach, 1985), Finnish (Lukka and Granlund, 1996) and Australian (Joye and Blayney, 1990) companies report the following usage rates:

	USA %	Finland %	Australia %
Process costing	36	32	63
Job costing	28	30	40
No process or job costing		38	
Process and Job combined	10		
Operation costing	18		

Presumably the Australian survey adopted a wider definition of process and job costing resulting in the respondents choosing one of the two categories whereas the Finnish study may have adopted a narrower definition. This may account for the fact that 38% of the organizations indicated that they adopted neither purely job nor process costing systems. These companies are likely to combine elements of both job and process costing.

Summary

The following items relate to the learning objectives listed at the beginning of the chapter.

- **Explain when process costing systems are appropriate.**

  A process costing system is appropriate in those situations where masses of identical units or batches are produced thus making it unnecessary to assign costs to individual or batches of output. Instead, the average cost per unit or batch of output is calculated by dividing the total costs assigned to a product or service for the period by the number of units or batches of output for that period. Industries using process costing systems include chemicals, textiles and oil refining.

- **Explain the accounting treatment of normal and abnormal losses.**

  Normal losses are inherent in the production process and cannot be eliminated: their cost should be borne by the good production. This is achieved by dividing the costs incurred for a period by the expected output rather than the actual output. Abnormal losses are avoidable, and the cost of these losses should not be assigned to products but recorded separately as an abnormal loss and written off as a period cost in the profit statement. Scrap sales (if any) that result from the losses should be allocated to the appropriate process account (for normal losses) and the abnormal loss account (for abnormal losses).

- **Prepare process, normal loss, abnormal loss and abnormal gain accounts when there is no ending work in progress.**

  The cost accumulation procedure follows the production flow. Control accounts are established for each process (or department) and costs are assigned (debited) to each process. Abnormal losses are credited to the process where they were incurred and debited to an abnormal loss account. Scrap sales arising from normal losses are credited to the process account and any sales of scrap arising from abnormal losses are credited to the abnormal losses account. The accounting entries were illustrated using Example 5.1.

- **Explain and calculate equivalent units.**

  Where stocks of work in progress are in existence, it is necessary in order to create homogeneous units of output to convert the work in progress into finished equivalent units of output. To do this we must estimate the percentage degree of completion of the work in progress and multiply this by the number of units in progress at the end of the accounting period. For example, if there are 5000 completed units estimated to be 40% complete this represents an equivalent production of 2000 completed units.

- **Compute the value of closing work in progress and completed production using the weighted average method and first in, first out methods of valuing work in progress.**

  There are two alternative methods of allocating opening work in progress costs to production: the weighted average and first in, first out methods. If the weighted average method is used, both the units and the value of opening work in progress are merged with the current period costs and production to calculate the average cost per unit. Using the first in, first out method, the opening work in progress is assumed to be the first group of units to be processed and completed during the current period. The opening work in progress is therefore assigned separately to completed production and the cost per unit is based only on current costs and production for the period. The closing work in progress is assumed to come from the new units that have been started during the period. The computations of closing work in progress and completed production using both methods together with the appropriate accounting entries were illustrated using Example 5.3.

- **Distinguish between the different costs per unit that are necessary for inventory valuation, decision-making and performance reporting for cost control.**

  For inventory valuation an average cost per unit of output is calculated by dividing process costs by the output of the process. Any costs incurred in the previous period (i.e. opening work in progress) and units in progress are merged with current period costs and production to compute the average cost per unit of completed production. The objective is to match the costs incurred with the associated production and this may entail the carrying forward of costs incurred in previous periods. For decision-making the focus is on the additional future costs and revenues resulting from a decision. Therefore only incremental costs (often represented by variable costs) may be relevant for short-term decisions. In respect of cost control, it is only current costs and production that should be included in the performance reports, since the focus should be on a manager's performance for the current period. Thus, performance reports should not be distorted with costs carried forward from previous periods.

- **Additional learning objectives specified in Appendix 5.1.**

  The appendix to this chapter includes one additional objective: to compute the value of normal and abnormal losses when there is ending work in progress. Because accounting for losses when all of the output is not fully complete is a complex topic that does not form part of the curriculum for many courses, this topic is dealt with in Appendix 5.1. You should check your course curriculum to ascertain if you need to read Appendix 5.1.

Appendix 5.1: Losses in process and partially completed units

Normal losses

Earlier in this chapter, we established that normal losses should be considered as part of the cost of the good production. We need to know, however, at what stage in the process the loss occurs so that we can determine whether the whole loss should be allocated to completed production or whether some of the loss should also be allocated to the closing work in progress. If the loss occurs near the end of the process, or is discovered at the point of inspection, only the units which have reached the inspection point should be allocated with the cost of the loss. Alternatively, the loss could be assumed to occur at a specific point, earlier in the process.

Generally, it is assumed that normal losses take place at the stage of completion where inspection occurs. Where such an assumption is made, the normal loss will not be allocated to the closing work in progress, since the loss is related only to units that have reached the inspection point. Consider Example 5A.1.

To calculate the value of the normal loss, we prepare the normal unit cost statement, but with a separate column for the number of units lost:

Element of cost	Total cost (£)	Completed units	Normal loss	WIP equiv. units	Total equiv. units	Cost per unit (£)
Materials	5000	600	100	300	1000	5.0
Conversion cost	3400	600	100	150	850	4.0
	8400					9.0

	(£)	(£)
Value of work in progress:		
Materials (300 units at £5)	1500	
Conversion cost (150 units at £4)	600	2100
Completed units (600 units at £9)	5400	
Normal loss (100 units at £9)	900	6300
		8400

EXAMPLE 5A.1

A department with no opening work in progress introduces 1000 units into the process; 600 are completed, 300 are half-completed and 100 units are lost (all normal). *Losses are detected upon completion.* Material costs are £5000 (all introduced at the start of the process) and conversion costs are £3400.

Note here that all of the cost of the normal loss is added to the completed production, since it is detected at the completion stage. The closing work in progress will not have reached this stage, and therefore does not bear any of the loss. The cost per unit completed after the allocation of the normal loss is £10.50 (£6300/600 units).

Some writers suggest that if the equivalent units computation for normal losses is ignored, the cost of the normal loss will be automatically apportioned to the good production. However, the results from adopting this short-cut are not as accurate. The calculations adopting this short-cut approach are as follows:

	Total cost (£)	Completed units	WIP equiv. units	Total equiv. units	Cost per unit (£)	WIP (£)
Materials	5000	600	300	900	5.5555	1666.65
Conversion cost	3400	600	150	750	4.5333	680.00
					10.0888	2346.65
			Completed units (600 × £10.0888)			6053.35
						8400.00

You can see that ignoring equivalent units for the normal loss decreased equivalent units and thus increases the cost per unit. The values of work in progress and completed production using each approach are as follows:

	Normal loss charged to good production (£)	Short-cut method (£)	Difference (£)
Work in progress	2100	2347	+247
Completed units	6300	6053	–247

If the short-cut approach is used, the work in progress valuation includes £247 normal loss that is not attributable to these units because they have not reached the inspection point. The £247 should be charged only to completed units that have reached the inspection point. It is therefore recommended that the cost of the normal loss is calculated and charged only to those units that have reached the inspection point.

Let us now assume for Example 5A.1 that the loss is detected when the process has reached the 50% stage of completion. The revised cost per unit will be as follows:

Element of cost	Total cost (£)	Completed units	Normal loss	WIP equiv. units	Total equiv. units	Cost per unit
Materials	5000	600	100	300	1000	5.00
Conversion cost	3400	600	50	150	800	4.25
	8400					9.25

The 100 lost units will not be processed any further once the loss is detected at the 50% completion stage. Therefore 50 units equivalent production (100 units × 50%) is entered in the normal loss column for conversion cost equivalent production. Note that materials are introduced at the start of the process and are fully complete when the loss is detected. The cost of the normal loss is

	£
Materials (100 × £5)	500.00
Conversion cost (50 × £4.25)	212.50
	712.50

When losses are assumed to occur at a specific point in the production process, you should allocate the normal loss over all units that have reached this point. In our example the loss is detected at the 50% stage of completion, and the work in progress has reached this point. Therefore the loss should be allocated between completed production and work in progress. If the losses were detected at the 60% stage, all of the normal loss would be allocated to completed production. Alternatively, if losses were detected before the 50% stage, the normal loss would be allocated to completed production and work in progress.

The question is: how should we allocate the normal loss between completed production and work in progress? Several different approaches are advocated, but the most accurate is to apportion the normal loss in the ratio of completed units and incompleted units in progress. In Example 5A.1, 600 units are completed and 300 units are partly complete. It is assumed that the units lost at the inspection were intended to be produced in the same ratio (6/9 to completed production and 3/9 to work in progress). The normal loss is therefore apportioned as follows:

	(£)
Completed units (600/900 × £712.50)	475.00
WIP (300/900 × £712.50)	237.50
	712.50

The cost of completed production and WIP when the loss is detected at the 50% stage is

	(£)	(£)
Completed units (600 × £9.25)	5550.00	
Share of normal loss	475.00	6025.00
Work in progress:		
Materials (300 × £5)	1500.00	
Conversion cost (150 × 4.25)	637.50	
Share of normal loss	£237.50	2375.00
		8400.00

When the lost units have a scrap value, the sales revenue should be deducted from the normal loss, and the net cost should be allocated to units which have passed the inspection point.

Abnormal losses

Where abnormal losses are incurred, the correct procedure is to produce the normal unit cost statement, but with the addition of two separate columns for the units lost; one for normal losses and one for abnormal losses. Consider Example 5A.2.

EXAMPLE 5A.2

A department with no opening work in progress introduced 1000 units into the process; 600 are completed, 250 are 20% complete, and 150 units are lost consisting of 100 units of normal loss and 50 units of abnormal loss. Losses are detected *upon completion.* Material costs are £8000 (all introduced at the start of the process) and conversion costs are £4000.

The unit cost calculations are as follows:

Element of cost	Total cost (£)	Completed units	Normal loss	Abnormal loss	WIP equiv. units	Total equiv. units	Cost per unit (£)
Materials	8 000	600	100	50	250	1000	8
Conversion cost	4 000	600	100	50	50	800	5
	12 000						13

	(£)	(£)
Value of work in progress:		
Materials (250 units at £8)	2000	
Conversion cost (50 units at £5)	250	2 250
Completed units (600 units at £13)	7800	
Add normal loss (100 units at £13)	1300	9 100
Abnormal loss (50 units at £13)		650
		12 000

You can see that the normal loss has been charged to completed units only. The abnormal loss is charged to a separate account and written off as a period cost to the profit and loss account. The entries in the process account will be as follows:

Process account

Materials	8 000	Transfer to next process	9 100
Conversion cost	4 000	Abnormal loss written off to profit and loss account	650
		Closing work in progress c/fwd	2 250
	12 000		12 000

Note that there is an argument for allocating the normal loss of £1300 between the completed units and the abnormal loss. If the normal loss is of a significant value then there are strong arguments for doing this, since the normal loss is part of the cost of production. The abnormal loss should therefore be valued at the cost per unit of *normal output*. In the unit cost statement for Example 5A.2 you will see that the completed production is 600 units and the abnormal loss is 50 units. The normal loss of £1300 is therefore apportioned pro rata to completed production and the abnormal loss. The calculations are as follows:

completed units (600/650 × £1300) = 1200

abnormal loss (50/650 × £1300) = 100

The revised value for completed production would then be £9000 (£7800 + £1200), while for the abnormal loss the value would be £750 (£650 + £100). For most examination questions it is unlikely that you will be expected to allocate the normal loss between completed units and the abnormal loss.

Normal and abnormal losses when they occur part way through the process

This section is more appropriate for an advanced course and may be omitted if you are pursuing an introductory or first level course. In Example 5A.1 we considered a situation where a normal loss was detected at the end of the process. In this section we shall consider a more complex problem when normal and abnormal losses are detected part way through the process. Consider the information presented in Example 5A.3.

The unit cost calculations are as follows:

(1) Element of cost	(2) Total cost (£)	(3) Completed units	(4) Normal loss	(5) Abnormal loss	(6) WIP equiv. units	(7) Total equiv. units	(8) Cost per unit (£)
Previous process cost	10 000	600	100	50	250	1000	10.000
Materials	8 000	600	100	50	250	1000	8.000
Conversion cost	2 900	600	50	25	150	825	3.515
	20 900						21.515

From this calculation you can see that materials and the previous process cost are 100% complete when the loss is discovered. However, spoilt units will not be processed any further once the loss is detected, and the lost units will be 50% complete in respect of conversion costs. Note that the closing work in progress is 60% complete, and has thus passed the point where the loss is detected. Therefore the normal loss should be allocated between the completed units and work in progress. The cost of the normal loss is

	(£)
Previous process cost (100 units at £10)	1000
Materials (100 units at £8)	800
Conversion cost (50 units at £3.515)	176
	1976

EXAMPLE 5A.3

A department with no opening work in progress introduces 1000 units into the process: 600 are completed, 250 are 60% complete and 150 units are lost, consisting of 100 units normal loss and 50 units abnormal loss. Losses are detected *when production is 50% complete*. Material costs are £8000 (all introduced at the start of the process), conversion costs are £2900 and the previous process cost is £10 000.

The normal loss is allocated in the ratio of completed units and units in progress as follows:

	(£)
Completed units (600/850 × £1976)	1395
Work in progress (250/850 × £1976)	581
	1976

The costs are accounted for as follows:

	(£)	(£)
Value of work in progress:		
Previous process cost (250 units at £10)	2 500	
Materials (250 units at £8)	2 000	
Conversion cost (150 units at £3.515)	527	
Share of normal loss	581	5 608
Completed units:		
600 units at £21.515	12 909	
Share of normal loss	1 395	14 304
Abnormal loss:		
Previous process cost (50 units at £10)	500	
Materials (50 units at £8)	400	
Conversion cost (25 units at £3.515)	88	988
		20 900

You will remember from our earlier discussion that there is an argument for allocating a share of the normal loss to the abnormal loss. If this approach is adopted, the cost of the normal loss would be apportioned as follows:

Completed production	600/900 × normal loss
WIP	250/900 × normal loss
Abnormal loss	50/900 × normal loss

If the short-cut method is applied, the normal loss is automatically allocated between completed units, work in progress and abnormal loss in the ratio of equivalent units (columns 3, 5 and 6 shown in the unit cost calculations) for each element of cost.

Key terms and concepts

abnormal gain (p. 160)
abnormal or controllable losses (p. 156)
batch costing (p. 172)
conversion cost (p. 155)
equivalent production (p. 162)
first in, first out method (p. 165)
normal or uncontrollable losses (p. 156)
operation costing (p. 172)
previous process cost (p. 164)
weighted average method (p. 165)

Key examination points

Process costing questions require many calculations and there is a possibility that you will make calculation errors. Make sure that your answer is clearly presented so that the examiner can ascertain whether or not you are using correct methods to calculate the cost per unit. Questions can generally be classified by three categories. First, all output is fully complete and the problem of equivalent production does not arise (see answer to Review problem 5.23 for an example). Second, work in progress (WIP) output is partially complete and there are no losses in process. Third, losses in process apply when WIP is partially complete. Review problems 5.24 and 5.26 fall within the second category with the former assuming the weighted average and the latter FIFO method of stack valuation. Review problem 5.27 involves equivalent production and losses in process. Sometimes examination questions do not indicate the stage in the process that losses occur. In this situation you are recommended to assume that the loss occurs at the end of the process and allocate the normal loss to completed production. Do not forget to state this assumption in your answer. The short-cut method should not be used if the loss occurs at the end of the process because this method assumes that the loss is to be shared between WIP and completed units.

Assessment material

Review questions

The review questions are short questions that enable you to assess your understanding of the main topics included in the chapter. The numbers in parentheses provide you with the page numbers to refer to if you cannot answer a specific question.

Review problems

The review problems are more complex and require you to relate and apply the chapter content to various business problems. The problems are graded by their level of difficulty. The multiple-choice questions are the least demanding and normally take less than 10 minutes to complete. Fully worked solutions to the review problems are provided in a separate section at the end of the book. For those questions in the white box the worked solutions are provided in the *Student's Manual* accompanying this book. Further review problems for this chapter are available on the accompanying website www.drury-online.com. The answers to these problems are available for lecturers on the lecturer's password protected section of the website.

Case studies

The website also includes over 30 case study problems. A list of these cases is provided in Part Seven of this book.

Review questions

5.1 Describe the differences between process costing and job costing. (*p. 153*)

5 2 Provide examples of industries that use process costing. (*p. 153*)

5.3 Why is cost accumulation easier with a process costing system compared with a job costing system? (*p. 154*)

5.4 Distinguish between normal and abnormal losses and explain how their accounting treatment differs. (*pp. 156–57*)

5.5 What are equivalent units? Why are they needed with a process costing system? (*p. 162*)

5.6 Why is it necessarily to treat 'previous process cost' as a separate element of cost in a process costing system? (*pp. 164–65*)

5.7 How is the equivalent unit cost calculation affected when materials are added at the beginning or at a later stage of the process rather than uniformly throughout the process? (*p. 165*)

5.8 Describe how the weighted average and FIFO methods differ in assigning costs to units completed and closing work in progress. (*pp. 167–68*)

5.9 Under what conditions will the weighted average and FIFO methods give similar results? (*p. 169*)

5.10 When a process costing system is used, explain how cost information requirements differ for inventory valuation/profit measurement, decision-making and performance reporting for cost control. (*pp. 170–71*)

5.11 Explain the distinguishing features of a batch/operating costing system. (*p. 171–72*)

5.12 What are the implications for the accounting treatment of normal and abnormal losses if losses are assumed to be detected (a) at the end of the process, and (b) before the end of the process? (*pp. 176–79*)

Review problems

5.13 **Intermediate**

AK Chemicals produces high-quality plastic sheeting in a continuous manufacturing operation. All materials are input at the beginning of the process. Conversion costs are incurred evenly throughout the process. A quality control inspection occurs 75% through the manufacturing process, when some units are separated out as inferior quality. The following data are available for December.

Materials costs	£90 000
Conversion costs	£70 200
Units started	40 000
Units completed	36 000

There is no opening or closing work in progress. Past experience indicates that approximately 7.5% of the units started are found to be defective on inspection by quality control.

What is the cost of abnormal loss for December?

A £3 600
B £4 050
C £4 680
D £10 800

ACCA Paper 3

5.14 **Intermediate**

KL Processing Limited has identified that an abnormal gain of 160 litres occurred in its refining process last week. Normal losses are expected and have a scrap value of £2.00 per litre. All losses are 100% complete as to material cost and 75% complete as to conversion costs.

The company uses the weighted average method of valuation and last week's output was valued using the following costs per equivalent unit:

Materials	£9.40
Conversion costs	£11.20

The effect on the profit and loss account of last week's abnormal gain is

A Debit £2528
B Debit £2828
C Credit £2528
D Credit £2848
E Credit £3168

CIMA Stage 2

5.15 **Intermediate**

The following details relate to the main process of W Limited, a chemical manufacturer:

Opening work in progress	2000 litres, fully complete as to materials and 40% complete as to conversion
Material input	24 000 litres
Normal loss is 10% of input	
Output to process 2	19 500 litres
Closing work in progress	3000 litres, fully complete as to materials and 45% complete as to conversion

The number of equivalent units to be included in W Limited's calculation of the cost per equivalent unit using a FIFO basis of valuation are:

	Materials	Conversion
A	19 400	18 950
B	20 500	20 050
C	21 600	21 150
D	23 600	20 750
E	23 600	21 950

CIMA Stage 2

5.16 **Intermediate**

Process B had no opening stock. 13 500 units of raw material were transferred in at £4.50 per unit. Additional material at £1.25 per unit was added in process. Labour and overheads were £6.25 per completed unit and £2.50 per unit incomplete.

If 11 750 completed units were transferred out, what was the closing stock in process B?

A £77 625.00
B £14 437.50
C £141 000.00
D £21 000.00

CIMA Stage 1

5.17 **Intermediate**

A chemical process has a normal wastage of 10% of input. In a period, 2500 kgs of material were input and there was an abnormal loss of 75 kgs.

What quantity of good production was achieved?

A 2175 kg
B 2250 kg
C 2325 kg
D 2475 kg

CIMA Stage 1 Cost Accounting

5.18 **Intermediate**

KL Processing operates the FIFO method of accounting for opening work in process in its mixing process. The following data relates to April:

Opening work in process	1 000 litres valued at	£1 500
Input	30 000 litres costing	£15 000
Conversion costs		£10 000
Output	24 000 litres	
Closing work in process	3 500 litres	

Losses in processes are expected to be 10% of period input. They are complete as to input material costs but are discovered after 60% conversion. Losses have a scrap value of £0.20 per litre.

Opening work in process was 100% complete as to input materials, and 70% complete as to conversion. Closing work in process is complete as to input materials and 80% complete as to conversion.

A The number of material-equivalent units was
(i) 26 300 litres
(ii) 26 600 litres
(iii) 27 000 litres
(iv) 28 000 litres
(v) 29 000 litres

B The number of conversion-equivalent units was
(i) 26 400 litres
(ii) 26 600 litres
(iii) 26 800 litres
(iv) 27 000 litres
(v) 27 400 litres

(Total 20 marks)

CIMA Stage 1 Operational Cost Accounting

5.19 **Intermediate**

The following details relate to the main process of Z Limited, a paint manufacturer:

Opening work in process	2 400 litres	fully complete as to materials and 30% complete as to conversion
Material input	58 000 litres	
Normal loss is 5% of input		
Output to next process	52 500 litres	
Closing work in process	3 000 litres	fully complete as to materials and 50% complete as to conversion

All losses occur at the end of the process.

The numbers of equivalent units to be included in Z Limited's calculation of the cost per equivalent unit, using a *weighted average basis* of valuation, are

	Materials	**Conversion**
A	53 100	51 600
B	55 500	54 000
C	55 500	53 300
D	57 500	56 000
E	57 500	55 300

CIMA Stage 2 – Operational Cost Accounting

5.20 Intermediate

The following information is required for sub-questions (a) to (c)

The incomplete process account relating to period 4 for a company which manufactures paper is shown below:

Process account

	Units	$		Units	$
Material	4000	16 000	Finished goods	2750	
Labour		8 125	Normal loss	400	700
Production overhead		3 498	Work in progress	700	

There was no opening work in process (WIP). Closing WIP, consisting of 700 units, was complete as shown:

Material	100%
Labour	50%
Production overhead	40%

Losses are recognised at the end of the production process and are sold for $1.75 per unit.

(a) Given the outcome of the process, which ONE of the following accounting entries is needed to complete the double entry to the process account?

	Debit	Credit
A	Abnormal Loss account	Process account
B	Process account	Abnormal Loss account
C	Abnormal Gain account	Process account
D	Process account	Abnormal Gain account

(b) The value of the closing WIP was

A $3868 B $4158 C $4678 D $5288

(c) The total value of the units transferred to finished goods was

A $21 052.50 B $21 587.50 C $22 122.50 D $22 656.50

CIMA – Management Accounting Fundamentals

5.21 Intermediate

The following process account has been drawn up for the last month:

Process account

	Units	£		Units	£
Opening WP	250	3 000	Normal loss	225	450
Input:			Output	4100	
Materials	4500	22 500	Abnormal Loss	275	
Labour		37 500	Closing WIP	150	
	4750			4750	

Work in progress has the following level of completion:

	Material	Labour
Opening WIP	100%	40%
Closing WIP	100%	30%

The company uses the FIFO method for valuing the output from the process and all losses occurred at the end of the process.

What were the equivalent units for labour?

A 4380 units
B 4270 units
C 4320 units
D 4420 units.

ACCA Paper 1.2 – Financial information for Management

5.22 Intermediate

Perth operates a process costing system. The process is expected to lose 25% of input and this can be sold for £8 per kg.

Input for the month were:

Direct materials	3500 kg at a total cost of £52 500
Direct labour	£9625 for the period

There is no opening or closing work in progress in the period. Actual output was 2800 kg.

What is the valuation of the output?

A £44 100
B £49 700
C £58 800
D £56 525.

ACCA Paper 1.2 – Financial information for Management

5.23 Intermediate: Preparation of process accounts with all output fully complete

'No Friction' is an industrial lubricant, which is formed by subjecting certain crude chemicals to two successive processes. The output of process 1 is passed to process 2, where it is blended with other chemicals. The process costs for period 3 were as follows:

Process 1
Material: 3000 kg @ £0.25 per kg
Labour: £120
Process plant time: 12 hours @ £20 per hour

Process 2
Material: 2000 kg @ £0.40 per kg
Labour: £84
Process plant time: 20 hours @ £13.50 per hour

General overhead for period 3 amounted to £357 and is absorbed into process costs on a process labour basis.

The normal output of process 1 is 80% of input, while that of process 2 is 90% of input.

Waste matter from process 1 is sold for £0.20 per kg, while that from process 2 is sold for £0.30 per kg.

The output for period 3 was as follows:

Process 1	2300 kg
Process 2	4000 kg

There was no stock or work in process at either the beginning or the end of the period, and it may be assumed that all available waste matter had been sold at the prices indicated.

You are required to show how the foregoing data would be recorded in a system of cost accounts.

5.24 Intermediate: Equivalent production with no losses (weighted average)

A cleansing agent is manufactured from the input of three ingredients. At 1 December there was no work in progress. During December the ingredients were put into the process in the following quantities:

A 2000 kg at 0.80 per kg
B 3000 kg at 0.50 per kg
C 6000 kg at 0.40 per kg

Additionally, labour working 941 hours and being paid £4 per hour was incurred, and overheads recovered on the basis of 50% of labour cost. There was no loss in the process. Output was 8600 kg.

The remaining items in work in progress were assessed by the company's works manager as follows:

Complete so far as materials were concerned:

One quarter of the items were 60% complete for labour and overheads;

Three-quarters were 25% complete for labour and overheads.

Required:

(a) A cleansing agent process account, showing clearly the cost of the output and work in progress carried forward.

(16 marks)

(b) Define the following terms, give examples and explain how they would be accounted for in process costing:

(i) By-products

(6 marks)

(ii) Abnormal gain

(3 marks)

(iii) Equivalent units

(3 marks)
(Total 28 marks)
AAT

5.25 Intermediate: Losses in process (weighted average)

A company operates expensive process plant to produce a single product from one process. At the beginning of October, 3400 completed units were still in the processing plant, awaiting transfer to finished stock. They were valued as follows:

	(£)
Direct material	25 500
Direct wages	10 200
Production overhead	20 400 (200% of direct wages)

During October, 37 000 further units were put into process and the following costs charged to the process:

	(£)
Direct materials	276 340
Direct wages	112 000
Production overhead	224 000

36 000 units were transferred to finished stock and 3200 units remained in work-in-progress at the end of October which were complete as to material and half-complete as to labour and production overhead. A loss of 1200 units, being normal, occurred during the process.

The average method of pricing is used.

You are required to

(a) prepare for the month of October, a statement (or statements) showing
   (i) production cost per unit in total and by element of cost;
   (ii) the total cost of production transferred to finished stock;
   (iii) the valuation of closing work-in-progress in total and by element of cost;

(15 marks)

(b) describe five of the characteristics which distinguish process costing from job costing.

(10 marks)

(Total 25 marks)

CIMA Stage 2 Cost Accounting

5.26 Intermediate: Equivalent production with no losses (FIFO Method)

A company operates a manufacturing process where six people work as a team and are paid a weekly group bonus based upon the actual output of the team compared with output expected.

A basic 37 hour week is worked during which the expected output from the process is 4000 equivalent units of product. Basic pay is £5.00 per hour and the bonus for the group, shared equally, is £0.80 per unit in excess of expected output.

In the week just ended, basic hours were worked on the process. The following additional information is provided for the week:

Opening work in process (1000 units):
  Materials £540 (100% complete)
  Labour and overheads £355 (50% complete).
During the week:
  Materials used £2255
  Overheads incurred £1748
  Completed production 3800 units
Closing work in process (1300 units)
  Materials (100% complete)
  Labour and overheads (75% complete).
There are no process losses.
The FIFO method is used to apportion costs.

Required:

(a) Prepare the process account for the week just ended.

(10 marks)

(b) Explain the purpose of the following documents which are used in the control of, and accounting for, the materials used in the process described in part (a)
   (i) purchase requisition
   (ii) materials (stores) requisition.

(4 marks)

(14 marks)

ACCA Foundation Stage Paper 3

5.27 **Intermediate: Equivalent production and losses in process**

A concentrated liquid fertilizer is manufactured by passing chemicals through two consecutive processes. Stores record cards for the chemical ingredients used exclusively by the first process show the following data for May 2000:

Opening stock	4 000 litres	£10 800
Closing stock	8 000 litres	£24 200
Receipts into store	20 000 litres	£61 000

Other process data for May is tabulated below:

	Process 1	Process 2
Direct labour	£4880	£6000
Direct expenses	£4270	—
Overhead absorption rates	250% of direct labour	100% of direct labour
Output	8000 litres	7500 litres
Opening stock of work in process	—	—
Closing stock of work in process	5600 litres	—
Normal yield	85% of input	90% of input
Scrap value of loss	—	—

In process 1 the closing stock of work in process has just passed through inspection, which is at the stage where materials and conversion costs are 100% and 75% completed respectively.

In process 2 inspection is the final operation.

Required:

(a) Prepare the relevant accounts to show the results of the processes for May 2000 and present a detailed working paper showing your calculations and any assumptions in arriving at the data shown in those accounts.

(18 marks)

(b) If supplies of the required chemicals are severely restricted and all production can be sold immediately, briefly explain how you would calculate the total loss to the company if, at the beginning of June, 100 litres of the correct mix of chemicals were spilt on issue to process 1.

(4 marks)
(Total 22 marks)
ACCA Foundation Costing

Review problems (with answers in the Student's Manual)

5.28 **Intermediate: Preparation of process accounts with all output fully completed**

A chemical compound is made by raw material being processed through two processes. The output of Process A is passed to Process B where further material is added to the mix. The details of the process costs for the financial period number 10 were as shown below:

Process A	
Direct material	2000 kilograms at 5 per kg
Direct labour	£7200
Process plant time	140 hours at £60 per hour

Process B	
Direct material	1400 kilograms at £12 per kg
Direct labour	£4200
Process plant time	80 hours at £72.50 per hour

The departmental overhead for Period 10 was £6840 and is absorbed into the costs of each process on direct labour cost.

	Process A	Process B
Expected output was	80% of input	90% of input
Actual output was	1400 kg	2620 kg

Assume no finished stock at the beginning of the period and no work in progress at either the beginning or the end of the period.

Normal loss is contaminated material which is sold as scrap for £0.50 per kg from Process A and £1.825 per kg from Process B, for both of which immediate payment is received.

You are required to prepare the accounts for Period 10, for

(i) Process A,
(ii) Process B,
(iii) Normal loss/gain,
(iv) Abnormal loss/gain,
(v) Finished goods,
(vi) Profit and loss (extract).

(15 marks)
CIMA Stage 2 Cost Accounting

5.29 Intermediate: Equivalent production and no losses

A firm operates a process, the details of which for the period were as follows. There was no opening work-in-progress. During the period 8250 units were received from the previous process at a value of £453 750, labour and overheads were £350 060 and material introduced was £24 750. At the end of the period the closing work-in-progress was 1600 units, which were 100% complete in respect of materials, and 60% complete in respect of labour and overheads. The balance of units were transferred to finished goods.

Requirements:

(a) Calculate the number of equivalent units produced.
(3 marks)

(b) Calculate the cost per equivalent unit.
(2 marks)

(c) Prepare the process account.
(7 marks)

(d) Distinguish between joint products and by-products, and briefly explain the difference in accounting treatment between them.
(3 marks)
(Total 15 marks)
CIMA Stage 1 Cost Accounting and Quantitative Methods

5.30 Intermediate: Losses in process (weighted average)

A company manufactures a product that requires two separate processes for its completion. Output from Process 1 is immediately input to Process 2.

The following information is available for Process 2 for a period:

(i) Opening work-in-progress units:
12 000 units: 90% complete as to materials, 50% complete as to conversion costs.

(ii) Opening work-in-progress value:
Process 1 output: £13 440
Process 2 materials added: £4970
Conversion costs: £3120.

(iii) Costs incurred during the period:
Process 1 output: £107 790 (95 000 units)
Process 2 materials added: £44 000
Conversion costs: £51 480.

(iv) Closing work-in-progress units
10 000 units: 90% complete as to materials, 70% complete as to conversion costs.

(v) The product is inspected when it is complete. 200 units of finished product were rejected during the period, in line with the normal allowance. Units rejected have no disposal value.

Required:

(a) Calculate the unit cost of production for the period in Process 2 (to three decimal places of £), using the periodic weighted average method.

(7 marks)

(b) Prepare the Process 2 Account for the period using the unit cost of production calculated in (a) above.

(5 marks)

(c) Explain why, and how, the Process 2 Account would be different if there was no normal allowance for rejects. NB The process account should not be reworked.

(5 marks)

(d) Explain how the process account workings, required in (a) above to calculate the unit cost, would differ if the FIFO valuation method was used instead.

(3 marks)
(Total 20 marks)
ACCA Management Information – Paper 3

5.31 Intermediate: Losses in process (weighted average)

Chemical Processors manufacture Wonderchem using two processes, mixing and distillation. The following details relate to the distillation process for a period

No opening work in progress (WIP)

Input from mixing	36 000 kg at a cost of	£166 000
Labour for period		£43 800
Overheads for period		£29 200

Closing WIP of 8000 kg, which was 100% complete for materials and 50% complete for labour and overheads.

The normal loss in distillation is 10% of fully complete production. Actual loss in the period was 3600 kg, fully complete, which were scrapped.

Required:

(a) Calculate whether there was a normal or abnormal loss or abnormal gain for the period.

(2 marks)

(b) Prepare the distillation process account for the period, showing clearly weights and values.

(10 marks)

(c) Explain what changes would be required in the accounts if the scrapped production had a resale value, *and* give the accounting entries.

(3 marks)

(Total 15 marks)

CIMA Stage 1 Cost Accounting

5.32 **Intermediate: Preparation of process accounts with output fully completed and a discussion of FIFO and average methods of WIP valuation**

(a) Z Ltd manufactures metal cans for use in the food processing industry. The metal is introduced in sheet form at the start of the process. Normal wastage in the form of offcuts is 2% of input. The offcuts can be sold for £0.26 per kilo. Each metal sheet weighs 2 kilos and is expected to yield 80 cans. In addition to wastage through offcuts, 1% of cans manufactured are expected to be rejected. These rejects can also be sold at £0.26 per kilo.

Production, and costs incurred, in the month just completed, were as follows:

Production:	3 100 760 cans
Costs incurred:	
Direct materials:	39 300 metal sheets at £2.50 per sheet
Direct labour and overhead:	£33 087

There was no opening or closing work in process.

Required:

Prepare the process accounts for the can manufacturing operation for the month just completed.

(15 marks)

(b) Another of the manufacturing operations of Z Ltd involves the continuous processing of raw materials with the result that, at the end of any period, there are partly completed units of product remaining.

Required:

With reference to the general situation outlined above

(i) explain the concept of equivalent units

(3 marks)

(ii) describe, and contrast, the FIFO and average methods of work in process valuation.

(7 marks)

(Total 25 marks)

ACCA Level 1 Costing

5.33 Intermediate: FIFO method and losses in process

The manufacture of one of the products of A Ltd requires three separate processes. In the last of the three processes, costs, production and stock for the month just ended were:

(1) Transfers from Process 2: 180 000 units at a cost of £394 200.

(2) Process 3 costs: materials £110 520, conversion costs £76 506.

(3) Work in process at the beginning of the month: 20 000 units at a cost of £55 160 (based on FIFO pricing method). Units were 70% complete for materials, and 40% complete for conversion costs.

(4) Work in process at the end of the month: 18 000 units which were 90% complete for materials, and 70% complete for conversion costs.

(5) Product is inspected when it is complete. Normally no losses are expected but during the month 60 units were rejected and sold for £1.50 per unit.

Required:

(a) Prepare the Process 3 account for the month just ended.

(15 marks)

(b) Explain how, and why, your calculations would be affected if the 60 units lost were treated as normal losses.

(5 marks)

(c) Explain how your calculations would be affected by the use of weighted average pricing instead of FIFO.

(5 marks)
(Total 25 marks)
ACCA Cost and Management Accounting 1

5.34 Intermediate: FIFO method and losses in process

A company operates several production processes involving the mixing of ingredients to produce bulk animal feedstuffs. One such product is mixed in two separate process operations. The information below is of the costs incurred in, and output from, Process 2 during the period just completed.

Costs incurred:	£
Transfers from Process 1	187 704
Raw materials costs	47 972
Conversion costs	63 176
Opening work in process	3 009
Production:	Units
Opening work in process (100% complete, apart from Process 2 conversion costs which were 50% complete)	1 200
Transfers from Process 1	112 000
Completed output	105 400
Closing work in process (100% complete, apart from Process 2 conversion costs which were 75% complete)	1 600

Normal wastage of materials (including product transferred from Process 1), which occurs in the early stages of Process 2 (after all materials have been added), is expected to be 5% of input. Process 2 conversion costs are all apportioned to units of good output. Wastage materials have no saleable value.

Required:

(a) Prepare the Process 2 account for the period, using FIFO principles.

(15 marks)

(b) Explain how, and why, your calculations would have been different if wastage occurred at the end of the process.

(5 marks)

(Total 20 marks)

ACCA Cost and Management Accounting

5.35 Advanced: FIFO stock valuation, standard costing and cost-plus pricing

Campex Ltd uses a dyeing and waterproofing process for its fabrics which are later made up into tents and other outdoor pursuit items, or sold to other manufacturers. Each roll of fabric is subject to the same process, with dyeing and waterproofing materials being added at specific times in the process. The direct labour costs are incurred uniformly throughout the process.

Inspection of the fabric for spoilage can take place only at the end of the process when it can be determined whether or not there has been any spoilage. Amounts of up to 10% of good output are acceptable as normal spoilage. Any abnormal spoilage is treated as a period loss. Some spoiled fabric can be reworked and it is saved up until a batch of 500 rolls can be reprocessed.

The reworking costs are charged to process overheads, and any reworked goods will not usually need the full cost of conversion spent on them. The work in progress is valued using the FIFO method.

At the beginning of the month of June the work in progress in the dyeing and waterproofing department was 1000 rolls which were valued at £12 000 direct materials and £4620 direct labour. The work in progress has had all the direct materials added, but was only 60% complete as far as the direct labour was concerned. During the month 5650 rolls were started from new, and 500 rolls were reworked. The rolls being reworked require 60% of direct materials and 50% of direct labour to bring them up to standard. By the end of the month 550 rolls had been found to be spoiled. The work in progress at the end of the month amounted to 800 rolls of which 80% were complete for direct materials and 40% were complete for direct labour. All other rolls were completed satisfactorily and transferred to stores to await further processing. The costs for June were direct materials £72 085, direct labour £11 718. The departmental overhead recovered was £3.5 for every £1 direct labour, whilst actual overhead expenditure amounted to £34 110 for the month (excluding the reworking costs).

Requirements:

(a) Prepare a schedule showing the actual equivalent units processed for each cost element in the processing department for the month of June and the costs per roll for the direct material used and the direct labour and applied overheads.

(7 marks)

(b) Prepare a schedule showing the allocation of the costs of production to the various cost headings for the month of June, including the value of closing work in progress using the FIFO method.

(6 marks)

(c) Discuss the usefulness of converting the system used above to a standard cost based system.

(4 marks)

(d) Comment on the use of the actual costs you have computed above in (a) and (b) for product pricing.

(4 marks)

(e) Comment briefly on the implications of using replacement costs in a process costing system including valuation of month end work in progress.

(4 marks)

(Total 25 marks)

ICAEW Paper 2/Management Accounting

Joint and by-product costing

6

A distinguishing feature of the production of joint and by-products is that the products are not identifiable as different products until a specific point in the production process is reached. Before this point joint costs are incurred on the production of all products emerging from the joint production process. It is therefore not possible to trace joint costs to individual products.

To meet internal and external profit measurement and inventory valuation requirements, it is necessary to assign all product-related costs (including joint costs) to products so that costs can be allocated to inventories and cost of goods sold. The assignment of joint costs, however, is of little use for decision-making. We shall begin by distinguishing between joint and by-products. This will be followed by an examination of the different methods that can be used to allocate joint costs to products for inventory valuation. We shall then go on to discuss which costs are relevant for decision-making.

LEARNING OBJECTIVES

After studying this chapter, you should be able to:

- distinguish between joint products and by-products;
- explain and identify the split-off point in a joint-cost situation;
- explain the alternative methods of allocating joint costs to products;
- discuss the arguments for and against each of the methods of allocating joint costs to products;
- present relevant financial information for a decision as to whether a product should be sold at a particular stage or further processed;
- describe the accounting treatment of by-products.

Distinguishing between joint products and by-products

Joint products and by-products arise in situations where the production of one product makes inevitable the production of other products. When a group of individual products is simultaneously produced, and each product has a significant relative sales value, the outputs are usually called **joint products**. Those products that are part of the simultaneous production process and have a minor sales value when compared with the joint products are called **by-products**.

As their name implies, by-products are those products that result incidentally from the main joint products. By-products may have a considerable absolute value, but the crucial classification test is that the sales value is small when compared with the values of the joint products. Joint products are crucial to the commercial viability of an organization, whereas by-products are incidental. In other words, by-products do not usually influence the decision as to whether or not to produce the main product, and they normally have little effect on the prices set for the main (joint) products. Examples of industries that produce both joint and by-products include chemicals, oil refining, mining, flour milling and gas manufacturing.

A distinguishing feature of the production of joint and by-products, is that the products are not identifiable as different individual products until a specific point in the production process is reached, known as the **split-off point**. All products may separate at one time, or different products may emerge at intervals. Before the split-off point, costs cannot be traced to particular products. For example, it is not possible to determine what part of the cost of processing a barrel of crude oil should be allocated to petrol, kerosene or paraffin. After the split-off point, joint products may be sold or subjected to further processing. If the latter is the case, any **further processing costs** can easily be traced to the specific products involved.

Figure 6.1 illustrates a simplified production process for joint and by-products. You will notice from this illustration that, at the split-off point, joint products A and B and by-product C all emerge, and that it is not possible to allocate costs of the joint process directly to the joint products or by-products. After the split-off point, further processing costs are added to the joint products before sale, and these costs can be specifically attributed to the joint products. By-product C in this instance is sold at the split-off point without further processing, although sometimes by-products may be further processed after the split-off point before they are sold on the outside market.

Methods of allocating joint costs

If all the production for a particular period was sold, the problem of allocating joint costs to products would not exist. Inventory valuations would not be necessary, and the calculation of profit would merely require the deduction of total cost from total sales. However, if inventories are in existence at the end of the period, cost allocation to products are necessary. As any such allocations are bound to be subjective and arbitrary, this area will involve the accountant in making decisions which are among the most difficult to defend. All one can do is to attempt to choose an allocation method that seems to provide a rational and reasonable method of cost distribution. The most frequently used methods that are used to allocate joint costs up to split-off point can be divided into the following two categories:

1 Methods based on physical measures such as weight, volume, etc.
2 Methods assumed to measure the ability to absorb joint costs based on allocating joint costs relative to the market values of the products.

FIGURE 6.1 *Production process for joint and by-products*

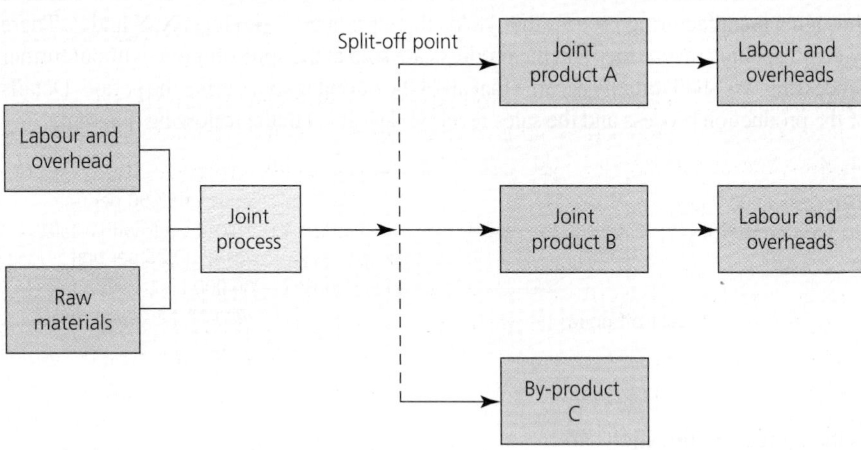

We shall now look at four methods that are used for allocating joint costs using the information given in Example 6.1. In Example 6.1 products X, Y and Z all become finished products at the split-off point. The problem arises as to how much of the £600 000 joint costs should be allocated to each individual product? The £600 000 cannot be specifically identified with any of the individual products, since the products themselves were not separated before the split-off point, but some method must be used to split the £600 000 among the three products so that inventories can be valued and the profit for the period calculated. The first method we shall look at is called the **physical measures method**.

Physical measures method

Using this method, the cost allocation is a simple allocation of joint costs in proportion to volume. Each product is assumed to receive similar benefits from the joint cost, and is therefore charged with its proportionate share of the total cost. The cost allocations using this method are as follows:

Product	Units produced	Proportion to total	Joint costs allocated (£)	Cost per unit (£)
X	40 000	1/3	200 000	5
Y	20 000	1/6	100 000	5
Z	60 000	1/2	300 000	5
	120 000		600 000	

Note that this method assumes that the cost per unit is the same for each of the products. Therefore an alternative method of allocating joint costs is as follows:

cost per unit = £5 (£600 000/120 000)

EXAMPLE 6.1

During the month of July the Van Nostrand Company processes a basic raw material through a manufacturing process that yields three products – products X, Y and Z. There were no opening inventories and the products are sold at the split-off point without further processing. We shall initially assume that all of the output is sold during the period. Details of the production process and the sales revenues are given in the following diagram.

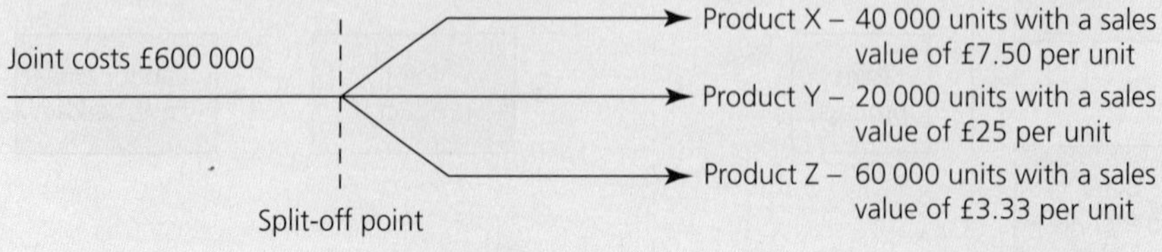

Thus the joint cost allocations are:

Product X: 40 000 × £5 = £200 000

Product Y: 20 000 × £5 = £100 000

Product Z: 60 000 × £5 = £300 000

Where market prices of the joint products differ, the assumptions of identical costs per unit for each joint product will result in some products showing high profits while others may show losses. This can give misleading profit calculations. Let us look at the product profit calculations using the information given in Example 6.1.

Product	Sales revenue (£)	Total cost (£)	Profit (loss) (£)	Profit/sales (%)
X	300 000	200 000	100 000	33 1/3
Y	500 000	100 000	400 000	80
Z	200 000	300 000	(100 000)	(50)
	1 000 000	600 000	400 000	40

You will see from these figures that the allocation of the joint costs bears no relationship to the revenue-producing power of the individual products. Product Z is allocated with the largest share of the joint costs but has the lowest total sales revenue; product Y is allocated with the lowest share of the joint costs but has the highest total sales revenue. The physical measures method is not therefore very satisfactory, and its weakness can be further highlighted if we assume that 80% of the production X, Y and Z were sold during the period. The appropriate inventory valuations and corresponding sales value of each product would be as follows:

Product	Inventory valuations cost[a] (£)	Sales values[a] (£)
X	40 000	60 000
Y	20 000	100 000
Z	60 000	40 000
	120 000	200 000

[a]20% of total cost and sales revenue.

Joint product costing in the semiconductor industry

In the semiconductor industry, the production of memory chips may be viewed as a joint processing situation because the output consists of different quality chips from a common production run. The manufacturing operation is composed of three phases: fabrication, assembly, and a 'stress test'. The first and second steps are mandatory. The third is optional and necessary to produce memory with a longer life expectancy. Of the three cases, only fabrication represents a joint production process; assembly and stress testing are separable steps.

The input to the fabrication phase is raw silicon wafers, which are first photolithographed and then baked at high temperatures. Each wafer will yield multiple chips of identical design. Upon completion of the fabrication process, the finished wafer is tested to identify usable and unusable chips. The test also classifies usable chips according to density (the number of good memory bits) and speed (the time required to access those bits.)

The input to the assembly process is usable chips, which are encapsulated in ceramic and wired for use on a memory board. The encapsulation process varies according to the number of chips, which constitute a finished module. Modules of a given density may be composed of one all-good chip or multiple partially-good chips. The finished modules are subjected to a nondestructive functional test to identify defective output.

If an extended life expectancy is not required, the good modules are not processed any further. A small sample of the good modules is subjected to the destructive reliability test before the finished product is considered salable. This destructive reliability test is a traditional quality control step designed to establish the 'time-to-failure' distribution of the output. The profile of this distribution will depend, in part, upon whether the modules were subjected to the optional stress test.

Source: Corbis

If a longer life expectancy is desired, the modules are stressed before being tested for reliability. This optional step exposes the modules to extreme conditions and those that survive are labelled extended-life modules. The proportion of the modules selected to undergo the stress test is under management control and can be varied with market conditions.

The final output of the process differs in quality according to a variety of dimensions. These include number of chips per module, speed, life expectancy, and temperature tolerance.

Source: Adapted from Cats-Baril *et al.*, Joint product costing in the semiconductor industry, *Management Accounting (USA)*, pp. 28–35.

It appears inappropriate to value the stock of product Z at a price higher than its market value and at a valuation three times higher than that of product Y, when in fact product Y is more valuable in terms of potential sales revenue. A further problem is that the joint products must be measurable by the same unit of measurement. Difficult measurement problems arise in respect of products emerging from the joint process consisting of solids, liquids and gases, and it is necessary to find some common base. For example, in the case of coke, allocations can be made on the basis of theoretical yields extracted from a ton of coke.

The main advantage of using the physical measures method is simplicity, but this is outweighed by its many disadvantages.

Sales value at split-off point method

When the **sales value at split-off point method** is used, joint costs are allocated to joint products in proportion to the estimated sales value of production on the assumption that higher selling prices indicate higher costs. To a certain extent, this method could better be described as a means of apportioning profits or losses, according to sales value, rather than a method for allocating costs. Using the information in Example 6.1, the allocations under the sales value method would be as follows:

Product	Units produced	Sales value (£)	Proportion of sales value to total (%)	Joint costs allocated (£)
X	40 000	300 000	30	180 000
Y	20 000	500 000	50	300 000
Z	60 000	200 000	20	120 000
		1 000 000		600 000

The revised product profit calculations would be as follows:

Product	Sales revenue (£)	Total cost (£)	Profit (loss) (£)	Profit/sales (%)
X	300 000	180 000	120 000	40
Y	500 000	300 000	200 000	40
Z	200 000	120 000	80 000	40
	1 000 000	600 000	400 000	

If we assume that 80% of the production is sold, the stock valuations would be as follows:

Product	Inventory valuations Cost[a]	Sales values[a]
X	36 000	60 000
Y	60 000	100 000
Z	24 000	40 000
	120 000	200 000

[a]20% of total cost and sales revenue.

The sales value method ensures that the inventory valuation does not exceed the net realizable value, but can itself be criticized since it is based on the assumption that sales revenue determines prior costs. For example, an unprofitable product with low sales revenue will be allocated with a small share of joint cost, thus giving the impression that it is generating profits.

In our discussion so far, relating to inventory valuations, we have assumed that inventories represented 20% of total production for each product. Therefore the total inventory valuation was £120 000 for both the physical measures and sales value at split-off methods of allocating joint costs. However, significant differences in the allocation of joint costs to inventories and cost of sales can occur between the two allocation methods. Consider a situation where the proportions of output for each product shown in Example 6.1 is as follows:

	Proportion of joint output sold (%)	Proportion of joint output included in the closing inventory (%)
Product X	90	10
Product Y	70	30
Product Z	90	10

Using the joint-cost allocations that we have already computed the allocations to inventories and cost of goods sold are as follows:

	Physical measures method			Sales value at split-off point method		
	Total joint costs allocated (£)	Allocated to inventories (£)	Allocated to cost of goods sold (£)	Total joint costs allocated (£)	Allocated to inventories (£)	Allocated to cost of good sold (£)
Product X	200 000	20 000 (10%)	180 000 (90%)	180 000	18 000 (10%)	162 000 (90%)
Product Y	100 000	30 000 (30%)	70 000 (70%)	300 000	90 000 (30%)	210 000 (70%)
Product Z	300 000	30 000 (10%)	270 000 (90%)	120 000	12 000 (10%)	108 000 (90%)
Total	600 000	80 000	520 000	600 000	120 000	480 000

There is a difference of £40 000 between the two methods in the costs allocated to inventories and cost of goods sold. Hence, reported profits will also differ by £40 000. The method chosen to allocate joint costs to products thus has a significant effect both on profit measurement and inventory valuation.

Net realizable value method

In Example 6.1 we have assumed that all products are sold at the split-off point and that no additional costs are incurred beyond that point. In practice, however, it is likely that joint products will be processed individually beyond the split-off point, and market values may not exist for the products at this stage. To estimate the sales value at the split-off point, it is therefore necessary to use the estimated sales value at the point of sale and work backwards. This method is called the **net realizable value method**. The net realizable value at split-off point can be estimated by deducting from the sales revenues the further processing costs at the point of sale. This approach is illustrated with the data given in Example 6.2 which is the same as Example 6.1 except that further processing costs beyond split-off point are now assumed to exist. You should now refer to Example 6.2.

EXAMPLE 6.2

Assume the same situation as Example 6.1 except that further processing costs now apply. Details of the production process and sales revenues are given in the following diagram:

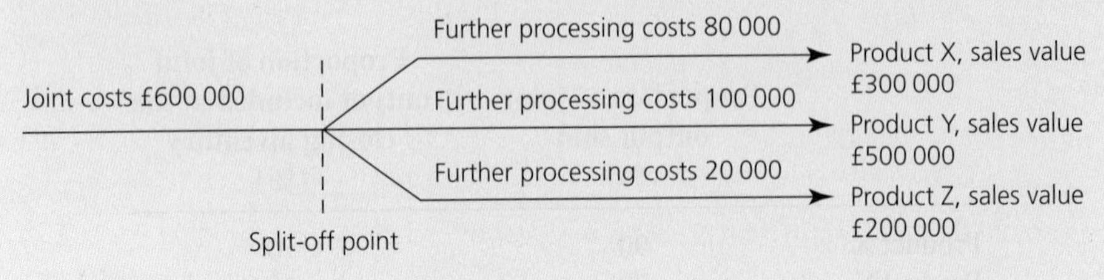

The calculation of the net realizable value and the allocation of joint costs using this method is as follows:

Product	Sales value (£)	Costs beyond split-off point (£)	Estimated net realizable value at split-off point (£)	Proportion to total (%)	Joint costs allocated (£)	Profit (£)	Gross profit (%)
X	300 000	80 000	220 000	27.5	165 000	55 000	18.33
Y	500 000	100 000	400 000	50.0	300 000	100 000	20.00
Z	200 000	20 000	180 000	22.5	135 000	45 000	22.50
	1 000 000	200 000	800 000		600 000	200 000	20.00

Note that the joint costs are allocated in proportion to each product's net realizable value at split-off point.

Constant gross profit percentage method

When the products are subject to further processing after split-off point and the net realizable method is used, the gross profit percentages are different for each product. In the above illustration they are 18.33% for product X, 20% for Y and 22.5% for Z. It could be argued that, since the three products arise from a single productive process, they should earn identical gross profit percentages. The **constant gross profit percentage method** allocates joint costs so that the overall gross profit percentage is identical for each individual product. From the information contained in Example 6.2 the joint costs would be allocated in such a way that the resulting gross profit percentage for each of the three products is equal to the overall gross profit percentage of 20%. Note that the gross profit percentage is calculated by deducting the *total* costs of the three products (£800 000) from the *total* sales (£1 000 000) and expressing the profit (£200 000) as a percentage of sales. The calculations are as follows:

	Product X (£)	Product Y (£)	Product Z (£)	Total (£)
Sales value	300 000	500 000	200 000	1 000 000
Gross profit (20%)	60 000	100 000	40 000	200 000
Cost of goods sold	240 000	400 000	160 000	800 000
Less separable further processing costs	80 000	100 000	20 000	200 000
Allocated joint costs	160 000	300 000	140 000	600 000

You can see that the required gross profit percentage of 20% is computed for each product. The additional further processing costs for each product are then deducted, and the balance represents the allocated joint costs.

The constant gross profit percentage method implicitly assumes that there is a uniform relationship between cost and sales value for each individual product. However, such an assumption is questionable, since we do not observe identical gross profit percentages for individual products in multi-product companies that do not involve joint costs.

Comparison of methods

What factors should be considered in selecting the most appropriate method of allocating joint costs? The cause-and-effect criterion, described in Chapter 3, cannot be used because there is no cause-and-effect relationship between the *individual* products and the incurrence of joint costs. Joint costs are caused by *all* products and not by individual products. Where cause-and-effect relationships cannot be established allocations ought to based on the benefits received criterion. If benefits received cannot be measured costs should be allocated based on the principle of equity or fairness. The net realizable method or the sales value at split-off point are the methods that best meet the benefits received criterion. The latter also has the added advantage of simplicity if sales values at the split-off point exists. It is also difficult to estimate the net realizable value in industries where there are numerous subsequent further processing stages and multiple split-off points. Similar measurement problems can also apply with the physical measures methods. In some industries a common denominator for physical measures for each product does not exist. For example, the output of the joint process may consist of a combination of solids, liquids and gases.

The purpose for which joint-cost allocations are used is also important. Besides being required for inventory valuation and profit measurement joint-cost allocations may be used as a mechanism for setting selling prices. For example, some utilities recharge their customers for usage of joint facilities. If market prices do not exist selling prices are likely to be determined by adding a suitable profit margin to the costs allocated to the products. The method used to allocate joint costs will therefore influence product costs, and in turn, the selling price. If external market prices do not exist it is illogical to use sales value methods to allocate joint costs. This would involve what is called circular reasoning because cost allocations determine selling prices, which in turn affect cost allocations, which will also lead to further changes in selling prices and sales revenues. For pricing purposes a physical measures method should be used if external market prices do not exist. What methods do companies actually use? Little empirical evidence exists apart from a UK survey by Slater and Wootton (1984). Their survey findings are presented in Exhibit 6.1. You will see that a physical measures method is most widely used. In practice firms are likely to use a method where the output from the joint process can be measured without too much difficulty. Establishing a common output measure is extremely difficult in some organizations. To overcome this problem they value inventories at their estimated net realizable value minus a normal profit margin.

EXHIBIT 6.1
Surveys of company practice

A survey of UK chemical and oil refining companies by Slater and Wootton (1984) reported the following methods of allocating joint costs:

	%
Physical measures method	76
Sales value method	5
Negotiated basis	19
Other	14

Note

The percentages add up to more than 100% because some companies used more than one method.

The analysis by industry indicated that the following methods were used:

Type of company	Predominant cost allocation method used
Petrochemicals	Sales value at split-off point or estimated net realizable method
Coal processing	Physical measures method
Coal chemicals	Physical measures method
Oil refining	No allocation of joint costs

The authors of the survey noted that it was considered by the majority of oil refineries that the complex nature of the process involved, and the vast number of joint product outputs, made it impossible to establish any meaningful cost allocation between products.

Irrelevance of joint cost allocations for decision-making

Our previous discussion has concentrated on the allocation of joint costs for inventory valuation and profit measurement. Joint product costs that have been computed for inventory valuation are entirely inappropriate for decision-making. For decision-making relevant costs should be used – these represent the incremental costs relating to a decision. Therefore costs that will be unaffected by a decision are classed as irrelevant. Joint-cost allocations are thus irrelevant for decision-making. Consider the information presented in Example 6.3.

The joint cost of £1 000 000 will be incurred irrespective of which decision is taken, and is not relevant for this decision. The information which is required for the decision is a comparison of the additional costs with the additional revenues from converting product Y into product Z. The following information should therefore be provided:

Additional revenue and costs from converting product Y into product Z	(£)
Additional revenues (50 000 × £2)	100 000
Additional conversion costs	60 000
Additional profit from conversion	40 000

EXAMPLE 6.3

The Adriatic Company incurs joint product costs of £1 000 000 for the production of two joint products, X and Y. Both products can be sold at split-off point. However, if additional costs of £60 000 are incurred on product Y then it can be converted into product Z and sold for £10 per unit. The joint costs and the sales revenue at split-off point are illustrated in the following diagram:

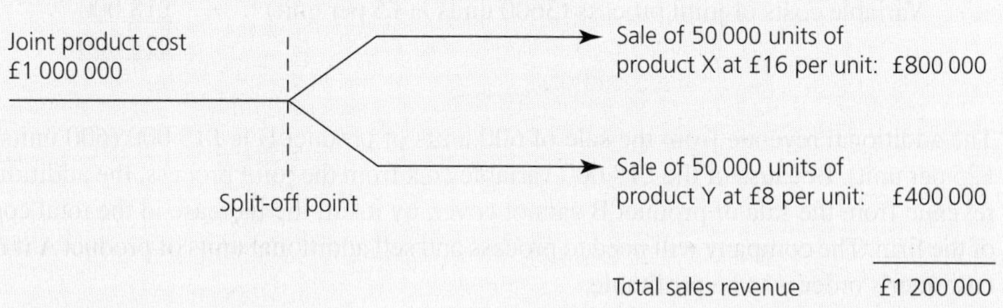

You are requested to advise management whether or not product Y should be converted in product Z.

The proof that profits will increase by £40 000 if conversion takes place is as follows:

	Convert to product Z (£)	Do not convert (£)
Sales	1 300 000	1 200 000
Total costs	1 060 000	1 000 000
Profits	240 000	200 000

The general rule is that it will be profitable to extend the processing of a joint product so long as the additional revenues exceed the additional costs, but note that the variable portion of the joint costs will be relevant for some decisions. For an illustration of a situation where joint variable costs are relevant for decision-making see Example 6.4.

You can see from Example 6.4 that the *further* processing variable costs of joint product A and B are £8 and £10 per unit respectively. The fixed portion of the joint costs of £240 000 will remain unchanged even if the customer's order is accepted, and any allocation of these costs should be excluded for decision-making. However, the variable costs of the joint process of £5 per unit will lead to additional costs if the customer's order is accepted, and so should be included in our analysis. Nevertheless, such costs should not be allocated to the products for decision-making. To decide whether or not to accept the offer, we must compare the incremented costs with the incremented revenues.

Unless we are sure that we can sell as much of product A as we produce, we cannot analyse the potential sale of an additional 600 units of product B by comparing the revenue and cost of product B itself. To increase production of product B, we need to incur additional variable costs of £5 per unit of output in the joint production process. As the production of 600 units of product B will lead to an output of 3000 units of product A in the joint process, the variable costs of the joint process will be £18 000 (3600 × £5). The additional costs associated with the production of 600 units of product B will therefore be:

Further processing variable costs of product B (600 units at £10 per unit)	£6 000
Variable costs of joint process (3600 units at £5 per unit)	£18 000
	£24 000

The additional revenue from the sale of 600 units of product B is £15 000 (600 units at £25 per unit). Because of the £18 000 variable cost from the joint process, the additional revenue from the sale of product B cannot cover, by itself, the increase in the total costs of the firm. The company will need to process and sell additional units of product A if the customer's order is to be profitable.

Producing an additional 3000 units of product A will increase the variable costs of product A by £24 000 (3000 units at £8 per unit) after the split-off point. The additional costs arising from acceptance of the customer's order will therefore be

Excess of variable costs over revenues from sale of product B (£24 000 – £15 000)	£9 000
Variable costs of product A (3000 units at £8)	£24 000
	£33 000

To cover these costs, the company must obtain additional sales revenue from product A. If a separate market can be found, the selling price of the 3000 units of product A must be in excess of £11 (£33 000/3000 units) if acceptance of the customer's order is to be profitable. This analysis, of course, assumes that the agreed price will not affect the selling price to existing customers. Alternatively, if the company cannot find a market for the 3000 units of product A at a selling price that is in excess of £11 per unit, it could consider selling the 3000 units at the split-off point rather than after further processing. The company would then have to find a market at the split-off point to cover the £9000 excess of variable costs over revenues from the sale of product B at the split-off point.

Accounting for by-products

By-products are products that have a minor sales value and that emerge incidentally from the production of the major product. As the major objective of the company is to produce the joint products, it can justifiably be argued that the joint costs should be allocated only to the joint products and that the by-products should not be allocated with any portion of the joint cost that are incurred before the split-off point. Any costs that are incurred in producing by-products after the split-off point can justifiably be charged to the by-product, since such costs are incurred for the benefit of the by-product only.

By-product revenues or by-product net revenues (the sales revenue of the by-product less the additional further processing costs after the split-off point) should be deducted from the cost of the joint products or the main product from which it emerges. Consider Example 6.5.

EXAMPLE 6.4

The Tivoli Company incurs joint production costs of £300 000 for the production of two joint products, A and B. Both products require further processing before they can be sold. Details of the expected costs and revenues of the joint products are given in the following diagram:

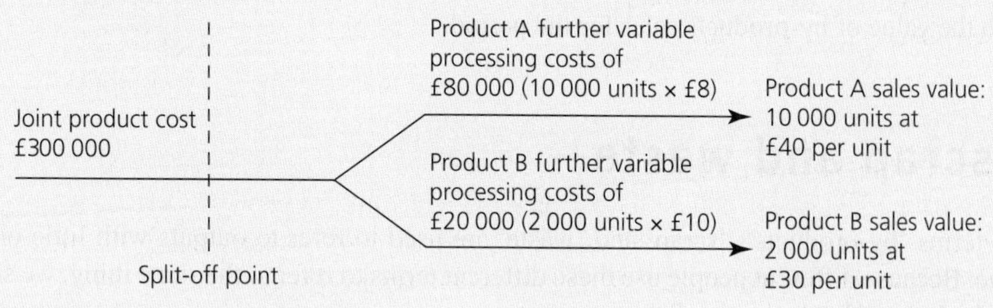

The joint costs of £300 000 consist of £240 000 fixed costs and a variable cost of £5 per unit of output. A new customer has approached the company with an offer to purchase 600 units of product B at a price of £25 per unit. The sale will not affect the market price to the other customers. Should the company accept this offer?

EXAMPLE 6.5

The Neopolitan Company operates a manufacturing process which produces joint products A and B and by-product C. The joint costs of the manufacturing process are £3 020 000, incurred in the manufacture of:

Product A	30 000 kg
Product B	50 000 kg
Product C	5 000 kg

By-product C requires further processing at a cost of £1 per kg, after which it can be sold at £5 per kg.

None of the joint costs shown in Example 6.5 is allocated to the by-product but the further processing costs of £5000 (5000 kg × £1) are charged to the by-product. The net revenues from the by-product of £20 000 (sales revenue of £25 000 less further processing costs of £5000) are deducted from the costs of the joint process (£3 020 000). Thus joint costs of £3 000 000 will be allocated to joint products A and B using one of the allocation methods described in this chapter. The accounting entries for the by-product will be as follows:

Dr By-product stock (5000 × £4)	20 000	
Cr Joint process WIP account		20 000

With the net revenue due from the production of the by-product:

Dr By-product stock	5000	
Cr Cash		5000

With the separable manufacturing costs incurred:

Dr Cash	25 000	
Cr By-product stock		25 000

With the value of by-products sales for the period.

By-products, scrap and waste

The terms 'by-products', 'scrap' and 'waste' are used to refer to outputs with little or no value. Because different people use these different terms to refer to the same thing, we shall briefly discuss the distinction between them.

Waste is a term used to describe material that has no value, or even negative value if it has to be disposed of at some cost. Examples include gases, sawdust, smoke and other unsaleable residues from the manufacturing process. Waste presents no accounting problems because it has no sales value, and therefore it is not included in the stock valuation.

By-products, as we have already seen, are those products that have a minor sales value and that emerge incidentally from the production of the major products.

Scrap also emerges as a consequence of the joint production process, but it is distinct from by-products in the sense that it is the leftover part of raw materials, whereas by-products are different from the material that went into the production process. The term 'scrap' is usually limited to material that has some minor sales value. Metal shavings with a minor sales value would normally be classified as scrap. When a product of minor sales value is processed beyond the split-off point, it should be considered as a by-product and not scrap, although the fact that a product will not be processed beyond the split-off point does not necessarily mean that it should be considered as scrap. The major distinguishing feature is that by-products are different from the materials that went into the production process.

The accounting procedures for scrap and by-products are fairly similar, and the accounting treatment which has already been outlined for by-products can also be applied to scrap.

Summary

The following items relate to the learning objectives listed at the beginning of the chapter.

- **Distinguish between joint products and by-products.**

  Both joint products and by-products arise from a joint production process whereby the products are not separately identifiable until after they have emerged from this joint process. Joint products have relatively high sales value whereas by-products have a low sales value compared with the sales value of a joint product. Joint products are also crucial to the commercial viability of an organization, whereas by-products are incidental.

- **Explain and identify the split-off point in a joint cost situation.**

  The split-off point is the point in the process when products become separately identifiable.

- **Explain the alternative methods of allocating joint costs to products.**

  Four different methods of allocating joint costs to products were described – physical measures, sales value at split-off point, net realizable value and gross profit percentage methods. The physical measures method simply allocates joint costs to individual products in proportion to their production volumes. The second method allocates joint costs to individual products based on their sales value at split-off point. If market prices of products at the split-off point do not exist, the sales value can be estimated using the net realizable method. With this method the net realizable values of the joint products at split-off point are estimated by deducting the further processing costs from the sales value at the point of sale. The gross profit percentage method allocates joint costs so that the overall gross profit percentage is identical for each product.

- **Discuss the arguments for and against each of the methods of allocating joint costs to products.**

  Cost should be allocated based on cause-and-effect relationships. Such relationships cannot be observed with joint products. When this situation occurs it is recommended that joint costs should be allocated based on the benefits received criterion. The advantage of the physical measures method is its simplicity but it suffers from the disadvantage that it can lead to a situation where the recorded joint cost inventory valuation for a product is in excess of its net realizable value. The sales value at split-off point suffers from the disadvantage that sales values for many joint products do not exist at the split-off point. The gross profit percentage method assumes that there is a uniform relationship between cost and sales value for each product. However, such a relationship is questionable since identical gross profit percentages for individual products in multiproduct companies that do not have joint costs are not observed. Both the sales value at split-off point and the net realizable value methods most closely meet the benefits received criterion but the latter is likely to be the preferred method if sales values at the split-off point do not exist.

- **Present relevant financial information for a decision as to whether a product should be sold at a particular stage or further processed.**

  The joint costs allocated to products are irrelevant for decisions relating to further processing. Such decisions should be based on a comparison of the incremental costs with the incremental revenues arising from further processing. The presentation of relevant financial information for further processing decisions was illustrated using the data presented in Examples 6.3 and 6.4.

- **Describe the accounting treatment of by-products.**

  By-product net-revenues should be deducted from the cost of the joint production process prior to allocating the costs to the individual joint products. The accounting treatment of by-products was illustrated with the data presented in Example 6.5.

Key terms and concepts

by-products (p. 198, p. 208, p. 210)
constant gross profit percentage method (p. 204)
further processing costs (p. 198)
joint products (p. 198)
net realizable value method (p. 203)
physical measures method (p. 199)
sales value at split-off point method (p. 202)
scrap (p. 210)
split-off point (p. 198)
waste (p. 210)

Recommended reading

For a description of a system of joint product costing involving the production of memory chips of differing quality in the semi-conductor industry in the USA you should refer to Cats-Baril *et al.* (1986). Research publications relating to the costs and joint products of English teaching hospitals and joint blood product costs are reported respectively in

Perrin (1987) and Trenchard and Dixon (2003). For a more detailed discussion of cost allocations in general you should refer to Ahmed and Scapens (1991) and Young (1985).

Key examination points

It is necessary to apportion joint costs to joint products for inventory valuation and profit measurement purposes. Remember that the costs calculated for inventory valuation purposes should not be used for decision-making purposes. Examination questions normally require joint product cost calculations and the presentation of information as to whether a product should be sold at split-off point or further processed (see the answers to Review problems 6.16 and 6.17). A common mistake with the latter requirement is to include joint cost apportionments. You should compare incremental revenues with incremental costs and indicate that, in the short term, joint costs are not relevant to the decision to sell at the split-off point or process further.

Assessment material

Review questions

The review questions are short questions that enable you to assess your understanding of the main topics included in the chapter. The numbers in parentheses provide you with the page numbers to refer to if you cannot answer a specific question.

Review problems

The review problems are more complex and require you to relate and apply the chapter content to various business problems. The problems are graded by their level of difficulty. The multiple-choice questions are the least demanding and normally take less than 10 minutes to complete. Fully worked solutions to the review problems are provided in a separate section at the end of the book. For those questions in the white box the worked solutions are provided in the *Student's Manual* accompanying this book. Further review problems for this chapter are available on the accompanying website www.drury-online.com. The answers to these problems are available for lecturers on the lecturer's password protected section of the website.

Case studies

The website also includes over 30 case study problems. A list of these cases is provided in Part Seven of this book.

Review questions

6.1 Define joint costs, split-off point and further processing costs. (*p. 198*)

6.2 Distinguish between joint products and by-products. (*p. 198*)

6.3 Provide examples of industries that produce both joint products and by-products. (*p. 198*)

6.4 Explain why it is necessary to allocate joint costs to products. (*p. 198*)

6.5 Describe the four different methods of allocating joint costs to products. (*pp. 199–205*)

6.6 Why is the physical measure method considered to be an unsatisfactory joint-cost allocation method? (*pp. 200–201*)

6.7 Explain the factors that should influence the choice of method when allocating joint costs to products. (*p. 205*)

6.8 Explain the financial information that should be included in a decision as to whether a product should be sold at the split-off point or further processed. (*pp. 206–07*)

6.9 Describe the accounting treatment of by-products. (*pp. 208–09*)

6.10 Distinguish between by-products, waste and scrap. (*p. 210*)

Review problems

6.11 Intermediate

A company operates a process which produces three joint products – K, P and Z. The costs of operating this process during September amounted to £117 000. During the month the output of the three products was:

K	2000 litres
P	4500 litres
Z	3250 litres

P is further processed at a cost of £9.00 per litre. The actual loss of the second process was 10% of the input which was normal. Products K and Z are sold without further processing.

The final selling prices of each of the products are:

K	£20.00 per litre
P	£25.00 per litre
Z	£18.00 per litre

Joint costs are attributed to products on the basis of output volume.

The profit attributed to product P was:

A £6750
B £12 150
C £13 500
D £16 200
E £18 000

CIMA Stage 2 Specimen Paper

6.12 Intermediate

The output of a process consists of two joint products, Jointpro A and Jointpro B, and a by-product. Jointpro B could go through a further process in order to increase its sales value. To assist management in making the decision whether to carry out further processing, which ONE of the following is relevant?

A The share of the total processing cost which has been allocated to Jointpro B.
B The sales value of Jointpro A and the by-product.
C The physical quantities of all three products at separation point.
D The cost of further processing Jointpro B and the increase in sales value that will result.

CIMA – Management Accounting Fundamentals

6.13 Intermediate

Charleville operates a continuous process producing three products and one by-product. Output from the process for a month was as follows:

Product	Selling price per unit	Units of output from process
1	£18	10 000
2	£25	20 000
3	£20	20 000
4 (by-product)	£2	3 500

Total output costs were £277 000.

What was the unit valuation for product 3 using the sales revenue basis for allocating joint cost?

A £4.70
B £4.80
C £5.00
D £5.10.

ACCA Paper 1.2 – Financial information for Management

6.14 Intermediate: Preparation of process accounts and apportionment of joint costs

(a) Distinguish between the cost accounting treatment of joint products and of by-products.

(3 marks)

(b) A company operates a manufacturing process which produces joint products A and B and by-product C.

Manufacturing costs for a period total £272 926, incurred in the manufacture of:

Product A 16 000 kg (selling price £6.10/kg)
Product B 53 200 kg (selling price £7.50/kg)
Product C 2 770 kg (selling price £0.80/kg)

Required:

Calculate the cost per kg (to three decimal places of a pound £) of products A and B in the period, using market values to apportion joint costs.

(5 marks)

(c) In another of the company's processes, product X is manufactured using raw materials P and T, which are mixed in the proportions 1:2.

Material purchase prices are:

P £5.00 per kg
T £1.60 per kg

Normal weight loss 5% is expected during the process.

In the period just ended 9130 kg of Product X were manufactured from 9660 kg of raw materials. Conversion costs in the period were £23 796. There was no work in progress at the beginning or end of the period.

Required:

Prepare the product X process account for the period.

(6 marks)
(Total 14 marks)
ACCA Foundation Paper 3

6.15 Intermediate: Apportionment of joint costs

The marketing director of your company has expressed concern about product X, which for some time has shown a loss, and has stated that some action will have to be taken.

Product X is produced from material A which is one of two raw materials jointly produced by passing chemicals through a process.

Representative data for the process is as follows:

Output (kg):	
Material A	10 000
Material B	30 000
Process B (£):	
Raw material	83 600
Conversion costs	58 000

Joint costs are apportioned to the two raw materials according to the weight of output. Production costs incurred in converting material A into product X are £1.80 per kg of material A used. A yield of 90% is achieved. Product X is sold for £5.60 per kg. Material B is sold without further processing for £6.00 per kg.

Required:

(a) Calculate the profit/loss per kg of product X and material B, respectively.
(7 marks)

(b) Comment upon the marketing director's concern, advising him whether you consider any action should be taken.
(7 marks)

(c) Demonstrate an alternative joint cost apportionment for product X and comment briefly upon this alternative method of apportionment.
(8 marks)

(Total 22 marks)

ACCA Level 1 Costing

6.16 Intermediate: Joint cost apportionment and decisions on further processing

A process costing £200 000 produces 3 products – A, B and C. Output details are as follows:

Product A	6 000 litres
Product B	10 000 litres
Product C	20 000 tonnes

Each product may be sold at the completion of the process as follows:

	Sales value at the end of the first process
Product A	£10 per litre
Product B	£4 per litre
Product C	£10 per tonne

Alternatively, further processing of each individual product can be undertaken to produce an enhanced product thus:

	Subsequent processing costs	Sales value after final process
Enhanced Product A	£14 per litre	£20 per litre
Enhanced Product B	£2 per litre	£8 per litre
Enhanced Product C	£6 per tonne	£16 per tonne

Required:

(a) Explain the following terms:
(i) normal process loss;
(ii) joint product;
(iii) by-product;
and state the appropriate costing treatments for normal process loss and for by-products.

(10 marks)

(b) Calculate the apportionment of joint process costs to products A, B and C above.

(8 marks)

(c) Explain whether the initial process should be undertaken and which, if any, of the enhanced products should be produced.

(7 marks)
(Total 25 marks)
AAT

6.17 **Intermediate: Preparation of profit statements and decision on further processing**

(a) Polimur Ltd operates a process that produces three joint products, all in an unrefined condition. The operating results of the process for October 2000 are shown below.

Output from process:

Product A	100 tonnes
Product B	80 tonnes
Product C	80 tonnes

The month's operating costs were £1 300 000. The closing stocks were 20 tonnes of A, 15 tonnes of B and 5 tonnes of C. The value of the closing stock is calculated by apportioning costs according to weight of output. There were no opening stocks and the balance of the output was sold to a refining company at the following prices:

Product A	£5 per kg
Product B	£4 per kg
Product C	£9 per kg

Required:

Prepare an operating statement showing the relevant trading results for October 2000.

(6 marks)

(b) The management of Polimur Ltd have been considering a proposal to establish their own refining operations.

The current market prices of the refined products are:

Product A	£17 per kg
Product B	£14 per kg
Product C	£20.50 per kg

The estimated unit costs of the refining operation are:

	Product A (£ per kg)	Product B (£ per kg)	Product C (£ per kg)
Direct materials	0.50	0.75	2.50
Direct labour	2.00	3.00	4.00
Variable overheads	1.50	2.25	5.50

Prime costs would be variable. Fixed overheads, which would be £700 000 monthly, would be direct to the refining operation. Special equipment is required for refining product B and this would be rented at a cost, not included in the above figures, of £360 000 per month.

It may be assumed that there would be no weight loss in the refining process and that the quantity refined each month would be similar to October's output shown in (a) above.

Required:

Prepare a statement that will assist management to evaluate the proposal to commence refining operations. Include any further comments or observations you consider relevant.

(16 marks)

(Total 22 marks)

ACCA Foundation Costing

6.18 Advanced: Calculation of joint product costs and the evaluation of an incremental order

Rayman Company produces three chemical products, J1X, J2Y and B1Z. Raw materials are processed in a single plant to produce two intermediate products, J1 and J2, in fixed proportions. There is no market for these two intermediate products. J1 is processed further through process X to yield the product J1X, product J2 is converted into J2Y by a separate finishing process Y. The Y finishing process produces both J2Y and a waste material, B1, which has no market value. The Rayman Company can convert B1, after additional processing through process Z, into a saleable by-product, B1Z. The company can sell as much B1Z as it can produce at a price of £1.50 per kg.

At normal levels of production and sales, 600 000 kg of the common input material are processed each month. There are 440 000 kg and 110 000 kg respectively, of the intermediate products J1 and J2, produced from this level of input. After the separate finishing processes, fixed proportions of J1X, J2Y and B1Z emerge, as shown below with current market prices (all losses are normal losses):

Product	Quantity kg	Market Price per kg
J1X	400 000	£2.425
J2Y	100 000	£4.50
B1Z	10 000	£1.50

At these normal volumes, materials and processing costs are as follows:

	Common Plant Facility	Separate Finishing Processes		
		X	Y	Z
	(£000)	(£000)	(£000)	(£000)
Direct materials	320	110	15	1.0
Direct labour	150	225	90	5.5
Variable overhead	30	50	25	0.5
Fixed overhead	50	25	5	3.0
Total	550	410	135	10.0

Selling and administrative costs are entirely fixed and cannot be traced to any of the three products.

Required:

(a) Draw a diagram which shows the flow of these products, through the processes, label the diagram and show the quantities involved in normal operation.

(2 marks)

(b) Calculate the *cost per unit* of the finished products J1X and J2Y and the *total manufacturing profit*, for the month, attributed to each product assuming all joint costs are allocated based on:

(i) physical units

(3 marks)

(ii) net realizable value

(4 marks)

and comment briefly on the two methods.

(3 marks)

NB All losses are normal losses.

(c) A new customer has approached Rayman wishing to purchase 10 000 kg of J2Y for £4.00 per kg. This is extra to the present level of business indicated above.

Advise the management how they may respond to this approach by:

(i) Developing a financial evaluation of the offer.

(4 marks)

(ii) Clarifying any assumptions and further questions which may apply.

(4 marks)

(Total 20 marks)

ACCA Paper 8 Managerial Finance

Review problems (with answers in the Student's Manual)

6.19 Intermediate: Preparation of joint product account and a decision of further processing

PQR Limited produces two joint products – P and Q – together with a by-product R, from a single main process (process 1). Product P is sold at the point of separation for £5 per kg, whereas product Q is sold for £7 per kg after further processing into product Q2. By-product R is sold without further processing for £1.75 per kg.

Process 1 is closely monitored by a team of chemists, who planned the output per 1000 kg of input materials to be as follows:

Product P	500 kg
Product Q	350 kg
Product R	100 kg
Toxic waste	50 kg

The toxic waste is disposed of at a cost of £1.50 per kg, and arises at the end of processing.

Process 2, which is used for further processing of product Q into product Q2, has the following cost structure:

Fixed costs	£6000 per week
Variable costs	£1.50 per kg processed

The following actual data relate to the first week of accounting period 10:

Process 1	
Opening work in process	Nil
Materials input 10 000 kg costing	£15 000
Direct labour	£10 000
Variable overhead	£4 000
Fixed overhead	£6 000

Outputs:

Product P	4800 kg
Product Q	3600 kg
Product R	1000 kg
Toxic waste	600 kg
Closing work in progress	nil

Process 2	
Opening work in process	nil
Input of product Q	3600 kg
Output of product Q2	3300 kg
Closing work in progress	300 kg, 50% converted

Conversion costs were incurred in accordance with the planned cost structure.

Required:

(a) Prepare the main process account for the first week of period 10 using the final sales value method to attribute pre-separation costs to joint products.

(12 marks)

(b) Prepare the toxic waste accounts and process 2 account for the first week of period 10.

(9 marks)

(c) Comment on the method used by PQR Limited to attribute pre-separation costs to its joint products.

(4 marks)

(d) Advise the management of PQR Limited whether or not, on purely financial grounds, it should continue to process product Q into product Q2:

(i) if product Q could be sold at the point of separation for £4.30 per kg; *and*

(ii) if 60% of the weekly fixed costs of process 2 were avoided by not processing product Q further.

(5 marks)

(Total 30 marks)

CIMA Stage 2 Operational Cost Accounting

6.20 Intermediate: Flow chart and calculation of cost per unit for joint products

A distillation plant, which works continuously, processes 1000 tonnes of raw material each day. The raw material costs £4 per tonne and the plant operating costs per day are £2600. From the input of raw material the following output is produced:

	(%)
Distillate X	40
Distillate Y	30
Distillate Z	20
By-product B	10

From the initial distillation process, Distillate X passes through a heat process which costs £1500 per day and becomes product X which requires blending before sale.

Distillate Y goes through a second distillation process costing £3300 per day and produces 75% of product Y and 25% of product X1.

Distillate Z has a second distillation process costing £2400 per day and produces 60% of product Z and 40% of product X2. The three streams of products X, X1 and X2 are blended, at a cost of £1555 per day to become the saleable final product XXX.

There is no loss of material from any of the processes.

By-product B is sold for £3 per tonne and such proceeds are credited to the process from which the by-product is derived.

Joint costs are apportioned on a physical unit basis.

You are required to:

(a) draw a flow chart, flowing from left to right, to show for one day of production the flow of material and the build up of the operating costs for each product;

(18 marks)

(b) present a statement for management showing for *each* of the products XXX, Y and Z, the output for *one* day, the total cost and the unit cost per tonne;

(5 marks)

(c) suggest an alternative method for the treatment of the income receivable for by-product B than that followed in this question (figures are not required).

(2 marks)
(Total 25 marks)
CIMA Stage 2 Cost Accounting

6.21 Intermediate: Calculation of cost per unit and decision on further processing

A chemical company carries on production operations in two processes. Materials first pass through process I, where a compound is produced. A loss in weight takes place at the start of processing. The following data, which can be assumed to be representative, relates to the month just ended:

Quantities (kg):	
Material input	200 000
Opening work in process (half processed)	40 000
Work completed	160 000
Closing work in process (two-thirds processed)	30 000

Costs (£):	
Material input	75 000
Processing costs	96 000
Opening work in process:	
Materials	20 000
Processing costs	12 000

Any quantity of the compound can be sold for £1.60 per kg. Alternatively, it can be transferred to process II for further processing and packing to be sold as Starcomp for £2.00 per kg. Further materials are added in process II such that for every kg of compound used, 2 kg of Starcomp result.

Of the 160 000 kg per month of work completed in process I, 40 000 kg are sold as compound and 120 000 kg are passed through process II for sale as Starcomp. Process II has facilities to handle up to 160 000 kg of compound per month if required. The monthly costs incurred in process II (other than the cost of the compound) are:

	120 000 kg of compound input	**160 000 kg of compound input**
Materials (£)	120 000	160 000
Processing costs (£)	120 000	140 000

Required:

(a) Determine, using the average method, the cost per kg of compound in process I, and the value of both work completed and closing work in process for the month just ended.

(11 marks)

(b) Demonstrate that it is worth while further processing 120 000 kg of compound.

(5 marks)

(c) Calculate the minimum acceptable selling price per kg, if a potential buyer could be found for the additional output of Starcomp that could be produced with the remaining compound.

(6 marks)

(Total 22 marks)

ACCA Level 1 Costing

6.22 Intermediate: Profitability analysis and a decision on further processing

C Ltd operates a process which produces three joint products. In the period just ended costs of production totalled £509 640. Output from the process during the period was:

Product W	276 000 kilos
Product X	334 000 kilos
Product Y	134 000 kilos

There were no opening stocks of the three products. Products W and X are sold in this state. Product Y is subjected to further processing. Sales of Products W and X during the period were:

Product W	255 000 kilos at £0.945 per kilo
Product X	312 000 kilos at £0.890 per kilo

128 000 kilos of Product Y were further processed during the period. The balance of the period production of the three products W, X and Y remained in stock at the end of the period. The value of closing stock of individual products is calculated by apportioning costs according to weight of output.

The additional costs in the period of further processing Product Y, which is converted into Product Z, were:

Direct labour	£10 850
Production overhead	£7 070

96 000 kilos of Product Z were produced from the 128 000 kilos of Product Y. A by-product BP is also produced which can be sold for £0.12 per kilo. 8000 kilos of BP were produced and sold in the period.

Sales of Product Z during the period were 94 000 kilos, with a total revenue of £100 110. Opening stock of Product Z was 8000 kilos, valued at £8640. The FIFO method is used for pricing transfers of Product Z to cost of sales.

Selling and administration costs are charged to all main products when sold, at 10% of revenue.

Required:

(a) Prepare a profit and loss account for the period, identifying separately the profitability of each of the three main products.

(14 marks)

(b) C Ltd has now received an offer from another company to purchase the total output of Product Y (i.e. before further processing) for £0.62 per kilo. Calculate the viability of this alternative.

(5 marks)

(c) Discuss briefly the methods of, and rationale for, joint cost apportionment.

(6 marks)

(Total 25 marks)

ACCA Level 1 Cost and Management Accounting 1

6.23 Advanced: Preparation of profit statements and decision on further processing

A fish processing company has a contract to purchase all the fish caught by a fishing vessel. The processor removes the head and skeleton which are waste (Process 1) and is then able to sell the fish fillets which remain. The waste is estimated to be 40% by weight of the fish bought and is sold at 30p per kilo for animal food.

The fish fillets are inspected for quality and three categories are identified (standard, special and superior). Half the catch is expected to be of standard quality. Of the remainder there is twice as much special as superior.

For one contract period, the vessel contains a total of 36 000 kilos of whole fish and the contract price is £1.50 per kilo, irrespective of quality. The labour cost for Process 1 is £28 000 for this quantity.

As an alternative to sale as fresh produce, the fillets of fish may be cooked and coated in breadcrumbs (Process 2). The process of cooking the fillets and coating them in breadcrumbs cost 10p per kilo for material and 60p per kilo for labour. Current market prices of fresh fillets and the breadcrumbed alternatives are:

	£ per kilo	
Category	**Fresh**	**Breadcrumbed**
Superior	7.50	8.70
Special	6.80	7.50
Standard	4.00	5.20

In Process 1 the overhead costs are recovered based on 120% of labour costs; one third of these overheads are variable. In Process 2 the overhead rate set is 180% of labour costs, one quarter being variable.

Required:

(a) An often quoted phrase used in management accounting is 'different costs for different purposes'. To demonstrate the appropriateness of this phrase list and briefly describe three purposes of preparing product costs in a manufacturing organization.

(5 marks)

(b) Prepare statements of total net profit or loss per period for each category of fish if all sales are in the fresh state (i.e. after Process 1) and on the assumption that the total net cost is shared between the three categories based on:

(i) weight;

(ii) market value.

(6 marks)

(c) If a loss was revealed for a category under either (b) (i) or (ii) above, explain how the management should react.

(4 marks)

(d) Determine for each category whether it is profitable for the company to further process the fillets, and make brief comments.

(5 marks)

(Total 20 marks)

ACCA Paper 8 Managerial Finance

6.24 **Advanced: Joint cost apportionment and decision-making**

Hawkins Ltd produces two joint products, Boddie and Soull. A further product, Threekeys, is also made as a by-product of one of the processes for making Soull. Each product is sold in bottles of one litre capacity.

It is now January 2001. You are a cost accountant for Hawkins Ltd. You have been instructed to allocate the company's joint costs for 2000 between Boddie and Soull, but *not* to the by-product Threekeys.

During 2000, 2 000 000 litres of a raw material, Necktar, costing £3 000 000, were processed in Department Alpha with no wastage. The processing costs were £1 657 000.

50% of the output of Department Alpha was unfinished Boddie, for which there was no external market. It was transferred to Department Beta, where it was further processed at an additional cost of £8 100 000. Normal wastage by evaporation was 16% of the input of unfinished Boddie. The remaining good output of finished Boddie was sold for £10 per litre in the outside market.

The other 50% of the output from the joint process in Department Alpha was in the form of processed Necktar. It was all transferred to Department Gamma, as there was no outside market for processed Necktar. In Department Gamma it was further processed, with no wastage, at a cost of £30 900 000.

72% of the output of Department Gamma was in the form of unfinished Soull, for which there was no external market. It was transferred to Department Delta, where it was subjected to a finishing process at a further cost of £719 000. Normal spoilage of $16\frac{2}{3}$% of the input to the finishing process was experienced. The spoiled material was disposed of without charge, as effluent. The remaining finished Soull was sold in the outside market for £60 per litre.

The remaining 28% of the output of Department Gamma was in the form of finished Threekeys, the by-product. It was sold in the outside market for £8 per litre, but due to its dangerous nature special delivery costs of £70 000 were incurred in respect of it.

You are required:

(a) to allocate the appropriate joint costs between Boddie and Soull on the basis of relative sales value, treating the net realizable value of Threekeys as an addition to the sales value of Soull,

(6 marks)

(b) to prepare a statement showing the profit or loss attributed to each of the three products and the total profit or loss, for 2000, on the basis of the information above and allocating joint costs as in (a) above,

(4 marks)

(c) to show with reasons whether Hawkins Ltd should continue to produce all three products in 2001, assuming that input/output relationships, prices and sales volumes do not change.

(3 marks)
(Total 13 marks)
ICAEW Management Accounting

6.25 **Advanced: Profitability analysis including an apportionment of joint costs and identification of relevant costs/revenues for a price/output decision**

A company manufactures two joint products in a single process. One is sold as a garden fertilizer, the other is a synthetic fuel which is sold to external customers but which can also be used to heat greenhouses in which the company grows fruit and vegetables all year round as a subsidiary market venture. Information relating to the previous 12 month period is as follows:

(i) 1 600 000 kilos of garden fertilizer were produced and then sold at £3.00 per kilo. Joint costs are apportioned between the garden fertilizer and the synthetic fuel on a physical units (weight) basis. The fertilizer has a contribution to sales ratio of 40% after such apportionment. There are no direct costs of fertilizer sales or production.

(ii) The synthetic fuel represents 20% of the total weight of output from the manufacturing process. A wholesaler bought 160 000 kilos at £1.40 per kilo under a long-term contract which stipulates that its availability to him will not be reduced below 100 000 kilos per annum. There is no other external market for the fuel. Fixed administrative, selling and distribution costs incurred specifically as a result of the fuel sales to the wholesaler totalled £40 000. That part of the fuel production which was sold to the wholesaler, incurred additional variable costs for packaging of £1.20 per kilo.

(iii) The remaining synthetic fuel was used to heat the company greenhouses. The greenhouses produced 5 kilos of fruit and vegetables per kilo of fuel. The fruit and vegetables were sold at an average price of £0.50 per kilo. Total direct costs of fruit and vegetable production were £520 000. Direct costs included a fixed labour cost of £100 000 which is avoidable if fruit and vegetable production ceases, the remainder being variable with the quantity produced.

A notional fuel charge of £1.40 per kilo of fuel is made to fruit and vegetable production. This notional charge is in addition to the direct costs detailed above.

(iv) Further company fixed costs were apportioned to the products as follows:

	(£)
Garden fertilizer	720 000
Synthetic fuel	18 000
Fruit and vegetables	90 000

The above data were used to produce a profit and loss analysis for the 12 month period for each of three areas of operation viz.

1. Garden fertilizer.
2. Synthetic fuel (including external sales and transfers to the greenhouses at £1.40 per kilo).
3. Fruit and vegetables (incorporating the deduction of any notional charges).

Required:

(a) Prepare a summary statement showing the profit or loss reported in each of the three areas of operation detailed above.

(8 marks)

(b) Calculate the percentage reduction in the fixed costs of £40 000 which would have been required before the synthetic fuel sales for the previous 12 month period would have resulted in a net benefit to the company.

(3 marks)

(c) Calculate the net benefit or loss which sales of fruit and vegetables caused the company in the previous 12 month period.

(3 marks)

(d) Advise management on the fruit and vegetable price strategy for the coming year if fruit and vegetable production/sales could be expanded according to the following price/demand pattern:

Sales (000 kilos)	1200	1300	1400	1500	1600
Average selling price/kilo (£)	0.50	0.495	0.485	0.475	0.465

All other costs, prices and quantities will remain unchanged during the coming year. The wholesaler will continue to purchase all available synthetic fuel not used in the greenhouses.

(8 marks)
(Total 22 marks)
ACCA Level 2 Management Accounting

6.26 Advanced: Calculation of cost per unit, break-even point and recommended selling price

Amongst its products a chemical company markets two concentrated liquid fertilizers – type P for flowers and type Q for vegetables. In 2001 total sales are expected to be restricted by forecast sales of type Q which are limited to 570 000 litres for the year. At this level the plant capacity will be under-utilized by 20%.

The fertilizers are manufactured jointly as follows:

Mixing: Raw materials A and B are mixed together in equal amounts and filtered. After filtering there is a saleable residue, X, amounting to 5% of the input materials.

Distillation: The mixed materials are heated and there is an evaporation loss of 10%. The remaining liquid distils into one-third each of an extract P, an extract Q and a by-product Y.

Blending: Two parts of raw material C are blended with one part of extract P to form the fertilizer type P. One part of raw material D is blended with one part of extract Q to form the fertilizer type Q.

Fertilizer type P is filled into 3-litre cans and labelled. Fertilizer type Q is filled into 6-litre preprinted cans. Both are then ready for sale.

The costs involved are as under:

Raw material	**Cost per 100 litres (£)**
A	25
B	12
C	20
D	55

Cans	**Cost each (£)**
3-litre	0.32
6-litre	0.50

Labels	Cost per 1000 (£)
For 3-litre cans	3.33

Manufacturing costs:

	per 100 litres of input processed Direct wages (£)	Variable overhead (£)	Fixed overhead per year (£)
Mixing	2.75	1.00	6 000
Distilling	3.00	2.00	20 000
Blending	5.00	2.00	33 250

The residue X and by-product Y are both sold to local companies at £0.03 and £0.04 per litre respectively. Supplies are collected in bulk by the buyers using their own transport. The sales revenue is credited to the process at which the material arises.

Product costs are apportioned entirely to the two main products on the basis of their output from each process.

No inventories of part-finished materials are held at any time.

The fertilizers are sold through agents on the basis of list price less 25%. Of the net selling price, selling and distribution costs amount to $13^1/_3$% and profit to 20%. Of the selling and distribution costs 70% are variable and the remainder fixed.

You are required to:

(a) calculate separately for the fertilizers type P and type Q for the year 2001:
  (i) total manufacturing cost,
  (ii) manufacturing cost per litre,
  (iii) list price per litre,
  (iv) profit for the year

(18 marks)

(b) calculate the break-even price per litre to manufacture and supply an extra 50 000 litres of fertilizer type Q for export and which would incur variable selling and distribution costs of £2000;

(8 marks)

(c) state the price you would recommend the company should quote per litre for this export business, with a brief explanation for your decision.

(4 marks)

(Total 30 marks)

CIMA P3 Management Accounting

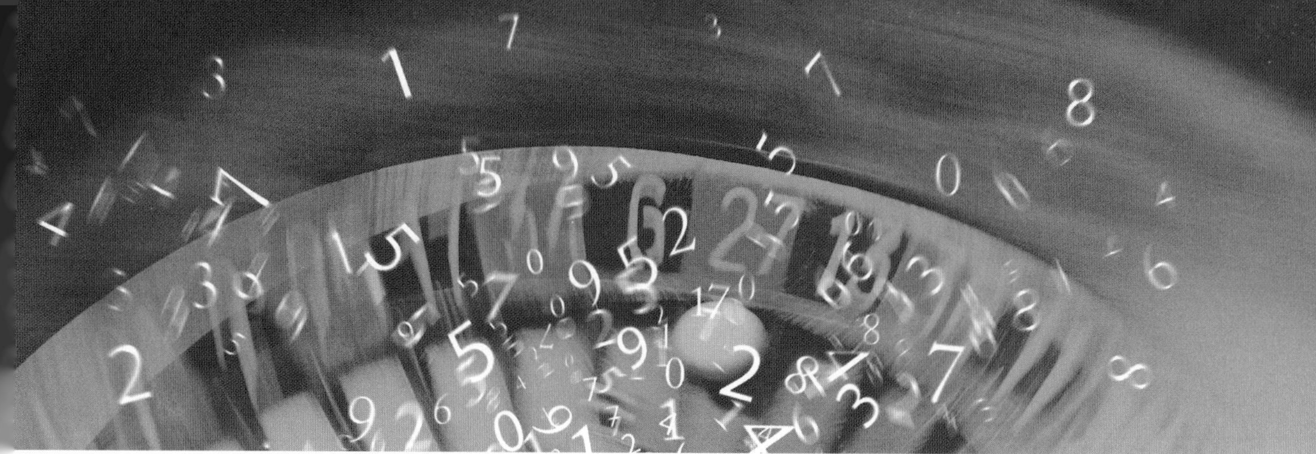

Income effects of alternative cost accumulation systems

7

In the previous chapters we looked at the procedures necessary to ascertain product or job costs for inventory valuation to meet the requirements of external reporting. The approach that we adopted was to allocate all manufacturing cost to products, and to value unsold stocks at their total cost of manufacture. Non-manufacturing costs were not allocated to the products but were charged directly to the profit statement and excluded from the inventory valuation. A costing system based on these principles is known as an **absorption** or **full costing** system.

In this chapter we are going to look at an alternative costing system known as **variable costing**, **marginal costing** or **direct costing**. Under this alternative system, only variable manufacturing costs are assigned to products and included in the inventory valuation. Fixed manufacturing costs are not allocated to the product, but are considered as period costs and charged directly to the profit statement. Both absorption costing and variable costing systems are in complete agreement regarding the treatment of non-manufacturing costs as period costs. The disagreement between the proponents of absorption costing and the proponents of variable costing is concerned with whether or not manufacturing fixed overhead should be regarded as a period cost or a product cost. An illustration of the

LEARNING OBJECTIVES

After studying this chapter, you should be able to:

- explain the differences between an absorption costing and a variable costing system;
- prepare profit statements based on a variable costing and absorption costing system;
- explain the difference in profits between variable and absorption costing profit calculations;
- explain the arguments for and against variable and absorption costing;
- describe the various denominator levels that can be used with an absorption costing system;
- explain why the choice of an appropriate denominator level is important.

different treatment of fixed manufacturing overhead for both absorption and variable costing systems is shown in Exhibit 7.1. You should note that in Exhibit 7.1 direct labour is assumed to be a variable cost. Generally direct labour is not a short term variable cost that varies in direct proportion to the volume of activity. It is a step fixed cost (see Chapter 2) that varies in the longer term. In other words, it is a long term variable cost. Because of this, variable costing systems generally assume that direct labour is a variable cost.

External and internal reporting

Many writers have argued the cases for and against variable costing for inventory valuation for external reporting. One important requirement for external reporting is consistency. It would be unacceptable if companies changed their methods of inventory valuation from year to year. In addition, inter-company comparison would be difficult if some companies valued their stocks on an absorption cost basis while others did so on a variable cost basis. Furthermore, the users of external accounting reports need reassurance that the published financial statements have been prepared in accordance with generally accepted standards of good accounting practice. Therefore there is a strong case for the acceptance of one method of stock valuation for external reporting. In the UK a Statement of Standard Accounting Practice on Stocks and Work in Progress was published by the Accounting Standards Committee (SSAP 9). This states:

> *In order to match costs and revenue, cost of stocks and work in progress should comprise that expenditure which has been incurred in the normal course of business in bringing the product or service to its present location and condition. Such costs will include all related production overheads, even though these may accrue on a time basis.*

The effect of this statement in SSAP 9 was to require absorption costing for external reporting and for non-manufacturing costs to be treated as period costs. The external financial reporting regulations in most other countries also require that companies adopt absorption costing. According to Virtanen (1996) one notable exception is Finland where the country's accounting regulations and institutions have not forced companies to adopt absorption costing for external reporting. As a result variable costing is extensively used by Finnish companies. However, it is not widely used in other countries (see Exhibit 7.4).

In spite of the fact that absorption costing is required for external reporting, the variable costing versus absorption costing debate is still of considerable importance for internal reporting. Management normally require profit statements at monthly or quarterly intervals, and will no doubt wish to receive separate profit statements for each major product group or segment of the business. This information is particularly useful in evaluating the performance of divisional managers. Management must therefore decide whether absorption costing or variable costing provides the more meaningful information in assessing the economic and managerial performance of the different segments of the business.

However, before discussing the arguments for and against absorption and variable costing, let us look at a simple illustration of both methods using Example 7.1. To keep things simple we shall assume that the company in this example produces only one product using a single overhead rate for the company as a whole, with units of output being used as the allocation base. These assumptions are very simplistic. As indicated in Chapter 3, most companies are multi-product companies and they do not use a single company or plant-wide overhead rate. Instead, many cost centres are established, each with their own allocation base. Nevertheless, the same general principles apply to both simplistic and complex product settings relating to the impact that variable and

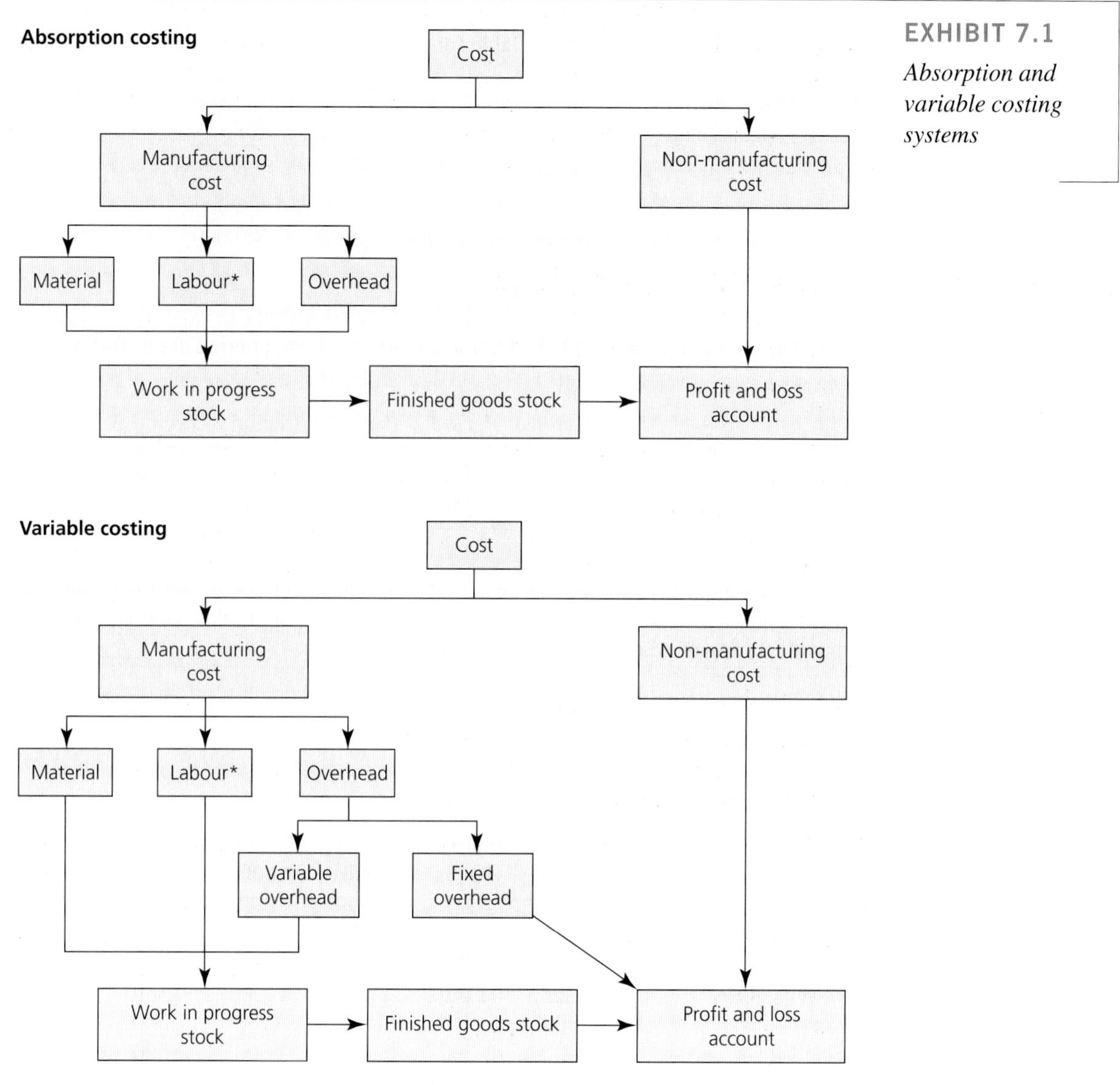

EXHIBIT 7.1
Absorption and variable costing systems

absorption costing have on profit measurement and inventory valuation. A more complex example would not enhance your understanding of the issues involved. You should now refer to Example 7.1.

Variable costing

The variable costing profit statements are shown in Exhibit 7.2. You will see that when a system of variable costing is used, the product cost is £6 per unit, and includes variable costs only since variable costs are assigned to the product. In period 1 production is 150 000 units at a variable cost of £6 per unit. The total fixed costs are then added separately to

EXAMPLE 7.1

The following information is available for periods 1–6 for the Samuelson Company:

	(£)
Unit selling price	10
Unit variable cost	6
Fixed costs per each period	300 000

The company produces only one product. Budgeted activity is expected to average 150 000 units per period, and production and sales for each period are as follows:

	Period 1	Period 2	Period 3	Period 4	Period 5	Period 6
Units sold (000's)	150	120	180	150	140	160
Units produced (000's)	150	150	150	150	170	140

There were no opening stocks at the start of period 1, and the actual manufacturing fixed overhead incurred was £300 000 per period. We shall also assume that non-manufacturing overheads are £100 000 per period.

EXHIBIT 7.2

Variable costing statements

	Period 1 (£000s)	Period 2 (£000s)	Period 3 (£000s)	Period 4 (£000s)	Period 5 (£000s)	Period 6 (£000s)
Opening stock	—	—	180	—	—	180
Production cost	900	900	900	900	1020	840
Closing stock	—	(180)	—	—	(180)	(60)
Cost of sales	900	720	1080	900	840	960
Fixed costs	300	300	300	300	300	300
Total costs	1200	1020	1380	1200	1140	1260
Sales	1500	1200	1800	1500	1400	1600
Gross profit	300	180	420	300	260	340
Less non-manufacturing costs	100	100	100	100	100	100
Net profit	200	80	320	200	160	240

produce a total manufacturing cost of £1 200 000. Note that the fixed costs of £300 000 are assigned to the period in which they are incurred.

In period 2, 150 000 units are produced but only 120 000 are sold. Therefore 30 000 units remain in stock at the end of the period. In order to match costs with revenues, the sales of 120 000 units should be matched with costs for 120 000. As 150 000 units were produced, we need to value the 30 000 units in stock and deduct this sum from the production cost. Using the variable costing system, the 30 000 units in stock are valued at

£6 per unit. A closing inventory of £180 000 will then be deducted from the production costs, giving a cost of sales figure of £720 000. Note that the closing inventory valuation does not include any fixed overheads.

The 30 000 units of closing inventory in period 2 becomes the opening inventory for period 3 and therefore an expense for this period. The production cost for the 150 000 units made in period 3 is added to this opening inventory valuation. The overall effect is that costs for 180 000 units are matched against sales for 180000 units. The profits for periods 4–6 are calculated in the same way.

Absorption costing

Let us now consider in Exhibit 7.3 the profit calculations when closing stocks are valued on an absorption costing basis. With the absorption costing method, a share of the fixed production overheads are allocated to individual products and are included in the products' production cost. Fixed overheads are assigned to products by establishing overhead absorption rates as described in Chapter 3. To establish the overhead rate we must divide the fixed overheads of £300 000 for the period by an appropriate denominator level. Most companies use an annual budgeted activity measure of the overhead allocation base as the denominator level (we shall discuss the different approaches that can be used for determining denominator levels later in the chapter). Our allocation base in Example 7.1 is units of output and we shall assume that the annual budgeted output is 1 800 000 units giving an average for each monthly period of 150 000 units. Therefore the budgeted fixed overhead rate is £2 per unit (£300 000/150 000 units). The product cost now consists of a variable cost (£6) plus a fixed manufacturing cost (£2), making a total of £8 per unit. Hence, the production cost for period 1 is £1 200 000 (150 000 units at £8).

Now compare the absorption costing statement (Exhibit 7.3) with the variable costing statement (Exhibit 7.2) for period 1. With absorption costing, the fixed cost is included in the production cost figure, whereas with variable costing only the variable cost is included. With variable costing, the fixed cost is allocated separately as a lump sum and is not included in the cost of sales figure. Note also that the closing inventory of 30 000 units for period 2 is valued at £8 per unit in the absorption costing statement, whereas the closing inventory is valued at only £6 in the variable costing statement.

In calculating profits, the matching principle that has been applied in the absorption costing statement is the same way as that described for variable costing. However, complications arise in periods 5 and 6; in period 5, 170 000 units were produced, so the production cost of £1 360 000 includes fixed overheads of £340 000 (170 000 units at £2). The total fixed overheads incurred for the period are only £300 000, so £40 000 too much has been allocated. This over recovery of fixed overhead is recorded as a **period cost adjustment**. (A full explanation of under and over recoveries of overheads and the reasons for period cost adjustments was presented in Chapter 3; if you are unsure of this concept, please refer back now to the section headed 'Under and over recovery of overheads'.) Note also that the under or over recovery of fixed overheads is also called **volume variance**.

In period 6, 140 000 units were produced at a cost of £1 120 000, which included only £280 000 (140 000 units at £2) for fixed overheads. As a result, there is an under recovery of £20 000, which is written off as a period cost. You can see that an under or over recovery of fixed overhead occurs whenever actual production differs from the budged average level of activity of 150 000 units, since the calculation of the fixed overhead rate of £2 per unit was based on the assumption that actual production would be 150 000 units per period. Note that both variable and absorption costing systems do not assign non-manufacturing costs to products for stock valuation.

EXHIBIT 7.3
Absorption costing statements

	Period 1 (£000s)	Period 2 (£000s)	Period 3 (£000s)	Period 4 (£000s)	Period 5 (£000s)	Period 6 (£000s)
Opening stock	—	—	240	—	—	240
Production cost	1200	1200	1200	1200	1360	1120
Closing stock	—	(240)	—	—	(240)	(80)
Cost of sales	1200	960	1440	1200	1120	1280
Adjustments for under/(over) recovery of overhead	—	—	—	—	(40)	20
Total costs	1200	960	1440	1200	1080	1300
Sales	1500	1200	1800	1500	1400	1600
Gross profit	300	240	360	300	320	300
Less non-manufacturing costs	100	100	100	100	100	100
Net profit	200	140	260	200	220	200

Variable costing and absorption costing: a comparison of their impact on profit

A comparison of the variable costing and absorption costing statements produced from the information contained in Example 7.1 reveals the following differences in profit calculations:

(a) The profits calculated under the absorption costing and variable costing systems are identical for periods 1 and 4.

(b) The absorption costing profits are higher than the variable costing profits in periods 2 and 5.

(c) The variable costing profits are higher than the absorption costing profits in periods 3 and 6.

Let us now consider each of these in a little more detail.

Production equals sales

In periods 1 and 4 the profits are the same for both methods of costing; in both periods production is equal to sales, and inventories will neither increase nor decrease. Therefore if opening inventories exist, the same amount of fixed overhead will be carried forward as an expense to be included in the current period in the opening inventory valuation as will be deducted in the closing inventory valuation from the production cost figure. The overall effect is that, with an absorption costing system, the only fixed overhead that will be included as an expense for the period will be the amount of fixed overhead that is incurred for the period. Thus, whenever sales are equal to production the profits will be the same for both the absorption costing and variable costing systems.

Production exceeds sales

In periods 2 and 5 the absorption costing system produces higher profits; in both periods production exceeds sales. Profits are higher for absorption costing when production is in excess of sales, because inventories are increasing. The effect of this is that a greater amount of fixed overheads in the closing inventory is being deducted from the expenses of the period than is being brought forward in the opening inventory for the period. For example, in period 2 the opening inventory is zero and no fixed overheads are brought forward from the previous period. However, a closing inventory of 30 000 units means that a £60 000 fixed overhead has to be deducted from the production cost for the period. In other words, only £240 000 is being allocated for fixed overhead with the absorption costing system, whereas the variable costing system allocates the £300 000 fixed overhead incurred for the period. The effect of this is that profits are £60 000 greater with the absorption costing system. As a general rule, if production is in excess of sales, the absorption costing system will show a higher profit than the variable costing system.

Sales exceed production

In periods 3 and 6 the variable costing system produces higher profits; in both periods sales exceed production. When this situation occurs, inventories decline and a greater amount of fixed overheads will need to be brought forward as an expense in the opening inventory than is being deducted in the closing inventory adjustment. For example, with the absorption costing system, in period 6, 30 000 units of opening inventory are brought forward, so that fixed costs of £60 000 are included in the inventory valuation. However, a closing inventory of 10 000 units requires a deduction of £20 000 fixed overheads from the production costs. The overall effect is that an additional £40 000 fixed overheads is included as an expense within the stock movements, and a total of £340 000 fixed overheads is allocated for the period. The variable costing system, on the other hand, would allocate fixed overheads for the period of only £300 000. As a result, profits are £40 000 greater with the variable costing system. As a general rule, if sales are in excess of production, the variable costing system will show a higher profit than the absorption costing system.

Impact of sales fluctuations

The profit calculations for an absorption costing system can produce some strange results. For example, in period 6 the sales volume has increased but profits have declined, in spite of the fact that both the selling price and the cost structure have remained unchanged. A manager whose performance is being judged in period 6 is likely to have little confidence in an accounting system that shows a decline in profits when sales volume has increased and the cost structure and selling price have not changed. The opposite occurs in period 5. In this period the sales volume declines but profit increases. The situations in periods 5 and 6 arise because the under or over recovery of fixed overhead is treated as a period cost, and such adjustments can at times give a misleading picture of profits.

In contrast, the variable costing profit calculations show that when sales volume increases profit also increases. Alternatively, when sales volume decreases, profit also decreases. These relationships continue as long as the selling price and cost structure remain unchanged. Looking again at the variable costing profit calculations, you will note that profit declines in period 5 when the sales volume declines, and increases in period 6 when the sales volume also increases. The reasons for these changes are that, with a system of variable costing, profit is a function of sales volume only, when the selling price and cost structure remain unchanged. However, with absorption costing, profit is a function of both sales volume and production volume.

A mathematical model of the profit functions

In Appendix 7.1 the following formula is developed to model the profit function for an absorption costing system when unit costs remain unchanged throughout the period:

$$OPBT_{AC} = (ucm - ufmc)Q_s + (ufmc \times Q_p) - FC \quad (7.1)$$

where

ucm = Contribution margin per unit (i.e. selling price per unit – variable cost per unit)
ufmc = Pre-determined fixed manufacturing overhead per unit of output
Q_p = Number of units produced
Q_s = Number of units sold
FC = Total fixed costs (manufacturing and non-manufacturing)
$OPBT_{AC}$ = Operating profit before taxes for the period (Absorption costing)
$OPBT_{VC}$ = Operating profit before taxes for the period (Variable costing)

Applying formula 7.1 to the data given in Example 7.1 gives the following profit function:

$$(£4 - £2)Q_s + (£2 \times Q_p) - £400\,000 = £2Q_s + £2Q_p - £400\,000$$

Applying the above profit function to periods 4–6 we get:

$$\text{Period 4} = £2(150\,000) + £2(150\,000) - £400\,000 = £200\,000$$
$$\text{Period 5} = £2(140\,000) + £2(170\,000) - £400\,000 = £220\,000$$
$$\text{Period 6} = £2(160\,000) + £2(140\,000) - £400\,000 = £200\,000$$

When production equals sales identical profits with an absorption and variable costing system are reported. Therefore formula 7.1 converts to the following variable costing profit function if we let $Q_s = Q_p$:

$$\text{Variable costing operating profit} = ucm \cdot Q_s - FC \quad (7.2)$$

Using the data given in Example 7.1 the profit function is:

$$£4Q_s - £400\,000$$

Applying the above profit function to periods 4–6 we get:

$$\text{Period 4} = £4(150\,000) - £400\,000 = £200\,000$$
$$\text{Period 5} = £4(140\,000) - £400\,000 = £160\,000$$
$$\text{Period 6} = £4(160\,000) - £400\,000 = £240\,000$$

The difference between the reported operating profits for an absorption costing and a variable costing system can be derived by deducting formulae 7.2 from 7.1 giving:

$$ufmc(Q_p - Q_s) \quad (7.3)$$

If you look closely at the above term you will see that it represents the inventory change (in units) multiplied by the fixed manufacturing overhead rate. Applying formula 7.3 to period 5 the inventory change ($Q_p - Q_s$) is 30 000 units (positive) so that absorption costing profits exceed variable costing profits by £60 000 (30 000 units at £2 overhead rate). For an explanation of how formulae (7.1) and (7.2) are derived you should refer to Appendix 7.1.

Some arguments in support of variable costing

Variable costing provides more useful information for decision-making

The separation of fixed and variable costs helps to provide relevant information about costs for making decisions. Relevant costs are required for a variety of short-term decisions, for example whether to make a component internally or to purchase externally, as well as problems relating to product-mix. These decisions will be discussed in Chapter 9. In addition, the estimation of costs for different levels of activities requires that costs be split into their fixed and variable elements. The assumption is that only with a variable costing system will such an analysis of costs be available. It is therefore assumed that projection of future costs and revenues for different activity levels, and the use of relevant cost decision-making techniques, are possible only if a variable costing system is adopted. There is no reason, however, why an absorption costing system cannot be used for profit measurement and inventory valuation and costs can be analysed into their fixed and variable elements for decision-making. The advantage of variable costing is that the analysis of variable and fixed costs is highlighted. (Such an analysis is not a required feature of an absorption costing system.)

Variable costing removes from profit the effect of inventory changes

We have seen that, with variable costing, profit is a function of sales volume, whereas, with absorption costing, profit is a function of both sales and production. We have also learned, using absorption costing principles, that it is possible for profit to decline when sales volumes increase. Where stock levels are likely to fluctuate significantly, profits may be distorted when they are calculated on an absorption costing basis, since the stock changes will significantly affect the amount of fixed overheads allocated to an accounting period.

Fluctuating stock levels are less likely to occur when one measures profits on an annual basis, but on a monthly or quarterly basis seasonal variations in sales may cause significant fluctuations. As profits are likely to be distorted by an absorption costing system, there are strong arguments for using variable costing methods when profits are measured at frequent intervals. Because frequent profit statements are presented only for management, the argument for variable costing is stronger for management accounting. A survey by Drury *et al.* (1993) relating to 300 UK companies reported that 97% of the companies prepared profit statements at monthly intervals. Financial accounts are presented for public release annually or at half-yearly intervals; because significant changes in stock levels are less likely on an annual basis, the argument for the use of variable costing in financial accounting is not as strong.

A further argument for using variable costing for internal reporting is that the internal profit statements may be used as a basis for measuring managerial performance. Managers may deliberately alter their inventory levels to influence profit when an absorption costing system is used; for example, it is possible for a manager to defer deliberately some of the fixed overhead allocation by unnecessarily increasing stocks over successive periods.

There is a limit, to how long managers can continue to increase stocks, and eventually the situation will arise when it is necessary to reduce them, and the deferred fixed overheads will eventually be allocated to the periods when the inventories are reduced. Nevertheless, there is likely to remain some scope for manipulating profits in the short term. Also senior management can implement control performance measures to guard against such behaviour. For example, the reporting of performance measures that monitor changes in inventory volumes will highlight those situations where managers are manipulating profits by unnecessarily increasing inventory levels.

Variable costing avoids fixed overheads being capitalized in unsaleable stocks

In a period when sales demand decreases, a company can end up with surplus stocks on hand. With an absorption costing system, only a portion of the fixed overheads incurred during the period will be allocated as an expense because the remainder of the fixed overhead will be included in the valuation of the surplus stocks. If these surplus stocks cannot be disposed of, the profit calculation for the current period will be misleading, since fixed overheads will have been deferred to later accounting periods. However, there may be some delay before management concludes that the stocks cannot be sold without a very large reduction in the selling price. The stocks will therefore be over-valued, and a stock write-off will be necessary in a later accounting period. The overall effect may be that the current period's profits will be overstated.

Some arguments in support of absorption costing

Absorption costing does not understate the importance of fixed costs

Some people argue that decisions based on a variable costing system may concentrate only on sales revenues and variable costs and ignore the fact that fixed costs must be met in the long run. For example, if a pricing decision is based on variable costs only, then sales revenue may be insufficient to cover all the costs. It is also argued that the use of an absorption costing system, by allocating fixed costs to a product, ensures that fixed costs will be covered. These arguments are incorrect. Absorption costing will not ensure that fixed costs will be recovered if actual sales volume is less than the estimate used to calculate the fixed overhead rate. For example, consider a situation where fixed costs are £100 000 and an estimated normal activity of 10 000 units is used to calculate the overhead rate. Fixed costs are recovered at £10 per unit. Assume that variable cost is £5 per unit and selling price is set at £20 (total cost plus one-third). If actual sales volume is 5000 units then total sales revenue will be £100 000 and total costs will be £125 000. Total costs therefore exceed total sales revenue. The argument that a variable costing system will cause managers to ignore fixed costs is based on the assumption that such managers are not very bright! A failure to consider fixed costs is due to faulty management and not to a faulty accounting system. Furthermore, using variable costing for inventory valuation and profit measurement still enables full cost information to be extracted for pricing decisions.

Absorption costing avoids fictitious losses being reported

In a business that relies on seasonal sales and in which production is built up outside the sales season to meet demand the full amount of fixed overheads incurred will be charged, in a variable costing system, against sales. However, in those periods where production is being built up for sales in a later season, sales revenue will be low but fixed costs will be recorded as an expense. The result is that losses will be reported during out-of-season periods, and large profits will be reported in the periods when the goods are sold.

By contrast, in an absorption costing system fixed overheads will be deferred and included in the closing inventory valuation, and will be recorded as an expense only in the period in which the goods are sold. Losses are therefore unlikely to be reported in the periods when stocks are being built up. In these circumstances absorption costing appears to provide the more logical profit calculation.

Fixed overheads are essential for production

The proponents of absorption costing argue that the production of goods is not possible if fixed manufacturing costs are not incurred. Consequently, fixed manufacturing overheads should be allocated to units produced and included in the inventory valuation.

Consistency with external reporting

Top management may prefer their internal profit reporting systems to be consistent with the external financial accounting absorption costing systems so that they will be congruent with the measures used by financial markets to appraise overall company performance. In a pilot study of six UK companies Hopper *et al.* (1992) observed that senior managers are primarily interested in financial accounting information because it is perceived as having a major influence on how financial markets evaluate companies and their management. If top management believe that financial accounting information does influence share prices then they are likely to use the same rules and procedures for both internal and external profit measurement and inventory valuation so that managers will focus on the same measures as those used by financial markets. Also the fact that managerial rewards are often linked to external financial measures provides a further motivation to ensure that internal accounting systems do not conflict with external financial accounting reporting requirements.

Alternative denominator level measures

When absorption costing systems are used estimated fixed overhead rates must be calculated. These rates will be significantly influenced by the choice of the activity level; that is the denominator activity level that is used to calculate the overhead rate. This problem applies only to fixed overheads, and the greater the proportion of fixed overheads in an organization's cost structure the more acute is the problem. Fixed costs arise from situations where resources must be acquired in discrete, not continuous, amounts in such a way that the supply of resources cannot be continuously adjusted to match the usage of resources. For example, a machine might be purchased that provides an annual capacity of 5000 machine hours but changes in sales demand may cause the annual usage to vary from 2500 to 5000 hours. It is not possible to match the supply and usage of the resource and unused capacity will arise in those periods where the resources used are less than the 5000 hours of capacity supplied.

In contrast, variable costs arise in those situations where the supply of resources can be continually adjusted to match the usage of resources. For example, the spending on energy costs associated with running machinery (i.e. the supply and resources) can be immediately reduced by 50% if resources used decline by 50% say, from 5000 hours to 2500 hours. There is no unused capacity in respect of variable costs. Consequently with variable cost the cost per unit of resource used will be constant.

With fixed overheads the cost per unit of resource used will fluctuate with changes in estimates of activity usage because fixed overhead spending remains constant over a wide range of activity. For example, if the estimated annual fixed overheads associated with the machine referred to above are £192 000 and annual activity is estimated to be 5000 hours then the machine hour rate will be £38.40 (£192 000/5000 hours). Alternatively if annual activity is estimated to be 2500 hours then the rate will be £76.80 (£192 000/2500 hours). Therefore the choice of the denominator capacity level can have a profound effect on product cost calculations.

Several choices are available for determining the denominator activity level when calculating overhead rates. Consider the situation described in Example 7.2.

There are four different denominator activity levels that can be used in Example 7.2. They are:

1 Theoretical maximum capacity of 6000 hours = £32 per hour (£192 000/6000 hours);
2 Practical capacity of 5000 hours = £38.40 per hour (£192 000/5000 hours);
3 Normal average long-run activity of 4800 hours = £40 per hour (£192 000/4800 hours);
4 Budgeted activity of 4000 hours = £48 per hour (£192 000/4000 hours).

Theoretical maximum capacity is a measure of maximum operating capacity based on 100% efficiency with no interruptions for maintenance or other factors. We can reject this measure on the grounds that it represents an activity level that is most unlikely to be achieved. The capacity was acquired with the expectation of supplying a maximum of 5000 hours rather than a theoretical maximum of 6000 hours. This former measure is called **practical capacity**. Practical capacity represents the maximum capacity that is likely to be supplied by the machine after taking into account unavoidable interruptions arising from machine maintenance and plant holiday closures. In other words, practical capacity is defined as theoretical capacity less activity lost arising from unavoidable interruptions. **Normal activity** is a measure of capacity required to satisfy average customer demand over a longer term period of, say, approximately three years after taking into account seasonal and cyclical fluctuations. Finally, **budgeted activity** is the activity level based on the capacity utilization required for the next budget period.

Assuming in Example 7.2 that actual activity and expenditure are identical to budget then, for each of the above denominator activity levels, the annual costs of £192 000 will be allocated as follows:

	Allocated to products	Volume variance (i.e. cost of unused capacity)	Total
Practical capacity	4000 hours × £38.40 = £153 600	1000 hours × £38.40 = £38 400	£192 000
Normal activity	4000 hours × £40 = £160 000	800 hours × £40 = £32 000	£192 000
Budgeted activity	4000 hours × £48 = £192 000	Nil	£192 000

EXAMPLE 7.2

The Green Company has established a separate cost centre for one of its machines. The annual budgeted fixed overheads assigned to the cost centre are £192 000. Green operates three shifts per day of 8 hours, five days per week for 50 weeks per year (the company closes down for holiday periods for two weeks per year). The maximum machine operating hours are 6000 hours per annum (50 weeks × 24 hrs × 5 days) but because of preventive maintenance the maximum practical operating usage is 5000 hours per annum. It is estimated that normal sales demand over the next three years will result in the machine being required for 4800 hours per annum. However, because of current adverse economic conditions budgeted usage for the coming year is 4000 hours. Assume that actual fixed overheads incurred are identical to the estimated fixed overheads and that there are no opening stocks at the start of the budget period.

Note that the overheads allocated to products consist of 4000 hours worked on products during the year multiplied by the appropriate overhead rate. The cost of unused capacity is the under-recovery of overheads arising from actual activity being different from the activity level used to calculate the overhead rate. If practical capacity is used the cost highlights that part of total capacity supplied (5000 hours) that has not been utilized. With normal activity the under-recovery of £32 000 represents the cost of failing to utilize the normal activity of 4800 hours. In Example 7.2 we assumed that actual activity was equivalent to budgeted activity. However, if actual activity is less than budgeted activity then the under-recovery can be interpreted as the cost of failing to achieve budgeted activity.

Impact on inventory valuation of profit computations

The choice of an appropriate activity level can have a significant effect on the inventory valuation and profit computation. Assume in Example 7.2 that 90% of the output was sold and the remaining 10% unsold and that there were no inventories at the start of the period. Thus 90% of the overheads allocated to products will be allocated to cost of sales, and 10% will be allocated to inventories. The volume variance arising from the under- or over-recovery of fixed overheads (i.e. the cost of unused capacity) is recorded as a period cost and therefore charged as an expense against the current period. It is not included in the inventory valuation. The computations are as follows:

	Allocated to cost of sales[a] (£)	Allocated to inventories[b] (£)	Total (£)
Practical capacity	176 640	15 360	192 000
Normal activity	176 000	16 000	192 000
Budgeted activity	172 800	19 200	192 000

[a]90% of overhead allocated to products plus cost of unused capacity.
[b]10% of overhead allocated to products.

In the above illustration the choice of the denominator level has not had an important impact on the inventory valuation and the cost of sales (and therefore the profit computation). Nevertheless, the impact can be material when inventories are of significant value.

Many service organizations, however, do not hold inventories and just-in-time manufacturing firms aim to maintain minimal inventory levels. In these situations virtually all of the expenses incurred during a period will be recorded as a period expense whatever denominator activity level is selected to calculate the overhead rate. We can therefore conclude that for many organizations the choice of the denominator activity level has little impact on profit measurement and inventory valuation. Therefore the impact of the chosen denominator level depends on the circumstances.

Even where the choice of the denominator level is not of significant importance for profit measurement and inventory valuation it can be of crucial importance for other purposes, such as pricing decisions and managing the cost of unused capacity. Since our objective in this chapter is to focus on the impact of the choice of denominator level on profit measurement and inventory measurement we shall defer a discussion of these other issues until Chapter 10.

Finally, what denominator levels do firms actually use? You will see from Exhibit 7.4 that budgeted activity is the most widely used rate. This preference for budgeted activity probably reflects a preference by firms to allocate fixed manufacturing overheads incurred during a period to products rather than writing off some of the costs as an excess capacity period cost. Also budgeted annual activity is readily available, being determined as part of the annual budgeting process. In contrast, normal activity and practical capacity are not readily available and cannot be precisely determined.

Summary

The following items relate to the learning objectives listed at the beginning of the chapter.

- **Explain the differences between an absorption costing and a variable costing system.**

  With an absorption costing system, fixed manufacturing overheads are allocated to the products and these are included in the inventory valuations. With a variable costing system, only variable manufacturing costs are assigned to the product; fixed manufacturing costs are regarded as period costs and written off as a lump sum to the profit and loss account. Both variable and absorption costing systems treat non-manufacturing overheads as period costs.

- **Prepare profit statements based on a variable costing and absorption costing system.**

  With a variable costing system manufacturing fixed costs are added to the variable manufacturing cost of sales to determine total manufacturing costs to be deducted from sales revenues. Manufacturing fixed costs are assigned to products with an absorption costing system. Therefore, manufacturing cost of sales is valued at full cost (manufacturing variable costs plus manufacturing fixed costs). With an absorption costing system fixed manufacturing costs are unitized by dividing the total manufacturing costs by estimated output. If actual output differs from estimated output an under- or over-recovery of overheads arises. This is recorded as a period cost adjustment in the current accounting period. The preparation of profit statements for absorption and variable costing systems was illustrated using Example 7.1.

- **Explain the difference in profits between variable and absorption costing profit calculations.**

  When production exceeds sales, absorption costing systems report higher profits. Variable costing systems yield higher profits when sales exceed production. Nevertheless, total profits over the life of the business will be the same for both systems. Differences arise merely in the profits attributed to each accounting period.

EXHIBIT 7.4

Surveys of company practice

Surveys have been undertaken in many countries relating to the use of variable costs and absorption costs. However, these surveys tend to focus on the information that is extracted from the costing system for decision-making rather than the costs that are used for inventory valuation and profit measurement. Many organizations accumulate and use absorption costs for inventory valuation but extract variable costs from the cost system for decision-making. Thus, the use of variable cost for decision-making does not imply that such costs are used for inventory valuation. Surveys that do not clearly indicate the costing method that is used for inventory valuation are therefore not included in the results reported below.

A UK study by Drury *et al.* (1993) indicated the following usage rates for internal profit measurement:

	(%)
Variable costing	13
Absorption costing	84
Other	3

A review of surveys of German organizations undertaken by Scherrer (1996) concluded that full costing is the most important system with only 12% of the responding organizations using only a variable costing system.

Similar results were observed in Spain by Saez-Torrecilla *et al.* (1996) who reported a 26% usage rate for variable costing.

In contrast, Virtanen *et al.* (1996) report that variable costing is widely used in Finland mainly because external financial accounting reporting regulations have not forced companies to use absorption costing for external reporting.

Little information is available relating to the denominator activity levels used. A UK study by Drury and Tayles (2000) reported the following usage rates:

	(%)
Budgeted annual activity	86
Practical capacity	4
Normal activity	8
Other	2

- **Explain the arguments for and against variable and absorption costing.**

The proponents of variable costing claim that it enables more useful information to be presented for decision-making but such claims are questionable since similar relevant cost information can easily be extracted from an absorption costing system. The major advantage of variable costing is that profit is reflected as a function of sales, whereas, with an absorption costing system, profit is a function of both sales and production. It is possible with absorption costing, when all other factors remain unchanged, for sales to increase and profit to decline. In contrast, with a variable costing system, when sales increase, profits also increase. A further advantage of variable costing is that fixed overheads are not capitalized in unsaleable stocks. The arguments that have been made supporting absorption costing include: (a) absorption costing does not understate the importance of fixed costs;

(b) absorption costing avoids the possibility of fictitious losses being reported; (c) fixed manufacturing overheads are essential to production and therefore should be incorporated in the product costs, and (d) internal profit measurement should be consistent with absorption costing profit measurement that is used for external reporting requirements.

- **Describe the various denominator levels that can be used with an absorption costing system.**

  Four different denominator levels were described. Theoretical maximum capacity is a measure of maximum operating capacity based on 100% efficiency with no interruptions for maintenance or machine breakdowns. Practical capacity represents the maximum capacity that is likely to be supplied after taking into account unavoidable interruptions such as machine maintenance and plant holiday closures. Normal capacity is a measure of capacity required to satisfy average demand over a long-term period (e.g. 3–5 years). Budgeted activity is the activity based on capacity utilization required for the next budget period.

- **Explain why the choice of an appropriate denominator level is important.**

  The use of each alternative measure results in the computation of a different overhead rate. This can result in significantly different reported product costs, profit levels and inventory valuations.

Appendix 7.1: Derivation of the profit function for an absorption costing system

Using the formulae listed in Exhibit 7A.1 the variable costing profit function can be expressed in equation form as follows:

$$\begin{aligned}\text{OPBT}_{\text{VC}} &= \text{Sales} - \text{Variable manufacturing costs of goods sold} \\ &\quad - \text{non-manufacturing variable costs} - \text{All fixed costs} \\ &= \text{usp} \cdot Q_s - \text{uvmc} \cdot Q_s - \text{uvnmc} \cdot Q_s - \text{FC} \qquad (7.\text{A1}) \\ &= \text{ucm} \cdot Q_s - \text{FC}\end{aligned}$$

(Note that the term contribution margin is used to describe unit selling price less unit variable cost)

The distinguishable feature between absorption costing and variable costing relates to the timing of the recognition of fixed manufacturing overheads (FC_m) as an expense. Variable costing expenses fixed manufacturing overheads in the period that they are incurred, whereas absorption costing assigns fixed manufacturing overheads to the units produced, thus recording them as an expense in the period in which the units are sold. The only difference between the two methods is that absorption costing incorporates some of the manufacturing fixed overheads in inventory. Therefore variable and absorption costing reported profits will differ by the amount of fixed manufacturing overheads that are included in the change in opening and closing inventories. This is equivalent to the difference between production and sales volumes multiplied by the manufacturing fixed overhead absorption rate.

We can therefore use equation (7.A1) as the basis for establishing the equation for the absorption costing profit function:

$$\begin{aligned}\text{OPBT}_{\text{AC}} &= \text{ucm} \cdot Q_s - \text{FC} + (Q_p - Q_s)\text{ufmc} \\ &= \text{ucm} \cdot Q_s - \text{FC} + (Q_p \times \text{ufmc}) - (Q_s \times \text{ufmc}) \qquad (7.\text{A2}) \\ &= (\text{ucm} - \text{ufmc})Q_s + (\text{ufmc} \times Q_p) - \text{FC}\end{aligned}$$

ucm = Contribution margin per unit (i.e. selling price per unit – variable cost per unit)
usp = Selling price per unit
uvmc = Variable manufacturing cost per unit
uvnmc = Variable non-manufacturing cost per unit
ufmc = Pre-determined fixed manufacturing overhead per unit of output
Q_p = Number of units produced
Q_s = Number of units sold
FC = Total fixed costs (manufacturing and non-manufacturing)
FC_m = Total fixed manufacturing costs
FCnmc = Total fixed manufacturing costs
$OPBT_{AC}$ = Operating profit before taxes for the period (Absorption costing)
$OPBT_{VC}$ = Operating profit before taxes for the period (Variable costing)

EXHIBIT 7.A1
Summary of notation used

Key terms and concepts

absorption costing (p. 229)
budgeted activity (p. 240)
direct costing (p. 229)
full costing (p. 229)
marginal costing (p. 229)
normal activity (p. 240)
period cost adjustment (p. 233)
practical capacity (p. 240)
theoretical maximum capacity (p. 240)
variable costing (p. 229)
volume variance (p. 233)

Key examination points

A common mistake is for students to calculate *actual* overhead rates when preparing absorption costing profit statements. Normal or budgeted activity should be used to calculate overhead absorption rates, and this rate should be used to calculate the production overhead cost for all periods given in the question. Do not calculate different actual overhead rates for each accounting period.

Remember not to include non-manufacturing overheads in the inventory valuations for both variable and absorption costing. Also note that variable selling overheads will vary with sales and not production. Another common mistake is not to include an adjustment for under-/over-recovery of fixed overheads when actual production deviates from the normal or budgeted production. You should note that under-/over-recovery of overhead arises only with fixed overheads and when an absorption costing system is used.

Assessment material

Review questions

The review questions are short questions that enable you to assess your understanding of the main topics included in the chapter. The numbers in parentheses provide you with the page numbers to refer to if you cannot answer a specific question.

Review problems

The review problems are more complex and require you to relate and apply the chapter content to various business problems. The problems are graded by their level of difficulty. The multiple-choice questions are the least demanding and normally take less than 10 minutes to complete. Fully worked solutions to the review problems are provided in a separate section at the end of the book. For those questions in the white box the worked solutions are provided in the *Student's Manual* accompanying this book. Further review problems for this chapter are available on the accompanying website www.drury-online.com. The answers to these problems are available for lecturers on the lecturer's password protected section of the website.

Case studies

The website also includes over 30 case study problems. A list of these cases is provided in Part Seven of this book. Bohemia Industries is a case study that is relevant to the content of this chapter.

Review questions

7.1 Distinguish between variable costing and absorption costing. *(pp. 229–30)*

7.2 How are non-manufacturing fixed costs treated under absorption and variable costing systems? *(p. 229)*

7.3 Describe the circumstances when variable and absorption costing systems will report identical profits. *(p. 234)*

7.4 Under what circumstances will absorption costing report higher profits than variable costing? *(p. 235)*

7.5 Under what circumstances will variable costing report higher profits than absorption costing? *(p. 235)*

7.6 What arguments can be advanced in favour of variable costing? *(p. 237–38)*

7.7 What arguments can be advanced in favour of absorption costing? *(p. 238–39)*

7.8 Explain how absorption costing can encourage managers to engage in behaviour that is harmful to the organization. *(p. 238)*

7.9 Why is it necessary to select an appropriate denominator level measure only with absorption costing systems? *(pp. 239–40)*

7.10 Identify and describe the four different denominator level measures that can be used to estimate fixed overhead rates. *(p. 240)*

7.11 Explain why the choice of an appropriate denominator level is important. *(p. 241)*

7.12 Why is budgeted activity the most widely used denominator measure? *(p. 242)*

Review problems

7.13 **Intermediate**

Z Limited manufactures a single product, the budgeted selling price and variable cost details of which are as follows:

	(£)
Selling price	15.00
Variable costs per unit:	
Direct materials	3.50
Direct labour	4.00
Variable overhead	2.00

Budgeted fixed overhead costs are £60 000 per annum, charged at a constant rate each month. Budgeted production is 30 000 units per annum.

In a month when actual production was 2400 units and exceeded sales by 180 units the profit reported under absorption costing was

A £6660
B £7570
C £7770
D £8200
E £8400

CIMA Stage 2

7.14 **Intermediate**

A company made 17 500 units at a total cost of £16 each. Three-quarters of the costs were variable and one-quarter fixed. 15 000 units were sold at £25 each. There were no opening stocks.

By how much will the profit calculated using absorption costing principles differ from the profit if marginal costing principles had been used?

A The absorption costing profit would be £22 500 less.
B The absorption costing profit would be £10 000 greater.
C The absorption costing profit would be £135 000 greater.
D The absorption costing profit would be £10 000 less.

CIMA Stage 1 Specimen Paper

7.15 Intermediate

A firm had opening stocks and purchases totalling 12 400 kg and closing stocks of 9600 kg. Profits using marginal costing were £76 456 and using absorption costing were £61 056.

What was the fixed overhead absorption rate per kilogram (to the nearest penny)?

A £1.60
B £5.50
C £6.17
D £6.36

CIMA Stage 1 Cost Accounting

7.16 Intermediate

Exe Limited makes a single product whose total cost per unit is budgeted to be £45. This includes fixed cost of £8 per unit based on a volume of 10 000 units per period. In a period, sales volume was 9000 units, and production volume was 11 500 units. The actual profit for the same period, calculated using absorption costing, was £42 000.

If the profit statement were prepared using marginal costing, the profit for the period

A would be £10 000
B would be £22 000
C would be £50 000
D would be £62 000
E cannot be calculated without more information

CIMA Stage 1 Operational Cost Accounting

7.17 Intermediate

In a period, opening stocks were 12 600 units and closing stocks 14 100 units. The profit based on marginal costing was £50 400 and profit using absorption costing was £60 150. The fixed overhead absorption rate per unit (to the nearest penny) is

A £4.00
B £4.27
C £4.77
D £6.50

CIMA Stage 1 Cost Accounting

7.18 Intermediate

The following data are to be used to answer questions (a) and (b) below.

SD plc is a new company. The following information relates to its first period:

	Budget	Actual
Production (units)	8000	9400
Sales (units)	8000	7100
Break-even point (units)	2000	
Selling price per unit	£125	£125
Fixed costs	£100 000	£105 000

The actual unit variable cost was £12 less than budgeted because of efficient purchasing.

(a) If SD plc had used standard absorption costing, the fixed overhead volume variance would have been

A £15 638 (F) B £17 500 (F) C £25 691 (F) D £28 750 (F)

(2 marks)

(b) If SD plc had used marginal costing, valuing finished goods stock at actual cost, the profit for the period would have been nearest to

A £335 200 B £337 600 C £340 200 D £450 400

(3 marks)

CIMA Management Accounting – Performance Management

7.19 **Intermediate**

Which of the following statements are correct with regard to marginal costing?

(i) Period costs are costs treated as expenses in the period incurred.
(ii) Product costs can be identified with goods produced.
(iii) Unavoidable costs are relevant for decision making.

A (i), (ii) and (iii)
B (i) and (ii) only
C (i) and (iii) only
D (ii) and (iii) only.

ACCA Paper 1.2 – Financial information for Management

7.20 **Intermediate: Preparation of variable costing and absorption costing profit statements and an explanation of the differences in profits**

The following data have been extracted from the budgets and standard costs of ABC Limited, a company which manufactures and sells a single product.

	£ per unit
Selling price	45.00
Direct materials cost	10.00
Direct wages cost	4.00
Variable overhead cost	2.50

Fixed production overhead costs are budgeted at £400 000 per annum. Normal production levels are thought to be 320 000 units per annum.

Budgeted selling and distribution costs are as follows:

Variable	£1.50 per unit sold
Fixed	£80 000 per annum

Budgeted administration costs are £120 000 per annum.

The following pattern of sales and production is expected during the first six months of the year:

	January–March	April–June
Sales (units)	60 000	90 000
Production (units)	70 000	100 000

There is to be no stock on 1 January.

You are required

(a) to prepare profit statements for each of the two quarters, in a columnar format, using
(i) marginal costing, and
(ii) absorption costing;

(12 marks)

(b) to reconcile the profits reported for the quarter January–March in your answer to (a) above;

(3 marks)

(c) to write up the production overhead control account for the quarter to 31 March, using absorption costing principles. Assume that the production overhead costs incurred amounted to £102 400 and the actual production was 74 000 units;

(3 marks)

(d) to state and explain briefly the benefits of using marginal costing as the basis of management reporting.

(5 marks)
(Total 23 marks)
CIMA Stage 1 Accounting

7.21 **Intermediate: Preparation of variable and absorption costing statements and an explanation of the differences in profits.**

Bittern Ltd manufactures and sells a single product at a unit selling price of £25. In constant-price-level terms its cost structure is as follows:

Variable costs:	
Production materials	£10 per unit produced
Distribution	£1 per unit sold
Semi-variable costs:	
Labour	£5000 per annum, plus £2 per unit produced
Fixed costs:	
Overheads	£5000 per annum

For several years Bittern has operated a system of variable costing for management accounting purposes. It has been decided to review the system and to compare it for management accounting purposes with an absorption costing system.

As part of the review, you have been asked to prepare estimates of Bittern's profits in constant-price-level terms over a three-year period in three different hypothetical situations, and to compare the two types of system generally for management accounting purposes.

(a) In each of the following three sets of hypothetical circumstances, calculate Bittern's profit in each of years t_1, t_2 and t_3, and also in total over the three year period t_1 to t_3, using first a variable costing system and then a full-cost absorption costing system with fixed cost recovery based on a normal production level of 1000 units per annum:

(i) Stable unit levels of production, sales and inventory

	t_1	t_2	t_3
Opening stock	100	100	100
Production	1000	1000	1000
Sales	1000	1000	1000
Closing stock	100	100	100

(5 marks)

(ii) Stable unit level of sales, but fluctuating unit levels of production and inventory

	t_1	t_2	t_3
Opening stock	100	600	400
Production	1500	800	700
Sales	1000	1000	1000
Closing stock	600	400	100

(5 marks)

(iii) Stable unit level of production, but fluctuating unit levels of sales and inventory

	t_1	t_2	t_3
Opening stock	100	600	400
Production	1000	1000	1000
Sales	500	1200	1300
Closing stock	600	400	100

(5 marks)

(Note that all the data in (i)–(iii) are volumes, not values.)

(b) Write a short comparative evaluation of variable and absorption costing systems for management accounting purposes, paying particular attention to profit measurement, and using your answer to (a) to illustrate your arguments if you wish.

(10 marks)

ICAEW Management Accounting

Review problems (with answers in the Student's Manual)

7.22 **Intermediate: Preparation of variable and absorption costing profit statements and an explanation of the change in profits**

A company sells a single product at a price of £14 per unit. Variable manufacturing costs of the product are £6.40 per unit. Fixed manufacturing overheads, which are absorbed into the cost of production at a unit rate (based on normal activity of 20 000 units per period), are £92 000 per period. Any over- or under-absorbed fixed manufacturing overhead balances are transferred to the profit and loss account at the end of each period, in order to establish the manufacturing profit.

Sales and production (in units) for two periods are as follows:

	Period 1	**Period 2**
Sales	15 000	22 000
Production	18 000	21 000

The manufacturing profit in Period 1 was reported as £35 800.

Required:

(a) Prepare a trading statement to identify the manufacturing profit for Period 2 using the existing absorption costing method.

(7 marks)

(b) Determine the manufacturing profit that would be reported in Period 2 if marginal costing was used.

(4 marks)

(c) Explain, with supporting calculations:

(i) the reasons for the change in manufacturing profit between Periods 1 and 2 where absorption costing is used in each period;

(5 marks)

(ii) why the manufacturing profit in (a) and (b) differs.

(4 marks)
(Total 20 marks)
ACCA Management Information – Paper 3

7.23 **Intermediate: Preparation of variable and absorption costing profit statements and CVP analysis**

R Limited is considering its plans for the year ending 31 December 2001. It makes and sells a single product, which has budgeted costs and selling price as follows:

	£ per unit
Selling price	45
Direct materials	11
Direct labour	8
Production overhead:	
variable	4
fixed	3
Selling overhead:	
variable	5
fixed	2
Administration overhead:	
fixed	3

Fixed overhead costs per unit are based on a normal annual activity level of 96 000 units. These costs are expected to be incurred at a constant rate throughout the year.

Activity levels during January and February 2001 are expected to be:

	January units	February units
Sales	7000	8750
Production	8500	7750

Assume that there will be no stocks held on 1 January 2001.

Required:

(a) Prepare, in columnar format, profit statements for each of the two months of January and February 2001 using:

(i) absorption costing;

(ii) marginal costing.

(12 marks)

(b) Reconcile and explain the reasons for any differences between the marginal and absorption profits for each month which you have calculated in your answer to (a) above.

(3 marks)

(c) Based upon marginal costing, calculate:
(i) the annual breakeven sales value; and
(ii) the activity level, in units, which will yield an annual profit of £122 800.

(6 marks)

(d) Explain 3 fundamental assumptions underpinning single product breakeven analysis.

(6 marks)
(Total 27 marks)
CIMA Stage 2 – Operational Cost Accounting

7.24 **Intermediate: Preparation of variable and absorption costing statements as a reconciliation of the profits**

The following budgeted profit statement has been prepared using absorption costing principles:

	January to June		July to December	
	(£000)	(£000)	(£000)	(£000)
Sales		540		360
Opening stock	100		160	
Production costs:				
Direct materials	108		36	
Direct labour	162		54	
Overhead	90		30	
	460		280	
Closing stock	160		80	
		300		200
GROSS PROFIT		240		160
Production overhead:				
(Over)/Under absorption	(12)		12	
Selling costs	50		50	
Distribution costs	45		40	
Administration costs	80		80	
		163		182
NET PROFIT/(LOSS)		77		(22)
Sales units	15 000		10 000	
Production units	18 000		6 000	

The members of the management team are concerned by the significant change in profitability between the two six-month periods. As management accountant, you have analysed the data upon which the above budget statement has been produced, with the following results:

1. The production overhead cost comprises both a fixed and a variable element, the latter appears to be dependent on the number of units

produced. The fixed element of the cost is expected to be incurred at a constant rate throughout the year.

2. The selling costs are fixed.
3. The distribution cost comprises both fixed and variable elements, the latter appears to be dependent on the number of units sold. The fixed element of the cost is expected to be incurred at a constant rate throughout the year.
4. The administration costs are fixed.

Required:

(a) Present the above budgeted profit statement in marginal costing format. *(10 marks)*

(b) Reconcile EACH of the six-monthly profit/loss values reported respectively under marginal and absorption costing. *(4 marks)*

(c) Reconcile the six-monthly profit for January to June from the absorption costing statement with the six-monthly loss for July to December from the absorption costing statement. *(4 marks)*

(d) Calculate the annual number of units required to break even. *(3 marks)*

(e) Explain briefly the advantages of using marginal costing as the basis of providing managers with information for decision making. *(4 marks)*

(Total 25 marks)

CIMA Stage 2 Operational Cost Accounting

7.25 Intermediate: Preparation of variable and absorption costing profit statements for FIFO and AVECO methods

The following information relates to product J, for quarter 3, which has just ended:

	Production (units)	Sales (units)	Fixed overheads (£000)	Variable costs (£000)
Budget	40 000	38 000	300	1800
Actual	46 000	42 000	318	2070

The selling price of product J was £72 per unit.

The fixed overheads were absorbed at a predetermined rate per unit.

At the beginning of quarter 3 there was an opening stock of product J of 2000 units, valued at £25 per unit variable costs and £5 per unit fixed overheads.

Required:

(a) (i) Calculate the fixed overhead absorption rate per unit for the last quarter, and present profit statements using FIFO (first in, first out) using:

(ii) absorption costing;

(iii) marginal costing; and

(iv) reconcile and explain the difference between the profits or losses.

(12 marks)

(b) Using the same data, present similar statements to those required in part (a). Using the AVECO (average cost) method of valuation, reconcile the profit or loss figures, and comment briefly on the variations between the profits or losses in (a) and (b).

(8 marks)

(Total 20 marks)

ACCA Paper 8 Managerial Finance

7.26 **Advanced: Explanation of absorption costing changes in profits and preparation of variable costing profit statements**

The Miozip Company operates an absorption costing system which incorporates a factory-wide overhead absorption rate per direct labour hour. For 1999 and 2000 this rate was £2.10 per hour. The fixed factory overhead for 2000 was £600 000 and this would have been fully absorbed if the company had operated at full capacity, which is estimated at 400 000 direct labour hours. Unfortunately, only 200 000 hours were worked in that year so that the overhead was seriously underabsorbed. Fixed factory overheads are expected to be unchanged in 2001 and 2002.

The outcome for 2000 was a loss of £70 000 and the management believed that a major cause of this loss was the low overhead absorption rate which had led the company to quote selling prices which were uneconomic.

For 2001 the overhead absorption rate was increased to £3.60 per direct labour hour and selling prices were raised in line with the established pricing procedures which involve adding a profit mark-up of 50% onto the full factory cost of the company's products. The new selling prices were also charged on the stock of finished goods held at the beginning of 2001.

In December 2001 the company's accountant prepares an estimated Profit and Loss Account for 2001 and a budgeted Profit and Loss Account for 2002. Although sales were considered to be depressed in 2000, they were even lower in 2001 but, nevertheless, it seems that the company will make a profit for that year. A worrying feature of the estimated accounts is the high level of finished goods stock held and the 2002 budget provides for a reduction in the stock level at 31 December 2002 to the (physical) level existing in January 2000. Budgeted sales for 2002 are set at the 2001 sales level.

The summarised profit statements for the three years to 31 December 2002 are as follows:

Summarized Profit and Loss Accounts

	Actual 2000		Estimated 2001		Budgeted 2002	
	(£)	(£)	(£)	(£)	(£)	(£)
Sales Revenue		1 350 000		1 316 250		1 316 250
Opening Stock of Finished Goods	100 000		200 000		357 500	
Factory Cost of Production	1 000 000		975 000		650 000	
	1 100 000		1 175 000		1 007 500	
Less: Closing Stock of Finished Goods	200 000		357 500		130 000	
Factory Cost of Goods Sold		900 000		817 500		877 500
		450 000		498 750		438 750
Less: Factory Overhead Under-Absorbed		300 000		150 000		300 000
		150 000		348 750		138 750
Administrative and Financial Costs		220 000		220 000		220 000
	Loss	(£70 000)		£128 750	Loss	(£81 250)

(a) You are required to write a short report to the board of Miozip explaining why the budgeted outcome for 2002 is so different from that of 2001 when the sales revenue is the same for both years.

(6 marks)

(b) Restate the Profit and Loss Account for 2000, the estimated Profit and Loss Account for 2001 and the Budgeted Profit and Loss Account for 2002 using marginal factory cost for stock valuation purposes.

(8 marks)

(c) Comment on the problems which *may* follow from a decision to increase the overhead absorption rate in conditions when cost plus pricing is used and overhead is currently underabsorbed.

(3 marks)

(d) Explain why the majority of businesses use full costing systems whilst most management accounting theorists favour marginal costing.

(5 marks)

NB Assume in your answers to this question that the value of the £ and the efficiency of the company have been constant over the period under review.

(Total 22 marks)

ACCA Level 2 Management Accounting

7.27 **Advanced: Explanation of absorption costing changes in profits and preparation of variable costing profit statements**

Mahler Products has two manufacturing departments each producing a single standardized product. The data for unit cost and selling price of these products are as follows:

	Department A (£)	Department B (£)
Direct material cost	4	6
Direct labour cost	2	4
Variable manufacturing overheads	2	4
Fixed manufacturing overheads	12	16
Factory cost	20	30
Profit mark-up	50% 10	25% 7.50
Selling price	30	37.50

The factory cost figures are used in the departmental accounts for the valuation of finished goods stock.

The departmental profit and loss accounts have been prepared for the year to 30 June. These are given below separately for the two halves of the year.

Departmental profit and loss accounts – year to 30 June

	1 July–31 December		1 January–30 June	
	Department A (£000)	Department B (000)	Department A (£000)	Department B (£000)
Sales revenue	300	750	375	675
Manufacturing costs:				
Direct material	52	114	30	132
Direct labour	26	76	15	88
Variable overheads	26	76	15	88
Fixed overheads	132	304	132	304
Factory cost of production	236	570	192	612
Add Opening stock of finished goods	60	210	120	180
	296	780	312	792
Less Closing stock of finished goods	120	180	20	300
Factory cost of goods sold	176	600	292	492
Administrative and selling costs	30	100	30	100
	206	700	322	592
Net profit	94	50	53	83

The total sales revenue was the same in each six monthly period but in the second half of the year the company increased the sales of department A (which has the higher profit mark-up) and reduced the sales of department B (which has the lower profit mark-up). An increase in company profits for the second six months was anticipated but the profit achieved was £8000 lower for the second half of the year than for the first half. The profit for department A fell by £41 000 while the profit for department B rose by £33 000. There has been no change in prices of inputs or outputs.

You are required:

(a) to explain the situation described in the last paragraph – illustrate your answer with appropriate supporting calculations,

(14 marks)

(b) to redraft the departmental profit and loss accounts using marginal cost to value unsold stock.

(8 marks)

(Total 22 marks)

ACCA Level 2 Management Accounting

PART 3

Information for Decision-making

The objective of this Part, which contains seven chapters, is to consider the provision of financial information that will help managers to make better decisions. Chapter 8–12 are concerned mainly with short-term decisions based on the environment of today, and the physical, human and financial resources that are presently available to a firm; these decisions are determined to a considerable extent by the quality of the firm's long-term decisions. An important distinction between the long-term and short-term decisions is that the former cannot easily be reversed whereas the latter can often be changed. The actions that follow short-term decisions are frequently repeated, and it is possible for different actions to be taken in the future. For example, the setting of a particular selling price or product mix can often be changed fairly quickly. With regard to long-term decisions, such as capital investment, which involves, for example, the purchase of new plant and machinery, it is not easy to change a decision in the short term. Resources may only be available for major investments in plant and machinery at lengthy intervals, and it is unlikely that plant replacement decisions will be repeated in the short term.

Chapters 8–12 concentrate mainly on how accounting information can be applied to different forms of short-term decisions. Chapter 8 focuses on what will happen to the financial results if a specific level of activity or volume fluctuates. This information is required for making optimal short-term output decisions. Chapter 9 examines how costs and revenues should be measured for a range of non-routine short-term and long-term decisions.

Chapter 10 focuses on an alternative approach for measuring resources consumed by cost objects. This approach is called activity-based costing. Chapter 11 is concerned with profitability analysis and the provision of financial information for pricing decisions. Chapters 8–11 assume a world of certainty, whereas Chapter 12 introduces methods of incorporating uncertainty into the analysis, and the topics covered in Chapters 8–11 are re-examined under conditions of uncertainty.

The final two chapters in this part are concerned with long-term decisions. Chapter 13 looks at the techniques that are used for evaluating capital investment decisions, and introduces the concept of the time value of money. A number of assumptions are made to simplify the discussion, but in Chapter 14 these assumptions are relaxed and we consider how capital investment techniques can be applied to more complex situations.

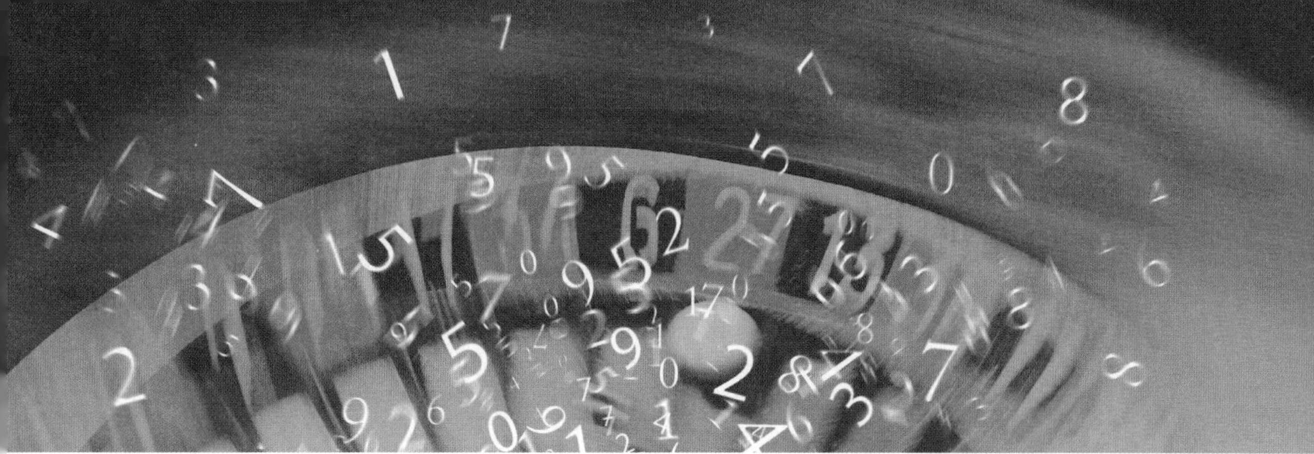

Cost–volume–profit analysis

8

In the previous chapters we have considered how costs should be accumulated for inventory valuation and profit measurement, and we have stressed that costs should be accumulated in a different way for decision-making and cost control. In the next seven chapters we shall look at the presentation of financial information for decision-making. We begin by considering how management accounting information can be of assistance in providing answers to questions about the consequences of following particular courses of action. Such questions might include 'How many units must be sold to break-even?' 'What would be the effect on profits if we reduce our selling price and sell more units?' 'What sales volume is required to meet the additional fixed charges arising from an advertising campaign?' 'Should we pay our sales people on the basis of a salary only, or on the basis of a commission only, or by a combination of the two?' These and other questions can be answered using cost–volume–profit (CVP) analysis.

This is a systematic method of examining the relationship between changes in activity (i.e. output) and changes in total sales revenue, expenses and net profit. As a model of these relationships CVP analysis simplifies the real-world conditions that a firm will face. Like most models, which are abstractions from reality, CVP analysis is subject to a number of

LEARNING OBJECTIVES

After studying this chapter, you should be able to:

- describe the differences between the accountant's and the economist's model of cost–volume–profit analysis;
- justify the use of linear cost and revenue functions in the accountant's model;
- apply the mathematical approach to answer questions similar to those listed in Example 8.1;
- construct break-even, contribution and profit–volume graphs;
- identify and explain the assumptions on which cost–volume–profit analysis is based;
- apply cost–volume–profit analysis in a multi-product setting.

underlying assumptions and limitations, which will be discussed later in this chapter; nevertheless, it is a powerful tool for decision-making in certain situations.

This objective of CVP analysis is to establish what will happen to the financial results if a specified level of activity or volume fluctuates. This information is vital to management, since one of the most important variables influencing total sales revenue, total costs and profits is output or volume. For this reason output is given special attention, since knowledge of this relationship will enable management to identify the critical output levels, such as the level at which neither a profit nor a loss will occur (i.e. the break-even point).

CVP analysis is based on the relationship between volume and sales revenue, costs and profit in the short run, the short run normally being a period of one year, or less, in which the output of a firm is restricted to that available from the current operating capacity. In the short run, some inputs can be increased, but others cannot. For example, additional supplies of materials and unskilled labour may be obtained at short notice, but it takes time to expand the capacity of plant and machinery. Thus output is limited in the short run because plant facilities cannot be expanded. It also takes time to reduce capacity, and therefore in the short run a firm must operate on a relatively constant stock of production resources. Furthermore, most of the costs and prices of a firm's products will have already been determined, and the major area of uncertainty will be sales volume. Short-run profitability will therefore be most sensitive to sales volume. CVP analysis thus highlights the effects of changes in sales volume on the level of profits in the short run.

The theoretical relationship between total sales revenue, costs and profits with volume has been developed by economists. In order to provide a theoretical basis for examining the accountant's approach to CVP analysis this chapter begins by describing the economist's model of CVP analysis.

The economist's model

An economist's model of CVP behaviour is presented in Figure 8.1. You will see that the total-revenue line is assumed to be curvilinear, which indicates that the firm is only able to sell increasing quantities of output by reducing the selling price per unit; thus the total revenue line does not increase proportionately with output. To increase the quantity of sales, it is necessary to reduce the unit selling price, which results in the total revenue line rising less steeply, and eventually beginning to decline. This is because the adverse effect of price reductions outweighs the benefits of increased sales volume.

The total cost line AD shows that, between points A and B, total costs rise steeply at first as the firm operates at the lower levels of the volume range. This reflects the difficulties of efficiently operating a plant designed for much larger volume levels. Between points B and C, the total cost line begins to level out and rise less steeply because the firm is now able to operate the plant within the efficient operating range and can take advantage of specialization of labour, and smooth production schedules. In the upper portion of the volume range the total cost line between points C and D rises more and more steeply as the cost per unit increases. This is because the output per direct labour hour declines when the plant is operated beyond the activity level for which it was designed: bottlenecks develop, production schedules become more complex, and plant breakdowns begin to occur. The overall effect is that the cost per unit of output increases and causes the total cost line to rise steeply.

The dashed horizontal line from point A represents the cost of providing the basic operating capacity, and is the economist's interpretation of the total fixed costs of the firm. Note

FIGURE 8.1 *Economist's cost–volume graph*

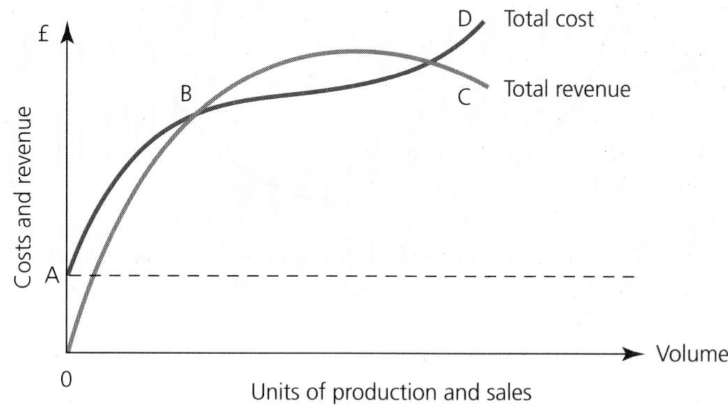

also from Figure 8.1 that the shape of the total revenue line is such that it crosses the total cost line at two points. In other words, there are two output levels at which the total costs are equal to the total revenues; or more simply, there are two break-even points.

It is the shape of the variable cost function in the economist's model that has the most significant influence on the total cost function; this is illustrated in Figure 8.2. The economist assumes that the average *unit* variable cost declines initially, reflecting the fact that, as output expands, a firm is able to obtain bulk discounts on the purchase of raw materials and can benefit from the division of labour; this results in the labour cost per unit being reduced. The economist refers to this situation as **increasing returns to scale**. The fact that *unit* variable cost is higher at lower levels of activity causes the total cost line between points A and B in Figure 8.1 to rise steeply. From Figure 8.2 you can see that the *unit* variable cost levels out between output levels Q_1 and Q_2 and then gradually begins to rise. This is because the firm is operating at its most efficient output level, and further economies of scale are not possible in the short term. However, beyond output level Q_2, the plant is being operated at a higher level than that for which it was intended, and bottlenecks and plant breakdowns occur. The effect of this is that output per direct labour hour declines, and causes the variable cost per unit to increase. The economist describes this situation as **decreasing returns to scale**.

It is the shape of the variable cost function that causes the total cost line to behave in the manner indicated in Figure 8.1. Between points B and C, the total cost line rises less steeply, indicating that the firm is operating in the range where unit variable cost is at its lowest. Between points C and D, the total cost line rises more steeply, since the variable cost per unit is increasing owing to decreasing returns to scale.

Marginal revenue and marginal cost presentation

The normal presentation of the economist's model is in terms of the marginal revenue and marginal cost curves. Marginal revenue represents the increase in total revenue from the sale of one additional unit. Figure 8.3 is in two parts, with the lower diagram presenting the traditional marginal revenue and marginal cost diagram; the top diagram repeats Figure 8.1. A comparison of the two diagrams in Figure 8.3 enables us to reconcile the traditional marginal revenue and marginal cost diagram with the total cost and total revenue presentation. Economic theory states that the profit maximizing output level is the

FIGURE 8.2 *Economist's variable cost function*

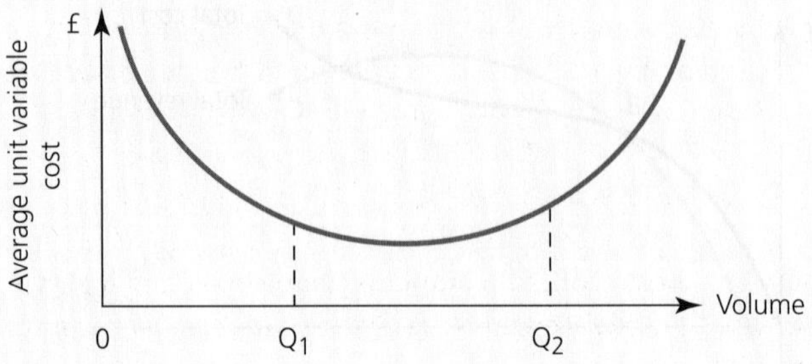

FIGURE 8.3 *Economist's marginal revenue and marginal costs diagrams, and total revenue and total costs diagrams*

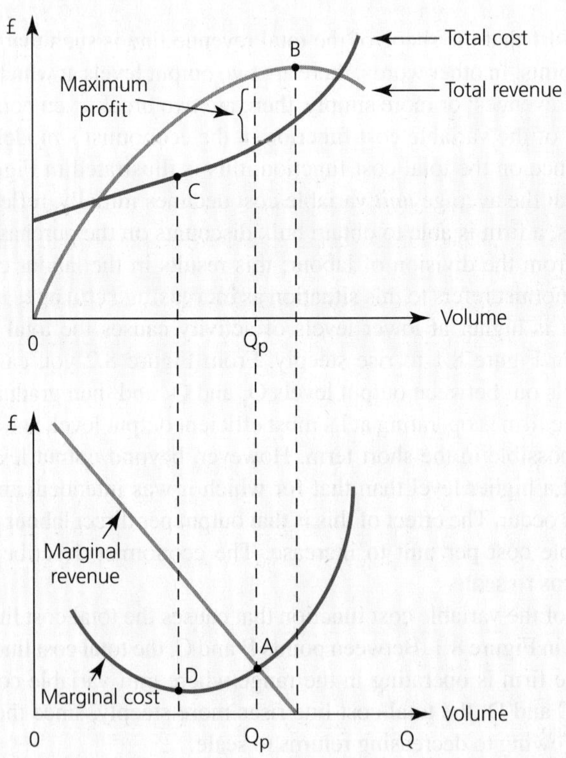

point at which marginal cost equals marginal revenue. This occurs at Point A on the lower diagram, at output level Q_p. Note that in the top diagram this is the point at which the difference between the total revenue and total cost lines is the greatest. The point where total revenue reaches a maximum, point B, is where marginal revenue is equal to zero. Also note that the marginal cost curve reaches a minimum at point D, where the total cost curve (at point C) changes from concave downwards to concave upwards. Let us now compare the accountant's CVP diagram, or break-even model as it is sometimes called, with the economist's model.

The accountant's cost–volume–profit model

The diagram for the accountant's model is presented in Figure 8.4. Note that the dashed line represents the economist's total cost function, which enables a comparison to be made with the accountant's total cost function. The accountant's diagram assumes a variable cost and a selling price that are constant per unit; this results in a linear relationship (i.e. a straight line) for total revenue and total cost as volume changes. The effect is that there is only one break-even point in the diagram, and the profit area widens as volume increases. The most profitable output is therefore at maximum practical capacity. Clearly, the economist's model appears to be more realistic, since it assumes that the total cost curve is non-linear.

Relevant range

How can we justify the accountant's assumption of linear cost and linear revenue functions? The answer is that the accountants' diagram is not intended to provide an accurate representation of total cost and total revenue throughout all ranges of output. The objective is to represent the behaviour of total cost and revenue over the range of output at which a firm expects to be operating within a short-term planning horizon. This range of output is represented by the output range between points X and Y in Figure 8.4. The term relevant range is used to refer to the output range at which the firm expects to be operating within a short-term planning horizon. This relevant range also broadly represents the output levels which the firm has had experience of operating in the past and for which cost information is available.

You can see from Figure 8.4 that, between points X and Y, the shape of the accountant's total cost line is very similar to that of the economist's. This is because the total cost line is only intended to provide a good approximation within the relevant range. Within this range, the accountant assumes that the variable cost per unit is the same throughout the entire range of output, and the total cost line is therefore linear. Note that the cost function is approximately linear within this range. It would be unwise, however, to make this assumption for production levels outside the relevant range. It would be more appropriate if the accountant's total cost line was presented for the relevant range of output only, and not extended to the vertical axis or to the output levels beyond Y in Figure 8.4.

Fixed cost function

Note also that the accountant's fixed cost function in Figure 8.4 meets the vertical axis at a different point to that at which the economist's total cost line meets the vertical axis. The reason for this can be explained from Figure 8.5. The fixed cost level of 0A may be applicable to, say, activity level Q_2 to Q_3, but if there were to be a prolonged economic recession then output might fall below Q_1, and this could result in redundancies and shutdowns. Therefore fixed costs may be reduced to 0B if there is a prolonged and a significant decline in sales demand. Alternatively, additional fixed costs will be incurred if long-term sales volume is expected to be greater than Q_3. Over a longer-term time horizon, the fixed cost line will consist of a series of step functions rather than the horizontal straight line depicted in Figure 8.4. However, since within its short-term planning horizon the firm expects to be operating between output levels Q_2 and Q_3, it will be committed, in the short term, to fixed costs of 0A; but you should remember that if there was a prolonged economic recession then in the longer term fixed costs may be reduced to 0B.

FIGURE 8.4 *Accountant's cost–volume–profit diagram*

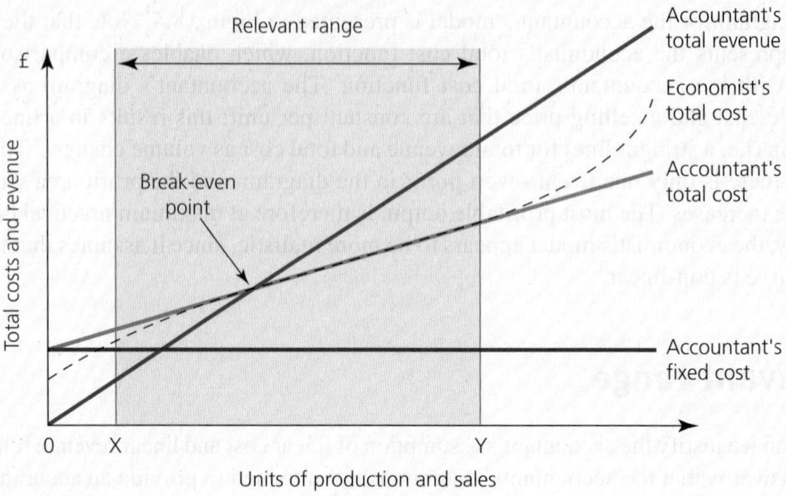

FIGURE 8.5 *Accountant's fixed costs*

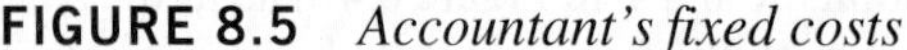

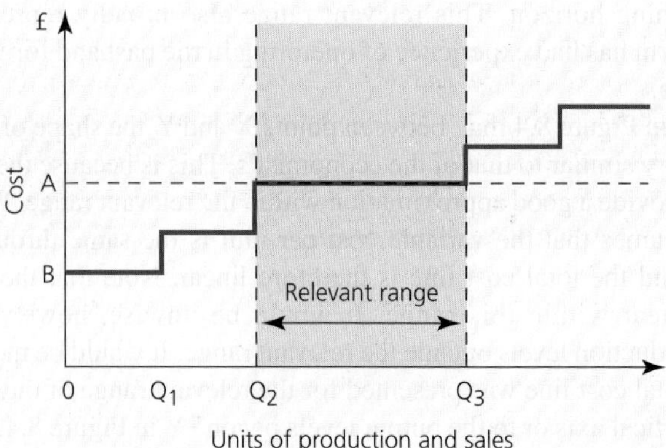

The fixed cost line for output levels below Q_1 (i.e. 0B) represents the cost of providing the basic operating capacity, and this line is the equivalent to the point where the economist's total cost line meets the vertical axis in Figure 8.4. Because the accountant assumes that in the short term the firm will operate in the relevant range between Q_2 and Q_3, the accountant's fixed cost line 0A in Figure 8.5 represents the fixed costs for the relevant output range only, which the firm is committed to in the current period and does not represent the fixed costs that would be incurred at the extreme levels of output beyond the shaded area in Figure 8.5.

Total revenue function

Let us now compare the total revenue line for the accountant and the economist. We have seen that the accountant assumes that selling price is constant over the relevant range of output, and therefore the total revenue line is a straight line. The accountant's assumption about the revenue line is a realistic one in those firms that operate in industries where selling prices tend to be fixed in the short term. A further factor reinforcing the assumption of a fixed selling price is that competition may take the form of non-price rather than price competition. Moreover, beyond the relevant range, increases in output may only be possible by offering substantial reductions in price. As it is not the intention of firms to operate outside the relevant range, the accountant makes no attempt to produce accurate revenue functions outside this range. It might be more meaningful in Figure 8.4 if the total revenue line was presented for output levels X and Y within the relevant range, instead of being extended to the left and right of these points.

Application to longer-term time horizons

CVP analysis becomes more complex and questionable if we extend our application to a longer term time horizon. Consider a capacity expansion decision. The expansion of output beyond certain points may require increments of fixed costs such as additional supervision and machinery, the appointment of additional sales persons and the expansion of the firm's distribution facilities. Such increases are incorporated in Figure 8.6. Note from this figure that if the current output level is OQ_1 then additional facilities are required, thus increasing fixed costs, if output is to be increased beyond this level. Similarly, additional fixed costs must be incurred to expand output beyond OQ_2.

At this point, for a capacity expansion decision, we are moving from beyond the short term to a longer term application of CVP analysis. In the longer term, other factors besides volume are likely to be important. For example, to utilize the additional capacity reductions in selling prices and alternative advertising strategies may be considered. Also consideration may be given to expanding the product range and mix. Therefore, for longer-term decisions other variables besides volume are likely to have an impact on total costs, total revenues and profits. These additional variables cannot be easily incorporated into the CVP analysis. Hence, the CVP analysis presented in Figure 8.6 is unlikely to be appropriate for long-term decisions because other variables, that are not captured by the CVP analysis, are unlikely to remain unchanged. CVP analysis is only appropriate if all variables, other than volume, remain unchanged.

Let us now assume that management has undertaken a detailed analysis, without using CVP analysis, that incorporates all of these other variables and has concluded that extra fixed costs should be incurred to expand output to a maximum level of OQ_2 as shown in Figure 8.6. For simplicity we shall also assume that the total cost functions are the same as those described in Figure 8.6.

Once a decision has been made to provide productive capacity equal to a maximum of OQ_2, a separate graph may be presented with a total cost function represented by line AB and maximum output of OQ_2. In this revised graph the step increases in fixed costs will not be included, since management has already made a decision to aim to operate within the output range Q_1 to Q_2. Assuming that the total revenue is the same as that depicted in Figure 8.6 the revised graph can now be used as a short-term planning tool to demonstrate the impact that short-term output decisions have on profits. It is this revised graph that was used as a basis for comparing the accountant's and the economist's CVP presentation earlier in this chapter.

A mathematical approach to cost–volume–profit analysis

Instead of using a diagram to present CVP information, we can use mathematical relationships. The mathematical approach is a quicker and more flexible method of producing the appropriate information than the graphical approach, and is a particularly appropriate form of input to a computer financial model.

FIGURE 8.6 *Increase in fixed costs*

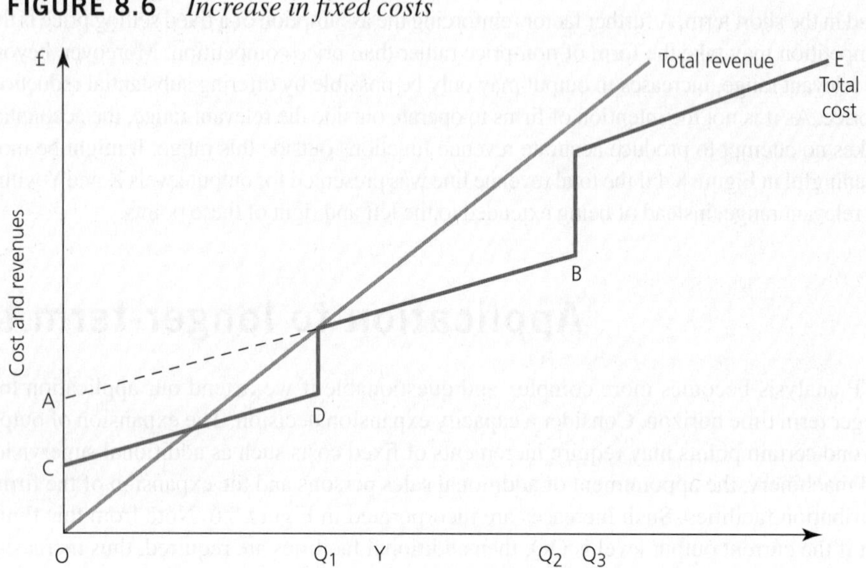

When developing a mathematical formula for producing CVP information, you should note that one is assuming that selling price and costs remain constant per unit of output. Such an assumption may be valid for unit selling price and variable cost, but remember that in Chapter 2 we noted that in the short run fixed costs are a constant *total* amount whereas *unit* cost changes with output levels. As a result, profit per *unit* also changes with volume. For example, if fixed costs are £10 000 for a period and output is 10 000 units, the fixed cost will be £1 per unit. Alternatively, if output is 5000 units, the fixed cost will be £2 per unit. Profit per unit will not therefore be constant over varying output levels and it is incorrect to unitize fixed costs for CVP decisions.

We can develop a mathematical formula from the following relationship:

$$\text{net profit} = (\text{units sold} \times \text{unit selling price}) - [(\text{units sold} \times \text{unit variable cost}) + \text{total fixed costs}]$$

The following symbols can be used to represent the various items in the above equation:

NP = net profit
x = units sold
P = selling price
b = unit variable cost
a = total fixed costs

The equation can now be expressed in mathematical terms as

$$NP = Px - (a + bx) \tag{8.1}$$

You should now refer to Example 8.1. This example will be used to illustrate the application of the mathematical approach to CVP analysis.

EXAMPLE 8.1

Norvik Enterprises operate in the leisure and entertainment industry and one of its activities is to promote concerts at locations throughout Europe. The company is examining the viability of a concert in Stockholm. Estimated fixed costs are £60 000. These include the fees paid to perfomers, the hire of the venue and advertising costs. Variable costs consist of the cost of a pre-packed buffet which will be provided by a firm of caterers at a price, which is currently being negotiated, but it is likely to be in the region of £10 per ticket sold. The proposed price for the sale of a ticket is £20. The management of Norvic have requested the following information:

1 The number of tickets that must be sold to break-even (that is, the point at which there is neither a profit or loss).
2 How many tickets must be sold to earn £30 000 target profit?
3 What profit would result if 8000 tickets were sold?
4 What selling price would have to be charged to give a profit of £30 000 on sales of 8000 tickets, fixed costs of £60 000 and variable costs of £10 per ticket?
5 How many additional tickets must be sold to cover the extra cost of television advertising of £8000?

Let us now provide the information requested in Example 8.1.

1 Break-even point in units (i.e. number of tickets sold)

Since $NP = Px - (a + bx)$, the break-even point is at a level of output (x) where

$$a + bx = Px - NP$$

Substituting the information in Example 8.1, we have

$$60\,000 + 10x = 20x - 0$$
$$60\,000 = 10x$$

and so $x = 6000$ tickets (or £120 000 total sales at £20 per ticket).

An alternative method, called the **contribution margin** approach, can also be used. Contribution margin is equal to sales minus variable expenses. Because the variable cost per unit and the selling price per unit are assumed to be constant the contribution margin per unit is also assumed to be constant. In Example 8.1 note that each ticket sold generates a contribution of £10, which is available to cover fixed costs and, after they are covered, to contribute to profit. When we have obtained sufficient total contribution to cover fixed costs, the break-even point is achieved, and the alternative formula is

$$\text{break-even point in units} = \frac{\text{fixed costs}}{\text{contribution per unit}}$$

The contribution margin approach can be related to the mathematical formula approach. Consider the penultimate line of the formula approach; it reads

$$£60\,000 = 10x$$

and so $$x = \frac{£60\,000}{£10}$$

giving the contribution margin formula

$$\frac{\text{fixed costs}}{\text{contribution per unit}}$$

The contribution margin approach is therefore a restatement of the mathematical formula, and either technique can be used; it is a matter of personal preference.

2 Units to be sold to obtain a £30 000 profit

Using the equation $NP = Px - (a + bx)$ and substituting the information in Example 8.1, we have

$$£30\,000 = £20x - (£60\,000 + £10x)$$
$$£90\,000 = £10x$$

and so $$x = 9000 \text{ tickets}$$

If we apply the contribution margin approach and wish to achieve the desired profit, we must obtain sufficient contribution to cover the fixed costs (i.e. the break-even point) plus a further contribution to cover the target profit. Hence we simply add the target profit to the fixed costs so that the equation using the contribution margin approach is

$$\text{units sold for target profit} = \frac{\text{fixed costs + target profit}}{\text{contribution per unit}}$$

This is merely a restatement of the penultimate line of the mathematical formula, which reads

$$£90\,000 = £10x$$

and so $$x = \frac{£90\,000}{£10}$$

3 Profit from the sale of 8000 tickets

Substituting in the equation $NP = Px - (a + bx)$, we have

$$NP = £20 \times 8000 - (£60\,000 + £10 \times 8000)$$
$$= £160\,000 - (£60\,000 + £80\,000)$$

and so $$NP = £20\,000$$

Let us now assume that we wish to ascertain the impact on profit if a further 1000 tickets are sold so that sales volume increases from 8000 to 9000 tickets. Assuming that fixed costs remain unchanged, the impact on a firm's profits resulting from a change in the number of units sold can be determined by multiplying the unit contribution margin by the change in units sold. Therefore the increase in profits will be £10 000 (1000 units times a unit contribution margin of £10).

4 Selling price to be charged to show a profit of £30 000 on sales of 8000 units

Applying the formula for net profit (i.e. Equation 8.1)

$$£30\,000 = 8000P - (60\,000 + (£10 \times 8000))$$
$$= 8000P - £140\,000$$

giving
$$8000P = £170\,000$$

and
$$P = £21.25 \text{ (i.e. an increase of £1.25 per ticket)}$$

5 Additional sales volume to meet £8000 additional fixed advertising charges

The contribution per unit is £10 and fixed costs will increase by £8000. Therefore an extra 800 tickets must be sold to cover the additional fixed costs of £8000.

The profit–volume ratio

The **profit–volume ratio** (also known as the **contribution margin ratio**) is the contribution divided by sales. It represents the proportion of each £1 sales available to cover fixed costs and provide for profit. In Example 8.1 the contribution is £10 per unit and the selling price is £20 per unit; the profit–volume ratio is 0.5. This means that for each £1 sale a contribution of £0.50 is earned. Because we assume that selling price and contribution per unit are constant, the profit–volume ratio is also assumed to be constant. Therefore the profit–volume ratio can be computed using either unit figures or total figures. Given an estimate of total sales revenue, it is possible to use the profit–volume ratio to estimate total contribution. For example, if total sales revenue is estimated to be £200 000, the total contribution will be £100 000 (£200 000 × 0.5). To calculate the profit, we deduct fixed costs of £60 000; thus a profit of £40 000 will be obtained from total sales revenue of £200 000.

Expressing the above computations in mathematical terms:

$$\text{NP} = (\text{Sales revenue} \times \text{PV ratio}) - \text{Fixed costs}$$
$$\text{NP} + \text{Fixed costs} = \text{Sales revenue} \times \text{PV ratio}$$

Therefore the break-even sales revenue (where NP = 0) = Fixed costs/PV ratio.

Relevant range

It is vital to remember that, as with the mathematical approach, the formulae method can only be used for decisions that result in outcomes within the relevant range. Outside this range the unit selling price and the variable cost are no longer deemed to be constant per unit, and any results obtained from the formulae that fall outside the relevant range will be incorrect. The concept of the relevant range is more appropriate for production settings but it can apply within non-production settings. Returning to Norvic Enterprises in Example 8.1, let us assume that the caterers' charges will be higher per ticket if ticket sales are below 4000 but lower if sales exceed 12 000 tickets. Thus, the £10 variable cost relates only to a sales volume within a range of 4000–12 000 tickets. Outside this range other costs apply. Also the number of seats made available at the venue is flexible and the hire cost will be reduced for sales of less than 4000 tickets and increased for sales beyond 12 000 tickets. In other words, we will assume that the relevant range is a sales volume of 4000–12 000 tickets and outside this range the results of our CVP analysis do not apply.

Margin of safety

The **margin of safety** indicates by how much sales may decrease before a loss occurs. Using Example 8.1, where unit selling price and variable cost were £20 and £10 respectively and fixed costs were £60 000, we noted that the break-even point was 6000 tickets or £120 000 sales value. If sales are expected to be 8000 tickets or £160 000, the margin of safety will be 2000 tickets or £40 000. Alternatively, we can express the margin of safety in a percentage form based on the following ratio:

$$\text{percentage margin of safety} = \frac{\text{expected sales} - \text{break-even sales}}{\text{expected sales}}$$

$$= \frac{£160\,000 - £120\,000}{£160\,000} = 25\%$$

Constructing the break-even chart

Managers may obtain a clearer understanding of CVP behaviour if the information is presented in graphical format. Using the data in Example 8.1, we can construct the **break-even chart** for Norvik Enterprises (Figure 8.7). In constructing the graph, the fixed costs are plotted as a single horizontal line at the £60 000 level. Variable costs at the rate of £10 per unit of volume are added to the fixed costs to enable the total cost line to be plotted. Two points are required to insert the total cost line. At zero sales volume total cost will be equal to the fixed costs of £60 000. At 12 000 units sales volume total costs will be £180 000 consisting of £120 000 variable cost plus £60 000 fixed costs. The total revenue line is plotted at the rate of £20 per unit of volume. The constraints of the relevant range consisting of two vertical lines are then added to the graph: beyond these lines we have little assurance that the CVP relationships are valid.

The point at which the total sales revenue line cuts the total cost line is the point where the concert makes neither a profit nor a loss. This is the break-even point and is 6000 tickets or £120 000 total sales revenue. The distance between the total sales revenue line and the total cost line at a volume below the break-even point represents losses that will occur for various sales levels below 6000 tickets. Similarly, if the company operates at a sales volume above the break-even point, the difference between the total revenue and the total cost lines represents the profit that results from sales levels above 6000 tickets.

Wyatt Earp's application of cost–volume–profit analysis to buffalo-hunting

Most people today know Wyatt Earp as one of the most respected and feared lawmen of the Old West. He helped bring law and order to Dodge City. Wyatt's earlier career pursuits as a buffalo hunter are not as well-known. By using cost–volume–profit analysis, he saw that by killing less buffalo, he could make more money. During the period 1871–74, he made a profit in buffalo hunting using methods that were revolutionary, at the time. To illustrate Wyatt's methods, we present here possible conversations between Wyatt and a more experienced hunter as they might have happened. We also include numeric schedules implied (not actual) from narrative accounts of buffalo hunting activities of Wyatt and other hunters.

"Wyatt Earp, you are the stubbornest cuss I've run up against. Why can't you listen to reason" thundered Link Barland. "There is no way you're gonna make any money buffalo hunting". Wyatt replied. "I know you don't approve of my methods, Link. But I've got it all figured out. I'll shoot fewer than half the buffalo you will and make more money doing it. Let me explain it to you."

The best hunters made money largely through sheer volume rather than smart business practices. Professional buffalo hunters typically used a large hunting party. There would be 12 men and four wagons, each pulled by a team of four horses, plus four more horses for riding, a total of 20 horses. The crew was comprised of the four drivers, the stock-tender, camp watchman, cook, four skinners and the hunter himself. The money received from selling the hides and meat was roughly split into two equal parts. One half went to the hunter, from which he paid all the expenses. The other half was divided into as many shares as there were drivers and skinners, and a share was paid to each helper as his seasonal wage.

Wyatt began his buffalo hunting venture with a budget (Table 1). He also developed certain theories concerning methods of hunting that he felt were the most efficient. First, he recognized that, although the typical hunting party was theoretically capable of shooting and skinning 100 buffalo per day, few were able to actually do this. Due to various uncontrollable factors, the average take was below 50. Wyatt saw that the typical hunting party had considerable idle capacity. So Wyatt scaled things down. He decided to use one wagon plus four horses and another horse for riding in place of the four wagons and 20 horses other hunters used. Wyatt hired one good skinner in a profit-sharing arrangement. The skinner would also drive and cook. After the season was over, Wyatt would keep the wagon and the horses, deduct all other expenses from the gross receipts, and share any net profit equally with his skinner.

Wyatt's sense of efficiency extended to his selection of a firearm. The weapon of choice for professional hunters was a heavy, expensive rifle using a massive .50-caliber bullet. The ammunition for the Sharps rifle was very expensive. Wyatt decided to shoot from a distance closer to the grazing buffalo than normal. This allowed him to use a shotgun in place of the Sharps. The shotgun used less expensive ammunition and could be fired more quickly without pause. "I understand what you're tellin' me, Wyatt. But there's just no way you can shoot more than 25 buffalo a day with that setup." "Link, my plans are based on 20 a day. I don't need to average 40 or 50 a day to cover my expenses. I'll show you the figures." Wyatt could indeed make more money in a day with his methods than his competitors (Table 2). Even though he was limited to 25 buffalo a day, his lower operating costs provided him a relatively stable profit opportunity with less financial risk. For example, Wyatt's investment in wagons and supplies was substantially lower, so a much smaller volume was needed. And the profit-sharing arrangement with his skinner reduced his exposure to unexpected downturns in volume. In today's parlance, he had a lower break-even point and a lower degree of operating leverage (i.e. the mix between fixed and variable costs). A higher degree of operating leverage – more reliance on fixed costs in the mix – leads to greater profits when volume is increasing but erodes profits faster when volume declines.

Wyatt only stayed in the buffalo hunting business for three years. But those years were enormously profitable. During his short stint as a hunter, he broke with traditional operating practices of the day and used financial information to make a variety of shrewd decisions that translated into higher profits. Wyatt had all the makings of a first class accountant . . . except that a new career beckoned.

Table 1 Budget based on a four-month season (66 shooting days)

Revenues		$4 620
Expenses:		
Horses and wagons	462	
Supplies	660	1 122
Profit		3 498
Skinner's share		1 749
Wyatt's share		1 749

Table 2 Comparative daily profits
(Typical hunt compared with Wyatt Earp hunt)

	Typical hunt	Wyatt Earp
Revenue	$150	$70.00
Expenses:		
Drivers, skinners and other helpers	75	
Horses and wagons	20	7.00
Supplies	30	10.00
Profit per day of trading	25	53.00
Less half for skinner		26.50
Wyatt Earp profit		26.50

Note that a portion of the supply costs (e.g. guns) and the remaining costs are fixed. The fixed element of the cost per day in Table 2 is derived from dividing the costs for a season by the number of days in the season.

Source: Adapted from Barton, T.L., Shenkir, W.G. and Hess, J.E., *CPA Journal*, June 1995, Vol. 65, Issue 6, pp. 48–50.

Alternative presentation of cost–volume–profit analysis

Contribution graph

In Figure 8.7 the fixed cost line is drawn parallel to the horizontal axis, and the variable cost is the difference between the total cost line and the fixed cost line. An alternative to

FIGURE 8.7 *Break-even chart for Example 8.1*

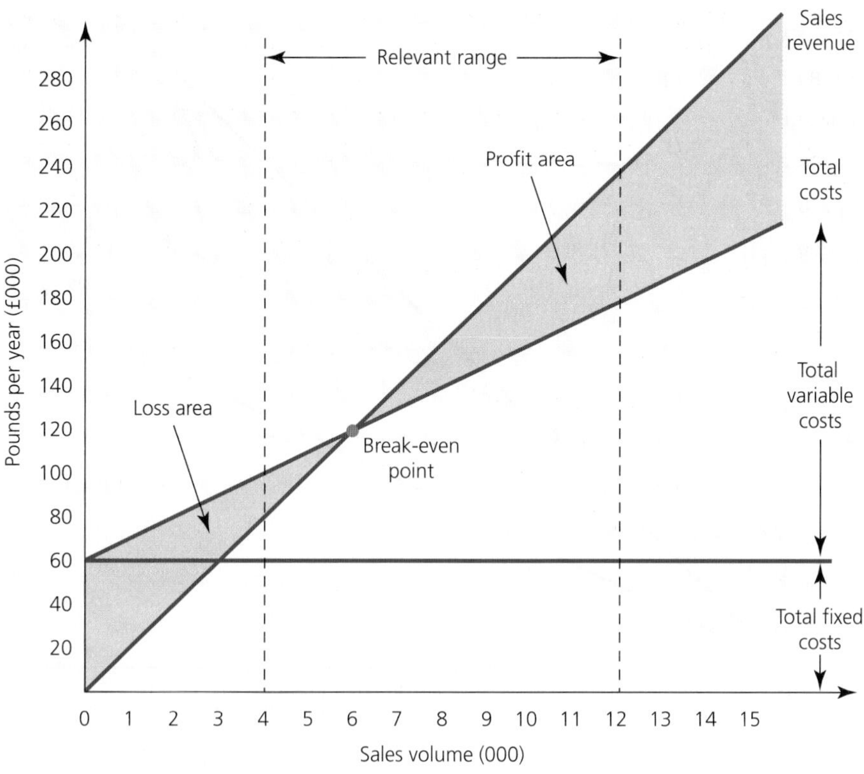

Figure 8.7 for the data contained in Example 8.1 is illustrated in Figure 8.8. This alternative presentation is called a **contribution graph**. In Figure 8.8 the variable cost line is drawn first at £10 per unit of volume. The fixed costs are represented by the difference between the total cost line and the variable cost line. Because fixed costs are assumed to be a constant sum throughout the entire output range, a constant sum of £60 000 for fixed costs is added to the variable cost line, which results in the total cost line being drawn parallel to the variable cost line. The advantage of this form of presentation is that the total contribution is emphasized in the graph, and is represented by the difference between the total sales revenue line and the total variable cost line.

Profit–volume graph

The break-even and contribution charts do not highlight the profit or loss at different volume levels. To ascertain the profit or loss figures from a break-even chart, it is necessary to determine the difference between the total-cost and total-revenue lines. The **profit–volume graph** is a more convenient method of showing the impact of changes in volume on profit. Such a graph is illustrated in Figure 8.9. The horizontal axis represents the various levels of sales volume, and the profits and losses for the period are recorded on the vertical scale. You will see from Figure 8.9 that profits or losses are plotted for each of the various sales levels, and these points are connected by a profit line. Two points are required to plot the profit line. When units sold are zero a

FIGURE 8.8 *Contribution chart for Example 8.1*

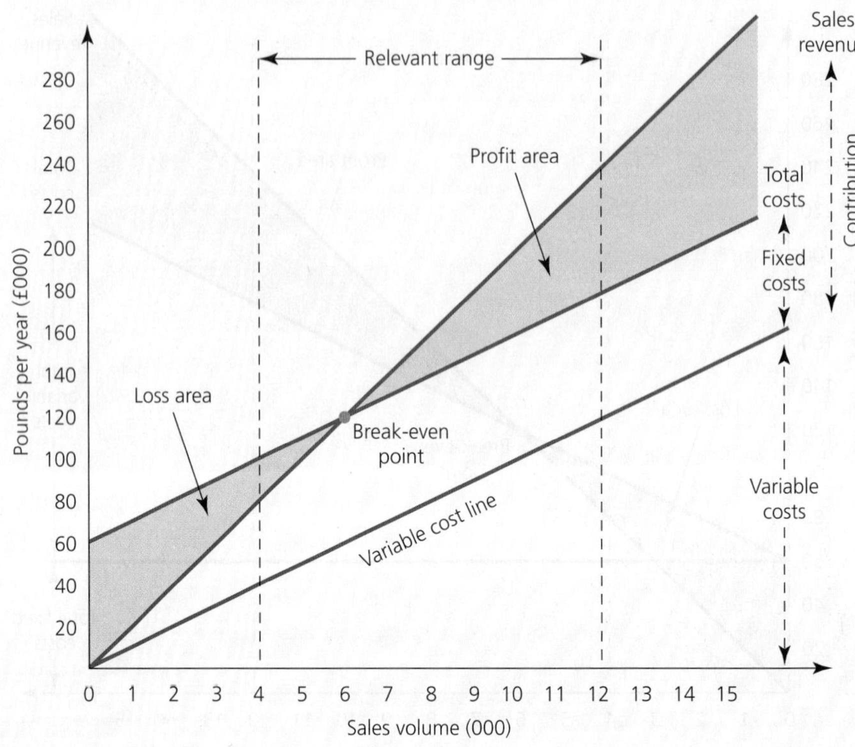

loss equal to the amount of fixed costs (£60 000) will be reported. At the break-even point (zero profits) sales volume is 6000 units. Therefore the break-even point is plotted at the point where the profit line intersects the horizontal line at a sales volume of 6000 tickets. The profit line is drawn between the two points. With each unit sold, a contribution of £10 is obtained towards the fixed costs, and the break-even point is at 6000 tickets, when the total contribution exactly equals the total of the fixed costs. With each additional unit sold beyond 6000 tickets, a surplus of £10 per ticket is obtained. If 10 000 tickets are sold, the profit will be £40 000 (4000 tickets at £10 contribution). You can see this relationship between sales and profit at 10 000 tickets from the dotted lines in Figure 8.9.

Multi-product cost–volume–profit analysis

Our analysis so far has assumed a single-product setting. However, most firms produce and sell many products or services. In this section we shall consider how we can adapt the analysis used for a single-product setting to a multi-product setting. Consider the situation presented in Example 8.2. You will see that the company sells two products so that there are two unit contribution margins. We can apply the same approach as that used for a single product if all of the fixed costs are directly attributable to products (i.e. there are no common fixed costs) or our analysis focuses only on the contribution to common fixed

FIGURE 8.9 *Profit–volume graph for Example 8.1*

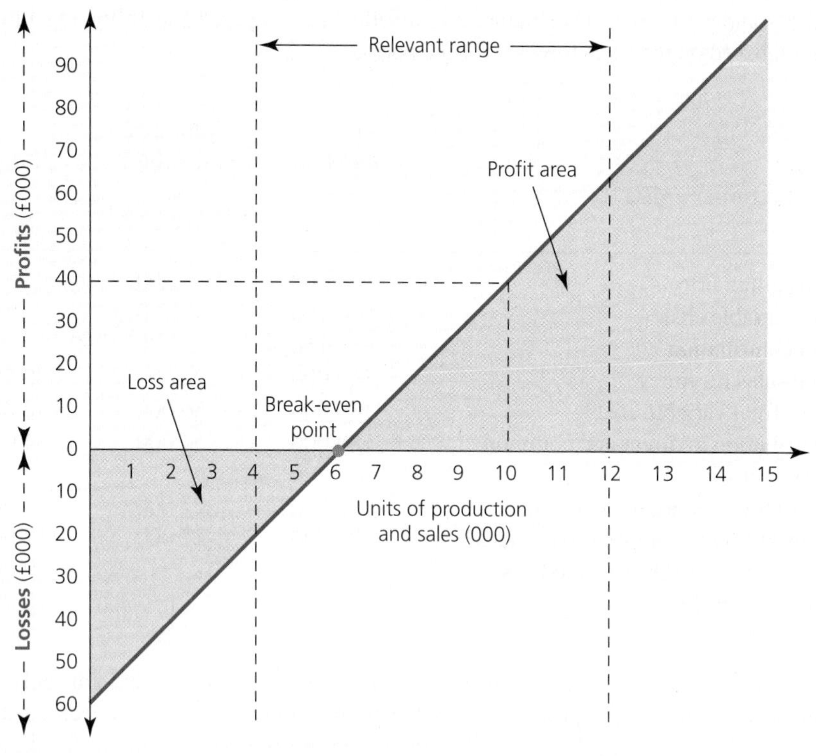

costs, rather than operating profit. We simply apply the analysis separately to each product as follows:

De-luxe washing machine break-even point

= Direct fixed costs (£90 000)/Unit contribution (£150)

= 600 units

Standard washing machine break-even point

= Direct fixed costs (£27 000)/Unit contribution (£90)

= 300 units

However, selling 600 de-luxe and 300 standard washing machines will generate a contribution that only covers direct fixed costs; the common fixed costs will not be covered. A loss equal to the common fixed costs will be reported. The break-even point for the firm as a whole has not been ascertained.

You may think that the break-even point for the firm as a whole can be derived if we allocate the common fixed costs to each individual product but this approach is inappropriate because the allocation will be arbitrary. The common fixed costs cannot be specifically identified with either of the products since they can only be avoided if *both* products are not sold. The solution to our problem is to convert the sales volume measure of the individual products into standard batches of products based on the planned sales mix. You will from see from Example 8.2 that Super Bright plans to sell 1200 de-luxe and 600 standard

EXAMPLE 8.2

The Super Bright Company sells two types of washing machines – a de-luxe model and a standard model. The financial controller has prepared the following information based on the sales forecast for the period:

Sales volume (units)	De-luxe machine 1200 (£)	Standard machine 600 (£)	Total (£)
Unit selling price	300	200	
Unit variable cost	150	110	
Unit contribution	150	90	
Total sales revenues	360 000	120 000	480 000
Less: Total variable cost	180 000	66 000	246 000
Contribution to direct and common fixed costs[a]	180 000	54 000	234 000
Less: Direct avoidable fixed costs	90 000	27 000	117 000
Contribution to common fixed costs[a]	90 000	27 000	117 000
Less common (indirect) fixed costs			39 000
Operating profit			78 000

The common fixed costs relate to the costs of common facilities and can only be avoided if neither of the products is sold. The managing director is concerned that sales may be less than forecast and has requested information relating to the break-even point for the activities for the period.

Note

[a]Contribution was defined earlier in this chapter as sales less variable costs. Where fixed costs are divided into direct and common (indirect) fixed costs it is possible to identify two separate contribution categories. The first is described as contribution to direct and common fixed costs and this is identical to the conventional definition, being equivalent to sales less variable costs. The second is after a further deduction of direct fixed costs and is described as 'Contribution to common or indirect fixed costs'.

machines giving a sales mix of 1200:600. Reducing this sales mix to the smallest whole number gives a mix of 2:1. In other words, for the sale of every two deluxe machines one standard machine is expected to be sold. We therefore define our standard batch of products as comprising two de-luxe and one standard machine giving a contribution of £390 per batch (two de-luxe machines at a contribution of £150 per unit sold plus and one standard machine at a contribution of £90).

The break-even point in standard batches can be calculated by using the same break-even equation that we used for a single product so that:

Break-even number of batches = Total fixed costs (£156 000)/Contribution margin per bath (£390)

= 400 batches

The sales mix used to define a standard batch (2:1) can be now be used to convert the break-even point (measured in standard batches) into a break-even point expressed in terms of the required combination of individual products sold. Thus, 800 de-luxe machines (2 × 400) and

400 (1 × 400) standard machines must be sold to break-even. The following profit statement verifies this outcome:

Units sold	De-luxe machine 800 (£)	Standard machine 400 (£)	Total (£)
Unit contribution margin	150	90	
Contribution to direct and common fixed costs	120 000	36 000	156 000
Less: Direct fixed costs	90 000	27 000	117 000
Contribution to common fixed costs	30 000	9 000	39 000
Less: Common fixed costs			39 000
Operating profit			0

Let us now assume that the actual sales volume for the period was 1200 units, the same total volume as the break-even volume, but consisting of a sales mix of 600 units of each machine. Thus, the actual sales mix is 1:1 compared with a planned sales mix of 2:1. The total contribution to direct and common fixed costs will be £144 000 ([150 × 600] + [£90 × 600]) and a loss of £12 000 (£144 000 contribution – £156 000 total fixed costs) will occur. It should now be apparent to you that the break-even point (or the sales volumes required to achieve a target profit) is not a unique number: it varies depending upon the composition of the sales mix. Because the actual sales mix differs from the planned sales mix, the sales mix used to define a standard batch has changed from 2:1 to 1:1 so that the contribution per batch changes from £390 to £240 ([1 × £150] + [1 × £90]). Therefore the revised break-even point will be 650 batches (£156 000 total fixed costs/£240 contribution per batch) which converts to a sales volume of 650 units of each machine based on a 1:1 sales mix. Generally, an increase in the proportion of sales of higher contribution margin products will decrease the break-even point whereas increases in sales of the lower margin products will increase the break-even point.

Cost–volume–profit analysis assumptions

It is essential that anyone preparing or interpreting CVP information is aware of the underlying assumptions on which the information has been prepared. If these assumptions are not recognized, serious errors may result and incorrect conclusions may be drawn from the analysis. We shall now consider these important assumptions. They are as follows:

1 All other variables remain constant.
2 A single product or constant sales mix.
3 Total costs and total revenue are linear functions of output.
4 Profits are calculated on a variable costing basis.
5 The analysis applies to the relevant range only.
6 Costs can be accurately divided into their fixed and variable elements.
7 The analysis applies only to a short-term time horizon.
8 Complexity-related fixed costs do not change.

1 All other variables remain constant

It has been assumed that all variables other than the particular one under consideration have remained constant throughout the analysis. In other words, it is assumed that volume is the only factor that will cause costs and revenues to change. However, changes in other variables such as production efficiency, sales mix, price levels and production methods can have an important influence on sales revenue and costs. If significant changes in these other variables occur the CVP analysis presentation will be incorrect.

2 Single product or constant sales mix

CVP analysis assumes that either a single product is sold or, if a range of products is sold, that sales will be in accordance with a predetermined sales mix. When a predetermined sales mix is used, it can be depicted in the CVP analysis by measuring sales volume using standard batch sizes based on a planned sales mix. Any CVP analysis must be interpreted carefully if the initial product mix assumptions do not hold.

3 Total costs and total revenue are linear functions of output

The analysis assumes that unit variable cost and selling price are constant. This assumption is only likely to be valid within the relevant range of production described on page 267.

4 Profits are calculated on a variable costing basis

The analysis assumes that the fixed costs incurred during the period are charged as an expense for that period. Therefore variable-costing profit calculations are assumed. If absorption-costing profit calculations are used, it is necessary to assume that production is equal to sales for the analysis to predict absorption costing profits. If this situation does not occur, the inventory levels will change and the fixed overheads allocated for the period will be different from the amount actually incurred during the period. Under absorption costing, only when production equals sales will the amount of fixed overhead incurred be equal to the amount of fixed overhead charged as an expense. For the application of CVP analysis with an absorption costing system you should refer to Appendix 8.1.

5 Analysis applies to relevant range only

Earlier in this chapter we noted that CVP analysis is appropriate only for decisions taken within the relevant production range, and that it is incorrect to project cost and revenue figures beyond the relevant range.

6 Costs can be accurately divided into their fixed and variable elements

CVP analysis assumes that costs can be accurately analysed into their fixed and variable elements. The separation of semi-variable costs into their fixed and variable elements is extremely difficult in practice. Nevertheless a reasonably accurate analysis is necessary if CVP analysis is to provide relevant information for decision-making.

7 The analysis applies only to a short-term time horizon

At the beginning of this chapter we noted that CVP analysis is based on the relationship between volume and sales revenue, costs and profits in the short-term, the short-term being typically a period of one year. In the short-term the costs of providing a firm's operating capacity, such as property taxes and the salaries of senior managers, are likely to be fixed in relation to changes in activity. Decisions on the firm's intended future potential level of operating capacity will determine the amount of capacity costs to be incurred. These decisions will have been made previously as part of the long-term planning process. Once these decisions have been made, they cannot easily be reversed in the short-term. It takes time to significantly expand the capacity of plant and machinery or reduce capacity. Furthermore, plant investment and abandonment decisions should not be based on short-term fluctuations in demand within a particular year. Instead, they should be reviewed periodically as part of the long-term planning process and decisions based on predictions of long-run demand over several years. Thus capacity costs will tend to be fixed in relation to changes of activity within short-term periods such as one year. However, over long-term periods significant changes in volume or product complexity will cause fixed costs to change.

It is therefore assumed that in the short term some costs will be fixed and unaffected by changes in volume whereas other (variable) costs will vary with changes in volume. In the short-run volume is the most important variable influencing total revenue, costs and profit. For this reason volume is given special attention in the form of CVP analysis. You should note, however, that in the long-term other variables, besides volume, will cause costs to change. Therefore, the long-term analysis should incorporate other variables, besides volume, and recognize that fixed costs will increase or decrease in steps in response to changes in the explanatory variables.

8 Complexity-related fixed costs do not change

CVP analysis assumes that **complexity-related costs** will remain unchanged. Cooper and Kaplan (1987) illustrate how complexity-related fixed costs can increase as a result of changes in the range of items produced, even though volume remains unchanged. They illustrate the relationship with an example of two identical plants. One plant produces one million units of product A. The second plant produces 100 000 units of A and 900 000 similar units of 199 similar products. The first plant has a simple production environment and requires limited manufacturing support facilities. Set-ups, expediting, inventory movements and schedule activities are minimal. The other plant has a much more complex production management environment. The 200 products must be scheduled through the plant, and this requires frequent set-ups, inventory movements, purchase receipts and inspections. To handle this complexity, the support departments' fixed costs must be larger.

Cooper and Kaplan use the above example to illustrate that many so-called fixed costs vary not with the volume of items manufactured but with the range of items produced (i.e. the complexity of the production process). Complexity-related costs do not normally vary significantly in the short-term with the volume of production. If a change in volume does not alter the range of products then it is likely that complexity-related fixed costs will not alter, but if volume stays constant and the range of items produced changes then support department fixed costs will eventually change because of the increase or decrease to product complexity.

CVP analysis assumptions will be violated if a firm seeks to enhance profitability by product proliferation: that is, by introducing new variants of products based on short-term contribution margins. The CVP analysis will show that profits will increase as sales volume increases and fixed costs remain constant in the short-term. The increased product diversity, however, will cause complexity-related fixed costs to increase in future periods, and there is a danger that long-term profits may decline as a result of product proliferation. The CVP analysis incorporates the fixed costs required to handle the diversity and complexity within the current product range, but the costs will remain fixed only if diversity and complexity are not increased further. Thus CVP analysis will not capture the changes in complexity-related costs arising from changes in the range of items produced.

Cost–volume–profit analysis and computer applications

The output from a CVP model is only as good as the input. The analysis will include assumptions about sales mix, production efficiency, price levels, total fixed costs, variable costs and selling price per unit. Obviously, estimates regarding these variables will be subject to varying degrees of uncertainty.

Sensitivity analysis is one approach for coping with changes in the values of the variables. Sensitivity analysis focuses on how a result will be changed if the original estimates or the underlying assumptions change. With regard to CVP analysis, sensitivity analysis answers questions such as the following:

1 What will the profit be if the sales mix changes from that originally predicted?

2 What will the profit be if fixed costs increase by 10% and variable costs decline by 5%?

The widespread use of spreadsheet packages has enabled management accountants to develop CVP computerized models. Managers can now consider alternative plans by keying the information into a computer, which can quickly show changes both graphically and numerically. Thus managers can study various combinations of changes in selling prices, fixed costs, variable costs and product mix, and can react quickly without waiting for formal reports from the management accountant.

Separation of semi-variable costs

CVP analysis assumes that costs can be accurately analysed into their fixed and variable elements. Direct material is generally presumed to be a variable cost, whereas depreciation, which is related to time and not usage, is a fixed cost. Semi-variable costs, however, include both a fixed and variable component. The cost of maintenance is a semi-variable cost consisting of planned maintenance which is undertaken whatever the level of activity, and a variable element which is directly related to activity. The separation of semi-variable costs into their fixed and variable elements is extremely difficult in practice, but an accurate analysis is necessary for CVP analysis.

Mathematical techniques should be used to separate costs accurately into fixed and variable elements. For a discussion of these techniques you should refer to Chapter 24. However, first-year cost and management accounting examinations sometimes require you to separate fixed and variable costs using a non-mathematical technique called the **high–low method**.

The high–low method consists of examining past costs and activity, selecting the highest and lowest activity levels and comparing the changes in costs which result from the two levels. Assume that the following activity levels and costs are extracted:

	Volume of production (units)	Indirect costs (£)
Lowest activity	5 000	22 000
Highest activity	10 000	32 000

If variable costs are constant per unit and the fixed costs remain unchanged the increase in costs will be due entirely to an increase in variable costs. The variable cost per unit is therefore calculated as follows:

$$\frac{\text{Difference in cost}}{\text{Difference in activity}} = \frac{\text{£10 000}}{\text{5000 units}}$$

$$= \text{£2 variable cost per unit of activity}$$

The fixed cost can be estimated at any level of activity by subtracting the variable cost portion from the total cost. At an activity level of 5000 units the total cost is £22 000 and the total variable cost is £10 000 (5000 units at 2 per unit). The balance of £12 000 is assumed to represent the fixed cost.

Summary

The following items relate to the learning objectives listed at the beginning of the chapter.

- **Describe the differences between the accountant's and the economist's model of cost–volume–profit analysis.**

  The major differences are that the total cost and total revenue functions are curvilinear in the economist's model whereas the accountant's model assumes linear relationships. However, the accountant's model is intended to predict CVP behaviour only within the relevant range, where a firm is likely to be operating on constant returns to scale. A comparison of the two models suggested that, within the relevant range of activity, the total costs and revenue functions are fairly similar.

- **Justify the use of linear cost and revenue functions in the accountant's model.**

  Within the relevant range it is generally assumed that cost and revenue functions are approximately linear. Outside the relevant range linearity is unlikely to apply. Care is therefore required in interpreting CVP relationships outside the relevant range.

- **Apply the mathematical approach to answer questions similar to those listed in Example 8.1.**

  In Example 8.1, the break-even point was derived by dividing fixed costs by the contribution per unit. To ascertain the number of units sold to achieve a target profit the sum of the fixed costs and the target profit is divided by the contribution per unit.

- **Construct break-even, contribution and profit–volume graphs.**

  Managers may obtain a clearer understanding of CVP behaviour if the information is presented in graphical format. With the break-even chart the fixed costs are plotted as a single horizontal line. The total cost line is plotted by adding variable costs to fixed costs. The reverse situation applies with a contribution graph. The variable costs are plotted first and the fixed costs are added to variable costs to plot the total cost line. Because fixed costs are assumed to be a constant sum throughout the output range, the total cost line is drawn parallel to the variable cost line. The break-even and contribution graphs do not highlight the profit or loss at different output levels and must be ascertained by comparing the differences between the total cost and total revenue lines. The profit–volume graph shows the impact of changes in volume on profits. The profits and losses are plotted for each of the various sales levels and these are connected by a profit line. You should refer to Figures 8.7–8.9 for an illustration of the graphs.

- **Identify and explain the assumptions on which cost–volume–profit analysis is based.**

  Cost–volume–profit analysis is based on the following assumptions: (a) all variables, other than volume, remain constant; (b) the sales mix remains constant; (c) total costs and revenues are linear functions of output; (d) profits are calculated on a variable costing basis; (e) the analysis applies only to the relevant range; (f) costs can be accurately divided into their fixed and variable elements; (g) the analysis applies only to a short-term horizon, and (h) complexity-related fixed costs do not change.

- **Apply cost–volume–profit analysis in a multi-product setting.**

  Multi-product CVP analysis requires that an assumption is made concerning the expected sales mix. The approach that is used is to convert the multi-product CVP analysis into a single product analysis based on the assumption that output consists of standard batches of the multiple products based on the expected sales mix. However, you should note that the answers change as the sales mix changes.

- **Additional learning objective presented in Appendix 8.1.**

  The appendix to this chapter includes an additional learning objective: to apply CVP analysis when profits are measured on an absorption costing basis. This topic has been presented in the appendix because it may not form part of your course curriculum. You should therefore check with your course curriculum to ascertain whether you need to study this topic.

Appendix 8.1: CVP analysis applied to absorption costing

You will recall from our discussion of CVP analysis assumptions that CVP analysis assumes that profits are measured using a variable costing system, or the special situation where sales volume equals production volume, so that absorption costing profits are equal to variable costing profits. In this appendix we are going to look at how CVP analysis can be adapted to be applied in situations when profits are measured on an absorption costing basis and sales volume does not equal production volume.

Where CVP analysis is used as an input to decision-making the analysis should be based on variable costing principles since inventory movements should not influence the underlying economic reality. However, the outcomes of decisions using CVP analysis are normally not separately reported. Instead, the estimated and actual outcomes arising from the decisions are merged with other activities and incorporated into the monthly budgeting and profit performance reporting system. The monthly profit reporting system in most organizations is based on absorption costing. This can result in situations where the profits reported within the monthly reporting system are different from those predicted by the variable costing CVP analysis. To ascertain how the consequences of decisions will be reported within the monthly reporting system management require CVP analysis based on absorption costing principles.

CVP analysis is more complex with absorption costing because profit is a function of both sales and production whereas with variable costing profit is a function of a single variable (sales volume). To apply CVP analysis to absorption costing the break-even curve will consist of a set of pairs of sales and production and we must assume that one of the variables remains a known, or constant, value.

We shall use the following terms to develop an absorption costing CVP analysis model:

ucm = Contribution margin per unit (i.e. selling price per unit – variable cost per unit)

ufmc = Pre-determined fixed manufacturing overhead per unit of output

Qp = Number of units produced

Qs = Number of units sold

FC = Total fixed costs (manufacturing and non-manufacturing)

$OPBT_{AC}$ = Operating profit before taxes for the period (Absorption costing)

Our starting point is to use the following absorption costing profit function that was derived in the appendix to the previous chapter

$$OPBT_{AC} = (ucm - ufmc)\,Qs + (ufmc \times Qp) - FC$$

(For an explanation of how this profit function was derived you should refer back to pages 244–245):

Setting profit equal to zero the net profit function is:

$$0 = (ucm - ufmc)\,Qs + (ufmc \times Qp) - FC$$
$$FC - (ufmc \times Qp) = (ucm - ufmc)\,Qs$$
$$BEP\ (Qs) = [FC - (ufmc \times Qp)]\ /\ (ucm - ufmc)$$

To illustrate the application of BEP (Qs) we shall use Example 7.1 from the previous chapter. This example is repeated in the form of Example 8A.1. You should now refer to Example 8A.1.

The absorption costing break-even point calculations are as follows:

BEP (Qs) Periods 1–4 = [£400 000 – (£2 × 150 000)] / (£4 – £2) = 50 000 units
BEP (Qs) Periods 5 = [£400 000 – (£2 × 170 000)] / (£4 – £2) = 30 000 units
BEP (Qs) Periods 6 = [£400 000 – (£2 × 140 000)] / (£4 – £2) = 60 000 units

Note that the break-even point remains unchanged in periods 1–4 because production is held constant at 150 000 units but changes in periods 5 and 6 because of changes in production. Given that absorption costing profit is a function of production volume, besides sales volume, the break-even sales volume changes when production volume changes.

Contrast the variable costing sales volume break-even point with the absorption costing break-even point. The former is 100 000 units (£400 000 fixed costs/£4 unit contribution) for all periods since the same amount of fixed costs are expensed each period whereas with the absorption costing system production volume is significantly in excess of sales volume. Consequently, a large proportion of fixed overheads is deferred to future periods. Hence, the absorption costing break-even point is significantly different from the variable costing break-even point.

The above analysis can be verified by preparing absorption costing profit statements adopting the same approach as that illustrated in Exhibit 7.3 in the previous chapter. If you

EXAMPLE 8A.1

The following information is available for periods 1–6 for the Samuelson Company:

	(£)
Unit selling price	10
Unit variable cost	6
Fixed manufacturing costs for each period	300 000
Unit fixed manufacturing cost	£2 (£300 000/150 000 units)

The company produces only one product. Budgeted activity is expected to average 150 000 units per period, and production and sales for each period are as follows:

	Period 1	Period 2	Period 3	Period 4	Period 5	Period 6
Units sold (000's)	150	120	180	150	140	160
Units produced (000's)	150	150	150	150	170	140

There were no opening stocks at the start of period 1, and the actual manufacturing fixed overhead incurred was £300 000 per period. We shall also assume that non-manufacturing overheads are £100 000 per period.

wish to verify the break-even point calculations, using the break-even sales volumes for each period, do remember to incorporate the opening and closing inventories that will result from the break-even sales volumes.

The same principles that are used in variable costing CVP analysis to determine the output levels to achieve target profit levels can also be applied here. Adding a target profit to the total fixed costs in the BEP(Qs) formula and assuming that production is held constant at 170 000 units, the sales volume to derive a target profit of £220 000 can be derived. The calculation is:

$$\text{BEP (Qs)} = [£400\,000 + £220\,000) - (£2 \times 170\,000)] / (£4 - £2) = 140\,000 \text{ units}$$

The above sales volume computation of 140 000 units is based on an assumed production volume of 170 000 units. If you look at the data shown in Example 8A.1 you will see that the production and sales volumes are identical to that of period 5. You should now refer back to Exhibit 7.3 in Chapter 7 and you will be able to verify that a production volume of 170 000 units and a sales volume of 140 000 units does result in a reported profit of £220 000.

The above analysis can also be reversed so that sales volume is a known constant and a break-even production point calculated. Setting operating profit equal to zero and assuming that sales volume (Qs) is known, the break-even point production level is:

$$\text{BEP (Qp)} = [\text{FC} - (\text{ucm} - \text{ufmc})\text{Qs}] / \text{ufmc}$$

However, since the impact of changes in sales volume is likely to be of greater importance to management the application of the above BEP (Qp) formula is not illustrated here.

Key terms and concepts

break-even chart (p. 274)
break-even point (p. 267)
complexity-related costs (p. 283)
contribution graph (p. 277)
contribution margin (p. 271)
contribution margin ratio (p. 273)
decreasing returns to scale (p. 265)
high-low method (p. 284)
increasing returns to scale (p. 265)
margin of safety (p. 274)
profit–volume graph (p. 277)
profit–volume ratio (p. 273)
relevant range (p. 267)
sensitivity analysis (p. 284)

Key examination points

Students tend to experience little difficulty in preparing break-even charts, but many cannot construct profit–volume charts. Remember that the horizontal axis represents the level of activity, while profit/losses are shown on the vertical axis. The maximum loss is at zero activity, and is equal to fixed costs. For practice on preparing a profit–volume chart you should attempt Review problem 8.24 and compare your answer with the solution. Students also experience difficulty with the following:

1 coping with multi-product situations;
2 calculating the break-even point when total sales and costs are given but no information is given on the unit costs;
3 explaining the assumptions of CVP analysis.

For multi-product situations you should base your answer on the average contribution per unit, using the approach shown in Example 8.2 Review problem 8.26 requires the computation of a break-even point in a multi-product setting. When unit costs are not given the break-even point in sales value can be calculated as follows:

$$\text{Fixed costs} \times \frac{\text{total estimated sales}}{\text{total estimated contribution}}$$

or

$$\frac{\text{Fixed costs}}{\text{profit} - \text{volume ratio}}$$

You should refer to the solutions to Review problems 8.13, 8.18 and 8.25 for an illustration of the application of the above approach. Sometimes questions will give details of costs but not the split into the fixed and variable elements. You can separate the total costs into their fixed and variable elements using the high–low method described in the chapter. This approach is required for review problems 8.14 and 8.25.

Assessment material

Review questions

The review questions are short questions that enable you to assess your understanding of the main topics included in the chapter. The numbers in parentheses provide you with the page numbers to refer to if you cannot answer a specific question.

Review problems

The review problems are more complex and require you to relate and apply the chapter content to various business problems. The problems are graded by their level of difficulty. The multiple-choice questions are the least demanding and normally take less than 10 minutes to complete. Fully worked solutions to the review problems are provided in a separate section at the end of the book. For those questions in the white box the worked solutions are provided in the *Student's Manual* accompanying this book. Further review problems for this chapter are available on the accompanying website www.drury-online.com. The answers to these problems are available for lecturers on the lecturer's password protected section of the website.

Case studies

The website also includes over 30 case study problems. A list of these cases is provided in Part Seven of this book. Several cases are relevant to the content of this chapter. Examples include Dunbellow Ltd., Hardhat Ltd. and Merrion Products Ltd.

Review questions

8.1 Provide examples of how cost–volume–profit analysis can be used for decision-making. *(p. 263)*

8.2 Distinguish between the economist's and the accountant's approach to cost–volume–profit analysis. *(pp. 267–69)*

8.3 Explain what is meant by the term 'relevant range'. *(p. 267)*

8.4 Define the term 'contribution margin'. *(p. 271)*

8.5 Define the term 'profit – volume ratio' and explain how it can be used for cost–volume–profit analysis. *(p. 273)*

8.6 Describe and distinguish between the three different approaches of presenting cost–volume–profit relationships in graphical format. *(pp. 274–78)*

8.7 Describe the assumptions underlying cost–volume–profit analysis. *(pp. 281–84)*

8.8 How can a company with multiple products use cost–volume–profit analysis? *(pp. 279–80)*

8.9 Explain why the break-even point changes when there is a change in sales mix. *(p. 281)*

8.10 How can sensitivity analysis be used in conjunction with cost–volume–profit analysis? *(p. 284)*

8.11 Why is cost–volume–profit analysis more complex with an absorption costing system? *(p. 287)*

Review problems

8.12 **Intermediate**

A company manufactures and sells two products, X and Y. Forecast data for a year are:

	Product X	Product Y
Sales (units)	80 000	20 000
Sales price (per unit)	£12	£8
Variable cost (per unit)	£8	3

Annual fixed costs are estimated at £273 000.

What is the break-even point in sales revenue with the current sales mix?

A £570 000
B £606 667
C £679 467
D £728 000

ACCA Foundation Paper 3 Sample Question

8.13 **Intermediate**

H Limited manufactures and sells two products, J and K. Annual sales are expected to be in the ratio of J:1, K:3. Total annual sales are planned to be £420 000. Product J has a contribution to sales ratio of 40%, whereas that of product K is 50%. Annual fixed costs are estimated to be £120 000.

The budgeted break-even sales value (to the nearest £1000):

A £196 000
B £200 000
C £253 000
D £255 000
E cannot be determined from the above data.

CIMA Stage 2

8.14 **Intermediate**

The following details relate to product R:

Level of activity (units)	1000 (£/unit)	2000 (£/unit)
Direct materials	4.00	4.00
Direct labour	3.00	3.00
Production overhead	3.50	2.50
Selling overhead	1.00	0.50
	11.50	10.00

The total fixed cost and variable cost per unit are:

	Total fixed cost (£)	Variable cost per unit (£)
A	2000	1.50
B	2000	7.00
C	2000	8.50
D	3000	7.00
E	3000	8.50

CIMA Stage 2

8.15 Intermediate

Z plc currently sells products Aye, Bee and Cee in equal quantities and at the same selling price per unit. The contribution to sales ratio for product Aye is 40%; for product Bee it is 50% and the total is 48%. If fixed costs are unaffected by mix and are currently 20% of sales, the effect of changing the product mix to:

Aye	40%
Bee	25%
Cee	35%

is that the total contribution/total sales ratio changes to:

A 27.4%
B 45.3%
C 47.4%
D 48.4%
E 68.4%

CIMA Stage 2

8.16 Intermediate

E plc operates a marginal costing system. For the forthcoming year, variable costs are budgeted to be 60% of sales value and fixed costs are budgeted to be 10% of sales value.

If E plc increases its selling prices by 10%, but if fixed costs, variable costs per unit and sales volume remain unchanged, the effect on E plc's contribution would be:

A a decrease of 2%
B an increase of 5%
C an increase of 10%
D an increase of 25%
E an increase of $66^2/_3$%

CIMA Stage 2

8.17 Intermediate

A Limited has fixed costs of £60 000 per annum. It manufactures a single product which it sells for £20 per unit. Its contribution to sales ratio is 40%.

A Limited's breakeven point in units is:

A 1200
B 1800
C 3000
D 5000
E 7500

CIMA Stage 2 Specimen Paper

8.18 Intermediate

Z plc makes a single product which it sells for £16 per unit. Fixed costs are £76 800 per month and the product has a contribution to sales ratio of 40%.

In a period when actual sales were £224 000, Z plc's margin of safety, in units, was

A 2 000
B 6 000
C 8 000
D 12 000
E 14 000

CIMA Stage 2

8.19 Intermediate

The following information is required for sub-questions (a) and (b)

W Ltd makes leather purses. It has drawn up the following budget for its next financial period:

Selling price per unit	$11.60
Variable production cost per unit	$3.40
Sales commission	5% of selling price
Fixed production costs	$430 500
Fixed selling and administration costs	$198 150
Sales	90 000 units

(a) The margin of safety represents

A 5.6% of budgeted sales
B 8.3% of budgeted sales
C 11.6% of budgeted sales
D 14.8% of budgeted sales

(b) The marketing manager has indicated that an increase in the selling price to $12.25 per unit would not affect the number of units sold, provided that the sales commission is increased to 8% of the selling price.

These changes will cause the break-even point (to the nearest whole number) to be

A 71 033 units B 76 016 units C 79 879 units D 87 070 units

CIMA – Management Accounting Fundamentals

8.20 Intermediate

The following information is required for sub-questions (a) and (b)

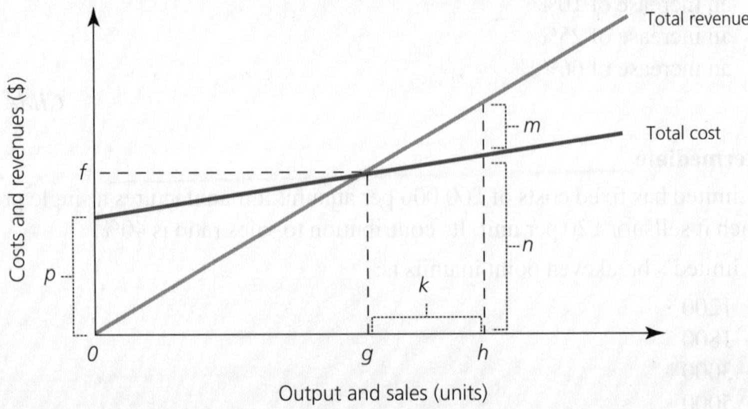

The company expects to sell *h* units in the next accounting period.

(a) The margin of safety is shown on the diagram by

A k B m C n D p

(b) The effect of an increase in fixed costs, with all other costs and revenues remaining the same, will be

A an increase in m
B an increase in k
C an increase in f
D a reduction in p

CIMA – Management Accounting Fundamentals

8.21 **Advanced**

Z plc provides a single service to its customers. An analysis of its budget for the year ending 31 December 2002 shows that in period 4, when the budgeted activity was 5220 service units with a sales value of £42 each, the margin of safety was 19.575%.

The budgeted contribution to sales ratio of the service is 40%.

Budgeted fixed costs in period 4 were nearest to

A £1700 B £71 000 C £88 000 D £176 000

(2 marks)

CIMA Management Accounting – Performance Management

8.22 **Advanced**

RT plc sells three products.

Product R has a contribution to sales ratio of 30%.

Product S has a contribution to sales ratio of 20%.

Product T has a contribution to sales ratio of 25%.

Monthly fixed costs are £100 000.

If the products are sold in the ratio:

R: 2 S: 5 T: 3

the monthly break-even sales revenue, to the nearest £1, is

A £400 000
B £411 107
C £425 532
D impossible to calculate without further information.

(2 marks)

CIMA Management Accounting – Performance Management

8.23 Intermediate

A break-even chart is shown below for Windhurst Ltd.

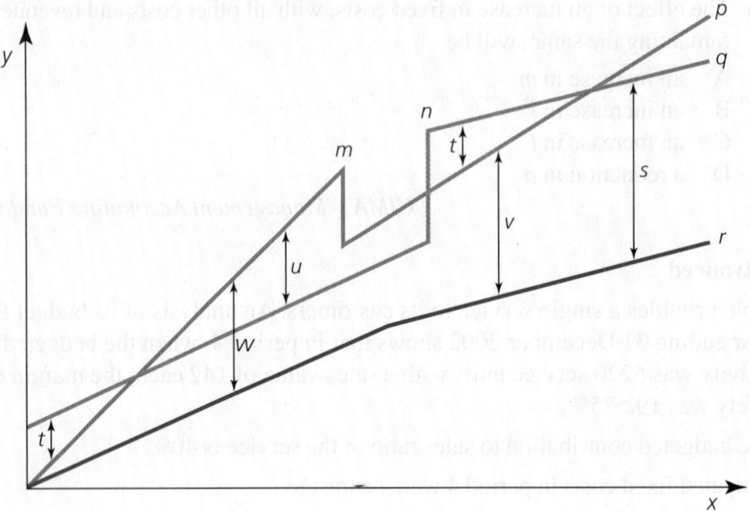

You are required:

(i) to identify the components of the break-even chart labelled *p*, *q*, *r*, *s*, *t*, *u*, *v*, *w*, *x* and *y*;

(5 marks)

(ii) to suggest what events are represented at the values of *x* that are labelled *m* and *n* on the chart;

(3 marks)

(iii) to assess the usefulness of break-even analysis to senior management of a small company.

(7 marks)

ICAEW Management Accounting

8.24 Intermediate: Preparation of break-even and profit–volume graphs

ZED plc manufactures one standard product, which sells at £10. You are required to:

(a) prepare from the data given below, a break-even and profit–volume graph showing the results for the six months ending 30 April and to determine:

(i) the fixed costs;
(ii) the variable cost per unit;
(iii) the profit–volume ratio;
(iv) the break-even point;
(v) the margin of safety;

Month	Sales (units)	Profit/(loss) (£)
November	30 000	40 000
December	35 000	60 000
January	15 000	(20 000)
February	24 000	16 000
March	26 000	24 000
April	18 000	(8 000)

(b) discuss the limitations of such a graph;

(c) explain the use of the relevant range in such a graph.

(20 marks)

CIMA Cost Accounting 2

8.25 Intermediate: Preparation of a contribution graph

Z plc operates a single retail outlet selling direct to the public. Profit statements for August and September are as follows:

	August	**September**
Sales	80 000	90 000
Cost of sales	50 000	55 000
Gross profit	30 000	35 000
Less:		
Selling and distribution	8 000	9 000
Administration	15 000	15 000
Net profit	7 000	11 000

Required:

(a) Use the high- and low-points technique to identify the behaviour of:
   (i) cost of sales;
   (ii) selling and distribution costs;
   (iii) administration costs.

(4 marks)

(b) Draw a contribution break-even chart and identify the monthly break-even sales value and area of contribution.

(10 marks)

(c) Assuming a margin of safety equal to 30% of the break-even value, calculate Z plc's annual profit.

(2 marks)

(d) Z plc is now considering opening another retail outlet selling the same products. Z plc plans to use the same profit margins in both outlets and has estimated that the specific fixed costs of the second outlet will be £100 000 per annum.

Z plc also expects that 10% of its annual sales from its existing outlet would transfer to this second outlet if it were to be opened.

Calculate the annual value of sales required from the new outlet in order to achieve the same annual profit as previously obtained from the single outlet.

(5 marks)

(e) Briefly describe the cost accounting requirements of organizations of this type.

(4 marks)

(Total 25 marks)

Chartered Institute of Management Accountants Operational Cost Accounting Stage 2

8.26 Intermediate: Changes in sales mix

XYZ Ltd produces two products and the following budget applies for 20 × 2:

	Product X (£)	Product Y (£)
Selling price	6	12
Variable costs	2	4
Contribution margin	4	8
Fixed costs apportioned	£100 000	£200 000
Units sold	70 000	30 000

You are required to calculate the break-even points for each product and the company as a whole and comment on your findings.

8.27 Intermediate: Non-graphical CVP analysis

The summarized profit and loss statement for Exewye plc for the last year is as follows:

	(£000)	(£000)
Sale (50 000 units)		1000
Direct materials	350	
Direct wages	200	
Fixed production overhead	200	
Variable production overhead	50	
Administration overhead	180	
Selling and distribution overhead	120	
		1100
Profit/(loss)		(100)

At a recent board meeting the directors discussed the year's results, following which the chairman asked for suggestions to improve the situation.

You are required as management accountant, to evaluate the following alternative proposals and to comment briefly on each:

(a) Pay salesmen a commission of 10% of sales and thus increase sales to achieve break-even point. *(5 marks)*

(b) Reduce selling price by 10%, which it is estimated would increase sales volume by 30%. *(3 marks)*

(c) Increase direct wage rates from £4 to £5 per hour, as part of a productivity/pay deal. It is hoped that this would increase production and sales by 20%, but advertising costs would increase by £50 000. *(4 marks)*

(d) Increase sales by additional advertising of £300 000, with an increased selling price of 20%, setting a profit margin of 10%. *(8 marks)*

(Total 20 marks)

CIMA P1 Cost Accounting

8.28 Advanced: Non-graphical CVP behaviour

Tweed Ltd is a company engaged solely in the manufacture of jumpers, which are bought mainly for sporting activities. Present sales are direct to retailers, but in recent years there has been a steady decline in output because of increased foreign competition. In the last trading year (2001) the accounting report indicated that the company produced the lowest profit for 10 years. The forecast for 2002 indicates that the present deterioration in profits is likely to continue. The company considers that a profit of £80 000 should be achieved to provide an adequate return on capital. The managing director has asked that a review be made of the present pricing and marketing policies. The marketing director has completed this review, and passes the proposals on to you for evaluation and recommendation, together with the profit and loss account for year ending 31 December 2001.

Tweed Ltd profit and loss account for year ending 31 December 2001

	(£)	(£)	(£)
Sales revenue			
(100 000 jumpers at £10)			1 000 000
Factory cost of goods sold:			
Direct materials	100 000		
Direct labour	350 000		
Variable factory overheads	60 000		
Fixed factory overheads	220 000	730 000	
Administration overhead		140 000	
Selling and distribution overhead			
Sales commission (2% of sales)	20 000		
Delivery costs (variable per unit sold)	50 000		
Fixed costs	40 000	110 000	980 000
Profit			20 000

The information to be submitted to the managing director includes the following three proposals:

(i) To proceed on the basis of analyses of market research studies which indicate that the demand for the jumpers is such that 10% reduction in selling price would increase demand by 40%.

(ii) To proceed with an enquiry that the marketing director has had from a mail order company about the possibility of purchasing 50 000 units annually if the selling price is right. The mail order company would transport the jumpers from Tweed Ltd to its own warehouse, and no sales commission would be paid on these sales by Tweed Ltd. However, if an acceptable price can be negotiated, Tweed Ltd would be expected to contribute £60 000 per annum towards the cost of producing the mail order catalogue. It would also be necessary for Tweed Ltd to provide special additional packaging at a cost of £0.50 per jumper. The marketing director considers that in 2002 the sales from existing business would remain unchanged at 100 000 units, based on a selling price of £10 if the mail order contract is undertaken.

(iii) To proceed on the basis of a view by the marketing director that a 10% price reduction, together with a national advertising campaign costing £30 000 may increase sales to the maximum capacity of 160 000 jumpers.

Required:

(a) The calculation of break-even sales value based on the 2001 accounts.

(b) A financial evaluation of proposal (i) and a calculation of the number of units Tweed Ltd would require to sell at £9 each to earn the target profit of £80 000.

(c) A calculation of the minimum prices that would have to be quoted to the mail order company, first, to ensure that Tweed Ltd would, at least, break even on the mail order contract, secondly, to ensure that the same overall profit is earned as proposal (i) and, thirdly, to ensure that the overall target profit is earned.

(d) A financial evaluation of proposal (iii).

Review problems (with answers in the Student's Manual)

8.29 Intermediate: Break-even, contribution and profit–volume graph

(a) From the following information you are required to construct:

(i) a break-even chart, showing the break-even point and the margin of safety;

(ii) a chart displaying the contribution level and the profit level;

(iii) a profit–volume chart.

Sales	6000 units at £12 per unit = £72 000
Variable costs	6000 units at £7 per unit = £42 000
Fixed costs	= £20 000

(9 marks)

(b) State the purposes of each of the three charts in (a) above.

(6 marks)

(c) Outline the limitations of break-even analysis.

(5 marks)

(d) What are the advantages of graphical presentation of financial data to executives?

(2 marks)
(Total 22 marks)
AAT

8.30 Intermediate: Profit–volume graph and changes in sales mix

A company produces and sells two products with the following costs:

	Product X	Product Y
Variable costs (per £ of sales)	£0.45	£0.6
Fixed costs	£1 212 000 per period	£1 212 000

Total sales revenue is currently generated by the two products in the following proportions:

Product X	70%
Product Y	30%

Required:

(a) Calculate the break-even sales revenue per period, based on the sales mix assumed above.

(6 marks)

(b) Prepare a profit–volume chart of the above situation for sales revenue up to £4 000 000. Show on the same chart the effect of a change in the sales mix to product X 50%, product Y 50%. Clearly indicate on the chart the break-even point for each situation.

(11 marks)

(c) Of the fixed costs £455 000 are attributable to product X. Calculate the sales revenue required on product X in order to recover the attributable fixed costs and provide a net contribution of £700 000 towards general fixed costs and profit.

(5 marks)
(Total 22 marks)
ACCA Level 1 Costing

8.31 Intermediate: Break-even chart with an increase in fixed costs and incorporating expected values

A manufacturer is considering a new product which could be produced in one of two qualities – Standard or De Luxe. The following estimates have been made:

	Standard (£)	De Luxe (£)
Unit labour cost	2.00	2.50
Unit material cost	1.50	2.00
Unit packaging cost	1.00	2.00
Proposed selling price per unit	7.00	10.00
Budgeted fixed costs per period:		
0–99 999 units	200 000	250 000
100 000 and above	350 000	400 000

At the proposed selling prices, market research indicates the following demand:

Standard

Quantity	Probability
172 000	0.1
160 000	0.7
148 000	0.2

De Luxe

Quantity	Probability
195 500	0.3
156 500	0.5
109 500	0.2

You are required

(a) to draw separate break-even charts for *each* quality, showing the break-even points;

(7 marks)

(b) to comment on the position shown by the charts and what guidance they provide for management;

(3 marks)

(c) to calculate, for *each* quality, the expected unit sales, expected profits and the margin of safety;

(3 marks)

(d) using an appropriate measure of risk, to advise management which quality should be launched.

(9 marks)
(Total 22 marks)
CIMA Stage 3 Management Accounting Techniques

8.32 **Intermediate: Calculation of break-even points based on different sales mix assumptions and a product abandonment decision**

M Ltd manufactures three products which have the following revenue and costs (£ per unit).

	Product 1	2	3
Selling price	2.92	1.35	2.83
Variable costs	1.61	0.72	0.96
Fixed costs:			
Product specific	0.49	0.35	0.62
General	0.46	0.46	0.46

Unit fixed costs are based upon the following annual sales and production volumes (thousand units):

Product 1	2	3
98.2	42.1	111.8

Required:

(a) Calculate:

(i) the break-even point sales (to the nearest £ hundred) of M Ltd based on the current product mix;

(9 marks)

(ii) the number of units of Product 2 (to the nearest hundred) at the break-even point determined in (i) above;

(3 marks)

(b) Comment upon the viability of Product 2.

(8 marks)
(Total 20 marks)
ACCA Cost and Management Accounting 1

8.33 Intermediate: Calculation of break-even points and limiting factor decision-making

You are employed as an accounting technician by Smith, Williams and Jones, a small firm of accountants and registered auditors. One of your clients is Winter plc, a large department store. Judith Howarth, the purchasing director for Winter plc, has gained considerable knowledge about bedding and soft furnishings and is considering acquiring her own business.

She has recently written to you requesting a meeting to discuss the possible purchase of Brita Beds Ltd. Brita Beds has one outlet in Mytown, a small town 100 miles from where Judith works. Enclosed with her letter was Brita Beds' latest profit and loss account. This is reproduced below.

Brita Beds Ltd
Profit and loss account – year to 31 May

Sales	(units)	(£)
Model A	1 620	336 960
Model B	2 160	758 160
Model C	1 620	1 010 880
Turnover		2 106 000
Expenses	(£)	
Cost of beds	1 620 000	
Commission	210 600	
Transport	216 000	
Rates and insurance	8 450	
Light heat and power	10 000	
Assistants' salaries	40 000	
Manager's salary	40 000	2 145 050
Loss for year		39 050

Also included in the letter was the following information:

1 Brita Beds sells three types of bed, models A to C inclusive.
2 Selling prices are determined by adding 30% to the cost of beds.
3 Sales assistants receive a commission of 10% of the selling price for each bed sold.
4 The beds are delivered in consignments of 10 beds at a cost of £400 per delivery. This expense is shown as 'Transport' in the profit and loss account.
5 All other expenses are annual amounts.
6 The mix of models sold is likely to remain constant irrespective of overall sales volume.

Task 1

In preparation for your meeting with Judith Howarth, you are asked to calculate:

(a) the minimum number of beds to be sold if Brita Beds is to avoid making a loss;

(b) the minimum turnover required if Brita Beds it to avoid making a loss.

At the meeting, Judith Howarth provides you with further information:

1 The purchase price of the business is £300 000.
2 Judith has savings of £300 000 currently earning 5% interest per annum, which she can use to acquire Beta Beds.
3 Her current salary is £36 550.

To reduce costs, Judith suggests that she should take over the role of manager as the current one is about to retire. However, she does not want to take a reduction in income. Judith also tells you that she has been carrying out some market research. The results of this are as follows:

1 The number of households in Mytown is currently 44 880.
2 Brita Beds Ltd is the only outlet selling beds in Mytown.
3 According to a recent survey, 10% of households change their beds every 9 years, 60% every 10 years and 30% every 11 years.
4 The survey also suggested that there is an average of 2.1 beds per household.

Task 2
Write a letter to Judith Howarth. Your letter should:

(a) identify the profit required to compensate for the loss of salary and interest;
(b) show the number of beds to be sold to achieve that profit;
(c) calculate the likely maximum number of beds that Brita Beds would sell in a year;
(d) use your answers in (a) to (c) to justify whether or not Judith Howarth should purchase the company and become its manager;
(e) give *two* possible reasons why your estimate of the maximum annual sales volume may prove inaccurate.

On receiving your letter, Judith Howarth decides she would prefer to remain as the purchasing director for Winter plc rather than acquire Brita Beds Ltd. Shortly afterwards, you receive a telephone call from her. Judith explains that Winter plc is redeveloping its premises and that she is concerned about the appropriate sales policy for Winter's bed department while the redevelopment takes place. Although she has a statement of unit profitability, this had been prepared before the start of the redevelopment and had assumed that there would be in excess of 800 square metres of storage space available to the bed department. Storage space is critical as customers demand immediate delivery and are not prepared to wait until the new stock arrives.

The next day, Judith Howarth sends you a letter containing a copy of the original statement of profitability. This is reproduced below:

Model	**A**	**B**	**C**
Monthly demand	**35**	**45**	**20**
(beds)	**(£)**	**(£)**	**(£)**
Unit selling price	240.00	448.00	672.00
Unit cost per bed	130.00	310.00	550.00
Carriage inwards	20.00	20.00	20.00
Staff costs	21.60	40.32	60.48
Department fixed overheads	20.00	20.00	20.00
General fixed overheads	25.20	25.20	25.20
Unit profit	23.20	32.48	(3.68)
Storage required per bed (square metres)	3	4	5

In her letter she asks for your help in preparing a marketing plan which will maximize the profitability of Winter's bed department while the redevelopment takes place. To help you, she has provided you with the following additional information:

1 Currently storage space available totals 300 square metres.
2 Staff costs represent the salaries of the sales staff in the bed department. Their total cost of £3780 per month is apportioned to units on the basis of planned turnover.
3 Departmental fixed overhead of £2000 per month is directly attributable to the department and is apportioned on the number of beds planned to be sold.
4 General fixed overheads of £2520 are also apportioned on the number of beds planned to be sold. The directors of Winter plc believe this to be a fair apportionment of the store's central fixed overheads.
5 The cost of carriage inwards and the cost of beds vary directly with the number of beds purchased.

Task 3

(a) Prepare a recommended monthly sales schedule in units which will maximize the profitability of Winter plc's bed department.
(b) Calculate the profit that will be reported per month if your recommendation is implemented.

AAT Technician's Stage

8.34 Intermediate: Decision-making and non-graphical CVP analysis

Fosterjohn Press Ltd is considering launching a new monthly magazine at a selling price of £1 per copy. Sales of the magazine are expected to be 500 000 copies per month, but it is possible that the actual sales could differ quite significantly from this estimate.

Two different methods of producing the magazine are being considered and neither would involve any additional capital expenditure. The estimated production costs for each of the two methods of manufacture, together with the additional marketing and distribution costs of selling the new magazine, are summarized below:

	Method A	Method B
Variable costs	0.55 per copy	0.50 per copy
Specific fixed costs	£80 000 per month	£120 000 per month
Semi-variable costs:		

The following estimates have been obtained:

350 000 copies	£55 000 per month	£47 500 per month
450 000 copies	£65 000 per month	£52 500 per month
650 000 copies	£85 000 per month	£62 500 per month

It may be assumed that the fixed cost content of the semi-variable costs will remain constant throughout the range of activity shown.

The company currently sells a magazine covering related topics to those that will be included in the new publication and consequently it is anticipated that sales of this existing magazine will be adversely affected. It is estimated that for every ten copies sold of the new publication, sales of the existing magazine will be reduced by one copy.

Sales and cost data of the existing magazine are shown below:

Sales	220 000 copies per month
Selling price	0.85 per copy
Variable costs	0.35 per copy
Specific fixed costs	£80 000 per month

Required:

(a) Calculate, for each production method, the net increase in company profits which will result from the introduction of the new magazine, at each of the following levels of activity:

500 000 copies per month
400 000 copies per month
600 000 copies per month

(12 marks)

(b) Calculate, for each production method, the amount by which sales volume of the new magazine could decline from the anticipated 500 000 copies per month, before the company makes no additional profit from the introduction of the new publication.

(6 marks)

(c) Briefly identify any conclusions which may be drawn from your calculations.

(4 marks)

(Total 22 marks)

ACCA Foundation Costing

8.35 Intermediate: Decision-making and non-graphical CVP analysis

Mr Belle has recently developed a new improved video cassette and shown below is a summary of a report by a firm of management consultants on the sales potential and production costs of the new cassette.

Sales potential: The sales volume is difficult to predict and will vary with the price, but it is reasonable to assume that at a selling price of £10 per cassette, sales would be between 7500 and 10 000 units per month. Alternatively, if the selling price was reduced to £9 per cassette, sales would be between 12 000 and 18 000 units per month.

Production costs: If production is maintained at or below 10 000 units per month, then variable manufacturing costs would be approximately £8.25 per cassette and fixed costs £12 125 per month. However, if production is planned to exceed 10 000 units per month, then variable costs would be reduced to £7.75 per cassette, but the fixed costs would increase to £16 125 per month.

Mr Belle has been charged £2000 for the report by the management consultants and, in addition, he has incurred £3000 development costs on the new cassette.

If Mr Belle decides to produce and sell the new cassette it will be necessary for him to use factory premises which he owns, but are leased to a colleague for a rental of £400 per month. Also he will resign from his current post in an electronics firm where he is earning a salary of £1000 per month.

Required:

(a) Identify in the question an example of

(i) an opportunity cost,

(ii) a sunk cost.

(3 marks)

(b) Making whatever calculations you consider appropriate, analyse the report from the consultants and advise Mr Belle of the potential profitability of the alternatives shown in the report.

Any assumptions considered necessary or matters which may require further investigation or comment should be clearly stated.

(19 marks)

(Total 22 marks)

ACCA Level 1 Costing

8.36 **Advanced: Decision-making and CVP analysis**

Bruno Ltd is considering proposals for design changes in one of a range of soft toys. The proposals are as follows:

(a) Eliminate some of the decorative stitching from the toy.

(b) Use plastic eyes instead of glass eyes in the toys (two eyes per toy).

(c) Change the filling material used. It is proposed that scrap fabric left over from the body manufacture be used instead of the synthetic material which is currently used.

The design change proposals have been considered by the management team and the following information has been gathered:

(i) Plastic eyes will cost £15 per hundred whereas the existing glass eyes cost £20 per hundred. The plastic eyes will be more liable to damage on insertion into the toy. It is estimated that scrap plastic eyes will be 10% of the quantity issued from stores as compared to 5% of issues of glass eyes at present.

(ii) The synthetic filling material costs £80 per tonne. One tonne of filling is sufficient for 2000 soft toys.

(iii) Scrap fabric to be used as filling material will need to be cut into smaller pieces before use and this will cost £0.05 per soft toy. There is sufficient scrap fabric for the purpose.

(iv) The elimination of the decorative stitching is expected to reduce the appeal of the product, with an estimated fall in sales by 10% from the current level. It is not felt that the change in eyes or filling material will adversely affect sales volume. The elimination of the stitching will reduce production costs by £0.60 per soft toy.

(v) The current sales level of the soft toy is 300 000 units per annum. Apportioned fixed costs per annum are £450 000. The net profit per soft toy at the current sales level is £3.

Required:

(a) Using the information given in the question, prepare an analysis which shows the estimated effect on annual profit if all three proposals are implemented, and which enables management to check whether each proposal will achieve an annual target profit increase of £25 000. The proposals for plastic eyes and the use of scrap fabric should be evaluated after the stitching elimination proposal has been evaluated.

(12 marks)

(b) Calculate the percentage reduction in sales due to the stitching elimination at which the implementation of all three design change proposals would result in the same total profit from the toy as that earned before the implementation of the changes in design.

(8 marks)

(c) Prepare a report which indicates additional information which should be obtained before a final decision is taken with regard to the implementation of the proposals.

(10 marks)

(Total 30 marks)

ACCA Level 2 Cost and Management Accounting II

8.37 Advanced: Cost–volume–profit analysis in a hospital

A private hospital is organised into separate medical units which offer specialised nursing care (e.g. maternity unit, paediatric unit). Figures for the paediatric unit for the year to 31 May 2001 have just become available. For the year in question the paediatric unit charged patients £200 per patient day for nursing care and £4.4m in revenue was earned.

Costs of running the unit consist of variable costs, direct staffing costs and allocated fixed costs. The charges for variable costs such as catering and laundry are based on the number of patient days spent in hospital. Staffing costs are established from the personnel requirements applicable to particular levels of patient days. Charges for fixed costs such as security, administration etc. are based on bed capacity, currently 80 beds.

The number of beds available to be occupied is regarded as bed capacity and this is agreed and held constant for the whole year. There was an agreement that a bed capacity of 80 beds would apply to the paediatric unit for the 365 days of the year to 31 May 2001.

The tables below show the variable, staffing and fixed costs applicable to the paediatric unit for the year to 31 Mary 2001.

Variable costs (based on patient days)	**£**
Catering	450 000
Laundry	150 000
Pharmacy	500 000
	1 100 000

Staffing costs

Each speciality recruits its own nurses, supervisors and assistants. The staffing requirements for the paediatric unit are based on the actual patient days, see the following table:

Patient Days per annum	Supervisors	Nurses	Assistants
up to 20 500	4	10	20
20 500 to 23 000	4	13	24
Over 23 000	4	15	28

The annual costs of employment are: supervisors £22 000 each, nurses £16 000 each and assistants £12 000 each.

Fixed costs (based on bed capacity)	£
Administration	850 000
Security	80 000
Rent and property	720 000
	1 650 000

During the year to 31 May 2001 the paediatric unit operated a 100% occupancy (i.e. all 80 beds occupied) for 100 days of the year. In fact, the demand on these days was for a least 20 beds more.

As a consequence of this, in the budget for the following year to 31 May 2002, an increase in the bed capacity has been agreed. 20 extra beds will be contracted for the whole of the year. It is assumed that the 100 beds will be fully occupied for 100 days, rather than being restricted to 80 beds on those days. An increase of 10% in employment costs for the year to 31 May 2002, due to wage rate rises, will occur for all personnel. The revenue per patient day, all other cost factors and the remaining occupancy will be the same as the year to 31 May 2001.

Required:

(a) Determine, for the year to 31 May 2001, the actual number of patient-days, the bed occupancy percentage, the net profit/loss and the break-even number(s) of patient days for the paediatric unit.

(6 marks)

(b) Determine the budget for the year to 31 May 2002 showing the revised number of patient-days, the bed occupancy percentage, the net profit/loss and the number of patient-days required to achieve the same profit/loss as computed in (a) above.

(5 marks)

(c) Comment on your findings from (a) and (b) offering advice to the management of the unit.

(6 marks)

(d) A business or operating unit can have both financial and social objectives and at times these can be in conflict. Briefly explain and give an example.

(3 marks)

(20 marks)

ACCA Paper 8 Managerial Finance

8.38 Advanced: CVP analysis and decision-making including a graphical presentation

In the last quarter it is estimated that YNQ will have produced and sold 20 000 units of their main product by the end of the year. At this level of activity it is estimated that the average unit cost will be:

	(£)
Direct material	30
Direct labour	10
Overhead: Fixed	10
Variable	10
	60

This is in line with the standards set at the start of the year. The management accountant of YNQ is now preparing the budget for the next year. He has incorporated into his preliminary calculations the following expected cost increases:

Raw material:	price increase of 20%
Direct labour:	wage rate increase of 5%
Variable overhead:	increase of 5%
Fixed overhead:	increase of 25%

The production manager believes that if a cheaper grade of raw material were to be used, this would enable the direct material cost per unit to be kept to £31.25 for the next year. The cheaper material would, however, lead to a reject rate estimated at 5% of the completed output and it would be necessary to introduce an inspection stage at the end of the manufacturing process to identify the faulty items. The cost of this inspection process would be £40 000 per year (including £10 000 allocation of existing factory overhead).

Established practice has been to reconsider the product's selling price at the time the budget is being prepared. The selling price is normally determined by adding a mark-up of 50% to unit cost. On this basis the product's selling price for last year has been £90 but the sales manager is worried about the implications of continuing the cost-plus 50% rule for next year. He estimates that demand for the product varies with price as follows:

Price:	£80	£84	£88	£90	£92	£96	£100
Demand (000)	25	23	21	20	19	17	15

(a) You are required to decide whether YNQ should use the regular or the cheaper grade of material and to calculate the best price for the product, the optimal level of production and the profit that this should yield. Comment briefly on the sensitivity of the solution to possible errors in the estimates. *(14 marks)*

(b) Indicate how one might obtain the answer to part (a) from an appropriately designed cost–volume–profit graph. You should design such a graph as part of your answer but the graph need not be drawn to scale providing that it demonstrates the main features of the approach that you would use. *(8 marks)*

(Total 22 marks)

ACCA Level 2 Management Accounting

8.39 Advanced: CVP analysis and changes in product mix

Dingbat Ltd is considering renting additional factory space to make two products, Thingone and Thingtwo. You are the company's management accountant and have prepared the following monthly budget:

	Thingone	Thingtwo	Total
Sales (units)	4000	2000	6000
	(£)	(£)	(£)
Sales revenue	80 000	100 000	180 000
Variable material and labour costs	(60 000)	(62 000)	(122 000)
Fixed production overheads (allocated on direct labour hours)	(9 900)	(18 000)	(27 900)
Fixed administration overheads (allocated on sales value)	(1 600)	(2 000)	(3 600)
Profit	8 500	18 000	26 500

The fixed overheads in the budget can only be avoided if neither product is manufactured. Facilities are fully interchangeable between products.

As an alternative to the manual production process assumed in the budget, Dingbat Ltd has the option of adopting a computer-aided process. This process would cut variable costs of production by 15% and increase fixed costs by £12 000 per month.

The management of Dingbat Ltd is confident about the cost forecasts, but there is considerable uncertainty over demand for the new products.

The management believes the company will have to depart from its usual cash sales policy in order to sell Thingtwo. An average of three months' credit would be given and bad debts and administration costs would probably amount to 4% of sales revenue for this product.

Both products will be sold at the prices assumed in the budget. Dingbat Ltd has a cost of capital of 2% per month. No stocks will be held.

Requirements:

(a) Calculate the sales revenues at which operations will break-even for each process (manual and computer-aided) and calculate the sales revenues at which Dingbat Ltd will be indifferent between the two processes:

(i) if Thingone alone is sold;

(4 marks)

(ii) if Thingone and Thingtwo units are sold in the ratio 4:1, with Thingtwo being sold on credit.

(6 marks)

(b) Explain the implications of your results with regard to the financial viability of Thingone and Thingtwo.

(5 marks)

(c) Discuss the major factors to be considered in the pricing and sales forecasting for new productions.

(10 marks)

(Total 25 marks)

ICAEW P2 Management Accounting

Measuring relevant costs and revenues for decision-making

9

In this chapter we are going to focus on measuring costs and benefits for non-routine decisions. The term **'special studies'** is sometimes used to refer to decisions that are not routinely made at frequent intervals. In other words, special studies are undertaken whenever a decision needs to be taken; such as discontinuing a product or a channel of distribution, making a component within the company or buying from an outside supplier, introducing a new product and replacing existing equipment. Special studies require only those costs and revenues that are relevant to the specific alternative courses of action to be reported. The term **'decision-relevant approach'** is used to describe the specific costs and benefits that should be reported for special studies. We shall assume that the objective when examining alternative courses of action is to maximize the present value of future net cash inflows. The calculations of present values will be explained in

LEARNING OBJECTIVES

After studying this chapter, you should be able to:

- distinguish between relevant and irrelevant costs and revenues;
- explain the importance of qualitative factors;
- distinguish between the relevant and irrelevant costs and revenues for the five decision-making problems described;
- describe the key concept that should be applied for presenting information for product-mix decisions when capacity constraints apply;
- explain why the book value of equipment is irrelevant when making equipment replacement decisions;
- describe the opportunity cost concept;
- explain the misconceptions relating to relevant costs and revenues.

Chapter 13. We also assume for this chapter that future costs and benefits are known with certainty; decision-making under conditions of uncertainty will be considered in Chapter 12. In Chapters 13 and 14 we shall concentrate on the special studies required for capital investment decisions.

It is important that you note at this stage that a decision-relevant approach adopts whichever planning time horizon the decision maker considers appropriate for a given situation. However, it is important not to focus excessively on the short term, since the objective is to maximize long-term net cash inflows. We begin by introducing the concept of relevant cost and applying this principle to special studies relating to the following:

1 special selling price decisions;
2 product-mix decisions when capacity constraints exist;
3 decisions on replacement of equipment;
4 outsourcing (make or buy) decisions;
5 discontinuation decisions.

We shall then consider in more detail the specific problems that arise in assessing the relevant costs of materials and labour.

The aim of this chapter is to provide you with an understanding of the principles that should be used to identify relevant costs and revenues. It is assumed that relevant costs can be easily measured but, in reality, some indirect relevant costs can be difficult to measure. The measurement of indirect relevant costs for decision-making using activity-based-costing techniques will be examined in the next chapter.

The meaning of relevance

The **relevant costs** and benefits required for decision-making are only those that will be affected by the decision. Costs and benefits that are independent of a decision are obviously not relevant and need not be considered when making that decision. The relevant financial inputs for decision-making purposes are therefore *future* cash flows, which will differ between the various alternatives being considered. In other words, only **differential** (or **incremental**) **cash flows** should be taken into account, and cash flows that will be the same for all alternatives are irrelevant. Since decision-making is concerned with choosing between future alternative courses of action, and nothing can be done to alter the past, then past costs (also known as sunk costs) are not relevant for decision-making. Consider a situation where an individual is uncertain as to whether he or she should purchase a monthly rail ticket to travel to work or use their car. Assuming that the individual will keep the car, whether or not he or she travels to work by train, the cost of the road fund licence and insurance will be irrelevant, since these costs remain the same irrespective of the mode of travel. The cost of petrol will, however, be relevant, since this cost will vary depending on which method of transport is chosen.

You will see that both depreciation and the allocation of common fixed costs are irrelevant for decision-making. Both are sunk costs. Depreciation represents the allocation of past costs to future periods. The original cost is unavoidable and common to all alternatives. Therefore it is irrelevant. Similarly, any allocation of common fixed costs will be irrelevant for decision-making since the choice of allocation method does not affect the level of cost to the company. It merely results in a redistribution of the same sunk cost between cost objects (e.g. products or locations within the organization).

Importance of qualitative factors

In many situations it is difficult to quantify in monetary terms all the important elements of a decision. Those factors that cannot be expressed in monetary terms are classified as qualitative factors. A decline in employee morale that results from redundancies arising from a closure decision is an example of a qualitative factor. It is essential that qualitative factors be brought to the attention of management during the decision-making process, since otherwise there may be a danger that a wrong decision will be made. For example, the cost of manufacturing a component internally may be more expensive than purchasing from an outside supplier. However, the decision to purchase from an outside supplier could result in the closing down of the company's facilities for manufacturing the component. The effect of such a decision might lead to redundancies and a decline in employees' morale, which could affect future output. In addition, the company will now be at the mercy of the supplier who might seek to increase prices on subsequent contracts and/or may not always deliver on time. The company may not then be in a position to meet customers' requirements. In turn, this could result in a loss of customer goodwill and a decline in future sales.

It may not be possible to quantify in monetary terms the effect of a decline in employees' morale or loss of customer goodwill, but the accountant in such circumstances should present the relevant quantifiable financial information and draw attention to those qualitative items that may have an impact on future profitability. In circumstances such as those given in the above example management must estimate the likelihood of the supplier failing to meet the company's demand for future supplies and the likely effect on customer goodwill if there is a delay in meeting orders. If the component can be obtained from many suppliers and repeat orders for the company's products are unlikely then the company may give little weighting to these qualitative factors. Alternatively, if the component can be obtained from only one supplier and the company relies heavily on repeat sales to existing customers then the qualitative factors will be of considerable importance. In the latter situation the company may consider that the quantifiable cost savings from purchasing the component from an outside supplier are insufficient to cover the risk of the qualitative factors occurring.

If it is possible qualitative factors should be expressed in quantitative non-financial terms. For example, the increase in percentage of on-time deliveries from a new production process, the reduction in customer waiting time from a decision to invest in additional cash dispensing machines and the reduction in the number of units of defective output delivered to customers arising from an investment in quality inspection are all examples of qualitative factors that can be expressed in non-financial numerical terms.

Let us now move on to apply the relevant cost approach to a variety of decision-making problems. We shall concentrate on measuring the financial outcomes but do remember that they do not always provide the full story. Qualitative factors should also be taken into account in the decision-making process.

Special pricing decisions

Special pricing decisions relate to pricing decisions outside the main market. Typically they involve one-time only orders or orders at a price below the prevailing market price. Consider the information presented in Example 9.1.

At first glance it looks as if the order should be rejected since the proposed selling price is less than the total cost of £33. A study of the cost estimates, however, indicates that during the next quarter, the direct labour, manufacturing (i.e. non-variable) fixed

EXAMPLE 9.1

The Caledonian Company is a manufacturer of clothing that sells its output directly to clothing retailers. One of its departments manufactures jumpers. The department has a production capacity of 50 000 jumpers per month. Because of the liquidation of one of its major customers the company has excess capacity. For the next quarter current monthly production and sales volume is expected to be 35 000 jumpers at a selling price of £40 per jumper. Expected costs and revenues for the next month at an activity level of 35 000 jumpers are as follows:

	(£)	(£)
Direct labour	420 000	12
Direct materials	280 000	8
Variable manufacturing overheads	70 000	2
Manufacturing non-variable overheads	280 000	8
Marketing and distribution costs	105 000	3
Total costs	1 155 000	33
Sales	1 400 000	40
Profit	245 000	7

Caledonian is expecting an upsurge in demand and considers that the excess capacity is temporary. A company in the leisure industry has offered to buy for its staff 3000 jumpers each month for the next three months at a price of £20 per jumper. The company would collect the jumpers from Caledonian's factory and thus no marketing and distribution costs will be incurred. No subsequent sales to this customer are anticipated. The company would require its company logo inserting on the jumper and Caledonian has predicted that this will cost £1 per jumper. Should Caledonian accept the offer from the company?

overheads and the marketing and distribution costs will remain the same irrespective of whether or not the order is accepted. These costs are therefore irrelevant for this decision. The direct material costs, variable manufacturing overheads and the cost of adding the leisure company's logo will be different if the order is accepted. Hence they are relevant for making the decision. The financial information required for the decision is shown in Exhibit 9.1.

You can see from Exhibit 9.1 that different approaches can be used for presenting relevant cost and revenue information. Information can be presented that includes both relevant and irrelevant costs or revenues for all alternatives under consideration. If this approach is adopted the *same* amount for the irrelevant items (i.e. those items that remain unchanged as a result of the decision which are direct labour, manufacturing non-variable overheads and the marketing and distribution costs in our example) are included for all alternatives, thus making them irrelevant to the decision. This information is presented in columns (1) and (2) in Exhibit 9.1. Alternatively, you can present cost information in columns (1) and (2) that excludes the irrelevant costs and revenues because they are identical for both alternatives. A third alternative is to present only the relevant (differential) costs. This approach is shown in column (3) of Exhibit 9.1. Note that column (3) represents the difference between columns (1) and (2). All of the methods show that the company is better off by £27 000 *per month* if the order is accepted.

EXHIBIT 9.1
Evaluation of three month order from the company in the leisure industry

	(1) Do not accept order (£ per month)	(2) Accept order (£ per month)	(3) Difference (relevant costs) (£ per month)
Direct labour	420 000	420 000	
Direct materials	280 000	304 000	24 000
Variable manufacturing overheads	70 000	76 000	6 000
Manufacturing non-variable overheads	280 000	280 000	
Inserting company logo		3 000	3 000
Marketing and distribution costs	105 000	105 000	
Total costs	1 155 000	1 188 000	33 000
Sales	1 400 000	1 460 000	60 000
Profit per month	245 000	272 000	27 000

Four important factors must be considered before recommending acceptance of the order. Most of these relate to the assumption that there are no long-run implications from accepting the offer at a selling price of £20 per jumper. First, it is assumed that the future selling price will not be affected by selling some of the output at a price below the going market price. If this assumption is incorrect then competitors may engage in similar practices of reducing their selling prices in an attempt to unload spare capacity. This may lead to a fall in the market price, which in turn would lead to a fall in profits from future sales. The loss of future profits may be greater than the short-term gain obtained from accepting special orders at prices below the existing market price. Given that Caledonian has found a customer in a different market from its normal market it is unlikely that the market price would be affected. However, if the customer had been within Caledonian's normal retail market there would be a real danger that the market price would be affected. Secondly, the decision to accept the order prevents the company from accepting other orders that may be obtained during the period at the going price. In other words, it is assumed that no better opportunities will present themselves during the period. Thirdly, it is assumed that the company has unused resources that have no alternative uses that will yield a contribution to profits in excess of £27 000 *per month*. Finally, it is assumed that the fixed costs are unavoidable for the period under consideration. In other words, we assume that the direct labour force and the fixed overheads cannot be reduced in the short term, or that they are to be retained for an upsurge in demand, which is expected to occur in the longer term.

It is important that great care is taken in presenting financial information for decision-making. For stock valuation, external financial regulations require that the jumpers must be valued at their manufacturing cost of £30. Using this cost would lead to the incorrect decision being taken. For decision-making purposes only future costs that will be relevant to the decision should be included. Costs that have been computed for meeting stock valuation requirements must not therefore be used for decision-making purposes.

When you are trying to establish which costs are relevant to a particular decision you may find that some costs will be relevant in one situation but irrelevant in another. In Example 9.1 we assumed that direct labour was not a relevant cost. The company wishes to retain the direct labour for an expected upsurge in demand and therefore the direct labour cost will be same whether or not the offer is accepted. Alternatively, Caledonian may have had an agreement with its workforce that entitled them to at least three months' notice in the event of any redundancies. Therefore, even if Caledonian was not expecting an upsurge in demand direct labour would have been a fixed cost within the three month time horizon. But now let us consider what the relevant cost would be if direct labour consisted of casual labour who are hired on a daily basis. In this situation direct labour will be a relevant cost, since the labour costs will not be incurred if the order is not accepted.

The identification of relevant costs depends on the circumstances. In one situation a cost may be relevant, but in another the same cost may not be relevant. It is not therefore possible to provide a list of costs that would be relevant in particular situations. In each situation you should follow the principle that the relevant costs are future costs that differ among alternatives. The important question to ask when determining the relevant cost is: What difference will it make? The accountant must be aware of all the issues relating to a decision and ascertain full details of the changes that will result, and then proceed to select the relevant financial information to present to management.

Evaluation of a longer-term order

In Example 9.1 we focused on a short-term time horizon of three months. Capacity cannot easily be altered in the short term and therefore direct labour and fixed costs are likely to be irrelevant costs with respect to short-term decisions. In the longer-term, however, it may be possible to reduce capacity and spending on fixed costs and direct labour. Let us now assume that for Example 9.1 that Caledonian's assumption about an expected upsurge in the market proved to be incorrect and that it estimates that demand in the foreseeable future will remain at 35 000 jumpers *per month*. Given that it has a productive capacity of 50 000 jumpers it has sought to develop a long-term market for the unutilized capacity of 15 000 jumpers. As a result of its experience with the one-time special order with the company in the leisure industry, Caledonian has sought to develop a market with other companies operating in the leisure industry. Assume that this process has resulted in potential customers that are prepared to enter into a contractual agreement for a three year period for a supply of 15 000 jumpers *per month* at an agreed price of £25 per jumper. The cost of inserting the insignia required by each customer would remain unchanged at £1 per jumper. No marketing and distribution costs would be incurred with any of the orders. Caledonian considers that it has investigated all other possibilities to develop a market for the excess capacity. Should it enter into contractual agreements with the suppliers at £25 per jumper?

If Caledonian does not enter into contractual agreement with the suppliers the direct labour required will be made redundant. No redundancy costs will be involved. Further investigations indicate that manufacturing non-variable costs of £70 000 *per month* could be saved if a decision was made to reduce capacity by 15 000 jumpers per month. For example, the rental contracts for some of the machinery will not be renewed. Also some savings will be made in supervisory labour and support costs. Savings in marketing and distribution costs would be £20 000 *per month*. Assume also that if the capacity was reduced factory rearrangements would result in part of the facilities being rented out at £25 000 *per month*. Note that because variable costs vary directly with changes in volume, direct materials and variable manufacturing overheads will decline by 30% if capacity is reduced by 30% from 50 000 to 35 000 jumpers.

We are now faced with a longer-term decision where some of the costs that were fixed in the short term can be changed in the longer term. The appropriate financial data for the analysis is shown in Exhibit 9.2. Note that in Exhibit 9.2 the information for an activity of 35 000 jumpers incorporates the changes arising from the capacity reduction whereas the information presented for the same activity level in Exhibit 9.1 is based on the assumption that capacity will be maintained at 50 000 jumpers. Therefore the direct labour cost in

Exhibit 9.1 is £420 000 because it represents the labour required to meet demand at full capacity. If capacity is permanently reduced from 50 000 to 35 000 jumpers (i.e. a 30% reduction) it is assumed that direct labour costs will be reduced by 30% from £420 000 to £294 000. This is the amount shown in Exhibit 9.2.

A comparison of the monthly outcomes reported in columns (1) and (2) of Exhibit 9.2 indicates that the company is better off by £31 000 *per month* if it reduces capacity to 35 000 jumpers, assuming that there are no qualitative factors. Instead of presenting the data in columns (1) and (2) you can present only the differential (relevant) costs and revenues shown in column (3). This approach also indicates that the company is better off by £31 000 per month. Note that the entry in column (3) of £25 000 is the lost revenues from the rent of the unutilized capacity if the company accepts the orders. This represents the opportunity cost of accepting the orders. We shall discuss opportunity costs later in the chapter.

Where the choice of one course of action requires that an alternative course of action is given up, the financial benefits that are forgone or sacrificed are known as **opportunity costs**. In other words, opportunity costs represent the lost contribution to profits arising from the best use of the alternative forgone. Opportunity costs only arise when resources are scarce and have alternative uses. Thus, in our illustration the capacity allocated to producing 15 000 jumpers results in an opportunity cost (i.e. the lost revenues from the rent of the capacity) of £25 000 per month.

In Exhibit 9.2 all of the costs and revenues are relevant to the decision because some of the costs that were fixed in the short term could be changed in the longer term. Therefore whether or not a cost is relevant often depends on the time horizon under consideration. Thus it is important that the information presented for decision-making relates to the appropriate time horizon. If inappropriate time horizons are selected there is a danger that misleading information will be presented. Remember that our aim should always be to maximize *long-term* net cash inflows.

Dangers of focusing excessively on a short-run time horizon

The problems arising from not taking into account the long-term consequences of accepting business that covers short-term incremental costs have been discussed by Kaplan (1990). He illustrates a situation where a company that makes pens has excess capacity, and a salesperson negotiates an order for 20 000 purple pens (a variation to the pens that are currently being made) at a price in excess of the incremental cost. In response to the question 'Should the order be accepted?' Kaplan states:

> *take the order. The economics of making the purple pen with the excess capacity are overwhelming. There's no question that if you have excess capacity, the workers are all hired, the technology exists, and you have the product designed, and someone says, let's get an order for 20 000 purple pens, then the relevant consideration is price less the material cost of the purple pens. Don't even worry about the labour cost because you're going to pay them anyway. The second thing we tell them, however, is that they are never to ask us this question again ... Suppose that every month managers see that they have excess capacity to make 20 000 more pens, and salespeople are calling in special orders for turquoise pens, for purple pens with red caps, and other such customised products. Why not accept all these orders based on short-run contribution margin? The answer is that if they do, then costs that appear fixed in the short-term will start to increase, or expenses currently being incurred will be incapable of being reduced (p. 14).*

Kaplan stresses that by utilizing the unused capacity to increase the range of products produced (i.e. different variations of pens in the above example), the production process

EXHIBIT 9.2
Evaluation of orders for the unutilized capacity over a three year time horizon

Monthly sales and production in units	(1) Do not accept orders 35 000 (£)	(2) Accept the orders 50 000 (£)	(3) Difference (relevant costs) 15 000 (£)
Direct labour	294 000	420 000	126 000
Direct materials	280 000	400 000	120 000
Variable manufacturing overheads	70 000	100 000	30 000
Manufacturing non-variable overheads	210 000	280 000	70 000
Inserting company logo		15 000	15 000
Marketing and distribution costs	85 000	105 000	20 000
Total costs	939 000	1 320 000	381 000
Revenues from rental of facilities	25 000		25 000
Sales revenues	1 400 000	1 775 000	(375 000)
Profit per month	486 000	455 000	31 000

becomes more complex and consequently the fixed costs of managing the additional complexity will eventually increase. Long-term considerations should therefore always be taken into account when special pricing decisions are being evaluated. In particular, there is a danger that a series of special orders will be evaluated independently as short-term decisions. Consequently, those resources that cannot be adjusted in the short term will be treated as irrelevant for each decision. However, the effect of accepting a series of consecutive special orders over several periods constitutes a long-term decision. If special orders are always evaluated as short-term decisions a situation can arise whereby the decision to reduce capacity is continually deferred. If demand from normal business is considered to be permanently insufficient to utilize existing capacity then a long-term capacity decision is required. This should be based on the long-term approach as illustrated in Exhibit 9.2 and not the short-term approach illustrated in Exhibit 9.1. In other words, this decision should be based on a comparison of the relevant revenues and costs arising from using the excess capacity for special orders with the capacity costs that can be eliminated if the capacity is reduced.

Product-mix decisions when capacity constraints exist

In the short term sales demand may be in excess of current productivity capacity. For example, output may be restricted by a shortage of skilled labour, materials, equipment or space. When sales demand is in excess of a company's productive capacity, the resources responsible for limiting the output should be identified. These scarce resources are known as **limiting factors**. Within a short-term time period it is unlikely that production constraints can be removed and additional resources acquired. Where limiting factors apply, profit is maximized when the greatest possible contribution to profit is obtained each time the scarce or limiting factor is used. Consider Example 9.2.

In this situation the company's ability to increase its output and profits/net cash inflows is limited in the short term by the availability of machine capacity. You may think, when first looking at the available information, that the company should give top priority to

EXAMPLE 9.2

Rhine Autos is a major European producer of automobiles. A department within one of its divisions supplies component parts to firms operating within the automobile industry. The following information is provided relating to the anticipated demand and the productive capacity for the next quarter in respect of three components that are manufactured within the department:

	Component X	Component Y	Component Z
Contribution per unit of output	£12	£10	£6
Machine hours required per unit of output	6 hours	2 hours	1 hour
Estimated sales demand	2 000 units	2000 units	2000 units
Required machine hours for the quarter	12 000 hours	4000 hours	2000 hours

Because of the breakdown of one of its special purpose machines capacity is limited to 12 000 machine hours for the period, and this is insufficient to meet total sales demand. You have been asked to advise on the mix of products that should be produced during the period.

producing component X, since this yields the highest contribution per unit sold, but this assumption would be incorrect. To produce each unit of component X, 6 scarce machine hours are required, whereas components Y and Z use only 2 hours and 1 hour respectively of scarce machine hours. By concentrating on producing components Y and Z, the company can sell 2000 units of each component and still have some machine capacity left to make component X. If the company concentrates on producing component X it will only be able to meet the maximum sales demand of component X, and will have no machine capacity left to make components Y or Z. The way in which you should determine the optimum production plan is to calculate the contribution per limiting factor for each component and then to rank the components in order of profitability based on this calculation.

Using the figures in the present example the result would be as follows:

	Component X	Component Y	Component Z
Contribution per unit	£12	£10	£6
Machine hours required	6 hours	2 hours	1 hour
Contribution per machine hour	£2	£5	£6
Ranking	3	2	1

The company can now allocate the 12 000 scarce machine hours in accordance with the above rankings. The first choice should be to produce as much as possible of component Z. The maximum sales are 2000 units, and production of this quantity will result in the use of 2000 machine hours, thus leaving 10 000 unused hours. The second choice should be to produce as much of component Y as possible. The maximum sales of 2000 units will result in the use of 4000 machine hours. Production of both components Z and Y require 6000 machine hours, leaving a balance of 6000 hours for the production of component X, which will enable 1000 units of component X to be produced.

We can now summarize the allocation of the scarce machine hours:

Production	Machine hours used	Balance of machine hours available
2000 units of Z	2000	10 000
2000 units of Y	4000	6 000
1000 units of X	6000	—

This production programme results in the following total contribution:

	(£)
2000 units of Z at £6 per unit contribution	12 000
2000 units of Y at £10 per unit contribution	20 000
1000 units of X at £12 per unit contribution	12 000
Total contribution	44 000

Always remember that it is necessary to consider other qualitative factors before the production programme is determined. For example, customer goodwill may be lost causing a fall in future sales if the company is unable to supply all three products to, say, 150 of its regular customers. Difficulties may arise in applying this procedure when there is more than one scarce resource. It could not be applied if, for example, labour hours were also scarce and the contribution per labour hour resulted in component Y being ranked first, followed by components X and Z. In this type of situation, where more than one resource is scarce, it is necessary to resort to linear programming methods in order to determine the optimal production programme. The application of linear programming to decision-making when there are several scarce resources will be examined in Chapter 26.

The approach described above can also be applied in non-manufacturing organizations. For example, in a major UK retail store display space is the limiting factor. The store maximizes its short-term profits by allocating shelving space on the basis of contribution per metre of shelving space. For an illustration of a product-mix decision with a capacity constraint within an agricultural setting you should refer to the solution to Review problem 9.33.

Finally, it is important that you remember that the approach outlined in this section applies only to those situations where capacity constraints cannot be removed in the short term. In the longer term additional resources should be acquired if the contribution from the extra capacity exceeds the cost of acquisition. You should note that the principles described in this section have also been applied to a new approach to production management known as the **theory of constraints** and **throughput accounting**. This approach is described in the appendix of this chapter.

Replacement of equipment – the irrelevance of past costs

Replacement of equipment is a capital investment or long-term decision that requires the use of discounted cash flow procedures. These procedures are discussed in detail in Chapter 13, but one aspect of asset replacement decisions which we will consider at this stage is how to deal with the book value (i.e. the **written-down value**) of old equipment. This is a problem that has been known to cause difficulty, but the correct approach is to apply relevant cost principles (i.e. past or sunk costs are irrelevant for decision-making). We shall now use Example 9.3 to illustrate the irrelevance of the book value of old equipment in a replacement decision. To avoid any possible confusion, it will be assumed here that £1 of cash inflow or outflow in year 1 is equivalent to £1 of cash inflow or outflow in, say, year 3. Such an assumption would in reality be incorrect and you will see why this is so in Chapter 13, but by adopting this assumption at this stage, the replacement problem can be simplified and we can focus our attention on the treatment of the book value of the old equipment in the replacement decision.

You can see from an examination of Example 9.3 that the total costs over a period of three years for each of the alternatives are as follows:

	(1) Retain present machine (£)	**(2) Buy replacement machine (£)**	**(3) Difference (relevant costs/ revenues) (£)**
Variable/incremental operating costs:			
20 000 units at £3 per unit for 3 years	180 000		
20 000 units at £2 per unit for 3 years		120 000	(60 000)
Old machine book value:			
3-year annual depreciation charge	90 000		
Lump sum write-off		90 000	
Old machine disposal value		(40 000)	(40 000)
Initial purchase price of new machine		70 000	70 000
Total cost	270 000	240 000	30 000

You can see from the above analysis that the £90 000 book value of the old machine is irrelevant to the decision. Book values are not relevant costs because they are past or sunk costs and are therefore the same for all potential courses of action. If the present machine is retained, three years' depreciation at £30 000 per annum will be written off annually whereas if the new machine is purchased the £90 000 will be written off as a lump sum if it is replaced. Note that depreciation charges for the new machine are not included in the analysis since the cost of purchasing the machine is already included in the analysis. The sum of the annual depreciation charges are equivalent to the purchase cost. Thus, including both items would amount to double counting.

The above analysis shows that the costs of operating the replacement machine are £30 000 less than the costs of operating the existing machine over the three year period. Again there are several different methods of presenting the information. They all show a £30 000 advantage in favour of replacing the machine. You can present the information shown in columns (1) and (2) above, as long as you ensure that the same amount for the irrelevant items is included for all alternatives. Instead, you can present columns (1) and (2) with the irrelevant item (i.e. the £90 000) omitted or you can present the differential items listed in column (3). However, if you adopt the latter approach you will probably find it more meaningful to restate column (3) as follows:

	(£)
Savings on variable operating costs (3 years)	60 000
Sale proceeds of existing machine	40 000
	100 000
Less purchase cost of replacement machine	70 000
Savings on purchasing replacement machine	30 000

EXAMPLE 9.3

A division within Rhine Autos purchased a machine three years ago for £180 000. Depreciation using the straight line basis, assuming a life of six years and with no salvage value, has been recorded each year in the financial accounts. The present written-down value of the equipment is £90 000 and it has a remaining life of three years. Management is considering replacing this machine with a new machine that will reduce the variable operating costs. The new machine will cost £70 000 and will have an expected life of three years with no scrap value. The variable operating costs are £3 per unit of output for the old machine and £2 per unit for the new machine. It is expected that both machines will be operated at a capacity of 20 000 units per annum. The sales revenues from the output of both machines will therefore be identical. The current disposal or sale value of the old machine is £40 000 and it will be zero in three years time.

Sometimes managers may make incorrect decisions, and not adopt the relevant cost approach, because of the method that is used to measure managerial performance. This is a major problem area for replacement decisions. For *profit measurement*, rather than the £90 000 book value being written off as a lump sum, it will be offset against the £40 000 sale proceeds of the old machine and written off as a loss on sale of £50 000. Therefore, if the machine is replaced the manager will be faced in the year of replacement with a profit report that includes a loss on sale of £50 000. The manager might be reluctant to take action to publicize such an event, particularly if he, or she, authorized the initial purchase. Furthermore, depreciation for the new machine may also be recorded as an expense in the year of purchase. The overall effect will be that significantly more expenses, and thus lower profits, will be recorded in the year of purchase if the manager makes the correct decision and replaces the machine. The adverse impact on short-term profits of purchasing the new machine will be counter-balanced in later years but if the manager places greater emphasis on short-term results the performance measurement system might motivate him, or her, not to replace the machine.

At this point in time our objective is not to focus on performance measurement. We shall look at how such problems might be overcome when we look at performance measurement in Chapter 20. The important point you should note is that only relevant costs should be incorporated into a financial appraisal. Note that the loss on sale is made up of the lump sum depreciation write-off and the sale proceeds. Only the latter is relevant, and depreciation and any profit or losses on sale of replaced assets, are irrelevant for replacement decisions.

Outsourcing and make or buy decisions

Outsourcing is the process of obtaining goods or services from outside suppliers instead of producing the same goods or providing the same services within the organization. Decisions on whether to produce components or provide services within the organization or to acquire them from outside suppliers are called outsourcing or make or buy decisions. Many organizations outsource some of their activities such as their payroll and purchasing functions or the purchase of speciality components. Increasingly municipal local services such as waste disposal, highways and property maintenance are being outsourced. Consider the information presented in Example 9.4 (Case A).

EXAMPLE 9.4

Case A

One of the divisions within Rhine Autos is currently negotiating with another supplier regarding outsourcing component A that it manufactures. The division currently manufactures 10 000 units per annum of the component. The costs currently assigned to the components are as follows:

	Total costs of producing 10 000 components (£)	Unit cost (£)
Direct materials	120 000	12
Direct labour	100 000	10
Variable manufacturing overhead costs (power and utilities)	10 000	1
Fixed manufacturing overhead costs	80 000	8
Share of non-manufacturing overheads	50 000	5
Total costs	360 000	36

The above costs are expected to remain unchanged in the foreseeable future if the Rhine Autos division continues to manufacture the components. The supplier has offered to supply 10 000 components per annum at price of £30 per unit guaranteed for a minimum of three years. If Rhine Autos outsources component A the direct labour force currently employed in producing the components will be made redundant. No redundancy costs will be incurred. Direct materials and variable overheads are avoidable if component A is outsourced. Fixed manufacturing overhead costs would be reduced by £10 000 per annum but non-manufacturing costs would remain unchanged. Assume initially that the capacity that is required for component A has no alternative use. Should the Division of Rhine Autos make or buy the component?

Case B

Assume now that the extra capacity that will be made available from outsourcing component A can be used to manufacture and sell 10 000 units of part B at a price of £34 per unit. All of the labour force required to manufacture component A would be used to make part B. The variable manufacturing overheads, the fixed manufacturing overheads and non-manufacturing overheads would be the same as the costs incurred for manufacturing component A. The materials required to manufacture component A would not be required but additional materials required for making part B would cost £13 per unit. Should Rhine Autos outsource component A?

At first glance it appears that the component should be outsourced since the purchase price of £30 is less than the current total unit cost of manufacturing. However, the unit costs include some costs that will be unchanged whether or not the components are outsourced. These costs are therefore not relevant to the decision. Assume also that there are no alternative uses of the

Measures of product attractiveness in retail operations

Shelf space limits the quantity and variety of products offered by a retail operation. The visibility of a particular stock-keeping unit (SKU) and probability of a stock-out are related to the space allocated to the SKU. Total contribution for the retail operation is influenced by how shelf space is allocated to the SKUs. For retailers, shelf space 'is their life blood – and it's very limited and expensive'. Shelf space, accordingly, can be treated as a constraint in retailing operations. The most attractive SKU is the SKU that generates the greatest contribution per unit of space (square foot or cubic foot). To calculate contribution, all incremental expenses are deducted from incremental revenue. Incremental revenues include retail price and other direct revenue such as deals, allowances, forward-buy and prompt-payment discounts. Incremental expenses include any money paid out as a result of selling one unit of a particular item. Included in the incremental expenses would be the invoice unit cost and other invoiced amounts (shipping charges, for example) that can be traced directly to the sale of the particular item. Incremental revenues and expenses are found by dividing case values by the number of units per case.

If capacity is not changed, then the relevant costs are the incremental costs rather than full costs. The choice of low direct product cost items (i.e. a full product cost including a share of the fixed warehouse, transport and storage costs) over high direct product cost items is essentially a choice to use less of the capacity that has already been paid for. If the costs of capacity are fixed, then using less capacity will not save money. Like the product mix problem, the answer to the space management problem is how to allocate existing capacity so that profit is maximized. To maximize profits where profits are constrained by space limitations, capacity should be allocated on the basis of the SKU that generates the greatest contribution per unit of space.

Source: © J Sainsbury plc 2003

Source: Adapted from Gardiner, S.C., Measures of product attractiveness and the theory of constraints, *International Journal of Retail and Distribution,* 1993, Vol. 21, No. 7, pp. 37–40.

released capacity if the components are outsourced. The appropriate cost information is presented in Exhibit 9.3 (Section A). Alternative approaches to presenting relevant cost and revenue information are presented. In columns (1) and (2) of Exhibit 9.3 cost information is presented that includes both relevant and irrelevant costs for both alternatives under consideration. The same amount for non-manufacturing overheads, which are irrelevant, is included for both alternatives. By including the same amount in both columns the cost is made irrelevant. Alternatively, you can present cost information in columns (1) and (2) that excludes any irrelevant costs and revenues because they are identical for both alternatives. Adopting either approach will result in a difference of £60 000 in favour of making component A.

The third approach is to list only the relevant costs, cost savings and any relevant revenues. This approach is shown in column (3) of Exhibit 9.3 (Section A). This column represents the differential costs or revenues and it is derived from the differences between columns (1) and (2). In column (3) only the information that is relevant to the decision is presented. You will see that this approach compares the relevant costs of making directly against outsourcing. It indicates that the additional costs of making component A are £240 000 but this enables

EXHIBIT 9.3
Evaluating a make or buy decision

Section A – Assuming there is no alternative use of the released capacity

	Total cost of continuing to make 10 000 components (1) (£ per annum)	Total cost of buying 10 000 components (2) (£ per annum)	Difference (relevant) (cost) (3) (£ per annum)
Direct materials	120 000		120 000
Direct labour	100 000		100 000
Variable manufacturing overhead costs (power and utilities)	10 000		10 000
Fixed manufacturing overhead costs	80 000	70 000	10 000
Non-manufacturing overheads	50 000	50 000	
Outside purchase cost incurred/(saved)		300 000	(300 000)
Total costs incurred/(saved) per annum	360 000	420 000	(60 000)

Column 3 is easier to interpret if it is restated as two separate alternatives as follows:

	Relevant cost of making component A (£ per annum)	Relevant cost of outsourcing component A (£ per annum)
Direct materials	120 000	
Direct labour	100 000	
Variable manufacturing overhead costs	10 000	
Fixed manufacturing overhead costs	10 000	
Outside purchase cost incurred		300 000
	240 000	300 000

Section B – Assuming the released capacity has alternative uses

	(1) Make component A and do not make part B (£ per annum)	(2) Buy component A and do not make part B (£ per annum)	(3) Buy component A and make part B (£ per annum)
Direct materials	120 000		130 000
Direct labour	100 000		100 000
Variable manufacturing overhead costs	10 000		10 000
Fixed manufacturing overhead costs	80 000	70 000	80 000
Non-manufacturing overheads	50 000	50 000	50 000
Outside purchase cost incurred		300 000	300 000
Revenues from sales of part B			(340 000)
Total net costs	360 000	420 000	330 000

purchasing costs of £300 000 to be saved. Therefore the company makes a net saving of £60 000 from making the components compared with outsourcing.

However, you will probably find column (3) easier to interpret if it is restated as two separate alternatives as shown in Exhibit 9.3. All of the approaches described in this and the preceding paragraph yield identical results. You can adopt any of them. It is a matter of personal preference.

Let us now re-examine the situation when the extra capacity created from not producing component A has an alternative use. Consider the information presented in Example 9.4 (Case B). The management of Rhine Autos now have three alternatives. They are:

1 Make component A and do not make part B.
2 Outsource component A and do not make part B.
3 Outsource component A and make and sell part B.

It is assumed there is insufficient capacity to make both component A and part B. The appropriate financial information is presented in Exhibit 9.3 (Section B). You will see that, with the exception of non-manufacturing costs, all of the items differ between the alternatives and are therefore relevant to the decision. Again we can omit the non-manufacturing costs from the analysis or include the same amount for all alternatives. Either approach makes them irrelevant. The first two alternatives that do not involve making and selling part B are identical to the alternatives considered in Case A so the information presented in columns (1) and (2) in sections A and B of Exhibit 9.3 are identical. In column 3 of section B the costs incurred in making part B in respect of direct labour, variable and fixed manufacturing overheads and non-manufacturing overheads are identical to the costs incurred in making component A. Therefore the same costs for these items are entered in column 3. However, different materials are required to make part B and the cost of these (10 000 units at £13) are entered in column 3. In addition, the revenues from the sales of part B are entered in column 3. Comparing the three columns in Section B of Exhibit 9.3 indicates that buying component A and using the extra capacity that is created to make part B is the preferred alternative.

The incremental costs of outsourcing are £60 000 more than making component B (see Section A of Exhibit 9.3) but the extra capacity released from outsourcing component A enables Rhine Autos to obtain a profit contribution of £90 000 (£340 000 incremental sales from part B less £250 000 incremental/relevant costs of making part B). The overall outcome is a £30 000 net benefit from outsourcing. Note that the relevant costs of making part B are the same as those of making component A, apart from direct materials, which cost £130 000. In other words, the relevant (incremental) costs of making part B (compared with outsourcing) are as follows:

	(£)
Direct materials	130 000
Direct labour	100 000
Variable manufacturing overhead costs	10 000
Fixed manufacturing overhead costs	10 000
	250 000

Discontinuation decisions

Most organizations periodically analyse profits by one or more cost objects, such as products or services, customers and locations. Periodic profitability analysis provides attention-directing information that highlights those unprofitable activities that require a more detailed appraisal (sometimes referred to as a special study) to ascertain whether or not they should be discontinued. In this section we shall illustrate how the principle of relevant costs can be applied to discontinuation decisions. Consider Example 9.5. You will see that it focuses on a decision whether to discontinue operating a sales territory, but the same principles can also be applied to discontinuing products, services or customers.

In Example 9.5 Euro Company analyses profits by locations. Profits are analysed by regions which are then further analysed by sales territories within each region. It is apparent from Example 9.5 that the Scandinavian region is profitable but the profitability analysis suggests that the Helsinki sales territory is unprofitable. A more detailed study is required to ascertain whether it should be discontinued. Let us assume that this study indicates that:

1 Discontinuing the Helsinki sales territory will eliminate cost of goods sold, salespersons salaries, sales office rent and regional and headquarters expenses arising from cause-and-effect cost allocations.
2 Discontinuing the Helsinki sales territory will have no effect on depreciation of sales office equipment, warehouse rent, depreciation of warehouse equipment and regional and headquarters expenses arising from arbitrary cost allocations. The same costs will be incurred by the company for all of these items even if the sales territory is discontinued.

Note that in the event of discontinuation the sales office will not be required and the rental will be eliminated whereas the warehouse rent relates to the warehouse for the region as a whole and, unless the company moves to a smaller warehouse, the rental will remain unchanged. It is therefore not a relevant cost. Discontinuation will result in the creation of additional space and if the extra space remains unused there are no financial consequences to take into account. However, if the additional space can be sub-let to generate rental income the income would be incorporated as an opportunity cost for the alternative of keeping the Helsinki territory.

Exhibit 9.4 shows the relevant cost computations. Column (1) shows the costs incurred by the company if the sales territory is kept open and column (2) shows the costs that would be incurred if a decision was taken to drop the sales territory. Therefore in column (2) only those costs that would be eliminated (i.e. those items listed in item (1) above) are deducted from column (1). You can see that the company will continue to incur some of the costs (i.e. those items listed in item (2) above) even if the Helsinki territory is closed and these costs are therefore irrelevant to the decision. Again you can either include, or exclude, the irrelevant costs in columns (1) and (2) as long as you ensure that the same amount of irrelevant costs is included for both alternatives if you adopt the first approach. Both approaches will show that future profits will decline by £154 000 if the Helsinki territory is closed. Alternatively, you can present just the relevant costs and revenues shown in column (3). This approach indicates that keeping the sales territory open results in additional sales revenues of £1 700 000 but additional costs of £1 546 000 are incurred giving a contribution of £154 000 towards fixed costs and profits.

You will have noted that we have assumed that the regional and headquarters costs assigned to the sales territories on the basis of cause-and-effect allocations can be eliminated if the Helsinki territory is discontinued. These are indirect costs that fluctuate in the longer-term according to the demand for them and it is assumed that the selected allocation base, or cost driver, provides a reasonably accurate measure of resources consumed by the sales territories. Cause-and-effect allocation bases assume that if the cause is eliminated or reduced, the effect (i.e. the costs) will be eliminated or reduced. If cost drivers are selected that result in allocations that are inaccurate measures of resources consumed by cost objects (i.e. sales territories) the relevant costs derived from these allocations will be incorrect and

EXAMPLE 9.5

The Euro Company is a wholesaler who sells its products to retailers throughout Europe. Euro's headquarters is in Brussels. The company has adopted a regional structure with each region consisting of 3–5 sales territories. Each region has its own regional office and a warehouse which distributes the goods directly to the customers. Each sales territory also has an office where the marketing staff are located. The Scandinavian region consists of three sales territories with offices located in Stockholm, Oslo and Helsinki. The budgeted results for the next quarter are as follows:

	Stockholm (£000s)	Oslo (£000s)	Helsinki (£000s)	Total (£000s)
Cost of goods sold	800	850	1000	2650
Salespersons salaries	160	200	240	600
Sales office rent	60	90	120	270
Depreciation of sales office equipment	20	30	40	90
Apportionment of warehouse rent	24	24	24	72
Depreciation of warehouse equipment	20	16	22	58
Regional and headquarters costs				
Cause-and-effect allocations	120	152	186	458
Arbitrary apportionments	360	400	340	1100
Total costs assigned to each location	1564	1762	1972	5298
Reported profit/(loss)	236	238	(272)	202
Sales	1800	2000	1700	5500

Assuming that the above results are likely to be typical of future quarterly performance should the Helsinki territory be discontinued?

incorrect decisions may be made. We shall explore this issue in some detail in the next chapter when we look at activity-based costing.

Determining the relevant costs of direct materials

So far in this chapter we have assumed, when considering various decisions, that any materials required would not be taken from existing stocks but would be purchased at a later date, and so the estimated purchase price would be the relevant material cost. Where materials are taken from existing stock do remember that the original purchase price represents a past or sunk cost and is therefore irrelevant for decision-making. If the materials are to be replaced then using the materials for a particular activity will necessitate their replacement. Thus, the decision to use the materials on an activity will result in additional acquisition costs compared with the situation if the materials were not used on that particular activity. Therefore the future **replacement cost** represents the relevant cost of the materials.

Consider now the situation where the materials have no further use apart from being used on a particular activity. If the materials have some realizable value, the use of the materials will result in lost sales revenues, and this lost sales revenue will represent an

EXHIBIT 9.4

Relevent cost analysis relating to the discontinuation of the Helsinki territory

	Total costs and revenues to be assigned		
	(1) Keep Helsinki territory open (£000s)	(2) Discontinue Helsinki territory (£000s)	(3) Difference incremental costs and revenues (£000s)
Cost of goods sold	2650	1650	1000
Salespersons salaries	600	360	240
Sales office rent	270	150	120
Depreciation of sales office equipment	90	90	
Apportionment of warehouse rent	72	72	
Depreciation of warehouse equipment	58	58	
Regional and headquarters costs			
Cause-and-effect allocations	458	272	186
Arbitrary apportionments	1100	1100	
Total costs to be assigned	5298	3752	1546
Reported profit	202	48	154
Sales	5500	3800	1700

opportunity cost that must be assigned to the activity. Alternatively, if the materials have no realizable value the relevant cost of the materials will be zero.

Determining the relevant costs of direct labour

Determining the direct labour costs that are relevant to short-term decisions depends on the circumstances. Where a company has temporary spare capacity and the labour force is to be maintained in the short term, the direct labour cost incurred will remain the same for all alternative decisions. The direct labour cost will therefore be irrelevant for short-term decision-making purposes. Consider now a situation where casual labour is used and where workers can be hired on a daily basis; a company may then adjust the employment of labour to exactly the amount required to meet the production requirements. The labour cost will increase if the company accepts additional work, and will decrease if production is reduced. In this situation the labour cost will be a relevant cost for decision-making purposes.

In a situation where full capacity exists and additional labour supplies are unavailable in the short term, and where no further overtime working is possible, the only way that labour resources could then be obtained for a specific order would be to reduce existing production. This would release labour for the order, but the reduced production would result in a lost contribution, and this lost contribution must be taken into account when ascertaining the relevant cost for the specific order. The relevant labour cost per hour where full capacity exists is therefore the hourly labour rate plus an opportunity cost consisting of the contribution per hour that is lost by accepting the order. Let us consider such a situation in Example 9.6.

EXAMPLE 9.6

A division of Rhine Autos has received an enquiry from one of its major customers for a special order for a component that will require 1000 skilled labour hours and that will incur other variable costs of £8000. Skilled labour is currently in short supply and if the company accepts the order then it will be necessary to reduce production of component P. Details of the cost per unit and the selling price of component P are as follows:

	(£)	(£)
Selling price		88
Less: Direct labour (4 hours at £10 per hour)	40	
Other variable costs	12	52
Contribution to profits		36

What is the minimum selling price the company should accept for the special order?

In this example the relevant labour cost is £19 per hour, consisting of the hourly wage rate of £10 plus the lost contribution of £9 per hour from component P (the contribution of component P is £36, and requires 4 direct labour hours, resulting in a contribution of £9 per hour). Hence the relevant costs for the special order are as follows:

	(£)
Variable cost (excluding direct labour)	8 000
Direct labour (1000 hours at £19 per hour)	19 000
	27 000

A selling price of £27 000 takes into account the lost contribution from component P and represents the minimum selling price that the company should accept if it wishes to ensure that future cash flows will remain unchanged. The acceptance of the special order means that production of component P must be reduced by 250 units (1000 hours/4 hours per unit). We can now check that the relevant cost calculation is correct by comparing the contribution from the special order with the contribution that would have been obtained from component P:

	Component P (250 units) (£)	Special order (£)
Sales (250 units at £88 per unit)	22 000	27 000
Less: direct labour (250 units at £40 per unit)	(10 000)	(10 000)
variable costs (250 units at £12 per unit)	(3 000)	(8 000)
Contribution to profits	9 000	9 000

This statement shows that the contribution to profits will be unchanged if the selling price of the special order is equivalent to the relevant cost of the order.

You may have noted that the hourly labour cost will continue whichever alternative is accepted, and you may therefore be concerned that the relevant cost consists of the hourly labour cost plus the lost contribution per hour. The reason for including the hourly labour cost is because a decision to create labour hours by reducing production of other work will result in a loss of sales and incremental/variable costs (excluding labour). That is, there will be a loss of contribution from component P of £76 (£88 selling price less £12 variable costs) before charging the labour costs giving a lost contribution of £19 per labour hour (£76/4 hours) in Example 9.6. This is just another way of saying that the relevant labour cost is the hourly wage rate of £10 plus the lost contribution per hour of £9.

Misconceptions about relevant costs

Until recently most textbooks have emphasized the contribution approach to decision-making. The term 'contribution' can have different meanings so it is important to precisely define the term. Traditionally contribution has been defined as sales revenues less variable costs. Using this definition the precise term is **variable contribution** which means the contribution that a product (or any other chosen cost object) makes to *all* fixed costs. This was the interpretation given to the term in the previous chapter. Sometimes contribution is defined as sales revenues less variable costs less direct fixed costs. Here the term 'contribution' represents the contribution to *indirect* fixed costs.

The traditional emphasis was on variable contribution for decision-making. This implies that only sales revenues and variable costs are relevant for decision-making and that all fixed costs are irrelevant. This assumption is only correct within a very short-term time horizon. We have seen in the illustrations used in this chapter that those fixed costs that differ among the alternatives are relevant for decision-making. In Example 9.5 the salaries of the salespersons was a relevant cost relating to a decision to discontinue a sales territory. Also variable costs are not always relevant for decision-making. If variable costs are the same for all alternatives they are clearly irrelevant. For example, if two alternative production methods are being considered that require identical direct materials then the direct material cost is irrelevant to both alternatives.

Another misconception is that all direct costs are relevant whereas all indirect costs are irrelevant. If a direct cost is a past/sunk cost it will be irrelevant. In Example 9.5 the depreciation of office equipment was a direct cost to each sales territory but was irrelevant to the discontinuation decision. Some non-variable indirect costs fluctuate according to the demand for them and they may be caused by factors other than volume. For example, a high volume product made in large batches may require less resources from the support activities than a low volume product that is made in small batches. Cost drivers that capture the demand that products place on support activities should be used to allocate indirect costs to products (or other chosen cost objects). If a low or high volume product is discontinued the cost system should accurately measure the reduced resource consumption so that estimates can be made of the costs that can be eliminated. For example, if as a result of a discontinuation decision the demand for the purchase activities is reduced by 10% then we would expect in the longer-term that some of the purchasing costs will be reduced by 10%. Hence, such indirect costs are relevant for decision-making. The measurement of relevant indirect costs for decision-making using activity-based costing systems will be dealt with in the next chapter.

Relevant costs are incremental or differential costs at the company level. You should always focus on the impact decisions will have on the future costs and revenues for the company as a whole and not parts within the company. Consider the arbitrary apportionment of central headquarters costs to the sales territories in Example 9.5. We assumed that the decision to discontinue the Helsinki territory would not affect these central headquarters costs. However, if as a result of the closure assume that the £340 000 costs that were allocated to the Helsinki territory would not be allocated to the Scandinavian region because they are apportioned on the basis of sales revenues. Therefore the costs would be allocated to other regions within the company. Now consider what could happen if the Scandinavian regional manager is responsible for making the decision. He or she might focus only on how the decision affects his or her region rather than the company as a whole. From a regional point of view the £340 000 would be interpreted as an incremental cost whereas from the company point of view it is not an incremental cost. Remember that when determining relevant costs always consider whether the cost is incremental at the company level and not at lower levels within the company.

Finally, always take care when using unit costs. If you turn back to Example 9.1 you will see that the direct labour costs for the period were £420 000 and this was the labour force required for an output level of 50 000 jumpers. However, there was a temporary decline in demand and the labour force was being maintained for the expected resurgence in demand. Current activity was 35 000 jumpers and the current unit labour cost was thus £12 (£420 000/35 000 jumpers). This unit cost only applies at an output level of 35 000 jumpers. At other output levels the unit cost will be different because the labour cost is fixed in the short-term. The example looked at a special one-off order of 3000 jumpers. Given that the labour cost is fixed in the short-term the incremental costs of the order will be zero but there is a real danger that the unit cost of £12 will be mistakenly used giving £36 000 incremental cost (3000 jumpers at a unit cost of £12) for the special one-off order. You can guard against this mistake by only including those future costs that will be incurred for the alternative course of action that is being evaluated.

Summary

The following items relate to the learning objectives listed at the beginning of the chapter.

- **Distinguish between relevant and irrelevant costs and revenues.**

  Relevant costs/revenues represent those future costs/revenues that will be changed by a particular decision, whereas irrelevant costs/revenues will not be affected by that decision. In the short-term total profits will be increased (or total losses decreased) if a course of action is chosen where relevant revenues are in excess of relevant costs.

- **Explain the importance of qualitative factors.**

  Quantitative factors refer to outcomes that can be measured in numerical terms. In many situations it is difficult to quantify all the important elements of a decision. Those factors that cannot be expressed in numerical terms are called qualitative factors. Examples of qualitative factors include changes in employee morale and the impact of being at the mercy of a supplier when a decision is made to close a company's facilities and subcontract components. Although qualitative factors cannot be quantified it is essential that they are taken into account in the decision-making process.

- **Distinguish between the relevant and irrelevant costs and revenues for the five decision-making problems described.**

  The five decision-making problems described were: (a) special selling price decisions; (b) product-mix decisions when capacity constraints apply; (c) decisions on the replacement of equipment; (d) outsourcing (make or buy) decisions; and (e) discontinuation decisions. Different approaches can be used for presenting relevant cost and revenue information. Information can be presented that includes both relevant and irrelevant items for all alternatives under consideration. If this approach is adopted the same amount for the irrelevant items (i.e. those items that remain unchanged as a result of the decision) are included for all alternatives thus making them irrelevant for the decision. Alternatively, information can be presented that lists only the relevant costs for the alternatives under consideration. Where only two alternatives are being considered a third approach is to present only the relevant (differential) items. You can adopt either approach. It is a matter of personal preference. All three approaches were illustrated for the five decision-making problems.

- **Describe the key concept that should be applied for presenting information for product-mix decisions when capacity constraints apply.**

  The information presented should rank the products by the contribution per unit of the constraining or limiting factor (i.e. the scarce resource). The capacity of the scarce resource should allocated according to this ranking.

- **Explain why the book value of equipment is irrelevant when making equipment replacement decisions.**

  The book value of equipment is a past (sunk) cost that cannot be changed for any alternative under consideration. Only future costs or revenues that will differ between alternatives are relevant for replacement decisions.

- **Describe the opportunity cost concept.**

  Where the choice of one course of action requires that an alternative course of action be given up the financial benefits that are forgone or sacrificed are known as opportunity costs. Opportunity costs thus represent the lost contribution to profits arising from the best alternative forgone. They arise only when the resources are scarce and have alternative uses. Opportunity costs must therefore be included in the analysis when presenting relevant information for decision-making.

- **Explain the misconceptions relating to relevant costs and revenues.**

  The main misconception relates to the assumption that only sales revenues and variable costs are relevant and that fixed costs are irrelevant for decision-making. Sometimes variable costs are irrelevant. For example, they are irrelevant when they are the same for all alternatives under consideration. Fixed costs are also relevant when they differ among the alternatives.

- **Additional learning objective presented in Appendix 9.1.**

  The appendix to this chapter includes the following additional learning objective: describe the theory of constraints and throughput accounting. This topic has been presented in the appendix because it is not vital to understanding the principles of measuring relevant costs and revenues for decision-making. The topic also tends to be covered on more advanced courses and may not form part of your course curriculum. You should therefore check with your course curriculum to ascertain whether you need to study this topic.

Appendix 9.1: The theory of constraints and throughput accounting

During the 1980s Goldratt and Cox (1984) advocated a new approach to production management called **optimized production technology (OPT)**. OPT is based on the principle that profits are expanded by increasing the throughput of the plant. The OPT approach determines what prevents throughput being higher by distinguishing

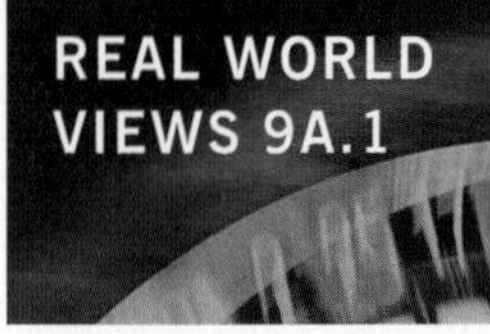

Throughput accounting: The Garrett Automative experience

Garrett Automative Ltd (GAL) is a UK subsidiary of an American parent company that manufactures turbochargers for the automative industry. Because of pressure from major customers for price reductions GAL investigated the impact of a small percentage change in total revenues and different categories of costs on profits. The conclusions from the analysis were that selling price, sales volume and material cost had by far the most dramatic effect on company profitability. There was a need for the management accounting system to highlight these aspects of the business.

GAL decided to begin its profit improvement programme by examining its factory throughput. Throughput was defined as the rate at which raw materials were turned into sales. In other words, throughput was defined as sales less material costs per period of time. All operating costs, other than direct materials were considered to be fixed in the short run. In conjunction with its new OPT scheduling system factory bottlenecks, defined as an activity within the organization where demand for the resource outstrips the capacity to supply, were identified. The bottlenecks became certain machines in the factory. The mechanism to improve profitability was to maximize throughput contribution by optimizing the use of bottleneck resources.

Management sought to alleviate the bottlenecks by making additional investments to improve bottleneck capacity and by shifting some of the operations from bottleneck to non-bottleneck machines. New investments to improve efficiency at non-bottleneck machines were rejected because this greater efficiency did nothing to improve throughput contribution. Priority was given to investments in bottlenecks. To motivate the employees to increase throughput the performance reporting system was changed. Less emphasis was given to labour efficiency and schedule adherence was introduced as a key performance measure. Employees at non-bottleneck operations were requested not to produce more than the scheduled quantity and use any surplus time on training and TQM initiatives.

GAL has found throughput accounting to be extremely helpful in its particular situation. By concentrating on managing its bottlenecks, GAL has been able to increase its production to meet its sales demand of many different types of turbochargers in relatively small batch sizes. During the two year period of operating throughput accounting, GAL has also seen a dramatic halving in its inventory.

Source: Adapted from Darlington, J. *et al.* (1992), Throughput accounting: the Garrett Automative experience, *Management Accounting (UK)*, April 1992, pp. 32–35, 38 and Coughlan, P. and Darlington, J. (1993), As fast as the slowest operations: the theory of constraints, *Management Accounting (UK)*, June 1993, pp. 14–17.

between bottleneck and non-bottleneck resources. A bottleneck might be a machine whose capacity limits the throughput of the whole production process. The aim is to identify bottlenecks and remove them or, if this is not possible, ensure that they are fully utilized at all times. Non-bottleneck resources should be scheduled and operated based on constraints within the system, and should not be used to produce more than the bottlenecks can absorb. The OPT philosophy therefore advocates that non-bottleneck resources should not be utilized to 100% of their capacity, since this would merely result in an increase in inventory. Thus idle time in non-bottleneck areas is not considered detrimental to the efficiency of the organization. If it were utilized, it would result in increased inventory without a corresponding increase in throughput for the plant.

With the OPT approach, it is vitally important to schedule all non-bottleneck resources within the manufacturing system based on the constraints of the system (i.e. the bottlenecks). For example, if only 70% of the output of a non-bottleneck resource can be absorbed by the following bottleneck then 30% of the utilization of the non-bottleneck is simply concerned with increasing inventory. It can therefore be argued that by operating at the 70% level, the non-bottleneck resource is achieving 100% efficiency.

Goldratt and Cox (1992) describe the process of maximizing operating profit when faced with bottleneck and non-bottleneck operations as the **theory of constraints (TOC)**. The process involves five steps:

1 identify the system's bottlenecks;
2 decide how to exploit the bottlenecks;
3 subordinate everything else to the decision in step 2;
4 elevate the system's bottlenecks;
5 if, in the previous steps, a bottleneck has been broken go back to step 1.

The first step involves identifying the constraint which restricts output from being expanded. Having identified the bottleneck it becomes the focus of attention since only the bottleneck can restrict or enhance the flow of products. It is therefore essential to ensure that the bottleneck activity is fully utilized. Decisions regarding the optimum mix of products to be produced by the bottleneck activity must be made. Step 3 requires that the optimum production of the bottleneck activity determines the production schedule of the non-bottleneck activities. In other words, the output of the non-bottleneck operations are linked to the needs of the bottleneck activity. There is no point in a non-bottleneck activity supplying more than the bottleneck activity can consume. This would merely result in an increase in WIP inventories and no increase in sales volume. The TOC is a process of continuous improvement to clear the throughput chain of all constraints. Thus, step 4 involves taking action to remove (that is, elevate) the constraint. This might involve replacing a bottleneck machine with a faster one, or increasing the bottleneck efficiency and capacity by providing additional training for a slow worker or changing the design of the product to reduce the processing time required by the activity. When a bottleneck activity has been elevated and replaced by a new bottleneck it is necessary to return to step 1 and repeat the process.

To apply TOC ideas Goldratt and Cox advocate the use of three key measures.

1 *Throughput contribution* which is the rate at which the system generates profit through sales. It is defined as sales less direct materials.
2 *Investments* (inventory) which is the sum of inventories, research and development costs and the costs of equipment and buildings.
3 *Other operational expenses* which include all operating costs (other than direct materials) incurred to earn throughput contribution.

The TOC aims to increase throughput contribution while simultaneously reducing inventory and operational expenses. However, the scope for reducing the latter is limited since they must be maintained at some minimum level for production to take place at all. In other words, operational expenses are assumed to be fixed costs. Goldratt and Cox argue that traditional management accounting is obsessed by the need to reduce operational expenses, which results in a declining spiral of cost-cutting, followed by falling production and a further round of cost-cutting. Instead, they advocate a throughput orientation whereby throughput must be given first priority, inventories second and operational expenses last.

The TOC adopts a short-run time horizon and treats all operating expenses (including direct labour but excluding direct materials) as fixed, thus implying that variable costing should be used for decision-making, profit measurement and inventory valuation. It emphasizes the management of bottleneck activities as the key to improving performance by focusing on the short-run maximization of throughput contribution. Adopting the throughput approach to implement the TOC, however, appears to be merely a restatement of the contribution per limiting factor that was described in this chapter. Consider the situation outlined in Example 9A.1.

You can see from Example 9A.1 that the required machine utilization is as follows:

Machine	1	112%	(1800/1600 × 100)
	2	178%	(2850/1600 × 100)
	3	56%	(900/1600 × 100)

Machine 2 represents the bottleneck activity because it has the highest machine utilization. To ascertain the optimum use of the bottleneck activity we calculate the contribution per hour for machine 2 for each product and rank the products in order of profitability based on this calculation. Using the figures in the present example the result would be as follows:

	Product X	Product Y	Product Z
Contribution per unit	£12	£10	£6
Machine 2 hours required	9	3	1.5
Contribution per machine hour	£1.33	£3.33	£4
Ranking	3	2	1

The allocation of the 1600 hours for the bottleneck activity is:

	Machine hours used	Balance of hours available
Production		
200 units of Z	300	1300
200 units of Y	600	700
77 units of X	700	—

Following the five step TOC process outlined earlier, action should be taken to remove the constraint. Let us assume that a financial analysis indicates that the purchase of a second 'Type 2' machine is justified. Machine capacity will now be increased by 1600 hours to 3200 hours and Machine 2 will no longer be a constraint. In other words, the bottleneck will have been elevated and Machine 1 will now become the con-straint. The above process must now be repeated to determine the optimum output for Machine 1.

Galloway and Waldron (1988) advocate an approach called **throughput accounting** to apply the TOC philosophy. To ascertain the optimum use of the bottleneck activity

EXAMPLE 9A.1

A company produces three products using three different machines. The following information is available for a period.

Product	X	Y	Z	Total
Contribution (Sales – direct materials)	£12	£10	£6	
Machine hours required per unit:				
Machine 1	6	2	1	
Machine 2	9	3	1.5	
Machine 3	3	1	0.5	
Estimated sales demand	200	200	200	
Required machine hours				
Machine 1	1200	400	200	1800
Machine 2	1800	600	450	2850
Machine 3	600	200	100	900

Machine capacity is limited to 1600 hours for each machine.

they rank the products according to a measure they have devised called the throughput accounting (TA) ratio. They define the TA ratio as:

$$\text{TA Ratio} = \frac{\text{Return per factory hour}}{\text{Cost per factory hour}}$$

$$\text{where Return per factory hour} = \frac{\text{Sales price} - \text{Material cost}}{\text{Time on key resource}}$$

$$\text{and Cost per factory hour} = \frac{\text{Total factory cost}}{\text{Total time available on key resource}}$$

Note that sales less direct material cost is equal to throughput contribution, total factory cost is defined in exactly the same way as other operational expenses and return per factory hour is identical to contribution per hour of the bottleneck activity. Let us assume for Example 9A.1 that the total factory cost for the period is £3200. The TA ratios and product rankings for the bottleneck activity (Machine 2), using the data shown in Example 9A.1, are as follows:

	Product X	Product Y	Product Z
1. Return per factory hour	£1.33	£3.33	£4
2. Cost per factory hour (£3200/1600 hours)	£2	£2	£2
3. TA ratio (Row 1/Row 2)	0.665	1.665	2
4. Ranking	3	2	1

The rankings are identical to the contribution per bottleneck hour calculated earlier. Given that the TA ratio is calculated by dividing the contribution per bottleneck hour (described as return per factory hour) by a constant amount (cost per factory hour) the TA ratio appears merely to represent a restatement of the contribution per limiting factor described in the main body of this chapter.

Goldratt (1993) rejects the use of throughput accounting. He does not advocate any specific accounting practices. Instead, accountants are encouraged to learn TOC ideas and apply them to accounting in ways that suit their own circumstances. However, traditional techniques that have been described in management accounting textbooks for many years, such as linear programming (see Chapter 26) for allocating the optimum use of bottleneck resources and the use of shadow prices for decision-making and variance analysis (see Chapter 19), can be viewed as an attempt to apply TOC ideas. Thus, applying TOC ideas to accounting does not represent a radical innovation in accounting but a move towards the widespread adoption of short-run variable costing techniques. Hence, the same criticisms that have been applied to variable costing can also be made to the application of TOC ideas. That is, all expenses other than direct materials are assumed to be fixed and unavoidable. For a more detailed discussion of the TOC and throughput accounting you should refer to Dugdale and Jones (1998) and Jones and Dugdale (1998).

Key terms and concepts

decision-relevant approach (p. 313)
differential cash flow (p. 314)
incremental cash flow (p. 314)
limiting factor (p. 320)
opportunity cost (p. 319)
optimized production technology (p. 335)
outsourcing (p. 324)
qualitative factors (p. 315)
relevant cost (p. 314)
replacement cost (p. 330)
special studies (p. 313)
theory of constraints (pp. 322, 337)
throughput accounting (pp, 322, 338)
written-down value (p. 322)
variable contribution (p. 333)

Recommended reading

For a discussion of the arguments for and against using the contribution analysis approach you should refer to the *Journal of Management Accounting Research* (USA) Fall 1990, 1–32, 'Contribution margin analysis: no longer relevant. Strategic cost management: the new paradigm', which reproduces the contributions from a panel of speakers at the American Accounting Association Annual Meeting: Ferrara (pp. 1–2) Kaplan (pp. 2–15), Shank (pp. 15–21), Horngren (pp. 21–4), Boer (pp. 24–7), together with concluding remarks (pp. 27–32). For a detailed discussion of the theory of constraints and throughput accounting you should refer to Jones and Dugdale (1998) and Dugdale and Jones (1998).

Key examination points

A common mistake that students make when presenting information for decision-making is to compare *unit* costs. With this approach, there is a danger that fixed costs will be unitized and treated as variable costs. In most cases you should compare total amounts of costs and revenues rather than unit amounts. Many students do not present the information clearly and concisely. There are many alternative ways of presenting the information, but the simplest approach is to list future costs and revenues for each alternative in a format similar to Exhibit 9.1. You should exclude irrelevant items or ensure that the same amount for irrelevant items is included for each alternative. To determine the amount to be entered for each alternative, you should ask yourself what difference it will make if the alternative is selected.

Never allocate common fixed costs to the alternatives. You should focus on how each alternative will affect future cash flows of the organization. Changes in the apportionment of fixed costs will not alter future cash flows of the company. Remember that if a resource is scarce, your analysis should recommend the alternative that yields the largest contribution per limiting factor. You should now attempt the Review problems and compare your answers with the solutions that are provided. These problems will test your understanding of a variety of decision problems that have been covered in Chapter 9. Pay particular attention to Review problem 9.32 since this includes many of the aspects that were discussed in the chapter.

Assessment material

Review questions

The review questions are short questions that enable you to assess your understanding of the main topics included in the chapter. The numbers in parentheses provide you with the page numbers to refer to if you cannot answer a specific question.

Review problems

The review problems are more complex and require you to relate and apply the chapter content to various business problems. The problems are graded by their level of difficulty. The multiple-choice questions are the least demanding and normally take less than 10 minutes to complete. Fully worked solutions to the review problems are provided in a separate section at the end of the book. For those questions in the white box the worked solutions are provided in the *Student's Manual* accompanying this book. Further review problems for this chapter are available on the accompanying website www.drury-online.com. The answers to these problems are available for lecturers on the lecturer's password protected section of the website.

Case studies

The website also includes over 30 case study problems. A list of these cases is provided in Part Seven of this book. Several cases are relevant to the content of this chapter. Examples include Baldwin Bicycle Company, Fleet Ltd. and High Street Reproduction Furniture Ltd.

Review questions

9.1 What is a relevant cost? (*p. 314*)

9.2 Why is it important to recognize qualitative factors when presenting information for decision-making? Provide examples of qualitative factors. (*p. 315*)

9.3 What underlying principle should be followed in determining relevant costs for decision-making? (*p. 318*)

9.4 Explain what is meant by special pricing decisions. (*p. 315*)

9.5 Describe the important factors that must be taken into account when making special pricing decisions. (*p. 317*)

9.6 Describe the dangers involved in focusing excessively on a short-run decision-making time horizon. (*pp. 319–20*)

9.7 Define limiting factors. (*p. 320*)

9.8 How should a company determine its optimal product mix when a limiting factor exists? (*p. 321*)

9.9 Why is the written down value and depreciation of an asset being considered for replacement irrelevant when making replacement decisions? (*p. 323*)

9.10 Explain the importance of opportunity costs for decision-making. (*p. 319*)

9.11 Explain the circumstances when the original purchase price of materials are irrelevant for decision-making. (*pp. 330–31*)

9.12 Why does the relevant cost of labour differ depending upon the circumstances? (*p. 331*)

9.13 Why are variable costs and direct costs sometimes irrelevant for decision-making? (*p. 333*)

9.14 Are fixed costs always irrelevant for decision-making? (*p. 333*)

9.15 Describe the five steps involved in applying the theory of constraints. (*p. 337*)

9.16 Describe throughput accounting and explain how it can be used to determine the optimum use of a bottleneck activity. (*pp. 338–40*)

Review problems

9.17 **Intermediate**

Z Limited manufactures three products, the selling price and cost details of which are given below:

	Product X (£)	Product Y (£)	Product Z (£)
Selling price per unit	75	95	95
Direct materials (£5/kg)	10	5	15
Direct labour (£4/hour)	16	24	20
Variable overhead	8	12	10
Fixed overhead	24	36	30

In a period when direct materials are restricted in supply, the most and the least profitable uses of direct materials are

	Most profitable	Least profitable
A	X	Z
B	Y	Z
C	X	Y
D	Z	Y
E	Y	X

CIMA Stage 2

9.18 Intermediate

Your company regularly uses material X and currently has in stock 600 kg, for which it paid £1500 two weeks ago. It this were to be sold as raw material it could be sold today for £2.00 per kg. You are aware that the material can be bought on the open market for £3.25 per kg, but it must be purchased in quantities of 1000 kg.

You have been asked to determine the relevant cost of 600 kg of material X to be used in a job for a customer. The relevant cost of the 600 kg is:

(a) £1200
(b) £1325
(c) £1825
(d) £1950
(e) £3250

CIMA Stage 2

9.19 Intermediate

Q plc makes two products – Quone and Qutwo – from the same raw material. The selling price and cost details of these products are as shown below:

	Quone (£)	Qutwo (£)
Selling price	20.00	18.00
Direct material (£2.00/kg)	6.00	5.00
Direct labour	4.00	3.00
Variable overhead unit	2.00	1.50
	12.00	9.50
Contribution per unit	8.00	8.50

The maximum demand for these products is:

Quone	500 units per week
Qutwo	unlimited number of units per week

If materials were limited to 2000 kg per week, the shadow price (opportunity cost) of these materials would be:

(a) nil;
(b) £2.00 per kg;
(c) £2.66 per kg;
(d) £3.40 per kg;
(e) none of these.

CIMA Stage 2

9.20 Intermediate

BB Limited makes three components: S, T and U. The following costs have been recorded:

	Component S Unit cost (£)	Component T Unit cost (£)	Component U Unit cost (£)
Variable cost	2.50	8.00	5.00
Fixed cost	2.00	8.30	3.75
Total cost	4.50	16.30	8.75

Another company has offered to supply the components to BB Limited at the following prices:

	Component S	Component T	Component U
Price each	£4	£7	£5.50

Which component(s), if any, should BB Limited consider buying in?

(a) Buy in all three components.
(b) Do not buy any.
(c) Buy in S and U.
(d) Buy in T only.

CIMA Stage 1 Specimen Paper

9.21 Intermediate

A company is considering accepting a one-year contract which will require four skilled employees. The four skilled employees could be recruited on a one-year contract at a cost of £40 000, per employee. The employees would be supervised by an existing manager who earns £60 000 per annum. It is expected that supervision of the contract would take 10% of the manager's time.

Instead of recruiting new employees, the company could retrain some existing employees who currently earn £30 000 per year. The training would cost £15 000 in total. If these employees were used they would need to be replaced at a total cost of £100 000.

The relevant labour cost of the contract is:

A £100 000
B £115 000
C £135 000
D £141 000
E £166 000

CIMA Stage 2

9.22 Intermediate

An engineering firm has surplus capacity and wishes to secure a short-term contract to supply components. It has decided to bid for a contract at a price which will just cover all relevant costs.

Which ONE of the following costs should be included in the calculation of the minimum price it can bid?

A The cost of a research project undertaken last year which has resulted in an improved method of manufacturing the components.
B The cost of hiring a supervisor to oversee the contract's progress.
C The cost of labour which will be transferred to the contract from another production line where it is currently idle.
D The depreciation charge on existing machinery owned by the firm which will be used to manufacture the components.

CIMA – Management Accounting Fundamentals

9.23 Intermediate

A company is considering the costs for a special order. The order would require 1250 kg of material D. This material is readily available and regularly used by the company. There are 265 kg of material D in stock which cost £795 last week. The current market price is £3.24 per kg.

Material D is normally used to make product X. Each unit of X requires 3 kg of material D and, if material D is costed at £3 per kg, each unit of X yields a contribution of £15.

The cost of material D to be included in the costing of the special order is nearest to

A £3990 B £4050 C £10 000 D £10 300

CIMA Management Accounting – Performance Management

9.24 Intermediate

Camden has three divisions. Information for the year ended 30 September is as follows:

	Division A £'000	Division B £'000	Division C £'000	Total £'000
Sales	350	420	150	920
Variable costs	280	210	120	610
Contribution	70	210	30	310
Fixed costs				262.5
Net profit				47.5

General fixed overheads are allocated to each division on the basis of sales revenue; 60% of the total fixed costs incurred by the company are specific to each division being split equally between them.

Using relevant costing techniques, which divisions should remain open if Camden wishes to maximise profits?

A A, B and C
B A and B only
C B only
D B and C only.

ACCA Paper 1.2 – Financial information for Management

9.25 Intermediate

The following data is to be used to answer questions (a), (b) and (c) below.

HG plc manufactures four products. The unit cost, selling price and bottleneck resource details per unit are as follows:

	Product W £	Product X £	Product Y £	Product Z £
Selling price	56	67	89	96
Material	22	31	38	46
Labour	15	20	18	24
Variable overhead	12	15	18	15
Fixed overhead	4	2	8	7
	Minutes	**Minutes**	**Minutes**	**Minutes**
Bottleneck resource time	10	10	15	15

(a) Assuming that labour is a unit variable cost, if the products are ranked according to their contribution to sales ratios, the most profitable product is

(A) W (B) X (C) Y (D) Z

(b) Assuming that labour is a unit variable cost, if budgeted unit sales are in the ratio W:2; X:3; Y:3; Z:4 and monthly fixed costs are budgeted to be £15 000, the number of units of W that would be sold at the budgeted breakeven point is nearest to

(A) 106 units. (B) 142 units. (C) 212 units. (D) 283 units.

(c) If the company adopted throughput accounting and the products were ranked according to 'product return per minute', the highest ranked product would be

(A) W (B) X (C) Y (D) Z

CIMA Management Accounting – Performance Management

9.26 Advanced

A company manufactures four products – J, K, L and M. The products use a series of different machines but there is a common machine, X, which causes a bottleneck. The standard selling price and standard cost per unit for each product for the forthcoming year are as follows:

	J £	K £	L £	M £
Selling price	2000	1500	1500	1750
Cost:				
Direct materials	410	200	300	400
Labour	300	200	360	275
Variable overheads	250	200	300	175
Fixed overheads	360	300	210	330
Profit	680	600	330	570
Machine X – minutes per unit	120	100	70	110

Direct materials is the only unit-level manufacturing cost.

Using a throughput accounting approach, the ranking of the products would be:

	J	K	L	M
A	1st	2nd	3rd	4th
B	1st	2nd	4th	3rd
C	2nd	1st	4th	3rd
D	2nd	3rd	1st	4th
E	3rd	2nd	1st	4th

(3 marks)

CIMA Management Accounting – Decision Making

9.27 Intermediate: Special pricing and make or buy decisions

Two decision-making problems are faced by a company which produces a range of products and absorbs production overhead using a rate of 200% on direct wages. This rate was calculated from the following budgeted figures:

	(£)
Variable production costs	64 000
Fixed production costs	96 000
Direct labour costs	80 000

Problem 1
The normal selling price of product X is £22 and production cost for one unit is:

	(£)
Raw materials	8
Direct labour	4
Production overhead	8
	£20

There is a possibility of supplying a special order for 2000 units of product X at £16 each. If the order were accepted the normal budgeted sales would not be affected and the company has the necessary capacity to produce the additional units.

Problem 2
The cost of making component Q, which forms part of product Y, is stated below:

	(£)
Raw materials	4
Direct labour	8
Production overhead	16
	£28

Component Q could be bought from an outside supplier for £20. You are required, assuming that fixed production costs will not change, to:

(a) State whether the company should:
  (i) accept the special order in problem 1;
  (ii) continue making component Q or buy it from outside in Problem 2;
  (Both your statements must be supported by details of cost.)

(b) Comment on the principle you have followed in your cost analysis to arrive at your answers to the two problems.

CIMA Cost Accounting 1

9.28 Intermediate: Key/limiting factors

Due to a national wage agreement, you find that wage rates for skilled workers are to increase by 50% over the budget figures. There is a shortage of such skilled workers and it takes over a year to train new recruits adequately. The managing director has asked you for advice as to which order of priority on the product range would give best use of the skilled labour resources available. The cost of unskilled labour, of which there is no shortage, will go up by 20% over budget.

The original budget figures for the next period before allowing for the increase in labour cost detailed above, were:

Product	V	W	X	Y	Z
Maximum production in units	3000	4000	6000	7000	9000
Selling price per unit	£16	£15	£18	£15	£30
Variable costs per unit					
Material	3	5	4	7	6
Skilled labour £4 per hour	4	4	6	2	8
Unskilled labour £2 per hour	2	2	1	1	4

Variable overheads are recovered at the rate of £1 per labour hour. The skilled labour available amounts to 30 000 hours in the period and there are fixed costs of £22 800.

You are required to:

(a) calculate the product mix which would result in the maximum profit; *(12 marks)*

(b) comment on the results of the revised budget. *(6 marks)*

(Total 18 marks)

AAT

9.29 Intermediate: Acceptance of a special order

The production manager of your organization has approached you for some costing advice on project X, a one-off order from overseas that he intends to tender for. The costs associated with the project are as follows:

	(£)
Material A	4 000
Material B	8 000
Direct labour	6 000
Supervision	2 000
Overheads	12 000
	32 000

You ascertain the following:

(i) Material A is in stock and the above was the cost. There is now no other use for material A, other than the above project, within the factory and it would cost £1750 to dispose of. Material B would have to be ordered at the cost shown above.

(ii) Direct labour costs of £6000 relate to workers that will be transferred to this project from another project. Extra labour will need to be recruited to the other project at a cost of £7000.

(iii) Supervision costs have been charged to the project on the basis of $33^1/_3$% of labour costs and will be carried out by existing staff within their normal duties.

(iv) Overheads have been charged to the project at the rate of 200% on direct labour.

(v) The company is currently operating at a point above break-even.

(vi) The project will need the utilization of machinery that will have no other use to the company after the project has finished. The machinery will have to be purchased at a cost of £10 000 and then disposed of for £5250 at the end of the project.

The production manager tells you that the overseas customer is prepared to pay up to a maximum of £30 000 for the project and a competitor is prepared to accept the order at that price. He also informs you the minimum that he can charge is £40 000 as the above costs show £32 000, and this does not take into consideration the cost of the machine and profit to be taken on the project.

Required:

(a) Cost the project for the production manager, clearly stating how you have arrived at your figures and giving reasons for the exclusion of other figures. *(12 marks)*

(b) Write a report to the production manager stating whether the organization should go ahead with the tender for the project, the reasons why and the price, bearing in mind that the competitor is prepared to undertake the project for £30 000. *(8 marks)*

Note: The project should only be undertaken if it shows a profit.

(c) State four non-monetary factors that should be taken into account before tendering for this project.

(2 marks)

(d) What would be your advice if you were told that the organization was operating below break-even point? Give reasons for your advice.

(3 marks)

(Total 25 marks)

AAT Cost Accounting and Budgeting

9.30 Intermediate: Decision on which of two mutually exclusive contracts to accept

A company in the civil engineering industry with headquarters located 22 miles from London undertakes contracts anywhere in the United Kingdom.

The company has had its tender for a job in north-east England accepted at £288 000 and work is due to begin in March. However, the company has also been asked to undertake a contract on the south coast of England. The price offered for this contract is £352 000. Both of the contracts cannot be taken simultaneously because of constraints on staff site management personnel and on plant available. An escape clause enables the company to withdraw from the contract in the north-east, provided notice is given before the end of November and an agreed penalty of £28 000 is paid.

The following estimates have been submitted by the company's quantity surveyor:

Cost estimates	North-east (£)	South coast (£)
Materials:		
In stock at original cost, Material X	21 600	
In stock at original cost, Material Y		24 800
Firm orders placed at original cost, Material X	30 400	
Not yet ordered – current cost, Material X	60 000	
Not yet ordered – current cost, Material Z		71 200
Labour – hired locally	86 000	110 000
Site management	34 000	34 000
Staff accommodation and travel for site management	6 800	5 600
Plant on site – depreciation	9 600	12 800
Interest on capital, 8%	5 120	6 400
Total local contract costs	253 520	264 800
Headquarters costs allocated at rate of 5% on total contract costs	12 676	13 240
	266 196	278 040
Contract price	288 000	352 000
Estimated profit	21 804	73 960

Notes:

1. X, Y and Z are three building materials. Material X is not in common use and would not realize much money if re-sold; however, it could be used on other contracts but only as a substitute for another material currently quoted at 10% less than the original cost of X. The price of Y, a material in common use, has doubled since it was purchased; its net realizable value if re-sold would be its

new price less 15% to cover disposal costs. Alternatively it could be kept for use on other contracts in the following financial year.

2. With the construction industry not yet recovered from the recent recession, the company is confident that manual labour, both skilled and unskilled, could be hired locally on a subcontracting basis to meet the needs of each of the contracts.
3. The plant which would be needed for the south coast contract has been owned for some years and £12 800 is the year's depreciation on a straight-line basis. If the north-east contract is undertaken, less plant will be required but the surplus plant will be hired out for the period of the contract at a rental of £6000.
4. It is the company's policy to charge all contracts with notional interest at 8% on estimated working capital involved in contracts. Progress payments would be receivable from the contractee.
5. Salaries and general costs of operating the small headquarters amount to about £108 000 each year. There are usually ten contracts being supervised at the same time.
6. Each of the two contracts is expected to last from March to February which, coincidentally, is the company's financial year.
7. Site management is treated as a fixed cost.

You are required, as the management accountant to the company,

(a) to present comparative statements to show the net benefit to the company of undertaking the more advantageous of the two contracts;

(12 marks)

(b) to explain the reasoning behind the inclusion in (or omission from) your comparative financial statements, of each item given in the cost estimates and the notes relating thereto.

(13 marks)
(Total 25 marks)
CIMA Stage 2 Cost Accounting

9.31 Intermediate: Deletion of a product

Blackarm Ltd makes three products and is reviewing the profitability of its product line. You are given the following budgeted data about the firm for the coming year.

Product	**A**	**B**	**C**
Sales (in units)	**100 000**	**120 000**	**80 000**
	(£)	**(£)**	**(£)**
Revenue	1 500 000	1 440 000	880 000
Costs:			
Material	500 000	480 000	240 000
Labour	400 000	320 000	160 000
Overhead	650 000	600 000	360 000
	1 550 000	1 400 000	760 000
Profit/(Loss)	(50 000)	40 000	120 000

The company is concerned about the loss on product A. It is considering ceasing production of it and switching the spare capacity of 100 000 units to Product C.

You are told:

(i) All production is sold.

(ii) 25% of the labour cost for each product is fixed in nature.

(iii) Fixed administration overheads of £900 000 in total have been apportioned to each product on the basis of units sold and are included in the overhead costs above. All other overhead costs are variable in nature.

(iv) Ceasing production of product A would eliminate the fixed labour charge associated with it and one-sixth of the fixed administration overhead apportioned to product A.

(v) Increasing the production of product C by 100 000 units would mean that the fixed labour cost associated with product C would double, the variable labour cost would rise by 20% and its selling price would have to be decreased by £1.50 in order to achieve the increased sales.

Required:

(a) Prepare a marginal cost statement for a unit of each product on the basis of:
  (i) the original budget;
  (ii) if product A is deleted.

(12 marks)

(b) Prepare a statement showing the total contribution and profit for each product group on the basis of:
  (i) the original budget;
  (ii) if product A is deleted.

(8 marks)

(c) Using your results from (a) and (b) advise whether product A should be deleted from the product range, giving reasons for your decision.

(5 marks)
(Total 25 marks)
AAT Cost Accounting and Budgeting

9.32 **Advanced: Alternative uses of obsolete materials**

Brown Ltd is a company that has in stock some materials of type XY that cost £75 000 but that are now obsolete and have a scrap value of only £21 000. Other than selling the material for scrap, there are only two alternative uses for them.

Alternative 1: Converting the obsolete materials into a specialized product, which would require the following additional work and materials:

Material A	600 units
Material B	1 000 units
Direct labour:	
5000 hours unskilled	
5000 hours semi-skilled	
5000 hours highly skilled	15 000 hours
Extra selling and delivery expenses	£27 000
Extra advertising	£18 000

The conversion would produce 900 units of saleable product, and these could be sold for £400 per unit.

Material A is already in stock and is widely used within the firm. Although present stocks together with orders already planned will be sufficient to facilitate normal activity, any extra material used by adopting this alternative will necessitate such materials being replaced immediately. Material B is also in stock, but it is unlikely that any additional supplies can be obtained for some considerable time because of an industrial dispute. At the present time material B is normally used in the production of product Z, which sells at £390 per unit and incurs total variable cost (excluding material B) of £210 per unit. Each unit of product Z uses four units of material B.

The details of materials A and B are as follows:

	Material A (£)	Material B (£)
Acquisition cost at time of purchase	100 per unit	10 per unit
Net realizable value	85 per unit	18 per unit
Replacement cost	90 per unit	—

Alternative 2: Adapting the obsolete materials for use as a substitute for a sub-assembly that is regularly used within the firm. Details of the extra work and materials required are as follows:

Material C	1000 units
Direct labour:	
4000 hours unskilled	
1000 hours semi-skilled	
4000 hours highly skilled	9000 hours

1200 units of the sub-assembly are regularly used per quarter, at a cost of £900 per unit. The adaptation of material XY would reduce the quantity of the sub-assembly purchased from outside the firm to 900 units for the next quarter only. However, since the volume purchased would be reduced, some discount would be lost, and the price of those purchased from outside would increase to £950 per unit for that quarter.

Material C is not available externally, but is manufactured by Brown Ltd. The 1000 units required would be available from stocks, but would be produced as extra production. The standard cost per unit of material C would be as follows:

	(£)
Direct labour, 6 hours unskilled labour	36
Raw materials	13
Variable overhead, 6 hours at £1	6
Fixed overhead, 6 hours at £3	18
	73

The wage rates and overhead recovery rates for Brown Ltd are:

Variable overhead	£1 per direct labour hour
Fixed overhead	£3 per direct labour hour
Unskilled labour	£6 per direct labour hour
Semi-skilled labour	£8 per direct labour hour
Highly skilled labour	£10 per direct labour hour

The unskilled labour is employed on a casual basis and sufficient labour can be acquired to exactly meet the production requirements. Semi-skilled labour is part of the permanent labour force, but the company has temporary excess supply of this type of labour at the present time. Highly skilled labour is in short supply and cannot be increased significantly in the short term; this labour is presently engaged in meeting the demand for product L, which requires 4 hours of highly skilled labour. The contribution (sales less direct labour and material costs and variable overheads) from the sale of one unit of product L is £24.

Given this information, you are required to present cost information advising whether the stocks of material XY should be sold, converted into a specialized product (alternative 1) or adapted for use as a substitute for a sub-assembly (alternative 2).

9.33 Advanced: Limiting factors and optimal production programme

A market gardener is planning his production for next season, and he has asked you as a cost accountant, to recommend the optimal mix of vegetable production for the coming year. He has given you the following data relating to the current year.

	Potatoes	Turnips	Parsnips	Carrots
Area occupied (acres)	25	20	30	25
Yield per acre (tonnes)	10	8	9	12
Selling price per tonne (£)	100	125	150	135
Variable cost per acre (£):				
Fertilizers	30	25	45	40
Seeds	15	20	30	25
Pesticides	25	15	20	25
Direct wages	400	450	500	570
Fixed overhead per annum £54 000				

The land that is being used for the production of carrots and parsnips can be used for either crop, but not for potatoes or turnips. The land being used for potatoes and turnips can be used for either crop, but not for carrots or parsnips. In order to provide an adequate market service, the gardener must produce each year at least 40 tonnes each of potatoes and turnips and 36 tonnes each of parsnips and carrots.

(a) You are required to present a statement to show:

(i) the profit for the current year;

(ii) the profit for the production mix that you would recommend.

(b) Assuming that the land could be cultivated in such a way that any of the above crops could be produced and there was no market commitment, you are required to:

(i) advise the market gardener on which crop he should concentrate his production;

(ii) calculate the profit if he were to do so;

(iii) calculate in sterling the break-even point of sales.

(25 marks)
CIMA Cost Accounting 2

9.34 Advanced: Throughput accounting

(a) Flopro plc make and sell two products A and B, each of which passes through the same automated production operations. The following estimated information is available for period 1:

(i) Product unit data:

	A	B
Direct material cost (£)	2	40
Variable production overhead cost (£)	28	4
Overall hours per product unit (hours)	0.25	0.15

(ii) Production/sales of products A and B are 120 000 units and 45 000 units respectively. The selling prices per unit for A and B are £60 and £70 respectively.

(iii) Maximum demand for each product is 20% above the estimated sales levels.

(iv) Total fixed production overhead cost is £1 470 000. This is absorbed by products A and B at an average rate per hour based on the estimated production levels.

Required:

Using net profit as the decision measure, show why the management of Flopro plc argues that it is indifferent on financial grounds as to the mix of products A and B which should be produced and sold, and calculate the total net profit for period 1.

(6 marks)

(b) One of the production operations has a maximum capacity of 3075 hours which has been identified as a bottleneck which limits the overall production/sales of products A and B. The bottleneck hours required per product unit for products A and B are 0.02 and 0.015 respectively.

All other information detailed in (a) still applies.

Required:

Calculate the mix (units) of products A and B which will maximize net profit and the value (£) of the maximum net profit.

(8 marks)

(c) The bottleneck situation detailed in (b) still applies. Flopro plc has decided to determine the profit maximizing mix of products A and B based on the Throughput Accounting principle of maximizing the throughput return per production hour of the bottleneck resource. This may be measured as:

$$\textit{Throughput return per production hour} = \frac{\textit{(selling price} - \textit{material cost)}}{\textit{bottleneck hours per unit.}}$$

All other information detailed in (a) and (b) still applies, except that the variable overhead cost as per (a) is now considered to be fixed for the short/intermediate term, based on the value (£) which applied to the product mix in (a).

Required:

(i) Calculate the mix (units) of products A and B which will maximize net profit and the value of that net profit.

(8 marks)

(ii) Calculate the throughput accounting ratio for product B which is calculated as:

$$\frac{\textit{throughput return per hour of bottleneck resource for product B}}{\textit{overall total overhead cost per hour of bottleneck resource.}}$$

(3 marks)

(iii) Comment on the interpretation of throughput accounting ratios and their use as a control device. You should refer to the ratio for product B in your answer.

(6 marks)

(iv) It is estimated that the direct material cost per unit of product B may increase by 20% due to shortage of supply.

Calculate the revised throughput accounting ratio for product B and comment on it.

(4 marks)

(35 marks)

ACCA Paper 9 Information for Control and Decision Making

Review problems (with answers in the Student's Manual)

9.35 Intermediate: Make or buy decision

The management of Springer plc is considering next year's production and purchase budgets.

One of the components produced by the company, which is incorporated into another product before being sold, has a budgeted manufacturing cost as follows:

	(£)
Direct material	14
Direct labour (4 hours at £3 per hour)	12
Variable overhead (4 hours at £2 per hour)	8
Fixed overhead (4 hours at £5 per hour)	20
Total cost	54 per unit

Trigger plc has offered to supply the above component at a guaranteed price of £50 per unit.

Required:

(a) Considering cost criteria only, advise management whether the above component should be purchased from Trigger plc. Any calculations should be shown and assumptions made, or aspects which may require further investigation should be clearly stated.

(6 marks)

(b) Explain how your above advice would be affected by each of the two *separate* situations shown below.

(i) As a result of recent government legislation if Springer plc continues to manufacture this component the company will incur additional inspection and testing expenses of £56 000 per annum, which are not included in the above budgeted manufacturing costs.

(3 marks)

(ii) Additional labour cannot be recruited and if the above component is not manufactured by Springer plc the direct labour released will be employed in increasing the production of an existing product which is sold for £90 and which has a budgeted manufacturing cost as follows:

	(£)
Direct material	10
Direct labour (8 hours at £3 per hour)	24
Variable overhead (8 hours at £2 per hour)	16
Fixed overhead (8 hours at £5 per hour)	40
	90 per unit

All calculations should be shown.

(4 marks)

(c) The production director of Springer plc recently said:

> 'We must continue to manufacture the component as only one year ago we purchased some special grinding equipment to be used exclusively by this component. The equipment cost £100 000, it cannot be resold or used elsewhere and if we cease production of this component we will have to write off the written down book value which is £80 000.'

Draft a brief reply to the production director commenting on his statement.

(4 marks)

(Total 17 marks)

ACCA Level 1 Costing

9.36 **Intermediate: Calculation of minimum selling price**

You have received a request from EXE plc to provide a quotation for the manufacture of a specialized piece of equipment. This would be a one-off order, in excess of normal budgeted production. The following cost estimate has already been prepared:

		Note	(£)
Direct materials:			
Steel	10 m^2 at £5.00 per sq. metre	1	50
Brass fittings		2	20
Direct labour			
Skilled	25 hours at £8.00 per hour	3	200
Semi-skilled	10 hours at £5.00 per hour	4	50
Overhead	35 hours at £10.00 per hour	5	350
Estimating time		6	100
			770
Administrative overhead at 20% of production cost		7	154
			924
Profit at 25% of total cost		8	231
Selling price			1155

Notes:

1. The steel is regularly used, and has a current stock value of £5.00 per sq. metre. There are currently 100 sq. metres in stock. The steel is readily available at a price of £5.50 per sq. metre.
2. The brass fittings would have to be bought specifically for this job: a supplier has quoted the price of £20 for the fittings required.
3. The skilled labour is currently employed by your company and paid at a rate of £8.00 per hour. If this job were undertaken it would be necessary either to work 25 hours overtime which would be paid at time plus one

half *or* to reduce production of another product which earns a contribution of £13.00 per hour.

4. The semi-skilled labour currently has sufficient paid idle time to be able to complete this work.
5. The overhead absorption rate includes power costs which are directly related to machine usage. If this job were undertaken, it is estimated that the machine time required would be ten hours. The machines incur power costs of £0.75 per hour. There are no other overhead costs which can be specifically identified with this job.
6. The cost of the estimating time is that attributed to the four hours taken by the engineers to analyse the drawings and determine the cost estimate given above.
7. It is company policy to add 20% on to the production cost as an allowance against administration costs associated with the jobs accepted.
8. This is the standard profit added by your company as part of its pricing policy.

Required:

(a) Prepare, on a relevant cost basis, the lowest cost estimate that could be used as the basis for a quotation. Explain briefly your reasons for using *each* of the values in your estimate.

(12 marks)

(b) There may be a possibility of repeat orders from EXE plc which would occupy part of normal production capacity. What factors need to be considered before quoting for this order?

(7 marks)

(c) When an organisation identifies that it has a single production resource which is in short supply, but is used by more than one product, the optimum production plan is determined by ranking the products according to their contribution per unit of the scarce resource.

Using a numerical example of your own, reconcile this approach with the opportunity cost approach used in (a) above.

(6 marks)
(Total 25 marks)
CIMA Stage Operational Cost Accounting

9.37 Intermediate: Impact of a product abandonment decision and CVP analysis

(a) Budgeted information for A Ltd for the following period, analysed by product, is shown below:

	Product I	Product II	Product III
Sales units (000s)	225	376	190
Selling price (£ per unit)	11.00	10.50	8.00
Variable costs (£ per unit)	5.80	6.00	5.20
Attributable fixed costs (£000s)	275	337	296

General fixed costs, which are apportioned to products as a percentage of sales, are budgeted at £1 668 000.

Required:

(i) Calculate the budgeted profit of A Ltd, and of each of its products. *(5 marks)*

(ii) Recalculate the budgeted profit of A Ltd on the assumption that Product III is discontinued, with no effect on sales of the other two products. State and justify other assumptions made. *(5 marks)*

(iii) Additional advertising, to that included in the budget for Product I, is being considered.

Calculate the minimum extra sales units required of Product I to cover additional advertising expenditure of £80 000. Assume that all other existing fixed costs would remain unchanged. *(3 marks)*

(iv) Calculate the increase in sales volume of Product II that is necessary in order to compensate for the effect on profit of a 10% reduction in the selling price of the product. State clearly any assumptions made. *(5 marks)*

(b) Discuss the factors which influence cost behaviour in response to changes in activity. *(7 marks)*

(Total 25 marks)

ACCA Cost and Management Accounting 1

9.38 Intermediate Price/output and key factor decisions

You work as a trainee for a small management consultancy which has been asked to advise a company, Rane Limited, which manufactures and sells a single product. Rane is currently operating at full capacity producing and selling 25 000 units of its product each year. The cost and selling price structure for this level of activity is as follows:

	At 25 000 units output (£ per unit)	(£ per unit)
Production costs		
Direct material	14	
Direct labour	13	
Variable production overhead	4	
Fixed production overhead	8	
Total production cost		39
Selling and distribution overhead:		
Sales commission – 10% of sales value	6	
Fixed	3	
		9
Administration overhead:		
Fixed		2
Total cost		50
Mark up – 20%		10
Selling price		60

A new managing director has recently joined the company and he has engaged your organization to advise on his company's selling price policy. The sales price of £60 has been derived as above from a cost-plus pricing policy. The price was viewed as satisfactory because the resulting demand enabled full capacity operation.

You have been asked to investigate the effect on costs and profit of an increase in the selling price. The marketing department has provided you with the following estimates of sales volumes which could be achieved at the three alternative sales prices under consideration.

Selling price per unit	£70	£80	£90
Annual sales volume (units)	20 000	16 000	11 000

You have spent some time estimating the effect that changes in output volume will have on cost behaviour patterns and you have now collected the following information.

Direct material: The loss of bulk discounts means that the direct material cost per unit will increase by 15% for all units produced in the year if activity reduces below 15 000 units per annum.

Direct labour: Savings in bonus payments will reduce labour costs by 10% for all units produced in the year if activity reduces below 20 000 units per annum.

Sales commission: This would continue to be paid at the rate of 10% of sales price.

Fixed production overhead: If annual output volume was below 20 000 units, then a machine rental cost of £10 000 per annum could be saved. This will be the only change in the total expenditure on fixed production overhead.

Fixed selling overhead: A reduction in the part-time sales force would result in a £5000 per annum saving if annual sales volume falls below 24 000 units. This will be the only change in the total expenditure on fixed selling and distribution overhead.

Variable production overhead: There would be no change in the unit cost for variable production overhead.

Administration overhead: The total expenditure on administration overhead would remain unaltered within this range of activity.

Stocks: Rane's product is highly perishable, therefore no stocks are held.

Task 1

(a) Calculate the annual profit which is earned with the current selling price of £60 per unit.

(b) Prepare a schedule to show the annual profit which would be earned with each of the three alternative selling prices.

Task 2

Prepare a brief memorandum to your boss, Chris Jones. The memorandum should cover the following points:

(a) Your recommendation as to the selling price which should be charged to maximize Rane Limited's annual profits.

(b) *Two* non-financial factors which the management of Rane Limited should consider before planning to operate below full capacity.

Another of your consultancy's clients is a manufacturing company, Shortage Limited, which is experiencing problems in obtaining supplies of a major component. The component is used in all of its four products and there is a labour dispute at the supplier's factory, which is restricting the component's availability.

Supplies will be restricted to 22 400 components for the next period and the company wishes to ensure that the best use is made of the available components. This is the only component used in the four products, and there are no alternatives and no other suppliers.

The components cost £2 each and are used in varying amounts in each of the four products.

Shortage Limited's fixed costs amount to £8000 per period. No stocks are held of finished goods or work in progress.

The following information is available concerning the products.

Maximum demand per period	**Product A 4000 units (£ per unit)**	**Product B 2500 units (£ per unit)**	**Product C 3600 units (£ per unit)**	**Product D 2750 units (£ per unit)**
Selling price	14	12	16	17
Component costs	4	2	6	8
Other variable costs	7	9	6	4

Task 3

(a) Prepare a recommended production schedule for next period which will maximize Shortage Limited's profit.

(b) Calculate the profit that will be earned in the next period if your recommended production schedule is followed.

AAT Technicians Stage

9.39 **Intermediate: Limiting factor optimum production and the use of simultaneous equations where more than one scarce factor exists**

A company manufactures two products (X and Y) in one of its factories. Production capacity is limited to 85 000 machine hours per period. There is no restriction on direct labour hours.

The following information is provided concerning the two products:

	Product X	**Product Y**
Estimated demand (000 units)	315	135
Selling price (per unit)	£11.20	£15.70
Variable costs (per unit)	£6.30	£8.70
Fixed costs (per unit)	£4.00	£7.00
Machine hours (per 000 units)	160	280
Direct labour hours (per 000 units)	120	140

Fixed costs are absorbed into unit costs at a rate per machine hour based upon full capacity.

Required:

(a) Calculate the production quantities of Products X and Y which are required per period in order to maximize profit in the situation described above.

(5 marks)

(b) Prepare a marginal costing statement in order to establish the total contribution of each product, and the net profit per period, based on selling the quantities calculated in (a) above.

(4 marks)

(c) Calculate the production quantities of Products X and Y per period which would fully utilize both machine capacity and direct labour hours, where the available direct labour hours are restricted to 55 000 per period. (The limit of 85 000 machine hours remains.)

(5 marks)
(Total 14 marks)
ACCA Foundation Paper 3

9.40 **Advanced: Assessing a number of options using relevant costs**

MOV plc produces custom-built sensors. Each sensor has a standard circuit board (SCB) in it. The current average contribution from a sensor is £400. MOV plc's business is steadily expanding and in the year just ending (2001/2002), the company will have produced 55 000 sensors. The demand for MOV plc's sensors is predicted to grow over the next three years:

Year	Units
2002/03	58 000
2003/04	62 000
2004/05	65 000

The production of sensors is limited by the number of SCBs the company can produce. The present production level of 55 000 SCBs is the maximum that can be produced without overtime working. Overtime could increase annual output to 60 500, allowing production of sensors to also increase to 60 500. However, the variable cost of SCBs produced in overtime would increase by £75 per unit.

Because of the pressure on capacity, the company is considering having the SCBs manufactured by another company, CIR plc. This company is very reliable and produces products of good quality. CIR plc has quoted a price of £116 per SCB, for orders greater than 50 000 units a year.

MOV plc's own costs per SCB are predicted to be:

	£	
Direct material	28	
Direct labour	40	
Variable overhead	20	(based on labour cost)
Fixed overhead	24	(based on labour cost and output of 55 000 units)
Total cost	112	

The fixed overheads directly attributable to SCBs are £250 000 a year; these costs will be avoided if SCBs are not produced. If more than 59 000 units are produced, SCBs' fixed overheads will increase by £130 000.

In addition to the above overheads, MOV plc's fixed overheads are predicted to be:

Sensor production, in units:	*54 001 to 59 000*	*59 001 to 64 000*	*64 001 to 70 000*
Fixed overhead:	£2 600 000	£2 900 000	£3 100 000

MOV plc currently holds a stock of 3500 SCBs but the production manager feels that a stock of 8000 should be held if they are bought-in; this would increase stockholding costs by £10 000 a year. A purchasing officer, who is paid £20 000 a year, spends 50% of her time on SCB duties. If the SCBs are bought-in, a liaison officer will have to be employed at a salary of £30 000 in order to liaise with CIR plc and monitor the quality and supply of SCBs. At present, 88 staff are involved in the production of SCBs at an average salary of £25 000 a year: if the SCBs were purchased, 72 of these staff would be made redundant at an average cost of £4000 per employee.

The SCB department, which occupies an area of 240 × 120 square metres at the far end of the factory, could be rented out, at a rent of £45 per square metre a year. However, if the SCBs were to be bought-in, for the first year only MOV plc would need the space to store the increased stock caused by outsourcing, until the main stockroom had been reorganized and refurbished. From 2003/04, the space could be rented out; this would limit the annual production of sensors to 60 500 units. Alternatively, the space could be used for the production of sensors, allowing annual output to increase to 70 000 units if required.

Required:

(a) Critically discuss the validity of the following statement. It was produced by Jim Elliott, the company's accountant, to show the gain for the coming year (2002/2003) if the SCBs were to be bought-in.

Saving in:	**£**
Manufacturing staff – salaries saved: 72 staff × £25 000	1 800 000
Purchasing officer – time saved	10 000
Placing orders for SCB materials: 1000 orders × £20 per order	20 000
Transport costs for raw materials for SCBs	45 000
Cost saved	1 875 000
Additional cost per SCB: (£116 – £112) × 58 000 units	232 000
Net gain if SCBs purchased	1 643 000

(10 marks)

(b) (i) Produce detailed calculations that show which course of action is the best financial option for the three years under consideration. (Ignore the time value of money.)

(12 marks)

(ii) Advise the company of the long-term advantages and disadvantages of buying-in SCBs.

(3 marks)

(Total 25 marks)

CIMA Management Accounting – Decision Making

9.41 **Advanced: Optimal production programme, shadow prices and relevant costs for pricing decisions**

Rosehip has spare capacity in two of its manufacturing departments – Department 4 and Department 5. A five day week of 40 hours is worked but there is only enough internal work for three days per week so that two days per week (16 hours) could be available in each department. In recent months Rosehip has sold this time to another manufacturer but there is some concern about the profitability of this work.

The accountant has prepared a table giving the hourly operating costs in each department. The summarized figures are as follows:

	Department 4 (£)	Department 5 (£)
Power costs	40	60
Labour costs	40	20
Overhead costs	40	40
	120	120

The labour force is paid on a time basis and there is no change in the weekly wage bill whether or not the plant is working at full capacity. The overhead figures are taken from the firm's current overhead absorption rates. These rates are designed to absorb all budgeted overhead (fixed and variable) when the departments are operating at 90% of full capacity (assume a 50 week year). The budgeted fixed overhead attributed to Department 4 is £36 000 p.a. and that for Department 5 is £50 400 p.a.

As a short term expedient the company has been selling processing time to another manufacturer who has been paying £70 per hour for time in either department. This customer is very willing to continue this arrangement and to purchase any spare time available but Rosehip is considering the introduction of a new product on a minor scale to absorb the spare capacity.

Each unit of the new product would require 45 minutes in Department 4 and 20 minutes in Department 5. The variable cost of the required input material is £10 per unit. It is considered that:

with a selling price of £100 the demand would be 1500 units p.a.;
with a selling price of £110 the demand would be 1000 units p.a.; and
with a selling price of £120 the demand would be 500 units p.a.

(a) You are required to calculate the best weekly programme for the slack time in the two manufacturing departments, to determine the best price to charge for the new product and to quantify the weekly gain that this programme and this price should yield.

(12 marks)

(b) Assume that the new product has been introduced successfully but that the demand for the established main products has now increased so that all available time could now be absorbed by Rosehip's main-line products. An optimal production plan for the main products has been obtained by linear programming and the optimal LP. tableau shows a shadow price of £76 per hour in Department 4 and of £27 per hour in

Department 5. The new product was not considered in this exercise. Discuss the viability of the new product under the new circumstances.

(5 marks)

(c) Comment on the relationship between shadow prices and opportunity costs.

(5 marks)

(Total 22 marks)

ACCA Level 2 Management Accounting

9.42 **Advanced: Decision relating to the timing of the conversion of a production process**

A company extracts exhaust gases from process ovens as part of the manufacturing process. The exhaust gas extraction is implemented by machinery which cost £100 000 when bought five years ago. The machinery is being depreciated at 10% per annum. The extraction of the exhaust gases enhances production output by 10 000 units per annum. This production can be sold at £8 per unit and has variable costs of £3 per unit. The exhaust gas extraction machinery has directly attributable fixed operating costs of £16 000 per annum.

The company is considering the use of the exhaust gases for space heating. The existing space heating is provided by ducted hot air which is heated by equipment with running costs of £10 000 per annum. This equipment could be sold now for £20 000 but would incur dismantling costs of £3000. If retained for one year the equipment could be sold for £18 000 with dismantling costs of £3500.

The conversion to the use of the exhaust gases for space heating would involve the following:

(i) The removal of the existing gas extraction machinery. This could be implemented now at a dismantling cost of £5000 with sale of the machinery for £40 000. Alternatively it could be sold in one year's time for £30 000 with dismantling costs of £5500.

(ii) The leasing of alternative gas extraction equipment at a cost of £4000 per annum with annual fixed running costs of £12 000.

(iii) The conversion would mean the loss of 30% of the production enhancement which the exhaust gas extraction provides for a period of one year only, until the new system is 'run-in'.

(iv) The company has a spare electric motor in store which could be sold to company X for £3500 in one year's time. It could be fitted to the proposed leased gas extraction equipment in order to reduce the impact of the production losses during the running-in period. This course of action would reduce its sales value to company X in one year's time to £2000 and would incur £2500 of fitting and dismantling costs. It would, however, reduce the production enhancement loss from 30% to 10% during the coming year (year 1). This would not be relevant in year 2 because of an anticipated fall in the demand for the product.The electric motor originally cost £5000. If replaced today it would cost £8000. It was purchased for another process which has now been discontinued. It could also be used in a cooling process for one year if modified at a cost of £1000, instead of the company hiring cooling equipment at a cost of

£3000 per annum. Because of its modification, the electric motor would have to be disposed of in one year's time at a cost of £250.

Ignore the time value of money.

Required:

(a) Prepare an analysis indicating all the options available for the use of the spare electric motor and the financial implications of each. State which option should be chosen on financial grounds.

(8 marks)

(b) Prepare an analysis on an incremental opportunity cost basis in order to decide on financial grounds whether to convert immediately to the use of exhaust gases for space heating or to delay the conversion for one year.

(18 marks)

(Total 26 marks)

ACCA Paper 9 Information for Control and Decision Making

9.43 Advanced: Decision on whether to subcontract an appliance repair service or do own maintenance

A company producing and selling a range of consumer durable appliances has its after-sales service work done by local approved sub-contractors.

The company is now considering carrying out all or some of the work itself and it has chosen one area in which to experiment with the new routine.

Some of the appliances are so large and bulky that repair/service work can only be done at the customers' homes. Others are small enough for sub-contractors to take them back to their local repair workshops, repair them, and re-deliver them to the customer. If the company does its own after-sales service, it proposes that customers would bring these smaller items for repair to a local company service centre which would be located and organized to deal with visitors.

There is a *list price* to customers for the labour content of any work done and for materials used. However, the majority of the after-sales service work is done under an annual maintenance contract taken out by customers on purchasing the product; this covers the labour content of any service work to be done, but customers pay for materials used.

Any labour or materials needed in the first six months are provided to the customer free of charge under the company's product guarantee and *sub-contractors* are allowed *by the company a fixed sum of 3.5% of the selling price* for each appliance to cover this work. These sums allowed have proved closely in line with the work needed over the past few years. The price structure is:

For materials:

Price to sub-contractor:	Company cost plus 10%
Price to customer:	Sub-contractor's price plus 25%

For labour: Price to sub-contractor:

Work done under maintenance contract:	90% of list price
Ad hoc work (i.e. work NOT done under maintenance contract):	85% of list price

Records show that 60% by value of the work has to be carried out at customers' homes, whilst the remainder can be done anywhere appropriate.

The annual income that the company currently receives from sub-contractors for the area in which the experiment is to take place is:

		(£)
Labour	– under maintenance contract	30 000
	– ad hoc	12 000
Materials	– under maintenance contract	18 000
	– ad hoc	6 000
		£66 000

The company expects the volume of after-sales work to remain the same as last year for the period of the experiment.

The company is considering the following options:

1. Set up a local service centre at which it can service small appliances only.

   Work at customers' houses would continue to be done under sub-contract.
2. Set up a local service centre to act only as a base for its own employees who would only service appliances at customers' homes.

   Servicing of small appliances would continue to be done under sub-contract.
3. Set up a local combined service centre plus base for all work. No work would be sub-contracted.

If the company were to do service work, annual fixed costs are budgeted to be:

	Option 1 (£000)	Option 2 (£000)	Option 3 (£000)
Establishment costs			
(rent, rates, light, etc.)	40	15	45
Management costs	20	15	30
Storage staff costs	10	10	15
Transport costs			
(all vans/cars hired)	8	65	70
Repair/service staff	70	180	225

You are required

(a) to recommend which of the three options the company should adopt from a financial viewpoint;

(18 marks)

(b) in relation to the data provided in order to make the recommendation required in (a) above, to comment critically in respect of non-financial features that might favourably or adversely affect the customer.

(7 marks)

(Total 25 marks)

CIMA Stage 4 Management Accounting Decision Making

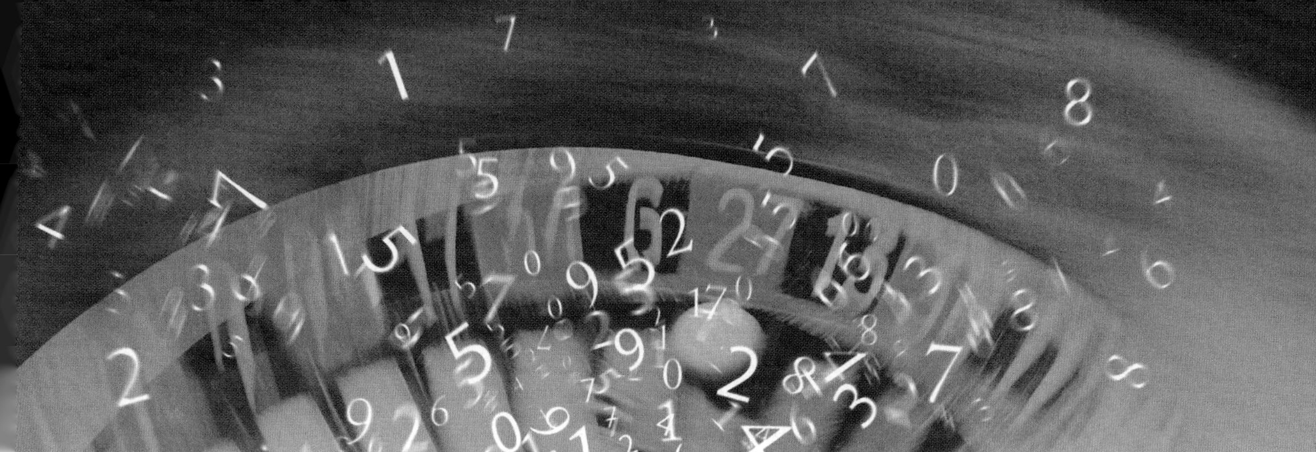

Activity-based costing

10

The aim of the previous chapter was to provide you with an understanding of the principles that should be used to identify relevant costs and revenues for various types of decisions. It was assumed that relevant costs could easily be measured but, in reality, it was pointed out that indirect relevant costs can be difficult to identify and measure. The measurement of indirect relevant costs for decision-making using activity-based costing (ABC) techniques will be examined in this chapter. The aim of this chapter is to provide you with a conceptual understanding of ABC. Some of the issues explored are complex and therefore much of the content of this chapter is appropriate for a second year management accounting course. If you are pursuing a first year course the content relating to ABC that was presented in Chapter 3 should meet your requirements. In addition, you may wish to read this chapter and omit those sections that are labelled advanced reading.

Because this chapter extends the material covered in Chapter 3 you are recommended to refresh your memory by reading pages 72–76 prior to reading this chapter.

LEARNING OBJECTIVES

After studying this chapter you should be able to:

- explain why a cost accumulation system is required for generating relevant cost information for decision-making;
- describe the differences between activity-based and traditional costing systems;
- explain why traditional costing systems can provide misleading information for decision-making;
- identify and explain each of the four stages involved in designing ABC systems;
- describe the ABC cost hierarchy;
- describe the ABC profitability analysis hierarchy;
- describe the ABC resource consumption model;
- justify the choice of practical capacity as the denominator level for estimating cost driver rates.

Our focus will be on an organization's *existing* products or services. There is also a need to manage *future* activities to ensure that only profitable products and services are launched. Here the emphasis is on providing cost information using techniques such as target costing, life cycle costing and value engineering. These issues will be explored in Chapter 22 and the mechanisms for appraising investments in new products, services or locations will be described in Chapters 13 and 14. We shall also defer our discussion of the relevant cost information that is required for pricing decisions until the next chapter.

Unless otherwise stated we shall assume that products are the cost objects but the techniques used, and the principles established, can also be applied to other cost objects such as customers, services and locations. We begin with an examination of the role that a cost accumulation system plays in generating relevant cost information for decision-making.

The need for a cost accumulation system in generating relevant cost information for decision-making

There are three main reasons why a cost accumulation system is required to generate relevant cost information for decision-making. They are:

1. many indirect costs are relevant for decision-making;
2. an attention-directing information system is required that periodically identifies those potentially unprofitable products that require more detailed special studies;
3. product decisions are not independent.

There is a danger that only those incremental costs that are uniquely attributable to individual products will be classified as relevant and indirect costs will be classified as irrelevant for decision-making. Direct costs are transparent and how they will be affected by decisions is clearly observable. In contrast, how indirect costs will be affected by decisions is not clearly observable. There has been a tendency in the past to assume that these costs are fixed and irrelevant for decision-making. In many organizations, however, these are costs that have escalated over the years. The message is clear – they cannot be assumed to be fixed and irrelevant for decision-making.

The costs of many joint resources fluctuate in the long term according to the demand for them. The cost of support functions fall within this category. They include activities such as materials procurement, materials handling, production scheduling, warehousing, expediting and customer order processing. The costs of these activities are either not directly traceable to products, or would involve such detailed tracing, the costs of doing so would far exceed their benefits. Product introduction, discontinuation, redesign and mix decisions determine the demand for support function resources. For example, if a decision results in a 10% reduction in the demand for the resources of a support activity then we would expect, in the long term, for some of the costs of that support activity to decline by 10%. Therefore, to estimate the impact that decisions will have on the support activities (and their future costs) a cost accumulation system is required that assigns those indirect costs, using cause-and-effect allocations, to products.

The second reason relates to the need for a periodic attention-directing reporting system. For decision-making it could be argued that relevant/incremental costs need only be ascertained when the need arises. For example, why not undertake special studies involving incremental cost/revenue analysis at periodic intervals to make sure that each product is still profitable? Estimates could be made only when undertaking a special study of those relevant costs that would be avoided if a product was discontinued. This approach is fine for highly simplified situations where an organization only produces a few products and where all relevant costs are uniquely attributable to individual products. However, most organizations produce hundreds of products and the range of potential decisions to explore undertaking special studies is enormous and unmanageable. For example, Kaplan (1990) considers a situation where a company has 100 products and outlines the difficulties of determining which product, or product combinations, should be selected for undertaking special studies. Kaplan states:

> *First how do you think about which product you should even think about making a decision on? There are 100 different products to consider. But think about all the combinations of these products: which two products, three products or groupings of 10 or 20 products should be analyzed? It's a simple exercise to calculate that there are 2^{100} different combinations of the 100 products ... so there is no way to do an incremental revenue/incremental analysis on all relevant combinations (p. 13).*

To cope with the vast number of potential product combinations organizations need attention-directing information to highlight those specific products, or combination of products, that appear to be questionable and which require further detailed special studies to ascertain their viability. Periodic product profitability analysis meets this requirement. A cost accumulation system is therefore required to assign costs to products for periodic profitability analysis.

The third reason for using a cost accumulation system is that many product related decisions are not independent. Consider again those joint resources shared by most products and that fluctuate in the longer term according to the demand for them. If we focus only on individual products and assume that they are independent, decisions will be taken in isolation of decisions made on other products. For joint resources the incremental/avoidable costs relating to a decision to add or drop a *single* product may be zero. Assuming that 20 products are viewed in this manner then the sum of the incremental costs will be zero. However, if the 20 products are viewed as a *whole* there may be a significant change in resource usage and incremental costs for those joint resources that fluctuate according to the demand for them.

Cooper (1990b) also argues that decisions should not be viewed independently. He states:

> *The decision to drop one product will typically not change 'fixed' overhead spending. In contrast, dropping 50 products might allow considerable changes to be made. Stated somewhat tritely, the sum of the parts (the decision to drop individual products) is not equal to the sum of the whole (the realisable savings from having dropped 50 products). To help them make effective decisions, managers require cost systems that provide insights into the whole, not just isolated individual parts (p. 58).*

Thus, where product decisions are not independent the multiplication of product costs, that include the cost of joint resources, by the units lost from ceasing production (or additional units from introducing a new product) may provide an approximation of the change in the long term of total company costs arising from the decisions. The rationale for this is that the change in resource consumption will ultimately be followed by a change in the cash flow pattern of the organization because organizations make product introduction or abandonment decisions for many products rather than just a single product. These issues are complex and will be explained in more detail later in the chapter.

Types of cost systems

Costing systems can vary in terms of which costs are assigned to cost objects and their level of sophistication. Typically cost systems are classified as follows:

1. direct costing systems;
2. traditional absorption costing systems;
3. activity-based costing systems.

Direct costing systems only assign direct costs to cost objects. Because they do not assign indirect costs to cost objects they report contributions to indirect costs. Direct costing systems can therefore be classified as partial costing systems. They are appropriate for decision-making where the cost of those joint resources that fluctuate according to the demand for them are insignificant. Negative or low contribution items should then be highlighted for special studies. An estimate of those indirect costs that are relevant to the decision should be incorporated within the analysis at the special study stage. The disadvantage of direct costing systems is that systems are not in place to measure and assign indirect costs to cost objects. Thus any attempt to incorporate indirect costs into the analysis at the special studies stage must be based on guesswork and arbitrary estimates. Direct costing systems can therefore only be recommended where indirect costs are a low proportion of an organization's total costs.

Both traditional and ABC systems assign indirect costs to cost objects. The major features of these systems were described in Chapter 3 and the assignment of costs to products was illustrated for both systems. In the next section the major features that were described in Chapter 3 are briefly summarized but the assignment of costs to products will not be repeated. If you wish to renew your understanding of the detailed cost assignment process you should refer back to Chapter 3 for an illustration of the application of the two-stage allocation process for both traditional and ABC systems.

A comparison of traditional and ABC systems

Figure 3.3 was used in Chapter 3 to illustrate the major differences between traditional costing and ABC systems. This diagram is repeated in the form of Figure 10.1 to provide you with an overview of both systems. Both use a two-stage allocation process. In the first stage a traditional system allocates overheads to production and service departments and then reallocates service department costs to the production departments. An ABC system assigns overheads to each major activity (rather than departments). With ABC systems, many activity-based cost centres (alternatively known as activity cost pools) are established, whereas with traditional systems overheads tend to be pooled by departments, although they are normally described as cost centres.

Activities consist of the aggregation of many different tasks and are described by verbs associated with objects. Typical support activities include: schedule production, set-up machines, move materials, purchase materials, inspect items, process supplier records, expedite and process customer orders. Production process activities include machine products and assemble products. Within the production process, activity cost centres are often identical to the cost centres used by traditional cost systems. Support activities are also sometimes identical to cost centres used by traditional systems, such as when the purchasing department and activity are both treated as cost centres. Overall, however, ABC systems will normally have a greater number of cost centres.

The second stage of the two-stage allocation process allocates costs from cost centres (pools) to products or other chosen cost objects. Traditional costing systems trace overheads to products using a small number of second stage allocation bases (normally described as overhead allocation rates), which vary directly with the volume produced. Instead of using the terms 'allocation bases' or 'overhead allocation rates' the term **'cost driver'** is used by ABC systems. Direct labour and machine hours are the allocation bases that are normally used by traditional costing systems. In contrast, ABC systems use many different types of second-stage cost drivers, including non-volume-based drivers, such as the number of production runs for production scheduling and the number of purchase orders for the purchasing activity. A further distinguishing feature is that traditional systems normally allocate service/support costs to production centres. Their costs are merged with the production cost centre costs and

FIGURE 10.1 *An illustration of the two-stage allocation process for traditional and activity-based costing systems*

(a) Traditional costing systems

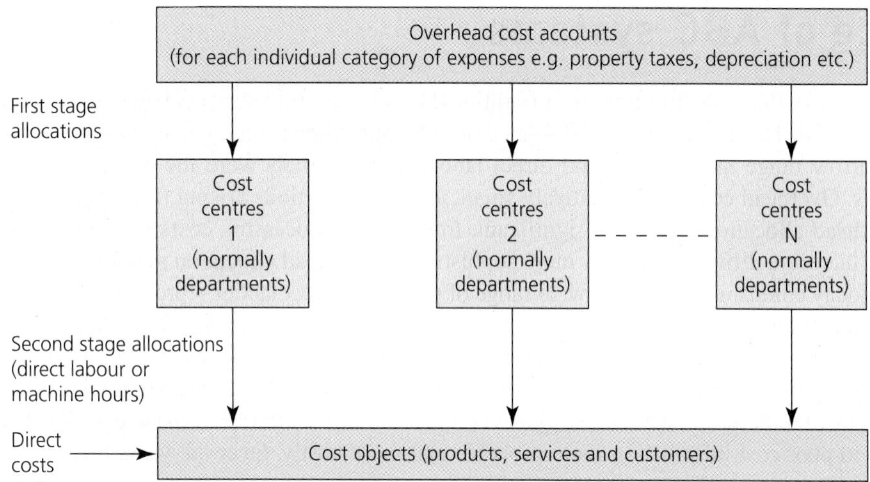

(b) Activity-based costing systems

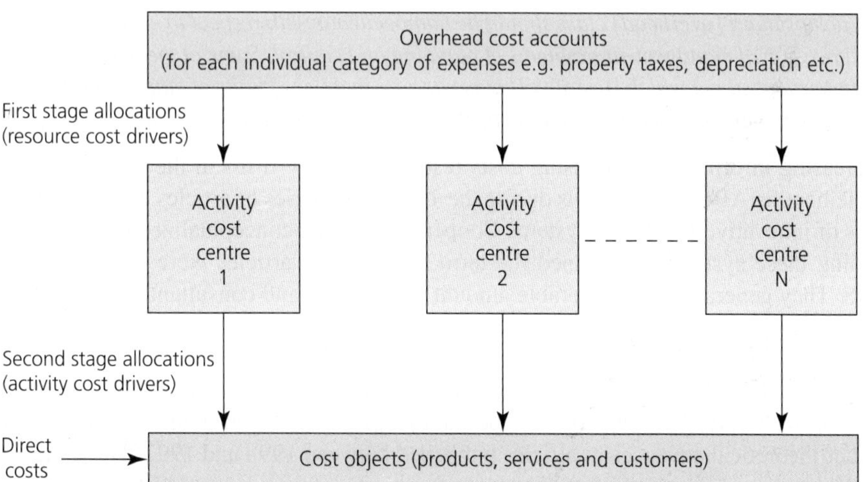

thus included within the production centre overhead rates. In contrast, ABC systems tend to establish separate cost driver rates for support centres, and assign the cost of support activities directly to cost objects without any reallocation to production centres.

Therefore the major distinguishing features of ABC systems are that within the two-stage allocation process they rely on:

1 a greater number of cost centres;

2 a greater number and variety of second stage cost drivers.

By using a greater number of cost centres and different types of cost drivers that cause activity resource consumption, and assigning activity costs to cost objects on the basis of cost driver usage, ABC systems can more accurately measure the resources consumed by cost objects. Traditional cost systems report less accurate costs because they use cost drivers where no cause-and-effect relationships exist to assign support costs to cost objects.

The emergence of ABC systems

During the 1980s the limitations of traditional product costing systems began to be widely publicized. These systems were designed decades ago when most companies manufactured a narrow range of products, and direct labour and materials were the dominant factory costs. Overhead costs were relatively small, and the distortions arising from inappropriate overhead allocations were not significant. Information processing costs were high, and it was therefore difficult to justify more sophisticated overhead allocation methods.

Today companies produce a wide range of products; direct labour represents only a small fraction of total costs, and overhead costs are of considerable importance. Simplistic overhead allocations using a declining direct labour base cannot be justified, particularly when information processing costs are no longer a barrier to introducing more sophisticated cost systems. Furthermore, the intense global competition of the 1980s has made decision errors due to poor cost information more probable and more costly. Over the years the increased opportunity cost of having poor cost information, and the decreased cost of operating more sophisticated cost systems, increased the demand for more accurate product costs (Holzer and Norreklit, 1991). It is against this background that ABC has emerged. ABC, however, is not a recent innovation. Fifty years ago Goetz (1949) advocated ABC principles when he wrote:

> *Each primary [overhead] class should be homogeneous with respect to every significant dimension of management problems of planning and control. Some of the major dimensions along which [overhead] may vary are number of units of output, number of orders, number of operations, capacity of plant, number of catalogue items offered (p. 142).*

Decreasing information processing costs resulted in a few firms in the USA and Europe implementing ABC type systems during the 1980s. In a series of articles based on observations of innovative ABC type systems Cooper and Kaplan conceptualized the ideas underpinning these systems and coined the term ABC. These articles were first published in 1988. They generated a considerable amount of publicity and consultants began to market and implement ABC systems before the end of the decade. In a survey of UK companies Innes and Mitchell (1991) reported that approximately 10% of the surveyed companies had implemented, or were in the process of implementing ABC. Based on their experience of working with early US adopters, Cooper and Kaplan articulated their ideas and reported further theoretical advances in articles published between 1990 and 1992. These ideas and the theoretical advances are described in the remainder of this chapter. ABC ideas have now become firmly embedded in the management accounting literature and educational courses and many practitioners have attended courses and conferences on the topic.

Volume-based and non-volume-based cost drivers

Our comparison of ABC systems with traditional costing systems indicated that ABC systems rely on a greater number and variety of second stage cost drivers. The term 'variety of cost drivers' refers to the fact that ABC systems use both volume-based and non-volume-based cost drivers. In contrast, traditional systems use only volume-based cost drivers. **Volume-based cost drivers** assume that a product's consumption of overhead resources is directly related to units produced. In other words, they assume that the overhead consumed by products is highly correlated with the number of units produced. Typical volume-based cost drivers used by traditional systems are units of output, direct labour hours and machine hours. These cost drivers are appropriate for measuring the consumption of expenses such as machine energy costs, depreciation related to machine usage, indirect labour employed in production centres and inspection costs where each item produced is subject to final inspection. For example, machine hours are an appropriate cost driver for energy costs since if volume is increased by 10%, machine hours are likely to increase by 10%, thus causing 10% more energy costs to be consumed. Similarly, an increase in volume of 10% is likely to increase the consumption of direct labour hours by 10% and, assuming that indirect labour hours are correlated with direct labour hours, 10% more indirect labour costs will be consumed.

Volume-based drivers are appropriate in the above circumstances because activities are performed each time a unit of the product or service is produced. In contrast, non-volume related activities are not performed each time a unit of the product or service is produced. Consider, for example, two activities – setting up a machine and re-engineering products. Set-up resources are consumed each time a machine is changed from one product to another. It costs the same to set-up a machine for 10 or 5000 items. As more set-ups are done more set-up resources are consumed. The number of set-ups, rather than the number of units produced, is a more appropriate measure of the consumption of the set-up activity. Similarly, product re-engineering costs may depend upon the number of different engineering works orders and not the number of units produced. For both of these activities, **non-volume-based cost drivers** such as number of set-ups and engineering orders are needed for the accurate assignment of the costs of these activities.

Using only volume-based cost drivers to assign non-volume related overhead costs can result in the reporting of distorted product costs. The extent of distortion depends on what proportion of total overhead costs the non-volume based overheads represent and the level of product diversity. If a large proportion of an organization's costs are unrelated to volume there is danger that inaccurate product costs will be reported. Conversely, if non-volume related overhead costs are only a small proportion of total overhead costs, the distortion of product costs will not be significant. In these circumstances traditional product costing systems are likely to be acceptable.

Product diversity applies when products consume different overhead activities in dissimilar proportions. Differences in product size, product complexity, sizes of batches and set-up times cause product diversity. If all products consume overhead resources in similar proportions product diversity will be low and products will consume non-volume related activities in the same proportion as volume-related activities. Hence, product cost distortion will not occur with traditional product costing systems. Two conditions are therefore necessary for product cost distortion – non-volume-related overhead costs are a large proportion of total overhead costs and product diversity applies. Where these two conditions exist traditional product costing systems can result in the overcosting of high volume products and undercosting of low volume products. Consider the information presented in Example 10.1.

The reported product costs and profits for the two products are as follows:

	Traditional system		ABC system	
	Product HV (£)	Product LV (£)	Product HV (£)	Product LV (£)
Direct costs	310 000	40 000	310 000	40 000
Overheads allocated[a]	300 000 (30%)	50 000 (5%)	150 000 (15%)	150 000 (15%)
Reported profits/(losses)	(10 000)	60 000	140 000	(40 000)
Sales revenues	600 000	150 000	600 000	150 000

Note

[a]Allocation of £1 million overheads using direct labour hours as the allocation base for the traditional system and number of batches processed as the cost driver for the ABC system.

EXAMPLE 10.1

Assume that the Balearic company has only one overhead cost centre or cost pool. It currently operates a traditional costing system using direct labour hours to allocate overheads to products. The company produces several products, two of which are products HV and LV. Product HV is made in high volumes whereas product LV is made in low volumes. Product HV consumes 30% of the direct labour hours and product LV consumes only 5%. Because of the high volume production product HV can be made in large production batches but the irregular and low level of demand for product LV requires it to be made in small batches. A detailed investigation indicates that the number of batches processed causes the demand for overhead resources. The traditional system is therefore replaced with an ABC system using the number of batches processed as the cost driver. You ascertain that each product accounts for 15% of the batches processed during the period and the overheads assigned to the cost centre that fluctuate in the long term according to the demand for them amount to £1 million. The direct costs and sales revenues assigned to the products are as follows:

	Product HV (£)	**Product LV (£)**
Direct costs	310 000	40 000
Sales revenues	600 000	150 000

Show the product profitability analysis for products HV and LV using the traditional and ABC systems.

Because product HV is a high volume product that consumes 30% of the direct labour hours whereas product LV, the low volume product consumes only 5%, the traditional system that uses direct labour hours as the allocation base allocates six times more overheads to product HV. However, ABC systems recognize that overheads are caused by other factors, besides volume. In our example, all of the overheads are assumed to be volume unrelated. They are caused by the number of batches processed and the ABC system establishes a cause-and-effect allocation relationship by using the number of batches processed as the cost driver. Both products require 15% of the total number of batches so they are allocated with an equal amount of overheads.

It is apparent from the consumption ratios of the two products that the traditional system based on direct labour hours will overcost high volume products. **Consumption ratios** represent the proportion of each activity consumed by a product. The consumption ratios if direct labour hours are used as the cost driver are 0.30 for product HV and 0.05 for product LV so that six times more overheads will be assigned to product HV. When the number of batches processed are used as the cost driver the consumption ratios are 0.15 for each product and an equal amount of overhead will be assigned to each product. Distorted product costs are reported with the traditional costing system that uses the volume-based cost driver because the two conditions specified above apply. First, non-volume related overheads are a large proportion of total overheads, being 100% in our example. Second, product diversity exists because the product consumption ratios for the two identified cost drivers are significantly different. Our illustration shows that if the consumption ratios for batches processed had been the same as the ratios for direct labour the traditional and ABC systems would report identical product costs.

With the traditional costing system misleading information is reported. A small loss is reported for product HV and if it were discontinued the costing system mistakenly gives the impression that overheads will decline in the longer term by £300 000. Furthermore, the message from the costing system is to concentrate on the more profitable speciality products like product LV. In reality this strategy would be disastrous because low volume products like product LV are made in small batches and require more people for scheduling production, performing set-ups, inspection of the batches and handling a large number of customer requests for small orders. The long-term effect would be escalating overhead costs.

In contrast, the ABC system allocates overheads on a cause-and-effect basis and more accurately measures the relatively high level of overhead resources consumed by product LV. The message from the profitability analysis is the opposite from the traditional system; that is, product HV is profitable and product LV is unprofitable. If product LV is discontinued, and assuming that the cost driver is the cause of all the overheads then a decision to discontinue product LV should result in the reduction in resource spending on overheads by £150 000.

Example 10.1 is very simplistic. It is assumed that the organization has established only a single cost centre or cost pool, when in reality many will be established with a traditional system, and even more with an ABC system. Furthermore, the data have been deliberately biased to show the superiority of ABC. The aim of the illustration has been to highlight the potential cost of errors that can occur when information extracted from simplistic and inaccurate cost systems is used for decision-making.

Designing ABC systems

The discussion so far has provided a broad overview of ABC. We shall now examine ABC in more detail by looking at the design of ABC systems. Four steps are involved. They are:

1 identifying the major activities that take place in an organization;
2 assigning costs to cost pools/cost centres for each activity;
3 determining the cost driver for each major activity;
4 assigning the cost of activities to products according to the product's demand for activities.

The first two steps relate to the first stage, and the final two steps to the second stage, of the two-stage allocation process shown in Figure 10.1. Let us now consider each of these stages in more detail.

Step 1: Identifying activities

Activities are composed of the aggregation of units of work or tasks and are described by verbs associated with tasks. For example, purchasing of materials might be identified as a separate activity. This activity consists of the aggregation of many different tasks, such as receiving a purchase request, identifying suppliers, preparing purchase orders, mailing purchase orders and performing follow-ups.

Activities are identified by carrying out an activity analysis. Innes and Mitchell (1995b) suggest that a useful starting point is to examine a physical plan of the workplace (to identify how all work space is being used) and the payroll listings (to ensure all relevant personnel have been taken into account). This examination normally has to be supplemented by a series of interviews with the staff involved, or having staff complete a time

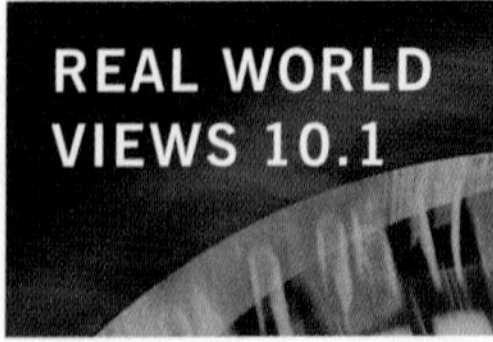

Implementing ABC in a service driven business – DHL Worldwide Express

DHL Worldwide Express is one of the world's leading air express companies. It picks up shipments from premises and flies them to a hub, where the shipments are sorted overnight. They are then flown to the destination country where the import procedures are carried out, and the shipments are delivered to their consignees. By the mid-1980s DHL was going through a period where profitability was not growing at the rate expected. When we tried to analyse the results, the information was not readily available. Without knowing which parts of our business were profitable and which were not, it was difficult to know where growth was improving profitability, and where it was making the situation worse. Another burning question we could not answer was how the growth in direct costs compared with the growth in overhead costs. We carried out a quick exercise. The results showed that while operation costs per shipment had grown by 4%, sales and customer services had grown by 25% and IT accounting, management and administration had grown by a massive 67%. We were definitely in need of a good ABC system.

After building an initial ABC model in 1987, a second generation model was later developed. One of the most fundamental choices was the level of detail to be used in defining activities. The number of activities was finally settled at 106 primary activities. These standard activities are documented in our 'Chart of Activities' and coded in such a way that they can be easily consolidated into 15 activity categories. We also needed to sort out the issue of whether to focus on product costing or customer costing. We found that from a costing point of view, products were not a significant driver of cost. It was the customer characteristics that made the overwhelming difference in cost.

Our cost model defines front-line activities which are driven by such things as courier stops, shipments, kilos, invoices, phone calls, sales visits, etc. All these cost drivers can be directly linked to customers and the cost of any given customer calculated according to their consumption of these drivers. Having mentioned front-line activities, the ones driven directly by customers, I should now mention that our cost model also recognizes that some activities are support activities. You could think of the front-line activities as being driven by external customers and the support activities as being driven by internal customers. So instead of being linked to customers through cost drivers, the support activities are reallocated over the activities that they support according to how those activities drive the support activities.

Let us take salary administration. It is a support activity which is clearly not driven directly by customers. However, it is driven by the number of DHL staff who have their salaries administered. Therefore the front-line activity of picking up shipments will not only include personnel costs, the vehicle costs, etc. coming directly from the general ledger, but it will also be loaded with the reallocated cost of salary administration based on the number of heads involved in the pick-up activity.

Having discussed front-line and support activities we come to the third and final type of activity, the unattributable (or overhead) activities. They are activities, which are not in any way driven by customers. Therefore none of these activities can be attributed to customers. Examples of these unattributable activities are the costs of the business infrastructure. We considered the possibility of simply leaving out the unattributable costs but were concerned that they should be included in the results of our cost model as a reminder that they do have to be recovered. Driven by our intention to give users the best information possible to support decision-making, we decided to show two results. First, the profitability of a customer based solely on the costs actually driven by the customer, i.e. the front-line costs loaded by the appropriate support costs. Then a second result showing the profitability with the unattributable cost spread back as a percentage mark-up on the costs actually driven by the customer. In practice our costing system says 'This customer's consumption of cost drivers will drive our costs by a given amount. If the revenue exceeds that amount, the customer is making a contribution to overheads and profits. However, do not forget that on average each customer will have to contribute another "X" percent to cover the overhead before they start to generate a profit.'

The original idea behind building our ABC system was to provide us with customer profitability data to support marketing decisions such as pricing, discounting, customer targeting, etc. We used it extensively to evaluate the potential profitability of new business, identifying which business we should take at what price and which business we should avoid. However, when we discovered in some cases our existing customers were unprofitable and that simply hitting them with a price increase was not an option, we were faced with the question of what we could do to reduce the cost of servicing these customers. If we were to identify opportunities for reducing customer costs we needed to improve our understanding of how our costs were being driven through the interface with our customers. Thus, since we started using ABC there has been a change in focus. It started originally as a methodology for costing products. Then we moved to customers, then as a basis for cost management and more recently, as a means of facilitating business process improvement.

Source: Adapted from Holton, M. in Innes, J. (ed), *Handbook of Management Accounting*, Gee, 1998, Chapter 23.

sheet for a specific time period explaining how their time is spent. Interviewers will ask managers and employees questions such as what staff work at the location and what tasks are performed by the persons employed at the location.

Many detailed tasks are likely to be identified in the first instance, but after further interviews, the main activities will emerge. The activities chosen should be at a reasonable level of aggregation based on costs versus benefits criteria. For example, rather than classifying purchasing of materials as an activity, each of its constituent tasks could be classified as separate activities. However, this level of decomposition would involve the collection of a vast amount of data and is likely to be too costly for product costing purposes. Alternatively, the purchasing activity might be merged with the materials receiving, storage and issuing activities to form a single materials procurement and handling activity. This is likely to represent too high a level of aggregation because a single cost driver is unlikely to provide a satisfactory determinant of the cost of the activity. For example, selecting the number of purchase orders as a cost driver may provide a good explanation of purchasing costs but may be entirely inappropriate for explaining costs relating to receiving and issuing. Therefore, instead of establishing materials procurement and handling as a single activity it may be preferable to decompose it into three separate activities; namely purchasing, receiving and issuing activities, and establish separate cost drivers for each activity.

In some of the early ABC systems hundreds of separate activity cost centres were established but recent studies suggest that between twenty and thirty activity centres tend to be the norm. The final choice of activities must be a matter of judgement but it is likely to be influenced by factors such as the total cost of the activity centre (it must be of significance to justify separate treatment) and the ability of a single driver to provide a satisfactory determinant of the cost of the activity. Where the latter is not possible further decomposition of the activity will be necessary. Activities with the same product consumption ratios can use the same cost driver to assign costs to products. Thus, all activities that have the same cost driver can be merged to form a single activity cost centre. However, if there are significant differences in activity product consumption ratios products will consume activities in dissimilar proportions and the activities should not be aggregated.

Step 2: Assigning costs to activity cost centres

After the activities have been identified the cost of resources consumed over a specified period must be assigned to each activity. The aim is to determine how much the organization is spending on each of its activities. Many of the resources will be directly attributable to specific activity centres but others (such as labour and lighting and heating costs) may be indirect and jointly shared by several activities. These costs should be assigned to activities on the basis of cause-and-effect cost drivers, or interviews with staff who can provide reasonable estimates of the resources consumed by different activities. Arbitrary allocations should not be used. The greater the amount of costs traced to activity centres by cost apportionments at this stage the more arbitrary and less reliable will be the product cost information generated by ABC systems. Cause-and-effect cost drivers used at this stage to allocate shared resources to individual activities are called **resource cost drivers**.

Step 3: Selecting appropriate cost drivers for assigning the cost of activities to cost objects

In order to assign the costs attached to each activity cost centre to products a cost driver must be selected for each activity centre. Cost drivers used at this stage are called **activity cost drivers**. Several factors must be borne in mind when selecting a suitable cost driver. First, it should provide a good explanation of costs in each activity cost pool. Second, a cost driver should be easily measurable, the data should be relatively easy to obtain and be identifiable with products. The costs of measurement should therefore be taken into account.

Activity cost drivers consist of three types.

1 transaction drivers;
2 duration drivers;
3 intensity drivers.

Transaction drivers, such as the number of purchase orders processed, number of customer orders processed, number of inspections performed and the number of set-ups undertaken, all count the number of times an activity is performed. Transaction drivers are the least expensive type of cost driver but they are also likely to be the least accurate because they assume that the same quantity of resources is required every time an activity is performed. However, if the variation in the amount of resources required by individual cost objects is not great transaction drivers will provide a reasonably accurate measurement of activity resources consumed. If this condition does not apply then duration cost drivers should be used.

Duration drivers represent the amount of time required to perform an activity. Examples of duration drivers include set-up hours and inspection hours. For example, if one product requires a short set-up time and another requires a long time then using set-up hours as the cost driver will more accurately measure activity resource consumption than the transaction driver (number of set-ups) which assumes that an equal amount of activity resources are consumed by both products. Using the number of set-ups will result in the product that requires a long set-up time being undercosted whereas the product that requires a short set-up will be overcosted. This problem can be overcome by using set-up hours as the cost driver, but this will increase the measurement costs.

Intensity drivers directly charge for the resources used each time an activity is performed. Whereas duration drivers establish an average hourly rate for performing an activity, intensity drivers involve direct charging based on the actual activity resources committed to a product. For example, if activities require unskilled and skilled personnel a duration driver would establish an average hourly rate to be assigned to products whereas an intensity driver would record the actual or estimated time for each type of personnel and assign the specific resources directly to the products.

Kaplan and Cooper (1998) illustrate how duration and intensity drivers can be simulated by using a weighted index approach. This involves asking individuals to estimate the relative difficulty of performing a task for different types of customers or products. An appropriate numerical scale is used such that standard low complexity products/customers are awarded low scores, medium complexity products/customers are awarded medium scores and highly complex products/customers attract high scores. The aim is to capture the variation in demands for an activity by products or customers without an over-expensive measurement system.

Innes and Mitchell (1995b) provide an illustration of the weighting approach where purchasing is an activity cost centre and the number of purchase orders represent a potential cost driver. Orders are made both domestically and overseas but the overseas orders involve considerably more administrative work. Rather than split the purchasing cost centre into two separate centres (home and overseas purchasing) and have separate cost drivers for each (home purchase orders and overseas purchase orders) the costs of measurement can be reduced by weighting the overseas orders relative to the home orders. For example, after undertaking an assessment of the work required to make the respective orders it might be decided that each overseas order be weighted 1.5 (relative to 1 for a home order) before determining the total weighted volume of the cost driver to be used in calculating the appropriate cost driver rate.

In most situations data will not initially be available relating to the past costs of activities or potential cost driver volumes. To ascertain potential cost drivers interviews will be required with the personnel involved with the specific activities. The interviews will seek to ascertain what causes the particular activity to consume resources and incur costs. The final choice of a cost driver is likely to be based on managerial judgement after taking into account the factors outlined above.

Step 4: Assigning the cost of the activities to products

The final stage involves applying the cost driver rates to products. Therefore the cost driver must be measurable in a way that enables it to be identified with individual products. Thus, if set-up hours are selected as a cost driver, there must be a mechanism for measuring the set-up hours consumed by each product. Alternatively, if the number of set-ups is selected as the cost driver measurements by products are not required since all products that require a set-up are charged with a constant set-up cost. The ease and cost of obtaining data on cost driver consumption by products is therefore a factor that must be considered during the third stage when an appropriate cost driver is being selected.

Activity hierarchies

Early ABC systems were subject to a number of criticisms, particularly relating to theoretical aspects. As a response to these criticisms a number of theoretical developments emerged during the 1990s.

The first theoretical development was reported by Cooper (1990a) who classified manufacturing activities along a cost hierarchy dimension consisting of:

1 unit-level activities;
2 batch-level activities;
3 product-sustaining activities;
4 facility-sustaining activities.

Unit-level activities (also known as volume-related activities) are performed each time a unit of the product or service is produced. Expenses in this category include direct labour, direct materials, energy costs and expenses that are consumed in proportion to machine processing time (such as maintenance). Unit-level activities consume resources in proportion to the number of units of production and sales volume. For example, if a firm produces 10% more units it will consume 10% more labour cost, 10% more machine hours and 10% more energy costs. Typical cost drivers for unit level activities include labour hours, machine hours and the quantity of materials processed. These cost drivers are also used by traditional costing systems. Traditional systems are therefore also appropriate for assigning the costs of unit-level activities to cost objects.

Batch-related activities, such as setting up a machine or processing a purchase order, are performed each time a batch of goods is produced. The cost of batch-related activities varies with the number of batches made, but is common (or fixed) for all units within the batch. For example, set-up resources are consumed when a machine is changed from one product to another. As more batches are produced, more set-up resources are consumed. It costs the same to set-up a machine for 10 or 5000 items. Thus the demands for the set-up resources are independent of the number of units produced after completing the set-up. Similarly, purchasing resources are consumed each time a purchasing order is processed, but the resources consumed are independent of the number of units included in the purchase order. Other examples of batch-related costs include resources devoted to production scheduling, first-item inspection and materials movement. Traditional costing systems treat batch-related expenses as fixed costs. However, the more the batch-related activities are required the more the organization must eventually spend to supply resources to perform these activities. Thus ABC systems assume that batch-related expenses vary with the number of batches processed and provide a mechanism for assigning some of the costs of complexity (such as set-ups, customer ordering and purchasing) to the products or services that cause the activity.

Product-sustaining activities or **service-sustaining activities** are performed to enable the production and sale of individual products (or services). Examples of product-sustaining activities provided by Kaplan and Cooper (1998) include maintaining and updating product specifications and the technical support provided for individual products and services. Other examples are the resources to prepare and implement engineering change notices (ECNs), to design processes and test routines for individual products, and to perform product enhancements. The costs of product-sustaining activities are incurred irrespective of the number of units of output or the number of batches processed and their expenses will tend to increase as the number of products manufactured is increased. ABC uses product-level bases such as number of active part numbers and number of ECNs to assign these costs to products. Kaplan and Cooper (1998) have extended their ideas to situations where customers are the cost objects with the equivalent term for product-sustaining being **customer-sustaining activities**. Customer market research and support for an individual customer, or groups of customers if they represent the cost object, are examples of customer-sustaining activities.

The final activity category is **facility-sustaining** (or **business-sustaining**) **activities**. They are performed to support the facility's general manufacturing process and include general administrative staff, plant management and property costs. They are incurred to support the organization as a whole and are common and joint to all products manufactured in the plant. There would have to be a dramatic change in activity, resulting in an expansion or contraction in the size of the plant, for facility-sustaining costs to change. Such events are most unlikely in most organizations. Therefore the ABC literature advocates that these costs should not be assigned to products since they are unavoidable and irrelevant for most decisions. Instead, they are regarded as common costs to *all* products made in the plant and deducted as a lump sum from the total of the operating margins from *all* products.

Activity-based costing profitability analysis

The second theoretical development was first highlighted by Kaplan (1990) and Cooper and Kaplan (1991). They apply the ABC hierarchical activity classification to profitability analysis. In addition, they stress that the reported ABC product costs do not provide information that can be used directly for decision-making. Instead, they report attention-directing information by highlighting those potentially unprofitable products or services that require more detailed special studies. Cooper (1997) has stressed that a major role of ABC is to develop profitability maps (i.e. periodic profitability analysis by cost objects) that are used to focus managerial attention. He argues that because the cost of special studies are high the number performed has to be carefully controlled; hence the need for good attention-directing information. He concludes that the primary value of ABC systems lies in the quality of the profitability analysis generated. Their greater accuracy increases the probability that when the special study is undertaken, its findings will support the message sent by the cost system. In other words, profitable products will be found to be profitable, and unprofitable products will be found to be unprofitable. Traditional cost systems often result in inaccurate profitability analysis resulting in special studies being at odds with the message sent by the cost system. In the extreme the cost system may be ignored.

Kaplan and Cooper (1998) extended cost hierarchies to develop activity-profitability maps by different cost objects. The general principles of activity profitability maps (or profitability analysis) analysed by different cost objects is illustrated in Figure 10.2. This approach categorizes costs according to the causes of their variability at different hierarchical levels. Hierarchies identify the lowest level to which cost can meaningfully be assigned without relying on arbitrary allocations. In Figure 10.2 the lowest hierarchical levels (shown at the top of the diagram) are product, customer and facility contributions and, ignoring the business unit level the highest levels (shown at the bottom of the diagram) are product lines, distribution channels and country profits.

Let us initially focus on products as the cost object. Look at the column for products as the cost object in Figure 10.2. You will see that a unit-level contribution margin is calculated for each *individual* product. This is derived by deducting the cost of unit-level activities from sales revenues. From this unit-level contribution expenses relating to batch-related activities are deducted. Next the cost of product-sustaining activities are deducted. Thus, three different contribution levels are reported at the *individual* product level. Differentiating contributions at these levels provides a better understanding of the implications of product-mix and discontinuation decisions in terms of cost and profit behaviour.

In Figure 10.2 there are two further levels within the product hierarchy. They are the product brand level and the product line level. Some organizations do not market their products by brands and therefore have only one further level within the product hierarchy. A product line consists of a group of similar products. For example, banks have product lines such as savings accounts, lending services, currency services, insurance services and brokering services. Each product line contains individual product variants. The savings product line would include low balance/low interest savings accounts, high balance/high interest accounts, postal savings accounts and other product variants. The lending services product line would include personal loans, house mortgage loans, business loans and other product variants within the product line.

Some organizations market groupings of products within their product lines as separate brands. A typical example of the difference between product brands and product lines is Procter and Gamble who market some of their products within their detergent product line under the Tide label and others without this label.

Where products are marketed by brands, all expenditure relating to a brand, such as management and brand marketing is for the benefit of all products within the brand and not for any specific individual product. Therefore, such **brand-sustaining expenses** should be attributed to the brand and not to individual products within the brand.

The same reasoning can be applied to the next level in the hierarchy. For example, marketing, research and development and distribution expenses might be incurred for the benefit of the whole product line and not for any specific brands or products within the line. Therefore these **product line-sustaining expenses** should be attributed to the product line but no attempt should be made to allocate them to individual products or brands. Finally, the profit for the organizational unit as a whole can be determined by deducting facility-sustaining expenses from the sum of the individual product line contributions.

A similar approach to the one described above for products can also be applied to other cost objects. The two final columns shown in Figure 10.2 illustrate how the approach can be applied to customers and locations. The aim of ABC hierarchical profitability analysis is to assign all organizational expenses to a particular hierarchical or organizational level where cause-and-effect cost assignments can be established so that arbitrary allocations are non-existent. The hierarchical approach helps to identify the impact on resource consumption by adding or dropping items at each level of the hierarchy. For example, if a brand is dropped activities at the brand level and below (i.e. above the brand profits row in Figure 10.2) which are uniquely associated with the brand will be affected, but higher level activities (i.e. at the product line level) will be unaffected. Similarly, if a product within a particular brand is dropped then all unit, batch and product-sustaining activities uniquely associated with that product will be affected but higher level brand and product-level activities will be unaffected.

Resource consumption models

The third, and possibly the most important theoretical advance in ABC systems was reported by Cooper and Kaplan (1992) in a paper which emphasized that ABC systems are **models of resource consumption**. The paper showed how ABC systems measure the cost of using resources and not the cost of supplying resources and highlighted the critical role played by unused capacity. To have a good conceptual grasp of ABC it is essential that you understand the content of this section.

Kaplan (1994) used the following equation to formalize the relationship between activity resources supplied and activity resources used for each activity:

$$\text{Cost of resources supplied} = \text{Cost of resources used} + \text{Cost of unused capacity} \quad (10.1)$$

To illustrate the application of the above formula we shall use Example 10.2. The left-hand side of the above equation indicates that the amount of expenditure on an activity

FIGURE 10.2 *An illustration of hierarchical profitability analysis*

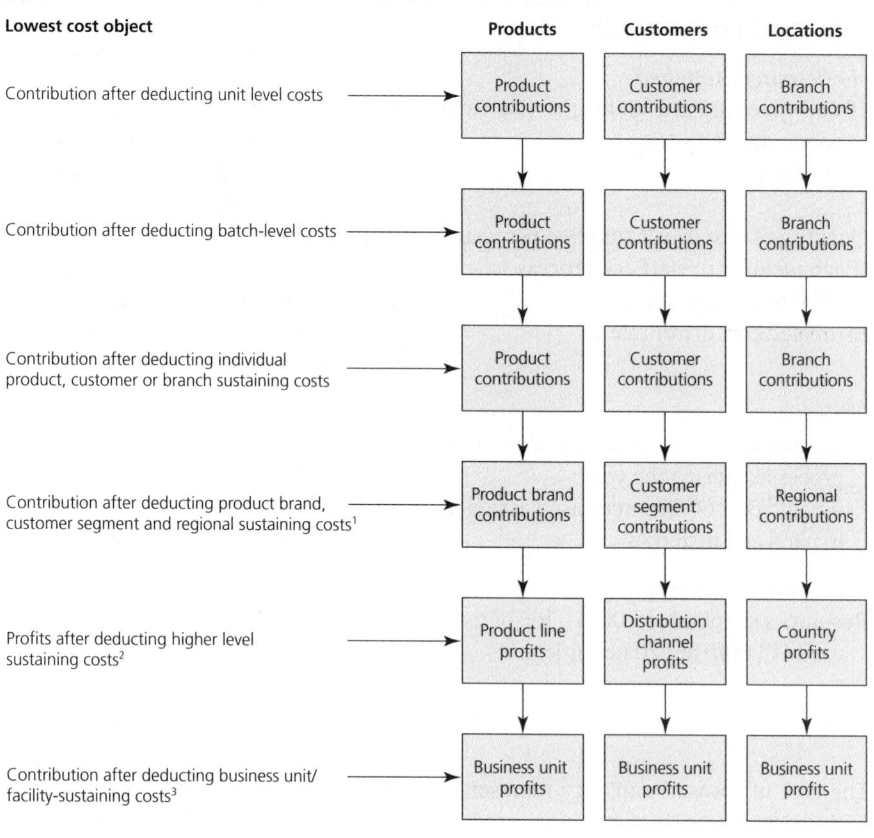

Notes

[1] Consists of expenses dedicated to sustaining specific product brands or customer segments or regions but which cannot be attributed to individual products, customers or branches.

[2] Consists of expenses dedicated to sustaining the product lines or distribution channels or countries but which cannot be attributed to lower items within the hierarchy.

[3] Consists of expenses dedicated to the business as a whole and not attributable to any lower items within the hierarchy.

depends on the cost of resources supplied rather than the cost of resources used. Example 10.2 contains data relating to the processing of purchase orders activity in which the equivalent of ten full-time staff are committed to the activity. You will see that the estimated annual cost is £300 000. This represents the **cost of resources supplied**. This expenditure provides the capacity to process 15 000 purchase orders (i.e. the quantity of resources supplied of the cost driver) per annum. Therefore the estimated cost of processing each purchase order is £20 (£300 000/15 000 orders that can be processed).

Periodic financial accounting profit statements measure the expenses incurred to make resources available (i.e. the cost of resources supplied) whereas ABC systems measure the cost of resources used by individual products, services or customers. During any particular period the number of orders processed will vary. In Example 10.2 it is assumed that the Etna Company expects to process 13 000 purchase orders (i.e. the quantity of resources used). The ABC system will therefore assign £260 000 (13 000 orders at £20 per order) to the parts and materials ordered during the year. This represents the **cost of resources used**.

EXAMPLE 10.2

The following information relates to the purchasing activity in a division of the Etna Company for the next year:

(1) Resources supplied	
10 full-time staff at £30 000 per year (including employment costs)	= £300 000 annual activity cost
Cost driver	= Number of purchase orders processed
Quantity of cost driver supplied per year: (Each member of staff can process 1500 orders per year)	= 15 000 purchase orders
Estimated cost driver rate	= £20 per purchase order (£300 000/15 000 orders)
(2) Resources used	
Estimated number of purchase orders to be processed during the year	= 13 000
Estimated cost of resources used assigned to parts and materials	= £260 000 (13 000 × £20)
(3) Cost of unused capacity	
Resources supplied (15 000) – Resources used (13 000) at £20 per order	= £40 000 (2000 × £20)

The **cost of unused capacity** represents the difference between the cost of resources supplied and the cost of resources used. Resources have been acquired to enable 15 000 purchase orders to be processed but during the year only 13 000 orders will be processed giving an unused capacity of 2000 purchase orders. Hence the predicted cost of the unused capacity will be £40 000 (2000 orders at £20 per order).

Unused capacity arises because the supply of some resources has to be acquired in discrete amounts in advance of usage such that the supply cannot be continually adjusted in the short run to match exactly the usage of resources. Typical expenses in this category include the acquisition of equipment or the employment of non-piecework employees. The expenses of supplying these resources are incurred independently of usage in the short run and this independence has led to them being categorized as fixed costs. Kaplan and Cooper (1998) describe such resources as **committed resources**. In contrast, there are other types of resources whose supply can be continually adjusted to match exactly the usage of resources. For example, materials, casual labour and the supply of energy for running machinery can be continually adjusted to match the exact demand. Thus the cost of supplying these resources will generally equal the cost of resources used and the resources will have no unused capacity. Kaplan and Cooper classify these resources as **'flexible resources'** although they have traditionally been categorized as variable costs.

The problem of adjusting the supply of resources to match the usage of resources and eliminating unused capacity therefore applies only to committed resources. Where the cost of supplying resources in the short run is fixed, the quantity used will fluctuate each period based on the activities performed for the output produced. Activity-based systems measure the cost of *using* these resources, even though the cost of supplying them will not vary with short-run usage.

Managers make decisions (for example, changes in output volume and mix, process changes and improvements and changes in product and process design) that result in changes in activity resource usage. Assuming that such decisions result in a decline in the demand for activity resources then the first term on the right-hand side of equation 10.1 will decline (the cost of resources used) but the cost of unused capacity (the second term on the right-hand side of the equation) will increase to offset exactly the lower resource usage cost. To translate the benefits of reduced activity demands into cash flow savings management action is required. They must permanently remove the unused capacity by reducing spending on the supply of the resources. Thus to make a resource variable in the downward direction requires two management decisions first to reduce the demand for the resource and, second, to lower the spending on the resource.

Demands for activity resources can also increase because of decisions to introduce new products, expand output and create greater product variety. Such decisions can lead to situations where activity resource usage exceeds the supply of resources. In the short term the excess demand might be absorbed by people working longer or faster or delaying production. Eventually, however, additional spending will be required to increase the supply of activity resources. Thus, even if permanent changes in activity resource consumption occur that result in either unused or excess capacity there may be a significant time lag before the supply of activity resources is adjusted to match the revised predicted activity usage. Indeed, there is always a danger that managers may not act to reduce the spending on the supply of resources to match a reduction in demand. They may keep existing resources in place even when there has been a substantial decline in demands for the activities consuming the resources. Consequently, there will be no benefits arising from actions to reduce activity usage. However, if decisions are made based on reported ABC costs it is implicitly assumed that predicted changes in activity resource usage will be translated into equivalent cash flow changes for the resources supplied.

A major feature of ABC systems is therefore that reported product, service or customer costs represent estimates of the cost of resources used. In a period, many decisions are made that affect the usage of resources. It is not feasible to link the required changes in the supply of resources with the change in usage predicted by each *individual* decision. The periodic reporting of both the predicted quantity and the cost of unused capacity for each activity signals the need for management to investigate the potential for reducing the activity resources supplied. In the case of flexible resources cash flow changes will soon follow decisions to reduce activity usage, such as dropping a product, but for committed resources performing one less set-up, ordering one less batch of materials or undertaking one fewer engineering change notice will not result in an automatic reduction in spending. It will create additional capacity and changes in spending on the supply of resources will often be the outcome of the totality of many decisions rather than focusing on a one-off product decision. Such ideas are considered to be of such vital importance by Kaplan and Cooper that they conclude that managing used and unused capacity is the central focus of ABC.

Selecting the cost driver denominator level

In Example 10.2 there are two potential denominator levels that can be used to establish cost driver rates. They are the capacity supplied (described as **practical capacity**) and the budgeted activity level. If practical capacity is used the cost driver rate will be £20 per purchase order processed (£300 000/15 000 orders) whereas the cost driver rate will be £23.08 (£300 000/13 000 orders) if the budgeted activity level is used as the denominator level.

Support activity costs are caused by the level of capacity that is made available (i.e. the capacity supplied) rather than the budgeted activity level of usage. Therefore the correct denominator activity level to use for calculating activity cost driver rates is practical capacity and not the anticipated activity usage. Furthermore, the use of budgeted activity will mean that the budgeted cost of unused capacity cannot be separately reported. This is the mechanism that is used to translate decisions that result in changes in activity usage into alterations in the supply of resources and thus changes in future spending. Using budgeted activity also means that the cost of unused capacity is also hidden in the cost driver rate and charged to products. Finally, anticipated capacity usage can lead to higher cost driver rates in periods of low sales demand when capacity is being maintained for an expected upsurge in demand. This will result in the cost of unused capacity being assigned to products and the higher cost driver rates will result in an increase in the reported product costs. Hence, there is a danger that bid prices will be increased when demand is depressed and at the time when a firm should be considering lowering prices.

In Example 10.2 practical capacity was measured in human resources which can be acquired and reduced in relatively discrete amounts. Human resources tend to be flexible in the longer term. It is therefore realistic to plan to adjust the practical capacity supplied for an activity to the planned demand for the activity resources. However, physical resources such as machinery and equipment are less flexible because they often can only be acquired in large discrete amounts. It is not possible, even in the longer term, to adjust the supply of capacity resources to exactly match the usage of resources. For example, consider a situation where the maximum demand for a machine might only be 80% of its practical maximum capacity. If the next smaller version of the machine has a capacity of only 60% of the larger machine, the larger machine must be acquired but there will be no expectation of utilizing the practical capacity. In these circumstances Kaplan and Cooper (1998) suggest that if the machine was purchased in the full knowledge that the maximum utilization would be 80% of its potential maximum capacity then the denominator level that should be used for measuring practical capacity is the 80% level. Hence, practical capacity should be defined as 80% of the machine's maximum capacity.

An alternative measure of physical capacity is **normal activity**. We looked at this measure in Chapter 7 when our objective was to focus on the factors which should influence the choice of capacity levels for profit measurement and inventory valuation. Normal activity is defined as the capacity required to satisfy average customer demand over a longer-term period of, say, approximately three years after taking into account seasonal and cyclical fluctuations. In many situations organizations will have invested in physical assets to provide capacity that is required to match long-run demand (i.e. normal activity). In other words, normal activity may be close to the 80% level for the machine quoted in the preceding paragraph. The end result is that a measure of normal capacity may be approximately similar to the measure of practical capacity as defined in the previous paragraph.

The message from the above discussion relating to the choice of denominator levels is that practical capacity ought to be used for measuring human resources. For physical resources it is recommended that the modified measure of practical capacity that has been described, or normal activity, should be used. Budgeted activity is not recommended on the grounds that it is a short-term measure which can lead to fluctuating cost driver rates if budgeted activity varies from period to period. However, a survey by Drury and Tayles (2000) of 186 UK organizations indicated that for both traditional and ABC systems budgeted annual activity was used by 86% of the responding organizations. Only 4% and 8% respectively used practical capacity and normal activity. The preference for budgeted annual activity may reflect the fact that the measure is readily available, being determined as part of the annual budgeting process whereas practical capacity and normal activity are not readily available and cannot be precisely determined.

Cost versus benefits considerations

In Chapter 3 it was pointed out that the design of a cost system should be based on cost versus benefit considerations. A sophisticated ABC system should generate the most accurate product costs. However, the cost of implementing and operating an ABC system is significantly more expensive than operating a direct costing or a traditional costing system. In particular, the training and software requirements may prohibit its adoption by small organizations. The partial costs reported by direct costing systems, and the distorted costs reported by traditional systems, may result in significant mistakes in decisions (such as selling unprofitable products or dropping profitable products) arising from the use of this information. If the cost of errors arising from using partial or distorted information generated from using these systems exceeds the additional costs of implementing and operating an ABC system then an ABC system ought to be implemented. In other words ABC must meet the cost/benefit criterion and improvements should be made in the level of sophistication of the costing system up to the point where the marginal cost of improvement equals the marginal benefit from improvement.

The optimal costing system is different for different organizations. A simplistic traditional costing system may report reasonably accurate product costs in organizations that have the following characteristics:

1 low levels of competition;
2 non-volume related indirect costs that are a low proportion of total indirect costs;
3 a fairly standardized product range all consuming organizational resources in similar proportions (i.e. low product diversity).

In contrast, a sophisticated ABC system may be optimal for organizations having following characteristics:

1 intensive competition;
2 non-volume related indirect costs that are a high proportion of total indirect costs;
3 a diverse range of products, all consuming organizational resources in significantly different proportions (i.e. high product diversity).

Single product firms and multiple-product firms that have entire facilities dedicated to the production of a single product have few problems with costing accuracy. With the former all costs will be directly attributable to the single product and with the latter only the costs of central facilities, such as central headquarter costs, will be indirect. All of the costs of the dedicated facilities will be directly attributable to products and therefore indirect costs will be a low proportion of total costs.

In Chapter 22 the major features of a just-in-time (JIT) manufacturing system will be described and we shall also look at how JIT affects management accounting. At this stage, however, you should note that JIT manufacturing systems result in the establishment of production cells that are dedicated to the manufacturing of a single product or a family of similar products. With JIT firms many of the support activities can be directly traced to the product dedicated cells. Thus, a high proportion of costs can be directly assigned to products. We can conclude that the benefits from implementing ABC product costing will be lower for single products or firms that have product dedicated facilities.

Periodic review of an ABC data base

The detailed tracking of costs is unnecessary when ABC information is used for decision-making. A data base should be maintained that is reviewed periodically, say once or twice a year. In addition periodic cost and profitability audits (similar to that illustrated in Figure 10.2) should be undertaken to provide a strategic review of the costs and profitability of a firm's products, customers and sales outlets. The data base and periodic cost and profitability review can be based on either past or future costs. Early adopters, and firms starting off with ABC initially analysed past costs. Besides being historical the disadvantage of this approach is that actual cost driver usage is used as the denominator level to calculate the cost driver rates. Thus cost driver rates and product costs will include the cost of unused capacity. Hence the cost of unused capacity for each activity is not highlighted for management attention. Nevertheless, the information provided for the first time an insight into the resources consumed by products and customers and their profitability based on measuring the resource usage rather than arbitrary allocations.

However, rather than focusing on the past it is preferable to concentrate on the future profitability of products and customers using estimated activity-based costs. It is therefore recommended that an activity-cost data base is maintained at estimated standard costs that are updated on an annual or semi-annual basis.

ABC in service organizations

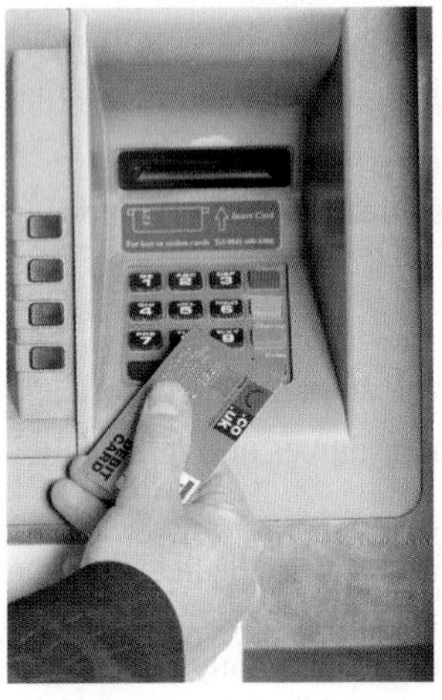

Kaplan and Cooper (1998) suggest that service companies are ideal candidates for ABC, even more than manufacturing companies. Their justification for this statement is that most of the costs in service organizations are indirect. In contrast, manufacturing companies can trace important components (such as direct materials and direct labour) of costs to individual products. Therefore indirect costs are likely to be a much smaller proportion of total costs. Service organizations must also supply most of their resources in advance and fluctuations in the usage of activity resources by individual services and customers does not influence short-term spending to supply the resources. Such costs are treated by traditional costing systems as fixed and irrelevant for most decisions. This resulted in a situation where profitability analysis was not considered helpful for decision-making. Furthermore, until recently many service organizations were either government owned monopolies or operated in a highly regulated, protected and non-competitive environment. These organizations were not subject to any great pressures to improve profitability by identifying and eliminating non-profit making activities. Cost increases could also be absorbed by increasing the prices of services to customers. Little attention was therefore given to developing cost systems that accurately measured the costs and profitability of individual services.

Privatization of government owned monopolies, deregulation, intensive competition and an expanding product range created the need for service organizations to develop management accounting systems that enabled them to understand their cost base and determine the sources of profitability for their products/services, customers and markets. Many service organizations have therefore only recently implemented management accounting systems. They have had the advantage of not having to meet some of the constraints imposed on manufacturing organizations, such as having to meet financial accounting stock valuation requirements or the reluctance to scrap or change existing cost systems that might have become embedded in organizations. Furthermore, service organizations have been implementing new costing systems at the same time as the deficiencies of traditional systems were being widely publicized. Also new insights were beginning to emerge on how cost systems could be viewed as resource consumption models which could be used to make decisions on adjusting the spending on the supply of resources to match resource consumption.

A UK survey by Drury and Tayles (2000) suggests that service organizations are more likely to implement ABC systems. They reported that 51% of the financial and service organizations surveyed, compared with 15% of manufacturing organizations, had implemented ABC. Kaplan and Cooper (1998) illustrate how ABC was applied in The Co-operative Bank, a medium sized UK bank. ABC was used for product and customer profitability analysis. The following are some of the activities and cost drivers that were identified:

Activity	Cost driver
Provide ATM services	Number of ATM transactions
Clear debit items	Number of debits processed
Clear credit items	Number of credits processed
Issue chequebooks	Number of chequebooks issued
Computer processing	Number of computer transactions
Prepare statements of account transactions	Number of statements issued
Administer mortgages	Number of mortgages maintained

Activity costs were allocated to the different savings and loans products based on their demand for the activities using the cost drivers as a measure of resource consumption. Some expenses, such as finance and human resource management, were not assigned to products because they were considered to be for the benefit of the organization as a whole and not attributable to individual products. These business sustaining costs represented approximately 15% of total operating expenses. Profitability analysis was extended to customer segments within product groups. The study revealed that approximately half of the current accounts, particularly those with low balances and high transactions were unprofitable. By identifying the profitable customer segments the marketing function was able to direct its effort to attracting more new customers, and enhancing relationships with those existing customers, whose behaviour would be profitable to the bank.

ABC cost management applications

Our aim in this chapter has been to look at how ABC can be used to provide information for decision-making by more accurately assigning costs to cost objects, such as products, customers and locations. In addition, ABC can be used for a range of cost management applications. They include cost reduction, activity-based budgeting, performance measurement, benchmarking of activities, process management and business process re-engineering. Figure 10.3 illustrates the product costing and cost management applications of ABC. The vertical box relates to product costing where costs are first assigned to activities and then to cost objects. The horizontal box relates to cost management. Here a process approach is adopted and costs are assigned to activities which then represent the basis for cost management applications. Thus, ABC can be adopted for both product costing and cost management or applied only to product costing or cost management. If ABC is only applied to cost management the second stage of assigning costs from activities to cost objects is omitted.

The decision to implement ABC should not, therefore, be based only on its ability to produce more accurate and relevant decision-making information. Indeed, surveys by Innes and Mitchell (1995a) and Innes *et al.* (2000) on ABC applications suggests that the

FIGURE 10.3 *Product costing and cost management applications of ABC*

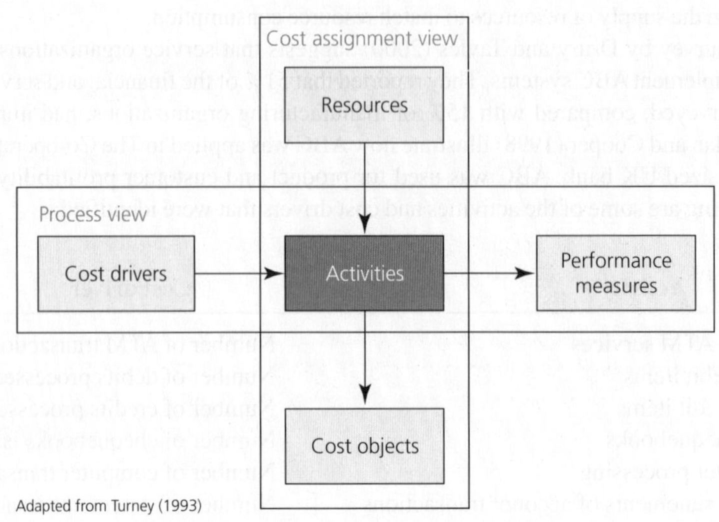

Adapted from Turney (1993)

cost management applications tend to outweigh the product costing applications which were central to ABC's initial development. We shall examine ABC applications to cost management in Chapter 22.

Pitfalls in using ABC information

Where unit costs are calculated, ABC systems suffer from the same disadvantages as traditional cost systems by suggesting an inappropriate degree of variability. For example, to calculate unit product costs, batch level activity costs are divided by the number of units in the batch and product sustaining costs are divided by the number of products produced. This unitizing approach is an allocation which yields a constant average cost per unit of output which will differ depending on the selected output level. For decision-making there is a danger that what started out as a non-volume-related activity cost will be translated into a cost which varies with production volume. Consider a situation where the cost per set-up is £1000 for a standard batch size of 100 units for a particular part, giving an average set-up cost per part of £10. If a special order requiring the part is received for 50 units then the batch size will differ from the standard batch size and the average cost of the set-up for processing the parts of £10 is not the appropriate cost to use for decision-making. There is a danger that costs of £500 could be assigned to the order. However, if the special order requires one set-up then the activity resources consumed will be £1000 for an additional set-up, and not £500. Care must therefore be taken when using ABC information.

A further problem is that the concept of managing unused capacity is fine for human resources but it does not have the same impact for physical resources, such as the acquisition of plant and equipment. Human resources are more flexible and can be adjusted in small increments. Therefore the supply of resources can more easily be adjusted to the usage of resources. In contrast, physical resources are acquired or removed in lumpy amounts and large increments. If resources are supplied to cover a wide range of activity usage there would have to be a dramatic change in activity for the supply to be changed. Therefore changes in resource usage would tend not be matched by a change in supply of resources and spending would remain unchanged. Care must therefore be taken to ensure that the cost of human and physical resources are not merged (so that they can be separately reported) when costs are assigned to activity cost centres within the first stage of the two-stage allocation process.

If the changes in physical resource usage arising from potential decisions do not have future cash flow consequences there is unlikely to be a link between resource usage and spending and the future cash flow impact for most decisions will be zero. In other words, the cost of resource usage would be treated as fixed and unavoidable for most decisions which is identical to how these costs would be treated adopting traditional costing systems. Also traditional costing systems accurately trace the cost of unit-level activities to products and facility-sustaining costs cannot accurately be assigned to cost objects by any costing system. Thus, for many organizations the proportion of costs that can be more accurately assigned to cost objects by ABC systems, and that can be expected to have a future cash flow impact, might be quite small. For such organizations this would imply that appropriate cost information extracted from simplistic costing systems may be sufficiently accurate for decision-making purposes.

Summary

The following items relate to the learning objectives listed at the beginning of the chapter.

- **Explain why a cost accumulation system is required for generating relevant cost information for decision-making.**

  There are three main reasons why a cost accumulation system is required for generating relevant cost information. First, many indirect costs are relevant for decision-making and a costing system is therefore required that provides an estimate of resources consumed by cost objects using cause-and-effect allocations to allocate indirect costs. Second, an attention-directing information system is required that periodically identifies those potentially unprofitable products that require more detailed special studies. Third, many product decisions are not independent and to capture product interdependencies those joint resources that fluctuate in the longer-term according to the demand for them should be assigned to products.

- **Describe the differences between activity-based and traditional costing systems.**

  The major differences relate to the two-stage allocation process. In the first-stage, traditional systems allocate indirect costs to cost centres (normally departments) whereas activity-based systems allocate indirect costs to cost centres based on activities rather than departments. Since there are many more activities than departments a distinguishing feature is that activity-based systems will have a greater number of cost centres in the first stage of the allocation process. In the second stage, traditional systems use a limited number of different types of second stage volume-based allocation bases (cost drivers) whereas activity-based systems use many different types of volume-based and non-volume-based cause-and-effect second stage drivers.

- **Explain why traditional costing systems can provide misleading information for decision-making.**

  Traditional systems often tend to rely on arbitrary allocations of indirect costs. In particular, they rely extensively on volume-based allocations. Many indirect costs are not volume-based but, if volume-based allocation bases are used, high volume products

EXHIBIT 10.1
Surveys of company practice

Significant variations in the usage of ABC both within the same country and across different countries have been reported. These differences may arise from the difficulty in precisely defining the difference between traditional costing systems and ABC systems and the specific time period when the surveys were actually undertaken.

Survey evidence suggests that over the last decade there has been an increasing interest in ABC. In the UK, surveys in the early 1990s reported adoption rates around 10% (Innes and Mitchell, 1991; Nicholls, 1992; Drury *et al.*, 1993). Similar adoption rates of 10% were found in Ireland (Clarke, 1992) and 14% in Canada (Armitage and Nicholson, 1993). In the USA Green and Amenkhienan (1992) claimed that 45% of firms used ABC to some extent. More recent surveys suggest higher ABC adoption rates. In the UK reported usage was 18% (Innes *et al.*, 2000), 22% (Banerjee and Kane, 1996), 21% (Evans and Ashworth, 1996) and 23% (Drury and Tayles, 2000). In the USA Shim and Stagliano (1997) reported a usage rate of 27%.

Reported usage rates for mainland Europe are 19% in Belgium (Bruggeman *et al.*, 1996) and 6% in Finland in 1992, 11% in 1993 and 24% in 1995 (Virtanen *et al.*, 1996). Low usage rates have been reported in Denmark (Israelsen *et al.*, 1996), Sweden (Ask *et al.*, 1996) and Germany (Scherrer, 1996). Activity-based techniques do not appear to have been adopted in Greece (Ballas and Venieris, 1996), Italy (Barbato *et al.*, 1996) or Spain (Saez-Torrecilla *et al.*, 1996).

Other studies have examined the applications of ABC. Innes and Mitchell (1995a) and Innes *et al.* (2000) found that cost reduction was the most widely used application. Other widely used applications included product/service pricing, cost modelling and performance measurement/improvement. ABC was used for stock valuation by 29% of ABC adopters thus suggesting that the majority of ABC users have separate systems for stock valuation and management accounting applications.

According to Bjornenak (1997a) there has been little research on who adopts ABC and for what reasons. His survey indicated that 40% of the responding Norwegian companies had adopted ABC as an idea (i.e. they had implemented ABC or planned to do so). Different variables relating to cost structure, competition, existing cost systems, size and product diversity were tested as explanatory factors for the adoption of ABC but only cost structure and size were found to be statistically significant. The UK study by Drury and Tayles indicated that company size and business sector had a significant impact on ABC adoption rates. The adoption rates were 45% for the largest organizations and 51% for financial and service organizations. Although the ABC adopters used significantly more cost pools and cost drivers than the non-adopters most adopters used fewer cost pools and drivers compared with what is recommended in the literature. Approximately, 50% of the ABC adopters used less than 50 cost centres and less than 10 separate types of cost driver rates.

Friedman and Lyne (1995, 1999) used longitudinal case studies to study the factors influencing ABC success and failure in 12 UK companies. They observed that top management support was a significant factor influencing the success or failure of ABC systems. Implementation problems identified by the various studies included the amount of work in setting up the system and data collection, difficulties in identifying activities and selecting cost drivers, lack of resources and inadequate computer software. The benefits reported by the studies included more accurate cost information for product pricing, more accurate profitability analysis, improved cost control and a better understanding of cost causation.

Studies in the USA by Shields (1995) and McGowan and Klammer (1997) indicated that ABC success was linked to six behavioural and organizational variables. They were top management support; integration with competitive strategy initiatives (e.g. total quality management and just-in-time); performance evaluation and compensation; non-accounting ownership of the ABC project; training provided in designing, implementing and using ABC; and the provision of adequate resourcing. Technical characteristics of the systems had no influence.

are likely to be assigned with a greater proportion of indirect costs than they have consumed whereas low volume products will be assigned a lower proportion. In these circumstances traditional systems will overcost high volume products and undercost low volume products. In contrast, ABC systems recognize that many indirect costs vary in proportion to changes other than production volume. By identifying the cost drivers that cause the costs to change and assigning costs to cost objects on the basis of cost driver usage, costs can be more accurately traced. It is claimed that this cause-and-effect relationship provides a superior way of determining relevant costs.

- **Identify and explain each of the four stages involved in designing ABC systems.**

  The design of ABC systems involves the following four stages: (a) identify the major activities that take place in the organization; (b) create a cost centre/cost pool for each activity; (c) determine the cost driver for each major activity; and (d) trace the cost of activities to the product according to a product's demand (using cost drivers as a measure of demand) for activities.

- **Describe the ABC cost hierarchy.**

  ABC systems classify activities along a cost hierarchy consisting of unit-level, batch-level, product-sustaining and facility-sustaining activities. Unit-level activities are performed each time a unit of the product or service is produced. Examples include direct labour and energy costs. Batch-level activities are performed each time a batch is produced. Examples include setting up a machine or processing a purchase order. Product-sustaining activities are performed to enable the production and sale of individual products. Examples include the technical support provided for individual products and the resources required performing product enhancements. Facility-sustaining activities are performed to support the facility's general manufacturing process. They include general administrative staff and property support costs.

- **Describe the ABC profitability analysis hierarchy.**

  The ABC profitability analysis hierarchy categorizes costs according to their variability at different hierarchical levels to report different hierarchical contribution levels. At the final level, facility or business-sustaining costs are deducted from the sum of the product contributions to derive a profit at the business unit level. In other words, facility/business sustaining costs are not allocated to individual products. The aim of hierarchical profitability analysis is to assign all organizational expenses to a particular hierarchical or organizational level where cause-and-effect cost assignments can be established so that arbitrary apportionments are non-existent.

- **Describe the ABC resource consumption model.**

  ABC systems are models of resource consumption. They measure the cost of using resources and not the cost of supplying resources. The difference between the cost of resources supplied and the cost of resources used represents the cost of unused capacity. The cost of unused capacity for each activity is the reporting mechanism for identifying the need to adjust the supply of resources to match the usage of resources. However, to translate the benefits of reduced activity demands into cash flow savings, management action is required to remove the unused capacity by reducing the spending on the supply of resources.

- **Justify the choice of practical capacity as the denominator level for estimating cost driver rates.**

  There are two potential denominator levels that can be used to establish cost driver rates – practical capacity and the budgeted activity level. Practical capacity represents the choice of capacity that is made available (i.e. the capacity supplied). Practical capacity is preferred because support activity costs are caused by the level of capacity that is made available rather than the budgeted level of usage. The major disadvantages of using the budgeted level of usage are that (a) the budgeted costs of unused capacity cannot be separately reported and (b) the cost of unused capacity is hidden in the cost diver rates.

Key terms and concepts

activities (p. 372)
activity cost drivers (p. 380)
batch-related activities (p. 382)
brand-sustaining expenses (p. 384)
business-sustaining activities (p. 382)
committed resources (p. 386)
consumption ratios (p. 376)
cost drivers (p. 372)
cost of resources supplied (p. 385)
cost of resources used (p. 385)
cost of unused capacity (p. 386)
customer-sustaining activities (p. 382)
duration drivers (p. 380)
facility-sustaining activities (p. 382)
flexible resources (p. 386)
intensity drivers (p. 381)
models of resource consumption (p. 384)
non-volume based cost drivers (p. 375)
normal activity (p. 388)
practical capacity (p. 387)
product line-sustaining activities (p. 384)
product-sustaining activities (p. 382)
resource cost drivers (p. 380)
service-sustaining activities (p. 382)
transaction drivers (p. 380)
unit-level activities (p. 382)
volume-based cost drivers (p. 374)

Recommended reading

Kaplan and Cooper have been the major contributors to the development of activity-based costing. Much of this chapter has therefore drawn off their ideas. For a detailed description of activity-based costing which incorporates all of Kaplan and Cooper's ideas you should consult *Cost and Effect: Using Integrated Systems to Drive Profitability and Performance* (1998). You should refer to the bibliography at the end of this book for the detailed reference. Other interesting articles that comment on developments in the ABC literature are Jones and Dugdale (2002) and Lukka and Granlund (2002).

Key examination points

ABC did not emerge until the late 1980s, and therefore fewer questions have been set on this topic. As a result a smaller number of questions are included in this chapter. It is likely that most questions will require you to compute product costs for a traditional system and an activity-based system and explain the difference between the product costs. It is also likely that examiners will require you to outline the circumstances where ABC systems are likely to prove most beneficial.

Assessment material

Review questions

The review questions are short questions that enable you to assess your understanding of the main topics included in the chapter. The numbers in parentheses provide you with the page numbers to refer to if you cannot answer a specific question.

Review problems

The review problems are more complex and require you to relate and apply the chapter content to various business problems. The problems are graded by their level of difficulty. The multiple-choice questions are the least demanding and normally take less than 10 minutes to complete. Fully worked solutions to the review problems are provided in a separate section at the end of the book. For those questions in the white box the worked solutions are provided in the *Student's Manual* accompanying this book. Further review problems for this chapter are available on the accompanying website www.drury-online.com. The answers to these problems are available for lecturers on the lecturer's password protected section of the website.

Case studies

The website also includes over 30 case study problems. A list of these cases is provided in Part Seven of this book.

Review questions

10.1 Explain why a cost accumulation system is required for generating relevant cost information for decision-making. (*pp. 370–71*)

10.2 Describe the three different types of cost systems that can be used to assign costs to cost objects. (*pp. 371–72*)

10.3 What are the fundamental differences between a traditional and an ABC system? (*pp. 372–74*)

10.4 Define activities and cost drivers. (*p. 372*)

10.5 What factors led to the emergence of ABC systems? (*p. 374*)

10.6 Distinguish between volume-based and non-volume-based cost drivers. (*pp. 374–75*)

10.7 Describe the circumstances when traditional costing systems are likely to report distorted costs. (*p. 375, p. 389*)

10.8 Explain how low volume products can be undercosted and high volume products overcosted when traditional costing systems are used. *(pp. 376–77)*

10.9 What is meant by 'product diversity' and why is it important for product costing? *(p. 375)*

10.10 Describe each of the four stages involved in designing ABC systems. *(pp. 377–81)*

10.11 Distinguish between resource cost drivers and activity cost drivers. *(p. 380)*

10.12 Distinguish between transaction and duration cost drivers. *(pp. 380–81)*

10.13 Describe the ABC manufacturing cost hierarchy. *(p. 382)*

10.14 Describe the ABC profitability analysis hierarchy. *(pp. 383-84)*

10.15 What is an ABC resource consumption model? *(pp. 384–87)*

10.16 Distinguish between the cost of resources supplied, the cost of resources used and the cost of unused capacity. *(pp. 385–86)*

10.17 Why is the choice of a denominator level important with ABC systems? *(pp. 387–88)*

10.18 Distinguish between practical capacity and normal activity and explain the circumstances when each denominator measured is preferred. *(pp. 387–88)*

10.19 Explain the circumstances when ABC is likely to be preferred to traditional costing systems. *(p. 389)*

10.20 Provide examples of how ABC can be used in service organizations. *(pp. 390–91)*

10.21 Describe some of the limitations of information generated from ABC systems. *(pp. 392–93)*

Review problems

10.22 Intermediate

S Ltd manufactures components for the aircraft industry. The following annual information regarding three of its key customers is available:

	W	X	Y
Gross margin	£1 100 000	£1 750 000	£1 200 000
General administration costs	£40 000	£80 000	£30 000
Units sold	1 750	2 000	1 500
Orders placed	1 000	1 000	1 500
Sales visits	110	100	170
Invoices raised	900	1 200	1 500

The company uses an activity based costing system and the analysis of customer-related costs is as follows:

Sales visits	£500 per visit
Order processing	£100 per order placed
Despatch costs	£100 per order placed
Billing and collections	£175 per invoice raised

Using customer profitability analysis, the ranking of the customers would be:

	W	X	Y
A	1st	2nd	3rd
B	1st	3rd	2nd
C	2nd	1st	3rd
D	2nd	3rd	1st
E	3rd	2nd	1st

(4 marks)

CIMA Management Accounting – Decision Making

10.23 **Intermediate**

DRP Limited has recently introduced an Activity Based Costing system. It manufactures three products, details of which are set out below:

	Product D	Product R	Product P
Budgeted annual production (units)	100 000	100 000	50 000
Batch size (units)	100	50	25
Machine set-ups per batch	3	4	6
Purchase orders per batch	2	1	1
Processing time per unit (minutes)	2	3	3

Three cost pools have been identified. Their budgeted costs for the year ending 30 June 2003 are as follows:

Machine set-up costs	£150 000
Purchasing of materials	£70 000
Processing	£80 000

The budgeted machine set-up cost per unit of product R is nearest to

A £0.52 B £0.60 C £6.52 D £26.09

(3 marks)

CIMA Management Accounting – Performance Management

10.24 **Intermediate**

It is now fairly widely accepted that conventional cost accounting distorts management's view of business through unrepresentative overhead allocation and inappropriate product costing.

This is because the traditional approach usually absorbs overhead costs across products and orders solely on the basis of the direct labour involved in their manufacture. And as direct labour as a proportion of total manufacturing cost continues to fall, this leads to more and more distortion and misrepresentation of the impact of particular products on total overhead costs.

(From an article in *The Financial Times*)

You are required to discuss the above and to suggest what approaches are being adopted by management accountants to overcome such criticism.

(15 marks)

CIMA Stage 2 Cost Accounting

10.25 **Advanced**

Large service organisations, such as banks and hospitals, used to be noted for their lack of standard costing systems, and their relatively unsophisticated budgeting and control systems compared with large manufacturing organisations. But this is changing and many large service organisations are now revising their use of management accounting techniques.

Requirements:

(a) Explain which features of large-scale service organisations encourage the application of activity-based approaches to the analysis of cost information. *(6 marks)*

(b) Explain which features of service organisations may create problems for the application of activity-based costing. *(4 marks)*

(c) Explain the uses for activity-based cost information in service industries. *(4 marks)*

(d) Many large service organisations were at one time state-owned, but have been privatised. Examples in some countries include electricity supply and telecommunications. They are often regulated. Similar systems of regulation of prices by an independent authority exist in many countries, and are designed to act as a surrogate for market competition in industries where it is difficult to ensure a genuinely competitive market.

Explain which aspects of cost information and systems in service organisations would particularly interest a regulator, and why these features would be of interest. *(6 marks)*

(Total 20 marks)

CIMA Stage 4 Management Accounting Control Systems

10.26 Intermediate: Comparison of traditional product costing with ABC

Having attended a CIMA course on activity-based costing (ABC) you decide to experiment by applying the principles of ABC to the four products currently made and sold by your company. Details of the four products and relevant information are given below for one period:

Product	A	B	C	D
Output in units	120	100	80	120
Costs per unit:	(£)	(£)	(£)	(£)
Direct material	40	50	30	60
Direct labour	28	21	14	21
Machine hours (per unit)	4	3	2	3

The four products are similar and are usually produced in production runs of 20 units and sold in batches of 10 units.

The production overhead is currently absorbed by using a machine hour rate, and the total of the production overhead for the period has been analysed as follows:

	(£)
Machine department costs (rent, business rates, depreciation and supervision)	10 430
Set-up costs	5 250
Stores receiving	3 600
Inspection/Quality control	2 100
Materials handling and despatch	4 620

You have ascertained that the 'cost drivers' to be used are as listed below for the overhead costs shown:

Cost	Cost Driver
Set up costs	Number of production runs
Stores receiving	Requisitions raised
Inspection/Quality control	Number of production runs
Materials handling and despatch	Orders executed

The number of requisitions raised on the stores was 20 for each product and the number of orders executed was 42, each order being for a batch of 10 of a product. You are required

(a) to calculate the total costs for each product if all overhead costs are absorbed on a machine hour basis;

(4 marks)

(b) to calculate the total costs for each product, using activity-based costing;

(7 marks)

(c) to calculate and list the unit product costs from your figures in (a) and (b) above, to show the differences and to comment briefly on any conclusions which may be drawn which could have pricing and profit implications.

(4 marks)

(Total 15 marks)

CIMA Stage 2 Cost Accounting

10.27 Advanced: Computation of product costs for traditional and ABC systems

The following information provides details of the costs, volume and cost drivers for a particular period in respect of ABC plc, a hypothetical company:

	Product X	Product Y	Product Z	Total
1. Production and sales (units)	30 000	20 000	8 000	
2. Raw material usage (units)	5	5	11	
3. Direct material cost	£25	£20	£11	£1 238 000
4. Direct labour hours	$1^1/_3$	2	1	88 000
5. Machine hours	$1^1/_3$	1	2	76 000
6. Direct labour cost	8	£12	£6	
7. Number of production runs	3	7	20	30
8. Number of deliveries	9	3	20	32
9. Number of receipts (2 × 7)[a]	15	35	220	270
10. Number of production orders	15	10	25	50
11. Overhead costs:				
Set-up	30 000			
Machines	760 000			
Receiving	435 000			
Packing	250 000			
Engineering	373 000			
	£1 848 000			

[a]The company operates a just-in-time inventory policy, and receives each component once per production run.

In the past the company has allocated overheads to products on the basis of direct labour hours.

However, the majority of overheads are more closely related to machine hours than direct labour hours.

The company has recently redesigned its cost system by recovering overheads using two volume-related bases: machine hours and a materials handling overhead rate for recovering overheads of the receiving department. Both the current and the previous cost system reported low profit margins for product X, which is the company's highest-selling product. The management accountant has recently attended a conference on activity-based costing, and the overhead costs for the last period have been analysed by the major activities in order to compute activity-based costs.

From the above information you are required to:

(a) Compute the product costs using a traditional volume-related costing system based on the assumptions that:
   (i) all overheads are recovered on the basis of direct labour hours (i.e. the company's past product costing system);
   (ii) the overheads of the receiving department are recovered by a materials handling overhead rate and the remaining overheads are recovered using a machine hour rate (i.e. the company's current costing system).

(b) Compute product costs using an activity-based costing system.

(c) Briefly explain the differences between the product cost computations in (a) and (b).

10.28 Advanced: ABC product cost computation and discussion relating to ABC, JIT and TQM

During the last 20 years, KL's manufacturing operation has become increasingly automated with computer-controlled robots replacing operatives. KL currently manufactures over 100 products of varying levels of design complexity. A single, plant-wide overhead absorption rate (OAR), based on direct labour hours, is used to absorb overhead costs.

In the quarter ended March, KL's manufacturing overhead costs were:

	(£000)
Equipment operation expenses	125
Equipment maintenance expenses	25
Wages paid to technicians	85
Wages paid to storemen	35
Wages paid to dispatch staff	40
	310

During the quarter, RAPIER Management Consultants were engaged to conduct a review of KLs cost accounting systems. RAPIERs report includes the following statement:

In KL's circumstances, absorbing overhead costs in individual products on a labour hour absorption basis is meaningless. Overhead costs should be attributed to products using an activity based costing (ABC) system. We have identified the following as being the most significant activities:

(1) receiving component consignments from suppliers
(2) setting up equipment for production runs
(3) quality inspections
(4) dispatching goods orders to customers.

Our research has indicated that, in the short term, KL's overheads are 40% fixed and 60% variable. Approximately half the variable overheads vary in relation to direct labour hours worked and half vary in relation to the number of quality inspections. This model applies only to relatively small changes in the level of output during a period of two years or less.

Equipment operation and maintenance expenses are apportionable as follows:

- component stores (15%), manufacturing (70%) and goods dispatch (15%).

Technician wages are apportionable as follows:

- equipment maintenance (30%), setting up equipment for production runs (40%) and quality inspections (30%).

During the quarter

- a total of 2000 direct labour hours were worked (paid at £12 per hour),
- 980 component consignments were received from suppliers,
- 1020 production runs were set up,
- 640 quality inspections were carried out, and
- 420 goods orders were dispatched to customers.

Part One

KL's production during the quarter included components *r*, *s* and *t*. The following information is available:

	Component r	Component s	Component t
Direct labour hours worked	25	480	50
Direct material costs	£1 200	£2 900	£1 800
Component consignments received	42	24	28
Production runs	16	18	12
Quality inspections	10	8	18
Goods orders dispatched	22	85	46
Quantity produced	560	12 800	2 400

In April 2001 a potential customer asked KL to quote for the supply of a new component (*z*) to a given specification. 1000 units of *z* are to be supplied each quarter for a two-year period. They will be paid for in equal instalments on the last day of each quarter. The job will involve an initial design cost of £40 000 and production will involve 80 direct labour hours, £2000 materials, 20 component consignments, 15 production runs, 30 quality inspections and 4 goods dispatches per quarter.

KL's Sales Director comments:

Now we have a modern ABC system, we can quote selling prices with confidence. The quarterly charge we quote should be the forecast ABC production cost of the units plus the design cost of the z *depreciated on a straight-line basis over the two years of the job – to which we should add a 25% mark-up for profit. We can base our forecast on costs experienced in the quarter ended March.*

Requirements:

(a) Calculate the unit cost of components *r*, *s* and *t*, using KLs existing cost accounting system (single factory labour hour OAR).

(5 marks)

(b) Explain how an ABC system would be developed using the information given. Calculate the unit cost of components *r*, *s* and *t*, using this ABC system.

(11 marks)

(c) Calculate the charge per quarter that should be quoted for supply of component *z* in a manner consistent with the Sales Directors comments. Advise KL's management on the merits of this selling price, having regard to factors you consider relevant.
Note: KL's cost of capital is 3% per quarter.

(9 marks)
(Total 25 marks)

Part Two

It is often claimed that ABC provides better information concerning product costs than traditional management accounting techniques. It is also sometimes claimed that ABC provides better information as a guide to decision-making. However, one should treat these claims with caution. ABC may give a different impression of product costs but it is not necessarily a better impression. It may be wiser to try improving the use of traditional techniques before moving to ABC.

Comment by KL's management accountant on the RAPIER report

Requirements:

(a) Explain the ideas concerning cost behaviour which underpin ABC. Explain why ABC may be better attuned to the modern manufacturing environment than traditional techniques. Explain why KL might or might not obtain a more meaningful impression of product costs through the use of ABC.

(10 marks)

(b) Explain how the traditional cost accounting system being used by KL might be improved to provide more meaningful product costs.

(6 marks)

(c) Critically appraise the reported claim that ABC gives better information as a guide to decision-making than do traditional product costing techniques.

(9 marks)
(Total 25 marks)

Part Three

The lean enterprise *[characterised by just-in-time (JIT), total quality management (TQM) and supportive supplier relations] is widely considered a better approach to manufacturing. Some have suggested, however, that ABC hinders the spread of the lean enterprise by making apparent the cost of small batch sizes.*

Comment by an academic accountant

Requirements:

(a) Explain the roles that JIT, TQM and supportive supplier relations play in a modern manufacturing management. How might the adoption of such practices improve KLs performance?

(10 marks)

(b) Explain what the writer of the above statement means by 'the cost of small batch sizes'. Critically appraise the manner in which this cost is treated by KLs existing (single OAR-based) cost accounting system. Explain the benefits that KL might obtain through a full knowledge and understanding of this cost.

(10 marks)

(c) Explain and discuss the extent to which academic research in the area of management accounting is likely to influence the practice of management accounting.

(5 marks)
(Total 25 marks)

CIMA Stage 3 Management Accounting Applications

Review problems (with answers in the Student's Manual)

10.29 **Intermediate: Preparation of conventional costing and ABC profit statements**

The following budgeted information relates to Brunti plc for the forthcoming period:

	Products		
	XYI (000)	YZT (000)	ABW (000)
Sales and production (units)	50	40	30
	(£)	(£)	(£)
Selling price (per unit)	45	95	73
Prime cost (per unit)	32	84	65
	Hours	Hours	Hours
Machine department (machine hours per unit)	2	5	4
Assembly department (direct labour hours per unit)	7	3	2

Overheads allocated and apportioned to production departments (including service cost centre costs) were to be recovered in product costs as follows:

Machine department at
£1.20 per machine hour
Assembly department at
£0.825 per direct labour hour

You ascertain that the above overheads could be re-analysed into 'cost pools' as follows:

Cost pool	£000	Cost driver	Quantity for the period
Machining services	357	Machine hours	420 000
Assembly services	318	Direct labour hours	530 000
Set-up costs	26	Set-ups	520
Order processing	156	Customer orders	32 000
Purchasing	84	Suppliers orders	11 200
	941		

You have also been provided with the following estimates for the period:

	Products		
	XYI	YZT	ABW
Number of set-ups	120	200	200
Customer orders	8000	8000	16 000
Suppliers' orders	3000	4000	4 200

Required:

(a) Prepare and present profit statements using:
  (i) conventional absorption costing;

(5 marks)

  (ii) activity-based costing;

(10 marks)

(b) Comment on why activity-based costing is considered to present a fairer valuation of the product cost per unit.

(5 marks)
(Total 20 marks)
ACCA Paper 8 Managerial Finance

10.30 **Advanced: Computation of ABC and traditional product costs plus a discussion of ABC**

Repak Ltd is a warehousing and distribution company which receives products from customers, stores the products and then re-packs them for distribution as required. There are three customers for whom the service is provided – John Ltd, George Ltd and Paul Ltd. The products from all three customers are similar in nature but of varying degrees of fragility. Basic budget information has been gathered for the year to 30 June and is shown in the following table:

	Products handled (cubic metres)
John Ltd	30 000
George Ltd	45 000
Paul Ltd	25 000
	Costs (£000)
Packaging materials (see note 1)	1 950
Labour – basic	350
– overtime	30
Occupancy	500
Administration and management	60

Note 1: Packaging materials are used in re-packing each cubic metre of product for John Ltd, George Ltd and Paul Ltd in the ratio 1:2:3 respectively. This ratio is linked to the relative fragility of the goods for each customer.

Additional information has been obtained in order to enable unit costs to be prepared for each of the three customers using an activity-based costing approach. The additional information for the year to 30 June has been estimated as follows:

(i) Labour and overhead costs have been identified as attributable to each of three work centres – receipt and inspection, storage and packing as follows:

	Cost allocation proportions		
	Receipt and inspection %	Storage %	Packing %
Labour – basic	15	10	75
– overtime	50	15	35
Occupancy	20	60	20
Administration and management	40	10	50

(ii) Studies have revealed that the fragility of different goods affects the receipt and inspection time needed for the products for each customer. Storage required is related to the average size of the basic incoming product units from each customer. The re-packing of goods for distribution is related to the complexity of packaging required by each customer. The relevant requirements per cubic metre of product for each customer have been evaluated as follows:

	John Ltd	George Ltd	Paul Ltd
Receipt and inspection (minutes)	5	9	15
Storage (square metres)	0·3	0·3	0·2
Packing (minutes)	36	45	60

Required:

(a) Calculate the budgeted average cost per cubic metre of packaged products for each customer for each of the following two circumstances:

(i) where only the basic budget information is to be used,

(6 marks)

(ii) where the additional information enables an activity-based costing approach to be applied.

(14 marks)

(b) Comment on the activities and cost drivers which have been identified as relevant for the implementation of activity-based costing by Repak Ltd and discuss ways in which activity-based costing might improve product costing and cost control in Repak Ltd. Make reference to your answer to part (a) of the question, as appropriate.

(10 marks)
(Total 30 marks)
ACCA Level 2

10.31 **Advanced: Comparison of ABC with traditional product costing**

(a) In the context of activity-based costing (ABC), it was stated in *Management Accounting – Evolution not Revolution* by Bromwich and Bhimani, that 'Cost drivers attempt to link costs to the scope of output rather than the scale of output thereby generating less arbitrary product costs for decision making.' You are required to explain the terms 'activity-based costing' and 'cost drivers'.

(13 marks)

(b) XYZ plc manufactures four products, namely A, B, C and D, using the same plant and processes. The following information relates to a production period:

Product	Volume	Material cost per unit	Direct labour per unit	Machine time cost per unit	Labour
A	500	£5	½ hour	¼ hour	£3
B	5000	£5	½ hour	¼ hour	£3
C	600	£16	2 hours	1 hour	£12
D	7000	£17	1½ hours	1½ hours	£9

Total production overhead recorded by the cost accounting system is analysed under the following headings:

Factory overhead applicable to machine-oriented activity is £37 424

Set-up costs are £4355

The cost of ordering materials is £1920

Handling materials – £7580

Administration for spare parts – £8600.

These overhead costs are absorbed by products on a machine hour rate of £4.80 per hour, giving an overhead cost per product of:

A £1.20 B £1.20 C £4.80 D £7.20

However, investigation into the production overhead activities for the period reveals the following totals:

Product	Number of set-ups	Number of material orders	Number of times material was handled	Number of spare parts
A	1	1	2	2
B	6	4	10	5
C	2	1	3	1
D	8	4	12	4

You are required:

(i) to compute an overhead cost per product using activity-based costing, tracing overheads to production units by means of cost drivers.

(6 marks)

(ii) to comment briefly on the differences disclosed between overheads traced by the present system and those traced by activity-based costing.

(6 marks)

(Total 25 marks)

CIMA Stage 4 Management Accounting – Control and Audit

10.32 **Intermediate**

In a marginal costing system only variable costs would be assigned to products or services, in which case management may rely on a *contribution approach to decisions*.

Required:

(a) Explain and discuss the contribution approach to decisions giving brief examples and drawing attention to any limitations.

(6 marks)

A full absorption costing system would involve the assignment of both variable and fixed overhead costs to products. A traditional full absorption costing system typically uses a *single volume related allocation base* (*or cost driver*) to assign overheads to products. An activity based costing (ABC) system would use *multiple allocation bases* (*or cost drivers*), taking account of *different categories of activities and related overhead costs* such as unit, batch, product sustaining and facility sustaining.

Required:

(b) Describe the likely stages involved in the design and operation of an ABC system.

(4 marks)

(c) Explain and discuss volume related allocation bases (or cost drivers), giving an example of one within a traditional costing system. Contrast this with the multiple allocation bases (or cost drivers) of an ABC system.

(6 marks)

(d) Briefly elaborate on the different categories of activities and related overhead costs, such as unit, batch, product sustaining and facility sustaining, which may be used in an ABC system.

(4 marks)

(Total 20 marks)

ACCA Paper 8 Managerial Finance

Pricing decisions and profitability analysis

11

Accounting information is often an important input to pricing decisions. Organizations that sell products or services that are highly customized or differentiated from each other by special features, or who are market leaders, have some discretion in setting selling prices. In these organizations the pricing decision will be influenced by the cost of the product. The cost information that is accumulated and presented is therefore important for pricing decisions. In other organizations prices are set by overall market and supply forces and they have little influence over the selling prices of their products and services. Nevertheless, cost information is still of considerable importance in these organizations for determining the relative profitability of different products and services so that management can determine the target product mix to which its marketing effort should be directed.

In this chapter we shall focus on both of the above situations. We shall consider the role that accounting information plays in determining the selling price by a price setting firm.

LEARNING OBJECTIVES:

After studying this chapter, you should be able to:

- describe how the optimum output and selling price is determined using economic theory;
- calculate the optimum selling price using differential calculus;
- explain the relevant cost information that should be presented in price setting firms for both short-term and long-term decisions;
- describe product and customer profitability analysis and the information that should be included for managing the product and customer mix;
- describe the target costing approach to pricing;
- describe the different cost-plus pricing methods for deriving selling prices;
- explain the limitations of cost-plus pricing;
- justify why cost-plus pricing is widely used;
- identify and describe the different pricing policies.

Where prices are set by the market our emphasis will be on examining the cost information that is required for product-mix decisions. In particular, we shall focus on both product and customer profitability analysis. The content of this chapter is normally applicable only to second year management accounting courses.

The theoretical solution to pricing decisions is derived from economic theory, which explains how the optimal selling price is determined. A knowledge of economic theory provides a suitable framework for considering the cost information that is appropriate for pricing decisions. This chapter therefore begins with a description of economic theory.

Economic theory

The central feature of the economic model is the assumption that the firm will attempt to set the selling price at a level where profits are maximized. For **monopolistic/imperfect competition** the model assumes that the lower the price, the larger will be the volume of sales.[1] This relationship is depicted in Figure 11.1, which is known as a demand curve.

Points A and B represent two of many possible price/quantity combinations. You will see that at a price P_a, the quantity demanded will be Q_a, while at the lower price of P_b the quantity demanded will increase to Q_b. The economist describes the sensitivity of demand to changes in price as the **price elasticity of demand**. Demand is elastic when there are substitutes for a product, or when customers do not value the product very highly; the result is that a small increase/decrease in price causes a large decrease/increase in the quantity demanded. Alternatively, demand is inelastic when customers place a high value on the product, or when no close substitutes exist; the result is that a small increase/decrease in price causes only a small decrease/increase in the quantity demanded (see Figure 11.2).

If you compare the two graphs in Figure 11.2, you will see that in (a) an increase in price from P_A to P_B results in only a small reduction in the quantity demanded, whereas in (b) the same increase in price results in a large reduction in the quantity demanded.

Establishing the optimum selling price

The precise quantification of the relationship between the selling price and the quantity demanded is very difficult in practice, but let us assume here that management has produced an estimate of the sales demand at various selling prices, as shown in Exhibit 11.1.

You will note that if the price is reduced from £40 to £38 the total revenue will increase by £18, and that each successive price reduction causes incremental or marginal revenue to increase by successively smaller amounts. This process eventually results in a decline in total revenue when the price per unit is reduced from £30 to £28.

To determine the optimum selling price (i.e. the price at which total profits are maximized), it is also necessary for management to estimate the total costs for each of the sales levels given in Exhibit 11.1; this cost information is set out in Exhibit 11.2.

The final stage is to calculate the profit for each sales level and select the most profitable price–volume combination. The profit calculations are obtained by combining the information given in Exhibits 11.1 and 11.2 (see Exhibit 11.3).

You can see from Exhibit 11.3 that profits are maximized at a selling price of £34 when 13 units are sold.

FIGURE 11.1 *A demand curve*

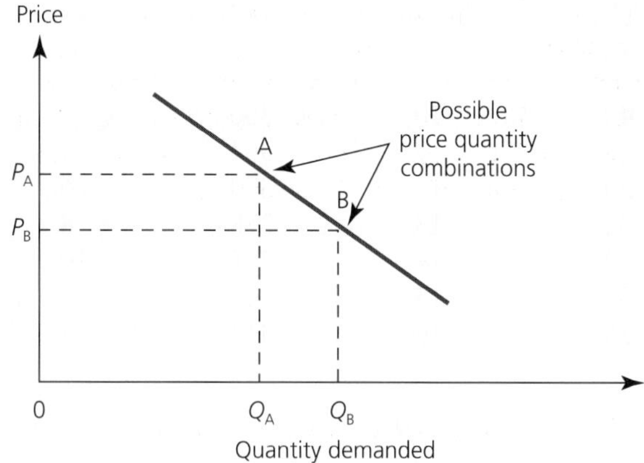

FIGURE 11.2 *Price elasticity of demand: (a) inelastic demand; (b) elastic demand*

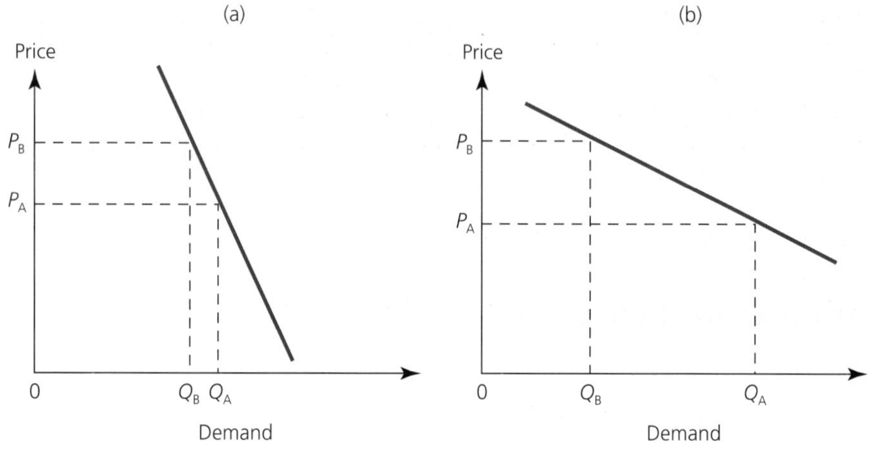

EXHIBIT 11.1

Estimate of sales demand at different price levels

Price (£)	Unit of sales demand	Total revenue (£)	Marginal revenue (£)
40	10	400	
38	11	418	18
36	12	432	14
34	13	442	10
32	14	448	6
30	15	450	2
28	16	448	–2

EXHIBIT 11.2
Estimate of total costs at different volume levels

Price (£)	Demand and output	Total costs (£)	Marginal cost (£)
40	10	360	
38	11	364	4
36	12	370	6
34	13	378	8
32	14	388	10
30	15	400	12
28	16	414	14

EXHIBIT 11.3
Estimate of profits at different output levels

Price (£)	Units sold	Total revenue (£)	Total cost (£)	Profit (£)
40	10	400	360	40
38	11	418	364	54
36	12	432	370	62
34	13	442	378	64
32	14	448	388	60
30	15	450	400	50
28	16	448	414	34

Graphical presentation

Economic theory would normally present the information contained in Exhibits 11.1 to 11.3 in graphical form as shown in Figure 11.3.

The shape of the graphs for the total revenue and the total cost lines is based on the explanations outlined in Chapter 8. If you refer to the top diagram in Figure 11.3, you will see that it indicates that the difference between total revenue and total cost increases as long as total revenue is climbing more rapidly than total cost. When total cost is climbing more rapidly than total revenue (i.e. unit marginal cost exceeds unit marginal revenue), a decision to increase the number of units sold will actually reduce the total profit. The difference between total cost and total revenue is the greatest at a volume level of 13 units; the price required to generate this demand is £34 and this is the optimum selling price.

The lower part of Figure 11.3 shows the cost and revenue information in terms of marginal revenue and marginal cost. Marginal revenue represents the increase in total revenue from the sale of one additional unit, and marginal cost represents the increase in total cost when output is increased by one additional unit. Note that the marginal revenue line slopes downwards to the right as demand increases, reflecting the fact that the slope of the total revenue line decreases as demand increases. Similarly, the marginal cost line slopes upwards because of the assumption that total cost increases as output increases.

Exhibit 11.1 and the demand/price curve in the lower part of Figure 11.3 indicates that to increase sales demand from 10 units to 11 units it is necessary to reduce the selling price

FIGURE 11.3 *Economist's model for establishing optimum price. MC, marginal cost; MR, marginal revenue; TC, total cost; TR, total revenue*

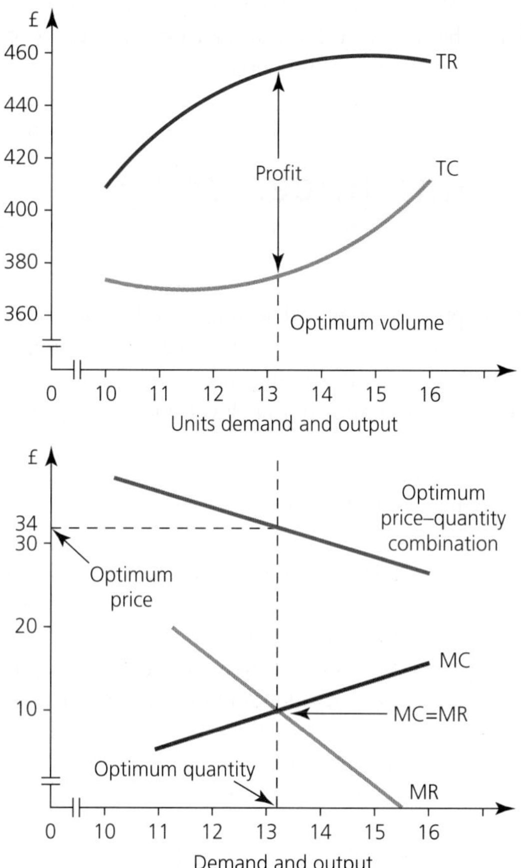

from £40 to £38. This increases total revenue from £400 to £418, the difference of £18 being the marginal revenue of the eleventh unit (shown in the graph as the height of the marginal revenue line at that point). The marginal revenues for the 12th, 13th and 14th units are £14, £10 and £6 respectively. The marginal cost is calculated by assessing the cost of one extra unit (or batch, etc.), and this information is presented in Exhibit 11.2. For example, the marginal cost is £4 for the eleventh unit and £6 for the twelfth unit. The marginal cost is plotted in Figure 11.3, and the optimum price is determined by the intersection of the marginal revenue and marginal cost curves; this is at a price of £34, when sales demand will be 13 units. Note that the intersection of the graphs occurs at a demand just in excess of 13 units. Clearly, we must work in whole units demanded, and therefore the optimal output is 13 units.

The demand curve is also included in the lower part of Figure 11.3, and to obtain the optimum price it is necessary to extend a vertical line upwards from the intersection of the marginal cost and marginal revenue curves. The point where this line cuts the demand curve provides us with the optimum selling price.

Note that if the vertical line at the point of intersection of the marginal cost and marginal revenue curve is extended further upwards into the top part of the graph, it will cut the total cost and the total revenue curves at the point where the difference between these two lines is the greatest. In other words, it cuts the total cost and total revenue curves at the points where the profits are maximized. The graphs in the lower and upper sections of Figure 11.3 are therefore related, and this dual presentation clearly indicates that the point where the difference between total cost and total revenue is the greatest is where marginal revenue is equal to marginal cost. The selling price that causes marginal revenue to be equal to marginal cost represents the optimum selling price.

Calculating optimum selling prices using differential calculus

We have established that optimal output is determined at the point where marginal revenue equals marginal cost. The highest selling price at which the optimum output can be sold determines the optimal selling price. If demand and cost schedules are known, it is possible to derive simultaneously the optimum output level and selling price using differential calculus. Consider Example 11.1.

The first step when calculating the optimum selling price is to calculate total cost and revenue functions. The total cost (TC) function is

$$TC = £700\,000 + £70x$$

where x is the annual level of demand and output.

At present the selling price is £160 and demand is 10 000 units. Each increase or decrease in price of £2 results in a corresponding decrease or increase in demand of 500 units. Therefore, if the selling price were increased to £200, demand would be zero. To increase demand by one unit, selling price must be reduced by £0.004 (£2/500 units). Thus the maximum selling price (SP) for an output of x units is

$$SP = £200 - £0.004x$$

Assuming that the output demanded is 10 000 units SP = £200 – £0.004 (10 000) = £160. Therefore if demand is 10 000 units, the maximum selling price is £160, the same selling price given in Example 11.1. We shall now use differential calculus to derive the optimal selling price:

$$TC = £700\,000 + £70x$$
$$SP = £200 - £0.004x$$

Therefore total revenue (TR) for an output of x units = $£200x - £0.004x^2$

$$\text{marginal cost (MC)} = \frac{dTC}{dx} = £70$$

$$\text{marginal revenue (MR)} = \frac{dTR}{dx} = £200 - £0.008x$$

At the optimum output level

$$\frac{dTC}{dx} = \frac{dTR}{dx}$$

EXAMPLE 11.1

A division within the Caspian Company sells a single product. Divisional fixed costs are £700 000 per annum and a variable cost of £70 is incurred for each additional unit produced and sold over a very large range of outputs. The current selling price for the product is £160, and at this price 10 000 units are demanded per annum. It is estimated that for each successive increase in price of £2 annual demand will be reduced by 500 units. Alternatively, for each £2 reduction in price demand will increase by 500 units.

Calculate the optimum output and price for the product assuming that if prices are set within each £2 range there will be a proportionate change in demand.

And so

$$£70 = £200 - £0.008x$$

$$x = 162\,500 \text{ units}$$

The highest selling price at which this output can be sold is

$$SP = £200 - £0.004\,(16\,250)$$

so

$$SP = £135$$

Thus optimum selling price and output are £135 and 16.250 units respectively.

For a more detailed example of setting optimal selling prices using differential calculus you should refer to Review problem 11.20 at the end of this chapter and to its solution.

Difficulties with applying economic theory

Economic theory is extremely difficult to apply in practice. The difficulties can be grouped into three categories. First, economic theory assumes that a firm can estimate a demand curve for its products. Techniques have been developed for estimating demand curves at the industry, or aggregate level for undifferentiated products such as automobiles, coffee and crude oil but consider the difficulties of estimating demand curves below the aggregate level. Most firms have hundreds of different products and varieties, some with complex inter-relationships, and it is therefore an extremely difficult task to estimate demand curves at the individual product level. The problem becomes even more complex when competitive reactions are taken into account since these are likely to impact on the price/demand estimates that have been incorporated in the demand curve.

Secondly, the basic model of economic theory assumes only price influences the quantity demanded. In practice, product quality and packaging, advertising and promotion, the credit terms offered and the after-sales service provided all have an important influence on price. Thus a model that includes only price will fail to capture all of the factors that determine customer demand.

Thirdly, the marginal cost curve for each individual product can only be determined after considerable analysis and the final result may only represent an approximation of the true marginal cost function particularly where significant joint product costs exist. However, whilst an approximation of the cost function may suffice for the application of economic theory the estimation of demand curves for each major product represents the major reason why many firms do not directly apply economic theory in practice.

Nevertheless, economic theory does provide useful insights and stresses the need for managers to think about price/demand relationships, even if the relationships cannot be precisely measured. For example, we shall see that many firms add a profit margin to a product's cost. If managers can identify products or customers where demand is inelastic they can add higher margins to a product's costs. Alternatively, where demand is elastic price changes are likely to be crucial and accurate cost measurement becomes vital. There is a danger where profit margins are reduced to minimal percentage figures that any under-costing of products may result in acceptance of unprofitable business whereas overcosting may result in the loss of profitable business to competitors.

The role of cost information in pricing decisions

Most organizations need to make decisions about setting or accepting selling prices for their products or services. In some firms prices are set by overall market supply and demand forces and the firm has little or no influence over the selling prices of its products or services. This situation is likely to occur where there are many firms in an industry and there is little to distinguish their products from each other. No one firm can influence prices significantly by its own actions. For example, in commodity markets such as wheat, coffee, rice and sugar prices are set for the market as a whole based on the forces of supply and demand. Also, small firms operating in an industry where prices are set by the dominant market leaders will have little influence over the price of their products or services. Firms that have little or no influence over the prices of their products or services are described as **price takers**.

In contrast firms selling products or services which are highly customized or differentiated from each other by special features, or who are market leaders, have some discretion in setting prices. Here the pricing decision will be influenced by the cost of the product, the actions of competitors and the extent to which customers value the product. We shall describe those firms that have some discretion over setting the selling price of their products or services as **price setters**. In practice, firms may be price setters for some of their products and price takers for others.

Where firms are price setters cost information is often an important input into the pricing decision. Cost information is also of vital importance to price takers in deciding on the output and mix of products and services to which their marketing effort should be directed, given their market prices. For both price takers and price setters the decision time horizon determines the cost information that is relevant for product pricing or output-mix decisions. We shall therefore consider the following four different situations:

1. a price setting firm facing short-run pricing decisions;
2. a price setting firm facing long-run pricing decisions;
3. a price taker firm facing short-run product-mix decisions;
4. a price taker firm facing long-run product-mix decisions.

A price setting firm facing short-run pricing decisions

Companies can encounter situations where they are faced with the opportunity of bidding for a one-time special order in competition with other suppliers. In this situation only the incremental costs of undertaking the order should be taken into account. It is likely that most of the resources required to fill the order will have already been acquired and the cost of these resources will be incurred whether or not the bid is accepted by the customer. Typically, the incremental costs are likely to consist of:

- extra materials that are required to fulfil the order;
- any extra part-time labour, overtime or other labour costs;
- the extra energy and maintenance costs for the machinery and equipment required to complete the order.

The incremental costs of one-off special orders in service companies are likely to be minimal. For example, the incremental cost of accepting one-off special business for a hotel may consist of only the cost of additional meals, laundering and bathroom facilities. In most cases, incremental costs are likely to be confined to items within unit-level activities. Resources for batch, product and service-sustaining activities are likely to have already been acquired and in most cases no extra costs on the supply of activities are likely to be incurred.

Bids should be made at prices that exceed incremental costs. Any excess of revenues over incremental costs will provide a contribution to committed fixed costs which would not otherwise have been obtained. Given the short-term nature of the decision long-term considerations are likely to be non-existent and, apart from the consideration of bids by competitors, cost data are likely to be the dominant factor in determining the bid price.

Any bid for one-time special orders that is based on covering only short-term incremental costs must meet all of the following conditions:

- Sufficient capacity is available for all resources that are required to fulfil the order. If some resources are fully utilized, opportunity costs (see Chapter 9 for an illustration) of the scarce resources must be covered by the bid price.
- The bid price will not affect the future selling prices and the customer will not expect repeat business to be priced to cover short-term incremental costs.
- The order will utilize unused capacity for only a short period and capacity will be released for use on more profitable opportunities. If more profitable opportunities do not exist and a short-term focus is always adopted to utilize unused capacity then the effect of pricing a series of special orders over several periods to cover incremental costs constitutes a long-term decision. Thus, the situation arises whereby the decision to reduce capacity is continually deferred and short-term incremental costs are used for long-term decisions.

A price setting firm facing long-run pricing decisions

In this section we shall focus on three approaches that are relevant to a price setting firm facing long-run pricing decisions. They are:

1. Pricing customized products
2. Pricing non-customized products
3. Target costing for pricing non-customized products

Pricing customized products

In the long run firms can adjust the supply of virtually all of their activity resources. Therefore a product or service should be priced to cover all of the resources that are committed to it. If a firm is unable to generate sufficient revenues to cover the long-run costs of all its products, and its business sustaining costs, then it will make losses and will not be able to survive. Setting prices to cover all of the resources that are committed to each individual product (or service) requires a costing system that accurately measures resources consumed by each product. If inaccurate costs are used undercosting or overcosting will occur. In the former situation there is a danger that prices will be set that fail to cover the long-run resources committed to a product. Conversely, with the latter situation profitable business may be lost because overstated product costs have resulted in excessive prices being set that adversely affect sales volumes and revenues. Where firms are price setters there are stronger grounds for justifying the adoption of ABC systems.

The terms **full cost** or **long-run cost** are used to represent the sum of the cost of all those resources that are committed to a product in the long-term. The term is not precisely defined and may include or exclude facility/business sustaining costs. Let us now consider a full cost computation for a product pricing decision using an ABC system. You should now refer to the data presented in Example 11.2.

The estimate of the cost of the resources required to fulfil the order is as follows:

Unit-level expenses		
Direct materials (500 × £22)	11 000	
Direct labour (500 × 2 hours × £10)	10 000	
Machining (500 × 1 hour × £30)	15 000	36 000
Batch-level expenses		
Purchasing and receiving materials and components (6 × £100)	600	
Scheduling production (4 production runs × £250)	1 000	
Setting-up machines (4 production runs × 3 hours × £120)	1 440	
Packaging and delivering (1 delivery at £400)	400	3 440
Product-sustaining expenses		
Engineering design and support (50 hours × £80)		4 000
Customer-sustaining expenses		
Marketing and order negotiation (2 visits × £300 per visit)	600	
Customer support (50 support hours × £50)	2 500	3 100
Total cost of resources (excluding facility-sustaining costs)		46 540

The full cost (excluding facility-sustaining costs) of the order is £46 540. It was pointed out in the previous chapter that facility-sustaining costs are incurred to support the organization as a whole and not for individual products. Therefore they should not be allocated to products for most decisions. Any allocation will be arbitrary. However, such costs must be covered by sales revenues, and for pricing purposes their allocation can be justified as long as they are separately reported.

What allocation base should be used for facility-sustaining costs? The answer is a base that will influence behaviour that the organization wishes to encourage. For example, if the organization has adopted a strategy of standardizing and reducing the number of separate parts maintained it could choose the number of parts as the allocation base. Thus, the facility-sustaining costs allocated to a product would increase with the number of parts used for an order and product designers would be motivated to use standard parts. If a behaviourally desirable allocation base cannot be established then a base should be selected that has a neutral effect and which does not encourage undesirable behaviour. Reporting facility-sustaining costs as a separate category should reduce, or eliminate, the behavioural impact of the chosen allocation base since this provides a clear signal to management that it is an arbitrary allocation, and not a cause-and-effect allocation. We shall look at the behavioural impact of cost drivers in more detail in Chapter 22.

EXAMPLE 11.2

The Kalahari Company has received a request for a price quotation from one of its regular customers for an order of 500 units with the following characteristics:

Direct labour per unit produced	2 hours
Direct materials per unit produced	£22
Machine hours per unit produced	1 hour
Number of component and material purchases	6
Number of production runs for the components prior to assembly	4
Average set-up time per production run	3 hours
Number of deliveries	1
Number of customer visits	2
Engineering design and support	50 hours
Customer support	50 hours

Details of the activities required for the order are as follows:

Activity	Activity cost driver rate
Direct labour processing and assembly activities	£10 per labour hour
Machine processing	£30 per machine hour
Purchasing and receiving materials and components	£100 per purchase order
Scheduling production	£250 per production run
Setting-up machines	£120 per set-up hour
Packaging and delivering orders to customers	£400 per delivery
Invoicing and accounts administration	£120 per customer order
Marketing and order negotiation	£300 per customer visit
Customer support activities including after sales service	£50 per customer service hour
Engineering design and support	£80 per engineering hour

To determine a proposed selling price an appropriate percentage mark-up is added to the estimated cost. In our example facility-sustaining costs have not been allocated to the order. Thus the mark-up that is added should be sufficient to cover a fair share of facility-sustaining costs and provide a profit contribution. Where facility-sustaining costs are allocated a smaller percentage mark-up would be added since the mark-up is required to provide only a profit contribution. Let us assume that the Kalahari Company adds a mark-up of 20%. This would result in a mark-up of £9308 (20% × £46 540) being added to the cost estimate of £46 540, giving a proposed selling price of £55 848. The approach that we have adopted here is called **cost-plus pricing**. We shall discuss cost-plus pricing and the factors influencing the determination of the profit mark-ups later in the chapter.

Note that the activity-based cost information provides a better understanding of cost behaviour. The batch, product and customer-sustaining costs are unrelated to quantity ordered whereas the unit-level costs are volume related. This provides useful information for salespersons in negotiations with the customer relating to the price and size of the order. Assume that the customer considers purchasing 3000 units, instead of the 500 units originally quoted. If the larger order will enable the company to order 3000 components, instead of 500, and each production run for a component processes 3000 units instead of 500, the batch-level expenses will remain unchanged. Also the cost of the product and customer-sustaining activities will be the same for the larger order but the cost of the unit-level activity resources required will increase by a factor of six because six times the amount of resources will be required for the larger order. Thus the cost of the resources used for an order of 3000 units will be:

	(£)
Unit-level expenses (6 × £36 000[a])	216 000
Batch-level expenses	3 440
Product-sustaining expenses	4 000
Customer-sustaining expenses	3 100
Total cost of resources (excluding facility-sustaining costs)	226 540

Note
[a]Unit-level expenses for an order of 500 units multiplied by a factor of 6.

The cost per unit for a 500 unit order size is £93.08 (£46 540/500) compared with £75.51 (£226 540/3000) for a 3000 unit order size and the resulting proposed unit selling prices are £111.70 (£93.08 × 120%) and £90.61 (£75.51 × 120%) respectively.

Pricing non-customized products

In Example 11.2 the Kalahari Company was faced with a pricing decision for the sale of a highly customized product to a single customer. The pricing decision would have been based on direct negotiations with the customer for a known quantity. In contrast, a market leader must make a pricing decision, normally for large and unknown volumes, of a single product that is sold to thousands of different customers. To apply cost-plus pricing in this situation an estimate is required of sales volume to determine a unit cost which will determine the cost-plus selling price. This circular process occurs because we are now faced with two unknowns which have a cause-and-effect relationship, namely selling price and sales volume. In this situation it is recommended that cost-plus selling prices are estimated for a range of potential sales volumes. Consider the information presented in Example 11.3 (Case A).

You will see that the Auckland Company has produced estimates of total costs for a range of activity levels. Ideally, the cost estimates should be built up in a manner similar to the activity-based cost estimates that were used by the Kalahari Company in Example 11.2. However, for brevity the cost build-up is not shown. Instead of adding a percentage profit margin the Auckland Company has added a fixed lump sum target profit contribution of £2 million.

The information presented indicates to management the sales volumes, and their accompanying selling prices, that are required to generate the required profit contribution. The unit cost calculation indicates the break-even selling price at each sales volume that is required to cover the cost of the resources committed at that particular volume. Management must assess the likelihood of selling the specified volumes at the designated prices and choose the price which they consider has the highest probability of generating at least the specified sales volume. If none of the sales volumes are likely to be achieved at the designated selling prices management must consider how demand can be stimulated and/or costs reduced to make the product viable. If neither of these, or other strategies, are successful the product should not be launched. The final decision must be based on management judgement and knowledge of the market.

The situation presented in Example 11.3 represents the most extreme example of the lack of market data for making a pricing decision. If we reconsider the pricing decision faced by the company it is likely that similar products are already marketed and information may be

EXAMPLE 11.3

Case A

The Auckland Company is launching a new product. Sales volume will be dependent on the selling price and customer acceptance but because the product differs substantially from other products within the same product category it has not been possible to obtain any meaningful estimates of price/demand relationships. The best estimate is that demand is likely to range between 100 000 and 200 000 units provided that the selling price is less than £100. Based on this information the company has produced the following cost estimates and selling prices required to generate a target profit contribution of £2 million from the product.

Sales volume (000's)	100	120	140	160	180	200
Total cost (£000's)	10 000	10 800	11 200	11 600	12 600	13 000
Required profit contribution (£000's)	2 000	2 000	2 000	2 000	2 000	2 000
Required sales revenues (£000's)	12 000	12 800	13 200	13 600	14 600	15 000
Required selling price to achieve target profit contribution (£)	120.00	106.67	94.29	85.00	81.11	75.00
Unit cost (£)	100.00	90.00	80.00	72.50	70.00	65.00

Case B

Assume now an alternative scenario for the product in Case A. The same cost schedule applies but the £2 million minimum contribution no longer applies. In addition, Auckland now undertakes market research. Based on this research, and comparisons with similar product types and their current selling prices and sales volumes, estimates of sales demand at different selling prices have been made. These estimates, together with the estimates of total costs obtained in Case A are shown below:

Potential selling price	£100	£90	£80	£70	£60
Estimated sales volume at the potential selling price (000's)	120	140	180	190	200
Estimated total sales revenue (£000's)	12 000	12 600	14 400	13 300	12 000
Estimated total cost (£000's)	10 800	11 200	12 600	12 800	13 000
Estimated profit (loss) contribution (£000's)	1 200	1 400	1 800	500	(1 000)

available relating to their market shares and sales volumes. Assuming that Auckland's product is differentiated from other similar products a relative comparison should be possible of its strengths and weaknesses and whether customers would be prepared to pay a price in excess of the prices of similar products. It is therefore possible that Auckland may be able to undertake market research to obtain rough approximations of demand levels at a range of potential selling prices. Let us assume that Auckland adopts this approach, and apart from this, the facts are the same as those given in Example 11.3 (Case A).

Now look at Case B in Example 11.3. The demand estimates are given for a range of selling prices. In addition the projected costs, sales revenues and profit contribution are shown. You can see that profits are maximized at a selling price of £80. The information also shows the effect of pursuing other pricing policies. For example, a lower selling price of £70 might be selected to discourage competition and ensure that a larger share of the market is obtained in the future. Where demand estimates are available ABC cost information should be presented for different potential volume levels and compared with projected sales revenues derived from estimated price/output relationships. Ideally, the cost projections should be based on a life-cycle costing approach to ensure that costs incurred over the whole of a product's life cycle are taken into account in the pricing decision. We shall look at life-cycle costing in Chapter 22.

Pricing non-customized products using target costing

Instead of using cost-plus pricing approach described in Exhibit 11.3 (Case A) whereby cost is used as the starting point to determine the selling price, **target costing** is the reverse of this process. With target costing the starting point is the determination of the target selling price. Next a standard or desired profit margin is deducted to get a target cost for the product. The aim is to ensure that the future cost will not be higher than the target cost. The stages involved in target costing can be summarized as follows:

Stage 1: determine the target price which customers will be prepared to pay for the product;

Stage 2: deduct a target profit margin from the target price to determine the target cost;

Stage 3: estimate the actual cost of the product;

Stage 4: if estimated actual cost exceeds the target cost investigate ways of driving down the actual cost to the target cost.

The first stage requires market research to determine the customers' perceived value of the product, its differentiation value relative to competing products and the price of competing products. The target profit margin depends on the planned return on investment for the organization as a whole and profit as a percentage of sales. This is then decomposed into a target profit for each product which is then deducted from the target price to give the target cost. The target cost is compared with the predicted actual cost. If the predicted actual cost is above the target cost intensive efforts are made to close the gap. Product designers focus on modifying the design of the product so that it becomes cheaper to produce. Manufacturing engineers also concentrate on methods of improving production processes and efficiencies.

The aim is to drive the predicted actual cost down to the target cost but if the target cost cannot be achieved at the pre-production stage the product may still be launched if management are confident that the process of continuous improvement and learning curve effects (see Chapter 24) will enable the target cost to be achieved early in the product's life. If this is not possible the product will not be launched.

The major attraction of target costing is that marketing factors and customer research provide the basis for determining selling price whereas cost tends to be the dominant factor with cost-plus pricing. A further attraction is that the approach requires the collaboration of product designers, production engineers, marketing and finance staff whose focus is on managing costs at the product design stage. At this stage costs can be most effectively managed because a decision to committing the firm to incur costs will not have been made.

Target costing is most suited for setting prices for non-customized and high sales volume products. It is also an important mechanism for managing the cost of future products. We shall therefore look at target costing in more detail when we focus on cost management in Chapter 22.

A price taker firm facing short-run product-mix decisions

Price taking firms may be faced with opportunities of taking on short-term business at a market determined selling price. In this situation the cost information that is required is no different from that of a price setting firm making a short-run pricing decision. In other words, accepting short-term business where the incremental sales revenues exceed incremental short-run costs will provide a contribution towards committed fixed costs which would not otherwise have been obtained. However, such business is acceptable only if the same conditions as those specified for a price setting firm apply. You should remember that these conditions are:

- sufficient capacity is available for all resources that are required from undertaking the business (if some resources are fully utilized, opportunity costs of the scarce resources must be covered by the selling price);
- the company will not commit itself to repeat longer-term business that is priced to cover only short-term incremental costs;
- the order will utilize unused capacity for only a short period and capacity will be released for use on more profitable opportunities.

Besides considering new short-term opportunities organizations may, in certain situations, review their existing product-mix over a short-term time horizon. Consider a situation where a firm has excess capacity which is being retained for an expected upsurge in demand. If committed resources are to be maintained then the product profitability analysis of existing products should be based on a comparison of incremental revenues with short-term incremental costs. The same principle applies as that which applied for accepting new short-term business where spare capacity exists. That is, in the short term products should be retained if their incremental revenues exceed their incremental short-term costs.

Where short-term capacity constraints apply, such that the firm has profitable products whose sales demand exceeds its productive capacity, the product-mix should be based on maximizing contribution per limiting production factor as described in Chapter 9. You may wish to refer back to Example 9.2 for an illustration of this approach. Do note, however, that in the longer-term capacity constraints can be removed.

A price taker firm facing long-run product-mix decisions

When prices are set by the market a firm has to decide which products to sell given their market prices. In the longer-term a firm can adjust the supply of resources committed to a product. Therefore the sales revenue from a service or product should exceed the cost of all the resources that are committed to it. Hence there is a need to undertake periodic profitability analysis to distinguish between profitable and unprofitable products in order to ensure that only profitable products are sold. Activity-based profitability analysis should be used to evaluate each product's long-run profitability. In the previous chapter Figure 10.2 was used to illustrate ABC hierarchical profitability analysis. This diagram is repeated in the form of Figure 11.4. You will see that where products are the cost object four different hierarchical levels have been identified – the individual products, the product brand groupings, the product line and finally the whole business unit. At the individual product level all of the resources required for undertaking the unit, batch and product-sustaining

FIGURE 11.4 *An illustration of hierarchical profitability analysis*

Lowest cost object	Products	Customers	Locations
Contribution after deducting unit level costs	Product contributions	Customer contributions	Branch contributions
Contribution after deducting batch-level costs	Product contributions	Customer contributions	Branch contributions
Contribution after deducting individual product, customer or branch sustaining costs	Product contributions	Customer contributions	Branch contributions
Contribution after deducting product brand, customer segment and regional sustaining costs[1]	Product brand contributions	Customer segment contributions	Regional contributions
Profits after deducting higher level sustaining costs[2]	Product line profits	Distribution channel profits	Country profits
Contribution after deducting business unit/ facility-sustaining costs[3]	Business unit profits	Business unit profits	Business unit profits

Notes

[1] Consists of expenses dedicated to sustaining specific product brands or customer segments or regions but which cannot be attributed to individual products, customers or branches.

[2] Consists of expenses dedicated to sustaining the product lines or distribution channels or countries but which cannot be attributed to lower items within the hierarchy.

[3] Consists of expenses dedicated to the business as a whole and not attributable to any lower items within the hierarchy.

activities that are associated with a product would no longer be required if that product were discontinued. Thus, if the product's sales revenues do not exceed the cost of the resources of these activities it should be subject to a special study for a discontinuation decision.

If product groups are marketed as separate brands the next level within the profitability hierarchy is brand profitability. The sum of the individual product profit contributions (that is, sales revenues less the cost of the unit, batch and product-sustaining activities) within a brand must be sufficient to cover those brand-sustaining expenses that can be attributed to the brand but not the individual products within the brand. Thus it is possible for each individual product within the product brand to generate positive contributions but for the brand grouping to be unprofitable because the brand-sustaining expenses exceed the sum of individual product contributions. In these circumstances a special study is required to consider alternative courses of action that can be undertaken to make the brand profitable.

Product line profitability is the next level in the hierarchy in Figure 11.4. The same principle applies. That is, if the product line consists of a number of separate groupings of branded and non-branded products the sum of their contributions (that is, sales revenues less the cost of the unit, batch, product-sustaining and brand-sustaining activities) should exceed those product-line sustaining expenses that are attributable to the product line as a whole but not the individual groupings of branded and non-branded products within the product line. Here a negative profit contribution would signal the need to undertake a major special study to investigate alternative courses of action relating to how the product line can be made profitable.

The final level in the profitability hierarchy shown in Figure 11.4 relates to the profitability of the business unit as a whole. Here the profit for the business unit can be determined by deducting the facility or business-sustaining expenses that are attributable to the business unit as a whole, but not to lower levels within the hierarchy, from the sum of the product line contributions. Clearly a business must generate profits in the long term if it is to survive.

Most of the decisions are likely to be made at the individual product level. Before discontinuing a product other alternatives or considerations must be taken into account at the special study stage. In some situations it is important to maintain a full product line for marketing reasons. For example, if customers are not offered a full product line to choose from they may migrate to competitors who offer a wider choice. By reporting individual product profitability the cost of maintaining a full product line, being the sum of unprofitable products within the product line, is highlighted. Where maintaining a full product line is not required managers should consider other options before dropping unprofitable products. They should consider re-engineering or redesigning the products to reduce their resource consumption.

If a product cannot be made profitable and it is discontinued do remember our discussion in the previous chapter. That is, dropping products based on ABC information will improve overall profitability only if managers either eliminate the spending on the supply of activity resources that are no longer required to support the discontinued product or redeploy the released resources to produce more of other profitable products. If management does not adopt either of these courses of action the resources will remain in place, the cost of unused capacity will increase and the supply of resources will remain unchanged but sales revenues from the discontinued products will be lost.

The above discussion has concentrated on product profitability analysis. You will see from Figure 11.4 that the same principles can be applied to other cost objects, such as customers or locations. Increasing attention is now being given to customer profitability analysis. Given the importance of this topic we shall consider customer profitability analysis later in the chapter. However, at this stage it is more appropriate to examine cost-plus pricing in more detail.

Cost-plus pricing

Our earlier discussion relating to short-run and long-run pricing suggested that, where it was virtually impossible to estimate demand, cost-plus pricing should be used by a price-setter. Cost-plus pricing was illustrated using the data presented in Examples 11.2 and 11.3.

SUMITOMO ELECTRIC OLYMPUS SONY CITIZEN

Pricing and target costing in Japanese organizations adopting a confrontation strategy

The following relates to extracts from an article by Cooper (1996) based on case studies of Japanese companies:

Nearly every firm studied competed in intensely competitive markets where prices were set by the market. For these firms, even the most revolutionary products had a counterpart that could be identified and used to establish a price for the new product. Under these conditions, cost-plus pricing was almost unheard of. For example, at *Citizen*:

> *Cost-plus pricing was rarely used at* Citizen *because most products were sold into competitive markets where the competitors had similar product offerings. Occasionally,* Citizen *would bring out a watch or movement for which there was no direct competitive offering. In these cases, where there was no market price, the selling price was determined using a 'to be accepted' market price. This price was determined by market savings and analysis that consisted of an evaluation of the attractiveness of the product and a comparison with other watches and other products (Cooper, R.,* Citizen Watch Co., Ltd., *Harvard Business School Case series 9–194–033, p. 5).*

A similar perspective was adopted at *Olympus*:

> *The role of other consumer products was important because some of them competed for the same segment of the consumer's disposable income. For example, consumer research had shown that many consumers were trying to choose between buying a compact disc player or a compact camera. Therefore,* Olympus *viewed compact disc players as competitive products (Cooper, R.,* Olympus Optimal Company, Ltd. (A), *Harvard Business School Case series 9–195–072, p. 4).*

When such a wide view of competitive products is adopted, it is almost impossible to introduce a product that does not have another product against which it is competing. Under these conditions, the competing product sets the price at which the new product must be introduced. Consequently, cost plus pricing is rarely undertaken by firms adopting a confrontation strategy.[1] The only exception was when the product was truly 'unique'. For example, at *Sumitomo Electric Industries,* the length of wire ordered varied by customer. Therefore, costs played an important role in setting prices.

Thus, under confrontational strategies prices are typically set by the market and the purpose of reported product costs is to determine the profitability of products not, typically, to set prices.

To ensure that new products were profitable, many firms have rules against introducing and selling unprofitable products. These rules were modified when complementary products were encountered. The target costing systems acted as the primary mechanism to identify unprofitable products before they were launched. For example, at *Citizen,* the target costing system includes procedures to ensure that unprofitable products are not introduced:

> *Reported product costs played an important part in product introduction because products would be introduced only if they could be sold at a profit.*

Once a new product had been designed, a market analysis was undertaken. This analysis identified the likely selling price of the new product and its potential sales volumes. The next step was to estimate the full cost of production.

The final step was to estimate the profitability of the new watch, which was determined by subtracting the expected costs from the selling price and multiplying the result by the anticipated volume. If the watch was profitable it was introduced and orders accepted from Citizen Trading Company *and other customers. If the watch was unprofitable, then the selling price, production cost, and design were reviewed. If there was no way for the product to be made profitable it was never introduced (*Citizen, *p. 5).*

Sony's rule, included a minimum acceptable profit:

The product planners did not have absolute freedom in relaxing a product's target cost. As a matter of policy, Sony *would not sell products at a loss and, under most conditions, would not sell them below the minimum profit margin established by the appropriate business group's manager. The only exceptions to this rule were strategic products, which* Sony *top management viewed as investments necessary to create or expand markets and which would pay off in the long run (Cooper, R.,* Sony Corporation, *Harvard Business School Case series, 9–195–076 p. 7).*

*The estimated cost of the new product was continuously compared to its target cost. If it appeared that the new product would fail to meet the firm's minimum profit margin requirement or would adversely affect the ability of the group to meet its profit target, then the product would be redesigned (*Sony, *p. 7).*

The addition of a minimum acceptable profit at *Sony* indicates that an important purpose of the firm's target costing system was to ensure that *adequate* profits were generated by all new products. The only major exception to the 'no unprofitable launches' rule was when not introducing a product would have major deleterious effects or when the product was considered strategically important. The following two paragraphs illustrate this exception at *Citizen* and *Olympus,* respectively:

If there was no way for the product to be made profitable (at Citizen*) it was never introduced. The only exceptions to this rule were products that were considered strategically important to* Citizen's *corporate image, such as the perpetual calendar watch (*Citizen, *p. 6).*

If the estimated costs were still too high (at Olympus*), the product was abandoned unless some strategic reason for keeping the product could be identified. Such considerations typically focused on maintaining a full product line (of electronic camera) or creating a 'flagship' product that demonstrated technological leadership (*Olympus, *A, p. 7).*

Note:
[1] Under a confrontational strategy firms cannot create sustainable competitive advantages. They are forced to compete head-on because all competitors sell essentially the same product at the same price.

Source: Adapted from Cooper, R. (1996), Costing techniques to support corporate strategy: evidence from Japan, *Management Accounting Research,* 7, pp. 219–246.

We shall now look at cost-plus pricing in more detail. Companies use different cost bases and mark-ups to determine their selling prices. Consider the information presented below:

Cost base	(£)	Mark-up percentage	Cost-plus selling price (£)
(1) Direct variable costs	200	150	500
(2) Direct non-variable costs	100		
(3) Total direct costs	300	70	510
(4) Indirect costs	80		
(5) Total cost (excluding higher level sustaining costs)	380	40	532
(6) Higher level sustaining costs	60		
(7) Total cost	440	20	528

In the above illustration four different cost bases are used resulting in four different selling prices. In row (1) only direct variable costs are assigned to products for cost-plus pricing and a high percentage mark-up (150%) is added to cover direct non-variable costs, indirect costs and higher level sustaining costs and also to provide a contribution towards profit. Where products are the cost object higher level sustaining costs would include brand, product line and business-sustaining costs. This approach is best suited to short-term pricing decisions.

The second cost base is row (3). Here a smaller percentage margin (70%) is added to cover indirect costs, the higher level sustaining costs and to provide a contribution to profit. Indirect costs are not therefore assigned to products for cost-plus pricing. This cost base is appropriate if indirect costs are a small percentage of an organization's total costs. The disadvantage of adopting this approach is that the consumption of joint resources by products is not measured. By adding a percentage mark-up to direct costs indirect costs are effectively allocated to products using direct costs as the allocation base. Hence, the approach implicitly uses arbitrary apportionments.

The third cost base is 'Total cost' (excluding higher level sustaining costs). With this base a lower profit margin (40%) is added to cover higher level sustaining costs and a profit contribution. This cost base is recommended for long-run pricing and was the approach illustrated in Examples 11.2 and 11.3. Ideally, ABC systems should be used to compute total (full) costs.

The final cost base is row (7) which includes an allocation of all costs but do remember that higher level sustaining costs cannot be allocated to products on a cause-and-effect basis. Some organizations, however, may wish to allocate all costs to products to ensure that all costs are covered in the cost base. The lowest percentage mark-up (20%) is therefore added since the aim is to provide only a profit contribution.

Some manufacturing organizations also use total manufacturing cost as the cost base and add a mark-up to cover non-manufacturing costs and a contribution to profit. The use of this method reflects the fact that many organizations choose to use the same costs as they use for stock valuation for other purposes, including product pricing. Also traditional costing systems are widely used for stock valuation. These systems were not designed to assign non-manufacturing costs to products and organizations. Therefore many organizations do not allocate non-manufacturing costs to products.

Establishing target mark-up percentages

Mark-ups are related to the demand for a product. A firm is able to command a higher mark-up for a product that has a high demand. Mark-ups are also influenced by the elasticity of demand with higher mark-ups being applicable to products which are subject to inelastic demand. Mark-ups are also likely to decrease when competition is intensive. Target mark-up percentages tend to vary from product line to product line to correspond with well-established differences in custom, competitive position and likely demand. For example, luxury goods with a low sales turnover may attract high profit margins whereas non-luxury goods with a high sales turnover may attract low profit margins.

Another approach is to choose a mark-up to earn a **target rate of return on invested capital**. This approach seeks to estimate the amount of investment attributable to a product and then set a price that ensures a satisfactory return on investment for a given volume. For example, assume that cost per unit for a product is £100 and that the annual volume is 10 000 units. If the product requires an investment of £1 million and the target rate of return is 15%, the target mark-up will be

$$\frac{15\% \times £1\ 000\ 000}{10\ 000 \text{ units}} = £15 \text{ per unit}$$

The target price will be £100 plus £15, or £115 per unit. The major problem of applying this approach is that it is difficult to determine the capital invested to support a product. Assets are normally used for many different products and therefore it is necessary to allocate investments in assets to different products. This process is likely to involve arbitrary allocations.

Note that once the target selling price has been calculated, it is rarely adopted without amendment. The price is adjusted upwards or downwards depending on such factors as the future capacity that is available, the extent of competition from other firms, and management's general knowledge of the market. For example, if the price calculation is much lower than that which management considers the customer will be prepared to pay, the price may be increased.

We may ask ourselves the question 'Why should cost-based pricing formulae be used when the final price is likely to be altered by management?' The answer is that cost based pricing formulae provide an initial approximation of the selling price. It is a target price and is important information, although by no means the only information that should be used when the final pricing decision is made. Management should use this information, together with their knowledge of the market and their intended pricing strategies, before the final price is set.

Limitations of cost-plus pricing

The main criticism that has been made against cost-plus pricing is that demand is ignored. The price is set by adding a mark-up to cost, and this may bear no relationship to the price-demand relationship. It is assumed that prices should depend solely on costs. For example, a cost-plus formula may suggest a price of £20 for a product where the demand is 100 000 units, whereas at a price of £25 the demand might be 80 000 units. Assuming that the variable cost for each unit sold is £15, the total contribution will be £500 000 at a selling price of £20, compared with a total contribution of £800 000 at a selling price of £25. Thus cost-plus pricing formulae might lead to incorrect decisions. The following statement made over forty years ago by Baxter and Oxenfeldt (1961) highlights the major weakness of cost-plus pricing. They state:

> *On the other hand, inability to estimate demand accurately scarcely excuses the substitution of cost information for demand information. Crude estimates of demand may serve instead of careful estimates of demand but cost gives remarkably little insight into demand.*

It is often claimed that cost-based pricing formulae serve as a pricing 'floor' shielding the seller from a loss. This argument, however, is incorrect since it is quite possible for a firm to lose money even though every product is priced higher than the estimated unit cost. The reason for this is that if sales demand falls below the activity level that was used to calculate the fixed cost per unit, the total sales revenue may be insufficient to cover the total fixed costs. Cost-plus pricing will only ensure that all the costs will be met, and the target profits earned, if the sales volume is equal to, or more than, the activity level that was used to estimate total unit costs.

Consider a hypothetical situation where all of the costs attributable to a product are fixed in the short-term and amount to £1 million. Assume that the cost per unit is £100 derived from an estimated volume of 10 000 units. The selling price is set at £130 using the cost-plus method and a mark-up of 30%. If actual sales volume is 7000 units, sales revenues will be £910 000 compared with total costs of £1 million. Therefore the product will incur a loss of £90 000 even though it is priced above full cost.

Reasons for using cost-plus pricing

Considering the limitations of cost-plus pricing, why is it that these techniques are frequently used in practice? Baxter and Oxenfeldt (1961) suggest the following reasons:

> *They offer a means by which plausible prices can be found with ease and speed, no matter how many products the firm handles. Moreover, its imposing computations look factual and precise, and its prices may well seem more defensible on moral grounds than prices established by other means. Thus a monopolist threatened by a public inquiry might reasonably feel that he is safeguarding his case by cost-plus pricing.*

Another major reason for the widespread use of cost-plus pricing methods is that they may help a firm to predict the prices of other firms. For example, if a firm has been operating in an industry where average mark-ups have been 40% in the past, it may be possible to predict that competitors will be adding a 40% mark-up to their costs. Assuming that all the firms in the industry have similar cost structures, it will be possible to predict the price range within which competitors may price their products. If all the firms in an industry price their products in this way, it may encourage price stability.

In response to the main objection that cost-based pricing formulae ignore demand, we have noted that the actual price that is calculated by the formula is rarely adopted without amendments. The price is adjusted upwards or downwards after taking account of the number of sales orders on hand, the extent of competition from other firms, the importance of the customer in terms of future sales, and the policy relating to customer relations. Therefore it is argued that management attempts to adjust the mark-up based on the state of sales demand and other factors which are of vital importance in the pricing decision.

Pricing policies

Cost information is only one of many variables that must be considered in the pricing decision. The final price that is selected will depend upon the pricing policy of the company. A price-skimming or pricing penetration policy might be selected.

A **price-skimming policy** is an attempt to exploit those sections of the market that are relatively insensitive to price changes. For example, high initial prices may be charged to take advantage of the novelty appeal of a new product when demand is initially inelastic. A skimming pricing policy offers a safeguard against unexpected future increases in costs, or a large fall in demand after the novelty appeal has declined. Once the market becomes saturated, the price can be reduced to attract that part of the market that has not yet been exploited. A skimming pricing policy should not be adopted when a number of close substitutes are already being marketed. Here the demand curve is likely to be elastic, and any price in excess of that being charged for a substitute product by a competitor is likely to lead to a large reduction in sales.

A **penetration pricing policy** is based on the concept of charging low prices initially with the intention of gaining rapid acceptance of the product. Such a policy is appropriate when close substitutes are available or when the market is easy to enter. The low price discourages potential competitors from entering the market and enables a company to establish a large share of the market. This can be achieved more easily when the product is new, than later on when buying habits have become established.

Many products have a **product life cycle** consisting of four stages: introductory, growth, maturity and decline. At the introductory stage the product is launched and there is minimal awareness and acceptance of it. Sales begin to expand rapidly at the growth stage because of introductory promotions and greater customer awareness, but this begins to taper off at the maturity stage as potential new customers are exhausted. At the decline stage sales diminish as the product is gradually replaced with new and better versions.

Sizer (1989) suggests that in the introductory stage it may be appropriate to shade upwards or downwards the price found by normal analysis to create a more favourable demand in future years. For example, he suggests that limited production capacity may rule out low prices. Therefore a higher initial price than that suggested by normal analysis may be set and progressively reduced, if and when (a) price elasticity of demand increases or (b) additional capacity becomes available. Alternatively if there is no production capacity constraint, a lower price than that suggested by normal analysis may be preferred. Such a price may result in a higher sales volume and a slow competitive reaction, which will enable the company to establish a large market share and to earn higher profits in the long term.

At the maturity stage a firm will be less concerned with the future effects of current selling prices and should adopt a selling price that maximizes short-run profits.

Customer profitability analysis

In the past, management accounting reports have tended to concentrate on analysing profits by products. Increasing attention is now being given to analysing profits by customers using an activity-based costing approach. **Customer profitability analysis** provides important information that can be used to determine which classes of customers should be emphasized or de-emphasized and the price to charge for customer services. Kaplan and Cooper (1998) use Kanthal – a Harvard Business School case study – to illustrate the benefits of customer profitability analysis. Kanthal is a Swedish company that sells electric heating elements. Customer-related selling costs represent 34% of total costs. Until recently, Kanthal allocated these costs on the basis of sales value when special studies of customer profitability analysis were undertaken. An activity-based costing system was introduced that sought to explain the resources consumed by different customers. A detailed study of the resources used to service different types of customers identified two cost drivers:

1. Number of orders placed: each order had a large fixed cost, which did not vary with the quantity of items purchased. Thus a customer who placed 10 orders of 100 items per order generated 10 times more ordering cost than a customer who placed a single order of 1000 units.
2. Non-standard production items: these items were more costly to produce than standard items.

Kanthal estimated the cost per order and the cost of handling standard and non-standard items. A customer profitability analysis was prepared based on the sales for the previous year. This analysis revealed that only 40% of its customers were profitable and a further 10% lost 120% of the profits. In other words, 10% incurred losses equal to 120% of Kanthal's total profits. Two of the most unprofitable customers turned out to be among the top three in total sales volume. These two companies made many small orders of non-standard items.

Let us now look at an illustration of customer profitability analysis. Consider the information presented in Example 11.4. The profitability analysis in respect of the four customers is as follows:

	A	B	Y	Z
Customer attributable costs:				
Sales order processing	60 000	30 000	15 000	9 000
Sales visits	4 000	2 000	1 000	1 000
Normal deliveries	30 000	10 000	2 500	1 250
Special (urgent) deliveries	10 000	2 500	0	0
Credit collection[a]	24 658	8 220	1 370	5 480
	128 658	52 720	19 870	16 730
Operating profit contribution	90 000	120 000	70 000	200 000
Contribution to higher level sustaining expenses	(38 658)	67 280	50 130	183 270

Note

[a](Annual sales revenue × 10%) × (Average collection period/365)

You can see from the above analysis that A and B are high cost to serve whereas Y and Z are low cost to serve customers. Customer A provides a positive operating profit contribution but is unprofitable when customer attributable costs are taken into account. This is because customer A requires more sales orders, sales visits and normal and urgent deliveries than the other customers. In addition, the customer is slow to pay and has higher delivery costs than the other customers. Customer profitability analysis identifies the characteristics of high cost and low cost to serve customers and shows how customer profitability can be increased. The information should be used to persuade high cost to serve customers to modify their buying behaviour away from placing numerous small orders and/or purchasing non-standard items that are costly to make. For example, customer A can be made profitable if action is taken to persuade the customer to place a smaller number of larger quantity orders, avoid special deliveries and reduce the credit period. If unprofitable customers cannot be persuaded to change their buying behaviour selling prices should be increased (or discounts on list prices reduced) to cover the extra resources consumed. Thus ABC is required for customer profitability analysis so that the resources consumed by customers can be accurately measured.

The customer profitability analysis can also be used to rank customers by order of profitability based on **Pareto analysis**. This type of analysis is based on observations by Pareto that a very small proportion of items usually account for the majority of the value. For example, the Darwin Company might find that 20% of the customers account for 80% of the profits. Special attention can then be given to enhancing the relationships with the most profitable customers to ensure that they do not migrate to other competitors. In addition greater emphasis can be given to attracting new customers that have the same attributes as the most profitable customers.

Organizations, such as banks, often with a large customer base in excess of one million customers cannot apply customer profitability analysis at the individual customer level.

EXAMPLE 11.4

The Darwin Company has recently adopted customer profitability analysis. It has undertaken a customer profitability review for the past 12 months. Details of the activities and the cost driver rates relating to those expenses that can be attributed to customers are as follows:

Activity	Cost driver rate
Sales order processing	£300 per sales order
Sales visits	£200 per sales visit
Normal delivery costs	£1 per delivery kilometre travelled
Special (urgent) deliveries	£500 per special delivery
Credit collection costs	10% per annum on average payment time

Details relating to four of the firm's customers are as follows:

Customer	A	B	Y	Z
Number of sales orders	200	100	50	30
Number of sales visits	20	10	5	5
Kilometres per delivery	300	200	100	50
Number of deliveries	100	50	25	25
Total delivery kilometres	30 000	10 000	2 500	1 250
Special (urgent deliveries)	20	5	0	0
Average collection period (days)	90	30	10	10
Annual sales	£1 million	£1 million	£0.5 million	£2 million
Annual operating profit contribution[a]	£90 000	£120 000	£70 000	£200 000

Note

[a] Consists of sales revenues less cost of unit-level and batch-related activities

Instead, they concentrate on customer segment profitability analysis by combining groups of customers into meaningful segments. This enables profitable segments to be highlighted where customer retention is particularly important and provides an input for determining the appropriate marketing strategies for attracting the new customers that have the most profit potential. Segment groupings that are used by banks include income classes, age bands, socio-economic categories and family units.

Summary

The following items relate to the learning objectives listed at the beginning of the chapter.

- **Describe how the optimum output and selling price is determined using economic theory.**

  Economic theory assumes that demand and costs can be estimated at each potential demand level. The optimum output is determined at the point where marginal cost equals

EXHIBIT 11.4
Surveys of practice

A survey of 187 UK organizations by Drury and Tayles (2000) indicated that 60% used cost-plus pricing. Most of the organizations that used cost-plus pricing indicated that it was applied selectively. It accounted for less than 10% of total sales revenues for 26% of the respondents and more than 50% for 39% of the organizations. Most of the firms (85%) used full cost and the remaining 15% used direct cost as the pricing base. The survey also indicated that 74% analysed profits either by customers or customer categories.

An earlier UK study by Innes and Mitchell (1995a) reported that 50% of the respondents had used customer profitability analysis and a further 12% planned to do so in the future. Of those respondents that ranked customer profitability 60% indicated that the Pareto 80/20 rule broadly applied (that, is 20% of the customers were generating 80% of the profits).

Dekker and Smidt (2003) undertook a survey of 32 Dutch firms on the use of costing practices that resembled the Japanese target costing concept. They reported that 19 out of the 32 firms used these practices, although they used different names for them. Adoption was highest among assembling firms and was related to a competitive and unpredictable environment.

marginal revenue. The selling price at which the optimum output can be sold determines the optimum price. Economic theory is difficult to apply in practice because it is difficult for a firm to estimate demand at different selling prices for all of its products.

- **Calculate the optimal selling price using differential calculus.**

If demand and cost schedules are known it is possible to derive simultaneously the optimum output and selling price using differential calculus. The calculation of the optimum selling price was illustrated using Example 11.1.

- **Explain the relevant cost information that should be presented in price setting firms for both short-term and long-term decisions.**

For short-term decisions the incremental costs of accepting an order should be presented. Bids should then be made at prices that exceed incremental costs. For short-term decisions many costs are likely to be fixed and irrelevant. Short-term pricing decisions should meet the following conditions: (a) spare capacity should be available for all of the resources that are required to fulfil an order; (b) the bid price should represent a one-off price that will not be repeated for future orders; and (c) the order will utilize unused capacity for only a short period and capacity will be released for use on more profitable opportunities. For long-term decisions a firm can adjust the supply of virtually all of the resources. Therefore, cost information should be presented providing details of all of the resources that are committed to a product or service. Since facility-sustaining costs should be covered in the long-term by sales revenues there are strong arguments for allocating such costs for long-run pricing decisions. To determine an appropriate selling price a mark-up is added to the total cost of the resources assigned to the product/service to provide a contribution to profits. If facility-sustaining costs are not allocated the mark-up must be sufficient to provide a contribution to covering facility-sustaining costs and a contribution to profit.

- **Describe product and customer profitability analysis and the information that should be included for managing the product and customer mix.**

Price-taking firms have to decide which products to sell, given their market prices. A mechanism is therefore required that ascertains whether or not the sales revenues from

Assessment material

Review questions

The review questions are short questions that enable you to assess your understanding of the main topics included in the chapter. The numbers in parentheses provide you with the page numbers to refer to if you cannot answer a specific question.

Review problems

The review problems are more complex and require you to relate and apply the chapter content to various business problems. The problems are graded by their level of difficulty. The multiple-choice questions are the least demanding and normally take less than 10 minutes to complete. Fully worked solutions to the review problems are provided in a separate section at the end of the book. For those questions in the white box the worked solutions are provided in the *Student's Manual* accompanying this book. Further review problems for this chapter are available on the accompanying website www.drury-online.com. The answers to these problems are available for lecturers on the lecturer's password protected section of the website.

Case studies

The website also includes over 30 case study problems. A list of these cases is provided in Part Seven of this book. Several cases are relevant to the content of this chapter. Examples include Lynch Printers, Reichard Maschinen and Sheridan Carpet Company.

Review questions

11.1 What does the price elasticity of demand measure? *(p. 412)*

11.2 Distinguish between elastic and inelastic demand. *(p. 412)*

11.3 How can the optimum selling price for a product or service be determined? *(pp. 412–16)*

11.4 Explain why economic theory is difficult to apply in practice. *(pp. 417–18)*

11.5 Distinguish between a price taker and a price setter. *(p. 418)*

11.6 What costs are likely to be relevant for (a) a short-run pricing decision, and (b) a long-run pricing decision? *(pp. 419–20)*

11.7 What is meant by the term 'full cost'? *(p. 420)*

11.8 What is meant by cost-plus pricing? *(p. 421, p. 430)*

11.9 Distinguish between cost-plus pricing and target costing. (*p. 424*)

11.10 Describe the four stages involved with target costing. (*pp. 424–25*)

11.11 What role does cost information play in price taking firms? (*p. 425*)

11.12 Describe the alternative cost bases that can be used with cost-plus pricing. (*p. 430*)

11.13 What are the limitations of cost-plus pricing? (*pp. 431–32*)

11.14 Why is cost-plus pricing frequently used in practice? (*p. 432*)

11.15 Describe the different kinds of pricing policies that an organization can apply. (*pp. 432–33*)

11.16 Why is customer profitability analysis important? (*pp. 433–34*)

Review problems

11.17 **Intermediate**

ABC plc is about to launch a new product. Facilities will allow the company to produce up to 20 units per week. The marketing department has estimated that at a price of £8000 no units will be sold, but for each £150 reduction in price one additional unit per week will be sold.

Fixed costs associated with manufacture are expected to be £12 000 per week.

Variable costs are expected to be £4000 per unit for each of the first 10 units; thereafter each unit will cost £400 more than the preceding one.

The most profitable level of output per week for the new product is

A 10 units.
B 11 units.
C 13 units.
D 14 units.
E 20 units.

(3 marks)

CIMA Management Accounting – Decision Making

11.18 **Intermediate: Calculation of different cost-plus prices**

Albany has recently spent some time on researching and developing a new product for which they are trying to establish a suitable price. Previously they have used cost plus 20% to set the selling price.

The standard cost per unit has been estimated as follows:

	£	
Direct materials		
Material 1	10	(4 kg at £2.50/kg)
Material 2	7	(1 kg at £7/kg)
Direct labour	13	(2 hours at £6.50/hour)
Fixed overheads	7	(2 hours at £3.50/hour)
	37	

Required:

(a) Using the standard costs calculate two different cost plus prices using two different bases and explain an advantage and disadvantage of each method. *(6 marks)*

(b) Give two other possible pricing strategies that could be adopted and describe the impact of each one on the price of the product.

(4 marks)
(Total 10 marks)
ACCA Paper 1.2 – Financial information for Management

11.19 **Advanced: Limiting factor resource allocation and comparison of marginal revenue to determine optimum output and price**

(a) A manufacturer has three products, A, B, and C. Currently sales, cost and selling price details and processing time requirements are as follows:

	Product A	Product B	Product C
Annual sales (units)	6000	6000	750
Selling price (£)	20.00	31.00	39.00
Unit cost (£)	18.00	24.00	30.00
Processing time required per unit (hours)	1	1	2

The firm is working at full capacity (13 500 processing hours per year). Fixed manufacturing overheads are absorbed into unit costs by a charge of 200% of variable cost. This procedure fully absorbs the fixed manufacturing overhead. Assuming that:

(i) processing time can be switched from one product line to another,
(ii) the demand at current selling prices is:

Product A	Product B	Product C
11 000	8 000	2 000

and

(iii) the selling prices are not to be altered. You are required to calculate the best production programme for the next operating period and to indicate the increase in net profit that this should yield. In addition identify the shadow price of a processing hour.

(11 marks)

(b) A review of the selling prices is in progress and it has been estimated that, for each product, an increase in the selling price would result in a fall in demand at the rate of 2000 units for an increase of £1 and similarly, that a decrease of £1 would increase demand by 2000 units. Specifically the following price/demand relationships would apply:

Product A		Product B		Product C	
Selling price (£)	Estimated demand	Selling price (£)	Estimated demand	Selling price (£)	Estimated demand
24.50	2 000	34.00	2 000	39.00	2 000
23.50	4 000	33.00	4 000	38.00	4 000
22.50	6 000	32.00	6 000	37.00	6 000
21.50	8 000	31.00	8 000	36.00	8 000
20.50	10 000	30.00	10 000	35.00	10 000
19.50	12 000	29.00	12 000	34.00	12 000
18.50	14 000	28.00	14 000	33.00	14 000

From this information you are required to calculate the best selling prices, the revised best production plan and the net profit that this plan should produce.

(11 marks)

(Total 22 marks)

ACCA Level 2 Management Accounting

11.20 Advanced: Calculation of optimum selling price using differential calculus

(a) Scott St Cyr wishes to decide whether to lease a new machine to assist in the manufacture of his single product for the coming quarter, and also to decide what price to charge for his product in order to maximize his profit (or minimize his loss).

In the quarter just ended his results were as follows:

		(£000)	(£000)
Sales (200 000 units)			600
Less: Cost of goods sold			
Production wages: fixed		20	
piecework		90	
		110	
Materials		400	
			510
Gross profit			90
Less royalties (£0.50 per unit sold)		100	
Less administration (fixed cost)		30	
			130
Loss			(40)

St Cyr expects that, during the coming quarter,

(i) fixed basic wages (£20 000), fixed administration costs (£30 000) and the royalty rate will not change;

(ii) the piecework rate will increase to £0.50 per unit.

Quality control is very difficult and a high proportion of material is spoiled. A new machine has become available that can be delivered immediately. Tests have shown that it will eliminate the quality control problems, resulting in a halving of the usage of materials. It cannot be bought but can be leased for £115 000 per quarter.

The product has a very short shelf life, and is produced only to order. St Cyr estimates that if he were to change the unit selling price, demand for the product would increase by 1000 units per quarter for each one penny (£0.01) decrease in the selling price (so that he would receive orders for 500 000 units if he were to offer them free of charge), and would decrease by 1000 units per quarter for each one penny (£0.01) increase in the unit selling price (so that at a price of £5 his sales would be zero).

You are required to advise Scott St Cyr whether, in the coming quarter, he should lease the new machine and also the price that he should charge for his product, in order to maximize his profit.

(15 marks)

(b) Christian Pass Ltd operates in an entirely different industry. However, it also produces to order, and carries no inventory.

Its demand function is estimated to be $P = 100 - 2Q$ (where P is the unit selling price in £ and Q is the quantity demanded in thousands of units).

Its total costs function is estimated to be $C = Q^2 + 10Q + 500$ (where C is the total cost in £000 and Q is as above).

You are required in respect of Christian Pass Ltd to

(i) calculate the output in units that will maximize total profit, and to calculate the corresponding unit selling price, total profit, and total sales revenue.

(5 marks)

(ii) calculate the output in units that will maximize total revenues, and to calculate the corresponding unit selling price, total loss, and total sales revenue.

(5 marks)
(Total 25 marks)
ICAEW Management Accounting

11.21 **Advanced**

Discuss the extent to which cost data is useful in the determination of pricing policy. Explain the advantages and disadvantages of presenting cost data for possible utilization in pricing policy determination using an absorption, rather than a direct, costing basis.

(14 marks)
ACCA P2 Management Accounting

11.22 **Advanced**

At one of its regular monthly meetings the board of Giant Steps Ltd was discussing its pricing and output policies. Giant Steps Ltd is a multi-product firm, operating in several distinct but related competitive markets. It aims to maximize profits.

You are required to comment critically and concisely on any four of the following six statements which were included in the taped record of the meeting:

(a) Profit is maximized by charging the highest possible price.

(b) The product manager's pricing policy should be to set a price which will maximize demand, by ensuring that contribution per unit is maximized.

(c) Allocation of overheads and joint costs enables management to compare performance between products, projects, or divisions.

(d) Allocation of overheads and joint costs is a way of accountants grabbing power and influence from marketing and production people.

(e) Our management accounts must be consistent with our published external accounts, so we must follow SSAP 9 on overhead allocation.

(f) Expenditure on Research and Development would be a past or sunk cost, and no matter what decision about output or price was eventually made it would have no bearing on the recovery of that expenditure.

(12 marks)
ICAEW Management Accounting

11.23 **Advanced**

'In providing information to the product manager, the accountant must recognize that decision-making is essentially a process of choosing between competing alternatives, each with its own combination of income and costs; and that the relevant concepts to employ are future incremental costs and revenues and opportunity cost, not full cost which includes past or sunk costs.' (Sizer)

Descriptive studies of pricing decisions taken in practice have, on the other hand, suggested that the inclusion of overhead and joint cost allocations in unit product costs is widespread in connection with the provision of information for this class of decision. Furthermore, these costs are essentially historic costs.

You are required to:

(a) explain the reasoning underlying the above quotation;

(10 marks)

(b) suggest reasons why overhead and joint cost allocation is nevertheless widely used in practice in connection with information for pricing decisions;

(10 marks)

(c) set out your own views as to the balance of these arguments.

(5 marks)

(Total 25 marks)

ICAEW Management Accounting

Review problems (with answers in the Student's Manual)

11.24 **Advanced: Calculation of cost-plus selling price and an evaluation of pricing decisions**

A firm manufactures two products EXE and WYE in departments dedicated exclusively to them. There are also three service departments, stores, maintenance and administration. No stocks are held as the products deteriorate rapidly.

Direct costs of the products, which are variable in the context of the whole business, are identified to each department. The step-wise apportionment of service department costs to the manufacturing departments is based on estimates of the usage of the service provided. These are expressed as percentages and assumed to be reliable over the current capacity range. The general factory overheads of £3.6m, which are fixed, are apportioned based on floor space occupied. The company establishes product costs based on budgeted volume and marks up these costs by 25% in order to set target selling prices.

Extracts from the budgets for the forthcoming year are provided below:

	Annual volume (units)	
	EXE	**WYE**
Max capacity	200 000	100 000
Budget	150 000	70 000

	EXE	WYE	Stores	Maintenance	Admin
Costs (£m)					
Material	1.8	0.7	0.1	0.1	
Other variable	0.8	0.5	0.1	0.2	0.2
Departmental usage (%)					
Maintenance	50	25	25		
Administration	40	30	20	10	
Stores	60	40			
Floor space (sq m)					
	640	480	240	80	160

Required:

Workings may be £000 with unit prices to the nearest penny.

(a) Calculate the budgeted selling price of one unit of EXE and WYE based on the usual mark up.

(5 marks)

(b) Discuss how the company may respond to each of the following independent events, which represent additional business opportunities.

(i) an enquiry from an overseas customer for 3000 units only of WYE where a price of £35 per unit is offered

(ii) an enquiry for 50 000 units of WYE to be supplied in full at regular intervals during the forthcoming year at a price which is equivalent to full cost plus 10%

In both cases support your discussion with calculations and comment on any assumptions or matters on which you would seek clarification.

(11 marks)

(c) Explain the implications of preparing product full costs based on maximum capacity rather than annual budget volume.

(4 marks)

(Total 20 marks)

ACCA Paper 8 Managerial Finance

11.25 **Advanced: Preparation of full cost and marginal cost information**

A small company is engaged in the production of plastic tools for the garden. Sub-totals on the spreadsheet of budgeted overheads for a year reveal:

	Moulding Department	Finishing Department	General Factory Overhead
Variable overhead (£000)	1600	500	1050
Fixed overhead (£000)	2500	850	1750
Budgeted activity			
Machine hours (000)	800	600	
Practical capacity			
Machine hours (000)	1200	800	

For the purposes of reallocation of general factory overhead it is agreed that the variable overheads accrue in line with the machine hours worked in each department. General factory fixed overhead is to be reallocated on the basis of the practical machine hour capacity of the two departments.

It has been a long-standing company practice to establish selling prices by applying a mark-up on full manufacturing cost of between 25% and 35%.

A possible price is sought for one new product which is in a final development stage. The total market for this product is estimated at 200 000 units per annum. Market research indicates that the company could expect to obtain and hold about 10% of the market. It is hoped the product will offer some improvement over competitors' products, which are currently marketed at between £90 and £100 each.

The product development department have determined that the direct material content is £9 per unit. Each unit of the product will take two labour hours (four machine hours) in the moulding department and three labour hours (three machine hours) in finishing. Hourly labour rates are £5.00 and £5.50 respectively.

Management estimate that the annual fixed costs which would be specifically incurred in relation to the product are: supervision £20 000, depreciation of a recently acquired machine £120 000 and advertising £27 000. It may be assumed that these costs are included in the budget given above. Given the state of development of this new product, management do not consider it necessary to make revisions, to the budgeted activity levels given above, for any possible extra machine hours involved in its manufacture.

Required:

(a) Briefly explain the role of costs in pricing.

(6 marks)

(b) Prepare full cost and marginal cost information which may help with the pricing decision.

(9 marks)

(c) Comment on the cost information and suggest a price range which should be considered.

(5 marks)
(Total 20 marks)
ACCA Paper 8 Managerial Finance

11.26 Advanced: Impact of a change in selling price on profits based on a given elasticity of demand

You are the management accountant of a medium-sized company. You have been asked to provide budgetary information and advice to the board of directors for a meeting where they will decide the pricing of an important product for the next period.

The following information is available from the records:

Sales		Previous period (£000)		Current period (£000)
(100 000 units at £13 each)		1300	(106 000 units at £13 each)	1378.0
Costs		1000		1077.4
Profit		300		300.6

You find that between the previous and current periods there was 4% general cost inflation and it is forecast that costs will rise a further 6% in the next period. As a matter of policy, the firm did not increase the selling price in the current period although competitors raised their prices by 4% to allow for the increased costs. A survey by economic consultants was commissioned and has found that the demand for the product is elastic with an estimated price elasticity of demand of 1.5. This means that volume would fall by 1½ times the rate of real price increase.

Various options are to be considered by the board and you are required

(a) to show the budgeted position if the firm maintains the £13 selling price for the next period (when it is expected that competitors will increase their prices by 6%);

(10 marks)

(b) to show the budgeted position if the firm also raises its price by 6%;

(6 marks)

(c) to write a short report to the board, with appropriate figures, recommending whether the firm should maintain the £13 selling price or raise it by 6%;

(3 marks)

(d) to state what assumptions you have used in your answers.

(3 marks)

(Total 22 marks)

CIMA Stage 3 Management Accounting Techniques

11.27 **Advanced: Recommendation of which market segment to enter and selling price to charge**

AB Ltd is a well-established company producing high quality, technically advanced, electronic equipment.

In an endeavour to diversify, it has identified opportunities in the hi-fi industry. After some preliminary market research it has decided to market a new product that incorporates some of the most advanced techniques available together with a very distinctive design.

AB Ltd's special skill is that it can apply these techniques economically to medium-sized quantities and offer a product of excellent design with an advanced degree of technology.

The new product faces three categories of competition:

Category	Technology	Design	Quantities sold per annum	Number of models	Retail selling price range (£)
1	Good	Standard	22 000	4	600–1050
2	Good	Good	6 000	5	1450–1900
3	Advanced	Good	750	2	2500–3000

The product will be distributed through a range of specialist retailers who have undertaken not to discount prices. Their commission will be 25% on retail selling price. AB Ltd has also acquired the rights to sell the product under the name of a prestigious hi-fi manufacturer who does not offer this type of product. For this it will pay a royalty of 5% of the retail selling price.

AB Ltd assesses that its direct cost per product will be £670 (excluding the royalty and the retailers' commission) and the annual fixed costs relevant to the project are budgeted at:

	(£)
Production	250 000
Research and development	50 000
Marketing	200 000
Finance and administration	50 000

You are required, from the data provided and making such assumptions as you consider reasonable,

(a) to suggest a range of retail prices (i.e. to the consumer) from which AB Ltd should choose the eventual price for its product. Explain briefly why you have suggested that range of prices;

(10 marks)

(b) to select *one* particular price from the range in (a) above that you would recommend AB Ltd to choose. Explain, with any relevant calculations, why you have recommended that price. Mention any assumptions that you have made.

(15 marks)

Note: The prices suggested should be rounded to the nearest £100. Ignore VAT (or sales taxes), taxation and inflation.

(Total 25 marks)

CIMA Stage 4 Management Accounting – Decision Making

11.28 **Advanced: Pricing strategies and calculation of optimum selling price**

Just over two years ago, R Ltd was the first company to produce a specific 'off-the-shelf' accounting software packages. The pricing strategy, decided on by the Managing Director, for the packages was to add a 50% mark-up to the budgeted full cost of the packages. The company achieved and maintained a significant market share and high profits for the first two years.

Budgeted information for the current year (Year 3) was as follows:

Production and sales	15 000 packages
Full cost	£400 per package

At a recent Board meeting, the Finance Director reported that although costs were in line with the budget for the current year, profits were declining. He explained that the full cost included £80 for fixed overheads. The figure had been calculated by using an overhead absorption rate based on labour hours and the budgeted level of production which, he pointed out, was much lower than the current capacity of 25 000 packages.

The Marketing Director stated that competitors were beginning to increase their market share. He also reported the results of a recent competitor analysis which showed that when R Ltd announced its prices for the current year, the competitors responded by undercutting them by 15%. Consequently, he commissioned an investigation of the market. He informed the Board that the market research showed that at a price of £750 there would be no demand for the packages but for every £10 reduction in price the demand would increase by 1000 packages.

The Managing Director appeared to be unconcerned about the loss of market share and argued that profits could be restored to their former level by increasing the mark-up.

Note: If price $= a - bx$

then marginal revenue $= a - 2bx$

Required:

(a) Discuss the Managing Director's pricing strategy in the circumstances described above. Your appraisal must include a discussion of the alternative strategies that could have been implemented at the launch of the packages.

(*10 marks*)

(b) (i) Based on the data supplied by the market research, calculate the maximum annual profit that can be earned from the sale of the packages from year 3 onwards.

(*6 marks*)

(ii) A German computer software distribution company, L, which is interested in becoming the sole distributor of the accounting software packages, has now approached R Ltd. It has offered to purchase 25 000 accounting packages per annum at a fixed price of €930 per package. If R Ltd were to sell the packages to L, then the variable costs would be £300 per package.

The current exchange rate is €1 = £0.60.

Required:

Draw a diagram to illustrate the sensitivity of the proposal from the German company to changes in the exchange rate and then state and comment on the minimum exchange rate needed for the proposal to be worthwhile.

(*7 marks*)

(c) R Ltd has signed a contract with L to supply the accounting packages. However, there has been a fire in one of the software manufacturing departments and a machine has been seriously damaged and requires urgent replacement.

The replacement machine will cost £1 million and R Ltd is considering whether to lease or buy the machine. A lease could be arranged under which R Ltd would pay £300 000 per annum for four years with each payment being made annually in advance. The lease payments would be an allowable expense for taxation purposes.

Corporation tax is payable at the rate of 30% per annum in two equal instalments: one in the year that profits are earned and the other in the following year. Writing-down allowances are allowed at 25% each year on a reducing balance basis. It is anticipated that the machine will have a useful economic life of four years, at the end of which there will be no residual value.

The after-tax cost of capital is 12%.

Required:
Evaluate the acquisition of the new machine from a financial viewpoint.

(7 marks)

(Total 30 marks)

CIMA Management Accounting – Decision Making

11.29 Advanced: Calculation of optimum selling prices using differential calculus

Alvis Taylor has budgeted that output and sales of his single product, flonal, will be 100 000 for the forthcoming year. At this level of activity his unit variable costs are budgeted to be £50 and his unit fixed costs £25. His sales manager estimates that the demand for flonal would increase by 1000 units for every decrease of £1 in unit selling price (and vice-versa), and that at a unit selling price of £200 demand would be nil.

Information about two price increases has just been received from suppliers. One is for materials (which are included in Alvis Taylor's variable costs), and one is for fuel (which is included in his fixed costs). Their effect will be to increase both the variable costs and the fixed costs by 20% in total over the budgeted figures.

Alvis Taylor aims to maximize profits from his business.
You are required, in respect of Alvis Taylor's business:

(a) to calculatc, *before the cost increases*:
  (i) the budgeted contribution and profit at the budgeted level of sales of 100 000 units, and
  (ii) the level of sales at which profits would be maximized, and the amount of those maximum profits,

(7 marks)

(b) to show whether and by how much Alvis Taylor should adjust his selling price, in respect of the increases in, respectively:
  (i) fuel costs
  (ii) materials costs,

(6 marks)

(c) to show whether and by how much it is worthwhile for Alvis Taylor, following the increases in costs, to spend £1 000 000 on a TV advertising campaign if this were confidently expected to have the effect during the next year (but not beyond then) that demand would still fall by 1000 units for every increase of £1 in unit selling price (and vice-versa), but that it would not fall to nil until the unit selling price was £210,

(5 marks)

(d) to comment on the results which you have obtained in (a)–(c) above and on the assumptions underlying them.

(7 marks)

(Total 25 marks)

ICAEW Management Accounting

Decision-making under conditions of risk and uncertainty

12

In Chapters 8–11 we considered the use of a single representative set of estimates for predicting future costs and revenues when alternative courses of action are followed. For example, in Chapter 11 we used a single representative estimate of demand for each selling price. However, the outcome of a particular decision may be affected by an uncertain environment that cannot be predicted, and a single representative estimate does not therefore convey all the information that might reasonably influence a decision.

Let us now look at a more complicated example; consider a situation where a company has two mutually exclusive potential alternatives, A and B, which each yield receipts of £50 000. The estimated costs of alternative A can be predicted with considerable confidence, and are expected to fall in the range of £40 000–£42 000; £41 000 might be considered a reasonable estimate of cost. The estimate for alternative B is subject to much greater uncertainty, since this alternative requires high-precision work involving operations that are unfamiliar to the company's labour force. The estimated costs are between £35 000 and £45 000, but £40 000 is selected as a representative estimate. If we consider single representative estimates alternative B appears preferable,

LEARNING OBJECTIVES

After studying this chapter, you should be able to:

- calculate and explain the meaning of expected values;
- explain the meaning of the terms standard deviation and coefficient of variation as measures of risk and outline their limitations;
- construct a decision tree when there is a range of alternatives and possible outcomes;
- describe and calculate the value of perfect and imperfect information;
- explain and apply the maximin, maximax and regret criteria;
- explain the implications of portfolio analysis.

since the estimated profit is £10 000 compared with an estimated profit of £9000 for alternative A; but a different picture may emerge if we take into account the range of possible outcomes.

Alternative A is expected to yield a profit of between £8000 and £10 000 whereas the range of profits for alternative B is between £5000 and £15 000. Management may consider it preferable to opt for a fairly certain profit of between £8000 and £10 000 for alternative A rather than take the chance of earning a profit of £5000 from alternative B (even though there is the possibility of earning a profit of £15 000 at the other extreme).

This example demonstrates that there is a need to incorporate the uncertainty relating to each alternative into the decision-making process, and in this chapter we shall consider the various methods of doing this. We shall then look at the application of these methods to pricing decisions and CVP analysis under conditions of uncertainty.

A decision-making model

It is possible to develop a model of decision-making since all decision problems have some definable structure containing certain basic elements. Figure 12.1 shows the elements of a decision model under conditions of risk and uncertainty.

You can see that a decision model has the following characteristics:

1 An objective or target that a decision-maker is hoping to achieve, for example maximization of profits, or present value of cash flows. The quantification of an objective is often called an **objective function**; it is used to evaluate the alternative courses of action and to provide the basis of choosing the best alternative.

2 The search for alternative courses of action that will enable the objective to be achieved.

3 Because decision problems exist in an uncertain environment, it is necessary to consider those uncontrollable factors that are outside the decision-maker's control and that may occur for each alternative course of action. These uncontrollable factors are called **events** or **states of nature**. For example, in a product launch situation possible states of nature could consist of events such as a similar product being launched by a competitor at a lower price, or no similar product being launched.

4 A set of **outcomes** for the various possible combinations of actions and events. Each outcome is conditionally dependent on a specific course of action and a specific state of nature.

5 A measure of the value or **payoff** of each possible outcome in terms of the decision-maker's objectives. Payoffs are normally expressed in monetary terms such as profits or cash flows, but in some problems we may be interested in other payoffs such as time, market share, and so on.

6 Selection of a course of action.

The essential characteristics of a decision model are illustrated from the information shown in Example 12.1.

The elements of the decision model for Example 12.1 and the hypothetical possible outcomes from each state of nature are illustrated in Figure 12.2. This is known as a **decision tree**. In this diagram we have not measured the value (i.e. the payoff) for each possible course of action, but in the remainder of the chapter we shall look at ways of measuring the payoff where various outcomes are possible. Let us begin by discussing some of the concepts and techniques which are necessary for analysing risk and uncertainty.

FIGURE 12.1 *A decision-making model under conditions of uncertainty*

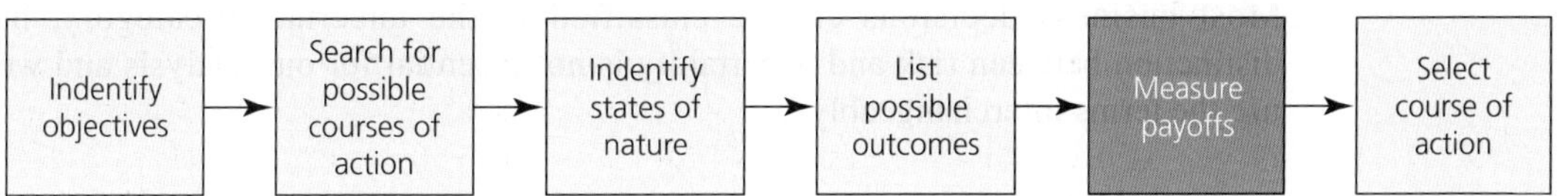

EXAMPLE 12.1

The Pretorian Company is reviewing its marketing policy for the next budget period. It has developed two new products, X and Y, but it only has sufficient resources to launch one of them. The appropriate states of nature relate to the activities of its competitors and are as follows:

1 competitors do nothing;
2 competitors introduce a comparable product;
3 competitors introduce a superior product.

FIGURE 12.2 *A decision tree*

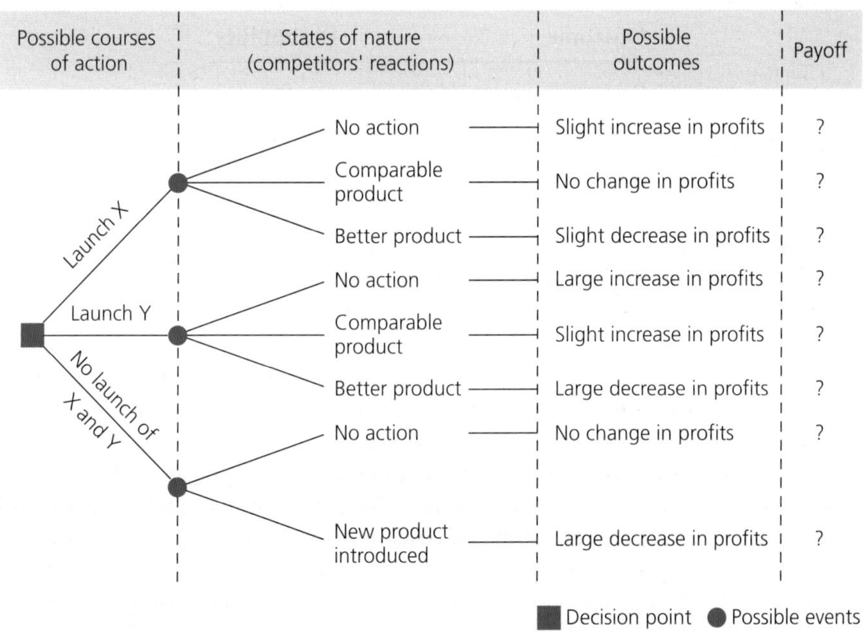

Risk and uncertainty

A distinction is often drawn by decision theorists between risk and uncertainty. **Risk** is applied to a situation where there are several possible outcomes and there is relevant past experience to enable statistical evidence to be produced for predicting the possible outcomes. Uncertainty exists where there are several possible outcomes, but there is little previous statistical evidence to enable the possible outcomes to be predicted. Most business decisions can be classified in the uncertainty category, but the distinction between risk and uncertainty is not essential for our analysis and we shall use the terms interchangeably.

Probabilities

The likelihood that an event or state of nature will occur is known as its probability, and this is normally expressed in decimal form with a value between 0 and 1. A value of 0 denotes a nil likelihood of occurrence whereas a value of 1 signifies absolute certainty – a definite occurrence. A probability of 0.4 means that the event is expected to occur four times out of ten. The total of the probabilities for events that can possibly occur must sum to 1.0. For example, if a tutor indicates that the probability of a student passing an examination is 0.7 then this means that the student has a 70% chance of passing the examination. Given that the pass/fail alternatives represent an exhaustive listing of all possible outcomes of the event, the probability of not passing the examination is 0.3.

The information can be presented in a probability distribution. A probability distribution is a list of all possible outcomes for an event and the probability that each will occur. The probability distribution for the above illustration is as follows:

Outcome	Probability
Pass examination	0.7
Do not pass examination	0.3
Total	1.0

Some probabilities are known as objective probabilities because they can be established mathematically or compiled from historical data. Tossing a coin and throwing a die are examples of objective probabilities. For example, the probability of heads occurring when tossing a coin logically must be 0.5. This can be proved by tossing the coin many times and observing the results. Similarly, the probability of obtaining number 1 when a die is thrown is 0.166 (i.e. one-sixth). This again can be ascertained from logical reasoning or recording the results obtained from repeated throws of the dice.

It is unlikely that objective probabilities can be established for business decisions, since many past observations or repeated experiments for particular decisions are not possible; the probabilities will have to be estimated based on managerial judgement. Probabilities established in this way are known as subjective probabilities because no two individuals will necessarily assign the same probabilities to a particular outcome. Subjective probabilities are based on an individual's expert knowledge, past experience, and observations of current variables which are likely to have an impact on future events. Such probabilities are unlikely to be estimated correctly, but any estimate of a future uncertain event is bound to be subject to error.

The advantage of this approach is that it provides more meaningful information than stating the most likely outcome. Consider, for example, a situation where a tutor is asked to state whether student A and student B will pass an examination. The tutor may reply that both students are expected to pass the examination. This is the tutor's estimate of the most likely outcome. However, the following probability distributions are preferable:

Outcome	Student A probability	Student B probability
Pass examination	0.9	0.6
Do not pass examination	0.1	0.4
Total	1.0	1.0

Such a probability distribution requires the tutor to specify the degree of confidence in his or her estimate of the likely outcome of a future event. This information is clearly more meaningful than a mere estimate of the most likely outcome that both students are expected to pass the examination, because it indicates that it is most unlikely that A will fail, whereas there is a possibility that B will fail. Let us now apply the principles of probability theory to business decision-making.

Probability distributions and expected value

The presentation of a probability distribution for each alternative course of action can provide useful additional information to management, since the distribution indicates the degree of uncertainty that exists for each alternative course of action. Probability distributions enable management to consider not only the possible profits (i.e. the payoff) from each alternative course of action but also the amount of uncertainty that applies to each alternative. Let us now consider the situation presented in Example 12.2.

From the probability distributions shown in Example 12.2 you will see that there is a 1 in 10 chance that profits will be £6000 for product A, but there is also a 4 in 10 chance that profits will be £8000. A more useful way of reading the probability distribution is to state that there is a 7 in 10 chance that profits will be £8000 or less. This is obtained by adding together the probabilities for profits of £6000, £7000 and £8000. Similarly, there is a 3 in 10 chance that profits will be £9000 or more.

Expected values

The **expected value** (sometimes called expected payoff) is calculated by weighting each of the profit levels (i.e. possible outcomes) in Example 12.2 by its associated probability. The sum of these weighted amounts is called the expected value of the probability distribution. In other words, the expected value is the weighted arithmetic mean of the possible outcomes. The expected values of £8000 and £8900 calculated for products A and B take into account a range of possible outcomes rather than using a **single most likely estimate**. For example, the single most likely estimate is the profit level with the highest probability attached to it. For both products A and B in Example 12.2 the single most likely estimate is £8000, which appears to indicate that we may be indifferent as to which product should be made. However the expected value calculation takes into account the possibility that a range of different profits are possible and weights these profits by the probability of their occurrence. The weighted calculation indicates that product B is expected to produce the highest average profits in the future.

The expected value of a decision represents the long-run average outcome that is expected to occur if a particular course of action is undertaken many times. For example, if the decision to make products A and B is repeated on, say, 100 occasions in the future then product A will be expected to give an average profit of £8000 whereas product B would be expected to give an average profit of £8900. The expected values are the averages of the possible outcomes based on management estimates. There is no guarantee that the actual

EXAMPLE 12.2

A manager is considering whether to make product A or product B, but only one can be produced. The estimated sales demand for each product is uncertain. A detailed investigation of the possible sales demand for each product gives the following probability distribution of the profits for each product.

Product A probability distribution

(1) Outcome	(2) Estimated probability	(3) Weighted (col. 1 amount × col. 2) (£)
Profits of £6000	0.10	600
Profits of £7000	0.20	1400
Profits of £8000	0.40	3200
Profits of £9000	0.20	1800
Profits of £10 000	0.10	1000
	1.00	
	Expected value	8000

Product B probability distribution

(1) Outcome	(2) Estimated probability	(3) Weighted (col. 1 amount × col. 2) (£)
Profits of £4000	0.05	200
Profits of £6000	0.10	600
Profits of £8000	0.40	3200
Profits of £10 000	0.25	2500
Profits of £12 000	0.20	2400
	1.00	
	Expected value	8900

Which product should the company make?

outcome will equal the expected value. Indeed, the expected value for product B does not appear in the probability distribution.

Measuring the amount of uncertainty

In addition to the expected values of the profits for the various alternatives, management is also interested in the degree of uncertainty of the expected future profits. For example, let us assume that another alternative course of action, say, product C, is added to the alternatives in Example 12.2 and that the probability distribution is as follows:

Product C probability distribution

Outcome	Estimated probability	Weighted amount (£)
Loss of £4000	0.5	(2000)
Profit of £22 000	0.5	11 000
	Expected value	9 000

Product C has a higher expected value than either product A or product B, but it is unlikely that management will prefer product C to product B, because of the greater variability of the possible outcomes. In other words, there is a greater degree of uncertainty attached to product C.

The conventional measure of the dispersion of a probability distribution is the **standard deviation**. The standard deviation (σ) is the square root of the mean of the squared deviations from the expected value and is calculated from the following formula:

$$\sigma = \sqrt{\sum_{x=1}^{n} (A_x - \bar{A})^2 P_x} \tag{12.1}$$

where A_x are the profit-level observations, $\bar{A}$ is the expected or mean value, P_x is the probability of each outcome, and the summation is over all possible observations, where n is the total number of possibilities.

The square of the standard deviation σ^2 is known as the statistical variance of the distribution, and should not be confused with the variance from budget or standard cost, which will be discussed in subsequent chapters. The calculations of the standard deviations for products A and B in Example 12.2 are set out in Exhibit 12.1.

If we are comparing the standard deviations of two probability distributions with different expected values, we cannot make a direct comparison. Can you see why this should be so? Consider the following probability distribution for another product, say product D.

Product D probability distribution

Outcome	Estimated probability	Weighted amount (£)
Profits of £40 000	0.05	2 000
Profits of £60 000	0.10	6 000
Profits of £80 000	0.40	32 000
Profits of £100 000	0.25	25 000
Profits of £120 000	0.20	24 000
	Expected value	89 000

The standard deviation for product D is £21 424, but all of the possible outcomes are ten times as large as the corresponding outcomes for product B. The outcomes for

EXHIBIT 12.1
Calculation of standard deviations

Product A

(1) Profit (£)	(2) Deviation from expected value, $A_x - \overline{A}$ (£)	(3) Squared deviation $(A_x - \overline{A})^2$ (£)	(4) Probability	(5) Weighted amount (col. 3 × col. 4) (£)
6 000	−2000	4 000 000	0.1	400 000
7 000	−1000	1 000 000	0.2	200 000
8 000	0	–	0.4	–
9 000	+1000	1 000 000	0.2	200 000
10 000	+2000	4 000 000	0.1	400 000
			Sum of squared deviations	1 200 000
			Standard deviation	£1095.40
			Expected value	£8000

Product B

(1) Profit (£)	(2) Deviation $A_x - \overline{A}$ (£)	(3) Squared deviation $(A_x - \overline{A})^2$ (£)	(4) Probability	(5) Weighted amount (col. 3 × col. 4) (£)
4 000	−4900	24 010 000	0.05	1 200 500
6 000	−2900	8 410 000	0.10	841 000
8 000	−900	810 000	0.40	324 000
10 000	1100	1 210 000	0.25	302 500
12 000	3100	9 610 000	0.20	1 922 000
			Sum of squared deviations	4 590 000
			Standard deviation	£2142.40
			Expected value	£8900

product D also have the same pattern of probabilities as product B, and we might conclude that the two projects are equally risky. Nevertheless, the standard deviation for product D is ten times as large as that for product B. This scale effect can be removed be replacing the standard deviation with a relative measure of dispersion. The relative amount of dispersion can be expressed by the **coefficient of variation**, which is simply the standard deviation divided by the expected value. The coefficient of variation for product B is 2142.40/8900 = 0.241 (or 24.1%), and for product D it is also 0.241 (21 424/89 000), thus indicating that the relative amount of dispersion is the same for both products.

In our discussion so far we have defined risk in terms of the spread of possible outcomes, so that risk may be large even if all the possible outcomes involve earning high profits. However, the risk attached to possible profits/losses obtained from alternative courses of action is not dispersion *per se* but the possibility of deviations *below* the expected value of the profits. A decision-maker would hardly consider large possible deviations *above* the expected value undesirable. Consider the following probability distributions:

Product X probability distribution

Outcome	Estimated probability	Weighted amount (£)
Profits of £4000	0.1	400
Profits of £6000	0.3	1800
Profits of £8000	0.6	4800
	Expected value	7000

Product Y probability distribution

Outcome	Estimated probability	Weighted amount (£)
Profits of £6000	0.2	1200
Profits of £8000	0.5	4000
Profits of £12 000	0.3	3600
	Expected valuc	8800

The standard deviations are £1342 for X and £2227 for Y, giving coefficients of variations of 0.19 for X and 0.28 for Y. These measures indicate that the estimates of product Y are subject to a greater variability, but product X appears to be the riskier product since the probability of profits being less that £7000 (the expected value of X) is 0.4 for product X but only 0.2 for product Y. Clearly, the standard deviation and coefficient of variation are not perfect measures of risk, but the mathematical complexities of measuring only those deviations below the expected value are formidable for anything beyond the simplest situation. Measures such as expected values, standard deviations or coefficient of variations are used to summarize the characteristics of alternative courses of action, but they are poor substitutes for representing the probability distributions, since they do not provide the decision-maker with all the relevant information. There is an argument for presenting the entire probability distribution directly to the decision-maker. Such an approach is appropriate when management must select one from a small number of alternatives, but in situations where many alternatives need to be considered the examination of many probability distributions is likely to be difficult and time-consuming. In such situations management may have no alternative but to compare the expected values and coefficients of variation.

Attitudes to risk by individuals

How do we determine whether or not a risky course of action should be undertaken? The answer to this question depends on the decision-maker's attitude to risk. We can identify three possible attitudes: an aversion to risk, a desire for risk and an indifference to risk. Consider two alternatives, A and B, which have the following possible outcomes, depending on the state of the economy (i.e. the state of nature):

Possible returns

State of the economy	A (£)	B (£)
Recession	90	0
Normal	100	100
Boom	110	200

If we assume that the three states of the economy are equally likely then the expected value for each alternative is £100. A **risk-seeker** is one who, given a choice between more or less risky alternatives with identical expected values, prefers the riskier alternative (alternative B). Faced with the same choice, a **risk-averter** would select the less risky alternative (alternative A). The person who is indifferent to risk (**risk neutral**) would be indifferent to both alternatives because they have the same expected values. With regard to investors in general, studies of the securities markets provide convincing evidence that the majority of investors are risk-averse.

Let us now reconsider how useful expected value calculations are for choosing between alternative courses of action. Expected values represent a long-run average solution, but decisions should not be made on the basis of expected values alone, since they do not enable the decision-maker's attitude towards risk to be taken into account. Consider for example, a situation where two individuals play a coin-tossing game, with the loser giving the winner £5000. The expected value to the player who calls heads is as follows:

Outcome	Cash flow (£)	Probability	Weighted amount (£)
Heads	+5000	0.5	+2500
Tails	–5000	0.5	–2500
		Expected value	0

The expected value is zero, but this will not be the actual outcome if only one game is played. The expected-value calculation represents the average outcome only if the game is repeated on many occasions. However, because the game is to be played only once, it is unlikely that each player will find the expected value calculation on its own to be a useful calculation for decision-making. In fact, the expected value calculation implies that each player is indifferent to playing the game, but this indifference will only apply if the two players are neutral to risk. However, a risk-averter will find the game most unattractive. As most business managers are unlikely to be neutral towards risk, and business decisions are rarely repeated, it is unwise for decisions to be made solely on the basis of expected values. At the very least, expected values should be supplemented with measures of dispersion and, where possible, decisions should be made after comparing the probability distributions of the various alternative courses of action.

Decision-tree analysis

In the examples earlier in this chapter we have assumed that profits were uncertain because of the uncertainty of sales demand. In practice, more than one variable may be uncertain (e.g. sales and costs), and also the value of some variables may be dependent on the values of other variables. Many outcomes may therefore be possible, and some outcomes may be dependent on previous outcomes. A useful analytical tool for clarifying the range of alternative courses of action and their possible outcomes is a **decision tree**.

A decision tree is a diagram showing several possible courses of action and possible events (i.e. states of nature) and the potential outcomes for each course of action. Each alternative course of action or event is represented by a branch, which leads to subsidiary branches for further courses of action or possible events. Decision trees are designed to illustrate the full range of alternatives and events that can occur, under all envisaged conditions. The value of a decision tree is that its logical analysis of a problem enables a complete strategy to be drawn up to cover all eventualities before a firm becomes committed to a scheme. Let us now consider Example 12.3. This will be used to illustrate how decision trees can be applied to decision-making under conditions of uncertainty.

The decision tree for Example 12.3 is set out in Figure 12.3. The boxes indicate the point at which decisions have to be taken, and the branches emanating from it indicate the available alternative courses of action. The circles indicate the points at which there are environmental changes that affect the consequences of prior decisions. The branches from these points indicate the possible types of environment (states of nature) that may occur.

Note that the joint probability of two events occurring together is the probability of one event times the probability of the other event. For example, the probability of the development effort succeeding and the product being very successful consists of the products of the probabilities of these two events, i.e. 0.75 times 0.4, giving a probability of 0.30. Similarly, the probability of the development effort being successful and the product being moderately successful is 0.225 (0.75 × 0.3). The total expected value for the decision to develop the product consists of the sum of all the items in the expected value column on the 'Develop product' branch of the decision tree, i.e. £49 500. If we assume that there are no other alternatives available, other than the decision not to develop, the expected value of £49 500 for developing the product can be compared with the expected value of zero for not developing the product. Decision theory would suggest that the product should be developed because a positive expected value occurs. However, this does not mean that an outcome of £49 500 profit is guaranteed. The expected-value calculation indicates that if the probabilities are correct and this decision was repeated on many occasions an average profit of £49 500 would result.

Unfortunately, the decision will not be repeated on many occasions, and a run of repeated losses could force a company out of business before it has the chance to repeat similar decisions. Management may therefore prefer to examine the following probability distribution for developing the product shown in Figure 12.3:

Outcome	Probability
Loss of £400 000	0.225
Loss of £180 000	0.25
Profit of £100 000	0.225
Profit of £540 000	0.30

Management may decide that the project is too risky, since there is nearly a 0.5 probability of a loss occurring.

The decision tree provides a convenient means of identifying all the possible alternative courses of action and their interdependencies. This approach is particularly useful for assisting in the construction of probability distributions when many combinations of events are possible.

EXAMPLE 12.3

A company is considering whether to develop and market a new product. Development costs are estimated to be £180 000, and there is a 0.75 probability that the development effort will be successful and a 0.25 probability that the development effort will be unsuccessful. If the development is successful, the product will be marketed, and it is estimated that:

1 if the product is very successful profits will be £540 000;
2 if the product is moderately successful profits will be £100 000;
3 if the product is a failure, there will be a loss of £400 000.

Each of the above profit and loss calculations is after taking into account the development costs of £180 000. The estimated probabilities of each of the above events are as follows:

1 Very successful	0.4
2 Moderately successful	0.3
3 Failure	0.3

FIGURE 12.3 *A simple decision tree*

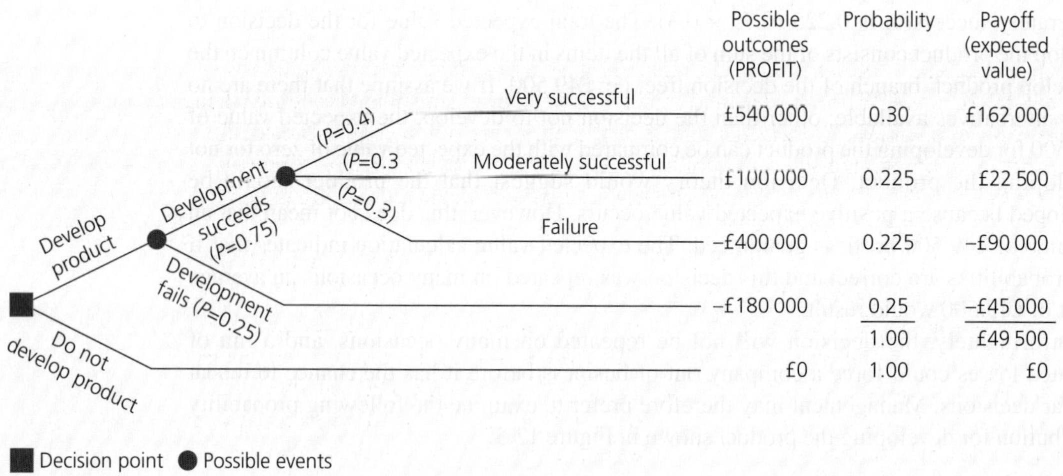

Cost–volume–profit analysis under conditions of uncertainty

In Chapter 8 our discussion of cost–volume–profit analysis was based on single value estimates. In other words, we assumed that all costs and revenues were known with certainty. Clearly, this assumption is unrealistic, and therefore the traditional CVP model suffers from the limitation of not including any adjustments for risk and uncertainty. You should note, however, that some writers have extended CVP analysis to allow for uncertainty in the parameters of the model. We shall not consider CVP analysis and uncertainty at this stage, since the objective of this chapter is to provide a general explanation of how adjustments for uncertainty can be incorporated into decision models. CVP analysis under conditions of uncertainty is therefore dealt with in the Appendix to this chapter.

Buying perfect and imperfect information

When a decision-maker is faced with a series of uncertain events that might occur, he or she should consider the possibility of obtaining additional information about which event is likely to occur. This section considers how we can calculate the maximum amount it would be worth paying to acquire additional information from a particular source. The approach we shall take is to compare the expected value of a decision if the information is acquired against the expected value with the absence of the information. The difference represents the maximum amount it is worth paying for the additional information. Consider Example 12.4.

Without the additional information, machine A will be purchased using the expected-value decision rule. If the additional information is obtained then this will give a perfect prediction of the level of demand, and the size of the machine can be matched with the level of demand. Therefore if demand is predicted to be low, machine A will be purchased, whereas if demand is predicted to be high, machine B will be purchased. The revised expected value is

$$(0.5 \times £100\,000) + (0.5 \times £200\,000) = £150\,000$$

You can see that the expected value is calculated by taking the highest profit in the case of low and high demand. When the decision to employ the market consultants is being taken, it is not known which level of demand will be predicted. Therefore the best estimate of the outcome from obtaining the additional information is a 0.5 probability that it will predict a low demand and a 0.5 probability that it will predict a high demand. (These are the probabilities that are currently associated with low and high demand.)

The value of the additional information is ascertained by deducting the expected value without the market survey (£130 000) from the expected value with the survey (£150 000). Thus the additional information increases expected value from £130 000 to £150 000 and the **expected value of perfect information** is £20 000. As long as the cost of obtaining the information is less than £20 000, the firm of market consultants should be employed.

In the above illustration it was assumed that the additional information would give a 100% accurate prediction of the expected demand. In practice, it is unlikely that *perfect* information is obtainable, but *imperfect* information (for example, predictions of future demand may be only 80% reliable) may still be worth obtaining. However, the value of imperfect information will always be less than the value of perfect information except when both equal zero. This would occur where the additional information would not change the decision. Note that the principles that are applied for calculating the value of imperfect information are the same as those we applied for calculating the value of perfect information, but the calculations are more complex. For an illustration see Scapens (1991).

Maximin, maximax and regret criteria

In some situations it might not be possible to assign meaningful estimates of probabilities to possible outcomes. Where this situation occurs managers might use any of the following criteria to make decisions: maximin, maximax or the criterion of regret.

EXAMPLE 12.4

The Boston Company must choose between one of two machines – machine A has low fixed costs and high unit variable costs whereas machine B has high fixed costs and low unit variable costs. Consequently, machine A is most suited to low-level demand whereas machine B is suited to high-level demand. For simplicity assume that there are only two possible demand levels – low and high – and the estimated probability of each of these events is 0.5. The estimated profits for each demand level are as follows:

	Low demand (£)	High demand (£)	Expected value (£)
Machine A	100 000	160 000	130 000
Machine B	10 000	200 000	105 000

There is a possibility of employing a firm of market consultants who would be able to provide a perfect prediction of the actual demand. What is the maximum amount the company should be prepared to pay the consultants for the additional information?

The assumption underlying the **maximin criterion** is that the worst possible outcome will always occur and the decision-maker should therefore select the largest payoff under this assumption. Consider the Boston Company in Example 12.4. You can see that the worst outcomes are £100 000 for machine A and £10 000 for machine B. Consequently, machine A should be purchased using the maximin decision rule.

The **maximax criterion** is the opposite of maximin, and is based on the assumption that the best payoff will occur. Referring again to Example 12.4, the highest payoffs are £160 000 for machine A and £200 000 for machine B. Therefore machine B will be selected under the maximax criterion.

The **regret criterion** is based on the fact that, having selected an alternative that does not turn out to be the best, the decision-maker will regret not having chosen another alternative when he or she had the opportunity. Thus if in Example 12.4 machine B has been selected on the assumption that the high level of demand would occur, and the high level of demand actually did occur, there would be no regret. However, if machine A has been selected, the company would lose £40 000 (£200 000 – £160 000). This measures the amount of the regret. Similarly, if machine A was selected on the assumption that demand would be low, and the low level of demand actually did occur, there would be no regret; but if machine B was selected, the amount of the regret would be £90 000 (£100 000 – £10 000). This information is summarized in the following regret matrix:

	State of nature	
	Low demand (£)	High demand (£)
Choose machine A	0	40 000
Choose machine B	90 000	0

The aim of the regret criterion is to minimize the maximum possible regret. The maximum regret for machine A is £40 000 while that for Machine B is £90 000. Machine A would therefore be selected using the regret criterion.

Portfolio analysis

It is unwise for a firm to invest all its funds in a single project, since an unfavourable event may occur that will affect this project and have a dramatic effect on the firm's total financial position. A better approach would be for the firm to invest in a number of different projects. If this strategy is followed, an unfavourable event that affects one project may have relatively less effect on the remaining projects and thus have only a small impact on the firm's overall financial position. That is, a firm should not put all of its eggs in one basket, but should try to minimize risk by spreading its investments over a variety of projects.

The collection of investments held by an individual investor or the collection of projects in which a firm invests is known as a **portfolio**. The objective in selecting a portfolio is to achieve certain desirable characteristics regarding risk and expected return. Let us now consider Example 12.5. From Example 12.5 it can be seen that both the existing activities (umbrella manufacturing) and the proposed new project (ice-cream manufacturing) are risky when considered on their own, but when they are combined, the risk is eliminated because whatever the outcome the cash inflow will be £20 000. Example 12.5 tells us that we should not only consider the risk of individual projects but should also take into account how the risks of potential new projects and existing activities co-vary with each other. Risk is eliminated completely in Example 12.5 because perfect negative correlation (i.e. where the correlation coefficient is –1) exists between the cash flows of the proposed project and the cash flows of the existing activities. When the cash flows are perfectly positively correlated (where the correlation is +1), risk reduction cannot be achieved when the projects are combined. For all other correlation values risk reduction advantages can be obtained by investing in projects that are not perfectly correlated with existing activities.

The important point that emerges from the above discussion is that it is not the risk of individual projects in isolation that is of interest but rather the incremental risk that each project will contribute to the overall risk of the firm.

EXAMPLE 12.5

A firm which currently manufactures umbrellas is considering diversifying and investing in the manufacture of ice-cream. The predicted cash flows for the existing activities and the new project are shown below.

States of nature	Existing activities (Umbrella manufacturing) (£)	Proposed project (Ice-cream manufacturing) (£)	Combination of existing activities and the proposed project (£)
Sunshine	–40 000	+60 000	+20 000
Rain	+60 000	–40 000	+20 000

To simplify the illustration it is assumed that only two states of nature exist (rain or sunshine) and each has a probability of 0.5.

A more complex illustration

We shall now use Example 12.6 to illustrate the application of the principles described in this chapter to a more complex situation relating to a pricing decision. To keep things simple Example 12.6 assumes that only three selling prices are being considered and that only sales demand and variable costs are subject to uncertainty. You should now refer to Example 12.6 and then to the decision tree shown in Figure 12.4.

You will see from the decision tree that there are three possible demands and two possible variable costs, giving six possible outcomes for each selling price, and 18 possible outcomes when all three prices are considered. These 18 possible outcomes are included in the decision tree. The expected value for each selling price is calculated by multiplying the contribution to general fixed costs column in Figure 12.4 by the combined probability column for each possible outcome. The probability distribution for each possible selling price has been extracted from the decision tree in Figure 12.4 and is presented in ascending order of contribution in Exhibit 12.2.

An examination of Exhibit 12.2 indicates that management would be wise not to choose a selling price of £20, since this price gives the lowest expected value. Also, the probability distribution for a selling price of £20 indicates that the probability of a contribution of £210 000 or less is 0.40 compared with zero for a selling price of £18 and £19. However, it may be useful to present salient information from Exhibit 12.2 to management to assist them in deciding whether to choose a selling price of £18 or £19. The following information could be presented:

	Selling price of £18	Selling price of £19
Probability of a contribution of £590 000 or less	0.30	0.32
Probability of a contribution of £850 000 or more	0.12	0.20
Maximum possible contribution	£850 000	£940 000
Minimum possible contribution	£520 000	£540 000
Expected value	£675 400	£680 000

There would be little difference between adopting a selling price of £18 or £19, but a selling price of £19 appears to be slightly more attractive. There are strong arguments for presenting to management all the information contained in Exhibit 12.2 plus the salient information extracted above for selling prices of £18 and £19. This would enable management to choose the selling price with a probability distribution which most closely matches their attitude towards risk. It is important to note, however, that if a single value estimate approach is adopted that ignores the range of possible outcomes, management will be presented with contribution calculations based on the most likely outcomes, that is, those variables that have the highest probabilities attached to them.

The most likely sales demands and unit variable costs are therefore as follows:

Selling price (£)	Sales demand (units)	Unit variable cost (£)
18	80 000	5
19	70 000	5
20	60 000	5

EXAMPLE 12.6

The Sigma Company is introducing a new product. The company has carried out some market research studies and analysed the selling prices of similar types of competitive products that are currently being sold. The information suggests that a selling price of £18, £19 or £20 is appropriate. The company intends to hire machinery to manufacture the product at a cost of £200 000 per annum, but if annual production is in excess of 60 000 units then additional machinery will have to be hired at a cost of £80 000 per annum. The variable cost is expected to be either £5 or £6 per unit produced, depending on the outcome of negotiations with suppliers. The market research department has produced the following estimates of sales demand for each possible selling price. These estimates are based on pessimistic, most likely and optimistic forecasts, and subjective probabilities have been attached to them. The estimates are as follows:

	£18		£19		£20	
	Units sold	Probability	Units sold	Probability	Units sold	Probability
Pessimistic	70 000	0.3	60 000	0.1	30 000	0.4
Most likely	80 000	0.5	70 000	0.7	60 000	0.5
Optimistic	90 000	0.2	90 000	0.2	70 000	0.1

The probabilities for the unit variable cost are 0.6 for a variable cost of £5 per unit and 0.4 for a variable cost of £6 per unit. The company has also committed itself to an advertising contract of £40 000 per annum.

EXHIBIT 12.2
Probability distribution for each possible selling price

	Selling price of £18			Selling price of £19			Selling price of £20	
Out-come	Contribution to general fixed costs (£)	Probability	Out-come	Contribution to general fixed costs (£)	Probability	Out-come	Contribution to general fixed costs (£)	Probability
2	520 000	0.12	8	540 000	0.04	14	180 000	0.16
1	590 000	0.18	10	590 000	0.28	13	210 000	0.24
4	640 000	0.20	7	600 000	0.06	16	600 000	0.20
3	720 000	0.30	9	660 000	0.42	15/18	660 000	0.34
6	760 000	0.08	12	850 000	0.08	17	730 000	0.06
5	850 000	0.12	11	940 000	0.12			1.00
		1.00			1.00			
	Expected value £675 400			Expected value £680 800			Expected value £467 000	

FIGURE 12.4 *Decision tree and probability distributions for various selling prices*

(1) Selling price	(2) Demand	(3) Variable cost	(4) (col.2×col.3) Combined probability	(5) Total contribution (£)	(6) Hire of machinery (£)	(7) Advertising (£)	(8) (col.5–col.6+7) Contribution to general fixed costs (£)	(9) (col.8×col.4) Expected value (£)	Outcome number
£18	70 000 units P=0.3	P=0.6 (£5)	0.18	910 000*	280 000	40 000	590 000	106 200	1
		P=0.4 (£6)	0.12	840 000**	280 000	40 000	520 000	62 400	2
	80 000 units P=0.5	P=0.6 (£5)	0.30	1 040 000	280 000	40 000	720 000	216 000	3
		P=0.4 (£6)	0.20	960 000	280 000	40 000	640 000	128 000	4
	90 000 units P=0.2	P=0.6 (£5)	0.12	1 170 000	280 000	40 000	850 000	102 000	5
		P=0.4 (£6)	0.08	1 080 000	280 000	40 000	760 000	60 800	6
			1.00					675 400	
£19	60 000 units P=0.1	P=0.6 (£5)	0.06	840 000	200 000	40 000	600 000	36 000	7
		P=0.4 (£6)	0.04	780 000	200 000	40 000	540 000	21 600	8
	70 000 units P=0.7	P=0.6 (£5)	0.42	980 000	280 000	40 000	660 000	277 200	9
		P=0.4 (£6)	0.28	910 000	280 000	40 000	590 000	165 200	10
	90 000 units P=0.2	P=0.6 (£5)	0.12	1 260 000	280 000	40 000	940 000	112 800	11
		P=0.4 (£6)	0.08	1 170 000	280 000	40 000	850 000	68 000	12
			1.00					680 800	
£20	30 000 units P=0.4	P=0.6 (£5)	0.24	450 000	200 000	40 000	210 000	50 400	13
		P=0.4 (£6)	0.16	420 000	200 000	40 000	180 000	28 800	14
	60 000 units P=0.5	P=0.6 (£5)	0.30	900 000	200 000	40 000	660 000	198 000	15
		P=0.4 (£6)	0.20	840 000	200 000	40 000	600 000	120 000	16
	70 000 units P=0.1	P=0.6 (£5)	0.06	1 050 000	280 000	40 000	730 000	43 800	17
		P=0.4 (£6)	0.04	980 000	280 000	40 000	660 000	26 400	18
			1.00					467 400	

■ Decision point ● Possible events

*70 000 unit sales at a unit contribution of £13 (£18 selling price £5 variable cost)
**70 000 unit sales at a unit contribution of £12 (£18 selling price less £6 variable cost)

The contribution to general fixed costs for the most likely outcomes can be obtained from outcomes 3, 9 and 15 in the decision tree (Figure 12.4), and are as follows:

Selling price of £18	Total contribution of £720 000
Selling price of £19	Total contribution of £660 000
Selling price of £20	Total contribution of £660 000

You will see that a single-value-estimate presentation provides rather misleading information. It appears that a selling price of £20 should be seriously considered and that the highest contribution is obtained from a selling price of £18. The expected value and probability-distribution approach provides a more revealing picture and indicates that management would be unwise to adopt a selling price of £20. Furthermore, a selling price of £19 is shown to be preferable to £18 when all the possible outcomes are considered.

You should also note that Example 12.6 contained only two variables with uncertain values: sales demand and variable cost per unit. In practice, several variables may be uncertain, and this can lead to a decision tree having hundreds of branches, thus causing difficulties in constructing probability distributions on a manual basis. We shall see in Chapter 14 that this problem can be overcome by using a computer and applying simulation techniques.

EXAMPLE 12A.1

The selling price of a product for the next accounting period is £100, and the variable cost is estimated to be £60 per unit. The budgeted fixed costs for the period are £36 000. Estimated sales for the period are 1000 units, and it is assumed that the probability distribution for the estimated sales quantity is normal with a standard deviation of 90 units. The selling price, variable cost and total fixed cost are assumed to be certain.

FIGURE 12A.1 *Normal distribution for the sales quantity in Example 12A.1*

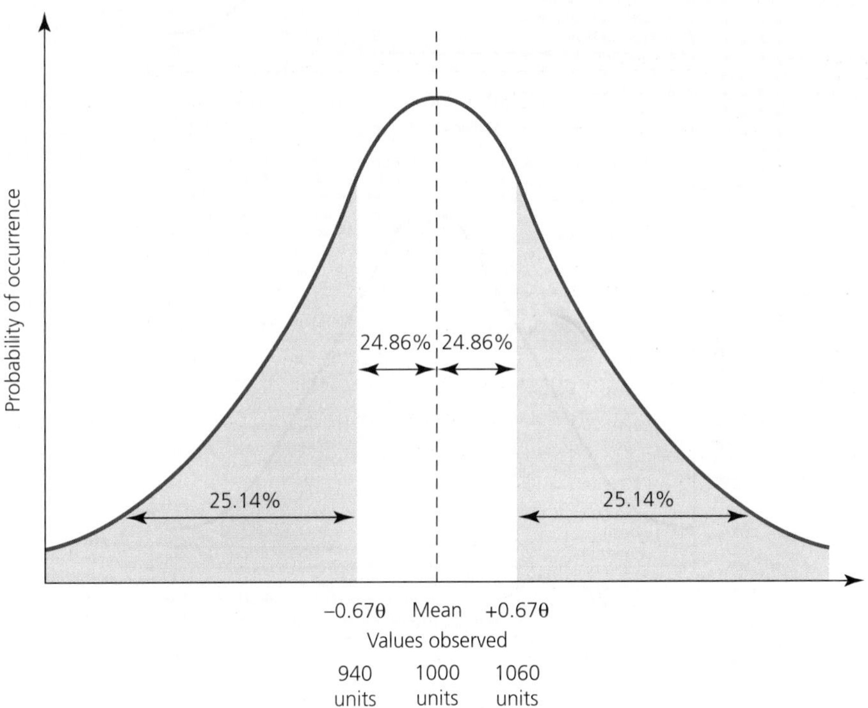

This calculation indicates that a profit of zero lies –1.11 standard deviations from the mean. To determine the probability that profit will be zero or less, we consult the normal probability distribution table in Appendix C at the end of this book. We find from the table that there is a 0.1335 probability that an observation will be less than –1.11 standard deviations from the mean of the distribution (Figure 12A.2(a)). The blue shaded area indicates that 13.35% of the observations will fall to the left of –1.11 standard deviations. Therefore the probability of a loss occurring is 13.35% (or 0.1335). The pink shaded area indicates that the probability of an observation to the right of –1.11 standard deviations from the mean is 86.65% (or 0.8665). Note that the total area under the normal curve is 1.0.

The probability that profits will be in excess of £7600 will result in an observation of one standard deviation from the mean. This is calculated as follows:

$$\frac{7600 - 4000}{3600} = +\ 1.0 \text{ standard deviation}$$

FIGURE 12A.2 *Probability distributions for various profit levels*

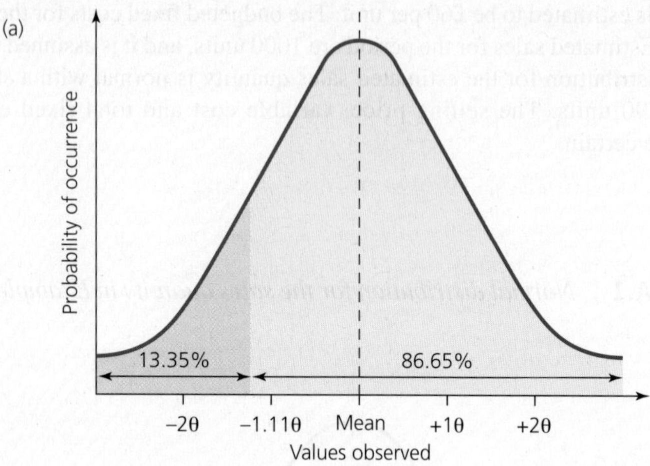

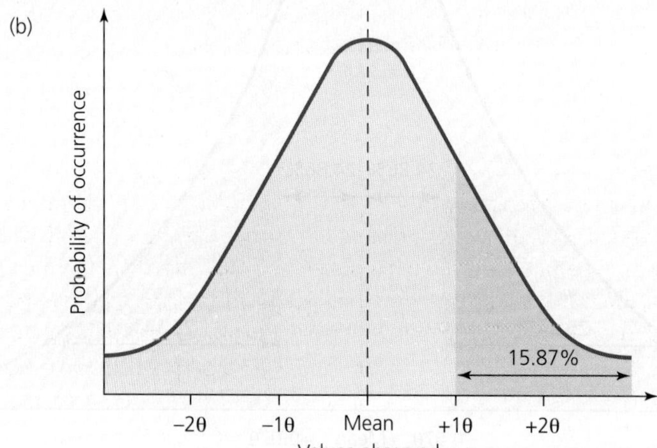

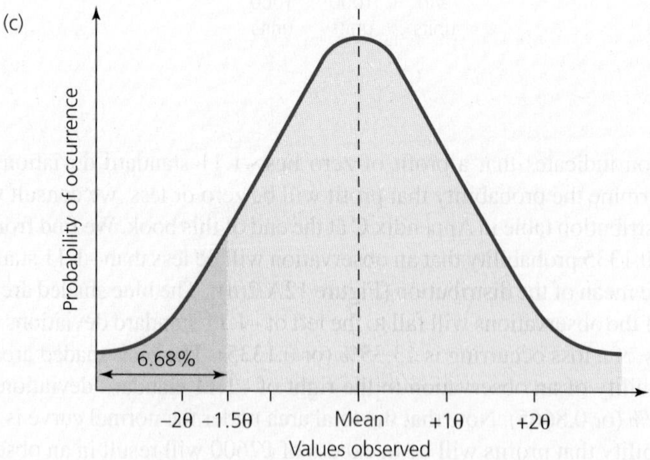

From the normal probability table in Appendix C you will see that the probability of an observation of +1.0 standard deviation from the mean is 0.1587, represented by the blue shaded area in Figure 12A.2(b). The probability of profits being greater than £7600 is therefore 15.87%.

Finally, the probability of a loss in excess of £1400 results in an observation of −1.5 standard deviations from the mean, calculated as follows:

$$\frac{-1400-4000}{3600} = -1.5 \text{ standard deviations}$$

This is represented by the blue shaded area in Figure 12A.2(c). Consequently, the probability of a loss in excess of £1400 is 0.0668.

The question now arises as to how this information that we have obtained can be used. The manager knows that the estimated break-even sales are 900 units (£36 000 fixed costs divided by a contribution of £40 per unit) and that the expected sales are 1000 units, giving a profit of £4000. In addition, normal distribution theory enables the following information to be presented:

1 The probability of a loss occurring is 0.1335 and the probability of a profit is 0.8665.
2 The probability of profits being at least £7600 is 0.1587.
3 The probability of a loss in excess of £1400 is 0.0668.

If the manager is comparing this product with other products then this approach will enable him or her to assess the risk involved for each product, as well as to compare the relative break-even points and expected profits. The analysis can be modified to include fixed cost, variable cost and selling price as uncertain variables. The effect of treating these variables as uncertain will lead to an increase in the standard deviation because the variability of the variable cost, fixed cost and selling price will add to the variability of profits. For a description of CVP analysis when more than one variable is uncertain see Jaedicke and Robichek (1964).

Normality assumption

Of vital importance to our discussion so far is the assumption that the distribution of possible outcomes is normal. It is possible to construct an estimate so that it represents a normal distribution. Consider an estimate of future sales quantity for a product. The marketing department are requested to produce an estimate based on the assumption that there is a 50% probability that actual sales will be above or below the estimated sales. Let us assume that this gives an estimated sales volume of 1000 units. Next we ask for an estimate of the quantity on either side of the mean of 1000 that is expected to result in sales quantity falling in this range 50% of the time. Let us assume the estimate is 60 units. In other words, we expect sales to fall within the range of 940 units to 1060 units 50% of the time. From the normal probability tables in Appendix C we know that one-half of the area under the normal curve lies within ± 0.67 standard deviations from the mean (i.e. 1000 units ± 60 units lies within 0.67 standard deviations from the mean). Therefore 0.67 standard deviations represents 60 units. Thus

$$2/3\ \sigma = 60 \text{ units}$$
$$\sigma = 90 \text{ units}$$

In other words, we have constructed the estimate in such a way that it meets the requirements of a normal distribution. The process can be illustrated by reference to Figure 12A.1.

The normal probability table in Appendix C indicates that the area to the right of +0.67 standard deviations from the mean is 25.14%. Similarly, the area to the left of –0.67 standard deviations is also 25.14%. The area between the mean and ±0.67 standard deviations represents the balance and is 49.72% or approximately 50%. In other words, for a normal distribution there is a probability of approximately 0.50 that observations will fall between ± 0.67 standard deviations from the mean.

By ensuring that estimates are established in such a way that they represent a normal distribution, it is possible to estimate probabilities for any possible outcome. However, it is important to note that the resulting probabilities are only as good as the estimates. Like any projection of future outcomes, the projected results are likely to be subject to error.

Note

1 Fixed costs will remain unchanged when activity changes. Consequently the standard deviation calculated is the standard deviation of sales volume multiplied by the unit contribution.

Key terms and concepts

coefficient of variation (p. 458)
decision tree (pp. 452, 461)
events (p. 452)
expected value (p. 455)
expected value of perfect information (p. 463)
maximax criterion (p. 464)
maximin criterion (p. 464)
objective function (p. 452)
objective probabilities (p. 454)
outcomes (p. 452)
payoff (p. 452)
portfolio (p. 465)
portfolio analysis (p. 465)
probability (p. 454)
probability distribution (p. 454)
regret criterion (p. 464)
risk (p. 453)
risk-averter (p. 460)
risk neutral (p. 460)
risk-seeker (p. 460)
single most likely estimate (p. 455)
standard deviation (p. 457)
states of nature (p. 452)
subjective probabilities (p. 454)
uncertainty (p. 454)

Recommended reading

A more detailed treatment of decision trees can be found in Chapter 4 of Moore and Thomas (1991). For an explanation and illustration of how imperfect information can be valued you should refer to Chapter 7 of Scapens (1991).

Key examination points

When you are faced with problems requiring an evaluation of alternatives with uncertain outcomes, you should calculate expected values and present probability distributions.

Note that expected values on their own are unlikely to be particularly useful and there is a need to supplement this measure with a probability distribution. Avoid calculating standard deviations, since they are rarely required and are a poor substitute for probability distributions.

It is particularly important with this topic that you plan your answer carefully. Once you have started your answer, it is difficult to remedy the situation if you initially adopt the wrong approach. A rough sketch of a decision tree at the start of your answer will force you to analyse the problem and identify all the alternatives and possible outcomes.

Most examination questions on this topic also include a requirement as to whether additional perfect information should be purchased. Do make sure that you understand how to calculate the value of perfect information.

Assessment material

Review questions

The review questions are short questions that enable you to assess your understanding of the main topics included in the chapter. The numbers in parentheses provide you with the page numbers to refer to if you cannot answer a specific question.

Review problems

The review problems are more complex and require you to relate and apply the chapter content to various business problems. The problems are graded by their level of difficulty. The multiple-choice questions are the least demanding and normally take less than 10 minutes to complete. Fully worked solutions to the review problems are provided in a separate section at the end of the book. For those questions in the white box the worked solutions are provided in the *Student's Manual* accompanying this book. Further review problems for this chapter are available on the accompanying website www.drury-online.com. The answers to these problems are available for lecturers on the lecturer's password protected section of the website.

Case studies

The website also includes over 30 case study problems. A list of these cases is provided in Part Seven of this book.

Review questions

12.1 Distinguish between risk and uncertainty. (*pp. 453–54*)

12.2 What is a probability distribution? (*p. 454*)

12.3 How do subjective probabilities differ from objective probabilities? (*p. 454*)

12.4 Distinguish between expected value and the single most likely estimate. (*p. 455*)

12.5 Distinguish between the standard deviation and the coefficient of variation. (*pp. 457–58*)

12.6 What are the disadvantages of the standard deviation as a measure of risk? (*p. 459*)

12.7 What is a decision tree and what purpose does it serve? (*pp. 460–61*)

12.8 What is the expected value of perfect information and how can it be determined? (*p. 463*)

12.9 Distinguish between maximin, maximax and regret criteria. When might it be appropriate to apply these criteria? *(pp. 463–64)*

12.10 Why is it important to measure risk using a portfolio analysis approach? *(p. 465)*

Review problems

12.11 Intermediate

Which of the following are true with regard to expected values?

Expected values

(i) represents the single most likely estimate of an outcome.
(ii) take no account of decision-maker's risk.
(iii) are reliant on the accuracy of the probability distribution.

A (i), (ii) and (iii)
B (i) and (ii) only
C (i) and (iii) only
D (ii) and (iii) only.

ACCA Paper 1.2 – Financial information for Management

12.12 Intermediate

Darwin uses decision tree analysis in order to evaluate potential projects. The company has been looking at the launch of a new product which it believes has a 70% probability of success. The company is, however, considering undertaking an advertising campaign costing £50 000, which would increase the probability of success to 95%.

If successful the product would generate income of £200 000 otherwise £70 000 would be received.

What is the maximum that the company would be prepared to pay for the advertising?

A £32 500
B £29 000
C £17 500
D £50 000.

ACCA Paper 1.2 – Financial information for Management

12.13 Advanced

The following data relate to both questions (a) and (b)

X Ltd can choose from five mutually exclusive projects. The projects will each last for one year only and their net cash inflows will be determined by the prevailing market conditions. The forecast annual cash inflows and their associated probabilities are shown below:

Market conditions	Poor	Good	Excellent
Probability	0.20	0.50	0.30
	£000	£000	£000
Project L	500	470	550
Project M	400	550	570
Project N	450	400	475
Project O	360	400	420
Project P	600	500	425

(a) Based on the expected value of the net cash inflows, which project should be undertaken?

A L
B M
C N
D O
E P

(2 marks)

(b) The value of perfect information about the state of the market is

A Nil
B £5 000
C £26 000
D £40 000
E £128 000

(3 marks)

CIMA Management Accounting – Decision Making

12.14 **Advanced: Expected values, probability distributions and regret criterion**

Central Ltd has developed a new product, and is currently considering the marketing and pricing policy it should employ for this. Specifically, it is considering whether the sales price should be set at £15 per unit or at the higher level of £24 per unit. Sales volumes at these two prices are shown in the following table:

Sales price £15 per unit		Sales price £24 per unit	
Forecast sales volume (000)	Probability	Forecast sales volume (000)	Probability
20	0.1	8	0.1
30	0.6	16	0.3
40	0.3	20	0.3
		24	0.3

The fixed production costs of the venture will be £38 000.

The level of the advertising and publicity costs will depend on the sales price and the market aimed for. With a sales price of £15 per unit, the advertising and publicity costs will amount to £12 000. With a sales price of £24 per unit, these costs will total £122 000.

Labour and variable overhead costs will amount to £5 per unit produced. Each unit produced requires 2 kg of raw material and the basic cost is expected to be £4 per kg. However, the suppliers of the raw materials are prepared to lower the price in return for a firm agreement to purchase a guaranteed minimum quantity. If Central Ltd contracts to purchase at least 40 000 kg then the price will be reduced to £3.75 per kg for *all* purchases. If Central contracts to purchase a minimum of 60 000 kg then the price will be reduced to £3.50 per kg for all purchases. It is only if Central Ltd guarantees either of the above minimum levels of purchases in advance that the appropriate reduced prices will be operative.

If Central Ltd were to enter into one of the agreements for the supply of raw material and was to find that it did not require to utilize the entire quantity of materials purchased then the excess could be sold. The sales price will depend upon the quantity that is offered for sale. If 16 000 kg or more are sold, the sales price will be £2.90 per kg for all sales. If less than 16 000 kg are offered, the sales price will be only £2.40 per kg.

Irrespective of amount sold, the costs incurred in selling the excess raw materials will be, per kg, as follows:

Packaging	£0.30
Delivery	£0.45
Insurance	£0.15

Central's management team feels that losses are undesirable, while high expected money values are desirable. Therefore it is considering the utilization of a formula that incorporated both aspects of the outcome to measure the desirability of each strategy. The formula to be used to measure the desirability is:

$$\text{desirability} = L + 3E$$

where L is the lowest outcome of the strategy and E is the expected monetary value of the strategy. The higher this measures, the more desirable the strategy.

The marketing manager seeks the advice of you, the management accountant, to assist in deciding the appropriate strategy. He says 'we need to make two decisions now:

(i) Which price per unit should be charged: £15 or £24?

(ii) Should all purchases of raw materials be at the price of £4 per kg, or should we enter into an agreement for a basic minimum quantity? If we enter into an agreement then what minimum level of purchases should we guarantee?

As you are the management accountant, I expect you to provide me with some useful relevant figures.'

Required:

(a) Provide statements that show the various expected outcomes of each of the choices open to Central Ltd.

(10 marks)

(b) Advise on its best choice of strategies if Central Ltd's objective is

(i) to maximize the expected monetary value of the outcomes;

(ii) to minimize the harm done to the firm if the worst outcome of each choice were to eventuate;

(iii) to maximize the score on the above mentioned measure of desirability.

(6 marks)

(c) Briefly comment on either

(i) two other factors that may be relevant in reaching a decision; OR

(ii) the decision criteria utilized in (b) above.

(4 marks)

(Total 20 marks)

ACCA P2 Management Accounting

12.15 Advanced: Expected values, maximin criterion and value of perfect information

Recyc plc is a company which reprocesses factory waste in order to extract good quality aluminium. Information concerning its operations is as follows:

(i) Recyc plc places an advance order each year for chemical X for use in the aluminium extraction process. It will enter into an advance contract for the coming year for chemical X at one of three levels – high, medium or low, which correspond to the requirements of a high, medium or low level of waste available for reprocessing.

(ii) The level of waste available will not be known when the advance order for chemical X is entered into. A set of probabilities have been estimated by management as to the likelihood of the quantity of waste being at a high, medium or low level.

(iii) Where the advance order entered into for chemical X is lower than that required for the level of waste for processing actually received, a discount from the original demand price is allowed by the supplier for the total quantity of chemical X actually required.

(iv) Where the advance order entered into for chemical X is in excess of that required to satisfy the actual level of waste for reprocessing, a penalty payment in excess of the original demand price is payable for the total quantity of chemical X actually required.

A summary of the information relating to the above points is as follows:

			Chemical X costs per kg		
Level of reprocessing	**Waste available (000 kg)**	**Probability**	**Advance order (£)**	**Conversion discount (£)**	**Conversion premium (£)**
High	50 000	0.30	1.00		
Medium	38 000	0.50	1.20		
Low	30 000	0.20	1.40		
Chemical X: order conversion:					
Low to medium				0.10	
Medium to high				0.10	
Low to high				0.15	
Medium to low					0.25
High to medium					0.25
High to low					0.60

Aluminium is sold at £0.65 per kg. Variable costs (excluding chemical X costs) are 70% of sales revenue.

Aluminium extracted from the waste is 15% of the waste input. Chemical X is added to the reprocessing at the rate of 1 kg per 100 kg of waste.

Required:

(a) Prepare a summary which shows the budgeted contribution earned by Recyc plc for the coming year for each of nine possible outcomes.

(14 marks)

(b) On the basis of maximizing expected value, advise Recyc plc whether the advance order for chemical X should be at low, medium or high level.

(3 marks)

(c) State the contribution for the coming year which corresponds to the use of (i) maximax and (ii) maximin decision criteria, and comment on the risk preference of management which is indicated by each.

(6 marks)

(d) Recyc plc are considering employing a consultant who will be able to say with certainty in advance of the placing of the order for chemical X, which level of waste will be available for reprocessing.

On the basis of expected value, determine the maximum sum which Recyc plc should be willing to pay the consultant for this information.

(6 marks)

(e) Explain and comment on the steps involved in evaluating the purchase of imperfect information from the consultant in respect of the quantity of waste which will be available for reprocessing.

(6 marks)

(Total 35 marks)

ACCA Paper 9 Information for Control and Decision Making

12.16 Advanced: Decision tree, expected value and maximin criterion

(a) The Alternative Sustenance Company is considering introducing a new franchised product, Wholefood Waffles.

Existing ovens now used for making some of the present 'Half-Baked' range of products could be used instead for baking the Wholefood Waffles. However, new special batch mixing equipment would be needed. This cannot be purchased, but can be hired from the franchiser in three alternative specifications, for batch sizes of 200, 300 and 600 units respectively. The annual cost of hiring the mixing equipment would be £5000, £15 000 and £21 500 respectively.

The 'Half-Baked' product which would be dropped from the range currently earns a contribution of £90 000 per annum, which it is confidently expected could be continued if the product were retained in the range.

The company's marketing manager considers that, at the market price for Wholefood Waffles of £0.40 per unit, it is equally probable that the demand for this product would be 600 000 or 1 000 000 units per annum.

The company's production manager has estimated the variable costs per unit of making Wholefood Waffles and the probabilities of those costs being incurred, as follows:

Batch size:	**200 units**	**300 units**	**600 units**	**600 units**
Cost per unit (pence)	**Probability if annual sales are either 600 000 or 1 000 000 units**	**Probability if annual sales are either 600 000 or 1 000 000 units**	**Probability if annual sales are 600 000 units**	**Probability if annual sales are 1 000 000**
£0.20	0.1	0.2	0.3	0.5
£0.25	0.1	0.5	0.1	0.2
£0.30	0.8	0.3	0.6	0.3

You are required:

(i) to draw a decision tree setting out the problem faced by the company,

(12 marks)

(ii) to show in each of the following three independent situations which size of mixing machine, if any, the company should hire:

(1) to satisfy a 'maximin' (or 'minimax' criterion),

(2) to maximize the expected value of contribution per annum,

(3) to minimize the probability of earning an annual contribution of less than £100 000.

(7 marks)

(b) You are required to outline briefly the strengths and limitations of the methods of analysis which you have used in part (a) above.

(6 marks)

(Total 25 marks)

ICAEW Management Accounting

Review problems (with answers in the Student's Manual)

12.17 **Advanced: Calculation of expected value and the presentation of a probability distribution**

The Dunburgh Bus Company operated during the year ended 31 May 2000 with the following results:

(i) Average variable costs were £0.75 per bus mile.

(ii) Total fixed costs were £1 750 000.

(iii) The fare structure per journey was as follows:

Adults 0 to 3 miles	£0.20
4 to 5 miles	£0.30
over 5 miles	£0.50
Juveniles (any distance)	£0.15
Senior citizens (any distance)	£0.10

(iv) Total passenger journeys paid for were 24 000 000 which represented 60% capacity utilization. The capacity utilized comprised 60% adult, 20% juvenile and 20% senior citizen journeys. The adult journeys were broken down into 0–3 miles: 50%, 4–5 miles: 30%, over 5 miles: 20%.

(v) Twenty routes were operated with four buses per route, each bus covering 150 miles per day for 330 days of the year. The remaining days were taken up with maintenance work on the buses.

(vi) Advertising revenue from displays inside and outside the buses totalled £250 000 for the year. This is a fixed sum from contracts which will apply to each year up to 31 May 2002.

It is anticipated that all costs will increase by 10% due to inflation during the year to 31 May 2001 and that fares will be increased by 5% during the year. Whilst the fare increase of 5% has already been agreed and cannot be altered, it is possible that inflation might differ from the 10% rate anticipated.

Required:

(a) Prepare a statement showing the calculation of the net profit or loss for the year ended 31 May 2000

(5 marks)

(b) Calculate the average percentage capacity utilization at which the company will break even during the forthcoming year to 31 May 2001 if all fares are increased by 5%, cost inflation is 10% as anticipated and the passenger mix and bus operating activity are the same as for the year to 31 May 2000.

(5 marks)

(c) Now assume that management have some doubts about the level of capacity utilization and rate of cost inflation which will apply in the year to 31 May 2001. Other factors are as previously forecast. Revised estimates of the likely levels of capacity utilization and inflation are as follows:

Capacity utilization	Probability	Inflation	Probability
70%	0.1	8%	0.3
60%	0.5	10%	0.6
50%	0.4	12%	0.1

(Capacity utilization rates and inflation rates are independent of each other.)

(i) Calculate the expected value of net profit or loss for the year to 31 May 2001 and show the range of profits or losses which may occur.

(9 marks)

(ii) Draw up a table of the possible profits and losses and their probabilities as calculated in (i) for the year ended 31 May 2001 in a way which brings to the attention of management the risks and opportunities which are implied and comment briefly on the figures.

(5 marks)

(d) Comment on factors which have not been incorporated into the model used in (c) above which may affect its usefulness to management in profit forecasting.

(6 marks)

(Total 30 marks)

ACCA Level 2 Cost Accounting II

12.18 **Advanced: Pricing decision and the calculation of expected profit and margin of safety**

E Ltd manufactures a hedge-trimming device which has been sold at £16 per unit for a number of years. The selling price is to be reviewed and the following information is available on costs and likely demand.

The standard variable cost of manufacture is £10 per unit and an analysis of the cost variances for the past 20 months show the following pattern which the production manager expects to continue in the future.

Adverse variances of +10% of standard variable cost occurred in ten of the months.

Nil variances occurred in six of the months.

Favourable variances of –5% of standard variable cost occurred in four of the months.

Monthly data
Fixed costs have been £4 per unit on an average sales level of 20 000 units but these costs are expected to rise in the future and the following estimates have been made for the total fixed cost:

	(£)
Optimistic estimate (Probability 0.3)	82 000
Most likely estimate (Probability 0.5)	85 000
Pessimistic estimate (Probability 0.2)	90 000

The demand estimates at the two new selling prices being considered are as follows:

If the selling price/unit is demand would be:	£17	£18
Optimistic estimate (Probability 0.2)	21 000 units	19 000 units
Most likely estimate (Probability 0.5)	19 000 units	17 500 units
Pessimistic estimate (Probability 0.3)	16 500 units	15 500 units

It can be assumed that all estimates and probabilities are independent.

You are required to

(a) advise management, based only on the information given above, whether they should alter the selling price and, if so, the price you would recommend;

(6 marks)

(b) calculate the expected profit at the price you recommend and the resulting margin of safety, expressed as a percentage of expected sales;
(6 marks)

(c) criticise the method of analysis you have used to deal with the probabilities given in the question;

(4 marks)

(d) describe briefly how computer assistance might improve the analysis.
(4 marks)
(Total 20 marks)
CIMA Stage 3 Management Accounting Techniques

12.19 **Advanced: Machine hire decision based on uncertain demand and calculation of maximum price to pay for perfect information**

Siteraze Ltd is a company which engages in site clearance and site preparation work. Information concerning its operations is as follows:

(i) It is company policy to hire all plant and machinery required for the implementation of all orders obtained, rather than to purchase its own plant and machinery.

(ii) Siteraze Ltd will enter into an advance hire agreement contract for the coming year at one of three levels – high, medium or low, which correspond to the requirements of a high, medium or low level of orders obtained.

(iii) The level of orders obtained will not be known when the advance hire agreement contract is entered into. A set of probabilities have been estimated by management as to the likelihood of the orders being at a high, medium or low level.

(iv) Where the advance hire agreement entered into is lower than that required for the level of orders actually obtained, a premium rate must be paid to obtain the additional plant and machinery required.

(v) No refund is obtainable where the advance hire agreement for plant and machinery is at a level in excess of that required to satisfy the site clearance and preparation orders actually obtained.

A summary of the information relating to the above points is as follows:

Level of orders	Turnover (£000)	Probability	Plant and machinery hire costs: Advance hire (£000)	Plant and machinery hire costs: Conversion premium (£000)
High	15 000	0.25	2300	
Medium	8 500	0.45	1500	
Low	4 000	0.30	1000	
Low to medium				850
Medium to high				1300
Low to high				2150

Variable cost (as percentage of turnover) 70%

Required: Using the information given above:

(a) Prepare a summary which shows the forecast net margin earned by Siteraze Ltd for the coming year for each possible outcome.

(6 marks)

(b) On the basis of maximizing expected value, advise Siteraze whether the advance contract for the hire of plant and machinery should be at the low, medium or high level.

(5 marks)

(c) Explain how the risk preferences of the management members responsible for the choice of advance plant and machinery hire contract may alter the decision reached in (b) above.

(6 marks)

(d) Siteraze Ltd are considering employing a market research consultant who will be able to say with certainty in advance of the placing of the plant and machinery hire contract, which level of site clearance and preparation orders will be obtained. On the basis of expected value, determine the maximum sum which Siteraze Ltd should be willing to pay the consultant for this information.

(5 marks)

(Total 22 marks)

ACCA Level 2: Cost and Management Accounting 11

12.20 Advanced: Pricing decisions under conditions of uncertainty

(a) Allegro Finishes Ltd is about to launch an improved version of its major product – a pocket size chess computer – onto the market. Sales of the original model (at £65 per unit) have been at the rate of 50 000 per annum but it is now planned to withdraw this model and the company is now deciding on its production plans and pricing policy.

The standard variable cost of the new model will be £50 which is the same as that of the old, but the company intends to increase the selling price 'to recover the research and development expenditure that has been incurred'. The research and development costs of the improved model are estimated at £750 000 and the intention is that these should be written off over 3 years. Additionally there are annual fixed overheads of approximately £800 000 allocated to this product line.

The sales director has estimated the maximum annual demand figures that would obtain at three alternative selling prices. These are as follows:

Selling price (£)	Estimated maximum annual demand (physical units)
70	75 000
80	60 000
90	40 000

You are required to prepare a cost–volume–profit chart that would assist the management to choose a selling price and the level of output at which to operate. Identify the best price and the best level of output. Outline briefly any reservations that you have with this approach.

(5 marks)

(b) With the facts as stated for part (a), now assume the sales director is considering a more sophisticated approach to the problem. He has estimated, for each selling price, an optimistic, a pessimistic and a most likely demand figure and associated probabilities for each of these. For the £90 price the estimates are:

	Annual demand	Probability of demand
Pessimistic	20 000	0.2
Most likely	35 000	0.7
Optimistic	40 000	0.1
		1.0

On the cost side, it is clear that the standard unit variable cost of £50 is an 'ideal' which has rarely been achieved in practice. An analysis of the past 20 months shows that the following pattern of variable cost variances (per unit of output) has arisen:
an adverse variance of around £10 arose on 4 occasions,
an adverse variance of around £5 arose on 14 occasions
and a variance of around 0 arose on 2 occasions.

There is no reason to think that the pattern for the improved model will differ significantly from this or that these variances are dependent upon the actual demand level.

From the above, calculate the expected annual profit for a selling price of £90.

(6 marks)

(c) A tabular summary of the result of an analysis of the data for the other two selling prices (£70 and £80) is as follows:

	£70	£80
Probability of a loss of £500 000 or more	0.02	0
Probability of a loss of £300 000 or more	0.07	0.05
Probability of a loss of £100 000 or more	0.61	0.08
Probability of break-even or worse	0.61	0.10
Probability of break-even or better	0.39	0.91
Probability of a profit of £100 000 or more	0.33	0.52
Probability of a profit of £300 000 or more	0.03	0.04
Probability of a profit of £500 000 or more	0	0.01
Expected value of profit (loss)	55 750	68 500

You are required to compare your calculations in part (b) with the above figures and to write a short memo to the sales director outlining your advice and commenting on the use of subjective discrete probability distributions in problems of this type.

(9 marks)

(d) Assume that there is a 10% increase in the fixed overheads allocated to this product line and a decision to write off the research and development costs in one year instead of over 3 years. Indicate the general effect that this would have on your analysis of the problem.

(2 marks)
(Total 22 marks)
ACCA Level 2 Management Accounting

12.21 **Advanced: Expected value comparison of low and high price alternatives**

The research and development department of Shale White has produced specifications for two new products for consideration by the company's production director. The director has received detailed costings which can be summarized as follows:

	Product newone (£)	Product newtwo (£)
Direct costs:		
Material	64	38
Labour (£3 per hour)	18	6
	82	44
Factory overheads		
(£3 per machine hour)	18	6
Total estimated unit cost	100	50

The sales department has provided estimates of the probabilities of various levels of demand for two possible selling prices for each product. The details are as follows:

	Product newone	Product newtwo
Low price alternative		
Selling price	£120	£60
Demand estimates:		
Pessimistic – probability 0.2	1000	3000
Most likely – probability 0.5	2000	4000
Optimistic – probability 0.3	3000	5000
High price alternative		
Selling price	£130	£70
Demand estimates:		
Pessimistic – probability 0.2	500	1500
Most likely – probability 0.5	1000	2500
Optimistic – probability 0.3	1500	3500

It would be possible to adopt the low price alternative for product newone together with the high price alternative for newtwo, or the high price alternative for product newone with the low price alternative for newtwo (demand estimates are independent for the two products).

The factory has 60 000 machine hours available during the year. For some years past it has been working at 90% of practical capacity making a standardized product. This product is very profitable and it is only the availability of 6000 hours of spare machine capacity that has made it necessary to search for additional product lines to use the machines fully. The actual level of demand will be known at the time of production.

A statistical study of the behaviour of the factory overhead over the past year has indicated that it can be regarded as a linear function of factory machine time worked. The monthly fixed cost is estimated at £10 000 and the variable cost at £1 per machine hour with a coefficient of correlation of 0.8.

You are required:

(a) to identify the best plan for the utilization of the 6000 machine hours, to comment on the rational selling price alternatives that exist for this plan and to calculate the expected increase in annual profit which would arise for each alternative,

(17 marks)

(b) to discuss the relevance of regression analysis for problems of this type.

(5 marks)

(Total 22 marks)

ACCA Level 2 Management Accounting

12.22 Advanced: Pricing decision based on competitor's response

In the market for one of its products, MD and its two major competitors (CN and KL) together account for 95% of total sales.

The quality of MD's products is viewed by customers as being somewhat better than that of its competitors and therefore at similar prices it has an advantage.

During the past year, however, when MD raised its price to £1.2 per litre, competitors kept their prices at £1.0 per litre and MD's sales declined even though the total market grew in volume.

MD is now considering whether to retain or reduce its price for the coming year. Its expectations about its likely volume at various prices charged by itself and its competitors are as follows:

Prices per litre			
MD (£)	CN (£)	KL (£)	MD's expected sales million litres
1.2	1.2	1.2	2.7
1.2	1.2	1.1	2.3
1.2	1.2	1.0	2.2
1.2	1.1	1.1	2.4
1.2	1.1	1.0	2.2
1.2	1.1	1.0	2.1
1.1	1.1	1.1	2.8
1.1	1.0	1.0	2.4
1.1	1.0	1.0	2.3
1.0	1.0	1.0	2.9

Experience has shown that CN tends to react to MD's price level and KL tends to react to CN's price level. MD therefore assesses the following probabilities:

If MD's price per litre is (£)	there is a probability of	that CN's price per litre will be (£)
1.2	0.2	1.2
	0.4	1.1
	0.4	1.0
	1.0	
1.1	0.3	1.1
	0.7	1.0
	1.0	
1.0	1.0	1.0

If CN's price per litre is (£)	there is a probability of	that KL's price per litre will be (£)
1.2	0.1	1.2
	0.6	1.1
	0.3	1.0
	1.0	
1.1	0.3	1.1
	0.7	1.0
	1.0	
1.0	1.0	1.0

Costs per litre of the product are as follows:

Direct wages	£0.24
Direct materials	£0.12
Departmental expenses:	
Indirect wages, maintenance and supplies	$16^2/_3$% of direct wages
Supervision and depreciation	£540 000 per annum
General works expenses (allocated)	$16^2/_3$% of prime cost
Selling and administration expenses (allocated)	50% of manufacturing cost

You are required to state whether, on the basis of the data given above, it would be most advantageous for MD to fix its price per litre for the coming year at £1.2, £1.1 or £1.0.

Support your answer with relevant calculations.

(20 marks)

CIMA P3 Management Accounting

12.23 **Advanced: Expected value, maximin and regret criterion**

Stow Health Centre specialises in the provision of sports/exercise and medical/dietary advice to clients. The service is provided on a residential basis and clients stay for whatever number of days suits their needs.

Budgeted estimates for the next year ending 30 June are as follows:

(i) The maximum capacity of the centre is 50 clients per day for 350 days in the year.

(ii) Clients will be invoiced at a fee per day. The budgeted occupancy level will vary with the client fee level per day and is estimated at different percentages of maximum capacity as follows:

Client fee per day	Occupancy level	Occupancy as percentage of maximum capacity
£180	High	90%
£200	Most likely	75%
£220	Low	60%

(iii) Variable costs are also estimated at one of three levels per client day. The high, most likely and low levels per client day are £95, £85 and £70 respectively.

The range of cost levels reflect only the possible effect of the purchase prices of goods and services.

Required:

(a) Prepare a summary which shows the budgeted contribution earned by Stow Health Centre for the year ended 30 June for each of nine possible outcomes.

(6 marks)

(b) State the client fee strategy for the next year to 30 June which will result from the use of each of the following decision rules: (i) *maximax*; (ii) *maximin*; (iii) *minimax* regret.

Your answer should explain the basis of operation of each rule. Use the information from your answer to (a) as relevant and show any additional working calculations as necessary.

(9 marks)

(c) The probabilities of variable cost levels occurring at the high, most likely and low levels provided in the question are estimated as 0.1, 0.6 and 0.3 respectively.

Using the information available, determine the client fee strategy which will be chosen where maximisation of expected value of contribution is used as the decision basis.

(5 marks)

(d) The calculations in (a) to (c) concern contribution levels which may occur given the existing budget.

Stow Health Centre has also budgeted for fixed costs of £1 200 000 for the next year to 30 June.

Discuss ways in which Stow Health Centre may instigate changes, in ways other than through the client fee rate, which may influence client demand, cost levels and profit.

Your answer should include comment on the existing budget and should incorporate illustrations which relate to each of four additional performance measurement areas appropriate to the changes you discuss.

(15 marks)

(Total 35 marks)

ACCA Paper 9 Information for Control and Decision Making

Capital investment decisions: 1

13

Capital investment decisions are those decisions that involve current outlays in return for a stream of benefits in future years. It is true to say that all of the firm's expenditures are made in expectation of realizing future benefits. The distinguishing feature between short-term decisions and capital investment (long-term) decisions is time. Generally, we can classify short-term decisions as those that involve a relatively short time horizon, say one year, from the commitment of funds to the receipt of the benefits. On the other hand, capital investment decisions are those decisions where a significant period of time elapses between the outlay and the recoupment of the investment. We shall see that this commitment of funds for a significant period of time involves an interest cost, which must be brought into the analysis. With short-term decisions, funds are committed only for short periods of time, and the interest cost is normally so small that it can be ignored.

Capital investment decisions normally represent the most important decisions that an organization makes, since they commit a substantial proportion of a firm's resources to

LEARNING OBJECTIVES

After studying this chapter, you should be able to:

- explain the opportunity cost of an investment;
- distinguish between compounding and discounting;
- explain the concepts of net present value (NPV), internal rate of return (IRR), payback method and accounting rate of return (ARR);
- calculate NPV, IRR, the payback period and ARR;
- justify the superiority of NPV over the IRR;
- explain the limitations of payback and ARR;
- justify why the payback and ARR methods are widely used in practice;
- describe the effect of performance measurement on capital investment decisions;
- describe the capital investment process.

actions that are likely to be irreversible. Such decisions are applicable to all sectors of society. Business firms' investment decisions include investments in plant and machinery, research and development, advertising and warehouse facilities. Investment decisions in the public sector include new roads, schools and airports. Individuals' investment decisions include house-buying and the purchase of consumer durables. In this and the following chapter we shall examine the economic evaluation of the desirability of investment proposals. We shall concentrate on the investment decisions of business firms, but the same principles, with modifications, apply to individuals, and the public sector.

To simplify the introduction to capital investment decision, we shall assume initially that all cash inflows and outflows are known with certainty, and that sufficient funds are available to undertake all profitable investments. We will also assume a world where there are no taxes and where there is an absence of inflation. These factors will be brought into the analysis in the next chapter.

Objectives of capital budgeting

Capital investment decisions are part of the **capital budgeting process**, which is concerned with decision-making in the following areas:

1 determining which specific projects a firm should accept;

2 determining the total amount of capital expenditure which the firm should undertake;

3 determining how the total amount of capital expenditure should be financed.

In this and the following chapter we shall concentrate on the first two items. Financing decisions are normally considered to be part of the corporate finance literature. Therefore, the third topic will not be covered in this book.

Each of the above decisions should be evaluated on the basis of their estimated contribution towards the achievement of the goals of the organization. In Chapter 1 it was pointed out that although organizations may pursue a variety of goals the theory of finance generally assumes that, broadly, firms seek to maximize shareholder value. The theory of capital budgeting specifies that shareholder value is maximized by applying the principle that a firm should operate at the point where marginal cost is equal to marginal revenue. Marginal revenue is represented by the percentage return on investment, while marginal cost is represented by the marginal cost of capital (MCC). By cost of capital we mean the cost of the funds to finance the projects. The application of this theory is illustrated in Figure 13.1.

The horizontal axis measures the total funds invested during a year, while the vertical axis shows both the percentage rate of return on the available projects and the percentage cost of capital used in financing these projects. The available projects are denoted by bands. For example, project A requires an outlay of £5 million and provides a 20% rate of return, project B requires a £2 million outlay and yields a return of 16% and so on.

Figure 13.1 illustrates that the firm should accept projects A to D because the return on investment is in excess of the cost of capital, and that projects E and F should be rejected because the return on investment is less than the cost of raising the capital. Throughout this chapter, we are assuming that the cost of capital is constant (i.e. the MCC curve is perceived by the suppliers of capital. These assumptions enable the firm's financing decision to be held constant so that we can concentrate on the investment decision. Note that the cost of capital is constant at 12%.

The major aim of this chapter is to provide you with an understanding of capital investment appraisal methods that should generally result in the maximizing of shareholder value. In addition, those appraisal methods that are also widely used by firms and that cannot be guaranteed to maximize shareholder value are explained. The reasons why firms

FIGURE 13.1 *Determining the total amounts of capital expenditure that a firm should undertake*

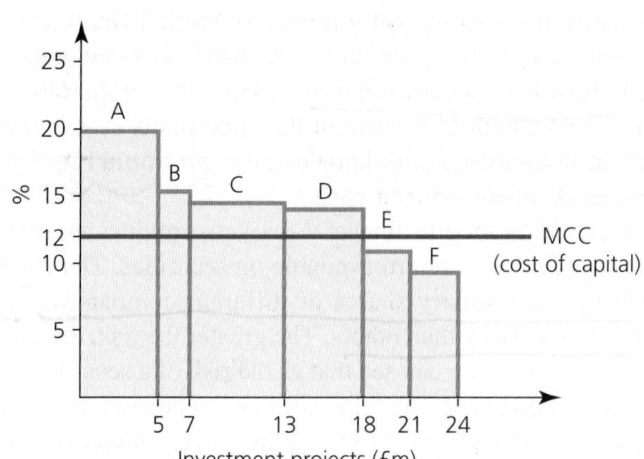

continue to use these methods are also examined. Because managers' personal goals may not be in alignment with shareholders' goals of maximizing shareholder value, the influence of managerial performance measurement systems on capital investment decisions are briefly examined. The chapter concludes with a description of the processes that firms use for authorizing capital investments and reviewing whether investment projects achieve the results that were specified in the investment proposals.

To understand the investment appraisal techniques that are consistent with maximizing shareholders' value it is important that you acquire an understanding of the term 'opportunity cost of an investment' and the principles of compounding and discounting. These topics are discussed in the following sections prior to a discussion of the various investment appraisal techniques.

The opportunity cost of an investment

Investors can invest in securities traded in financial markets. If you prefer to avoid risk, you can invest in government securities, which will yield a *fixed* return. On the other hand, you may prefer to invest in *risky* securities such as the ordinary shares of companies quoted on the stock exchange. If you invest in the ordinary shares of a company, you will find that the return will vary from year to year, depending on the performance of the company and its future expectations. Investors normally prefer to avoid risk if possible, and will generally invest in risky securities only if they believe that they will obtain a greater return for the increased risk. Suppose that **risk-free gilt-edged securities** issued by the government yield a return of 10%. You will therefore be prepared to invest in ordinary shares only if you expect the return to be greater than 10%; let us assume that you require an *expected* return of 15% to induce you to invest in ordinary shares in preference to a risk-free security. Note that expected return means the average return. You would expect to earn, on average, 15%, but in some years you might earn more and in others considerably less.

Suppose you invest in company X ordinary shares. Would you want company X to invest your money in a capital project that gives less than 15%? Surely not, assuming the project has the same risk as the alternative investments in shares of other companies that are yielding a return of 15%. You would prefer company X to invest in other companies' ordinary shares at 15% or, alternatively, to repay your investment so that you could invest yourself at 15%.

The rates of return that are available from investments in securities in financial markets such as ordinary shares and government gilt-edged securities represent the **opportunity cost of an investment** in capital projects; that is, if cash is invested in the capital project, it cannot be invested elsewhere to earn a return. A firm should therefore invest in capital projects only if they yield a return in excess of the opportunity cost of the investment. The opportunity cost of the investment is also known as the **minimum required rate of return**, **cost of capital**, **discount rate** or **interest rate**.

The return on securities traded in financial markets provides us with the opportunity costs, that is the required rates of return available on securities. The expected returns that investors require from the ordinary shares of different companies vary because some companies' shares are more risky than others. The greater the risk, the greater the expected returns. Consider Figure 13.2. You can see that as the risk of a security increases the return that investors require to compensate for the extra risk increases. Consequently, investors will expect to receive a return in excess of 15% if they invest in securities that have a higher risk than company X ordinary shares. If this return was not forthcoming, investors would not purchase high-risk securities. It is therefore important that companies investing in high-risk capital projects earn higher returns to compensate investors for this risk. You can also see that a risk-free security such as a gilt-edged government security yields the lowest return, i.e. 10%. Consequently, if a firm invests in a project with zero risk, it should earn a return in excess of 10%. If the project does not yield this return and no other projects are available then the funds earmarked for the project should be repaid to the shareholders as dividends. The shareholders could then invest the funds themselves at 10%.

Compounding and discounting

Our objective is to calculate and compare returns on an investment in a capital project with an alternative equal risk investment in securities traded in the financial markets. This comparison is made using a technique called **discounted cash flow (DCF)** analysis. Because a DCF analysis is the opposite of the concept of **compounding interest**, we shall initially focus on compound interest calculations.

Suppose you are investing £100 000 in a risk-free security yielding a return of 10% payable at the end of each year. Exhibit 13.1 shows that if the interest is reinvested, your investment will accumulate to £146 410 by the end of year 4. Period 0 in the first column of Exhibit 13.1 means that no time has elapsed or the time is *now*, period 1 means one year later, and so on. The values in Exhibit 13.1 can also be obtained by using the formula:

$$FV_n = V_0 (1 + K)^n \qquad (13.1)$$

where FV_n denotes the future value of an investment in n years, V_0 denotes the amount invested at the beginning of the period (year 0), K denotes the rate of return on the investment and n denotes the number of years for which the money is invested. The calculation for £100 000 invested at 10% for two years is

$$FV_2 = £100\,000\,(1 + 0.10)^2 = £121\,000$$

In Exhibit 13.1 all of the year-end values are equal as far as the time value of money is concerned. For example, £121 000 received at the end of year 2 is equivalent to £100 000 received today and invested at 10%. Similarly, £133 100 received at the end of year 3 is

FIGURE 13.2 *Risk–return trade-off*

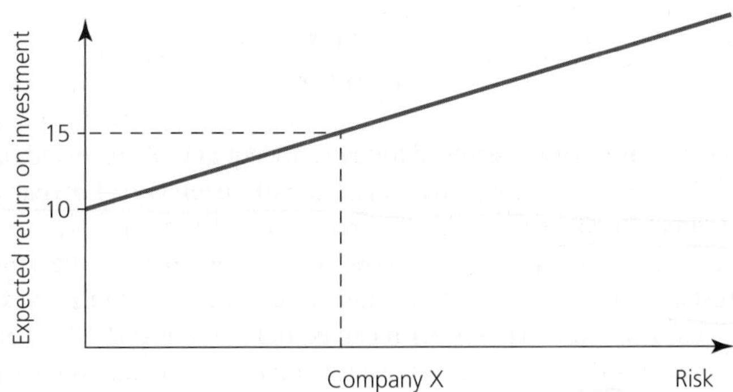

EXHIBIT 13.1 *The value of £100 000 invested at 10%, compounded annually, for four years*

End of year	Interest earned (£)	Total investment (£)
0		100 000
	0.10 × 100 000	10 000
1		110 000
	0.10 × 110 000	11 000
2		121 000
	0.10 × 121 000	12 100
3		133 100
	0.10 × 133 100	13 310
4		146 410

equivalent to £121 000 received at the end of year 2, since £121 000 can be invested at the end of year 2 to accumulate to £133 100. Unfortunately, none of the amounts are directly comparable at any single moment in time, because each amount is expressed at a different point in time.

When making capital investment decisions, we must convert cash inflows and outflows for different years into a common value. This is achieved by converting the cash flows into their respective values at the same point in time. Mathematically, any point in time can be chosen, since all four figures in Exhibit 13.1 are equal to £100 000 at year 0, £110 000 at year 1, £121 000 at year 2, and so on. However, it is preferable to choose the point in time at which the decision is taken, and this is the present time or year 0. All of the values in Exhibit 13.1 can therefore be expressed in values at the present time (i.e. '**present value**') of £100 000.

The process of converting cash to be received in the future into a value at the present time by the use of an interest rate is termed **discounting** and the resulting present value is the **discounted present value**. Compounding is the opposite of discounting, since it is the future value of present value cash flows. Equation (13.1) for calculating future values can be rearranged to produce the present value formula:

$$V_0 \text{ (present value)} = \frac{FV_n}{(1+K)^n} \qquad (13.2)$$

By applying this equation, the calculation for £121 000 received at the end of year 2 can be expressed as

$$\text{present value} = \frac{£121\,000}{(1 + 0.10)^2} = £100\,000$$

You should now be aware that £1 received today is not equal to £1 received one year from today. No rational person will be equally satisfied with receiving £1 a year from now as opposed to receiving it today, because money received today can be used to earn interest over the ensuing year. Thus one year from now an investor can have the original £1 plus one year's interest on it. For example, if the interest rate is 10% each £1 invested now will yield £1.10 one year from now. That is, £1 received today is equal to £1.10 one year from today at 10% interest. Alternatively, £1 one year from today is equal to £0.9091 today, its present value because £0.9091, plus 10% interest for one year amounts to £1. The concept that £1 received in the future is not equal to £1 received today is known as the **time value of money**.

We shall now consider five different methods of appraising capital investments: the net present value, internal rate of return, profitability index, accounting rate of return and payback methods. We shall see that the first three methods take into account the time value of money whereas the accounting rate of return and payback methods ignore this factor.

The concept of net present value

By using discounted cash flow techniques and calculating present values, we can compare the return on an investment in capital projects with an alternative equal risk investment in securities traded in the financial market. Suppose a firm is considering four projects (all of which are risk-free) shown in Exhibit 13.2. You can see that each of the projects is identical with the investment in the risk-free security shown in Exhibit 13.1 because you can cash in this investment for £110 000 in year 1, £121 000 in year 2, £133 100 in year 3 and £146 410 in year 4. In other words your potential cash receipts from the risk-free security are identical to the net cash flows for projects A, B, C and D shown in Exhibit 13.2. Consequently, the firm should be indifferent as to whether it uses the funds to invest in the projects or invests the funds in securities of identical risk traded in the financial markets.

The most straightforward way of determining whether a project yields a return in excess of the alternative equal risk investment in traded securities is to calculate the **net present value (NPV)**. This is the present value of the net cash inflows less the project's initial investment outlay. If the rate of return from the project is greater than the return from an equivalent risk investment in securities traded in the financial market, the NPV will be positive. Alternatively, if the rate of return is lower, the NPV will be negative. A positive NPV therefore indicates that an investment should be accepted, while a negative value indicates that it should be rejected. A zero NPV calculation indicates that the firm should be indifferent to whether the project is accepted or rejected.

You can see that the present value of each of the projects shown in Exhibit 13.2 is £100 000. You should now deduct the investment cost of £100 000 to calculate the project's NPV. The NPV for each project is zero. The firm should therefore be indifferent to whether it accepts any of the projects or invests the funds in an equivalent risk-free security. This was our conclusion when we compared the cash flows of the projects with the investments in a risk-free security shown in Exhibit 13.1.

You can see that it is better for the firm to invest in any of the projects shown in Exhibit 13.2 if their initial investment outlays are less than £100 000. This is because we have to

EXHIBIT 13.2
Evaluation of four risk-free projects

	A (£)	B (£)	C (£)	D (£)
Project investment outlay	100 000	100 000	100 000	100 000
End of year cash flows:				
Year 1	110 000	0	0	0
2	0	121 000	0	0
3	0	0	133 100	0
4	0	0	0	146 410
present value =	$\frac{110\,000}{1.10}$	$\frac{121\,000}{(1.10)^2}$	$\frac{133\,000}{(1.10)^3}$	$\frac{146\,410}{(1.10)^4}$
	= 100 000	= 100 000	= 100 000	= 100 000

pay £100 000 to obtain an equivalent stream of cash flows from a security traded in the financial markets. Conversely, we should reject the investment in the projects if their initial investment outlays are greater than £100 000. You should now see that the NPV rule leads to a direct comparison of a project with an equivalent risk security traded in the financial market. Given that the present value of the net cash inflows for each project is £100 000, their NPVs will be positive (thus signifying acceptance) if the initial investment outlay is less than £100 000 and negative (thus signifying rejection) if the initial outlay is greater than £100 000.

Calculating net present values

You should now have an intuitive understanding of the NPV rule. We shall now learn how to calculate NPVs. The NPV can be expressed as:

$$NPV = \frac{FV_1}{1+K} + \frac{FV_2}{(1+K)^2} + \frac{FV_3}{(1+K)^3} + \cdots + \frac{FV_n}{(1+K)^n} - I_0 \qquad (13.3)$$

where I_0 represents the investment outlay and FV represents the future values received in years 1 to n. The rate of return K used is the return available on an equivalent risk security in the financial market. Consider the situation in Example 13.1.

The net present value calculation for Project A is:

$$NPV = \frac{£300\,000}{(1.10)} + \frac{£1\,000\,000}{(1.10)^2} + \frac{£400\,000}{(1.10)^3} - £1\,000\,000 = +£399\,700$$

Alternatively, the net present value can be calculated by referring to a published table of present values. You will find examples of such a table if you refer to Appendix A (see pages 1174–7). To use the table, simply find the discount factors by referring to each year of the cash flows and the appropriate interest rate.

For example, if you refer to year 1 in Appendix A, and the 10% column, this will show a discount factor of 0.9091. For years 2 and 3 the discount factors are 0.8264 and 0.7513. You then multiply the cash flows by the discount factors to find the present value of the cash flows. The calculation is as follows:

EXAMPLE 13.1

The Bothnia Company is evaluating two projects with an expected life of three years and an investment outlay of £1 million. The estimated net cash inflows for each project are as follows:

	Project A (£)	Project B (£)
Year 1	300 000	600 000
Year 2	1 000 000	600 000
Year 3	400 000	600 000

The opportunity cost of capital for both projects is 10%. You are required to calculate the net present value for each project.

Year	Amount (£000's)	Discount factor	Present value (£)
1	300	0.9091	272 730
2	1000	0.8264	826 400
3	400	0.7513	300 520
			1 399 650
		Less initial outlay	1 000 000
		Net present value	399 650

The difference between the two calculations is due to rounding differences.

Note that the discount factors in the present value table are based on £1 received in *n* years time calculated according to the present value formula (equation 13.2). For example, £1 received in years 1, 2 and 3 when the interest rate is 10% is calculated as follows:

$$\text{Year } 1 = £1/1.10 = 0.9091$$

$$\text{Year } 2 = £1(1.10)^2 = 0.8264$$

$$\text{Year } 3 = £1(1.10)^3 = 0.7513$$

The positive net present value from the investment indicates the increase in the market value of the shareholders' funds which should occur once the stock market becomes aware of the acceptance of the project. The net present value also represents the potential increase in present consumption that the project makes available to the ordinary shareholders, after any funds used have been repaid with interest. For example, assume that the firm finances the investment of £1 million in Example 13.1 by borrowing £1 399 700 at 10% and repays the loan and interest out of the project's proceeds as they occur. You can see from the repayment schedule in Exhibit 13.3 that £399 700 received from the loan is available for current consumption, and the remaining £1 000 000 can be invested in the project. The cash flows from the project are just sufficient to repay the loan. Therefore acceptance of the project enables the ordinary shareholders' present consumption to be increased by the net present value of £399 700. Hence the acceptance of all available projects with a positive net present value should lead to the maximization of shareholders' wealth.

EXHIBIT 13.3

The pattern of cash flows assuming that the loan is repaid out of the proceeds of the project

Year	Loan outstanding at start of year (1) (£)	Interest at 10% (2) (£)	Total amount owed before repayment (3) = (1) + (2) (£)	Proceeds from project (4) (£)	Loan outstanding at year end (5) = (3) – (4) (£)
1	1 399 700	139 970	1 539 670	300 000	1 239 670
2	1 239 670	123 967	1 363 637	1 000 000	363 637
3	363 637	36 363	400 000	400 000	0

Let us now calculate the net present value for Project B. When the annual cash flows are constant, the calculation of the net present value is simplified. The discount factors when the cash flows are the same each year (that is, an annuity) are set out in Appendix B (see pages 1178–81). We need to find the discount factor for 10% for three years. If you refer to Appendix B, you will see that it is 2.487. The NPV is calculated as follows:

Annual cash inflow	Discount factor	Present value (£)
£600 000	2.487	1 492 200
	Less investment cost	1 000 000
	Net present value	492 200

You will see that the total present value for the period is calculated by multiplying the cash inflow by the discount factor. It is important to note that the annuity tables shown in Appendix B can only be applied when the annual cash flows are the same each year.

The internal rate of return

The **internal rate of return (IRR)** is an alternative technique for use in making capital investment decisions that also takes into account the time value of money. The internal rate of return represents the true interest rate earned on an investment over the course of its economic life. This measure is sometimes referred to as the **discounted rate of return**. The internal rate of return is the interest rate K that when used to discount all cash flows resulting from an investment, will equate the present value of the cash receipts to the present value of the cash outlays. In other words, it is the discount rate that will cause the net present value of an investment to be zero. Alternatively, the internal rate of return can be described as the maximum cost of capital that can be applied to finance a project without causing harm to the shareholders. The internal rate of return is found by solving for the value of K from the following formula:

$$I_0 = \frac{FV_1}{1+K} + \frac{FV_2}{(1+K)^2} + \frac{FV_3}{(1+K)^3} + \cdots + \frac{FV_n}{(1+K)^n} \qquad (13.4)$$

It is easier, however, to use the discount tables. Let us now calculate the internal rate of return for Project A in Example 13.1.

The IRR can be found by trial and error by using a number of discount factors until the NPV equals zero. For example, if we use a 25% discount factor, we get a positive NPV of £84 800. We must therefore try a higher figure. Applying 35% gives a negative NPV of £66 530. We know then that the NPV will be zero somewhere between 25% and 35%. In fact, the IRR is approximately 30%, as indicated in the following calculation:

Year	Net cash flow (£)	Discount factor (30%)	Present value of cash flow (£)
1	300 000	0.7692	230 760
2	1 000 000	0.5917	591 700
3	400 000	0.4552	182 080
		Net present value	1 004 540
		Less initial outlay	1 000 000
		Net present value	4 540

It is claimed that the calculation of the IRR does not require the prior specification of the cost of capital. The decision rule is that if the IRR is greater than the opportunity cost of capital, the investment is profitable and will yield a positive NPV. Alternatively, if the IRR is less than the cost of capital, the investment is unprofitable and will result in a negative NPV. Therefore any interpretation of the significance of the IRR will still require that we estimate the cost of capital. The calculation of the IRR is illustrated in Figure 13.3.

The dots in the graph represent the NPV at different discount rates. The point where the line joining the dots cuts the horizontal axis indicates the IRR (the point at which the NPV is zero). Figure 13.3 indicates that the IRR is 30%, and you can see from this diagram that the interpolation method can be used to calculate the IRR without carrying out trial and error calculations. When we use interpolation, we infer the missing term (in this case the discount rate at which NPV is zero) from a known series of numbers. For example, at a discount rate of 25% the NPV is +£84 800 and for a discount rate of 35% the NPV is –£66 530. The total distance between these points is £151 330 (+£84 800 and –£66 530). The calculation for the approximate IRR is therefore

$$25\% + \frac{84\ 800}{151\ 330} \times (35\% - 25\%) = 30.60\%$$

In other words, if you move down line A in Figure 13.3 from a discount rate of 25% by £84 800, you will reach the point at which NPV is zero. The distance between the two points on line A is £151 330, and we are given the discount rates of 25% and 35% for these points. Therefore 84 800/151 330 represents the distance that we must move between these two points for the NPV to be zero. This distance in terms of the discount rate is 5.60% [(84 800/151 330) × 10%], which, when added to the starting point of 25%, produces an IRR of 30.60%. The formula using the interpolation method is as follows:

$$A + \frac{C}{C - D}(B - A) \qquad (13.5)$$

where A is the discount rate of the low trial, B is the discount rate of the high trial, C is the NPV of cash inflow of the low trial and D is the NPV of cash inflow of the high trial. Thus

FIGURE 13.3 *Interpretation of the internal rate of return*

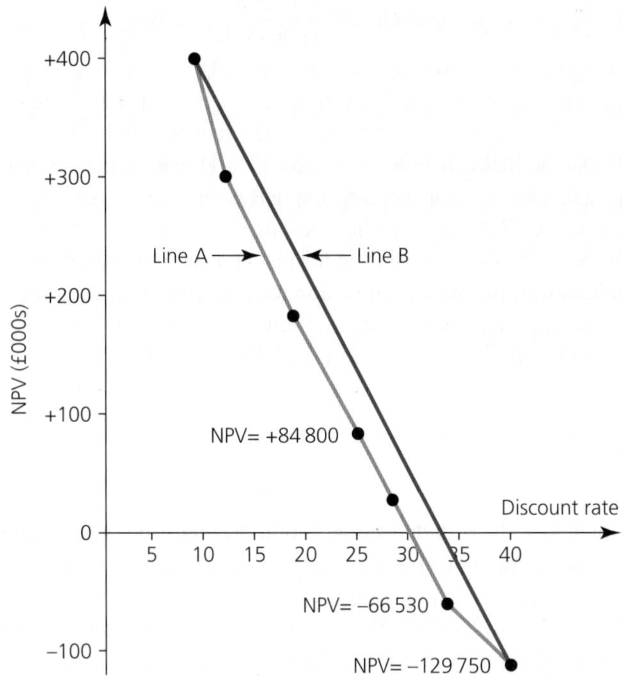

$$25\% + \left[\frac{84\,800}{84\,800 - (-66\,530)} \times 10\% \right]$$

$$= 25\% + \left[\frac{84\,800}{151\,330} \times 10\% \right]$$

$$= 30.60\%$$

Note that the interpolation method only gives an approximation of the IRR. The greater the distance between any two points that have a positive and a negative NPV, the less accurate is the IRR calculation. Consider line B in Figure 13.3. The point where it cuts the horizontal axis is approximately 33%, whereas the actual IRR is 30.60%.

The calculation of the IRR is easier when the cash flows are of a constant amount each year. Let us now calculate the internal rate of return for project B in Example 13.1. Because the cash flows are equal each year, we can use the annuity table in Appendix B. When the cash flows are discounted at the IRR, the NPV will be zero. The IRR will therefore be at the point where

$$[\text{annual cash flow}] \times \left[\begin{array}{c} \text{discount factor for number of years} \\ \text{for which cash flow is received} \end{array} \right] - \left[\begin{array}{c} \text{investment} \\ \text{cost} \end{array} \right] = 0$$

Rearranging this formula, the internal rate of return will be at the point where

$$\text{discount factor} = \frac{\text{investment cost}}{\text{annual cash flow}}$$

Substituting the figures for project B in Example 13.1,

$$\text{discount factor} = \frac{£1\,000\,000}{£600\,000} = 1.666$$

We now examine the entries for the year 3 row in Appendix B to find the figures closest to 1.666. They are 1.673 (entered in the 36% column) and 1.652 (entered in the 37% column). We can therefore conclude that the IRR is between 36% and 37%. However, because the cost of capital is 10%, an accurate calculation is unnecessary; the IRR is far in excess of the cost of capital.

The calculation of the IRR can be rather tedious (as the cited examples show), but the trial-and-error approach can be programmed for fast and accurate solution by a computer or calculator. The calculation problems are no longer a justification for preferring the NPV method of investment appraisal. Nevertheless, there are theoretical justifications, which we shall discuss later in this chapter, that support the NPV method.

Relevant cash flows

Investment decisions, like all other decisions, should be analysed in terms of the cash flows that can be directly attributable to them. These cash flows should include the incremental cash flows that will occur in the future following acceptance of the investment. The cash flows will include cash inflows and outflows, or the inflows may be represented by savings in cash outflows. For example, a decision to purchase new machinery may generate cash savings in the form of reduced out-of-pocket operating costs. For all practical purposes such cost savings are equivalent to cash receipts.

It is important to note that depreciation is not included in the cash flow estimates for capital investment decisions, since it is a non-cash expense. This is because the capital investment cost of the asset to be depreciated is included as a cash outflow at the start of the project, and depreciation is merely a financial accounting method for allocating past capital costs to future accounting periods. Any inclusion of depreciation will lead to double counting.

Timing of cash flows

Our calculations have been based on the assumption that any cash flows in future years will occur in one lump sum at the year end. Obviously, this is an unrealistic assumption, since cash flows are likely to occur at various times throughout the year, and a more accurate method is to assume monthly cash flows and use monthly discount rates. However, the use of annual cash flows enables all cash flows which occur in a single year to be combined and discounted in one computation. Even though the calculated results that are obtained are not strictly accurate, they are normally accurate enough for most decisions.

Comparison of net present value and internal rate of return

In many situations the internal rate of return method will result in the same decision as the net present value method. In the case of conventional projects (in which an initial cash outflow is followed by a series of cash inflows) that are independent of each other (i.e. where the selection of a particular project does not preclude the choice of the other), both NPV and IRR rules will lead to the same accept/reject decisions. However, there are also situations where the IRR method may lead to different decisions being made from those that would follow the adoption of the NPV procedure.

Mutually exclusive projects

Where projects are **mutually exclusive**, it is possible for the NPV and the IRR methods to suggest different rankings as to which project should be given priority. Mutually exclusive projects exist where the acceptance of one project excludes the acceptance of another project, for example the choice of one of several possible factory locations, or the choice of one of many different possible machines. Example 13.2 illustrates how the application of the IRR and the NPV rules can lead to different decisions.

The NPV and IRR calculations are as follows:

	IRR (%)	NPV (£)
Project X	22	153 041
Project Y	18	172 824

You can see that the IRR ranks X first, but the NPV rate ranks Y first. If the projects were independent, this would be irrelevant, since both would be accepted and the firm would be indifferent as to the order in which they were accepted. However, in the case of mutually exclusive projects the ranking is crucial, since only one project can be accepted and we cannot be indifferent to the outcome of applying the NPV and the IRR rules. The reasons for the different rankings are shown in Figure 13.4.

The NPV ranking depends on the discount rate used. For a discount rate greater than 12% no contradictions arise, since both the NPV and the IRR rules rank X first. However, the two methods give different ranking for discount rates that are less than 12%: project Y has a higher NPV, but project X has a higher IRR. Logically such a situation should not exist, and the only explanation seems to be that one of the methods must indicate an incorrect ranking. In fact, the IRR method gives an incorrect ranking, and we can prove this by considering the increments of cash flows of project Y over project X. The increments are as follows:

	Years 0 (£)	1 (£)	2 (£)	3 (£)
Project Y	1 200 000	552 000	552 000	552 000
Project X	700 000	343 000	343 000	343 000
Incremental cash flow (Y – X)	500 000	209 000	209 000	209 000

If we assume that the firm adopts the IRR method and initially chooses project X, we can consider whether it is worthwhile to add the hypothetical incremental investment (Y–X). The acceptance of the initial investment plus the hypothetical incremental investment is X+(Y–X) and this is the equivalent of accepting project Y. Therefore if the firm is prepared to accept the incremental investment, using the IRR rule, this is equivalent to the

EXAMPLE 13.2

The Bothnia Company is also evaluating two alternative mutually exclusive methods of improving the marketing of its products which it has described as project X and project Y. The estimated incremental cash flows from each alternative are as follows:

	Initial Investment outlay (£)	Net inflow at the end of years 1–3 (£)		
		1	2	3
Project X	700 000	343 000	343 000	343 000
Project Y	1 200 000	552 000	552 000	552 000

The company's estimated cost of capital is 10%. Which project should the company accept?

FIGURE 13.4 *Net present values at different discount rates for projects X and Y (Example 13.2)*

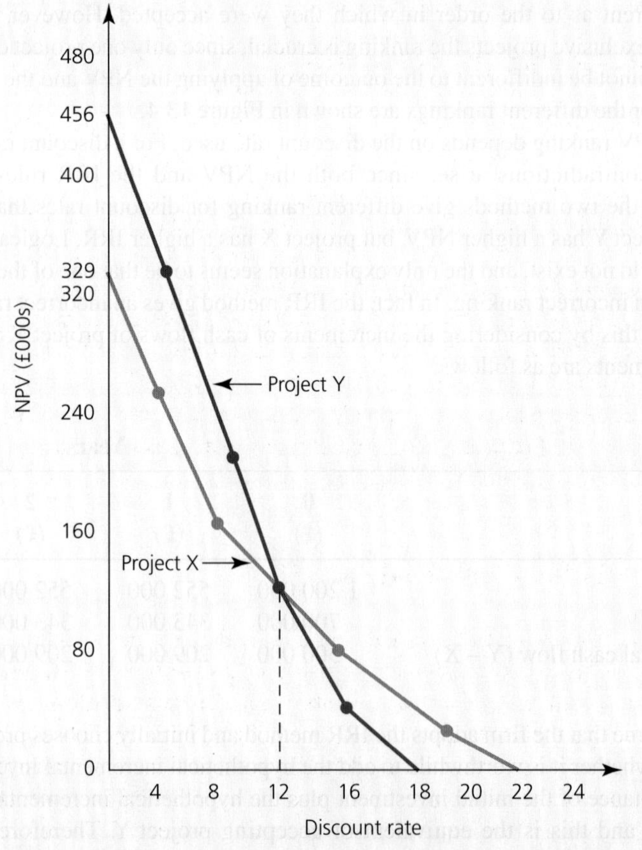

firm shifting from X to Y. The IRR of the incremental investment (Y–X) is 12%. As the cost of capital is 10%, the incremental project should be accepted. In other words, the IRR has indicated that we should move from project X to project Y, and the superiority of the NPV method has been established by using the IRR analysis to contradict the IRR rule.

Note also that if the cost of capital is greater than 12%, it does not pay to invest in the incremental project (Y–X), and the firm should not shift from project X to project Y. This is exactly what the NPV method prescribes in Figure 13.4.

Percentage returns

Another problem with the IRR rule is that it expresses the result as a percentage rather than in monetary terms. Comparison of percentage returns can be misleading; for example, compare an investment of £10 000 that yields a return of 50% with an investment of £100 000 that yields a return of 25%. If only one of the investments can be undertaken, the first investment will yield £5000 but the second will yield £25 000. If we assume that the cost of capital is 10%, and that no other suitable investments are available, any surplus funds will be invested at the cost of capital (i.e. the returns available from equal risk securities traded in financial markets). Choosing the first investment will leave a further £90 000 to be invested, but this can only be invested at 10%, yielding a return of £9000. Adding this to the return of £5000 from the £10 000 investment gives a total return of £14 000. Clearly, the second investment, which yields a return of £25 000, is preferable. Thus, if the objective is to maximize the shareholders' wealth then NPV provides the correct measure.

Reinvestment assumptions

The assumption concerning the reinvestment of interim cash flows from the acceptance of projects provides another reason for supporting the superiority of the NPV method. The implicit assumption if the NPV method is adopted is that the cash flows generated from an investment will be reinvested at the cost of capital (i.e. the returns available from equal risk securities traded in financial markets). However, the IRR method makes a different implicit assumption about the reinvestment of the cash flows. It assumes that all the proceeds from a project can be reinvested to earn a return equal to the IRR of the original project. In Example 13.2 the NPV method assumes that the annual cash inflows of £343 000 for project X will be reinvested at a cost of capital of 10%, whereas the IRR method assumes that they will be reinvested at 22%. In theory, a firm will have accepted all projects which offer a return in excess of the cost of capital, and any other funds that become available can only be reinvested at the cost of capital. This is the assumption that is implicit in the NPV rule.

Unconventional cash flows

Where a project has unconventional cash flows, the IRR has a technical shortcoming. Most projects have conventional cash flows that consist of an initial negative cash flow followed by positive cash inflows in later years. In this situation the algebraic sign changes, being negative at the start and positive in all future periods. If the sign of the net cash flows changes in successive periods, it is possible for the calculations to produce as many internal rates of return as there are sign changes. While multiple rates of return are mathematically possible, only one rate of return is economically significant in determining whether or not the investment is profitable.

EXAMPLE 13.3

The Bothnia Company has the following series of cash flows for a specific project:

Year 0	−£400 000 (Investment outlay)
Year 1	+£1 020 000 (Net cash inflows)
Year 2	−£630 000 (Environmental and disposal costs)

You are required to calculate the internal rate of return.

FIGURE 13.5 *Net present values for unconventional cash flows*

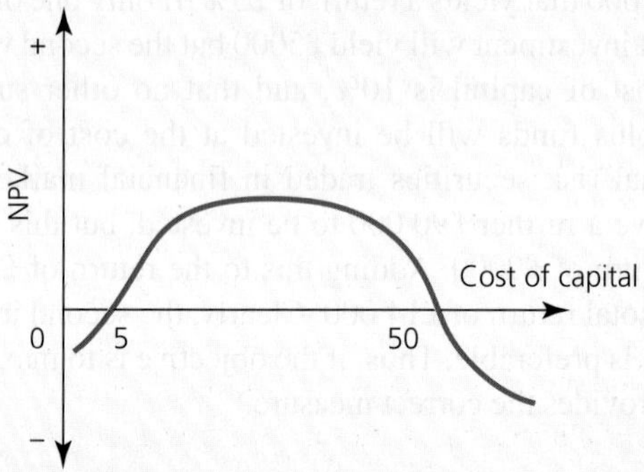

Fortunately, the majority of investment decisions consist of conventional cash flows that produce a single IRR calculation. However, the problem cannot be ignored, since unconventional cash flows are possible and, if the decision-maker is unaware of the situation, serious errors may occur at the decision-making stage. Example 13.3 illustrates a situation where two internal rates of return occur.

You will find that the cash flows in Example 13.3 give internal rates of return of 5% and 50%. The effect of multiple rates of return on the NPV calculations is illustrated in Figure 13.5.

When the cost of capital is between 5% and 50%, the NPV is positive and, following the NPV rule, the project should be accepted. However, if the IRR calculation of 5% is used, the project may be incorrectly rejected if the cost of capital is in excess of 5%. You can see that the graph of the NPV in Figure 13.5 indicates that this is an incorrect decision when the cost of capital is between 5% and 50%. Alternatively, if the IRR of 50% is used, this will lead to the same decision being made as if the NPV rule were adopted, provided that the cost of capital is greater than 5%. Note that the NPV is negative if the cost of capital is less than 5%.

Profitability index

The **profitability index** is the third method of evaluating capital investment proposals that takes into account the time value of money. The method is simply a variation of the NPV method, and it is computed by dividing the present value of the cash proceeds by the initial cost of the investment. If the profitability index is less than 1, the investment should be rejected. Conversely, if it is greater than 1, the investment should be accepted. This method is consistent with the NPV method, since the index can only be less than 1 when the NPV is negative. Similarly, an index greater than 1 only arises when the NPV is positive.

In the case of independent projects and where the company is not restricted from accepting profitable projects because of the shortage of funds the profitability index will yield the same acceptance/rejection decision as the NPV method. For mutually exclusive investments the profitability index will not always result in the same rankings as the NPV method. Consider the following situation, where projects C and D are mutually exclusive:

	PV of cash flow (£)	Initial investment outlay (£)	Profitability index
Project C	100 000	50 000	2.0
Project D	180 000	100 000	1.8

According to the profitability index, project C is to be preferred, but, given that only one of these two projects can be chosen, project D should be the one. This is because D gives the largest absolute NPV. Therefore the profitability index is a weak measure for selecting between mutually exclusive investment projects in a situation when a company can accept all investments that yield a positive NPV. However, we shall see in the next chapter that when a firm cannot accept all of those projects with positive NPVs because of the unavailability of funds, the profitability index can be a useful method for determining how the scarce funds can best be allocated.

Techniques that ignore the time value of money

In addition to those methods that take into account the time value of money two other methods that ignore this factor are frequently used in practice. These are the payback method and the accounting rate of return method. Methods that ignore the time value of money are theoretically weak, and they will not necessarily lead to the maximization of the market value of ordinary shares. Nevertheless, the fact that they are frequently used in practice means that we should be aware of these techniques and their limitations.

Payback method

The payback method is one of the simplest and most frequently used methods of capital investment appraisal. It is defined as the length of time that is required for a stream of cash proceeds from an investment to recover the original cash outlay required by the investment. If the stream of cash flows from the investment is constant each year, the payback period can be calculated by dividing the total initial cash outlay by the amount of the expected annual cash proceeds. Therefore if an investment requires an initial outlay of £60 000 and is expected to produce annual cash inflows of £20 000 per year for five years, the payback period will be £60 000 divided by £20 000, or three years. If the stream of expected proceeds is not constant from year to year, the payback period is determined by adding up the cash inflows expected in successive years until the total is equal to the original outlay. Example 13.4 illustrates two projects, A and B, that require the same initial outlay of £50 000 but that display different time profiles of benefits.

In Example 13.4 project A pays back its initial investment cost in three years, whereas project B pays back its initial cost in four years so that project A would be ranked in preference to project B. However, project B has a higher NPV, and the payback method incorrectly ranks project A in preference to project B. Two obvious deficiencies are apparent from these calculations. First, the payback method does not take into account cash flows that are earned after the payback period and, secondly, it fails to take into account the differences in the timing of the proceeds which are earned before the payback period. Payback computations ignore the important fact that future cash receipts cannot be validly compared with an initial outlay until they are discounted to their present values.

Not only does the payback period incorrectly rank project A in preference to project B, but the method can also result in the acceptance of projects that have a negative NPV. Consider the cash flows for project C in Example 13.5.

The payback period for project C is three years, and if this was within the time limit set by management, the project would be accepted in spite of its negative NPV. Note also that the payback method would rank project C in preference to project B in Example 13.4, despite the fact that B would yield a positive NPV.

The payback period can only be a valid indicator of the time that an investment requires to pay for itself, if all cash flows are first discounted to their present values and the discounted values are then used to calculate the payback period. This adjustment gives rise to what is known as the adjusted or **discounted payback method**. Even when such an adjustment is made, the adjusted payback method cannot be a complete measure of an investment's profitability. It can estimate whether an investment is likely to be profitable, but it cannot estimate how profitable the investment will be.

Despite the theoretical limitations of the payback method it is the method most widely used in practice (see Exhibit 13.4). Why, then, is payback the most widely applied formal investment appraisal technique? It is a particularly useful approach for ranking projects where a firm faces liquidity constraints and requires a fast repayment of investments. The payback method may also be appropriate in situations where risky investments are made in uncertain markets that are subject to fast design and product changes or where future cash flows are extremely difficult to predict. The payback method assumes that risk is time-related: the longer the period, the greater the chance of failure. By concentrating on the early cash flows, payback uses data in which managers have greater confidence. Thus, the payback period can be used as a rough measure of risk, based on the assumption that the longer it takes for a project to pay for itself, the riskier it is. Managers may also choose projects with quick payback periods because of self-interest. If a manager's performance is measured using short-term criteria, such as net profits, there is a danger that he or she may choose projects with quick paybacks to show improved net profits as soon as possible. The payback method is also frequently used in conjunction with the NPV or IRR methods. It serves as a simple first-level screening device that identifies those projects that should be subject to more rigorous investigation. A further attraction of payback is that it is easily understood by all levels of management and provides an important summary measure: how quickly will the project recover its initial outlay? Ideally, the payback method should be used in conjunction with the NPV method, and the cash flows discounted before the payback period is calculated.

It is apparent from the above surveys that firms use a combination of appraisal methods. The studies by Pike indicate a trend in the increasing usage of discount rates. The Drury *et al.* study suggests that larger organizations use net present value and internal rate of return to a greater extent than the smaller organizations. The Drury *et al.* study also asked the respondents to rank the appraisal methods in order of importance for evaluating major projects. The larger organizations ranked internal rate of return first, followed by payback

EXAMPLE 13.4

The cash flows and NPV calculations for two projects are as follows:

	Project A		Project B	
	(£)	(£)	(£)	(£)
Initial cost				
Net cash inflows		50 000		50 000
Year 1	10 000		10 000	
Year 2	20 000		10 000	
Year 3	20 000		10 000	
Year 4	20 000		20 000	
Year 5	10 000		30 000	
Year 6	–		30 000	
Year 7	–	80 000	30 000	140 000
NPV at a 10% cost capital		10 500		39 460

EXAMPLE 13.5

The cash flows and NPV calculation for project C are as follows:

	(£)	(£)
Initial cost		
Net cash inflows		50 000
Year 1	10 000	
Year 2	20 000	
Year 3	20 000	
Year 4	3 500	
Year 5	3 500	
Year 6	3 500	
Year 7	3 500	64 000
NPV (at 10% cost of capital)		(–1 036)

and net present value whereas the smaller organizations ranked payback first, internal rate of return second and intuitive management judgement third.

The use of the accounting rate of return probably reflects the fact that it is a widely used external financial accounting measure by financial markets and managers therefore wish to assess what impact a project will have on the external reporting of this measure. Also it is a widely used measure for evaluating managerial performance.

Accounting rate of return

The **accounting rate of return** (also known as the **return on investment** and **return on capital employed**) is calculated by dividing the average annual profits from a project into

EXHIBIT 13.4
Surveys of practice

Surveys conducted by Pike relating to the investment appraisal techniques by 100 large UK companies between 1975 and 1992 provide an indication of the changing trends in practice in large UK companies. Pike's findings relating to the percentage of firms using different appraisal methods are as follows:

	1975 %	1981 %	1986 %	1992 %
Payback	73	81	92	94
Accounting rate of return	51	49	56	50
DCF methods (IRR or NPV)	58	68	84	88
Internal rate of return (IRR)	44	57	75	81
Net present value (NPV)	32	39	68	74

Source: Pike (1996)

A study of 300 UK manufacturing organizations by Drury *et al.* (1993) sought to ascertain the extent to which particular techniques were used. The figures below indicate the percentage of firms that often or always used a particular technique:

	All organizations %	Smallest organizations %	Largest organizations %
Payback (unadjusted)	63	56	55
Discounted payback	42	30	48
Accounting rate of return	41	35	53
Internal rate of return	57	30	85
Net present value	43	23	80

More recently a UK study by Arnold and Hatzopoulos (2000) reported that NPV has overtaken IRR as the most widely used method by larger firms. They reported that 97% of large firms use NPV compared with 84% which employ IRR.

Few studies have been undertaken in mainland Europe. The following usage rates relate to surveys undertaken in the USA and Belgium. For comparative purposes Pike's UK study is also listed:

	UK[a] %	USA[b] %	Belgium[c] %
Payback	94	72	50
Accounting rate of return	50	65	65
Internal rate of return	81	91	77
Net present value	74	88	60
Discounted payback		65	68

[a]Pike (1996)
[b]Trahan and Gitman (1995)
[c]Dardenne (1998)

the average investment cost. It differs from other methods in that profits rather than cash flows are used. Note that profits are not equal to cash flows because financial accounting profit measurement is based on the accruals concept. Assuming that depreciation represents the only non-cash expense, profit is equivalent to cash flows less depreciation. The use of accounting rate of return can be attributed to the wide use of the return on investment measure in financial statement analysis.

When the average annual net profits are calculated, only additional revenues and costs that follow from the investment are included in the calculation. The average annual net profit is therefore calculated by dividing the difference between incremental revenues and costs by the estimated life of the investment. The incremental costs include either the *net* investment cost or the total depreciation charges, these figures being identical. The average investment figure that is used in the calculation depends on the method employed to calculate depreciation. If straight-line depreciation is used, it is presumed that investment will decline in a linear fashion as the asset ages. The average investment under this assumption is one-half of the amount of the initial investment plus one-half of the scrap value at the end of the project's life.[1]

For example, the three projects described in Examples 13.4 and 13.5 for which the payback period was computed required an initial outlay of £50 000. If we assume that the projects have no scrap values and that straight-line depreciation is used, the average investment for each project will be £25 000. The calculation of the accounting rate of return for each of these projects is as follows:

$$\text{accounting rate of return} = \frac{\text{average annual profits}}{\text{average investment}}$$

$$\text{project A} = \frac{6\,000}{25\,000} = 24\%$$

$$\text{project B} = \frac{12\,857}{25\,000} = 51\%$$

$$\text{project C} = \frac{2\,000}{25\,000} = 8\%$$

For project A the total profit over its five-year life is £30 000 (£80 000 – £50 000), giving an average annual profit of £6000. The average annual profits for projects B and C are calculated in a similar manner.

It follows that the accounting rate of return is superior to the payback method in one respect; that is, it allows for differences in the useful lives of the assets being compared. For example, the calculations set out above reflect the high earnings of project B over the whole life of the project, and consequently it is ranked in preference to project A. Also, projects A and C have the same payback periods, but the accounting rate of return correctly indicates that project A is preferable to project C.

However, the accounting rate of return suffers from the serious defect that it ignores the time value of money. When the method is used in relation to a project where the cash inflows do not occur until near the end of its life, it will show the same accounting rate of return as it would for a project where the cash inflows occur early in its life, providing that the average cash inflows are the same. For this reason the accounting rate of return cannot be recommended. Nevertheless, the accounting rate of return is widely used in practice (see Exhibit 13.4). This is probably due to the fact that the annual accounting rate of return is frequently used to measure the managerial performance of different business units within a company. Therefore, managers are likely to be interested in how any new investment contributes to the business unit's overall accounting rate of return.

The effect of performance measurement on capital investment decisions

The way that the performance of a manager is measured is likely to have a profound effect on the decisions he or she will make. There is a danger that, because of the way performance is measured, a manager may be motivated to take the wrong decision and not follow the NPV rule. Consider the information presented in Exhibit 13.5 in respect of the net cash inflows and the annual reported profits or losses for projects J and K. The figures without the parentheses refer to the cash inflows whereas the figures within the parentheses refer to annual reported profit. You will see that the total cash inflows over the five year lives for projects J and K are £11 million and £5 million respectively. Both projects require an initial outlay of £5 million. Assuming a cost of capital of 10%, without undertaking any calculations it is clear that project J will have a positive NPV and project K will have a negative NPV.

If the straight line method of depreciation is used the annual depreciation for both projects will be £1 million (£5 million investment cost/5 years). Therefore the reported profits are derived from deducting the annual depreciation charge from the annual net cash inflows. For decision-making the focus is on the entire life of the projects. Our objective is to ascertain whether the present value of the cash inflows exceeds the present value of the cash outflows over the entire life of a project, and not allocate the NPV to different accounting periods as indicated by the dashed vertical lines in Exhibit 13.5. In other words we require an answer to the question will the project add value?

In contrast, a company is required to report on its performance externally at annual intervals and managerial performance is also often evaluated on an annual or more frequent basis. Evaluating managerial performance at the end of the five year project lives is clearly too long a time scale since managers are unlikely to remain in the same job for such lengthy periods. Therefore, if a manager's performance is measured using short-term criteria, such as annual profits, he or she may choose projects that have a favourable impact on short-term financial performance. Because Project J will have a negative impact on performance in its early years (i.e. it contributes losses) there is a danger that a manager who is anxious to improve his or her short-term performance might reject project J even though it has a positive impact on the performance measure in the long-term.

The reverse may happen with project K. This has a favourable impact on the short-term profit performance measure in years one and two but a negative impact in the longer-term so the manager might accept the project to improve his or her short-term performance measure.

It is thus important to avoid an excessive focus on short-term profitability measures since this can have a negative impact on long-term profitability. Emphasis should also be given to measuring a manager's contribution to an organization's long-term objectives. These issues are discussed in Chapter 20 when we shall look at performance measurement in more detail. However, at this point you should note that the way in which managerial performance is measured will influence their decisions and may motivate them to work in their own best interests, even when this is not in the best interest of the organization.

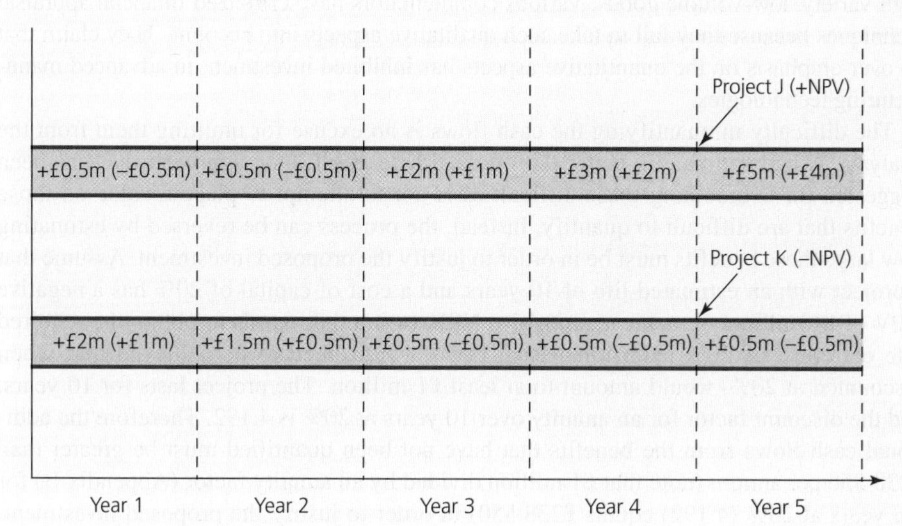

EXHIBIT 13.5

Annual net cash inflows (profits/losses) for two projects each with an initial outlay of £5 million

Qualitative factors

Not all investment projects can be described completely in terms of monetary costs and benefits (e.g. a new cafeteria for the employees or the installation of safety equipment). Nevertheless, the procedures described in this chapter may be useful by making the value placed by management on quantitative factors explicit. For example, if the present value of the cash outlays for a project is £100 000 and the benefits from the project are difficult to quantify, management must make a value judgement as to whether or not the benefits are in excess of £100 000. In the case of capital expenditure on facilities for employees, or expenditure to avoid unpleasant environmental effects from the company's manufacturing process, one can take the view that the present value of the cash outlays represents the cost to shareholders of the pursuit of goals other than the maximization of shareholders' funds. In other words, ordinary shareholders, as a group in the bargaining coalition, should know how much the pursuit of other goals is costing them.

Capital investment decisions are particularly difficult in non-profit organizations such as national and local government organizations, since it is not always possible to quantify the costs and benefits of a project. **Cost–benefit analysis (CBA)**, which is an investment appraisal technique for analysing and measuring the costs and benefits to the community of capital projects, has been developed to resolve this problem, and it seeks to determine the incidence of costs and benefits between different sectors of the community. CBA attempts to take into account all the costs and benefits that accrue from a project by defining the costs and benefits in much wider terms than those that would be included in traditional accounting measures. A wider range of factors is therefore included in the analysis than those that would be incorporated in the traditional accounting investment appraisal. For example, when CBA was applied to the appraisal of a new metro service in London attempts were made to set a monetary value on the travelling time saved by users.

There is also a danger that those aspects of a new investment that are difficult to quantify may be omitted from the financial appraisal. This applies particularly to investments in advanced manufacturing technologies that yield benefits such as improved quality and delivery times and a greater flexibility that provides the potential for low cost production of high-variety, low-volume goods. Various commentators have criticized financial appraisal techniques because they fail to take such qualitative aspects into account. They claim that an over-emphasis on the quantitative aspects has inhibited investment in advanced manufacturing technologies.

The difficulty in quantifying the cash flows is no excuse for omitting them from the analysis. A bad estimate is better than no estimate at all. One approach that has been suggested for overcoming these difficulties is not to attempt to place a value on those benefits that are difficult to quantify. Instead, the process can be reversed by estimating how large these benefits must be in order to justify the proposed investment. Assume that a project with an estimated life of 10 years and a cost of capital of 20% has a negative NPV of £1 million. To achieve a positive NPV, or in other words to obtain the required rate of return of 20%, additional cash flows would need to be achieved that when discounted at 20%, would amount to at least £1 million. The project lasts for 10 years, and the discount factor for an annuity over 10 years at 20% is 4.192. Therefore the additional cash flows from the benefits that have not been quantified must be greater than £238 550 per annum (note that £1 million divided by an annuity factor (Appendix B) for ten years at 20% (4.192) equals £238 550) in order to justify the proposed investment. Discussions should then take place to consider whether benefits that have not been quantified, such as improved flexibility, rapid customer service and market adaptability, are worth more than £238 550 per year.

The capital investment process

The capital investment process should aim to ensure that projects are accepted that contribute to achieving an organization's objectives and that are also closely related to its strategies. Strategy refers to the basis on which a firm will compete to sustain a superior level of performance. We shall focus on the identification of strategies in Chapter 15. The capital investment process entails several stages including:

1 the search for investment opportunities;
2 initial screening;
3 project authorizations;
4 controlling the capital expenditure during the installation stage;
5 post-completion audit of the cash flows.

It is essential to implement a sound system for approving capital investment proposals. Capital investment decisions frequently require the commitment of a large amount of funds for many years, and, once approval has been obtained and initial outlays have been incurred, there is normally no turning back on the decision. A detailed scrutiny of capital investment proposals by top management is therefore essential. A process should be established that encourages managers to submit investment proposals, since only by managers constantly reviewing future opportunities and threats can a company prosper in the long term. However, approval should not be merely a rubber-stamping of the managers' proposals, since there is a danger that managers' favourite proposals will be implemented when they do not provide a sound financial return. It is therefore important that top management establishes a capital investment process that both encourages managers to submit capital investment proposals and also ensures that such proposals meet the long-term objectives of the company. In addition, when capital investments have been approved and are being undertaken, it is important to implement a system of reviewing the investments. Let us now examine each of the above stages in more detail.

Search for investment opportunities

Potential investment projects are not just born – someone has to suggest them. Without a creative search of new investment opportunities, even the most sophisticated appraisal techniques are worthless. A firm's prosperity depends far more on its ability to create investments than on its ability to appraise them. Thus it is important that a firm scans the environment for potential opportunities or takes action to protect itself against potential threats. This process is closely linked to the strategies of an organization. An important task of senior management is therefore to promote a culture that encourages the search for and promotion of new investment opportunities.

Initial screening

During this stage projects are examined and subject to preliminary assessment to ascertain if they are likely to warrant further attention through the application of more sophisticated analysis. Projects that are not considered to warrant further attention are normally discarded. The preliminary assessment involves an examination of whether projects satisfy strategic criteria and conform to initial risk requirements. At this stage projects may also be subject to an assessment as to whether they satisfy simplistic financial criteria, such as meeting required payback periods. Because different criteria may be applied to different types of investments, many firms require that projects be classified by different categories. Classification also enables managers to focus their attention on those categories that are of greatest importance to the success of the organization. Typical categories include cost reduction and replacement, expansion of existing product lines, introduction of new product lines, and statutory, welfare and health and safety projects. For most large firms, those projects that meet the initial screening requirements are included in an annual **capital budget**, which is a list of projects planned for the coming year. However, it should be noted that the inclusion of a project in the capital project does not provide an authorization for the final go-ahead for the investment.

Project authorizations

Many organizations require that project proposals are presented in a formalized manner by submitting capital appropriation request forms for each project. These requests include descriptions of the projects, detailed cash flow forecasts, the investment required and a financial appraisal incorporating discounted cash flow analyses. Other financial criteria also may be presented such as the payback period and the annual accounting rates of return. Because investment decisions are of vital importance appropriation requests are generally submitted for approval to a top management committee. Companies normally set ceilings for investments so that only those projects that exceed the ceiling are submitted to the top management committee. Investments below the ceiling are normally subject to approval at lower management levels.

Controlling the capital expenditure during the installation stage

Capital expenditure is difficult to control because each investment is usually unique, and therefore no predetermined standards or past experience will be available for establishing what the cash outflows should be. When the actual capital expenditure costs are different from

Post-completion auditing within Heineken

At Heineken the Executive Board of Heineken NV (the corporate head office) encourages the conducting of post-completion audits (PCAs). It is made clear that a PCA is something that can help everyone. Another major requirement is that the objectives of the investment project must be clear from the start, as a PCA is impossible without an adequate investment proposal. Included in that proposal there should be a statement of the concrete goals of the investment. The PCA can then be conducted on the basis of those goals. In that respect the prospect of a PCA immediately heightens awareness when drawing up an investment proposal. If the goals have to be clearly stated, people will think more about the reasons and motives for the investment.

We shall now describe the content of the PCA report of one of the first PCAs carried out at Heineken Nederland, which is the Dutch regional division of Heineken NV. The PCA relates to the replacement of an old bottling line dating from 1976 at the Den Bosch brewery. The PCA-report starts with project information like the approval dates and planned investment expenditures. These are followed by a summary of the goals of the capital investment and the experience and problems in implementing the investment programme. Next, the 'outcomes' of the project, e.g. efficiency achieved, number of people employed, maintenance time, the quality of filling and working conditions, are described. The audit report then looks at the financial results and the departures from the planned expenditures. The results of the new bottling line are then compared with the planned objectives. The audit report concludes with what could be learned from the investment project.

One of the lessons learned from this PCA within Heineken Nederland was that the variables which are less easily quantified (e.g. working conditions) must be defined as far as is possible in a quantifiable form. This means that not only must the objectives be stated in the investment proposal, but they should also be stated, wherever possible, in terms which are measurable. PCAs can be classified as being oriented to:

(a) project control;

(b) improving the investment system;

(c) the performance of future projects.

A PCA of type A is used to control current investment project outlays and thus must take place during the implementation phase. However, this is similar to normal project monitoring procedures. At Heineken Nederland, as such procedures are already available, the new PCA-procedure was primarily aimed at learning from the outcomes of past projects in order to improve the selection and performance of future projects (type C). But in addition, improvements in the investment system (type B) also emerged. At Heineken Nederland a PCA is conducted some months after the end of the implementation phase of the investment project. It is still impossible to evaluate whether all the cash flow projections are actually working out; this often depends on various external circumstances. What, however, can be evaluated is whether the project budget was properly estimated, what can be improved in the implementation phase of subsequent investments, how the installation is functioning at that time and whether the expected savings and improvements seem realistic.

It will never be possible to evaluate an investment completely objectively. This leaves room for personal interpretation and perhaps portraying the results in a better light. It is therefore better to separate responsibility for the investment decision from that of the PCA. This means that the line management involved will not conduct the PCA. It is those who are most involved in the investment who have the knowledge needed to undertake a good PCA. For this reason the staff of the Planning and Control departments are also responsible for the PCA. The justification for this internal audit is based on the nation that a professional controller works autonomously and an attempt is made to establish quantifiable objectives which limit the necessary qualitative evaluations.

The procedure implies that all capital investments are not necessarily subject to a PCA and that business unit managers can be selective. Self-selection bias is, however, reduced because senior management can also ask for a PCA of a specific investment. Finally, as a result of the experiences described in this article, the Executive Board of Heineken NV has, in the context of promoting 'best practices', called for PCAs to be conducted within the entire group worldwide.

Source: Adapted from Mathijs Brantjes; Henk von Eije; Frans Eusman and Wout Prins, Post-completion auditing within Heineken, *Management Accounting (UK)*, April, 1999, pp. 20–22.

the amount originally estimated, the difference may be due to an incorrect original estimate and/or inefficiency in controlling the actual costs. Unfortunately, it is very difficult, and sometimes impossible, to isolate a variance (i.e. the difference between the actual and the estimated expenditure) into a forecasting element and an efficiency element. However, the originator of a project will have prepared an estimate and defended it at the approval stage. This estimate forms a major component in determining whether or not the project should be approved, and there are sound reasons for comparing this estimate with the actual expenditures and requiring the individual responsible to explain any variances. This comparison may also indicate inefficiencies that will enable action to be taken to avoid overspending on the uncompleted part of the project. In addition, a comparison of actual costs with estimated costs will provide an incentive for the proposers of future projects to make careful estimates, and will also provide an incentive to control the costs and the date of completion.

Comparisons should take place at periodic intervals during the installation and construction stage of the project. Reports should be prepared giving details of the percentage completion, over- or under-spending relative to the stage of completion, the estimated costs to complete compared with the original estimate, the time taken compared with the estimate for the current stage of completion, and also the estimated completion date compared with the original estimate. This information will enable management to take corrective cost-saving action such as changing the construction schedule.

Post-completion audit of cash flows

When the investment is in operation, **post-completion audits** should be undertaken whereby the actual results are compared with the estimated results that were included in the investment proposal. The comparison should be based on the same method of evaluation as was used in making the investment decision. Whenever possible, actual cash flows plus estimated cash flows for the remainder of the project's life should be compared with the cash flows that were included in the original estimate. However, the feasibility of making such a comparison will depend on the ease and cost of estimating future cash flows.

The problem is that normally no pre-set standards or past information will be available as to what the cash inflows and outflows should be, and a comparison of actual and estimated cash flows will be difficult to evaluate. Furthermore, except for the very large projects, the portion of cash flows that stem from a specific capital investment is very difficult to isolate. All one can do in such situations is to scrutinize carefully the investment at the approval stage and incorporate the estimated results into departmental operating budgets. Although the results of individual projects cannot be isolated, their combined effect can be examined as part of the conventional periodic performance review.

A post-audit of capital investment decisions is a very difficult task, and any past investment decisions that have proved to be wrong should not be interpreted in isolation. It is important to remind oneself that capital investment decisions are made under uncertainty. For example, a good decision may turn out to be unsuccessful yet may still have been the correct decision in the light of the information and alternatives available at the time. We would agree that a manager should undertake a project that costs £100 000 and has a 0.9 probability of a positive NPV of £20 000 and a 0.1 probability of a negative NPV of £5000. However, if the event with a 0.1 probability occurred, a post-completion audit would suggest that the investment has been undesirable.

Care should be taken to ensure that post-audits are not conducted as recriminatory 'post-mortems'. Adopting such an approach can discourage initiative and produce a policy of over-caution. There is a danger that managers will submit only safe investment proposals. The problem is likely to be reduced if managers know their selections will be fairly judged.

In spite of all the problems a post-audit comparison should be undertaken. A record of past performance and mistakes is one way of improving future performance and ensuring that fewer mistakes are made. In addition, the fact that the proposers of capital investment projects are aware that their estimates will be compared with actual results encourages them to exercise restraint and submit more thorough and realistic appraisals of future investment projects. The survey evidence indicates that post-audits are used by the majority of UK companies. A survey by Arnold and Hatzopoulos (2000) reported that 28% of the surveyed companies always, and a further 59% sometimes, conducted post-audits of major capital expenditure.

Summary

The following items relate to the learning objectives listed at the beginning of the chapter.

- **Explain the opportunity cost of an investment.**

  The rates of return that are available from investments in financial markets in securities with different levels of risk (e.g. company shares, company and government bonds) represent the opportunity cost of an investment. In other words, if cash is invested in a capital project it cannot be invested elsewhere to earn a return. A firm should therefore only invest in projects that yield a return in excess of the opportunity cost of investment.

- **Distinguish between compounding and discounting.**

  The process of converting cash invested today at a specific interest rate into a future value is known as compounding. Discounting is the opposite of compounding and refers to the process of converting cash to be received in the future into the value at the present time. The resulting present value is called the discounted present value.

- **Explain the concepts of net present value (NPV), internal rate of return (IRR), payback method and accounting rate of return (ARR).**

  Both NPV and IRR are methods of determining whether a project yields a return in excess of an equal risk investment in traded financial securities. A positive NPV provides an absolute value of the amount by which an investment exceeds the return available from an alternative investment in financial securities of equal risk. Conversely, a negative value indicates the amount by which an investment fails to match an equal risk investment in financial securities. In contrast, the IRR indicates the true percentage return from an investment after taking into account the time value of money. To ascertain whether an investment should be undertaken, the percentage internal rate of return on investment should be compared with the returns available from investing in equal risk in financial securities. Investing in all projects that have positive NPV's or IRR's in excess of the opportunity cost of capital should maximize shareholder value. The payback method is the length of time that is required for a stream of cash proceeds from an investment to recover the original cash outflow required by the investment. The ARR expresses the annual average profits arising from a project as a percentage return on the average investment required for the project.

- **Calculate NPV, IRR, the payback period and ARR.**

  The NPV is calculated by discounting the net cash inflows from a project and deducting the investment outlay. The IRR is calculated by ascertaining the discount rate that will cause the NPV of a project to be zero. The payback period is calculated by adding up the cash flows expected in successive years until the total is equal to the original outlay. The ARR is calculated by dividing the average annual profits estimated from a project by the average investment cost. The calculation of NPV and IRR was illustrated using Example 13.1 and Examples 13.4 and 13.5 were used to illustrate the calculations of the payback period and the ARR.

- **Justify the superiority of NPV over the IRR.**

  NPV is considered to be theoretically superior to IRR because: (a) unlike the NPV method the IRR method cannot be guaranteed to rank mutually exclusive projects correctly; (b) the percentage returns generated by the IRR method can be misleading when choosing between alternatives; (c) the IRR method makes incorrect reinvestment assumptions by assuming that the interim cash flows can be reinvested at the IRR rather than the cost of capital; and (d) where unconventional cash flows occur multiple IRR's are possible.

- **Explain the limitations of payback and ARR.**

  The major limitations of the payback method are that it ignores the time value of money and it does not take into account the cash flows that are earned after the payback period. The ARR also fails to take into account the time value of money and relies on a percentage return rather than an absolute value.

- **Justify why the payback and ARR methods are widely used in practice.**

  The payback method is frequently used in practice because (a) it is considered useful when firms face liquidity constraints and require a fast repayment of their investments; (b) it serves as a simple first-level screening device that identifies those projects that should be subject to more rigorous investigations; and (c) it provides a rough measure of risk, based on the assumption that the longer it takes for a project to pay for itself, the riskier it is. The ARR is a widely-used financial accounting measure of managerial and company performance. Therefore, managers are likely to be interested in how any new investment contributes to the business unit's overall accounting rate of return.

- **Describe the effect of performance measurement on capital investment decisions.**

  Managerial and company performance is normally evaluated using short-term financial criteria whereas investment appraisal decisions should be based on the cash flows over the whole life of the projects. Thus, the way that performance is evaluated can have a profound influence on investment decisions and there is a danger that managers will make decisions on the basis of an investment's impact on the short-term financial performance evaluation criteria rather than using the NPV decision rule.

- **Describe the capital investment process.**
  The capital investment process entails several stages including: (a) the search for investment opportunities; (b) initial screening of the projects; (c) project authorizations; (d) controlling the capital expenditure during the installation stage; and (e) a post-completion audit of the cash flows. You should refer to the end of Chapter 13 for an explanation of each of these stages.

Note

1 Consider a project that costs £10 000 and has a life of four years and an estimated scrap value of £2000. The following diagram illustrates why the project's scrap value is added to the initial outlay to calculate the average capital employed. You can see that at the mid-point of the project's life the capital employed is equal to £6000 (i.e. ½ (10 000 + £2000)).

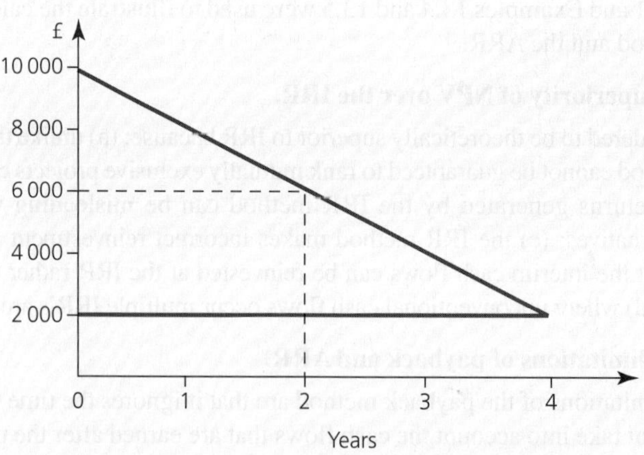

Key terms and concepts

accounting rate of return (p. 511)
capital budget (p. 517)
capital budgeting process (p. 494)
compounding interest (p. 496)
cost–benefit analysis (p. 515)
cost of capital (p. 496)
discount rate of return (p. 501)
discounted cash flow (p. 496)
discounted payback method (p. 510)
discounted present value (p. 497)
discounted rate (p. 496)
discounting (p. 497)
interest rate (p. 496)
internal rate of return (p. 501)
minimum required rate of return (p. 496)
mutually exclusive projects (p. 505)
net present value (p. 498)
opportunity cost of an investment (p. 496)
payback method (p. 509)
post-completion audits (p. 519)
present value (p. 497)
profitability index (p. 508)
return on capital employed (p. 511)
return on investment (p. 511)
risk-free gilt-edged securities (p. 495)
time value of money (p. 498)

Recommended reading

The financing of capital projects is normally part of a corporate finance course. If you wish to undertake further reading relating to the financing of capital investments you should refer to Pike and Neale (2003) or Brealey and Myers (2003). For a discussion of the issues relating to appraising investments in advanced manufacturing technologies you should read the publications by Currie (1990, 1991a,b) and Sizer and Motteram, Chapter 15 (1996).

Key examination points

A common mistake is a failure to distinguish between relevant and irrelevant cash flows. Remember to include only incremental cash flows in a DCF analysis. Depreciation and reapportionments of overheads should not be included.

Another common error is to use the wrong present-value table. With unequal annual cash flows, use Appendix A (the discount factors will be less that 1), and if the cash flows are the same each year, use Appendix B (the discount factors will be greater than 1 from year 2 onwards). If you are required to evaluate mutually exclusive projects, use NPV, since IRR can give incorrect rankings. Where IRR calculations are required, check that the cash flows are conventional. For unconventional cash flows it is necessary to calculate more than one IRR. Normally, very accurate calculations of the IRR will not be required, and an approximate answer using the interpolation method should be appropriate.

Assessment material

Review questions

The review questions are short questions that enable you to assess your understanding of the main topics included in the chapter. The numbers in parentheses provide you with the page numbers to refer to if you cannot answer a specific question.

Review problems

The review problems are more complex and require you to relate and apply the chapter content to various business problems. The problems are graded by their level of difficulty. The multiple-choice questions are the least demanding and normally take less than 10 minutes to complete. Fully worked solutions to the review problems are provided in a separate section at the end of the book. For those questions in the white box the worked solutions are provided in the *Student's Manual* accompanying this book. Further review problems for this chapter are available on the accompanying website www.drury-online.com. The answers to these problems are available for lecturers on the lecturer's password protected section of the website.

Case studies

The website also includes over 30 case study problems. A list of these cases is provided in Part Seven of this book. The Rawhide Development Company is a case study that is relevant to the content of this chapter.

Review questions

13.1 What are the objectives of capital budgeting? (*p. 494*)

13.2 What is meant by the opportunity cost of an investment? What role does it play in capital investment decisions? (*pp. 495–96*)

13.3 Distinguish between compounding and discounting. (*pp. 496–97*)

13.4 Explain what is meant by the term 'time value of money'. (*p. 498*)

13.5 Describe the concept of net present value (NPV). (*p. 498*)

13.6 Explain what is meant by the internal rate of return (IRR). (*p. 501*)

13.7 Distinguish between independent and mutually exclusive projects. (*pp. 504–05*)

13.8 Explain the theoretical arguments for preferring NPV to IRR when choosing among mutually exclusive projects. (*pp. 505–08*)

13.9 Why might managers choose to use IRR in preference to NPV? *(p. 510)*

13.10 What is the profitability index? *(pp. 508–09)*

13.11 Describe the payback method. What are its main strengths and weaknesses? *(pp. 509–10)*

13.12 Describe the accounting rate of return. What are its main strengths and weaknesses? *(p. 513)*

13.13 Distinguish between the payback method and discounted payback method. *(p. 510)*

13.14 What impact can the way in which a manager's performance is measured have on capital investment decisions? *(p. 514)*

13.15 Describe the stages involved in the capital investment process. *(pp. 516–20)*

13.16 Explain what a post-completion audit is and how it can provide useful benefits. *(pp. 519–20)*

Review problems

13.17 Intermediate

Dalby is currently considering an investment that gives a positive net present value of £3664 at 15%. At a discount rate of 20% it has a negative net present value of £21 451. What is the internal rate of return of this investment?

A 15.7%
B 16.0%
C 19.3%
D 19.9%.

ACCA Paper 1.2 – Financial information for Management

13.18 Intermediate

Ayr is planning on paying £300 into a fund on a monthly basis starting 3 months from now, for 12 months. The interest earned will be at a rate of 3% per month.

What is the present value of these payments?

A £2816
B £2733
C £2541
D £2986.

ACCA Paper 1.2 – Financial information for Management

13.19 Intermediate: Calculation of payback, ARR and NPV

The following data are supplied relating to two investment projects, only one of which may be selected:

	Project A (£)	Project B (£)
Initial capital expenditure	50 000	50 000
Profit (loss) year 1	25 000	10 000
2	20 000	10 000
3	15 000	14 000
4	10 000	26 000
Estimated resale value at end of year 4	10 000	10 000

Notes

1 Profit is calculated after deducting straight-line depreciation.

2 The cost of capital is 10%.

Required:

(a) Calculate for each project:

(i) average annual rate of return on average capital invested;

(ii) payback period;

(iii) net present value.

(12 marks)

(b) Briefly discuss the relative merits of the three methods of evaluation mentioned in (a) above.

(10 marks)

(c) Explain which project you would recommend for acceptance.

(3 marks)

(Total 25 marks)

AAT

13.20 **Intermediate**

A machine with a purchase price of £14 000 is estimated to eliminate manual operations costing £4000 per year. The machine will last five years and have no residual value at the end of its life.

You are required to calculate:

(a) the internal rate of return (IRR);

(b) the level of annual saving necessary to achieve a 12% IRR;

(c) the net present value if the cost of capital is 10%.

13.21 **Advanced: Calculation of payback, ARR and NPV**

Stadler is an ambitious young executive who has recently been appointed to the position of financial director of Paradis plc, a small listed company. Stadler regards this appointment as a temporary one, enabling him to gain experience before moving to a larger organization. His intention is to leave Paradis plc in three years' time, with its share price standing high. As a consequence, he is particularly concerned that the reported profits of Paradis plc should be as high as possible in his third and final year with the company.

Paradis plc has recently raised £350 000 from a rights issue, and the directors are considering three ways of using these funds. Three projects (A, B and C) are being considered, each involving the immediate purchase of equipment costing £350 000. One project only can be undertaken, and the equipment for each project will have a useful life equal to that of the project, with no scrap value. Stadler favours project C because it is expected to show the highest accounting profit in the third year. However, he does not wish to reveal his real reasons for favouring project C, and so, in his report to the chairman, he recommends project C because it shows the highest internal rate of return. The following summary is taken from his report:

Project	Net cash flows (£000) Years									Internal rate of return (%)
	0	1	2	3	4	5	6	7	8	
A	−350	100	110	104	112	138	160	180	–	27.5
B	−350	40	100	210	260	160	–	–	–	26.4
C	−350	200	150	240	40	–	–	–	–	33.0

The chairman of the company is accustomed to projects being appraised in terms of payback and accounting rate of return, and he is consequently suspicious of the use of internal rate of return as a method of project selection. Accordingly, the chairman has asked for an independent report on the choice of project. The company's cost of capital is 20% and a policy of straight-line depreciation is used to write off the cost of equipment in the financial statements.

Requirements:

(a) Calculate the payback period for each project.

(3 marks)

(b) Calculate the accounting rate of return for each project.

(5 marks)

(c) Prepare a report for the chairman with supporting calculations indicating which project should be preferred by the ordinary shareholders of Paradis plc.

(12 marks)

(d) Discuss the assumptions about the reactions of the stock market that are implicit in Stadler's choice of project C.

(5 marks)

Note: ignore taxation. *(Total 25 marks)*

ICAEW P2 Financial Management

13.22 Advanced: Calculation of NPV and IRR, a discussion of the inconsistency in ranking and a calculation of the cost of capital at which the ranking changes

A company is considering which of two mutually exclusive projects it should undertake. The finance director thinks that the project with the higher NPV should be chosen whereas the managing director thinks that the one with the higher IRR should be undertaken especially as both projects have the same initial outlay and length of life. The company anticipates a cost of capital of 10% and the net after tax cash flows of the projects are as follows:

	Project X (£000)	Project Y (£000)
Year 0	−200	−200
1	35	218
2	80	10
3	90	10
4	75	4
5	20	3

You are required to:

(a) calculate the NPV and IRR of each project;

(6 marks)

(b) recommend, with reasons, which project you would undertake (if either);

(4 marks)

(c) explain the inconsistency in ranking of the two projects in view of the remarks of the directors;

(4 marks)

(d) identify the cost of capital at which your recommendation in (b) would be reversed.

(6 marks)
(Total 20 marks)
CIMA Stage 3 Management Accounting Techniques

13.23 Advanced: Evaluation of a proposed investment of computer integrated manufacturing equipment and a discussion of NPV and ARR

Abert, the production manager of Blom plc, a manufacturer of precision tools, has recently attended a major international exhibition on Computer Integrated Manufacturing (CIM). He has read of the improvements in product quality and profitability achieved by companies which have switched to this new technology. In particular, his Japanese competitors are believed to use CIM equipment extensively. Abert is sufficiently concerned about his company's future to commission a report from Saint-Foix Ltd, a vendor of CIM equipment, as to the appropriateness of utilising CIM for all his manufacturing operations.

The report, which has recently been prepared, suggests that the following costs and benefits will accrue to Blom plc as a result of investing in an appropriate CIM system:

(1) *Costs of implementing CIM*

(i) Capital equipment costs will be £40m. The equipment will have an estimated life of 10 years, after which time its disposal value will be £10m.

(ii) Proper use of the equipment will require the substantial re-training of current employees. As a result of the necessary changes in the production process, and the time spent on retraining, Blom plc will lose production (and sales) in its first two years of implementation. The lost production (and sales) will cost the company £10m per annum.

(iii) The annual costs of writing software and maintaining the computer equipment will be £4m.

(2) *Benefits of implementing CIM*

(i) The use of CIM will enhance the quality of Blom plc's products. This will lead to less reworking of products, and a consequent reduction in warranty costs. The annual cost savings are expected to be £12m per annum.

(ii) The CIM equipment will use less floor space than the existing machinery. As a result one existing factory will no longer be needed. It is estimated that the factory can be let at an annual rental of £2m.

(iii) Better planning and flow of work will result in an immediate reduction in the existing levels of working capital from £13m to £8m.

The directors of Blom plc currently require all investments to generate a positive net present value at a cost of capital of 15% *and* to show an accounting rate of return in the first year of at least 15%. You may assume that all cash flows arise at the end of the year, except for those relating to the equipment and re-training costs, and the reduction in working capital. It is Blom plc's intention to capitalise re-training costs for management accounting purposes. Requirements:

(a) Determine whether Blom plc should invest in the CIM technology on the basis of its existing investment criteria.

(10 marks)

(b) Discuss possible reasons as to why Blom plc currently requires its long-term investments to meet both the net present value *and* the accounting rate of return criteria.

(8 marks)

(c) Discuss the additional factors Blom plc should consider when deciding whether to switch to CIM technology.

(7 marks)
(Total 25 marks)
ICAEW P2 Financial Management

Review problems (with answers in the Student's Manual)

13.24 Intermediate

An investment project has the following expected cash flows over its economic life of three years:

	(£)
Year 0	(142 700)
1	51 000
2	62 000
3	73 000

Required:

(i) Calculate the net present value (NPV) of the project at discount rates of 0%, 10% and 20% respectively.

(ii) Draw a graph of the project NPVs calculated in (i) and use the graph to estimate, and clearly indicate, the project internal rate of return (IRR) to the nearest integer percentage.

(8 marks)
ACCA Foundation Stage Paper 3

13.25 Advanced: Calculation of payback, accounting rate of return and NPV

P, a multinational organization, is currently appraising a major capital investment project which will revolutionize its business. This investment involves the installation of an Intranet. *[An Intranet is a private Internet reserved for use by employees and/or customers who have been given the authority and passwords necessary to use that network. It is a private network environment built around Internet technologies and standards.]*

You have recently been appointed as the Management Accountant for this project and have been charged with the responsibility of preparing the financial evaluation of the proposed investment. You have carried out some initial investigations and find that management currently uses a target accounting rate of return of 25% and a target payback period of four years as the criteria for the acceptance or rejection of major capital investments.

You propose to use the net present value method of project appraisal and, having carried out some further investigations, you ascertain the following information for the project:

	£000
Initial outlay	2000
Cash savings:	
Years 1 to 3	400 per annum
Years 4 to 5	500 per annum
Years 6 to 8	450 per annum
Years 9 to 10	400 per annum

At the end of the project's life, no residual value is expected for the project.

The company's cost of capital is 15% per annum. All cash savings are assumed to occur at the end of each year.

Ignore taxation and inflation.

Required:

As Management Accountant for this project,

(a) write a report to the management of P which incorporates the following:

(i) a full analysis and evaluation of the existing methods of project appraisal and of your proposed method of project appraisal;

(ii) a recommendation on a purely financial basis as to whether or not the project should be undertaken;

(iii) a discussion of the difficulties associated with the net present value method when appraising this type of investment;

(15 marks)

(b) describe how you would undertake a post-completion appraisal for this project and discuss the benefits and drawbacks which the management of P might expect when undertaking such an exercise.

(10 marks)

(Total 25 marks)

CIMA Management Accountant – Decision Making

13.26 **Advanced: NPV calculation and identification of incremental cash flows**

LKL plc is a manufacturer of sports equipment and is proposing to start project VZ, a new product line. This project would be for the four years from the start of year 20X1 to the end of 20X4. There would be no production of the new product after 20X4.

You have recently joined the company's accounting and finance team and have been provided with the following information relating to the project:

Capital expenditure

A feasibility study costing £45 000 was completed and paid for last year. This study recommended that the company buy new plant and machinery costing £1 640 000 to be paid for at the start of the project. The machinery and plant would be depreciated at 20% of cost per annum and sold during year 20X5 for £242 000 receivable at the end of 20X5.

As a result of the proposed project it was also recommended that an old machine be sold for cash at the start of the project for its book value of £16 000. This machine had been scheduled to be sold for cash at the end of 20X2 for its book value of £12 000.

Other data relating to the new product line:

	20X1 (£000)	20X2 (£000)	20X3 (£000)	20X4 (£000)
Sales	1000	1300	1500	1800
Debtors (at the year end)	84	115	140	160
Lost contribution on existing products	30	40	40	36
Purchases	400	500	580	620
Creditors (at the year end)	80	100	110	120
Payments to sub-contractors,	60	90	80	80
including prepayments of	5	10	8	8
Net tax payable associated with this project	96	142	174	275
Fixed overheads and advertising:				
With new line	1330	1100	990	900
Without new line	1200	1000	900	800

Notes

- The year-end debtors and creditors are received and paid in the following year.
- The next tax payable has taken into account the effect of any capital allowances. There is a one year time-lag in the payment of tax.
- The company's cost of capital is a constant 10% per annum.
- It can be assumed that operating cash flows occur at the year end.
- Apart from the data and information supplied there are no other financial implications after 20X4.

Labour costs

From the start of the project, three employees currently working in another department and earning £12 000 each would be transferred to work on the new product line, and an employee currently earning £20 000 would be promoted to work on the new line at a salary of £30 000 per annum. The effect on the transfer of employees from the other department to the project is included in the lost contribution figures given above.

As a direct result of introducing the new product line, four employees in another department currently earning £10 000 each would have to be made redundant at the end of 20X1 and paid redundancy pay of £15 500 each at the end of 20X2.

Agreement had been reached with the trade unions for wages and salaries to be increased by 5% each year from the start of 20X2.

Material costs

Material XNT which is already in stock, and for which the company has no other use, cost the company £6400 last year, and can be used in the manufacture of the new product. If it is not used the company would have to dispose of it at a cost to the company of £2000 in 20X1.

Material XPZ is also in stock and will be used on the new line. It cost the company £11 500 some years ago. The company has no other use for it, but could sell it on the open market for £3000 in 20X1.

Required

(a) Prepare and present a cash flow budget for project VZ, for the period 20X1 and 20X5 and calculate the net present value of the project.

(14 marks)

(b) Write a short report for the board of directors which:

  (i) explains why certain figures which were provided in (a) were excluded from your cash flow budget, and

  (ii) advises them on whether or not the project should be undertaken, and lists other factors which would also need to be considered.

(7 marks)

(Total 21 marks)

ACCA Paper 8 Managerial Finance

13.27 Advanced: Comparison of NPV and IRR and relationship between profits and NPV

Khan Ltd is an importer of novelty products. The directors are considering whether to introduce a new product, expected to have a very short economic life. Two alternative methods of promoting the new product are available, details of which are as follows:

Alternative 1 would involve heavy initial advertising and the employment of a large number of agents. The directors expect that an immediate cash outflow of £100 000 would be required (the cost of advertising) which would produce a net cash inflow after one year of £255 000. Agents' commission, amounting to £157 500, would have to be paid at the end of two years.

Alternative 2 would involve a lower outlay on advertising (£50 000, payable immediately), and no use of agents. It would produce net cash inflows of zero after one year and £42 000 at the end of each of the subsequent two years.

Mr Court, a director of Khan Ltd, comments, 'I generally favour the payback method for choosing between investment alternatives such as these. However, I am worried that the advertising expenditure under the second alternative will reduce our reported profit next year by an amount not compensated by any net revenues from sale of the product in that year. For that reason I do not think we should even consider the second alternative.'

The cost of capital of Khan Ltd is 20% per annum. The directors do not expect capital or any other resource to be in short supply during the next three years.

You are required to:

(a) calculate the net present values and estimate the internal rates of return of the two methods of promoting the new product;

(10 marks)

(b) advise the directors of Khan Ltd which, if either, method of promotion they should adopt, explaining the reasons for your advice and noting any additional information you think would be helpful in making the decision; *(8 marks)*

(c) comment on the views expressed by Mr Court. *(7 marks)*

Ignore taxation.

(Total 25 marks)
ICAEW Financial Management

13.28 **Advanced: NPV evaluation of alternative options**

All of the 100 accountants employed by X Ltd are offered the opportunity to attend six training courses per year. Each course lasts for several days and requires the delegates to travel to a specially selected hotel for the training. The current costs incurred for each course are:

Delegate costs:

	£ per delegate per course
Travel	200
Accommodation, food and drink	670
	870

It is expected that the current delegate costs will increase by 5% per annum.

Course costs:

	£ per course
Room hire	1 500
Trainers	6 000
Course material	2 000
Equipment hire	1 500
Course administration	750
	11 750

It is expected that the current course costs will increase by 2.5% per annum.

The Human Resources Director of X Ltd is concerned at the level of costs that these courses incur and has recently read an article about the use of the Internet for the delivery of training courses (e-learning). She decided to hire an external consultant at a cost of £5000 to advise the company on how to implement an e-learning solution. The consultant prepared a report which detailed the costs of implementing and running an e-learning solution:

	Notes	£
Computer hardware	(1)	1 500 000
Software licences	(2)	35 000 per annum
Technical Manager	(3)	30 000 per annum
Camera and sound crew	(4)	4 000 per course
Trainers and course material	(5)	2 000 per course
Broadband connection	(6)	300 per delegate per annum

Notes

(1) The computer hardware will be depreciated on a straight-line basis over five years. The scrap value at the end of the five years is expected to be £50 000.

(2) The company would sign a software licence agreement which fixes the annual software licence fee for five years. This fee is payable in advance.

(3) An employee working in the IT Department currently earning £20 000 per annum will be promoted to Technical Manager for this project. This employee's position will be replaced. The salary of the Technical Manager is expected to increase by 6% per annum.

(4) The company supplying the camera and sound crew for recording the courses for Internet delivery has agreed to hold its current level of pricing for the first two years but then it will increase costs by 6% per annum. All courses will be recorded in the first quarter of the year of delivery.

(5) The trainers will charge a fixed fee of £2000 per course for the delivery and course material in the first year and expect to increase this by 6% per annum thereafter. The preparation of the course material and the recording of the trainers delivering the courses will take place in the first quarter of the year of delivery.

(6) All of the accountants utilizing the training courses will be offered £300 towards broadband costs which will allow them to access the courses from home. They will claim this expense annually in arrears. Broadband costs are expected to decrease by 5% per annum after the first year as it becomes more widely used by Internet users.

X Ltd uses a 14% cost of capital to appraise projects of this nature.

Ignore taxation.

Required:

As the Management Accountant for X Ltd,

(a) prepare a financial evaluation of the options available to the company and advise the directors on the best course of action to take, from a purely financial point of view; (Your answer should state any assumptions you have made.)

(16 marks)

(b) (i) using the annual equivalent technique, calculate the breakeven number of delegates per annum taking each of the six e-learning courses that is required to justify the implementation of the e-learning solution;

(Note that you should assume that the number of delegates taking the e-learning courses will be the same in each of the five years.)

(6 marks)

(ii) comment on the implications of the breakeven number you have calculated in your answer to (b) (i).

(3 marks)

(Total 25 marks)

CIMA Management Accounting – Decision Making

13.29 Advanced: Evaluation of alternative options based on NPVs

CAF plc is a large multinational organization that manufactures a range of highly engineered products/components for the aircraft and vehicle industries. The directors are considering the future of one of the company's factories in the UK which manufactures product A. Product A is coming to the end of its life but another two years' production is planned. This is expected to produce a net cash inflow of £3 million next year and £2.3 million in the product's final year.

Product AA

CAF plc has already decided to replace product A with product AA which will be ready to go into production in two years' time. Product AA is expected to have a life of eight years. It could be made either at the UK factory under consideration or in an Eastern European factory owned by CAF plc. The UK factory is located closer to the markets and therefore if product AA is made in Eastern Europe, the company will incur extra transport costs of £10 per unit. Production costs will be the same in both countries. Product AA will require additional equipment and staff will need training; this will cost £6 million at either location. 200 000 units of product AA will be made each year and each unit will generate a net cash inflow of £25 before extra transport costs. If product AA is made in the UK, the factory will be closed and sold at the end of the product's life.

Product X

Now, however, the directors are considering a further possibility: product X could be produced at the UK factory and product AA at the Eastern European factory. Product X must be introduced in one year's time and will remain in production for three years. If it is introduced, the manufacture of product A will have to cease a year earlier than planned. If this happened, output of product A would be increased by 12.5% to maximum capacity next year, its last year, to build stock prior to the product's withdrawal. The existing staff would be transferred to product X.

The equipment needed to make product X would cost £4 million. 50 000 units of product X would be made in its first year; after that, production would rise to 75 000 units a year. Product X would earn a net cash flow of £70 per unit. After three years' production of product X, the UK factory would be closed and sold. (Product AA would not be transferred back to the factory in the UK at that stage; production would continue at the Eastern European site.)

Sale of factory

It is expected that the UK factory could be sold for £5.5 million at any time between the beginning of year 2 and the end of year 10. If the factory is sold, CAF plc will make redundancy payments of £2 million and the sale of equipment will raise £350 000.

CAF plc's cost of capital is 5% each year.

Required:

(a) Prepare calculations that show which of the three options is financially the best.

(15 marks)

(b) The directors of CAF plc are unsure whether their estimates are correct. Calculate and discuss the sensitivity of your choice of option in (a) to:

(i) changes in transport costs;

(3 marks)

(ii) changes in the selling price of the factory.

(3 marks)

(c) Briefly discuss the business issues that should be considered before relocating to another country.

(4 marks)

(Total 25 marks)

CIMA Management Accounting – Decision Making

13.30 **Advanced: NPV calculations for alternative options**

Amber plc operates a daily return high speed train service between the UK and mainland Europe, via the channel tunnel. In an attempt to reduce overheads, the company is considering using an outside supplier to take over responsibility for all on-train catering services. Amber invited tenders for a five-year contract, and at the same time the senior management accountant drafted a schedule of costs for in-house provision of an equivalent service. This cost schedule, together with the details of the lowest price tender which was received, are given below. (See Table 1 and additional information.)

TABLE 1 *In-House Provision of Train Catering Services Schedule of Costs, Amber plc*

Variable Costs	Pence Per £ Sales
Direct material	55
Variable overhead	12
Fixed Costs (allocated to products)	
Labour (Year 1)	10
Purchase/storage management	3
Depreciation (catering equipment)	4
Insurance	2
Total cost	86

The train service operates 360 days per year and a single restaurant carriage is adequate to service the catering needs of a train carrying up to 600 passengers. The tendered contract (and the in-house schedule of costs) is for the provision of one catering carriage per train. Past sales data indicates that 45% of passengers will use the catering service, spending an average of £4.50 each per single journey, or £9.00 per return journey. This is expected to remain unchanged over the next five years, unless Amber invests in quality improvements.

Statistical forecasts of the level of demand for the train service, under differing average weather conditions and average exchange rates over the next five years are shown in Table 2.

TABLE 2 *Forecast Passenger Figures (per single journey)*

	UK weather conditions		
Exchange rate Euro/£	Poor	Reasonable	Good
1.52	500	460	420
1.54	550	520	450
1.65	600	580	500

The differing weather conditions are all assumed to be equally likely.

Based upon historical trends, the probability of each different exchange rate occurring is estimated as follows:

Rate Euro/£	Probability
1.52	0.2
1.54	0.5
1.65	0.3

Additional information

1 Labour costs are expected to rise at a rate of 5% per year over the next five years.

2 Variable costs per £ sales are expected to remain unchanged over the next five years.

3 Some catering equipment will need to be replaced at the end of Year 2 at a cost of £500 000. This would increase the depreciation charge on catering equipment to 5 pence per £ sales. The equipment value at the end of Year 5 is estimated to be £280 000.

4 The outside supplier (lowest price tender) has agreed to purchase immediately (for cash) the existing catering equipment owned by Amber plc at a price equal to the current book value i.e. £650 000. The supplier would charge Amber a flat fee of £250 per day for the provision of this catering service, and Amber would receive 5% of gross catering receipts where these exceeded an average of £2200 per day in each 360 day period. The quality of the catering service is expected to be unaffected by the contracting out.

5 In the event of Amber deciding to contract out the catering, the following fixed costs will be saved:

Depreciation	£35 000 per year
Purchasing/storage costs	£18 000 per year
Insurance	£3 000 per year
Labour costs	£74 844 (Year 1)

6 The cost of capital for Amber plc is 12%.

Assume that all cash flows occur at the end of each year. Taxation may be ignored in answering this question.

Required:

(a) Calculate the expected number of passengers per single journey for the train service.

(5 marks)

(b) Draft a table of annual cash flows and, using discounted cash flow analysis, determine which of the two alternatives (in-house provision or contracting out) is preferred.

(16 marks)

(c) Calculate and comment upon the financial effect on the decision of a forecast 10% increase in the *number* of passengers purchasing food and beverages on each train if the in-house catering service were to be improved. Any such improvement would require Amber investing £10 000 per year over five years on staff training.

(7 marks)

(d) Comment on the limitations of using demand forecasts, such as that given in Table 2, for the purposes of the decision in question.

(5 marks)

(e) Identify and critically comment upon three non-financial factors which need to be taken into account when a business is considering this type of decision.

(7 marks)
(Total 40 marks)

Capital investment decisions: 2

14

In the previous chapter the major techniques that can be used for evaluating capital investment decisions were introduced and their relative merits were assessed. To simplify the discussion, we made a number of assumptions: first, that cash inflows and outflows were known with certainty; secondly that sufficient funds were available to enable acceptance of all those projects with positive net present values; thirdly, that firms operated in an environment where there was no taxation and no inflation; and finally, that the cost of capital was the risk-free rate.

In this chapter we shall relax these assumptions and discuss how capital investment techniques can be applied to more complicated situations. Many of the topics included in this chapter are more appropriate to a second year management accounting course. Also some of the topics may be incorporated in a corporate finance course rather than a management accounting course. Therefore, you should check whether the topics are included in your course curriculum prior to reading this chapter.

LEARNING OBJECTIVES

After studying this chapter, you should be able to:

- evaluate mutually exclusive projects with unequal lives;
- explain capital rationing and select the optimum combination of investments when capital is rationed for a single period;
- calculate the incremental taxation payments arising from a proposed investment;
- describe the two approaches for adjusting for inflation when appraising capital projects;
- explain how risk-adjusted discount rates are calculated;
- identify and describe the traditional methods of measuring risk.

The evaluation of mutually exclusive investments with unequal lives

The application of the net present value method is complicated when a choice must be made between two or more projects, where the projects have unequal lives. A perfect comparison requires knowledge about future alternatives that will be available for the period of the difference in the lives of the projects that are being considered. Let us look at the situation in Example 14.1.

In Example 14.1 it is assumed that both machines produce exactly the same output. Therefore only cash outflows will be considered, because revenue cash inflows are assumed to be the same whichever alternative is selected. Consequently our objective is to choose the alternative with the lower present value of cash outflows. Revenue cash inflows should only be included in the analysis if they differ for each alternative. Suppose we compute the present value (PV) of the cash outflows for each alternative.

	End of year cash flows (£000)				
Machine	Year 0	Year 1	Year 2	Year 3	PV at 10%
X	1200	240	240	240	1796.832
Y	600	360	360		1224.78

Machine Y appears to be the more acceptable alternative, but the analysis is incomplete because we must consider what will happen at the end of year 2 if machine Y is chosen. For example, if the life of the task to be performed by the machines is in excess of three years, it will be necessary to replace machine Y at the end of year 2; whereas if machine X is chosen, replacement will be deferred until the end of year 3. We shall consider the following methods of evaluating projects with unequal lives:

1. Evaluate the alternatives over an interval equal to the lowest common multiple of the lives of the alternatives under consideration.
2. Equivalent annual cash flow method by which the cash flows are converted into an equivalent annual annuity.
3. Estimate a terminal value for one of the alternatives.

1. Lowest common multiple method

Assume that the life of the task to be performed by the machines is a considerable period of time, say in excess of six years. Consequently, both machines will be replaced at the end of their useful lives. If machine X is replaced by an identical machine then it will be replaced every three years, whereas machine Y will be replaced every two years. A correct analysis therefore requires that a sequence of decisions be evaluated over a common time horizon so that the analysis of each alternative will be comparable. The common time horizon can be determined by setting the time horizon equal to the **lowest common multiple** of the lives of the alternatives under consideration. In Example 14.1, where the lives of the alternatives are two and three years, the lowest common multiple is six years. The analysis for the sequence of replacements over a six-year period is as follows:

EXAMPLE 14.1

The Bothnia Company is choosing between two machines, X and Y. They are designed differently but have identical capacity and do exactly the same job. Machine X costs £1 200 000 and will last three years, costing £240 000 per year to run. Machine Y is a cheaper model costing £600 000 but will last only two years and costs £360 000 per year to run. The cost of capital is 10%. Which machine should the firm purchase?

	End-of-year cash flows (£000)						
	0	1	2	3	4	5	6
Sequence of type X machines							
Capital investment	1200			1200			
Operating costs		240	240	240	240	240	240
PV at 10%	–3146.76						
Sequence of type Y machines							
Capital investment	600		600		600		
Operating costs		360	360	360	360	360	360
PV at 10%	–3073.44						

By year 6 machine X is replaced twice and machine Y three times. At this point the alternatives are comparable, and a replacement must be made in year 6 regardless of the initial choice of X or Y. We can therefore compare the present value of the cost of these two sequences of machines. Thus it is better to invest in a sequence of type Y machines, since this alternative has the lowest present value of cash outflows. Note that another decision must be made in year 6. This will depend on the sequence of machines that is then available and how much longer is the life of the task that is to be performed by the machines.

2. Equivalent annual cash flow method

Comparing projects over a span of time equal to the lowest common multiple of their individual life spans is often tedious. Instead, we can use the second method – the **equivalent annual cash flow method**. The costs for the different lives of machines X and Y are made comparable if they are converted into an equivalent annuity. The present value of the costs of machine X is £1 796 832 for a three-year time horizon and £3 146 760 for a six-year time horizon. The equivalent annual cash outflows for the machine can be solved from the following formula:

$$\text{present value of cash flows} = \text{equivalent annual cost} \times \text{annuity factor for } N \text{ years of R\%} \tag{14.1}$$

Solving for the equivalent annual cost, we have

$$\text{equivalent annual cash flow} = \frac{\text{present value of costs}}{\text{annuity factor for } N \text{ years at R\%}} \tag{14.2}$$

Using the data for machine X, the equivalent annual cost is

$$\frac{£1\,796\,832}{2.4869} = £722\,519 \text{ (using a 3-year time horizon)}$$

or

$$\frac{£3\,146\,760}{4.3553} = £722\,519 \text{ (using a 6-year time horizon)}$$

The present values in the above calculations are obtained from our earlier calculations for three- and six-year time horizons. The annuity factors are obtained from annuity (i.e. cumulative discount) tables shown in Appendix B for three and six years and a 10% discount rate. We get the same equivalent annual cash flows for both time horizons. To simplify calculations, we can always use the first purchase in the sequence to calculate the equivalent annual cost.

What does the equivalent annual cost represent? Merely that the sequence of machine X cash flows is exactly like a sequence of cash flows of £722 519 a year. Calculating the equivalent annual cost for machine Y, you will find that it is £705 678 a year. A stream of machine X cash flows is the costlier; therefore we should select machine Y. Using this method, our decision rule is to choose the machine with the lower annual equivalent cost.

Note that when we used the common time horizon method the present value of a sequence of machine Xs was £3 146 760 compared with £3 073 440 for a sequence of machine Ys; a present value cost saving of £73 320 in favour of machine Y. The equivalent annual cost saving for machine Y was £16 841 (£722 519 – £705 678). If we discount this saving for a time horizon of six years, the present value is £73 320, the same as the saving we calculated using the lowest common multiple method.

The equivalent annual cash flow method simplifies handling different multiples of lives. For example, if two alternative machines have lives of three and eight years respectively, the least common time horizon method requires combined calculations over 24 years. In contrast, the equivalent annual cash flow method only requires calculations for the initial life of each machine. You should note, however, that the equivalent annual cash flow method should only be used when there is a sequence of identical replacements for each alternative and this process continues until a common time horizon is reached.

3. Estimate terminal values

Consider a situation where machines A and B have lives of six and eight years respectively. Assume that the life of the task to be performed by the machines is ten years. Because the task life is shorter than the lowest common multiple (24 years), we cannot use either of the first two methods. An alternative approach is to assume that each machine will be replaced once (machine X at the end of year 6 and machine Y at the end of year 8) and incorporate estimates of the disposal values into the analysis for both machines at the end of the 10 year task life.

Capital rationing

In our previous discussions it has been suggested that all investments with positive net present values should be undertaken. For mutually exclusive projects the project with the highest net present value should be chosen. However, situations may occur where there are insufficient funds available to enable a firm to undertake all those projects that yield a positive net present value. The situation is described as **capital rationing**.

Capital rationing occurs whenever there is a budget ceiling, or a market constraint on the amount of funds that can be invested during a specific period of time. For various reasons top management may pursue a policy of limiting the amount of funds available for investment in any one period. Such policies may apply to firms that finance all their capital investment with internal funds. Alternatively, in a large decentralized organization top management may limit the funds available to the divisional managers for investment. Such restrictions on available funds may be for various reasons. For example, top management may be reluctant to issue additional share capital because they may be concerned that this will lead to outsiders gaining control of the business, or because a share issue may lead to a dilution of earnings per share. Alternatively, they may be reluctant to raise additional debt capital beyond a certain point because they do not wish to be committed to large fixed interest payments. Note that whenever a firm adopts a policy that restricts funds available for investment, such a policy may be less than optimal, as the firm may reject projects with a positive net present value and forgo opportunities that would have enhanced the market value of the firm.

The term **'soft capital rationing'** is often used to refer to situations where, for various reasons the firm *internally* imposes a budget ceiling on the amount of capital expenditure. On the other hand, where the amount of capital investment is restricted because of *external* constraints such as the inability to obtain funds from the financial markets, the term **'hard capital rationing'** is used.

Whenever capital rationing exists, management should allocate the limited available capital in a way that maximizes the NPVs of the firm. Thus it is necessary to rank all investment opportunities so that the NPV can be maximized from the use of the available funds. The analytical techniques used must therefore be capable of ranking the various alternatives or of determining the optimal combination of investments that meet the constraint of limited capital. Ranking in terms of absolute NPVs will normally give incorrect results, since this method leads to the selection of large projects, each of which has a high individual NPV but that have in total a lower NPV than a large number of smaller projects with lower individual NPVs. For example, the ranking of projects by NPV will favour a project that yields an NPV of £1000, for an investment of £10 000, over two projects of £5000 that each yield an individual NPV of £800. Clearly, if funds are restricted to £10 000, it is better to accept the two smaller projects, which will yield a total NPV of £1600. Consider the situation presented in Example 14.2.

Our aim is to select the projects in descending order of profitability until the investment funds of £20 million have been exhausted. If we use the net present value method of ranking, the following projects will be selected:

Projects selected in order of ranking	Investment cost (£m)	New present value (£m)
C	5	2.575
D	10	2.350
G	5	0.900
	Total net present value	5.825

If, on the other hand, we adopt the profitability index method of ranking, the selected projects will be as follows:

EXAMPLE 14.2

A division of the Bothnia Company that operates under the constraint of capital rationing has identified seven independent investments from which to choose. The company has £20 million available for capital investment during the current period. Which projects should the company choose? The net present values and profitability index ratios for each of the projects are as follows:

Projects	Investment required (£m)	Present value, PV (£m)	Net present value (£m)	Profitability index, PV/investment cost	Ranking as per NPVs	Ranking as per profitability index
A	2.5	3.25	0.75	1.30	6	2
B	10.0	10.825	0.825	1.08	5	6
C	5.0	7.575	2.575	1.51	1	1
D	10.0	12.35	2.35	1.23	2	3
E	12.5	13.35	0.85	1.07	4	7
F	2.5	3.0	0.5	1.20	7	4
G	5.0	5.9	0.9	1.18	3	5

Projects selected in order of ranking	Investment cost (£m)	Net present value (£)
C	5.0	2.575
A	2.5	0.750
D	10.0	2.350
F	2.5	0.500
	Total net present value	6.175

You can see that the ranking of projects by the profitability index gives the highest NPV.

Our discussion so far has assumed that investment funds are restricted for one period only. This is most unlikely. Also, the cost of certain investment projects may be spread over several periods. In addition, a one-period analysis does not take into account the intermediate cash flows generated by a project. Some projects may provide relatively high cash flows in the early years, and these can then be used to increase the availability of funds for investment in further projects in those early years. We should therefore consider more than just a one-period constraint in the allocation of limited capital to investment projects. To cope with such problems, it is necessary to use mathematical techniques, but we shall defer our discussion of the application of such techniques until Chapter 26.

Taxation and investment decisions

In our discussions so far we have ignored the impact of taxation. Taxation rules differ between countries but in most countries similar principles tend to apply relating to the taxation allowances available on capital investment expenditure. Companies rarely pay taxes on the profits that are disclosed in their annual published accounts, since certain expenses that are deducted in the published accounts are not allowable deductions for taxation purposes. For example, depreciation is not an allowable deduction; instead, taxation legislation enables **capital allowances** (also known as **writing-down allowances** or **depreciation tax shields**) to be claimed on capital expenditure that is incurred on plant and machinery and other fixed assets. Capital allowances represent standardized depreciation allowances granted by the tax authorities. These allowances vary from country to country but their common aim is to enable the *net* cost of assets to be deducted as an allowable expense, either throughout their economic life or on an accelerated basis which is shorter than an asset's economic life.

Taxation laws in different countries typically specify the amount of capital expenditure that is allowable (sometimes this exceeds the cost of the asset where a government wishes to stimulate investment), the time period over which the capital allowances can be claimed and the depreciation method to be employed. Currently in the UK, larger companies can claim annual capital allowances of 25% on the written-down value of plant and equipment based on the reducing balance method of depreciation. Different percentage capital allowances are also available on other assets such as industrial buildings where an allowance of 4% per annum based on straight line depreciation can be claimed.[1]

Let us now consider how taxation affects the NPV calculations. You will see that the calculation must include the incremental tax cash flows arising from the investment. Consider the information presented in Example 14.3.

The first stage is to calculate the annual writing down allowances (i.e. the capital allowances). The calculations are as follows:

End of year	Annual writing-down allowance (£)	Written-down value (£)
0	0	1 000 000
1	250 000 (25% × £1 000 000)	750 000
2	187 500 (25% × £750 000)	562 500
3	140 630 (25% × £562 500)	421 870
4	105 470 (25% × £421 870)	316 400
	683 600	

Next we calculate the additional taxable profits arising from the project. The calculations are as follows:

	Year 1 (£)	Year 2 (£)	Year 3 (£)	Year 4 (£)
Incremental annual profits	500 000	500 000	500 000	500 000
Less annual writing-down allowance	250 000	187 500	140 630	105 470
Incremental taxable profits	250 000	312 500	359 370	394 530
Incremental tax at 35%	87 500	109 370	125 780	138 090

You can see that for each year the incremental tax payment is calculated as follows:

corporate tax rate × (incremental profits – capital allowance)

Note that depreciation charges should not be included in the calculation of incremental cash flows or taxable profits. We must now consider the timing of the taxation payments. In the UK taxation payments vary depending on the end of the accounting year, but they are

EXAMPLE 14.3

The Sentosa Company operates in Ruratania where investments in plant and machinery are eligible for 25% annual writing-down allowances on the written-down value using the reducing balance method of depreciation. The corporate tax rate is 35%. The company is considering whether to purchase some machinery which will cost £1 million and which is expected to result in additional net cash inflows and profits of £500 000 per annum for four years. It is anticipated that the machinery will be sold at the end of year 4 for its written-down value for taxation purposes. Assume a one year lag in the payment of taxes. Calculate the net present value assuming a cost of capital of 10%.

generally paid approximately one year after the end of the company's accounting year. We shall apply this rule to our example. This means that the tax payment of £87 500 for year 1 will be paid at the end of year 2, £109 370 tax will be paid at the end of year 3 and so on.

The incremental tax payments are now included in the NPV calculation:

Year	Cash flow (£)	Taxation	Net cash flow (£)	Discount factor	Present value (£)
0	−1 000 000	0	−1 000 000	1.0000	−1 000 000
1	+500 000	0	+500 000	0.9091	+454 550
2	+500 000	−87 500	+412 500	0.8264	+348 090
3	+500 000	−109 370	+390 630	0.7513	+293 480
4	+500 000 +316 400[a]	−125 780	+690 620	0.6830	+471 690
5	0	−138 090	−138 090	0.6209	−85 740
				Net present value	+482 070

[a]Sale of machinery for written down value of £316 400.

The taxation rules in most countries allow capital allowances to be claimed on the *net* cost of the asset. In our example the machine will be purchased for £1 million and the estimated realizable value at the end of its life is its written-down value of £316 400. Therefore the estimated net cost of the machine is £683 600. You will see from the above calculations that the total of the writing-down allowances amount to the net cost. How would the analysis change if the estimated realizable value for the machine was different from its written-down value, say £450 000? The company will have claimed allowances of £683 600 but the estimated net cost of the machine is £550 000 (£1 million – £450 000 estimated net realizable value). Therefore excess allowances of £133 600 (£683 600 – £550 000) will have been claimed and an adjustment must be made at the end of year 4 so that the tax authorities can claim back the excess allowance. This adjustment is called a **balancing charge**.

Note that the above calculation of taxable profits for year 4 will now be as follows:

Incremental annual profits	500 000
Less annual writing-down allowance	(105 470)
Add balancing charge	133 600
Incremental taxable profits	528 130
Incremental taxation at 35%	184 845

An alternative calculation is to assume that a writing-down allowance will not be claimed in year 4. The balancing charge is now calculated by deducting the written-down value at the end of year 3 of £421 870 from the *actual* sales value at the time of sale (i.e. £450 000 sale proceeds). The balancing charge is now £28 130. This is the same as the net charge incorporated in the above calculation (£133 600 – £105 470 = £28 130). You can adopt either method. It is a matter of personal preference.

Let us now assume that the estimated disposal value is less than the written-down value for tax purposes, say £250 000. The net investment cost is £750 000 (£100 0000 – £250 000), but you will see that our calculations at the start of this section indicate that estimated taxation capital allowances of £683 600 will have been claimed by the end of year 4. Therefore an adjustment of £66 400 (£750 000 – £683 600) must be made at the end of year 4 to reflect the fact that insufficient capital allowances have been claimed. This adjustment is called a **balancing allowance**.

Thus in year 4 the total capital allowance will consist of an annual writing-down allowance of £105 470 plus a balancing allowance of £66 400, giving a total of £171 870. Taxable profits for year 4 are now £328 130 (500 000 – £171 870), and tax at the rate of 35% on these profits will be paid at the end of year 5.

Do note that in the UK, and some other countries, it is possible to combine similar types of assets into asset pools and purchases and sales of assets are added to the pool so that balancing allowances and charges on individual assets do not arise. However, similar outcomes are likely to occur. Accordingly, it is essential when appraising investment proposals to be fully aware of the specific taxation legislation that applies so that you can precisely determine the taxation impact. In most cases taxation is likely to have an important effect on the NPV calculation. For an illustration of the treatment of asset acquisitions and disposals when asset are incorporated into a general pool you should refer to the article by Franklin (1998).

The effect of inflation on capital investment appraisal

In the 1970s the annual rate of inflation in many European countries exceeded 10%. What impact does inflation have on capital investment decisions? We shall see that inflation affects future cash flows and the return that shareholders require on the investment (i.e. the discount rate). The discount rate consists of the required rate of return on a riskless investment plus a risk premium that is related to a project's risk. Inflation affects both the risk-free interest rate and the risk premium. How does inflation affect the risk-free interest rate? According to Fisher (1930), interest rates quoted on risk-free investments such as treasury bills fully reflect anticipated inflation. Note that interest rates quoted on securities are known as **nominal or money rates of interest**, whereas the **real rate of interest** represents the rate of interest that would be required in the absence of inflation. Fisher proposed the following equation relating to the nominal rate of interest to the real rate of interest and the rate of inflation:

$$\left(1+\begin{matrix}\text{nominal rate}\\\text{of interest}\end{matrix}\right)=\left(1+\begin{matrix}\text{real rate}\\\text{of interest}\end{matrix}\right)\times\left(1+\begin{matrix}\text{expected rate}\\\text{of inflation}\end{matrix}\right) \tag{14.3}$$

Suppose that the real rate of interest is expected to be 2% and the anticipated rate of inflation 8%. Applying Fisher's equation, the nominal or money rate of interest would be

$$(1+0.02)(1+0.08)=1.1016$$

The nominal rate of interest would therefore be 10.16% (i.e. 1.1016 – 1). In the absence of inflation, an individual who invests £100 in a risk-free security will require a 2% return of £102 to compensate for the time value of money. Assuming that the expected rate of inflation is 8%, then to maintain the return of £102 in real terms this return will have to grow by 8% to £110.16 (i.e. £102 + 8%). Therefore a real rate of interest of 2% requires a nominal rate of interest of 10.16% when the expected rate of inflation is 8%.

Inflation also affects future cash flows. For example, assume that you expect a cash flow of £100 in one year's time when there is no inflation. Now assume that that the predicted annual inflation rate is 10%. Your expected cash flow at the end of the year will now be £110, instead of £100. However, you will be no better off as a result of the 10% increase in cash flows. Assume that you can buy physical goods, say widgets, at £1 each when there is no inflation so that at the end of the year you can buy 100 widgets. With an annual inflation rate of 10% the cost of a widget will increase to £1.10 and your cash flow will be £110, but your purchasing power will remain unchanged because you will still only be able to buy 100 widgets.

The increase in cash flows from £100 to £110 is an illusion because it is offset by a decline in the purchasing power of the monetary unit. Rather than expressing cash flows in year one monetary units it is more meaningful to express the cash flows in today's purchasing power or monetary unit (that is, in real cash flows). Thus, £110 receivable at the end of year one is equivalent to £100 in today's purchasing power. When cash flows are expressed in monetary units at the time when they are received they are described as **nominal cash flows** whereas cash flows expressed in today's (that is, time zero) purchasing power are known as **real cash flows**. Therefore the £110 cash flow is a nominal cash flow but if it is expressed in today's purchasing power it will be equivalent to a real cash flow of £100.

Real cash flows can be converted to nominal cash flows using the following formula:

$$\text{Nominal cash flow} = \text{Real cash flow}\ (1 + \text{the anticipated rate of inflation})^n \quad (14.4)$$

where n = the number of periods that the cash flows are subject to inflation.

Alternatively, we can rearrange formula (14.4) to restate it in terms of real cash flows:

$$\text{Real cash flow} = \text{Nominal cash flow}/(1 + \text{the anticipated rate of inflation})^n \quad (14.5)$$

Therefore if a real cash flow expressed in today's purchasing power is £100 and the anticipated annual rate of inflation is 10% then the nominal value at the end of year 2 will be:

$$£100(1 + 0.10)^2 = £121$$

or a nominal cash flow of £121 receivable at the end of year 2 will be equivalent to a real cash flow of:

$$£121/(1 + 0.10)^2 = £100$$

The average rate of inflation for all goods and services traded in an economy is known as the **general rate of inflation**. Assume that your cash flow of £100 has increased at exactly the same rate as the general rate of inflation (in other words, the general rate of inflation is 10%). Therefore your purchasing power has remained unchanged and you will be no better or worse off if all your cash flows increase at the general rate of inflation. Indeed, we would expect the same result to apply when we calculate NPVs. If project cash flows increase at exactly the same rate as the general rate of inflation we would expect NPV to be identical to what the NPV would be if there was no inflation. Consider Example 14.4.

EXAMPLE 14.4

A division within the Bothnia Company is considering whether to undertake a project that will cost £1 million and will have the following cash inflows:

Year 1	£600 000
Year 2	£400 000
Year 3	£1 000 000

The cost of capital (i.e. the required rate of return) is 10% and the expected rate of inflation is zero. Ignore taxation. Calculate the net present value.

You should recall from Chapter 13 that the NPV can be expressed in formula terms as:

$$\frac{FV_1}{1+K} + \frac{FV_2}{(1+K)^2} + \frac{FV_3}{(1+K)^3} + \cdots + \frac{FV_n}{(1+K)^n} - I_0$$

where FV_n are future values, K is the cost of capital and I_0 is the initial investment cost. The NPV calculation is

$$\frac{£600\,000}{1.10} + \frac{£400\,000}{(1.10)^2} + \frac{£1\,000\,000}{(1.10)^3} - £1\,000\,000 = £627\,347$$

Let us now adjust Example 14.4 and incorporate the effects of inflation. Suppose that an annual inflation rate of 8% is expected during the three years of the project. In this situation the stock market data that are used to calculate the rate of return required by investors will include a premium for anticipated inflation. Hence this premium will be incorporated in the required rate of return on the project (i.e. the applicable cost of capital for the project). The revised required rate of return (RRR) is calculated using Fisher's formula:

$$\begin{aligned} 1 + \text{nominal RRR} &= [1 + \text{real RRR } (0.10)] \times [1 + \text{rate of inflation}(0.08)] \\ &= (1 + 0.10)(1 + 0.08) \\ &= 1.188 \end{aligned}$$

Therefore the RRR is now 18.8% (i.e. 1.188 – 1). It is also necessary to adjust the cash flows for inflation. The revised NPV calculation is

$$\frac{£600\,000(1.08)}{(1.10)(1.08)} + \frac{£400\,000(1.08)^2}{(1.10)^2(1.08)^2} + \frac{£1\,000\,000(1.08)^3}{(1.10)^3(1.08)^3} - £1\,000\,000 = £627\,347$$

You can see in the numerator of the NPV calculation that the real cash flows are adjusted at the compound rate of inflation of 8%. In the denominators of the calculation Fisher's equation is shown to calculate the discount rate assuming an expected inflation rate of 8%. Consequently, the inflation factors of 1.08 cancel out. Therefore if the cash flows and the required rate of return are subject to the same rate of inflation then the project's NPV will be unaffected by expected changes in the level of inflation. For example, if inflation is now expected to be 5% instead of 8% then the inflation factor of 1.08 in the numerator and denominator of the NPV calculation would be replaced by 1.05. However, the revised inflation factors would still cancel out, and NPV would remain unchanged.

Looking at the NPV calculation, you should see that there are two correct approaches for adjusting for inflation which will lead to the same answer. They are:

Method 1: Predict *nominal cash flows* (i.e. adjust the cash flows for inflation) and use a *nominal discount rate*.

Method 2: Predict *real cash flows* at today's prices and use a *real discount rate.*

You will have noted that the approach outlined above used Method 1. Can you see that if we use Method 2 the inflation factors of 1.08 will be omitted from the above NPV calculation but the NPV will remain unchanged? The NPV calculation will thus be identical to the calculation shown earlier, which assumed zero inflation.

The correct treatment of inflation therefore requires that the assumptions about inflation that enter the cash flow forecasts are consistent with those that enter into the discount rate calculation. You must avoid the mistakes that are commonly made of discounting real cash flows at nominal discount rates or the discounting of nominal cash flows at real discount rates.

If *all* cash flows increase at the same rate as the general level of inflation, we could estimate cash flows in todays (*current*) prices, since such estimates would represent real cash flows. In other words, cash flows would be estimated without considering inflation. Applying the real discount rate would result in the correct treatment of inflation. However, the taxation rules in many countries can result in taxation cash flows not increasing at the general rate of inflation. This is because capital allowances remain constant, and thus taxation cash flows will not change in line with inflation. When cash flows do not increase at the general rate of inflation, we cannot use current price estimates to represent real cash flows. Real cash flows can then only be estimated by first expressing them in nominal terms and deflating them by the general rate of inflation. Because of these difficulties, you are recommended to use Method 1 if all of the cash flows do not increase at the same rate as the general level of inflation.

Calculating risk-adjusted discount rates

In Chapter 13 we noted that a company should only invest in new projects if the returns are greater than those that the shareholders could obtain from investing in securities of the same risk traded in the financial markets. If we can measure the returns that investors require for different levels of risk, we can use these rates of return as the discount rates for calculating net present values.

Exhibit 14.1 shows the *average* returns from investing in treasury bills and ordinary shares (common stocks) in the USA. Investing in treasury bills is nearly risk-free, but investing in ordinary shares is risky.[2] There is a possibility that you could earn very low or very high returns. You can see from Exhibit 14.1 that the safest investment gives the lowest average rate of return.

The average return on ordinary shares represents the average return that you would have obtained if you invested in a proxy portfolio of 500 companies listed on the USA stock exchange. We shall describe this portfolio as being representative of investing in the **market portfolio** (i.e. all shares listed in the USA Stock Exchange). It is unlikely that any investor could invest in the market portfolio, but it is possible to invest in a portfolio of shares (or a unit trust) that in terms of risk and return is virtually identical with the market portfolio.

From Exhibit 14.1 you can see that in the past investors who invested in the market portfolio obtained on average a return of 9.2% (13% – 3.8%) in excess of the risk-free

EXHIBIT 14.1

% Average rates of return on Treasury bills, government bonds, and common stocks (ordinary shares) 1926–1997

Portfolio	Average annual rate of return: Nominal	Average annual rate of return: Real	Average risk premium (extra return versus Treasury bills)
Treasury bills	3.8	.7	0
Government bonds	5.6	2.6	1.8
Common stocks/ordinary shares (S+P 500)	13.0	9.7	9.2

Source: Ibbotson Associates, Inc., *1998 Yearbook.*

(treasury bill) investment. This extra return is called the **risk premium**. Suppose a firm has a project that in terms of risk is identical with the market portfolio. What is the *current* required rate of return on this project? We calculate this by taking the current interest rate on treasury bill securities (called the risk-free rate) and adding the average past risk premium of 9.2%. Assume that the current interest rate is 4%. The required rate of return (RRR) is calculated as follows:

$$\begin{matrix}\text{RRR on an equivalent} \\ \text{investment to the market portfolio}\end{matrix} = \begin{matrix}\text{risk-free} \\ \text{rate (4\%)}\end{matrix} + \begin{matrix}\text{average past risk} \\ \text{premium (9.2\%)}\end{matrix} \qquad (14.6)$$

Therefore the project's cash flows should be discounted at 13.2% and a project that is risk free should be discounted at the same rate as that available from investing in treasury bills (i.e. 4%).

We have now established two benchmarks: the discount rate for risk-free projects and the discount rate for investments that have a risk equivalent to the market portfolio. However, we have not established how discount rates can be estimated for projects that do not fall into these categories. To do this, we must consider the relationship between risk and return.

Let us consider the risk and return from holding the market portfolio. Assume that the expected return from holding the market portfolio is 13% and the risk-free rate of interest is 4%. Therefore the risk premium required for holding the market portfolio is 9%. We shall also assume that the standard deviation from investing in the market portfolio is 16% and that from investing in the risk-free security is zero. These risk–return relationships are plotted in Figure 14.1. Note that the return on the market portfolio is represented by R_m and the return on the risk-free security as R_f.

You can see that an investor can invest in any portfolio that falls on the line between points R_f and R_m. For example, if you invest in portfolio X consisting of £500 in the market portfolio and £500 in the risk-free investment, your *expected* return will be 8.5% (£500 at 4% plus £500 at 13%). Note that the standard deviation from investing in portfolio X is

$$\left(\begin{matrix}1/2 \times \text{standard deviation of} \\ \text{risk-free security (0)}\end{matrix}\right) + \left(\begin{matrix}1/2 \times \text{standard deviation of} \\ \text{market portfolio (16\%)}\end{matrix}\right) = 8\% \qquad (14.7)$$

In other words, investing in portfolio X is half as risky as investing in the market portfolio. We can now establish a formula for calculating the *expected* return on portfolios of different levels of risk:

FIGURE 14.1 *Risk–return relationship from combining borrowing and lending with the market portfolio*

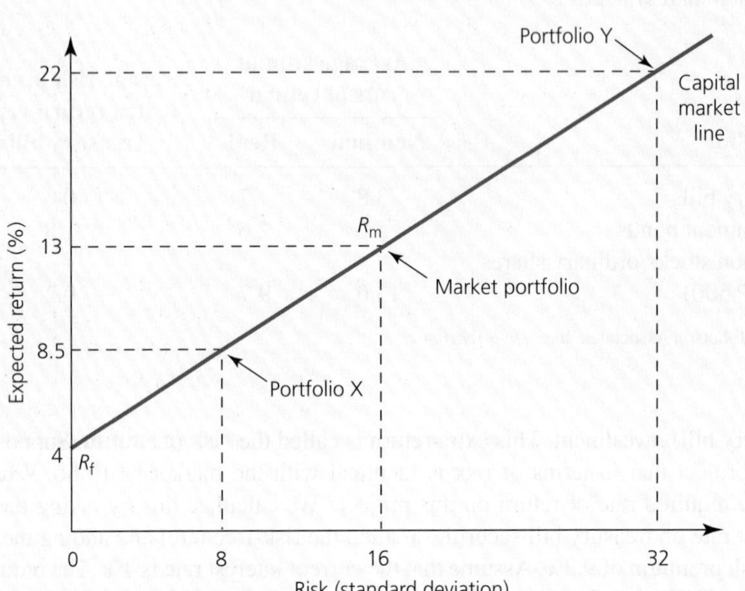

$$\text{expected return} = \frac{\text{risk-free}}{\text{return}} + \left(\text{risk premium} \times \frac{\text{risk of selected portfolio}}{\text{risk of market portfolio}}\right) \quad (14.8)$$

$$= 4 + (9\% \times 8/16) = 8.5\%$$

Using this formula, we can calculate the expected return for any point along the line R_f to R_m in Figure 14.1. How can you invest in a portfolio that falls on the line above R_m? Such a position is achieved by borrowing and investing your funds in the market portfolio. Suppose you invest £1000 of your own funds and borrow £1000 at the risk-free rate of 4% and invest the combined funds of £2000 in the market portfolio. We shall call this portfolio Y. Your *expected* annual return will be £260 from investing in the market portfolio (£2000 × 13%) less £40 interest on the £1000 loan. Therefore your return will be £220 from investing £1000 of your own funds, i.e. 22%. However, this is the *expected* return, and there is a possibility that the return on the market portfolio could be zero, but you would have to repay the borrowed funds. In other words, by borrowing you increase the variability of your potential returns and therefore the standard deviation. The calculation of the standard deviation for portfolio Y is

$$\frac{(£2000 \times 16\%) - (£1000 \times 0\%)}{£1000} = 32\%$$

We can also use equation (14.8) to calculate the expected return on portfolio Y. It is

$$4\% + (9\% \times 32/16) = 22\%$$

We have now established that an investor can achieve any point along the sloping line in Figure 14.1 by combining lending (i.e. investing in the risk-free security) and investing in the market portfolio or borrowing and investing in the market portfolio.

The sloping line shown in Figure 14.1 that indicates the risk return relationship from combining lending or borrowing with the market portfolio is called the **capital market line**.

The market portfolio can now be used as a benchmark for determining the expected return on *individual* securities, rather than portfolios of securities. Consider three securities – the ordinary shares of companies A, B and C. Let us assume that, relative to the variability of the market portfolio, the risk of security A is identical, B is half as risky and C is twice as risky. In other words, in terms of risk, security A is identical with the market portfolio, B is equivalent to portfolio X and C is equivalent to portfolio Y. Consequently the required rates of return are 13% for A, 8.5% for B and 22% for C.

The returns available from combining investing in the market portfolio with borrowing and lending represent the most efficient investment portfolios, and determines the risk/return relationships for all securities traded in the market. The relationship between the risk of a security and the risk of the market portfolio is called **beta**. The beta of the market portfolio is 1.0, and the beta of a security that is half as risky as the market is 0.5 whereas the beta of a security that is twice as risky as the market portfolio is 2.0. The relationship between risk (measured in terms of beta) and expected return is shown by the sloping line in Figure 14.2. This sloping line is called the **security market line**.

Beta measures the sensitivity of the return on a security with market movements. For example, if the return on the market portfolio increased by 10%, the *expected* return on portfolio X and security B will be expected to increase by 5%. Similarly, if the return on the market portfolio decreased by 10%, the *expected* return on portfolio X and security B will be expected to decline by 5%. Both portfolio X and security B have a beta of 0.5, and this indicates that for a market increase/decrease of 1% any security with a beta of 0.5 is expected to increase/decrease by 0.5%. Consider now a security with a beta of 2.0 (e.g. security C or portfolio Y). If the market increases/decreases by 1%, the security will be expected *on average* to increase/decrease by 2%.

The model described above is called the **capital asset pricing model (CAPM)**. The equation for the CAPM is the equation for the security market line shown in Figure 14.2, and can be used to establish the expected return on any security. The equation is

$$\begin{matrix}\text{expected}\\ \text{return on a}\\ \text{security}\end{matrix} = \begin{matrix}\text{risk-free}\\ \text{rate}\end{matrix} + \left(\begin{matrix}\text{expected return}\\ \text{on the market}\\ \text{portfolio}\end{matrix} - \begin{matrix}\text{risk-free}\\ \text{rate}\end{matrix}\right) \times \text{beta} \qquad (14.9)$$

Therefore

$$\text{security A} = 4\% + (13\% - 4\%) \times 1.0 = 13\%$$
$$\text{security B} = 4\% + (13\% - 4\%) \times 0.5 = 8.5\%$$
$$\text{security C} = 4\% + (13\% - 4\%) \times 2.0 = 22\%$$

How is beta calculated? For the answer to this question you should consult the business finance literature (see Brealey and Myers, 2003, Chs 7–9). Calculating betas in practice is very tedious, and is normally based on comparing 60 monthly returns from a security with the market portfolio. Fortunately, it is unnecessary to calculate betas, since their values are published in various risk measurement publications relating to securities traded in financial markets.

FIGURE 14.2 *Risk–return relationship expressed in terms of beta*

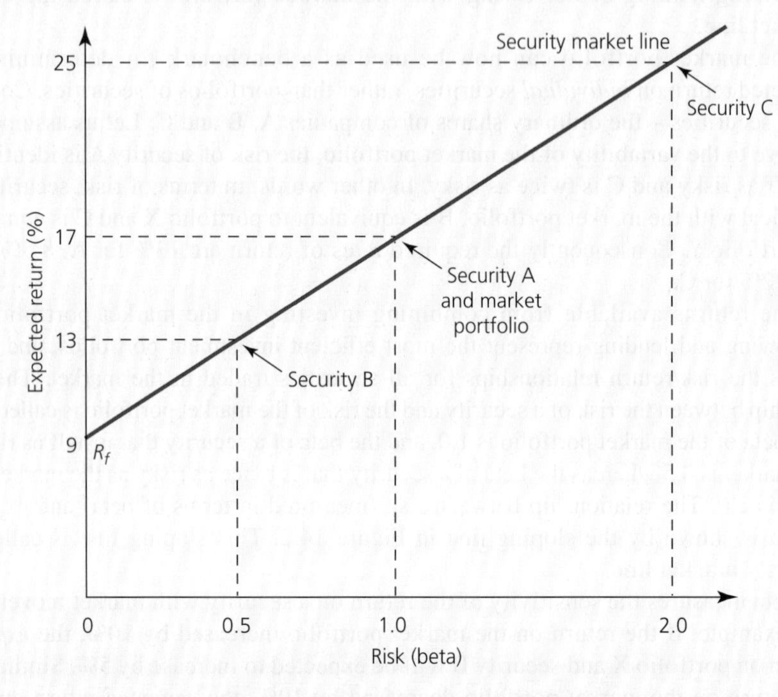

Calculating the required rates of returns on a firm's securities

You should now know how to calculate the required rates of returns for securities: simply multiply the average risk premium from investing in the market portfolio (9.2% shown in Exhibit 14.1) by the beta for the security, and add this to the current interest rate on gilt-edged securities. The required rate of return is the cost of capital or discount rate, which should be used to calculate the NPVs of projects that are just as risky as the firm's existing business.[3] For projects that are more or less risky than a firm's existing business it will be necessary to use the beta of companies that specialize in the projects being evaluated. For a detailed explanation of this approach you should refer to Brealey and Myers (2003, Ch. 9) or Pike and Neale (2003, Ch. 12).

Weighted average cost of capital

So far we have assumed that firms are financed only by equity finance (i.e. ordinary share capital and retained earnings). However, most companies are likely to be financed by a combination of debt and equity capital. These companies aim to maintain target proportions of debt and equity.

The cost of *new* debt capital is simply the after tax interest cost of raising new debt. Assume that the after tax cost of new debt capital is 6% and the required rate of return on equity capital is 14% and that the company intends to maintain a capital structure of 50% debt and 50% equity. The overall cost of capital for the company is calculated as follows:

$$= \begin{pmatrix} \text{proportion of debt capital} \\ \times \text{ cost of debt capital} \\ (0.5 \times 6\%) \end{pmatrix} + \begin{pmatrix} \text{proportion of equity capital} \\ \times \text{ cost of equity capital} \\ (0.5 \times 14\%) \end{pmatrix} = 10\% \quad (14.10)$$

The overall cost of capital is also called the **weighted average cost of capital**. Can we use the weighted average cost of capital as the discount rate to calculate a project's NPV? The answer is yes, provided that the project is of equivalent risk to the firm's existing assets and the firm intends to maintain its target capital structure of 50% debt and 50% equity.

In practice, a firm will not finance every single project with 50% debt and 50% equity. For example, project X costing £5 million might be all equity financed. The firm should maintain its target capital structure by issuing debt to finance future projects of £5 million. In this way the firm maintains its target capital structure. Therefore the weighted average cost of capital that should be used for evaluating investment proposals should be an incremental cost based on the firm's target capital structure. Do not use the specific cost of the funds that have been used to finance the project.

We have now established how to calculate the discount rate for projects that are of similar risk to the firm's existing assets and to incorporate the financing aspects. It is the weighted average cost of equity and debt capital.

Traditional methods of measuring risk

In this section we shall consider some of the traditional methods used by companies to measure the risk of a project. These measures were developed before we knew how to introduce risk into the calculation of NPV using the capital asset pricing model. Because these methods continue to be used, it is important that you understand their limitations. We shall consider the following methods of quantifying risk:

1 standard deviations and probability distributions;
2 simulation;
3 sensitivity analysis.

1 Standard deviation and probability distributions

In Chapter 12 we discussed standard deviations, the coefficient of variation and probability distributions as methods of comparing the risk characteristics of various alternative courses of action. We shall now consider how these methods can be used to assess the risk of various capital projects. Consider the situation presented in Example 14.5.

The expected values of the cash flows can be used to calculate the project's **expected net present value** by adding together the discounted net present values of the expected values for each year. That is,

$$\text{Expected NPV} = \frac{£20\,000}{1.10} + \frac{£5000}{(1.10)^2} + \frac{£0}{(1.10)^3} - £20\,000 = £2314$$

One method of describing the uncertainty associated with this project is to construct the entire probability distribution for the project's NPV. Unfortunately, the calculations are rather tedious, since there are 125 possibilities (i.e. 5^3) in Example 14.5. We could summarize the 125 possibilities in a probability distribution of several possible

EXAMPLE 14.5

A firm is considering a capital investment proposal that requires an immediate cash outlay of £20 000. The project has an estimated life of three years and the forecast cash flows and their estimated probabilities are as follows:

Year 1		Year 2		Year 3	
Probability	Net Cash flow (£)	Probability	Net Cash flow (£)	Probability	Net Cash flow (£)
0.10	10 000	0.10	(–5 000)	0.10	(–10 000)
0.25	15 000	0.25	0	0.25	(–5 000)
0.30	20 000	0.30	5 000	0.30	0
0.25	25 000	0.25	10 000	0.25	5 000
0.10	30 000	0.10	15 000	0.10	10 000
Expected value	20 000	Expected value	5 000	Expected value	0

The operating cash flows in any one year do not depend on the operating cash flows of previous years. The risk-free cost of capital is 10%.

outcomes, but the 125 NPVs must still initially be calculated. To avoid all these calculations, an indication of the risk may be obtained by calculating the standard deviation of the NPV. The formula for the calculation of the variance of the NPV is given below. The standard deviation is the square root of the variance.

$$V_{\mathrm{p}} = \sum_{t=0}^{n} \frac{V_t}{(1+r)^{2t}} \tag{14.11}$$

where V_{p} is the variance of the project's NPV and V_t is the variance of the project's cash flow in year t. The discount factor is squared so that it is in the same terms as the variance of the cash flows. The cash flow variances for each of the three years are £32 500 000.[4] The variances are identical because the probability distributions have the same dispersion about their expected values. Let us now apply equation (14.9) to calculate the variance of the project's NPV:

$$V_{\mathrm{p}} = \frac{£32\,500\,000}{(1.10)^2} + \frac{£32\,500\,000}{(1.10)^4} + \frac{£32\,500\,000}{(1.10)^6} = £67\,402\,844$$

The standard deviation is the square root of the variance (i.e. £8210), so the expected value of the NPV of the project is £2314 and the standard deviation about the expected NPV is £8210. Note that the risk-free rate has been used in the above calculations. Our objective is to measure the risk of investment proposals, but if we use a discount rate which embodies a premium for risk then this would result in an adjustment for risk within the discounting process and would lead to double counting and the prejudging of risk.

It is difficult to interpret expected NPVs and the standard deviations. The expected NPV and standard deviation for the project in Example 14.5 are £2314 and £8210 respectively. However, we have no means of ascertaining whether an NPV of £2314 is sufficient to compensate for the risk involved (i.e. a standard deviation of £8210).

Consider also a situation where the firm has a second, alternative project that has an expected NPV of £5000 with a standard deviation of £10 000. Assume that the two projects are mutually exclusive. It is unclear from the analysis whether the increase in the expected NPV of £2686 is sufficient to justify the increase in risk (i.e. an increase in standard deviation of £1790). In contrast, the capital asset pricing model incorporates risk in the discounting process and clearly indicates whether a project's return is in excess of the risk adjusted return required by shareholders.

2 Simulation

To produce a probability distribution for the possible NPVs in Example 14.5, it is necessary to construct a decision tree with 125 different outcomes, even though the example was based on some very simple assumptions. In practice, it may be necessary to produce separate probabilities for alternative sales revenue outcomes, different items of costs, and different possible life spans. Consequently, a decision tree will consist of thousands of different branches. In addition, the cash flows may be correlated over the years; for example, if a new product is successful in the early years then it is also likely to be successful in later years. When the cash flows are correlated over time, the standard deviation calculation in equation (14.9) will not give a correct calculation of the variation of the project's NVP.

A way in which these problems can be overcome is to use **Monte Carlo simulation analysis**. We can use Example 14.5 to illustrate the simulation process. The first step is to construct a probability distribution for each factor that influences the capital investment decision, for example market share, selling price, operating costs and the useful life of the facilities. For Example 14.5 we shall only use probability distributions for the cash flows in each year of the project's life. The next step is to assign numbers (from 1 to 100) to the cash flows in the probability distributions to exactly match their respective probabilities. This is achieved by working upwards cumulatively from the lowest to the highest cash flow values and assigning numbers that will correspond to probability groupings. The numbers for the cash flows in Example 14.5 for each year are as follows:

Year 1		Year 2		Year 3	
Assigned numbers	Cash flow (£)	Assigned numbers	Cash flow (£)	Assigned numbers	Cash flow (£)
1–10	10 000	1–10	(–5 000)	1–10	(–10 000)
11–35	15 000	11–35	0	11–35	(–5 000)
36–65	20 000	36–65	5 000	36–65	0
66–90	25 000	66–90	10 000	66–90	5 000
91–100	30 000	91–100	15 000	91–100	10 000

For year 1 the selection of a number at random between 1 and 10 obtained from between 1 and 100 has a probability of 0.1. In the above schedule this represents a cash flow of £10 000. Similarly, the selection of a number at random between 11 and 35 has a probability of 0.25, and this represents a cash flow of £15 000. Numbers have been assigned to cash flows so that when numbers are selected at random the cash flows have exactly the same probability of being selected as is indicated in their respective probability distribution in Example 14.5.

Simulation trials are now carried out by computer. The computer selects one number at random for each of the relevant distributions (i.e. each probability distribution for years 1–3 in our example) and produces an estimated NPV. For example, if random numbers of 26, 8 and 85 respectively are selected for each of the three distributions for each year, this will indicate cash flows of +£15 000 in year 1, –£5000 in year 2 and +£5000 in year 3 and the resulting NPV will be calculated. This particular NPV is only one of a particular combination of values from a computer run. The computer will select many other sets of random numbers, convert them into cash flows and compute other NPVs repeatedly, for perhaps several thousand trials. A count is kept of the number of times each NPV is computed; and when the computer run has been completed, it can be programmed to produce an expected value, probability distribution and standard deviation. A graph of the probability distribution can also be plotted.

Note that the cash flows for each computer run are discounted at the risk-free rate for the reasons described earlier (namely to avoid double counting and prejudging risk). It is therefore very difficult to interpret the probability distribution of NPVs discounted at the risk-free rate. We still lack a clear-cut answer to the basic question: should the project be accepted or rejected?

The advantage of simulation analysis is that it compels decision-makers to look carefully at the relationships between the factors affecting the cash flows. Brealey and Myers (2003) conclude:

> *By considering a detailed Monte Carlo simulation model, you will get a better understanding of how a project works and what could go wrong with it. You will have confirmed, or improved, your forecasts of future cash flows, and your calculations of project NPV will be more confident ... Don't use simulation just to generate a distribution of NPVs. Use it to understand the project, forecast its expected cash flows, and assess its risk. Then calculate the NPV the old fashioned way, by discounting expected cash flows at a discount rate appropriate for the project's risk.*

Computer simulation is not always feasible for risk analysis. The technique requires that probability distributions be established for a number of variables such as sales volume, selling prices, various input prices and asset lives. Therefore full-scale simulation may only be appropriate for the most important projects that involve large sums of money.

3 Sensitivity analysis

Sensitivity analysis enables managers to assess how responsive the NPV is to changes in the variables which are used to calculate it. Figure 14.3 illustrates that the NPV calculation is dependent on several independent variables, all of which are uncertain. The approach requires that the NPVs are calculated under alternative assumptions to determine how sensitive they are to changing conditions.

The application of sensitivity analysis can indicate those variables to which the NPV is most sensitive, and the extent to which these variables may change before the investment results in a negative NPV. In other words, sensitivity analysis indicates why a project might fail. Management should review any critical variables to assess whether or not there is a strong possibility of events occurring which will lead to a negative NPV. Management should also pay particular attention to controlling those variables to which NPV is particularly sensitive, once the decision has been taken to accept the investment. Sensitivity analysis is illustrated with Example 14.6.

FIGURE 14.3 *Sensitivity of NPV to changes in independent variables*

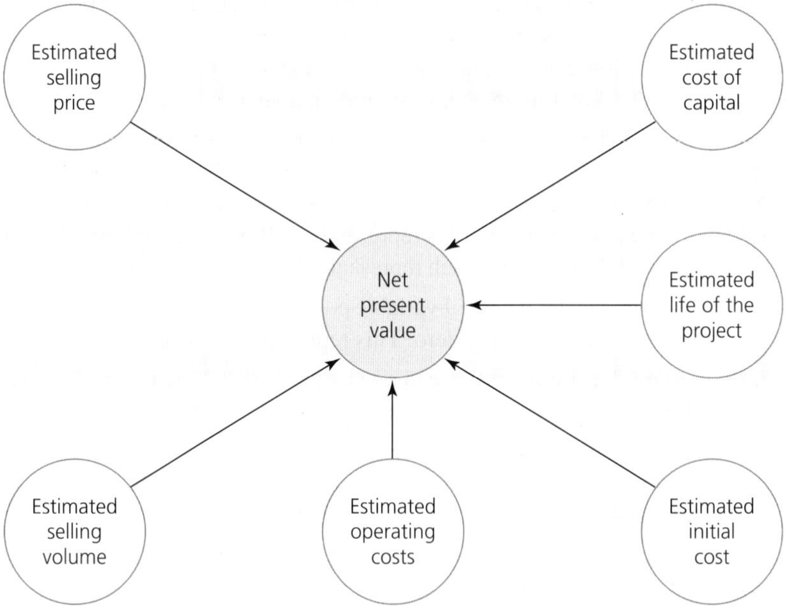

EXAMPLE 14.6

One of the divisions of the Bothnia Company is considering the purchase of a new machine, and estimates of the most likely cash flows are as follows:

	Year 0 (£)	Year 1 (£)	Year 2 (£)	Year 3 (£)
Initial outlay	–2 000 000			
Cash inflows				
(100 000 units at £30 per unit)		3 000 000	3 000 000	3 000 000
Variable costs		2 000 000	2 000 000	2 000 000
Net cash flows	–2 000 000	+1 000 000	+1 000 000	+1 000 000

The cost of capital is 15% and the net present value is £283 000.

Some of the variables referred to in Example 14.6 to which sensitivity analysis can be applied are as follows.

1 *Sales volume*: The net cash flows will have to fall to £876 040 (£2 000 000/2.283 discount factor) for the NPV to be zero, because it will be zero when the present value of the future cash flows is equal to the investment cost of £2 000 000. As the cash flows are equal each year, the cumulative discount tables in Appendix B can be used. The discount factor for 15% and year 3 is 2.283. If the discount factor is divided into the required present value of £2 000 000, we get an annual

cash flow of £876 040. Given that the most likely *net* cash flow is £1 000 000, the *net* cash flow may decline by approximately £124 000 each year before the NPV becomes zero. Total sales revenue may therefore decline by £372 000 (assuming that net cash flow is 33.1/3% of sales). At a selling price of £30 per unit, this represents 12 400 units, or alternatively we may state that the sales volume may decline by 12.4% before the NPV becomes negative.

2 *Selling price*: When the sales volume is 100 000 units per annum, total annual sales revenue can fall to approximately £2 876 000 (£3 000 000 – £124 000) before the NPV becomes negative (note that it is assumed that total variable costs and units sold will remain unchanged). This represents a selling price per unit of £28.76, or a reduction of £1.24 per unit, which represents a 4.1% reduction in the selling price.

3 *Variable costs*: The total annual variable costs can increase by £124 000 or £1.24 per unit before NPV becomes zero. This represents an increase of 6.2%.

4 *Initial outlay*: The initial outlay can rise by the NPV before the investment breaks even. The initial outlay may therefore increase by £283 000 or 14.15%.

5 *Cost of capital*: We calculate the internal rate of return for the project, which is 23%. Consequently, the cost of capital can increase by 53% before the NPV becomes negative.

The elements to which the NPV appears to be most sensitive are the items with the lowest percentage changes. They are selling price followed by the variable costs, and it is important for the manager to pay particular attention to these items so that they can be carefully monitored.

Sensitivity analysis can take various forms. In our example, for the selected variables, we focused on the extent to which each could change for NPV to become zero. Another form of sensitivity analysis is to examine the impact on NPV of a specified percentage change in a selected variable. For example, what is the impact on NPV if sales volume falls by 10%? A third approach is to examine the impact on NPV of pessimistic, most likely and optimistic estimates for each selected variable.

Sensitivity analysis has a number of serious limitations. In particular, the method requires that changes in each key variable be isolated, but management is more interested in the combination of the effect of changes in two or more key variables. In addition, the method gives no indication of the probability of key variables or a combination of these variables occurring. For example, the sensitivity analysis may indicate that one key variable may change by 25% and another may change by 10%. This suggests that we should concentrate on the latter, but if the former has a probability of occurring of 0.5 and the latter has a probability of 0.01 then clearly the key variable change of 25% is more important. You will see from Exhibit 14.2 (Surveys of company practice) that sensitivity analysis is the most frequently used formal risk measurement technique.

A summary of risk measurement techniques

There are three different approaches that can be adopted to measure the risk of a project. Project risk can be measured by viewing the investment:

1 As part of a well-diversified investment portfolio held by shareholders (i.e. a *capital asset pricing model approach*).

2 On its own and ignoring its relationship with either the shareholders' or the firm's other investments (i.e. a *stand-alone risk measure*).

3 As part of the firm's total investment in assets (i.e. *corporate portfolio risk measure*).

We adopted the **capital asset pricing model (CAPM)** approach when we described the method of computing risk-adjusted discount rates. With this approach, risk is measured by comparing the risk of a project relative to the market portfolio. Investors are assumed to hold an efficiently diversified portfolio (this can normally be achieved by investing in about 15 securities) that approximates the market portfolio. The CAPM approach assumes that the *overall* risk incurred by shareholders falls into two categories:

1. **Specific (diversifiable) risk**, which is specific to an *individual* company such as the impact on cash flows arising from a new competitor entering the market or when a technological change makes one of the firm's major products obsolete.
2. **Market (non-diversifiable) risk**, which is due to macroeconomic factors that affect the returns of *all* companies, such as changes in interest or corporate tax rates or changes in overall consumer demand.

The *CAPM approach* assumes that specific risk is irrelevant in determining the returns required by shareholders because they can diversify it away (and thus avoid it) by investing in a well-diversified portfolio of securities. Consider a situation where you invest in a company whose main activity is ice-cream manufacturing. You will be exposed to specific company risk, since a rainy summer will adversely affect the company's profitability and share price. You can eliminate much of this specific risk by also investing in a company that manufactures rainwear, assuming that a rainy summer will have a favourable impact on company profitability and share price. By investing in a well-diversified portfolio of securities, an unfavourable event affecting the value of any one company in the portfolio will have a small impact on the value of the entire portfolio because much of the investment will be unaffected by the occurrence of the event.

If investors do hold well-diversified portfolios (and the major investors such as the financial institutions certainly do) then the market will only reward investors for bearing risk that cannot be avoided (i.e. market risk). The CAPM approach measures the *market* risk of a project relative to the market portfolio. This is expressed in the form of the beta measure, which can then be used to derive the *expected* returns for different levels of market risk (Figure 14.2). The CAPM approach implies that investors are saying: 'These are the *expected* returns that can be obtained from securities traded in financial markets for different levels of *market* risk. If you (the firm) can invest in projects that earn returns in excess of returns available from securities with the same level of market risk then invest the funds on my behalf.'

The *stand-alone risk measurement approach* measures the *total* risk of a project in isolation from either the shareholders' or the firm's other investments. The standard deviation, probability distributions and simulation methods described earlier are stand-alone measures of risk. They measure the dispersion of the outcomes for a specific project, but do not distinguish between specific and market risk. If only market risk is rewarded by the stock market then stand-alone risk measures will be inappropriate, since they include specific firm risk that is not rewarded by the stock market. A further problem is that stand-alone risk measures merely measure risk. They do not provide a basis for determining the rates of return required for different levels of risk.

The *corporate portfolio risk measurement approach* measures the incremental risk arising from the acceptance of a project. The incremental risk may not be the same as the individual risk of a project measured on a stand-alone approach. For example, the standard deviation of the cash flows from the firm's existing assets might be £100 000

EXAMPLE 14.7

Assume that a firm operates in an environment in which there are only two potential states of nature. There is an equal probability that each state of nature will occur. The estimated cash flow from the existing projects and a proposed investment project are as follows:

	Existing projects (£)	Proposed project (£)	Existing projects combined with proposed project (£)
State of nature 1	–40 000	+20 000	–20 000
State of nature 2	+60 000	–10 000	+50 000
Expected value	+10 000	+5 000	+15 000
Standard deviation	50 000	15 000	35 000

and the standard deviation of the cash flows of a proposed project £60 000 on a stand-alone basis. If the proposed project is not highly correlated with the firm's existing projects, it is possible that the total standard deviation of the cash flows from the firm's assets might increase to, say, £120 000. Thus the incremental standard deviation arising from the acceptance of the project is only £20 000 whereas the stand-alone measure is £60 000.

You can see why stand-alone risk can differ from incremental risk by considering Example 14.7. The stand-alone standard deviation of the cash flows from the proposed project is +£15 000 but the incremental standard deviation of the cash flow is –£15 000 (£35 000 – £50 000). Thus acceptance of the project *reduces* the dispersion of the total cash flows of the firm, and therefore has risk reduction properties. However, when viewed on a stand-alone basis the proposed project appears to involve a high level of risk. The analysis suggests that we should not focus on the risk of individual projects in isolation, but we should consider the impact of a project on the total risk of the firm.

The corporate portfolio risk approach can merely measure incremental risk. As with stand-alone measures, there is no mechanism for determining the required rate of return for different levels of risk. It is also extremely difficult to compute the standard deviation from the firm's existing assets and thus measure incremental risk. In Example 14.7 we illustrated how diversification by the firm can reduce risk. However, shareholders can do this themselves by investing in well-diversified portfolios. The firm has reduced specific (diversifiable) risk, but if investors can do this themselves then risk reduction by the firm will be of no value. The corporate portfolio approach therefore fails to distinguish between specific and market risk.

Finally, you should note that, unlike the other methods described in this chapter, sensitivity analysis does not measure risk. It shows the impact on NPV from making alternative assumptions in the variables that were used to calculate it, and can also be used to indicate the extent to which each variable can change before the investment results in a negative NPV. Sensitivity analysis should be used to complement the CAPM risk-adjusted discount approach. Its real value is that it helps managers to delve into the cash flow estimates and understand what could go wrong and what opportunities are available to modify the project.

EXHIBIT 14.2

Surveys of company practice

Surveys conducted by Pike (1996) on the use of risk analysis techniques by 100 large UK companies between 1975 and 1992 provide an indication of the changing trends in practice in large UK companies. Pike's findings are as follows:

	1975 %	1980 %	1986 %	1992 %
Sensitivity analysis	28	42	71	86
Best/worse case analysis	N/A	N/A	93	85
Reduced payback period	25	30	51	69
Risk adjusted discount rate	37	41	61	64
Probability analysis	9	10	40	47
Beta analysis (based on the CAPM)	–	–	16	20

Source: Pike (1996)

A USA study by Trahan and Gitman (1995) reported that 52% adjusted the discount rate and 72% used sensitivity analysis.

The UK study of 300 UK manufacturing organizations by Drury *et al.* (1993) sought to ascertain the extent to which particular risk adjustment techniques were used. The figures below indicate the percentage of firms that often or always used a particular technique:

Require a shorter payback period	37
Increase/decrease discount rate	18
Probability analysis	14
Monte Carlo simulation	1
Sensitivity analysis	51
Conservative cash flow forecasts	32
Beta analysis (based on the CAPM)	1

Dardenne (1998) reported that 42% of Belgian companies regularly used sensitivity analysis, 16% regularly used the simulation approach and 35% raised the discount rate.

The most recent UK study by Arnold and Hatzopoulos (2000) reported that sensitivity analysis was the most widely used technique (85% of firms). Other reported usage rates were raising the required rate of return (52%), subjective assessment (46%), probability analysis (31%), shortening the payback period (20%) and beta analysis (3%).

The Drury *et al.* (1993) study also examined the methods that firms used to incorporate inflation into the investment appraisal. They reported that 44% of the responding firms incorrectly discounted real cash flows at a nominal discount rate and a further 11% incorrectly discounted nominal cash flows at a real discount rate.

The conclusions that emerge from the above studies is that there has been a dramatic increase over the years in the usage of formal risk analysis techniques and that the CAPM approach is not widely used in practice.

Summary

The following items relate to the learning objectives listed at the beginning of the chapter.

- **Evaluate mutually exclusive projects with unequal lives.**

  The application of the net present value method is complicated when a choice must be made between two or more projects, where the projects have unequal lives. For equipment replacement decisions it is necessary to compare the alternatives over equal time periods. This is achieved by converting the time periods into a common time horizon such that a series of replacements of identical equipment occurs until a common time horizon is reached. One approach is to list the series of cash flows for the alternatives under consideration until the common time horizon is reached and calculate the net present values. A simpler approach is to use the equivalent annual cash flow method whereby the cash flows for the alternatives under consideration are converted into an annuity (i.e. equivalent annual cash flows). The approaches can only be used when there is a series of identical replacements for each alternative and this process continues until a common time horizon is reached.

- **Explain capital rationing and select the optimum combination of investments when capital is rationed for a single period.**

  Capital rationing applies to a situation where there is a constraint on the amount of funds that can be invested during a specific period of time. In this situation the net present value is maximized by adopting the profitability index method (i.e. the present value of cash flows divided by the investment outlay) of ranking and using this ranking to select investments up to the total investment funds that are available for the period. The selection of the optimum combination of investments based on single period capital rationing was illustrated using Example 14.2.

- **Calculate the incremental taxation payments arising from a proposed investment.**

  The cash flows from a project must be reduced by the amount of taxation payable on these cash flows. However, the taxation savings arising from the capital allowances (i.e. annual writing down allowances) reduce the taxation payments. Because taxation payments do not occur at the same time as the associated cash flows, the precise timing of the taxation payments should be identified to calculate NPV. You should refer to the section headed 'Taxation and investment decisions' for an illustration of the computation of the incremental taxation payment.

- **Describe the two approaches for adjusting for inflation when appraising capital projects.**

  The net present value can be adjusted by two basic ways to take inflation into account. First, a discount rate can be used, based on the required rate of return, that includes an allowance for inflation. Remember that cash flows must also be adjusted for inflation. Secondly, the anticipated rate of inflation can be excluded from the discount rate, and the cash flows can be expressed in real terms. In other words, the first method discounts nominal cash flows at a nominal discount rate and the second method discounts real cash flows at a real discount rate.

- **Explain how risk-adjusted discount rates are calculated.**

  Risk-adjusted discount rates for a firm can be calculated using the capital asset pricing model (CAPM). The CAPM uses beta as a measure of risk. Beta is a measure of the sensitivity of the returns on a firm's securities relative to a proxy market portfolio (e.g. the Financial Times all-share index). The risk-adjusted return is derived by adding a risk premium for a firm's securities to a risk free rate (normally represented by government treasury bills). The risk premium is derived by estimating the return on the market portfolio over the risk free rate and multiplying this premium by the beta of a firm's shares.

- **Identify and describe the traditional methods of measuring risk.**

  Traditional methods of measuring risk include (a) expected values, standard deviations and probability distributions; (b) simulation; and (c) sensitivity analysis. The first method involves weighting the estimated annual outcomes of the cash flows by their associated probabilities to derive the annual expected value of the cash flows. The cash flows are then discounted to derive the expected net present value. The dispersion of the NPV's is determined by calculating the standard deviation of the net present values. Instead of presenting summary measures of the probability distribution in the form of the expected value and standard deviation the entire probability distribution for the project's NPVs can be presented. However, it is extremely difficult to derive a probability distribution because of the many outcomes that are possible. To overcome this problem Monte Carlo simulation can be used. Sensitivity analysis can be used to determine how responsive the NPV is to changes in the variables that are used to calculate it. Sensitivity analysis can take various forms but the most popular form is to ascertain the percentage change that can take place for each selected variable for NPV to become zero. The major weakness of the first two traditional methods described above is that they cannot be used to determine a risk-adjusted discount rate. They require that the risk free discount rate be used to discount the cash flows. Therefore, they fail to deal with the risk–return trade-off and do not provide a clear-cut answer to the basic question: Should the project be accepted or rejected?

Notes

1 In 2003 the profits of UK companies were subject to a corporate tax rate of 30%. For small companies with annual profits of less than £300 000 the corporate tax rate was 19%.

2 Future payments of interest and the principal repayment on maturity are fixed and known with certainty. Gilt-edged securities are therefore risk-free in nominal terms. However, they are not risk-free in real terms because changes in interest rates will result in changes in the market values.

3 It is assumed that the company does not intend to change its target financing mix of debt and equity.

4 The calculation of the variance of the cash flows for year 1 is as follows:

Cash flow	Deviation from expected value	Squared deviation	Probability	Weighted amount
10 000	–10 000	100 000 000	0.10	10 000 000
15 000	–5 000	25 000 000	0.25	6 250 000
20 000	0	0	0.30	0
25 000	5 000	25 000 000	0.25	6 250 000
30 000	10 000	100 000 000	0.10	10 000 000
	Sum of squared deviation (variance)			32 500 000

Key terms and concepts

balancing allowance (p. 549)
balancing charge (p. 548)
beta (p. 555)
capital allowances (p. 547)
capital asset pricing model (pp. 555, 563)
capital market line (p. 555)
capital rationing (p. 545)
depreciation tax shields (p. 547)
equivalent annual cash flow method (p. 543)
expected net present value (p. 557)
general rate of inflation (p. 550)
hard capital rationing (p. 545)
lowest common multiple method (p. 542)
market (non-diversifiable) risk (p. 563)
market portfolio (p. 552)
Monte Carlo simulation analysis (p. 559)
nominal or money rates of interest (p. 549)
nominal cash flows (p. 550)
real cash flows (p. 550)
real rate of interest (p. 549)
risk premium (p. 553)
security market line (p. 555)
sensitivity analysis (p. 560)
soft capital rationing (p. 545)
specific (diversifiable) risk (p. 563)
weighted average cost of capital (p. 557)
writing-down allowances (p. 547)

Recommended reading

This chapter has provided an outline of the capital asset pricing model and the calculation of risk-adjusted discount rate. These topics are dealt within more depth in the business finance literature. You should refer to Brealey and Myers (2003, Chs 7–10) for a description of the capital asset pricing model and risk-adjusted discount rates. For a discussion of the differences between company, divisional and project cost of capital and an explanation of how project discount rates can be calculated when project risk is different from average overall firm risk see Pike and Neale (2003, Ch. 12).

Key examination points

A common error is for students to include depreciation and apportioned overheads in the DCF analysis. Remember that only incremental cash flows should be included in the analysis. Where a question includes taxation, you should separately calculate the incremental taxable profits and then work out the tax payment. You should then include the tax payment in the DCF analysis. Incremental taxable profits are normally incremental cash flows less capital allowances on the project. To simplify the calculations, questions sometimes indicate that capital allowances should be calculated on a straight-line depreciation method.

Do not use accounting profits instead of taxable profits to work out the tax payment. Taxable profits are calculated by adding back depreciation to accounting profits and then deducting capital allowances. Make sure that you include any balancing allowance or charge and disposal value in the DCF analysis if the asset is sold.

With inflation, you should discount nominal cash flows at the nominal discount rate. Most questions give the nominal discount rate (also called the money discount rate). You should then adjust the cash flows for inflation. If you are required to choose between alternative projects, check that they have equal lives. If not, use one of the methods described in this chapter.

Assessment material

Review questions

The review questions are short questions that enable you to assess your understanding of the main topics included in the chapter. The numbers in parentheses provide you with the page numbers to refer to if you cannot answer a specific question.

Review problems

The review problems are more complex and require you to relate and apply the chapter content to various business problems. The problems are graded by their level of difficulty. The multiple-choice questions are the least demanding and normally take less than 10 minutes to complete. Fully worked solutions to the review problems are provided in a separate section at the end of the book. For those questions in the white box the worked solutions are provided in the *Student's Manual* accompanying this book. Further review problems for this chapter are available on the accompanying website www.drury-online.com. The answers to these problems are available for lecturers on the lecturer's password protected section of the website.

Case studies

The website also includes over 30 case study problems. A list of these cases is provided in Part Seven of this book. Cases that are relevant to the content of this chapter include Foster Construction Company and Rawhide Development Company.

Review questions

14.1 Explain the special considerations that should be taken into account when evaluating projects with unequal lives. (*p. 542*)

14.2 Describe the methods of evaluating projects with unequal lives. (*pp. 542–44*)

14.3 What is capital rationing? Distinguish between hard and soft capital rationing. (*pp. 544–45*)

14.4 Explain how the optimum investment programme should be determined when capital is rationed for a single period. (*pp. 545–46*)

14.5 How does taxation affect the appraisal of capital investments? (*pp. 546–48*)

14.6 Define writing-down-allowances (also known as depreciation tax shields or capital allowances), balancing allowances and balancing charges. (*pp. 547–49*)

14.7 How does the presence of inflation affect the appraisal of capital investments? (*pp. 549–50*)

14.8 Distinguish between nominal cash flows and real cash flows and nominal discount rates and real discount rates. *(p. 550)*

14.9 Why is it necessary to use risk-adjusted discount rates to appraise capital investments? *(pp. 552–54)*

14.10 Explain how risk-adjusted discount rates are calculated. *(pp. 552–53)*

14.11 Describe the traditional methods of dealing with risk. What are their limitations? *(pp. 557–62)*

14.12 How can sensitivity analysis help in appraising capital investments? What are the limitations of sensitivity analysis? *(pp. 560–62)*

14.13 Describe the different forms of sensitivity analysis. *(p. 562)*

14.14 Describe the three broad approaches that can be adopted to measure the risk of a project. *(pp. 562–64)*

14.15 Distinguish between specific (diversifiable) and market (non-diversifiable) risk. *(p. 563)*

Review problems

14.16 Advanced

A supermarket is trying to determinc the optimal replacement policy for its fleet of delivery vehicles. The total purchase price of the fleet is £220 000.

The running costs and scrap values of the fleet at the end of each year are:

	Year 1	Year 2	Year 3	Year 4	Year 5
Running costs	£110 000	£132 000	£154 000	£165 000	£176 000
Scrap value	£121 000	£88 000	£66 000	£55 000	£25 000

The supermarket's cost of capital is 12% per annum.

Ignore taxation and inflation.

The supermarket should replace its fleet of delivery vehicles at the end of

A year 1.
B year 2.
C year 3.
D year 4.
E year 5.

(4 marks)

CIMA Management Accounting – Decision Making

14.17 Advanced

R Ltd is deciding whether to launch a new product. The initial outlay for the product is £20 000. The forecast possible annual cash inflows and their associated probabilities are shown below.

	Probability	Year 1	Year 2	Year 3
Optimistic	0.20	£10 000	£12 000	£9 000
Most likely	0.50	£7 000	£8 000	£7 600
Pessimistic	0.30	£6 400	£7 200	£6 200

The company's cost of capital is 10% per annum.

Assume the cash inflows are received at the end of the year and that the cash inflows for each year are independent.

for the product is

(3 marks)

CIMA Management Accounting – Decision Making

oth questions (a) and (b)

esting in a manufacturing project that would have a stment would involve an immediate cash outflow of lual value. In each of the three years, 4000 units The contribution per unit, based on current prices, is ual cost of capital of 8%. It is expected that the ach of the next three years.

the project (to the nearest £500) is

(3 marks)

rate is now projected to be 4%, the maximum monetary project to remain viable, is (to the nearest 0.5%)

(2 marks)

CIMA Management Accounting – Decision Making

14.19 **Advanced: Inflation and taxation**

Assume that you have been appointed finance director of Breckall plc. The company is considering investing in the production of an electronic security device, with an expected market life of five years.

The previous finance director has undertaken an analysis of the proposed project; the main features of his analysis are shown below. He has recommended that the project should not be undertaken because the estimated annual accounting rate of return is only 12.3%.

Proposed electronic security device project

	Year 0 (£000)	Year 1 (£000)	Year 2 (£000)	Year 3 (£000)	Year 4 (£000)	Year 5 (£000)
Investment in depreciable fixed assets	4500					
Cumulative investment in working capital	300	400	500	600	700	700
Sales		3500	4900	5320	5740	5320
Materials		535	750	900	1050	900
Labour		1070	1500	1800	2100	1800
Overhead		50	100	100	100	100
Interest		576	576	576	576	576
Depreciation		900	900	900	900	900
		3131	3826	4276	4726	4276
Taxable profit		369	1074	1044	1014	1044
Taxation		129	376	365	355	365
Profit after tax		240	698	679	659	679

Total initial investment is £4 800 000
Average annual after tax profit is £591 000

All the above cash flow and profit estimates have been prepared in terms of present day costs and prices, since the previous finance director assumed that the sales price could be increased to compensate for any increase in costs.

You have available the following additional information:

(a) Selling prices, working capital requirements and overhead expenses are expected to increase by 5% per year.

(b) Material costs and labour costs are expected to increase by 10% per year.

(c) Capital allowances (tax depreciation) are allowable for taxation purposes against profits at 25% per year on a reducing balance basis.

(d) Taxation on profits is at a rate of 35%, payable one year in arrears.

(e) The fixed assets have no expected salvage value at the end of five years.

(f) The company's real after-tax weighted average cost of capital is estimated to be 8% per year, and nominal after-tax weighted average cost of capital 15% per year.

Assume that all receipts and payments arise at the end of the year to which they relate, except those in year 0, which occur immediately.

Required:

(a) Estimate the net present value of the proposed project. State clearly any assumptions that you make.

(13 marks)

(b) Calculate by how much the discount rate would have to change to result in a net present value of approximately zero.

(4 marks)

(c) Describe how sensitivity analysis might be used to assist in assessing this project. What are the weaknesses of sensitivity analysis in capital investment appraisal? Briefly outline alternative techniques of incorporating risk into capital investment appraisal.

(8 marks)
(Total 25 marks)
ACCA Level 3 Financial Management

14.20 **Advanced: Replacement decision**

Ceder Ltd has details of two machines that could fulfil the company's future production plans. Only one of these will be purchased.

The 'standard' model costs £50 000, and the 'de luxe' £88 000, payable immediately. Both machines would require the input of £10 000 working capital throughout their working lives, and both have no expected scrap value at the end of their expected working lives of 4 years for the standard machine and 6 years for the de luxe machine.

The forecast pre-tax operating net cash flows (£) associated with the two machines are

	Years hence					
	1	2	3	4	5	6
Standard	20 500	22 860	24 210	23 410		
De luxe	32 030	26 110	25 380	25 940	38 560	35 100

The de luxe machine has only recently been introduced to the market, and has not been fully tested in operating conditions. Because of the higher risk involved, the appropriate discount rate for the de luxe machine is believed to be 14% per year, 2% higher than the discount rate for the standard machine.

The company is proposing to finance the purchase of either machine with a term loan at a fixed interest rate of 11% per year.

Taxation at 35% is payable on operating cash flows one year in arrears, and capital allowances are available at 25% per year on a reducing balance basis.

Required:

(a) For both the standard and the de luxe machines calculate:

(i) payback period;

(ii) net present value.

Recommend, with reasons, which of the two machines Ceder Ltd should purchase.

(Relevant calculations must be shown.)

(13 marks)

(b) Surveys have shown that the accounting rate of return and payback period are widely used by companies in the capital investment decision process. Suggest reasons for the widespread use of these investment appraisal techniques.

(6 marks)
(Total 19 marks)
ACCA Level 3 Financial Management

14.21 Advanced: Single period capital rationing

Banden Ltd is a highly geared company that wishes to expand its operations. Six possible capital investments have been identified, but the company only has access to a total of £620 000. The projects are not divisible and may not be postponed until a future period. After the projects end it is unlikely that similar investment opportunities will occur.

Expected net cash inflows (including salvage value)

Project	Year 1 (£)	2 (£)	3 (£)	4 (£)	5 (£)	Initial Outlay (£)
A	70 000	70 000	70 000	70 000	70 000	246 000
B	75 000	87 000	64 000			180 000
C	48 000	48 000	63 000	73 000		175 000
D	62 000	62 000	62 000	62 000		180 000
E	40 000	50 000	60 000	70 000	40 000	180 000
F	35 000	82 000	82 000			150 000

Projects A and E are mutually exclusive. All projects are believed to be of similar risk to the company's existing capital investments.

Any surplus funds may be invested in the money market to earn a return of 9% per year. The money market may be assumed to be an efficient market.

Banden's cost of capital is 12% per year.

Required:

(a) Calculate:

(i) The expected net present value;

(ii) The expected profitability index associated with each of the six projects, and rank the projects according to both of these investment appraisal methods.

Explain briefly why these rankings differ.

(8 marks)

(b) Give reasoned advice to Banden Ltd recommending which projects should be selected.

(6 marks)

(c) A director of the company has suggested that using the company's normal cost of capital might not be appropriate in a capital rationing situation. Explain whether you agree with the director.

(4 marks)

(d) The director has also suggested the use of linear or integer programming to assist with the selection of projects. Discuss the advantages and disadvantages of these mathematical programming methods to Banden Ltd.

(7 marks)

(Total 25 marks)

ACCA Level 3 Financial Management

14.22 Advanced: NPV calculation, choice of discount rate and sensitivity analysis

The managing director of Tigwood Ltd believes that a market exists for 'microbooks'. He has proposed that the company should market 100 best-selling books on microfiche which can be read using a special microfiche reader that is connected to a television screen. A microfiche containing an entire book can be purchased from a photographic company at 40% of the average production cost of best-selling paperback books.

It is estimated that the average cost of producing paperback books is £1.50, and the average selling price of paperbacks is £3.95 each. Copyright fees of 20% of the average selling price of the paperback books would be payable to the publishers of the paperbacks plus an initial lump sum which is still being negotiated, but is expected to be £1.5 million. No tax allowances are available on this lump sum payment. An agreement with the publishers would be signed for a period of six years. Additional variable costs of staffing, handling and marketing are 20 pence per microfiche, and fixed costs are negligible.

Tigwood Ltd has spent £100 000 on market research, and expects sales to be 1 500 000 units per year at an initial unit price of £2.

The microfiche reader would be produced and marketed by another company.

Tigwood would finance the venture with a bank loan at an interest rate of 16% per year. The company's money (nominal) cost of equity and real cost of equity are estimated to be 23% per year and 12.6% per year respectively. Tigwood's money weighted average cost of capital and real weighted average cost of capital are 18% per year and 8% per year respectively. The risk free rate of interest is 11% per year and the market return is 17% per year.

Corporate tax is at the rate of 35%, payable in the year the profit occurs. All cash flows may be assumed to be at the year end, unless otherwise stated.

Required

(a) Calculate the expected net present value of the microbooks project.

(5 marks)

(b) Explain the reasons for your choice of discount rate in your answer to part (a). Discuss whether this rate is likely to be the most appropriate rate to use in the analysis of the proposed project.

(5 marks)

(c) (i) Using sensitivity analysis, estimate by what percentage each of the following would have to change before the project was no longer expected to be viable:
- initial outlay
- annual contribution
- the life of the agreement
- the discount rate.

(ii) What are the limitations of this sensitivity analysis?

(10 marks)

(d) What further information would be useful to help the company decide whether to undertake the microbook project?

(5 marks)

(Total 25 marks)

ACCA Level 3 Financial Management

Review problems (with answers in the Student's Manual)

14.23 Advanced: Equivalent annual cost to determine optimum replacement cycle

(a) Explain and illustrate (using simple numerical examples) the Accounting Rate of Return and Payback approaches to investment appraisal, paying particular attention to the limitations of each approach.

(6 marks)

(b) (i) Explain the differences between NPV and IRR as methods of Discounted Cash Flow analysis.

(6 marks)

(ii) A company with a cost of capital of 14% is trying to determine the optimal replacement cycle for the laptop computers used by its sales team. The following information is relevant to the decision:

The cost of each laptop is £2400. Maintenance costs are payable at the end of *each full year* of ownership, but not in the year of replacement e.g. if the laptop is owned for two years, then the maintenance cost is payable at the end of year 1.

Interval between Replacement (years)	Trade-in Value (£)	Maintenance cost (£)
1	1200	Zero
2	800	75 (payable at end of Year 1)
3	300	150 (payable at end of Year 2)

Required:

Ignoring taxation, calculate the equivalent annual cost of the three different replacement cycles, and recommend which should be adopted. What other factors should the company take into account when determining the optimal cycle?

(8 marks)

(Total 20 marks)

ACCA Paper 8 – Managerial Finance

14.24 Advanced: Expected NPV and capital rationing

The Independent Film Company plc is a film distribution company which purchases distribution rights on films from small independent producers, and sells the films on to cinema chains for national and international screening. In recent years the company has found it difficult to source sufficient films to maintain profitability. In response to the problem, the Independent Film Company has decided to invest in commissioning and producing films in its own right. In order to gain the expertise for this venture, the Independent Film Company is considering purchasing an existing filmmaking concern, at a cost of £400 000. The main difficulty that is anticipated for the business is the increasing uncertainty as to the potential success/failure rate of independently produced films. Many cinema chains are adopting a policy of only buying films from large international film companies, as they believe that the market for independent films is very limited and specialist in nature. The Independent Film Company is prepared for the fact that they are likely to have more films that fail than that succeed, but believe that the proposed film production business will nonetheless be profitable.

Using data collected from the existing distribution business and discussions with industry experts, they have produced cost and revenue forecasts for the five years of operation of the proposed investment. The company aims to complete the production of three films per year. The after tax cost of capital for the company is estimated to be 14%.

Year 1 sales for the new business are uncertain, but expected to be in the range of £4–10 million. Probability estimates for different forecast values are as follows:

Sales (£ Million)	Probability
4	0.2
5	0.4
7	0.3
10	0.1

Sales are expected to grow at an annual rate of 5%.

Anticipated costs related to the new business are as follows:

Cost Type	£'000
Purchase of film-making company	400
Annual legal and professional costs	20
Annual lease rental (office equipment)	12
Studio and set hire (per film)	180
Camera/specialist equipment hire (per film)	40
Technical staff wages (per film)	520
Screenplay (per film)	50
Actors' salaries (per film)	700
Costumes and wardrobe hire (per film)	60
Set design and painting (per film)	150
Annual non-production staff wages	60

Additional information

(i) No capital allowances are available.

(ii) Tax is payable one year in arrears, at a rate of 33% and full use can be made of tax refunds as they fall due.

(iii) Staff wages (technical and non-production staff) and actors' salaries, are expected to rise by 10% per annum.

(iv) Studio hire costs will be subject to an increase of 30% in Year 3.

(v) Screenplay costs per film are expected to rise by 15% per annum due to a shortage of skilled writers.

(vi) The new business will occupy office accommodation which has to date been let out for an annual rent of £20 000. Demand for such accommodation is buoyant and the company anticipates no problems in finding future tenants at the same annual rent.

(vii) A market research survey into the potential for the film production business cost £25 000.

Required:

(a) Using DCF analysis, calculate the expected Net Present Value of the proposed investment. (Workings should be rounded to the nearest £'000.) *(15 marks)*

(b) Outline the main limitations of using expected values when making investment decisions. *(6 marks)*

(c) In addition to the possible purchase of the film-making business, the company has two other investment opportunities, the details of which are given below:

	Post-Tax Cash Flows, £'000						
	Year 0	**Year 1**	**Year 2**	**Year 3**	**Year 4**	**Year 5**	**Year 6**
Investment X	(200)	200	200	150	100	100	100
Investment Y	(100)	80	80	40	40	40	40

The Independent Film Company has a total of £400 000 available for capital investment in the current year. No project can be invested in more than once.

Required:

(i) Define the term profitability index, and briefly explain how it may be used when a company faces a problem of capital rationing in any single accounting period. *(4 marks)*

(ii) Calculate the profitability index for each of the investment projects available to the Independent Film Company, i.e. purchase of the film production company, Investment X and Investment Y, and outline the optimal investment strategy. Assume that all of the projects are indivisible. *(6 marks)*

(iii) Explain the limitations of using a profitability index in a situation where there is capital rationing. *(4 marks)*

(d) Briefly explain how the tax treatment of capital purchases can affect an investment decision. *(5 marks)*

(Total 40 marks)

ACCA Paper 8 – Managerial Finance

14.25 Advanced: Inflation adjustments and sensitivity analysis

(a) Burley plc, a manufacturer of building products, mainly supplies the wholesale trade. It has recently suffered falling demand due to economic recession, and thus has spare capacity. It now perceives an opportunity to produce designer ceramic tiles for the home improvement market. It has already paid £0.5m for development expenditure, market research and a feasibility study.

The initial analysis reveals scope for selling 150 000 boxes per annum over a five-year period at a price of £20 per box. Estimated operating costs, largely based on experience, are as follows:

Cost per box of tiles (£) (at today's prices):

Material cost	8.00
Direct labour	2.00
Variable overhead	1.50
Fixed overhead (allocated)	1.50
Distribution, etc.	2.00

Production can take place in existing facilities although initial re-design and set-up costs would be £2m after allowing for all relevant tax reliefs. Returns from the project would be taxed at 33%.

Burley's shareholders require a nominal return of 14% per annum after tax, which includes allowance for generally-expected inflation of 5.5% per annum. It can be assumed that all operating cash flows occur at year ends.

Required:

Assess the financial desirability of this venture in *real* terms, finding both the Net Present Value and the Internal Rate of Return to the nearest 1%) offered by the project.

Note: Assume no tax delay.

(*7 marks*)

(b) Briefly explain the purpose of sensitivity analysis in relation to project appraisal, indicating the drawbacks with this procedure.

(*6 marks*)

(c) Determine the values of
   (i) price
   (ii) volume

   at which the project's NPV becomes zero.

   Discuss your results, suggesting appropriate management action.

(*7 marks*)

(*Total 20 marks*)

ACCA Paper 8 Managerial Finance

14.26 Advanced: Calculation of expected NPV and impact of writing down allowances

CH Ltd is a swimming club. Potential exists to expand the business by providing a gymnasium as part of the facilities at the club. The Directors believe that this will stimulate additional membership of the club.

The expansion project would require an initial expenditure of £550 000. The project is expected to have a disposal value at the end of 5 years which is equal to 10% of the initial expenditure.

The following schedule reflects a recent market research survey regarding the estimated annual sales revenue from additional memberships over the project's five-year life:

Level of demand	£000	Probability
High	800	0.25
Medium	560	0.50
Low	448	0.25

It is expected that the contribution to sales ratio will be 55%. Additional expenditure on fixed overheads is expected to be £90 000 per annum.

CH Ltd incurs a 30% tax rate on corporate profits. Corporation tax is to be paid in two equal instalments: one in the year that profits are earned and the other in the following year.

CH Ltd's after-tax nominal (money) discount rate is 15.5% per annum. A uniform inflation rate of 5% per annum will apply to all costs and revenues during the life of the project.

All of the values above have been expressed in terms of current prices.

You can assume that all cash flows occur at the end of each year and that the initial investment does not qualify for capital allowances.

Required:

(a) Evaluate the proposed expansion from a financial perspective.

(13 marks)

(b) Calculate and then discuss the sensitivity of the project to changes in the expected annual contribution.

(5 marks)

You have now been advised that the capital cost of the expansion will qualify for writing down allowances at the rate of 25% per annum on a reducing balance basis. Also, at the end of the project's life, a balancing charge or allowance will arise equal to the difference between the scrap proceeds and the tax written down value.

Required:

(c) Calculate the financial impact of these allowances.

(7 marks)

(Total 25 marks)

CIMA Management Accounting – Decision Making

14.27 **Advanced: Expected NPV calculation and taxes on cashflows**

Blackwater plc, a manufacturer of speciality chemicals, has been reported to the anti-pollution authorities on several occasions in recent years, and fined substantial amounts for making excessive toxic discharges into local rivers. Both the environmental lobby and Blackwaters shareholders demand that it clean up its operations.

It is estimated that the total fines it may incur over the next four years can be summarized by the following probability distribution (all figures are expressed in present values):

Level of fine	Probability
£0.5m	0.3
£1.4m	0.5
£2.0m	0.2

Filta & Strayne Ltd (FSL), a firm of environmental consultants, has advised that new equipment costing £1m can be installed to virtually eliminate illegal discharges. Unlike fines, expenditure on pollution control equipment is tax-allowable via a 25% writing-down allowance (reducing balance). The rate of corporate tax is 33%, paid with a one-year delay. The equipment will have no resale value after its expected four-year working life, but can be in full working order immediately prior to Blackwater's next financial year.

A European Union Common Pollution Policy grant of 25% of gross expenditure is available, but with payment delayed by a year. Immediately on receipt of the grant from the EU, Blackwater will pay 20% of the grant to FSL as commission. These transactions have no tax implications for Blackwater.

A disadvantage of the new equipment is that it will raise production costs by £30 per tonne over its operating life. Current production is 10 000 tonnes per annum, but is expected to grow by 5% per annum compound. It can be assumed that other production costs and product price are constant over the next four years. No change in working capital is envisaged.

Blackwater applies a discount rate of 12% after all taxes to investment projects of this nature. All cash inflows and outflows occur at year ends.

Required:

(a) Calculate the expected net present value of the investment assuming a four-year operating period.

Briefly comment on your results.

(12 marks)

(b) Write a memorandum to Blackwater's management as to the desirability of the project, taking into account both financial and non-financial criteria.

(8 marks)
(Total 20 marks)
ACCA Paper 8 Managerial Finance

14.28 **Advanced: Expected NPV and decision trees**

NP plc is a company that operates a number of different businesses. Each separate business operates its own costing system, which has been selected to suit the particular needs of that business. Data is transferred to Head Office for weekly management control purposes.

NP plc is considering investing in a project named Fantazia, which is a pleasure park consisting of a covered dome and external fun rides. The cost of the dome, which is a covered frame that can be dismantled and erected elsewhere or stored, is £20 million. NP plc is considering two sites for the dome: London or Manchester. The cost of acquiring the land and installing the equipment is expected to be £20 million for the London site and £9 million for the Manchester site.

A market research survey shows that if Fantazia were to be situated in London, there is a 0.5 chance of getting 1.2 million visitors a year for the next four years and a 0.5 chance of getting only 0.8 million visitors a year. Each visitor to the London site is expected to spend £25 on average. This comprises a £10 entrance fee which includes access to fun rides, £10 on souvenir merchandise and £5 on food and drink.

If Fantazia were to be situated in Manchester, there is a 0.4 chance of getting 1.2 million visitors a year for the next four years and a 0.6 chance of getting only 0.8 million visitors. Each visitor to the Manchester site is expected to spend £23 on average. This comprises £9 entrance fee, £10 on merchandise and £4 on food and drink.

The average cost of servicing each visitor (that is, providing rides, merchandise and food and drink) at both sites is estimated to be £10.

After four years, the dome could be kept in operation for a further four years or dismantled. If the dome is kept on the same site, it is estimated that visitor numbers will fall by 0.1 million a year. This means that London would have a 0.5 chance of 1.1 million visitors and a 0.5 chance of 0.7 million visitors in each of years 5 to 8, and Manchester a 0.4 chance of 1.1 million visitors and a 0.6 chance of 0.7 million visitors.

If the dome were to be dismantled after four years, it could be stored at a cost of £0.5 million a year, sold for £4 million or transferred to the other site. The number of visitors and revenue received at this site would be as predicted for years 1 to 4.

The cost of dismantling the dome and equipment would be £3 million and the cost of moving and re-erecting it would be £9 million.

The purchase or sale price of the land at the end of year 4 would be: London £14 million and Manchester £10 million. At the end of year 8, the dome's resale value would be zero and all land values would be as four years previously.

The final cost of dismantling the dome and equipment would be £2 million.

NP plc uses a discount rate of 10% when evaluating all projects.

Required:

(a) Assuming that NP plc intends to terminate the Fantazia project *after four years*:

(i) draw a decision tree to show the options open to NP plc;

(3 marks)

(ii) calculate which option would generate the highest net present value. (Use either the decision tree or another method.)

(5 marks)

(b) Assuming that NP plc chose the most advantageous option for years 1 to 4, determined in your answer to (a)(ii) above,

(i) draw a decision tree for years 5 to 8, showing the options open to NP plc if Fantazia is not terminated after 4 years;

(3 marks)

(ii) calculate which of these options generates the highest net present value over years 5 to 8.

(5 marks)

(c) Advise the company which options it should select in order to maximize net present value over the full 8 years of the project. State what that net present value would be.

(5 marks)

(d) NP plc recommends that Fantazia adopts activity based costing (ABC) in order to cost its activities. Discuss whether this would be a suitable system for Fantazia to use in order to assess visitor profitability. If you feel that ABC is not an appropriate system for Fantazia, suggest alternative(s).

(9 marks)

(Total 30 marks)

CIMA Management Accounting – Decision Making

14.29 Advanced: Relevant cash flows and taxation plus a calculation of the weighted average cost of capital

Ceely plc is evaluating a high risk project in a new industry. The company is temporarily short of accountants, and has asked an unqualified trainee to produce a draft financial evaluation of the project. This draft is shown below:

				(£000)			
Year[1]	**0**	**1**	**2**	**3**	**4**	**5**	**6**
Cash outflows							
Long term capital:							
Land and buildings	500	600					
Plant and machinery	700	1700					
Working capital (cumulative requirement)	230	570	680	700	720	740	740
Sales		2950	3820	5200	5400	5600	5800
Direct costs:							
Materials		487	630	858	891	924	957
Labour		805	1043	1420	1474	1529	1583
Selling and distribution		207	267	364	378	392	406
		1499	1940	2642	2743	2845	2946
Overheads		370	480	630	642	655	660
Interest		214	610	610	610	610	610
Depreciation		240	700	700	700	700	460
Total cost		2323	3730	4582	4695	4810	4676
Net profit before tax		627	90	618	705	790	1124
Taxation at 40%		251	36	247	282	316	450
Net profit after taxation		376	54	371	423	474	674
Net cash flows	(1200)	(1924)	54	371	423	474	674
Cash flows discounted at 30% per year	(1200)	(1480)	32	169	148	124	140

The net present value is – £2 067 000

Conclusion: The project is not financially viable and should not be undertaken.

Notes:
[1] Year 0 is the present time, year 1 one year in the future etc.

Cash flows have been discounted at a high rate because of the high risk of the project.

Assume that you have been engaged as a financial consultant to Ceely plc. The following additional information is made available to you.

(i) The company has a six year planning horizon for capital investments. The value of the investment at the end of six years is estimated to be five times the after tax operating cash flows of the sixth year.

(ii) The project would be financed by two 15% debentures, one issued almost immediately and one in a year's time. The debentures would both have a maturity of 10 years.

(iii) 50% of the overheads would be incurred as a direct result of undertaking this project.

(iv) Corporate taxation is at the rate of 40% payable one year in arrears.

(v) Tax allowable depreciation is on a straight-line basis at a rate of 20% per year on the full historic cost of depreciable fixed assets. Land and buildings are not depreciable fixed assets and their total value is expected to be £1.1 million at the end of year six.

(vi) The company is listed on the USM. Its current share price is £2.73, and its equity beta coefficient value is 1.1.

(vii) The yield on Treasury Bills is 12% per year, and the average total yield from companies forming the Financial Times Actuaries All Share Index is 20% per year.

(viii) Interest rates are not expected to change significantly.

(ix) The equity beta value of a company whose major activity is the manufacture of a similar product to that proposed in Ceely's new project is 1.5. Both companies have gearing levels of 60% equity and 40% debt (by market values). Ceely's gearing includes the new debenture issues.

Required:

(a) Modify the draft financial evaluation of the project, where appropriate, to produce a revised estimate of the net present value of the project. Recommend whether the project should be accepted, and briefly discuss any reservations you have about the accuracy of your revised appraisal. State clearly any assumptions that you make.

(20 marks)

(b) You are later told that the draft cash flow estimates did not include the effects of changing prices. Discuss whether, on the basis of this new information, any further amendments to your analysis might be necessary.

(5 marks)

(Total 25 marks)

ACCA Level 3 Financial Management

PART 4

Information for Planning, Control and Performance Measurement

The objective in this section is to consider the implementation of decisions through the planning and control process. Planning involves systematically looking at the future, so that decisions can be made today which will bring the company its desired results. Control can be defined as the process of measuring and correcting actual performance to ensure that plans for implementing the chosen course of action are carried out.

Part Four contains seven chapters. Chapter 15 considers the role of budgeting within the planning process and the relationship between the long-range plan and the budgeting process. The budgeting process in profit-oriented organizations is compared with that in non-profit organizations.

Chapters 16–19 are concerned with the control process. To fully understand the role that management accounting control systems play in the control process, it is necessary to be aware of how they relate to the entire array of control mechanisms used by organizations. Chapter 16 describes the different types of controls that are used by companies. The elements of management accounting control systems are described within the context of the overall control process. To design effective management accounting control systems it is necessary to consider the circumstances in which they will be used. There is no universally best management accounting control system which can be applied to all organizations. The applicability of a management accounting control system is contingent on the circumstances faced by organizations. Chapter 17 describes the contingency theory of management accounting. In addition, the role of management accounting is examined within a social, organizational and political context. Chapters 18 and 19 focus on the technical aspects of accounting control systems. They describe the major features of a standard costing system: a system that enables the differences between the planned and actual outcomes to be analysed in detail. Chapter 18 describes the operation of a standard costing system and explains the procedure for calculating the variances. Chapter 19 examines the difficulties that arise from using standard costing in today's environment, and looks at some suggestions for overcoming them.

Chapters 20 and 21 examine the special problems of control and measuring performance of divisions and other decentralized units within an organization. Chapter 20 considers how divisional financial performance measures might be devised which will motivate managers to pursue overall organizational goals. Chapter 21 focuses on the transfer pricing problem and examines how transfer prices can be established that will motivate managers to make optimal decisions and also ensure that the performance measures derived from using the transfer prices represent a fair reflection of managerial performance.

The budgeting process

15

In the previous seven chapters we have considered how management accounting can assist managers in making decisions. The actions that follow managerial decisions normally involve several aspects of the business, such as the marketing, production, purchasing and finance functions, and it is important that management should coordinate these various interrelated aspects of decision-making. If they fail to do this, there is a danger that managers may each make decisions that they believe are in the best interests of the organization when, in fact, taken together they are not; for example, the marketing department may introduce a promotional campaign that is designed to increase sales demand to a level beyond that which the production department can handle. The various activities within a company should be coordinated by the preparation of plans of actions for future periods. These detailed plans are usually referred to as **budgets**.

Our objective in this chapter is to focus on the planning process within a business organization and to consider the role of budgeting within this process. What do we mean

LEARNING OBJECTIVES

After studying this chapter, you should be able to:

- explain how budgeting fits into the overall planning and control framework;
- identify and describe the six different purposes of budgeting;
- identify and describe the various stages in the budget process;
- prepare functional and master budgets;
- describe the use of computer-based financial models for budgeting;
- describe the limitations of incremental budgeting;
- describe activity-based budgeting;
- describe budgeting and planning, programming budgeting systems (PPBS) in non-profit organizations;
- describe zero-base budgeting (ZBB).

by planning? Planning is the design of a desired future and of effective ways of bringing it about (Ackoff, 1981). A distinction is normally made between short-term planning (budgeting) and **long-range planning**, alternatively known as **strategic** or **corporate planning**. How is long-range planning distinguished from other forms of planning? Sizer (1989) defines long-range planning as a systematic and formalized process for purposely directing and controlling future operations towards desired objectives for periods extending beyond one year. Short-term planning or budgeting, on the other hand, must accept the environment of today, and the physical, human and financial resources at present available to the firm. These are to a considerable extent determined by the quality of the firm's long-range planning efforts.

Stages in the planning process

To help you understand the budgetary process we shall begin by looking at how it fits into an overall general framework of planning, decision-making and control. The framework outlined in this model will be used to illustrate the role of long-term and short-term planning within the overall planning and control process (Figure 15.1). The first stage involves establishing the objectives of the organization.

Stage 1: Establishing objectives

Establishing **objectives** is an essential pre-requisite of the planning process. In all organizations employees must have a good understanding of what the organization is trying to achieve. Strategic or long-range planning therefore begins with the specification of the objectives towards which future operations should be directed. The attainment of objectives should be measurable in some way and ideally people should be motivated by them. Johnson and Scholes (2002) distinguish between three different objectives, which form a hierarchy: the 'mission' of an organization, corporate objectives and unit objectives.

The **mission** of an organization describes in very general terms the broad purpose and reason for an organization's existence, the nature of the business(es) it is in and the customers it seeks to serve and satisfy. It is a visionary projection of the central and overriding concepts on which the organization is based. Objectives tend to be more specific, and represent desired states or results to be achieved.

Corporate objectives relate to the organization as a whole. They are normally measurable and are expressed in financial terms such as desired profits or sales levels, return on capital employed, rates of growth or market share. Corporate objectives are normally formulated by members of the board of directors and handed down to senior managers. It is important that senior managers in an organization understand clearly where their company is going and why and how their own role contributes to the attainment of corporate objectives. Once the overall objectives of the organization have been established they must be broken down into subsidiary objectives relating to areas such as product range, market segmentation, customer service and so on. Objectives must also be developed for the different parts of an organization. **Unit objectives** relate to the specific objectives of individual units within the organization, such as a division or one company within a holding company. Corporate objectives are normally set for the organization as a whole and are then translated into unit objectives, which become the targets for the individual units. You should note that the expression **aims** is sometimes used as an alternative to mission and the term **goals** is synonymous with objectives.

FIGURE 15.1 *The role of long- and short-term planning within the planning, decision-making and control process*

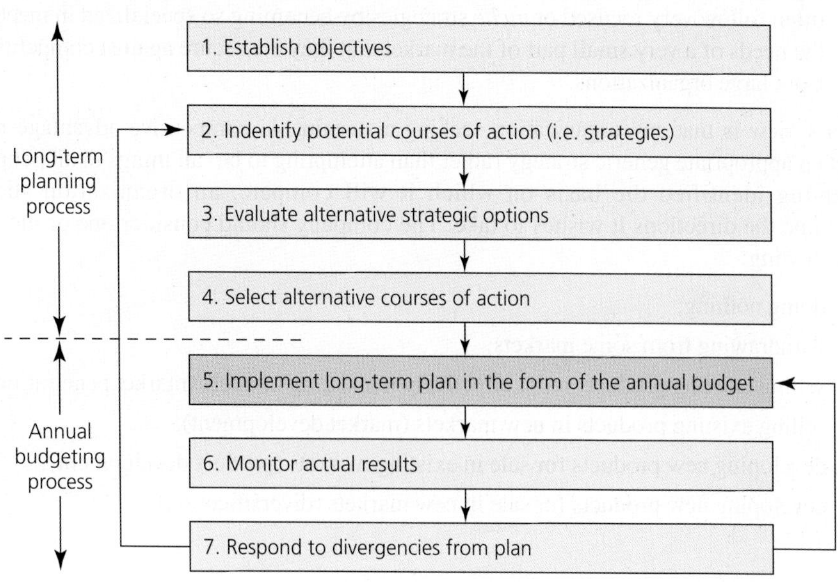

Stage 2: Identify potential strategies

The next stage shown in Figure 15.1 is to identify a range of possible courses of action (or strategies) that might enable the company's objectives to be achieved. The corporate strategy literature advocates that, prior to developing strategies, it is necessary to undertake a strategic analysis to become better informed about the organization's present strategic situation. This involves understanding the company's present position, its strengths and weaknesses and its opportunities and risks.

Having undertaken a strategic analysis, the next stage is to identify alternative strategies. The identification of strategies should take into account the following:

1 the generic strategy to be pursued (i.e. the basis on which the organization will compete or sustain excellence).

2 the alternative directions in which the organization may wish to develop.

An organization should determine the basis on which it will compete and/or sustain a superior level of performance (i.e. the generic strategy that it will follow). The purpose is to ensure that deliberate choices are made regarding the type of competitive advantage it wishes to attain. Porter (1985) has identified three generic strategies that an organization can follow:

1 *cost leadership*, whereby the organization aims to be the lowest cost producer within the industry;

2 *differentiation*, through which the organization seeks some unique dimension in its product/service that is valued by consumers, and which can command a premium price;

3 *focus*, whereby the organization determines the way in which the strategy is focused at particular parts of the market. For example, a product or service may be aimed at a particular buyer group, segment of the product line or smaller geographical area.

An organization that adopts a focused strategy aimed at narrow segments of the market to the exclusion of others also needs to determine whether within the segment it will compete through cost leadership or differentiation. Small companies often follow very focused or *niche* strategies by becoming so specialized in meeting the needs of a very small part of the market that they are secure against competition from large organizations.

Porter's view is that any organization seeking a sustainable competitive advantage must select an appropriate generic strategy rather than attempting to be 'all things to all people'.

Having identified the basis on which it will compete, an organization should determine the directions it wishes to take. The company should consider one or more of the following:

1 doing nothing;
2 withdrawing from some markets;
3 selling existing products more effectively in existing markets (market penetration);
4 selling existing products in new markets (market development);
5 developing new products for sale in existing markets (product development);
6 developing new products for sale in new markets (diversification).

Stage 3: Evaluation of strategic options

The alternative strategies should be examined based on the following criteria:[1]

1 *suitability*, which seeks to ascertain the extent to which the proposed strategies fit the situation identified in the strategic analysis. For example, does the strategy exploit the company strengths and environmental opportunities, avoid the weaknesses and counter the environmental threats?
2 *feasibility*, which focuses on whether the strategy can be implemented in resource terms. For example, can the strategy be funded? Can the necessary market position be achieved? Can the company cope with the competitive reactions?
3 *acceptability*, which is concerned with whether a particular strategy is acceptable. For example, will it be sufficiently profitable? Is the level of risk acceptable?

The above criteria represent a broad framework of general criteria against which strategic options can be judged. The criteria narrow down the options to be considered for a detailed evaluation. The evaluation of the options should be based on the approaches described in Chapters 13 and 14 and will not be repeated here. Management should select those strategic options that have the greatest potential for achieving the company's objectives. There could be just one strategy chosen or several.

Stage 4: select course of action

When management has selected those strategic options that have the greatest potential for achieving the company's objectives, long-term plans should be created to implement the strategies. A **long-term plan** is a statement of the preliminary targets and activities required by an organization to achieve its strategic plans together with a broad estimate for each year of the resources required.

Because long-term planning involves 'looking into the future' for several years ahead the plans tend to be uncertain, general in nature, imprecise and subject to change.

Stage 5: implementation of the long-term plans

Budgeting is concerned with the implementation of the long-term plan for the year ahead. Because of the shorter planning horizon budgets are more precise and detailed. Budgets are a clear indication of what is expected to be achieved during the budget period whereas long-term plans represent the broad directions that top management intend to follow.

The budget is not something that originates 'from nothing' each year – it is developed within the context of ongoing business and is ruled by previous decisions that have been taken within the long-term planning process. When the activities are initially approved for inclusion in the long-term plan, they are based on uncertain estimates that are projected for several years. These proposals must be reviewed and revised in the light of more recent information. This review and revision process frequently takes place as part of the annual budgeting process, and it may result in important decisions being taken on possible activity adjustments within the current budget period. The budgeting process cannot therefore be viewed as being purely concerned with the current year – it must be considered as an integrated part of the long-term planning process.

Stages 6 and 7: Monitor actual outcomes and respond to divergencies from planned outcomes

The final stages in the decision-making, planning and control process outlined in Figure 15.1 are to compare the actual and the planned outcomes, and to respond to any divergencies from the plan. These stages represent the control process of budgeting, but a detailed discussion of this process will be deferred until Chapter 16. Let us now consider the short-term budgeting process in more detail.

The multiple functions of budgets

Budgets serve a number of useful purposes. They include:

1. *planning* annual operations;
2. *coordinating* the activities of the various parts of the organization and ensuring that the parts are in harmony with each other;
3. *communicating* plans to the various responsibility centre managers;
4. *motivating* managers to strive to achieve the organizational goals;
5. *controlling* activities;
6. *evaluating* the performance of managers.

Let us now examine each of these six factors.

Planning

The major planning decisions will already have been made as part of the long-term planning process. However, the annual budgeting process leads to the refinement of those plans, since managers must produce detailed plans for the implementation of the long-range plan. Without the annual budgeting process, the pressures of day-to-day operating problems may tempt managers not to plan for future operations. The budgeting process ensures that managers do plan for future operations, and that they consider how conditions in the next year might change and what steps they should take now to respond to these changed conditions. This process encourages managers to anticipate problems before they arise, and hasty decisions that are made on the spur of the moment, based on expediency rather than reasoned judgement, will be minimized.

Coordination

The budget serves as a vehicle through which the actions of the different parts of an organization can be brought together and reconciled into a common plan. Without any guidance, managers may each make their own decisions, believing that they are working in the best interests of the organization. For example, the purchasing manager may prefer to place large orders so as to obtain large discounts; the production manager will be concerned with avoiding high stock levels; and the accountant will be concerned with the impact of the decision on the cash resources of the business. It is the aim of budgeting to reconcile these differences for the good of the organization as a whole, rather than for the benefit of any individual area. Budgeting therefore compels managers to examine the relationship between their own operations and those of other departments, and, in the process, to identify and resolve conflicts.

Communication

If an organization is to function effectively, there must be definite lines of communication so that all the parts will be kept fully informed of the plans and the policies, and constraints, to which the organization is expected to conform. Everyone in the organization should have a clear understanding of the part they are expected to play in achieving the annual budget. This process will ensure that the appropriate individuals are made accountable for implementing the budget. Through the budget, top management communicates its expectations to lower level management, so that all members of the organization may understand these expectations and can coordinate their activities to attain them. It is not just the budget itself that facilitates communication – much vital information is communicated in the actual act of preparing it.

Motivation

The budget can be a useful device for influencing managerial behaviour and motivating managers to perform in line with the organizational objectives. A budget provides a standard that under certain circumstances, a manager may be motivated to strive to achieve. However, budgets can also encourage inefficiency and conflict between managers. If individuals have actively participated in preparing the budget, and it is used as a tool to assist managers in managing their departments, it can act as a strong motivational device by providing a challenge. Alternatively, if the budget is dictated from above, and imposes a threat rather than a challenge, it may be resisted and do more harm than good. We shall discuss the dysfunctional motivational consequence of budgets in Chapter 16.

Control

A budget assists managers in managing and controlling the activities for which they are responsible. By comparing the actual results with the budgeted amounts for different categories of expenses, managers can ascertain which costs do not conform to the original plan and thus require their attention. This process enables management to operate a system of **management by exception** which means that a manager's attention and effort can be concentrated on significant deviations from the expected results. By investigating the reasons for the deviations, managers may be able to identify inefficiencies such as the purchase of inferior quality materials. When the reasons for the inefficiencies have been found, appropriate control action should be taken to remedy the situation.

Performance evaluation

A manager's performance is often evaluated by measuring his or her success in meeting the budgets. In some companies bonuses are awarded on the basis of an employee's ability to achieve the targets specified in the periodic budgets, or promotion may be partly dependent upon a manager's budget record. In addition, the manager may wish to evaluate his or her own performance. The budget thus provides a useful means of informing managers of how well they are performing in meeting targets that they have previously helped to set. The use of budgets as a method of performance evaluation also influences human behaviour, and for this reason we shall consider the behavioural aspects of performance evaluation in Chapter 16.

Conflicting roles of budgets

Because a single budget system is normally used to serve several purposes there is a danger that they may conflict with each other. For instance the planning and motivation roles may be in conflict with each other. Demanding budgets that may not be achieved may be appropriate to motivate maximum performance, but they are unsuitable for planning purposes. For these a budget should be set based on easier targets that are expected to be met.

There is also a conflict between the planning and performance evaluation roles. For planning purposes budgets are set in advance of the budget period based on an anticipated set of circumstances or environment. Performance evaluation should be based on a comparison of actual performance with an adjusted budget to reflect the circumstances under which managers actually operated. In practice, many firms compare actual performance with the original budget (adjusted to the actual level of activity, i.e. a flexible budget), but if the circumstances envisaged when the original budget was set have changed then there will be a planning and evaluation conflict.

The budget period

The conventional approach is that once per year the manager of each budget centre prepares a detailed budget for one year. The budget is divided into either twelve monthly or thirteen four-weekly periods for control purposes. The preparation of budgets on an annual basis has been strongly criticized on the grounds that it is too rigid and ties a company to a twelve month commitment, which can be risky because the budget is based on uncertain forecasts.

An alternative approach is for the annual budget to be broken down by months for the first three months, and by quarters for the remaining nine months.The quarterly budgets are then developed on a monthly basis as the year proceeds. For example, during the first quarter, the monthly budgets for the second quarter will be prepared; and during the second quarter, the monthly budgets for the third quarter will be prepared. The quarterly budgets may also be reviewed as the year unfolds. For example, during the first quarter, the budget for the next three quarters may be changed as new information becomes available. A new budget for a fifth quarter will also be prepared. This process is known as **continuous** or **rolling budgeting**, and ensures that a twelve month budget is always available by adding a quarter in the future as the quarter just ended is dropped. Contrast this with a budget prepared once per year. As the year goes by, the period for which a budget is available will shorten until the budget for next year is prepared. Rolling budgets also ensure that planning is not something that takes place once a year when the budget is being formulated. Instead, budgeting is a continuous process, and managers are encouraged to constantly look ahead and review future plans. Furthermore, it is likely that actual performance will be compared with a more realistic target, because budgets are being constantly reviewed and updated. The main disadvantage of a rolling budget is that it can create uncertainty for managers because the budget is constantly being changed.

Irrespective of whether the budget is prepared on an annual or a continuous basis, it is important that monthly or four-weekly budgets be used for *control* purposes.

Administration of the budgeting process

It is important that suitable administration procedures be introduced to ensure that the budget process works effectively. In practice, the procedures should be tailor-made to the requirements of the organization, but as a general rule a firm should ensure that procedures are established for approving the budgets and that the appropriate staff support is available for assisting managers in preparing their budgets.

The budget committee

The budget committee should consist of high-level executives who represent the major segments of the business. Its major task is to ensure that budgets are realistically established and that they are coordinated satisfactorily. The normal procedure is for the functional heads to present their budget to the committee for approval. If the budget does not reflect a reasonable level of performance, it will not be approved and the functional head will be required to adjust the budget and re-submit it for approval. It is important that the person whose performance is being measured should agree that the revised budget can be achieved; otherwise, if it is considered to be impossible to achieve, it will not act as a motivational device. If budget revisions are made, the budgetees should at least feel that they were given a fair hearing by the committee. We shall discuss budget negotiation in more detail later in this chapter.

The budget committee should appoint a budget officer, who will normally be the accountant. The role of the budget officer is to coordinate the individual budgets into a budget for the whole organization, so that the budget committee and the budgetee can see the impact of an individual budget on the organization as a whole.

Accounting staff

The accounting staff will normally assist managers in the preparation of their budgets; they will, for example, circulate and advise on the instructions about budget preparation, provide past information that may be useful for preparing the present budget, and ensure that managers submit their budgets on time. The accounting staff do not determine the content of the various budgets, but they do provide a valuable advisory and clerical service for the line managers.

Budget manual

A budget manual should be prepared by the accountant. It will describe the objectives and procedures involved in the budgeting process and will provide a useful reference source for managers responsible for budget preparation. In addition, the manual may include a timetable specifying the order in which the budgets should be prepared and the dates when they should be presented to the budget committee. The manual should be circulated to all individuals who are responsible for preparing budgets.

Stages in the budgeting process

The important stages are as follows:

1. communicating details of budget policy and guidelines to those people responsible for the preparation of budgets;
2. determining the factor that restricts output;
3. preparation of the sales budget;
4. initial preparation of various budgets;
5. negotiation of budgets with superiors;
6. coordination and review of budgets;
7. final acceptance of budgets;
8. ongoing review of budgets.

Let us now consider each of these stages in more detail.

Communicating details of the budget policy

Many decisions affecting the budget year will have been taken previously as part of the long-term planning process. The long-range plan is therefore the starting point for the preparation of the annual budget. Thus top management must communicate the policy effects of the long-term plan to those responsible for preparing the current year's budgets. Policy effects might include planned changes in sales mix, or the expansion or contraction of certain activities. In addition, other important guidelines that are to govern the preparation of the budget should be specified – for example the allowances that are to be made for price and wage increases, and the expected changes in productivity. Also, any expected changes in industry demand and output should be communicated by top management to the managers responsible for budget preparation. It is essential that all managers be made aware of the policy of top management for implementing the long-term plan in the current year's budget so that common guidelines can be established. The process also indicates to the managers responsible for preparing the budgets how they should respond to any expected environmental changes.

Determining the factor that restricts performance

In every organization there is some factor that restricts performance for a given period. In the majority of organizations this factor is sales demand. However, it is possible for production capacity to restrict performance when sales demand is in excess of available capacity. Prior to the preparation of the budgets, it is necessary for top management to determine the factor that restricts performance, since this factor determines the point at which the annual budgeting process should begin.

Preparation of the sales budget

The volume of sales and the sales mix determine the level of a company's operations, when sales demand is the factor that restricts output. For this reason, the sales budget is the most important plan in the annual budgeting process. This budget is also the most difficult plan to produce, because total sales revenue depends on the actions of customers. In addition, sales demand may be influenced by the state of the economy or the actions of competitors.

Initial preparation of budgets

The managers who are responsible for meeting the budgeted performance should prepare the budget for those areas for which they are responsible. The preparation of the budget should be a 'bottom-up' process. This means that the budget should originate at the lowest levels of management and be refined and coordinated at higher levels. The justification for this approach is that it enables managers to participate in the preparation of their budgets and increases the probability that they will accept the budget and strive to achieve the budget targets.

There is no single way in which the appropriate quantity for a particular budget item is determined. Past data may be used as the starting point for producing the budgets, but this does not mean that budgeting is based on the assumption that what has happened in the past will occur in the future. Changes in future conditions must be taken into account, but past information may provide useful guidance for the future. In addition, managers may look to the guidelines provided by top management for determining the content of their budgets. For example, the guidelines may provide specific instructions as to the content of their budgets and the permitted changes that can be made in the prices of purchases of materials and services. For production activities standard costs may be used as the basis for costing activity volumes which are planned in the budget.

Negotiation of budgets

To implement a participative approach to budgeting, the budget should be originated at the lowest level of management. The managers at this level should submit their budget to their superiors for approval. The superior should then incorporate this budget with other budgets for which he or she is responsible and then submit this budget for approval to his or her superior. The manager who is the superior then becomes the budgetee at the next higher level. The process is illustrated in Figure 15.2. Sizer (1989) describes this approach as a two-way process of a top-down statement of objectives and strategies, bottom-up budget preparation and top-down approval by senior management.

The lower-level managers are represented by boxes 1–8. Managers 1 and 2 will prepare their budgets in accordance with the budget policy and the guidelines laid down by top management. The managers will submit their budget to their supervisor, who is in charge of the whole department (department A). Once these budgets have been agreed by the manager of department A, they will be combined by the departmental manager, who will then present this budget to his or her superior (manager of plant 1) for approval. The manager of plant 1 is also responsible for department B, and will combine the agreed budgets for departments A and B before presenting the combined budget to his or her supervisor (the production manager). The

FIGURE 15.2 *An illustration of budgets moving up the organization hierarchy*

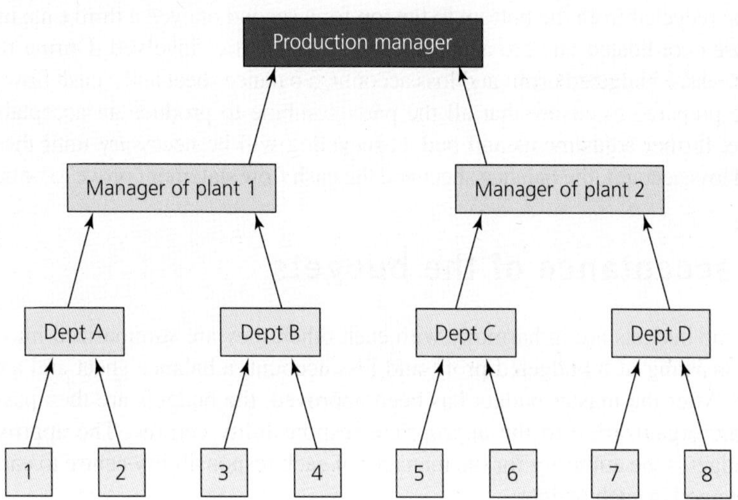

production manager will merge the budget for plants 1 and 2, and this final budget will represent the production budget that will be presented to the budget committee for approval.

At each of these stages the budgets will be negotiated between the budgetees and their superiors, and eventually they will be agreed by both parties. Hence the figures that are included in the budget are the result of a bargaining process between a manager and his or her superior. It is important that the budgetees should participate in arriving at the final budget and that the superior does not revise the budget without giving full consideration to the subordinates' arguments for including any of the budgeted items. Otherwise, real participation will not be taking place, and it is unlikely that the subordinate will be motivated to achieve a budget that he or she did not accept.

It is also necessary to be watchful that budgetees do not deliberately attempt to obtain approval for easily attainable budgets, or attempt to deliberately understate budgets in the hope that the budget that is finally agreed will represent an easily attainable target. It is equally unsatisfactory for a superior to impose difficult targets in the hope that an authoritarian approach will produce the desired results. The desired results may be achieved in the short term, but only at the cost of a loss of morale and increased labour turnover in the future.

The negotiation process is of vital importance in the budgeting process, and can determine whether the budget becomes a really effective management tool or just a clerical device. If managers are successful in establishing a position of trust and confidence with their subordinates, the negotiation process will produce a meaningful improvement in the budgetary process and outcomes for the period.

Coordination and review of budgets

As the individual budgets move up the organizational hierarchy in the negotiation process, they must be examined in relation to each other. This examination may indicate that some budgets are out of balance with other budgets and need modifying so that they will be compatible with other conditions, constraints and plans that are beyond a manager's knowledge or control. For example, a plant manager may include equipment replacement in his or her budget when funds are simply not available. The accountant must identify such inconsistencies and bring them to the attention of the appropriate manager. Any changes in the budgets should be made by the responsible managers, and this may require that the budgets be recycled from the bottom to the top for a second or even a third time until all the budgets are coordinated and are acceptable to all the parties involved. During the coordination process, a budgeted profit and loss account, a balance sheet and a cash flow statement should be prepared to ensure that all the parts combine to produce an acceptable whole. Otherwise, further adjustments and budget recycling will be necessary until the budgeted profit and loss account, the balance sheet and the cash flow statement prove to be acceptable.

Final acceptance of the budgets

When all the budgets are in harmony with each other, they are summarized into a **master budget** consisting of a budgeted profit and loss account, a balance sheet and a cash flow statement. After the master budget has been approved, the budgets are then passed down through the organization to the appropriate responsibility centres. The approval of the master budget is the authority for the manager of each responsibility centre to carry out the plans contained in each budget.

Budget review

The budget process should not stop when the budgets have been agreed. Periodically, the actual results should be compared with the budgeted results. These comparisons should normally be made on a monthly basis and a report sent to the appropriate budgetees in the first week of the following month, so that it has the maximum motivational impact. This will enable management to identify the items that are not proceeding according to plan and to investigate the reasons for the differences. If these differences are within the control of management, corrective action can be taken to avoid similar inefficiencies occurring again in the future. However, the differences may be due to the fact that the budget was unrealistic to begin with, or that the actual conditions during the budget year were different from those anticipated; the budget for the remainder of the year would than be invalid.

During the budget year, the budget committee should periodically evaluate the actual performance and reappraise the company's future plans. If there are any changes in the actual conditions from those originally expected, this will normally mean that the budget plans should be adjusted. This revised budget then represents a revised statement of formal operating plans for the remaining portion of the budget period. The important point to note is that the budgetary process does not end for the current year once the budget has begun; budgeting should be seen as a continuous and dynamic process.

A detailed illustration

Let us now look at an illustration of the procedure for constructing budgets in a manufacturing company, using the information contained in Example 15.1. Note that the level of detail included here is much less than that which would be presented in practice. A truly realistic illustration would fill many pages, with detailed budgets being analysed in various ways. We shall consider an annual budget, whereas a realistic illustration would analyse the annual budget into twelve monthly periods. Monthly analysis would considerably increase the size of the illustration, but would not give any further insight into the basic concepts or procedures. In addition,

EXAMPLE 15.1

The Enterprise Company manufactures two products, known as alpha and sigma. Alpha is produced in department 1 and sigma in department 2. The following information is available for 200X.

Standard material and labour costs:

	(£)
Material X	7.20 per unit
Material Y	16.00 per unit
Direct labour	12.00 per hour

Overhead is recovered on a direct labour hour basis.

The standard material and labour usage for each product is as follows:

	Model alpha	Model sigma
Material X	10 units	8 units
Material Y	5 units	9 units
Direct labour	10 hours	15 hours

The balance sheet for the previous year end 200X was as follows:

	(£)	(£)	(£)
Fixed assets:			
Land		170 000	
Buildings and equipment	1 292 000		
Less depreciation	255 000	1 037 000	1 207 000
Current assets:			
Stocks, finished goods	99 076		
raw materials	189 200		
Debtors	289 000		
Cash	34 000		
	611 276		
Less current liabilities			
Creditors	248 800		362 476
Net assets			1 569 476
Represented by shareholder's interest:			
1 200 000 ordinary shares of £1 each		1 200 000	
Reserves		369 476	
			1 569 476

Other relevant data is as follows for the year 200X:

	Finished product	
	Model alpha	Model sigma
Forecast sales (units)	8500	1600
Selling price per unit	£400	£560
Ending inventory required (units)	1870	90
Beginning inventory (units)	170	85

	Direct material	
	Material X	Material Y
Beginning inventory (units)	8 500	8 000
Ending inventory required (units)	10 200	1 700

	Department 1 (£)	Department 2 (£)
Budgeted variable overhead rates		
(per direct labour hour):		
Indirect materials	1.20	0.80
Indirect labour	1.20	1.20
Power (variable portion)	0.60	0.40
Maintenance (variable portion)	0.20	0.40
Budgeted fixed overheads		
Depreciation	100 000	80 000
Supervision	100 000	40 000
Power (fixed portion)	40 000	2 000
Maintenance (fixed portion)	45 600	3 196

	(£)
Estimated non-manufacturing overheads:	
Stationery etc. (Administration)	4 000
Salaries	
Sales	74 000
Office	28 000
Commissions	60 000
Car expenses (Sales)	22 000
Advertising	80 000
Miscellaneous (Office)	8 000
	276 000

Budgeted cash flows are as follows:

	Quarter 1 (£)	Quarter 2 (£)	Quarter 3 (£)	Quarter 4 (£)
Receipts from customers	1 000 000	1 200 000	1 120 000	985 000
Payments:				
Materials	400 000	480 000	440 000	547 984
Payments for wages	400 000	440 000	480 000	646 188
Other costs and expenses	120 000	100 000	72 016	13 642

You are required to prepare a master budget for the year 200X and the following budgets:

1 sales budget;

2 production budget;

3 direct materials usage budget;
4 direct materials purchase budget;
5 direct labour budget;
6 factory overhead budget;
7 selling and administration budget;
8 cash budget.

we shall assume in this example that the budgets are prepared for only two responsibility centres (namely departments 1 and 2). In practice, many responsibility centres are likely to exist.

Sales budget

The sales budget shows the quantities of each product that the company plans to sell and the intended selling price. It provides the predictions of total revenue from which cash receipts from customers will be estimated, and it also supplies the basic data for constructing budgets for production costs, and for selling, distribution and administrative expenses. The sales budget is therefore the foundation of all other budgets, since all expenditure is ultimately dependent on the volume of sales. If the sales budget is not accurate, the other budget estimates will be unreliable. We will assume that the Enterprise Company has completed a marketing analysis and that the following annual sales budget is based on the result:

Schedule 1 – Sales budget for year ending 200X

Product	Units sold	Selling price (£)	Total revenue (£)
Alpha	8500	400	3 400 000
Sigma	1600	560	896 000
			4 296 000

Schedule 1 represents the *total* sales budget for the year. In practice, the *total* sales budget will be supported by detailed *subsidiary* sales budgets where sales are analysed by areas of responsibility, such as sales territories, and into monthly periods analysed by products. The detailed *subsidiary* sales budget could be set out as shown on page 601.

Note that with the detailed subsidiary monthly budgets the total budgeted sales of £4 296 000 is analysed by each sales territory for each month of the budget period. The detailed analysis assumes that sales are divided among the four sales territories as follows:

	Alpha	Sigma
North	3000 units	500 units
South	2500 units	600 units
East	1000 units	200 units
West	2000 units	300 units
	8500 units	1600 units

Detailed monthly budgets for North, South, East and West sales territories

		North		South		East		West		Total	
		Units	Value (£)	Units	Value (£)	Units	Value (£)	Units	Value (£)	Units	Value (£)
Month 1	Alpha										
	Sigma										
	Total										
Month 2											
Month 3											
Month 4											
Month 5											
Month 6											
Month 7											
Month 8											
Month 9											
Month 10											
Month 11											
Month 12											
Total months 1–12											
	Alpha	3000	1 200 000	2500	1 000 000	1000	400 000	2000	800 000	8500	3 400 000
	Sigma	500	280 000	600	336 000	200	112 000	300	168 000	1600	896 000
			1 480 000		1 336 000		512 000		968 000		4 296 000

Production budget and budgeted stock levels

When the sales budget has been completed, the next stage is to prepare the production budget. This budget is expressed in *quantities only* and is the responsibility of the production manager. The objective is to ensure that production is sufficient to meet sales demand and that economic stock levels are maintained. The production budget (schedule 2) for the year will be as follows:

Schedule 2 – Annual production budget

	Department 1 (alpha)	Department 2 (sigma)
Units to be sold	8 500	1600
Planned closing stock	1 870	90
Total units required for sales and stocks	10 370	1690
Less planned opening stocks	170	85
Units to be produced	10 200	1605

The total production for each department should also be analysed on a monthly basis.

Direct materials usage budget

The supervisors of departments 1 and 2 will prepare estimates of the materials which are required to meet the production budget. The materials usage budget for the year will be as follows:

Schedule 3 – Annual direct material usage budget

	Department 1			Department 2					
	Units	Unit price (£)	Total (£)	Units	Unit price (£)	Total (£)	Total units	Total unit price (£)	Total (£)
Material X	102 000[a]	7.20	734 400	12 840[c]	7.20	92 448	114 840	7.20	826 848
Material Y	51 000[b]	16.00	816 000	14 445[d]	16.00	231 120	65 445	16.00	1 047 120
			1 550 400			323 568			1 873 968

[a]10 200 units production at 10 units per unit of production.
[b]10 200 units production at 5 units per unit of production.
[c]1605 units production at 8 units per unit of production.
[d]1605 units production at 9 units per unit of production.

Direct materials purchase budget

The direct materials purchase budget is the responsibility of the purchasing manager, since it will be he or she who is responsible for obtaining the planned quantities of raw materials to meet the production requirements. The objective is to purchase these materials at the right time at the planned purchase price. In addition, it is necessary to take into account the planned raw material stock levels. The annual materials purchase budget for the year will be as follows:

Schedule 4 – Direct materials purchase budget

	Material X (units)	Material Y (units)
Quantity necessary to meet production requirements as per material usage budget	114 840	65 445
Planned closing stock	10 200	1 700
	125 040	67 145
Less planned opening stock	8 500	8 000
Total units to be purchased	116 540	59 145
Planned unit purchase price	£7.20	£16
Total purchases	£839 088	£946 320

Note that this budget is a summary budget for the year, but for detailed planning and control it will be necessary to analyse the annual budget on a monthly basis.

Direct labour budget

The direct labour budget is the responsibility of the respective managers of departments 1 and 2. They will prepare estimates of the departments' labour hours required to meet the planned production. Where different grades of labour exist, these should be specified separately in the budget. The budget rate per hour should be determined by the industrial relations department. The direct labour budget will be as follows:

Schedule 5 – Annual direct labour budget

	Department 1	Department 2	Total
Budgeted production (units)	10 200	1 605	
Hours per unit	10	15	
Total budgeted hours	102 000	24 075	126 075
Budgeted wage rate per hour	£12	£12	
Total wages	£1 224 000	£288 900	£1 512 900

Factory overhead budget

The factory overhead budget is also the responsibility of the respective production department managers. The total of the overhead budget will depend on the behaviour of the costs of the individual overhead items in relation to the anticipated level of production. The overheads must also be analysed according to whether they are controllable or non-controllable for the purpose of cost control. The factory overhead budget will be as follows:

Schedule 6 – Annual factory overhead budget
Anticipated activity – 102 000 direct labour hours (department 1)
24 075 direct labour hours (department 2)

	Variable overhead rate per direct labour hour		Overheads		
	Department 1 (£)	Department 2 (£)	Department 1 (£)	Department 2 (£)	Total (£)
Controllable overheads:					
Indirect material	1.20	0.80	122 400	19 260	
Indirect labour	1.20	1.20	122 400	28 890	
Power (variable portion)	0.60	0.40	61 200	9 630	
Maintenance (variable portion)	0.20	0.40	20 400	9 630	
			326 400	67 410	393 810
Non-controllable overheads:					
Depreciation			100 000	80 000	
Supervision			100 000	40 000	
Power (fixed portion)			40 000	2 000	
Maintenance (fixed portion)			45 600	3 196	
			285 600	125 196	410 796
Total overhead			612 000	192 606	804 606
Budgeted departmental overhead rate			£6.00[a]	8.00[b]	

[a]£612 000 total overheads divided by 102 000 direct labour hours.
[b]£192 606 total overheads divided by 24 075 direct labour hours.

The budgeted expenditure for the variable overhead items is determined by multiplying the budgeted direct labour hours for each department by the budgeted variable overhead rate per hour. It is assumed that all variable overheads vary in relation to direct labour hours.

Selling and administration budget

The selling and administration budgets have been combined here to simplify the presentation. In practice, separate budgets should be prepared: the sales manager will be responsible for the selling budget, the distribution manager will be responsible for the distribution expenses and the chief administrative officer will be responsible for the administration budget.

Schedule 7 – Annual selling and administration budget

	(£)	(£)
Selling:		
Salaries	74 000	
Commission	60 000	
Car expenses	22 000	
Advertising	80 000	236 000
Administration:		
Stationery	4 000	
Salaries	28 000	
Miscellaneous	8 000	40 000
		276 000

Departmental budgets

For cost control the direct labour budget, materials usage budget and factory overhead budget are combined into separate departmental budgets. These budgets are normally broken down into twelve separate monthly budgets, and the actual monthly expenditure is compared with the budgeted amounts for each of the items concerned. This comparison is used for judging how effective managers are in controlling the expenditure for which they are responsible. The departmental budget for department 1 will be as follows:

Department 1 – Annual departmental operating budget

	(£)	Budget (£)	Actual (£)
Direct labour (from schedule 5):			
102 000 hours at £12		1 224 000	
Direct materials (from schedule 3):			
102 000 units of material X at £7.20 per unit	734 400		
51 000 units of material Y at £16 per unit	816 000	1 550 400	
Controllable overheads (from schedule 6):			
Indirect materials	122 400		
Indirect labour	122 400		
Power (variable portion)	61 200		
Maintenance (variable portion)	20 400	326 400	

Uncontrollable overheads (from schedule 6):		
Depreciation	100 000	
Supervision	100 000	
Power (fixed portion)	40 000	
Maintenance (fixed portion)	45 600	285 600
		3 386 400

Master budget

When all the budgets have been prepared, the budgeted profit and loss account and balance sheet provide the overall picture of the planned performance for the budget period.

Budgeted profit and loss account for the year ending 200X

		(£)	(£)
Sales (schedule 1)			4 296 000
Opening stock of raw materials (from opening balance sheet)		189 200	
Purchases (schedule 4)		1 785 408[a]	
		1 974 608	
Less closing stock of raw materials (schedule 4)		100 640[b]	
Cost of raw materials consumed		1 873 968	
Direct labour (schedule 5)		1 512 900	
Factory overheads (schedule 6)		804 606	
Total manufacturing cost		4 191 474	
Add opening stock of finished goods (from opening balance sheet)	99 076		
Less closing stock of finished goods	665 984[c]		
		(566 908)	
Cost of sales			3 624 566
Gross profit			671 434
Selling and administration expenses (schedule 7)			276 000
Budgeted operating profit for the year			395 434

[a]£839 088 (X) + £946 320 (Y) from schedule 4.

[b]10 200 units at £7.20 plus 1700 units at £16 from schedule 4.

[c]1870 units of alpha valued at £332 per unit, 90 units of sigma valued at £501.60 per unit. The product unit costs are calculated as follows:

	Alpha		Sigma	
	Units	(£)	Units	(£)
Direct materials				
X	10	72.00	8	57.60
Y	5	80.00	9	144.00
Direct labour	10	120.00	15	180.00
Factory overheads:				
Department 1	10	60.00	—	—
Department 2	—	—	15	120.00
		332.00		501.60

Budgeted balance sheet as at 31 December

	(£)	(£)
Fixed assets:		
Land		170 000
Building and equipment	1 292 000	
Less depreciation[a]	435 000	857 000
		1 027 000
Current assets:		
Raw material stock	100 640	
Finished good stock	665 984	
Debtors[b]	280 000	
Cash[c]	199 170	
	1 245 794	
Current liabilities:		
Creditors[d]	307 884	937 910
		1 964 910
Represented by shareholders' interest:		
1 200 000 ordinary shares of £1 each	1 200 000	
Reserves	369 476	
Profit and loss account	395 434	1 964 910

[a]£255 000 + £180 000 (schedule 6) = £435 000.
[b]£289 000 opening balance + £4 296 000 sales – £4 305 000 cash.
[c]Closing balance as per cash budget.
[d]£248 800 opening balance + £1 785 408 purchases + £141 660 indirect materials – £1 876 984 cash.

Cash budgets

The objective of the cash budget is to ensure that sufficient cash is available at all times to meet the level of operations that are outlined in the various budgets. The cash budget for Example 15.1 is presented below and is analysed by quarters, but in practice monthly or weekly budgets will be necessary. Because cash budgeting is subject to uncertainty, it is necessary to provide for more than the minimum amount required, to allow for some margin of error in planning. Cash budgets can help a firm to avoid cash balances that are surplus to its requirements by enabling management to take steps in advance to invest the surplus cash in short-term investments. Alternatively, cash deficiencies can be identified in advance, and steps can be taken to ensure that bank loans will be available to meet any temporary cash deficiencies. For example, by looking at the cash budget for the Enterprise Company, management may consider that the cash balances are higher than necessary in the second and third quarters of the year, and they may invest part of the cash balance in short-term investments.

The overall aim should be to manage the cash of the firm to attain maximum cash availability and maximum interest income on any idle funds.

Cash budget for year ending 200X

	Quarter 1 (£)	Quarter 2 (£)	Quarter 3 (£)	Quarter 4 (£)	Total (£)
Opening balance	34 000	114 000	294 000	421 984	34 000
Receipts from debtors	1 000 000	1 200 000	1 120 000	985 000	4 305 000
	1 034 000	1 314 000	1 414 000	1 406 984	4 339 000
Payments:					
Purchase of materials	400 000	480 000	440 000	547 984	1 867 984
Payment of wages	400 000	440 000	480 000	646 188	1 966 188
Other costs and expenses	120 000	100 000	72 016	13 642	305 658
	920 000	1 020 000	992 016	1 207 814	4 139 830
Closing balance	114 000	294 000	421 984	199 170	199 170

Final review

The budgeted profit and loss account, the balance sheet and the cash budget will be submitted by the accountant to the budget committee, together with a number of budgeted financial ratios such as the return on capital employed, working capital, liquidity and gearing ratios. If these ratios prove to be acceptable, the budgets will be approved. In Example 15.1 the return on capital employed is approximately 20%, but the working capital ratio is over 4:1, so management should consider alternative ways of reducing investment in working capital before finally approving the budgets.

Computerized budgeting

In the past, budgeting was a task dreaded by many management accountants. You will have noted from Example 15.1 that many numerical manipulations are necessary to prepare the budget. In the real world the process is far more complex, and, as the budget is being formulated, it is altered many times since some budgets are found to be out of balance with each other or the master budget proves to be unacceptable.

In today's world, the budgeting process is computerized instead of being primarily concerned with numerical manipulations, the accounting staff can now become more involved in the real planning process. Computer-based financial models normally consist of mathematical statements of inputs and outputs. By simply altering the mathematical statements budgets can be quickly revised with little effort. However, the major advantage of computerized budgeting is that management can evaluate many different options before the budget is finally agreed. Establishing a model enables 'What-if?' analysis to be employed. For example, answers to the following questions can be displayed in the form of a master budget: What if sales increase or decrease by 10%? What if unit costs increase or decrease by 5%? What if the credit terms for sales were reduced from 30 to 20 days?

In addition, computerized models can incorporate actual results, period by period, and carry out the necessary calculations to produce budgetary *control* reports. It is also possible to adjust the budgets for the remainder of the year when it is clear that the circumstances on which the budget was originally set have changed.

Using Web technology for the budget process

An e-budgeting solution completely automates the development of an organization's budget and forecast. From anywhere in the world, at all times, participants in the process can log through the Internet to access their budget and any pertinent related information so they can work on their plans. Web-based enterprise budgeting systems offer a centrally administered system that provides easy-to-use flexible tools for the end users who are responsible for budgeting. The Web functionality of these applications allows constant monitoring, updates and modelling.

E-budgeting provides the flexibility demanded by modern organizations. For example, the finance department can request across-the-board reallocations of expenditures and model the result immediately. No longer do management accountants have to go back and forth with other managers reinputing data and retallying results. E-budgeting can eliminate the cumbersome accounting tasks of pulling numbers from disparate files, cutting and pasting, entering and uploading, and constantly performing reconciliation. Also, a Web-based budgeting application lets managers access data from office or home – wherever they happen to be working. It broadens the system's availability to the user community.

When executives at Toronto-Dominion Bank were searching for a new solution capable of handling the bank's enterprise budgeting and planning function, they turned to the Internet. The company selected Clarus Corporation's Web-deployed, enterprise Clarus™ Budget solution. Its accountant stated 'in the past, we have compiled our business plan using hundreds of spreadsheets, and our analysts have spent a disproportionate amount of their time compiling and verifying data from multiple sources. Implementing a Web-based, enterprise-wide budgeting solution will help us to develop our business plans and allow our analysts to be proactive in monitoring quarterly results.'

Source: Adapted from Hornyak, S. (2000), Budgeting made easy, in Reeve, J.M. (ed.), *Readings and Issues in Cost Management,* South Western College Publishing, pp. 341–346.

Activity-based budgeting

The conventional approach to budgeting works fine for unit level activity costs where the consumption of resources varies proportionately with the volume of the final output of products or services. However, for those indirect costs and support activities where there are no clearly defined input–output relationships, and the consumption of resources does not vary with the final output of products or services, conventional budgets merely serve as authorization levels for certain levels of spending for each budgeted item of expense. Budgets that are not based on well-understood relationships between activities and costs are poor indicators of performance and performance reporting normally implies little more than checking whether the budget has been exceeded. Conventional budgets therefore provide little relevant information for managing the costs of support activities.

With conventional budgeting indirect costs and support activities are prepared on an incremental basis. This means that existing operations and the current budgeted allowance for existing activities are taken as the starting point for preparing the next annual budget. The base is then adjusted for changes (such as changes in product mix, volumes and prices) which are expected to occur during the new budget period. This approach is called **incremental budgeting**, since the budget process is concerned mainly with the increment in operations or expenditure that will occur during the forthcoming budget period. For example, the allowance for budgeted expenses may be based on the previous budgeted allowance plus an increase to cover higher prices caused by inflation. The major disadvantage of the incremental approach is that the majority of expenditure, which is associated with the 'base level' of activity, remains unchanged. Thus, the cost of non-unit level activities become fixed and past inefficiencies and waste inherent in the current way of doing things is perpetuated.

To manage costs more effectively organizations that have implemented activity-based costing (ABC) have also adopted **activity-based budgeting (ABB)**. The aim of ABB is to authorize the supply of only those resources that are needed to perform activities required to meet the budgeted production and sales volume. Whereas ABC assigns resource expenses to activities and then uses activity cost drivers to assign activity costs to cost objects (such as products, services or customers), ABB is the reverse of this process. Cost objects are the starting point. Their budgeted output determines the necessary activities which are then used to estimate the resources that are required for the budget period. ABB involves the following stages:

1 estimate the production and sales volume by individual products and customers;
2 estimate the demand for organizational activities;
3 determine the resources that are required to perform organizational activities;
4 estimate for each resource the quantity that must be supplied to meet the demand;
5 take action to adjust the capacity of resources to match the projected supply.

The first stage is identical to conventional budgeting. Details of budgeted production and sales volumes for individual products and customer types will be contained in the sales and production budgets. Next, ABC extends conventional budgeting to support activities such as ordering, receiving, scheduling production and processing customers' orders. To implement ABB a knowledge of the activities that are necessary to produce and sell the products and services and service customers is essential. Estimates of the quantity of activity cost drivers must be derived for each activity. For example, the number of purchase orders, the number of receipts, the number of set-ups and the number of customer orders processed are estimated using the same approach as that used by conventional budgeting to determine the quantity of direct labour and materials that are incorporated into the direct labour and materials purchase budgets. Standard cost data incorporating a bill of activities is maintained for each product indicating the different activities, and the quantity of activity drivers that are required, to produce a specified number of products. Such documentation provides the basic information for building up the activity-based budgets.

The third stage is to estimate the resources that are required for performing the quantity of activity drivers demanded. In particular, estimates are required of each type of resource, and their quantities required, to meet the demanded quantity of activities. For example, if the number of customer orders to be processed is estimated to be 5000 and each order takes 30 minutes processing time then 2500 labour hours of the customer processing activity must be supplied.

Next, the resources demanded (derived from the third stage) are converted into an estimate of the total resources that must be supplied for each type of resource used by an activity. The quantity of resources supplied depends on the cost behaviour of the resource. For flexible resources where the supply can be matched exactly to meet demand, such as direct materials and energy costs, the quantity of resources supplied will be identical to the quantity demanded. For example, if customer processing were a flexible resource exactly 2500 hours would be purchased. However, a more likely assumption is that customer processing labour will be a step cost function in relation to the volume of the activity (see Chapter 2 for a description of step cost functions).

Assuming that each person employed is contracted to work 1500 hours per year then 1.67 persons (2500/1500) represents the quantity of resources required, but because resources must be acquired in uneven amounts, two persons must be employed. For other resources, such as equipment, resources will tend to be fixed and committed over a very wide range of volume for the activity. As long as demand is less than the capacity supplied by the committed resource no additional spending will be required.

The final stage is to compare the estimates of the quantity of resources to be supplied for each resource with the quantity of resources that are currently committed. If the estimated supply of a resource exceeds the current capacity additional spending must be authorized within the budgeting process to acquire additional resources. Alternatively, if the demand for resources is less than the projected supply, the budgeting process should result in management taking action to either redeploy or reduce those resources that are no longer required.

Exhibit 15.1 illustrates an activity-based budget for an order receiving process or department. You will see that the budget is presented in a matrix format with the major activities being shown for each of the columns and the resource inputs are listed by rows. The cost driver activity levels are also highlighted. A major feature of ABB is the enhanced visibility arising from showing the outcomes, in terms of cost drivers, from the budgeted expenditure. This information is particularly useful for planning and estimating future expenditure.

Let us now look at how ABB can be applied using the information presented in Exhibit 15.1. Assume that ABB stages one and two as outlined above result in an estimated annual demand of 2800 orders for the processing of the receipt of the standard customers' order activity (column 6 in Exhibit 15.1). For the staff salaries row (that is, the processing of customers' orders labour resource) assume that each member of staff can process on average 50 orders per month, or 600 per year. Therefore 4.67 (2800 orders/600 orders) persons are required for the supply of this resource (that is, stage three as outlined above). The fourth stage converts the 4.67 staff resources into the amount that must be supplied, that is 5 members of staff. Let us assume that the current capacity or supply of resources committed to the activity is 6 members of staff at £25 000 per annum, giving a total annual cost of £150 000. Management is therefore made aware that staff resources can be reduced by £25 000 per annum by transferring one member of staff to other activities where staff resources need to be expanded or, more drastically, making them redundant.

Some of the other resource expenses (such as office supplies and telephone expenses) listed in Exhibit 15.1 for the processing of customers' order activity represent flexible resources which are likely to vary in the short-term with the number of orders processed. Assuming that the budget for the forthcoming period represents 80% of the number of orders processed during the previous budget period then the budget for those resource expenses that vary in the short-term with the number of orders processed should be reduced by 20%.

With conventional budgeting the budgeted expenses for the forthcoming budget for support activities are normally based on the previous year's budget plus an adjustment for inflation. Support costs are therefore considered to be fixed in relation to activity volume. In contrast, ABB provides a framework for understanding the amount of resources that are required to achieve the budgeted level of activity. By comparing the amount of resources that are required with the amount of resources that are in place, upwards or downwards adjustments can be made during the budget setting phase.

Periodically actual results should be compared with a budget adjusted (flexed) to the actual output for the activities (in terms of cost drivers) to highlight both in financial and non-financial terms those activities with major discrepancies from budget. Assume that practical capacity for salaries for the processing of customers' standard orders activity was set at 3000 orders (5 staff at 600 orders per member of staff), even though budgeted activity was only 2800 orders, and the actual number of orders processed during the

EXHIBIT 15.1
Activity-based budget for an order receiving process

Activities →	Handle import goods	Execute express orders	Special Deliveries	Distribution administration	Order receiving (standard products)	Order receiving (non-standard products)	Execute rush orders	Total cost
Resource expense accounts:								
Office supplies								
Telephone expenses								
Salaries								
Travel								
Training								
Total cost								
Activity cost driver → measures	Number of customs documents	Number of customer bills	Number of letters of credit	Number of consignment notes	Number of standard orders	Number of non-standard orders	Number of rush orders	

period was 2500 orders. Also assume that the actual resources committed to the activity in respect of salaries was £125 000 (all fixed in the short term). The following information should be presented in the performance report:

Flexed budget based on the number of orders processed (2500 orders at £41.67)	104 175
Budgeted unused capacity (3000 – 2800) × £41.67	8 334
Actual unplanned unused capacity (2800 – 2500) × £41.67	12 491
	125 000

The cost driver rate of £41.67 per order processed is calculated by dividing the £125 000 budgeted cost of supplying the resources by the capacity supplied (3000 orders). The above activity performance information highlights for management attention the potential reduction in the supply of resources of £20 825 (£8334 expected and £12 491 unexpected) or, alternatively, the additional business that can be accommodated with the existing supply of resources.

A survey of UK organizations by Innes *et al.* (2000) found that 55% of the respondents that had adopted ABC used the activity-based approach for budgeting and 76% of these users rated the ability to set more realistic budgets as the most important benefit from ABB. Other benefits identified by the survey respondents included the better identification of resource needs and the identification of budget slack. In an earlier survey of organizations in the financial services sector Innes and Mitchell (1997) found that these organizations also derived similar benefits from ABB.

The budgeting process in non-profit-making organizations

The budgeting process in a non-profit-making organization normally begins with the managers of the various activities calculating the expected costs of maintaining current ongoing activities and then adding to those costs any further developments of the services that are considered desirable. For example, the education, health, housing and social services departments of a municipal authority will propose specific activities and related costs for the coming year. These budgets are coordinated by the accounting department into an overall budget proposal.

The available resources for financing the proposed level of public services should be sufficient to cover the total costs of such services. In the case of a municipal authority the resources will be raised by local taxes and government grants. Similar procedures are followed by churches, hospitals, charities and other non-profit-making organizations, in that they produce estimates for undertaking their activities and then find the means to finance them, or reduce the activities to realistic levels so that they can be financed from available financial resources.

One difficulty encountered in non-profit-making organizations is that precise objectives are difficult to define in a quantifiable way, and the actual accomplishments are even more difficult to measure. In most situations outputs cannot be measured in monetary terms. By 'outputs' we mean the quality and amount of the services rendered. In profit-oriented organizations output can be measured in terms of sales revenues. The effect of this is that budgets in non-profit organizations, tend to be mainly concerned with the input of resources (i.e. expenditure), whereas budgets in profit organizations focus on the relationships between inputs (expenditure) and outputs (sales revenue). In non-profit organizations there is not the same emphasis on what was intended to be achieved for a given input of resources. The budgeting process tends to compare what is happening in cash input terms with the estimated cash inputs. In other words, there is little emphasis on measures of managerial performance in terms of the results achieved. The reason for this is that there is no clear relationship between resource inputs and the benefits flowing from the use of these resources. However, we shall see that increasing efforts have been made in recent years to overcome these deficiencies by developing measures of output that can be used to compare budgeted and actual accomplishments.

Line item budgets

The traditional format for budgets in non-profit organizations is referred to as **line item budgets**. A line item budget is one in which the expenditures are expressed in considerable detail, but the activities being undertaken are given little attention. In other words, line item budgeting shows the nature of the spending but not the purpose. A typical line item budget is illustrated in Exhibit 15.2.

The amounts in this type of budget are frequently established on the basis of historical costs that have been adjusted for anticipated changes in costs and activity levels. When they are compared with the actual expenditures, line item budgets provide a basis for comparing whether or not the authorized budgeted expenditure has been exceeded or whether underspending has occurred. Note that data for the current year and for the previous year are included to indicate how the proposed budget differs from current spending patterns. However, such line item budgets fail to identify the costs of *activities* and the *programmes* to be implemented. In addition, compliance with line item budgets provides no assurance that resources are used wisely, effectively or efficiently in financing the various activities in a non-profit organization.

EXHIBIT 15.2
Typical line item budget

	Actual 20X2 (£)	Original budget 20X3 (£)	Revised budget 20X3 (£)	Proposed budget 20X4 (£)
Employees	1 292 000	1 400 000	1 441 000	1 830 000
Premises	3 239	12 000	10 800	14 200
Supplies and services	34 735	43 200	44 900	147 700
Transport	25 778	28 500	28 700	30 700
Establishment expenses	123 691	120 000	116 000	158 600
Agency charges	10 120	10 000	9 800	13 300
Financing charges	2 357	2 700	2 800	114 800
Other expenses	1 260	1 350	1 400	1 600
	1 493 180	1 617 750	1 655 400	2 310 900

Planning, programming budgeting systems

Non-profit organizations have found line item budgets to be unsatisfactory mainly because they fail to provide information on planned and actual accomplishments. In addition, such budgets do not provide information on the efficiency with which the organization's activities have been performed, or its effectiveness in achieving its objectives. A further deficiency with line item budgets is that they fail to provide a sound basis for deciding how the available resources should be allocated. **Planning, programming budgeting systems (PPBS)** are intended to overcome these deficiencies.

The aim of PPBS is to enable the management of a non-profit organization to make more informed decisions about the allocation of resources to meet the overall objectives of the organization. First, overall objectives are established. Secondly, the programmes that might achieve these objectives are identified. Programmes normally relate to the major activities undertaken by municipal or government organizations. Finally the costs and benefits of each programme are determined so that budget allocations can be made on the basis of the cost–benefits of the different programmes. PPBS is the counterpart of the long-term planning process operated in profit-oriented organizations. We can relate PPBS to the long-term planning process outlined in Figure 15.1 for profit-oriented companies. The first stage in the process of PPBS is to review the organizational objectives for the activities which it performs (i.e. stage 1 in Figure 15.1). Stage 2 involves identifying programmes that can be undertaken to achieve the organization's objectives. Examples of programmes include extending childcare facilities, improvement of health care for senior citizens and the extension of nursery facilities (see Exhibit 15.3 for an illustration of a childcare programme). The third stage involves identifying and evaluating alternative methods of achieving the objectives for each specific programme. Such a comparison and evaluation will show the costs of each alternative course of action and the benefits which result. The final stage (stage 4) is to select the appropriate programmes on the basis of cost–benefit principles. At this stage it would be useful if the programmes could be ranked, but this is extremely difficult. It is therefore necessary for a subjective judgement to be made by the top management of the organization on the amount of resources to be allocated to the various programmes.

PPBS involves the preparation of a *long-term* corporate plan that clearly establishes the objectives that the organization aims to achieve. These objectives do not necessarily follow

EXHIBIT 15.3
Illustration of a childcare programme

- The construction of three new kindergartens.
- The repair and extension of five existing kindergartens.
- The employment of ten new nursery school teachers.
- The establishment of a child-minding scheme that is based in the homes of mothers with young children of their own.
- The setting up of an occasional childcare centre.
- The introduction of an hourly baby-sitting service.

Source: Wilson and Chua (1993).

the existing organizational structure. For example, one objective of a local authority may be the care of the elderly. The following services may contribute to this objective:

1 provision of sheltered accommodation;
2 erection of aged-persons dwellings;
3 provision of domestic health services;
4 provision of home nursing services;
5 provision of social and recreational facilities.

The provision of these activities may be undertaken by separate departments, such as housing, health and social services. However, PPBS relates the estimates of total costs to the care of the elderly programme, rather than relating costs to the various departments. A programme budget cuts across departmental barriers by providing estimates of the programme for the provision of the elderly rather than these estimates being included within the three budgets for each of the housing, health and social welfare departments.

PPBS forces management to identify the activities, functions or programmes to be provided, thereby establishing a basis for evaluating their worthiness. In addition, PPBS provides information that will enable management to assess the effectiveness of its plans; for example, is the provision of the services for the elderly as well developed as it should be for an expenditure of X thousand pounds? The programme structure should correspond to the principal objectives of the organization and enable management to focus on the organization's outputs (the objectives to be achieved) rather than just the inputs (the resources available to be used). Hence a more effective allocation of scarce resources can be achieved. Within the overall programme budget, apart from the main objectives of the programme, there will be a series of sub-objectives reaching down to the lower levels of management.

Because the programme structure is unlikely to match the organization's structure, a particular individual must be made responsible for controlling and supervising the programme. Anthony and Young (1988) suggest that one possibility is to adopt a matrix type of organizational structure, with a matrix consisting of programme managers in one dimension and functionally organized responsibility centres in the other. This process is illustrated in Figure 15.3. The programmes are represented by horizontal bars and the budgets by vertical dashed lines. The budget for year 1 has been analysed by six responsibility centres (A to F). Such an organizational structure requires that the budgeted and the actual accomplishments be compared by *programmes*. In addition information must be accumulated by department or responsibility centre (i.e. responsibility centres A to F in Figure 15.3) and line item budgets must be used for controlling expenditure. Note that the budgeting process in this illustration focuses on a single year, whereas PPBS focuses on

FIGURE 15.3 *A matrix organizational structure*

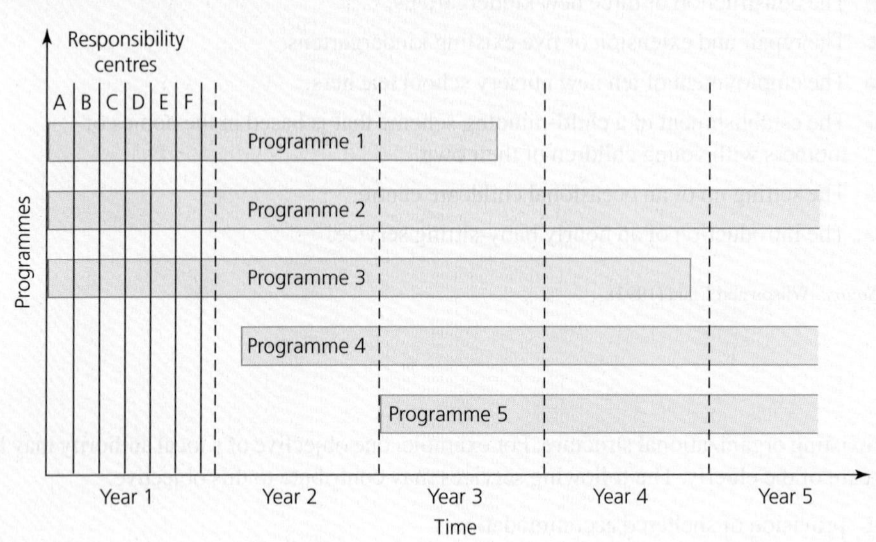

activities extending over a period of several years. A budget is, in effect, one slice of the organization's programmes where costs are related to departments or responsibility centres, rather than programmes.

In the 1960s and early 1970s efforts were made to implement PPBS into US government budgeting, but by the mid 1970s the attempt had been abandoned. Pendlebury (1996) concludes that efforts to implement PPBS failed because much of the data that were required on outputs were unobtainable. He states:

> *Although the philosophy behind PPBS was good, practical difficulties and organizational realities led to its demise. One influence that it did have, however, and that still remains, is to have reinforced the advantages of a programme structure. In other words even though programme impacts might not be measurable and the establishment of cost/benefit relationships not possible, the budget might at least show the proposed spending on different activities or programmes (page 287).*

Zero-based budgeting

Zero-based budgeting (also known as **priority-based budgeting**) emerged in the late 1960s as an attempt to overcome the limitations of **incremental budgets**. This approach requires that all activities are justified and prioritized before decisions are taken relating to the amount of resources allocated to each activity. Besides adopting a 'zero-based' approach zero-base budgeting (ZBB) also focuses on programmes or activities instead of functional departments based on line-items which is a feature of traditional budgeting.

ZBB works from the premise that projected expenditure for existing programmes should start from base zero, with each year's budgets being compiled as if the programmes were being launched for the first time. The budgetees should present their requirements for appropriations in such a fashion that all funds can be allocated on the basis of cost–benefit or some similar kind of evaluative analysis. The cost–benefit approach is an attempt to

The implementation of a zero base budgeting approach in a UK local authority

The social services department of a local authority decided in 1990 to implement a system of devolved budgeting. Prior to these initiatives, budget preparation had been largely centralized with input from the social services department coming primarily from the director and the assistant directors. In social services departments, the major divisions of service are: juvenile justice and services for adolescents; children and families; elderly; elderly mental infirm; learning difficulties; mental health; and physical disability. In the authority under review, each of these divisions of service was under the control of an assistant director and in addition there was an assistant director responsible for finance and administration. As a result of the devolved budgeting initiative, the number of budget holders increased to over 70, and over 300 cost centres were established.

A zero based approach to budget preparation was introduced for the financial year 1992/93. Prior to the introduction of zero base budgeting (ZBB) the budget allocations available to each cost centre and budget holder were based on an incremental budgeting system which meant that past histories of spending patterns determined current resource allocations. It was anticipated that the increased budget involvement would make it difficult on occasions to justify historically based allocations and the move to zero base budgeting (ZBB) was seen as a means of providing the opportunity for the base to be challenged and redistributions brought about. In its pure form, ZBB requires each budget request to be built up from zero. For large complex organizations this would clearly be close to impossible. The social services department's attempt at ZBB for the financial year 1992/93 adopted the philosophy of starting from some point within the base, rather than from zero, and followed loosely a decision package approach. The process was bottom-up with budgets being built up from cost centres to arrive at a budget holder's budget. The aggregate of each budget holder's budget gave the budget for the division of service, and the aggregate of each division of service budget gave the total social services department budget. (For 1992/93, the gross revenue budget was over £50 million.)

Each budget holder was required to compile three incremental decision packages for the group of cost centres they were responsible for. These were:

current provision,
statutory provision,
90 per cent provision.

The purpose of the 90 per cent package was to release a notional amount from each budget holder which would be available for redistribution on a prioritized basis. The 90 per cent target was not required for each cost centre but for the group of cost centres under the budget holder's control, thus providing scope to move money around. ZBB does, of course, require not only the inputs for each decision package to be determined but also the outputs. A careful analysis of the needs of the community for personal social services was required in order to establish the demand for services and the level of service that could be provided at each level of funding.

Source: Adapted from Pendlebury, M.E., Management accounting in local government, *Financial Accountability & Management*, May 1994, pp. 117–129.

ensure 'value for money'; it questions long-standing assumptions and serves as a tool for systematically examining and perhaps abandoning any unproductive projects.

ZBB is best suited to discretionary costs and support activities. With **discretionary costs** management has some discretion as to the amount it will budget for the particular activity in question. Examples of discretionary costs include advertising, research and development and training costs. There is no optimum relationship between inputs (as measured by the costs) and outputs (measured by revenues or some other objective function) for these costs. Furthermore, they are not predetermined by some previous commitment. In effect, management can determine what quantity of service it wishes to purchase and there is no established method for determining the appropriate amount to be spent in particular periods. ZBB has mostly been applied in local and government organizations where the predominant costs are of a discretionary nature. In contrast, direct production and service costs, where input–output relationships exist, are more suited to traditional budgeting using standard costs.

ZBB involves the following three stages:

- a description of each organizational activity in a decision package;
- the evaluation and ranking of decision packages in order of priority;
- allocation of resources based on order of priority up to the spending cut-off level.

Decision packages are identified for each decision unit. Decision units represent separate programmes or groups of activities that an organization undertakes. A decision package represents the operation of a particular programme with incremental packages reflecting different levels of effort that may be expended on a specific function. One package is usually prepared at the 'base' level for each programme. This package represents the minimum level of service or support consistent with the organization's objectives. Service or support higher than the base level is described in one or more incremental packages. For example, managers might be asked to specify the base package in terms of level of service that can be provided at 70% of the current cost level and incremental packages identify higher activity or cost levels.

Once the decision packages have been completed, management is ready to start to review the process. To determine how much to spend and where to spend it, management will rank all packages in order of decreasing benefits to the organization. Theoretically, once management has set the budgeted level of spending, the packages should be accepted down to the spending level based on cost–benefit principles.

The benefits of ZBB over traditional methods of budgeting are claimed to be as follows:

1. Traditional budgeting tends to extrapolate the past by adding a percentage increase to the current year. ZBB avoids the deficiencies of incremental budgeting and represents a move towards the allocation of resources by need or benefit. Thus, unlike traditional budgeting the level of funding is not taken for granted.
2. ZBB creates a questioning attitude rather than one that assumes that current practice represents value for money.
3. ZBB focuses attention on outputs in relation to value for money.

ZBB was first applied in Texas Instruments in 1969. It quickly became one of the fashionable management tools of the 1970s and, according to Phyrr (1976), there were 100 users in the USA in the early 1970s, including the State of Georgia whose governor was ex-president Jimmy Carter. When he became the US President, he directed that all federal agencies adopt ZBB.

During the 1970s many articles on ZBB were published but they declined rapidly towards the end of the decade, and by the 1980s they had become a rarity. ZBB has never achieved the widespread adoption that its proponents envisaged. The major reason for its lack of success would appear to be that it is too costly and time-consuming. The process of identifying decision packages and determining their purpose, cost and benefits is extremely time-consuming. Furthermore, there are often too many decision packages to evaluate and there is frequently insufficient information to enable them to be ranked.

Research suggests that many organizations tend to approximate the principles of ZBB rather than applying the full-scale approach outlined in the literature. For example, it does not have to be applied throughout the organization. It can be applied selectively to those areas about which management is most concerned and used as a one-off cost reduction programme. Some of the benefits of ZBB can be captured by using **priority-based incremental budgets**. Priority incremental budgets require managers to specify what incremental activities or changes would occur if their budgets were increased or decreased by a specified percentage (say 10%). Budget allocations are made by comparing the change in costs with the change in benefits. Priority incremental budgets thus represent an economical compromise between ZBB and incremental budgeting.

Summary

The following items relate to the learning objectives listed at the beginning of the chapter.

- **Explain how budgeting fits into the overall planning and control framework.**

  The annual budget should be set within the context of longer-term plans, which are likely to exist even if they have not been made explicit. A long-term plan is a statement of the preliminary targets and activities required by an organization to achieve its strategic plans together with a broad estimate for each year of the resources required. Because long-term planning involves 'looking into the future' for several years, the plans tend to be uncertain, general in nature, imprecise and subject to change. Annual budgeting is concerned with the detailed implementation of the long-term plan for the year ahead. As the year progresses the control process involves comparing planned and actual outcomes and responding to any deviations by taking appropriate remedial action to ensure that future results will conform to the annual budget. Alternatively, the annual budget may have to be changed if remedial action cannot be taken. Budgeting is therefore a continuous and dynamic process, and should not end once the annual budget has been prepared.

- **Identify and describe the six different purposes of budgeting.**

  Budgets are used for the following purposes: (a) planning annual operations; (b) coordinating the activities of the various parts of the organization and ensuring that the parts are in harmony with each other; (c) communicating the plans to the managers of the various responsibility centres; (d) motivating managers to strive to achieve organizational goals; (e) controlling activities; and (f) evaluating the performance of managers.

- **Identify and describe the various stages in the budget process.**

  The important stages are as follows: (a) communicating details of the budget policy and guidelines to those people responsible for the preparation of the budgets; (b) determining the factor that restricts output (normally sales volume); (c) preparation of the sales budget (assuming that sales demand is the factor that restricts output); (d) initial preparation of the various budgets; (e) negotiation of budgets with superiors; (f) coordination and review of budgets; (g) final acceptance of budgets; and (h) ongoing review of budgets. Each of the above stages is described in the chapter.

- **Prepare functional and master budgets.**

  When all of the budgets have been prepared they are summarized into a master budget consisting in a budgeted profit and loss account, a balance sheet and a cash budget statement. The preparation of functional and master budgets was illustrated using Example 15.1.

- **Describe the use of computer-based financial models for budgeting.**

  Computer-based financial models are mathematical statements of the inputs and output relationships that affect the budget. These models allow management to conduct sensitivity analysis to ascertain the effects on the master budget of changes in the original predicted data or changes in the assumptions that were used to prepare the budgets.

- **Describe the limitations of incremental budgeting.**

  With incremental budgeting indirect costs and support activities are prepared on an incremental basis. This means that existing operations and the current budgeted allowance for existing activities are taken as the starting point for preparing the next annual budget. The base is then adjusted for changes (such as changes in product mix, volumes and prices) which are expected to occur during the new budget period. When this approach is adopted the concern is mainly with the increment in operations or expenditure that will occur during the forthcoming budget period. The major disadvantage of the incremental approach is that the majority of expenditure, which is associated with the 'base level' of activity, remains unchanged. Thus, past inefficiencies and waste inherent in the current way of doing things are perpetuated.

- **Describe activity-based budgeting.**

  With conventional budgeting the budgeted expenses for the forthcoming budget for support activities are normally based on the previous year's budget plus an adjustment for inflation. Support costs are therefore considered to be fixed in relation to activity volume. Activity-based budgeting (ABB) aims to manage costs more effectively by authorizing the supply of only those resources that are needed to perform activities required to meet the budgeted production and sales volume. Whereas ABC assigns resource expenses to activities and then uses activity cost drivers to assign activity costs to cost objects (such as products, services or customers) ABB is the reverse of this process. Cost objects are the starting point. Their budgeted output determines the necessary activities which are then used to estimate the resources that are required for the budget period. ABB involves the following stages: (a) estimate the production and sales volume by individual products and customers; (b) estimate the demand for organizational activities; (c) determine the resources that are required to perform organizational activities; (d) estimate for each resource the quantity that must be supplied to meet the demand; and (e) take action to adjust the capacity of resources to match the projected supply.

- **Describe budgeting and planning, programming and budgeting systems (PPBS) in non-profit organizations.**

  In non-profit organizations the annual budgeting process compares budgeted and actual inputs, but does not provide information on the efficiency with which activities have been performed, or the effectiveness in achieving objectives. The aim of PPBS is to enable the management of a non-profit organization to make more informed decisions about the allocation of resources to meet the objectives of the organization. PPBS involves the following stages: (a) establishing the overall objectives; (b) identifying the programmes to achieve these objectives; and (c) determining the costs and benefits of the programmes so that budget allocations can be made on the basis of cost–benefits of the different programmes. Each of these stages is illustrated in Chapter 15. PPBS is the counterpart of the long-term planning process in profit-oriented companies.

- **Describe zero-base budgeting (ZBB).**

  ZBB is a method of budgeting that is mainly used in non-profit organizations but it can also be applied to discretionary costs and support activities in profit organizations. It seeks to overcome the deficiencies of incremental budgeting. ZBB works from the premise that projected expenditure for existing programmes should start from base zero, with each year's budgets being compiled as if the programmes were being launched for the first time. The budgetees should present their requirements for appropriations in such a fashion that all funds can be allocated on the basis of cost–benefit or some similar kind of evaluative analysis. The cost–benefit approach is an attempt to ensure 'value for money'; it questions long-standing assumptions and serves as a tool for systematically examining and perhaps abandoning any unproductive projects.

Note

1 The criteria specified are derived from Johnson and Scholes (2002), ch 9.

Key terms and concepts

activity-based budgeting (p. 612)
aims (p. 590)
budgeting (p. 593)
budgets (p. 589)
cash budgets (p. 609)
continuous budgeting (p. 596)
corporate objectives (p. 590)
corporate planning (p. 590)
decision package (p. 620)
discretionary costs (p. 620)
generic strategies (p. 591)
goals (p. 590)
incremental budgeting (pp. 611, 618)
line item budgets (p. 615)
long-range planning (p. 590)
long-term plan (p. 592)
management by exception (p. 595)
master budget (p. 600)
mission (p. 590)
objectives (p. 590)
planning, programming budgeting systems (PPBS) (p. 616)
priority based budgets (p. 618)
priority based incremental budgets (p. 621)
rolling budgeting (p. 596)
strategic analysis (p. 591)
strategic planning (p. 590)
strategies (p. 591)
unit objectives (p. 590)
zero-based budgeting (p. 618)

Recommended reading

In this chapter we have provided a very brief summary of the process for selecting alternative strategies. A detailed explanation of strategy formulation can be found in the corporate strategy literature. Predominant texts on this area include Johnson and Scholes (2002) and Thompson (2001). For a more detailed discussion of budgeting in the public sector see Pendlebury (1996). You should refer to Kennedy and Dugdale (1999) for a discussion of the reasons for the dissatisfaction with the budgeting process and suggestions for ways in which they can be eliminated. Other relevant articles relating to the criticisms of budgeting include Ekholm and Wallin (2000) and Hope and Fraser (2001).

Key examination points

Examination questions on budgeting frequently require the preparation of functional or cash budgets. A common mistake is to incorrectly deduct closing stocks and add opening stocks when preparing production and material purchase budgets. Examination questions are also set frequently on zero-base budgeting (ZBB). Do make sure that you can describe and discuss the advantages and disadvantages of ZBB. You should refer to the solution to Review problem 15.26 for the application of activity-based budgeting.

Assessment material

Review questions

The review questions are short questions that enable you to assess your understanding of the main topics included in the chapter. The numbers in parentheses provide you with the page numbers to refer to if you cannot answer a specific question.

Review problems

The review problems are more complex and require you to relate and apply the chapter content to various business problems. The problems are graded by their level of difficulty. The multiple-choice questions are the least demanding and normally take less than 10 minutes to complete. Fully worked solutions to the review problems are provided in a separate section at the end of the book. For those questions in the white box the worked solutions are provided in the *Student's Manual* accompanying this book. Further review problems for this chapter are available on the accompanying website www.drury-online.com. The answers to these problems are available for lecturers on the lecturer's password protected section of the website.

Case studies

The website also includes over 30 case study problems. A list of these cases is provided in Part Seven of this book. Several cases are relevant to the content of this chapter. Examples include Endeavour Toplise Ltd., Global Ltd. and Integrated Technology Ltd.

Review questions

15.1 Define the term 'budget'. How are budgets used in planning? (*pp. 589–90*)

15.2 Describe the different stages in the planning and control process. (*pp. 590–93*)

15.3 Distinguish between budgeting and long-range planning. How are they related? (*p. 590, p. 593*)

15.4 Describe the different purposes of budgeting. (*pp. 593–95*)

15.5 Explain what is meant by the term 'management by exception'. (*p. 595*)

15.6 Describe how the different roles of budgets can conflict with each other. (*p. 595*)

15.7 Distinguish between continuous and rolling budgets. (*pp. 595–96*)

15.8 Describe the different stages in the budgeting process. (*pp. 597–600*)

15.9 All budgets depend on the sales budget. Do you agree? Explain. (*pp. 597–98*)

15.10 What is a master budget? (*p. 600*)

15.11 Define incremental budgeting. (*pp. 611–12*)

15.12 What are the distinguishing features of activity-based budgeting? (*pp. 611–12*)

15.13 Describe the five different stages that are involved with activity-based-budgeting. (*pp. 612–13*)

15.14 What are the distinguishing features of budgeting in non-profit-making organizations? (*p. 615*)

15.15 What are line item budgets? (*pp. 615–16*)

15.16 Explain what is meant by the term 'planning, programming budgeting systems'. (*pp. 616–18*)

15.17 How does zero-based budgeting differ from traditional budgeting? (*p. 618, p. 620*)

15.18 What are discretionary costs? (*p. 620*)

15.19 Distinguish between zero-based budgeting and priority-based incremental budgeting. (*p. 621*)

Review problems

15.20 **Intermediate**

When preparing a production budget, the quantity to be produced equals

A sales quantity + opening stock + closing stock
B sales quantity – opening stock + closing stock
C sales quantity – opening stock – closing stock
D sales quantity + opening stock – closing stock
E sales quantity

CIMA Stage 2

15.21 **Intermediate**

BDL plc is current preparing its cash budget for the year to 31 March 2003. An extract from its sales budget for the same year shows the following sales values:

	£
March	60 000
April	70 000
May	55 000
June	65 000

40% of its sales are expected to be for cash. Of its credit sales, 70% are expected to pay in the month after sale and take a 2% discount; 27% are expected to pay in the second month after the sale, and the remaining 3% are expected to be bad debts.

The value of sales receipts to be shown in the cash budget for May 2002 is:

A £38 532
B £39 120
C £60 532
D £64 220
E £65 200

CIMA Stage 2

15.22 **Intermediate**

The following data is to be used to answer questions (a) and (b) below

A division of PLR plc operates a small private aircraft that carries passengers and small parcels for other divisions.

In the year ended 31 March 2002, it carried 1024 passengers and 24 250 kg of small parcels. It incurred costs of £924 400.

The division has found that 70% of its total costs are variable, and that 60% of these vary with the number of passengers and the remainder varies with the weight of the parcels.

The company is now preparing its budget for the 3 months ending 30 September 2002 using an incremental budgeting approach. In this period it expects:

- All prices to be 3% higher than the average paid in the year ended 31 March 2002;
- Efficiency levels to be unchanged;
- Activity levels to be:
  - 209 passengers;
  - 7200 kg of small parcels.

(a) The budgeted passenger related cost (to the nearest £100) for the **three months** ending 30 September 2002 is

A £81 600
B £97 100
C £100 000
D £138 700

(2 marks)

(b) The budgeted small parcel related cost (to the nearest £100) for the **three months** ending 30 September 2002 is

A £64 700
B £66 600
C £79 200
D £95 213

(2 marks)

CIMA Management Accounting – Performance Management

15.23 Intermediate: Preparation of functional budgets, cash budget and master budget

The budgeted balance sheet data of Kwan Tong Umbago Ltd is as follows:

1 March

	Cost (£)	Depreciation to date (£)	Net (£)
Fixed assets			
Land and buildings	500 000	—	500 000
Machinery and equipment	124 000	84 500	39 500
Motor vehicles	42 000	16 400	25 600
	666 000	100 900	565 100
Working capital:			
Current assets			
Stock of raw materials (100 units)		4 320	
Stock of finished goods (110 units)[a]		10 450	
Debtors (January £7680 February £10 400)		18 080	
Cash and bank		6 790	
		39 640	
Less current liabilities			
Creditors (raw materials)		3 900	35 740
			600 840
Represented by:			
Ordinary share capital (fully paid) £1 shares			500 000
Share premium			60 000
Profit and loss account			40 840
			600 840

[a]The stock of finished goods was valued at marginal cost

The estimates for the next four-month period are as follows:

	March	April	May	June
Sales (units)	80	84	96	94
Production (units)	70	75	90	90
Purchases of raw materials (units)	80	80	85	85
Wages and variable overheads at £65 per unit	£4550	£4875	£5850	£5850
Fixed overheads	£1200	£1200	£1200	£1200

The company intends to sell each unit for £219 and has estimated that it will have to pay £45 per unit for raw materials. One unit of raw material is needed for each unit of finished product.

All sales and purchases of raw materials are on credit. Debtors are allowed two months' credit and suppliers of raw materials are paid after one month's credit. The wages, variable overheads and fixed overheads are paid in the month in which they are incurred.

Cash from a loan secured on the land and buildings of £120 000 at an interest rate of 7.5% is due to be received on 1 May. Machinery costing £112 000 will be received in May and paid for in June.

The loan interest is payable half yearly from September onwards. An interim dividend to 31 March of £12 500 will be paid in June.

Depreciation for the four months, including that on the new machinery is:

Machinery and equipment	£15 733
Motor vehicles	£3 500

The company uses the FIFO method of stock valuation. Ignore taxation.

Required:

(a) Calculate and present the raw materials budget and finished goods budget in terms of units, for each month from March to June inclusive.

(5 marks)

(b) Calculate the corresponding sales budgets, the production cost budgets and the budgeted closing debtors, creditors and stocks in terms of value.

(5 marks)

(c) Prepare and present a cash budget for each of the four months.

(6 marks)

(d) Prepare a master budget, i.e. a budgeted trading and profit and loss account, for the four months to 30 June, and budgeted balance sheet as at 30 June.

(10 marks)

(e) Advise the company about possible ways in which it can improve its cash management.

(9 marks)
(Total 35 marks)
ACCA Paper 8 Managerial Finance

15.24 **Intermediate: Budget preparation and comments on sales forecasting methods**

You have recently been appointed as the management accountant to Alderley Ltd, a small company manufacturing two products, the Elgar and the Holst. Both products use the same type of material and labour but in different proportions. In the past, the company has had poor control over its working capital. To remedy this, you have recommended to the directors that a budgetary control system be introduced. This proposal has, now, been agreed.

Because Alderley Ltd's production and sales are spread evenly over the year, it was agreed that the annual budget should be broken down into four periods, each of 13 weeks, and commencing with the 13 weeks ending 4 April. To help you in this task, the sales and production directors have provided you with the following information:

1. Marketing and production data

	Elgar	Holst
Budgeted sales for 13 weeks (units)	845	1235
Material content per unit (kilograms)	7	8
Labour per unit (standard hours)	8	5

2. Production labour
The 24 production employees work a 37-hour, five-day week and are paid £8 per hour. Any hours in excess of this involve Alderley in paying an overtime premium of 25%. Because of technical problems, which will continue over the next 13 weeks, employees are only able to work at 95% efficiency compared to standard.
3. Purchasing and opening stocks
The production director believes that raw material will cost £12 per kilogram over the budget period. He also plans to revise the amount of stock being kept. He estimates that the stock levels at the commencement of the budget period will be as follows:

Raw materials	Elgar	Holst
2328 kilograms	163 units	361 units

4. Closing stocks
At the end of the 13-week period closing stocks are planned to change. On the assumption that production and sales volumes for the second budget period will be similar to those in the first period:
   - raw material stocks should be sufficient for 13 days' production;
   - finished stocks of the Elgar should be equivalent to 6 days' sales volume;
   - finished stocks of the Holst should be equivalent to 14 days' sales volume.

Task 1

Prepare in the form of a statement the following information for the 13-week period to 4 April:

(a) the production budget in units for the Elgar and Holst;

(b) the purchasing budget for Alderley Ltd in units;

(c) the cost of purchases for the period;

(d) the production labour budget for Alderley Ltd in hours;

(e) the cost of production labour for the period.

Note: Assume a five-day week for both sales and production.

The managing director of Alderley Ltd, Alan Dunn, has also only recently been appointed. He is keen to develop the company and has already agreed to two new products being developed. These will be launched in 18 months' time. While talking to you about the budget, he mentions that the quality of sales forecasting will need to improve if the company is to grow rapidly. Currently, the budgeted sales figure is found by initially adding 5% to the previous year's sales volume and then revising the figure following discussions with the marketing director. He believes this approach is increasingly inadequate and now requires a more systematic approach.

A few days later, Alan Dunn sends you a memo. In that memo, he identifies three possible strategies for increasing sales volume. They are:

- more sales to existing customers;
- the development of new markets;
- the development of new products.

He asks for your help in forecasting likely sales volumes from these sources.

Task 2

Write a brief memo to Alan Dunn. Your memo should:

(a) identify *four* ways of forecasting future sales volume;

(b) show how each of your four ways of forecasting can be applied to *one* of the sales strategies identified by Alan Dunn and justify your choice;

(c) give *two* reasons why forecasting methods might not prove to be accurate.

AAT Technicians Stage

15.25 **Intermediate: Preparation of cash budgets**

The management of Beck plc have been informed that the union representing the direct production workers at one of their factories, where a standard product is produced, intends to call a strike. The accountant has been asked to advise the management of the effect the strike will have on cash flow.

The following data has been made available:

	Week 1	Week 2	Week 3
Budgeted sales	400 units	500 units	400 units
Budgeted production	600 units	400 units	Nil

The strike will commence at the beginning of week 3 and it should be assumed that it will continue for at least four weeks. Sales at 400 units per week will continue to be made during the period of the strike until stocks of finished goods are exhausted. Production will stop at the end of week 2. The current stock level of finished goods is 600 units. Stocks of work in progress are not carried.

The selling price of the product is £60 and the budgeted manufacturing cost is made up as follows:

	(£)
Direct materials	15
Direct wages	7
Variable overheads	8
Fixed overheads	18
Total	£48

Direct wages are regarded as a variable cost. The company operates a full absorption costing system and the fixed overhead absorption rate is based upon a budgeted fixed overhead of £9000 per week. Included in the total fixed overheads is £700 per week for depreciation of equipment. During the period of the strike direct wages and variable overheads would not be incurred and the cash expended on fixed overheads would be reduced by £1500 per week.

The current stock of raw materials are worth £7500; it is intended that these stocks should increase to £11 000 by the end of week 1 and then remain at this level during the period of the strike. *All direct materials are paid for one week after they have been received. Direct wages are paid one week in arrears. It should be assumed that all relevant overheads are paid for immediately the expense is incurred.* All sales are on credit, 70% of the sales value is received in cash from the debtors at the end of the first week after the sales have been made and the balance at the end of the second week.

The current amount outstanding to material suppliers is £8000 and direct wage accruals amount to £3200. Both of these will be paid in week 1. The current balance owing from debtors is £31 200, of which £24 000 will be received during week 1 and the remainder during week 2. The current balance of cash at bank and in hand is £1000.

Required:

(a) (i) Prepare a cash budget for weeks 1 to 6 showing the balance of cash at the end of each week together with a suitable analysis of the receipts and payments during each week.

(13 marks)

(ii) Comment upon any matters arising from the cash budget which you consider should be brought to management's attention.

(4 marks)

(b) Explain why the reported profit figure for a period does not normally represent the amount of cash generated in that period.

(5 marks)

(Total 22 marks)

ACCA Level 1 Costing

15.26 **Advanced: Activity-based budgeting**

Flosun plc makes and sells a range of products. Management has carried out an analysis of the total cost of production. The information in Appendix 3.1 reflects this analysis of budgeted costs for the six month period to 30 June 2004. The analysis has identified that the factory is organized in order to permit the operation of three production lines X, Y and Z. Each production line facilitates the production of two or more products. Production line X is only used for the production of products A and B. The products are manufactured in batches on a just-in-time basis in order to fulfil orders from customers. Only one product can be manufactured on the production line at any one time. Materials are purchased and received on a just-in-time basis. Additional information is available for production line X as follows:

(i) Production line machine costs including labour, power, etc., vary in proportion to machine hours.

(ii) Costs incurred for production scheduling, WIP movement, purchasing and receipt of materials are assumed to be incurred in proportion to the number of batches of product which are manufactured. Machine set-up costs vary in proportion to the number of set-ups required and are linked to a batch throughput system.

(iii) Costs for material scheduling systems and design/testing routines are assumed to be incurred by each product in proportion to the total quantity of components purchased and the total number of types of component used respectively. The number of different components designed/tested for products A and B are 12 and 8 respectively.

(iv) Product line development cost is identified with changes in product design and production method. At present such costs for production line X are apportioned 80%:20% to products A and B respectively. Production line maintenance costs are assumed to vary in proportion to the maintenance hours required for each product.

(v) General factory costs are apportioned to each of production lines X, Y and Z in the ratio 25%:30%:45% respectively. Such costs are absorbed by product units at an average rate per unit through each production line.

Required:

(a) Prepare an activity based budget for production line X for the six month period to 30 June 2004 analysed into sub-sets for activities which are product unit based, batch based, product sustaining, production line sustaining and factory sustaining.

The budget should show:

(i) Total cost for each activity sub-set grouped to reflect the differing operational levels at which each sub-set is incurred/controlled.

(ii) Average cost per unit for each of products A and B analysed by activity sub-set.

(24 marks)

(b) Discuss the incidence and use of each of the following terms in relation to Flosun plc, giving examples from the question to illustrate your answer:

(i) hierarchy of activities

(ii) cost pools

(iii) cost drivers.

(6 marks)

(c) Prepare a sequential set of steps which may be included in an investigation of activities in order to improve company profitability.

This should be a general list of steps and not specifically relating to Flosun plc.

(5 marks)

(35 marks)

ACCA Paper 9 Information for Control and Decision Making

Appendix 3.1

Flosun plc – Budget data six months to 30 June 2004

	Product A	Product B
Material cost per product unit	£60	£45
Production line X – machine hours per unit	0.8	0.5
Production batch size (units)	100	200
Total production (units)	9 000	15 000
Components per product unit (quantity)	20	12
Number of customers	5	10
Number of production line set-ups	15	25
Production line X – maintenance hours	300	150

Cost category	Production line X £	Factory total £
Labour, power, etc.	294 000	
Set-up of machines	40 000	
Production scheduling	29 600	
WIP movement	36 400	
Purchasing and receipt of material	49 500	
Material scheduling system	18 000	
Design/testing routine	16 000	
Production line development	25 000	
Production line maintenance	9 000	
General factory administration		500 000
General factory occupancy		268 000

15.27 Advanced

You are the management accountant of a group of companies and your managing director has asked you to explore the possibilities of introducing a zero-base budgeting system experimentally in one of the operating companies in place of its existing orthodox system. You are required to prepare notes for a paper for submission to the board that sets out:

(a) how zero-base budgeting would work within the company chosen;
(6 marks)

(b) what advantages it might offer over the existing system;
(5 marks)

(c) what problems might be faced in introducing a zero-base budgeting scheme;
(5 marks)

(d) the features you would look for in selecting the operating company for the introduction in order to obtain the most beneficial results from the experiment.
(4 marks)

(Total 20 marks)

CIMA P3 Management Accounting

15.28 Advanced

A company that has hitherto prepared its operating budgets on a single target level of performance is considering changing to one of the following:

(i) a three-level budget;

(ii) a decision tree analysis leading to a calculation of joint probabilities of budget levels;

(iii) a simulation of probabilities of budget levels (probably computer-based).

You are required to:

(a) explain briefly the method of constructing budgets for (i), (ii) and (iii) above;

(b) comment briefly on the advantages that would result from choosing:
method (i) over the existing method;
method (ii) over method (i);
method (iii) over method (ii).

(20 marks)

CIMA P3 Management Accounting

15.29 Advanced

Various attempts have been made in the public sector to achieve a more stable, long-term planning base in contrast to the traditional short-term annual budgeting approach, with its emphasis on 'flexibility'.

You are required to:

(a) explain the deficiencies of the traditional approach to planning which led to the attempts to introduce PPBS (programme budgeting);
(6 marks)

(b) give an illustration of how a PPBS plan could be drawn up in respect of one sector of public authority activity;
(8 marks)

(c) discuss the problems which have made it difficult in practice to introduce PPBS.
(6 marks)

(Total 20 marks)

CIMA Stage 4: Management Accounting

Review problems (with answers in the Student's Manual)

15.30 **Advanced**

Traditional budgeting systems are incremental in nature and tend to focus on cost centres. Activity based budgeting links strategic planning to overall performance measurement aiming at continuous improvement.

(a) Explain the weaknesses of an incremental budgeting system.

(5 marks)

(b) Describe the main features of an activity based budgeting system and comment on the advantages claimed for its use.

(10 marks)
(Total 15 marks)
ACCA Paper 9 Information for Control and Decision Making

15.31 **Advanced**

Budgeting has been criticized as

- a cumbersome process which occupies considerable management time;
- concentrating unduly on short-term financial control;
- having undesirable effects on the motivation of managers;
- emphasizing formal organization structure.

Requirements:

(a) Explain these criticisms.

(8 marks)

(b) Explain what changes can be made in response to these criticisms to improve the budgeting process.

(12 marks)
(Total 20 marks)
CIMA Stage 4 Management Accounting

15.32 **Advanced**

For a number of years, the research division of Z plc has produced its annual budget (for new and continuing projects) using incremental budgeting techniques. The company is now under new management and the annual budget for 2004 is to be prepared using zero based budgeting techniques.

Required:

(a) Explain the differences between incremental and zero based budgeting techniques.

(5 marks)

(b) Explain how Z plc could operate a zero based budgeting system for its research projects.

(8 marks)

The operating divisions of Z plc have in the past always used a traditional approach to analysing costs into their fixed and variable components. A single measure of activity was used, which, for simplicity, was the number of units produced. The new management does not accept that such a simplistic approach is appropriate for budgeting in the modern environment and has requested that the managers adopt an activity-based approach to their budgets for 2004.

Required:

(c) (i) Briefly explain activity-based budgeting (ABB).

(3 marks)

(ii) Explain how activity-based budgeting would be implemented by the operating divisions of Z plc.

(9 marks)

(Total 25 marks)

CIMA Management Accounting – Performance Management

15.33 **Intermediate: Preparation of functional budgets**

Wollongong wishes to calculate an operating budget for the forthcoming period. Information regarding products, costs and sales levels is as follows:

Product	A	B
Materials required		
X (kg)	2	3
Y (litres)	1	4
Labour hours required		
Skilled (hours)	4	2
Semi skilled (hours)	2	5
Sales level (units)	2000	1500
Opening stocks (units)	100	200

Closing stock of materials and finished goods will be sufficient to meet 10% of demand. Opening stocks of material X was 300 kg and for material Y was 1000 litres. Material prices are £10 per kg for material X and £7 per litre for material Y. Labour costs are £12 per hour for the skilled workers and £8 per hour for the semi skilled workers.

Required:

Produce the following budgets:

(a) production (units);

(b) materials usage (kg and litres);

(c) materials purchases (kg, litres and £); and

(d) labour (hours and £).

(10 marks)

ACCA Paper 1.2 – Financial information for Management

15.34 **Intermediate: Preparation of functional budgets and budgeted profit statement**

A division of Bud plc is engaged in the manual assembly of finished products F1 and F2 from bought-in components. These products are sold to external customers. The budgeted sales volumes and prices for Month 9 are as follows:

Product	Units	Price
F1	34 000	£50.00
F2	58 000	£30.00

Finished goods stockholding budgeted for the end of Month 9, is 1000 units of F1 and 2000 units of F2, with no stock at the beginning of that month. The purchased components C3 and C4 are used in the finished products in the quantities shown below. The unit price is for just-in-time delivery of the components; the company holds no component stocks.

Product	Component C3	C4
F1 (per unit)	8 units	4 units
F2 (per unit)	4 units	3 units
Price (each)	£1.25	£1.80

The standard direct labour times and labour rates and the budgeted monthly manufacturing overhead costs for the assembly and finishing departments for Month 9 are given below:

Product	Assembly	Finishing
F1 (per unit)	30 minutes	12 minutes
F2 (per unit)	15 minutes	10 minutes
Labour rate (per hour)	£5.00	£6.00
Manufacturing overhead cost for the month	£617 500	£204 000

Every month a predetermined direct labour hour recovery rate is computed in each department for manufacturing overhead and applied to items produced in that month.

The selling overhead of £344 000 per month is applied to products based on a predetermined percentage of the budgeted sales value in each month.

Required:

(a) Prepare summaries of the following budgets for Month 9:

(i) component purchase and usage (units and value);

(ii) direct labour (hours and value);

(iii) departmental manufacturing overhead recovery rates;

(iv) selling overhead recovery rate;

(v) stock value at the month-end.

(8 marks)

(b) Tabulate the standard unit cost and profit of each of F1 and F2 in Month 9.

(3 marks)

(c) Prepare a budgeted profit and loss account for Month 9 which clearly incorporates the budget values obtained in (a) above.

(3 marks)

(d) Explain clearly the implications of the company's treatment of manufacturing overheads, i.e. computing a monthly overhead rate, compared to a predetermined overhead rate prepared annually.

(6 marks)

(Total 20 marks)

ACCA Paper 8 Managerial Finance

15.35 Intermediate: Preparation of production budget and key factor analysis

The management team at MN Limited is considering the budgets it prepared for the year ending 31 December 2003. It has now been revealed that in June 2003 the company will be able to purchase only 10 000 litres of material Q (all other resources will be fully available). In the light of this new information, the management team wants to revise its plans for June to ensure that profits are maximized for that month.

MN Limited can produce three products from the same labour and main raw material Q, though different amounts are required for each product. The standard resource requirements, costs and selling prices, and the customer demand for delivery in June (including those orders already accepted) for each of its finished products are as follows:

	Product V	Product S	Product T
Resources per unit:			
Material Q	10 litres	8 litres	5 litres
Direct labour	8 hours	9 hours	6 hours
	£ per unit	**£ per unit**	**£ per unit**
Selling prices and costs:			
Selling price	145.00	134.00	99.00
Material Q	25.00	20.00	12.50
Other materials	10.00	4.00	8.50
Direct labour	40.00	45.00	30.00
Overheads:			
Variable	10.00	11.25	7.50
Fixed*	24.00	30.00	12.00
	109.00	110.25	70.50
Customer demand	1100 units	950 units	1450 units

*based on budgeted costs of £95 000 per month.

MN Limited has already accepted customer orders for delivery in June 2003 as follows:

Product V	34 units
Product S	75 units
Product T	97 units

The management team has decided that these customer orders must be satisfied as the financial and non-financial penalties that would otherwise arise are very significant.

Given the shortage of material Q, the management team has now set the following stock levels for June:

	Opening stock	Closing stock
Material Q**	621 litres	225 litres
Product V	20 units	10 units
Product S	33 units	25 units
Product T	46 units	20 units

**This would mean that 10 396 litres of material Q would be available during the period.

Required:

(a) Prepare a production budget for June 2003 that clearly shows the number of units of each product that should be produced to maximize the profits of MN Limited for June 2003.

(12 marks)

(b) Using your answer to requirement (a) above, calculate the number of units of each product that will be sold in June 2003.

(3 marks)

(c) Using your answer to requirement (b) above, calculate the profit for June 2003 using:

(i) marginal costing;

(ii) absorption costing.

(5 marks)

The Managing Director of MN Limited is concerned about the effect on cashflow caused by the scarcity of material Q during June 2003. She is aware that monthly profit and cashflow are often unequal and has heard that marginal costing profits more closely resemble cashflow than do absorption costing profits.

Required:

(d) (i) Explain briefly why there is a difference between cashflow and profit.

(ii) Briefly discuss the assertion that marginal costing profits are a better indicator of cashflow than absorption costing profits.

(5 marks)

(Total 25 marks)

CIMA Management Accounting – Performance Management

15.36 **Advanced: Comments on budget preparation and zero-based budgeting**

A Public Sector Organization is extending its budgetary control and responsibility accounting system to all departments. One such department concerned with public health and welfare is called 'Homecare'. The department consists of staff who visit elderly 'clients' in their homes to support them with their basic medical and welfare needs.

A monthly cost control report is to be sent to the department manager, a copy of which is also passed to a Director who controls a number of departments. In the system, which is still being refined, the budget was set by the Director and the manager had not been consulted over the budget or the use of the monthly control report.

Shown below is the first month's cost control report for the Homecare department.

Cost Control Report – Homecare Department
Month ending May 2000

	Budget	Actual	(Overspend)/ Underspend
Visits	10 000	12 000	(2 000)
	£	£	£
Department expenses:			
Supervisory salary	2 000	2 125	(125)
Wages (Permanent staff)	2 700	2 400	300
Wages (Casual staff)	1 500	2 500	(1 000)
Office equipment depreciation	500	750	(250)
Repairs to equipment	200	20	180
Travel expenses	1 500	1 800	(300)
Consumables	4 000	6 000	(2 000)
Administration and telephone	1 000	1 200	(200)
Allocated administrative costs	2 000	3 000	(1 000)
	15 400	19 795	(4 395)

In addition to the manager and permanent members of staff, appropriately qualified casual staff are appointed on a week to week basis to cope with fluctuations in demand. Staff use their own transport and travel expenses are reimbursed. There is a central administration overhead charge over all departments. Consumables consist of materials which are used by staff to care for clients. Administration and telephone are costs of keeping in touch with the staff who often operate from their own homes.

As a result of the report, the Director sent a memo to the manager of the Homecare department pointing out that the department must spend within its funding allocation and that any spending more than 5% above budget on any item would not be tolerated. The Director requested an immediate explanation for the serious overspend.

You work as the assistant to the Directorate Management Accountant. On seeing the way the budget system was developing, he made a note of points he would wish to discuss and develop further, but was called away before these could be completed.

Required:

(a) Develop and explain the issues concerning the budgetary control and responsibility accounting system which are likely to be raised by the management accountant. You should refer to the way the budget was prepared, the implications of a 20% increase in the number of visits, the extent of controllability of costs, the implications of the funding allocation, social aspects and any other points you think appropriate. You may include numerical illustrations and comment on specific costs, but you are not required to reproduce the cost control report. *(14 marks)*

(b) Briefly explain Zero-Based Budgeting (ZBB), describe how (in a situation such as that above) it might be implemented, and how as a result it could improve the budget setting procedure.

(6 marks)
(Total 20 marks)
ACCA Paper 8 Managerial Finance

15.37 **Advanced: Preparation of activity-based and flexible budgets**

AHW plc is a food processing company that produces high-quality, part-cooked meals for the retail market. The five different types of meal that the company produces (Products A to E) are made by subjecting ingredients to a series of processing activities. The meals are different, and therefore need differing amounts of processing activities.

Budget and actual information for October 2002 is shown below:

Budgeted data

	Product A	Product B	Product C	Product D	Product E
Number of batches	20	30	15	40	25
Processing activities per batch:					
Processing activity W	4	5	2	3	1
Processing activity X	3	2	5	1	4
Processing activity Y	3	3	2	4	2
Processing activity Z	4	6	8	2	3

Budgeted costs of processing activities:

	£000
Processing activity W	160
Processing activity X	130
Processing activity Y	80
Processing activity Z	200

All costs are expected to be variable in relation to the number of processing activities.

Actual data

Actual output during October 2002 was as follows:

	Product A	Product B	Product C	Product D	Product E
Number of batches	18	33	16	35	28

Actual processing costs incurred during October 2002 were:

	£000
Processing activity W	158
Processing activity X	139
Processing activity Y	73
Processing activity Z	206

Required:

(a) Prepare a budgetary control statement (to the nearest £000) that shows the original budget costs, flexible budget costs, the actual costs, and the total variances of each processing activity for October 2002.

(15 marks)

Your control statement has been issued to the Managers responsible for each processing activity and the Finance Director has asked each of them to explain the reasons for the variances shown in your statement. The Managers are not happy about this as they were not involved in setting the budgets and think that they should not be held responsible for achieving targets that were imposed upon them.

Required:

(b) Explain briefly the reasons why it might be preferable for Managers **not** to be involved in setting their own budgets.

(5 marks)

(c) (i) Explain the difference between fixed and flexible budgets and how each may be used to control production costs and non-production costs (such as marketing costs) within AHW plc.

(4 marks)

(ii) Give two examples of costs that are more appropriately controlled using a fixed budget, and explain why a flexible budget is less appropriate for the control of these costs.

(3 marks)

Many organizations use linear regression analysis to predict costs at different activity levels. By analysing past data, a formula such as

$$y = ax + b$$

is derived and used to predict future cost levels.

Required:

(d) Explain the meaning of the terms *y, a, x* and *b* in the above equation.

(3 marks)

(Total 30 marks)

CIMA Management Accounting – Performance Management

Management control systems

16

Control is the process of ensuring that a firm's activities conform to its plan and that its objectives are achieved. There can be no control without objectives and plans, since these predetermine and specify the desirable behaviour and set out the procedures that should be followed by members of the organization to ensure that a firm is operated in a desired manner.

Drucker (1964) distinguishes between 'controls' and 'control'. **Controls** are measurement and information, whereas control means direction. In other words, 'controls' are purely a means to an end; the end is control. **'Control'** is the function that makes sure that actual work is done to fulfil the original intention, and 'controls' are used to provide information to assist in determining the control action to be taken. For example, material costs may be greater than budget. 'Controls' will indicate that costs exceed budget and that this

LEARNING OBJECTIVES:

After studying this chapter you should be able to:

- describe the three different types of controls used in organizations;
- describe a cybernetic control system;
- distinguish between feedback and feed-forward controls;
- explain the potential harmful side-effects of results controls;
- define the four different types of responsibility centres;
- explain the different elements of management accounting control systems;
- describe the controllability principle and the methods of implementing it;
- describe the different approaches that can be used to determine financial performance targets and discuss the impact of their level of difficulty on motivation and performance;
- describe the influence of participation in the budgeting process;
- distinguish between the three different styles of evaluating performance and identify the circumstances when a particular style is most appropriate.

may be because the purchase of inferior quality materials causes excessive wastage. 'Control' is the action that is taken to purchase the correct quality materials in the future to reduce excessive wastage.

'Controls' encompasses all the methods and procedures that direct employees towards achieving the organization objectives. Many different control mechanisms are used in organizations and the management accounting control system represents only one aspect of the various control mechanisms that companies use to control their managers and employees. To fully understand the role that management accounting control systems play in the control process, it is necessary to be aware of how they relate to the entire array of control mechanisms used by organizations.

This chapter begins by describing the different types of controls that are used by companies. The elements of management accounting control systems will then be described within the context of the overall control process.

Control at different organizational levels

Control is applied at different levels within an organization. Merchant (1998) distinguishes between strategic control and management control. **Strategic control** has an external focus. The emphasis is on how a firm, given its strengths and weaknesses and limitations can compete with other firms in the same industry. We shall explore some of these issues in Chapter 23 within the context of strategic management accounting. In this, and the next four chapters, our emphasis will be on **management control systems** which consist of a collection of control mechanisms that primarily have an internal focus. The aim of management control systems is to influence employee behaviours in desirable ways in order to increase the probability that an organization's objectives will be achieved.

The terms 'management accounting control systems', 'accounting control systems' and 'management control systems' are often used interchangeably. Both management accounting and accounting control systems refer to the collection of practices such as budgeting, standard costing and periodic performance reporting that are normally administered by the management accounting function. Management control systems represent a broader term that encompasses management accounting/accounting control systems but it also includes other controls such as action, personnel and social controls. These controls are described in the following section.

Different types of controls

Companies use many different control mechanisms to cope with the problem of organizational control. To make sense of the vast number of controls that are used we shall classify them into three categories using approaches that have been adopted by Ouchi (1979) and Merchant (1998). They are:

1 action (or behavioural) controls;
2 personnel and cultural (or clan and social) controls;
3 results (or output) controls.

The terms in parentheses refer to the classification used by Ouchi whereas the other terms refer to the categories specified by Merchant. Because the classifications used by both authors are compatible we shall use the terms interchangeably. You should note that management accounting systems are normally synonymous with output controls whereas management control systems encompass all of the above categories of controls.

Action or behavioural controls

Behavioural controls involve observing the actions of individuals as they go about their work. They are appropriate where cause and effect relationships are well understood, so that if the correct means are followed, the desired outcomes will occur. Under these circumstances effective control can be achieved by having superiors watch and guide the actions of subordinates. For example, if the foreman watches the workers on the assembly line and ensures that the work is done exactly as prescribed then the expected quality and quantity of work should ensue.

Instead of using the term behavioural controls Merchant uses the term action controls. He defines **action controls** as applying to those situations where the actions themselves are the focus of control. They are usable and effective only when managers know what actions are desirable (or undesirable) and have the ability to make sure that the desirable actions occur (or that the undesirable actions do not occur). Forms of action controls described by Merchant include behavioural constraints, preaction reviews and action accountability.

The aim of *behavioural constraints* is to prevent people from doing things that should not be done. They include physical constraints, such as computer passwords that restrict accessing or updating information sources to authorized personnel, and administrative constraints. Imposing ceilings on the amount of capital expenditure that managers may authorize is an example of an administrative constraint. For example, managers at lower levels may be able to authorize capital expenditure below £10 000 within a total annual budget of, say, £100 000. The aim is to ensure that only those personnel with the necessary expertise and authority can authorize major expenditure and that such expenditure remains under their control.

Preaction reviews involve the scrutiny and approval of action plans of the individuals being controlled before they can undertake a course of action. Examples include the approval by municipal authorities of plans for the construction of properties prior to building commencing or the approval by a tutor of a dissertation plan prior to the student being authorized to embark on the dissertation.

Action accountability involves defining actions that are acceptable or unacceptable, observing the actions and rewarding acceptable or punishing unacceptable actions. Examples of action accountability include establishing work rules and procedures and company codes of conduct that employees must follow. Line item budgets that were described in the previous chapter are another form of action accountability whereby an upper limit on an expense category is given for the budget period. If managers exceed these limits they are held accountable and are required to justify their actions. The purpose of action accountability is to set limits on employee behaviour. Direct observation of employees' actions by superiors to ensure that they are following prescribed rules represents the main form of ensuring action accountability. Other forms include internal audits which involve checks on transaction records and compliance with pre-set action standards.

Action/behavioural controls can only be used effectively when managers know what actions are desirable (or undesirable). In other words, they are appropriate only when cause-and-effect work relationships are well understood such as when a supervisor can observe the actions of workers on a production line to ensure that work is done exactly as prescribed. In contrast, the application of action controls is limited where the work of employees is complex and uncertain and cause-and-effect relationships cannot be precisely described. For action controls to be effective a second requirement must also be met.

Managers must also be able to ensure that desired actions are taken. There must be some means of action tracking so that managers can distinguish between good and bad actions. If both of the above conditions do not apply then action controls are inappropriate.

Action controls that focus on *preventing* undesirable behaviour are the ideal form of control because their aim is to prevent the behaviour from occurring. They are preferable to *detection* controls that are applied after the occurrence of the actions because they avoid the costs of undesirable behaviour. Nevertheless, detection controls can still be useful if they are applied in a timely manner so that they can lead to the early cessation of undesirable actions. Their existence also discourages individuals from engaging in such actions.

Personnel, cultural and social controls

Clan and social controls are the second types of controls described by Ouchi. **Clan controls** are based on the belief that by fostering a strong sense of solidarity and commitment towards organizational goals people can become immersed in the interests of the organization. Macintosh (1985) illustrates an extreme example of clan controls by describing the exploits of the Japanese *kamikaze* pilots during World War II. He describes how each pilot fervently believed his individual interests were served best by complete personal immersion in the needs of Japan and the Emperor. It was understood that each pilot would sacrifice himself and his plane by crashing into an enemy warship. National ruin without resistance represented public disgrace. These beliefs were shared by each pilot.

The main feature of clan controls is the high degree of employee discipline attained through the dedication of each individual to the interests of the whole. At a less extreme level clan controls can be viewed as corporate cultures or a special form of **social control** such as the selection of people who have already been socialized into adopting particular norms and patterns of behaviour to perform particular tasks. For example, if the only staff promoted to managerial level are those who display a high commitment to the firm's objectives then the need for other forms of controls can be reduced, provided that the managers are committed to achieving the 'right' objectives.

Merchant adopts a similar approach to Ouchi and classifies personnel and cultural controls as a second form of control. He defines **personnel controls** as helping employees do a good job by building on employees' natural tendencies to control themselves. In particular, they ensure that the employees have the capabilities (in terms of intelligence, qualifications and experience) and the resources needed to do a good job. Merchant identifies three major methods of implementing personnel controls. They are selection and placement, training and job design and the provision of the necessary resources. Selection and placement involves finding the right people to do a specified job. Training can be used to ensure that employees know how to perform the assigned tasks and to make them fully aware of the results and actions that is expected from them. Job design entails designing jobs in such a way that enable employees to undertake their tasks with a high degree of success. This requires that jobs are not made too complex, onerous or badly defined so that employees do not know what is expected of them.

Cultural controls represent a set of values, social norms and beliefs that are shared by members of the organization and that influence their actions. Cultural controls are exercised by individuals over one another – for example, procedures used by groups within an organization to regulate performance of their own members and to bring them into line when they deviate from group norms. It is apparent from the above description that cultural controls are virtually the same as social controls.

Merchant suggest that a number of methods can be employed to shape culture and thus effect cultural controls. They include codes of conduct, group based rewards, and interorganizational transfers. Codes of conduct are formal written documents that incorporate general statements of corporate values and commitments to stakeholders and ways in which top management would like the organization to function. They are designed to indicate to employees what behaviours are expected in the absence of clearly defined rules or controls. Group based rewards consist of rewards based on collective achievements such as group bonuses and profit sharing schemes. They encourage mutual-monitoring by members of the group and reduce measurement costs because individual performance does not have to be measured. Interorganizational transfers involve moving managers between different functions and divisions in order to give them a better understanding of the organization as a whole. This practice is frequently used by Japanese firms to improve their sense of belonging to an organization rather than to the sub-units and also to ensure that managers are aware of the problems experienced by different parts of the organization.

In recent years working practices have begun to change and managers are now relying on people closest to the operating processes and customers to take actions without authorization from superiors. This approach is known as employee empowerment and places greater emphasis on shared organizational values for ensuring that everyone is acting in the organization's best interests. A strong internal firm culture can decrease the need for other control mechanisms since employee beliefs and norms are more likely to coincide with firm goals. They can also be used to some extent in many different organizational settings and are less costly to operate than other types of controls. They also tend to have less harmful side-effects than other control mechanisms.

Results or output controls

Output or **results controls** involve collecting and reporting information about the outcomes of work effort. The major advantage of results controls is that senior managers do not have to be knowledgeable about the means required to achieve the desired results or be involved in directly observing the actions of subordinates. They merely rely on output reports to ascertain whether or not the desired outcomes have been achieved. Management accounting control systems can be described as a form of output controls. They are mostly defined in monetary terms such as revenues, costs, profits and ratios such as return on investment. Results measures also include non-accounting measures such as the number of units of defective production, the number of loan applications processed or ratio measures such as the number of customer deliveries on time as a percentage of total deliveries.

Results controls involve the following stages:

1 establishing results (i.e. performance) measures that minimize undesirable behaviour;
2 establishing performance targets;
3 measuring performance;
4 providing rewards or punishment.

Ideally desirable behaviour should improve the performance measure and undesirable behaviour should have a detrimental effect on the measure. A performance measure that is not a good indicator of what is desirable to achieve the organization's objectives might actually encourage employees to take actions that are detrimental to the organization. The term 'What you measure is what you get' can apply whereby employees concentrate on improving the performance measures even when they are aware that their actions are not in the firm's best interests. For example, a divisional manager whose current return on investment (ROI) is 30% might reject a project which yields an ROI of 25% because it will lower the division's average ROI, even though the project has a positive NPV, and acceptance is in the best interests of the organization.

Without the *second-stage* requirement of a pre-set performance target individuals do not know what to aim for. Various research studies suggest that the existence of a clearly defined quantitative target is likely to motivate higher performance than vague statements such as 'do your best'. It is also difficult for employees or their superiors to interpret performance unless actual performance can be compared against predetermined standards.

The *third stage* specified above relates to measuring performance. Ability to measure some outputs effectively constrains the use of results measures. In the previous chapter you will remember that it was pointed out that the outputs in non-profit organizations are extremely difficult to measure and inhibit the use of results controls. Another example relates to measuring the performance of support departments. Consider a personnel department. The accomplishments of the department can be difficult to measure and other forms of control might be preferable. Merchant suggests that to evoke the right behaviours results measures should be precise, objective, timely and understandable.

Whilst 100% accuracy is not essential, measurements should be sufficiently accurate for the purpose required. If measures are not sufficiently precise they will have little information value and may lead to managers misevaluating performance. Measures should also be objective and free from bias. Where performance is self-measured and reported there is a danger that measures will be biased. Objectivity can be increased by performance being measured by people who are independent of the process being measured. Timeliness relates to the time lag between actual performance and the reporting of the results. Significant delays in reporting will result in the measures losing most of their motivational impact and a lengthy delay in taking remedial action when outcomes deviate from target. Finally, measures should be understandable by the individuals whose behaviours are being controlled. If measures are not understandable it is unlikely that managers will know how their actions will effect the measure and there is a danger that the measures will lose their motivational impact.

For results measures to work effectively the individuals whose behaviours are being controlled must be able to control and influence the results. Where factors outside the control of the individuals affect the results measures it is difficult to determine whether the results are the outcome of actions taken or from the impact of uncontrollable factors. If uncontrollable factors cannot be separated from controllable factors results controls measures are unlikely to provide useful information for evaluating the actions taken. Note also that if the outcomes of desirable behaviours are offset by the impact of uncontrollable factors results measures will lose their motivational impact and create the impression that the results measures are unjust. The term **controllability principle** is used to refer to the extent that individuals whose behaviours are being controlled can influence the results controls measures. We shall examine the controllability principle in more detail later in this chapter.

The *final stage* of results controls involves encouraging employees to achieve organizational goals by having rewards (or punishments) linked to their success (or failure) in achieving the results measures. Organizational rewards include salary increases, bonuses, promotions and recognition. Employees can also derive intrinsic rewards through a sense of accomplishment and achievement. Punishments include demotions, failure to obtain the rewards and possibly the loss of one's job.

Cybernetic control systems

The traditional approach in the management control literature has been to view results controls as a simple **cybernetic system**. In describing this process authors often use a mechanical model such as a thermostat that controls a central heating system as a resemblance. This process is illustrated in Figure 16.1. You will see that the control system consists of the following elements:

FIGURE 16.1 *A cybernetic control system*

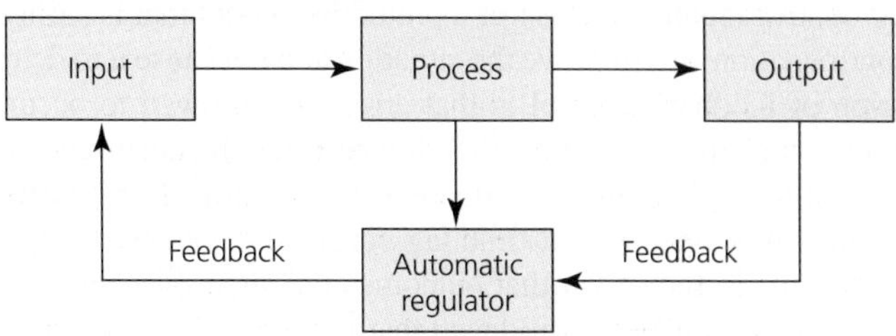

1 The process (the room's temperature) is continually monitored by an automatic regulator (the thermostat).
2 Deviations from a predetermined level (the desired temperature) are identified by the automatic regulator.
3 Corrective actions are started if the output is not equal to the predetermined level. The automatic regulator causes the input to be adjusted by turning the heater on if the temperature falls below a predetermined level. The heater is turned off when the output (temperature) corresponds with the predetermined level.

The output of the process is monitored, and whenever it varies from the predetermined level, the input is automatically adjusted. Emmanuel *et al.* (1990) state that four conditions must be satisfied before any process can be said to be controlled. First, objectives for the process being controlled must exist. Without an aim or purpose control has no meaning. Secondly, the output of the process must be measurable in terms of the dimensions defined by the objectives. In other words, there must be some mechanism for ascertaining whether the process is attaining its objectives. Thirdly, a predictive model of the process being controlled is required so that causes for the non-attainment can be identified and proposed corrective actions evaluated. Finally, there must be a capability for taking action so that deviations from objectives can be reduced. Emmanuel *et al.* stress that if any of these conditions are not met the process cannot be considered to be 'in control'.

Result controls and therefore management accounting controls resemble the thermostat control model. Standards of performance are determined, measurement systems monitor performance, comparisons are made between the standard and actual performance and feedback provides information on the variances. Note that the term **variance** is used to describe the difference the standard and actual performance of the actions that are being measured.

Feedback and feed-forward controls

The cybernetic system of control described in Figure 16.1 is that of feedback control. **Feedback control** involves monitoring outputs achieved against desired outputs and taking whatever corrective action is necessary if a deviation exists. In **feed-forward control** instead of actual outputs being compared against desired outputs, predictions are made of what outputs are expected to be at some future time. If these expectations differ from what is desired, control actions are taken that will minimize these differences. The objective is for control to be achieved before any deviations from desired outputs actually occur. In other words, with feed-forward controls likely errors can be anticipated and steps taken to avoid them, whereas with feedback controls actual errors are identified after the event and corrective action is taken to implement future actions to achieve the desired outputs.

Feed-forward control requires the use of a predictive model that is sufficiently accurate to ensure that control action will improve the situation and not cause it to deteriorate further. A major limitation of feedback control is that errors are allowed to occur. This is not a significant problem when there is a short time lag between the occurrence of an error and the identification and implementation of corrective action. Feed-forward control is therefore preferable when a significant time lag occurs. The budgeting process is a feed-forward control system. To the extent that outcomes fall short of what is desired, alternatives are considered until a budget is produced that is expected to achieve what is desired. The comparison of actual results with budget, in identifying variances and taking remedial action to ensure that future outcomes will conform with budgeted outcomes is an illustration of a feedback control system. Thus accounting control systems consist of both feedback and feed-forward controls.

Harmful side-effects of controls

Harmful side-effects occur when the controls motivate employees to engage in behaviour that is not organizationally desirable. In this situation the control system leads to a lack of goal congruence. Alternatively, when controls motivate behaviour that is organizationally desirable they are described as encouraging goal congruence.

Results controls can lead to a lack of goal congruence if the results that are required can only be partially specified. Here there is a danger that employees will concentrate only on what is monitored by the control system, regardless of whether or not it is organizationally desirable. In other words, they will seek to maximize their individual performance according to the rules of the control system irrespective of whether their actions contribute to the organization's objectives. In addition, they may ignore other important areas, if they are not monitored by the control system. The term 'What you measure is what you get' applies in these circumstances.

Figure 16.2, derived from Otley (1987) illustrates the problems that can arise when the required results can only be partially specified. You will see that those aspects of behaviour on which subordinates are likely to concentrate to achieve their personal goals (circle B) do not necessarily correspond with those necessary for achieving the wider organizational goals (circle A). In an ideal system the measured behaviour (represented by circle C) should completely cover the area of desired behaviour (represented by circle A). Therefore if a manager maximizes the performance measure, he or she will also maximize his or her contribution to the goals of the organization. In other words, the performance measures encourage goal congruence. In practice, it is unlikely that perfect performance measures can be constructed that measure all desirable organizational behaviour, and so it is unlikely that all of circle C will cover circle A. Assuming that managers desire the rewards offered by circle C, their actual behaviour (represented by circle B) will be altered to include more of circle C and, to the extent that C coincides with A, more of circle A.

However, organizational performance will be improved only to the extent that the performance measure is a good indicator of what is desirable to achieve the firm's goals. Unfortunately, performance measures are not perfect and, as an ideal measure of overall performance, is unlikely to exist. Some measures may encourage goal congruence or organizationally desirable behaviour (the part of circle C that coincides with A), but other measures will not encourage goal congruence (the part of circle C that does not coincide with A). Consequently, there is a danger that subordinates will concentrate only on what is measured, regardless of whether or not it is organizationally desirable. Furthermore, actual

FIGURE 16.2 *The measurement and reward process with imperfect measures*

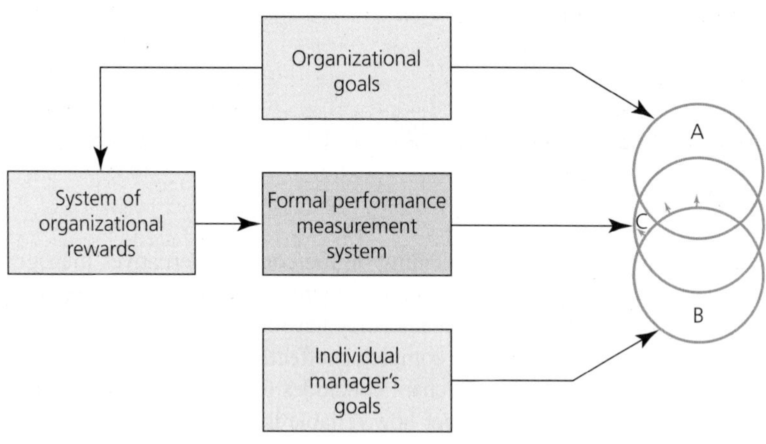

A Behaviour necessary to achieve organizational goals
B Behaviour actually engaged in by an individual manager
C Behaviour formally measured by control systems

behaviour may be modified so that desired results appear to be obtained, although they may have been achieved in an undesirable manner which is detrimental to the firm.

There is also a tendency for results controls to focus mainly on controlling behaviours that are quantifiable and easily measurable and ignore those behaviours that are less quantifiable. For example, less attention may be given to employee morale and welfare, personnel development or public responsibility because actions relating to these areas are difficult to quantify. A possible solution is to develop appropriate surrogate measures such as conducting attitude surveys to measure employee welfare. However, care must be taken not to overuse results measures in circumstances where the results that are required cannot be specified in quantitative terms. Instead, other types of controls should be used.

The evidence suggests that data manipulation is common with results controls (Merchant, 1990). Data manipulation occurs where individuals try and distort the data in order to improve the performance measure. For example, where individuals have some influence in the setting of performance targets there is a danger that they will seek to obtain easier targets by deliberately underperforming so that their targets will not be increased in the forthcoming period. Merchant (1990) also reported the widespread use of shifting funds between different budget items in order to avoid adverse budget variances.

Another harmful side effect of controls is that they can cause negative attitudes towards the control system. If controls are applied too rigorously they can result in job-related tensions, conflict and a deterioration in relationships with managers. To a certain extent people do not like being subject to controls so that negative attitudes may be unavoidable. Nevertheless, they can be minimized if care is taken in designing control systems. Results controls can cause negative attitudes when targets are set which are considered to be too difficult and unachievable. Negative attitudes can also be exacerbated by a failure to apply the controllability principle. Performance evaluations are likely to be considered unfair where managers are held accountable for outcomes over which they have little control. Another potential cause of negative attitudes is the way in which results controls are applied. If they are applied in an insensitive and rigid manner and used mainly as punitive devices they are likely to provoke negative reactions. The way that a control system is applied can be just as important as the design issues in determining the success of a control system. Negative attitudes are likely to be the cause of many of the harmful side-effects that have been described above. Thus, if the negative attitudes can be minimized the harmful side-effects are likely to be minimized.

Advantages and disadvantages of different types of controls

Merchant (1998) suggests that when deciding on the control alternatives managers should start by considering whether *personnel* or *cultural controls* will be sufficient. He suggests that they are worthy of first consideration because they have relatively few harmful side-effects. Also in small organizations they may be completely effective without the need to supplement them with other forms of controls. Merchant concludes that considering personnel/cultural controls first allows managers to consider how reliable these controls are and the extent to which it is necessary to supplement them with other forms of control. However, he points out that these controls are appropriate only if the people in their particular roles understand what is required, are capable of performing well, and are motivated to perform well without additional rewards or punishments provided by the organization.

Action controls are the most effective form of control because there is a direct link between the control mechanism and the action and also a high probability that desirable outcomes will occur. They dispense with the need to measure the results and measurement problems do not therefore apply. The major limitation of action controls is that because they are dependent on cause-and-effect work relationships that are well understood they are not feasible in many situations. These requirements are likely to be applicable only with highly routinized jobs. A second limitation is that they tend to be best suited to stable situations. They can discourage creativity and the ability to adapt to changing circumstances and are therefore likely to be unsuitable in a changing environment.

The major attraction of *results controls* is that they can be applied where knowledge of what actions are desirable is lacking. This situation applies in most organizations. A second attraction of results controls is that their application does not restrict individual autonomy. The focus is on the outcomes thus giving individuals the freedom to determine how they can best achieve the outcomes. Individuals are not burdened with having to follow prescribed rules and procedures.

The major disadvantages of results controls have already been discussed in the previous section. In many cases the results required can only be partially specified, there can be difficulties in separating controllable and uncontrollable factors and measurement problems in the form of precision, objectivity, timeliness and understandability may inhibit their ability to satisfactorily measure performance.

Management accounting control systems

Although output controls predominantly consist of management accounting controls the latter have not been examined in detail. To enable you to understand the role that management accounting control systems play within the overall control process this chapter has initially adopted a broad approach to describing management control systems. We shall now concentrate on management accounting control systems which represent the predominant controls in most organizations.

Why are accounting controls the predominant controls? There are several reasons. First, all organizations need to express and aggregate the results of a wide range of dissimilar activities using a common measure. The monetary measure meets this requirement. Second, profitability and liquidity are essential to the success of all organizations and financial measures relating to these and other areas are closely monitored by stakeholders. It is therefore natural that managers will wish to monitor performance in monetary terms. Third, financial measures also enable a common decision rule to be applied by all managers when considering alternative courses of action. That is, a course of action will normally benefit a firm only if it results in an improvement in its financial performance. Fourth, measuring results in financial terms enables managers to be given more autonomy. Focusing on the outcomes of managerial actions, summarized in financial terms, gives managers the freedom to take whatever actions they consider to be appropriate to achieve the desired results. Finally, outputs expressed in financial terms continue to be effective in uncertain environments even when it is unclear what course of action should be taken. Financial results provide a mechanism to indicate whether the actions benefited the organization.

Responsibility centres

The complex environment in which most businesses operate today makes it virtually impossible for most firms to be controlled centrally. This is because it is not possible for central management to have all the relevant information and time to determine the detailed plans for all the organization. Some degree of decentralization is essential for all but the smallest firms. Organizations decentralize by creating responsibility centres. A **responsibility centre** may be defined as a unit of a firm where an individual manager is held responsible for the unit's performance. There are four types of responsibility centres. They are:

1. cost or expense centres;
2. revenue centres;
3. profit centres;
4. investment centres.

The creation of responsibility centres is a fundamental part of management accounting control systems. It is therefore important that you can distinguish between the various forms of responsibility centres.

Cost or expense centres

Cost or **expense centres** are responsibility centres whose managers are normally accountable for only those costs that are under their control. We can distinguish between two types of cost centres – standard cost centres and discretionary cost centres. The main features of **standard cost centres** are that output can be measured and the input required to produce each unit of output can be specified. Control is exercised by comparing the standard cost (that is, the cost of the inputs that *should* have been consumed in producing the output) with the cost that was *actually* incurred. The difference between the actual cost and the standard cost is described as the **variance**. Standard cost centres and variance analysis will be discussed extensively in Chapters 18 and 19.

Standard cost centres are best suited to units within manufacturing firms but they can also be established in service industries such as units within banks, where output can be measured in terms of the number of cheques or the number of loan applications processed, and there are also well defined input–output relationships. Although cost centre managers are not accountable for sales revenues they can affect the amount of sales revenue generated if quality standards are not met and outputs are not produced according to schedule. Therefore quality and timeliness non-financial performance measures are also required besides financial measures.

Discretionary expense centres are those responsibility cost centres where output cannot be measured in financial terms and there are no clearly observable relationships between inputs (the resources consumed) and the outputs (the results achieved). Control normally takes the form of ensuring that actual expenditure adheres to budgeted expenditure for each expense category and also ensuring that the tasks assigned to each centre have been successfully accomplished. Examples of discretionary centres include advertising and publicity and research and development departments. You should note that in discretionary centres underspending against budget may not necessarily be a good thing since this may result in a lower level of service than that originally planned by management. For example, underspending on research and development may indicate that the amount to be spent on research and development has not been followed. One of the major problems arising in discretionary expense centres is measuring the effectiveness of expenditures. For example, the marketing support department may not have exceeded an advertising budget but this does not mean that the advertising expenditure has been effective. The advertising may have been incorrectly timed, it may have been directed to the wrong audience, or it may have contained the wrong message. Determining the effectiveness and efficiency of discretionary expense centres is one of the most difficult areas of management control.

Revenue centres

Revenue centres are responsibility centres where managers are accountable only for financial outputs in the form of generating sales revenues. Typical examples of revenue centres are where regional sales managers are accountable for sales within their regions. In some organizations revenue centres acquire finished goods from a manufacturing division and are responsible for selling and distributing these goods. Where managers are evaluated solely on the basis of sales revenues there is a danger that they may concentrate on maximizing sales revenues at the expense of profitability. This can occur when all sales are not equally profitable and managers can achieve higher sales revenues by promoting low-profit products.

Revenue centre managers may also be held accountable for selling expenses, such as salesperson salaries, commissions and order-getting costs. They are not, however, made accountable for the cost of the goods and services that they sell. Revenue centres can be distinguished from profit centres by the fact that revenue centres are accountable for only a small proportion of the total costs of manufacturing and selling products and services, namely selling costs, whereas profit centre managers are responsible for the majority of the costs including both manufacturing and selling costs.

Profit centres

Both cost and revenue centre managers have limited decision-making authority. Cost centre managers are accountable only for managing inputs of their centres and decisions relating to outputs are made by other units within the firm. Revenue centres are accountable for selling the products or services but they have no control over their manufacture. A significant increase in managerial autonomy occurs when unit managers are given responsibility for both production and sales. In this situation managers are normally free to set selling prices, choose which markets to sell in, make product-mix and output decisions and select suppliers. Units within an organization whose managers are accountable for both revenues and costs are called profit centres.

In practice many firms create profit centres that do not conform to the above requirements. They are more limited in scope and can be described as pseudo-profit centres. For example, selling units might be made profit centres by charging the units with the standard cost of the products or services sold, thus making the unit manager accountable for gross margin. Making selling units pseudo-profit centres overcomes a major limitation of revenue centres whereby managers can be motivated to maximize sales revenues rather than profits.

Sometimes manufacturing and administrative units that supply products or services to other units are allocated sales revenues derived from internal transfer prices that are established for the goods or services. If established external market prices can be used as a benchmark for setting the transfer prices and the buying units can outsource their purchases, rather than buying internally, then the selling units are likely to have some influence over the revenues generated and thus resemble true profit centres. If these conditions do not apply and inter-unit trading is not subject to external competitive forces the responsibility centres will be merely pseudo-profit centres. You should note, however, that many profit centres do in fact derive most, or sometimes all, of their revenues by selling their products or services to other units within the same firm.

Investment centres

Investment centres are responsibility centres whose managers are responsible for both sales revenues and costs and, in addition, have responsibility and authority to make working capital and capital investment decisions. Typical investment centre performance measures include return on investment and economic value added. These measures are influenced by revenues, costs and assets employed and thus reflect the responsibility that managers have for both generating profits and managing the investment base.

Investment centres represent the highest level of managerial autonomy. They include the company as a whole, operating subsidiaries, operating groups and divisions. You will find that many firms are not precise in their terminology and call their investment centres profit centres. Profit and investment centres will be discussed extensively in Chapter 20.

The nature of management accounting control systems

Management accounting control systems have two core elements. The first is the formal planning processes such as budgeting and long-term planning that were described in the previous chapter. These processes are used for establishing performance expectations for evaluating performance. The second is responsibility accounting which involves the creation of responsibility centres. Responsibility centres enable accountability for financial results and outcomes to be allocated to individuals throughout the organization. The objective of responsibility accounting is to accumulate costs and revenues for each individual responsibility centre so that the deviations from a performance target (typically the budget) can be attributed to the individual who is accountable for the responsibility centre. For each responsibility centre the process involves setting a performance target, measuring performance, comparing performance against the target, analysing the variances and taking action where significant variances exist between actual and target performance. Financial performance targets for profit or investment centres are typically in terms of profits, return on investment or economic value added whereas performance targets for cost centres are defined in terms of costs.

Responsibility accounting is implemented by issuing performance reports at frequent intervals (normally monthly) that inform responsibility centre managers of the deviations from budgets for which they are accountable and are required to take action. An example of a performance report issued to a cost centre manager is presented in the lower section of Exhibit 16.1. You should note that at successively higher levels of management less detailed information is reported. You can see from the upper sections of Exhibit 16.1 that the information is condensed and summarized as the results relating to the responsibility centre are reported at higher levels. Exhibit 16.1 only includes financial information. In addition non-financial measures such as those relating to quality and timeliness may be reported. We shall look at non-financial measures in more detail in Chapter 23.

Responsibility accounting involves:

- distinguishing between those items which managers can control and for which they should be held accountable and those items over which they have no control and for which they are not held accountable;
- determining how challenging the financial targets should be;
- determining how much influence managers should have in the setting of financial targets.

We shall now examine each of these items in detail.

The controllability principle

Responsibility accounting is based on the application of the **controllability principle** which means that it is appropriate to charge to an area of responsibility only those costs that are significantly influenced by the manager of that responsibility centre. The controllability principle can be implemented by either eliminating the uncontrollable items from the areas for which managers are held accountable or calculating their effects so that the reports distinguish between controllable and uncontrollable items.

Applying the controllability principle is difficult in practice because many areas do not fit neatly into either controllable and uncontrollable categories. Instead, they are partially controllable. For example, even when outcomes may be affected by occurrences outside a manager's control; such as competitors' actions, price changes and supply shortages, managers can take action to reduce their adverse effects. They can substitute alternative materials where the prices of raw materials change or they can monitor and respond to competitors' actions. If these factors are categorized as uncontrollables managers will be motivated not to try and influence them. A further problem is that even when a factor is clearly uncontrollable, it is difficult to measure in order to highlight its impact on the reported outcomes.

Types of uncontrollable factors

Merchant (1998) identifies three types of uncontrollable factors. They are:

1. economic and competitive factors;
2. acts of nature;
3. interdependencies.

Both revenues and costs are affected by *economic and competitive factors*. Changes in customers' tastes, competitors' actions, business cycles and changing government regulations and foreign exchange rates affect sales revenues. Costs are affected by items such as changes

EXHIBIT 16.1

Responsibility accounting monthly performance reports

Performance report to managing director

		Budget		Variance[a] F (A)	
		Current month (£)	Year to date (£)	This month (£)	Year to date (£)
Managing director	Factory A	453 900	6 386 640	80 000(A)	98 000(A)
	Factory B	X	X	X	X
	Factory C	X	X	X	X
	Administration costs	X	X	X	X
	Selling costs	X	X	X	X
	Distribution costs	X	X	X	X
		2 500 000	30 000 000	400 000(A)	600 000(A)

Performance report to production manager of factory A

		Current month (£)	Year to date (£)	This month (£)	Year to date (£)
Production manager	Works manager's office	X	X	X	X
	Machining department 1	165 600	717 600	32 760(A)	89 180(A)
	Machining department 2	X	X	X	X
	Assembly department	X	X	X	X
	Finishing department	X	X	X	X
		453 900	6 386 640	80 000(A)	98 000(A)

Performance report to head of responsibility centre

		Current month (£)	Year to date (£)	This month (£)	Year to date (£)
Head of responsibility centre	Direct materials	X	X	X	X
	Direct labour	X	X	X	X
	Indirect labour	X	X	X	X
	Indirect materials	X	X	X	X
	Power	X	X	X	X
	Maintenance	X	X	X	X
	Idle time	X	X	X	X
	Other	X	X	X	X
		165 600	717 600	32 760(A)	89 180(A)

[a]F indicates a favourable variance (actual cost less than budgeted cost) and (A) indicates an adverse budget (actual cost greater than budget cost). Note that, at the lowest level of reporting, the responsibility centre head's performance report contains detailed information on operating costs. At successively higher levels of management less detail is reported. For example, the managing director's information on the control of activities consists of examining those variances that represent significant departures from the budget for each factory and functional area of the business and requesting explanations from the appropriate managers.

in input prices, interest and foreign exchange rates, government regulations and taxes. Although these items appear to be uncontrollable managers can respond to these changes to relieve their negative impacts. For example, they can respond to changes in customers' tastes by developing new products or redesigning existing products. They can respond to changes in exchange rates by changing their sources of supply and selling in different countries. Responding to such changes is an important part of a manager's job. Therefore most management accounting control systems do not shield managers completely from economic and competitive factors although they may not be required to bear all of the risk.

Acts of nature are usually large, one-time events with effects on performance that are beyond the ability of managers to anticipate. Examples are disasters such as fires, floods, riots, tornadoes, accidents and machine breakdowns. Most organizations protect managers from the adverse consequences of acts of nature by not making them accountable for them provided that the events are considered to be clearly uncontrollable. However, controllability can be an issue where accidents or machine breakdowns are avoidable. Also the extent of uncontrollability becomes questionable where managers have failed in their responsibility to reduce the adverse consequences of such events by not purchasing insurance protection.

The third type of uncontrollable relates to *interdependence* whereby a responsibility centre is not completely self-contained so that the outcomes are affected by other units within the organization. For example, responsibility centres use common/pooled firm resources such as shared administrative activities. Pooled interdependence is low when responsibility centres are relatively self-contained so that use of pooled resources has little impact on a unit's performance. The users of pooled resources should not have to bear any higher costs arising from the bad performance of the shared resource pools. Managers can be protected from inefficiencies of the shared resource pools to a certain extent by negotiations during the annual budgeting process whereby the quantities and amounts of services are agreed. Responsibility centre managers are charged with their usage of pooled resources at the budgeted rate and do not bear the cost of any inefficiencies incurred by the pooled resource centres during the current budget period.

Dealing with the distorting effects of uncontrollable factors before the measurement period

Management can attempt to deal with the distorting effects of uncontrollables by making adjustments either before or after the measurement period. Uncontrollable and controllable factors can be determined prior to the measurement period by specifying which budget line items are to be regarded as controllable and uncontrollable. Uncontrollable items can either be excluded from performance reports or shown in a separate section within the performance report so that they are clearly distinguishable from controllable items. The latter approach has the advantage of drawing managerial attention to those costs that a company incurs to support their activities. Managers may be able to indirectly influence these costs if they are made aware of the sums involved.

How do we distinguish between controllable and uncontrollable items? Merchant suggests that the following general rule should be applied to all employees – 'Hold employees accountable for the performance areas you want them to pay attention to.' Applying this rule explains why some organizations assign the costs of shared resource pools, such as administrative costs relating to personnel and data processing departments, to responsibility centres. Assigning these costs authorizes managers of the user responsibility centres to question the amount of the costs and the quantity and quality of services supplied. In addition, responsibility centres are discouraged from making unnecessary requests for the use of these services when they are aware that increases in costs will be assigned to the users of the services.

Care must be taken, however, in making responsibility heads accountable for many areas for which they do not have a significant influence. The additional costs arising from the harmful side-effects described earlier will be incurred and these must be offset against the benefits discussed above.

Dealing with the distorting effects of uncontrollable factors after the measurement period

Merchant identifies four methods of removing the effects of uncontrollable factors from the results measures after the measurement period and before the rewards are assigned. They are:

1 variance analysis;
2 flexible performance standards;
3 relative performance evaluations;
4 subjective performance evaluations.

Variance analysis seeks to analyse the factors that cause the actual results to differ from pre-determined budgeted targets. In particular, variance analysis helps to distinguish between controllable and uncontrollable items and identify those individuals who are accountable for the variances. For example, variances analysed by each type of cost, and by their price and quantity effects, enables variances to be traced to accountable individuals and also to isolate those variances that are due to uncontrollable factors. Variance analysis will be discussed extensively in Chapters 18 and 19.

Flexible performance standards apply when targets are adjusted to reflect variations in uncontrollable factors arising from the circumstances not envisaged when the targets were set. The most widely used flexible performance standard is to use **flexible budgets** whereby the uncontrollable volume effects on cost behaviour are removed from the manager's performance reports. Because some costs vary with changes in the level of activity, it is essential when applying the controllability principle to take into account the variability of costs. For example, if the actual level of activity is greater than the budgeted level of activity then those costs that vary with activity will be greater than the budgeted costs purely because of changes in activity. Let us consider the simplified situation presented in Example 16.1.

Assuming that the increase in activity was due to an increase in sales volume greater than that anticipated when the budget was set then the increases in costs arising from the volume change are beyond the control of the responsibility centre manager. It is clearly inappropriate to compare actual *variable* costs of £105 000 from an activity level of 24 000 units with budgeted *variable* costs of £100 000 from an activity level of 20 000 units. This would incorrectly suggest an overspending of £5000. If managers are to be made responsible for their costs, it is essential that they are responsible for performance under the conditions in which they worked, and not for a performance based on conditions when the budget was drawn up. In other words, it is misleading to compare actual costs at one level of activity with budgeted costs at another level of activity. At the end of the period the original budget must be adjusted to the actual level of activity to take into account the impact of the uncontrollable volume change on costs. This procedure is called flexible budgeting. In Example 16.1 the performance report should be as follows:

Budgeted expenditure	Actual expenditure
(flexed to 24 000 units)	(24 000 units)
£120 000	£105 000

EXAMPLE 16.1

An item of expense that is included in the budget for a responsibility centre varies directly in relation to activity at an estimated cost of £5 per unit of output. The budgeted monthly level of activity was 20 000 units and the actual level of activity was 24 000 units at a cost of £105 000.

The budget is adjusted to reflect what the costs should have been for an actual activity of 24 000 units. This indicates that the manager has incurred £15 000 less expenditure than would have been expected for the actual level of activity, and a favourable variance of £15 000 should be recorded on the performance report, not an adverse variance of £5000, which would have been recorded if the original budget had not been adjusted.

In Example 16.1 it was assumed that there was only one variable item of expense, but in practice the budget will include many different expenses including fixed, semi-variable and variable expenses. You should note that fixed expenses do not vary in the short-term with activity and therefore the budget should remain unchanged for these expenses. The budget should be flexed only for variable and semi-variable expenses.

Budgets may also be adjusted to reflect other uncontrollable factors besides volume changes. Budgets are normally set based on the environment that is anticipated during the budget setting process. If the budget targets are then used throughout the duration of the annual budget period for performance evaluation the managers will be held accountable for uncontrollable factors arising from forecasting errors. To remove the managerial exposure to uncontrollable risks arising from forecasting errors ***ex post* budget adjustments** can be made whereby the budget is adjusted to the environmental and economic conditions that the manager's actually faced during the period. An alternative view is that a manager's job is to respond to such uncertainties and that the uncontrollable effects should not be removed from the performance evaluation. This view has greater merit where managers have participated in the forecasting process. A further problem is that it is time-consuming and costly to isolate the effects of unforeseen events. The uncontrollable factors arising from forecasting errors can be substantially reduced by using the system of continuous or rolling budgets that was described in the previous chapter.

Relative performance evaluation relates to the situations where the performance of a responsibility centre is evaluated relative to the performance of similar centres within the same company or to similar units outside the organization. To be effective responsibility centres must perform similar tasks and face similar environmental and business conditions with the units that they are being benchmarked against. Such relative comparisons with units facing similar environmental conditions neutralizes the uncontrollable factors because they are in effect held constant when making the relative comparisons. The major difficulty relating to relative performance evaluations is finding benchmark units that face similar conditions and uncertainties.

Instead of making the formal and quantitative adjustments that are a feature of the methods that have been described so far **subjective judgements** are made in the evaluation process based on the knowledge of the outcome measures and the circumstances faced by the responsibility centre heads. The major advantage of subjective evaluations is that they can alleviate some of the defects of the measures used by accounting control systems. The disadvantages of subjective evaluations are that they are not objective, they tend not to provide the person being evaluated with a clear indication of how performance has been evaluated, they can create conflict with superiors resulting in a loss of morale and a decline in motivation and they are expensive in terms of management time.

Guidelines for applying the controllability principle

Dealing with uncontrollables represents one of the most difficult areas for the design and operation of management accounting control systems. The following guidelines published by the Report of the Committee of Cost Concepts and Standards in the United States in 1956 still continues to provide useful guidance:

1. If a manager *can control the quantity and price paid* for a service then the manager is responsible for all the expenditure incurred for the service.
2. If the manager *can control the quantity of the service but not the price paid* for the service then only that amount of difference between actual and budgeted expenditure that is due to usage should be identified with the manager.
3. If the manager *cannot control either the quantity or the price paid* for the service then the expenditure is uncontrollable and should not be identified with the manager.

An example of the latter situation is when the costs of an industrial relations department are apportioned to a department on some arbitrary basis; such arbitrary apportionments are likely to result in an allocation of expenses that the managers of responsibility centres may not be able to influence. In addition to the above guidelines Merchants's general rule should also be used as a guide – 'Hold employees accountable for the performance areas you want them to pay attention to.'

Setting financial performance targets

There is substantial evidence from a large number of studies that the existence of a defined, quantitative goal or target is likely to motivate higher levels of performance than when no such target is stated. People perform better when they have a clearly defined goal to aim for and are aware of the standards that will be used to interpret their performance. There are three approaches that can be used to set financial targets. They are targets derived from engineering studies of input–output relationships, targets derived from historical data and targets derived from negotiations between superiors and subordinates.

Engineered targets can be used when there are clearly defined and stable input–output relationships such that the inputs required can be estimated directly from product specifications. For example, in a fast-food restaurant for a given output of hamburgers it is possible to estimate the inputs required because there is a physical relationship between the ingredients such as meats, buns, condiments and packaging and the number of hamburgers made. Input–output relationships can also be established for labour by closely observing the processes to determine the quantity of labour that will be required for a given output.

Where clearly defined input–output relationships do not exist other approaches must be used to set financial targets. One approach is to use **historical targets** derived directly from the results of previous periods. Previous results plus an increase for expected price changes may form the basis for setting the targets or an improvement factor may be incorporated into the estimate, such as previous period costs less a reduction of 10%. The disadvantage of using historical targets is that they may include past inefficiencies or may encourage employees to underperform if the outcome of efficient performance in a previous period is used as a basis for setting a more demanding target in the next period.

Negotiated targets are set based on negotiations between superiors and subordinates. The major advantage of negotiated targets is that they address the information asymmetry gap that can exist between superior and subordinate. This gap arises because subordinates have more information than their superiors on the relationships between outputs and inputs and the constraints that exist at the operating level, whereas superiors have a broader view of the organization as a whole and the resource constraints that apply. Negotiated targets enable the information asymmetry gap to be reduced so that the targets set incorporate the constraints applying at both the operational level and the firm as a whole. You should refer back to the previous chapter for a more detailed discussion of the negotiation process.

Targets vary in their level of difficulty and the chosen level has a significant effect on motivation and performance. Targets are considered to be moderately difficult (or highly achievable) when they are set at the average level of performance for a given task. According to Merchant (1990) most companies set their annual profit budgets targets at levels that are highly achievable. Their budgets are set to be challenging but achievable 80–90 per cent of the time by an effective management team working at a consistently high level of effort. Targets set at levels above average are labelled as difficult, tight or high, and those set below average are classed as easy, loose or low (Chow, 1983).

The research evidence suggests that setting specific difficult budget targets leads to higher task performance than setting specific moderate or easy targets (Stedry and Kay, 1966; Hofstede, 1968; Chow, 1983). However, Hirst (1987) has advocated that the benefits arising from setting specific difficult budget goals are dependent on the level of task uncertainty. He suggests that where task uncertainty is low, setting specific difficult budget goals will promote performance, and the subsequent use of difficult budget goals to evaluate performance will minimize the incidence of dysfunctional behaviour, such as falsifying accounting information. In contrast, where task uncertainty is high, the beneficial effects arising from setting specific difficult goals are less likely to occur, and subsequent use of these difficult goals will promote dysfunctional behaviour.

The effect of the level of budget difficulty on motivation and performance

The fact that a financial target represents a specific quantitative goal gives it a strong motivational potential, but the targets set must be accepted if managers are to be motivated to achieve higher levels of performance. Unfortunately, it is not possible to specify exactly the optimal degree of difficulty for financial targets, since task uncertainty and cultural, organizational and personality factors all affect an individual manager's reaction to a financial target.

Figure 16.3, derived from Otley (1987), shows the theoretical relationship between budget difficulty, aspiration levels and performance. In Figure 16.3 it is assumed that performance and aspiration levels are identical. Note that the **aspiration level** relates to the personal goal of the budgetee (that is, the person who is responsible for the budget). In other words, it is the level of performance that they hope to attain. You will see from Figure 16.3 that as the level of budget difficulty is increased both the budgetees' aspiration level and performance increases. However, there becomes a point where the budget is perceived as impossible to achieve and the aspiration level and performance decline dramatically. It can be seen from Figure 16.3 that the budget level that motivates the best level of performance may not be achievable. In contrast, the budget that is expected to be achieved (that is, the expectations budget in Figure 16.3) motivates a lower level of performance.

Hofstede (1968) adopted a similar approach to illustrate a hypothesized relationship between the level of difficulty of an expense budget, the aspiration level and performance. His work is still relevant today. Hofstede uses the diagram reproduced in Figure 16.4 to illustrate an expense budget, where the level of expense is shown on the vertical axis and the degree of tightness of the budget is shown on the horizontal axis, going from very loose on the left to very tight on the right. The budget, aspiration levels and actual results are

FIGURE 16.3 *The effect of budget difficulty on performance. Source: Otley (1987)*

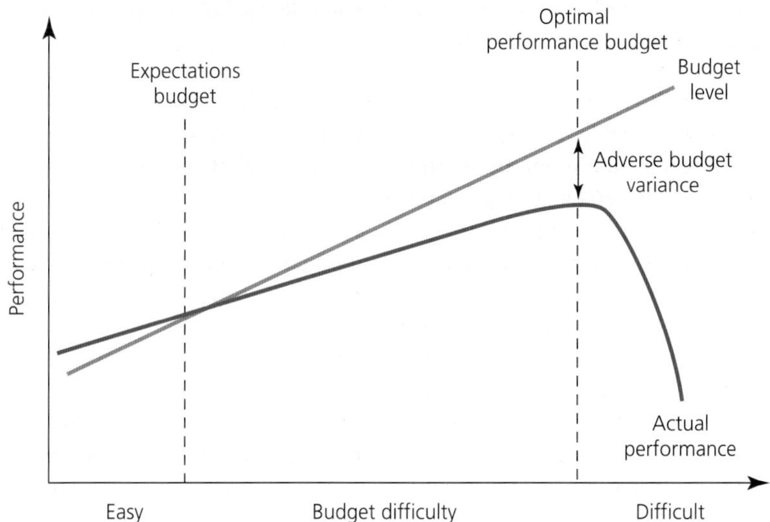

FIGURE 16.4 *The effect of budget levels on aspiration*

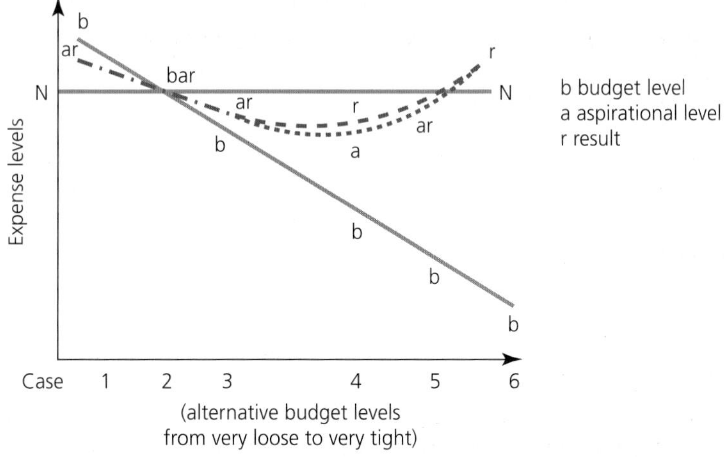

denoted by the letters b, a and r. In the absence of a budget the expense level is assumed to be N, and the diagram shows what will happen if we consider various alternative budget levels from very loose (case 1) to very tight (case 6). In case 1 the budget is too loose (i.e. above level N). The budgetee will not find the budget very challenging, and will set a higher aspiration level (lower than the budgeted cost) but still above N. The result r will be equal to the aspiration level.

In case 2 the budget is equal to N, and the aspiration level and the result coincide with the budget; the budget will not influence performance. In case 3, the budget is below N, and the budgetee responds by altering his aspiration level to below N but not to the budgeted level of expenditure. Because the aspiration level is not too difficult, the actual result will be equal to the aspiration level. In case 4 the budget is tighter still, and this results in an improvement in the aspiration level. However, since the budget and aspiration level are so tight, there is a strong possibility that the actual result will not be as good as the aspiration level. Therefore r is shown to be above a, but the highest level of performance will be achieved at this point. In case 5 the budget is very tight. The budgetee sees this is almost impossible, and sets an aspiration level that is easier than case 4. In this situation the actual result will be equal to the aspiration level. In case 6 the budget is so tight that the budgetee will regard it as impossible. He or she will stop trying, and will not attempt to set an aspiration level. The effect of this approach is that the actual result will be worse than that which would have been achieved had no budget been set.

A close examination of Figure 16.4 indicates that budgets do not always lead to improved performance. In cases 1 and 6 the budgets do more harm than good, and improvements occur only in cases 3 and 4. The problem is further complicated by the fact that failure to achieve the budget is likely to lead to a lowering of aspiration levels. Therefore in case 4, where the actual result is worse than the aspiration level, the budgetee might respond by setting a less ambitious aspiration level next time. The effect may be that case 4 will shift to case 5.

An interesting implication of the hypothesized relationships is that the budget level that motivates the best performance is unlikely to be achieved much of the time (case 4 in Figure 16.4 or the optimal performance budget in Figure 16.3). However, a budget that is usually achieved will motivate a lower level of performance (cases 1 and 2 in Figure 16.4 or the expectations budget in Figure 16.3). Therefore if budgets are to be set at a level that will motivate individuals to achieve maximum performance, adverse budget variances are to be expected. In such a situation it is essential that adverse budget variances are not used by management as a punitive device, since this is likely to encourage budgetees to attempt to obtain looser budgets by either underperforming or deliberately negotiating easily attainable budgets. This may lead to fewer adverse variances, but also to poorer overall performance.

To motivate the best level of actual performance, demanding budgets should be set and small adverse variances should be regarded as a healthy sign and not as something to be avoided. If budgets are always achieved with no adverse variances, this indicates that the standards are too loose to motivate the best possible results.

Arguments in favour of setting highly achievable budgets

It appears from our previous discussion that tight budgets should be established to motivate maximum performance, although this may mean that the budget has a high probability of not being achieved. Otley (1987) suggests that the optimum point may be at the point where individuals perceive there is significantly less than a 50% chance of target achievement. However, budgets are not used purely as a motivational device to maximize performance. They are also used for planning purposes and it is most unlikely that tight budgets will be suitable for planning purposes. Why? Tight budgets that have a high probability of not being achieved are most unsuitable for cash budgeting and for harmonizing the company plans in the form of a master budget. Because of this conflict, it has been suggested that separate budgets should be used for planning and for motivation purposes. The counter argument to this is that budgetees may react unfavourably to a situation where they believe that one budget is used to evaluate their performance and a second looser budget is used by top management.

Most companies use the same budgets for planning and motivational purposes (Umapathy, 1987). If only one set of budgets is used it is most unlikely that one set can, at the same time,

Key terms and concepts

action controls (p. 645)
aspiration level (p. 662)
behavioural controls (p. 645)
bottom-up budget setting (p. 665)
budget-constrained style (p. 668)
clan controls (p. 646)
control (p. 643)
controllability principle (pp. 648, 656)
controls (p. 643)
cost centres (p. 653)
cultural controls (p. 646)
cybernetic system (p. 648)
discretionary expense centres (p. 654)
engineered targets (p. 661)
expense centres (p. 653)
ex post budget adjustments (p. 660)
feedback control (p. 649)
feed-forward control (p. 649)
flexible budgets (p. 659)
goal congruence (p. 650)
historical targets (p. 661)
investment centres (p. 655)
management control systems (p. 644)
negotiated targets (p. 661)
non-accounting style (p. 668)
output controls (p. 647)
participation (p. 665)
personnel controls (p. 646)
profit centres (p. 655)
profit-conscious style (p. 668)
relative performance evaluation (p. 660)
responsibility accounting (p. 655)
responsibility centre (p. 653)
results controls (p. 647)
revenue centres (p. 654)
social control (p. 646)
standard cost centres (p. 653)
strategic control (p. 644)
subjective judgements (p. 660)
top-down budget setting (p. 665)
variance (pp. 649, 653)
variance analysis (p. 659)

Recommended reading

For a detailed study of the controllability principle you should refer to Merchant (1989). There are a number of important textbooks that specialize in management control. If you wish to study management control in more depth you are recommended to read Merchant (1998). For a discussion of performance measurement in the service industries you should refer to Fitzgerald and Moon (1996).

Key examination points

Essay questions are extensively used in second year management accounting courses. They tend not to be wisely used for first year courses. The most frequently examined topic on first year courses is to prepare flexible budgets (see Solutions to Review problems 16.22 and 16.24). If you are required to prepare flexible budgets remember to flex the budget on the basis of target cost for actual output rather than input measures, such as direct labour or input hours. Also questions requiring you to comment on, or redraft performance reports, are frequently set at all levels (e.g. Review problems 16.23 and 16.25). It is important that you distinguish between controllable and non-controllable expenses and stress the need to incorporate non-financial measures. A common error is to compare actual performance with an unflexed budget.

Assessment material

Review questions

The review questions are short questions that enable you to assess your understanding of the main topics included in the chapter. The numbers in parentheses provide you with the page numbers to refer to if you cannot answer a specific question.

Review problems

The review problems are more complex and require you to relate and apply the chapter content to various business problems. The problems are graded by their level of difficulty. Fully worked solutions to the review problems are provided in a separate section at the end of the book. For those questions in the white box the worked solutions are provided in the *Student's Manual* accompanying this book. Further review problems for this chapter are available on the accompanying website www.drury-online.com. The answers to these problems are available for lecturers on the lecturer's password protected section of the website.

Case studies

The website also includes over 30 case study problems. A list of these cases is provided in Part Seven of this book. Cases that are relevant to the content of this chapter include Airport Complex and Integrated Technology Services Ltd.

Review questions

16.1 Distinguish between 'controls' and 'control'. *(p. 643)*

16.2 Identify and describe three different types of control mechanisms used by companies. *(pp. 644–48)*

16.3 Provide examples of behavioural, action, social, personnel and cultural controls. *(pp. 644–48)*

16.4 Describe the different stages that are involved with output/results controls. *(pp. 647–48)*

16.5 Describe the elements of cybernetic control systems. How do they relate to results/output controls? *(pp. 648–49)*

16.6 Distinguish between feedback and feed-forward controls. Provide an example of each type of control. *(pp. 649–50)*

16.7 Describe some of the harmful side-effects that can occur with output/results controls. *(pp. 650–51)*

16.8 Explain the circumstances when it is appropriate or inappropriate to use personnel/cultural, behavioural/action and results/output controls. *(p. 652)*

16.9 Describe the four different types of responsibility centres. *(pp. 653–55)*

16.10 Explain what is meant by the term 'responsibility accounting'. *(pp. 655–56)*

16.11 What factors must be taken into account when operating a responsibility accounting system? *(p. 656)*

16.12 What is the 'controllability principle'? Describe the different ways in which the principle can be applied. *(pp. 656–60)*

16.13 Describe three different types of uncontrollable factors. *(pp. 656–58)*

16.14 What are flexible budgets? Why are they preferred to fixed (static budgets)? *(pp. 659–60)*

16.15 What is meant by the term 'aspiration level'? *(p. 662)*

16.16 Describe the effect of the level of budget difficulty on motivation and performance. *(pp. 662–64)*

16.17 Distinguish between participation and top-down budget setting. *(p. 665)*

16.18 Describe the factors influencing the effectiveness of participation in the budget process. *(pp. 666–67)*

16.19 What are the limitations of participation in the budget process? *(p. 667)*

16.20 Distinguish between budget-constrained, profit conscious and non-accounting styles of performance evaluation. *(p. 668)*

16.21 Under what circumstances is it considered appropriate to use (a) the budget constrained and (b) the profit conscious style of performance evaluation? *(p. 669)*

Review problems

16.22 Intermediate: Fixed and flexible budgets

(a) Explain what is meant by the terms 'fixed budget' and 'flexible budget', and state the main objective of preparing flexible budgets.

(5 marks)

(b) (i) Prepare a flexible budget for 20X5 for the overhead expenses of a production department at the activity levels of 80%, 90% and 100%, using the information listed below.

(12 marks)

1. The direct labour hourly rate is expected to be £3.75.
2. 100% activity represents 60 000 direct labour hours.
3. Variable costs:

Indirect labour	£0.75 per direct labour hour
Consumable supplies	£0.375 per direct labour hour
Canteen and other welfare services	6% of direct *and* indirect labour costs

4. Semi-variable costs are expected to correlate with the direct labour hours in the same manner as for the last five years, which was:

Year	Direct labour hours	Semi-variable costs (£)
20X0	64 000	20 800
20X1	59 000	19 800
20X2	53 000	18 600
20X3	49 000	17 800
20X4	40 000 (estimate)	16 000 (estimate)

5. Fixed costs:

	(£)
Depreciation	18 000
Maintenance	10 000
Insurance	4 000
Rates	15 000
Management salaries	25 000

6. Inflation is to be ignored.

(ii) Calculate the budgets cost allowance for 20X5 assuming that 57 000 direct labour hours are worked.

(3 marks)
(Total 20 marks)
CIMA Cost Accounting 1

16.23 **Intermediate: Comments on a performance report**

The Victorial Hospital is located in a holiday resort that attracts visitors to such an extent that the population of the area is trebled for the summer months of June, July and August. From past experience, this influx of visitors doubles the activity of the hospital during these months. The annual budget for the hospital's laundry department is broken down into four quarters, namely April–June, July–September, October–December and January–March, by dividing the annual budgeted figures by four. The budgeting work has been done for the current year by the secretary of the hospital using the previous year's figures and adding 3% for inflation. It is realized by the Hospital Authority that management information for control purposes needs to be improved, and you have been recruited to help to introduce a system of responsibility accounting.

You are required, from the information given, to:

(a) comment on the way in which the quarterly budgets have been prepared and to suggest improvements that could be introduced when preparing the budgets for 2001/2002;

(b) state what information you would like to flow from the actual against budget comparison (note that calculated figures are *not* required);

(c) state the amendments that would be needed to the current practice of budgeting and reporting to enable the report shown below to be used as a measure of the efficiency of the laundry manager.

Victorial Hospital – Laundry department
Report for quarter ended 30 September 2000

	Budget	Actual
Patients days	9 000	12 000
Weight processed (kg)	180 000	240 000
	(£)	(£)
Costs:		
Wages	8 800	12 320
Overtime premium	1 400	2 100
Detergents and other supplies	1 800	2 700
Water, water softening and heating	2 000	2 500
Maintenance	1 000	1 500
Depreciation of plant	2 000	2 000
Manager's salary	1 250	1 500
Overhead, apportioned:		
for occupancy	4 000	4 250
for administration	5 000	5 750

(15 marks)
CIMA Cost Accounting 1

16.24 **Intermediate: Flexible budgets and the motivational role of budgets**

Club Atlantic is an all-weather holiday complex providing holidays throughout the year. The fee charged to guests is fully inclusive of accommodation and all meals. However, because the holiday industry is so competitive, Club Atlantic is only able to generate profits by maintaining strict financial control of all activities. The club's restaurant is one area where there is a constant need to monitor costs. Susan Green is the manager of the restaurant. At the beginning of each year she is given an annual budget which is then broken down into months. Each month she receives a statement monitoring actual costs against the annual budget and highlighting any variances. The statement for the month ended 31 October is reproduced below along with a list of assumptions:

Club Atlantic Restaurant Performance Statement
Month to 31 October

	Actual	Budget	Variance (over)/ under
Number of guest days	11 160	9 600	(1 560)
	(£)	(£)	(£)
Food	20 500	20 160	(340)
Cleaning materials	2 232	1 920	(312)
Heat, light and power	2 050	2 400	350
Catering wages	8 400	7 200	(1 200)
Rent rates, insurance and depreciation	1 860	1 800	(60)
	35 042	33 480	(1 562)

Assumptions:

(a) The budget has been calculated on the basis of a 30-day calendar month with the cost of rents, insurance and depreciation being an apportionment of the fixed annual charge.

(b) The budgeted catering wages assume that:

(i) there is one member of the catering staff for every 40 guests staying at the complex;

(ii) the daily cost of a member of the catering staff is £30.

(c) All other budgeted costs are variable costs based on the number of guest days.

Task 1

Using the data above, prepare a revised performance statement using flexible budgeting. Your statement should show both the revised budget and the revised variances. Club Atlantic uses the existing budgets and performance statements to motivate its managers as well as for financial control. If manages keep expenses below budget they receive a bonus in addition to their salaries. A colleague of Susan is Brian Hilton. Brian is in charge of the swimming pool and golf course, both of which have high levels of fixed costs. Each month he manages to keep expenses below budget and in return enjoys regular bonuses. Under the current reporting system, Susan Green only rarely receives a bonus.

At a recent meeting with Club Atlantic's directors Susan Green expressed concern that the performance statement was not a valid reflection of her management of the restaurant. You are currently employed by Hall and Co., the club's auditors, and the directors of Club Atlantic have asked you to advice them whether there is any justification for Susan Green's concern.

At the meeting with the Club's directors, you were asked the following questions:

(a) Do budgets motivate managers to achieve objectives?

(b) Does motivating managers lead to improved performance?

(c) Does the current method of reporting performance motivate Susan Green and Brian Hilton to be more efficient?

Task 2

Write a *brief* letter to the directors of Club Atlantic addressing their question and justifying your answers.

Note: You should make use of the data given in this task plus your findings in Task 1.

AAT Technicians Stage

16.25 **Advanced: Recommendations for improvements to a performance report and a review of the management control system**

Your firm has been consulted by the managing director of Inzone plc, which owns a chain of retail stores. Each store has departments selling furniture, tableware and kitchenware. Departmental managers are responsible to a store manager, who is in turn responsible to head office (HO).

All goods for sale are ordered centrally and stores sell at prices fixed by HO. Store managers (aided by departmental managers) order stocks from HO and stores are charged interest based on month-end stock levels. HO appoints all permanent staff and sets all pay levels. Store managers can engage or dismiss temporary workers, and are responsible for store running expenses.

The introduction to Inzone plc's management accounting manual states:

'Budgeting starts three months before the budget year, with product sales projections which are developed by HO buyers in consultation with each store's departmental managers. Expense budgets, adjusted for expected inflation, are then prepared by HO for each store. Inzone plc's accounting year is divided into 13 four-weekly control periods, and the budgeted sales and expenses are assigned to periods with due regard to seasonal factors. The budgets are completed one month before the year begins on 1st January.

'All HO expenses are recharged to stores in order to give the clearest indication of the "bottom line" profit of each store. These HO costs are mainly buying expenses, which are recharged to stores according to their square footage.

'Store reports comparing actual results with budgets are on the desks of HO and store management one week after the end of each control period. Significant variations in performance are then investigated, and appropriate action taken.'

Ms Lewis is manager of an Inzone plc store. She is eligible for a bonus equal to 5% of the amount by which her store's 'bottom-line' profit exceeds the year's budget. However, Ms Lewis sees no chance of a bonus this year, because major roadworks near the store are disrupting trade. Her store report for the four weeks ending 21 June is as follows:

	Actual (£)	Budget (£)
Sales	98 850	110 000
Costs:		
Cost of goods (including stock losses)	63 100	70 200
Wages and salaries	5 300	5 500
Rent	11 000	11 000
Depreciation of store fittings	500	500
Distribution costs	4 220	4 500
Other store running expenses	1 970	2 000
Interest charge on stocks	3 410	3 500
Store's share of HO costs	2 050	2 000
Store profit	7 300	10 800
	98 850	110 000
Stocks held at end of period	341 000	350 000
Store fittings at written down value	58 000	58 000

Requirements:

(a) Make recommendations for the improvement of Inzone plc's store report, briefly justifying each recommendation.

(11 marks)

(b) Prepare a report for the managing director of Inzone plc reviewing the company's responsibility delegation, identifying the major strengths and weaknesses of Inzone plc's management control system, and recommending any changes you consider appropriate.

(14 marks)

(Total 25 marks)

ICAEW P2 Management Accounting

16.26 **Advanced**

A major feature of the world economy is the high proportion of employment in service industries, and the development of large service organizations such as banks, insurance companies, and hotel groups.

You are required to explain:

(a) how and why control of a large service organization differs from that of a large manufacturing organization;

(8 marks)

(b) the problems of tracing costs to products in service industries and the uses of the cost information that can be obtained;

(6 marks)

(c) how the control of quality in service industries differs from that in manufacturing industry, and suggest three appropriate measures for quality in a large-scale competitive service organization. Indicate briefly how the measurements would be made. *(Possible examples of such industries include banks, insurance companies and large professional firms, but an organization in another industry may be selected: the choice should be indicated.)*

(6 marks)
(Total 20 marks)
CIMA Stage 4 Management Accounting – Control and Audit

16.27 **Advanced**

One of the major practical difficulties of applying a financial reporting and control system based on flexible budgeting to a service or overhead department is in identifying and measuring an appropriate unit of activity with which to 'flex' the budget.

Required:

(a) Describe and comment on the desirable attributes of such a measure in the context of a valid application of flexible budgeting to a service centre or to a cost centre where standard costing is not applicable.

(c. 8 marks)

(b) Explain the difficulties in obtaining such a measure.

(c. 6 marks)

(c) List three suitable measures of activity, indicating the circumstances in which each would be suitable and the circumstances in which each of them would be misleading or unsuitable.

(c. 6 marks)
(Total 20 marks)
ACCA P2 Management Accounting

16.28 **Advanced**

One common approach to organizational control theory is to look at the model of a cybernetic system. This is often illustrated by a diagram of a thermostat mechanism.

You are required:

(a) to explain the limitations of the simple feedback control this model illustrates, as an explanation of the working of organizational control systems;

Note: A diagram is *not* required.

(7 marks)

(b) to explain

(i) the required conditions (pre-requisites) for the existence of control in an organization, which are often derived from this approach to control theory;

(5 marks)

(ii) the difficulties of applying control in a not-for-profit organization (NPO).

(8 marks)

(Total 20 marks)

CIMA Stage 4 Management Accounting – Control and Audit
May 1994

16.29 Advanced

Several assumptions are commonly made by accountants when preparing or interpreting budgetary information.

You are required to explain why each of the following five assumptions might be made by accountants when designing a system of budgeting, and to set out in each case also any arguments which, in your view, raise legitimate doubts about their validity:

(a) budgeted performance should be reasonably attainable but not too loose,

(5 marks)

(b) participation by managers in the budget-setting process leads to better performance,

(5 marks)

(c) management by exception is the most effective system of routine reporting,

(5 marks)

(d) a manager's budget reports should exclude all matters which are not completely under his control,

(5 marks)

(e) budget statements should include only matters which can be easily and accurately measured in monetary terms.

(5 marks)

(Total 25 marks)

ICAEW Management Accounting

16.30 Advanced

You are required to:

(i) discuss the factors that are likely to cause managers to submit budget estimates of sales and costs that do not represent their best estimates or expectations of what will actually occur,

(8 marks)

(ii) suggest, as a budget accountant, what procedures you would advise in order to minimize the likelihood of such biased estimates arising.

(4 marks)

ICAEW Management Accounting

16.31 **Advanced**

To focus on specific performance measures may lead employees or managers to take action which is not in the best interests of the organization. Examples of problems which may occur are:

(i) Over-emphasis on the short term
(ii) Over-emphasis on the achievement of specific measures
(iii) Over-simplification of the meaning of specific measures
(iv) Deliberate distortion

Required:

(a) Expand briefly on each of the above problems, giving a specific example to illustrate how each may occur.

(10 marks)

(b) Name and comment on any FOUR actions which may be implemented in order to overcome problems in the operations of a performance measurement system.

(5 marks)
(Total 15 marks)
ACCA Paper 8 – Managerial Finance

Review problems (with answers in the Student's Manual)

16.32 **Intermediate**

(a) Identify and explain the essential elements of an effective cost control system.

(13 marks)

(b) Outline possible problems which may be encountered as a result of the introduction of a system of cost control into an organization.

(4 marks)
(Total 17 marks)

16.33 **Advanced**

You are required, within the context of budgetary control, to:

(a) explain the specific roles of planning, motivation and evaluation;

(7 marks)

(b) describe how these roles may conflict with each other;

(7 marks)

(c) give *three* examples of ways by which the management accountant may resolve the conflict described in (b).

(6 marks)
CIMA P3 Management Accounting

16.34 **Advanced**

(a) Explain the ways in which the attitudes and behaviour of managers in a company are liable to pose more threat to the success of its budgetary control system than are minor technical inadequacies that may be in the system.

(15 marks)

(b) Explain briefly what the management accountant can do to minimize the disruptive effects of such attitudes and behaviour.

(5 marks)
CIMA P3 Management Accounting

16.35 **Advanced**

What are the behavioural aspects which should be borne in mind by those who are designing and operating standard costing and budgetary control systems?

(20 marks)
CIMA Cost Accounting 2

16.36 **Advanced**

One purpose of management accounting is to influence managers' behaviour so that their resulting actions will yield a maximum benefit to the employing organization. In the context of this objective, you are required to discuss:

(a) how budgets can cause behavioural conflict;

(b) how this behavioural conflict may be overcome;

(c) the importance of the feedback of information; and

(d) the purpose of goal congruence.

(20 marks)
CIMA P3 Management Accounting

16.37 **Advanced**

In his study of 'The Impact of Budgets on People', published in 1952, C. Argyris reported *inter alia* the following comment by a financial controller on the practice of participation in the setting of budgets in his company:

'We bring in the supervisors of budget areas, we tell them that we want their frank opinion, but most of them just sit there and nod their heads. We know they're not coming out with exactly how they feel. I guess budgets scare them.'

You are required to suggest reasons why managers may be reluctant to participate fully in setting budgets, and to suggest also unwanted side effects which may arise from the imposition of budgets by senior management.

(13 marks)
ICAEW Management Accounting

16.38 **Advanced**

The level of efficiency assumed in the setting of standards has important motivational implications – Discuss.

(8 marks)
ACCA Level 2 Management Accounting

16.39 **Advanced**

In discussing the standard setting process for use within budgetary control and/or standard costing systems, the following has been written: 'The level of standards appears to play a role in achievement motivation…'

Required:

(a) Briefly distinguish between the motivational and managerial reporting objectives of both budgetary control and standard costing. Describe the extent to which these two objectives place conflicting demands on the standard of performance utilized in such systems.

(6 marks)

(b) Describe three levels of efficiency which may be incorporated in the standards used in budgetary control and/or standard costing systems. Outline the main advantages and disadvantages of each of the three levels described.

(6 marks)

(c) Discuss the advantages and disadvantages of involving employees in the standard setting process.

(8 marks)
(Total 20 marks)
ACCA P2 Management Accounting

16.40 **Advanced**

The typical budgetary control system in practice does not encourage *goal congruence*, contains *budgetary slack*, ignores the *aspiration levels* of participants and attempts to control operations by *feedback*, when *feedforward* is likely to be more effective; in summary the typical budgetary control system is likely to have dysfunctional effects.

You are required to

(a) explain briefly *each* of the terms in italics;

(6 marks)

(b) describe how the major dysfunctional effects of budgeting could be avoided.

(11 marks)
(Total 17 marks)
CIMA Stage 3 Management Accounting Techniques

16.41 **Advanced**

Accounting information plays a major part in the planning and control activities of any organization. Often these planning and control activities, in which budgets feature prominently, are undertaken within a structure known as responsibility accounting.

Required:

(a) Briefly explain responsibility accounting and describe three potential difficulties with operating a system of responsibility accounting.

(6 marks)

(b) Explain 'feedback' and 'feed-forward' in the context of budgetary control. Present a simple diagram to illustrate each.

(7 marks)

(c) Typical purposes of budgets are
   (i) resource allocation
   (ii) authorization
   (iii) control

   Explain each of these giving an example from the setting of a non-profit organization.

(7 marks)
(Total 20 marks)
ACCA Paper 8 Managerial Finance

16.42 **Intermediate: Preparation of a flexible budget performance report**

The Viking Smelting Company established a division, called the reclamation division, two years ago, to extract silver from jewellers' waste materials. The waste materials are processed in a furnace, enabling silver to be recovered. The silver is then further processed into finished products by three other divisions within the company.

A performance report is prepared each month for the reclamation division which is then discussed by the management team. Sharon Houghton, the newly appointed financial controller of the reclamation division, has recently prepared her first report for the four weeks to 31 May. This is shown below:

Performance Report Reclamation Division
4 weeks to 31 May

	Actual	Budget	Variance	Comments
Production (tonnes)	200	250	50 (F)[a]	
	(£)	(£)	(£)	
Wages and social security costs	46 133	45 586	547 (A)	Overspend
Fuel	15 500	18 750	3 250 (F)	
Consumables	2 100	2 500	400 (F)	
Power	1 590	1 750	160 (F)	
Divisional overheads	21 000	20 000	1 000 (A)	Overspend
Plant maintenance	6 900	5 950	950 (A)	Overspend
Central services	7 300	6 850	450 (A)	Overspend
Total	100 523	101 386	863 (F)	

[a](A) = adverse, (F) = favourable

In preparing the budgeted figures, the following assumptions were made for May:

- the reclamation division was to employ four teams of six production employees;
- each employee was to work a basic 42-hour week and be paid £7.50 per hour for the four weeks of May;
- social security and other employment costs were estimated at 40% of basic wages;
- a bonus, shared amongst the production employees, was payable if production exceeded 150 tonnes. This varied depending on the output achieved;

1. if output was between 150 and 199 tonnes, the bonus was £3 per tonne produced;
2. if output was between 200 and 249 tonnes, the bonus was £8 per tonne produced;
3. if output exceeded 249 tonnes the bonus was £13 per tonne produced;
   - the cost of fuel was £75 per tonne;
   - consumables were £10 per tonne;
   - power comprised a fixed charge of £500 per four weeks plus £5 per tonne for every tonne produced;
   - overheads directly attributable to the division were £20 000;
   - plant maintenance was to be apportioned to divisions on the basis of the capital values of each division;
   - the cost of Viking's central services was to be shared equally by all four divisions.

You are the deputy financial controller of the reclamation division. After attending her first monthly meeting with the board of the reclamation division, Sharon Houghton arranges a meeting with you. She is concerned about a number of issues, one of them being that the current report does not clearly identify those expenses and variances which are the direct responsibility of the reclamation division.

Task 1

Sharon Houghton asks you to prepare a flexible budget report for the reclamation division for May in a form consistent with responsibility accounting.

On receiving your revised report. Sharon tells you about the other questions raised at the management meeting when the original report was presented. These are summarized below:

(i) Why are the budget figures based on 2-year-old data taken from the proposal recommending the establishment of the reclamation division?

(ii) Should the budget data be based on what we were proposing to do or what we actually did do?

(iii) Is it true that the less we produce the more favourable our variances will be?

(iv) Why is there so much maintenance in a new division with modern equipment and why should we be charged with the actual costs of the maintenance department even when they overspend?

(v) Could the comments, explaining the variances, be improved?

(vi) Should all the variances be investigated?

(vii) Does showing the cost of central services on the divisional performance report help control these costs and motivate the divisional managers?

Task 2

Prepare a memo for the management of the reclamation division. Your memo should:

(a) answer their queries and justify your comments;

(b) highlight the main objective of your revised performance report developed in Task 1 and give two advantages of it over the original report

AAT Technicians Stage

16.43 **Intermediate: Sales forecasting removing seasonal variations, flexible budgets and budget preparation**

You work as the assistant to the management accountant for Henry Limited, a medium-sized manufacturing company. One of its products, product P, has been very successful in recent years, showing a steadily increasing trend in sales volumes. Sales volumes for the four quarters of last year were as follows:

	Quarter 1	Quarter 2	Quarter 3	Quarter 4
Actual sales volume (units)	420 000	450 000	475 000	475 000

A new assistant has recently joined the marketing department and she has asked you for help in understanding the terminology which is used in preparing sales forecasts and analysing sales trends. She has said: 'My main problem is that I do not see why my boss is so enthusiastic about the growth in product P's sales volume. It looks to me as though the rate of growth is really slowing down and has actually stopped in quarter 4. I am told that I should be looking at the deseasonalized or seasonally adjusted sales data but I do not understand what is meant by this.'

You have found that product P's sales are subject to the following seasonal variations:

	Quarter 1	Quarter 2	Quarter 3	Quarter 4
Seasonal variation (units)	+25 000	+15 000	0	–40 000

Task 1

(a) Adjust for the seasonal variations to calculate deseasonalized or seasonally adjusted sales volume (i.e. the trend figures) for each quarter of last year.

(b) Assuming that the trend and seasonal variations will continue, forecast the sales volumes for each of the four quarters of next year.

Task 2

Prepare a memorandum to the marketing assistant which explains:

(a) what is meant by seasonal variations and deseasonalized or seasonally adjusted data;

(b) how they can be useful in analysing a time series and preparing forecasts.

Use the figures for product P's sales to illustrate your explanations.

Task 3

Using the additional data below, prepare a further memorandum to the marketing assistant which explains the following:

(a) why fixed budgets are useful for planning but flexible budgets may be more useful to enable management to exercise reflective control over distribution costs,

(b) *two* possible activity indicators which could be used as a basis for flexing the budget for distribution costs,

(c) how a flexible budget cost allowance is calculated and used for control purposes. Use your own examples and figures where appropriate to illustrate your explanations.

Additional data:

The marketing assistant has now approached you for more help in understanding the company's planning and control systems. She has been talking with the distribution manager, who has tried to explain how flexible budgets are used to control distribution costs within Henry Limited. She makes the following comment. 'I thought that budgets were supposed to provide a target to plan our activities and against which to monitor our costs. How can we possibly plan and control our costs if we simply change the budgets when activity levels alter?'

Product Q is another product which is manufactured and sold by Henry Limited. In the process of preparing budgetary plans for next year the following information has been made available to you.

1. Forecast sales units of product Q for the year = 18 135 units.
2. Closing stocks of finished units of product Q at the end of next year will be increased by 15% from their opening level of 1200 units.
3. All units are subject to quality control check. The budget plans are to allow for 1% of all units checked to be rejected and scrapped at the end of the process. All closing stocks will have passed this quality control check.
4. Five direct labour hours are to be worked for each unit of product Q processed, including those which are scrapped after the quality control check. Of the total hours to be paid for, 7.5% are budgeted to be idle time.
5. The standard hourly rate of pay for direct employees is £6 per hour.
6. Material M is used in the manufacture of product Q. One finished unit of producing Q contains 9 kg of M but there is a wastage of 10% of input of material M due to evaporation and spillage during the process.
7. By the end of next year stocks of material M are to be increased by 12% from their opening level of 8000 kg. During the year a loss of 1000 kg is expected due to deterioration of the material in store.

Task 4

Prepare the following budgets for the forthcoming year:

(a) production budget for product Q, in units;

(b) direct labour budget for product Q, in hours and in £;

(c) material usage budget for material M, in kg;

(d) material purchases budget for material M, in kg.

Task 5

The supplier of material M was warned that available supplies will be below the amount indicated in your budget for Task 4 part (d) above. Explain the implications of this shortage and suggest *four* possible actions which could be taken to overcome the problem. For each suggestion, identify any problems which may arise.

AAT Technicians Stage

16.44 **Intermediate: Preparation of flexible budgets**

Data

Rivermede Ltd makes a single product called the Fasta. Last year, Steven Jones, the managing director of Rivermede Ltd, attended a course on budgetary control. As a result, he agreed to revise the way budgets were prepared in the company. Rather than imposing targets for managers, he encouraged participation by senior managers in the preparation of budgets.

An initial budget was prepared but Mike Fisher, the sales director, felt that the budgeted sales volume was set too high. He explained that setting too high a budgeted sales volume would mean his sales staff would be de-motivated because they would not be able to achieve that sales volume. Steven Jones agreed to use the revised sales volume suggested by Mike Fisher.

Both the initial and revised budgets are reproduced below complete with the actual results for the year ended 31 May.

Rivermede Ltd – budgeted and actual costs for the year ended 31 May

Fast production and sales (units)	Original budget 24 000 (£)	Revised budget 20 000 (£)	Actual results 22 000 (£)	Variances from revised budget 2000 (£)	(F)
Variable costs					
Material	216 000	180 000	206 800	26 800	(A)
Labour	288 000	240 000	255 200	15 200	(A)
Semi-variable costs					
Heat, light and power	31 000	27 000	33 400	6 400	(A)
Fixed costs					
Rent, rates and depreciation	40 000	40 000	38 000	2 000	(F)
	575 000	487 000	533 400	46 400	(A)

Assumptions in the two budgets

1. No change in input prices
2. No change in the quantity of variable inputs per Fasta

As the management accountant at Rivermede Ltd, one of your tasks is to check that invoices have been properly coded. On checking the actual invoices for heat, light and power for the year to 31 May, you find that one invoice for £7520 had been incorrectly coded. The invoice should have been coded to materials.

Task 1

(a) Using the information in the original and revised budgets, identify:
- the variable cost of material and labour per Fasta;
- the fixed and unit variable cost within heat, light and power.

(b) Prepare a flexible budget, including variances, for Rivermede Ltd after correcting for the miscoding of the invoice.

Data

On receiving your flexible budget statement, Steven Jones states that the total adverse variance is much less than the £46 400 shown in the original statement. He also draws your attention to the actual sales volume being greater than in the revised budget. He believes these results show that a participative approach to budgeting is better for the company and wants to discuss this belief at the next board meeting. Before doing so, Steven Jones asked for your comments.

Task 2

Write a memo to Steven Jones. Your memo should:

(a) *briefly* explain why the flexible budgeting variances differ from those in the original statement given in the data to task 1;

(b) give *two* reasons why a favourable cost variance may have arisen other than through the introduction of participative budgeting;

(c) give *two* reasons why the actual sales volume compared with the revised budget's sales volume may not be a measure of improved motivation following the introduction of participative budgeting.

AAT Technicians Stage

16.45 **Intermediate: Demand forecasts and preparation of flexible budgets**

Data

Happy Holidays Ltd sells holidays to Xanadu through newspaper advertisements. Tourist are flown each week of the holiday season to Xanadu, where they take a 10-day touring holiday. In 2000, Happy Holidays began to use the least-squares regression formula to help forecast the demand for its holidays.

You are employed by Happy Holidays as an accounting technician in the financial controller's department. A colleague of yours has recently used the least-squares regression formula on a spreadsheet to estimate the demand for holidays per year. The resulting formula was:

$$y = 640 + 40x$$

where y is the annual demand and x is the year. The data started with the number of holidays sold in 1993 and was identified in the formula as year 1. In each subsequent year the value of x increases by 1 so, for example, 1998 was year 6. To obtain the *weekly* demand the result is divided by 25, the number of weeks Happy Holidays operates in Xanadu.

Task 1

(a) Use the least-squares regression formula developed by your colleague to estimate the weekly demand for holidays in Xanadu for 2001.

(b) In preparation for a budget meeting with the financial controller, draft a *brief* note. Your note should identify *three* weaknesses of the least-squares regression formula in forecasting the weekly demand for holidays in Xanadu.

Data

The budget and actual costs for holidays to Xanadu for the 10 days ended 27 November 2000 is reproduced below.

Happy Holidays Ltd Cost Statement
10 days ended 27 November 2000

	Fixed Budget (£)	Actual (£)	Variances (£)
Aircraft seats	18 000	18 600	600 A
Coach hire	5 000	4 700	300 F
Hotel rooms	14 000	14 200	200 A
Meals	4 800	4 600	200 F
Tour guide	1 800	1 700	100 F
Advertising	2 000	1 800	200 F
Total costs	45 600	45 600	0

Key: A = adverse, F = favourable

The financial controller gives you the following additional information:

Cost and volume information

- each holiday lasts 10 days;
- meals and hotel rooms are provided for each of the 10 days;
- the airline charges £450 per return flight per passenger for each holiday but the airline will only sell seats at this reduced price if Happy Holidays purchases seta in blocks of 20;
- the costs of coach hire, the tour guide and advertising are fixed costs;
- the cost of meals was budgeted at £12 per tourist per day;
- the cost of a single room was budgeted at £60 per day;
- the cost of a double room was budgeted at £70 per day;
- 38 tourists travelled on the holiday requiring 17 double rooms and 4 single rooms;

Sales information

- the price of a holiday is £250 more if using a single room.

Task 2

Write a memo to the financial controller. Your memo should:

(a) take account of the cost and volume information to prepare a revised cost statement using flexible budgeting and identifying any variances;

(b) state and justify which of the two cost statements is more useful for management control of costs;

(c) identify *three* factors to be taken into account in deciding whether or not to investigate individual variances.

AAT Technicians Stage

16.46 **Advanced: Impact of aggregating budget estimates and budget bias**

Devonshire Dairies plc sells a range of dairy products on a national basis through a direct sales force organized into four geographical regions. In December the sales director had received sales budgets for the next year from his four regional managers, and was concerned that they appeared to represent very different standards of attainment. He also thought it unlikely that the national budget (i.e. the sum of the four regional budgets) could be achieved, and so had made his own estimates of the sales revenue he expected each division to obtain, as shown below:

Region	Sales revenue budgets submitted (£m)	Sales director's own estimates (£m)
Northern	5.7	5.0
Southern	10.9	10.0
Eastern	7.9	8.0
Western	7.5	7.0
Total	32.0	30.0

The sales director recognized that his estimates were subject to some uncertainty due to random events, and believed this could be adequately modelled by assuming that they represented the means of normal distributions having a standard deviation of £1 million for each region and that actual sales in each region were statistically independent of each other. However, he was reluctant to amend the budgets submitted to him as he could see the motivational advantages in letting each regional sales manager aim for a target which he had set for himself, and to which he was committed.

Requirements

(a) Calculate the probability of each sales region achieving at least the budget submitted by its regional manager, on the assumption that the sales director's model is correct. Also calculate the probability that the total of the budget submissions will be at least achieved, and comment on your results.

(10 marks)

(b) Discuss the reasons why managers may submit budgets that differ from their superiors' estimates of outcomes. What action would you recommend the sales director to take in this case?

(8 marks)

(c) The company is considering implementing a system of performance-related pay whereby managers who achieve their annual sales budgets are rewarded by the payment of an annual bonus equivalent to one month's salary. Discuss the impact such a system could have on the operation of the budgeting system, and suggest ways in which the proposed bonus system could be amended to minimize any adverse effects.

(7 marks)

(Total 25 marks)

ICAEW P2 Management Accounting

Contingency theory and organizational and social aspects of management accounting

17

In the previous chapter the major features of management accounting control systems were described. To design effective management accounting control systems it is necessary to consider the circumstances in which they will be used. It should be apparent from the discussion in the previous chapter that there is no universally best management accounting control system which can be applied to all organizations. The applicability of a management accounting control system is contingent on the circumstances faced by organizations. This approach is known as the **contingency theory** approach to

LEARNING OBJECTIVES

After reading this chapter, you should be able to:

- describe the contingency theory of management accounting;
- provide illustrations of the relationship between the five broad contingent factors described in Exhibit 17.1 and features of the management accounting control system;
- describe the framework that links the appropriate types of controls to the interaction between ability to measure output and knowledge of the transformation process;
- distinguish between efficiency and effectiveness measures;
- describe the framework that links the appropriate type of assessment to the interaction between task instrumentality and beliefs about the clarity of organizational goals;
- distinguish between programmed and non-programmed decisions;
- describe the framework that links the uses of accounting information for decision-making to the interaction between the uncertainty of objectives and the uncertainty relating to cause-and-effect relationships;
- identify and explain the different purposes for which accounting information is used within organizations.

management accounting. A widely used contingency theory definition is that provided by Otley (1980). He states:

The contingency approach to management accounting is based on the premise that there is no universally appropriate accounting system applicable to all organizations in all circumstances. Rather a contingency theory attempts to identify specific aspects of an accounting system that are associated with certain defined circumstances and to demonstrate an appropriate matching. (page 413)

This chapter, all of which you should regard as advanced reading, will examine the contingency theory approach. In addition, the different roles that management accounting information plays in organizations will also be considered. In particular, the wider social and political roles of management accounting are discussed. We begin with a discussion of contingency theory.

An overview of contingency theory

Prior to the emergence of the contingency theory approach to management accounting in the mid-1970s, it was assumed that an optimal management accounting information system design existed that was applicable to some degree to all organizations. The contingency theory approach advocates that there is no one 'best' design for a management accounting information system, but that 'it all depends' upon the situational factors. The situational factors represent the contingent factors (also known as contingent variables or contextual factors). Figure 17.1 provides a simplified version of the contingency theory model. You will see from the first two boxes in Figure 17.1 that contingent factors are assumed to influence the design of the management accounting information system. Examples of the contingent factors are presented in Exhibit 17.1. They include the external environment faced by organizations, the type of competitive strategy they adopt and the nature of the production process. The characteristics of the management accounting information systems that contingency theory research has focused on include dimensions of budgeting (e.g. participation, importance of meeting budgets), reliance on accounting information for performance evaluation and dimensions of information (e.g. timeliness and level of aggregation). The linkage between the second and third boxes in Figure 17.1 implies that organizational performance or effectiveness depends on the level of fit or alignment between the contingent variables and the management accounting information system. In other words, organizations that achieve a fit between the contingent variables of the management accounting information system design achieve enhanced performance.

The contingency theory literature has two strands – theoretical and empirical. The early contingency theory studies were of a theoretical nature. They drew off the organizational theory contingency studies to speculate on the nature of a contingency theory of management accounting information systems. These early studies provided the impetus for later empirical studies that sought to investigate the relationship between some hypothesized contingent factors and the existence of certain features of the management accounting system. Most of the empirical studies have relied on large scale cross-sectional postal questionnaire studies to examine the relationships between the identified contingent variables and characteristics of management accounting information systems.

Researchers have faced a number of difficulties when undertaking empirical studies. Because each organization is unique, the potential range of situations or contingent

FIGURE 17.1 *An overview of the contingency theory framework*

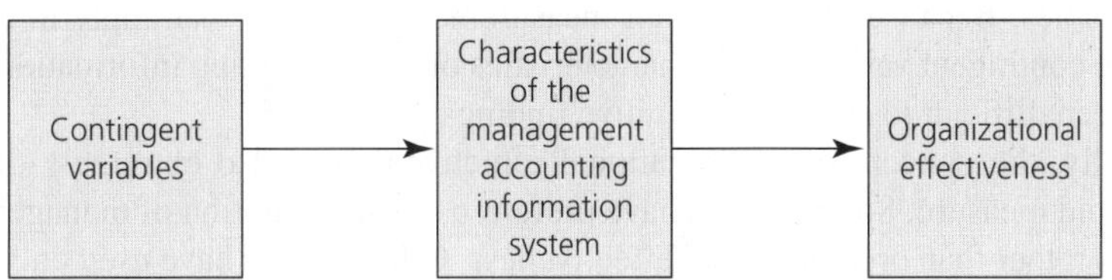

EXHIBIT 17.1
Contingent factors grouped by major categories

1 *The external environment*
Uncertain and certain
Static and dynamic
Simple and complex
Turbulent and calm

2 *Competitive strategy and strategic mission*
Low cost and differentiation
Defender and prospector
Product life cycle (build, hold, harvest and divest)

3 *Technology*
Small batch, large batch, process production, mass production
Interdependence (pooled, sequential, reciprocal)

4 *Business unit, firm and industry variables*
Firm size
Firm diversification (single product, related diversified and unrelated diversified)
Organizational structure
Industry variables

5 *Knowledge and observability factors*
Knowledge of the transformation process
Outcome (output) observability
Behaviour (effort) observability

(Adapted from Fisher, 1995)

factors is enormous and it is impossible to study each one separately. To overcome this problem, contingency factors are classified into categories that appear to make sense in terms of explaining differences in management accounting information systems. Exhibit 17.1 lists the major contingent factors, divided into five broad categories, that have been examined in the literature.

Problems also apply in defining and measuring the contingent variables. Many of the contingent variables are abstract or theoretical constructs that are not capable of direct measurement such as environmental uncertainty, intensity of competition and competitive strategy. Therefore the variables may be subject to measurement error and this has important implications when statistical analysis is undertaken to test the contingency theory models. Where there is measurement error there is a possibility that the observed relationships may be subject to a misstatement of the true relationship. This may have implications in terms of drawing incorrect inferences of the true relationships between the variables. Because of the difficult measurement problems that apply in measuring both the contingent variables and characteristics of the accounting information systems, it has been difficult to establish definitive findings.

Finally, the concept of organizational effectiveness is also extremely difficult to define and measure. Some studies have preferred to use the notion of managerial effectiveness rather than organizational effectiveness. Other studies have used only financial measures to measure effectiveness. Relying only on financial measures, however, has been widely criticized as a proxy measure of effectiveness because they tend to be short-term and adopt a narrow focus. Various researchers have called for the use of a multiplicity of dimensions to be incorporated in order to measure effectiveness. Because of the difficulties of measuring organizational effectiveness, and the fact that effectiveness is influenced by many other factors besides the match between contingent variables and the management accounting information system, many researchers have restricted their studies to examining only the relationship between the first two boxes shown in Figure 17.1 (i.e. the relationship between the contingent variables and characteristics of the management accounting information system). A further justification for not incorporating organizational effectiveness in the empirical studies is that researchers have argued that rational managers are unlikely to adopt or use management accounting information systems that do not assist in enhancing organizational performance (Chenhall, 2003).

Another important feature of the contingency theory literature is that the terms 'management accounting information systems', 'management accounting control systems' and 'management control systems' are often used interchangeably even though it is possible to distinguish between them. Management accounting information systems refer to a collection of practices that incorporate aspects of management accounting information for *both* decision making and control whereas management accounting control systems relate to the collection of accounting practices (typically results or output controls that were described in the previous chapter) that are used mainly for control purposes. 'Management control systems' represents a broader term that encompasses management accounting control systems but also includes other controls such as behavioural, personal and social controls. Most of the contingency theory accounting literature has concentrated on aspects of management accounting control systems. Therefore, this chapter is primarily concerned with management accounting control systems but it will also look at some of the contingency studies relating to management control systems and management accounting information systems that incorporate aspects of accounting information for both decision-making and control. Where the latter applies, the term management accounting information system will be used.

The impact of contingent factors on management accounting information systems

There is a vast amount of literature relating to the impact of each of the contingent factors listed in Exhibit 17.1 on management accounting information systems. A discussion of each factor is not possible within a general purpose management accounting textbook. The following sections will therefore attempt to provide only a broad overview of the contingency theory studies for each category listed in Exhibit 17.1

and describe the major theoretical and empirical studies that are of particular relevance to the content of this book.

The external environment

The first broad category listed in Exhibit 17.1 consists of variables relating to the external environment. Most of the variables within this category are concerned with the level of environmental uncertainty. Uncertainty relates to the level of change in the environment that occurs unexpectedly, such as unpredictable shifts in the economy or unexpected changes in customer demand or competitor actions.

An empirical study of eight firms in the USA by Govindarajan (1984) supported the hypothesis that superiors in business units which face higher environmental uncertainty use a more subjective performance appraisal approach whereas superiors of business units that face lower environmental uncertainty use a more formula-based performance evaluation approach. A formula-based approach was defined as an evaluation based solely on meeting various levels of financial performance.

The rationale for the hypothesis is that performance evaluation presupposes targets, and for targets to remain valid standards for subsequent performance appraisal, one must be able to predict the conditions that will exist during the coming year. It is possible to predict these conditions more accurately under stable environmental conditions than under dynamic and changing conditions. Thus, the greater the environmental uncertainty, the more difficult it is to prepare satisfactory targets which could then become the basis for performance evaluation. In addition, although managers have control over their actions they do not have control over the states of nature which combine with their actions to result in outcomes. In a situation with high environmental uncertainty, financial data alone will not, therefore, adequately reflect managerial performance whereas such data would be adequate for a situation with low environmental uncertainty.

Govindarajan related his findings to those of Hopwood (1976) and Otley (1978) described in the final section of the previous chapter. He suggests that Otley studied units which might have operated in relatively stable environmental conditions whereas Hopwood examined units which might have operated in relatively uncertain environmental conditions. Govindarajan concludes that, in the light of his findings, it is not surprising that Hopwood found dysfunctional effects for the budget constrained style whereas Otley did not. In other words, a budget constrained style was synonymous with a formula-based, rigid evaluation style and this style was inappropriate in units facing an uncertain environment. Therefore there was a mis-match and this caused the dysfunctional side-effects.

Gordon and Narayanan, Chenhall and Morris (1986) and Gul and Chia (1994) provide evidence to suggest that the greater the *perceived environmental uncertainty* the greater the need for more sophisticated management accounting information that has a broad scope. Broad scope was defined as information that was external, non-finical and future oriented whereas narrow scope relates to internal, financial and historical information. Chenhall and Morris also found that perceived environmental uncertainty was associated with the need for more timely information. The results from the study by Gul and Chia suggest that decentralization, and the availability of broad scope management accounting information, was also associated with higher managerial performance under conditions of perceived environmental uncertainty.

The hostility of the environment faced by organizations has also been associated with a strong emphasis on meeting budgets (Otley, 1978). Hostility in the form of organizations facing intense competition has also been related to reliance on formal control systems (Imoisili, 1985) and the use of more sophisticated formal controls (Khandwalla, 1972).

Competitive strategy and strategic mission

Competitive strategy describes how a business chooses to compete in its industry and tries to achieve a competitive advantage relative to its competitors. Strategic mission can be defined across a continuum from the early to the late stages of a product's life cycle from build, hold, harvest and divest. These variables indicate an organization's intended trade-off between market share growth and maximizing short-term profits. The contingency theory literature suggests that different types of strategies will cause different control system configurations and that the management control system should be tailored to support the strategy of the business to yield superior performance.

The research relating to corporate strategy has focused mainly on classifications proposed by Porter (1985) and Miles and Snow (1978). Most of the contingency theory research that has addressed Porter's strategy variables has examined the control differences between business units pursuing *low-cost* and *differentiation strategies*. A low cost strategy involves offering relatively standardized, undifferentiated products with an attempt to obtain high volume and routinized tasks to exploit economies of scale. A differentiation strategy involves the creation of something that is perceived by customers as being unique and valuable. Porter (1985) argues that the successful implementation of generic strategies requires different organizational arrangements, control procedures and incentive systems. He suggests that an overall cost leadership strategy requires intense supervision of labour, tight cost control, frequent and detailed control reports and structured organization and responsibility. In contrast, Porter suggests that a differentiation strategy requires strong coordination between various functions and subjective performance measurement and incentives instead of quantitative measures.

Miles and Snow distinguish between *defenders and prospectors*. Defenders operate in relatively stable areas, have limited product lines and employ a mass production routine technology. They compete through making operations efficient through cost, quality and service leadership, rather than innovation and product and market development. Prospectors perceive high uncertainty in their environment and compete through new product innovations and market development and are constantly looking for new market opportunities.

Merchant (1998) concludes that business units following a low-cost strategy, or those defending existing businesses, should control their lower level employees' behaviours through standardized operating procedures designed to maximize efficiency. For motivating managers their results measures should emphasize cost reductions and budget achievement. Alternatively, business units competing on the basis of differentiation and those prospecting for new markets, should have a more participative decision-making environment and should reward employees and managers based on any of a number of non-financial indicators, such as product innovation, market development, customer service and growth, as well as secondarily financial measures such as budget achievement. Simons (1987) found that business units that follow a defender strategy tend to place a greater emphasis on the use of financial measures (e.g. short-term budget targets) for compensating financial managers. Ittner *et al.* (1997) also found that the use of non-financial measures for determining executives' bonuses increases with the extent to which firms follow an innovation-oriented prospector strategy.

Building on the established linkages between competitive strategies and environmental uncertainty, and between uncertainty and performance evaluation, Govindarajan (1988) argued that firms pursuing a differentiation strategy face greater uncertainty than firms pursuing a low cost strategy. High uncertainty implies that it is difficult to predict future events, and arrive at a priori budget targets that can serve as satisfactory standards for performance evaluation. Moreover, uncertainty implies that cause–effect knowledge is incomplete for decision-makers. Thus, subjective approaches towards evaluating managerial performance are expected since financial measures (e.g. budgets) alone are not enough to reflect managerial performance. From these arguments, Govindarajan hypothesized that for business units employing a strategy of differentiation, de-emphasizing budgetary goals during performance evaluations, is likely to be associated with higher performance. Conversely, emphasizing budgetary goals is likely to be associated with higher performance in business units employing low cost strategy. Using data collected from 121 manufacturing business units in 24 large USA organizations, the findings supported the above hypothesis.

A study by Chenhall and Langfield-Smith (1998b) relating to a survey of 78 Australian companies hypothesized that higher performing firms that place a strong emphasis on product differentiation strategies will gain high benefits from the following management techniques and management accounting practices:

- quality systems;
- integrating systems;
- team-based structures;
- human resource management policies;
- balanced performance measures;
- benchmarking;
- strategic planning techniques.

To implement product differentiation strategies successfully, companies may employ manufacturing techniques which enhance their ability to persuade their customers that their products are of high quality. Therefore quality systems, such as statistical process control (see Chapter 23) may be used to provide a way to detect and correct process variations that may influence product quality.

The effective implementation of customer focused strategies may require employees at the operational level to adopt a strong customer orientation. Employees are more likely to develop a customer focus if a high degree of empowerment is encouraged. Two broad approaches are identified as being conducive to employee empowerment. First, team-based structures may be introduced to encourage employees to take ownership of customer-focused initiatives. Second, a range of human resource management policies may be introduced to establish a work environment that encourages employees to share the organization's customer-focused orientation. These include encouraging a participative culture, and providing focused training. In other words, effective implementation of customer strategies suggests that the personnel and cultural controls that were described in the previous chapter should be emphasized.

Balanced performance measurement systems provide a balanced focus on various aspects of differentiation strategies by linking measures of customer satisfaction (such as timely and reliable delivery) with other measures of key production strategies (such as cycle time and throughput rates) and also emphasizing financial outcomes. This balanced performance measurement approach is known as the balanced scorecard and represents an attempt to develop a broader and integrated set of financial and non-financial performance measures that provide a comprehensive view of the performance of the business. The balanced scorecard will be dealt with extensively in Chapter 23. Overall the results provided support for the proposed associations, described above.

Chenhall and Langfield-Smith also hypothesized that higher performing firms that place a strong emphasis on low cost/price strategies will gain high benefits from the following management techniques and management accounting practices:

- improving existing practices;
- manufacturing innovations;
- traditional accounting techniques;
- activity-based techniques.

To achieve cost efficiencies companies may focus on improving existing processes. This may involve reorganizing existing processes in order to improve efficiency and reduce waste. In addition, companies may reduce costs by outsourcing when external firms can supply at a lower cost. The type of formal performance measures appropriate for firms emphasizing low price strategies will focus mainly on controlling costs. Traditional management accounting techniques, such as budget performance measures and variance analysis, may be particularly suitable for these companies. Activity-based techniques are considered to be appropriate for companies pursuing a low cost strategy because they are a powerful mechanism for helping managers understand how their firms' activities affect costs. They also provide useful information for reducing costs by redesigning business processes. The results also provided support for the associations specified above relating to the second hypothesis.

In terms of the product life cycle Govindarajan and Gupta (1985) examined the impact of build and harvest strategies on managerial incentive component systems (an element of the management control system). A build strategy is concerned with improving market share and competitive position more than maximizing short-term profit or cash flow. In contrast, the harvest strategy is concerned more with maximizing short-term profit and cash flow. The components of incentive compensation system investigated were the relative importance given to long-run criteria (e.g. sales growth, market share, new product and market development) and short-run criteria (e.g. cost control, profit margins, return on investment) when determining managers' bonuses. The researchers found that business units following a build strategy rely more on non-financial measures for determining managers' bonuses. They also found that greater reliance on long-run criteria and a subjective (non-formula) method in determining managerial bonuses had a positive impact on the effectiveness of the business units adopting build strategy, whereas a negative effect applied relating to effectiveness within harvest organizations. However, they found no support for their other proposition that short-run criteria for bonus determination would make a greater contribution to effectiveness in the case of harvest rather than build SBUs. In other words, short-run financial and accounting measures of performance were found to be relevant for all firms regardless of their strategies, while long run (non-financial performance measures) are critical for the successful implementation of build strategies along with short-run financial measures of performance.

Firm technology and interdependence

Firm technology and interdependence includes Woodward's (1965) classification of technology into *small batch, large batch, process production and mass production categories.* The nature of the production process determines the type of costing system with process costing being used in process production and mass production technologies and job costing being used in batch production technologies.

In the previous chapter pooled interdependencies were described whereby responsibility centres use common/pooled firm resources, such as shared administrative units.

Pooled interdependence is low when responsibility centres are relatively self-contained so that use of pooled resources has little impact on a unit's performance. Therefore unsophisticated methods can be used for assigning the costs of pooled resources to the user responsibility centres. However, where pooled interdependence is high management accounting control systems must address the issue of how to protect managers from being assigned the costs of the inefficiencies incurred by the shared resource pools. You should refer back to the previous chapter (page 661) for a discussion of the methods that can be adopted. Based on a review of the contingency theory literature relating to the impact of technology on management control systems Chenhall (2003) developed the following propositions:

- The more technologies are characterized by standardized and automated processes the more formal the controls, including reliance on traditional budgets with less budgetary slack. Budget slack relates to the process by which managers obtain targets that can be easily achieved.
- The more technologies are characterized by high levels of task uncertainty the more informal the controls resulting in (i) less reliance on standard operating procedures, behavioural controls and accounting performance measures; (ii) higher participation in budgeting; and (iii) greater reliance on personal controls, clan controls and the use of broad scope management accounting control systems.
- The more technologies are characterized by high levels of interdependence the more informal the controls resulting in less emphasis on budgets and more frequent interactions between subordinates and superiors.

Firm size, industry type, firm diversification and firm structure

Studies indicate a positive relationship between *company size* and management accounting system sophistication. In particular, studies of ABC adoption rates have shown that adoption is much higher in larger organizations (Innes and Mitchell, 1995a; Bjornenak, 1997a). A possible reason for this is that larger organizations have relatively greater access to resources to experiment with the introduction of more sophisticated systems. Several surveys have also indicated that an important factor limiting the implementation of more sophisticated management accounting systems is the prohibitive cost (Innes and Mitchell, 1995a; Shields, 1995). As larger organizations have more resources to develop innovative systems it is also more likely that they will be able to implement more sophisticated costing systems.

The research evidence also suggests that generally large organizations are associated with more diversified operations, formalization of procedures and specialization of functions. In addition, large organizations are also associated with an emphasis on and participation in budgets and more sophisticated controls.

Control systems have been shown to differ by *industry type*. For example, controls differ in the manufacturing sector that have a large number of standard cost centres that rely extensively on detailed variance analysis. In contrast, costs in non-manufacturing industries tend to be mostly of a discretionary nature. You will remember from the previous chapter that different approaches were required for cost control in discretionary cost centres.

According to Chandler (1962) a diversification strategy can either be related or unrelated to a firm's existing products. With a *related diversification strategy* firms do not veer far from their core business activity. They diversify in order to obtain the benefits of economies of scope arising from relationships among the divisions. Firms pursuing an *unrelated diversification strategy* do not restrict their activities to their core business. A firm should adopt a management control system that is consistent with its diversification strategy. Because of the high interdependence among sub-units that exists when a firm pursues a related diversification strategy Merchant (1998) suggests that they should take advantage of this interdependence by using several features. First, they should rely on elaborate planning and budgeting systems requiring large amounts of interpersonal communication in order to encourage their managers to keep their interrelated activities coordinated so that they can find and exploit synergy. Second, they should also encourage coordination by using performance-dependent incentive compensation systems that base rewards to some extent on group performance. Third, they should devote considerable resources to solving transfer pricing problems so that they do not inhibit coordination. We shall focus on transfer pricing in Chapter 21.

The top-level corporate management of an organization with unrelated businesses are unable to remain informed about all of the activities of their diverse business units. Decentralization of decision-making to lower levels in the organization and a heavy reliance on financial controls are common responses to the information asymmetry. In particular, unrelated diversification leads to the creation of profit and investment centre responsibility structures and a greater reliance on the financial results controls, such as return on investment and economic value added, rather than other types of controls. Because corporate management do not have a detailed knowledge of the activities of the business units they are likely to judge their performance objectively and not rely on subjective evaluations. Lower-level managers will tend to be under considerable pressure to achieve financial performance although they will have a relatively high level of autonomy in terms of how they might achieve the financial targets.

There is evidence to suggest that the *structure of an organization* affects the manner in which budgetary information is best used. Hopwood's (1976) study, discussed in the previous chapter, indicated that a rigid budget constrained style of evaluation was associated with high degrees of job-related tension and dysfunctional behaviour (such as the manipulation of accounting data) whereas the more flexible profit-conscious style had no such associations. Adopting a universal approach suggests that a flexible profit conscious style is likely to lead to more effective organizational performance. A subsequent study by Otley (1978) yielded contradictory results and suggested that a rigid style was more likely to lead to a better performance than the more flexible style.

A comparison of the two findings indicates an important situational difference which suggests a contingent explanation. Hopwood's study was based on responsibility cost centres that were highly interdependent whereas Otley's study involved profit centres which were independent of each other. The contingency theory explanation is that an appropriate style of budget use depends upon the degree of interdependence that exists between responsibility centres. Because budgetary measures of performance are less appropriate as the degree of interdependence increases, managers tend to use the budgetary information in a more flexible manner. In contrast, in highly independent units where managers perceive themselves as having more control over their performance outcomes a rigid budget constrained style of evaluation is more appropriate.

Knowledge and observablility factors

The final category in Exhibit 17.1 consists of knowledge and observablility factors. Four areas that fall within this category will be examined in detail since they are of particular relevance to the content of this book. The first relates to the type controls that are appropriate in relation to the knowledge of the transformation process and the ability to measure output. The second examines the appropriate type of performance assessment and scorekeeping in relation to the extent to which task cause-and-effect relationships are well understood and the uncertainty concerning an organization's goals. Programmability of decisions, that is the extent to which a decision is sufficiently well understood for reliable predictions of the decision outcomes to be made, is the third area. Here we shall look on how programmability influences the type of controls that should be used. The final area examines the relationship between accounting information and uncertainty about objectives and the uncertainty about cause-and-effect relationships.

Types of controls in relation to the transformation process and output measurement

Ouchi (1979) considered the circumstances when behavioural, output and social controls should be employed. These controls were described in the previous chapter. You should be able to recall that **behavioural controls** involve observing the actions of individuals, **output controls** involve collecting and reporting information about the outcome of the work effort and **social controls** are concerned with the selection of people who have already been socialized into adopting particular norms and patterns of behaviour to perform particular tasks. Ouchi identified two basic conditions. First, the ability to measure outputs and second, knowledge of the transformation process. He combined these elements to derive a matrix containing four control situations. This matrix is reproduced in Figure 17.2.

The first cell shown in Figure 17.2 describes a situation where knowledge of the transformation process is perfect (i.e. task knowledge is high) and output measures are available. In this situation it is possible to measure both output and behaviour and so both behavioural and output controls are appropriate. An illustration of the conditions outlined in the first cell is in a production department where the process can be controlled by the foreman monitoring the actions of each of the employees. Alternatively, if it is possible to measure the output of each employee, control can be exercised by relying on information derived from reports relating to production qualities, spoilage and the efficiency of each worker.

In cell 2 the ability to measure output is high but knowledge of the transformation process is imperfect. Therefore observing behaviour is not beneficial and output control mechanisms are most appropriate. A good example of this type of situation is that described by Macintosh (1985). He illustrates a situation where a financial services company is selling life assurance. We do not know the 'correct' way of selling life assurance and it is not possible to create a set of rules which, if followed, would ensure success. However, the results of sales efforts, measured in terms of life assurance cover and premiums, can easily be measured. In this situation output controls should be used.

In cell 3 where the ability to measure output is low but knowledge of the transformation process is perfect, emphasis should shift from output to behavioural controls. Ouchi relates this situation to a tin can plant where it is impossible to measure the output of any individual working on the assembly line. Therefore output controls cannot be used. The technology, however, is well understood and supervisors can monitor both the actions of each employee and the workings of the machines to see if they accord with the proper action. If they do, they know without relying on output measures that the right

FIGURE 17.2 *Uncertainty situations and control measurements*

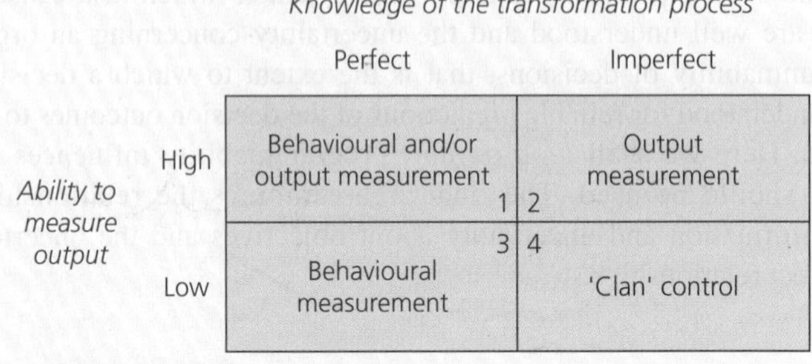

quantity and quality of tin cans are coming off the assembly line. Behavioural controls are therefore appropriate in this situation.

Finally, in cell 4 the ability to measure output is low and knowledge of the transformation process is imperfect. Under these conditions neither behavioural nor output controls are appropriate and Ouchi advocates the use of **clan controls** or corporate cultures as the most appropriate mode. He illustrates the use of clan controls in a multibillion dollar corporation that runs a research laboratory. The controls focused on the recruitment of only a few selected individuals, each of whom had been through a schooling and professionalization process which has taught them to internalize the desired values. This process includes encouraging attendance at seminars, writing articles for learned journals and awards for breakthroughs which will lead to marketable new products for the company. These and other social tests are used to reward researchers who display the underlying attitudes and values that are likely to lead to organizational success, thus reminding everyone of what they are supposed to be trying to achieve, even though it is almost impossible to determine what is being accomplished.

The above analysis indicates that if organizations concentrate only on accounting-based controls then this will result in all control situations being seen as occupying Ouchi's first two cells. The value of Ouchi's framework is that it draws attention to those conditions where accounting-based controls are inappropriate and places management accounting control systems within a broader framework of other organizational control systems.

Scorekeeping and uncertainty

In the previous section we looked at a framework used by Ouchi that identified the different circumstances where different types of controls should be used. Adopting a similar approach Macintosh (1985) uses a framework developed by Thompson (1967) that deals with the appropriate type of assessment and scorekeeping for different types of uncertainty.

The framework, reproduced in Figure 17.3, concentrates on the interaction of two antecedent conditions: task instrumentality and beliefs about the clarity of the organization's ends (goals), mission and purpose. **Task instrumentality** refers to the available means for task accomplishment. It is a continuum; at one end (represented by cells 1 and 3 in Figure 17.3) the ways of doing the work are well understood so that actions produce highly predictable results. An example falling within this category is an engineering factory where the correct sequencing of operations is well understood, the precise

FIGURE 17.3 *Assessment situations and appropriate tests*

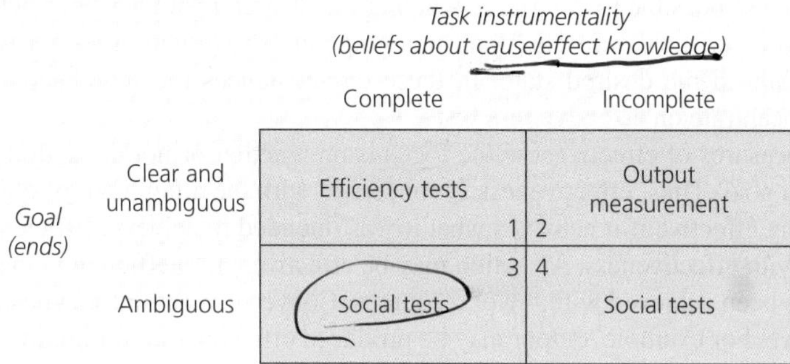

machine tolerances can be specified and the optimum inputs of labour and materials can be specified with a high degree of certainty.

At the other end of the continuum (cells 2 and 4) the optimum ways of doing the work are not known and the effect of actions cannot be predicted with any degree of certainty. For example, the sales revenues generated by a marketing department cannot be directly related to specific courses of action. The effect of pricing decisions, choice of distribution channels or methods of advertising cannot be traced directly to specific sales transactions. The actions of competitors and changes in the external economic environment also have a significant but indeterminate influence over the outcome.

The second area of uncertainty relates to beliefs about the organization's ends, mission and purpose. This is also a continuum. At one end (cells 1 and 2) goals are objectively determined and there are clear-cut preferences over other possible goals. For example, profit is preferable to market share, health is preferred to illness and wealth to poverty. The direction for improvement is also obvious moving from market share to profit and from poverty to wealth. When there is general agreement on one clear-cut end, goals can be viewed as being unambiguous.

At the other end of the continuum (cells 3 and 4) goals are ambiguous and involve a choice between two or more dimensions. Using Macintosh's illustration it is not merely a matter of health over illness, but rather a choice of health or wealth. Furthermore, there can also be shades of health and shades of wealth involved in the choice. In these circumstances there is no general agreement about which end(s) are preferred and goals are therefore ambiguous.

Macintosh combined the two continuums and used their extreme values to derive the four assessment situations depicted in Figure 17.3. In cell 1 where task instrumentality is well understood and goals are clear and unambiguous the optimum economic relationship between inputs and outputs can be derived. In such circumstances scorekeeping and assessment can rely on **efficiency tests**. Efficiency is concerned with achieving a given result with a minimum use of resources or, alternatively, achieving the maximum amount of output from a given level of input resources. Thus, efficiency measures imply that we have a means of determining the minimum resources necessary to produce a given effect or the maximum output that should be derived from a given level of resources. Efficiency measures, such as standard costing efficiency variances (discussed in the next chapter), are widely used accounting performance measures. However, the accuracy and usefulness of such measures is dependent on tasks being well understood and goals being clear and unambiguous.

In cell 2 uncertainty exists in relation to cause and effect knowledge such that the relationship of inputs and outputs cannot be ascertained with any degree of certainty. It is therefore not possible to determine whether the desired result has been achieved efficiently. However, goals are clear and unambiguous so we can ascertain whether the actions achieved the desired state. In these circumstances the scorekeeping question should concentrate on **effectiveness tests**.

With measures of effectiveness the focus is on whether or not the action resulted in the desired goal. Thus, effectiveness is concerned with the attainment of objectives; an action being effective if it achieves what it was intended to achieve. Efficiency is often confused with effectiveness. An action may be effective, but inefficient in that the result could have been achieved with fewer resources. Conversely, actions can be efficient but not effective. For example, output may be produced efficiently at minimum cost but this is ineffective if demand is depressed so that the output must be sold below cost.

Macintosh describes those tests that are intended to ascertain whether actions achieve the desired goals as **instrumental tests**. He illustrates how such tests are widely used in the public sector with scorekeeping being based on simple bottom-line assessments such as the ability to achieve the desired outputs for levels of employment, inflation and interest rates. Most large industrial organizations divide themselves into separate self-contained segments or divisions and use instrumental tests to measure the effectiveness of each division. Performance is deemed satisfactory if predetermined target profits are met. However, it is impossible to establish the level of optimum profits, or determine the extent to which profits may have been influenced by external factors, such as general changes in the economy.

In cells 3 and 4 goals are ambiguous. Efficiency measures can be computed for the situation depicted in cell 3 where task instrumentality is well understood but uncertainty exists about what output is desirable. Therefore in both situations efficiency and instrumental tests are unreliable and Macintosh suggests that organizations must use a less satisfactory but more appropriate measure of assessment: the **social test**. The basic idea of social tests is that accomplishment and fitness are judged by the collection of opinions and beliefs of one or more relevant groups. Macintosh illustrates how social tests can be used to assess the performance of a personnel department. The department provides various services to user departments such as advertising for new staff, hiring, firing, training and safety courses. The collective opinions of client departments provide useful information on the personnel department's performance and potential future action.

It is apparent from the above framework that there are many situations where efficiency and effectiveness measures are inappropriate and there is a danger that in such situations assessment and scorekeeping may be ignored. If the management accounting function is to continue to represent the dominant scorekeeping function in an organization it is important that it expands scorekeeping beyond measures of efficiency and effectiveness and gathers, stores and reports information on opinions and beliefs of relevant social groups within the organization.

Programmed and non-programmed decisions

Emmanuel *et al.* (1990) distinguish between programmed and non-programmed decisions. They define a **programmed decision** as one where the decision situation is sufficiently well understood for a reliable prediction of the decision outcome to be made. Programmed decisions are equivalent to the situations outlined in cell 1 of Figures 17.2 and 17.3 where knowledge of the transformation process is high and task instrumentality is well understood so that the optimum relationship between inputs and outputs can be derived. Because input/output relationships are well understood detailed line item budgets specifying an appropriate level of spending for each item of expenditure can be prepared. Variance analysis can be used as a tool to control spending of each item of expenditure. Behavioural controls and output controls in the form of efficiency tests can also be applied to programmed situations.

A **non-programmed decision** is defined by Emmanuel *et al.* as one that has to rely on the judgement of managers because there is no formal mechanism for predicting likely outcomes. In non-programmed decisions, the causal relationships are less well understood so that it is possible only to instruct a manager as to what he or she is expected to achieve. Managers can be held responsible for results; but how they are to be attained must be left to their discretion. Thus non-programmed decisions are equivalent to situations where knowledge of the transformation process and task cause-and-effect relationships are incomplete (that is, cells 2 and 4 in Figures 17.2 and 17.3). Where the ability to measure output is high and goals are clear and unambiguous then output controls should be used and scorekeeping measures should consist of instrumental tests.

Accounting information, decision-making and uncertainty

Earl and Hopwood (1981) and Burchell *et al.* (1980) examined the relationship between accounting information and decision-making. They use a framework developed from earlier work by Thompson and Tuden (1959) that characterized various states of uncertainty and, as a consequence, a range of possible approaches to decision-making. The framework, reproduced in Figure 17.4, distinguishes between uncertainty over the objectives (or disagreement which has the same effects at the organizational level) for organizational action and uncertainty over the patterns of cause and effect relations that determine the consequences of action. Earl and Hopwood contrast the potentially useful roles that accounting systems should play (that is, their ideal uses) with their actual uses.

Ideal uses

By referring to cell 1 in Figure 17.4 you will see that objectives are clear and undisputed and the consequences of action (i.e. the cause-and-effect relationship) are presumed to be known. In such circumstances it is possible to compute whether the consequences of action being considered will not satisfy objectives. Tasks can be programmed and algorithms, formulae and predetermined rules can be derived and decisions can be made by computation. Here accounting information systems can serve as **'answer machines'** to provide solutions to problems. Examples of accounting systems fulfilling this role include standard costing systems, discounted cash flow, linear programming and economic order inventory models. For these situations the accounting information system provides information that enables a clear and optimal decision to be made.

In cell 2 objectives are uncertain but cause-and-effect relationships are assumed to be known. Uncertainty over objectives may arise because they are simply unstated or, in a rapidly changing environment, there may be disagreement and conflict over which objectives should take precedence. Where objectives are uncertain Thompson and Tuden suggest that decision-making is a political rather than a computational process with a range of interests being articulated and the outcome being determined by bargaining and compromise.

FIGURE 17.4 *Uncertainty decision-making and ideal information systems*

		Uncertainty about objectives	
		Low	High
Uncertainty of cause and effect relationships	Low	– Decision by computation – Answer machines 1	2 – Decision by compromise – Dialogue machines
	High	3 – Decision by judgement – Learning machines	4 – Decision by inspiration – Idea machines

In these circumstances decision-making should be orientated towards opening up and maintaining channels of communication. Accounting information systems can facilitate this process by helping managers to develop and argue different points of view which are conflicting, but consistent with the underlying facts (Boland, 1979). Here the accounting system should serve as a **'dialogue machine'** designed to encourage exploration and debate, rather than providing answers.

The third cell relates to those situations where objectives are clear but cause-and-effect relationships are uncertain so we do not know which courses of action are likely to yield the optimum results. In these circumstances there is a need to explore problems, ask questions, investigate the analysable parts of decisions and finally resort to judgement. Here the accounting system can still provide considerable support during the decision-making process by serving as a **'learning machine'** that helps the managers to thoroughly assess the alternative courses of action. Examples of learning machines include computerized models with sensitivity analysis and 'what-if?' applications and inquiry systems for probing databases. These systems help managers to learn more about the possible alternatives and their consequences before making decisions.

Finally, in cell 4 both objectives and cause-and-effect relationships are uncertain. Here decision-making tends to be of an inspirational nature and accounting systems can serve as an **'idea machine'** by helping to stimulate and trigger creativity during brainstorming sessions where any idea is given serious consideration. It has been suggested that in changing environmental conditions semi-confusing accounting systems can be designed deliberately to shake organizations out of rigid behaviour patterns (Hedberg and Jonsson, 1978).

Actual uses

The above analysis suggests that decision-making requirements and the role of information systems should vary with the nature of the underlying uncertainty. However, in practice accounting information systems do not always follow the ideal uses depicted in Figure 17.4. There are no problems in cell 1 where objectives are certain and cause-and-effect relationships are well understood. Here decisions are programmable and the accounting information system can be used to generate answers.

In cell 2 where uncertainty over objectives applies but cause-and-effect relationships are well understood we find that **'ammunition machines'** are used instead of dialogue and compromise. In these situations political processes are important and accounting information is often used as ammunition through which interested parties seek to promote their own vested interests. Traditional management accounting systems are often used as ammunition machines. Reports containing only financial information are used to reduce multiple objectives to a single goal when, in reality organizational needs also include marketing, engineering and human relations aspects (Macintosh, 1994). By focusing on only one objective, information systems can be exploited to further the political ambitions of particular vested interest groups (Dirsmith and Jablonsky, 1979).

Macintosh illustrates how different parties can use the same information by quoting an example from politics where various parties try and influence the law-making in legislative assemblies. Using the same data base, one party develops an information system which supports a reduction in government meddling in the economy, while another using the very same data base, develops information which indicates the need for an increase in government planning. Ammunition machines are dangerous because they override the need for constructive dialogue and compromise.

In cell 3 learning machines are required but answer machines are often used instead. This situation can arise when accounting information is presented in such a way that it ignores or masks uncertainty when cause-and-effect relationships are uncertain. For example there is a danger that techniques, such as probability and risk analysis models which have been designed to incorporate uncertainty into the analysis, may produce answers that inadvertently create an aura of relative certainty. If these techniques are used purely as answer machines there is a possibility that opportunities to stimulate learning and exploit uncertainty will be lost (Macintosh, 1994).

Finally, in cell 4 where both objectives and cause-and-effect relationships are uncertain we often find that instead of using accounting information systems as idea machines they are used as **'rationalization machines'** that seek to justify and legitimize actions that have already been decided upon. For example, Bower (1970) has suggested that capital budgeting procedures are often used to justify decisions that have already been made, rather than as an aid to decision-making. Rationalization machines sometimes can have legitimate uses such as when it is appropriate to justify to others that decisions are being taken rationally. Accounting systems, however, should not be used to discourage creativity or always encourage the maintenance of the status quo.

The message from the analysis above is that the role of accounting information systems should be dependent on the type of uncertainty involved for the particular decision. An over-emphasis on formal systems and technical problems is inconsistent with the realities of organizational information flows. Unless accounting information system managers abandon their traditional narrow and technical perspective they will continue to be isolated from substantive organizational processes (Macintosh, 1985).

Purposes of management accounting

You should be aware from reading the previous section that management accounting information can be used for several different purposes. Drawing off earlier work by Earl and Hopwood (1981), Burchell *et al.* (1980) and Chua (1988), Kelly and Pratt (1992) review the different 'roles' or 'purposes' of management accounting. They include:

1. a rational/instrumental purpose;
2. a symbolic purpose;
3. a political/bargaining purpose;
4. a legitimate/retrospective rationalizing purpose;
5. a repressive/dominating/ideological purpose.

A rational/instrumental purpose

The conventional wisdom of management accounting, as portrayed in most management accounting textbooks, is derived from neo-classical economic theory. It is assumed that decision-making involves the formulation of goals (usually based on profit maximization), the identification of alternative courses of action, the evaluation of alternatives and a rational choice based on clearly defined criteria. The role of management accounting is to aid rational economic decision-making. The writings of Burchell *et al.* (1980) and Earl and Hopwood (1981), described in the previous section, suggest that when task instrumentality is well understood and objectives are clear, rational decision-making models can provide an accurate description of actual practice. In many situations, however, the assumption of rational economic decision-making does not reflect actual real world behaviour. For example, Cooper (1980) states:

> *Within a business context, it is perhaps unsurprising that the techniques that have been developed from neo-classical marginal theory are rarely implemented. Many managers recognize the simplistic and partial nature of the models and therefore have little confidence in the level of their prescriptions.*

As long ago as 1959, Simon drew attention to the many problems inherent in attempting to explain the organizational decision-making process purely in economic terms. He concluded that the normative microeconomist does not need a theory of human behaviour: he wants to know how people *ought* to behave, not how they *do* behave. Simon also attacked one of the most fundamental assumptions of neo-classical economics; that is that people are rational economic decision-makers. He argues that business people are content to find a plan that provides satisfactory profits rather than to maximize profits. Because the business environment is too complex to understand in its entirety and people can deal with only a limited amount of information at any one time (Simon uses the term **'bounded rationality'** to describe these constraints) they tend to search for solutions only until the first acceptable solution is found rather than continuing to search until the *best* solution is found.

It is also argued that the problem of resolving conflict between multiple goals is simplified by pursuing one goal at a time. At any one time, a particular goal is seen as being of prime importance, and action is taken to try and attain it. As time progresses other goals that have been neglected become of prime importance and attention is devoted to them in turn. This sequential attention to goals is a means of avoiding computing trade-offs between mutually exclusive goals and such behaviour has been described by Lindblom (1959) as 'muddling through'. Rather than the rational decision-making model this type of behaviour may be a more accurate description of actual behaviour in many organizations.

Other influential work based on bounded rationality is that of Cohen, March and Olsen (1972) who developed a **garbage can model of decision-making** in organizations that do not have clearly defined goals. They suggest that decisions are made in terms of the relatively random interaction of problems, solutions, participants and choice opportunities. A choice opportunity is modelled as a garbage can into which various problems and solutions are dumped by organizational participants.

Organizational life is seen as a continuous stream of problems that interact with an independent stream of possible solutions in an almost random manner. A given solution is chosen because it happens to be available and perceived at the time at which the problem emerges. This can result in solutions looking for problems as well as the more normal view of problems seeking solutions. Participants come and go and only chance attaches them to any particular decision opportunity. Choices are made only when problems, solutions and participants combine in such a way to make action possible.

In reviewing the garbage can model Ezzamel and Hart (1987) point out that in some cases goals may be pre-existent, well-ordered and antecedent to action. In these cases the emphasis is on interpreting actions and relating them to goals. In many cases, however, goals may be fluid, vague and ill-defined and discovered or reformulated as a consequence of action. The link between goals and actions will be ambiguous or even non-existent in these circumstances. In such cases emphasis is likely to shift from a preoccupation with ensuring that actions are consistent with goals to a concern with the processes through which actions are taken and possibly legitimized.

The conclusion that emerges from the literature is that where objectives can be clearly specified and input–output relationships are well understood, rational decision-making may represent a reasonable approximation to real world behaviour. In many situations, however, rationality is imperfect and actual behaviour is inconsistent with that assumed by neo-classical economic theory. To obtain a more complete understanding of management accounting there is a need to expand our knowledge, beyond adopting a universal theory that assumes rational decision-making, to approaches that incorporate what actually happens in practice. In the remaining part of this chapter we shall consider alternative roles that management accounting play in organizations.

A symbolic purpose

Organizations and managers gather and process far more information than they can possibly use for decision-making (Feldman and March, 1981). Furthermore, much of the information they collect is totally unconnected with decisions. The observations by Feldman and March that organizations overinvest in the amount of information they gather and process is in marked contrast to conventional wisdom which suggests that managers will collect and process information only if its marginal cost is less than its incremental value.

Why do managers collect more information than they need for decision-making? The answer is that information represents a means of signalling to others inside and outside the organization that decisions are being taken rationally and that managers in the organization are accountable. It is a representation to others of one's competence and is a symbol for all to see that one believes in intelligent choice. Accounting systems may be adopted ceremonially in order to convince the environment of the legitimacy and rationality of organizational activities.

Organizations without formal accounting systems are vulnerable to claims that they are negligent (Cooper *et al.*, 1981). Thus managers can find value in accounting information systems for symbolic purposes even when the information has little or no relation to decision-making. In its most extreme form it is more important to be perceived as being rational rather than actually being rational (Kelly and Pratt, 1992).

There is a mythical belief in Western society that more information leads to better decisions. Therefore the more information that a manager processes, the more impressive he or she is likely to be to others. Thus managers can establish their legitimacy, enhance their reputation and inspire confidence in others by displaying their command and use of the accounting information system. Therefore management accounting information can have a value to managers far beyond its worth as a basis for action (Macintosh, 1994).

Mackintosh also draws attention to the fact that managers use management accounting information for defensive purposes. There is a widespread practice within many organizations of criticizing decisions after the event. Because decisions are made under uncertainty a good decision may turn out to be unsuccessful yet it may still have been the correct one in the light of the information and alternatives available at the time.

Furthermore, managers may be criticized on the grounds that they should have collected more information prior to making the decision. To protect themselves against such criticisms, and to defend their actions, managers protect their interests by collecting all the information available before making a decision.

A political/bargaining purpose

Various writers have drawn attention to the fact that accounting information is widely used to achieve political power or a bargaining advantage. You will have already noted earlier in this chapter that when objectives are uncertain accounting information is often used as an ammunition machine through which interested parties seek to promote their own vested interests. Burchell *et al.* (1980) state:

> *Rather than creating a basis for dialogue and interchange where objectives are uncertain or in dispute, accounting systems are often used to articulate and promote particular interest positions and values ... Organizations are arenas in which people and groups participate with a diversity of interests with political processes being endemic features of organizational life ... The design of information and processing systems are also implicated in the management of these political processes ... The powerful are helped to observe the less powerful but not vice versa ... Moreover by influencing the accepted language of negotiation and debate, accounting systems can help to shape what is regarded as problematic, what can be deemed a credible solution and, perhaps most important of all, the criteria which are used for selection. For rather than being solely orientated towards the provision of information for decision-making, accounting systems can influence the criteria by which other information is sifted, marshalled and evaluated. (Page 17.)*

Cooper *et al.* (1981) also draw attention to the role of accounting systems as reflections of power and tools of internal disputes. Pfeffer and Salancik (1974) observed that university budget allocations can be understood in terms of the relative power of departments, such power deriving from research reputations and ability to generate external funds. Wildavsky (1974) cites numerous examples of the political aspects of budgeting at the government level, many of which have ready parallels with both public and business organizations. For example, he cites situations where successful arguments for funding are based on ignorance of sunk costs, and where combining budget estimates enables 'pet projects' to be slipped through the review process. Macintosh (1994) also concludes that management accounting and control systems are vitally involved in relations of domination and power. He states that

> *command over them is a key allocation resource used by upper-level executives to hold dominion over the organization's physical and technical assets. The master budget, for example, contains the detailed and all-encompassing blueprint for resource allocation for the entire organization and is a powerful lever in terms of ability to make a difference, to get things done and to dominate the organization. (Page 175.)*

The various studies that have examined the use of accounting information to achieve political power or a bargaining position have concluded that accounting systems are a significant component of the power system in the organization. In addition, these studies have also contributed to a wider understanding of how accounting operates in an organizational context and the ways in which accounting can be used by interested parties to reinterpret and modify existing perceptions of reality.

A legitimating/retrospective rationalizing purpose

This role relates to the use of accounting information to justify and legitimize actions that have already been decided upon. This role was briefly discussed when we considered how accounting information can be used as a 'rationalization machine'.

Weick (1969) maintains that the sequence whereby actions precede goals may well be a more accurate portrayal of organizational functioning than the more traditional goal–action paradigm. If goals are discovered through action and we make sense of actions retrospectively the notion of a budget as a quantified statement about future actions, as reflected by the conventional wisdom of management accounting, simply does not hold (Cooper *et al.*, 1981). Rather as part of the rationalization process of retrospective goal discovery, it appears that by performing the budget process an organization may be discovering its goals instead of achieving them because the exercise often involves looking backwards prior to extrapolation into the future. The budget process may be interpreted as a means of justifying past actions and making them appear sensible.

Attention has already been drawn to the observation by Bower (1970) that a major use of capital budgeting procedures is to justify decisions already made, rather than simply providing information prior to taking a particular decision. Similarly, Dirsmith and Jablonsky (1979) and Covaleski and Dirsmith (1980) suggest from their studies of budgetary systems in the governmental and health sectors, that systems such as planned programmed budgeting and management by objectives and budgets are used in large part to provide an appearance of rationality and a legitimation of activities. Earl and Hopwood (1981) and Burchell *et al.* (1980) also cite numerous instances in which managers utilize accounting data as *ex post* justification rather than as informational input. Cooper *et al.* (1981) state:

> *Accounting systems which record and report the results of activities provide an authoritative means of explaining the past and thereby providing a guide to the future. Such observations have led to the suggestion that sophisticated accounting systems may, rather than aiding efficiency itself, instead provide a dramatization of efficiency, maintaining a rational facade and thus providing a respectable identity for an organization. In general the processes associated with accounting in organizations may be interpreted as a way of facilitating what has happened in the past and attaching meaning to previous actions. Future actions may then be justified by the same explanations which have helped to make sense of previous action. The rituals of accounting may provide the legitimation for continuing current organizational activities. (Page 181.)*

In summary, Cooper *et al.* provide an insight into how accounting information can act as signals and symbols which can be used to endow past actions and decisions with legitimacy. In particular, they demonstrate that in organizations characterized by ambiguous goals and uncertain technologies (they refer to this situation as an organized anarchy) accounting systems represent an *ex post* rationalization of actions, rather than an *ex ante* statement of organization goals. In addition, they also highlight the role that accounting systems, and in particular budgets, play in providing a rationalization of behaviour rather than a decisional input.

A repressive/dominating/ideological purpose

This role is based on the labour process perspective of management control which views management accounting systems as playing a crucial role in preserving capitalist and class-based systems of domination. The labour process perspective sees management accounting as contributing to the institutional subordination of labour through a language that serves to legitimate sectional interests and which like other forms of management control has been fashioned largely to meet the perceived interests of capital (Hopper *et al.*, 1987). Puxty (1993) describes how management accounting and control systems developed during early capitalism to secure control over recalcitrant labour developed into sophisticated control mechanisms designed to ensure the institutionalized subordination of labour to the needs of capital.

The labour process scholars depict management accounting, supported with management science techniques, as a way for owners to deprive workers of the technical and financial knowledge of the production process, treat them as commodities and pressure them for even more productivity. Owners also use accounting systems as a way to legitimate grabbing the lion's share of any surplus value accruing to the enterprise (Mackintosh, 1994). Reviewing the literature relating to the repressive/dominating role of accounting Kelly and Pratt (1992) conclude that the labour process perspective views the managers of capital as being assessed, not in terms of how well they serve the labour entrusted to them, but how well they protect the interests of the absentee owners of the capital. In order to serve this end it is necessary for managers to initiate a surveillance system to monitor the performance of de-skilled labour.

The distinctly Marxist perspective adopted by labour process scholars arises from their concern with the role that accounting plays in the processes of social reproduction characteristics of advanced capitalism. In the hands of its more committed advocates the labour process perspective is an unashamedly partial perspective on work and organizations. It sets out from the premise that in a capitalist society work and employment, the organization and industrial relations are all shaped and structured to serve the interests of the capitalist class. The study of these aspects of social order is intended to demonstrate the substance of the founding assumption of this perspective (Roslender, 1992).

Summary

The following items relate to the learning objectives listed at the beginning of the chapter.

- **Describe the contingency theory of management accounting.**

  The contingency theory approach advocates that there is no one 'best' design for a management accounting information system, but that 'it all depends' upon the situational factors. The situational factors represent the contingent factors. Examples of contingent factors include the external environment faced by organizations, the type of competitive strategy they adopt, the nature of the production process and organizational structure (e.g. centralized or decentralized).

- **Provide illustrations of the relationship between the five broad contingent factors described in Exhibit 17.1 and features of the management accounting control system.**

  In terms of the external environment, studies indicate that a rigid budget style of evaluation is more appropriate in units facing low environmental uncertainty whereas a profit conscious flexible style of evaluation is more appropriate for organizations facing high levels of environmental uncertainty. A low cost competitive strategy requires a greater emphasis on cost controls and frequent and detailed performance reports whereas a differentiation strategy requires less emphasis on tight cost controls and greater reliance on non-financial performance measures. Within the technology category the nature of the production process determines the type of costing system with process costing being used in process production and mass production technologies and job costing being used in batch production technologies. Control systems have been shown to differ by industry type. For example, controls differ in the manufacturing sector that have a large number of standard cost centres. They rely extensively on detailed variance analysis. In contrast, costs in non-manufacturing industries tend to be mostly of a discretionary nature. Different approaches are required for cost control in discretionary cost centres (see Chapter 16). Relationships within the knowledge and observability category are discussed in learning objectives 3 and 5.

- **Describe the framework that links the appropriate types of controls to the interaction between ability to measure output and knowledge of the transformation process.**

  Where knowledge of the transformation process is near perfect, behavioural controls can be used. Alternatively, output controls are most appropriate if knowledge of the transformation process is imperfect but the ability to measure output is high. Where there is low ability to measure outputs coupled with imperfect knowledge of the transformation process, neither behaviour nor output controls are appropriate. Here clan/social controls are the most appropriate mode.

- **Distinguish between efficiency and effectiveness measures.**

  Efficiency is concerned with achieving a given result with a minimum amount of resources or, alternatively, achieving the maximum amount of output from a given level of input resources. Efficiency measures focus on the relationship between inputs and outputs. Effectiveness focuses on whether or not actions result in the desired goal. Thus, effectiveness is concerned with the attainment of objectives; an action being effective if it achieves what it was intended to achieve. Efficiency is often confused with effectiveness. An action may be effective, but inefficient in that the result could have been achieved with fewer resources. Conversely, actions can be efficient but not effective. For example, output may be produced efficiently but this is ineffective if the output cannot be sold.

- **Describe the framework that links the appropriate type of assessment to the interaction between task instrumentality and beliefs about the clarity of organizational goals.**

  Where goals are clear and unambiguous and task instrumentality (i.e. the ways of doing work) is well understood, so that the optimum economic relationship between inputs and outputs can be derived, scorekeeping and assessment can rely on efficiency tests. Alternatively, where task instrumentality is not well understood but goals are clear and unambiguous, we can ascertain whether the actions achieved the desired result. In these circumstances the scorekeeping question should focus on measures of effectiveness. Where goals are ambiguous both efficiency and effectiveness measures are unreliable and the use of social tests is appropriate. With social tests the performance of a department is based on the collective opinions and beliefs of one or more user groups.

- **Distinguish between programmed and non-programmed decisions.**

  A programmed decision is one where the decision situation is sufficiently well understood for a reliable prediction of the decision outcome to be made. Because input–output relationships are well understood, variance analysis (see Chapter 18) is an appropriate control technique. With non-programmed decisions one that has to rely on the judgement of managers because there is no formal mechanism for predicting likely outcomes. In non-programmed decisions, the causal relationships are less well understood so that it is possible only to instruct a manager as to what he or she is expected to achieve. Managers can be held responsible for results; but how they are to be attained must be left to their discretion.

- **Describe the framework that links the uses of accounting information for decision-making to the interaction between the uncertainty of objectives and the uncertainty relating to cause-and-effect relationships.**

  Four situations can be identified. When objectives are clear and the patterns of cause-and-effect relationships are known, tasks can be programmed and decisions can be made by computation. Here accounting systems can serve as 'answer machines' to provide solutions to problems. The second situation relates to where objectives are uncertain but cause-and-effect relations are still known. Accounting systems should serve as a 'dialogue machine' by providing information that helps managers to develop and argue different points of view. However, in these circumstances accounting information is often used as an 'ammunition machine' whereby interested parties seek to promote their own vested interests. The third situation applies to where objectives are clear but cause-and-effect relations are uncertain. Here there is a need to explore problems and use accounting systems as learning machines by providing information that helps managers to assess thoroughly the alternative courses of action. Examples include sensitivity analysis and inquiry systems for probing databases. In practice, however, accounting information is often used as an answer machine instead of a learning machine. The final situation relates to where both objectives and cause-and-effect relationships are uncertain. In these circumstances decision-making tends to be of an inspirational nature and accounting systems can serve as an 'idea machine' by helping to stimulate and trigger creativity. Instead, we often find that accounting information systems are used as 'rationalization machines' that seek to justify and legitimize actions that have already been decided upon.

- **Identify and explain the different purposes for which accounting information is used within organizations.**

  Five different purposes have been identified. They are: (a) a rational/instrumental purpose; (b) a symbolic purpose; (c) a political/bargaining purpose; (d) a legitimate/retrospective rationalizing purpose; and (e) a repressive/dominating/ideological purpose. Each purpose is described in detail within the chapter.

Key terms and concepts

ammunition machine (p. 710)
answer machine (p. 709)
behavioural controls (p. 705)
bounded rationality (p. 712)
clan controls (p. 706)
contingency theory (p. 695)
dialogue machine (p. 710)
effectiveness tests (p. 708)
efficiency tests (p. 707)
garbage can model of decision-making (p. 712)
idea machine (p. 710)
instrumental tests (p. 708)
learning machine (p. 710)
non-programmed decision (p. 709)
output controls (p. 705)
programmed decision (p. 708)
rationalization machine (p. 711)
social controls (p. 705)
social test (p. 708)
task instrumentality (p. 706)

Recommended reading

There are several textbooks that focus mainly on the organizational and social aspects of management accounting. You are recommended to read either Emmanuel *et al.* (1990),

Macintosh (1985), Macintosh (1994), Ezzamel and Hart (1987) or Roslender (1992). See Chenhall (2003) for a review and summary of the findings of contingency theory research. For a more in-depth understanding of some of the issues discussed in this chapter you should refer to the articles by Burchell *et al.* (1980), Cooper *et al.* (1981) and Kelly and Pratt (1992).

Key examination points

Most professional examining bodies rarely examine the content of this chapter. However, the content is likely to be examined in those courses that focus on management accounting within a wider social and organizational context. Examination questions are likely to consist of essays and be somewhat ill-defined. There will be no ideal answer. You should concentrate on reading widely and relating the literature to the question that is asked.

Assessment material

Review questions

The review questions are short questions that enable you to assess your understanding of the main topics included in the chapter. The numbers in parentheses provide you with the page numbers to refer to if you cannot answer a specific question.

Review problems

The review problems are more complex and require you to relate and apply the chapter content to various business problems. Fully worked solutions to the review problems are provided in a separate section at the end of the book.

Case studies

The website also includes over 30 case study problems. A list of these cases is provided in Part Seven of this book. The Mestral case is relevant to the content of this chapter.

Review questions

17.1 Explain what is meant by the contingency theory of management accounting. *(p. 696)*

17.2 Provide examples of three contingent factors and for each factor explain their potential influence on the nature of the management accounting control system. *(pp. 699–704)*

17.3 Explain the framework that links the appropriate types of controls (i.e. behavioural, social, output, etc.) to the interaction between the ability to measure output and knowledge of the transformation process. *(pp. 705–06)*

17.4 Explain what is meant by the term 'task instrumentality'. *(p. 706)*

17.5 Distinguish between efficiency, effectiveness and instrumental tests. *(pp. 707–08)*

17.6 Describe the framework that links the appropriate type of assessment (i.e. efficiency, effectiveness, etc.) to the interaction between task instrumentality and beliefs about the clarity of organizational goals. *(pp. 706–08)*

17.7 Distinguish between programmed and non-programmed decisions. *(pp. 708–09)*

17.8 Explain what is meant by the terms answer, dialogue, learning, ideas, ammunition and rationalization machines. *(pp. 709–11)*

17.9 Describe the framework that links the use of accounting information for decision-making to the interaction between the uncertainty of objectives and the uncertainty relating to the cause-and-effect relationships. (*pp. 709–11*)

17.10 Describe the different purposes for which accounting information is used within organizations. (*pp. 711–16*)

Review problems

17.11 Advanced

(a) Contingency theory has frequently been used to explain variations in the functioning of organizations. It has been criticized on a number of grounds, including whether sufficient attention has been given to people and culture.

Requirement:

Explain and discuss from a management control perspective, the criticism that contingency theory pays insufficient attention to the people in organizations and to organizational culture.

(10 marks)

(b) Some organizations have long-standing practices of promoting from existing staff, as a consequence of which they rarely recruit outsiders to any senior position. Staff turnover is very low. Other organizations have frequent management and structural changes, and often recruit senior managers from outside the organization.

Requirement:

Explain the differences in control systems and approaches to management control that could be expected with these alternative practices.

CIMA Stage 4
Management Accounting Control Systems

17.12 Advanced

Conventional approaches to the study of the organizational process emphasize economic reality, order and planned action as the basis of managerial decision-making. Outline the major limitations inherent in such a viewpoint, highlighted by research studies, and discuss the implications of your analysis for the management accountant.

17.13 Advanced

It has been argued that the further introduction of technical management accounting controls in the public sector and not-for-profit sector are doomed to failure. Evaluate possible grounds of such an argument.

17.14 Advanced

Describe the contingency theory of management accounting and discuss the relationship between various contingent factors and features of the management accounting system.

17.15 Advanced

Describe the different types of controls that can be used in organizations and discuss the factors that influence the choice of specific types of controls.

17.16 **Advanced**

Discuss the different 'roles' or 'purposes' for which management accounting information is used within organizations.

17.17 **Advanced**

Management accounting information is rarely used in the ways that are depicted in textbooks. Discuss.

17.18 **Advanced**

There is no universally best management accounting control system which can be applied to all organizations. Discuss.

Standard costing and variance analysis 1

18

In the previous two chapters the major features of management accounting control systems have been examined. Chapter 16 concentrated on the different types of controls used by companies so that the elements of management accounting control systems could be described within the context of the overall control process. Because there is no universally best management accounting control system that can be applied to all organizations Chapter 17 considered the relationship between contingent, or situational factors, and certain features of management accounting control systems. Both chapters adopted a broad approach to control and the detailed procedures of financial controls were not examined. In this, and the next two chapters we shall focus on the detailed financial controls that are used by organizations.

In this chapter we shall consider a financial control system that enables the deviations from budget to be analysed in detail, thus enabling costs to be controlled more effectively. This system of control is called standard costing. In particular, we shall examine how a

LEARNING OBJECTIVES

After studying this chapter, you should be able to:

- explain how a standard costing system operates;
- explain how standard costs are set;
- explain the meaning of standard hours produced;
- define basic, ideal and currently attainable standards;
- identify and describe the purposes of a standard costing system;
- calculate labour, material, overhead and sales margin variances and reconcile actual profit with budgeted profit;
- identify the causes of labour, material, overhead and sales margin variances;
- construct a departmental performance report;
- distinguish between standard variable costing and standard absorption costing.

standard costing system operates and how the variances are calculated. In the next chapter we shall consider some of the criticisms made against standard costing variance analysis, and look at various ways of overcoming the problems that arise. Standard costing systems are applied in standard cost centres which were described in Chapter 16. You will recall that the main features of standard cost centres are that output can be measured and the input required to produce each unit of output can be specified. Therefore standard costing is generally applied to manufacturing activities and non-manufacturing activities are not incorporated within the standard costing system. In addition, the sales variances that are described in this chapter can also be applied in revenue centres. In Chapter 20 we shall look at financial controls that are appropriate for measuring profit and investment centre performance.

Standard costs are predetermined costs; they are target costs that should be incurred under efficient operating conditions. They are not the same as **budgeted costs**. A budget relates to an entire activity or operation; a standard presents the same information on a per unit basis. A standard therefore provides cost expectations per unit of activity and a budget provides the cost expectation for the total activity. If the budget output for a product is for 10 000 units and the standard cost is £3 per unit, budgeted cost will be £30 000. We shall see that establishing standard costs for each unit produced enables a detailed analysis to be made of the difference between the budgeted cost and the actual cost so that costs can be controlled more effectively.

In the first part of the chapter (pages 726–48) we shall concentrate on those variances that are likely to be useful for cost control purposes. The final part describes those variances that are required for financial accounting purposes but that are not particularly useful for cost control. If your course does not relate to the disposition of variances for financial accounting purposes, you can omit pages 749–54.

Operation of a standard costing system

Standard costing is most suited to an organization whose activities consist of a series of *common* or *repetitive* operations and the input required to produce each unit of output can be specified. It is therefore relevant in manufacturing companies, since the processes involved are often of a repetitive nature. Standard costing procedures can also be applied in service industries such as units within banks, where output can be measured in terms of the number of cheques or the number of loan applications processed, and there are also well-defined input–output relationships. Standard costing cannot, however, be applied to activities of a non-repetitive nature, since there is no basis for observing repetitive operations and consequently standards cannot be set.

A standard costing system can be applied to organizations that produce many different products, as long as production consists of a series of common operations. For example, if the output from a factory is the result of five common operations, it is possible to produce many different product variations from these operations. It is therefore possible that a large product range may result from a small number of common operations. Thus standard costs should be developed for repetitive operations and product standard costs are derived simply by combining the standard costs from the operations which are necessary to make the product. This process is illustrated in Exhibit 18.1.

It is assumed that the standard costs are £20, £30, £40 and £50 for each of the operations 1 to 4. The standard cost for *product* 100 is therefore £110, which consists of £20 for operation 1, plus £40 and £50 for operations 3 and 4. The standard costs for each of the other products are calculated in a similar manner. In addition, the total standard cost for the total output of each operation for the period has been calculated. For example, six items of operation number 1 have been completed, giving a total standard cost of £120 for this operation (six items at £20 each). Three items of operation 2 have been completed, giving a total standard cost of £90, and so on.

Variances allocated to responsibility centres

You can see from Exhibit 18.1 that different responsibility centres are responsible for each operation. For example, responsibility centre A is responsible for operation 1, responsibility centre B for operation 2, and so on. Consequently, there is no point in comparing the actual cost of *product* 100 with the standard cost of £110 for the purposes of control, since responsibility centres A, C and D are responsible for the variance. None of the responsibility centres is solely answerable for the variance. Cost control requires that responsibility centres be identified with the standard cost for the output achieved. Therefore if the actual costs for responsibility centre A are compared with the standard cost of £120 for the production of the six items (see first row of Exhibit 18.1), the manager of this responsibility centre will be answerable for the full amount of the variance. Only by comparing total actual costs with total standard costs *for each operation or responsibility centre* for a period can control be effectively achieved. A comparison of standard *product* costs (i.e. the columns in Exhibit 18.1) with actual costs that involves several different responsibility centres is clearly inappropriate.

Figure 18.1 provides an overview of the operation of a standard costing system. You will see that the standard costs for the actual output for a particular period are traced to the managers of responsibility centres who are responsible for the various operations. The actual costs for the same period are also charged to the responsibility centres. Standard and actual costs are compared and the variance is reported. For example, if the actual cost for the output of the six items produced in responsibility centre A during the period is £220 and the standard cost is £120 (Exhibit 18.1), a variance of £100 will be reported.

Detailed analysis of variances

Figure 18.1 provides an overview of a standard costing system. You can see from the box below the first arrow in Figure 18.1 that the operation of a standard costing system also enables a detailed analysis of the variances to be reported. For example, variances for each responsibility centre can be identified by each element of cost and analysed according to the price and quantity content. The accountant assists managers by pinpointing where the variances have arisen and the responsibility managers can undertake to carry out the appropriate investigations to identify the reasons for the variance. For example, the accountant might identify the reason for a direct materials variance as being excessive usage of a certain material in a particular process, but the responsibility centre manager must investigate this process and identify the reasons for the excessive usage. Such an investigation should result in appropriate remedial action being taken or, if it is found that the variance is due to a permanent change in the standard, the standard should be changed.

Actual product costs are not required

It is questionable whether the allocation of actual costs to products serves any useful purpose. Because standard costs represent *future* target costs, they are preferable to actual *past* costs for decision-making. Also, the external financial accounting regulations in most countries specify that if standard product costs provide a reasonable approximation of actual product costs, they are acceptable for inventory valuation calculations for external reporting.

There are therefore strong arguments for not producing actual *product* costs when a standard costing system exists, since this will lead to large clerical savings. However, it

EXHIBIT 18.1
Standard costs analysed by operations and products

Responsibility centre	Operation no. and standard cost No.	(£)	Products 100	101	102	103	104	105	106	Total standard cost (£)	Actual cost
A	1	20	✓	✓		✓	✓	✓	✓	120	
B	2	30		✓		✓		✓		90	
C	3	40	✓		✓		✓			120	
D	4	50	✓	✓	✓				✓	200	
Standard product cost			£110	£100	£90	£50	£60	£50	£70	530	

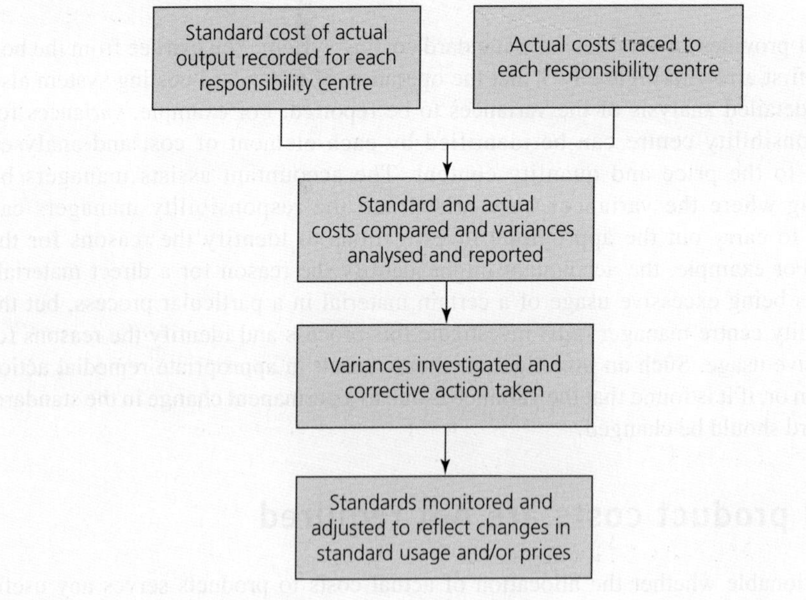

FIGURE 18.1 *An overview of a standard costing system*

must be stressed that actual costs must be accumulated periodically for each operation or responsibility centre, so that comparisons can be made with standard costs. Nevertheless, there will be considerably fewer responsibility centres than products, and the accumulation of actual costs is therefore much less time consuming.

Comparisons after the event

It may be argued that there is little point in comparing actual performance with standard performance, because such comparisons can only be made after the event. Nevertheless, if people know in advance that their performance is going to be judged, they are likely to act differently from the way they would have done if they were aware that their performance was not going to be measured. Furthermore, even though it is not possible for a manager to change his or her performance after the event, an analysis of how well a person has performed in the past may indicate – both to the person concerned and his or her superior – ways of obtaining better performance in the future.

Establishing cost standards

Control over costs is best effected through action at the point where the costs are incurred. Hence the standards should be set for the quantities of material, labour and services to be consumed in performing an *operation*, rather than the complete *product* cost standards. Variances from these standards should be reported to show causes and responsibilities for deviations from standard. Product cost standards are derived by listing and adding the standard costs of operations required to produce a particular product. For example, if you refer to Exhibit 18.1 you will see that the standard cost of product 100 is £110 and is derived from the sum of the standard costs of operations 1, 3 and 4.

There are two approaches that can be used to set standard costs. First, past historical records can be used to estimate labour and material usage. Secondly, standards can be set based on **engineering studies**. With engineering studies a detailed study of each operation is undertaken based on careful specifications of materials, labour and equipment and on controlled observations of operations. If historical records are used to set standards, there is a danger that the latter will include past inefficiencies. With this approach, standards are set based on average past performance for the same or similar operations. Known excess usage of labour or materials should be eliminated or the standards may be tightened by an arbitrary percentage reduction in the quantity of resources required. The disadvantage of this method is that, unlike the engineering method, it does not focus attention on finding the best combination of resources, production methods and product quality. Nevertheless, standards derived from average historical usage do appear to be widely used in practice. (See Exhibit 18.3.)

Let us now consider how standards are established for each operation for direct labour, direct materials and overheads using the engineering studies approach. Note that the standard cost for each operation is derived from multiplying the quantity of input that should be used per unit of output (i.e. the quantity standard) by the amount that should be paid for each unit of input (i.e. the price standard).

Direct material standards

These are based on product specifications derived from an intensive study of the input *quantity* necessary for each operation. This study should establish the most suitable materials for each product, based on product design and quality policy, and also the optimal quantity that should be used after taking into account any wastage or loss that is considered inevitable in the production process. Material quantity standards are usually recorded on a **bill of materials**. This describes and states the required quantity of materials for each operation to complete the product. A separate bill of materials is maintained for each product. The standard material product cost is then found by multiplying the standard quantities by the appropriate standard prices.

The standard *prices* are obtained from the purchasing department. The standard material prices are based on the assumption that the purchasing department has carried out a suitable search of alternative suppliers and has selected suppliers who can provide the required quantity of sound quality materials at the most competitive price. Normally, price standards take into account the advantages to be obtained by determining the most economical order quantity and quantity discounts, best method of delivery and the most favourable credit terms. However, consideration should also be given to vendor reliability with respect to material quality and meeting scheduled delivery dates. Standard prices then provide a suitable base against which actual prices paid for materials can be evaluated.

Direct labour standards

To set labour standards, activities should be analysed by the different operations. Each operation is studied and an allowed time computed, usually after carrying out a time and motion study. The normal procedure for such a study is to analyse each operation to eliminate any unnecessary elements and to determine the most efficient production method. The most efficient methods of production, equipment and operating conditions are then standardized. This is followed by time measurements that are made to determine the number of standard hours required by an average worker to complete the job. Unavoidable delays such as machine breakdowns and routine maintenance are included in the standard time. Wage rate standards are normally either a matter of company policy or the result of negotiations between management and unions. The agreed wage rates are applied to the standard time allowed to determine the standard labour cost for each operation.

Overhead standards

The procedure for establishing standard manufacturing overhead rates for a standard costing system is the same as that which is used for establishing predetermined overhead rates as described in Chapter 3. Separate rates for fixed and variable overheads are essential for planning and control. Normally the standard overhead rate will be based on a rate per direct labour hour or machine hour of input.

Fixed overheads are largely independent of changes in activity, and remain constant over wide ranges of activity in the short term. It is therefore inappropriate for short-term cost control purposes to unitize fixed overheads to derive a fixed overhead rate per unit of activity. However, in order to meet the external financial reporting stock valuation requirements, fixed manufacturing overheads must be traced to products. It is therefore necessary to unitize fixed overheads for stock valuation purposes.

The main difference with the treatment of overheads under a standard costing system as opposed to a non-standard costing system is that the product overhead cost is based on the hourly overhead rates multiplied by the *standard hours* (that is, hours which should have been used) rather than the *actual hours* used.

At this stage it is appropriate if we summarize the approach that should be used to establish cost standards. Control over costs is best effected through action at the point where they are incurred. Hence standards should be set for labour, materials and variable overheads consumed in performing an *operation*. For stock valuation purposes it is necessary to establish *product cost* standards. Standard manufacturing product costs consist of the total of the standard costs of operations required to produce the product plus the product's standard fixed overhead cost. Note that standard costs are not normally established for non-manufacturing activities. A standard cost card should be maintained for each product and operation. It reveals the quantity of each unit of input that should be used to produce one unit of output. A typical product standard cost card is illustrated in Exhibit 18.2. In most organizations standard cost cards are now stored on a computer. Standards should be continuously reviewed, and, where significant changes in production methods or input prices occur, they should be changed in order to ensure that standards reflect current targets. We shall discuss how the learning curve can be applied in standard setting in Chapter 24.

Standard hours produced

It is not possible to measure *output* in terms of units produced for a department making several different products or operations. For example, if a department produces 100 units of product X, 200 units of product Y and 300 units of product Z, it is not possible to add the production of these items together, since they are not homogeneous. This problem can be overcome by ascertaining the amount of time, working under efficient conditions, it should take to make each product. This time calculation is called **standard hours produced**. In other words, **standard hours** are an *output* measure that can act as a common denominator for adding together the production of unlike items.

Let us assume that the following standard times are established for the production of one unit of each product:

Product X	5 standard hours
Product Y	2 standard hours
Product Z	3 standard hours

This means that it should take five hours to produce one unit of product X under efficient production conditions. Similar comments apply to products Y and Z. The production for the department will be calculated in standard hours as follows:

Product	Standard time per unit produced (hours)	Actual output (units)	Standard hours produced
X	5	100	500
Y	2	200	400
Z	3	300	900
			1800

Remember that standard hours produced is an output measure, and flexible budget allowances should be based on this. In the illustration we should expect the *output* of 1800 standard hours to take 1800 direct labour hours of *input* if the department works at the prescribed level of efficiency. The department will be inefficient if 1800 standard hours of output are produced using, say, 2000 direct labour hours of input. The flexible budget allowance should therefore be based on 1800 standard hours produced to ensure that no extra allowance is given for the 200 excess hours of input. Otherwise, a manager will obtain a higher budget allowance through being inefficient.

EXHIBIT 18.2
An illustration of a standard cost card

Date standard set .... **Product: Sigma**

Direct materials

Operation no.	Item code	Quantity (kg)	Standard price (£)	Department A	B	C	D	Totals (£)
1	5.001	5	3		£15			
2	7.003	4	4			£16		
								31

Direct labour

Operation no.	Standard hours	Standard rate (£)	A	B	C	D	Totals (£)
1	7	9		£63			
2	8	9			£72		
							135

Factory overhead

Department	Standard hours	Standard rate (£)	A	B	C	D	Totals (£)
B	7	3		£21			
C	8	4			£32		
							53
Total manufacturing cost per unit (£)							219

Types of cost standards

The determination of standard costs raises the problem of how demanding the standards should be. Should they represent ideal or faultless performance or should they represent easily attainable performance? Standards are normally classified into three broad categories:

1 basic cost standards;

2 ideal standards;

3 currently attainable standards.

Basic cost standards

Basic cost standards represent constant standards that are left unchanged over long periods. The main advantage of basic standards is that a base is provided for a comparison with actual costs through a period of years with the same standard, and efficiency trends can be established over time. When changes occur in methods of production, price levels or other relevant factors, basic standards are not very useful, since they do not represent *current* target costs. For this reason basic cost standards are seldom used.

Ideal standards

Ideal standards represent perfect performance. Ideal standard costs are the minimum costs that are possible under the most efficient operating conditions. Ideal standards are unlikely to be used in practice because they may have an adverse impact on employee motivation. Such standards constitute goals to be aimed for rather than performance that can currently be achieved.

Currently attainable standard costs

These standards represent those costs that should be incurred under efficient operating conditions. They are standards that are difficult, but not impossible, to achieve. **Attainable standards** are easier to achieve than ideal standards because allowances are made for normal spoilage, machine breakdowns and lost time. The fact that these standards represent a target that can be achieved under efficient conditions, but which is also viewed as being neither too easy to achieve nor impossible to achieve, provides the best norm to which actual costs should be compared. Attainable standards can vary in terms of the level of difficulty. For example, if tight attainable standards are set over a given time period, there might only be a 70% probability that the standard will be attained. On the other hand, looser attainable standards might be set with a probability of 90% attainment. Attainable standards are equivalent to highly achievable standards described in Chapter 16.

Attainable standards that are likely to be achieved are preferable for planning and budgeting. It is preferable to prepare the master budget and cash budget using these standards. Clearly, it is inappropriate to use standards that may not be achieved for planning purposes. Hence attainable standards that are likely to be achieved lead to economies, since they can be used for both *planning* and *control*. However, easily attainable standards are unlikely to provide a challenging target that will motivate higher levels of efficiency.

For an indication of the types of cost standards that companies actually use you should refer to Exhibit 18.3.

Purposes of standard costing

Standard costing systems are widely used because they provide cost information for many different purposes such as the following.

- Providing a prediction of future costs that can be used for *decision-making purposes*. Standard costs can be derived from either traditional or activity-based costing systems. Because standard costs represent *future* target costs based on the elimination of avoidable inefficiencies they are preferable to estimates based on adjusted past costs which may incorporate inefficiencies. For example, in markets where competitive prices do not exist products may be priced on a bid basis. In these situations standard costs provide more appropriate information because efficient competitors will seek to eliminate avoidable costs. It is therefore unwise to assume that inefficiencies are recoverable within the bid price.
- Providing a *challenging target* which individuals are motivated to achieve. For example research evidence suggests that the existence of a defined quantitative goal or target is likely to motivate higher levels of performance than would be achieved if no such target was set.
- Assisting in *setting budgets* and evaluating managerial performance. Standard costs are particularly valuable for budgeting because a reliable and convenient source of data is provided for converting budgeted production into physical and monetary

EXHIBIT 18.3

Surveys of company practice

Since its introduction in the early 1900s standard costing has flourished and is now one of the most widely used management accounting techniques. Three independently conducted surveys of USA practice indicate highly consistent figures in terms of adopting standard costing systems. Cress and Pettijohn (1985) and Schwarzbach (1985) report an 85% adoption rate, while Cornick *et al.* (1988), found that 86% of the surveyed firms used a standard costing system. A Japanese survey by Scarborough *et al.* (1991) reported a 65% adoption rate. Surveys of UK companies by Drury *et al.* (1993) and New Zealand companies by Guilding *et al.* (1998) report adoption rates of 76% and 73% respectively.

In relation to the methods to set labour and material standards Drury *et al.* reported the following usage rates:

	Extent of use (%)				
	Never	**Rarely**	**Sometimes**	**Often**	**Always**
Standards based on design/ engineering studies	18	11	19	31	21
Observations based on trial runs	18	16	36	25	5
Work study techniques	21	18	19	21	21
Average of historic usage	22	11	23	35	9

In the USA Lauderman and Schaeberle (1983) reported that 43% of the respondents used average historic usage, 67% used engineering studies, 11% used trial runs under controlled conditions and 15% used other methods. The results add up to more than 100% because some companies used more than one method.

Drury *et al.* also reported that the following types of standards were employed:

Maximum efficiency standards	5%
Achievable but difficult to attain standards	44%
Average past performance standards	46%
Other	5%

resource requirements. Budgetary preparation time is considerably reduced if standard costs are available because the standard costs of operations and products can be readily built up into total costs of any budgeted volume and product mix.

- Acting as a *control device* by highlighting those activities which do not conform to plan and thus alerting managers to those situations that may be 'out of control' and in need of corrective action. With a standard costing system variances are analysed in great detail such as by element of cost, and price and quantity elements. Useful feedback is therefore provided in pinpointing the areas where variances have arisen.
- Simplifying the task of tracing costs to products for *profit measurement and inventory valuation* purposes. Besides preparing annual financial accounting profit statements most organizations also prepare monthly internal profit statements. If actual costs are used a considerable amount of time is required in tracking costs so that monthly costs can be allocated between cost of sales and inventories. A data processing system is required which can track monthly costs in a resource efficient manner. Standard costing systems meet this requirement You will see from Figure 18.2 that product costs

FIGURE 18.2 *Standard costs for inventory valuation and profit measurement*

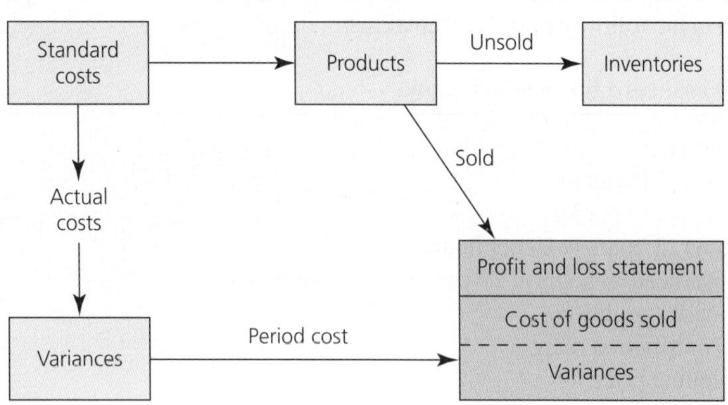

are maintained at standard cost. Inventories and cost of goods sold are recorded at standard cost and a conversion to actual cost is made by writing off all variances arising during the period as a period cost. Note that the variances from standard cost are extracted by comparing actual with standard costs at the responsibility centre level, and not at the product level, so that actual costs are not assigned to individual products.

Variance analysis

It is possible to compute variances simply by committing to memory a series of variance formulae. If you adopt this approach, however, it will not help you to understand what a variance is intended to depict and what the relevant variables represent. In our discussion of each variance we shall therefore concentrate on the fundamental meaning of the variance, so that you can logically deduce the variance formulae as we go along.

All of the variances presented in this chapter are illustrated from the information contained in Example 18.1 on page 736. Note that the level of detail presented is highly simplified. A truly realistic situation would involve many products, operations and responsibility centres but would not give any further insights into the basic concepts or procedures.

Figure 18.3 shows the breakdown of the profit variance (the difference between budgeted and actual profit) into the component cost and revenue variances that can be calculated for a standard variable costing system. We shall now calculate the variances set out in Figure 18.3 using the data presented in Example 18.1.

Material variances

The costs of the materials which are used in a manufactured product are determined by two basic factors: the price paid for the materials, and the quantity of materials used in production. This gives rise to the possibility that the actual cost will differ from the standard cost because the *actual quantity* of materials used will be different from the *standard quantity* and/or that the *actual price* paid will be different from the *standard price*. We can therefore calculate a material usage and a material price variance.

EXAMPLE 18.1

Alpha manufacturing company produces a single product, which is known as sigma. The product requires a single operation, and the standard cost for this operation is presented in the following standard cost card:

Standard cost card for product sigma	**(£)**
Direct materials:	
2 kg of A at £10 per kg	20.00
1 kg of B at £15 per kg	15.00
Direct labour (3 hours at £9 per hour)	27.00
Variable overhead (3 hours at £2 per direct labour hour)	6.00
Total standard variable cost	68.00
Standard contribution margin	20.00
Standard selling price	88.00

Alpha Ltd plan to produce 10 000 units of sigma in the month of April, and the budgeted costs based on the information contained in the standard cost card are as follows:

Budget based on the above standard costs and an output of 10 000 units	**(£)**	**(£)**	**(£)**
Sales (10 000 units of sigma at £88 per unit)			880 000
Direct materials:			
A: 20 000 kg at £10 per kg	200 000		
B: 10 000 kg at £15 per kg	150 000	350 000	
Direct labour (30 000 hours at £9 per hour)		270 000	
Variable overheads (30 000 hours at £2 per direct labour hour)		60 000	680 000
Budgeted contribution			200 000
Fixed overheads			120 000
Budgeted profit			80 000

Annual budgeted fixed overheads are £1 440 000 and are assumed to be incurred evenly throughout the year. The company uses a variable costing system for internal profit measurement purposes.

The actual results for April are:

	(£)	**(£)**
Sales (9000 units at £90)		810 000
Direct materials:		
A: 19 000 kg at £11 per kg	209 000	
B: 10 100 kg at £14 per kg	141 400	
Direct labour (28 500 hours at £9.60 per hour)	273 600	
Variable overheads	52 000	676 000
Contribution		134 000
Fixed overheads		116 000
Profit		18 000

Manufacturing overheads are charged to production on the basis of direct labour hours. Actual production and sales for the period were 9000 units.

FIGURE 18.3 *Variance analysis for a variable costing system*

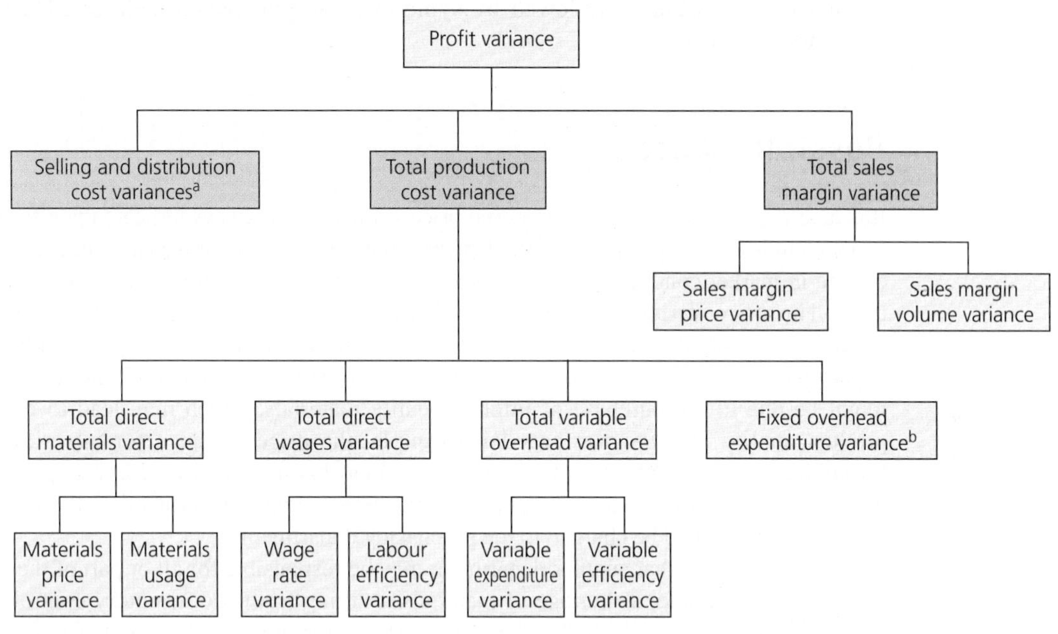

[a]Selling and distribution cost variances are not presented in this chapter. If activities are of a repetitive nature, standards can be established and variances can be calculated in a similar manner to production cost variances. If standards cannot be established, costs should be controlled by comparing budgeted and actual costs.

[b]With an absorption costing system, the summary of fixed overhead variances presented in Exhibit 18.6 would replace this box.

Material price variances

The starting point for calculating this variance is simply to compare the standard price per unit of materials with the actual price per unit. You should now read Example 18.1. You will see that the standard price for material A is £10 per kg, but the actual price paid was £11 per kg. The price variance is £1 per kg. This is of little consequence if the excess purchase price has been paid only for a small number of units or purchases. But the consequences are important if the excess purchase price has been paid for a large number of units, since the effect of the variance will be greater.

The difference between the standard material price and the actual price per unit should therefore be multiplied by the quantity of materials purchased. For material A the price variance is £1 per unit; but since 19 000 kg were purchased, the excess price was paid out 19 000 times. Hence the total material price variance is £19 000 adverse. The formula for the material price variance now follows logically:

the **material price variance** is equal to the difference between the standard price (SP) and the actual price (AP) per unit of materials multiplied by the quantity of materials purchased (QP):

$$(SP - AP) \times QP$$

Now refer to material B in Example 18.1. The standard price is £15, compared with an actual price of £14 giving a £1 saving per kg. As 10 100 kg were purchased, the total price variance will be £10 100 (10 100kg at £1). The variance for material B is favourable and that for material A is adverse. The normal procedure is to present the amount of the variances followed by symbols A or F to indicate either adverse or favourable variances.

Possible causes

It is incorrect to assume that the material price variance will always indicate the efficiency of the purchasing department. Actual prices may exceed standard prices because of a change in market conditions that causes a general price increase for the type of materials used. The price variance might therefore be beyond the control of the purchasing department. Alternatively, an adverse price variance may reflect a failure by the purchasing department to seek the most advantageous sources of supply. A favourable price variance might be due to the purchase of inferior quality materials, which may lead to inferior product quality or more wastage. For example, the price variance for material B is favourable, but we shall see in the next section that this is offset by excess usage. If the reason for this excess usage is the purchase of inferior quality materials then the material usage variance should be charged to the purchasing department.

It is also possible that another department may be responsible for all or part of the price variance. For example, a shortage of materials resulting from bad inventory control may necessitate an emergency purchase being made at short notice. The supplier may incur additional handling and freight charges on special rush orders, and may therefore charge a higher price for the materials. In this situation the price variance will be the responsibility of the stores department and not the purchasing department.

Calculation on quantity purchased or quantity used

We have noted that the price variance may be due to a variety of causes, some of which will be beyond a company's control, but others of which may be due to inefficiencies. It is therefore important that variances be reported as quickly as possible so that any inefficiencies can be identified and remedial action taken. A problem occurs, however, with material purchases in that the time of purchase and the time of usage may not be the same: materials may be purchased in one period and used in a subsequent period. For example, if 10 000 units of a material are purchased in period 1 at a price of £1 per unit over standard and 2000 units are used in each of periods 1 to 5, the following alternatives are available for calculating the price variance:

1 The full amount of the price variance of £10 000 is reported in *period 1* with quantity being defined as the *quantity purchased*.
2 The price variance is calculated with quantity being defined as the *quantity used*. The unit price variance of £1 is multiplied by the quantity used (i.e. 2000 units), which means that a price variance of £2000 will be reported for each of *periods 1 to 5*.

Method 1 is recommended, because the price variance can be reported in the period in which it is incurred, and reporting of the total variance is not delayed until months later when the materials are used. Also, adopting this approach enables corrective action to be taken earlier. For the sake of simplicity we shall assume in Example 18.1 that the actual purchases are identical with the actual usage.

Material usage variance

The starting point for calculating this quantity variance is simply to compare the standard quantity that should have been used with the actual quantity which has been used. Refer again to Example 18.1. You will see that the standard usage for the production of one unit of sigma is 2 kg for material A. As 9000 units of sigma are produced, 18 000 kg of material A should have been used; however, 19 000 kg are actually used, which means there has been an excess usage of 1000 kg.

The importance of this excess usage depends on the price of the materials. For example, if the price is £0.01 per kg then an excess usage of 1000 kg will not be very significant, but if the price is £10 per unit then an excess usage of 1000 kg will be very significant. It follows that to assess the importance of the excess usage, the variance should be expressed in monetary terms.

Calculation based on standard price or actual price

Should the standard material price per kg or the actual material price per kg be used to calculate the variance? The answer is the standard price. If the *actual* material price is used, the usage variance will be affected by the efficiency of the purchasing department, since any excess purchase price will be assigned to the excess usage. It is therefore necessary to remove the price effects from the usage variance calculation, and this is achieved by valuing the variance at the standard price. Hence the 1000 kg excess usage of material A is multiplied by the standard price of £10 per unit, which gives an adverse usage variance of £10 000. The formula for the variance is

the **material usage variance** is equal to the difference between the standard quantity (SQ) required for actual production and the actual quantity (AQ) used multiplied by the standard material price (SP):

$$(SQ - AQ) \times SP$$

For material B you will see from Example 15.1 that the standard quantity is 9000 kg (9000 units × 1 kg), but 10 100 kg have been used. The excess usage of 1100 kg is multiplied by the standard price of £15 per kg, which gives an adverse variance of £16 500. Note that the principles of flexible budgeting described in Chapter 16 also apply here, with *standard quantity being based on actual production and not budgeted production.* This ensures that a manager is evaluated under the conditions in which he or she actually worked and not those envisaged at the time the budget was prepared.

Possible causes

The material usage variance is normally controllable by the manager of the appropriate production responsibility centre. Common causes of material usage variances include the careless handling of materials by production personnel, the purchase of inferior quality materials, pilferage, changes in quality control requirements, or changes in methods of production. Separate material usage variances should be calculated for each type of material used and allocated to each responsibility centre.

Joint price usage variance

Note that the analysis of the material variance into the price and usage elements is not theoretically correct, since there may be a joint mutual price/quantity effect. The following information is extracted from Example 18.1 for material A:

1 18 000 kg of material A are required, at a standard price of £10 per kg.

2 19 000 kg are used, at a price of £11 per kg.

The purchasing officer might readily accept responsibility for the price variance of £1 per kg for 18 000kg, but may claim that the extra 1000 kg at £1 is more the responsibility of the production foreman. It may be argued that if the foreman had produced in accordance with the standard then the extra 1000 kg would not have been needed.

The foreman, on the other hand, will accept responsibility for the 1000 kg excess usage at a standard price of £10, but will argue that he should not be held accountable for the additional purchase price of £1 per unit.

One possible way of dealing with this would be to report the joint price/quantity variance of £1000 (1000 kg at £1) separately and not charge it to either manager. In other words, the original price variance of £19 000 would be analysed as follows:

	(£)
1. Pure price variance (18 000 kg at £1 per kg)	18 000A
2. Joint price/quantity variance (1000 kg at £1 per kg)	1 000A
	19 000A

The importance of this refinement depends on the significance of the joint variance and the purpose for which price variances are used. For example, if the purchasing officer is paid a bonus depending upon the value of the variance then conflict may arise where the purchasing officer's bonus is reduced because of the impact of an adverse joint price/quantity variance.

Most textbooks recommend that the material price variance be calculated by multiplying the difference between the standard and actual prices by the actual quantity, rather than the standard quantity. Adopting this approach results in the joint price/quantity variance being assigned to the materials price variance. This approach can be justified on the ground that the purchasing manager ought to be responsible for the efficient purchase of all material requirements, irrespective of whether or not the materials are used efficiently by the production departments.

Total material variance

From Figure 18.3 you will see that this variance is the total variance before it is analysed into the price and usage elements. The formula for the variance is

the **total material variance** is the difference between the standard material cost (SC) for the actual production and the actual cost (AC):

$$SC - AC$$

For material A the standard material cost is £20 per unit (see Example 18.1), giving a total standard material cost of £180 000 (9000 units × £20). The actual cost is £209 000, and therefore the variance is £29 000 adverse. The price variance of £19 000 plus the usage variance of £10 000 agrees with the total material variance. Similarly, the total material variance for material B is £6400, consisting of a favourable price variance of £10 100 and an adverse usage variance of £16 500.

Note that if the price variance is calculated on the actual quantity *purchased* instead of the actual quantity *used*, the price variance plus the usage variance will agree with the total variance only when the quantity purchased is equal to the quantity which is used in the particular accounting period. Reconciling the price and usage variance with the total variance is merely a reconciliation exercise, and you should not be concerned if reconciliation of the sub-variances with the total variance is not possible.

Labour variances

The cost of labour is determined by the price paid for labour and the quantity of labour used. Thus a price and quantity variance will also arise for labour. Unlike materials, labour cannot be stored, because the purchase and usage of labour normally takes place at the same time. Hence the actual quantity of hours *purchased* will be equal to the actual quantity of hours *used* for each period. For this reason the price variance plus the quantity variance should agree with the total labour variance.

Wage rate variance

This variance is calculated by comparing the standard price per hour with the actual price paid per hour. In Example 18.1 the standard wage rate per hour is £9 and the actual wage rate is £9.60 per hour, giving a wage rate variance of £0.60 per hour. To determine the importance of the variance, it is necessary to ascertain how many times the excess payment of £0.60 per hour is paid. As 28 500 labour hours are used (see Example 18.1), we multiply 28 500 hours by £0.60. This gives an adverse wage rate variance of £17 100. The formula for the wage rate variance is

the **wage rate variance** is equal to the difference between the standard wage rate per hour (SR) and the actual wage rate (AR) multiplied by the actual number of hours worked (AH):

$$(SR - AR) \times AH$$

Note the similarity between this variance and the material price variance. Both variances multiply the difference between the standard price and the actual price paid for a unit of a resource by the actual quantity of resources used.

Possible causes

The wage rate variance may be due to a negotiated increase in wage rates not yet having been reflected in the standard wage rate. In a situation such as this the variance cannot be regarded as controllable. Unexpected overtime can also be a cause of this variance. Labour rate variances may also occur because a standard is used that represents a single average rate for a given operation performed by workers who are paid at several different rates. In this situation part of all of the variance may be due to the assignment of skilled labour to work that is normally performed by unskilled labour. The variance may then be regarded as the responsibility of the foreman, because he should have matched the appropriate grade of labour to the task at hand. However, the wage rate variance is probably the one that is least subject to control by management. In most cases the variance is due to wage rate standards not being kept in line with changes in actual wage rates, and for this reason it is not normally controllable by departmental managers.

Labour efficiency variance

The labour efficiency variance represents the quantity variance for direct labour. The quantity of labour that should be used for the actual output is expressed in terms of *standard hours produced*. In Example 18.1 the standard time for the production of one unit of sigma is 3 hours. Thus a production level of 9000 units results in an output of 27 000 standard hours. In other words, working at the prescribed level of efficiency, it should take 27 000 hours to produce 9000 units. However, 28 500 direct labour hours are actually required to produce this output, which means that 1500 excess direct labour hours are used. We multiply the excess direct labour hours by the *standard* wage rate to calculate the variance. This gives an adverse variance of £13 500. The formula for calculating the labour efficiency variance is

the **labour efficiency variance** is equal to the difference between the standard labour hours for actual production (SH) and the actual labour hours worked (AH) during the period multiplied by the standard wage rate per hour (SR):

$$(SH - AH) \times SR$$

This variance is similar to the material usage variance. Both variances multiply the difference between the standard quantity and actual quantity of resources consumed by the standard price.

Possible causes

The labour efficiency variance is normally controllable by the manager of the appropriate production responsibility centre and may be due to a variety of reasons. For example, the use of inferior quality materials, different grades of labour, failure to maintain machinery in proper condition, the introduction of new equipment or tools and changes in the production processes will all affect the efficiency of labour. An efficiency variance may not always be controllable by the production foreman; it may be due, for example, to poor production scheduling by the planning department, or to a change in quality control standards.

Total labour variance

From Figure 18.3 you will see that this variance represents the total variance before analysis into the price and quantity elements. The formula for the variance is

the **total labour variance** is the difference between the standard labour cost (SC) for the actual production and the actual labour cost (AC):

$$SC - AC$$

In Example 18.1 the actual production was 9000 units, and, with a standard labour cost of £27 per unit, the standard cost is £243 000. The actual cost is £273 600, which gives an adverse variance of £30 600. This consists of a wage rate variance of £17 100 and a labour efficiency variance of £13 500.

Variable overhead variances

A total variable overhead variance is calculated in the same way as the total direct labour and material variances. In Example 18.1 the output is 9000 units and the standard variable overhead cost is £6 *per unit* produced. The standard cost of production for variable overheads is thus £54 000. The actual variable overheads incurred are £52 000, giving a favourable variance of £2000. The formula for the variance is

the **total variable overhead variance** is the difference between the standard variable overheads charged to production (SC) and the actual variable overheads incurred (AC):

$$SC - AC$$

Where variable overheads vary with direct labour or machine hours of *input* the total variable overhead variance will be due to one or both of the following:

1. A *price* variance arising from actual expenditure being different from budgeted expenditure.
2. A *quantity* variance arising from actual direct labour or machine hours of input being different from the hours of input, which *should* have been used.

These reasons give rise to the two sub-variances, which are shown in Figure 18.3: the variable overhead expenditure variance and the variable overhead efficiency variance.

Variable overhead expenditure variance

To compare the actual overhead expenditure with the budgeted expenditure, it is necessary to flex the budget. Because it is assumed in Example 18.1 that variable overheads will vary with direct labour hours of *input* the budget is flexed on this basis. Actual variable overhead expenditure is £52 000, resulting from 28 500 direct labour hours of input. For this level of activity variable overheads of £57 000, which consist of 28 500 input hours at £2 per hour, should have been spent. Spending was £5000 less than it should have been, and the result is a favourable variance.

If we compare the budgeted and the actual overhead costs for 28 500 direct labour hours of input, we shall ensure that any efficiency content is removed from the variance. This means that any difference must be due to actual variable overhead spending being different from the budgeted variable overhead spending. The formula for the variance is

the **variable overhead expenditure variance** is equal to the difference between the budgeted flexed variable overheads (BFVO) for the actual direct labour hours of input and the actual variable overhead costs incurred (AVO):

$$BFVO - AVO$$

Possible causes

Variable overhead represents the aggregation of a large number of individual items, such as indirect labour, indirect materials, electricity, maintenance and so on. The variable overhead variance can arise because the prices of individual items have changed. Alternatively, the variance can also be affected by how efficiently the individual variable overhead items are used. Waste or inefficiency, such as using more kilowatt-hours of power than should have been used will increase the cost of power and, thus, the total cost of variable overhead. The variable overhead expenditure on its own is therefore not very informative. Any meaningful analysis of this variance requires a comparison of the actual expenditure for each individual item of variable overhead expenditure against the budget. If you refer to the performance report presented in Exhibit 18.8 on pages 755–56, you can see how the £5000 variable overhead expenditure variance can be analysed by individual items of expenditure. Control should be exercised by focusing on the individual line items of the expenditure variances and not the total variance.

Variable overhead efficiency variance

In Example 18.1 it is assumed that variable overheads vary with direct labour hours of input. The variable overhead efficiency variance arises because 28 500 direct labour hours of input were required to produce 9000 units. Working at the prescribed level of efficiency, it should take 27 000 hours to produce 9000 units of output. Therefore an extra 1500 direct labour hours of input were required. Because variable overheads are assumed to vary with direct labour hours of input, an additional £3000 (1500 hours at £2) variable overheads will be incurred. The formula for the variance is

the **variable overhead efficiency variance** is the difference between the standard hours of output (SH) and the actual hours of input (AH) for the period multiplied by the standard variable overhead rate (SR):

$$(SH - AH) \times SR$$

You should note that if it is assumed that variable overheads vary with direct labour hours of input, this variance is identical to the labour efficiency variance. Consequently, the reasons for the variance are the same as those described previously for the labour efficiency variance. If you refer again to Figure 18.3, you will see that the variable overhead expenditure variance (£5000 favourable) plus the variable efficiency variance (£3000 adverse) add up to the total variable overhead variance of £2000 favourable.

Similarities between materials, labour and overhead variances

So far, we have calculated price and quantity variances for direct material, direct labour and variable overheads. You will have noted the similarities between the computations of the three quantity and price variances. For example, we calculated the quantity variances (i.e. material usage, labour efficiency and variable overhead efficiency variances) by multiplying the difference between the standard quantity (SQ) of resources consumed for the actual production and the actual quantity (AQ) of resources consumed by the standard price (SP) per unit of the resource. Thus, the three quantity variances can be formulated as

$$(SQ - AQ) \times SP$$

Note that the standard quantity is derived from determining the quantity that should be used *for the actual production* for the period so that the principles of flexible budgeting are applied.

The price variances (i.e. material price, wage rate and variable overhead expenditure variances) were calculated by multiplying the difference between the standard price (SP) and the actual price (AP) per unit of a resource by the actual quantity (AQ) of resources acquired/used. The price variances can be formulated as

$$(SP - AP) \times AQ$$

This can be re-expressed as

$$(AQ \times SP) - (AQ \times AP)$$

Note that the first term in this formula (with AQ representing actual hours) is equivalent to the budgeted flexed variable overheads that we used to calculate the variable overhead expenditure variance. The last term represents the actual cost of the resources consumed.

We can therefore calculate all the price and quantity variances illustrated so far in this chapter by applying the formulae outlined above.

Fixed overhead expenditure or spending variance

The final variance shown in Figure 18.3 is the fixed overhead expenditure variance. With a variable costing system, fixed manufacturing overheads are not unitized and allocated to products. Instead, the total fixed overheads for the period are charged as an expense to the period in which they are incurred. Fixed overheads are assumed to remain unchanged in the short term in response to changes in the level of activity, but they may change in response to other factors. For example, price increases may cause expenditure on fixed overheads to increase. The fixed overhead expenditure variance therefore explains the difference between budgeted fixed overheads and the actual fixed overheads incurred. The formula for the **fixed overhead expenditure variance** is the difference between the budgeted fixed overheads (BFO) and the actual fixed overhead (AFO) spending:

$$BFO - AFO$$

In Example 18.1 budgeted fixed overhead expenditure is £120 000 and actual fixed overhead spending £116 000. Therefore the fixed overhead expenditure variance is £4000. Whenever the actual fixed overheads are less than the budgeted fixed overheads, the variance will be favourable. The total of the fixed overhead expenditure variance on its own is not particularly informative. Any meaningful analysis of this variance requires a comparison of the actual expenditure for each individual item of fixed overhead expenditure against the budget. The difference may be due to a variety of causes, such as changes in salaries paid to supervisors, or the appointment of additional supervisors. Only by comparing individual items of expenditure and ascertaining the reasons for the variances, can one determine whether the variance is controllable or uncontrollable. Generally, this variance is likely to be uncontrollable in the short term.

Sales variances

Sales variances can be used to analyse the performance of the sales function or revenue centres on broadly similar terms to those for manufacturing costs. The most significant feature of sales variance calculations is that they are calculated in terms of profit or contribution margins rather than sales values. Consider Example 18.2.

You will see that when the variances are calculated on the basis of sales *value*, it is necessary to compare the budgeted sales *value* of £110 000 with the actual sales of £120 000. This gives a favourable variance of £10 000. This calculation, however, ignores the impact of the sales effort on profit. The budgeted profit contribution is £40 000, which consists of 10 000 units at £4 per unit, but the actual impact of the sales effort in terms of profit margins indicates a profit contribution of £36 000, which consists of 12 000 units at £3 per unit, indicating an adverse variance of £4000. If we examine Example 18.2, we can see that the selling prices have been reduced, and that this has led not only to an increase in the total sales revenue but also to a reduction in total profits. The objective of the selling function is to influence favourably total profits. Thus a more meaningful performance measure will be obtained by comparing the results of the sales function in terms of profit or contribution margins rather than sales revenues.

Note that with a standard absorption costing system, *profit* margins are used (selling price less total unit manufacturing cost), whereas with a standard variable costing system, *contribution* margins (selling price less unit manufacturing variable cost) are used to calculate the variances.

Let us now calculate the sales variances for a standard variable costing system from the information contained in Example 18.1.

Total sales margin variance

Where a variable costing approach is adopted, the total sales *margin* variance seeks to identify the influence of the sales function on the difference between budget and actual profit contribution. In Example 18.1 the budgeted profit contribution is £200 000, which consists of budgeted sales of 10 000 units at a contribution of £20 per unit. This is compared with the contribution from the actual sales volume of 9000 units. Because the sales function is responsible for the sales volume and the unit selling price, but not the unit manufacturing costs, the standard cost of sales and not the actual cost of sales is deducted from the actual sales revenue. The calculation of *actual* contribution for ascertaining the total sales margin variance will therefore be as follows:

	(£)
Actual sales revenue (9000 units at £90)	810 000
Standard variable cost of sales for actual sales volume (9000 units at £68)	612 000
Actual profit contribution margin	198 000

To calculate the total sales margin variance, we compare the budgeted contribution of £200 000 with the actual contribution of £198 000. This gives an adverse variance of £2000 because the actual contribution is less that the budgeted profit contribution.

EXAMPLE 18.2

The budgeted sales for a company are £110 000 consisting of 10 000 units at £11 per unit. The standard cost per unit is £7. Actual sales are £120 000 (12 000 units at £10 per unit) and the actual cost per unit is £7.

The formula for calculating the variance is as follows:

the **total sales margin variance** is the difference between the actual contribution (AC) and the budgeted contribution (BC) (both based on standard unit costs):

$$AC - BC$$

Using the standard cost to calculate both the budgeted and the actual contribution ensures that the production variances do not distort the calculation of the sales variances. The effect of using standard costs throughout the contribution margin calculations means that the sales variances arise because of changes in those variables controlled by the sales function (i.e. selling prices and sales quantity). Consequently, Figure 18.3 indicates that it is possible to analyse the total sales margin variance into two sub-variances – a sales margin price variance and a sales margin volume variance.

Sales margin price variance

In Example 18.1 the actual selling price is £90 but the budgeted selling price is £88. With a standard unit variable cost of £68, the change in selling price has led to an increase in the contribution margin from £20 per unit to £22 per unit. Because the actual sales volume is 9000 units, the increase in the selling price means that an increased contribution margin is obtained 9000 times, giving a favourable sales margin price variance of £18 000. The formula for calculating the variance is

the **sales margin price variance** is the difference between the actual contribution margin (AM) and the standard margin (SM) (both based on standard unit costs) multiplied by the actual sales volume (AV):

$$(AM - SM) \times AV$$

Sales margin volume variance

To ascertain the effect of changes in the sales volume on the difference between the budgeted and the actual contribution, we must compare the budgeted sales volume with the actual sales volume. You will see from Example 18.1 that the budgeted sales are 10 000 units but the actual sales are 9000 units, and to enable us to determine the impact of this reduction in sales volume on profit, we must multiply the 1000 units by the standard contribution margin of £20. This gives an adverse variance of £20 000.

The use of the standard margin (standard selling price less standard cost) ensures that the standard selling price is used in the calculation, and the volume variance will not be affected by any *changes* in the actual selling prices. The formula for calculating the variance is

the **sales margin volume variance** is the difference between the actual sales volume (AV) and the budgeted volume (BV) multiplied by the standard contribution margin (SM):

$$(AV - BV) \times SM$$

Difficulties in interpreting sales margin variances

The favourable sales margin price variance of £18 000 plus the adverse volume variance of £20 000 add up to the total adverse sales margin variance of £2000. It may be argued that it is not very meaningful to analyse the total sales margin variance into price and volume components, since changes in selling prices are likely to affect sales volume. Consequently, a favourable price variance will tend to be associated with an adverse volume variance, and vice versa. It may be unrealistic to sell more than the budgeted volume when selling prices have increased.

A further problem with sales variances is that the variances may arise from external factors and may not be controllable by management. For example, changes in selling prices may be the result of a response to changes in selling prices of competitors. Alternatively, a reduction in both selling prices and sales volume may be the result of an economic recession that was not foreseen when the budget was prepared. Manufacturing variances are not influenced as much by external factors, and for this reason management are likely to focus most of their attention on the control of the manufacturing variances. Nevertheless, sales margin variances provide useful information that enables the budgeted profit to be reconciled with the actual profit. However, for control and performance appraisal it is preferable to compare actual market share with target market share for each product. In addition, the trend in market shares should be monitored and selling prices should be compared with competitors' prices.

Reconciling budgeted profit and actual profit

Top management will be interested in the reason for the actual profit being different from the budgeted profit. By adding the favourable production and sales variances to the budgeted profit and deducting the adverse variances, the reconciliation of budgeted and actual profit shown in Exhibit 18.4 can be presented in respect of Example 18.1.

Example 18.1 assumes that Alpha Ltd produces a single product consisting of a single operation and that the activities are performed by one responsibility centre. In practice, most companies make many products, which require operations to be carried out in different responsibility centres. A reconciliation statement such as that presented in Exhibit 18.4 will therefore normally represent a summary of the variances for many responsibility centres. The reconciliation statement thus represents a broad picture to top management that explains the major reasons for any difference between the budgeted and actual profits.

Standard absorption costing

The external financial accounting regulations in most countries require that companies should value inventories at full absorption manufacturing cost. The effect of this is that

EXHIBIT 18.4
Reconciliation of budgeted and actual profits for a standard variable costing system

	(£)	(£)	(£)
Budgeted net profit			80 000
Sales variances:			
Sales margin price	18 000F		
Sales margin volume	20 000A	2 000A	
Direct cost variances:			
Material: Price	8 900A		
Usage	26 500A	35 400A	
Labour: Rate	17 100A		
Efficiency	13 500A	30 600A	
Manufacturing overhead variances:			
Fixed overhead expenditure	4 000F		
Variable overhead expenditure	5 000F		
Variable overhead efficiency	3 000A	6 000F	62 000A
Actual profit			18 000

fixed overheads should be allocated to products and included in the closing inventory valuations. With the variable costing system, fixed overheads are not allocated to products. Instead, the total fixed costs are charged as an expense to the period in which they are incurred. (For a discussion of the differences between variable and absorption costing systems you should refer back to Chapter 7.) With an absorption costing system, an additional fixed overhead variance is calculated. This variance is called a **volume variance**. In addition, the sales margin variances must be expressed in unit *profit* margins instead of *contribution* margins. These variances are not particularly useful for control purposes. If your course does not relate to the disposition of variances to meet financial accounting requirements, you can omit pages 749–53.

With a standard absorption costing system, predetermined fixed overhead rates are established by dividing annual budgeted fixed overheads by the budgeted annual level of activity. We shall assume that in respect of Example 18.1, budgeted annual fixed overheads are £1 440 000 (£120 000 per month) and budgeted annual activity is 120 000 units (10 000 units per month). The fixed overhead rate per unit of output is calculated as follows:

$$\frac{\text{budgeted fixed overheads (£1 440 000)}}{\text{budgeted activity (120 000 units)}} = \text{£12 per unit of sigma produced}$$

We have noted earlier in this chapter that in most situations more than one product will be produced. Where different products are produced, units of output should be converted to standard hours. In Example 18.1 the output of one unit of sigma requires 3 direct labour hours. Therefore, the budgeted output in standard hours is 360 000 hours (120 000 × 3 hours). The fixed overhead rate per standard hour of output is

$$\frac{\text{budgeted fixed overheads (£1 440 000)}}{\text{budgeted standard hours (360 000)}} = \text{£4 per standard hour}$$

By multiplying the number of hours required to produce one unit of Sigma by £4 per hour, we also get a fixed overhead allocation of £12 for one unit of Sigma (3 hours × £4). For the remainder of this chapter output will be measured in terms of standard hours produced.

We shall assume that production is expected to occur evenly throughout the year. Monthly budgeted production output is therefore 10 000 units, or 30 000 standard direct labour hours. At the planning stage an input of 30 000 direct labour hours (10 000 × 3 hours) will also be planned as the company will budget at the level of efficiency specified in the calculation of the product standard cost. Thus the **budgeted hours of input** and the **budgeted hours of output** (i.e. the standard hours produced) will be the same at the planning stage. In contrast, the *actual* hours of input may differ from the *actual* standard hours of output. In Example 18.1 the actual direct labour hours of input are 28 500, and 27 000 standard hours were actually produced.

With an absorption costing system, fixed overheads of £108 000 (27 000 standard hours of output at a standard rate of £4 per hour) will have been charged to products for the month of April. Actual fixed overhead expenditure was £116 000. Therefore, £8000 has not been allocated to products. In other words, there has been an under-recovery of fixed overheads. Where the fixed overheads allocated to products exceeds the overhead incurred, there will be an over-recovery of fixed overheads. The under- or over-recovery of fixed overheads represents the total fixed overhead variance for the period. The total fixed overhead variance is calculated using a formula similar to those for the total direct labour and total direct materials variances:

the **total fixed overhead variance** is the difference between the standard fixed overhead charged to production (SC) and the actual fixed overhead incurred (AC):

SC (£108 000) – AC (£116 000) = £8000A

Note that the standard cost for the actual production can be calculated by measuring production in standard hours of output (27 000 hours × £4 per hour) or units of output (9000 units × £12 per unit).

The under- or over-recovery of fixed overheads (i.e. the fixed overhead variance) arises because the fixed overhead rate is calculated by dividing *budgeted* fixed overheads by *budgeted* output. If actual output or fixed overhead expenditure differs from budget, an under- or over-recovery of fixed overheads will arise. In other words, the under- or over-recovery may be due to the following:

1. A fixed overhead expenditure variance of £4000 arising from actual *expenditure* (£116 000) being different from budgeted *expenditure* (£120 000).
2. A fixed overhead volume variance arising from actual *production* differing from budgeted production.

The fixed overhead expenditure variance also occurs with a variable costing system. The favourable variance of £4000 was explained earlier in this chapter. The volume variance arises only when inventories are valued on an absorption costing basis.

Volume variance

This variance seeks to identify the portion of the total fixed overhead variance that is due to actual production being different from budgeted production. In Example 18.1 the standard fixed overhead rate of £4 per hour is calculated on the basis of a normal activity of 30 000 standard hours per month. Only when actual standard hours produced are 30 000 will the budgeted monthly fixed overheads of £120 000 be exactly recovered. Actual output, however, is only 27 000 standard hours. The fact that the actual production is 3000 standard hours less than the budgeted output hours will lead to a failure to recover £12 000 fixed overhead (3000 hours at £4 fixed overhead rate per hour). The formula for the variance is

the **volume variance** is the difference between actual production (AP) and budgeted production (BP) for a period multiplied by the standard fixed overhead rate (SR):

$$(AP - BP) \times SR$$

The volume variance reflects the fact that fixed overheads do not fluctuate in relation to output in the short term. Whenever actual production is less than budgeted production, the fixed overhead charged to production will be less than the budgeted cost, and the volume variance will be adverse. Conversely, if the actual production is greater than the budgeted production, the volume variance will be favourable.

Sunk cost

Information indicating that actual production is 3000 standard hours less than budgeted production is useful to management, but to attach a fixed overhead rate to this figure is of little value for control because fixed costs represent sunk costs. The volume variance of £12 000 does not reflect the cost of the facilities that remain idle, since the fixed overhead cost will not change if production declines – at least in the short term. A cost of lost output only occurs if a firm has demand for the lost output. In this situation it is more meaningful to measure the cost of the lost output in terms of the lost contribution from a failure to produce the budgeted output. We shall consider this approach in the next chapter.

Possible causes

Changes in production volume from the amount budgeted may be caused by shifts in demand for products, labour disputes, material shortages, poor production scheduling, machine breakdowns, labour efficiency and poor production quality. Some of these factors may be controllable by production or sales management, while others may not.

When the adverse volume variance of £12 000 is netted with the favourable expenditure variance of £4000, the result is equal to the total fixed overhead adverse variance of £8000. It is also possible to analyse the volume variance into two further sub-variances – the volume efficiency variance and the capacity variance.

Volume efficiency variance

If we wish to identify the reasons for the volume variance, we may ask why the actual production was different from the budgeted production. One possible reason may be that the labour force worked at a different level of efficiency from that anticipated in the budget.

The actual number of direct labour hours of input was 28 500. Hence one would have expected 28 500 hours of output (i.e. standard hours produced) from this input, but only 27 000 standard hours were actually produced. Thus one reason for the failure to meet the budgeted output was that output in standard hours was 1500 hours less than it should have been. If the labour force had worked at the prescribed level of efficiency, an additional 1500 standard hours would have been produced, and this would have led to a total of £6000 (£1500 hours at £4 per standard hour) fixed overheads being absorbed. The inefficiency of labour is therefore one of the reasons why the actual production was less than the budgeted production, and this gives an adverse variance of £6000. The formula for the variance is

the **volume efficiency variance** is the difference between the standard hours of output (SH) and the actual hours of input (AH) for the period multiplied by the standard fixed overhead rate (SR):

$$(SH - AH) \times SR$$

You may have noted that the physical content of this variance is a measure of labour efficiency and is identical with the labour efficiency variance. Consequently, the reasons for this variance will be identical with those previously described for the labour efficiency variance. Note also that since this variance is a sub-variance of the volume variance, the same comments apply as to the usefulness of attaching a value for fixed overheads, because fixed overheads represent sunk costs. Total fixed overhead will not change because of the efficiency of labour. Again it would be better to measure this variance in terms of the lost contribution arising from lost sales.

Volume capacity variance

This variance indicates the second reason why the actual production might be different from the budgeted production. The budget is based on the assumption that the direct labour hours of input will be 30 000 hours, but the actual hours of input are 28 500 hours. The difference of 1500 hours reflects the fact that the company has failed to utilize the planned capacity. If we assume that the 1500 hours would have been worked at the prescribed level of efficiency, an additional 1500 standard hours could have been produced and an additional £6000 fixed overhead could have been absorbed. Hence the capacity variance is £6000 adverse.

Whereas the volume efficiency variance indicated a failure to utilize capacity *efficiently*, the volume capacity variance indicates a failure to utilize capacity *at all*. The formula is

the **volume capacity variance** is the difference between the actual hours of input (AH) and the budgeted hours of input (BH) for the period multiplied by the standard fixed overhead rate (SR):

$$(AH - BH) \times SR$$

A failure to achieve the budgeted capacity may be for a variety of reasons. Machine breakdowns, material shortages, poor production scheduling, labour disputes and a reduction in sales demand are all possible causes of an adverse volume capacity variance. Again it is better to express this variance in terms of lost contribution from lost sales caused by a failure to utilize the capacity. It is not very meaningful to attach fixed costs to the variance, since the total fixed costs will not be affected by a failure to utilize capacity.

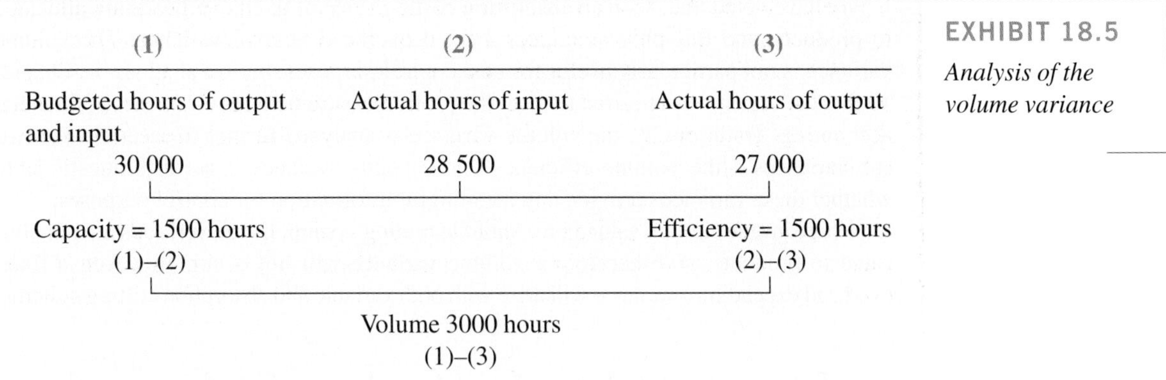

EXHIBIT 18.5 *Analysis of the volume variance*

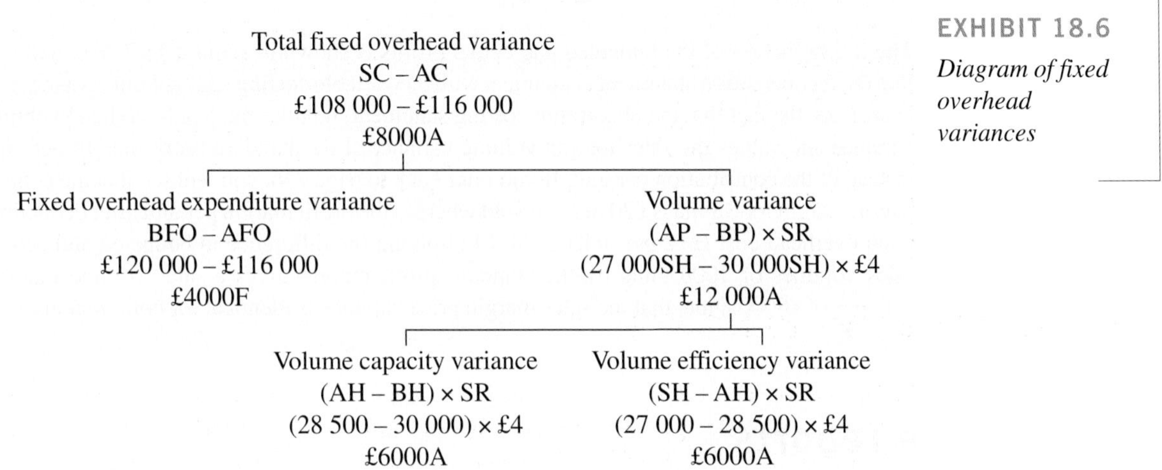

EXHIBIT 18.6 *Diagram of fixed overhead variances*

Summary of fixed overhead variances

The volume efficiency variance is £6000 adverse, and the volume capacity variance is also £6000 adverse. When these two variances are added together, they agree with the fixed overhead volume variance of £12 000. Exhibit 18.5 summarizes how the volume variance is analysed according to capacity and efficiency.

The actual *output* was 3000 hours less than the budget, giving an adverse volume variance. The capacity variance indicates that one reason for failing to meet the budgeted output was that 1500 hours of *capacity* were not utilized. In addition, those 28 500 hours that were utilized only led to 27 000 hours of output. An inefficient use of 1500 hours capacity therefore provides a second explanation as to why the budgeted output was not achieved. A fixed overhead rate of £4 per hour is applied to the physical quantity of the variances, so that fixed overhead variances may be presented in monetary terms. Exhibit 18.6 summarizes the variances we have calculated in this section.

In Example 18.1 we have assumed that fixed overheads are allocated to products on a direct labour hour basis. In automated production departments fixed overheads ought to be allocated on the basis of machine hours. Where machine hours are used as an allocation base, output should be measured in standard machine hours and the fixed overhead variances calculated by replacing direct labour hours with machine hours.

We have noted that, with an absorption costing system, fixed overheads are allocated to products, and this process creates a fixed overhead volume variance. The volume variance is not particularly useful for cost control purposes, but we shall see in Chapter 19 that the variance is required to meet the profit measurement requirements of financial accounting. Traditionally, the volume variance is analysed further to ascertain the two sub-variances – the volume efficiency and capacity variance – but it is questionable whether these variances provide any meaningful information for control purposes.

Where inventories are valued on a variable costing system, fixed overheads are not allocated to products, and therefore a volume variance will not occur. However, a fixed overhead expenditure variance will arise with both variable and absorption costing systems.

Reconciliation of budgeted and actual profit for a standard absorption costing system

The reconciliation of the budgeted and actual profits is shown in Exhibit 18.7. You will see that the reconciliation statement is identical with the variable costing reconciliation statement, apart from the fact that the absorption costing statement includes the fixed overhead volume variance and values the sales margin volume variance at the standard profit margin per unit instead of the contribution per unit. If you refer back to page 736, you will see that the contribution margin for Sigma is £20 per unit sold whereas the profit margin per unit after deducting fixed overhead cost (£12 per unit) is £8. Multiplying the difference in budgeted and actual sales volumes of 1000 units by the standard profit margin gives a sales volume margin variance of £8000. Note that the sales margin price variance is identical for both systems.

Performance reports

The managers of responsibility centres will require a more detailed analysis of the variances to enable them to exercise control, and detailed performance reports should be prepared at monthly or weekly intervals to bring to their attention any significant variances. A typical performance report based on the information contained in Example 18.1 is presented in Exhibit 18.8. A departmental performance report should include only those items that the responsibility manager can control or influence. The material price variance and the monetary amount of the volume variance are *not* presented, since these are not considered to be within the control of the manager of the responsibility centre. However, the volume variance and the two sub-variances (capacity and efficiency) are restated in non-monetary terms in Exhibit 18.8. You can see that these variances have been replaced by the following three control ratios:

$$\text{production volume ratio} = \frac{\text{standard hours of actual output (27 000)}}{\text{budgeted hours of output (30 000)}} \times 100$$
$$= 90\%$$

$$\text{production efficiency ratio} = \frac{\text{standard hours of actual output (27 000)}}{\text{actual hours worked (28 500)}} \times 100$$
$$= 94.7\%$$

$$\text{capacity usage ratio} = \frac{\text{actual hours worked (28 500)}}{\text{budgeted hours of input (30 000)}} \times 100$$
$$= 95\%$$

EXHIBIT 18.7

Reconciliation of budgeted and actual profit for a standard absorption costing system

		(£)	(£)	(£)	(£)
Budgeted net profit					80 000
Sales variances:					
Sales margin price			18 000F		
Sales margin volume			8 000A	10 000F	
Direct cost variances:					
Material – Price:	Material A	19 000A			
	Material B	10 100F	8 900A		
– Usage:	Material A	10 000A			
	Material B	16 500A	26 500A	35 400A	
Labour – Rate			17 100A		
Efficiency			13 500A	30 600A	
Manufacturing overhead variances:					
Fixed – Expenditure		4 000F			
Volume		12 000A	8 000A		
Variable – Expenditure		5 000F			
Efficiency		3 000A	2 000F	6 000A	62 000A
Actual profit					18 000

EXHIBIT 18.8

A typical departmental performance report

DEPARTMENTAL PERFORMANCE REPORT

Department.......................	Actual production	27 000 standard hours
Period........... April 20XX...........	Actual working hours	28 500 hours
	Budgeted hours	30 000 hours

Control ratios: Efficiency 94.7% Capacity 95% Volume 90%

DIRECT MATERIALS

Type	Standard quantity	Actual quantity	Difference	Standard price	Usage variance	Reason
A	18 000 kg	19 000	1000	£10.00	£10 000A	
B	9 000 kg	10 100	1100	£15.00	£16 500A	

DIRECT LABOUR

Grade	Standard hours	Actual hours	Difference	Standard cost	Actual cost	Total variance	Analysis: Efficiency	Analysis: Rate	Reason
	27 000	28 500	1500	£243 000	£273 600	£30 600	£13 500A	£17 100A	

OVERHEADS

	Allowed cost	Actual cost	Expenditure variance	Reason	Variable overhead efficiency variance (hours)	Variable overhead efficiency variance (£)
Controllable costs (variable):						
Indirect labour				Difference		
Power				between	1500	3000A
Maintenance				standard		
Indirect materials				hours and actual hours at £2 per hour		
Total	£57 000	£52 000	£5000F		1500	3000A
Uncontrollable costs (fixed):						
Lighting and heating						
Depreciation						
Supervision						
	£120 000	116 000	4000F			

SUMMARY

	Variances (£) This month (£)	Variances (£) Cumulative (£)	Variances as a % of a standard cost This month (%)	Variances as a % of a standard cost Cumulative (%)
Direct materials usage	26 500A			
Direct labour:				
Efficiency	13 500A			
Wage rate	17 100A			
Controllable overheads:				
Expenditure	5 000F			
Variable overhead	3 000A			
Total	55 100A			

Comments:

You can interpret these ratios in the same way as was described for the equivalent monetary variances. The ratios merely represent the replacement of an *absolute* monetary measure with a *relative* performance measure.

A comparison of current variances with those of previous periods and/or with those of the year to date is presented in the summary of the performance report. This information is often useful in establishing a framework within which current variances can be evaluated. In addition to weekly or monthly performance reports, the manager of a responsibility centre should receive daily reports on those variances that are controllable on a daily basis.

This normally applies to material usage and labour efficiency. For these variances the weekly or monthly performance reports will provide a summary of the information that has previously been reported on a daily basis.

Summary

The following items relate to the learning objectives listed at the beginning of the chapter.

- **Explain how a standard costing system operates.**

  Standard costing is most suited to an organization whose activities consist of a series of repetitive operations and the input required to produce each unit of output can be specified. A standard costing system involves the following: (a) the standard costs for the actual output are recorded for each operation for each responsibility centre; (b) actual costs for each operation are traced to each responsibility centre; (c) the standard and actual costs are compared; (d) variances are investigated and corrective action is taken where appropriate; and (e) standards are monitored and adjusted to reflect changes in standard usage and/or prices.

- **Explain how standard costs are set.**

  Standards should be set for the quantities and prices of materials, labour and services to be consumed in performing each operation associated with a product. Product standard costs are derived by listing and adding the standard costs of operations required to produce a particular product. Two approaches are used for setting standard costs. First, past historical records can be used to estimate labour and material usage. Secondly, standards can be set based on engineering studies. With engineering studies a detailed study of each operation is undertaken under controlled conditions, based on high levels of efficiency, to ascertain the quantities of labour and materials required. Target prices are then applied based on efficient purchasing to ascertain the standard costs.

- **Explain the meaning of standard hours produced.**

  It is not possible to measure output in terms of units produced for a department making several different products or operations. This problem is overcome by ascertaining the amount of time, working under efficient operating conditions, it should take to make each product. This time calculation is called standard hours produced. Standard hours thus represents an output measure that acts as a common denominator for adding together the production of unlike items.

- **Define basic, ideal and currently attainable standards.**

  Basic cost standards represent constant standards that are left unchanged over long periods. Ideal standards represent perfect performance. They represent the minimum costs that are possible under the most efficient operating conditions. Currently attainable standards represent those costs that should be incurred under efficient operating conditions. They are standards that are difficult, but not impossible, to achieve. Currently attainable standards are normally recommended for standard costing.

- **Identify and describe the purposes of a standard costing system.**

  Standard costing systems can be used for the following purposes: (a) providing a prediction of future costs that can be used for decision-making; (b) providing a challenging target which individuals are motivated to achieve; (c) providing a reliable and convenient source of data for budget preparation; (d) acting as a control device by highlighting those activities that do not conform to plan and thus alerting managers to those situations that may be 'out of control' and in need of corrective action; and (e) simplifying the task of tracing costs to products for profit measurement and inventory valuation purpose. Each purpose is described in more detail in Chapter 18.

- **Calculate labour, material, overhead and sales margin variances and reconcile actual profit with budgeted profit.**

  To reconcile actual profit with budget profit the favourable variances are added to the budgeted profit and adverse variances are deducted. The end result should be the actual profit. A summary of the formulae for the computation of the variances is presented in Exhibit 18.9. In each case the formula is presented so that so that a positive variance is favourable and a negative variance unfavourable.

- **Identify the causes of labour, material, overhead and sales margin variances.**

  Quantities cost variances arise because the actual quantity of resources consumed exceed actual usage. Examples include excess usage of materials and labour arising from the usage of inferior materials, careless handling of materials and failure to maintain machinery in proper condition. Price variances arise when the actual prices paid for resources exceed the standard prices. Examples include the failure of the purchasing function to seek the most efficient sources of supply or the use of a different grade of labour to that incorporated in the standard costs.

- **Construct a departmental performance report.**

  For an illustration of a departmental performance report you should refer to Exhibit 18.8.

- **Distinguish between standard variable costing and standard absorption costing.**

  With a standard variable costing system, fixed overheads are not allocated to products. Sales margin variances are therefore reported in terms of contribution margins and a single fixed overhead variance, that is, the fixed overhead expenditure variance is reported. With a standard absorption costing system, fixed overheads are allocated to products and this process leads to the creation of a fixed overhead volume variance and the reporting of sales margin variances measured in terms of profit margins. The fixed overhead volume variance is not particularly helpful for cost control purposes, but this variance is required for financial accounting purposes.

Key terms and concepts

attainable standards (p. 733)
basic cost standards (p. 732)
bill of materials (p. 729)
budgeted costs (p. 726)
budgeted hours of input (p. 750)
budgeted hours of output (p. 750)
capacity usage ratio (p. 754)
engineering studies (p. 729)
fixed overhead expenditure variance (p. 745)
ideal standards (p. 733)
labour efficiency variance (p. 742)
material price variance (p. 737)
material usage variance (p. 739)
production efficiency ratio (p. 754)
production volume ratio (p. 754)
sales margin price variance (p. 747)
sales margin volume variance (p. 748)
standard costs (p. 726)
standard hours (p. 731)
standard hours produced (p. 731)
total fixed overhead variance (p. 750)
total labour variance (p. 742)
total material variance (p. 740)
total sales margin variance (p. 747)
total variable overhead variance (p. 743)
variable overhead efficiency variance (p. 744)
variable overhead expenditure variance (p. 743)
volume capacity variance (p. 752)
volume efficiency variance (p. 752)
volume variance (pp. 749, 751)
wage rate variance (p. 741).

EXHIBIT 18.9

Summary of the formulae for the computation of the variances

The following variances are reported for both variable and absorption costing systems:

Materials and labour

1	Material price variance	=	(standard price per unit of material – actual price) × quantity of materials purchased
2	Material usage variance	=	(standard quantity of materials for actual production – actual quantity used) × standard price per unit
3	Total materials cost variance	=	(actual production × standard material cost per unit of production) – actual materials cost
4	Wage rate variance	=	(standard wage rate per hour – actual wage rate) × actual labour hours worked
5	Labour efficiency variance	=	(standard quantity of labour hours for actual production – actual labour hours) × standard wage rate
6	Total labour cost variance	=	(actual production × standard labour cost per unit of production) – actual labour cost

Fixed production overhead

7	Fixed overhead expenditure	=	budgeted fixed overheads – actual fixed overheads

Variable production overhead

8	Variable overhead expenditure variance	=	(budgeted variable overheads for actual input volume – actual variable overhead cost)
9	Variable overhead efficiency variance	=	(standard quantity of input hours for actual production – actual input hours) × variable overhead rate
10	Total variable overhead variance	=	(actual production × standard variable overhead rate per unit) – actual variable overhead cost

Sales margins

11	Sales margin price variance	=	(actual unit contribution margin* – standard unit contribution margin) × actual sales volume

(*Contribution margins are used with a variable standard costing system whereas profit margins are used with an absorption costing system. With both systems, actual margins are calculated by deducting *standard* costs from actual selling price.)

12	Sales margin volume variance	=	(actual sales volume – budgeted sales volume) × standard contribution margin
13	Total sales margin variance	=	total actual contribution – total budgeted contribution

With a standard absorption costing system the following additional variances can be reported:

14 Fixed overhead volume variance	=	(actual production – budgeted production) × standard fixed overhead rate
15 Volume efficiency variance	=	(standard quantity of input hours for actual production – actual input hours) × standard fixed overhead rate
16 Volume capacity variance	=	(actual hours of input – budgeted hours of input) × standard fixed overhead rate
17 Total fixed overhead variance	=	(actual production × standard fixed overhead rate per unit) – actual fixed overhead cost

Key examination points

A common error that students make is to calculate variances based on the original fixed budget. Remember to flex the budget. Therefore the starting point when answering a standard costing question should be to calculate actual production. If more than one product is produced, output should be expressed in standard hours. If standard overhead rates are not given, you can calculate the rates by dividing budgeted fixed and variable overheads by the budgeted output. Remember that output can be measured by units produced or standard hours produced. Make sure you are consistent and use overhead rates per standard hours if production is measured in standard hours, or overhead rates per unit produced if output is measured in terms of units produced. You should always express output in standard hours if the question requires the calculation of overhead efficiency variances. If the question does not specify whether you should calculate the variances on an absorption costing or variable costing basis, choose your preferred method and state the approach you have selected in your answer.

Frequently questions are set that give you the variances but require calculations of actual costs and inputs (see Review problems 18.25 and 18.26). Students who calculate variances simply by committing to memory a series of variance formulae experience difficulties in answering these questions. Make sure you understand how the variances are calculated, and check your answers with the solutions to the Review problems.

Assessment material

Review questions

The review questions are short questions that enable you to assess your understanding of the main topics included in the chapter. The numbers in parentheses provide you with the page numbers to refer to if you cannot answer a specific question.

Review problems

The review problems are more complex and require you to relate and apply the chapter content to various business problems. The problems are graded by their level of difficulty. The multiple-choice questions are the least demanding and normally take less than 10 minutes to complete. Fully worked solutions to the review problems are provided in a separate section at the end of the book. For those questions in the white box the worked solutions are provided in the *Student's Manual* accompanying this book. Further review problems for this chapter are available on the accompanying website www.drury-online.com. The answers to these problems are available for lecturers on the lecturer's password protected section of the website.

Case studies

The website also includes over 30 case study problems. A list of these cases is provided in Part Seven of this book. Several cases are relevant to the content of this chapter. Examples include Anjo Ltd., Boston Creamery and the Berkshire Toy Company.

Review questions

18.1 Describe the difference between budgeted and standard costs. (*p. 726*)

18.2 Explain how a standard costing system operates. (*pp. 726–28*)

18.3 Describe how standard costs are established using engineering studies. (*pp. 729–30*)

18.4 What are standard hours produced? What purpose do they serve? (*p. 731*)

18.5 What are basic, ideal and currently attainable standards? Which type of standards are usually adopted? Why? (*pp. 732–33*)

18.6 Describe the different purposes of a standard costing system. (*pp. 733–34*)

18.7 What are the possible causes of (a) material price and (b) material usage variances? (*pp. 737, 739*)

18.8 Explain why it is preferable for the material price variance to be computed at the point of purchase rather than the point of issue. (*p. 738*)

18.9 What are the possible causes of (a) wage rate and (b) labour efficiency variances? (*pp. 741–42*)

18.10 Explain how variable overhead efficiency and expenditure variances are computed. What are the possible causes of each of these variances? (*pp. 743–44*)

18.11 Why are sales variances based on contribution margins rather than sales revenues? (*p. 746*)

18.12 Distinguish between a standard absorption and a standard marginal costing system. (*p. 749*)

18.13 What additional variance arises with a standard absorption costing system? Why? (*p. 749*)

18.14 How do sales variances differ between a standard absorption and marginal costing system? (*p. 749*)

18.15 Explain what is meant by a volume variance. Does the volume variance provide any meaningful information for cost control? (*pp. 750–51*)

Review problems

18.16 Intermediate

During a period, 17 500 labour hours were worked at a standard cost of £6.50 per hour. The labour efficiency variance was £7800 favourable.

How many standard hours were produced?

A 1 200
B 16 300
C 17 500
D 18 700

18.17 Intermediate

T plc uses a standard costing system, which is material stock account being maintained at standard costs. The following details have been extracted from the standard cost card in respect of direct materials:

8 kg at £0.80/kg = £6.40 per unit
Budgeted production in April was 850 units.

The following details relate to actual materials purchased and issued to production during April, when actual production was 870 units:

Materials purchased	8200 kg costing £6888
Materials issued to production	7150 kg

Which of the following correctly states the material price and usage variance to be reported?

	Price	Usage
A	£286 (A)	£152 (A)
B	£286 (A)	£280 (A)
C	£286 (A)	£294 (A)
D	£328 (A)	£152 (A)
E	£328 (A)	£280 (A)

CIMA Stage 2

18.18 **Intermediate**

PQ Limited operates a standard costing system for its only product. The standard cost card is as follows:

Direct material (4 kg at £2/kg)	£8.00
Direct labour (4 hours at £4/hour)	£16.00
Variable overhead (4 hours at £3/hour)	£12.00
Fixed overhead (4 hours at £5/hour)	£20.00

Fixed overheads are absorbed on the basis of labour hours. Fixed overhead costs are budgeted at £12 000 per annum, arising at a constant rate during the year.

Activity in period 3 is budgeted to be 10% of total activity for the year. Actual production during period 3 was 500 units, with actual fixed overhead costs incurred being £9800 and actual hours worked being 1970.

The fixed overhead expenditure variance for period 3 was:

A £2200 (F)
B £200 (F)
C £50 (F)
D £200 (A)
E £2200 (A)

CIMA Stage 2

18.19 **Intermediate**

QR Limited uses a standard absorption costing system. The following details have been extracted from its budget for April:

Fixed production overhead cost	£48 000
Production (units)	4 800

In April the fixed production overhead cost was under-absorbed by £8000 and the fixed production overhead expenditure variance was £2000 adverse.

The actual number of units produced was:

A 3800
B 4000
C 4200
D 5400
E 5800

CIMA Stage 2

18.20 Intermediate

F Limited has the following budget and actual data:

Budget fixed overhead cost	£100 000
Budget production (units)	20 000
Actual fixed overhead cost	£110 000
Actual production (units)	19 500

The fixed overhead volume variance:

A is £500 adverse;
B is £2500 adverse;
C is £10 000 adverse;
D is £17 500 adverse;
E cannot be calculated from the data given.

CIMA Stage 2 Specimen Paper

18.21 Intermediate

J Limited operates a standard cost accounting system. The following information has been extracted from its standard cost card and budgets:

Budgeted sales volume	5000 units
Budgeted selling price	£10.00 per unit
Standard variable cost	£5.60 per unit
Standard total cost	£7.50 per unit

If it used a standard marginal cost accounting system and its actual sales were 4500 units at a selling price of £12.00, its sales volume variance would be:

A £1250 adverse
B £2200 adverse
C £2250 adverse
D £3200 adverse
E £5000 adverse

CIMA Stage 2 Specimen Paper

18.22 Intermediate

Bowen has established the following with regard to fixed overheads for the past month:

Actual costs incurred	£132 400
Actual units produced	5000 units
Actual labour hours worked	9750 hours
Budgeted costs	£135 000
Budgeted units of production	4500 units
Budgeted labour hours	9000 hours

Overheads are absorbed on a labour hour basis.

What was the fixed overhead capacity variance?

A £750 favourable
B £11 250 favourable
C £22 500 favourable
D £11 250 adverse.

ACCA Paper 1.2 – Financial information for Management

18.23 Intermediate

The following data are to be used to answer questions (a) and (b) below

W plc uses a standard absorption costing system. The absorption rate is based on labour hours. The following data relates to April 2003:

	Budget	Actual
Labour hours worked	10 000	11 135
Standard hours produced	10 000	10 960
Fixed overhead cost	£45 000	£46 200

(a) The fixed overhead capacity variance to be reported for April 2003 is nearest to

A £5110 (A) B £4710 (A) C £4710 (F) D £5110 (F)

(b) The fixed overhead efficiency variance to be reported for April 2003 is nearest to

A £710 (A) B £730 (A) C £740 (A) D £790 (A)

CIMA Management Accounting – Performance Management

18.24 Intermediate: Variance analysis and reconciliation of actual and budgeted profit

BS Limited manufactures one standard product and operates a system of variance accounting using a fixed budget. As assistant management accountant, you are responsible for preparing the monthly operating statements. Data from the budget, the standard product cost and actual data for the month ended 31 October are given below.

Using the data given, you are required to prepare the operating statement for the month ended 31 October to show the budgeted profit; the variances for direct materials, direct wages, overhead and sales, each analysed into causes; and actual profit.

Budgeted and standard cost data:

Budgeted sales and production for the month: 10 000 units
Standard cost for each unit of product:
Direct material: X: 10 kg at £1 per kg
Y: 5 kg at £5 per kg
Direct wages: 5 hours at £3 per hour
Fixed production overhead is absorbed at 200% of direct wages
Budgeted sales price has been calculated to give a profit of 20% of sales price

Actual data for month ended 31 October:

Production: 9500 units sold at a price of 10% higher than that budgeted
Direct materials consumed:
X: 96 000 kg at £1.20 per kg
Y: 48 000 kg at £4.70 per kg
Direct wages incurred 46 000 hours at £3.20 per hour
Fixed production overhead incurred £290 000

(30 marks)

CIMA Cost Accounting 2

18.25 Intermediate: Calculation of actual input data working back from variances

The following data relate to actual output, costs and variances for the four-weekly accounting period number 4 of a company that makes only one product. Opening and closing work in progress figures were the same.

	(£000)
Actual production of product XY	18 000 units
Actual costs incurred:	
Direct materials purchased and used (150 000 kg)	210
Direct wages for 32 000 hours	136
Variable production overhead	38

	(£000)
Variances:	
Direct materials price	15 F
Direct materials usage	9 A
Direct labour rate	8 A
Direct labour efficiency	16 F
Variable production overhead expenditure	6 A
Variable production overhead efficiency	4 F

Variable production overhead varies with labour hours worked.
A standard marginal costing system is operated.

You are required to:

(a) present a standard product cost sheet for one unit of product XY, *(16 marks)*

(b) describe briefly *three* types of standard that can be used for a standard costing system, stating which is usually preferred in practice and why. *(9 marks)*

(Total 25 marks)

CIMA Cost Accounting Stage 2

18.26 Intermediate: Calculation of actual quantities working backwards from variances

The following profit reconciliation statement summarizes the performance of one of SEWs products for March.

	(£)
Budgeted profit	4250
Sales volume variance	850A
Standard profit on actual sales	3400
Selling price variance	4000A
	(600)

Cost variances:	Adverse (£)	Favourable (£)	
Direct material price		1000	
Direct material usage	150		
Direct labour rate	200		
Direct labour efficiency	150		
Variable overhead expenditure	600		
Variable overhead efficiency	75		
Fixed overhead efficiency		2500	
Fixed overhead volume		150	
Actual profit	1175	3650	2475F
			1875

The budget for the same period contained the following data:

Sales volume		1500 units
Sales revenue	£20 000	
Production volume		1500 units
Direct materials purchased		750 kg
Direct materials used		750 kg
Direct material cost	£4 500	
Direct labour hours		1125
Direct labour cost	£4 500	
Variable overhead cost	£2 250	
Fixed overhead cost	£4 500	

Additional information:

- Stocks of raw materials and finished goods are valued at standard cost.
- During the month the actual number of units produced was 1550.
- The actual sales revenue was £12 000.
- The direct materials purchased were 1000 kg.

Required:

(a) Calculate

(i) the actual sales volume;

(ii) the actual quantity of materials used;

(iii) the actual direct material cost;

(iv) the actual direct labour hours;

(v) the actual direct labour cost;

(vi) the actual variable overhead cost;

(vii) the actual fixed overhead cost.

(19 marks)

(b) Explain the possible causes of the direct materials usage variance, direct labour rate variance and sales volume variance.

(6 marks)

(Total 25 marks)

CIMA Operational Cost Accounting Stage 2

18.27 Advanced: Reconciliation of budgeted and actual profits

The Britten Co. Ltd manufactures a variety of products of basically similar composition. Production is carried out by subjecting the various raw materials to a number of standardized operations, each major series of operations being carried out in a different department. All products are subjected to the same initial processing which is carried out in departments A, B and C; the order and extent of further processing then depending upon the type of end product to be produced.

It has been decided that a standard costing system could be usefully employed within Britten and a pilot scheme is to be operated for six months based initially only on department B, the second department in the initial common series of operations. If the pilot scheme produces useful results then a management accountant will be employed and the system would be incorporated as appropriate throughout the whole firm.

The standard cost per unit of output of department B is:

	(£)	(£)
Direct labour (14 hours at £2 per hour)		28
Direct materials:		
(i) output of department A (3 kg at £9 per kg)	27	
(ii) acquired by and directly input to department B material X (4 kg at £5 per kg)	20	47
Variable overhead (at £1 per direct labour hour worked)		14
Fixed production overheads		
(i) directly incurred by department B (note 1) manufacturing overhead (per unit)	3	
(ii) allocated to department B general factory overhead (per unit)	8	11
Standard cost per unit		£100

In the first month of operation of the pilot study (month 7 of the financial year), department B had no work in progress at the beginning and the end of the month. The actual costs allocated to department B in the first month of operation were:

	(£)	(£)
Direct labour (6500 hours)		14 000
Direct materials:		
(i) output of department A (1400 kg) (note 2)	21 000	
(ii) material X (1900 kg)	11 500	32 500
Variable overhead		8 000
Fixed overhead:		
(i) directly incurred manufacturing overhead	1 600	
(ii) allocated to department B (note 3)	2 900	4 500
		£59 000

Note 1 Based on normal monthly production of 400 units.
Note 2 Actual cost of output of department A.
Note 3 Based on the actual expenditure on joint manufacturing overheads and allocated to departments in accordance with labour hours worked.

The production manager feels that the actual costs of £59 000 for production of 500 units indicates considerable inefficiency on the part of department B. He says, 'I was right to request that the pilot standard costing system be carried out in department B as I have suspected that they are inefficient and careless – this overspending of £9000 proves I am right.'

Required:

(a) Prepare a brief statement which clearly indicates the reasons for the performance of department B and the extent to which that performance is attributable to department B. The statement should utilize variance analysis to the extent it is applicable and relevant.

(14 marks)

(b) Comment on the way the pilot standard costing system is currently being operated and suggest how its operation might be improved during the study period.

(6 marks)

(Total 20 marks)

ACCA P2 Management Accounting

18.28 **Advanced: Comparison of variable and absorption standard costing**

Chimera Ltd makes chimes, one of a variety of products. These products pass through several production processes.

The first process is moulding and the standard costs for moulding chimes are as follows:

	Standard costs per unit	**(£)**
Direct material X	7 kg at £7.00 per kg	49.00
Direct labour	5 hours at £5 per hour	25.00
Overhead (fixed and variable)	5 hours at £6.60 per hour	33.00
		107.00

The overhead allocation rate is based on direct labour hours and comprises an allowance for both fixed and variable overhead costs. With the aid of regression analysis the fixed element of overhead costs has been estimated at £9000 per week, and the variable element of overhead costs has been estimated at £0.60 per direct labour hour. The accounting records do not separate actual overhead costs between their fixed and variable elements.

The moulding department occupies its own premises, and all of the department's overhead costs can be regarded as being the responsibility of the departmental manager.

In week 27 the department moulded 294 chimes, and actual costs incurred were:

Direct material X (2030 kg used)	£14 125
Direct labour (1520 hours worked)	£7 854
Overhead expenditure	£10 200

The 1520 hours worked by direct labour included 40 hours overtime, which is paid at 50% above normal pay rates.

Requirements:

(a) Prepare a report for the moulding department manager on the results of the moulding department for week 27, presenting information in a way which you consider to be most useful.

(9 marks)

(b) Discuss the treatment of overheads adopted in your report and describe an alternative treatment, contrasting its use with the method adopted in your report.

(6 marks)

(c) Describe the approaches used for determining standards for direct costs and assess their main strengths and weaknesses.

(10 marks)

(Total 25 marks)

ICAEW P2 Management Accounting

18.29 Intermediate

A major information source within many businesses is a system of standard costing and variance analysis.

Required:

(a) Describe briefly four purposes of a system of standard costing.

(4 marks)

(b) Explain three different levels of performance which may be incorporated into a system of standard costing and comment on how these may relate to the purposes set out in (a) above.

(6 marks)

(c) Comment on whether standard costing applies in both manufacturing and service businesses and how it may be affected by modern initiatives of continuous performance improvement and cost reduction.

(4 marks)

(d) A standard costing system enables variances for direct costs, variable and fixed overheads to be extracted. Identify and briefly discuss some of the complexities and practical problems in calculation which may limit the usefulness of those variances.

(6 marks)

(Total 20 marks)

ACCA Paper 8 – Managerial Finance

Review problems (with answers in the Student's Manual)

18.30 Intermediate

Despite changes in the environment in which business operates, standard costing and variance analysis may continue to be used in a number of different ways in the operation of a management accounting system. An example of its use would be as a control aid in each accounting period through the investigation of variances.

Required:

Name and explain *five* applications (other than as a control aid each period) of standard costing and/or variance analysis in the operation of a management accounting system.

(15 marks)

ACCA Paper 8 – Managerial Finance

18.31 Intermediate

(a) Outline the uses of standard costing and discuss the reasons why standards have to be reviewed.

(13 marks)

(b) Standard costs are a detailed financial expression of organizational objectives. What non-financial objectives might organizations have? In your answer, identify any stakeholder group that may have a non-financial interest.

(12 marks)
(Total 25 marks)
ACCA Paper 2.4 – Financial Management and Control

18.32 Intermediate: Direct labour and material variances

Newcastle Limited uses variance analysis as a method of cost control. The following information is available for the year ended 30 September 2001:

Budget	Production for the year	12 000 units
	Standard cost per unit:	£
	Direct materials (3 kg at £10/kg)	30
	Direct labour (4 hours at £6/hour)	24
	Overheads (4 hours at £2/hour)	8
		62
Actual	Actual production units for year	11 500 units
	Labour – hours for the year	45 350 hours
	– cost for the year	£300 000
	Materials – kg used in the year	37 250 kg
	– cost for the year	£345 000

Required:

(a) Prepare a reconciliation statement between the original budgeted and actual prime costs.

(7 marks)

(b) Explain what the labour variances calculated in (a) show and indicate the possible interdependence between these variances.

(3 marks)
(Total 10 marks)
ACCA Paper 1.2 – Financial information for Management

18.33 Intermediate: Variance analysis and reconciliation of standard with actual cost

SK Limited makes and sells a single product 'Jay' for which the standard cost is as follows:

		£ per unit
Direct materials	4 kilograms at £12.00 per kg	48.00
Direct labour	5 hours at £7.00 per hour	35.00
Variable production overhead	5 hours at £2.00 per hour	10.00
Fixed production overhead	5 hours at £10.00 per hour	50.00
		143.00

The variable production overhead is deemed to vary with the hours worked.

Overhead is absorbed into production on the basis of standard hours of production and the normal volume of production for the period just ended was 20 000 units (100 000 standard hours of production).

For the period under consideration, the actual results were:

Production of 'Jay'	18 000 units (£)
Direct material used – 76 000 kg at a cost of	836 000
Direct labour cost incurred – for 84 000 hours worked	604 800
Variable production overhead incurred	172 000
Fixed production overhead incurred	1 030 000

You are required

(a) to calculate and show, by element of cost, the standard cost for the output for the period;

(2 marks)

(b) to calculate and list the relevant variances in a way which reconciles the standard cost with the actual cost (*Note*: Fixed production overhead sub-variances of capacity and volume efficiency (productivity) are *not* required).

(9 marks)

(c) to comment briefly on the usefulness to management of statements such as that given in your answer to (b) above.

(4 marks)

(Total 15 marks)

CIMA Stage 2 Cost Accounting

18.34 **Intermediate: Reconciliation of budgeted and actual contribution**

JK plc operates a chain of fast-food restaurants. The company uses a standard marginal costing system to monitor the costs incurred in its outlets. The standard cost of one of its most popular meals is as follows:

		£ per meal
Ingredients	(1.08 units)	1.18
Labour	(1.5 minutes)	0.15
Variable conversion costs	(1.5 minutes)	0.06
The standard selling price of this meal is		1.99

In one of its outlets, which has budgeted sales and production activity level of 50 000 such meals, the number of such meals that were produced and sold during April 2003 was 49 700. The actual cost data was as follows:

		£
Ingredients	(55 000 units)	58 450
Labour	(1 200 hours)	6 800
Variable conversion costs	(1 200 hours)	3 250
The actual revenue from the sale of the meals was		96 480

Required:

(a) Calculate

(i) the total budgeted contribution for April 2003;

(ii) the total actual contribution for April 2003.

(3 marks)

(b) Present a statement that reconciles the budgeted and actual contribution for April 2003. Show all variances to the nearest £1 and in as much detail as possible.

(17 marks)

(c) Explain why a marginal costing approach to variance analysis is more appropriate in environments such as that of JK plc, where there are a number of different items being produced and sold.

(5 marks)
(Total 25 marks)
CIMA Management Accounting – Performance Management

18.35 **Intermediate: Reconciliation of budgeted and actual profit**

ZED plc sells two products, the Alpha and the Beta. These are made from three different raw materials that are bought from local suppliers using a Just-in-Time (JIT) purchasing policy. Products Alpha and Beta are made to customer order using a JIT manufacturing policy. Overhead costs are absorbed using direct labour hours as appropriate.

The following information relates to October 2002:

	Alpha	Beta
Budgeted production (units)	2400	1800

Standard selling price

The standard selling price is determined by adding a 100% mark-up to the standard variable costs of each product.

Standard variable costs per unit	Alpha £	Beta £
Direct material X (£5 per metre)	10.00	12.50
Direct material Y (£8 per litre)	8.00	12.00
Direct material X (£10 per kg)	5.00	10.00
Direct labour (£7 per hour)	14.00	10.50
Variable overhead costs	3.00	2.25

Actual data for October 2002

Direct material X	10 150 metres	costing	£48 890
Direct material Y	5 290 litres	costing	£44 760
Direct material Z	2 790 kg	costing	£29 850
Direct labour	9 140 hours paid	costing	£67 980
Direct labour	8 350 hours worked		
Variable overhead			£14 300
Fixed overhead			£72 000
Actual production	Alpha 3000 units		
	Beta 1500 units		

Sales variances

The following sales variances have been calculated:

	Absorption costing		Marginal costing	
	Alpha	Beta	Alpha	Beta
	£	£	£	£
Selling price	6 000 (A)	4 500 (F)	6 000 (A)	4 500 (F)
Sales volume	18 000 (F)	11 925 (A)	24 000 (F)	14 175 (A)

Required:

(a) Calculate the budgeted fixed overhead cost for October 2002.
(3 marks)

(b) Calculate the budgeted profit for October 2002.
(2 marks)

(c) Calculate the actual profit for October 2002.
(2 marks)

(d) Prepare a statement, using absorption costing principles, that reconciles the budgeted and actual profits for October 2002, showing the variances in as much detail as possible. Do not calculate material mix and yield variances.
(15 marks)

(e) Explain why it would be inappropriate to calculate material mix and yield variances in requirement (d) above.
(3 marks)
(Total 25 marks)

CIMA Management Accounting – Performance Management

18.36 **Intermediate: Calculation of labour variances and actual material inputs working backwards from variances**

A company manufactures two components in one of its factories. Material A is one of several materials used in the manufacture of both components.

The standard direct labour hours per unit of production and budgeted production quantities for a 13-week period were:

	Standard direct labour hours	Budgeted production quantities
Component X	0.40 hours	36 000 units
Component Y	0.56 hours	22 000 units

The standard wage rate for all direct workers was £5.00 per hour. Throughout the 13-week period 53 direct workers were employed, working a standard 40-hour week.

The following actual information for the 13-week period is available:

Production:
Component X, 35 000 units
Component Y, 25 000 units
Direct wages paid, £138 500
Material A purchases, 47 000 kilos costing £85 110
Material A price variance, £430 F
Material A usage (component X), 33 426 kilos
Material A usage variance (component X), £320.32 A

Required:

(a) Calculate the direct labour variances for the period;

(5 marks)

(b) Calculate the standard purchase price for material A for the period and the standard usage of material A per unit of production of component X.

(8 marks)

(c) Describe the steps, and information, required to establish the material purchase quantity budget for material A for a period.

(7 marks)

(Total 20 marks)

ACCA Cost and Management Accounting 1

18.37 **Intermediate: Comparison of absorption and marginal costing variances**

You have been provided with the following data for S plc for September:

Accounting method: Variances:	Absorption (£)	Marginal (£)
Selling price	1900 (A)	1900 (A)
Sales volume	4500 (A)	7500 (A)
Fixed overhead expenditure	2500 (F)	2500 (F)
Fixed overhead volume	1800 (A)	n/a

During September production and sales volumes were as follows:

	Sales	Production
Budget	10 000	10 000
Actual	9 500	9 700

Required:

(a) Calculate:

(i) the standard contribution per unit;

(ii) the standard profit per unit;

(iii) the actual fixed overhead cost total.

(9 marks)

(b) Using the information presented above, explain why different variances are calculated depending upon the choice of marginal or absorption costing.

(8 marks)

(c) Explain the meaning of the fixed overhead volume variance and its usefulness to management.

(5 marks)

(d) Fixed overhead absorption rates are often calculated using a single measure of activity. It is suggested that fixed overhead costs should be attributed to cost units using multiple measures of activity (activity-based costing).

Explain 'activity-based costing' and how it may provide useful information to managers.

(Your answer should refer to both the setting of cost driver rates and subsequent overhead cost control.)

(8 marks)
(Total 30 marks)
CIMA Operational Cost Accounting Stage 2

18.38 Intermediate: Calculation of production ratios

NAB Limited has produced the following figures relating to production for the week ended 21 May:

	Production (in units)	
	Budgeted	**Actual**
Product A	400	400
Product B	400	300
Product C	100	140

Standard production times were:

	Standard hours per unit
Product A	5.0
Product B	2.5
Product C	1.0

During the week 2800 hours were worked on production.

You are required:

(a) (i) to calculate the production volume ratio and the efficiency ratio for the week ended 21 May;

(4 marks)

(ii) to explain the significance of the two ratios you have calculated and to state which variances may be related to each of the ratios;

(5 marks)

(b) to explain the three measures of capacity referred to in the following statement:

During the recent recession, increased attention was paid to 'practical capacity' and 'budgeted capacity' because few manufacturing companies could anticipate working again at 'full capacity'.

(6 marks)
(Total 15 marks)
CIMA Stage 2 Cost Accounting

Standard costing and variance analysis 2: further aspects

19

In the previous chapter we examined the principles of standard costing variance analysis. We are now going to consider how the material usage and the sales margin volume variance can be further analysed, and look at the accounting entries that are necessary to record the variances. We shall then turn our attention to considering more meaningful approaches to variance analysis and identify the factors that should be taken into account in deciding whether or not it is worthwhile investigating variances. Finally, we shall consider the future role of standard costing and examine the implications of ABC for traditional flexible budgeting and variance analysis.

With the exception of the accounting entries for a standard costing system all of the topics covered in this chapter are more appropriate to a second-year management accounting course. It is recommended that you read the relevant topics appropriate to your course of study rather than reading the chapter from start to finish. However, the sections

LEARNING OBJECTIVES

After studying this chapter, you should be able to:

- explain and calculate material mix and yield and sales mix and quantity variances;
- explain the criticisms of sales margin variances;
- prepare a set of accounts for a standard costing system;
- explain and calculate planning and operating variances;
- explain and calculate variances using the opportunity cost approach to variance analysis;
- explain the factors that influence the decision to investigate a variance and describe the different methods that can be used to determine whether an investigation is warranted;
- comment on the future role of standard costing;
- explain the role of standard costing within an ABC system.

relating to the future role of standard costing and the implications of ABC for traditional variance analysis should be regarded as essential reading for all second-year management accounting students.

Direct materials mix and yield variances

In many industries, particularly of the process type, it is possible to vary the mix of input materials and affect the yield. Where it is possible to combine two or more raw materials, input standards should be established to indicate the target mix of materials required to produce a unit, or a specified number of units, of output. Laboratory and engineering studies are necessary in order to determine the standard mix. The costs of the different material mixes are estimated, and a standard mix is determined based on the mix of materials that minimizes the cost per unit of output but still meets the quality requirements. Trade-offs may occur. For example, cost increases arising from using better quality materials may be offset by a higher yield, or vice versa.

By deviating from the standard mix of input materials, operating managers can affect the yield and cost per unit of output. Such deviations can occur as a result of a conscious response to changes in material prices, or alternatively may arise from inefficiencies and a failure to adhere to the standard mix. By computing mix and yield variances, we can provide an indication of the cost of deviating from the standard mix.

Mix variance

The **material mix variance** arises when the mix of materials used differs from the predetermined mix included in the calculation of the standard cost of an operation. If the mixture is varied so that a larger than standard proportion of more expensive materials is used, there will be an unfavourable variance. When a larger proportion of cheaper materials is included in the mixture, there will be a favourable variance. Consider Example 19.1.

The total input for the period is 100 000 litres, and, using the standard mix, an input of 50 000 litres of X (5/10 × 100 000), 30 000 litres of Y (3/10 × 100 000) and 20 000 litres of Z (2/10 × 100 000) should have been used. However, 53 000 litres of X, 28 000 litres of Y and 19 000 litres of Z were used. Therefore 3000 additional litres of X at a standard price of £7 per litre were substituted for 2000 litres of Y (at a standard price of £5 per litre) and 1000 litres of Z (at a standard price of £2 per litre). An adverse material mix variance of £9000 will therefore be reported. The formula for the material mix variance is as follows:

(actual quantity in standard mix proportions – actual quantity used) × standard price

If we apply this formula, the calculation is as follows:

Actual usage in standard proportions:

		(£)
X = 50 000 litres (5/10 × 100 000) at	£7	350 000
Y = 30 000 litres (3/10 × 100 000) at	£5	150 000
Z = 20 000 litres (2/10 × 100 000) at	£2	40 000
		540 000

EXAMPLE 19.1

The Milano company has established the following standard mix for producing 9 litres of product A:

	(£)
5 litres of material X at £7 per litre	35
3 litres of material Y at £5 per litre	15
2 litres of material Z at £2 per litre	4
	£54

A standard loss of 10% of input is expected to occur. Actual input was

	(£)
53 000 litres of material X at £7 per litre	371 000
28 000 litres of material Y at £5.30 per litre	148 400
19 000 litres of material Z at £2.20 per litre	41 800
100 000	£561 200

Actual output for the period was 92 700 litres of product A.

Actual usage in actual proportions:

	(£)
X = 53 000 litres at £7	371 000
Y = 28 000 litres at £5	140 000
Z = 19 000 litres at £2	38 000
	549 000
mix variance =	£9 000 A

Note that standard prices are used to calculate the mix variance to ensure that the price effects are removed from the calculation. An adverse mix variance will result from substituting more expensive higher quality materials for cheaper materials. Substituting more expensive materials may result in a boost in output and a favourable yield variance. On the other hand, a favourable mix variance will result from substituting cheaper materials for more expensive materials – but this may not always be in a company's best interests, since the quality of the product may suffer or output might be reduced. Generally, the use of a less expensive mix of inputs will mean the production of fewer units of output than standard. This may be because of excessive evaporation of the input units, an increase in rejects due to imperfections in the lower quality inputs, or other similar factors. To analyse the effect of changes in the quantity of outputs from a given mix of inputs, a yield variance can be calculated. It is important that the standard mix be continuously reviewed and adjusted where necessary, since price changes may lead to a revised standard mix.

Direct materials yield variance

The **materials yield variance** arises because there is a difference between the standard output for a given level of inputs and the actual output attained. In Example 19.1 an input of 100 000 litres should have given an output of 90 000 litres of product A. (Every 10 litres of input should produce 9 litres of output.) In fact, 92 700 litres were produced, which means that the output was 2700 litres greater than standard. This output is valued at the average standard cost per unit of *output*, which is calculated as follows.

Each 10 litres of *input* is expected to yield 9 litres of *output*.
The standard cost for this output is £54.
Therefore the standard cost for one litre of *output* = 54 × 1/9 = £6.

The yield variance will be £6 × 2700 = £16 200F. The formula is as follows:

(actual yield – standard yield from actual input of material)
× standard cost per unit of output
= (92 700 litres – 90 000 litres) × £6 = £16 200F

An adverse yield variance may arise from a failure to follow standard procedures. For example, in the steel industry a yield variance may indicate that the practice that was followed for pouring molten metal may have been different from that which was determined as being the most efficient when the standard yield was calculated. Alternatively, the use of inferior quality materials may result in an adverse yield variance.

The material mix variance in Example 19.1 is £9000 adverse, while the material yield variance is £16 200 favourable. There was a trade-off in the material mix, which boosted the yield. This trade-off may have arisen because the prices of materials Y and Z have increased whereas the actual price paid for material X is identical with the standard price. The manager of the production process may have responded to the different relative prices by substituting material X (the most expensive material) for materials Y and Z. This substitution process has resulted in an adverse mix variance and a favourable yield variance. Note, however, that actual material cost per unit of output is £6.05 (£561 200/92 700 litres) whereas the standard cost per unit is £6 (£54/9 litres). You will find that this difference has been partly caused by an adverse material price variance of £12 200.

At this stage you should be aware that materials price, mix and yield variances are inter-related and that individual variances should not be interpreted in isolation. Interdependencies should be recognized. You should also note that changes in relative input prices of materials will affect the optimal standard mix and yield of materials. Where significant changes in input prices occur, the actual mix and yield should be compared with a revised *ex post* standard mix and yield. We shall discuss the *ex post* approach later in this chapter.

Material usage variance

The material usage variance consists of the mix variance and the yield variance. The material usage variance is therefore a favourable variance of £7200, consisting of an adverse mix variance of £9000 and a favourable yield variance of £16 200. To calculate the material usage variance, we compare the standard quantity of materials for the actual production with the actual quantity of materials used and multiply by the standard material prices in the normal way. The calculations are as follows:

Standard quality for actual production at standard prices:

Actual production of 92 700 litres requires an input of 103 000 litres (92 700 × 10/9), consisting of

	(£)
51 500 litres of X (103 000 × 5/10) at £7 per litre	= 360 500
30 900 litres of Y (103 000 × 3/10) at £5 per litre	= 154 500
20 600 litres of Z (103 000 × 2/10) at £2 per litre	= 41 200
	556 200 (i)

Actual quantity at standard prices:

	(£)
53 000 litres of X at £7 per litre	= 371 000
28 000 litres of Y at £5 per litre	= 140 000
19 000 litres of Z at £2 per litre	= 38 000
	549 000 (ii)
Material usage variance (i) – (ii)	= £7 200 F

Note that the standard quantity for actual production at standard prices can also be calculated by multiplying the actual output by the standard cost per unit of output (92 700 × £6 = £556 200).

Summary of material variances

The total material variance and the price variances are calculated using the approaches described in the previous chapter. The calculations are as follows:

Total material variance:	
Standard cost for actual production (92 700 × £6)	= £556 200
– Actual cost	(£561 200)
	= £5 000 A

Material price variances, (standard price – actual price) × actual quantity:

Material X = (£7 – £7) × 53 000	= 0
Material Y = (£5 – £5.30) × 28 000	= £8 400 A
Material Z = (£2 – £2.20) × 19 000	= £3 800 A
	£12 200 A

We have already noted that these variances may be inter-related. The manager of the production process may have responded to the price increases by varying the mix of inputs, which in turn may affect the yield of the process. The decomposition of the total material variance into price, mix and yield components highlights different aspects of the production process and provides additional insights to help managers to attain the optimum combination of materials input.

You should note that mix and yield variances are appropriate only to those production processes where managers have the discretion to vary the mix of materials and deviate from engineered input–output relationships. Where managers control each input on an individual basis and have no discretion regarding the substitution of materials, it is inappropriate to calculate mix and yield variances. For example, there is often a predetermined mix of components needed for the assembly of washing machines, television sets and vacuum cleaners. In these production processes deviations from standard usage are related to efficiency of material usage rather than to changes in the physical mix of material inputs.

The same approach as that used to determine material mix and yield variances can also be applied to direct labour where it is possible to combine two or more grades of labour to perform specific operations. Given that the variance calculations for labour mix and yield variances are identical with the procedures described in this section, the computations will not be illustrated.

Sales mix and sales quantity variances

Where a company sells several different products that have different profit margins, the sales volume margin variance can be divided into a sales quantity (sometimes called a sales yield variance) and sales mix variance. This division is commonly advocated in textbooks. The quantity variance measures the effect of changes in physical volume on total profits, and the mix variance measures the impact arising from the actual sales mix being different from the budgeted sales mix. The variances can be measured either in terms of contribution margins or profit margins. However, contribution margins are recommended because changes in sales volume affect profits by the contribution per unit sold and not the profit per unit sold. Let us now calculate the sales margin mix and quantity variances. Consider Example 19.2.

The **total sales margin variance** is £4000 adverse, and is calculated by comparing the difference between the budgeted total contribution and the actual contribution. Contribution margins for the three products were exactly as budgeted. The total sales margin for the period therefore consists of a zero **sales margin price variance** and an adverse **sales margin volume variance** of £4000. Even through more units were sold than anticipated (22 000 rather than the budgeted 20 000), and budgeted and actual contribution margins were the same, the sales volume variance is £4000 adverse. The reasons for this arises from having sold fewer units of product X, the high margin product, and more units of product Z, which has the lowest margin.

We can explain how the sales volume margin variance was affected by the change in sales mix by calculating the **sales margin mix variance**. The formula for calculating this variance is

(actual sales quantity – actual sales quantity in budgeted proportions)
× standard margin

If we apply this formula, we will obtain the following calculations:

	Actual sales quantity	Actual sales in budgeted proportions	Difference	Standard margin (£)	Sales margin mix variance (£)
Product X	6 000 (27%)	8 800 (40%) =	–2800	20	56 000A
Y	7 000 (32%)	7 700 (35%) =	–700	12	8 400A
Z	9 000 (41%)	5 500 (25%) =	+3500	9	31 500F
	22 000	22 000			32 900A

EXAMPLE 19.2

The budgeted sales for the Milano company for a period were

	Units	Unit contribution margin (£)	Total contribution (£)
Product X	8 000 (40%)	20	160 000
Y	7 000 (35%)	12	84 000
Z	5 000 (25%)	9	45 000
	20 000		289 000

and the actual sales were

	Units (£)	Unit contribution margin (£)	Total contribution
Product X	6 000	20	120 000
Y	7 000	12	84 000
Z	9 000	9	81 000
	22 000		285 000

You are required to calculate the sales margin variances.

To compute the sales quantity component of the sales volume variance, we compare the budgeted and actual sales volumes (holding the product mix constant). The formula for calculating the **sales quantity variance** is

(actual sales quantity in budgeted proportion – budgeted sales quantity)
× standard margin

Applying this formula gives the following calculations:

	Actual sales in budgeted proportions	Budgeted sales quantity	Difference	Standard margin (£)	Sales margin quantity variance (£)
Product X	8 800 (40%)	8 000 (40%)	+800	20	16 000F
Y	7 700 (35%)	7 000 (35%)	+700	12	8 400F
Z	5 500 (25%)	5 000 (20%)	+500	9	4 500F
	22 000	20 000			28 900F

The sales quantity variance is sometimes further divided into a market size and a market share variance. A summary of the sales margin variances is presented in Figure 19.1. Before considering the market size and market share variances, we shall discuss the sales variances we have calculated so far in respect of Example 19.2.

By separating the sales volume variance into quantity and mix variances, we can explain how the sales volume variance is affected by a shift in the total physical volume of

FIGURE 19.1 *Summary of sales variances*

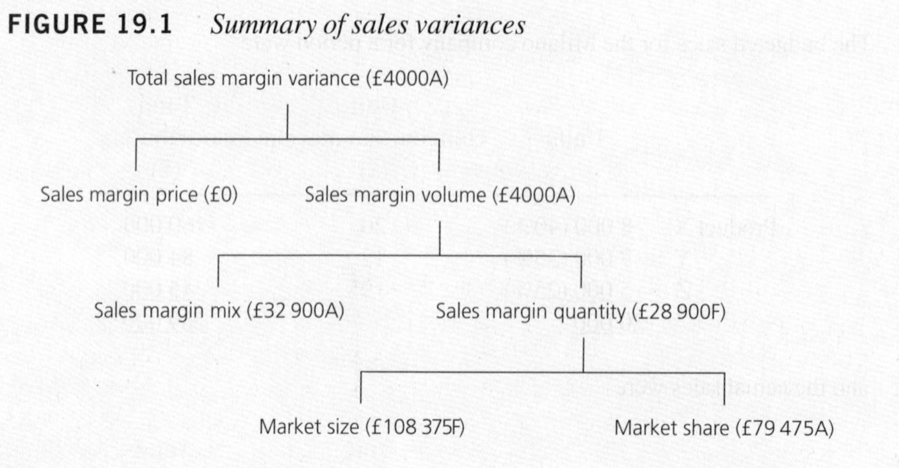

sales and a shift in the relative mix of products. The sales volume quantity variance indicates that if the original planned sales mix of 40% of X, 35% of Y and 25% of Z had been maintained then, for the actual sales volume of 22 000 units, profits would have increased by £28 900. In other words, the sales volume variance would have been £28 900 favourable instead of £4000 adverse. However, because the actual sales mix was not in accordance with the budgeted sales mix, an adverse mix variance of £32 900 occurred. The adverse sales mix variance has arisen because of an increase in the percentage of units sold of product Z, which has the lowest contribution margin, and a decrease in the percentage sold of units of product X, which has the highest contribution margin. An adverse mix variance will occur whenever there is an increase in the percentage sold of units with below average contribution margins or a decrease in the percentage sold of units with above average contribution margins. The division of the sales volume variance into quantity and mix components demonstrates that increasing or maximizing sales volume may not be as desirable as promoting the sales of the most desirable mix of products.

Market size and share variances

Where published industry sales statistics are readily available, it is possible to divide the sales quantity variance into a component due to changes in market size and a component due to changes in market share. Suppose that the budgeted industry sales volume for the illustrative company in Example 19.2 was 200 000 units and a market share of 10% was predicted. Assume also that the actual industry sales volume was 275 000 units and the company obtained a market share of 8 per cent (8% × 275 000 = 22 000 units). The formulae and calculations of the **market size** and **market share variances** are as follows:

$$\text{market size variance} = \begin{bmatrix}\text{budgeted}\\\text{market}\\\text{share}\\\text{percentage}\end{bmatrix} \times \begin{bmatrix}\text{actual} & & \text{budgeted}\\\text{industry} & & \text{industry}\\\text{sales} & - & \text{sales}\\\text{volume} & & \text{volume}\\\text{in units} & & \text{in units}\end{bmatrix} \times \begin{bmatrix}\text{budgeted}\\\text{average}\\\text{contribution}\\\text{margin}\\\text{per unit}\end{bmatrix}$$

$$= 10\% \times (275\,000 - 200\,000) \times £14.45^*$$

$$= £108\,375\text{F}$$

(*budgeted company total contribution (£289 000)/budgeted sales volume in units (20 000))

$$\text{market size variance} = \left[\begin{array}{c}\text{actual}\\\text{market}\\\text{share}\\\text{percentage}\end{array} - \begin{array}{c}\text{budgeted}\\\text{market}\\\text{share}\\\text{percentage}\end{array}\right] \times \left[\begin{array}{c}\text{actual}\\\text{industry}\\\text{sales}\\\text{volume}\\\text{in units}\end{array} \times \begin{array}{c}\text{budgeted}\\\text{average}\\\text{contribution}\\\text{margin}\\\text{per unit}\end{array}\right]$$

$$= (8\% - 10\%) \times 275\,000 \times £14.45$$

$$= £79\,475\text{A}$$

The market size variance indicates that an additional contribution of £108 375 was expected, given that the market expanded from 200 000 to 275 000 units. However, the company did not attain the predicted market share of 10%. Instead, a market share of only 8% was attained, and the 2% decline in market share resulted in a failure to obtain a contribution of £79 475. Hence the sum of the market size variance (£108 375F) and the market share variance (£79 475A) equals the sales margin quantity variance of £28 900.

Using the budgeted average contribution per unit in the formulae for the market size and share variances implies that we are assuming that budgeted and actual industry sales mix is the same as company's sales mix of 40% of X, 35% of Y and 25% of Z. Market size and share variances provide more meaningful information where the market size for each individual product can be ascertained.

Criticisms of sales margin variances

Sales margin price and volume variances and the decomposition of the volume variance into mix and yield variances are commonly advocated in textbooks. However, some writers (e.g. Manes, 1983) question the usefulness of sales variance analysis on the grounds that in an imperfectly competitive market structure, prices and quantities are interrelated. Given price elasticity, the logical consequence of lower/higher sales prices is higher/lower volume. Thus the relevant analysis based on these variances are also interrelated. Consequently, it is argued that sales margin variance analysis does not generate any meaningful results.

Several writers have also argued that it is inappropriate to separate the sales volume variance into mix and quantity variances. Bastable and Bao (1988) illustrate two different approaches advocated in the literature to calculate mix and yield variances. The first approach calculates weights in terms of physical quantities whereas the second uses sales dollars. Bastable and Bao show that the two approaches generate divergent results in many situations. Because of this deficiency they argue that decomposing the sales volume variance into mix and quantity variances is misleading and has the potential for more harm than good.

Gibson (1990) advocates that mix and quantity variances provide useful information only where there is an identifiable relationship between the products sold and these relationships are incorporated into the planning process. Where relationships between products are not expected, the budgeted contribution for a period is derived from separate estimates of physical volumes and prices of each product. The mix that emerges from the combination of the *separate* estimates for each product does not constitute a planned mix. Gibson therefore argues that providing management with mix and quantity variances, where there is no identified relationship between the sales volume of individual products, is misleading because it incorrectly implies that a possible cause of the sales volume variance is a change in mix. The only possible 'causes' that require investigation are simply deviations from planned volumes for the individual products. Gibson (1990) provides the following examples of situations where identifiable relationships exist:

the sale, by the firm of a number of similar products (differentiated by single characteristics such as size) where sales of individual products are expected *to vary proportionally with total sales; the sale of complementary products (where increased sales of one product are* expected *to result in increased sales in another); the sale of product substitutes (where increased sales of one product are expected to result in decreased sales of another); and the sale of heterogeneous products, the quantities of which are limited by factors of production (for example, where the sale of products with lower contribution margins per limiting resource factor is made only if products with higher contribution margins cannot be sold). (Page 38.)*

Gibson identifies two possible situations where a planned relationship between the sales of products could be incorporated into the planning model. The first relates to where the total sales of individual products are expected to occur in a constant mix, such as different sizes of a particular product. In this situation management would be interested in how the volume variance has been affected by deviations from the planned mix. The second relates to situations where sales of products in a group are expected to vary in proportion to sales of a 'critical' product, such as where other products are complementary to, or substitutes for, the 'critical' product.

Recording standard costs in the accounts

If you are not studying for a specialist accounting qualification it is possible that your curriculum may not include the recording of standard costs. You should therefore check whether or not this topic is included in your curriculum to ascertain if you need to read this section. Standard costs can be used for planning, control, motivation and decision-making purposes without being entered into the books. However, the incorporation of standard costs into the cost accounting system greatly simplifies the task of tracing costs for inventory valuation and saves a considerable amount of data processing time. For example, if raw material stocks are valued at standard cost, the stock records may be maintained in terms of physical quantities only. The value of raw materials stock may be obtained simply by multiplying the physical quantity of raw materials in stock by the standard cost per unit. This avoids the need to record stocks on a first-in, first-out or average cost basis. The financial accounting regulations in most countries specify that inventory valuations based on standard costs may be included in externally published financial statements, provided the standard costs used are current and attainable. Most companies that have established standard costs therefore incorporate them into their cost accounting recording system.

Variations exist in the data accumulation methods adopted for recording standard costs, but these variations are merely procedural and the actual inventory valuations and profit calculations will be the same whichever method is adopted. In this chapter we shall illustrate a standard absorption costing system that values all inventories at standard cost, and all entries that are recorded in the inventory accounts will therefore be at *standard prices*. Any differences between standard costs and actual costs are debited or credited to variance accounts. Adverse variances will appear as debit balances, since they are additional costs in excess of standard. Conversely, favourable variances will appear as credit balances. Only production variances are recorded, and sales variances are not entered in the accounts.

Let us now consider the cost accounting records, for Example 18.1, which was presented in the previous chapter. We shall assume that the company operates an integrated cost accounting system. The variances recorded in the accounts will be those we calculated in Chapter 18 for an absorption costing system, and we need not therefore explain them again here but if you cannot remember the variance calculations, turn back now to Chapter 18 to refresh your memory. To keep things simple and to avoid confusion, we shall now repeat Example 18.1 and the reconciliation of actual and budgeted profits for this example (which was Exhibit 18.7 in the previous chapter).

Let us now consider the accounting entries for Example 18.1. The appropriate ledger entries are presented in Exhibit 19.1. Each ledger entry and journal entry has been labelled with numbers from 1 to 13 to try to give you a clear understanding of each accounting entry.

Purchase of materials

19 000 kg of raw material A at £11 per kg and 10 100 kg of raw material B at £14 per kg were purchased. This gives a total purchase cost of £209 000 for A and £141 400 for B. The standard prices were £10 per kg for A and £5 per kg for B. The accounting entries for material A are

1. Dr Stores ledger control account (AQ × SP)	190 000	
1. Dr Material price variance account	19 000	
1. Cr Creditors control account (AQ × AP)		209 000

You will see that the stores ledger control account is debited with the standard price (SP) for the actual quantity purchased (AQ), and the actual price (AP) to be paid is credited to the creditors control account. The difference is the material price variance. The accounting entries for material B are

2. Dr Stores ledger control account (AQ × SP)	151 500	
2. Cr Material price variance account		10 100
2. Cr Creditors (AQ × AP)		141 400

Usage of materials

19 000 kg of A and 10 100 kg of B were actually issued, and the standard usage (SQ) was 18 000 and 9000 kg at standard prices of £10 and £15. The accounting entries for material A are

3. Dr Work in progress (SQ × SP)	180 000	
3. Dr Material usage variance	10 000	
3. Cr Stores ledger control account (AQ × SP)		190 000

Work in progress is debited with the standard quantity of materials at the standard price and the stores ledger account is credited with the actual quantity issued at the standard price. The difference is the material usage variance. The accounting entries for material B are

4. Dr Work in progress (SQ × SP)	135 000	
4. Dr Material usage variance	16 500	
4. Cr Stores ledger control account (AQ × SP)		151 500

EXAMPLE 18.1
[From Chapter 18]

Alpha manufacturing company produces a single product, which is known as sigma. The product requires a single operation, and the standard cost for this operation is presented in the following standard cost card:

Standard cost card for product sigma	(£)
Direct materials:	
2 kg of A at £10 per kg	20.00
1 kg of B at £15 per kg	15.00
Direct labour (3 hours at £9 per hour)	27.00
Variable overhead (3 hours at £2 per direct labour hour)	6.00
Total standard variable cost	68.00
Standard contribution margin	20.00
Standard selling price	88.00

Alpha Ltd plan to produce 10 000 units of sigma in the month of April, and the budgeted costs based on the information contained in the standard cost card are as follows:

Budget based on the above standard costs and an output of 10 000 units

	(£)	(£)	(£)
Sales (10 000 units of sigma at £88 per unit)			880 000
Direct materials:			
A: 20 000 kg at £10 per kg	200 000		
B: 10 000 kg at £15 per kg	150 000	350 000	
Direct labour (30 000 hours at £9 per hour)		270 000	
Variable overheads (30 000 hours at £2 per direct labour hour)		60 000	680 000
Budgeted contribution			200 000
Fixed overheads			120 000
Budgeted profit			80 000

Annual budgeted fixed overheads are £1 440 000 and are assumed to be incurred evenly throughout the year. The company uses a variable costing system for internal profit measurement purposes.

The actual results for April are:

	(£)	(£)
Sales (9000 units at £90)		810 000
Direct materials:		
A: 19 000 kg at £11 per kg	209 000	
B: 10 100 kg at £14 per kg	141 400	
Direct labour (28 500 hours at £9.60 per hour)	273 600	
Variable overheads	52 000	676 000
Contribution		134 000
Fixed overheads		116 000
Profit		18 000

Manufacturing overheads are charged to production on the basis of direct labour hours. Actual production and sales for the period were 9000 units.

		(£)	(£)	(£)	(£)
Budgeted net profit					80 000
Sales variances:					
Sales margin price			18 000 F		
Sales margin volume			8 000 A	10 000 F	
Direct cost variances					
Material – Price:	Material A	19 000 A			
	Material B	10 100 F	8 900 A		
Usage:	Material A	10 000 A			
	Material B	16 500 A	26 500 A	35 400 A	
Labour – Rate			17 100 A		
Efficiency			13 500 A	30 600 A	
Manufacturing overhead variances					
Fixed – Expenditure		4 000 F			
Volume		12 000 A	8 000 A		
Variable – Expenditure		5 000 F			
Efficiency		3 000 A	2 000 F	6 000 A	62 000 A
Actual profit					18 000

EXHIBIT 18.7
[from Chapter 18]
Reconciliation of budgeted and actual profits for April

Direct wages

The actual hours worked were 28 500 hours for the month. The standard hours produced were 27 000. The actual wage rate paid was £9.60 per hour, compared with a standard rate of £9 per hour. The actual wages cost is recorded in the same way in a standard costing system as an actual costing system. The accounting entry for the actual wages paid is

5. Dr Wages control account	273 600	
5. Cr Wages accrued account		273 600

The wages control account is then cleared as follows:

6. Dr Work in progress (SQ × SP)	243 000	
6. Cr Wages control account		243 000
6. Dr Wage rate variance	17 100	
6. Dr Labour efficiency variance	13 500	
6. Cr Wages control account		30 600

The wages control account is credited and the work in progress account is debited with the standard cost (i.e. standard hours produced times the standard wage rate). The wage rate and labour efficiency variance accounts are debited, since they are both adverse variances and account for the difference between the actual wages cost (recorded as a debit in the wages control account) and the standard wages cost (recorded as a credit in the wages control account).

Manufacturing overhead costs incurred

The actual manufacturing overhead incurred is £52 000 for variable overheads and £116 000 for fixed overheads. The accounting entries for actual overhead *incurred* are recorded in the same way in a standard costing system as in an actual costing system. That is,

7. Dr Factory variable overhead control account	52 000	
7. Dr Factory fixed overhead control account	116 000	
7. Cr Expense creditors		168 000

Absorption of manufacturing overheads and recording the variances

Work in progress is debited with the standard manufacturing overhead cost for the output produced. The standard overhead rates were £4 per standard hour for fixed overhead and £2 per standard hour for variable overheads. The actual output was 27 000 standard hours. The standard fixed overhead cost is therefore £108 000 (27 000 standard hours at £4 per hour) and the variable overhead cost is £54 000. The accounting entries for fixed overheads are

8. Dr Work in progress (SQ × SP)	108 000	
8. Dr Volume variance	12 000	
8. Cr Factory fixed overhead control account		120 000
8. Dr Factory fixed overhead control account	4 000	
8. Cr Fixed overhead expenditure variance		4 000

You will see that the debit of £108 000 to the work in progress account and the corresponding credit to the factory fixed overhead control account represents the standard fixed overhead cost of production. The difference between the debit entry of £116 000 in the factory fixed overhead control account in Exhibit 19.1 for the *actual* fixed overheads incurred, and the credit entry of £108 000 for the *standard* fixed overhead cost of production is the total fixed overhead variance, which consists of an adverse volume variance of £12 000 and a favourable expenditure variance of £4000. This is recorded as a debit to the volume variance account and a credit to the expenditure variance account. The accounting entries for variable overheads are

9. Dr Work in progress account (SQ × SP)	54 000	
9. Dr Variable overhead efficiency variance	3 000	
9. Cr Factory variable overhead control account		57 000
9. Dr Factory variable overhead control account	5 000	
9. Cr Variable overhead expenditure variance account		5 000

The same principles apply with variable overheads. The debit to work in progress account and the corresponding credit to the factory variable overhead control account of £54 000 is the standard variable overhead cost of production. The difference between the debit entry of £52 000 in the factory variable overhead account in Exhibit 19.1 for the *actual* variable overheads incurred and the credit entry of £54 000 for the *standard* variable overhead cost of production is the total variable overhead variance, which consists of an adverse efficiency variance of £3000 and a favourable expenditure variance of £5000.

EXHIBIT 19.1

Accounting entries for a standard costing system

Stores ledger control account

1. Creditors (material A)	190 000	3. Work in progress (material A)	180 000
2. Creditors (material B)	151 500		
		3. Material usage variance (material A)	10 000
		4. Work in progress (material B)	135 000
		4. Material usage variance (material B)	16 500
	341 500		341 500

Creditors control account

2. Material price variance (material B)	10 100	1. Stores ledger control (material A)	190 000
		1. Material price variance (material A)	19 000
		2. Stores ledger control (material B)	151 500

Variance accounts

1. Creditors (material A)	19 000	2. Creditors (material price B)	10 100
3. Stores ledger control (material A usage)	10 000	8. Fixed factory overhead (expenditure)	4 000
4. Stores ledger control (material B usage)	16 500	9. Variable factory overhead (expenditure)	5 000
6. Wages control (wage rate)	17 100		19 100
6. Wages control (lab. effic'y)	13 500	13. Costing P + L a/c (balance)	72 000
8. Fixed factory overhead (volume)	12 000		
9. Variable factory overhead (effic'y)	3 000		
	91 100		91 100

Work in progress control account

3. Stores ledger (material A)	180 000	10. Finished goods stock account	720 000
4. Stores ledger (material B)	135 000		
6. Wages control	243 000		
8. Fixed factory overhead	108 000		
9. Variable factory overhead	54 000		
	720 000		720 000

Wages control account

5. Wages accrued account	273 600	6. WIP	243 000
		6. Wage rate variance	17 100
		6. Labour efficiency variance	13 500
	273 600		273 600

Fixed factory overhead control account

7. Expense creditors	116 000	8. WIP	108 000
8. Expenditure variance	4 000	8. Volume variance	12 000
	120 000		120 000

Variable factory overhead control account

7. Expense creditors	52 000	9. WIP	54 000
9. Expenditure	5 000	9. Efficiency variance	3 000
	57 000		57 000

Finished goods stock control account

10. WIP	720 000	12. Cost of sales	720 000

Cost of sales account

12. Finish goods stock	720 000	13. Costing P + L a/c	720 000

Costing P + L Account

12. Cost of sales at standard cost	720 000	11. Sales	810 000
13. Variance account (net variances)	72 000		
Profit for period	18 000		
	810 000		810 000

Completion of production

In Exhibit 19.1 the total amount recorded on the debit side of the work in progress account is £720 000. As there are no opening or closing stocks, this represents the total standard cost of production for the period, which consists of 9000 units at £80 per unit. When the completed production is transferred from work in progress to finished goods stock, the accounting entries will be as follows:

10. Dr Finished stock account	720 000	
10. Cr Work in progress account		720 000

Because there are no opening or closing stocks, both the work in progress account and the stores ledger account will show a nil balance.

Sales

Sales variances are not recorded in the accounts, so actual sales of £810 000 for 9000 units will be recorded as

11. Dr Debtors	810 000	
11. Cr Sales		810 000

As all the production for the period has been sold, there will be no closing stock of finished goods, and the standard cost of production for the 9000 units will be transferred from the finished goods account to the cost of sales account:

12. Dr Cost of sales account	288 000	
12. Cr Finished goods account		288 000

Finally, the cost of sales account and the variance accounts will be closed by a transfer to the costing profit and loss account (the item labelled 13 in Exhibit 19.1). The balance of the costing profit and loss account will be the *actual* profit for the period.

Calculation of profit

To calculate the profit, we must add the adverse variances and deduct the favourable variances from the standard cost of sales, which is obtained from the cost of sales account. This calculation gives the actual cost of sales for the period, which is then deducted from the actual sales to produce the actual profit for the period. The calculations are as follows:

	(£)	(£)	(£)
Sales			810 000
Less standard cost of sales		720 000	
Plus adverse variances:			
Material A price variance	19 000		
Material usage variance	26 500		
Wage rate variance	17 100		
Labour efficiency variance	13 500		
Volume variance	12 000		
Variable overhead efficiency variance	3 000	91 100	
		811 100	
Less favourable variances:			
Material B price variance	10 100		
Fixed overhead expenditure variance	4 000		
Variable overhead expenditure variance	5 000	19 100	
Actual cost of sales			792 000
Actual profit			18 000

Accounting disposition of variances

At the end of an accounting period a decision must be made as to how the variances that have arisen during the period should be treated in the accounts. Variance may be disposed of in either of the following ways:

1. Adopt the approach illustrated in Exhibit 19.1 and charge the variances as expenses to the period in which they arise. With this approach, inventories are valued at standard cost.
2. Allocate the variances between inventories and cost of goods sold.

If standards are current and attainable then charging the total amount of the variances for the period to the profit and loss account is recommended, since the variances are likely to represent efficiencies or inefficiencies. This approach is justified on the grounds that the cost of inefficient operations is not recoverable in the selling price, and should not therefore be deferred and included in the inventory valuation, but should be charged to the period in which the inefficiency occurred.

Where standards are not current, the second method can be used and variances allocated between inventories and cost of goods sold. The effect is to include with the cost of inventories the portion of the variance that is applicable to the stocks in inventory, and thereby to arrive at the approximate actual cost of these stocks. In practice, a company may treat different types of variances in different ways. Some may be written off in their entirety against the current period, while others may be divided between inventories and cost of goods sold. For example, price variances are frequently not controllable by a firm because they can arise following changes in the external market prices. It can therefore be argued that those price variances that are unavoidable should be allocated between inventories and cost of goods sold.

To illustrate the method of allocating variances between inventories and cost of goods sold, consider a situation where the percentages of cost elements in the inventories and cost of goods sold are as follows:

	Materials (%)	Labour (%)	Factory overhead (%)
Raw material stocks	20	–	–
Work in progress	10	15	20
Finished goods stocks	15	25	30
Cost of goods sold	55	60	50
	100	100	100

Assume that the following variances for a particular period are to be allocated between inventories and cost of goods sold:

	(£)
Material price	30 000
Wage rate	20 000
Overhead expenditure	10 000

The variances would be allocated as follows:

	Material price (£)	Wage rate (£)	Overhead expenditure (£)	Total (£)
Raw material stocks	6 000	–	–	6 000
Work in progress	3 000	3 000	2 000	8 000
Finished goods stocks	4 500	5 000	3 000	12 500
Cost of goods sold	16 500	12 000	5 000	33 500
	30 000	20 000	10 000	60 000

At the end of the period the above figures are allocated to the cost of sales and inventory control accounts, but the subsidiary inventory accounts and records are not adjusted. At the beginning of the next period the inventory allocations are reversed (by crediting the inventory accounts and debiting the variance accounts) in order to return beginning inventories to standard costs. At the end of that period the amounts reversed plus new variances are allocated in the same manner as before, based on the standard cost of ending inventory and cost of goods sold balances.

Ex post variance analysis

Standard costing variance analysis has some recognized disadvantages. Most of the problems centre around the comparison of actual performance with the standard. If the standard is weak then the comparison is also likely to be weak. Standards or plans are normally based on the environment that is anticipated when the targets are set. However, Demski (1977) has argued that if the environment is different from that anticipated, actual performance should be compared with a standard which reflects these changed conditions (i.e. an ***ex post* variance analysis approach**). Clearly, to measure managerial performance, we should compare like with like and compare actual results with adjusted standards based on the conditions that managers actually operated during the period. Let us now apply this principle to a selection of cost variances. For a more detailed discussion of the items covered in the foregoing section you should refer to the answers to Questions 19.22 and 19.34. Consider Example 19.3.

The conventional material price variance is £1800 adverse (10 000 units at £0.18). However, this variance consists of an adverse planning variance of £2000 that is due to incorrect estimates of the target buying price and a favourable purchasing efficiency (operational) variance of £200. The planning variance is calculated as follows:

purchasing planning variance

= (original target price – general market price at the time of purchase) × quantity purchased

= (£5 – £5.20) × 10 000

= £2000 A

This planning variance is not controllable, but it does provide useful feedback information to management on how successful they are in forecasting material prices, thus helping managers to improve their future estimates of material prices.

The efficiency of the purchasing department is assessed by a purchasing efficiency variance. This variance measures the purchasing department's efficiency for the conditions that actually prevailed and is calculated as follows:

purchasing efficiency variance

= (general market price – actual price paid) × quantity purchased

= (£5.20 – £5.18) × 10 000

= £200F

EXAMPLE 19.3

The standard cost per unit of raw material was estimated to be £5 per unit. The general market price at the time of purchase was £5.20 per unit and the actual price paid was £5.18 per unit. 10 000 units of the raw materials were purchased during the period.

Hence the conventional price variance of £1800 adverse can be divided into an *uncontrollable* adverse material planning variance of £2000 and a *controllable* favourable purchasing efficiency variance of £200. This analysis give a clearer indication of the efficiency of the purchasing function, and avoids including an adverse uncontrollable planning variance in performance reports. If an adverse price variance of £1800 is reported, this is likely to lead to dysfunctional motivation effects if the purchasing department have performed the purchasing function efficiently.

In practice, standard prices are often set on an annual basis, with the target representing the average for the year. Price changes will occur throughout the year, and it is unlikely that the actual prices paid for the materials will be equal to the average for the year as a whole even if actual prices are equal to the prices used to set the average standard price. Consequently, with rising prices actual prices will be less than the average earlier in the year (showing favourable variances) and above average standard later in the year (showing adverse variances).

This problem can be overcome by calculating separate purchasing planning and efficiency variances.

Material usage variance

Part of the material usage variance may also be due to uncontrollable environmental changes. For example, materials may be in short supply and it may be necessary to purchase inferior substitute materials. The material usage variance should therefore be based on a comparison of actual usage with an adjusted standard that takes account of the change in environmental conditions. The difference between the original standard and the adjusted standard represents an uncontrollable planning variance. Example 19.4 illustrates the analysis of the material usage variance.

The conventional analysis would report an adverse material usage variance of £200 (200 kg at £1), but this is misleading if all or part of this variance is due to uncontrollable environmental changes. When the standard is adjusted to take into account the changed conditions, the standard quantity is 6 kg per unit, which gives a *revised* standard of 1500 kg for an output of 250 units. The difference between this revised standard and the original standard quantity of 1250 kg (250 units at 5 kg per unit) represents the **uncontrollable planning variance** due to environmental changes. The uncontrollable planning variance is therefore £250 adverse, and is calculated as follows:

(original standard quantity – revised standard quantity) × standard price
= (1250 – 1500) × £1

The revised **controllable usage variance** is the difference between the standard quantity of 1500 kg, based on the revised standard usage, and the actual usage of 1450 kg. Hence the controllable usage variance will be £50 favourable.

The conventional material usage variance of £200 adverse has been divided into an uncontrollable adverse planning variance of £250 and a revised controllable usage

EXAMPLE 19.4

The standard quantity of materials per unit of production for a product is 5 kg. Actual production for the period was 250 units and actual material usage was 1450 kg. The standard cost per kg of materials was £1. Because of a shortage of skilled labour, it has been necessary to use unskilled labour and it is estimated that this will increase the material usage by 20%.

variance of £50 favourable. This approach produces variance calculations that provide a truer representation of a manager's performance and avoids any uncontrollable elements being included in the material usage variance.

Labour variances

The criticisms we have identified for the material variances are also applicable to the labour variances. For example, the labour efficiency and wage rate variances should be adjusted to reflect changes in the environmental conditions that prevailed during the period. A situation where this might occur is when unskilled labour is substituted for skilled labour because of conditions in the labour market. It is necessary in these circumstances to adjust the standard and separate the labour efficiency and wage rate variances into the following components:

- an uncontrollable planning variance due to environmental changes;
- a controllable efficiency and wage rate variance.

The variance should be calculated in a similar manner to that described for material variances.

Sales variances

The conventional sales volume variance reports the difference between actual and budgeted sales priced at the budgeted contribution per unit. This variance merely indicates whether sales volume is greater or less than expected. It does not indicate how well sales management has performed. In order to appraise the performance of sales management, actual sales volume should be compared with an *ex post* estimate that reflects the market conditions prevailing during the period.

Consider a situation where the budgeted sales are 100 000 units at a standard contribution of £100 per unit. Assume that actual sales are 110 000 units and that actual selling price is identical with the budgeted selling price. The conventional approach would report a favourable sales volume variance of £1m (10 000 units at £100 contribution per unit). However, the market size was greater than expected and, if the company had attained its target market share for the period, sales volume should have been 120 000 units. In other words, the *ex post* standard sales volume is 120 000 units. Actual sales volume is 10 000 units less than would have been expected after the circumstances prevailing during the period are taken into account. The *ex post* variance approach would therefore report an adverse sales volume appraisal variance of £1m (10 000 units × £100). Conversely, if the total market demand had fallen because of reasons outside the control of sales management, actual sales volume would be assessed against a more realistic lower standard.

The difference between the original budgeted sales volume of 100 000 units and the *ex post* budgeted sales volume of 120 000 units, priced at the budgeted contribution, represents the planning variance. A planning variance of £2m (20 000 units at a contribution of £100 per unit) would therefore be reported. The sum of the planning variance (£2m favourable) and the *ex post* sales volume variance (£1m adverse) equals the conventional sales volume variance.

The *ex post* approach provides an opportunity cost view of the performance of sales management by reporting a forgone contribution of £1m. The conventional approach reports a favourable performance, whereas the *ex post* approach reports that sales management has under-performed by indicating the cost to the company of neglected opportunities. The conventional variance is irrelevant, since it merely indicates whether or not sales management has beaten an obsolete target.

In our illustration we have assumed that actual selling price was equal to the budgeted selling price. A zero sales price variance would therefore be reported, and the sales volume variance would be equal to the *total* sales margin variance. It is questionable whether separating the total sales margin variance into a volume and a price variance provides any meaningful extra information. We noted earlier in this chapter that selling prices and sales volumes are inter-related and that the logical consequence of lower/higher selling price is higher/lower sales volume. It is therefore recommended that only the total sales margin variance be reported. The variance should be separated into planning and appraisal elements using the following formulae:

Total sales margin variance (planing element):

ex post budgeted sales volume × (*ex post* selling price – standard cost)
– original budgeted sales volume × (budgeted selling price – standard cost)

Total sales margin variance (appraisal element):

actual sales volume × (actual selling price – standard cost)
– *ex post* budgeted sales volume × (*ex post* selling price – standard cost)

The *ex post* budgeted sales volume for a particular product can be determined by estimating the total market sales volume for the period and then multiplying this estimate by the target percentage market share. Where industry statistics are published, this calculation should be based on actual total industry sales volume.

Where a company markets several different product lines, separate variances should be calculated for each. Mix variances should only be reported where there are identifiable relationships between the volumes of each product sold and these relationships are incorporated into the budgeting process.

Variance analysis and the opportunity cost of scarce resources

We shall now consider situations where production resources are scarce. Thus any failure to use the scarce resources efficiently results in forgone profits that should be included in the appropriate variance analysis calculations. To keep things simple at this stage, we shall assume that only one production resource is scarce, the *ex post* standard is identical with the original standard and actual and budgeted input prices are identical. In order to provide an understanding of the computation of variances when resources are scarce, we shall compute the variances for the situation outlined in Example 19.5. An analysis of the variances and a reconciliation of the budgeted and actual profits is presented in Exhibit 19.2. Note that Example 19.5 has been designed so that all the price variances are zero. This will enable us to concentrate on the quantity variances. Let us now consider each of the columns in Exhibit 19.2.

1 Conventional method

The variances in column 1 are calculated according to the variable costing approach outlined in the previous chapter. Turn back to Chapter 18 if you need to refresh your memory on how these calculations are made.

2 Scarce materials

The material usage variance in column 2 is £6000 adverse, compared with £2000 adverse using the conventional method. The conventional method values the 1000 kg excess usage at the standard acquisition cost of £2 per unit.[1] However, because materials are scarce, the opportunity cost method includes the lost contribution that arises from the excess usage because the scarce resources were not used efficiently. The product contribution is £20 and each unit produced requires 5 scarce kg of materials, giving a planned contribution of £4 per kg. The excess usage of 1000 kg leads to a lost contribution of £4000. This contribution is added to the acquisition cost for the excess materials, giving a total variance of £6000.

Because labour hours are not scarce, the labour variances are identical with those from the conventional method. The computation of the sales margin volume variance, however, is different from the conventional method because the failure to achieve budgeted sales is due to a failure to use the scarce materials efficiently. Hence the cost should be charged to the responsible production manager and not the sales manager.

3 Scarce labour

Because it is assumed that materials are no longer scarce, the materials usage variance in column 3 is identical with the conventional method calculation in column 1. Since labour hours are scarce, the acquisition cost will not reflect the true economic cost for the labour efficiency variance. The conventional approach values the 800 excess hours at the standard acquisition cost of £9 per hour, but the opportunity cost method in column 3 adds the lost contribution from the excess usage of 800 scarce labour hours.[2] The product contribution is £20 and each unit produced required 4 scarce labour hours, so each labour hour is planned to yield a £5 contribution. Thus the 800 excess labour hours lead to a £4000 lost contribution. This lost contribution of £4000 is added to the acquisition cost for the excess labour hours, giving a variance of £11 200.

4 No scarce inputs

Where there are no scarce production inputs, the failure to achieve the budgeted sales volume is the responsibility of the sales manager. The lost sales volume of 200 units results in a lost contribution of £20 per unit, giving an adverse sales volume variance of £4000. In this situation there is no lost contribution arising from the inefficient use of resources, which are not scarce. Cost variances should therefore be priced at their standard acquisition cost. We can conclude that where production inputs are not scarce,

EXAMPLE 19.5

XYZ Ltd manufacture a single product, the standards of which are as follows:

	(£)	(£)
Standard per unit		
Standard selling price		72
Less standard cost		
Material (5 kg at £2 per kg)	10	
Labour (4 hours at £9 per hour)	36	
Variable overheads (4 hours at £1.50 per hour)[a]	6	52
Standard contribution		20

[a]Variable overheads are assumed to vary with direct labour hours

The following information relates to the previous month's activities.

	Budget	Actual
Production and sales	2000 units	1800 units
Direct materials	10 000 kg at £2 per kg	10 000 kg at £2 per kg
Direct labour	8000 hours at £9 per hour	8000 hours at £9 per hour
Variable overheads	£12 000	£12 000
Fixed overheads	£12 000	£12 000
Profit	£28 000	£13 600

The actual selling price was identical with the budgeted selling price and there were no opening or closing stocks during the period.

You are required to calculate the variances and reconcile the budgeted and actual profit for each of the following methods:

1 The traditional (or conventional) method.
2 The relevant cost method assuming *materials* are the limiting factor and materials are restricted to 10 000 kg for the period.
3 The relevant cost method assuming *labour hours* are the limiting factor and labour hours are restricted to 8000 hours for the period.
4 The relevant cost method assuming there are no scarce inputs.

and the *ex post* standards are identical with the original standards, variances should be reported adopting the conventional approach illustrated in column 1.

Conclusion

There are strong arguments for valuing variances at their opportunity cost. This approach requires that scarce resources be identified in advance of production, but this is not easy to do in practice. In addition, the approach must rely on linear programming techniques when more than one scarce resource exists. (Multiple resource constraints

	(1) Conventional method (£)	(2) Scarce materials (£)	(3) Scarce labour hours (£)
Budgeted profit	28 000	28 000	28 000
Direct material usage variance	2 000A	6 000A	2 000A
Labour efficiency variance	7 200A	7 200A	11 200A
Variable overhead efficiency	1 200A	1 200A	1 200A
Sales margin volume	4 000A	Nil	Nil
Actual profit	13 600	13 600	13 600

EXHIBIT 19.2
Variance analysis using a conventional and opportunity cost approach

are discussed in Chapter 26.) The important points that you should note from this discussion are, first, that if quantity variances are valued at the acquisition cost of resources, this may not be a true reflection of the correct economic cost. Secondly, standard costing variance analysis must not be viewed as a mechanical procedure, but rather as an intelligent approach to charging the controllable economic cost of the difference between actual and target performance to responsible individuals.

The investigation of variances

In Chapter 18 we noted that a standard costing system consists of the following:

1 setting standards for each operation;
2 comparing actual with standard performance;
3 analysing and reporting variances arising from the difference between actual and standard performance;
4 investigating significant variances and taking appropriate corrective action.

In the final stage of this process management must decide which variances should be investigated. They could adopt a policy of investigating every reported variance. Such a policy would, however, be very expensive and time-consuming, and would lead to investigating some variances that would not result in improvements in operations even if the cause of the variance was determined. If, on the other hand, management do not investigate reported variances, the control function would be ignored. The optimal policy lies somewhere between these two extremes. In other words, the objective is to investigate only those variances that yield benefits in excess of the cost of investigation.

We shall now consider some of the cost variance investigation models developed in the accounting literature. These models can be classified into the following categories.

1 *Simple rule of thumb models* based on arbitrary criteria such as investigating if the absolute size of a variance is greater than a certain amount or if the ratio of the variance to the total standard cost exceeds some predetermined percentage.
2 *Statistical models* that compute the probability that a given variance comes from an in-control distribution but that does not take into account the costs and benefits of investigation.
3 *Statistical decision models* that take into account the cost and benefits of investigation.

To help you to understand the variance investigation models, we shall start by considering the reasons why actual performance might differ from standard performance.

Types of variances

There are several reasons why actual performance might differ from standard performance. A variance may arise simply as a result of an error in measuring the actual outcome. A second cause relates to standards becoming out of date because of changes in production conditions. Thirdly, variances can result from efficient or inefficient operations. Finally, variances can be due to random or chance fluctuations for which no cause can be found.

Measurement errors

The recorded amounts for actual costs or actual usage may differ from the actual amounts. For example, labour hours for a particular operation may be incorrectly added up or indirect labour costs might be incorrectly classified as a direct labour cost. Unless an investigation leads to an improvement in the accuracy of the recording system, it is unlikely that any benefits will be obtained where the cause is found to be due to measurement errors.

Out-of-date standards

Where frequent changes in prices of inputs occur, there is a danger that standard prices may be out of date. Consequently any investigation of price variances will indicate a general change in market prices rather than any efficiencies or inefficiencies in acquiring the resources. Standards can also become out of date where operations are subject to frequent technological changes or fail to take into account learning-curve effects. Investigation of variances falling into this category will provide feedback on the inaccuracy of the standards and highlight the need to update the standard. Where standards are revised, it may be necessary to alter some of the firm's output or input decisions. Ideally, standards ought to be frequently reviewed and, where appropriate, updated in order to minimize variances being reported that are due to standards being out of date.

Out-of-control operations

Variances may result from inefficient operations due to a failure to follow prescribed procedures, faulty machinery or human errors. Investigation of variances in this category should pinpoint the cause of the inefficiency and lead to corrective action to eliminate the inefficiency being repeated.

Random or uncontrollable factors

These occur when a particular process is performed by the same worker under the same conditions, yet performance varies. When no known cause is present to account for this variability, it is said to be due to **random or uncontrollable factors**. A standard is determined from a series of observations of a particular operation. It is most unlikely that repeated observations of this operation will yield the same result, even if the operation consists of the same worker repeating the same task under identical conditions. The correct approach is to choose a representative reading from these observations to determine a standard. Frequently, the representative reading that is chosen is the average or some other measure of central tendency. The important point to note is that one summary reading has been chosen to represent the standard when in reality a range of outcomes is possible when the process is *under control*. Any observation that differs from the chosen standard when the process is under control can be described as a random uncontrollable variation around the standard.

Any investigation of variances due to random uncontrollable factors will involve a cost, and will not yield any benefits because no assignable cause for the variance is present. Furthermore, those variances arising from **assignable causes** (such as inaccurate data, out of date standards or out-of-control operations) do not necessarily warrant investigation. For example, such variances may only be worthy of investigation if the benefits expected from the investigation exceed the costs of searching for and correcting the sources of the variance.

Variances may therefore be due to the following causes:

1. random uncontrollable factors when the operation is under control;
2. assignable causes, but with the costs of investigation exceeding the benefits;
3. assignable causes, but with the benefits from investigation exceeding the cost of investigation.

A perfect cost investigation model would investigate only those variances falling in the third category.

Simple rule of thumb cost investigation models

In many companies managers use simple models based on arbitrary criteria such as investigating if the absolute size of a variance is greater than a certain amount or if the variance exceeds the standard cost by some predetermined percentage (say 10%). For example, if the standard usage for a particular component was 10 kilos and the actual output for a period was 1000 components then the variance would not be investigated if actual usage was between 9000 and 11 000 kilos.

The advantages of using simple arbitrary rules are their simplicity and ease of implementation. There are, however, several disadvantages. Simple rule of thumb models do not adequately take into account the statistical significance of the reported variances or consider the costs and benefits of an investigation. For example, investigating all variances that exceed the standard cost by a fixed percentage can lead to investigating many variances of small amounts.

Some of these difficulties can be overcome by applying different percentages or amounts for different expense items as the basis for the investigation decision. For example, smaller percentages might be used as a signal to investigate key expense items, and a higher percentage applied to less important items of expense. Nevertheless, such approaches still do not adequately take into account the statistical significance of the reported variances, or balance the cost and benefits of investigation. Instead, they rely on managerial judgement and intuition in selecting the 'cut-off' values.

Statistical models not incorporating costs and benefits of investigation

A number of cost variance investigation models have been proposed in the accounting literature that determine the statistical probability that a variance comes from an in-control distribution. An investigation is undertaken when the probability that an observation comes from an in-control distribution falls below some arbitrarily determined probability level. The statistical models that we shall consider assume that two mutually exclusive states are possible. One state assumes that the system is 'in control' and a variance is simply due to random fluctuations around the expected outcome. The second possible state is that the system is in some way 'out of control' and corrective action can be taken to remedy the situation. We shall also assume that the 'in-control' state can be expressed in the form of a known probability distribution such as a normal one.

Determining probabilities

Consider a situation where the standard material usage for a particular operation has been derived from the average (i.e. the expected value) of a series of past observations made under 'close' supervision to ensure they reflected operations under normal efficiency. The average usage is 10 kg per unit of output. We shall assume that the actual observations were normally distributed with a standard deviation of 1 kg. Suppose that the actual material usage for a period was 12 000 kg and that output was 1000 units. Thus average usage was 12 kg per unit of output. We can ascertain the probability of observing an average usage of 12 kg or more when the process is under control by applying normal distribution theory. An observation of an average usage of 12 kg per unit of output is 2 standard deviations from the expected value, where, for a normal distribution,

$$Z = \frac{\text{actual usage (12 kg)} - \text{expected usage (10 kg)}}{\text{standard deviation (1 kg)}} = 2.0$$

A table of areas under the normal distribution (see Appendix C shown on page 1182) indicates that there is a probability of 0.02275 that an observation from that distribution will occur at least 2 standard deviations above the mean. This is illustrated in Figure 19.2. The shaded area indicates that 2.275% of the area under the curve falls to the right of 2 standard deviations from the mean. Thus the probability of actual material usage per unit of output being 12 kg or more when the operation is under control is 2.275%. It is very unlikely that the observation comes from a distribution with a mean of 10 kg and a standard deviation of 1 kg. In other words, it is likely that this observation comes from another distribution and that the material usage for the period is out of control.

Where the standard is derived from a small number of observations, we only have an estimate of the standard deviation, rather than the true standard deviation, and the deviation from the mean follows a *t*-distribution rather than a normal distribution. The *t*-distribution has more dispersion than the normal distribution so as to allow for the additional uncertainty that exists where an estimate is used instead of the true standard deviation. However, as the number of observations increases, to about 30, the values of a *t*-distribution shown on a *t*-table approach the values on a table for a normal distribution. Assume that the mean and the standard deviation were derived from 10 observations when the process was under control. The probability that a random variable having a *t*-distribution with 9 degrees of freedom ($n - 1$) will exceed 2 standard deviations from the mean is still small, equal to approximately 0.025 (or 1 chance in 40).[3] Therefore it is

FIGURE 19.2 *A normal probability distribution for the in-control process*

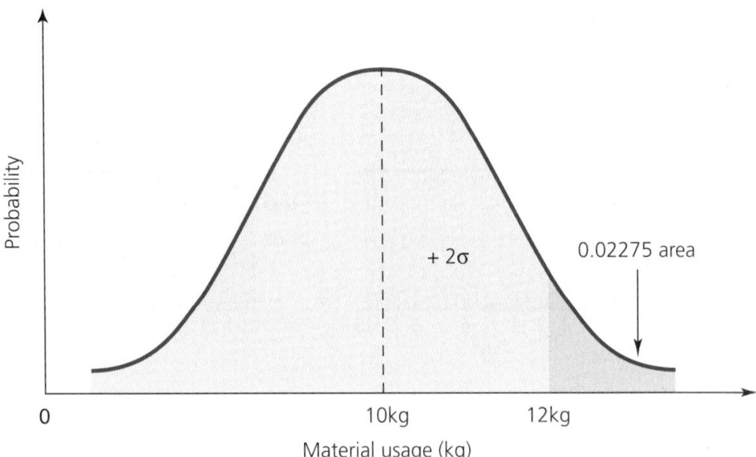

still likely that the observation comes from another distribution, and thus the material usage for the period is out of control.

Statistical control charts

Variances can be monitored by recording the number of standard deviations each observation is from the mean of the in-control distribution (10 kg in our illustration) on a statistical control chart. **Statistical quality control charts** are widely used as a quality control technique to test whether a batch of produced items is within pre-set tolerance limits. Usually samples from a particular production process are taken at hourly or daily intervals. The mean, and sometimes the range, of the sampled items are calculated and plotted on a quality control chart (Figure 19.3). A control chart is a graph of a series of past observations (which can be a single observation, a mean or a range of samples) in which each observation is plotted relative to pre-set points on the expected distribution. Only observations beyond specified pre-set control limits are regarded as worthy of investigation.

The control limits are set based on a series of past observations of a process when it is under control, and thus working efficiently. It is assumed that the past observations can be represented by a normal distribution.

The past observations are used to estimate the population mean and the population standard deviation σ. Assuming that the distribution of possible outcomes is normal, then, when the process is under control, we should expect

68.27% of the observations to fall within the range $+1\sigma$ from the mean;
95.45% of the observations to fall within the range $+2\sigma$ from the mean;
99.8% of the observations to fall within the range $+3\sigma$ from the mean.

Control limits are now set. For example, if control limits are set based on two standard deviations from the mean then this would indicate 4.55% (100% – 95.45%) of future observations would result from pure chance when the process is under control. Therefore there is a high probability that an observation outside the 2 control limits is out of control.

FIGURE 19.3 *Statistical quality control charts*

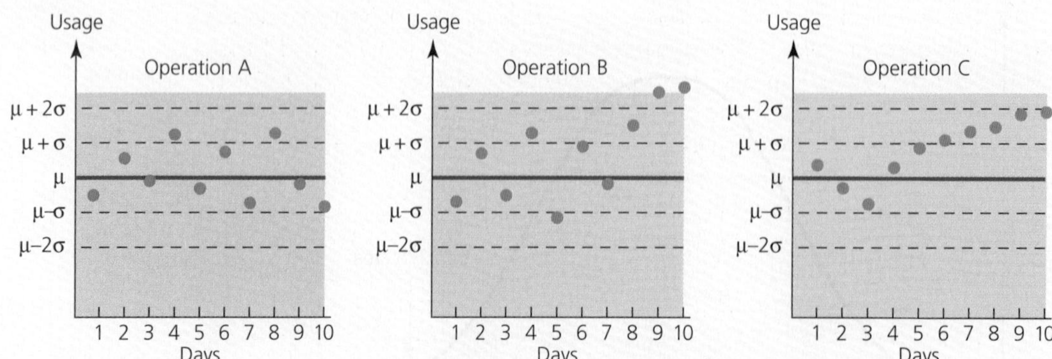

Figure 19.3 shows three control charts, with the outer horizontal lines representing a possible control limit of 2σ, so that all observations outside this range are investigated. You will see that for operation A the process is deemed to be in control because all observations fall within the control limits. For operation B the last two observations suggest that the operation is out of control. Therefore both observations should be investigated. With operation C the observations would not prompt an investigation because all the observations are within the control limits. However, the last six observations show a steadily increasing usage in excess of the mean, and the process may be out of control. Statistical procedures (called casum procedures) that consider the trend in recent usage as well as daily usage can also be used.

Statistical quality control is used mainly for product or quality control purposes, but within a standard costing context, statistical control charts can be used to monitor accounting variances. For example, labour usage and material usage could be plotted on a control chart on a hourly or daily basis for each operation. This process would consist of sampling the output from an operation and plotting on the chart the mean usage of resources per unit for the sample output.

Decision models with costs and benefits of investigation

Statistical decision models have been extended to incorporate the costs and benefits of investigation. A simple decision theory single-period model for the investigation of variances was advocated by Bierman *et al.* (1977). The model assumes that two mutually exclusive states are possible. One state assumes that the system is in control and a variance is simply due to a random fluctuation around the expected outcome. The second possible state is that the system is in some way out of control and corrective action can be taken to remedy this situation. In other words, it is assumed that if an investigation is undertaken when the process is out of control, the cause can be found and corrective action can always be taken to ensure that the process returns to its in-control state. This assumption is more appropriate for controlling the quality of output from a production process, but may not be appropriate when extended to the investigation of standard cost variances. For example, it does not capture situations where the investigation was signalled by measurement errors or the cause of the variance was due to out of date standards.

If the process is out of control, there is a benefit B associated with returning the process to its 'in-control' state. This benefit represents the cost saving that will arise through bringing the system back under control and thereby avoiding variances in future periods. However, if we do not investigate in this period, it is possible that an investigation may be undertaken in the next period. Therefore it is unlikely that the benefits will be equivalent to the savings for many periods in the future. Kaplan (1982) concludes that B should be defined as the expected one-period benefit from operating in control rather than out of control, recognizing that this will underestimate the actual benefits.

A cost of C will be incurred when an investigation is undertaken. This cost includes the manager's time spent on investigation, the cost of interrupting the production process, and the cost of correcting the process. We shall assume that the costs to correct of an investigation that discovers that the process is 'out of control' are identical with the costs associated with finding that the process is 'in control'. However, the model can be easily modified to incorporate the incremental correction costs if the process is found to be out of control.

To illustrate a one-period model let us assume that the incremental cost of investigating the material usage variance in our earlier illustration (see page 804) is £100. Assume also that the estimated benefit B from investigating a variance and taking corrective action is £400. We can therefore develop a simple decision rule: investigate if the expected benefit is greater than the expected cost. Denoting by P the probability that the process is *out* of control, the expected benefit can be expressed as

$$\begin{aligned}\text{expected benefit} &= PB + (1 - P)B \\ &= PB + (1 - P)0 \\ &= PB\end{aligned}$$

The probability that the system is *in* control is $1 - P$, and the benefit arising from investigating an 'in-control' situation is zero. Therefore PB represents the expected benefit of investigating a variance. Assuming that the cost of investigation C is known with certainty, the decision rule is to investigate if

$$PB > C, \text{ or } P > C/B$$

In our example we should investigate if

$$P > 100/400 = 0.25$$

The model requires an estimate of P, the probability that the process is out of control. Bierman *et al.* (1977) have suggested that the probabilities could be determined by computing the probability that a particular observation, such as a variance, comes from an 'in-control' distribution. They also assume that the 'in-control' state can be expressed in the form of a known probability distribution such as a normal distribution. Consider our earlier example shown on page 804, where the expected usage based on actual observation when the process in control was 10 kg per unit of output with a standard deviation of 1 kg. We noted that the recorded actual average usage of 12 kg for a particular period exceeded the mean of the distribution by 2 standard deviations. We referred to a normal probability table to ascertain that the probability of an observation of 12 kg (or larger) was 0.02275 (2.275%).[4] The probability of the process being out of control is 1 minus the probability of being in control.[5]

Thus $P = 1 - 0.02275 = 0.97725$. Recall that we ascertained that the variance should be investigated if the probability that the process is out of control is in excess of 0.25. The process should therefore be investigated. Instead of using the cost–benefit ratio *C/B*, we can ascertain whether

$$PB > C;$$
$$PB = 0.97725 \times £400 = £391$$
$$C = £100$$

Therefore the *expected value* of the benefits from investigation, *PB*, exceeds the cost of the investigation, *C*, and the variance should be investigated.

A major problem with decision theory models concerns the difficulty in determining the cost of investigation *C* and the benefits arising from the investigation *B*. Note that *B* is defined as the present value of the costs that will be incurred if an investigation is not made now. In situations where the inefficiency will be repeated there will be many opportunities in the future to correct the process, and the discounted future costs, assuming no future investigation, will be an overestimate of *B*. We have noted that Kaplan (1982) concludes that *B* should be defined as the expected one-period benefit from operating in control rather than out of control, but recognizing that this will be an underestimate of the actual benefits. It is also assumed that when an out-of-control situation is discovered, action can be taken so that the process will be in-control. In many situations the variance may have been caused by a permanent change in the process, such as a change in the production process or in raw material availability. In such instances the investigation will not exceed the expected benefit, since future operations will remain at the current cost level. The cost–benefit variance investigation model does not take such factors into account. Some benefits will be derived, however, since standards can be altered to reflect the permanent changes in the production process. This should lead to improvements in planning and control in future periods.

Problems also arise with determining the cost of investigating variances. The cost of an investigation will vary, depending upon the cause of the variance. Some assignable causes will be detected before others, depending upon the ordering of the stages in the investigation procedure. If the variance is not due to an assignable cause, the cost of investigation will be higher because the investigation must eliminate all other causes before it can be established that the variance is not due to an assignable cause. Also, *additional* costs of carrying out the investigation may not be incurred, since they may be carried out by existing staff at no extra cost to the organization. However, some opportunity cost is likely to be involved because of alternative work forgone while the investigation is being undertaken.

Quantity variances

Finally, it is important to note that the application of statistical techniques that incorporate random variations is only applicable to quantity variances – that is, labour efficiency and material usage variances. There is a fundamental difference between these variances and price variances. Efficiency cannot be predetermined in the same way as material prices and wage rates: first, because of the random variations inherent in the human element; and, secondly, because the resulting non-uniformity is more pronounced. One does not expect actual results to be equal to standard where the human element is involved, since some variances may be expected to occur even when no assignable cause is present. For this reason, statistical techniques should be applied only to quantity variances. For an indication of the extent to which statistical models are used in practice you should refer to Exhibit 19.3.

Criticisms of standard costing

Standard costing systems were developed to meet the needs of a business environment drastically different from that which exists today. The usefulness of standard costing variance analysis in a modern business environment has been questioned and several writers have predicted its demise because of the following:

- the changing cost structure;
- inconsistency with modern management approaches;
- over-emphasizes the importance of direct labour;
- delay in feedback reporting.

Impact of the changing cost structure

It is claimed that overhead costs have become the dominant factory costs, direct labour costs have diminished in importance and that most of a firm's costs have become fixed in the short-term. Given that standard costing is a mechanism that is most suited to the control of direct and variable costs, but not fixed or indirect costs, its usefulness has been questioned. However, recent surveys in many different countries have reported remarkably similar results in terms of cost structures. They all report that direct costs and overheads averaged approximately 75% and 25% respectively of total manufacturing costs with average direct labour costs varying from 10–15% of total manufacturing cost.

Clearly the claim by some commentators that overheads are the dominant factory costs is not supported by the survey evidence. Direct materials are the dominant costs in most manufacturing organizations and account for, on average, approximately 60% of total manufacturing costs. Direct labour costs are now of much less importance and tend to be fixed in the short-term. Direct materials and variable overheads (e.g. energy costs for running the machines) are now the only short-term variable costs. Thus, standard costing variance analysis for control purposes would appear to be only appropriate for direct materials and variable overheads, the latter being a small proportion of total manufacturing costs. However, the reporting of direct labour variances at periodic intervals is probably justified since efficiencies/inefficiencies in resource consumption are highlighted and provide useful feedback information for re-deploying labour or ensuring that in the longer-term changes in resource consumption are translated into changes in spending on the supply of direct labour resources.

Inconsistency with modern management approaches

In recent years many organizations have adopted new management approaches that focus on minimizing inventories, zero defective production, delivery of high quality products and services and a process of continuous improvement. Critics claim that variance analysis does not support today's management philosophy. For example, if

EXHIBIT 19.3
Survey of company practice

A USA survey by Lauderman and Schaeberle (1983) and two UK surveys (Puxty and Lyall, 1990; Drury *et al.*, 1993) indicate that the statistical models outlined in this chapter are rarely used and also that some firms use more than one method to determine when variances should be investigated.

	Lauderman and Schaeberle (1983) (%)	Puxty and Lyall (1990) (%)
Decision based on managerial judgement	72	81
Variances investigated beyond a certain monetary amount	54	36
Variances investigated beyond a certain percentage	43	26
Investigation based on statistical decision rules	4	–
Variances investigated in all cases	–	9
(– no details reported)		

Drury et al. *(1993) survey*	Extent to which method used				
	Never (%)	Rarely (%)	Sometimes (%)	Often (%)	Always (%)
Decision based on managerial judgement	8	5	12	53	22
Investigation where a variance exceeds a specific amount	12	17	31	34	6
Investigation where a variance exceeds a given percentage of standard	15	18	31	29	7
Statistical basis using control charts or other statistical models	60	25	12	2	1

purchase price variances are used to evaluate the performance of the purchasing function, it is likely that purchasing management will be motivated to focus entirely on obtaining the materials at the lowest possible prices even if this results in:

- the use of many suppliers (all of them selected on the basis of price);
- larger quantity purchases, thus resulting in larger inventories;
- delivery of lower quality goods;
- indifference to attaining on-time delivery.

Today, companies wish to focus on performance measures which emphasize all the factors important to the purchasing function, such as quality and reliability of suppliers, and not just price. Nevertheless, material price variances still have an important role to play.

It is also claimed that using the volume variance to measure unutilized capacity motivates managers to expand output and thus increase inventories. This is inconsistent with a philosophy of minimizing inventories. Favourable volume variances are reported whenever actual production exceeds budgeted production and therefore profit centre managers can manipulate monthly profits by expanding output and increasing profits. Attention has already been drawn to the fact that volume variances are inappropriate for short-term cost control and performance measurement purposes. If volume variances are being used for these purposes then the problem arises because of the faulty application, rather than the inadequacies, of standard costing.

Volume variances are required to meet financial accounting requirements. Even if standard costing is abandoned the under- or over-recovery of overheads is necessary to meet conventional absorption costing profit measurement requirements. It is therefore inappropriate to single out standard costing variance analysis as being responsible for the excess production. The solution is to replace absorption costing with a standard variable costing system for monthly internal reporting.

To compete successfully in today's global competitive environment organizations are adopting a philosophy of continuous improvement, an ongoing process that involves a continuous search to reduce costs, eliminate inefficiencies and improve the quality and performance of activities that increase customer satisfaction. It is claimed that when standards are set, a climate is created whereby the standards represent targets to be achieved and maintained, rather than a philosophy of continuous improvement. Standard costing can be made more consistent with a continuous improvement philosophy if variances are used to monitor the trend in performance and giving more emphasis to the rate of change in performance. In addition, standards should also be regularly reviewed and tightened as improvements occur.

Over-emphasis on direct labour

Some writers have criticized variance analysis on the grounds that it encourages too much attention to be focused on direct labour when direct labour has diminished in importance and is only a small proportion of total factory costs. Surveys, however, indicate that direct labour is the most widely used overhead allocation base. To reduce their allocated costs managers are motivated to reduce direct labour hours since this is the basis on which the overheads are allocated to cost centres. This process overstates the importance of direct labour and directs attention away from controlling escalating overhead costs. This overemphasis on direct labour arises, not from any inadequacies of standard costing, but from the faulty application of standard costing by focusing excessively on volume variances for short-term cost control and performance evaluation. Attention has already been drawn to the fact that volume variances should be used for meeting financial accounting requirements and not for cost control.

Delayed feedback reporting

A further criticism of variance reporting is that performance reports often arrive too late to be of value in controlling production operations. Performance reports are normally prepared weekly or monthly but such a lengthy time lag is not helpful for the daily control of operations. For operational control purposes labour and material quantity variances should be reported in physical terms in 'real time'. For example, most companies now use 'on line' computers to collect information at the point of manufacture so that variances can be reported and fed into the system instantaneously. Summary variance reports can still be prepared at appropriate periodic intervals if management wish to monitor deviations from standard and examine the trend in reported variances.

The future role of standard costing

Critics of standard costing question the relevance of traditional variance analysis for cost control and performance appraisal in today's manufacturing and competitive environment. Nevertheless, standard costing systems continue to be widely used. This is because standard costing systems provide cost information for many other purposes besides cost control and performance evaluation. Standard costs and variance analysis would still be required for other purposes; particularly inventory valuation, profit measurement and decision-making even if they were abandoned for cost control and performance evaluation. For example, the detailed tracking of costs is unnecessary for decision-making purposes. Product costs for decision-making should be extracted from a data base of standard costs reviewed periodically (say once or twice a year). A periodic cost audit should be undertaken to provide a strategic review of the standard costs and profitability of a firm's products. The review provides attention-directing information for signalling the need for more detailed studies to make cost reduction, discontinuation, redesign or outsourcing decisions. Standard costs thus provide the basis for such decisions and can be derived from a database of either traditional or activity-based systems.

Many organizations have adapted their variance reporting system to report on those variables that are particularly important to them. These variables are company specific and cannot be found in textbooks. For example, some organizations that pursue a zero production defects policy have sought to measure the cost of quality by reporting quality variances. They define the quality variance as the standard cost of the output that does not meet specification. In traditional variance analysis this variance is buried in the efficiency variances of the various inputs. To illustrate the computation of the variances we shall simplify it by ignoring direct labour and overhead variances and concentrate on direct materials and assume that the standard usage for the production of a product is 5 kg and the standard price is £10 per kg. Actual usage for an output of 5000 units (of which 400 were defective) was 24 800 kg. Traditional variance would report an adverse usage variance of £18 000, being the difference between the standard quantity of 23 000 kg for the good output of 4600 units and the actual usage of 24 800 kg priced at £10 per kg. The variance analysis is modified to report an adverse quality variance of £20 000 (400 defective units × 5 kg × £10) and a favourable usage variance of £2000 reflecting the fact that only 24 800kg were used to produce 5000 units with a standard usage of 25 000 kg. The fact that 400 units were defective is reflected in the quality variance.

In recent years there has been a shift from using variances generated from a standard costing system as the foundation for short-term cost control and performance measurement to treating them as one among a broader set of measures. Greater emphasis is now being placed on the frequent reporting of non-financial measures that provide feedback on the key variables required to compete successfully in today's competitive environment. These non-financial measures focus on such factors as quality, reliability, flexibility, after-sales service, customer satisfaction and delivery performance. Recognition is also being given to the fact that periodic short-term reporting may be inappropriate for controlling those costs that are fixed in the short-run but variable in the longer-term. Attention has already been drawn to the fact that variance reporting for long-term variable costs should be at less frequent intervals. However, standard costing on its own is insufficient for controlling these costs. Special cost reduction exercises (i.e. *kaizen* costing) for existing products, target costing for future products and activity-based cost management are now being increasingly used to manage future costs. In particular, an awareness that a significant proportion of a product's costs are determined by decisions made early in a product's life cycle has resulted in greater attention being given to feed-forward controls and managing the costs at the design stage rather than after production has commenced. The management of long-run variable costs using the above techniques will be examined in Chapter 22.

Most of the criticisms that have been levelled at standard costing relate to cost control and performance measurement. It remains to be seen whether standard costing will decline in importance as a cost control and a performance evaluation mechanism. The survey evidence, however, suggests that practitioners do consider that it is an important mechanism for controlling costs. A UK survey by Drury *et al.* (1993) reported that 76% of the responding organizations operated a standard costing system. When asked how important standard costing was for cost control and performance evaluation, 72% of the respondents whose organizations operated a standard costing system stated that it was 'above average' or of 'vital importance'.

The role of standard costing when ABC has been implemented

For those organizations that have implemented activity-based systems standard costing still has an important role to play in controlling the costs of unit-level activities. Unit-level activities can be defined as those activities that are performed each time a unit of product or service is produced. These activities consume resources in proportion to the number of units produced. For example, if a firm produces 10% more units, it will consume 10% more labour cost, 10% more materials, 10% more machine hours and 10% more energy costs. Expenses in this category include direct labour, direct materials, energy costs and expenses that are consumed in proportion to machine processing times (such as machine maintenance). Therefore traditional variance analysis can be applied for direct labour, direct materials and those variable overheads that vary with output, machine hours and direct labour hours.

Variance analysis is most suited to controlling the costs of unit-level activities but it can also provide meaningful information for managing those overhead costs that are fixed in the short-term but variable in the longer-term if traditional volume-based cost drivers are replaced with activity-based cost drivers that better reflect the causes of resource consumption. Variance analysis, however, cannot be used to manage all overhead costs. It is inappropriate for the control of facility-sustaining (infrastructure) costs because the costs of these resources do not fluctuate in the longer-term according to the demand for them.

Mak and Roush (1994) and Kaplan (1994b) have considered how variance analysis can be applied to incorporate activity costs and cost drivers for those overheads that are fixed in the short-term but variable in the long-term. The data presented in Example 19.6 illustrates their ideas relating to ABC overhead variance analysis for a set-up activity. You will see from this example that budgeted fixed costs of £80 000 provide a practical capacity to perform 2000 set-ups during the period. Assuming that the number of set-ups has been identified as the appropriate cost driver a cost of £40 per set-up (£80 000/2000) will be charged to products. For a discussion of the reasons for basing the cost driver rate on practical capacity, rather than budgeted usage, refer back to Chapter 10 (pages 387–388). Since budgeted capacity usage is 1600 set-ups not all of the capacity provided (2000 set-ups) will be used, and a budgeted cost of unused capacity of £16 000 (400 × £40), will be highlighted during the budget process. The actual number of set-ups performed was 1500 compared with a budget of 1600 and an unexpected capacity utilization variance of £4000 (100 × £40) will be reported at the end of the period. The traditional spending (expenditure) variance is £10 000, being the difference between budgeted and actual fixed costs incurred. We can now reconcile the fixed set-up expenses charged to products with the actual expenses incurred that are recorded in the financial accounts:

	£
Set-up expenses charged to products (1500 × £40)	60 000
Budgeted unused capacity variance (400 × £40)	16 000A
Capacity utilization variance (100 × £40)	4 000A
Expenditure variance	10 000F
Total actual expenses	70 000

The above capacity variances highlight for management attention the £20 000 unused capacity (£16 000 expected and £4000 unexpected) and thus signals the opportunity for actions such as reducing the supply of resources or using the surplus resources to generate additional revenues.

In Example 19.6 it is assumed that the variable set-up costs, such as the cost of supplies used in the set-up activity, varies with the number of set-ups. The variable cost driver rate of £25 per set-up has been calculated by dividing the budgeted variable cost of £40 000 by the budgeted number of set-ups of 1600. Note that the budgeted variable cost per set-up will be £25 for all activity levels. Thus the estimated set-up costs at the practical capacity of 2000 set-ups would be £50 000 (2500 × £25) but the cost per set-up would remain at £25. To calculate the set-up variable cost variance we must flex the budget. The actual number of set-ups performed were 1500 and the flexible budget allowance is £37 500 (1500 × £25). Actual expenditure is £39 000 and therefore an adverse variable cost variance of £1500 will be reported. The reconciliation between the variable set-up expenses charged to products and the actual expenses incurred is as follows:

Variable set-up expenses charged to products (1500 × £25)	37 500
Variable overhead variance	1 500A
Total actual expenses	39 000

In Example 19.6 we assumed that the number of set-ups was the cost driver. If set-ups take varying amounts of time they will not represent an homogeneous measure of output and thus may not provide a satisfactory measure of the cost of activity. To overcome this problem it may be preferable to use the number of set-up hours as the cost driver. Let us now assume in Example 19.6 that the cost driver is set-up hours and that the quantity of set-up hours is the same throughout as the number of set-ups. Therefore the variance analysis based on set-up hours will be identical to the variances that were computed when the number of set-ups was the cost driver.

Where cost drivers that capture the duration of the activity are used Mak and Roush (1994) advocate the reporting of separate efficiency variances for each activity. Assume in Example 19.6 that the standard activity level for the actual number of set-ups performed during the period was 1500 hours but the actual number of set-up hours required was 1660. The standard activity level represents the number of set-up hours that should have been required for the actual number of set-ups. The difference between the standard and the actual set-up hours thus arises because of efficiencies/inefficiencies in performing the

EXAMPLE 19.6

Assume the following information for the set-up activity for a period:

Budget	Actual
Activity level: 1600 set-ups	Total fixed costs: £70 000
Practical capacity supplied: 2000 set-ups	Total variable costs: £39 000
Total fixed costs: £80 000	
Total variable costs: £40 000	Number of set-ups 1500
Cost driver rates (variable): £25 per set-up	
(fixed): £40 per set-up	

set-up activities. Assuming that variable costs vary with the number of set-up hours then inefficiency in performing set-up activities has resulted in an extra 160 set-up hours (1660 – 1500) being used thus causing additional spending of £4000 (160 hours × £25). In addition, a favourable variable overhead expenditure variance of £2500 will be reported. This figure is derived in a manner similar to the traditional analysis by deducting the actual variable overhead expenditure of £39 000 from the flexible budget based on actual set-up hours (1660 × £25 = £41 500). Note that the sum of the efficiency variance (£4000A) and the expenditure variance (£2500F) is the same as the variable overhead variance of £1500 reported when the number of set-ups were used as the cost driver.

It is also possible to compute a capacity utilization and efficiency variance for fixed overheads. The efficiency variance is calculated by multiplying the 160 excess set-up hours by the fixed cost driver rate. Therefore an adverse efficiency variance of £6400 (160 × £40) and a favourable capacity utilization variance of £2400 (60 × £40) will be reported. The capacity utilization variance reflects the fact that the actual set-up capacity utilized was 60 hours in excess of the budget (assumed to be 1600 hours) but this was offset by the inefficiency in performing the activity which resulted in 160 hours in excess of requirements being utilized. The sum of the efficiency variance (£6400A) and the revised capacity utilization variance (£2400F) is identical to the capacity utilization variance reported when the number of set-ups was used as the cost driver.

The capacity utilization and efficiency variances relating to activity fixed costs are not particularly useful for short-term cost management. Mak and Roush conclude that they are more useful in a multi-period context whereby recurring adverse capacity variances (unused capacity) indicate the potential cost savings which can result from eliminating excess capacity.

Summary

The following items relate to the learning objectives listed at the beginning of the chapter.

- **Explain and calculate material mix and yield and sales mix and quantity variances.**

  In some production processes it is possible to vary the mix of materials used to make the final product. Any deviations from the standard mix will lead to a materials mix variance. A favourable mix variance will occur when cheaper materials are substituted for more expensive ones. This may not always be in the company's best interest, since product quality may suffer or output may be reduced, leading to an adverse yield variance. The yield variance arises because there is a difference between the standard output for a given level of input and the actual output attained. Part of the sales margin volume variance may be accounted for because the actual sales mix differs from the budgeted sales mix. Calculating a sales margin mix variance can isolate this element. The remaining part of the sales margin volume variance represents the sales quantity variance. Thus, separating the sales margin volume variance into quantity and mix variances provides an explanation of how the sales volume margin variance is affected by a shift in the total volume of sales and a shift in the relative mix of products. The calculations of the variances were illustrated using Examples 19.1 and 19.2.

- **Explain the criticisms of sales margin variances.**

  The decomposition of the sales margin variances into price and quantity variances has been criticized on the grounds that, in imperfectly competitive markets, prices and quantities are interrelated. The logical consequence of lower/higher sales prices is higher/lower volume. Thus, the relevant analyses based on these variances are also interrelated. Consequently, it is argued that the decomposition of the sales margin variance does not generate any meaningful results.

- **Prepare a set of accounts for a standard costing system.**

  The method used in the chapter to illustrate the recording of standard costs valued all inventories at standard cost with all entries being recorded in the inventory accounts at standard prices. Any differences between standard costs and actual costs are debited or credited to variance accounts. Adverse variances appear as debit balances and favourable variances as credit balances. The preparation of a set of accounts for a standard costing system was illustrated in Exhibit 19.1.

- **Explain and calculate planning and operating variances.**

  One of the criticisms of standard costing is that standards are normally based on the environment that was anticipated when the targets were set. To overcome this problem, whenever the actual environment is different from the anticipated environment, performance should be compared with a standard that reflects the changed conditions. One possible solution is to extract an uncontrollable planning or forecasting variance and report operating variances based on the changed conditions that applied during the period. The calculations of planning and operating variances were illustrated using Examples 19.3 and 19.4.

- **Explain and calculate variances using the opportunity cost approach to variance analysis.**

  Traditionally, quantity variances are calculated using standard acquisition costs but where resources are scarce such costs do not represent the economic cost arising from a failure to use scarce resources efficiently. In such cases it is preferable to value the quantity variances at their opportunity cost (i.e. the forgone profit contribution) of scarce resource. The forgone profit is computed by multiplying any excess usage by the standard contribution per unit of the scarce resource. The calculation of variances using the opportunity cost approach was illustrated using Example 19.5.

- **Explain the factors that influence the decision to investigate a variance and describe the different methods that can be used to determine whether an investigation is warranted.**

  The decision to investigate a variance should depend on whether the expected benefits are likely to exceed the costs of carrying out the investigation. Variances may be due to: (a) random uncontrollable variations when the variance is under control; (b) assignable causes but the costs of investigation exceed the benefits of investigation; and (c) assignable causes but the benefits from investigation exceed the costs of investigation.

The aim should be only to investigate those variances that fall into the latter category. Methods of investigating variances include (a) simple rule of the thumb models; (b) statistical models that focus on the probability of the variances being out of control; and (c) statistical decision models that take into account the cost and benefits of investigation. These methods are described in detail in Chapter 19.

- **Comment on the future role of standard costing.**

  Some writers have predicted the demise of standard costing on the following grounds: (a) the changing cost structure that has resulted in the growth of indirect costs (it is claimed that standard costing is not particularly suitable for controlling such costs); (b) the inconsistency of standard costing with modern management approaches; (c) the overemphasis of standard costing with direct labour, which is now a diminishing cost; and (d) the delay in feedback in variance reporting. Most of the criticisms relate to standard costing as a control mechanism but standard costing provides information for many other purposes (e.g. inventory valuation and providing a database for which information can be extracted for decision-making purposes). Many organizations have also adapted standard costing to meet their own specific requirements and standard costing is also being adapted to be operated within an activity-based costing system.

- **Explain the role of standard costing within an ABC system.**

  Within an ABC system variance analysis is most suited to controlling the costs of unit level activities. It can also provide meaningful information for managing those overhead costs that are fixed in the short-term but variable in the longer-term if traditional volume-based cost drivers are replaced with activity-based cost drivers that better reflect the causes of resource consumption. Variance analysis, however, cannot be used to manage all overhead costs. It is inappropriate for the control of facility-sustaining (infrastructure) costs because the cost of these resources does not fluctuate in the longer term according to the demand for them.

Notes

1 The standard quantity of materials for an actual production of 1800 units is 9000 kg. The actual usage of materials is 10 000 kg, which means an excess usage of 1000 kg.

2 For an output of 1800 units 7200 labour hours should have been used, but the actual number of hours used was 8000. Consequently, 800 excess labour hours were required.

3 The probability of 0.025 is derived from a *t*-distribution with 9 degrees of freedom.

4 It is assumed that the actual observations used to establish the standard performance can be represented by a normal distribution. There is no reason, however, why the analysis could not be modified to accommodate some other probability distribution.

5 We assume here that all favourable variances are in control or do not warrant an investigation. If favourable variances 2 standard deviations from the mean is deemed to be out of control then the probability of observing a variance plus or minus 2 standard deviations from the mean is 0.0455 (0.02275 × 2). Consequently, the probability that the process is out of control is 0.9545 (1 – 0.0455). The variance should still be investigated. Bierman *et al.* (1977) advocate a similar approach by stating that the probability of an event, given that another event (in this case an unfavourable variance) has already occurred, is based on considering only one-half of the probability distribution. Therefore the probabilities derived from normal probability tables should be divided by 0.5. Thus 0.02275/0.5 = 0.0455.

Key terms and concepts

assignable causes (p. 803)
controllable usage variance (p. 796)
ex post variance analysis (p. 795)
market share variance (p. 784)
market size variance (p. 784)
material mix variance (p. 778)
materials yield variance (p. 780)
purchasing efficiency variance (p. 795)
purchasing planning variance (p. 795)
random uncontrollable factors (p. 803)
sales margin mix variance (p. 782)
sales margin price variance (p. 782)
sales margin volume variance (p. 782)
sales quantity variance (p. 783)
statistical quality control charts (p. 805)
total sales margin variance (p. 782)
uncontrollable planning variance (p. 796)

Recommended reading

For a review of the research literature relating to variance investigation models you should refer to Scapens (1991, ch. 6) and Sen (1998). For further reading on ABC variance analysis see Kaplan (1994a) and Mak and Roush (1994, 1996). The future role of standard costing is addressed in the article by Cheatham and Cheatham (1996).

Two articles by Emsley (2000, 2001) describe field studies relating to the role of variance analysis in problem solving.

Key examination points

Questions on accounting entries for a standard costing system, variance investigation models and calculating planning and operating variance are frequently included in advanced management accounting examinations. Make sure you understand these topics and attempt the Review problems that relate to these topics. You should compare your answers with the Solutions to the Review problems.

Assessment material

Review questions

The review questions are short questions that enable you to assess your understanding of the main topics included in the chapter. The numbers in parentheses provide you with the page numbers to refer to if you cannot answer a specific question.

Review problems

The review problems are more complex and require you to relate and apply the chapter content to various business problems. The problems are graded by their level of difficulty. The multiple-choice questions are the least demanding and normally take less than 10 minutes to complete. Fully worked solutions to the review problems are provided in a separate section at the end of the book. For those questions in the white box the worked solutions are provided in the *Student's Manual* accompanying this book. Further review problems for this chapter are available on the accompanying website www.drury-online.com. The answers to these problems are available for lecturers on the lecturer's password protected section of the website.

Case studies

The website also includes over 30 case study problems. A list of these cases is provided in Part Seven of this book. Several cases are relevant to the content of this chapter. Examples include Anjo Ltd., Boston Creamery and the Berkshire Toy Company.

Review questions

19.1 Under what circumstances will a (a) material mix and (b) material yield variances arise? *(pp. 778–80)*

19.2 Distinguish between a sales margin mix and sales margin quantity variance. *(pp. 782–84)*

19.3 Why do some writers criticize separating sales variances into their price and quantity elements? *(pp. 785–86)*

19.4 Describe the two alternative way of accounting for the variances at the end of an accounting period. *(pp. 793–95)*

19.5 What are planning variances? Why are they separately identified? *(pp. 795–98)*

19.6 Why is it advocated that opportunity costs should be incorporated into variance analysis? *(pp. 798–99)*

19.7 Describe three approaches for determining when a variance should be investigated. *(p. 801)*

19.8 Explain why actual performance might differ from standard performance. *(pp. 802–03)*

19.9 When should a standard cost variance be investigated? *(p. 803)*

19.10 What is a statistical control chart? How can it be applied to determining when a variance should be investigated? *(pp. 805–06)*

19.11 Explain why the usefulness of standard costing in a modern business environment had been questioned. *(pp. 809–11)*

19.12 Explain the future potential role of standard costing in a modern business environment. *(pp. 812–13)*

19.13 How can standard costing be used when ABC has been implemented? *(pp. 813–15)*

19.14 Why is standard costing more suitable for controlling the cost of unit-level activities? *(p. 813)*

Review problems

19.15 Advanced

The following data are to be used to answer questions (a) and (b) below
SW plc manufactures a product known as the TRD100 by mixing two materials. The standard material cost per unit of the TRD100 is as follows:

		£
Material X	12 litres @ £2.50	30
Material Y	18 litres @ £3.00	54

In October 2002, the actual mix used was 984 litres of X and 1230 litres of Y. The actual output was 72 units of TRD100.

(a) The total material mix variance reported was nearest to

A £102 (F) B £49 (F) C £49 (A) D £151 (A)

(3 marks)

(b) The total material yield variance reported was nearest to

A £102 (F) B £49 (F) C £49 (A) D £151 (A)

(2 marks)

CIMA Management Accounting – Performance Management

19.16 Advanced

Company P sells 3 products – R, S and T. Sales information for April 2002 was as follows:

	Budgeted sales units	Budgeted price per unit	Actual sales units	Actual price per unit
R	100	£100	108	£104
S	150	£50	165	£47
T	250	£35	221	£37

The expected size of the market for April was 2500 units. The actual market size was 2650 units.

The market share variance and sales mix variance were:

	Market share variance	Sales mix variance
A	£1490 (A)	£1890 (A)
B	£1575 (F)	£850 (F)
C	£1575 (F)	£315 (A)
D	£1890 (A)	£315 (A)
E	£1890 (A)	£850 (F)

(4 marks)

CIMA Management Accounting – Decision Making

19.17 **Advanced**

The following data relate to both questions (a) and (b)

A company has budgeted to produce and sell 15 000 units per annum of a single product. The budgeted market size for this product is 75 000 units per annum. The budgeted information per unit is as follows:

	£
Selling price	125
Standard cost:	
Direct materials	20
Direct labour	15
Variable overhead	10
Fixed overhead	5
Standard profit	75

In the period covered by the budget, the following actual results were recorded:

Production and sales	13 000 units
Industry sales	10% lower than previously forecast

(a) The market size variance, calculated on a contribution per unit basis is

A £40 000 adverse
B £40 000 favourable
C £120 000 adverse
D £120 000 favourable
E £160 000 adverse

(2 marks)

(b) The market share variance, calculated on a contribution per unit basis is

A £40 000 adverse
B £40 000 favourable
C £120 000 adverse
D £120 000 favourable
E £160 000 favourable

(2 marks)

CIMA Management Accounting – Decision Making

19.18 Advanced

The following data relate to both questions (a) and (b)

P Ltd operates a standard costing system. The following information has been extracted from the standard cost card for one of its products:

Budgeted production		1 250 units
Direct material cost	7 kg @ £4.10 per kg	£28.70 per unit

Actual results for the period were as follows:

Production		1 000 units
Direct material (purchased and used)	7700 kg	£33 880

It has subsequently been noted that the market price of the material was £4.50 per kg during the period.

(a) The value of the planning variance is

A £1225 adverse.
B £2800 adverse.
C £3500 adverse.
D £4375 adverse.
E £5950 adverse.

(2 marks)

(b) The value of the material usage variance is

A £2870 adverse.
B £3080 adverse.
C £3150 adverse.
D £3587.50 adverse.
E £3937.50 adverse.

(2 marks)

CIMA Management Accounting – Decision Making

19.19 Advanced: Accounting entries for a standard costing system

Bronte Ltd manufactures a single product, a laminated kitchen unit with a standard cost of £80 made up as follows:

	(£)
Direct materials (15 sq. metres at £3 per sq. metre)	45
Direct labour (5 hours at £4 per hour)	20
Variable overheads (5 hours at £2 per hour)	10
Fixed overheads (5 hours at £1 per hour)	5
	80

The standard selling price of the kitchen unit is £100. The monthly budget projects production and sales of 1000 units. Actual figures for the month of April are as follows:

Sales 1200 units at £102
Production 1400 units
Direct materials 22 000 sq. metres at £4 per sq. metre
Direct wages 6800 hours at £5
Variable overheads £11 000
Fixed overheads £6000

You are required to prepare:

(a) a trading account reconciling actual and budgeted profit and showing all the appropriate variances

(13 marks)

(b) ledger accounts in respect of the above transactions.

*ICAEW Accounting Techniques**

(*The original examination question did not include part (b).)

19.20 **Advanced: Material mix and yield variances**

Acca-chem Co plc manufacture a single product, product W, and have provided you with the following information which relates to the period which has just ended:

Standard cost per batch of product W

	Materials:	Kilos	Price per kilo (£)	Total (£)
	F	15	4	60
	G	12	3	36
	H	8	6	48
		35		144
Less: Standard loss		3		
Standard yield		32		
Labour:		Hours	Rate per hour (£)	
Department P		4	10	40
Department Q		2	6	12
				196

Budgeted sales for the period are 4096 kilos at £16 per kilo. There were no budgeted opening or closing stocks of product W.

The actual materials and labour used for 120 batches were:

	Materials:	Kilos	Price per kilo (£)	Total (£)
	F	1680	4.25	7 140
	G	1650	2.80	4 620
	H	870	6.40	5 568
		4200		17 328
Less: Actual loss		552		
Actual yield		3648		
Labour:		Hours	Rate per hour (£)	
Department P		600	10.60	6 360
Department Q		270	5.60	1 512
				25 200

All of the production of W was sold during the period for £16.75 per kilo.

Required:

(a) Calculate the following material variances:
– price
– usage
– mix
– yield.

(5 marks)

(b) Prepare an analysis of the material mix and price variances for each of the materials used.

(3 marks)

(c) Calculate the following labour variances:
– cost
– efficiency
– rate
for each of the production departments.

(4 marks)

(d) Calculate the sales variances.

(3 marks)

(e) Comment on your findings to help explain what has happened to the yield variance.

(5 marks)
(Total 20 marks)
ACCA Paper 8 Managerial Finance

19.21 Advanced: Sales mix and quantity variances and planning and operating variances

Milbao plc make and sell three types of electronic game for which the following budget/standard information and actual information is available for a four-week period:

Model	Budget sales (units)	Standard unit data		Actual sales (units)
		Selling price (£)	Variable cost (£)	
Superb	30 000	100	40	36 000
Excellent	50 000	80	25	42 000
Good	20 000	70	22	18 000

Budgeted fixed costs are £2 500 000 for the four-week period. Budgeted fixed costs should be changed to product units at an overall budgeted average cost unit where it is relevant to do so.

Required:

(a) Calculate the sales volume variance for each model and in total for the four-week period where (i) turnover (ii) contribution and (iii) net profit is used as the variance valuation base.

(9 marks)

(b) Discuss the relative merits of each of the valuation bases of the sales volume variance calculated in (a) above.

(6 marks)

(c) Calculate the *total* sales quantity and sales mix variances for Milbao plc for the four-week period, using contribution as the valuation base. (Individual model variances are not required.)

(4 marks)

(d) Comment on why the individual model variances for sales mix and sales quantity may provide misleading information to management.
(No calculations are required.)

(4 marks)

(e) The following additional information is available for the four-week period:

1. The actual selling price and variable costs of Milbao plc are 10% and 5% lower respectively, than the original budget/standard.
2. General market prices have fallen by 6% from the original standard. Short-term strategy by Milbao plc accounts for the residual fall in selling price.
3. 3% of the variable cost reduction from the original budget/standard is due to an over-estimation of a wage award, the remainder (i.e. 2%) is due to short-term operational improvements.

(i) Prepare a summary for a four-week period for model 'Superb' *only*, which reconciles original budget contribution with actual contribution where planning and operational variances are taken into consideration.

(8 marks)

(ii) Comment on the usefulness to management of planning and operational variance analysis in feedback and feedforward control.

(4 marks)

(Total 35 marks)

ACCA Paper 9 Information for Control and Decision Making

19.22 **Advanced: Planning and operating variances**

A year ago Kenp Ltd entered the market for the manufacture and sale of a revolutionary insulating material. The budgeted production and sales volumes were 1000 units. The originally estimated sales price and standard costs for this new product were:

	(£)	(£)
Standard sales price (per unit)		100
Standard costs (per unit)		
Raw materials (Aye 10 kg at £5)	50	
Labour (6 hours at £4)	24	74
Standard contribution (per unit)		£26

Actual results were:

First year's results

	(£000)	**(£000)**
Sales (1000 units)		158
Production costs (1000 units)		
Raw materials (Aye 10 800 kg)	97.2	
Labour (5800 hours)	34.8	132
Actual contribution		£26

'Throughout the year we attempted to operate as efficiently as possible, given the prevailing conditions' stated the managing director. 'Although in total the performance agreed with budget, in every detailed respect, expect volume, there were large differences. These were due, mainly, to the tremendous success of the new insulating material which created increased demand both for the product itself and all the manufacturing resources used in its production. This then resulted in price rises all round.'

'Sales were made at what was felt to be the highest feasible price but, it was later discovered, our competitors sold for £165 per unit and we could have equalled this price. Labour costs rose dramatically with increased demand for the specialist skills required to produce the product and the general market rate was £6.25 per hour – although Kenp always paid below the general market rate whenever possible.'

'Raw material Aye was chosen as it appeared cheaper than the alternative material Bee which could have been used. The costs which were expected at the time the budget was prepared were (per kg): Aye, £5 and Bee, £6. However, the market prices relating to efficient purchases of the materials during the year were:

Aye £8.50 per kg, and
Bee £7.00 per kg.

Therefore it would have been more appropriate to use Bee, but as production plans were based on Aye it was Aye that was used.'

'It is not proposed to request a variance analysis for the first year's results as most of the deviations from budget were caused by the new products great success and this could not have been fully anticipated and planned for. In any event the final contribution was equal to that originally budgeted so operations must have been fully efficient.'

Required:

(a) Compute the traditional variances for the first year's operations. *(5 marks)*

(b) Prepare an analysis of variances for the first year's operations which will be useful in the circumstances of Kenp Ltd. The analysis should indicate the extent to which the variances were due to operational efficiency or planning causes. *(10 marks)*

(c) Using, for illustration, a comparison of the raw material variances computed in (a) and (b) above, briefly outline two major advantages and two major disadvantages of the approach applied in part (b) over the traditional approach. *(5 marks)*

(Total 20 marks)

ACCA P2 Management Accounting

19.23 Advanced: Traditional and activity-based variance analysis

Frolin Chemicals Ltd produces FDN. The standard ingredients of 1 kg of FDN are:

0.65 kg of ingredient F	@ £4.00 per kg
0.30 kg of ingredient D	@ £6.00 per kg
0.20 kg of ingredient N	@ £2.50 per kg
1.15 kg	

Production of 4000 kg of FDN was budgeted for April. The production of FDN is entirely automated and production costs attributed to FDN production comprise only direct materials and overheads. The FDN production operation works on a JIT basis and no ingredient or FDN inventories are held.

Overheads were budgeted for April for the FDN production operation as follows:

Activity		Total amount
Receipt of deliveries from suppliers	(standard delivery quantity is 460 kg)	£4 000
Despatch of goods to customers	(standard despatch quantity is 100 kg)	£8 000
		£12 000

In April, 4200 kg of FDN were produced and cost details were as follows:

- *Materials used:*
  2840 kg of F, 1210 kg of D and 860 kg of N
  total cost £20 380
- *Actual overhead costs*:
  12 supplier deliveries (cost £4800) were made, and 38 customer despatches (cost £7800) were processed.

Frolin Chemicals Ltd's budget committee met recently to discuss the preparation of the financial control report for April, and the following discussion occurred:

Chief Accountant: 'The overheads do not vary directly with output and are therefore by definition "fixed". They should be analysed and reported accordingly.'

Management Accountant: 'The overheads do not vary with output, but they are certainly not fixed. They should be analysed and reported on an activity basis.'

Requirements:

Having regard to this discussion,

(a) prepare a variance analysis for FDN production costs in April: separate the material cost variance into price, mixture and yield components; separate the overhead cost variance into expenditure, capacity and efficiency components using consumption of ingredient F as the overhead absorption base;

(11 marks)

(b) prepare a variance analysis for FDN production overhead costs in April on an activity basis;

(9 marks)

(c) explain how, in the design of an activity-based costing system, you would identify and select the most appropriate activities and cost drivers.

(5 marks)

(Total 25 marks)

CIMA Stage 3 Management Accounting Applications

19.24 Advanced: Investigation of variances

From past experience a company operating a standard cost system has accumulated the following information in relation to variances in its monthly management accounts:

Percentage of total number of variances

(1) Its variances fall into two categories:

Category 1: those which are not worth investigating	64
Category 2: those which are worth investigating	36
	100

(2) Of Category 2, corrective action has eliminated 70% of the variances, but the remainder have continued.

(3) The cost of investigation averages £350 and that of correcting variances averages £550.

(4) The average size of any variance not corrected is £525 per month and the company's policy is to assess the present value of such costs at 2% per month for a period of five months.

You are required to:

(a) prepare *two* decision trees, to represent the position if an investigation is:

(i) carried out;

(ii) not carried out;

(12 marks)

(b) recommend, with supporting calculations, whether or not the company should follow a policy of investigating variances as a matter of routine;

(3 marks)

(c) explain briefly *two* types of circumstance that would give rise to variances in Category 1 and *two* to those in Category 2;

(6 marks)

(d) mention any *one* variation in the information used that you feel would be beneficial to the company if you wished to improve the quality of the decision-making rule recommended in (b) above. Explain briefly why you have suggested it.

(4 marks)

(Total 25 marks)

CIMA P3 Management Accounting

19.25 Advanced

(a) In high technology small batch manufacture, accountants sometimes take the view that standard costing cannot be applied. The move into high technology is generally accompanied by a shift away from labour-dominated to capital-intensive processes.

You are required to appraise the application of standard costing in the circumstance described above.

(12 marks)

(b) In order to secure and direct employee motivation towards the achievement of a firm's goals, it may be considered that budget centres should be created at the lowest defined management level.

You are required to discuss the advantages and disadvantages of creating budget centres at such a level.

(12 marks)
(Total 24 marks)
CIMA Stage 4 Management Accounting – Control and Audit

19.26 **Advanced**

In recent years, writers have argued that standard costing and variance analysis should not be used for cost control and performance evaluation purposes in today's manufacturing world. Its use, they argue, is likely to induce behaviour which is inconsistent with the strategic manufacturing objectives that companies need to achieve in order to survive in today's intensely competitive international economic environment.

Requirements:

(a) Explain the arguments referred to in the above paragraph concerning the relevance of standard costing and variance analysis.

(10 marks)

(b) Explain the arguments in favour of the relevance of standard costing and variance analysis in the modern manufacturing environment.

(8 marks)

(c) Suggest methods that might be used by management accountants to control costs and evaluate efficiency as alternatives or complements to standard costing and variance analysis.

(7 marks)
(Total 25 marks)
CIMA Stage 3 Management Accounting Applications

19.27 **Advanced**

(a) The investigation of a variance is a fundamental element in the effective exercise of control through budgetary control and standard costing systems. The systems for identifying the variances may be well defined and detailed yet the procedures adopted to determine whether to pursue the investigation of variances may well not be formalized.

Critically examine this situation, discussing possible effective approaches to the investigation of variances.

(15 marks)

(b) Explain the major motivational factors which influence managers in their actions to eliminate variances from budget.

(10 marks)
(Total 25 marks)
CIMA Stage 4 Management Accounting Control and Audit

Review problems (with answers in the Student's Manual)

19.28 Advanced

(a) Outline the factors a management accountant should consider when deciding whether or not to investigate variances revealed in standard costing and budgetary control systems.

(b) Indicate briefly what action the management accountant can take to improve the chances of achieving positive results from investigating variances.

(20 marks)

CIMA P3 Management Accounting

19.29 Advanced

Explain:

(a) the problems concerning control of operations that a manufacturing company can be expected to experience in using a standard costing system during periods of rapid inflation;

(b) three methods by which the company could try to overcome the problems to which you have referred in your answer to (a) above, indicating the shortcomings of each method.

(20 marks)

CIMA P3 Management Accounting

19.30 Advanced

(a) Name three bases of valuation of the sales volume variance in a standard cost system and discuss the appropriateness of each valuation basis.

(9 marks)

(b) Expand on arguments supporting the view that the use of sales variances in a standard cost system could be enhanced through the use of a planning and operational approach to the valuation of sales price variances.

(6 marks)

(Total 15 marks)

ACCA Paper 9 – Information for Control and Decision Making

19.31 Advanced

(a) Discuss ways in which standards may be seen as useful aids in management accounting decision-making.

(6 marks)

(b) Suggest ways in which the use of standards may be seen as having a *dysfunctional effect* in relation to decision making about each of materials, labour and overhead cost.

(9 marks)

(Total 15 marks)

ACCA Paper 9 – Information for Control and Decision Making

19.32 Intermediate: Calculation of labour, material and overhead variances plus appropriate accounting entries

JC Limited produces and sells one product only, Product J, the standard cost for which is as follows for one unit.

	(£)
Direct material X – 10 kilograms at £20	200
Direct material Y – 5 litres at £6	30
Direct wages – 5 hours at £6	30
Fixed production overhead	50
Total standard cost	310
Standard gross profit	90
Standard selling price	400

The fixed production overhead is based on an expected annual output of 10 800 units produced at an even flow throughout the year; assume each calendar month is equal. Fixed production overhead is absorbed on direct labour hours.

During April, the first month of the financial year, the following were the actual results for an actual production of 800 units.

		(£)
Sales on credit:		320 000
800 units at £400		
Direct materials:		
X 7800 kilogrammes	159 900	
Y 4300 litres	23 650	
Direct wages: 4200 hours	24 150	
Fixed production overhead	47 000	
		254 700
Gross profit		65 300

The material price variance is extracted at the time of receipt and the raw materials stores control is maintained at standard prices. The purchases, bought on credit, during the month of April were:

X 9000 kilograms at £20.50 per kg from K Limited
Y 5000 litres at £5.50 per litre from C plc.

Assume no opening stocks.

Wages owing for March brought forward were £6000.

Wages paid during April (net) £20 150.

Deductions from wages owing to the Inland Revenue for PAYE and NI were £5000 and the wages accrued for April were £5000.

The fixed production overhead of £47 000 was made up of expense creditors of £33 000, none of which was paid in April, and depreciation of £14 000.

The company operates an integrated accounting system.

You are required to

(a) (i) calculate price and usage variances for each material,

(ii) calculate labour rate and efficiency variances,

(iii) calculate fixed production overhead expenditure, efficiency and volume variances;

(9 marks)

(b) show all the accounting entries in T accounts for the month of April – the work-in-progress account should be maintained at standard cost and each balance on the separate variance accounts is to be transferred to a Profit and Loss Account which you are also required to show;

(18 marks)

(c) explain the reason for the difference between the actual gross profit given in the question and the profit shown in your profit and loss account.

(3 marks)

(Total 30 marks)

CIMA Stage 2 Cost Accounting

19.33 **Advanced: Mix variances and reconciliation of actual and budgeted profit**

The budgeted income statement for one of the products of Derwen plc for the month of May was as follows:

Budgeted income statement – May

	(£)	(£)	(£)
Sales revenue:			
10 000 units at £5			50 000
Production costs:			
Budgeted production			
10 000 units			
Direct materials:			
Material			
A (5000 kg at £0.30)	1 500		
B (5000 kg at £0.70)	3 500		
		5 000	
Direct labour:			
Skilled (4500 hours at £3.00)	13 500		
Semi-skilled (2600 hours at £2.50)	6 500		
		20 000	
Overhead cost:			
Fixed		10 000	
Variable (10 000 units at £0.50)		5 000	
		40 000	
Add Opening stock (1000 units at £4)		4 000	
		44 000	
Deduct Closing stock (1000 units at £4)		4 000	
Cost of goods sold			40 000
Budgeted profit			10 000

During May production and sales were both above budget and the following income statement was prepared:

Income statement – May

	(£)	(£)	(£)
Sales revenue:			
7000 units at £5			35 000
4000 units at £4.75			19 000
			54 000
Production costs:			
Actual production			
12 000 units			
Direct materials:			
Material			
A (8000 kg at £0.20)	1 600		
B (5000 kg at £0.80)	4 000		
		5 600	
Direct labour:			
Skilled (6000 hours at £2.95)	17 700		
Semi-skilled (3150 hours at £2.60)	8 190		
		25 890	
Overhead cost:			
Fixed		9 010	
Variable		7 500	
(12 000 units at £0.625)			
		48 000	
Add Opening stock (1000 units at £4)		4 000	
		52 000	
Deduct Closing stock (2000 units at £4)		8 000	
Cost of goods sold			44 000
'Actual' profit			10 000

In the above statement stock is valued at the standard cost of £4 per unit.

There is general satisfaction because the budgeted profit level has been achieved but you have been asked to prepare a standard costing statement analysing the differences between the budget and the actual performance. In your analysis, include calculations of the sales volume and sales price variances and the following cost variances: direct material price, mix, yield and usage variances; direct labour rate, mix, productivity and efficiency variances: and overhead spending and volume variances.

(17 marks)

Provide a commentary on the variances and give your views on their usefulness.

(5 marks)

(Total 22 marks)

ACCA Level 2 Management Accounting

19.34 **Advanced: Planning and operating variances**

POV Ltd uses a standard costing system to control and report upon the production of its single product.

An abstract from the original standard cost card of the product is as follows:

	(£)	(£)
Selling price per unit		200
less: 4 kg materials @ £20 per kg	80	
6 hours labour @ £7 per hour	42	122
Contribution per unit		78

For Period 3, 2500 units were budgeted to be produced and sold but the actual production and sales were 2850 units.

The following information was also available:

(i) At the commencement of Period 3 the normal material became unobtainable and it was necessary to use an alternative. Unfortunately, 0.5 kg per unit extra was required and it was thought that the material would be more difficult to work with. The price of the alternative was expected to be £16.50 per kg. In the event, actual usage was 12 450 kg at £18 per kg.

(ii) Weather conditions unexpectedly improved for the period with the result that a £0.50 per hour bad weather bonus, which had been allowed for in the original standard, did not have to be paid. Because of thc difficulties expected with the alternative material, management agreed to pay the workers £8 per hour for Period 3 only. During the period 18 800 hours were paid for.

After using conventional variances for some time, POV Ltd is contemplating extending its system to include planning and operational variances.

You are required:

(a) to prepare a statement reconciling budgeted contribution for the period with actual contribution, using conventional material and labour variances;

(4 marks)

(b) to prepare a similar reconciliation statement using planning and operational variances;

(14 marks)

(c) to explain the meaning of the variances shown in statement (b).

(4 marks)

(Total 22 marks)

CIMA Stage 3 Management Accounting Techniques

19.35 **Advanced: Activity based standard costing**

X Ltd has recently automated its manufacturing plant and has also adopted a Total Quality Management (TQM) philosophy and a Just in Time (JIT) manufacturing system. The company currently uses a standard absorption costing system for the electronic diaries which it manufactures.

The following information for the last quarter has been extracted from the company records.

	Budget	Actual
Fixed production overheads	$100 000	$102 300
Labour hours	10 000	11 000
Output (electronic diaries)	100 000	105 000

Fixed production overheads are absorbed on the basis of direct labour hours.

The following fixed production overhead variances have been reported:

	$
Expenditure variance	2 300 (A)
Capacity variance	10 000 (F)
Efficiency variance	5 000 (A)
Total	2 700 (F)

If the fixed production overheads had been further analysed and classified under an Activity Based Costing (ABC) system, the above information would then have been presented as follows:

	Budget	Actual
Costs:		
Material handling	$30 000	$30 800
Set up	$70 000	$71 500
Output (electronic diaries)	100 000	105 000
Activity:		
Material handling (orders executed)	5 000	5 500
Set up (production runs)	2 800	2 600

The following variances would have been reported:

		$
Overhead expenditure variance	Material handling	2 200 (F)
	Set ups	6 500 (A)
Overhead efficiency variance	Material handling	1 500 (A)
	Set ups	8 500 (F)
Total		2 700 (F)

Required:

(a) Explain why and how X Ltd may have to adapt its standard costing system now that it has adopted TQM and JIT in its recently automated manufacturing plant.

(9 marks)

(b) Explain the meaning of the fixed overhead variances calculated under the standard absorption costing system and discuss their usefulness to the management of X Ltd for decision-making.

(6 marks)

(c) For the variances calculated under the ABC classification,

(i) explain how they have been calculated;

(ii) discuss their usefulness to the management of X Ltd for decision-making.

(10 marks)

(Total 25 marks)

CIMA Management Accounting – Decision Making

19.36 **Advanced: Investigation of variances**

(a) The Secure Locke Company operates a system of standard costing, which it uses amongst other things as the basis for calculating certain management bonuses.

In September the Company's production of 100 000 keys was in accordance with budget. The standard quantity of material used in each key is one unit; the standard price is £0.05 per unit. In September 105 000 units of material were used, at an actual purchase price of £45 per thousand units (which was also the replacement cost).

The materials buyer is given a bonus of 10% of any favourable materials price variance. The production manager is given a bonus of 10% of any favourable materials quantity variance.

You are required:

(i) to calculate the materials cost variances for September;

(4 marks)

(ii) to record all relevant bookkeeping entries in journal form;

(2 marks)

(iii) to evaluate the bonus system from the view-points of the buyer, the production manager, and the company.

(6 marks)

(b) In October there was an adverse materials quantity variance of £500. A decision has to be made as to whether to investigate the key-making process to determine whether it is out of control.

On the basis of past experience the cost of an investigation is estimated at £50. The cost of correcting the process if it is found to be out of control is estimated at £100. The probability that the process is out of control is estimated at .50.

You are required:

(i) to calculate the minimum present value of the expected savings that would have to be made in future months in order to justify making an investigation;

(6 marks)

(ii) to suggest why the monthly cost savings arising from a systematic investigation are unlikely to be as great as the adverse materials variance of £500 which was experienced in the month of October;

(3 marks)

(iii) to calculate, if the expected present value of cost savings were *first* £600 and *second* £250, the respective levels of probability that the process was out of control, at which the management would be indifferent about whether to conduct an investigation.

(4 marks)

ICAEW Management Accounting

Divisional financial performance measures

20

Large companies produce and sell a wide variety of products throughout the world. Because of the complexity of their operations, it is difficult for top management to directly control operations. It may therefore be appropriate to divide a company into separate self-contained segments or divisions and to allow divisional managers to operate with a great deal of independence. A divisional manager has responsibility for both the production and marketing activities of the division. The danger in creating autonomous divisions is that divisional managers might not pursue goals that are in the best interests of the company as a whole. The objective of this chapter is to consider financial performance measures that will motivate managers to pursue those goals that will best benefit the company as a whole. In other words, the objective is to develop performance measures that will achieve goal congruence.

In this chapter we shall focus on financial measures of divisional performance. However, financial measures cannot adequately measure all those factors that are critical to the success of a division. Emphasis should also be given to reporting key non-financial

LEARNING OBJECTIVES

After studying this chapter, you should be able to:

- distinguish between functional and divisionalized organizational structures;
- explain why it is preferable to distinguish between managerial and economic performance;
- explain the factors that should be considered in designing financial performance measures for evaluating divisional managers;
- explain the meaning of return on investment, residual income and economic value added;
- compute economic value added;
- explain why performance measures may conflict with the net present value decision model;
- justify the use of a risk-adjusted discount rate for determining the divisional cost of capital;
- identify and explain the approaches that can be used to reduce the dysfunctional consequences of short-term financial measures.

measures relating to such areas as competitiveness, product leadership, quality, delivery performance, innovation and flexibility to respond to changes in demand. In particular, performance measures should be developed that support the objectives and competitive strategies of the organization. Divisional financial performance measures should therefore be seen as one of a range of measures that should be used to measure and control divisional performance.

Functional and divisionalized organizational structures

A **functional organizational structure** is one in which all activities of a similar type within a company are placed under the control of the appropriate departmental head. A simplified organization chart for a functional organizational structure is illustrated in Figure 20.1(a). It is assumed that the company illustrated consists of five separate departments – production, marketing, financial administration, purchasing and research and development. In a typical functional organization none of the managers of the five departments is responsible for more than a part of the process of acquiring the raw materials, converting them into finished products, selling to customers, and administering the financial aspects of this process. For example, the production department is responsible for the manufacture of all products at a minimum cost, and of satisfactory quality, and to meet the delivery dates requested by the marketing department. The marketing department is responsible for the total sales revenue and any costs associated with selling and distributing the products, but not for the total profit. The purchasing department is responsible for purchasing supplies at a minimum cost and of satisfactory quality so that the production requirements can be met.

You will see from Figure 20.1 that the marketing function is a revenue centre and the remaining departments are cost centres. Revenues and costs (including the cost of investments) are combined together only at the chief executive, or corporate level, which is classified as an investment centre.

Let us now consider Figure 20.1(b), which shows a **divisionalized organizational structure**, which is split up into divisions in accordance with the products which are made. You will see from the diagram that each divisional manager is responsible for all of the operations relating to his or her particular product. To reflect this greater autonomy each division is either an investment centre or a profit centre. To simplify the presentation it is assumed that all of the divisions in Figure 20.1(b) are investment centres (we shall discuss the factors influencing the choice of investment or profit centres later in the chapter). Note that within each division there are multiple cost and revenue centres and also that a functional structure is applied within each division. Figure 20.1(b) shows a simplified illustration of a divisionalized organizational structure. In practice, however, only part of a company may be divisionalized. For example, activities such as research and development, industrial relations, and general administration may be structured centrally on a functional basis with a responsibility for providing services to all of the divisions.

The distinguishing feature between the functional structure (Figure 20.1(a)) and the divisionalized structure (Figure 20.1(b)) is that in the functional structure only the organization as a whole is an investment centre and below this level a functional structure applies throughout. In contrast, in a divisionalized structure the organization is divided into separate investment or profit centres and a functional structure applies below this level. In this chapter we shall focus on financial measures and controls at the profit or investment centre (i.e. divisional) level.

Generally, a divisionalized organizational structure will lead to a decentralization of the decision-making process. For example, divisional managers will normally be free to set

FIGURE 20.1 *A functional and divisionalized organizational structure*

(a) Functional organizational structure

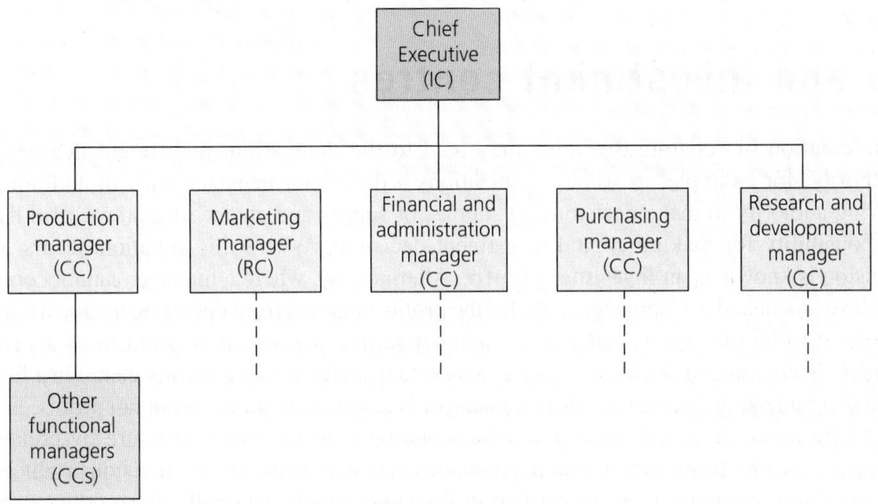

(b) Divisionalized organizational structure

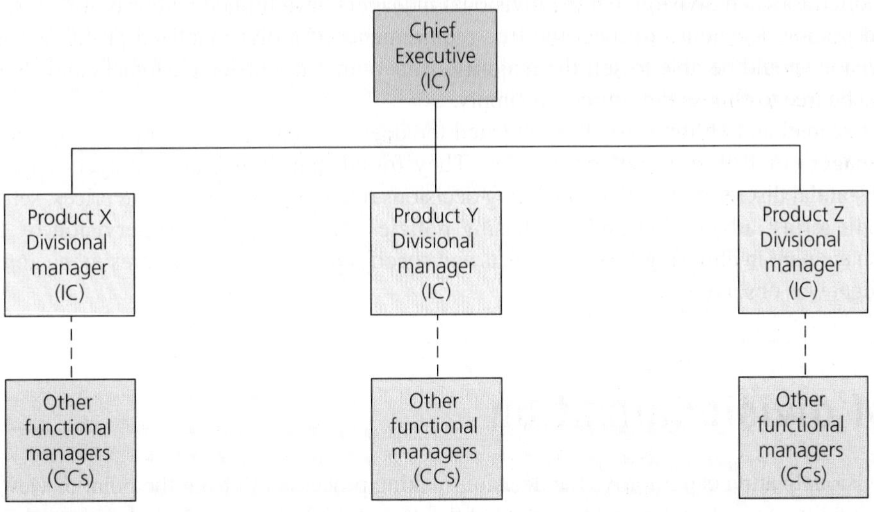

IC = Investment centres, CC = Cost centrres

selling prices, choose which market to sell in, make product mix and output decisions, and select suppliers (this may include buying from other divisions within the company or from other companies). In a functional organizational structure pricing, product mix and output decisions will be made by central management. Consequently, the functional managers in a centralized organization will have far less independence than divisional managers. One way to express the difference between the two organizational structures is to say that the divisional managers have profit responsibility. They are responsible for generating revenues, controlling costs and earning a satisfactory return on the capital invested in their operations.

The managers of the functional organizational structure do not have profit responsibility. For example, in Figure 20.1(a) the production manager has no control over sources of supply, selling prices, or product mix and output decisions.

Profit centres and investment centres

The creation of separate divisions may lead to the delegation of different degrees of authority; for example, in some organizations a divisional manager may, in addition to having authority to make decisions on sources of supply and choice of markets, also have responsibility for making capital investment decisions. Where this situation occurs, the division is known as an **investment centre**. Alternatively, where a manager cannot control the investment and is responsible only for the profits obtained from operating the fixed assets assigned to him or her by corporate headquarters, the segment is referred to as a **profit centre**. In contrast, the term **cost centre** is used to describe a responsibility centre in a functional organizational structure where a manager is responsible for costs but not profits.

Many firms attempt to simulate a divisionalized profit centre structure by creating separate manufacturing and marketing divisions in which the supplying division produces a product and transfers it to the marketing division, which then sells the product in the external market. Transfer prices are assigned to the products transferred between the divisions. This practice creates pseudo-divisionalized profit centres. Separate profits can be reported for each division, but the divisional managers have limited authority for sourcing and pricing decisions. To meet the true requirements of a divisionalized profit centre, a division should be able to sell the majority of its output to outside customers and should also be free to choose the sources of supply.

Ezzamel and Hilton (1980) investigated the degree of autonomy allowed to divisional managers in 129 large UK companies. They found that divisional managers enjoyed substantial discretion in taking operating decisions relating to output, selling prices, setting credit terms, advertising and purchasing policies. However, close supervision by top management in choosing capital projects and specifying capital expenditures in the annual budget was observed.

Advantages of divisionalization

Divisionalization can improve the decision-making process both from the point of view of the quality of the decision and the speed of the decision. The quality of the decisions should be improved because decisions can be made by the person who is familiar with the situation and who should therefore be able to make more informed judgements than central management who cannot be intimately acquainted with all the activities of the various segments of the business. Speedier decisions should also occur because information does not have to pass along the chain of command to and from top management. Decisions can be made on the spot by those who are familiar with the product lines and production processes and who can react to changes in local conditions in a speedy and efficient manner.

In addition, delegation of responsibility to divisional managers provides them with greater freedom, thus making their activities more challenging and providing the opportunity to achieve self-fulfilment. This process should mean that motivation and efficiency will be increased not just at the divisional manager level but throughout the whole division. A study by Dittman and Ferris (1978) of the attitudes of managers in companies in the USA found that those managers in charge of profit centres had greater job satisfaction than the managers of cost centres. They conclude that wherever possible, system designers ought to try to construct profit centres for organizational units.

Another important reason for adopting a divisionalized structure is that the distribution of decision-making responsibility to divisions frees top management from detailed involvement in day-to-day operations, and enables them to devote more effort to strategic planning. It is also claimed that divisions can provide an excellent training ground for future members of top management by enabling trainee managers to acquire the basic managerial skills and experience in an environment that is less complex than managing the company as a whole.

Disadvantages of divisionalization

If a company is divisionalized, there is a danger that divisions may compete with each other excessively and that divisional managers may be encouraged to take action which will increase their own profits at the expense of the profits of other divisions. This may adversely affect co-operation between the divisions and lead to a lack of harmony in achieving the overall organizational goals of the company. This in turn may lead to a reduction in total company profits.

It is also claimed that the costs of activities that are common to all divisions may be greater for a divisionalized structure than for a centralized structure. For example, a large central accounting department in a centralized organizational structure may be less costly to operate than separate accounting departments for each division within a divisionalized structure. If top management are contemplating a divisionalized structure, it is important that they assess whether the additional benefits will exceed the additional costs.

A further argument against divisionalization is that top management loses some control by delegating decision-making to divisional managers. It is argued that a series of control reports is not as effective as detailed knowledge of a company's activities. However, with a good system of performance evaluation together with appropriate control information, top management should be able to effectively control operations.

Pre-requisites for successful divisionalization

A divisionalized structure is most suited to companies engaged in several dissimilar activities. The reason is that it is difficult for top management to be intimately acquainted with all the diverse activities of the various segments of the business. On the other hand, when the major activities of a company are closely related, these activities should be carefully coordinated, and this coordination is more easily achieved in a centralized organizational structure. The results from a number of surveys suggest that divisionalization is more common in companies having diversified activities than when single or related activities are undertaken (Ezzamel and Hilton, 1980).

For successful divisionalization it is important that the activities of a division be as independent as possible of other activities. However, Solomons (1965) argues that even though substantial independence of divisions from each other is a necessary condition for divisionalization, if carried to the limit it would destroy the very idea that such divisions are an integral part of any single business. Divisions should be more than investments they should contribute not only to the success of the company but to the success of each other.

According to Solomons, a further condition for the success of divisionalization is that the relations between divisions should be regulated so that no one division, by seeking its own profit, can reduce that of the company as a whole. He states that this is not the same as seeking profit at the expense of other divisions, but the amount that a division adds to its own profit must exceed the loss that it inflicts on another division. Unfortunately, conflicts between divisions do arise, and one of the important tasks of the accountant is to design an accounting control system that will discourage a division from improving its own profit at the expense of the company as a whole.

Distinguishing between the managerial and economic performance of the division

Before discussing the factors to be considered in determining how divisional profitability should be measured, we must decide whether the primary purpose is to measure the performance of the division or that of the divisional manager. The messages transmitted from these two measures may be quite different. For example, a manager may be assigned to an ailing division to improve performance, and might succeed in substantially improving the performance of the division. However, the division might still be unprofitable because of industry factors, such as overcapacity and a declining market. The future of the division might be uncertain, but the divisional manager may well be promoted as a result of the outstanding managerial performance. Conversely, a division might report significant profits but, because of management deficiencies, the performance may be unsatisfactory when the favourable economic environment is taken into account.

If the purpose is to evaluate the divisional manager then only those items directly controllable by the manager should be included in the profitability measure. Thus all allocations of indirect costs, such as central service and central administration costs, which cannot be influenced by divisional managers, ought not to be included in the profitability measure. Such costs can only be controlled where they are incurred; which means that central service managers should be held accountable for them.

Corporate headquarters, however, will also be interested in evaluating a division's economic performance for decision-making purposes, such as expansion, contraction and divestment decisions. In this situation a measure that includes only those amounts directly controllable by the divisional manager would overstate the economic performance of the division. This overstatement occurs because, if the divisions were independent companies, they would have to incur the costs of those services provided by head office. Therefore, to measure the economic performance of the division many items that the divisional manager cannot influence, such as interest expenses, taxes and the allocation of central administrative staff expenses, should be included in the profitability measure.

Alternative divisional profit measures

There are strong arguments for computing two measures of divisional profitability – one to evaluate managerial performance and the other to evaluate the economic performance of the division. In this chapter we shall focus on both these measures. The most common measures of divisional profitability are return on investment (that is, profit as a percentage of the investment in a division) residual income and economic value added. The reported divisional profit is a component of each of these measures. At this stage we shall restrict our attention purely to problems that are encountered with divisional profit measurement before turning our attention to the above three common measures of divisional profitability.

Exhibit 20.1 presents a divisional profit statement. You can see that there are four different profit measures that we can use to measure divisional performance. We shall focus initially on measuring *managerial* performance. The **variable short-run contribution margin** is inappropriate for performance evaluation, because it does not include fixed costs that are controllable by the divisional manager. For example, a manager may not be motivated to control non-variable labour costs or equipment rentals, since they fall below the variable short-run contribution line and are not included in the performance measure.

The **controllable contribution** is computed by deducting from total divisional revenues all those costs that are controllable by the division manager. This measure therefore includes controllable fixed costs such as non-variable labour, equipment rental and the cost of utilities. These costs are fixed in the short term, but in the longer term the divisional manager has the option of reducing them by altering the scale of operations or reducing the complexity and diversity of product lines and distribution channels. Where a division is a profit centre, depreciation is not a controllable cost, since the manager does not have authority to make capital investment decisions. Depreciation, however, should be deemed to be a controllable expense for an investment centre in respect of those assets that are controllable by the divisional manager.

Controllable contribution is the most appropriate measure of a divisional manager's performance, since it measures the ability of managers to use the resources under their control effectively. It should not be interpreted in isolation if it is used directly to evaluate the performance of a divisional manager. Instead, the controllable contribution reported by a division should be evaluated relative to a budgeted performance, so that market conditions can be taken into account.

In practice, it is extremely difficult to distinguish between controllable and non-controllable costs. However, three situations can be identified that will assist us in overcoming this problem. Where a division is completely free to shop around for a service and there is no rule requiring the division to obtain the service from within the company, the expense is clearly controllable. Alternatively, a division may not be free to choose an outside source of supply for the service in question, but it may be able to decide how much of this service is utilized. In this latter situation the quantity is controllable by the division but the price is not. An appropriate solution here is for the division to be charged with the actual quantity at the standard or budgeted cost for the service that has been obtained. Thus any difference between the budget and actual performance would relate solely to excess usage by the division recorded at the standard price. Finally, the division may not be free to decide on either the quantity of the service it utilizes or the price it will be charged. Industrial relations costs may fall into this category. Here the divisions have no choice but to accept an apportioned cost for the benefits they have received (such apportionments may be made for external reporting purposes). In situations like this, the costs charged to the division for the service can only be regarded as a non-controllable item of divisional overhead. Another general rule that can be applied for distinguishing between controllable and non-controllable costs is to follow the guideline suggested by Merchant (1998) – that is, hold managers accountable for those costs that you want them to pay attention to.

Controllable contribution provides an incomplete measure of the *economic* performance of a division, since it does not include those costs that are attributable to the division but which are not controllable by the divisional manager. For example, depreciation of divisional assets, and head office finance and legal staff who are assigned to providing services for specific divisions, would fall into this category. These expenses would be avoidable if a decision were taken to close the division. Those non-controllable expenses that are attributable to a division, and which would be avoidable if the division was closed, are deducted from controllable contribution to derive the **divisional contribution**. This is clearly a useful figure for evaluating the *economic* contribution of the division, since it represents the contribution that a division is making to corporate profits and overheads. It should not be

EXHIBIT 20.1
Alternative divisional profit measures

Sales to outside customers	xxx
Transfers to other divisions	xxx
Total sales revenue	xxx
Less variable costs	xxx
1. Variable short-run contribution margin	xxx
Less controllable fixed costs	xxx
2. Controllable contribution	xxx
Less non-controllable avoidable costs	xxx
3. Divisional contribution	xxx
Less allocated corporate expenses	xxx
4. Divisional net profit before taxes	xxx

used, however, to evaluate managerial performance, since it includes costs that are not controllable by divisional managers.

Many companies allocate all corporate general and administrative expenses to divisions to derive a **divisional net profit before taxes**. From a theoretical point of view, it is difficult to justify such allocations since they tend to be arbitrary and do not have any connection with the manner in which divisional activities influence the level of these corporate expenses. Divisional contribution would therefore seem to be the most appropriate measure of divisions' *economic* performance, since it is not distorted by arbitrary allocations. We have noted, however, that corporate headquarters may wish to compare a division's economic performance with that of comparable firms operating in the same industry. The divisional contribution would overstate the performance of the division, because if the division were independent, it would have to incur the costs of those services performed by head office. The apportioned head office costs are an approximation of the costs that the division would have to incur if it traded as a separate company. Consequently, companies may prefer to use divisional net profit when comparing the economic performance of a division with similar companies.

For the reasons mentioned above, divisional net profit is not a satisfactory measure for evaluating *managerial* performance. Despite the many theoretical arguments against divisional net profit, the empirical evidence indicates that this measure is used widely to evaluate both divisional *economic* and *managerial* performance (Reece and Cool, 1978; Fremgen and Liao, 1981; Ramadan, 1989; Skinner, 1990; Drury *et al.*, 1993). In the Fremgen and Liao survey respondents were asked why they allocated indirect costs. The most important managerial performance evaluation reason was to 'remind profit centre managers that indirect costs exist and that profit centre earnings must be adequate to cover a share of these costs'. The counter-argument to this is that if central management wishes to inform managers that divisions must be profitable enough to cover not only their own operations but corporate expenses as well, it is preferable to set a high budgeted controllable contribution target that takes account of these factors. Divisional managers can then concentrate on increasing controllable contribution by focusing on those costs and revenues that are under their control and not be concerned with costs that they cannot control.

A further reason for cost allocations cited in the surveys by Fremgen and Liao and Skinner was that by allocating central overhead costs to divisions, divisional managers are made aware of these costs, so they will exert pressure on central management to minimize the costs of central staff departments. There is also some evidence to suggest that companies hold managers accountable for divisional net profit because this is equivalent to the measure that financial markets focus on to evaluate the performance of the company as a whole (Joseph *et al.*, 1996). Top management therefore require their divisional managers to concentrate on the same measures as those used by financial markets.

A more recent UK study by El-Shishini and Drury (2001) asked the respondents to rank in order of importance the factors influencing organizations to allocate the cost of shared resources to divisions. In rank order the highest rankings were attributed to the following factors:

1. to show divisional managers the total costs of operating their divisions;
2. to make divisional managers aware that such costs exist and must be covered by divisional profits;
3. divisional managers would incur such costs if they were independent units;
4. divisional managers should bear the full business risk as if they were managers of non-divisionalized companies.

Return on investment

Instead of focusing purely on the absolute size of a division's profits, most organizations focus on the **return on investment (ROI)** of a division. Note that ROI is synonymous with accounting rate of return (ARR) described as an investment appraisal technique in Chapter 13. In Chapter 13 our focus was on future estimates (i.e. an *ex ante* measure) for making investment decisions. In this chapter we are focusing on an historic after-the-event (i.e. *ex post*) performance measure. ROI expresses divisional profit as a percentage of the assets employed in the division. Assets employed can be defined as total divisional assets, assets controllable by the divisional manager or net assets. We shall consider the alternative measures of assets employed later in the chapter.

ROI is the most widely used financial measure of divisional performance. Why? Consider a situation where division A earns a profit of £1 million and division B a profit of £2 million. Can we conclude that Division B is more profitable than Division A? The answer is no, since we should consider whether the divisions are returning a sufficiently high return on the capital invested in the division. Assume that £4 million capital is invested in division A and £20 million in division B. Division A's ROI is 25% (£1m/£4m) whereas the return for division B is 10% (£2m/£20m). Capital invested has alternative uses, and corporate management will wish to ascertain whether the returns being earned on the capital invested in a particular division exceeds the division's opportunity cost of capital (i.e. the returns available from the alternative use of the capital). If, in the above illustration, the return available on similar investments to that in division B is 15% then the economic viability of division B is questionable if profitability cannot be improved. In contrast, the ROI measure suggests that division A is very profitable.

ROI provides a useful overall approximation on the success of a firm's past investment policy by providing a summary measure of the *ex post* return on capital invested. Kaplan and Atkinson (1998) also draw attention to the fact that, without some form of measurement of the *ex post* returns on capital, there is little incentive for accurate estimates of future cash flows during the capital budgeting process. Measuring returns on invested capital also focuses managers' attention on the impact of levels of working capital (particularly stocks and debtors) on the ROI.

Another feature of the ROI is that it can be used as a common denominator for comparing the returns of dissimilar businesses, such as other divisions within the group or outside competitors. ROI has been widely used for many years in all types of organizations so that most managers understand what the measure reflects and consider it to be of considerable importance.

Despite the widespread use of ROI, a number of problems exist when this measure is used to evaluate the performance of divisional managers. For example, it is possible that divisional ROI can be increased by actions that will make the company as a whole worse off, and conversely, actions that decrease the divisional ROI may make the company as a whole better off. In other words, evaluating divisional managers on the basis of ROI may not encourage goal congruence. Consider the following example:

	Division X	Division Y
Investment project available	£10 million	£10 million
Controllable contribution	£2 million	£1.3 million
Return on the proposed project	20%	13%
ROI of divisions at present	25%	9%

It is assumed that neither project will result in any changes in non-controllable costs and that the overall cost of capital for the company is 15%. The manager of division X would be reluctant to invest the additional £10 million because the return on the proposed project is 20%, and this would reduce the existing overall ROI of 25%. On the other hand, the manager of division Y would wish to invest the £10 million because the return on the proposed project of 13% is in excess of the present return of 9%, and it would increase the division's overall ROI. Consequently, the managers of both divisions would make decisions that would not be in the best interests of the company. The company should accept only those projects where the return is in excess of the cost of capital of 15%, but the manager of division X would reject a potential return of 20% and the manager of division Y would accept a potential return of 13%. ROI can therefore lead to a lack of goal congruence.

Managers can also be motivated to make incorrect asset disposal decisions. Consider the situation where the manager of division X has an asset that generates a return of 19% and the manager of division Y has an asset that yields a return of 12%. The manager of division X can increase ROI by disposing of the asset, whereas the ROI of division Y will decline if the asset is sold. Asset disposals are appropriate where assets earn a return less than the cost of capital. Hence the asset in division X should be kept and division Y's asset sold (assuming that the assets can be sold for their book values). Both managers can therefore increase their ROI by making decisions that are not in the best interest of the company.

Residual income

To overcome some of the dysfunctional consequences of ROI, the residual income approach can be used. For the purpose of evaluating the performance of *divisional managers*, **residual income** is defined as controllable contribution less a cost of capital charge on the investment controllable by the divisional manager. For evaluating the *economic performance* of the division residual income can be defined as divisional contribution (see Exhibit 20.1) less a cost of capital charge on the total investment in assets employed by the division. If residual income is used to measure the managerial performance of investment centres, there is a greater probability that managers will be encouraged, when acting in their own best interests, also to act in the best interests of the company. Returning to our previous illustration in respect of the investment decision for divisions X and Y, the residual income calculations are as follows:

	Division X (£)	Division Y (£)
Proposed investment	10 million	10 million
Controllable contribution	2 million	1.3 million
Cost of capital charge (15% of the investment cost)	1.5 million	1.5 million
Residual income	0.5 million	– 0.2 million

This calculation indicates that the residual income of division X will increase and that of division Y will decrease if both managers accept the project. Therefore the manager of division X would invest, whereas the manager of division Y would not. These actions are in the best interests of the company as a whole.

Residual income would also encourage both managers to make the correct asset disposal decisions. Consider again the asset disposal example in the previous section. The manager of division X would avoid a cost of capital charge of 15% on the asset by disposing of it, but this would also result in a loss of the return of 19%. In contrast, the manager of division Y would also avoid a cost of capital charge of 15% on the asset, but would lose a return of 12%. Therefore the residual income measure would lead to the manager of division Y disposing of the asset and the manager of division X retaining the asset.

A further reason cited in favour of residual income over the ROI measure is that residual income is more flexible, because different cost of capital percentage rates can be applied to investments that have different levels of risk. Not only will the cost of capital of divisions that have different levels of risk differ – so may the risk and cost of capital of assets within the same division. The residual income measure enables different risk-adjusted capital costs to be incorporated in the calculation, whereas the ROI cannot incorporate these differences.

Residual income suffers from the disadvantages of being an absolute measure, which means that it is difficult to compare the performance of a division with that of other divisions or companies of a different size. For example, a large division is more likely to earn a larger residual income than a small division. To overcome this deficiency, targeted or budgeted levels of residual income should be set for each division that are consistent with asset size and the market conditions of the divisions.

In the case of profit centres, where divisional managers are not authorized to make capital investment decisions and where they cannot influence the investment in working capital, ROI is a satisfactory performance measure, because if the return on investment is maximized on a fixed quantity of capital, the absolute return itself will also be maximized. However, in the case of investment centres, or profit centres where managers can significantly influence the investment in working capital, ROI appears to be an unsatisfactory method of measuring managerial performance, and in these circumstances the residual income is preferable.

Surveys of methods used by companies to evaluate the performance of divisional managers indicate a strong preference for ROI over residual income. For example, the UK survey by Drury *et al.* (1993) reported that the following measures were used:

	(%)
A target ROI set by the group	55
Residual income	20
A target profit *before* charging interest on investment	61
A target cash flow figure	43

Why is ROI preferred to residual income? Skinner (1990) found evidence to suggest that firms prefer to use ROI because, being a ratio, it can be used for inter-division and inter-firm comparisons. ROI for a division can be compared with the return from other divisions within the group or with whole companies outside the group, whereas absolute monetary measures such as residual income are not appropriate in making such comparisons. A second possible reason for the preference for ROI is that 'outsiders' tend to use ROI as a measure of a company's overall performance. Corporate managers therefore want their divisional managers to focus on ROI so that their performance measure is congruent with outsiders' measure of the company's overall economic performance. A further reason, suggested by Kaplan and Atkinson (1998), is that managers find percentage measures of profitability such as ROI more convenient, since they enable a division's profitability to be compared with other financial measures (such as inflation rates, interest rates, and the ROI rates of other divisions and comparable companies outside the group).

Economic value added (EVA(TM))

During the 1990s residual income has been refined and renamed as **economic value added (EVA(TM))** by the Stern Stewart consulting organization and they have registered EVA(TM) as their trademark. An article in an issue of *Fortune* magazine (1993) described the apparent success that many companies had derived from using EVA(TM) to motivate and evaluate corporate and divisional managers. *The Economist* (1997) reported that more than 300 firms world-wide had adopted EVA(TM) including Coca-Cola, AT&T, ICL, Boots and the Burton Group. A UK study by El-shishini and Drury (2001) reported that 23% of the responding organizations used EVA(TM) to evaluate divisional performance.

The EVA(TM) concept extends the traditional residual income measure by incorporating adjustments to the divisional financial performance measure for distortions introduced by generally accepted accounting principles (GAAP). EVA(TM) can be defined as:

EVA(TM) = Conventional divisional profit ± accounting adjustments – cost of capital charge on divisional assets

Our earlier discussion relating to which of the conventional alternative divisional profit measures listed in Exhibit 20.1 should be used also applies here. There are strong theoretical arguments for using controllable contribution as the divisional profit measure for *managerial* performance and divisional contribution for measuring *economic* performance. Many companies, however, use divisional net profit (after allocated costs) to evaluate both divisional managerial and economic performance.

Adjustments are made to the chosen conventional divisional profit measure in order to replace historic accounting data with a measure that attempts to approximate economic profit and asset values. Stern Stewart have stated that they have developed approximately 160 accounting adjustments that may need to be made to convert the conventional accounting profit into a sound measure of EVA(TM) but they have indicated that most organizations will only need to use about 10 of the adjustments. These adjustments result in the capitalization of many discretionary expenditures, such as research and development, marketing and advertising, by spreading these costs over the periods in which the benefits are received. Therefore adopting EVA(TM) should reduce some of the harmful side-effects arising from using financial measures that were discussed in Chapter 16. This is because managers will not bear the full costs of the discretionary expenditures in the period in which they are incurred if the expenses are capitalized. Instead, the cost will be spread across the periods when the benefits from the expenditure are estimated to be received. Also because it is a restatement of the residual income measure, compared with ROI, EVA(TM) is more likely to encourage goal congruence in terms of asset acquisition and disposal decisions. By making cost of capital visible managers are made aware that capital has a cost and they are thus encouraged to dispose of underutilized assets that do not generate sufficient income to cover their cost of capital.

Stern Stewart developed EVA(TM) with the aim of producing an overall financial measure that encourages senior managers to concentrate on the delivery of shareholder value. They consider that the aim of managers of companies, whose shares are traded in the stock market, should be to maximize shareholder value. It is therefore important that

How the use of EVA analysis transformed Armstrong's financial performance

The financial mission of a company should be to invest and create cash flows in excess of the cost of capital. Why? The marketplace values corporate assets in such a way that, given the known investment strategies of the company, the expected return on the market price of those assets equals the cost of capital. As a result, if an investment is announced that is expected to earn in excess of the cost of capital, then the value of the firm will immediately rise by the present value of that excess – as long as the market understands and believes the available projections. The question is: What is the best way to measure this?

The creation of corporate value should be measured by increases in the total market value of the company. Traditional measures of return, such as ROI, actually could unwittingly motivate and reward managers to shrink the value of the company. Therefore, the concept EVA, was developed. In a nutshell, EVA is designed to measure the degree to which a company's after-tax operating profits exceed – or fall short of – the cost of capital invested in the business. It makes managers think more about the use of capital and the amount of capital in each business.

Armstrong World Industries Inc. is a multibillion-dollar manufacturer and supplier of floor coverings, insulation products, ceiling and wall systems, and installation products. During the 1970s and 1980s, the company's financial performance was inconsistent and highly cyclical, with long periods of underperforming stock returns. While the company used standard measures such as ROI for its annual goals, there was less focus on shareholder value creation. In 1992, the company came to the conclusion that traditional accounting measures were totally inconclusive in explaining relative stock performance. The company looked at 10-year historical comparisons of its total stock return with accounting-based return measures and growth measures (sales, EBIT, EPS, and so on), along with those of 40 peer companies. As a result of this analysis, the company realized that accounting based goals alone do not necessarily lead to value creation. The use of accounting measures for annual performance goals and discounted cash flow techniques for investment decisions create disconnected and potentially competing objectives. The company also came to the conclusion that the value of its stock is a function of the market's perception of a company's future cash flows discounted to present value at a market-derived cost of capital. Therefore, the company needed to focus on one of the several value-based performance metric systems available, the essence of which apply discounted cash-flow techniques to entire business units and companies in addition to individual projects.

In 1993 the decision was made to discontinue the ROI concept and use EVA for strategic planning, performance measurement, and compensation. EVA is the profit earned in excess of the minimum return required by all contributors of debt and equity capital. It is computed from straightforward adjustments to convert book values on the income statement and balance sheet to an economic basis. There are many such adjustments, from the capitalization and amortization of advertising and R&D to the special treatment of strategic investments to encourage growth. Armstrong used about a dozen adjustments.

Importantly, in analysing potential investments, valuation by discounting EVA to present value is equal to the traditional net present value of cash flows, but EVA provides the added benefit of giving managers a clear view of how investment decisions impact incentive awards. Armstrong considered EVA to be the best financial measure for accurately linking accounting measures to stock market value and performance, making it ideal for setting financial targets. At the senior-management level, straight salary accounted for less than 30% of total pay, with the balance at risk in EVA and stock incentives. Changes in behaviour have become focused on three basic actions: (1) improving profit without more capital; (2) investing in projects earning above the cost of capital; and (3) eliminating operations unable to earn above the cost of capital.

On a higher strategic level, EVA allowed Armstrong to step back to see where the company was losing value. In what the company called its 'sunken ship' chart it was clear that businesses earning above the cost of capital were providing huge amounts of EVA. However, the ship was being dragged down because actual EVA was only 50%. The trouble was negative EVA businesses and corporate overheads. By benchmarking 'the best' companies, Armstrong found it needed to improve its organizational effectiveness and dramatically reduce worldwide overhead. By selling or combining negative EVA businesses and by growing and further reducing costs in its positive EVA businesses, the company provided the potential to more than double its EVA.

EVA serves as the basis for communicating financial objectives and results to both employees and the investment community. Employees receive ongoing training, and continual progress reports on EVA performance are prepared. In the end, EVA helped Armstrong stand out in the competition for global capital and gives the company a better chance of adding 'let the investor have faith' to its list of corporate principles. In today's environment, that principle is especially timely.

Source: Adapted from Institute of Management & Administration Report on Financial Analysis Planning and Reporting, September, 2002.

the key financial measure that is used to measure divisional or company performance should be congruent with shareholder value. Stern Stewart claim that, compared with other financial measures, EVA(TM) is more likely to meet this requirement and also to reduce dysfunctional behaviour.

There are a number of issues that apply to ROI, residual income or its replacement EVA(TM). They concern determining which assets should be included in a division's asset base, and the adjustments that should be made to financial accounting practices to derive managerial information that is closer to economic reality.

Determining which assets should be included in the investment base

We must determine which assets to include in a division's asset base to compute both ROI and EVA(TM). (Note that for the remainder of the chapter we shall use the term EVA(TM) to incorporate residual income.) If the purpose is to evaluate the performance of the divisional manager then only those assets that can be directly traced to the division and that are controllable by the divisional manager should be included in the asset base. Assets managed by central headquarters should not be included. For example, if debtors and cash are administered centrally, they should not be included as part of the asset base. On the other hand, if a divisional manager can influence these amounts, they should be included in the investment base. If they were not included, divisional managers could improve their profits by granting over-generous credit terms to customers; they would obtain the rewards of the additional sales without being charged with any cost for the additional capital that would be tied up in debtors.

Any liabilities that are within the control of the division should be deducted from the asset base. For example, a division may finance its investment in stocks by the use of trade creditors; this liability for creditors should therefore be deducted. The term **controllable investment** is used to refer to the net asset base that is controllable by divisional managers. Our overall aim in analysing controllable and non-controllable investment is to produce performance measures that will encourage a manager to behave in the best interests of the organization and also to provide a good approximation of managerial performance. It is therefore appropriate to include in the investment base only those assets that a manager can influence, and any arbitrary apportionments should be excluded.

If the purpose is to evaluate the economic performance of the division, the profitability of the division will be overstated if controllable investment is used. This is because a division could not operate without the benefit of corporate assets such as buildings, cash and debtors managed at the corporate level. These assets would be included in the investment base if the divisions were separate independent companies. Therefore many divisionalized companies allocate corporate assets to divisions when comparing divisional profitability with comparable firms in the same industry.

The impact of inflation

Both ROI and EVA(TM) are likely to be distorted if there is no attempt to adjust for inflation. This is because cash costs and revenues are measured in current prices, whereas fixed assets and depreciation charges are measured in historical prices of the year in which the assets were acquired. Depreciation and fixed assets should be adjusted by a price index to reflect inflationary price movements. If these adjustments are not made then both depreciation and fixed assets will be understated. Therefore divisional profits will be overstated and the divisional investment will be understated. The combination of overstated profits and understated investment causes ROI and EVA(TM) to be overstated. The increased ROI and EVA(TM) result from a failure to adjust for inflationary price changes, and do not represent an increase in economic wealth. A discussion of the alternative accounting approaches for incorporating inflationary price changes is outside the scope of this book. Readers interested in this topic should refer to financial accounting textbooks such as Lee (1996).

The impact of depreciation

It is common to find fixed assets valued at either their original cost or their written down value for the purpose of calculating return on investment and EVA(TM), but both of these valuation methods are weak. Consider, for example, an investment in an asset of £1 million with a life of five years with annual cash flows of £350 000 and a cost of capital of 10%. This investment has a positive NPV of £326 850, and should be accepted. You can see from Exhibit 20.2 that the annual profit is £150 000 when straight line depreciation is used. If the asset is *valued at original cost*, there will be a return of 15% per annum for five years. This will understate the true return, because the economic valuation is unlikely to remain at £1 million each year for five years and then immediately fall to zero. If ROI is based on the *written-down value*, you can see from Exhibit 20.2 that the investment base

EXHIBIT 20.2
Profitability measures using straight-line depreciation

	1 (£)	2 (£)	3 (£)	4 (£)	5 (£)
Net cash flow	350 000	350 000	350 000	350 000	350 000
Depreciation	200 000	200 000	200 000	200 000	200 000
Profit	150 000	150 000	150 000	150 000	150 000
Cost of capital (10% of WDV)	100 000	80 000	60 000	40 000	20 000
EVA(TM)	50 000	70 000	90 000	110 000	130 000
Opening WDV of the asset	1 000 000	800 000	600 000	400 000	200 000
ROI	15%	18.75%	25%	37.5%	75%

will decline each year – and, with constant profits, the effect will be to show a steady increase in return on investment. This steady increase in return on investment will suggest an improvement in managerial performance when the economic facts indicate that performance has remained unchanged over the five-year period.

Similar inconsistencies will also occur if the EVA(TM) method is used. If the asset is valued at the original cost, EVA(TM) of £50 000 will be reported each year (£150 000 profit – (10% cost of capital × 1 million)). On the other hand, if the cost of capital charge is based on the written-down value of the asset, the investment base will decline each year, and EVA(TM) will increase.

Exhibit 20.2 serves to illustrate that if asset written-down values are used to determine the division's investment base, managers can improve their ROI or EVA(TM) by postponing new investments and operating with older assets with low written-down values. In contrast, divisional managers who invest in new equipment will have a lower ROI or EVA(TM). This situation arises because financial accounting depreciation methods (including the reducing balance method) produce lower profitability measures in the earlier years of an asset's life.

To overcome this problem, it has been suggested that ROI or EVA(TM) calculations should be based on the original cost (i.e. gross book value) of the assets. When assets are measured at gross book value, managers will have an incentive to replace existing assets with new assets. This is because the increase in the investment base is only the difference between the original cost of the old asset and the purchase cost of the new asset. This difference is likely to be significantly less than the incremental cash flow (purchase cost less sale proceeds of the old asset) of the new asset. Managers may therefore be motivated to replace old assets with new ones that have a negative NPV.

To overcome the problems created by using financial accounting depreciation methods, alternative depreciation models have been recommended. These methods are discussed in the Appendix to this chapter. The theoretically correct solution to the problem is to value assets at their economic cost (i.e. the present value of future net cash inflows) but this presents serious practical difficulties. An appropriate solution to the practical problems is to value assets at their replacement cost (see Lee, 1996 for a discussion of this topic). Although this method is conceptually distinct from the present value method of valuation, it may provide answers which are reasonable approximations of what would be obtained using a present value approach. In addition, replacement cost is conceptually superior to the historical cost method of asset valuation. It follows that the depreciation charge on controllable investment based on replacement cost is preferable to a charge based on historical cost. The ROI and EVA(TM) would then be calculated on controllable investment valued at replacement cost.

The effect of performance measurement on capital investment decisions

Capital investment decisions are the most important decisions that a divisional manager will have to make. We noted in Chapter 13 that these decisions should be taken on the basis of the net present value (NPV) decision rule. The way in which the performance of the divisional manager is measured, however, is likely to have a profound effect on the decisions that he or she will make. There is a danger that, because of the way in which divisional performance is measured, the manager may be motivated to take the wrong decision and not follow the NPV rule. We noted in an earlier example (page 846) that the residual income (or EVA$^{(TM)}$) method of evaluation appeared to encourage a divisional manager to make capital investment decisions that are consistent with the NPV rule, but there is no guarantee that this or any other financial measure will in fact motivate the manager to act in this way. Consider the information presented in Exhibit 20.3, which relates to three mutually exclusive projects: X, Y and Z. Applying the NPV rule, you will see from the information presented that the manager should choose project X in preference to project Z, and should reject project Y.

Profits and return on investment

Divisional managers are likely to estimate the outcomes from alternative investments and choose the investment that maximizes their performance measure. Exhibit 20.4 shows the estimated profits and ROI's for projects X, Y and Z. The calculations in Exhibit 20.4 are based on the net cash flows for each year presented in Exhibit 20.3, less straight-line depreciation of £287 000 per year. The ROI is calculated on the *opening* written-down value at the start of the year. From the calculation in Exhibit 20.4 you will see that a manager who is anxious to improve his or her *short-term* performance will choose project Y if he or she is evaluated on total profits or return on investment, since project Y earns the largest profits and ROI in year 1; but project Y has a negative net present value, and should be rejected. Alternatively, a manager who assesses the impact of the project on his or her performance measure *over the three years* will choose project Z, because this yields the highest total profits and average ROI.

Economic value added (EVA$^{(TM)}$)

Let us now consider whether the EVA$^{(TM)}$ calculations are consistent with the NPV calculations. Exhibit 20.5 presents the estimated EVA$^{(TM)}$ calculations for project X.

The total present value of EVA$^{(TM)}$ for project X is £77 000 and this is identical with the NPV of project X which was calculated in Exhibit 20.3. EVA$^{(TM)}$ is therefore the long-term counterpart of the discounted NPV. Thus, given that maximizing NPV is equivalent to maximizing shareholder value, then maximizing the present value of EVA$^{(TM)}$ is also equivalent to maximizing shareholder value and Stern Stewart's claim that EVA$^{(TM)}$ is congruent with shareholder value would appear to be justified. Consequently, if divisional managers are evaluated on the basis of the long-run present value of EVA$^{(TM)}$, their capital investment decisions should be consistent with the decisions that would be taken using the NPV rule.

However, there is no guarantee that the short-run EVA$^{(TM)}$ measure will be consistent with the longer-run measure if conventional depreciation methods are used. To ensure consistency with the long-run measure and NPV an adjustment must be made within the

EXHIBIT 20.3

Mutually exclusive capital projects NPV ranking[1]

	X (£000s)	Y (£000s)	Z (£000s)
Machine cost initial outlay (time zero)	861	861	861
Estimated net cash flow (year 1)	250	390	50
Estimated net cash flow (year 2)	370	250	50
Estimated net cash flow (year 3)	540	330	1100
Estimated net present value at 10% cost of capital[a]	77	(52)	52
Ranking on the basis of NPV	1	3	2

Note

[a] The net present value calculations are to the nearest £000.

EXHIBIT 20.4

Estimated profit and ROI from mutually exclusive projects

Profits	X (£000s)	Y (000s)	Z (£000s)
Year 1	(37)	103	(237)
Year 2	83	(37)	(237)
Year 3	253	43	813
Total profits	299	109	339

ROI	X (%)	Y (%)	Z (%)
Year 1	(4.3)	11.9	(27.5)
Year 2	14.5	(6.4)	(41.3)
Year 3	88.1	15.0	283.2
Average	32.8	6.8	71.5

EVA(TM) accountancy adjustments so that depreciation is based on economic values and not historic book values. For example, if conventional depreciation is used the EVA(TM) for year 1 for each of the projects will be as follows:

	(£000s)
Project X	(–123)
Project Y	17
Project Z	(–323)

The *short-term* measure of EVA(TM) may lead to acceptance of project Y. In addition, a manager concerned about a possible deterioration in his or her expected EVA(TM) may reject project X even when he or she is aware that acceptance will mean an increase in long-term EVA(TM).

Let us now repeat the facts that we have established in our discussion so far. Decisions taken on the basis of a project's impact on divisional profit and return on investment are not

EXHIBIT 20.5
Estimated EVA(TM) calculations for project X[a]

	Year 1 (£000s)	Year 2 (£000s)	Year 3 (£000s)	Total (£000s)
Profit before interest	(37)	83	253	
10% interest on opening written-down value	86	57	29	
EVA(TM)	(123)	26	224	
PV of EVA(TM)	(112)	21	168	77

Note
[a] All calculations are to the nearest £000

consistent with the NPV rule. If managerial performance is evaluated on this basis of either of these two measures, there is a danger that managers will make decisions that will improve their own performance measure, even if such decisions are not in the best interests of the organization. The present value of EVA(TM) is the long-run counterpart of the discounted NPV, but the short-run measure may not signal the same decision as the long-run measure. Hence there is a need to establish a short-term measure of EVA(TM) that signals the same decision as the long-run measure. If this can be achieved and managers are evaluated on this basis, decisions based on improving their own short-term performance will be consistent with decisions taken using the NPV rule. In the Appendix to this chapter alternative depreciation models are explained that ensure that the short-term EVA(TM) measure does not conflict with the long-term measure and that are therefore consistent with the NPV rule. These models are not widely used in practice. The theoretical conclusion reached in the Appendix is that a comparison of budgeted and actual cash flows is the most appropriate method of measuring divisional performance, but, for various reasons, managers may prefer to use accounting methods based on the accruals concept. Where accruals based accounting is employed, the EVA(TM) approach should be used to measure managerial performance.[2]

Determining the divisional cost of capital charge

To calculate NPV and EVA(TM), we must ascertain the cost of capital for each division. The use of a single corporate cost of capital that is applied to all divisions within the group appears to be widespread in computing EVA(TM). The survey by Drury *et al.* (1993) reported that 74% of the firms used the same cost of capital for all divisions within the group. The use of a uniform cost of capital is probably due to the fact that divisional managers consider this to be a fairer method of comparing their results with other divisions. In addition, it is claimed that the use of uniform rates avoids friction and has a more favourable impact on the morale of managers.

It appears, however, that the use of a uniform cost of capital may lead to incorrect decisions. The theory of business finance supports the use of a different cost of capital being used for different divisions. The various divisions of a company can be viewed as a collection of different investments whose income streams result from different risks. In Chapter 14 we established that the cost of capital is a function of risk, and, since various divisions face different risks, a different cost of capital should be used for each division, based on the relative investment risk of each division.

Figure 20.2 shows how the use of a uniform company cost of capital for appraising capital investments can lead to incorrect decisions. The horizontal line AC represents the overall cost of capital of the company and the sloping line BD represents the risk-adjusted

FIGURE 20.2 *Risk-adjusted discount rates*

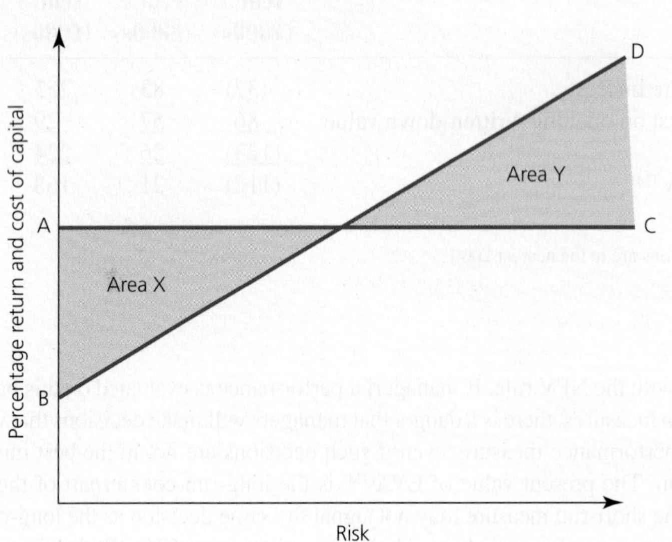

cost of capital. If the overall cost of capital is used as a discount rate then only those projects that yield an internal rate of return in excess of AC (which is equivalent to having a positive NPV at this cost of capital) will be accepted. You can see that low-risk projects that yield an internal rate of return in excess of the risk-adjusted discount rate (i.e. those that fall in area X) will be *incorrectly* rejected. Projects falling in this area will have a negative NPV when discounted at the company's overall cost of capital (AC) but a positive NPV when discounted at the risk adjusted cost of capital. Furthermore if an overall cost of capital is used, there is a danger that high-risk projects that yield a lower return than the risk-adjusted discount rate (i.e. projects that fall in area Y) will be incorrectly accepted.

To establish the cost of capital to be used for each division, quoted companies should be identified that are engaged solely in the same line of business as the division. The cost of capital of the identified companies can then be used as an approximation of the division's cost of capital. A full discussion of the appropriate cost of capital that should be used is beyond the scope of this book, but for a detailed discussion of this topic you should refer to Pike and Neale (2003, ch. 12). The important point to note when measuring managerial performance is that we have attempted to establish a measure that is consistent with the NPV rule. If the chosen measure requires that a manager be charged with the cost of capital on the division investment (i.e. EVA(TM)), the cost of capital which is used in this calculation should be the same rate as that used for capital investment decisions. Only by using the same cost of capital can the success of a manager's past investment decisions be truly established.

Addressing the dysfunctional consequences of short-term financial performance measures

The primary objective of profit-making organizations is to maximize shareholder value. Therefore performance measures should be based on the value created by each division. Unfortunately, direct measures of value creation are not possible because the shares for only the business as a whole are traded on the stockmarket. It is not possible to derive stock market values at the segmental or business unit level of an organization. Instead, most firms use accounting profit or ROI measures as a surrogate for changes in market values. Also, even if market measures could be derived, they may not be ideal performance measures because they are affected by many factors that managers cannot control (such as changes in investor expectations, interest rate changes and rumours). In contrast, accounting performance measures are not affected to the same extent by some of the uncontrollable factors that cause the volatile changes in share values.

Unfortunately, using accounting measures such as ROI or EVA(TM) as performance measures can encourage managers to become short-term oriented. For example, it has been shown that in the short term managers can improve both of these measures, by rejecting profitable long-term investments. By not making the investments, they can reduce expenses in the current period and not suffer the lost revenues until future periods. Managers can also boost their performance measure in a particular period by destroying customer and employee goodwill. For example, they can force employees to work excessive overtime towards the end of a measurement period so that goods can be delivered and their sales revenues and profits reported for the period. If the products are of lower quality, customer satisfaction (and future sales) may diminish. In addition, the effects of increased work pressure may result in staff absenteeism, demotivation and increased labour turnover. These harmful effects are unlikely to have much impact on the financial performance measure in the short term and will only become apparent in future periods. You will also remember from Chapter 7 that where profits are measured on an absorption costing basis it is possible to defer expenses to future reporting periods, and increase profits, by deliberately increasing inventories.

Consider also the situation where two divisional managers using exactly the same amount of investment produce exactly the same EVA(TM) or ROI. Does this mean that their performances are the same? The answer is no. Even though their performance measures would be identical this does not mean their performances are the same. One manager may have built up customer goodwill by offering excellent customer service, and also have paid great attention to training, education, research and development, etc., while another may not have given these items any consideration. Differences such as these would not show up initially in financial performance measures.

Return on investment and EVA(TM) are short-run concepts that deal only with the current reporting period, whereas managerial performance measures should focus on future results that can be expected because of present actions. Ideally, divisional performance should be evaluated on the basis of economic income by estimating future cash flows and discounting them to their present value. This calculation could be made for a division at the beginning and the end of a measurement period. The difference between the beginning and ending values represents the estimate of economic income.

The main problem with using estimates of economic income to evaluate performance is that it lacks precision and objectivity. It is also inconsistent with external financial accounting information that is used by financial markets to evaluate the performance of the company as a whole. It is likely that corporate managers may prefer their divisional managers to focus on the same financial reporting measures that are used by financial markets to evaluate the company as a whole. A final difficulty with measuring economic income is that the individual that is most knowledgeable and in the best position to provide the cash flow estimates is usually the individual whose performance is being evaluated. Thus, managers will be tempted to bias their estimates.

Various approaches can be used to overcome the short-term orientation that can arise when accounting profit-related measures are used to evaluate divisional performance. One possibility is to improve the accounting measures. EVA(TM) represents such an approach. If you refer back to the formula for calculating EVA(TM) you will see that it is computed by making accounting adjustments to the conventional financial accounting divisional profit calculation. These adjustments, such as capitalizing research and development and advertising expenditure, represent an attempt to approximate economic income. Incorporating a cost of capital charge is also a further attempt to approximate economic income. However, it should be noted that conventional accounting profits are the starting point for calculating EVA(TM) and these are based on historic costs, and not future cash flows, so that EVA(TM) can only provide a rough approximation of economic income.

Another alternative for reducing the short-term orientation, and increasing congruence of accounting measures with economic income is to lengthen the measurement period. The longer the measurement period, the more congruent accounting measures of performance are with economic income. For example, profits over a three-year measurement period are a better indicator of economic income than profits over a six-monthly period. The disadvantage of lengthening the measurement period is that rewards are tied to the performance evaluation, and if they are provided a long time after actions are taken, there is a danger that they will lose much of their motivational effects.

Probably the most widely used approach to mitigate against the dysfunctional consequences that can arise from relying excessively on financial measures is to supplement them with non-financial measures that measure those factors that are critical to the long-term success and profits of the organization. These measures focus on areas such as competitiveness, product leadership, productivity, quality, delivery performance, innovation and flexibility in responding to changes in demand. If managers focus excessively on the short-term, the benefits from improved short-term financial performance may be counter-balanced by a deterioration in the non-financial measures. Such non-financial measures should provide a broad indication of the contribution of a divisional manager's current actions to the long-term success of the organization.

The incorporation of non-financial measures creates the need to link financial and non-financial measures of performance. In particular, there is a need for a balanced set of measures that provide both short-term performance measures and also leading indicators of future financial performance from current actions. The **balanced scorecard** emerged in the 1990s to meet these requirements. The balanced scorecard will be covered extensively in Chapter 23 but at this stage you should note that the financial performance evaluation measures discussed in this chapter ought to be seen as one of the elements within the balanced scorecard. Divisional performance evaluation should be based on a combination of financial and non-financial measures using the balanced scorecard approach.

Summary

The following items relate to the learning objectives listed at the beginning of the chapter.

- **Distinguish between functional and divisionalized organizational structures.**

  A functional structure is one in which all activities of a similar type within a company are placed under the control of a departmental head. The organization as a whole is an investment centre. With a divisionalized structure, the organization is split up into divisions that consist of either investment centres or profit centres. Thus, the distinguishing feature is that in a functional structure only the organization as a whole is an investment centre and below this level a functional structure applies throughout. In contrast, in a divisionalized structure the organization is divided into separate profit or investment centres, and a functional structure applies below this level.

- **Explain why it is preferable to distinguish between managerial and economic performance.**

  Divisional economic performance can be influenced by many factors beyond the control of divisional managers. For example, good or bad economic performance may arise mainly from a favourable or unfavourable economic climate faced by the division rather than the specific contribution of the divisional manager. To evaluate the performance of divisional managers an attempt ought to be made to distinguish between the economic and managerial performance.

- **Explain the factors that should be considered in designing financial performance measures for evaluating divisional managers.**

  To evaluate the performance of a divisional manager only those items directly controllable by the manager should be included in the divisional managerial performance financial measures. Thus, all allocations of indirect costs, such as those central service and administration costs that cannot be influenced by divisional managers, ought not to be included in the performance measure. Such costs can only be controlled where they are incurred, which means those central service managers should be held accountable for them.

- **Explain the meaning of return on investment (ROI), residual income and economic value added (EVA™).**

  ROI expresses divisional profit as a percentage of the assets employed in a division. Residual income is defined as divisional profit less a cost of capital charge on divisional investment (e.g. net assets or total assets). During the 1990s, residual income was refined and renamed as EVA™. It extends the traditional residual income measure by incorporating adjustments to the divisional financial performance measure for distortions introduced by using generally accepted accounting principles that are used for external financial reporting. Thus, EVA™ consists of a divisional profit measure plus or minus the accounting adjustments less a cost of capital charge. All three measures can be used either as measures of managerial or economic performance. For managerial performance controllable profit should be used whereas for economic performance divisional net profit can be used. To derive the ROI or cost of capital charge, controllable investment (e.g. controllable net assets) can be used for measuring managerial performance and total divisional investment can be used to measure economic performance.

- **Compute economic value added (EVA™).**

  EVA™ is computed by starting with a conventional divisional profit measure and (a) adding or deducting adjustments for any distortions to divisional profit measures arising from using generally accepted accounting principles for external reporting, and (b) deducting a cost of capital charge on divisional assets. The measure can be used either as a measure of managerial or economic performance as described in (4) above. Typical accounting adjustments include the capitalization of discretionary expenditures, such as research and development expenditure. A detailed calculation of EVA™ is provided in the solution to Review problem 20.21.

- **Explain why performance measures may conflict with the net present value decision model.**

  Divisional managerial and economic performance is normally evaluated using short-term financial criteria whereas investment appraisal decisions using NPV are based on the cash flows over the whole life of the projects. Thus, the way that performance is evaluated can have a profound influence on investment decisions and there is a danger that managers will make decisions on the basis of an investment's impact on the short-term financial performance evaluation criteria rather than using the NPV decision rule. A conflict may arise between the measures because performance measures are short-term, multi-period and historical whereas NPV is a future single period measure over the whole life of the investment.

- **Justify the use of a risk-adjusted discount rate for determining the divisional cost of capital.**

  Investors require a greater expected return for more risky investments. It was therefore pointed out in Chapter 13 that risk adjusted discount rates should be used for investment appraisal. Thus, when measuring divisional financial performance the measure used to derive the cost of capital should be consistent with the measure used to compute net present value for divisional investment appraisal. One of the functions of divisional financial performance measures is to provide an overall approximation of the success of a division's past investment record by providing periodically summary measures of the *ex post* return on capital invested. Thus an attempt should be made to make the performance measurement criteria consistent with investment appraisal criteria.

- **Identify and explain the approaches that can be used to reduce the dysfunctional consequences of short-term financial measures.**

  Methods suggested for reducing the dysfunctional consequences include (a) use of improved financial performance measures such as EVA™ that incorporate accounting adjustments that attempt to overcome the deficiencies of conventional accounting measures; (b) lengthen the performance measurement period; and (c) do not rely excessively on accounting measures and incorporate non-financial measures using the balanced scorecard approach described in Chapter 23.

- **Additional learning objective presented in Appendix 20.1**

  The appendix to this chapter includes an additional learning objective: to explain how the short- and long-term measures of residual income or EVA™ can be reconciled. This topic has been presented in the appendix because it is not essential to an understanding to the chapter content. It examines one aspect of the chapter in more depth and should be regarded as further reading, based on your personal interest in the topic, rather than essential reading.

Appendix 20.1: Reconciling short- and long-term residual income/EVA(TM) measures

In this Appendix alternative depreciation models are examined that seek to ensure that the short-term residual income measure does not conflict with the long-term measure.

Valuing assets at NPV of future cash flows

It is not easy to design a short-term measure of performance that does not conflict with decisions based on the NPV rule. One approach is to value the assets at the present value of the future cash flows. This is illustrated in Exhibit 20A.1 in respect of the information presented in Exhibit 20.3 in the main body of this chapter for project X.

You will see that the asset is valued at £938 000 at the start, and because it is purchased for £861 000, an immediate profit of £77 000 is recognized. This is identical with the NPV calculated in Exhibit 20.3. EVA(TM) of zero will then be recorded for the next three years. This approach recognizes that the firm will be better off at the time of the acquisition by £77 000. However, because of the difficulty of valuing an asset at the present value of future cash flows, and writing the asset up in value above cost at the start, it is unlikely that this approach will be acceptable to accountants and managers.

EXHIBIT 20A.1

Effect of valuing assets at NPV of future cash flows (000s)[a]

	(£000s)
Value of asset at start (£) (250 × 0.909) + (370 × 0.826) + (540 × 0.751)	= 938
Value at end of year 1 (£) (370 × 0.909) + (540 × 0.826)	= 782
Value at end of year 2 (£) (540 × 0.909)	= 491
Value at end of year 3 (£)	= nil

	Year 1 (£000)	Year 2 (£000)	Year 3 (£000)
Cash inflow	250	370	540
Depreciation	156[b]	291	491
Profit before interest	94	79	49
Interest (at 10%)	94[c]	79	49
EVA(TM)	—	—	—

[a]All calculations are to the nearest (£000s)
[b]Value at start (£938) less value at end of year 1 (£782)
[c]Calculated on opening written-down value (10% of £938)

Annuity depreciation

When the cash inflows are constant and the **annuity method of depreciation** is used, the short-term EVA(TM) will also be constant. In addition, the total present value of the EVA(TM) will be equal to the NPV calculation. In other words, decisions taken on the basis of the short-term measure will be consistent with decisions taken on the basis of the long-term measure or the NPV rule. Let us illustrate the procedure using the annuity method of depreciation. Consider Example 20A.1.

There is a danger that this project will be rejected on the basis of the first year's EVA(TM) calculation if the straight-line method of depreciation is used.

If we use the annuity method of depreciation, the annual depreciation will be equivalent to the capital element of an annuity required to redeem £100 000 borrowed at 10% over five years.

If you refer to Appendix D (see page 1183), you will see that the capital recovery factor for five years at 10% is 0.2638 for £1; look at the entry in the five-year row and the 10% column. A repayment of £26 380 per annum is therefore required to repay £100 000 borrowed for five years. The repayment schedule is set out in Exhibit 20A.2.

The £100 000 will be repaid with interest, and the capital repayment column represents the annual depreciation charge. The EVA(TM) calculation using this depreciation charge is shown in Exhibit 20A.3.

The annual cash inflow is constant, and the EVA(TM) is also constant at £2620 per annum for five years. The present value of £2620, which is received annually for five years, is equal to the net present value calculation of £9939. The short-term measure should therefore lead to decisions being made that are consistent with decisions that would be taken on the basis of NPV calculations, when the cash inflows are constant and the annuity method of depreciation is used. A manager will undertake the machinery purchase, even if he or she places great emphasis on the impact of the purchase on the first year's performance. The manager may, however, reject the purchase if straight-line depreciation is used because a negative figure for EVA(TM) is reported.

EXAMPLE 20A.1

A division has the opportunity to acquire a new machine for £100 000. The machine is expected to produce cash savings of £29 000 every year for five years. The cost of capital is 10%.

The net present value for the new machine is £9939 and is calculated as follows:

	(£)
Investment cost	100 000
Present value of cash savings (29 000 × 3.791)	109 939
Net present value	9 939

The EVA(TM) for year 1 using the straight-line method of depreciation is:

	(£)	(£)
Annual cash inflow		29 000
Less Depreciation	20 000	
Interest on capital (10% of £100 000)	10 000	30 000
EVA(TM)		(1 000)

EXHIBIT 20A.2
Capital repayment schedule

Year	Annual repayment (1) (£)	10% interest on capital outstanding (2) (£)	Capital repayment (3) = (1) – (2) (£)	Capital outstanding (4) = (4) – (3) (£)
0				100 000
1	26 380	10 000	16 380	83 620
2	26 380	8 362	18 018	65 602
3	26 380	6 560	19 820	45 782
4	26 380	4 578	21 802	23 980
5	26 380	2 398	23 982	(2)

Uneven cash flows

Unfortunately, the annuity method of depreciation only produces a short-term measure that will lead to decisions consistent with the NPV rule when the net cash inflows are equal each year. Example 20A.1 has been amended so that the total net cash inflows of £145 000 fluctuate between years. All other items remain unchanged. The revised problem is presented in Example 20A.2.

The EVA(TM) for this example, using the annuity method of depreciation that was calculated in Exhibit 20A.2, is presented in Exhibit 20A.4.

The present value of the EVA(TM) in Exhibit 20A.4 is £9938, which is identical with the NPV calculation. There is, however, a danger that the manager may reject the

EXHIBIT 20A.3

EVA(TM) calculation

Year	Opening written down value (1) (£)	Cash inflow (2) (£)	Depreciation (3) (£)	Interest on capital (10%) (4) (£)	EVA(TM) (2) – [(3) + (4)] (5) (£)
1	100 000	29 000	16 380	10 000	2620
2	83 620	29 000	18 018	8 362	2620
3	65 602	29 000	19 820	6 560	2620
4	45 782	29 000	21 802	4 578	2620
5	23 980	29 000	23 982	2 398	2620

EXAMPLE 20A.2

A division has the opportunity to acquire a new machine for £100 000. The machine has expected cash savings of £145 000 over five years. The timing of the expected cash savings is as follows:

	(£)
Year 1	20 000
Year 2	25 000
Year 3	50 000
Year 4	40 000
Year 5	10 000

The cost of capital is 10% and the NPV is £9938.

EXHIBIT 20A.4

EVA(TM) with unequal cash flows

Year	Opening written-down value (£)	Cash inflow (£)	Depreciation (£)	Interest on capital (£)	EVA(TM) (£)
1	100 000	20 000	16 380	10 000	(6 380)
2	83 620	25 000	18 018	8 362	(1 380)
3	65 602	50 000	19 820	6 560	23 620
4	45 782	40 000	21 802	4 578	13 620
5	23 980	10 000	23 982	2 398	(16 380)

investment because of the negative EVA(TM) calculations in years 1 and 2. This means that *the short-term EVA(TM) measure may be in conflict with the NPV rule when the annuity method of depreciation is used and unequal cash flows occur.*

Tomkins (1975) shows that it is possible to construct a depreciation schedule that avoids negative or EVA(TM) calculations and that will motivate managers to accept projects yielding positive NPVs. He suggests that, instead of using the annuity method

EXHIBIT 20A.5
Depreciation based on interest deducted from cash flows

Year	Cash inflow (1) (£)	Capital outstanding (written-down value) (2) (£)	Interest (10%) (3) (£)	Depreciation (4) = (1) – (3) (£)	EVA(TM) (5) = (1) – [(3) + (4)] (£)
0		100 000			
1	20 000	90 000	10 000	10 000	0
2	25 000	74 000	9 000	16 000	0
3	50 000	31 400	7 400	42 600	0
4	40 000	0	3 140	31 400	5 460
5	10 000	0	0	0	10 000

of depreciation, a depreciation figure should be calculated by deducting the interest on the written-down value of the asset from the expected cash inflows for the year, instead of deducting it from the annuity required to redeem the loan. This procedure is illustrated in Exhibit 20A.5.

You will see that the interest is calculated on the opening written-down value. For example, the £9000 interest charge for year 2 is based on 10% of the opening written-down value for year 2 of £90 000. (This is represented by the written-down value at the end of year 1.) Depreciation is then calculated by deducting interest from the cash inflow. In year 4 the depreciation charge is limited to the written-down value of £31 400. The effect of the depreciation charge being based on a deduction of interest from the cash flow means that EVA(TM) is zero each year until the asset is completely written off. Any cash inflows received after this point will result in a positive EVA(TM) calculation. The present value of the EVA(TM) in years 4 and 5 is £9931, compared with the capital investment net present value calculation of £9938.

If a divisional manager is evaluated with EVA(TM) calculated in the manner illustrated in Exhibit 20A.5, he or she will recognize that in the short term EVA(TM) will remain unchanged, and that by years 4 and 5 the benefits will be reflected in the performance measure. The manager will be motivated to accept the project. It remains doubtful, though, whether widespread adoption of this method can be achieved, since the depreciation is merely a balancing figure that does not conform to any of the usual notions of depreciation. The calculations also indicate that the EVA(TM) does not become positive until the initial investment cost topped up with interest cost has been recovered. Tomkins suggests that a better description of the concept would be capital surplus rather than residual income.

Comparison of actual with budget

When considering performance evaluation, the *actual* EVA(TM) must be compared with a *predetermined* standard such as budgeted EVA(TM). If we use the procedure suggested in Exhibit 20A.5, however, we shall obtain a zero EVA(TM) calculation in the early years of a project's life for both the actual and budgeted results. Consequently, there are no benefits to be derived from making such a comparison between budgeted and actual EVA(TM). Tomkins suggests that the relevant yardstick of performance in this situation is a comparison between the budgeted capital outstanding at the end of the year and the actual capital outstanding. Any difference, though, between budgeted and actual capital outstanding can only result from actual cash flows being different from budgeted cash flows, since both interest and depreciation charges will be dependent on actual cash flows.[3] Tomkins therefore concludes that calculating residual income (and therefore EVA(TM)) and comparing budgeted and actual capital outstanding is only an elaborate way of achieving what can be attained far more simply merely by comparing actual cash flows with those budgeted in the capital investment proposals.

It appears that the choice is between using an accounting method based on the accruals concept, which will lead to the correct decision more often than other methods, or comparing budgeted and actual cash flows. If the former method is preferred, EVA(TM) is the most appropriate method of measuring the performance of divisional managers.

Notes

1 This exhibit and subsequent comments were adapted from Flower, J.F. (1977). Measurement of divisional performance, *Readings in Accounting and Business Research, Accounting and Business Research Special Issue*, pp. 121–30.

2 Amey argues that residual income is an inappropriate measure for profit centres and investment centres, whereas for practical reasons Tomkins argues that performance should be measured by a comparison of budgeted and actual cash flows. However, for profit centres where the manager can control the amount invested in working capital Tomkins suggests that residual income is an appropriate measure. For a discussion of each writer's views see Amey (1975), Tomkins (1975), Emmanuel and Otley (1976).

3 Assuming that the actual cash flows in Exhibit 20A.5 were £15 000 for year 1, instead of £20 000, the capital outstanding will be as follows:

Year	Cash inflow	Capital outstanding (WDV)	Interest (10%)	Depreciation	Residual income
	(1)	(2)	(3)	(4) = (1) – (3)	(5) = (1) – [(3) + (4)]
	(£)	(£)	(£)	(£)	(£)
0		100 000			
1	15 000	95 000	10 000	5 000	0

You will see that the capital outstanding is £95 000 compared with £90 000 in Exhibit 20A.5. Any difference between this calculation of capital outstanding and Exhibit 20A.5 will be due entirely to the actual cash inflow (£15 000) being different from the budgeted cash inflow (£20 000).

Key terms and concepts

annuity method of depreciation (p. 861)
balanced scorecard (p. 858)
controllable contribution (p. 843)
controllable investment (p. 851)
cost centre (p. 840)
divisional contribution (p. 843)
divisional net profit before taxes (p. 844)
divisionalized organizational structure (p. 838)
economic value added (EVA™) (p. 848)
functional organizational structure (p. 838)
investment centre (p. 840)
profit centre (p. 840)
residual income (p. 846)
return on investment (ROI) (p. 845)
risk-adjusted cost of capital (p. 855)
single corporate cost of capital (p. 855)
variable short-run contribution margin (p. 843)

Recommended reading

You should refer to an article by Keef and Roush (2002) for a discussion of the criticisms of economic value added. Lovata and Costigan (2002) report on a survey relating to the adopters of economic value added. For a theoretical review of economic value added see O'Hanlon and Peasnell (1998). See also Bromwich and Walker (1998) for a discussion of residual income in relation to its past and future. A discussion of the computation of divisional cost of capital is presented in De Bono (1997).

Key examination points

Most examination questions include a comparison of residual income (RI) (or EVA(TM)) and return on investment (ROI). Make sure you can calculate these measures and discuss the merits and deficiencies of RI and ROI. You should emphasize that when evaluating short-term divisional performance, it is virtually impossible to capture in one financial measure all the variables required to measure the performance of a divisional manager. It is also necessary to include in the performance reports other non-financial performance measures.

Typical examination questions require you to consider whether a manager will undertake various transactions when he or she is evaluated on RI/EVA(TM) or ROI. For each transaction you should state which course of action is in the best interests of the company as a whole. You should then state which course of action is likely to maximize a managers performance rating. Goal congruence will only exist when actions that are in the best interests of the company also lead to an improvement in the performance measures used to evaluate the divisional managers. A typical requirement is to compare the change in RI or ROI when the assets are valued at original cost or written-down value (see Review problem 20.20). Note that neither method of valuation is satisfactory (you should therefore pay particular attention to the section on 'The Impact of Depreciation' (see pages 851–52).

Economic value added is a recent development and is likely to feature more prominently (instead of residual income) in future examinations. You should refer to the solution to Review problem 20.21 for an illustration of the computation of EVA.

Assessment material

Review questions

The review questions are short questions that enable you to assess your understanding of the main topics included in the chapter. The numbers in parentheses provide you with the page numbers to refer to if you cannot answer a specific question.

Review problems

The review problems are more complex and require you to relate and apply the chapter content to various business problems. The problems are graded by their level of difficulty. The multiple-choice questions are the least demanding and normally take less than 10 minutes to complete. Fully worked solutions to the review problems are provided in a separate section at the end of the book. For those questions in the white box the worked solutions are provided in the *Student's Manual* accompanying this book. Further review problems for this chapter are available on the accompanying website www.drury-online.com. The answers to these problems are available for lecturers on the lecturer's password protected section of the website.

Case studies

The website also includes over 30 case study problems. A list of these cases is provided in Part Seven of this book. EVA Ault Foods Ltd. is a case study that is relevant to the content of this chapter.

Review questions

20.1 Distinguish between a functional and divisionalized organizational structure. (*pp. 838–39*)

20.2 Distinguish between profit centres and investment centres. (*p. 840*)

20.3 What are the advantages and disadvantages of divisionalization? (*pp. 840–41*)

20.4 What are the pre-requisites for successful divisionalization? (*pp. 841–42*)

20.5 Why might it be appropriate to distinguish between the managerial and economic performance of a division? (*p. 842*)

20.6 Describe the four alternative profit measures that can be used to measure divisional performance. Which measures are preferable for (a) measuring divisional *managerial* performance and (b) measuring divisional *economic* performance? (*pp. 842–45*)

20.7 Why is it common practice not to distinguish between managerial and economic performance? (*pp. 844–45*)

20.8 Why is it common practice to allocate central costs to measure divisional managerial performance? (*p. 845*)

20.9 Distinguish between return on investment, residual income and economic value added. (*pp. 845–48*)

20.10 How does the use of return on investment as a performance measure lead to bad decisions? How do residual income and economic value added overcome this problem? (*pp. 846–47*)

20.11 Explain how economic value added is calculated. (*p. 848*)

20.12 Describe the effect of performance measurement on capital investment decisions. (*pp. 853–55*)

20.13 Explain why a risk adjusted discount rate should be used for determining the divisional cost of capital (i.e. the cost of capital that is used as an input to compute residual income or economic value added). (*pp. 855–56*)

20.14 Explain the approaches that can be used to reduce the dysfunctional consequences of short-term financial measures. (*pp. 857–58*)

Review problems

20.15 Intermediate

Bollon uses residual income to appraise its divisions using a cost of capital of 10%. It gives the managers of these divisions considerable autonomy although it retains the cash control function at head office.

The following information was available for one of the divisions:

	Net profit after tax £'000	Profit before interest and tax £'000	Divisional net assets £'000	Cash/ (overdraft) £'000
Division 1	47	69	104	(21)

What is the residual income for this division based on controllable profit and controllable net assets?

A £36 600
B £56 500
C £58 600
D £60 700.

ACCA Paper 1.2 – Financial information for Management

20.16 Advanced

Division Q makes a single product. Information for the division for the year just ended is:

Sales	30 000 units
Fixed costs	£487 000
Depreciation	£247 500
Residual income	£47 200
Net assets	£1 250 000

Head Office assesses divisional performance by the residual income achieved. It uses a cost of capital of 12% a year.

Division Q's average contribution per unit was

A £14.82
B £22.81
C £28.06
D £31.06
E £32.81

(2 marks)
CIMA Management Accounting – Decision Making

20.17 **Advanced: Impact of various transactions on divisional profitability measure**

Theta Ltd compares the performance of its subsidiaries by return on capital employed (ROCE), using the following formula.

Profit: Depreciation is calculated on a straight-line basis. Losses on sale of assets are charged against profit in the year of the sale.

Capital employed: Net current assets – at the average value throughout the year. Fixed assets – at original cost less accumulated depreciation as at the end of the year.

Theta Ltd, whose cost of capital is 14% per annum, is considering acquiring Alpha Ltd, whose performance has been calculated on a similar basis to that shown above except that fixed assets are valued at original cost.

During the past year, apart from normal trading, Alpha Ltd was involved in the following separate transactions:

(a) It bought equipment on 1 November 2000 (the start of its financial year) at a cost of £120 000. Resulting savings were £35 000 for the year; these are expected to continue at that level throughout the six-year expected life of the asset, after which it will have no scrap value.

(b) On 1 November 2000 it sold a piece of equipment that had cost £200 000 when bought exactly three years earlier. The expected life was four years, with no scrap value. This equipment has been making a contribution to profit of £30 000 per annum before depreciation, and realized £20 000 on sale.

(c) It negotiated a bank overdraft of £20 000 for the year to take advantage of quick payment discounts offered by creditors; this reduced costs by £4000 per annum.

(d) To improve liquidity, it reduced stocks by an average of £25 000 throughout the year. This resulted in reduced sales with a reduction of £6000 per annum contribution.

The financial position of Alpha Ltd for the year from 1 November 1999 to 31 October 2000 *excluding the outcomes of transactions (a)–(d)* above, was as follows:

	(£000)
Profit for the year	225
Fixed assets:	
Original cost	1000
Accumulated depreciation	475
Net current assets (average for the year)	250

You are required to:

(a) Calculate the ROCE of Alpha Ltd using its present basis of calculation:
  (i) if none of the transactions (A)–(D) had taken place;
  (ii) if transaction (A) had taken place by not (B), (C) or (D);
  (iii) if transaction (B) had taken place but not (A), (C), or (D);
  (iv) if transaction (C) had taken place but not (A), (B) or (D);
  (v) if transaction (D) had taken place but not (A), (B) or (C).

(b) Calculate the ROCE as in (a) (i)–(v) above using Theta Ltd's basis of calculation.

(c) Explain briefly whether there would have been any lack of goal congruence between Theta Ltd and the management of Alpha Ltd (assuming that Alpha Ltd has been acquired by Theta Ltd on 1 November 1999 and that Theta Ltd's basis of calculation was used) in respect of
  (i) transaction (A);
  (ii) transaction (B).

Taxation is to be ignored.

(25 marks)
CIMA P3 Management Accounting

20.18 Advanced: Accounting, motivational and ethical issues arising from divisional actions

Within a large group, divisional managers are paid a bonus which can represent a large proportion of their annual earnings. The bonus is paid when the budgeted divisional profit for the financial year is achieved or exceeded.

Meetings of divisional boards are held monthly and attended by the senior management of the division, and senior members of group management.

With the aid of the financial year approaching, there had been discussion in all divisional board meetings of forecast profit for the year, and whether budgeted profit would be achieved. In three board meetings, for divisions which were having difficulty in achieving budgeted profits, the following divisional actions had been discussed. In each case, the amounts involved would have been material in determining whether the division would achieve its budget:

- Division A had severely cut spending on training, and postponed routine re-painting of premises.
- Division B had re-negotiated a contract for consultancy services. It was in the process of installing Total Quality Management (TQM) systems, and had originally agreed to pay progress payments to the consultants, and had budgeted to make these payments. It had re-negotiated that the consultancy would invoice the division with the total cost only when the work was completed in the next financial year.
- Division C had persuaded some major customers to take early delivery, in the current financial year, of products originally ordered for delivery early in the next financial year. This would ensure virtually nil stock at year end.

Requirement:

Discuss the financial accounting, budgeting, ethical and motivational issues which arise from these divisional actions.

Comment on whether any group management action is necessary.

(20 marks)
CIMA Stage 4 Management Accounting Control Systems

20.19 Advanced: Conflict between NPV and performance measurement

Linamix is the chemicals division of a large industrial corporation. George Elton, the divisional general manager, is about to purchase new plant in order to manufacture a new product. He can buy either the Aromatic or the Zoman plant, each of which have the same capacity and expected four year life, but which differ in their capital costs and expected net cash flows, as shown below:

	Aromatic	Zoman
Initial capital investment	£6 400 000	£5 200 000
Net cash flows (before tax)		
2001	£2 400 000	£2 600 000
2002	£2 400 000	£2 200 000
2003	£2 400 000	£1 500 000
2004	£2 400 000	£1 000 000
Net present value (@ 16% p.a.)	£315 634	£189 615

In the above calculations it has been assumed that the plant will be installed and paid for by the end of December 2000, and that the net cash flows accrue at the end of each calendar year. Neither plant is expected to have a residual value after decommissioning costs.

Like all other divisional managers in the corporation, Elton is expected to generate a before tax return on his divisional investment in excess of 16% p.a., which he is currently just managing to achieve. Anything less than a 16% return would make him ineligible for a performance bonus and may reduce his pension when he retires in early 2003. In calculating divisional returns, divisional assets are valued at net book values at the beginning of the year. Depreciation is charged on a straight line basis.

Requirements:

(a) Explain, with appropriate calculations, why neither return on investment nor residual income would motivate Elton to invest in the process showing the higher net present value. To what extent can the use of alternative accounting techniques assist in reconciling the conflict between using accounting-based performance measures and discounted cash flow investment appraisal techniques?

(12 marks)

(b) Managers tend to use post-tax cash flows to evaluate investment opportunities, but to evaluate divisional and managerial performance on the basis of pre-tax profits. Explain why this is so and discuss the potential problems that can arise, including suggestions as to how such problems can be overcome.

(8 marks)

(c) Discuss what steps can be taken to avoid dysfunctional behaviour which is motivated by accounting-based performance targets.

(5 marks)

(Total 25 marks)

ICAEW Management Accounting and Financial Management 2

20.20 Advanced: Calculation and comparison of ROI and RI using straight line and annuity depreciation

Alpha division of a retailing group has five years remaining on a lease for premises in which it sells self-assembly furniture. Management are considering the investment of £600 000 on immediate improvements to the interior of the premises in order to stimulate sales by creating a more effective selling environment.

The following information is available:

(i) The expected increased sales revenue following the improvements is £500 000 per annum. The average contribution: sales ratio is expected to be 40%.

(ii) The cost of capital is 16% and the division has a target return on capital employed of 20%, using the net book value of the investment at the beginning of the year in its calculation.

(iii) At the end of the five year period the premises improvements will have a nil residual value.

Required:

(a) Prepare *two* summary statements for the proposal for years 1 to 5, showing residual income and return on capital employed for each year. Statement 1 should incorporate straight-line depreciation. Statement 2 should incorporate annuity depreciation at 16%.

(12 marks)

(b) Management staff turnover at Alpha division is high. The divisions investment decisions and management performance measurement are currently based on the figures for the first year of a proposal.

(i) Comment on the use of the figures from statements 1 and 2 in (a) above as decision-making and management performance measures.

(ii) Calculate the net present value (NPV) of the premises improvement proposal and comment on its compatibility with residual income as a decision-making measure for the proposals acceptance or rejection

(8 marks)

(c) An alternative forecast of the increase in sales revenue per annum from the premises improvement proposal is as follows:

Year:	**1**	**2**	**3**	**4**	**5**
Increased sales revenue (£000)	700	500	500	300	200

All other factors remain as stated in the question.

(i) Calculate year 1 values for residual income and return on capital employed where (1) straight-line depreciation and (2) annuity depreciation at 16% are used in the calculations.

(ii) Calculate the net present value of the proposal.

(iii) Comment on managements evaluation of the amended proposal in comparison with the original proposal using the range of measures calculated in (a), (b) and (c).

(10 marks)

(Total 30 marks)

ACCA Level 2 Cost and Management Accounting II

20.21 Advanced: Economic valued added approach to divisional performance measurement

The most recent published results for V plc are shown below:

	Published (£m)
Profit before tax for year ending 31 December	13.6
Summary consolidated balance sheet at 31 December	
Fixed assets	35.9
Current assets	137.2
Less: Current liabilities	(95.7)
Net current assets	41.5
Total assets *less* current liabilities	77.4
Borrowings	(15.0)
Deferred tax provisions	(7.6)
Net assets	54.8
Capital and reserves	54.8

An analyst working for a stockbroker has taken these published results, made the adjustments shown below, and has reported his conclusion that 'the management of V plc is destroying value'.

Analyst's adjustments to profit before tax:

	(£m)
Profit before tax	13.6
Adjustments	
Add: Interest paid (net)	1.6
R&D (Research and Development)	2.1
Advertising	2.3
Amortization of goodwill	1.3
Less: Taxation paid	(4.8)
Adjusted profit	16.1

Analyst's adjustments to summary consolidated balance sheet at 31 December

	(£m)	
Capital and reserves	54.8	
Adjustments		
Add: Borrowings	15.0	
Deferred tax provisions	7.6	
R&D	17.4	Last 7 years' expenditure
Advertising	10.5	Last 5 years' expenditure
Goodwill	40.7	Written off against reserves on acquisitions in previous years
Adjusted capital employed	146.0	
Required return	17.5	12% cost of capital
Adjusted profit	16.1	
Value destroyed	1.4	

The Chairman of V plc has obtained a copy of the analyst's report.

Requirement:

(a) Explain, as management accountant of V plc, in a report to your Chairman, the principles of the approach taken by the analyst. Comment on the treatment of the specific adjustments to R&D, Advertising, Interest and Borrowings and Goodwill.

(12 marks)

(b) Having read your report, the Chairman wishes to know which division or divisions are 'destroying value', when the current internal statements show satisfactory returns on investment (ROIs). The following summary statement is available:

Divisional performance, year ending 31 December

	Division A (Retail) (£m)	**Division B (Manufacturing) (£m)**	**Division C (Services) (£m)**	**Head office (£m)**	**Total (£m)**
Turnover	81.7	63.2	231.8	–	376.7
Profit before interest and tax	5.7	5.6	5.8	(1.9)	15.2
Total assets *less* current liabilities	27.1	23.9	23.2	3.2	77.4
ROI	21.0%	23.4%	25.0%		

Some of the adjustments made by the analyst can be related to specific divisions:

- Advertising relates entirely to Division A (Retail)
- R&D relates entirely to Division B (Manufacturing)
- Goodwill write-offs relate to
  - Division B (Manufacturing) £10.3m
  - Division C (Services) £30.4m
- The deferred tax relates to
  - Division B (Manufacturing) £1.4m
  - Division C (Services) £6.2m
- Borrowings and interest, per divisional accounts, are:

	Division A (Retail) (£m)	**Division B (Mfg) (£m)**	**Division C (Services) (£m)**	**Head office (£m)**	**Total (£m)**
Borrowings	–	6.6	6.9	1.5	15.0
Interest paid/ (received)	(0.4)	0.7	0.9	0.4	1.6

Requirement:

Explain, with appropriate comment, in a report to the Chairman, where 'value is being destroyed'. Your report should include

- a statement of divisional performance,
- an explanation of any adjustments you make,
- a statement and explanation of the assumptions made, and
- comment on the limitations of the answers reached.

(20 marks)

(c) The use of ROI has often been criticized as emphasizing short-term profit, but many companies continue to use the measure. Explain the role of ROI in managing business performance, and how the potential problems of short-termism may be overcome.

(8 marks)
(Total 40 marks)
CIMA State 4 Management Accounting Control Systems

20.22 **Advanced**

(a) 'Because of the possibility of goal incongruence, an optimal plan can only be achieved if divisional budgets are constructed by a central planning department, but this means that divisional independence is a pseudo-independence.'

Discuss the problems of establishing divisional budgets in the light of this quotation.

(9 marks)

(b) 'Head Office' will require a division to submit regular reports of its performance.

Describe, discuss and compare three measures of divisional operating performance that might feature in such reports.

(8 marks)
ACCA Level 2 Management Accounting

20.23 **Advanced**

A long-established, highly centralized company has grown to the extent that its chief executive, despite having a good supporting team, is finding difficulty in keeping up with the many decisions of importance in the company.

Consideration is therefore being given to re-organizing the company into profit centres. These would be product divisions, headed by a divisional managing director, who would be responsible for all the divisions activities relating to its products.

You are required to explain, in outline:

(a) the types of decision areas that should be transferred to the new divisional managing directors if such a reorganization is to achieve its objectives;

(b) the types of decision areas that might reasonably be retained at company head office;

(c) the management accounting problems that might be expected to arise in introducing effective profit centre control.

(20 marks)
CIMA P3 Management Accounting

20.24 **Advanced**

(a) Explain the meaning of each of the undernoted measures which may be used for divisional performance measurement and investment decision-making. Discuss the advantages and problems associated with the use of each.

(i) Return on capital employed.

(ii) Residual income.

(iii) Discounted future earnings.

(9 marks)

(b) Comment on the reasons why the measures listed in (a) above may give conflicting investment decision responses when applied to the same set of data. Use the following figures to illustrate the conflicting responses which may arise:

Additional investment of £60 000 for a 6 year life with nil residual value.

Average net profit per year: £9000 (after depreciation).

Cost of capital: 14%.

Existing capital employed: £300 000 with ROCE of 20%.

(8 marks)

(Solutions should ignore taxation implications.)

(Total 17 marks)

ACCA Level 2 Management Accounting

Review problems (with answers in the Student's Manual)

20.25 Advanced

A recently formed group of companies is proposing to use a single return on capital employed (ROCE) rate as an index of the performance of its operating companies which differ considerably from one another in size and type of activities.

It is, however, particularly concerned that the evaluations it makes from the use of this rate should be valid in terms of measurement of performance.

You are required to:

(a) mention *four* considerations in calculating the ROCE rate to which the group will need to attend, to ensure that its intentions are achieved; for each consideration give an example of the type of problem that can arise;

(8 marks)

(b) mention *three* types of circumstance in which a single ROCE rate might not be an adequate measure of performance and, for each, explain what should be done to supplement the interpretation of the results of the single ROCE rate.

(12 marks)

CIMA P3 Management Accounting

20.26 Advanced

Residual Income and Return on Investment are commonly used measures of performance. However, they are frequently criticized for placing too great an emphasis on the achievement of short-term results, possibly damaging longer-term performance.

You are required to discuss

(a) the issues involved in the long-term:short-term conflict referred to in the above statement;

(11 marks)

(b) suggestions which have been made to reconcile this difference.

(11 marks)

(Total 22 marks)

CIMA Stage 4 Management Accounting – Control and Audit

20.27 Advanced: Impact of various transactions on ROCE and a discussion whether ROCE leads to goal congruence

G Limited, one of the subsidiaries of GAP Group plc., produces the following condensed data in respect of its budgeted performance for the year to 31 December:

	(£000)
Profit	330
Fixed assets:	
Original cost	1500
Accumulated depreciation (as at 31 December)	720
Net current assets (average for the year)	375

In addition, it is considering carrying out the following separate non-routine transactions:

A. It would offer its customers cash discounts that would cost £8000 per annum.

   This would reduce the level of its debtors by an average of £30 000 over the year. This sum would be used to increase the dividend to GAP Group plc. payable at the end of the year.

B. It would increase its average stocks by £40 000 throughout the year and reduce by that amount the dividend payable to GAP Group plc. at the end of the year.

   This is expected to yield an increased contribution of £15 000 per annum resulting from larger sales.

C. At the start of the year it would sell for £35 000 a fixed asset that originally cost £300 000 and which has been depreciated by 4/5ths of its expected life.

   If not sold, this asset would be expected to earn a profit contribution of £45 000 during the year.

D. At the start of the year it would buy for £180 000 plant that would achieve reductions of £52 500 per annum in revenue costs. This plant would have a life of five years, after which it would have no resale value.

The chief accountant of GAP Group plc. has the task of recommending to the Group management committee whether the non-routine transactions should go ahead. The Groups investment criterion is to earn 15% DCF and where no time period is specified, four years is the period assumed.

In measuring the comparative performance of its subsidiaries, GAP Group plc. uses return on capital employed (ROCE) calculated on the following basis:

Profit:	Depreciation of fixed assets is calculated on a straight-line basis. Profit or loss on sale of assets is respectively added to or deducted from operating profits in the year of sale.
Capital employed:	
Fixed assets:	Valued at original cost less accumulated depreciation as at the end of the year.
Net current assets:	At the average value for the year.

You are required

(a) as managing director of G Ltd, to recommend whether *each* of the *four* non-routine transactions (A to D) should independently go ahead;

(*8 marks*)

(b) as chief accountant of GAP Group plc.,

(i) to state whether you expect there to be goal congruence between G Limited and GAP Group plc. in respect of *each* of the *four* non-routine transactions considered separately;

(*8 marks*)

(ii) to state whether you would support a proposal to substitute a Group ROCE investment criterion in place of the existing DCF investment criterion.

(*4 marks*)

Note: You should give supporting calculations and/or explanations in each part of your answer. Ignore taxation.

(*Total 20 marks*)

CIMA Stage 4 Management Accounting – Decision Making

20.28 **Advanced: Appropriate performance measures for different goals**

The executive directors and the seven divisional managers of Kant Ltd spent a long weekend at a country house debating the company's goals. They concluded that Kant had multiple goals, and that the performance of senior managers should be assessed in terms of all of them.

The goals identified were:

(i) to generate a reasonable financial return for shareholders;

(ii) to maintain a high market share;

(iii) to increase productivity annually;

(iv) to offer an up-to-date product range of high quality and proven reliability;

(v) to be known as responsible employers;

(vi) to acknowledge social responsibilities;

(vii) to grow and survive autonomously.

The finance director was asked to prepare a follow-up paper, setting-out some of the implications of these ideas. He has asked you, as his personal assistant, to prepare comments on certain issues for his consideration.

You are required to set out briefly, with reasons:

(a) suitable measures of performance for each of the stated goals for which you consider this to be possible.

(*18 marks*)

(b) an outline of your view as to whether any of the stated goals can be considered to be sufficiently general to incorporate all of the others.

(*7 marks*)

(*Total 25 marks*)

ICAEW Management Accounting

20.29 Advanced: Calculation and comparison of ROI and residual income using straight line and annuity methods of depreciation

The CP division of R plc. had budgeted a net profit before tax of £3 million per annum over the period of the foreseeable future, based on a net capital employed of £10 million.

Plant replacement anticipated over this period is expected to be approximately equal to the annual depreciation each year. These figures compare well with the organization's required rate of return of 20% before tax.

CP's management is currently considering a substantial expansion of its manufacturing capacity to cope with the forecast demands of a new customer. The customer is prepared to offer a five-year contract providing CP with annual sales of £2 million.

In order to meet this contract, a total additional capital outlay of £2 million is envisaged, being £1.5 million of new fixed assets plus £0.5 million working capital. A five-year plant life is expected.

Operating costs on the contract are estimated to be £1.35 million per annum, excluding depreciation.

This is considered to be a low-risk venture as the contract would be firm for five years and the manufacturing processes are well understood within CP.

You are required

(a) to calculate the impact of accepting the contract on the CP divisional Return on Capital Employed (ROCE) and Residual Income (RI), indicating whether it would be attractive to CP's management;
(8 marks)

(b) to repeat (a) using annuity depreciation for the newly acquired plant;
(7 marks)

(c) to explain the basis of the calculations in the statements you have produced and discuss the suitability of each method in directing divisional management toward the achievement of corporate goals.
(10 marks)

(Total 25 marks)

CIMA Stage 4 – Control and Audit

20.30 Advanced: Computation of divisional performance measures and NPV and impact on bonuses

Tannadens Division is considering an investment in a quality improvement programme for a specific product group which has an estimated life of four years. It is estimated that the quality improvement programme will increase saleable output capacity and provide an improved level of customer demand due to the enhanced reliability of the product group.

Forecast information about the programme in order that it may be evaluated at each of best, most likely and worst scenario levels is as follows:

(i) There will be an initial investment of £4 000 000 on 1 January, year 1, with a programme life of four years and nil residual value. Depreciation will be calculated on a straight line basis.

(ii) Additional costs of staff training, consultancy fees and the salary of the programme manager are estimated at a most likely level of £100 000 per annum for each year of the proposal. This may vary by ±2.5%. This is the only relevant fixed cost of the proposal.

(iii) The most likely additional output capacity which will be sold is 1000 standard hours in year 1 with further increases in years 2, 3 and 4 of 300, 400 and 300 standard hours respectively. These values may vary by ±5%.

(iv) The most likely contribution per standard hour of extra capacity is £1200. This may vary by ±10%.

(v) The most likely cost of capital is 10%. This may vary from 8% to 12%.

Assume that all cash flows other than the initial investment take place at the end of each year. Ignore taxation.

Required:

(a) Present a table (including details of relevant workings) showing the net profit, residual income and return on investment for each of years 1 to 4 and also the net present value (NPV) for the BEST OUTCOME situation of the programme.

(10 marks)

Using the information provided above, the net profit, residual income (RI), and return on investment (ROI) for each year of the programme have been calculated for the most likely outcome and the worst outcome as follows:

Most likely outcome:	Year 1	Year 2	Year 3	Year 4
Net profit (£)	100 000	460 000	940 000	1 300 000
Residual income (£)	–300 000	160 000	740 000	1 200 000
Return on investment	2.5%	15.3%	47.0%	130.0%

Worst outcome:	Year 1	Year 2	Year 3	Year 4
Net profit (£)	–76 500	231 300	641 700	949 500
Residual income (£)	–556 500	–128 700	401 700	829 500
Return on investment	–1.9%	7.7%	32.1%	95.0%

In addition, the net present value (NPV) of the programme has been calculated as most likely outcome: £1 233 700 and worst outcome: £214 804.

It has been decided that the programme manager will be paid a bonus in addition to the annual salary of £40 000 (assume that this salary applies to the best, most likely and worst scenarios). The bonus will be paid on **ONE** of the following bases:

(A) Calculated and paid each year at 1.5% of any profit in excess of £250 000 for the year.

(B) Calculated and paid each year at 5% of annual salary for each £100 000 of residual income in excess of £250 000.

(C) Calculated and paid at 15% of annual salary in each year in which a positive ROI (%) is reported.

(D) Calculated and paid at the end of year 4 as 2.5% of the NPV of the programme.

Required:

(b) Prepare a table showing the bonus to be paid in each of years 1 to 4 and in total for each of methods (A) to (D) above, where the MOST LIKELY outcome situation applies.

(9 marks)

(c) Discuss which of the bonus methods is likely to be favoured by the programme manager at Tannadens Division. You should refer to your calculations in (b) above as appropriate. You should also consider the total bonus figures for the best outcome and worst outcome situations which are as follows:

	Total bonus	
	Best outcome	Worst outcome
	£	£
Net profit basis	43 890	16 368
Residual income basis	48 150	14 624
ROI basis	24 000	18 000
NPV basis	60 323	5 370

(11 marks)

(d) 'The achievement of the quality improvement programme will be influenced by the programme manager's:

(i) level of effort

(ii) attitude to risk, and

(iii) personal expectations from the programme'.

Discuss this statement.

(5 marks)

(Total 35 marks)

ACCA Paper 9 Information for Control and Decision Making

20.31 Computation and discussion of economic value added

The managers of Toutplut Inc were surprised at a recent newspaper article which suggested that the company's performance in the last two years had been poor. The CEO commented that turnover had increased by nearly 17% and pre-tax profit by 25% between the last two financial years, and that the company compared well with others in the same industry.

	$ million	
	Profit and loss account extracts for the year	
	2000	2001
Turnover	326	380
Pre-tax accounting profit[1]	67	84
Taxation	23	29
Profit after tax	44	55
Dividends	15	18
Retained earnings	29	37

	Balance sheet extracts for the year ending	
	2000	**2001**
Fixed assets	120	156
Net current assets	130	160
	250	316
Financed by:		
Shareholders' funds	195	236
Medium- and long-term bank loans	55	80
	250	316

[1]After deduction of the economic depreciation of the company's fixed assets. This is also the depreciation used for tax purposes.

Other information:

(i) Toutplut had non-capitalized leases valued at $10 million in each year 1999–2001.

(ii) Balance Sheet capital employed at the end of 1999 was $223 million.

(iii) The company's pre-tax cost of debt was estimated to be 9% in 2000, and 10% in 2001.

(iv) The company's cost of equity was estimated to be 15% in 2000 and 17% in 2001.

(v) The target capital structure is 60% equity, 40% debt.

(vi) The effective tax rate was 35% in both 2000 and 2001.

(vii) Economic depreciation was $30 million in 2000 and $35 million in 2001.

(viii) Other non-cash expenses were $10 million per year in both 2000 and 2001.

(ix) Interest expense was $4 million in 2000 and $6 million in 2001.

Required:

(a) Estimate the Economic Valued Added (EVA) for Toutplut Inc for both 2000 and 2001. State clearly any assumptions that you make.

Comment upon the performance of the company.

(7 marks)

(b) Explain the relationship between economic value added and net present value.

(2 marks)

(c) Briefly discuss the advantages and disadvantages of EVA.

(6 marks)

(Total 15 marks)

ACCA Paper 3.7 Strategic Financial Management

Both divisions pursuing their own best interests in isolation will not therefore arrive at the optimal company solution that is, the sale of 3 units of the intermediate product and 3 units of the final product. A conflict occurs because what is in the best interests of a specific division is not in the best interests of the company as a whole. One way of ensuring that the optimal solution is achieved is for central headquarters to obtain information from the supplying and the receiving divisions and to work out the optimal production programme for each division. However, such an approach strikes at the very heart of the transfer price problem, because the optimal production programme has been achieved by an infringement of divisional autonomy.

Summary relating to an imperfect market for the intermediate product

Let us now summarize our findings where there is an imperfect market for the intermediate product. Where the supplying division has no capacity constraints, the theoretically correct transfer price is the marginal cost of producing the intermediate product at the optimal output level for the company as a whole. Where unit marginal cost is constant (and thus equals variable cost) and fixed costs remain unchanged, this rule will give a transfer price equal to the variable cost per unit of the supplying division. However, when capacity constraints apply and the profit maximizing output cannot be achieved, transfer prices based on marginal cost will not ensure that optimal output is achieved, and in this situation it may be necessary for staff at the central headquarters to establish the optimum production programme for each division based on the output derived from a linear programming model. The application of linear programming to management accounting is presented in Chapter 26.

Summary

The following items relate to the learning objectives listed at the beginning of the chapter.

- **Describe the different purposes of a transfer pricing system.**

  Transfer pricing can be used for the following purposes: (a) to provide information that motivates divisional managers to make good economic decisions; (b) to provide information that is useful for evaluating the managerial and economic performance of a division; (c) to intentionally move profits between divisions or locations; and (d) to ensure that divisional autonomy is not undermined.

- **Identify and describe the five different transfer pricing methods.**

  The five main transfer pricing methods are (a) market-based transfer prices; (b) marginal cost transfer prices; (c) full cost transfer prices; (d) cost-plus a mark-up transfer prices; and (e) negotiated transfer prices.

- **Explain why the correct transfer price is the external market price when there is a perfectly competitive market for the intermediate product.**

  If there is a perfectly competitive market for the intermediate product transfers recorded at market, prices are likely to represent the real economic contribution to total company profits. If the supplying division did not exist, the intermediate product would have to be purchased on the outside market at the current market price. Alternatively, if the receiving division did not exist, the intermediate product would have to be sold on the outside market at the current market price. Divisional profits are therefore likely to be similar to the profits that would be calculated if the divisions were separate organizations. For decision-making, if the receiving division does not acquire the intermediate product internally it would be able to acquire the product at the competitive external market price. Similarly, if the supplying division does transfer internally it will be able to sell the product at the external market price. Thus, the market price represents the opportunity cost of internal transfers.

- **Explain why cost-plus transfer prices will not result in the optimum output being achieved.**

  If cost-plus transfer prices are used, the receiving division will determine its optimal output at the point where the marginal cost of its transfers is equal to its net marginal revenue (i.e. marginal revenue less marginal conversion costs, excluding the transfer price). However, the marginal cost of the transfers (i.e. the cost-plus transfer price) will be in excess of the marginal cost of producing the intermediate product for the company as a whole. Thus, marginal cost will be overstated and the receiving division manager will restrict output to the point where net marginal revenue equals the transfer price, rather than the marginal cost to the company of producing the intermediate product.

- **Explain the two methods of transfer pricing that have been advocated to resolve the conflicts between the decision-making and performance evaluation objectives.**

  To overcome the decision-making and performance evaluation conflicts that can occur with cost-based transfer pricing two methods have been proposed – a dual-rate transfer pricing system and a two-part transfer pricing system. With a dual rate transfer pricing system the receiving division is charged with the marginal cost of the intermediate product and the supplying division is credited with the full cost per unit plus a profit margin. Therefore, the receiving division should choose the output level at which the marginal cost of the intermediate product is equal to the net marginal revenue of the final product. Also, the supplying division will earn a profit on inter-divisional transfers. Any inter-divisional profits are written off by an accounting adjustment. The two-part transfer pricing system involves transfers being made at the marginal cost per unit of output of the supplying division plus a lump-sum fixed fee charged by the supplying division to the receiving division for the use of the capacity allocated to the intermediate product. This transfer pricing system should also motivate the receiving division to choose the optimal output level and enable the supplying division to obtain a profit on inter-divisional trading.

- **Describe the additional factors that must be considered when setting transfer prices for multinational transactions.**

  When divisions operate in different countries, taxation implications can be a dominant influence. The aim is to set transfer prices at levels which will ensure that most of the profits are allocated to divisions operating in low taxation counties. However, taxation authorities in the countries where the divisions are located and the OECD have introduced guidelines and legislation to ensure that companies do not use the transfer prices for taxation manipulation purposes. Transfer pricing can also have an impact on import duties and dividend repatriations. Import duties can be minimized by transferring products at low prices to a division located in a country with high import duties. Some countries also restrict dividend repatriations. By increasing the transfer prices of the goods transferred into divisions operating with these restrictions, it is possible to increase the funds repatriated without appearing to violate dividend restrictions.

- **Calculate optimum output and transfer prices when there is no external market or an imperfect external market for the intermediate product.**

  The theoretically correct transfer price for both of the above situations, when there are no capacity constraints, is the marginal cost of producing the intermediate product at the optimum output level for the company as a whole. The application of this rule was illustrated with Exhibits 21.4 and 21.5 when there is no external market and with Exhibits 21.6 and 21.7 when there is an imperfect market for the intermediate product.

- **Additional learning objective presented in Appendix 21.1**

  The appendix to this chapter includes an additional learning objective: to explain how optimal transfer prices can be determined using economic analysis. The economic analysis is normally presented in diagrammatic form. Appendix 21.1 has been included for those readers who prefer this form of presentation, but if you prefer the non-diagrammatic form you can omit reading the appendix.

Appendix 21.1: Economic analysis of transfer pricing

It is difficult to discuss the economic analysis of transfer pricing in purely verbal terms without some loss of rigour. To overcome this difficulty, a number of theoretical transfer pricing models applicable to different situations are presented in diagrammatic form in this Appendix.[3] These are based upon principles first suggested by Hirshleifer (1956) and Gould (1964). For simplicity, we shall assume that the company consists of only two divisions: a supplying division and a receiving division. The theoretically correct transfer price that will induce divisions to arrive at the optimum output for the company as a whole, when operating in their own best interests, is presented in the foregoing analysis.

Perfect external market for the intermediate product

In our previous discussion in the main body of the chapter we established that where a perfect market for an intermediate product exists, the correct transfer price is the intermediate external market price. This situation is presented in Figure 21A.1.

The external market price for the intermediate product is OP, and, because the external market for the intermediate product is assumed to be perfect, the marginal revenue for the intermediate product (MR_S) is constant and is represented by the horizontal line PE. The NMR line refers to the net marginal revenue of the receiving division, and consists of the marginal revenue of the receiving division (MR_R) less the marginal conversion cost (MC_R) but excludes the transfer price paid to the supplying division.

The transfer price will be set equal to the market price of the intermediate product on the external perfect market at OP. At this transfer price the receiving division will require quantity OQ_1 (this is where NMR is equal to the transfer price) and will be indifferent as to whether it obtains this supply from the supplying division or the external market. The supplying division will also be indifferent as to whether it sells this quantity to the receiving division or the external market. However, the supplying division will wish to sell a total quantity of OQ_2, and will sell an additional quantity Q_1Q_2 externally if it supplies OQ_1 internally. (Total quantity OQ_2 is where the marginal cost of the supplying division (MC_S) is equal to its marginal revenue (MR_S).) Note that the NMR schedule for the company as a whole is BCDE, and the most profitable output is where it intersects the company's marginal cost schedule ADE at point D. This requires an output of OQ_2, which is identical with the amount produced by the supplying division.

FIGURE 21A.1 *Perfect external market for the intermediate product*

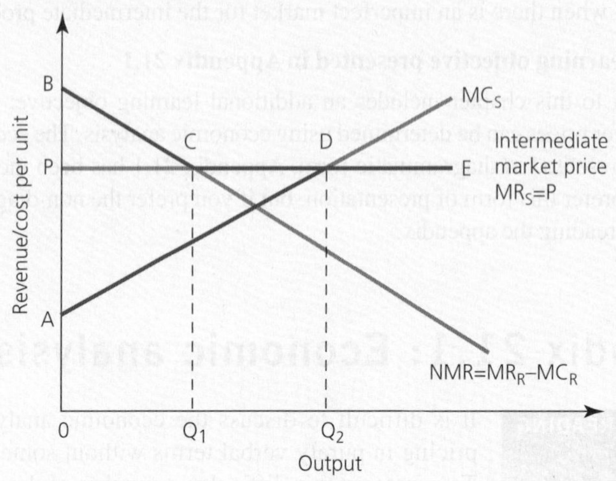

A transfer price of OP, which is equal to the market price of the intermediate product, will mean that the divisions will achieve the total company's optimal output, and it will also allow them to deal with each other as they please.

A perfect market for the intermediate product and the present of selling costs

Gould (1964) considers the situation where a company incurs transportation and selling costs such that there might be a difference between the net price received for the sale of the intermediate product externally and the price at which the product is purchased on the external market. Also, if the intermediate product is transferred internally, some selling costs might be avoided. Under these circumstances an optimal production policy may not be achieved if the divisions are allowed to ignore each other's request for the transfer of intermediate products.

Figure 21A.2 contains information identical with that presented in Figure 21A.1, with the exception that the market price line is replaced by two lines – a buying price and a selling price. Figure 21A.2(a) represents the situation where the NMR and MCS lines intersect below the net selling price for the intermediate product. You will see that it is cheaper for the company to manufacture the intermediate product internally so long as the marginal cost of the supplying division (MC_S) is below the buying price of the intermediate product on the external market. Beyond B it is cheaper to purchase the intermediate product on the external market. The company as a whole therefore faces a marginal cost schedule equal to FBC.

So long as the company can obtain a larger marginal revenue by converting the intermediate product into the final product, it should do so. This situation applies so long as the NMR line lies above the net selling price for the intermediate product. This is represented by the segment AD of the NMR line, giving an output of OQ_1 of the *final* product for sale in the external final product market. Additional output of the intermediate product beyond OQ_1 can be sold profitability on the external markets; so in this case Q_1Q_2 of the intermediate product will be sold on the external market at a price of OP_s. The effect of this is that

FIGURE 21A.3 *No external market for the intermediate product*

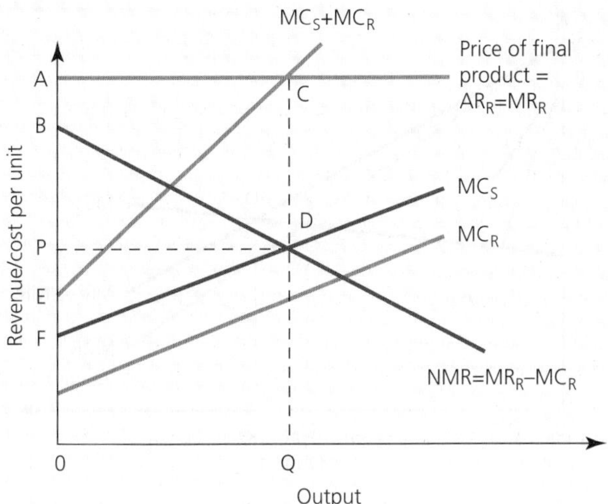

revenue. This is also quantity OQ. So both divisions will want quantity OQ to be transferred between them, and the sum of their respective profits will be equal to the total company's maximum profit. The supplying division's profit is represented by the area FDP and the receiving division's profit by the area BDP, which together equal BDF; the area BDF is equal to the area ACE that represents total company profits.

Imperfect market for the intermediate product

In an imperfect market the quantity of the intermediate product that is sold externally will influence the market price, and the marginal revenue for the sale of the intermediate product (MR_S) will decline as output increases (Figure 21A.4). The marginal cost and marginal revenue schedules for the company as a whole are represented by the MC_S and MR_S + NMR schedules. The latter represents the marginal revenue of the supplying division plus the net marginal revenue of the receiving division. The optimum output for the company as a whole will therefore occur where the MC_S and MR_S + NMR schedules intersect; that is, at level OQ_3.

The optimal transfer price that induces the supplying and receiving divisions to operate in this output level is shown by the point on the vertical axis where the MC_S and the MR_S+ NMR schedules intersect. The correct transfer price is therefore OP_T (i.e. the MC of the supplying division at the optimum output level). At this price the receiving division will view the horizontal line P_TD as its marginal cost of supply and require output OQ_2 from the supplying division. At this point its NMR schedule intersects the horizontal line P_TD. The supplying division will face a marginal revenue schedule equal to BED (it will prefer to sell at a transfer price P_T beyond point E, since this is in excess of the marginal revenue line below E). This means that the supplying division will prefer to sell OQ_1 of the intermediate product on the external market at a price OP_E (the selling price at which its marginal revenue line is equal to or above E). In addition, the supplying division will wish to supply Q_1Q_3 at the transfer price OP_T to the receiving division. This will give a total output by the supplying division of OQ_3 (i.e. the optimal output for the

FIGURE 21A.4 *Imperfect market for the intermediate product*

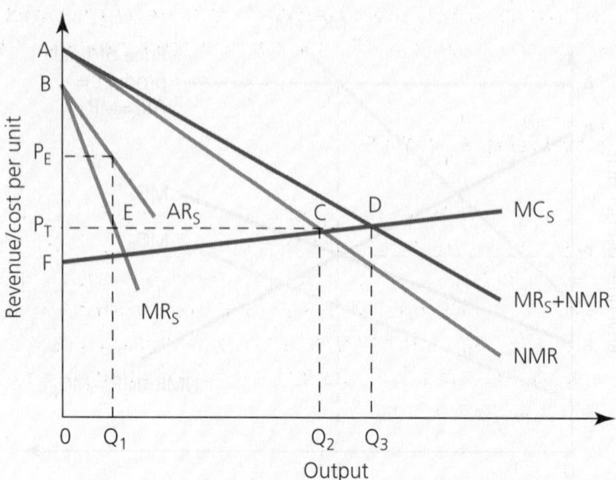

company as a whole), being the quantity of output at which its marginal cost MCS is equal to its marginal revenue BED. This is consistent with the receiving division's demand for OQ_2, because OQ_1 is equal to Q_2Q_3. Therefore, OQ_2 equals Q_1Q_3.

Notes

1 Exhibits 21.4 and 21.6 are adapted from illustrations first presented by Solomons (1965).

2 The supplying division will obtain marginal revenue in excess of the transfer price of £27.01/£27.49 for the sale of the first five units on the external market and it will not be motivated to follow the optimal company plan for the company as a whole. Similarly, the receiving division will maximize its own profits by accepting, all transfers until the net marginal revenue equals the transfer price, and it will therefore wish to sell six units of the final product.

3 The models presented in this appendix are adapted from Tomkins, C., *Financial Planning in Divisionalised Companies*, Haymarket, 1973, Ch. 3.

Key terms and concepts

cost-plus a mark-up transfer prices (p. 885)
dual-rate transfer pricing (p. 899)
final products (p. 884)
full cost transfer prices (p. 885)
intermediate products (p. 884)
marginal cost transfer prices (p. 885)
market-based transfer prices (p. 885)
negotiated transfer prices (p. 885)
net marginal revenue (pp. 890, 908)
perfectly competitive market (p. 886)
two-part transfer pricing system (p. 900)

Recommended reading

A book authoured by Emmanuel and Mehafdi (1994) focuses exclusively on transfer pricing. For research studies relating primarily to domestic transfer pricing you should refer to Perera *et al.* (2003), Boyns *et al.*(1999) and Chan (1998). Shorter articles by Atkinson and Tyrrall (1997) and Elliott (1998a) provide further insights into international transfer pricing issues and research relating to surveys of international transfer practices is presented in the articles by Elliott (1998b) and Oyelere and Emmanuel (1998).

Key examination points

When discussing a transfer pricing system, you should indicate that the proposed system should motivate managers to make correct decisions, provide a reasonable measure of performance and ensure that divisional autonomy is not undermined. It is not possible for a single transfer price to meet all three of these requirements. Most examination questions require you to recommend an optimal transfer price. It is particularly important that you understand how optimal transfer prices should be set when there is an imperfect market or no market for the intermediate product.

Assessment material

Review questions

The review questions are short questions that enable you to assess your understanding of the main topics included in the chapter. The numbers in parentheses provide you with the page numbers to refer to if you cannot answer a specific question.

Review problems

The review problems are more complex and require you to relate and apply the chapter content to various business problems. The problems are graded by their level of difficulty. The multiple-choice questions are the least demanding and normally take less than 10 minutes to complete. Fully worked solutions to the review problems are provided in a separate section at the end of the book. For those questions in the white box the worked solutions are provided in the *Student's Manual* accompanying this book. Further review problems for this chapter are available on the accompanying website www.drury-online.com. The answers to these problems are available for lecturers on the lecturer's password protected section of the website.

Case studies

The website also includes over 30 case study problems. A list of these cases is provided in Part Seven of this book.

Review questions

21.1 Distinguish between intermediate products and final products. (*p. 884*)

21.2 Explain the four purposes for which transfer pricing can be used. (*pp. 884–85*)

21.3 Explain why a single transfer pricing method cannot serve all four purposes. (*p. 885*)

21.4 If an external, perfectly competitive market exists for an intermediate product what should be the transfer price? Why? (*p. 886*)

21.5 Define the term 'net marginal revenue'. (*p. 890*)

21.6 If there is no external market for the intermediate product what is the optimal transfer price? Why? (*pp. 890–91*)

21.7 Why are full cost and cost-plus a mark-up transfer prices unlikely to result in the optimum output? (*p. 891–93*)

21.8 Why are marginal cost transfer prices not widely used in practice? (*p. 891*)

21.9 Why are transfer prices based on full cost widely used in practice? *(pp. 891–92)*

21.10 Discuss the advantages and disadvantages of negotiated transfer prices. *(pp. 893–94)*

21.11 What are the circumstances that favour the use of negotiated transfer prices? *(pp. 893–94)*

21.12 Describe the two proposals that have been recommended for resolving transfer pricing conflicts. *(pp. 898–901)*

21.13 What are the special considerations that must be taken into account with international transfer pricing? *(pp. 904–07)*

21.14 When there is an imperfect market for the intermediate product what is the optimal transfer price? *(p. 910)*

Review problems

21.15 **Advanced**

X plc, a manufacturing company, has two divisions: Division A and Division B. Division A produces one type of product, ProdX, which it transfers to Division B and also sells externally. Division B has been approached by another company which has offered to supply 2500 units of ProdX for £35 each.

The following details for Division A are available:

	£
Sales revenue	
Sales to Division B @ £40 per unit	400 000
External sales @ £45 per unit	270 000
Less:	
Variable cost @ £22 per unit	352 000
Fixed costs	100 000
Profit	218 000

If Division B decides to buy from the other company, the impact of the decision on the profits of Division A and X plc, assuming external sales of ProdX cannot be increased, will be

	Division A	X plc
A	£12 500 decrease	£12 500 decrease
B	£15 625 decrease	£12 500 increase
C	£32 500 decrease	£32 500 increase
D	£45 000 decrease	£32 500 decrease
E	£45 000 decrease	£45 000 decrease

(3 marks)

CIMA Management Accounting – Decision Making

21.16 **Advanced**

Division A transfers 100 000 units of a component to Division B each year.

The market price of the component is £25.

Division A's variable cost is £15 per unit.

Division A's fixed costs are £500 000 each year.

What price would be credited to Division A for each component that it transfers to Division B under

(i) dual pricing (based on marginal cost and market price)?

(ii) two-part tariff pricing (where the Divisions have agreed that the fixed fee will be £200 000)?

	Dual pricing	Two-part tariff pricing
A	£15	£15
B	£25	£15
C	£15	£17
D	£25	£17
E	£15	£20

(2 marks)
CIMA Management Accounting – Decision Making

21.17 **Advanced: Determining optimal transfer prices for three different scenarios**

Manuco Ltd has been offered supplies of special ingredient Z at a transfer price of £15 per kg by Helpco Ltd which is part of the same group of companies. Helpco Ltd processes and sells special ingredient Z to customers external to the group at £15 per kg. Helpco Ltd bases its transfer price on cost plus 25% profit mark-up. Total cost has been estimated as 75% variable and 25% fixed.

Required:

Discuss the transfer prices at which Helpco Ltd should offer to transfer special ingredient Z to Manuco Ltd in order that group profit maximizing decisions may be taken on financial grounds in each of the following situations:

(i) Helpco Ltd has an external market for all of its production of special ingredient Z at a selling price of £15 per kg. Internal transfers to Manuco Ltd would enable £1.50 per kg of variable packing cost to be avoided.

(ii) Conditions are as per (i) but Helpco Ltd has production capacity for 3000 kg of special ingredient Z for which no external market is available.

(iii) Conditions are as per (ii) but Helpco Ltd has an alternative use for some of its spare production capacity. This alternative use is equivalent to 2000 kg of special ingredient Z and would earn a contribution of £6000.

(13 marks)
ACCA Paper 9 Information for Control and Decision Making

21.18 **Impact of cost-plus transfer price on decision making and divisional profits**

Enormous Engineering (EE) plc is a large multidivisional engineering company having interests in a wide variety of product markets. The Industrial Products Division (IPD) sells component parts to consumer appliance manufacturers, both inside and outside the company. One such part, a motor unit, it sells solely to external customers, but buys the motor itself internally from the Electric Motor Division. The Electric Motor Division (EMD) makes the motor to IPD specifications and it does not expect to be able to sell it to any other customers.

In preparing the 2001 budgets IPD estimated the number of motor units it expects to be able to sell at various prices as follows:

Price (ex works) (£)	Quantity sold (units)
50	1000
40	2000
35	3000
30	4000
25	6000
20	8000

It then sought a quotation from EMD, who offered to supply the motors at £16 each based on the following estimate:

	(£)
Materials and bought-in parts	2
Direct labour costs	4
Factory overhead (150% of direct labour costs)	6
Total factory cost	12
Profit margin ($33^1/_3$% on factory cost)	4
Quoted price	£16

Factory overhead costs are fixed. All other costs are variable.

Although it considered the price quoted to be on the high side, IPD nevertheless believed that it could still sell the completed unit at a profit because it incurred costs of only £4 (material £1 and direct labour £3) on each unit made. It therefore placed an order for the coming year.

On reviewing the budget for 2001 the finance director of EE noted that the projected sales of the motor unit were considerably less than those for the previous year, which was disappointing as both divisions concerned were working well below their capacities. On making enquiries he was told by IPD that the price reduction required to sell more units would reduce rather than increase profit and that the main problem was the high price charged by EMD. EMD stated that they required the high price in order to meet their target profit margin for the year, and that any reduction would erode their pricing policy.

You are required to:

(a) develop tabulations for each division, and for the company as a whole, that indicate the anticipated effect of IPD selling the motor unit at each of the prices listed,

(10 marks)

(b) (i) show the selling price which IPD should select in order to maximize its own divisional profit on the motor unit,

(2 marks)

(ii) show the selling price which would be in the best interest of EE as a whole,

(2 marks)

(iii) explain why this latter price is not selected by IPD,

(1 mark)

(c) state:

(i) what changes you would advise making to the transfer pricing system so that it will motivate divisional managers to make better decisions in future, *(5 marks)*

(ii) what transfer price will ensure overall optimality in this situation. *(5 marks)*

(Total 25 marks)

ICAEW Management Accounting

21.19 Advanced: Calculating the effects of a transfer pricing system on divisional and company profits

Division A of a large divisionalized organization manufactures a single standardized product. Some of the output is sold externally whilst the remainder is transferred to Division B where it is a subassembly in the manufacture of that divisions product. The unit costs of Division A's product are as follows:

	(£)
Direct material	4
Direct labour	2
Direct expense	2
Variable manufacturing overheads	2
Fixed manufacturing overheads	4
Selling and packing expense – variable	1
	15

Annually 10 000 units of the product are sold externally at the standard price of £30.

In addition to the external sales, 5000 units are transferred annually to Division B at an internal transfer charge of £29 per unit. This transfer price is obtained by deducting variable selling and packing expense from the external price since this expense is not incurred for internal transfers.

Division B incorporates the transferred-in goods into a more advanced product. The unit costs of this product are as follows:

	(£)
Transferred-in item (from Division A)	29
Direct material and components	23
Direct labour	3
Variable overheads	12
Fixed overheads	12
Selling and packing expense – variable	1
	80

Division B's manager disagrees with the basis used to set the transfer price. He argues that the transfers should be made at variable cost plus an agreed (minimal) mark-up since he claims that his division is taking output that Division A would be unable to sell at the price of £30.

Partly because of this disagreement, a study of the relationship between selling price and demand has recently been made for each division by the company's sales director. The resulting report contains the following table:

Customer demand at various selling prices:

Division A			
Selling price	£20	£30	£40
Demand	15 000	10 000	5000
Division B			
Selling price	£80	£90	£100
Demand	7 200	5 000	2800

The manager of Division B claims that this study supports his case. He suggests that a transfer price of £12 would give Division A a reasonable contribution to its fixed overheads while allowing Division B to earn a reasonable profit. He also believes that it would lead to an increase of output and an improvement in the overall level of company profits.

You are required:

(a) to calculate the effect that the transfer pricing system has had on the company's profits, and

(16 marks)

(b) to establish the likely effect on profits of adopting the suggestion by the manager of Division B of a transfer price of £12.

(6 marks)
(Total 22 marks)
ACCA Level 2 Management Accounting

21.20 **Advanced: Make or buy decision and intercompany trading**

Companies RP, RR, RS and RT are members of a group. RP wishes to buy an electronic control system for its factory and, in accordance with group policy, must obtain quotations from companies inside and outside of the group.

From outside of the group the following quotations are received:

Company A quoted £33 200.
Company B quoted £35 000 but would buy a special unit from RS for £13 000. To make this unit, however, RS would need to buy parts from RR at a price of £7500.

The inside quotation was from RS whose price was £48 000. This would require RS buying parts from RR at a price of £8000 and units from RT at a price of £30 000. However, RT would need to buy parts from RR at a price of £11 000.

Additional data are as follows:

(1) RR is extremely busy with work outside the group and has quoted current market prices for all its products.

(2) RS costs for the RP contract, including purchases from RR and RT, total £42 000. For the Company B contract it expects a profit of 25% on the cost of its own work.

(3) RT prices provide for a 20% profit margin on total costs.

(4) The variable costs of the group companies in respect of the work under consideration are:

RR: 20% of selling price

RS: 70% of own cost (excluding purchases from other group companies)

RT: 65% of own cost (excluding purchases from other group companies)

You are required, from a group point of view, to:

(a) recommend, with appropriate calculations, whether the contract should be placed with RS or Company A or Company B;

(b) state briefly *two* assumptions you have made in arriving at your recommendations.

(30 marks)
CIMA P3 Management Accounting

21.21 **Advanced: Setting an optimal transfer price when there is an intermediate imperfect market**

(a) Memphis plc is a multi-division firm operating in a wide range of activities. One of its divisions, Division A, produces a semi-finished product Alpha, which can be sold in an outside market at a price P_S. It can also be sold to Division B, which can use it in manufacturing its finished product Beta. The outside market in which Alpha is traded is perfect in all respects, except in so far as the buying division would have to incur transportation costs, which are included in the buying price P_B if it buys Alpha in the open market. The finished product of Division B, Beta, can be sold only in another perfect external market. Assume also that the marginal cost of each division is a rising linear function of output, and that the goal for Memphis plc is to maximize its total profits.

You are required to explain how the optimal transfer price for Alpha should be derived in these circumstances, and to outline any rules which should be stipulated by the management of Memphis plc to ensure attaining its goal of profit maximization.

(15 marks)

(b) Assume that Divisions A and B as above, except (i) that Division A is a monopolist facing a downward sloping demand curve and (ii) that it can sell Alpha externally at a price higher than the price it charges internally to Division B. Relevant information about both divisions is given below.

Output of Alpha (units)	Total cost of Alpha (£000)	Revenue from outside selling of Alpha (£000)	Net marginal revenue of Beta (£000)
60	112	315	47
70	140	350	45
80	170	380	43
90	203	405	40
100	238	425	36
110	275	440	33
120	315	450	30
130	359	455	25

You are required to calculate the optimal transfer price for Alpha and the optimal activity level for each division.

(10 marks)
(Total 25 marks)
ICAEW Management Accounting

21.22 Advanced: Calculation of optimal selling price using calculus and the impact of using the imperfect market price as the transfer price

AB Ltd has two Divisions – A and B. Division A manufactures a product called the aye and Division B manufactures a product called the bee. Each bee uses a single aye as a component. A is the only manufacturer of the aye and supplies both B and outside customers.

Details of A's and B's operations for the coming period are as follows:

	Division A	Division B
Fixed costs	£7 500 000	£18 000 000
Variable costs per unit	£280	£590*
Capacity – units	30 000	18 000

*Note: Excludes transfer costs

Market research has indicated that demand for AB Ltd's products from outside customers will be as follows in the coming period:

- *the aye*: at unit price £1000 no ayes will be demanded but demand will increase by 25 ayes with every £1 that the unit price is reduced below £1000;
- *the bee*: at unit price £4000 no bees will be demanded, but demand will increase by 10 bees with every £1 that the unit price is reduced below £4000.

Requirements:

(a) Calculate the unit selling price of the bee (accurate to the nearest £) that will maximize AB Ltd's profit in the coming period.

(10 marks)

(b) Calculate the unit selling price of the bee (accurate to the nearest £) that is likely to emerge if the Divisional Managers of A and B both set selling prices calculated to maximize Divisional profit from sales to outside customers and the transfer price of ayes going from A to B is set at 'market selling price'.

(10 marks)

(c) Explain why your answers to parts (a) and (b) are different, and propose changes to the system of transfer pricing in order to ensure that AB Ltd is charging its customers at optimum prices.

(5 marks)

(Total 25 marks)

CIMA Stage 3 Management Accounting Applications

21.23 Advanced

P plc is a multi-national conglomerate company with manufacturing divisions, trading in numerous countries across various continents. Trade takes place between a number of the divisions in different countries, with partly-completed products being transferred between them. Where a transfer takes place between divisions trading in different countries, it is the policy of the Board of P plc to determine centrally the appropriate transfer price without reference to the divisional managers concerned. The Board of plc justifies this policy to divisional managers on the grounds that its objective is to maximize the conglomerate's post-tax profits and that the global position can be monitored effectively only from the Head Office.

Requirements:

(a) Explain and critically appraise the possible reasoning behind P plc's policy of centrally determining transfer prices for goods traded between divisions operating in different countries.

(10 marks)

(b) Discuss the ethical implications of P plc's policy of imposing transfer prices on its overseas divisions in order to maximize post-tax profits.

(10 marks)
(Total 20 marks)
CIMA Stage 4 Strategic Management Accounting and Marketing

Review problems (with answers in the Student's Manual)

21.24 **Advanced**

(a) Transfers between processes in a manufacturing company can be made at (i) cost or (ii) sales value at the point of transfer.

Discuss how each of the above methods might be compatible with the operation of a responsibility accounting system.

(8 marks)

(b) Shadow prices (net opportunity costs or dual prices) may be used in the setting of transfer prices between divisions in a group of companies, where the intermediate products being transferred are in short supply.

Explain why the transfer prices thus calculated are more likely to be favoured by the management of the divisions supplying the intermediate products rather than the management of the divisions receiving the intermediate products.

(9 marks)
(Total 17 marks)
ACCA Level 2 Management Accounting

21.25 **Advanced**

SK plc is divided into five divisions that provide consultancy services to each other and to outside customers. The divisions are Computing and Information Technology, Human Resources, Legal, Engineering, and Finance.

It has been company policy for all budgets to be prepared centrally with each division being given Sales and Profit targets. However, the divisional managers feel that the targets are unrealistic, as they do not consider the individual circumstances of each division, or the effects on profitability of providing services to other divisions. The current basis of charging for these services is to use the actual marginal cost of the supplying division.

In response to the comments made by the divisional managers, SK plc has now asked the managers to prepare their own budgets for next year and to submit proposals for a new internal charging system.

Required:

(a) (i) State why organizations prepare budgets.

(3 marks)

(ii) Explain the arguments for and against the involvement of managers in the preparation of their budgets.

(7 marks)

(b) Discuss the implications for SK plc, and the consequences for the managers of the supplying and receiving divisions, of each of the following possible cost-based approaches to setting a transfer price:

(i) marginal cost;

(ii) total cost;

(iii) cost plus;

(iv) opportunity cost.

(10 marks)

(c) Discuss whether standard costs or actual costs should be used as the basis for cost-based transfer prices.

(5 marks)

(Total 25 marks)

CIMA Management Accounting – Performance Management

21.26 **Advanced: The effect of alternative transfer prices on the divisional performance measure**

MCP plc specializes in providing marketing, data collection, data processing and consulting services. The company is divided into divisions that provide services to each other and also to external clients. The performance of the Divisional Managers is measured against profit targets that are set by central management.

During October, the Consulting division undertook a project for AX plc. The agreed fee was £15 500 and the costs excluding data processing were £2600. The data processing, which needed 200 hours of processing time, was carried out by the Data Processing (DP) division. An external agency could have been used to do the data processing, but the DP division had 200 chargeable skilled hours available in October.

The DP division provides data processing services to the other divisions and also to external customers. The budgeted costs of the DP division for the year ending 31 December 2002, which is divided into 12 equal monthly periods, are as follows:

	£
Variable costs:	
Skilled labour (6000 hours worked)	120 000
Semi-skilled labour	96 000
Other processing costs	60 000
Fixed costs	240 000

These costs are recovered on the basis of chargeable skilled labour hours (data processing hours) which are budgeted to be 90% of skilled labour hours worked. The DP division's external pricing policy is to add a 40% mark-up to its total budgeted cost per chargeable hour.

During October 2002, actual labour costs incurred by the DP division were 10% higher than expected, but other costs were 5% lower than expected.

Required:

(a) Calculate the total transfer value that would have been charged by the DP division to the Consulting division for the 200 hours on its AX plc project, using the following bases:

(i) actual variable cost;

(ii) standard variable cost + 40% mark-up;

(iii) market price.

(6 marks)

(b) Prepare statements to show how the alternative values calculated in answer to requirement (a) above would be reflected in the performance measurement of the DP division and the Consulting division.

(12 marks)

(c) Recommend, with supporting calculations, explanations and assumptions, the transfer value that should be used for the 200 hours of processing time in October. Your answer need not be one of those calculated in your answer to requirement (a) above.

(7 marks)

(Total 25 marks)

CIMA Management Accounting – Performance Management

21.27 **Advanced: ABC implementation and evaluation of a cost-plus transfer pricing system**

M Ltd has two divisions, X and Y. Division X is a chip manufacturer and Division Y assembles mobile phones. Division X currently manufactures many different types of chip, one of which is used in the manufacture of the mobile phones. Division X has no external market for the chips that are used in the mobile phones and currently sets the transfer price on the basis of total cost plus 20% mark-up.

The budgeted profit and loss statement for Division Y for next year shows the following results:

Mobile phone range	P	Q	R
	£000	£000	£000
Sales	10 000	9 500	11 750
Less: Total costs	7 200	11 700	9 250
Profit/(loss)	2 800	(2 200)	2 500
Fixed costs	2 000	5 400	5 875

The total costs shown above include the cost of the chips.

Division Y uses a traditional absorption costing system based on labour hours.

M Ltd operates a performance measurement system based on divisional profits. In order to increase profit for the forthcoming year, Division Y has asked permission to buy chips from an external supplier.

The accountant of M Ltd has recently attended a course on activity based costing (ABC) and has recommended that the divisions should implement an ABC system rather than continue to operate the traditional absorption costing system.

Required:

(a) A presenter at the conference stated that 'ABC provides information that is more relevant for decision making than traditional forms of costing'. Discuss this statement, using Division Y when appropriate to explain the issues you raise.

(8 marks)

(b) The management team of M Ltd has decided to implement ABC in all of the divisions. Discuss any difficulties which might be experienced when implementing ABC in the divisions.

(6 marks)

(c) (i) Discuss the current transfer pricing system and explain alternative systems that might be more appropriate for the forthcoming year.

(7 marks)

(ii) Explain the impact that the introduction of an ABC system could have on the transfer price and on divisional profits.

(4 marks)

(Total 25 marks)

CIMA Management Accounting – Decision Making

21.28 Advanced: Impact of transfer price on bonus payments and recommendation of transfer price to maximize group profits

CTD Ltd has two divisions – FD and TM. FD is an iron foundry division which produces mouldings that have a limited external market and are also transferred to TM division. TM division uses the mouldings to produce a piece of agricultural equipment called the 'TX' which is sold externally. Each TX requires one moulding. Both divisions produce only one type of product.

The performance of each Divisional Manager is evaluated individually on the basis of the residual income (RI) of his or her division. The company's average annual 12% cost of capital is used to calculate the finance charges. If their own target residual income is achieved, each Divisional Manager is awarded a bonus equal to 5% of his or her residual income. All bonuses are paid out of Head Office profits.

The following budgeted information is available for the forthcoming year:

	TM division TX per unit £	FD division Moulding per unit £
External selling price	500	80
Variable production cost	366*	40
Fixed production overheads	60	20
Gross profit	74	20
Variable selling and distribution cost	25	4**
Fixed administration overhead	25	4
Net profit	24	12
Normal capacity (units)	15 000	20 000
Maximum production capacity (units)	15 000	25 000
Sales to external customers (units)	15 000	5 000
Capital employed	£1 500 000	£750 000
Target RI	£105 000	£85 000

*The variable production cost of TX includes the cost of an FD moulding.

**External sales only of the mouldings incur a variable selling and distribution cost of £4 per unit.

FD division currently transfers 15 000 mouldings to TM division at a transfer price equal to the total production cost plus 10%.

Fixed costs are absorbed on the basis of normal capacity.

Required:

(a) Calculate the bonus each Divisional Manager would receive under the current transfer pricing policy and discuss any implications that the current performance evaluation system may have for each division and for the company as a whole.

(7 marks)

(b) Both Divisional Managers want to achieve their respective residual income targets. Based on the budgeted figures, calculate

(i) the maximum transfer price per unit that the Divisional Manager of TM division would pay.

(ii) the minimum transfer price per unit that the Divisional Manager of FD division would accept.

(6 marks)

(c) Write a report to the management of CTD Ltd that explains, and recommends, the transfer prices which FD division should set in order to maximize group profits. Your report should also

- consider the implications of actual external customer demand exceeding 5000 units; and
- explain how alternative transfer pricing systems could overcome any possible conflict that may arise as a result of your recommended transfer prices.

Note: your answer must be related to CTD Ltd. You will not earn marks by just describing various methods for setting transfer prices.

(12 marks)

(Total 25 marks)

CIMA Management Accounting – Decision Making

21.29 Advanced: Determining optimal transfer prices to influence optimal sourcing decisions

Business Solutions is a firm of management consultants which experienced considerable business growth during the last decade. By 2000 the firm's senior managers were beginning to experience difficulties in managing the business. During 2001 the firm was reorganized and a regional divisional structure was introduced with individual profit targets being set for each of the semi-autonomous profit centres. Although North division has its own customer base that is distinct from that of its sister division South, it does occasionally call upon the services of a South consultant to assist with its projects. North has to pay a cross charge to South per consulting day. The amount of the charge is determined by HQ. North is free to choose whether it employs a South consultant or subcontracts the project to an external consultant. The manager of North division believes that the quality of the external consultant and the one from South division are identical and on this basis will always employ the one who is prepared to work for the lower fee.

The following information is also available:

- North division is very busy and it charges its clients £1200 per consulting day
- North division pays its external consultant £500 per consulting day
- The variable cost per internal consulting day is £100

Required:

(a) Determine a possible optimal daily cross charge that should be paid by North for the services of a consultant from South in the scenarios outlined below. The charges that you select must induce both divisional managers to arrive at the same decision independently. Explain how you have determined your cross charges and state any assumptions that you think necessary.

Scenario (i)

- South division has spare consulting capacity.

Scenario (ii)

- South division is fully occupied earning fees of £400 per consulting day.

Scenario (iii)

- South division is fully occupied earning fees of £700 per consulting day.

(10 marks)

(b) Identify the possible factors that may have prompted the senior management to introduce a divisional structure in 2001 and suggest some potential problems that may arise.

(10 marks)

(Total 20 marks)

ACCA Paper 3.3 – Performance Management

21.30 Advanced: Scarce capacity and the use of shadow prices

Black and Brown are two divisions in a group of companies and both require intermediate products Alpha and Beta which are available from divisions A and B respectively. Black and Brown divisions convert the intermediate products into products Blackalls and Brownalls respectively. The market demand for Blackalls and Brownalls considerably exceeds the production possible, because of the limited availability of intermediate products Alpha and Beta.

No external market exists for Alpha and Beta and no other intermediate product market is available to Black and Brown divisions.

Other data are as follows:

Black division

Blackalls: Selling price per unit £45
Processing cost per unit £12
Intermediate products required per unit:
Alpha: 3 units
Beta: 2 units

Brown division

Brownalls: Selling price per unit £54
Processing cost per unit £14
Intermediate products required per unit:
Alpha: 2 units
Beta: 4 units

A division

Alpha: Variable cost per unit £6
Maximum production capacity 1200 units

B division

Beta: Variable cost per unit £4
Maximum production capacity 1600 units

The solution to a linear programming model of the situation shows that the imputed scarcity value (shadow price) of Alpha and Beta is £0.50 and £2.75 per unit respectively and indicates that the intermediate products be transferred such that 200 units of Blackalls and 300 units of Brownalls are produced and sold.

Required:

(a) Calculate the contribution earned by the group if the sales pattern indicated by the linear programming model is implemented.

(3 marks)

(b) Where the transfer prices are set on the basis of variable cost plus shadow price, show detailed calculations for

(i) the contribution per unit of intermediate product earned by divisions A and B and

(ii) the contribution per unit of final product earned by Black and Brown divisions.

(4 marks)

(c) Comment on the results derived in (b) and on the possible attitude of management of the various divisions to the proposed transfer pricing and product deployment policy.

(6 marks)

(d) In the following year the capacities of divisions A and B have each doubled and the following changes have taken place:

1. *Alpha*: There is still no external market for this product, but A division has a large demand for other products which could use the capacity and earn a contribution of 5% over cost. Variable cost per unit for the other products would be the same as for Alpha and such products would use the capacity at the same rate as Alpha.
2. *Beta*: An intermediate market for this product now exists and Beta can be bought and sold in unlimited amounts at £7.50 per unit. External sales of Beta would incur additional transport costs of £0.50 per unit which are not incurred in inter-divisional transfers.

The market demand for Blackalls and Brownalls will still exceed the production availability of Alpha and Beta.

(i) Calculate the transfer prices at which Alpha and Beta should now be offered to Black and Brown divisions in order that the transfer policy implemented will lead to the maximization of group profit.

(ii) Determine the production and sales pattern for Alpha, Beta, Blackalls and Brownalls which will now maximize group contribution and calculate the group contribution thus achieved. It may be assumed that divisions will make decisions consistent with the financial data available.

(9 marks)

(Total 22 marks)

ACCA Level 2 Management Accounting

PART 5

Cost Management and Strategic Management Accounting

In Part Four the major features of traditional management accounting control systems and the mechanisms that can be used to control costs were described. The focus was on comparing actual results against a pre-set standard (typically the budget), identifying and analysing variances and taking remedial action to ensure that future outcomes conform with budgeted outcomes. Traditional cost control systems tend to be based on the preservation of the *status-quo* and the ways of performing existing activities are not reviewed. The emphasis is on cost containment rather than cost reduction. In contrast, cost management focuses on cost reduction rather than cost containment. Chapter 22 examines the various approaches that fall within the area of cost management

During the late 1980s criticisms of traditional management accounting practices were widely publicized and new approaches were advocated which are more in tune with today's competitive and business environment. In particular, strategic management accounting has been identified as a way forward. However, there is still no comprehensive framework as to what constitutes strategic management accounting. Chapter 23 examines the elements of strategic management accounting and describes the different contributions that have been made to its development. In addition, recent developments that seek to incorporate performance measurement within the strategic management process are described.

Cost management

22

In Chapters 16–19 the major features of traditional management accounting control systems and the mechanisms that can be used to control costs were described. The focus was on comparing actual results against a pre-set standard (typically the budget), identifying and analysing variances and taking remedial action to ensure that future outcomes conform with budgeted outcomes. Traditional cost control systems tend to be based on the preservation of the *status quo* and the ways of performing existing activities are not reviewed. The emphasis is on cost containment rather than cost reduction.

Cost management focuses on cost reduction and continuous improvement and change rather than cost containment. Indeed, the term cost reduction could be used instead of cost

LEARNING OBJECTIVES

After studying this chapter, you should be able to:

- distinguish between the features of a traditional management accounting control system and cost management;
- explain life-cycle costing and describe the typical pattern of cost commitment and cost incurrence during the three stages of a product's life cycle;
- describe the target costing approach to cost management;
- describe tear-down analysis, value engineering and functional analysis;
- distinguish between target costing and *kaizen* costing;
- describe activity-based cost management;
- distinguish between value added and non-value added activities;
- explain the purpose of a cost of quality report;
- describe how value chain analysis can be used to increase customer satisfaction and manage costs more effectively;
- explain the role of benchmarking within the cost management framework;
- outline the main features of a just-in-time philosophy.

management but the former is an emotive term. Therefore cost management is preferred. Whereas traditional cost control systems are routinely applied on a continuous basis, cost management tends to be applied on an *ad hoc* basis when an opportunity for cost reduction is identified. Also many of the approaches that are incorporated within the area of cost management do not necessarily involve the use of accounting techniques. In contrast, cost control relies heavily on accounting techniques.

Cost management consists of those actions that are taken by managers to reduce costs, some of which are prioritized on the basis of information extracted from the accounting system. Other actions, however, are undertaken without the use of accounting information. They involve process improvements, where an opportunity has been identified to perform processes more effectively and efficiently, and which have obvious cost reduction outcomes. It is important that you are aware of all the approaches that can be used to reduce costs even if these methods do not rely on accounting information. You should also note that although cost management seeks to reduce costs, it should not be at the expense of customer satisfaction. Ideally, the aim is to take actions that will both reduce costs and enhance customer satisfaction.

Life-cycle costing

Traditional management accounting control procedures have focused primarily on the manufacturing stage of a product's life cycle. Pre-manufacturing costs, such as research and development and design and post-manufacturing abandonment and disposal costs are treated as period costs. Therefore they are not incorporated in the product cost calculations, nor are they subject to the conventional management accounting control procedures.

Life-cycle costing estimates and accumulates costs over a product's entire life cycle in order to determine whether the profits earned during the manufacturing phase will cover the costs incurred during the pre- and post-manufacturing stages. Identifying the costs incurred during the different stages of a product's life cycle provides an insight into understanding and managing the total costs incurred throughout its life cycle. In particular, life-cycle costing helps management to understand the cost consequences of developing and making a product and to identify areas in which cost reduction efforts are likely to be most effective.

Most accounting systems report on a period-by-period basis, and product profits are not monitored over their life cycles. In contrast, product life-cycle reporting involves tracing costs and revenues on a product-by-product basis over several calendar periods throughout their life cycle. A failure to trace all costs to products over their life cycles hinders management's understanding of product profitability, because a product's actual life-cycle profit is unknown. Consequently, inadequate feedback information is available on the success or failure in developing new products.

Figure 22.1 illustrates a typical pattern of cost commitment and cost incurrence during the three stages of a product's life cycle – the planning and design stage, the manufacturing stage and the service and abandonment stage. **Committed** or **locked-in costs** are those costs that have not been incurred but that will be incurred in the future on the basis of decisions that have already been made. Costs are incurred when a resource is used or sacrificed. Costing systems record costs only when they have been incurred. It is difficult to significantly alter costs after they have been committed. For example, the product design specifications determine a product's material and labour inputs and the production process. At this stage costs become committed and broadly determine the future costs that will be incurred during the manufacturing stage.

FIGURE 22.1 *Product life-cycle phases: relationship between costs committed and costs incurred*

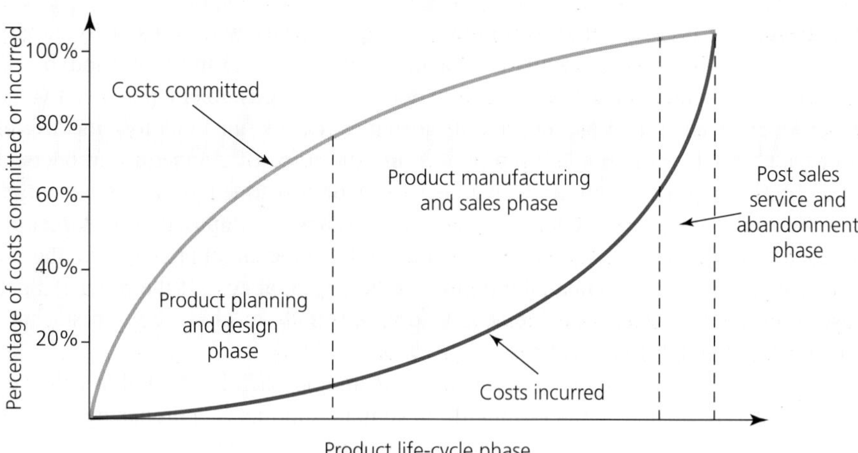

You will see from Figure 22.1 that approximately 80% of a product's costs are *committed* during the planning and design stage. At this stage product designers determine the product's design and the production process. In contrast, the majority of costs are *incurred* at the manufacturing stage, but they have already become locked-in at the planning and design stage and are difficult to alter.

The pattern of cost commitment and incurrence will differ based on the industry and specific product introduced. For example, cost incurrence is high at the planning and development stage for manufacturing new aeroplanes or large product abandonment costs may be incurred for those products whose disposal involves harmful effects to the environment, such as nuclear waste or other toxic chemicals.

It is apparent from Figure 22.1 that cost management can be most effectively exercised during the planning and design stage and not at the manufacturing stage when the product design and processes have already been determined and costs have been committed. At this latter stage the focus is more on cost containment than cost management. An understanding of life-cycle costs and how they are committed and incurred at different stages throughout a product's life cycle led to the emergence of **target costing**, a technique that focuses on managing costs during a product's planning and design phase.

Target costing

In Chapter 11 we briefly looked at target costing as a mechanism for determining selling prices. We shall now consider how target costing can be used as a cost management tool. Target costing involves the following stages:

Stage 1: Determine the target price which customers will be prepared to pay for the product.

Stage 2: Deduct a target profit margin from the target price to determine the target cost.

Stage 3: Estimate the actual cost of the product.

Stage 4: If estimated actual cost exceeds the target cost investigate ways of driving down the actual cost to the target cost.

Target costing is a customer-oriented technique that is widely used by Japanese companies and which has recently been adopted by companies in Europe and the USA. The first stage requires market research to determine the customers' perceived value of the product based on its functions and its attributes (i.e. its functionality), its differentiation value relative to competing products and the price of competing products. The target profit margin depends on the planned return on investment for the organization as a whole and profit as a percentage of sales. This is then decomposed into a target profit for each product which is subsequently deducted from the target price to give the target cost. The target cost is compared with the predicted actual cost. If the predicted actual cost is above the target cost intensive efforts are made to close the gap so that the predicted cost equals the target cost.

A major feature of target costing is that a team approach is adopted to achieve the target cost. The team members include designers, engineers, purchasing, manufacturing, marketing and management accounting personnel. Their aim is to achieve the target cost specified for the product at the prescribed level of functionality and quality. The discipline of a team approach ensures that no particular group is able to impose their functional preferences. For example, design engineers pursuing their flair for design may design into products features that increase a product's costs but which customers do not value, or features that require the use of unique parts when alternative designs requiring standardized parts may meet customer requirements. Similarly, without a multi-functional team approach a marketing emphasis might result in the introduction of product features that customers find attractive, but not essential, and so they are not prepared to pay to have them included in the product's design. Therefore the aim during the product design process is to eliminate product functions that add cost but which do not increase the market price.

In some organizations representatives from the suppliers are included in the design team in order to obtain their expertise. They can often provide suggestions of design changes that will enable standard parts to replace custom-designed parts, thus reducing the product's cost. Alternatively, suppliers have the expertise to suggest alternative parts or components at the lowest cost for a given level of functionality.

The major advantage of adopting target costing is that it is deployed during a product's design and planning stage so that it can have a maximum impact in determining the level of the locked-in costs. It is an iterative process with the design team, which ideally should result in the design team continuing with its product and process design attempts until it finds designs that give an expected cost that is equal or less than the target cost. If the target cost cannot be attained then the product should not be launched. Design teams should not be allowed to achieve target costs by eliminating desirable product functions. Thus, the aim is to design a product with an expected cost that does not exceed target cost and that also meets the target level of functionality. Design teams use tear-down analysis and value engineering to achieve the target cost.

Tear-down analysis

Tear-down analysis (also known as **reverse engineering**) involves examining a competitor's product in order to identify opportunities for product improvement and/or cost reduction. The competitor's product is dismantled to identify its functionality and design and to provide insights about the processes that are used and the cost to make the product. The aim is to benchmark provisional product designs with the designs of competitors and to incorporate any observed relative advantages of the competitor's approach to product design.

Value engineering

Value engineering (also known as **value analysis**) is a systematic interdisciplinary examination of factors affecting the cost of a product or service in order to devise means of achieving the specified purpose at the required standard of quality and reliability at the target cost. The aim of value engineering is to achieve the assigned target cost by (i) identifying improved product designs that reduce the product's cost without sacrificing functionality and/or (ii) eliminating unnecessary functions that increase the product's costs and for which customers are not prepared to pay extra for.

Value engineering requires the use of **functional analysis**. This process involves decomposing the product into its many elements or attributes. For example, in the case of automobiles, functions might consist of style, comfort, operability, reliability, quality, attractiveness and many others (Kato, 1993). A price, or value, for each element is determined which reflects the amount the customer is prepared to pay. To obtain this information companies normally conduct surveys and interviews with customers. The total of the values for each function gives the estimated selling price from which the target profit is deducted to derive the target cost. The cost of each function of a product is compared with the benefits perceived by the customers. If the cost of the function exceeds the benefit to the customer, then the function should be either eliminated, modified to reduce its cost, or enhanced in terms of its perceived value so that its value exceeds the cost. Also by focusing on the product's functions, the design team will often consider components that perform the same function in other products, thus increasing the possibility of using standard components and reducing costs.

The need for accurate cost measurement systems

It is important that target costing is supported by an accurate cost system. In particular, cost drivers should be established that are the significant determinants of the costs of the activities so that cause-and-effect allocations are used. Arbitrary cost allocations should be avoided. If arbitrary cost allocations are used the allocation base will not be a significant determinant of cost. Let us assume that an arbitrary allocation base, say direct labour hours, is used to allocate support costs to products. To reduce the projected cost towards the target cost the target costing team will be motivated to focus on reducing direct labour hours. Why? Because this will result in a smaller proportion of the support costs being assigned to the product. However, the support costs incurred by the organization will not be reduced because there is no cause-and-effect relationship between direct labour hours and the resulting costs. Therefore the target costing exercise will merely result in a reduction in the costs that are allocated to the product but organizational costs will not be reduced. In contrast, if cause-and-effect allocation bases (i.e. cost drivers) are established, reductions in cost driver usage should be followed by a reduction in organizational support costs.

Therefore it is very important that cost systems use cost drivers that are the determinants of costs so that they will motivate designers to take actions that will reduce organizational costs. Decisions taken at the design stage lead to the committed usage of cost drivers which can be difficult to change in the future.

An illustration of target costing

Example 22.1 is used to illustrate the target costing process. You will have noted from reading the information presented in this example that the projected cost of the product is £700 compared with a target cost of £560. To achieve the target cost the company establishes a project team to undertake an intense target costing exercise. Example 22.1 indicates that the end result of the target costing exercise is a projected cost of £555 which is marginally below the target cost of £560. Let us now look at how the company has achieved the target cost and also how the costs shown in Example 22.1 have been derived.

In response to the need to reduce the projected cost the project team starts by purchasing video cameras from its main competitors and undertaking a tear-down analysis. This process involves dismantling the cameras to provide insights into potential design improvements for the new camera that will be launched. Value engineering is also undertaken with the project team working closely with the design engineers. Their objective is to identify new designs that will accomplish the same functions at a lower cost and also to eliminate any functions that are deemed to be unnecessary. This process results in a simplified design, the reduction in the number of parts and the replacement of some customized parts with standard parts. The outcome of the tear-down analysis and value engineering activities is a significant reduction in the projected direct materials, labour and rework costs, but the revised cost estimates still indicate that the projected cost exceeds the target cost.

Next the team engages in functional analysis. They identify the different elements, functions and attributes of the camera and potential customers are interviewed to ascertain the values that they place on each of the functions. This process indicates that several functions that have been included in the prototype are not valued by customers. The team therefore decide to eliminate these functions. The functional analysis results in further cost reductions being made, principally in the areas of materials and direct labour assembly costs but the revised cost estimates still indicate that the target cost has not been attained.

The team now turn their attention to redesigning the production and support processes. They decide to redesign the ordering and receiving process by reducing the number of suppliers and working closely with a smaller number of suppliers. The suppliers are prepared to enter into contractual arrangements whereby they are periodically given a pre-determined production schedule and in return they will inspect the shipments and guarantee quality prior to delivery. In addition, the marketing, distribution and customer after-sales services relating to the product are subject to an intensive review, and process improvements are made that result in further reductions in costs that are attributable to the camera. The projected cost after undertaking all of the above activities is £555 compared with the target cost of £560 and at this point the target costing exercise is concluded.

Having described the target costing approach that the Digital Electronics Company has used let us now turn our attention to the derivation of the projected costs shown in Example 22.1. The projected cost for direct materials prior to the target costing exercise is £390 but value engineering and the functional analysis have resulted in a reduction in the number of parts that are required to manufacture the video camera. The elimination of most of the unique parts, and the use of standard parts that the company currently purchases in large volumes, also provides scope for further cost savings. The outcome of the redesign process is a direct material cost of £325.

EXAMPLE 22.1

The Digital Electronics Company manufactures cameras and video equipment. It is in the process of introducing a new state-of-the art combined digital video and still camera. The company has undertaken market research to ascertain the customers' perceived value of the product based on its special features and a comparison with competitors' products. The results of the survey, and a comparison of the new camera with competitors' products and market prices, have been used to establish a target selling price and projected lifetime volume. In addition, cost estimates have been prepared based on the proposed product specification. The company has set a target profit margin of 30% on the proposed selling price and this has been deducted from the target selling price to determine the target cost. The following is a summary of the information that has been presented to management:

Projected lifetime sales volume	300 000 units
Target selling price	£800
Target profit margin (30% of selling price)	£240
Target cost (£800 – £240)	£560
Projected cost	£700

The excess of the projected cost over the target cost results in an intensive target costing exercise. After completing the target costing exercise the projected cost is £555 which is marginally below the target cost of £560. The analysis of the projected cost before and after the target costing exercise is as follows:

	Before		After	
	(£)	(£)	(£)	(£)
Manufacturing cost				
Direct material (bought in parts)	390		325	
Direct labour	100		80	
Direct machining costs	20		20	
Ordering and receiving	8		2	
Quality assurance	60		50	
Rework	15		6	
Engineering and design	10	603	8	491
Non-manufacturing costs				
Marketing	40		25	
Distribution	30		20	
After-sales service and warranty costs	27	97	19	64
Total cost		700		555

The simplified product design enables the assembly time to be reduced thus resulting in the reduction of direct labour costs from £100 to £80. The direct machine costs relate to machinery that will be used exclusively for the production of the new product. The estimated cost of acquiring, maintaining and operating the machinery throughout the product's life cycle is £6 million. This is divided by the projected lifetime sales volume of the camera (300 000 units) giving a unit cost of £20. However, it has not been possible to reduce the unit cost because the machinery costs are committed, and fixed, and the target costing exercise has not resulted in a change in the predicted lifetime volume.

Prior to the target costing exercise 80 separate parts were included in the product specification. The estimated number of orders placed for each part throughout the product's life cycle is 150 and the predicted cost per order for the order and receiving activity is £200. Therefore the estimated lifetime costs are £2.4 million (80 parts × 150 orders × £200 per order) giving a unit cost of £8 (£2.4 million/300 000 units). The simplified design, and the parts standardization arising from the functional analysis and the value engineering activities, have enabled the number of parts to be reduced to 40. The redesign of the ordering and receiving process has also enabled the number of orders and the ordering cost to be reduced (the former from 150 to 100 and the latter from £200 to £150 per order). Thus the projected lifetime ordering and receiving costs after the target costing exercise are £600 000 (40 parts × 100 orders × £150 per order) giving a revised unit cost of £2 (£600 000/300 000 units).

Quality assurance involves inspecting and testing the cameras. Prior to the target costing exercise the projected cost was £60 (12 hours at £5 per hour) but the simplified design means that the camera will be easier to test resulting in revised cost of £50 (10 hours at £5 per hour). Rework costs of £15 represent the average rework costs per camera. Past experience with manufacturing similar products suggests that 10% of the output will require rework. Applying this rate to the estimated total lifetime volume of 300 000 cameras results in 30 000 cameras requiring rework at an estimated average cost of £150 per reworked camera. The total lifetime rework cost is therefore predicted to be £4.5 million (30 000 × £150) giving an average cost per unit of good output of £15 (£4.5 million/300 000). Because of the simplified product design the rework rate and the average rework cost will be reduced. The predicted rework rate is now 5% and the average rework cost will be reduced from £150 to £120. Thus, the revised estimate of the total lifetime cost is £1.8 million (15 000 reworked units at £120 per unit) and the projected unit cost is £6 (£1.8 million/300 000 units).

The predicted total lifetime engineering and design costs and other product sustaining costs are predicted to be £3 million giving a unit cost of £10. The simplified design and reduced number of parts enables the lifetime cost to be reduced by 20%, to £2.4 million, and the unit cost to £8. The planned process improvements have also enabled the predicted marketing, distribution and after-sales service costs to be reduced. In addition, the simplified product design and the use of fewer parts has contributed to the reduction to the after-sales warranty costs. However, to keep our example brief the derivation of the non-manufacturing costs will not be presented, other than to note that the company uses an activity-based-costing system. All costs are assigned using cost drivers that are based on established cause-and-effect relationships.

Kaizen costing

In addition to target costing ***kaizen* costing** is widely used by Japanese organizations as a mechanism for reducing and managing costs. *Kaizen* is the Japanese term for making improvements to a process through small incremental amounts, rather than through large innovations. The major difference between target and *kaizen* costing is that target costing is applied during the design stage whereas *kaizen* costing is applied during the manufacturing stage of the product life cycle. With target costing the focus is on the product, and cost reductions are achieved primarily through product design. In contrast, *kaizen* costing focuses on the production processes and cost reductions are derived primarily through the increased efficiency of the production process. Therefore the potential cost reductions are smaller with *kaizen* costing because the products are already in the manufacturing stage of their life cycles and a significant proportion of the costs will have become locked-in.

The aim of *kaizen* costing is to reduce the cost of components and products by a pre-specified amount. Monden and Hamada (1991) describe the application of *kaizen* costing in a Japanese automobile plant. Each plant is assigned a target cost reduction ratio and this is applied to the previous year's actual costs to determine the target cost reduction. *Kaizen* costing relies heavily on employee empowerment. They are assumed to have superior knowledge about how to improve processes because they are closest to the manufacturing processes and customers and are likely to have greater insights into how costs can be reduced. Thus, a major feature of *kaizen* costing is that workers are given the responsibility to improve processes and reduce costs. Unlike target costing it is not accompanied by a set of techniques or procedures that are automatically applied to achieve the cost reductions.

Source: Image supplied by Toyota Manufacturing UK Ltd

Activity-based management

The early adopters of activity-based costing (ABC) used it to produce more accurate product (or service) costs but it soon became apparent to the users that it could be extended beyond purely product costing to a range of cost management applications. The terms **activity-based management (ABM)** or **activity-based cost management (ABCM)** are used to describe the cost management applications of ABC. To implement an ABM system only the first three of the four stages described in Chapter 10 for designing an activity-based product costing system are required. They are:

1. identifying the major activities that take place in an organization;
2. assigning costs to cost pools/cost centres for each activity;
3. determining the cost driver for each major activity.

Thus, firms can omit the final stage of assigning activity costs to products and adopt ABC solely for cost management without activity-based product costing. Alternatively, organizations can design an activity-based system that incorporates both ABM and activity-based product costing but note that only the first three stages are required for ABM. Where a firm does use an activity-based system for both cost management and product costing it may choose to create a large number of activity cost pools to monitor the costs of the many different activities but aggregate the pools so that a smaller number is used for product costing purposes.

ABM views the business as a set of linked activities that ultimately add value to the customer. It focuses on managing the business on the basis of the activities that make up the organization. ABM is based on the premise that activities consume costs. Therefore by managing activities costs will be managed in the long term. The goal of ABM is to enable customer needs to be satisfied while making fewer demands on organizational resources. Besides providing information on what activities are performed, ABM provides information on the cost of activities, why the activities are undertaken, and how well they are performed.

The impact of ABC at Insteel Industries

Insteel Industries, Inc., manufactures and markets concrete reinforcing products, industrial wire, bulk nails, collated fasteners, PC strand and tire bead wire. This paper studies the managerial and organizational issues related to ABC at the Andrews, South Carolina, plant of Insteel Industries. Four product lines are produced at the Andrews plant. In 1996, about 477 individual products were spread across these four product lines.

In 1996, after years of product and customer proliferation, Insteel decided to implement an ABC system The ABC team took their first ABC snapshot of operations at the Andrews plant in the summer of 1996 with the assistance of a big-six accounting firm. The ABC team analysed Andrews' operations and identified 12 business processes. Within each business process, a number of activities were identified – a total of 146 activities. Next, 426 employees were surveyed to estimate how they allocated their time to different activities. All overhead resources were then collected in 80 cost pools and assigned to cost objects such as products and customers (some cost pools included multiple activities). This assignment was done by selecting cost drivers that link the performance of activities to demands made by individual products. For example, the cost of the material-handling activity was assigned to products based on the number of moves for that product, on the ground that it is the number of times raw materials and work-in-process is moved that cause material handling resources to be consumed, rather than the weight of materials moved. A second ABC snapshot was developed in the summer of 1997, by which time Insteel had its own staff group collecting the data.

Insteel managers indicated that the new ABC system influenced operations and also product portfolio, product pricing and customer portfolio decisions. The effect of ABC on operations (process improvements) appears to be its first benefit. Internal reports at Insteel prepared in 1996 and 1997 document the use of ABC information for process improvements. The first ABC study, in 1996, reveals that the 20 most expensive activities accounted for 87% of Andrews' total physical and people resource cost of \$21.4 million. Within the top 20 activities, almost \$5 million pertained to quality-related activities such as reactive maintenance, management of by-products and scrap, and preventive maintenance. Analysis of the top 20 activities also revealed that material-handling costs, including freight costs, consumed \$4.6 million. Activities were further classified into value-added and non-value-added or resource-draining activities. Nearly \$4.9 million was spent on resource-draining activities such as reactive maintenance, management of by-products and scrap, moving materials and resources, processing returns and claims, reworking products, managing customer complaints, and handling warranties, claims and returns. These activities, within the 20 most expensive activities, were targeted for cost reduction and process improvement.

The 1996 ABC reports also list improvement opportunities and identify teams of senior and middle managers responsible for each broad opportunity. For example, separate teams were formed for managing quality costs, material handling and preventive maintenance. As a part of the 1997 study, Insteel followed up on the process improvement opportunities identified in the 1996 study. The company estimates that within a year of the first ABC study, \$1.8 million had been saved in quality costs, mainly through a reduction of scrap and reactive maintenance costs. Freight costs were reduced \$555 000 in a year in the Andrews plant alone. Resource-draining activities were reduced from 22% of activity costs to 17%.

Insteel focused on freight because delivering products to customers showed up as the most expensive activity following the 1996 ABC study. It represented 16% of the total people and physical resources cost at the Andrews plant. We believe that prior to the ABC study this cost would not have been apparent, because it would have been billed to the customer. As a part of the ABC study, Insteel started tracking freight cost per pound shipped. This directed attention to ways in which these costs could be reduced. In 1997, by changing the layout of boxes within each truck, the Andrews plant was able to ship 7400 pounds more per truckload than in 1996. This represented a 20% reduction in freight expense, from about $31/ton to about $25/ton. Subsequently, all of Insteel's other manufacturing facilities also converted to heavier loads, emulating the results achieved at Andrews. The resulting savings were significant in comparison with Insteel's after-tax income of $4.2 million in 1996.

When Insteel realized after the 1996 ABC study how much they were actually incurring in quality costs, they put in place a team responsible for probing deeper and understanding better what was causing the quality costs to be incurred in the first place and for suggesting steps to reduce them. Insteel realized that certain foreign suppliers of rods were lower in price but supplied poorer-quality rods that caused breakdowns in Insteel's manufacturing process. The lower price of those suppliers did not compensate for the quality costs. Insteel switched to higher-quality rod suppliers. Insteel also realized that smaller-diameter wire products are more likely to break and disrupt the manufacturing process. Insteel migrated its product mix to more large-diameter wire products. Such initiatives led to a reduction in quality costs from $6.7 million in 1996 to $4.9 million in 1997.

It is hard to estimate how much of these savings would have been realized had Insteel not conducted an ABC analysis. From interviews with Insteel managers and sitting in on senior management meetings, it appears that the activity analysis gave them an appreciation of the scope and quantified the magnitude of the improvement potential, thereby allowing them to prioritize among various process improvement possibilities. In the opinion of the senior management, the ABC system also helped them keep track of the savings and ensure that the promised payback was actually realized. Clearly ABC served as a focusing device at Insteel by providing cost data by activity rather than by department, directing attention to the top 20 activities, and by labelling some of them as resource-draining activities.

Source: Adapted from Narayanan, V.G. and Sarkar, R.G., The impact of activity-based costing on managerial decisions at Insteel industries: A field study, *Journal of Economics and Management Strategy*, Vol. 11, No. 2, Summer 2002, pp. 257–288.

Traditional budget and control reports analyse costs by types of expense for each responsibility centre. In contrast, ABM analyses costs by activities and thus provides management with information on why costs are incurred and the output from the activity (in terms of cost drivers). Exhibit 22.1 illustrates the difference between the conventional analysis and the activity-based analysis in respect of customer order processing. The major differences are that the ABM approach reports by *activities* whereas the traditional analysis is by *departments*. Also ABM reporting is by sub-activities but traditional reporting is by expense categories. Another distinguishing feature of ABM reporting is that it often reports information on activities that cross departmental boundaries. For example, different production departments and the distribution department might undertake customer processing activities. They may

EXHIBIT 22.1
Customer order processing activity

	(£000s)
Traditional analysis	
Salaries	320
Stationery	40
Travel	140
Telephone	40
Depreciation of equipment	40
	580
ABM analysis	
Preparing quotations	120
Receiving customer orders	190
Assessing the creditworthiness of customers	100
Expediting	80
Resolving customer problems	90
	580

resolve customer problems by expediting late deliveries. The finance department may assess customer credit worthiness and the remaining customer processing activities might be undertaken by the customer service department. Therefore the total cost of the customer processing activity could be considerably in excess of the costs that are assigned to the customer service department. However, to simplify the presentation it is assumed in Exhibit 22.1 that the departmental and activity costs are identical but if the cost of the customer order processing activity was found to be, say, three times the amount assigned to the customer service department, this would be important information because it may change the way in which the managers view the activity. For example, the managers may give more attention to reducing the costs of the customer processing activity.

It is apparent from an examination of Exhibit 22.1 that the ABM approach provides more meaningful information. It gives more visibility to the cost of undertaking the activities that make up the organization and may raise issues for management action that are not highlighted by the traditional analysis. For example, why is £90 000 spent on resolving customer problems? Attention-directing information such as this is important for managing the cost of the activities.

Johnson (1990) suggests that knowing costs by activities is a catalyst that eventually triggers the action necessary to become competitive. Consider a situation where salespersons, as a result of costing activities, are informed that it costs £50 to process a customer's order. They therefore become aware that it is questionable to pursue orders with a low sales value. By eliminating many small orders, and concentrating on larger value orders, the demand for customer-processing activities should decrease, and future spending on this activity should be reduced.

Prior to the introduction of ABM most organizations have been unaware of the cost of undertaking the activities that make up the organization. Knowing the cost of activities enables those activities with the highest cost to be highlighted so that they can be prioritized for detailed studies to ascertain whether they can be eliminated or performed more efficiently. In a study of a UK-based multinational bank Soin *et al.* (2002) reported that ABM was used to establish which activities were expensive and why they were being used, and to ascertain whether increased volumes would or would not increase costs. No attempt was made to link costs to products or customers.

To identify and prioritize the potential for cost reduction many organizations have found it useful to classify activities as either value added or non-value added. Definitions of what constitutes value added and non-value added activities vary. A common definition is that a **value added activity** is an activity that customers perceive as adding usefulness to the product or service they purchase. For example, painting a car would be a value added activity in an organization that manufactures cars. Other definitions are an activity that is being performed as efficiently as possible or an activity that supports the primary objective of producing outputs.

In contrast, a **non-value added activity** is an activity where there is an opportunity for cost reduction without reducing the product's service potential to the customer. Examples of non-value added activities include inspecting, storing and moving raw materials. The cost of these activities can be reduced without reducing the value of the products to the customers. Non-value added activities are essentially those activities that customers should not be expected to pay for. Reporting the cost of non-value added activities draws management's attention to the vast amount of waste that has been tolerated by the organization. This should prioritize those activities with the greatest potential for cost reduction by eliminating or carrying them out more effectively, such as reducing material movements, improving production flows and taking actions to reduce stock levels. Taking action to reduce or eliminate non-value added activities is given top priority because by doing so the organization permanently reduces the cost it incurs without reducing the value of the product to the customer.

Kaplan and Cooper (1998) criticize the classification of activities by simplistic value added and non-value added categories. They point out, that apart from the extreme examples similar to the ones illustrated above, people cannot consistently define what constitutes a value added or non-value added activity. To reinforce this point they discuss whether the activity of setting up a machine is value added or non-value added. One view is that customers do not perceive performing set-ups as adding usefulness to products and the activity is non-value added. However, without set-ups a plant can only produce single products. If customers value customized or diverse products, changing machine settings to produce different product varieties creates value for customers. Kaplan and Cooper also point out the demotivating impact when employees are informed that they are performing non-value added activities.

To overcome the above problems Kaplan and Cooper advocate that instead of using a value added/non-value added classification the following simple five point scale should be used to summarize an ABC project team's initial judgement about the current efficiency of an activity:

1 highly efficient, with little (less than 5%) apparent opportunity for improvement;
2 modestly efficient, some (5–15%) opportunity for improvement;
3 average efficiency, good opportunities (15–25%) for improvement;
4 inefficient, major opportunities (25–50%) for improvement;
5 highly inefficient, perhaps should not be done at all; 50–100% opportunity for improvement.

By identifying the cost of activities that make up their organization and classifying them into the above five categories, opportunities for cost reduction can be prioritized. Cost reduction can be achieved by either eliminating the activities, performing them more efficiently with fewer organizational resources or redesigning them so that they are performed in an entirely different and more cost efficient way. We shall consider how activities can be redesigned later in the chapter.

Our discussion so far has related to the application of ABM during the manufacturing or service phase of a product's life cycle. However, some organizations have used their activity-based costing systems to influence future costs at the design stage within the target costing process. In particular, they have opted for behaviourally orientated cost systems that are less accurate than costing technology allows in order to induce desired behavioural responses (Merchant and Shields, 1993). Hiromoto (1991) illustrated how a Japanese company used cost drivers to implement a policy of parts standardization as one component of a cost reduction strategy. The manufacturer identified the number of part numbers as its key cost driver, or strategic behavioural cost driver, to implement the chosen strategy of standardizing and reducing parts, simplifying the manufacturing process and decreasing manufacturing costs. Management devised a method of allocating manufacturing overhead so that product costs increased with the number of parts used and with the number of non-standard parts used. The standardization rate (number of common parts/total number of parts) increased steadily over a 12-year period, despite increasing product variety, from 20% to 68%.

A further example that is cited in the literature is the cost system operated by Tektronix Portable Instruments Division. The company assigned material support expenses using a single cost driver-number of part numbers. The company wanted to encourage design engineers to focus their attention on reducing the number of part numbers, parts and vendors in future generations of products. Product timeliness was seen as a critical success factor and this was facilitated by designs which simplified parts procurement and production processes. The cost system motivated engineers to design simpler products requiring less development time because they had fewer parts and part numbers. The cost system designers knew that most of the material support expenses were not incurred in direct proportion to the single cost driver chosen, but the simplified and imprecise cost system focused attention on factors deemed to be most critical to the division's future success.

A survey of activity-based costing applications by Innes and Mitchell (1995a) indicated that many organizations use cost driver rates as a measure of cost efficiency and performance for the activity concerned. The cost driver rate is computed by dividing the activity costs by the cost driver volume. For example, if the cost of processing 10 000 purchase orders is £100 000, the cost per purchasing order is £10. Assume now that improvements in procedures in the purchasing activity enable costs to be reduced to £80 000. If the same number of orders can be processed with fewer resources the cost of processing an order will be reduced to £8. Reporting and focusing on cost driver rates can thus be used to motivate managers to reduce the cost of performing activities.

There is a danger, however, that cost driver rates can encourage dysfunctional behaviour. An improvement in the cost driver rate can be achieved by splitting some purchase orders and increasing the orders processed to, say, 12 000. Assuming that the cost of the activity remains unchanged at £100 000 the cost per purchasing order will be reduced from £10 to £8.33 if all costs are fixed in the short term. The overall effect is that the workload will be increased and, in the long term, this could result in an increase in costs. Care should therefore be taken to avoid these dysfunctional consequences by using cost driver rates as feedback information to guide employees in improving the efficiency of performing activities. If the measures are interpreted in a recriminatory or threatening manner, there is a danger that they will lead to dysfunctional behaviour.

Business process re-engineering

Business process re-engineering involves examining business processes and making substantial changes to how the organization currently operates. It involves the redesign of how work is done through activities. A business process consists of a collection of activities that are linked together in a co-ordinated manner to achieve a specific objective. For example, material handling might be classed as a business process consisting of separate activities relating to scheduling production, storing materials, processing purchase orders, inspecting materials and paying suppliers.

The aim of business process re-engineering is to improve the key business processes in an organization by focusing on simplification, cost reduction, improved quality and enhanced customer satisfaction. Consider the materials handling process outlined in the above paragraph. The process might be re-engineered by sending the production schedule direct to nominated suppliers and entering into contractual agreements to deliver the materials in accordance with the production schedule and also guaranteeing their quality by inspecting them prior to delivery. The end result might be the elimination, or a permanent reduction, of the storing, purchasing and inspection activities. These activities are non-value added activities since they represent an opportunity for cost reduction without reducing the products' service potentials to customers.

A distinguishing feature of business process re-engineering is that it involves radical and dramatic changes in processes by abandoning current practices and reinventing completely new methods of performing business processes. The focus is on major changes rather than marginal improvements. A further example of business process re-engineering is moving from a traditional functional plant layout to a just-in-time cellular product layout and adopting a just-in-time philosophy. Adopting a just-in-time (JIT) system and philosophy has important implications for cost management and performance reporting. It is therefore important that you understand the nature of such systems and how they differ from traditional systems, but rather than deviating at this point from our discussion of cost management the description of a JIT system will be deferred until the end of the chapter.

Cost of quality

To compete successfully in today's global competitive environment companies are becoming 'customer-driven' and making customer satisfaction an overriding priority. Customers are demanding ever-improving levels of service regarding cost, quality, reliability, delivery and the choice of innovative new products. Quality has become one of the key competitive variables and this has created the need for management accountants to become more involved in the provision of information relating to the quality of products and services and activities that produce them. In the UK quality related costs have been reported to range from 5 to 15% of total company sales revenue (Plunkett *et al.*, 1985). Eliminating inferior quality can therefore result in substantial savings and higher revenues.

Total quality management (TQM), a term used to describe a situation where *all* business functions are involved in a process of continuous quality improvement, has been adopted by many companies. TQM has broadened, from its early concentration on the statistical monitoring of manufacturing processes, to a customer-oriented process of continuous improvement that focuses on delivering products or services of consistent high quality in a timely fashion. In the 1980s most European and American companies considered quality to be an additional cost of manufacturing, but by the end of the decade they began to realize that quality saved money. The philosophy of emphasizing production volume over quality resulted in high levels of stocks at each production stage in order to protect against shortages caused by inferior quality at previous stages and excessive expenditure on inspection, rework, scrap and warranty repairs. Companies discovered that it was cheaper to produce the items correctly the first time rather than wasting resources by making substandard items that have to be detected, reworked,

The quality cost report at Gilroy Foods

Prepared monthly, Gilroy's Quality Cost Report (QCR) is divided into two parts: a narrative and the data. We consider the narrative to be as important as the data. It is divided into two sections: an Executive Summary and the Monthly Topic. The Executive Summary discusses monthly results in total and highlights major factors contributing to quality costs. The Monthly Topic addresses ideas for improvement, implemented improvements, areas needing attention, explanation of prior events and other areas prime for management focus. Sometimes supplemental schedules are provided to help explain a concern or to highlight a topic. Some recent subjects include onion/garlic slicing thickness, garlic mill capital audit, utilizing packaging drums more efficiently, worker safety and overtime concerns.

The narrative process is the tool we use to involve the entire company. Each month different individuals are interviewed and requested to provide input. Ultimately all functions and departments are represented. The topic and the focus it receives can become an instant way to reduce costs, or it can be used to mobilize a group to attack a specific problem.

For the data part we currently include nearly 40 items in our QCR segregated into the four cost categories, and the list is growing. Month and year-to-date numbers are included and expressed as a percent of sales. Prior year-to-date numbers and a variance column comparing this year vs. last are also shown. The far right of the report displays sources for the data.

It is our opinion that our report understates quality costs in spite of our best efforts. We continually encounter new areas ripe for improvement. Our first report included 33 items; the most recent included 38. Our cost systems are continually being refined to capture costs more clearly, and we expect the number of items to grow.

Nonetheless, we feel the Total Quality Cost Report is superior to traditional accounting information for several reasons:

- It clearly segregates costs and identifies them as non-value added, which allows the organization to focus on the reduction or elimination of those items.
- It is a true barometer for the current health of the company because the cost data are not embedded in cost of sales, which can mask current performance.
- Because of the segregation of costs into prevention, appraisal, internal failure and external failure categories, the impact is magnified, and the focus is improved.
- It provides a target that can be shared with the entire company that really measures progress of the total quality programme in concrete terms.
- It encourages the development of more meaningful measurements, which forces all who participate to learn more about the operation.

Source: Adapted from Brinkman, S.L. and Appelbaum, M.A. (1994), The quality cost report: It is alive and well at Gilroy Foods, *Management Accounting (USA)*, September, pp. 61–65.

scrapped or returned by customers. In other words, the emphasis of TQM is to design and build quality in, rather than trying to inspect it in, by focusing on the causes rather than the symptoms of poor quality.

Management accounting systems can help organizations achieve their quality goals by providing a variety of reports and measures that motivate and evaluate managerial efforts to improve quality. These will include financial and non-financial measures. Many companies are currently not aware of how much they are spending on quality because they are incurred across many different departments and not accumulated as a separate cost object within the costing system. Managers need to know the costs of quality and how they are changing over time. A **cost of quality report** should be prepared to indicate the total cost to the organization of producing products or services that do not conform with quality requirements. Four categories of costs should be reported.

1 **Prevention costs** are the costs incurred in preventing the production of products that do not conform to specification. They include the costs of preventive maintenance, quality planning and training and the extra costs of acquiring higher quality raw materials.
2 **Appraisal costs** are the costs incurred to ensure that materials and products meet quality conformance standards. They include the costs of inspecting purchased parts, work in process and finished goods, quality audits and field tests.
3 **Internal failure costs** are the costs associated with materials and products that fail to meet quality standards. They include costs incurred before the product is despatched to the customer, such as the costs of scrap, repair, downtime and work stoppages caused by defects.
4 **External failure costs** are the costs incurred when products or services fail to conform to requirements or satisfy customer needs after they have been delivered. They include the costs of handling customer complaints, warranty replacement, repairs of returned products and the costs arising from a damaged company reputation. Costs within this category can have a dramatic impact on future sales.

Exhibit 22.2 presents a typical cost of quality report. Note that some of the items in the report will have to be estimated. For example, included in the external failure costs category is the forgone contribution from lost sales arising from poor quality. This cost is extremely difficult to estimate. Nevertheless, the lost contribution can be substantial and it is preferable to include an estimate rather than omit it from the report. By expressing each category of costs as a percentage of sales revenues comparisons can be made with previous periods, other organizations and divisions within the same group. Such comparisons can highlight problem areas. For example, comparisons of external failure costs with other companies can provide an indication of the current level of customer satisfaction.

The cost of quality report can be used as an attention-directing device to make the top management of a company aware of how much is being spent on quality-related costs. The report can also draw management's attention to the possibility of reducing total quality costs by a wiser allocation of costs among the four quality categories. For example, by spending more on the prevention costs, the amount of spending in the internal and external failure categories can be substantially reduced, and therefore total spending can be lowered. Also, by designing quality into the products and processes, appraisal costs can be reduced, since far less inspection is required.

Prevention and appraisal costs are sometimes referred to as the **costs of quality conformance** or **compliance** and internal and external failure costs are also known as the **costs of non-conformance** or **non-compliance**. Costs of compliance are incurred with the intention of eliminating the costs of failure. They are discretionary in the sense that they do not have to be incurred whereas costs of non-compliance are the result of production imperfections and can only be reduced by increasing compliance expenditure. The optimal investment in compliance costs is when total costs of quality reach a minimum. This can occur when 100 per cent quality compliance has not been achieved. It is virtually impossible to measure accurately all quality costs (particularly the lost contribution from forgone sales) and determine the optimal investment in conformance costs. However, some people argue that a failure to achieve 100 per cent quality

EXHIBIT 22.2
Cost of quality report

	(£000s)		% of sales (£50 million)
Prevention costs			
Quality training	1000		
Supplier reviews	300		
Quality engineering	400		
Preventive maintenance	500		
		2 200	4.4
Appraisal costs			
Inspection of materials received	500		
Inspection of WIP and completed units	1000		
Testing equipment	300		
Quality audits	800		
		2 600	5.2
Internal failure costs			
Scrap	800		
Rework	1000		
Downtime due to quality problems	600		
Retesting	400	2 800	5.6
External failure costs			
Returns	2000		
Recalls	1000		
Warranty repairs	800		
Handling customer complaints	500		
Foregone contribution from lost sales	3000		
		7 300	14.6
		14 900	29.8

compliance is non-optimal and that a **zero-defects policy** is optimal. With a zero-defects policy the focus is on continuous improvement with the ultimate aim of achieving zero-defects and eliminating all internal and external failure costs.

A zero-defects policy does not use percentages as the unit of measurement because a small percentage defect rate can result in a large number of defects. For example, a 1% defect rate from an output of 1 million units results in 10 000 defective units. To overcome this problem the attainment of a zero-defects goal is measured in parts per million (PPM) so that seemingly small numbers can be transferred into large numbers. Thus, instead of reporting a 1% defect rate, a measure of 10 000 PPM is more likely to create pressure for action and highlight the trend in defect rates. Cost of quality reports provide a useful summary of quality efforts and progress to top management, but at lower management levels non-financial quality measures provide more timely and appropriate target measures for quality improvement. These measures will be discussed in the next chapter.

Besides using non-financial measures **statistical quality control charts** are used as a mechanism for distinguishing between random and non-random variations in operating processes. A control chart is a graph of a series of successive observations of operations taken at regular intervals of time to test whether a batch of produced items is within pre-set tolerance limits. Usually samples from a particular production process are taken at hourly or daily intervals. The mean, and sometimes the range, of the sampled items are calculated and plotted on a quality control chart (see Figure 22.2). Each observation is plotted relative to pre-set points on the expected distribution. Only observations beyond specified pre-set control limits are regarded as worthy of investigation.

The control limits are based on a series of past observations of a process when it is under control, and thus working efficiently. It is assumed that the past observations can be represented by a normal distribution. The past observations are used to estimate the population mean and the population standard deviation. Assuming that the distribution of possible outcomes is normal, then, when the process is under control, we should expect

68.27% of the observation to fall within the range $+1\sigma$ from the mean;

95.45% of the observation to fall within the range $+2\sigma$ from the mean.

Control limits are now set. For example, if control limits are set based on two standard deviations from the mean then this would indicate 4.55% (100% – 95.45%) of future observations would result from pure chance when the process is under control. Therefore there is a high probability that an observation outside the 2σ control limits is out of control.

Figure 22.2 shows three control charts, with the outer horizontal lines representing a possible control limit of 2σ, so that all observations outside this range are investigated. You will see that for operation A the process is deemed to be in control because all observations fall within the control limits. For operation B the last two observations suggest that the operation is out of control. Therefore both observations should be investigated. With operation C the observations would not prompt an investigation because all the observations are within the control limits. However, the last six observations show a steadily increasing usage in excess of the mean, and the process may be out of control. Statistical procedures (called casum procedures) that consider the trend in recent usage as well as daily usage can also be used.

Cost management and the value chain

Increasing attention is now being given to **value-chain analysis** as a means of increasing customer satisfaction and managing costs more effectively. The value chain is illustrated in Figure 22.3. It is the linked set of value-creating activities all the way from basic raw material sources for component suppliers through to the ultimate end-use product or service delivered to the customer. A value-chain analysis is used to analyse, coordinate and optimize linkages in the value chain. Coordinating the individual parts of the value chain together creates the conditions to improve customer satisfaction, particularly in terms of cost efficiency, quality and delivery. A firm which performs the value chain activities more efficiently, and at a lower cost, than its competitors will gain a competitive advantage. Therefore it is necessary to understand how value chain activities are performed and how they interact with each other. The activities are not just a collection of independent activities but a system of inter-dependent activities in which the performance of one activity affects the performance and cost of other activities.

The linkages in the value chain express the relationships between the performance of one activity and its effects on the performance of another activity. A linkage occurs when interdependence exists between activities and the higher the interdependence between activities the greater is the required coordination. Thus, it is appropriate to view the value chain from the customer's perspective, with each link being seen as the customer of the previous link. If each link in the value chain is designed to meet the needs of its customers, then end-customer satisfaction should ensue. Furthermore, by viewing each link in the value chain as a supplier–customer relationship, the opinions of the customers

FIGURE 22.2 *Statistical quality control charts*

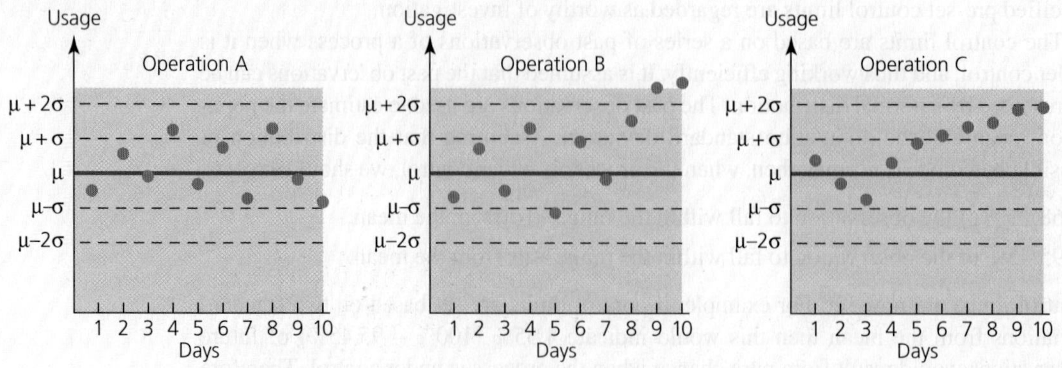

FIGURE 22.3 *The value chain*

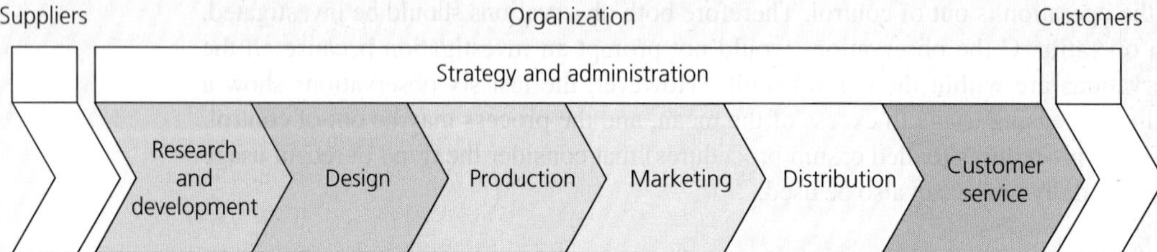

can be used to provide useful feedback information on assessing the quality of service provided by the supplier. Opportunities are thus identified for improving activities throughout the entire value chain.

Shank and Govindarajan (1992) advocate that a company should evaluate its value chain relative to the value chains of its competitors or the industry. They suggest that the following methodology should be adopted:

1 Identify the industry's value chain. This is composed of all the value-creating activities within the industry, beginning with the basic raw material and ending with delivery of the product to the final customer. Based on the industry's value chain, a company's internal value chain should be identified. This is composed of all value-creating activities within a particular firm. They represent the activities that are the building blocks with which firms in the industry have created a product that buyers find valuable. Costs, revenues and assets should then be assigned to activities to ascertain their value.
2 Diagnose the cost drivers regulating each value activity.
3 Develop sustainable cost advantage, either through controlling cost drivers better than competitors or by reconfiguring the chain value. By systematically analysing costs, revenues and assets in each activity, a firm can achieve low cost. This is achieved by comparing the firm's value chain with the value chains of a few major competitors and identifying actions needed to manage the firm's value chain better than competitors manager their value chains.

Value chain analysis in interfirm relationships

The following presents extracts from a case study on the use of an ABC cost model by a large UK retail firm (Sainsburys) and a group of suppliers for supporting their supply chain management practices. This cost model was based on the principles of value chain analysis and integrated cost information across the supply chain. It was used to improve supply chain operations by performing benchmark analyses, strategic what-if analyses and cost monitoring. The model was used to identify opportunities to reduce supply chain costs.

Source: ©J Sainsbury plc 2003

To be able to analyse the supply chain costs, cost and cost driver data were required from both Sainsbury and suppliers. Suppliers were free to choose whether or not they would participate in this initiative. When they decided to participate, they were required to deliver cost data and cost driver quantities to Sainsbury for feeding the supplier section of the model.

Benchmarking was used to compare suppliers' activity costs with the average of their network. In addition, cost comparisons were made between networks, regions and store types. By clustering suppliers into different networks the most important differences between their operations were eliminated, as suppliers within a network performed fairly comparable activities. The most important measure for the benchmark analysis was the cost per cost driver (i.e. the cost driver rate), as this measure could be compared directly with other suppliers. The benchmark analysis revealed the suppliers' relative performance against the network average. When a supplier deviated significantly from the average, the Logistics Operations department would initiate a discussion with the supplier to find out the cause(s) of the difference, by analysing the underlying activities, and to assess whether and how performance could be improved. In addition, as suppliers in different networks faced no competition, comparing the costs of their activities and analysing the differences in their operations could be used to transfer efficient supply chain practices across networks.

Strategic what-if analyses were performed to analyse the effects of changes in the supply chain on supply chain costs. When, for example, as a result of a benchmark analysis, Sainsbury and a supplier developed ideas or scenarios for improving supply chain processes, the model was used to calculate the expected changes in costs of each scenario. An example of a benchmark and a strategic what-if analysis that were performed relates to the use of plastic crates for chilled products. Before the model was developed, Sainsbury and a large supplier discussed the use of these crates to improve the efficiency of product handling activities. As the cost consequences of adopting the crates were unknown to the supplier, Sainsbury was not able to persuade the firm to adopt them. After developing the model, it was used to calculate the supply chain costs related to suppliers using the crates and the costs of the non-adopting supplier. The differences that came out of this benchmark analysis revealed a clear cost advantage for the adopting suppliers. The next step was to analyse what changes would occur in the supply chain activities, if the supplier were to adopt the plastic crates. For instance, while the adoption of plastic crates was expected to result in a cost reduction for the supply chain as a whole, it was predicted to result in increasing costs for the supplier, while the benefits of enhanced efficiency would be reaped mainly by Sainsbury. A possible solution in the negotiations with the supplier about adopting the plastic crates was that Sainsbury would invest in the required handling equipment for the supplier. Another solution was that Sainsbury would agree on a price increase for the supplier's product, which for Sainsbury would be more than offset by the efficiency gains.

Source: Adapted from Dekker, H.C. (2003), Value chain analysis in interfirm relationships: a field study, *Management Accounting Research*, Vol. 14, No. 1, pp. 1–23.

Shank and Govindarajan also point out that focusing on the value chain results in the adoption of a broader strategic approach to cost management. Analysing the industry value chain helps a company evaluate its strategic position in the industry, whereas the analysis of its internal value chain enables a company to take advantage of its strategic internal value chain activities. They also argue that traditional management accounting adopts an internal focus which, in terms of the value chain, starts too late and stops too soon. Starting cost analysis with purchases misses all the opportunities for exploiting linkages with the firm's suppliers and stopping cost analysis at the point of sale eliminates all opportunities for exploiting linkages with customers. Shank (1989) illustrates how an American automobile company failed to use the value chain approach to exploit links with suppliers and enhance profitability. The company had made significant internal savings from introducing JIT manufacturing techniques, but, at the same time, price increases from suppliers more than offset these internal cost savings. A value chain perspective revealed that 50% of the firm's costs related to purchases from parts suppliers. As the automobile company reduced its own need for buffer stocks, it placed major new strains on the manufacturing responsiveness of suppliers. The increase in the suppliers' manufacturing costs was greater than the decrease in the automobile company's internal costs. Shank states:

> *For every dollar of manufacturing cost the assembly plants saved by moving towards JIT management concepts, the suppliers' plant spent much more than one dollar extra because of schedule instability arising from the introduction of JIT. Because of its narrow value added perspective, the auto company had ignored the impact of its changes on its suppliers' costs. Management had ignored the idea that JIT involves a partnership with suppliers (Shank, 1989: 51).*

Managing linkages in the value chain is also the central idea of the concept of **supply chain management**. By examining potential linkages with suppliers and understanding supplier costs it may be possible for the buying organization to change its activities in order to reduce the supplier's costs. For example, cost generating activities in the supplying organizations are often triggered by purchasing parameters (e.g. design specifications, lot size, delivery schedule, number of shipments, design changes and level of documentation). However, the buying organization can only be sensitive to these issues if it understands how supplier costs are generated (Seal *et al.*, 1999). In many organizations materials purchased from suppliers account for more than 60% of total manufacturing costs (Drury *et al.*, 1993) and therefore managing supply chain costs has become a critical element in overall cost management. Because of this some companies have established strategic supply partnerships. Seal *et al.* (1999) describe the attempt at a strategic supply partnership between two UK companies and how the buying company was seeking information sharing and research and development collaboration with the supplier for strategic components. In return the supplier was wishing to develop a higher level of cooperation and trust. Such developments represent an attempt to apply cost management throughout the entire value chain.

Similarly, by developing linkages with customers mutually beneficial relationships can be established. For example, Shank and Govindarajan (1992), drawing off research by Hergert and Morris (1989) point out that some container producers in the USA have constructed manufacturing facilities near beer breweries and deliver the containers through overhead conveyers directly onto the customers' assembly lines. This practice results in significant cost reductions for both the container producers and their customers by expediting the transport of empty containers, which are bulky and heavy.

Benchmarking

In order to identify the best way of performing activities and business processes organizations are turning their attention to **benchmarking**, which involves comparing key activities with world-class best practices. Benchmarking attempts to identify an activity, such as customer order processing, that needs to be improved and finding a non-rival organization that is considered to represent world-class best practice for the activity and studying how it performs the activity. The objective is to find out how the activity can be improved and ensure that the improvements are implemented.

Benchmarking is cost beneficial since an organization can save time and money avoiding mistakes that other companies have made and/or the organization can avoid duplicating the efforts of other companies. The overall aim should be to find and implement best practice.

Environmental cost management

Environmental cost management is becoming increasingly important in many organizations. There are several reasons for this. First, environmental costs can be large for some industrial sectors. For example, Ranganathan and Ditz (1996) reported that Amoco's environmental costs at its Yorktown refinery were at least 22% of operating costs. Second, regulatory requirements involving huge fines for non-compliance have increased significantly over the past decade. Therefore, selecting the least costly method of compliance has become a major objective. Third, society is demanding that companies focus on becoming more environmentally friendly. Companies are finding that becoming a good social citizen and being environmentally responsible improves their image and enhances their ability to sell their products and services. These developments have created the need for companies to develop a system of measuring, reporting and monitoring environmental costs.

According to Epstein and Roy (1997) many companies cannot identify their total environmental costs and do not recognize that they can be controlled and reduced. In most cost accounting systems, environmental costs are hidden within general overheads and are either not allocated to cost objects, or they are allocated on an arbitrary basis within the allocation of general overheads. Thus, crucial relationships are not identified between environmental costs and the responsible products, processes and underlying activities. For example, Ranganathan and Ditz point out that the principal environmental issue facing Spectrum Glass, a major manufacturer of specialty sheet glass, is the use and release of cadmium. It discovered that only one product (Ruby red glass) was responsible for all of its cadmium emissions but the cost accounting system allocated a portion of this cost to all products. This process resulted in ruby red glass being undercosted and other products being overcosted.

Environmental costs should be accumulated by separate cost pools, analysed by appropriate categories and traced to the products or processes that caused the costs using ABC concepts. Knowledge of the amount and categories of environmental costs, and their causes, provides the information that managers need to not only manage environmental costs more effectively by process redesign but to also reduce the pollutants emitted to the environment.

Hansen and Mendoza (1999) point out that environmental costs are incurred because poor environmental quality exists and thus are similar in nature to quality costs discussed earlier in this chapter. They advocate that an environmental cost report should be periodically produced, based on the principles of a cost of quality report (see Exhibit 22.2) to indicate the total environmental costs to the organization associated with the creation, detection, remedy and prevention of environmental degradation. Adopting a similar classification as that used for quality costs, the following four categories of environmental costs can be reported:

1 **Environmental prevention costs** are the costs of activities undertaken to prevent the production of waste that could cause damage to the environment. Examples include the costs associated with the design and operation of processes to reduce contaminants, training employees, recycling products and obtaining certification relating to meeting the requirements of international and national standards.
2 **Environmental appraisal costs** are the costs incurred to ensure that a firm's activities, products and processes conform to regulatory laws and voluntary standards. Examples include inspection of products and processes to ensure regulatory compliance, auditing environmental activities and performing contamination tests.
3 **Environmental internal failure costs** are the costs incurred from performing activities that have been produced but not discharged into the environment. Such costs are incurred to eliminate or reduce waste to levels that comply with regulatory requirements. Examples include the costs of disposing of toxic materials and recycling scrap.
4 **Environmental external failure costs** are the costs incurred on activities performed after discharging waste into the environment. Examples include the costs of cleaning up contaminated soil, restoring land to its natural state and cleaning up oil spills and waste discharges. Clearly this category of costs has the greatest impact on a company in terms of adverse publicity.

The environmental cost report should be similar in format to the cost of quality report (see Exhibit 22.2) with each category of costs expressed as a percentage of sales revenues (or operating costs) so that comparisons can be made with previous periods, other organizations and divisions within the same group. The environmental cost report should be used as an attention-directing device to make top management aware of how much is being spent on environmental costs and the relative amount in each category. The report also draws management's attention to those areas that have the greatest potential for cost reduction. A major limitation of environmental cost reports is that they only report those environmental costs for which the company is responsible. The report does not include costs that are caused by a firm but borne by society. Examples include losing land for recreational use and damaging ecosystems from solid waste disposal. Attempts should be made to develop non-financial and/or qualitative measures that draw attention to how an organization is contributing to becoming environmentally responsible and a good social citizen.

In addition to the approaches described above, the environmental consequences of products should be evaluated using the life-cycle costing approach described at the beginning of this chapter. In other words, the environmental consequences should be managed at the planning and design stage and not at the manufacturing stage when a substantial proportion of the environmental costs and outcomes will already have been determined. Finally, you should note at this point that incorporating an environmental perspective within a balanced scorecard framework has been adopted by some companies to link their environmental strategy to concrete performance measures. The balanced scorecard framework requires that within the scorecard the environmental objectives are clearly specified and that these objectives should be translated into specific performance measures. In addition, within the scorecard, firms should describe the major initiatives for achieving each objective and also establish targets for each performance measure. For feedback reporting, actual performance measures should also be added. The balanced scorecard framework is described in the next chapter.

Just-in-time systems

Earlier in this chapter it was pointed out that re-organizing business processes and adopting a just-in-time (JIT) system was an illustration of business process engineering but so far a JIT system has not been explained. Given that implementing a JIT system is a mechanism for reducing non-value added costs and long-run costs it is important that you understand the nature of such a system and its cost management implications.

The success of Japanese firms in international markets generated interest among many Western companies as to how this success was achieved. The implementation of **just-in-time (JIT) production methods** was considered to be one of the major factors contributing to this success. The JIT approach involves a continuous commitment to the pursuit of excellence in all phases of manufacturing systems design and operations. The aims of JIT are to produce the required items, at the required quality and in the required quantities, at the precise time they are required. In particular, JIT seeks to achieve the following goals:

- elimination of non-value added activities;
- zero inventory;
- zero defects;
- batch sizes of one;
- zero breakdowns;
- a 100% on-time delivery service.

The above goals represent perfection, and are most unlikely to be achieved in practice. They do, however, offer targets, and create a climate for continuous improvement and excellence. Let us now examine the major features of a JIT manufacturing philosophy.

Elimination of non-value added activities

JIT manufacturing is best described as a philosophy of management dedicated to the elimination of waste. Waste is defined as anything that does not add value to a product. The lead or cycle time involved in manufacturing and selling a product consists of process time, inspection time, move time, queue time and storage time. Of these five steps, only process time actually adds value to the product. All the other activities add cost but no value to the product, and are thus deemed non-value added processes within the JIT philosophy. According to Berliner and Brimson (1988), process time is less than 10% of total manufacturing lead time in many organizations in the USA. Therefore 90% of the manufacturing lead time associated with a product adds costs, but no value, to the product. By adopting a JIT philosophy and focusing on reducing lead times, it is claimed that total costs can be significantly reduced. The ultimate goal of JIT is to convert raw materials to finished products with lead times equal to processing times, thus eliminating all non-value added activities.

Factory layout

The first stage in implementing JIT manufacturing techniques is to rearrange the production process away from a **batch production functional layout** towards a product layout using flow lines. With a functional plant layout products pass through a number of specialist departments that normally contain a group of similar machines. Products are processed in large batches so as to minimize the set-up times when machine settings are changed between processing batches of different products. Batches move via different and complex routes through the various departments, travelling over much of the factory floor before they are completed. Each process normally involves a considerable amount of waiting time. In addition, much time is taken transporting items from one process to another. A further problem is that it is not easy at any point in time to determine what progress has been made on individual batches. Therefore detailed cost accumulation records are necessary to track work in progress. The consequences of this complex routing process are high work in progress stock levels and long manufacturing cycle times.

The JIT solution is to reorganize the production process by dividing the many different products that an organization makes into families of similar products or components. All of the products in a particular group will have similar production requirements and routings. Production is rearranged so that each product family is manufactured in a well-defined production cell based on flow line principles. The production layout thus resembles a 'mini' factory for each product family. In a **product flow line**, specialist departments containing *similar* machines no longer exist. Instead groups of *dissimilar* machines are organized into product or component family flow lines that function like an assembly line. For each product line the machines are placed close together in the order in which they are required by the group of products to be processed. Items in each product family can now move, one at a time, from process to process more easily, thereby reducing work in progress stocks and lead times. The aim is to produce products or components from start to finish without returning to the stock room.

The ideal layout of each flow line is normally U-shaped. This layout, which is called **cellular manufacturing**, allows the operatives access to a number of machines, thus enabling each to operate several machines. Operatives are trained to operate all machines on the line and undertake routine preventive maintenance. Any worker can stop the production line if a problem arises. The emphasis is on employee empowerment, involving a high level of trust and greater responsibility for workers. It is assumed that workers will perform better when they are given greater authority to control their activities.

JIT manufacturing aims to produce the right parts at the right time, only when they are needed, and only in the quantity needed. This philosophy has resulted in a **pull manufacturing system**, which means that parts move through the production system based on end-unit demand, focusing on maintaining a constant flow of components rather than batches of WIP. With the pull system, work on components does not commence until specifically requested by the next process. JIT techniques aim to keep the materials moving in a continuous flow with no stoppages and no storage. Material movements between operations are minimized by eliminating space between work stations and grouping dissimilar machines into manufacturing cells on the basis of product groups and functioning like an assembly line.

The pull system is implemented by monitoring the consumption of parts at each operation stage and using various types of visible signalling systems (known as **Kanbans**) to authorize production and movement of the part to the using location. The producing cell cannot run the parts until authorized to do so. The signalling mechanism usually involves the use of *Kanban* containers. These containers hold materials or parts for movement from one work centre to another. The capacity of *Kanban* containers tends to vary from two to five units. They are just big enough to permit the production line to operate smoothly despite minor interruptions to individual work centres within the cell. To illustrate how the system works consider three machines forming part of a cell where the parts are first processed by machine A before being further processed on machine B and then machine C. The *Kanban*s are located between the machines. As long as the *Kanban* container is not full, the worker at machine A continues to produce parts, placing them in the *Kanban* container. When the container is full the worker stops producing and recommences when a part has been removed from the container by the worker operating machine B. A similar process applies between the operations of machines B and C. This process can result in idle time within certain locations within the cell, but the JIT philosophy considers that it is more beneficial to absorb short-run idle time rather than add to inventory during these periods. During idle time the workers perform preventive maintenance on the machines.

With a pull system problems arising in any part of the system will immediately halt the production line because work centres at the earlier stages will not receive the pull signal (because the *Kanban* container is full) if a problem arises at a later stage. Alternatively, work centres at a later stage will not have their pull signal answered (because of empty *Kanban* containers) when problems arise with work centres at the earlier stages of the production cycle. Thus attention is drawn immediately to production problems so that appropriate remedial action can be taken. This is deemed to be preferable to the approach adopted in a traditional manufacturing system where large stock levels provide a cushion for production to continue. This can lead to a situation where major problems can remain hidden, or deferred indefinitely, rather than triggering a search for immediate long-term solutions.

In contrast, the traditional manufacturing environment is based on a **push manufacturing system**. With this system, machines are grouped into work centres based on the similarity of their functional capabilities. Each manufactured part has a designated routing, and the preceding process supplies parts to the subsequent process without any consideration being given to whether the next process is ready to work on the parts or not. Hence the use of the term 'push-through system'.

Batch sizes of one

Set-up time is the amount of time required to adjust equipment and to retool for a different product. Long set-up and changeover times make the production of batches with a small number of units uneconomic. However, the production of large batches leads to substantial throughput delays and the creation of high inventory levels. Throughput delays arise because several lengthy production runs are required to process larger batches through the factory. A further problem with large batches is that they often have to wait for lengthy periods before they are processed by the next process or before they are sold. The JIT philosophy is to reduce and eventually eliminate set-up times. For example, by investing in advanced manufacturing technologies some machine settings can be adjusted automatically instead of manually. Alternatively, some set-up times can be eliminated entirely by redesigning products so that machines do not have to be reset each time a different product has to be made.

If set-up times are approaching zero, this implies that there are no advantages in producing in batches. Therefore the optimal batch size can be one. With a batch size of one, the work can flow smoothly to the next stage without the need for storage and to schedule the next machine to accept this item. In many situations set-up times will not be approaching zero, but by significantly reducing set-up times, small batch sizes will be economical. Small batch sizes, combined with short throughput times, also enable a firm to adapt more readily to short-term fluctuations in market demand and respond faster to customer requests, since production is not dependent on long planning lead times.

JIT purchasing arrangements

The JIT philosophy also extends to adopting JIT purchasing techniques, whereby the delivery of materials immediately precedes their use. By arranging with suppliers for more frequent deliveries, stocks can be cut to a minimum. Considerable savings in material handling expenses can be obtained by requiring suppliers to inspect materials before their delivery and guaranteeing their quality. This improved service is obtained by giving more business to fewer suppliers and placing longer-term purchasing orders. Therefore the supplier has an assurance of long-term sales, and can plan to meet this demand.

Companies that have implemented JIT purchasing techniques claim to have substantially reduced their investment in raw materials and work in progress stocks. Other advantages include a substantial saving in factory space, large quantity discounts, savings in time from negotiating with fewer suppliers and a reduction in paperwork arising from issuing blanket long-term orders to a few suppliers rather than individual purchase orders to many suppliers.

JIT and management accounting

Management accountants in many organizations have been strongly criticized because of their failure to alter the management accounting system to reflect the move from a traditional manufacturing to a just-in-time manufacturing system. Conventional management accounting systems can encourage behaviour that is inconsistent with a just-in-time manufacturing philosophy. Management accounting must support just-in-time manufacturing by monitoring, identifying and communicating to decision-makers any delay, error and waste in the system. Modern management accounting systems are now placing greater emphasis on providing information on supplier reliability, set-up times, throughput cycle times, percentage of deliveries that are on time and defect rates. All of these measures are critical to supporting a just-in-time manufacturing philosophy and are discussed in more detail in the next chapter.

Because JIT manufacturing systems result in the establishment of production cells that are dedicated to the manufacturing of a single product or a family of similar products many of the support activities can be directly traced to the product dedicated cells. Thus, a high proportion of costs can be directly assigned to products. Therefore the benefits from implementing ABC product costing will be lower in JIT organizations.

Summary

The following items relate to the learning objectives listed at the beginning of the chapter.

- **Distinguish between the features of a traditional management accounting control system and cost management.**

  A traditional management accounting control system tends to be based on the preservation of the status quo and the ways of performing existing activities are not reviewed. The emphasis is on cost containment rather than cost reduction. Cost management focuses on cost reduction rather than cost containment. Whereas traditional cost control systems are routinely applied on a continuous basis, cost management tends to be applied on an ad-hoc basis when an opportunity for cost reduction is identified. Also many of the approaches that are incorporated within the area of cost management do not involve the use of accounting techniques. In contrast, cost control relies heavily on accounting techniques.

- **Explain life-cycle costing and describe the typical pattern of cost commitment and cost incurrence during the three stages of a product's life cycle.**

  Life-cycle costing estimates and accumulates costs over a product's entire life cycle in order to determine whether the profits earned during the manufacturing phase will cover the costs incurred during the pre- and post-manufacturing stages. Three stages of a product's life cycle can be identified – the planning and design stage, the manufacturing stage and the service and abandonment stage. Approximately 80% of a product's costs are committed during the planning and design stage. At this stage product designers determine the product's design and the production process. In contrast, the majority of costs are incurred at the manufacturing stage, but they have already become locked-in at the planning and design stage and are difficult to alter. Cost management can be most effectively exercised during the planning and design stage and not at the manufacturing stage when the product design and processes have already been determined and costs have been committed.

- **Describe the target costing approach to cost management.**

  Target costing is a customer-oriented technique that is widely used by Japanese companies and which has recently been adopted by companies in Europe and the USA. The first stage requires market research to determine the target selling price for a product. Next a standard or desired profit margin is deducted to establish a target cost for the product. The target cost is compared with the predicted actual cost. If the predicted actual cost is above the target cost intensive efforts are made to close the gap. Value engineering and functional analysis are used to drive the predicted actual cost down to the target cost. The major advantage of adopting target costing is that it is deployed during a product's design and planning stage so that it can have a maximum impact in determining the level of the locked-in costs.

- **Describe tear-down analysis, value engineering and functional analysis.**

  Tear-down analysis involves examining a competitor's product in order to identify opportunities for product improvement and/or cost reduction. The aim of value engineering is to achieve the assigned target cost by (a) identifying improved product designs that reduce the product's cost without sacrificing functionality and/or (b) eliminating unnecessary functions that increase the product's costs and for which customers are not prepared to pay extra. Value engineering requires the use of functional analysis. This involves decomposing the product into its many elements or attributes. A value for each element is determined which reflects the amount the customer is prepared to pay. The cost of each function of a product is compared with the benefits perceived by the customers. If the cost of the function exceeds the benefit to the customer, then the function is either eliminated, modified to reduce its cost, or enhanced in terms of its perceived value so that its value exceeds the cost.

- **Distinguish between target costing and *kaizen* costing.**

  The major difference between target and *kaizen* costing is that target costing is applied during the design stage whereas *kaizen* costing is applied during the manufacturing stage of the product life cycle. With target costing, the focus is on the product and cost reductions are achieved primarily through product design. In contrast, *kaizen* costing focuses on the production processes and cost reductions are derived primarily through the increased efficiency of the production process. The aim of *kaizen* costing is to reduce the cost of components and products by a pre-specified amount. A major feature is that workers are given the responsibility to improve processes and reduce costs. Unlike target costing it is not accompanied by a set of techniques or procedures that are automatically applied to achieve the cost reductions.

- **Describe activity-based cost management.**

  Activity-based management (ABM) focuses on managing the business on the basis of the activities that make up the organization. It is based on the premise that activities consume costs. Therefore, by managing activities, costs will be managed in the long term. The goal of ABM is to enable customer needs to be satisfied while making fewer demands on organization resources. Prior to the introduction of ABM most organizations have been unaware of the cost of undertaking the activities that make up the organization. Knowing the cost of activities enables those activities with the highest cost to be highlighted so that they can be prioritized for detailed studies to ascertain whether they can be eliminated or performed more efficiently.

- **Distinguish between value added and non-value added activities.**

  To identify and prioritize the potential for cost reduction using ABM, many organizations have found it useful to classify activities as either value added or non-value added. A value added activity is an activity that customers perceive as adding usefulness to the product or service they purchase whereas a non-value added activity is an activity where there is an opportunity for cost reduction without reducing the product's service potential to the customer. Taking action to reduce or eliminate non-value added activities is given top priority because by doing so the organization permanently reduces the cost it incurs without reducing the value of the product to the customer.

- **Explain the purpose of a cost of quality report.**

  A cost of quality report indicates the total cost to the organization of producing products or services that do not conform with quality requirements. Quality costs are analysed by four categories for reporting purposes (prevention, appraisal, and internal and external failure costs). The report draws management's attention to the possibility of reducing total quality costs by a wiser allocation of costs among the four quality categories.

- **Describe how value chain analysis can be used to increase customer satisfaction and manage costs more effectively.**

  Increasing attention is now being given to value chain analysis as a means of increasing customer satisfaction and managing costs more effectively. The value chain is the linked set of value-creating activities all the way from basic raw material sources from component suppliers through to the ultimate end-use product or service delivered to the customer. Understanding how value chain activities are performed and how they interact with each other creates the conditions to improve customer satisfaction, particularly in terms of cost efficiency, quality and delivery.

- **Explain the role of benchmarking within the cost management framework.**

  Benchmarking involves comparing key activities with world-class best practices by identifying an activity that needs to be improved, finding a non-rival organization that is considered to represent world-class best practice for the activity, and studying how it performs the activity. The objective is to establish how the activity can be improved and ensure that the improvements are implemented. The outcome should be reduced costs for the activity or process or performing the activity more effectively, thus increasing customer satisfaction.

- **Outline the main features of a just-in-time philosophy.**

  In recent years many companies have sought to eliminate and/or reduce the costs of non-value added activities by introducing just-in-time (JIT) systems. The aims of a JIT system are to produce the required items, at the required quality and in the required quantities, at the precise time they are required. In particular, JIT aims to eliminate waste by minimizing inventories and reducing cycle or throughput times (i.e. the time elapsed from when customers place an order until the time when they receive the desired product or service). Adopting a JIT manufacturing system involves moving from a batch production functional layout to a cellular flow line manufacturing system. The JIT philosophy also extends to adopting JIT purchasing techniques, whereby the delivery of materials immediately precedes their use. By arranging with suppliers for more frequent deliveries, stocks can be cut to a minimum.

Key terms and concepts

activity-based cost management (p. 951)
activity-based management (p. 951)
appraisal costs (p. 959)
batch production functional layout (p. 968)
benchmarking (p. 965)
business process re-engineering (p. 956)
cellular manufacturing (p. 968)
committed costs (p. 944)
costs of non-compliance (p. 959)
costs of non-conformance (p. 959)
costs of quality compliance (p. 959)
costs of quality conformance (p. 959)
cost of quality report (p. 959)
environmental appraisal costs (p. 966)
environmental external failure costs (p. 966)
environmental internal failure costs (p. 966)
environmental prevention costs (p. 966)
external failure costs (p. 959)
functional analysis (p. 947)
internal failure costs (p. 959)
just-in-time (JIT) production methods (p. 967)
kaizen costing (p. 950)
Kanbans (p. 969)
life-cycle costing (p. 944)
locked-in costs (p. 944)
non-value added activity (p. 955)
prevention costs (p. 959)
product flow line (p. 968)
pull manufacturing system (p. 968)
push manufacturing system (p. 969)
reverse engineering (p. 946)
statistical quality control charts (p. 960)
supply chain management (p. 964)
target costing (p. 945)
tear-down analysis (p. 946)
total quality management (p. 957)
value added activity (p. 955)
value analysis (p. 947)
value-chain analysis (p. 961)
value engineering (p. 947)
zero-defects policy (p. 960)

Recommended reading

You should refer to Kato (1993) and Tani *et al.* (1994) for a description of target costing in Japanese companies. For a survey of target costing in Dutch firms you should refer to Dekker and Smidt (2003). A more detailed description of activity-based cost management can be found in Chapter 8 of Kaplan and Cooper (1998). For a description of the application of value chain analysis to cost management see Shank and Govindarajan (1992). See also McNair and Polutnik (2001) for a discussion of a value creation model.

Key examination points

Much of the content of this chapter relates to relatively new topics. Therefore fewer examination questions have been set by the professional examining bodies on the content of this chapter. The questions that follow provide an illustration of the type of questions that have been set. It is likely that most of the questions that will be set on cost management topics will be essays and will require students to demonstrate that they have read widely on the various topics covered in this chapter. Questions set are likely to be open-ended and there will be no ideal answer.

Assessment material

Review questions

The review questions are short questions that enable you to assess your understanding of the main topics included in the chapter. The numbers in parentheses provide you with the page numbers to refer to if you cannot answer a specific question.

Review problems

The review problems are more complex and require you to relate and apply the chapter content to various business problems. Fully worked solutions to the review problems are provided in a separate section at the end of the book. For those questions in the white box the worked solutions are provided in the *Student's Manual* accompanying this book. Further review problems for this chapter are available on the accompanying website www.drury-online.com. The answers to these problems are available for lecturers on the lecturer's password protected section of the website.

Case studies

The website also includes over 30 case study problems. A list of these cases is provided in Part Seven of this book.

Review questions

22.1 How does cost management differ from traditional management accounting control systems? (*pp. 943–44*)

22.2 What are committed (locked-in) costs? (*p. 944*)

22.3 Explain the essential features of life-cycle costing. (*pp. 944–45*)

22.4 Describe the stages involved with target costing. Describe how costs are reduced so that the target cost can be achieved. (*pp. 945–46*)

22.5 What is *kaizen* costing? (*pp. 950–51*)

22.6 What are the distinguishing features of activity based management? (*pp. 951–56*)

22.7 Distinguish between value added and non-value added activities. (*p. 955*)

22.8 What is business process re-engineering? (*pp. 956–57*)

22.9 Identify and discuss the four kinds of quality costs that are included in a cost of quality report. Give examples of costs that fall within each category. *(p. 959)*

22.10 Discuss the value of a cost of quality report. *(pp. 959–61)*

22.11 Describe what is meant by a zero-defects policy. *(p. 960)*

22.12 Explain what is meant by value-chain analysis. Illustrate how value-chain analysis can be applied. *(pp. 961–65)*

22.13 Explain how benchmarking can be used to manage costs and improve activity performance. What are the major features of a just-in-time manufacturing philosophy? *(p. 965, pp. 968–69)*

22.14 Distinguish between a pull and push manufacturing system. *(pp. 968–69)*

22.15 What are the essential features of just-in-time purchasing arrangements? *(p. 970)*

Review problems

22.16 **Advanced: Cost of quality reporting**

Burdoy plc has a dedicated set of production facilities for component X. A just-in-time system is in place such that no stock of materials; work-in-progress or finished goods are held.

At the beginning of period 1, the planned information relating to the production of component X through the dedicated facilities is as follows:

(i) Each unit of component X has input materials: 3 units of material A at £18 per unit and 2 units of material B at £9 per unit.

(ii) Variable cost per unit of component X (excluding materials) is £15 per unit worked on.

(iii) Fixed costs of the dedicated facilities for the period: £162 000.

(iv) It is anticipated that 10% of the units of X worked on in the process will be defective and will be scrapped.

It is estimated that customers will require replacement (free of charge) of faulty units of component X at the rate of 2% of the quantity invoiced to them in fulfilment of orders.

Burdoy plc is pursuing a total quality management philosophy. Consequently all losses will be treated as abnormal in recognition of a zero defect policy and will be valued at variable cost of production.

Actual statistics for each periods 1 to 3 for component X are shown in Appendix 3.1. No changes have occurred from the planned price levels for materials, variable overhead or fixed overhead costs.

Required:

(a) Prepare an analysis of the relevant figures provided in Appendix 3.1 to show that the period 1 actual results were achieved at the planned level in respect of (i) quantities and losses and (ii) unit cost levels for materials and variable costs. *(5 marks)*

(b) Use your analysis from (a) in order to calculate the value of the planned level of each of internal and external failure costs for period 1. *(3 marks)*

(c) Actual free replacements of component X to customers were 170 units and 40 units in periods 2 and 3 respectively. Other data relating to periods 2 and 3 is shown in Appendix 3.1.

Burdoy plc authorized additional expenditure during periods 2 and 3 as follows:
Period 2: Equipment accuracy checks of £10 000 and staff training of £5000.
Period 3: Equipment accuracy checks of £10 000 plus £5000 of inspection costs; also staff training costs of £5000 plus £3000 on extra planned maintenance of equipment.

Required:

(i) Prepare an analysis for EACH of periods 2 and 3 which reconciles the number of components invoiced to customers with those worked-on in the production process. The analysis should show the changes from the planned quantity of process losses and changes from the planned quantity of replacement of faulty components in customer hands;
(All relevant working notes should be shown)

(8 marks)

(ii) Prepare a cost analysis for EACH of periods 2 and 3 which shows actual internal failure costs, external failure costs, appraisal costs and prevention costs;

(6 marks)

(iii) Prepare a report which explains the meaning and inter-relationship of the figures in Appendix 3.1 and in the analysis in (a), (b) and (c) (i)/(ii). The report should also give examples of each cost type and comment on their use in the monitoring and progressing of the TQM policy being pursued by Burdoy plc.

(13 marks)
(Total 35 marks)

Appendix 3.1
Actual statistics for component X

	Period 1	Period 2	Period 3
Invoiced to customers (units)	5 400	5 500	5 450
Worked-on in the process (units)	6 120	6 200	5 780
Total costs:			
Materials A and B (£)	440 640	446 400	416 160
Variable cost of production (£)			
(excluding material cost)	91 800	93 000	86 700
Fixed cost (£)	162 000	177 000	185 000

ACCA Paper 9 Information for Control and Decision Making

22.17 Advanced: Calculation of total savings from introducing a JIT system and determination of optimal selling price

X Ltd manufactures and distributes three types of car (the C1, C2 and C3). Each type of car has its own production line. The company is worried by extremely difficult market conditions and forecasts losses for the forthcoming year.

Current operations

The budgeted details for next year are as follows:

	C1 £	C2 £	C3 £
Direct materials	2 520	2 924	3 960
Direct labour	1 120	1 292	1 980
Total direct cost per car	3 640	4 216	5 940
Budgeted production (cars)	75 000	75 000	75 000
Number of production runs	1 000	1 000	1 500
Number of orders executed	4 000	5 000	5 600
Machine hours	1 080 000	1 800 000	1 680 000

Annual overheads

	Fixed £000	Variable £
Set ups	42 660	13 000 per production run
Materials handling	52 890	4 000 per order executed
Inspection	59 880	18 000 per production run
Machining	144 540	40 per machine hour
Distribution and warehousing	42 900	3 000 per order executed

Proposed JIT system

Management has hired a consultant to advise them on how to reduce costs. The consultant has suggested that the company adopts a just-in-time (JIT) manufacturing system. The introduction of the JIT system would have the following impact on costs (fixed and variable):

Direct labour	Increase by 20%
Set ups	Decrease by 30%
Materials handling	Decrease by 30%
Inspection	Decrease by 30%
Machining	Decrease by 15%
Distribution and warehousing	Eliminated

Required:

(a) Based on the budgeted production levels, calculate the total annual savings that would be achieved by introducing the JIT system.

(6 marks)

The following table shows the price/demand relationship for each type of car per annum.

C1		C2		C3	
Price £	Demand	Price £	Demand	Price £	Demand
5000	75 000	5750	75 000	6500	75 000
5750	65 000	6250	60 000	6750	60 000
6000	50 000	6500	45 000	7750	45 000
6500	35 000	7500	35 000	8000	30 000

Required:

(b) Assuming that X Ltd adopts the JIT system and that the revised variable overhead cost per car remains constant (as per the proposed JIT system budget), calculate the profit-maximizing price and output level for each type of car.

(12 marks)

Investigations have revealed that some of the fixed costs are directly attributable to the individual production lines and could be avoided if a line is closed down for the year. The specific fixed costs for each of the production lines, expressed as a percentage of the total fixed costs, are:

C1	4%
C2	5%
C3	8%

Required:

(c) Determine the optimum production plan for the forthcoming year (based on the JIT cost structure and the prices and output levels you recommended in answer to requirement (b)).

(4 marks)

(d) Write a report to the management of X Ltd which explains the conditions that are necessary for the successful implementation of a JIT manufacturing system.

(8 marks)
(Total 30 marks)
CIMA Management Accounting – Decision Making

22.18 Advanced: Traditional and activity-based budget statements and life-cycle costing

The budget for the Production, Planning and Development Department of Obba plc, is currently prepared as part of a traditional budgetary planning and control system. The analysis of costs by expense type for the period ended 30 November 2000 where this system is in use is as follows:

Expense type	Budget %	Actual %
Salaries	60	63
Supplies	6	5
Travel cost	12	12
Technology cost	10	7
Occupancy cost	12	13

The total budget and actual costs for the department for the period ended 30 November 2000 are £1 000 000 and £1 060 000 respectively.

The company now feels that an Activity Based Budgeting approach should be used. A number of activities have been identified for the Production, Planning and Development Department. An investigation has indicated that total budget and actual costs should be attributed to the activities on the following basis:

	Budget %	Actual %
Activities		
1. Routing/scheduling – new products	20	16
2. Routing/scheduling – existing products	40	34
3. Remedial re-routing/scheduling	5	12
4. Special studies – specific orders	10	8
5. Training	10	15
6. Management & administration	15	15

Required:

(a) (i) Prepare *two* budget control statements for the Production Planning and Development Department for the period ended 30 November 2000 which compare budget with actual cost and show variances using
1. a traditional expense based analysis and
2. an activity based analysis.

(6 marks)

(ii) Identify and comment on *four* advantages claimed for the use of Activity Based Budgeting over traditional budgeting using the Production Planning and Development example to illustrate your answer.

(12 marks)

(iii) Comment on the use of the information provided in the activity based statement which you prepared in (i) in activity based performance measurement and suggest additional information which would assist in such performance measurement.

(8 marks)

(b) Other activities have been identified and the budget quantified for the three months ended 31 March 2001 as follows:

Activities	Cost Driver Unit basis	Units of Cost Driver	Cost (£000)
Product design	design hours	8 000	2000 (see note 1)
Purchasing	purchase orders	4 000	200
Production	machine hours	12 000	1500 (see note 2)
Packing	volume (cu.m.)	20 000	400
Distribution	weight (kg)	120 000	600

Note 1: this includes all design costs for new products released this period.

Note 2: this includes a depreciation provision of £300 000 of which £8000 applies to 3 months' depreciation on a straight line basis for a new product (NPD). The remainder applies to other products.

New product NPD is included in the above budget. The following additional information applies to NPD:

(i) Estimated total output over the product life cycle: 5000 units (4 years life cycle).

(ii) Product design requirement: 400 design hours

(iii) Output in quarter ended 31 March 2001: 250 units

(iv) Equivalent batch size per purchase order: 50 units

(v) Other product unit data: production time 0.75 machine hours: volume 0.4 cu. metres; weight 3 kg.

Required:

Prepare a unit overhead cost for product NPD using an activity based approach which includes an appropriate share of life cycle costs using the information provided in (b) above.

(9 marks)
(Total 35 marks)
ACCA Paper Information for Control and Decision Making

22.19 **Advanced**

The implementation of budgeting in a world class manufacturing environment may be affected by the impact of (i) a total quality ethos (ii) a just-in-time philosophy and (iii) an activity based focus.

Briefly describe the principles incorporated in EACH of (i) to (iii) and discuss ways in which each may result in changes in the way in which budgets are prepared as compared to a traditional incremental budgeting system.

(15 marks)
ACCA Paper 9 Information for Control and Decision Making

22.20 **Advanced**

New techniques are often described as contributing to cost reduction, but when cost reduction is necessary it is not obvious that such new approaches are used in preference to more established approaches. Three examples are:

new technique	compared with	*established approach*
(a) benchmarking		interfirm comparison
(b) activity based budgeting		zero base budgeting
(c) target costing		continuous cost improvement

You are required, for two of the three newer techniques mentioned above:

- to explain its objectives
- to explain its workings
- to differentiate it from the related approach identified
- to explain how it would contribute to a cost reduction programme.

(20 marks)
CIMA Stage 4 Management Accounting – Control and Audit

22.21 **Advanced**

'ABC is still at a relatively early stage of its development and its implications for process control may in the final analysis be more important than its product costing implications. It is a good time for every organization to consider whether or not ABC is appropriate to its particular circumstances.'

J. Innes & F. Mitchell, *Activity Based Costing, A Review with Case Studies*, CIMA, 1990.

You are required:

(a) to contrast the feature of organizations which would benefit from ABC with those which would not;

(8 marks)

(b) to explain in what ways ABC may be used to manage costs, and the limitations of these approaches;

(11 marks)

(c) to explain and to discuss the use of target costing to control product costs.

(6 marks)

(Total 25 marks)

CIMA Stage 4 Management Accounting – Control and Audit

22.22 **Advanced**

You are Financial Controller of a medium-sized engineering business. This business was family-owned and managed for many years but has recently been acquired by a large group to become its Engineering Division.

The first meeting of the management board with the newly appointed Divisional Managing Director has not gone well.

He commented on the results of the division:

- Sales and profits were well below budget for the month and cumulatively for the year, and the forecast for the rest of the year suggested no improvement.
- Working capital was well over budget.
- Even if budget were achieved the return on capital employed was well below group standards.

He proposed a Total Quality Management (TQM) programme to change attitudes and improve results.

The initial responses of the managers to these comments were:

- The Production Director said there was a limit to what was possible with obsolete machines and facilities and only a very short-term order book.
- The Sales Director commented that it was impossible to get volume business when deliveries and quality were unreliable and designs out of date.
- The Technical Director said that there was little point in considering product improvements when the factory could not be bothered to update designs and the sales executives were reluctant to discuss new ideas with new potential customers.

You have been asked to prepare reports for the next management board meeting to enable a more constructive discussion.

You are required:

(a) to explain the critical success factors for the implementation of a programme of Total Quality Management. Emphasize the factors that are crucial in changing attitudes from those quoted;

(11 marks)

(b) to explain how you would measure quality cost, and how the establishment of a system of measuring quality costs would contribute to a TQM programme.

(9 marks)

(Total 20 marks)

CIMA Stage 4 Management Accounting – Control and Audit

22.23 **Advanced**

Explain your answers to (a) and (b) with figures/calculations where appropriate.

(a) Many manufacturing companies in different countries throughout the world have sought to influence managers' behaviour by the method(s) they employ to charge overheads to products.

Required:

Discuss how overhead systems may be used to:

(i) direct or manipulate decisions made by departmental managers;

(ii) influence product design decisions that affect costs occurring during the product's life cycle.

(15 marks)

(b) Certain types of costing system encourage operational managers to produce in excess of both budget and demand.

Required:

Discuss the statement made above. Your answer should cover the following areas:

- the types of costing system that encourage this behaviour;
- how these costing systems encourage over-production;
- what can be done to overcome the problem of over-production created by a costing system.

(10 marks)

(Total 25 marks)

CIMA Management Accounting – Decision Making

22.24 **Advanced**

A traditional view of the environment in which goods are manufactured and sold is where stocks of materials and components are held. Such stocks are then used to manufacture products to agreed standard specifications, aiming at maximizing the use of production capacity. Finished goods are held in stock to satisfy steady demand for the product range at agreed prices.

Required:

(a) Discuss aspects of the operation of the management accounting function which are likely to apply in the above system.

(5 marks)

(b) Describe an alternative sequence from purchasing to the satisfaction of customer demand, which may be more applicable in the current business environment. Your answer should refer to the current 'techniques or philosophies' which are likely to be in use.

(5 marks)

(c) Name specific ways in which changes suggested in (b) will affect the operation of the management accounting function.

(5 marks)
(Total 15 marks)
ACCA Paper 9 Information for Control and Decision Making

Review problems (with answers in the Student's Manual)

22.25 **Advanced**

Traditional cost control systems focused on cost containment rather than cost reduction. Today, cost management focuses on process improvement and the identification of how processes can be more effectively and efficiently performed to result in cost reductions.

Required:

Discuss how *each* of the following cost management techniques differs from the traditional cost containment approach and how each seeks to achieve cost reduction:

- Just-in-time;
- Target costing;
- Life cycle costing;
- Activity based management.

(25 marks)
CIMA Management Accounting – Decision Making

22.26 **Advanced**

Within a diversified group, one division, which operates many similar branches in a service industry, has used internal benchmarking and regards it as very useful.

Group central management is now considering the wider use of benchmarking.

Requirement:

(a) Explain the aims, operation, and limitations of internal benchmarking, and explain how external benchmarking differs in these respects.

(10 marks)

(b) A multinational group wishes to internally benchmark the production of identical components made in several plants in different countries. Investments have been made with some plants in installing new Advanced Manufacturing Technology (AMT) and supporting this with manufacturing management systems such as just-in-time (JIT) and Total Quality Management (TQM). Preliminary comparisons suggest that the standard cost in plants using new technology is no lower than that in plants using older technology.

Requirement:

Explain possible reasons for the similar standard costs in plants with differing technology. Recommend appropriate benchmarking measures, recognizing that total standard costs may not provide the most useful measurement of performance.

(10 marks)
(Total 20 marks)
CIMA Stage 4 Management Accounting – Control Systems

22.27 **Advanced**

SG plc is a long-established food manufacturer which produces semi-processed foods for fast food outlets. While for a number of years it has recognized the need to produce good quality products for its customers, it does not have a formalized quality management programme.

A director of the company has recently returned from a conference, where one of the speakers introduced the concept of Total Quality Management (TQM) and the need to recognize and classify quality costs.

Required:

(a) Explain what is meant by TQM and use examples to show how it may be introduced into different areas of SG plc's food production business.
(12 marks)

(b) Explain why the adoption of TQM is particularly important within a just-in-time (JIT) production environment.
(5 marks)

(c) Explain four quality cost classifications, using examples relevant to the business of SG plc.
(8 marks)

(Total 25 marks)
CIMA Management Accounting – Performance Management

22.28 **Advanced**

PG plc manufactures gifts and souvenirs for both the tourist and commercial promotions markets. Many of the items are similar except that they are overprinted with different slogans, logos, and colours for the different customers and markets. For many years, it has been PG plc's policy to produce the basic items in bulk and then overprint them as required, but this policy has now been questioned by the company's new Finance Director.

She has also questioned the current policy of purchasing raw materials in bulk from suppliers whenever the periodic stock review system indicates that the re-order level has been reached.

She has said that it is most important in this modern environment to be as efficient as possible, and that bulk purchasing and production strategies are not necessarily the most efficient strategies to be adopted. She has suggested that the company must carefully consider its approaches to production, and the associated costs.

Required:

(a) Compare and contrast the current strategies of PG plc for raw materials purchasing and production with those that would be associated with a just-in-time (JIT) philosophy.

(15 marks)

(b) Explain what is meant by cost reduction.

(3 marks)

(c) Explain how PG plc might introduce a cost reduction programme without affecting its customers' perceptions of product values.

(7 marks)

(Total 25 marks)

CIMA Management Accounting – Performance Management

22.29 **Advanced**

Standard costing and target costing have little in common for the following reasons:

- the former is a costing system and the latter is not;
- target costing is proactive and standard costing is not;
- target costs are agreed by all and are rigorously adhered to whereas standard costs are usually set without wide consultation.

Required:

(a) Discuss the comparability of standard costing and target costing by considering the validity of the statements above.

(18 marks)

A pharmaceutical company, which operates a standard costing system, is considering introducing target costing.

Required:

(b) Discuss whether the company should do this and whether the two systems would be compatible.

(7 marks)

(Total 25 marks)

CIMA Management Accounting – Decision Making

22.30 **Advanced: Construction of life cycle curves, investment appraisal and sensitivity analysis**

(a) Scovet plc uses its production capacity in dedicated product line format to satisfy demand for a rolling range of products. Such products have limited life cycles. A turnover value of £20m is taken as a measure of the annual production capacity of the company. The turnover figures (actual and forecast) are shown below for each of products A, B and C from the beginning of the life cycle of each product up to 2004. These are the only products for which Scovet plc has sales (actual or forecast) for the years 2001 to 2004.

Scovet plc

Sales Turnover (£ million) – actual or forecast

Product	1996	1997	1998	1999	2000	2001	2002	2003	2004
	A	A	A	A	A	F	F	F	F
A	2.0	4.0	6.0	7.0	4.5	3.0	2.0	1.5	nil
B	nil	nil	3.0	6.0	8.0	9.0	3.0	1.0	nil
C	nil	nil	nil	4.0	5.0	6.5	7.5	8.0	7.0

Note A = actual; F = forecast

Other relevant information (forecast) relating to the products for the years 2001 and 2002 is as follows:

1 Contribution to Sales ratios (%): product A (70%); product B (75%); product C (60%).

2 Product specific fixed costs:

	2001 £m	2002 £m
Product A	2.0	1.1
Product B	4.0	1.8
Product C	2.8	3.0

3 Company fixed costs for year; £2.5m.

Required:

(i) Using the graph paper provided, show the life cycle pattern for EACH of products A, B and C expressed in terms of turnover (£m). *(4 marks)*

(ii) Comment on the shape of the life cycle curves in the graphs prepared in (i). *(5 marks)*

(iii) Prepare a profit/loss analysis for each of years 2001 and 2002 which shows the analysis by product including product turnover, contribution and profit and also company net profit or loss. *(4 marks)*

(iv) Comment briefly on the figures in the analysis which you prepared in (iii) above. *(4 marks)*

(b) Scovet plc has identified a market for a new product D for which the following estimated information is available:

1 Sales turnover for the years 2002, 2003 and 2004 of £6m, £7m and £6m respectively. No further sales are expected after 2004.

2 Contribution to sales percentage of 60% for each year.

3 Product specific fixed costs in the years 2002, 2003 and 2004 of £2.5m, £2.2m and £1.8m respectively.

4 Capital investment of £4.5m on 1 January 2002 with nil residual value at 31 December 2004. The cost of capital from 1 January 2002 is expected to be 10% per annum.

Assume all cash flows (other than the initial investment) take place on 31 December of each year. Ignore taxation.

Required:

(i) Determine whether the new product is viable on financial grounds.

(4 marks)

(ii) Calculate the minimum target contribution to sales ratio (%) at which product D will be viable in financial terms where all other factors remain unchanged.

(3 marks)

(iii) Suggest actions which should allow the investigation of variable cost in order that the target contribution to sales ratio (%) calculated in (ii) may be achieved.

(3 marks)

(c) Suggest alternative strategies which may be formulated by Scovet plc in order to improve the overall financial position in the period 2002 to 2004 inclusive where only products A, B, C and D are available for incorporation in the calculations. Comment on the extent of the need for such strategies and include an explanation of any cost/benefit information which would be required.

(8 marks)

(Total 35 marks)

ACCA Paper 9 Information of Control and Decision Making

22.31 **Advanced: Calculation of costs before and after introduction of a quality management programme**

Calton Ltd make and sell a single product. The existing product unit specifications are as follows:

Direct material X:	8 sq. metres at £4 per sq. metre
Machine time:	0.6 running hours
Machine cost per gross hour:	£40
Selling price:	£100

Calton Ltd require to fulfil orders for 5000 product units per period. There are no stocks of product units at the beginning or end of the period under review. The stock level of material X remains unchanged throughout the period.

The following additional information affects the costs and revenues:

1. 5% of incoming material from suppliers is scrapped due to poor receipt and storage organization.
2. 4% of material X input to the machine process is wasted due to processing problems.
3. Inspection and storage of material X costs £0.10 pence per sq. metre purchased.
4. Inspection during the production cycle, calibration checks on inspection equipment, vendor rating and other checks cost £25 000 per period.
5. Production quantity is increased to allow for the downgrading of 12.5% of product units at the final inspection stage. Downgraded units are sold as 'second quality' units at a discount of 30% on the standard selling price.

6. Production quantity is increased to allow for returns from customers which are replaced free of charge. Returns are due to specification failure and account for 5% of units initially delivered to customers. Replacement units incur a delivery cost of £8 per unit. 80% of the returns from customers are rectified using 0.2 hours of machine running time per unit and are re-sold as 'third quality' products at a discount of 50% on the standard selling price. The remaining returned units are sold as scrap for £5 per unit.
7. Product liability and other claims by customers is estimated at 3% of sales revenue from standard product sales.
8. Machine idle time is 20% of gross machine hours used (i.e. running hours = 80% of gross hours).
9. Sundry costs of administration, selling and distribution total £60 000 per period.
10. Calton Ltd is aware of the problem of excess costs and currently spends £20 000 per period in efforts to prevent a number of such problems from occurring.

Calton Ltd is planning a quality management programme which will increase its excess cost prevention expenditure from £20 000 to £60 000 per period. It is estimated that this will have the following impact:

1. A reduction in stores losses of material X to 3% of incoming material.
2. A reduction in the downgrading of product units at inspection to 7.5% of units inspected.
3. A reduction in material X losses in process to 2.5% of input to the machine process.
4. A reduction in returns of products from customers to 2.5% of units delivered.
5. A reduction in machine idle time to 12.5% of gross hours used.
6. A reduction in product liability and other claims to 1% of sales revenue from standard product sales.
7. A reduction in inspection, calibration, vendor rating and other checks by 40% of the existing figure.
8. A reduction in sundry administration, selling and distribution costs by 10% of the existing figure.
9. A reduction in machine running time required per product unit to 0.5 hours.

Required:

(a) Prepare summaries showing the calculation of (i) total production units (pre-inspection), (ii) purchases of material X (sq. metres), (iii) gross machine hours. In each case the figures are required for the situation both before and after the implementation of the additional quality management programme, in order that the orders for 5000 product units may be fulfilled.

(10 marks)

(b) Prepare profit and loss accounts for Calton Ltd for the period showing the profit earned both before and after the implementation of the additional quality management programme.

(10 marks)

(c) Comment on the relevance of a quality management programme and explain the meaning of the terms internal failure costs, external failure costs, appraisal costs and prevention costs giving examples for each, taken where possible from the information in the question.

(10 marks)

(Total 30 marks)

ACCA Level 2 Cost and Management Accounting II

Strategic management accounting

23

During the late 1980s criticisms of traditional management accounting practices were widely publicized and new approaches were advocated which are more in tune with today's competitive and business environment. In particular, strategic management accounting has been identified as a way forward. However, there is still no comprehensive framework as to what constitutes strategic management accounting. In this chapter we shall examine the elements of strategic management accounting and describe the different contributions that have been made to its development.

One of the elements of strategic management accounting involves the provision of information for the formulation of an organization's strategy and managing strategy implementation. To encourage behaviour that is consistent with an organization's strategy, attention is now being given to developing an integrated framework of performance measurement that can be used to clarify, communicate and manage strategy. In the latter part of this chapter recent developments that seek to incorporate performance measurement within the strategic management process are described.

LEARNING OBJECTIVES:

After studying this chapter, you should be able to:

- describe the different elements of strategic management accounting;
- describe the balanced scorecard;
- explain each of the four perspectives of the balanced scorecard;
- provide illustrations of performance measures for each of the four perspectives;
- describe the distinguishing characteristics of service organizations that influence performance measurement.

What is strategic management accounting?

For many years **strategic management accounting** has been advocated as a potential area of development that would enhance the future contribution of management accounting. In the late 1980s the UK Chartered Institute of Management Accountants commissioned an investigation to review the current state of development of management accounting. The findings were published in a report entitled *Management Accounting: Evolution not Revolution*, authoured by Bromwich and Bhimani (1989). In the report, and a follow-up report (*Management Accounting: Pathways to Progress*, 1994) Bromwich and Bhimani drew attention to strategic management accounting as an area for future development. Despite the publicity that strategic management accounting has received there is still no comprehensive conceptual framework of what strategic management accounting is (Tomkins and Carr, 1996). For example, Coad (1996) states:

> *Strategic management accounting is an emerging field whose boundaries are loose and, as yet, there is no unified view of what it is or how it might develop. The existing literature in the field is both disparate and disjointed (Coad, 1996: 392)*

Innes (1998) defines strategic management accounting as the provision of information to support the strategic decisions in organizations. Strategic decisions usually involve the longer-term, have a significant effect on the organization and, although they may have an internal element, they also have an external element. Adopting this definition suggests that the provision of information that supports an organization's major long-term decisions, such as the use of activity-based costing information for providing information relating to product mix, introduction and abandonment decisions falls within the domain of strategic management accounting. This view is supported by Cooper and Kaplan (1988) who state that strategic accounting techniques are designed to support the overall competitive strategy of the organization, principally by the power of using information technology to develop more refined product and service costs. Various writers have suggested that other management accounting techniques that fall within the domain of strategic management accounting are target costing, life-cycle costing and activity-based management (see Chapter 22 for a discussion of these techniques).

Other writers, however, have adopted definitions that emphasize that strategic management accounting is externally focused. Simmonds (1981, 1982), who first coined the term strategic management accounting, views it as the provision and analysis of management accounting data about a business and its competitors which is of use in the development and monitoring of the strategy of that business. He views profits as emerging not from internal efficiencies but from the firm's competitive position in its markets. More recently, Bromwich (1990), a principal advocate of strategic management accounting, has provided the following definition:

> *The provision and analysis of financial information on the firm's product markets and competitors' costs and cost structures and the monitoring of the enterprise's strategies and those of its competitors in these markets over a number of periods (Bromwich, 1990: 28).*

The Chartered Institute of Management Accountants (CIMA) in the UK defines strategic management accounting as:

> *A form of management accounting in which emphasis is placed on information which relates to factors external to the firm, as well as non-financial information and internally generated information (CIMA Official Terminology, 2000: 50).*

Because of the lack of consensus on what constitutes strategic management accounting Lord (1996) reviewed the literature and identified several strands that have been used to characterize strategic management accounting. They include:

1. The extension of traditional management accounting's internal focus to include external information about competitors.
2. The relationship between the strategic position chosen by a firm and the expected emphasis on management accounting (i.e. accounting in relation to strategic positioning).
3. Gaining competitive advantage by analysing ways to decrease costs and/or enhance the differentiation of a firm's products, through exploiting linkages in the value chain and optimizing cost drivers.

Let us now examine each of the above characteristics in more detail.

External information about competitors

Much of the early work relating to strategic management accounting can be attributed to the writings of Simmonds (1981, 1982 and 1986). He argued that management accounting should be more outward looking and should help the firm evaluate its competitive position relative to the rest of the industry by collecting data on costs and prices, sales volumes and market shares, and cash flows and resources availability for its main competitors. To protect an organization's strategic position and determine strategies to improve its future competitiveness managers require information that indicates by whom, by how much and why they are gaining or being beaten. This information provides advance warning of the need for a change in competitive strategy. Competitive information is available from public sources such as company annual reports, press, official institutions and informal sources (e.g. sales personnel, analysing competitors' products, industry specialists, consultants, etc.).

Simmonds also stressed the importance of the **learning curve** (see Chapter 24) as a means of obtaining strategic advantage by forecasting cost reductions and consequently selling price reductions of competitors. He also drew attention to the importance of early experience with a new product as a means of conferring an unbeatable lead over competitors. The leading competitor should be able to reduce its selling price for the product (through the learning curve effect) which should further increase its volume and market share and eventually force some lagging competitors out of the industry.

An organization may also seek to gain strategic advantage by its pricing policy. Here the management accounting function can assist by attempting to assess each major competitor's cost structure and relate this to their prices. In particular, Simmonds suggests that it may be possible to assess the cost–volume–profit relationship of competitors in order to predict their pricing responses. He states:

> *Clearly, competitor reactions can substantially influence the outcome of a price move. Moreover, likely reactions may not be self-evident when each competitor faces a different cost–volume–profit situation. Competitors may not follow a price lead nor even march in perfect step as they each act to defend or build their own positions. For an adequate assessment of the likelihood of competitor price reactions, then, some calculation is needed of the impact of possible price moves on the performance of individual competitors. Such an assessment in turn requires an accounting approach that can depict both competitor cost–volume–profit situations and their financial resources (Simmonds: 1982: 207).*

Besides dealing with costs and prices Simmonds focused on volume and market share. By monitoring movements in market share for its major products, an organization can see whether it is gaining or losing position, and an examination of relative market shares will indicate the strength of different competitors. Including market-share details in management accounting reports helps to make management accounting more strategically relevant. Competitor information may be obtained through public, formal sources, such as published reports and the business press, or through informal channels, such as the firm's salesforce, its customers and its suppliers.

Simmonds (1981) also suggested some changes and additions to traditional management accounting reporting systems in order to include the above information. Market share statements could be incorporated into management accounts. In addition, budgets could be routinely presented in a strategic format with columns for Ourselves, Competitor A, Competitor B, etc. According to Ward (1992) very few firms regularly report competitor information.

Accounting in relation to strategic positioning

Various classifications of strategic positions that firms may choose have been identified in the strategic management literature. Porter (1985) suggests that a firm has a choice of three generic strategies in order to achieve sustainable competitive advantage. They are:

- *cost leadership*, whereby an enterprise aims to be the lowest-cost producer within the industry thus enabling it to compete on the basis of lower selling prices rather than providing unique products or services. The source of this competitive advantage may arise from factors such as economies of scale, access to favourable raw materials prices and superior technology (Langfield-Smith, 1997).
- *differentiation*, whereby the enterprise seeks to offer products or services that are considered by its customers to be superior and unique relative to its competitors. Examples include the quality or dependability of the product, after-sales service, the wide availability of the product and product flexibility (Langfield-Smith, 1997).
- *focus*, which involves seeking advantage by focusing on a narrow segment of the market that has special needs that are poorly served by other competitors in the industry. Competitive advantage is based on either cost leadership or product differentiation.

Miles and Snow (1978) distinguish between *defenders* and *prospectors*. Defenders operate in relatively stable areas, have limited product lines and employ a mass production routine technology. They compete through making operations efficient through cost, quality and service leadership, and engage in little product/market development. Prospectors compete through new product innovations and market development and are constantly looking for new market opportunities. Hence, they face a more uncertain task environment.

The accounting literature suggests that firms will place more emphasis on particular accounting techniques, depending on which strategic position they adopt. For example, Porter (1980) suggested that tight cost controls are more appropriate when a cost leadership strategy is followed. Simons (1987) found that business units that follow a defender strategy tend to place a greater emphasis on the use of financial measures (e.g., short-term budget targets) for compensating financial managers. Prospector firms placed a greater emphasis on forecast data and reduced importance on cost control. Ittner *et al.* (1997) also found that the use of non-financial measures for determining executive's bonuses increases with the extent to which firms follow an innovation-oriented prospector strategy. Shank (1989) stresses the need for management accounting to support a firm's competitive strategies, and illustrates how two different competitive strategies – cost leadership and product differentiation – demand different cost analysis perspectives. For example, carefully engineered product cost standards are likely to be a very important management control tool for a firm that pursues a cost leadership strategy in a mature commodity business. In contrast, carefully engineered manufacturing cost standards are likely to be less important for a firm following a product differentiation strategy in a market-driven, rapidly changing and fast-growing business. A firm pursuing a product differentiation strategy is likely to require more information than a cost leader about new product innovations, design cycle times, research and development expenditures and marketing cost analysis. Exhibit 23.1 illustrates some potential differences in cost management emphasis, depending on the primary strategic thrust of the firm. For additional discussion relating to accounting and strategic positioning you should refer back to the section titled 'Competitive strategy and strategic mission' in Chapter 17.

Gaining competitive advantage

Porter (1985) advocated using **value-chain analysis** (see Chapter 22) to gain competitive advantage. The aim of value chain analysis is to find linkages between value-creating activities which result in lower cost and/or enhanced differentiation. These linkages can be within the firm or between the firm and its suppliers, and customers. The value chain comprises five primary activities and a number of support activities. The primary activities are defined sequentially as inbound logistics, operations, outbound logistics, marketing and sales and services. The secondary activities exist to support the primary activities and include the firm's infrastructure, human resource management, technology and procurement. Costs and assets are assigned to each activity in the value chain. The cost behaviour pattern of each activity depends on a number of causal factors which Porter calls cost drivers. These cost drivers operate in an interactive way and it is management's success in coping with them which determines the cost structure.

Strategic cost analysis also involves identifying the value chain and the operation of cost drivers of competitors in order to understand relative competitiveness. Porter advocates that organizations should use this information to identify opportunities for cost reduction, either by improving control of the cost drivers or reconfiguring the value chain. The latter involves deciding on those areas of the value chain where the firm has a comparative advantage and those which it should source to suppliers. It is essential that the cost reduction performance of both the organization and its principal competitors is continually monitored if competitive advantage is to be sustained.

You may be able to remember the illustration in the previous chapter relating to how an American automobile company failed to use the value chain approach to exploit links with suppliers and enhance profitability.[1] The company had made significant internal savings from introducing JIT manufacturing techniques, but, at the same time, price increases from suppliers more than offset these internal cost savings. A value chain perspective revealed that 50% of the firm's costs related to purchases from parts suppliers. As the automobile company reduced its own need for buffer stocks, it placed major new strains on the manufacturing responsiveness of suppliers. The increase in the suppliers' manufacturing costs was greater than the decrease in the automobile company's internal costs. Shank (1989) states:

> *For every dollar of manufacturing cost the assembly plants saved by moving towards JIT management concepts, the suppliers' plant spent much more than one dollar extra because of schedule instability arising from the introduction of JIT.*

EXHIBIT 23.1

Relationship between strategies and cost management emphasis

	Product differentiation	Cost leadership
Role of standard costs in assessing performance	Not very important	Very important
Importance of such concepts as flexible budgeting for manufacturing cost control	Moderate to low	High to very high
Perceived importance of meeting budgets	Moderate to low	High to very high
Importance of marketing cost analysis	Critical to success	Often not done at all on a formal basis
Importance of product cost as an input to pricing decisions	Low	High
Importance of competitor cost analysis	Low	High

Source: Shank (1989)

> *Because of its narrow value added perspective, the auto company had ignored the impact of its changes on its suppliers' costs. Management had ignored the idea that JIT involves a partnership with suppliers (Shark, 1989: 51).*

Other contributions to strategic management accounting

In this section we shall briefly consider further approaches to strategic management accounting which have not been included within Lord's classification of the literature. Bromwich (1990) has attempted to develop strategic management accounting to consider the benefits which products offer to customers, and how these contribute to sustainable competitive advantage. Bromwich sought to compare the relative cost of product attributes or characteristics with what the customer is willing to pay for them. Products are seen as comprising of a package of attributes which they offer to customers. It is these attributes that actually constitute commodities, and which appeal to customers so that they buy the product. The attributes might include a range of quality elements (such as operating performance variables, reliability and warranty arrangements, physical features – including the degree of finish and trim, and service factors – such as the assurance of supply and after-sales service). A firm's market share depends on the match between the attributes provided by its products and consumers' tastes and on the supply of attributes by competitors. Bromwich argues that it is the product attributes which need to be the subject of appropriate analysis. The purpose of the analysis should be to attribute those costs which are normally treated as product costs to the benefits they provide to the consumer for each of those attributes which are believed to be of strategic importance. By matching costs with benefits firms can compare whether revenues generated from the benefits exceed their costs.

Bromwich concludes that information about a number of demand and cost factors appertaining to attributes possessed by a firm's products and those of its rivals is needed for optimal decision-making. Management accountants can play an important role here in costing the characteristics provided and in monitoring and reporting on these costs regularly. Similarly, they need to be involved in determining the cost of any package of attributes which is being considered for introduction to the market because deciding to provide a product with a particular configuration of attributes or characteristics requires the organization to achieve this at a competitive cost level.

Roslender (1995) has identified **target costing** as falling within the domain of strategic management accounting. The justification for this is the external focus and that it is a market driven approach to product pricing and cost management. In addition it involves the diffusion of management accounting information throughout the organization and the active involvement of staff from across a broad spectrum of management functions. Their aim is to achieve the target cost which involves identifying, valuing and costing product attributes using functional analysis and examining cost reduction opportunities throughout the entire value chain. For a detailed explanation of target costing you should refer back to Chapter 22.

Surveys of strategic management accounting practices

Little research has been undertaken on the extent to which companies use strategic management accounting practices. A notable exception is a survey undertaken by Guilding *et al.* (2000). The survey consisted of a sample of 312 large companies comprising 63 from the UK, 127 from the USA and 124 from New Zealand.

Guilding *et al.* acknowledge the difficulty in identifying what are generally accepted as constituting strategic management accounting practices. Based on a review of the literature they identified 12 strategic management accounting practices. The criteria that they used for identifying the practices were that they must exhibit one or more of the following characteristics: environmental or marketing orientation; focus on competitors; and long-term, forward-looking orientation. The average usage of the identified practices and their perceived merits are reported in Exhibit 23.2. You will see that attribute costing is one of the 12 identified practices. This practice, based on the views promoted by Bromwich (1990) was described in the previous section. Three of the 12 listed practices; namely quality costing (involving the use of cost of quality reports), life-cycle costing and target costing were described in the previous chapter. Although some of the remaining eight practices have been described in this chapter they can be subject to different interpretations and definitions. The following represent the definitions of these eight terms given to the respondents participating in the survey:

- *Competitive position monitoring* The analysis of competitor positions within the industry by assessing and monitoring trends in competitor sales, market share, volume, unit costs and return on sales. This information can provide a basis for the assessment of a competitor's market strategy.
- *Strategic pricing* The analysis of strategic factors in the pricing decision process. These factors may include: competitor price reaction; price elasticity; market growth; economies of scale and experience.
- *Competitor performance appraisal based on published financial statements* The numerical analysis of a competitor's published statements as part of an assessment of the competitor's key sources of competitive advantage.

EXHIBIT 23.2

Usage and perceived merit of strategic management accounting practices

Strategic management accounting practice	Average usage score[a]	Ranking	Average perceived merit score[b]	Ranking
Competitive position monitoring	4.99	1	5.73	1
Strategic pricing	4.54	2	5.45	2
Competitor performance appraisal based on published financial statements	4.42	3	5.31	3
Competitor cost assessment	4.07	4	5.27	4
Strategic costing	3.49	5	4.91	5
Quality costing	3.22	6	4.29	6
Target costing	3.12	7	3.94	8
Value-chain costing	3.04	8	4.27	7
Brand value monitoring	2.73	9	3.38	11
Life-cycle costing	2.60	10	3.58	9
Attribute costing	2.33	11	3.49	10
Brand value budgeting	2.32	12	3.33	12

Notes
[a]All items scored on a Likert scale where 1 denotes used 'not at all' and 7 denotes used 'to a great extent'.
[b]All items scored on a Likert scale where 1 denotes 'not at all helpful' and 7 denotes 'helpful to a great extent'.

- *Competitor cost assessment* The provision of regularly updated estimates of a competitor's costs based on, for example, appraisal of facilities, technology, economies of scale. Sources include direct observation, mutual suppliers, mutual customers and ex-employees.
- *Strategic costing* The use of cost data based on strategic and marketing information to develop and identify superior strategies that will sustain a competitive advantage.
- *Value-chain costing* An activity-based costing approach where costs are allocated to activities required to design, procure, produce, market, distribute and service a product or service.
- *Brand value monitoring* The financial valuation of a brand through the assessment of brand strength factors such as: leadership; stability; market; internationality; trend; support; and protection combined with historical brand profits.
- *Brand value budgeting* The use of brand value as a basis for managerial decisions on the allocation of resources to support/enhance a brand position, thus placing attention on management dialogue on brand issues.

It is apparent from Exhibit 23.2 that the three competitor accounting practices and strategic pricing are the most popular strategic management accounting practices. They all have average scores above the mid-point on the seven-point scale for the 'not at all/to

incorporate measures of these characteristics in the operation processes component of the balanced scorecard. These developments have created the need to focus on measures relating to achieving excellence in terms of time, quality and cost.

Cycle time measures

Many customers place a high value on short and reliable lead times, measured from the time elapsed from when they place an order until the time when they receive the desired product or service. Traditionally companies met this requirement by holding large inventories of many different products but, as indicated in the previous chapter, this approach is not consistent with being a low-cost supplier. Because of this many companies are adopting just-in-time (JIT) production systems with the aim of achieving both the low-cost and short lead time objectives. Reducing cycle or throughput times is therefore of critical importance for JIT companies.

Delivery performance can focus on **cycle time measures** and supplier delivery performance. Cycle times can be measured in various ways. Total cycle time measures the length of time required from the placing of an order by a customer to the delivery of the product or service to the customer. Manufacturing cycle time measures the time it takes from starting and finishing the production process. Cycle times should be measured and monitored and trends observed.

The total manufacturing cycle time consists of the sum of processing time, inspection time, wait time and move time. Only processing time adds value, and the remaining activities are non-value added activities. The aim is to reduce the time spent on non-value added activities and thus minimize manufacturing cycle time. A measure of cycle time that has been adopted is **manufacturing cycle efficiency (MCE):**

$$\text{MCE} = \frac{\text{processing time}}{\text{processing time} + \text{inspection time} + \text{wait time} + \text{move time}}$$

The MCE measure is particularly important for JIT manufacturing companies. With a computerized manufacturing process, it may be possible to report the time taken on each of the above non-value added activities. This will pinpoint those activities that are causing excessive manufacturing cycle times. At the operational level, cycle times should be measured for each product or product line, and trends reported. The emphasis should be on continuous improvements and a shortening of the cycle times.

Reducing set-up times enables manufacturing lot sizes to be reduced, thus leading to shorter manufacturing cycles and greater flexibility. Set-up times should therefore also be measured at the operational level for each process and monitored over time. Modern nanufacturing techniques also advocate preventive maintenance to ensure that machines working effectively at all times, so that quality problems and late deliveries do not ır. A useful measure of machine downtime is the number of lost machine hours in manufacturing cell. However, downtime when a machine is not needed is not ıt. The focus should be on downtime when a machine is needed but is not ready. In leneck operations should be monitored. The aim is to obtain 100% ipment where bottleneck occurs.

so lengthens the cycle time. The time required to inspect parts, rework wait for a machine breakdown to be repaired result in lengthening nce there is a need to measure and reduce the incidence of these ler appropriate performance measures later within this section asurements are discussed.

n processes and MCE measures were initially developed for hey are also applicable to service companies. For example, many customers are forced to queue to receive a service. Companies that can eliminate waiting time for a service will find it easier to attract customers. The time taken to process mortgage and loan applications by financial institutions can take a considerable time period involving a considerable amount of non-value added waiting time. Thus, reducing the time to process the applications enhances customer satisfaction and creates the potential for increasing sales revenues.

Quality measures

Besides time, **quality measures** should also be included in the measures relating to operating processes. Most organizations now have established quality programmes and use all, or some of the following process quality measurements:

- process parts-per-million (PPM) defect rates
- yields (ratio of good items produced to good items entering the process)
- first-pass yields
- waste
- scrap
- rework
- returns
- percentages of processes under statistical process control.

In many companies suppliers also have a significant influence on the ability of a company to achieve its time, quality and cost objectives. Performance measures relating to suppliers' performance include the frequency of defects, the number of late deliveries and price trends.

Cost measurement

Kaplan and Norton recommend that activity-based costing should be used to produce **cost measures** of the important internal business processes. These costs, together with measurements relating time and quality should be monitored over time and/or benchmarked with a view to continuous improvement or process re-engineering.

The above measures represent generic measures but aspects of quality, time and cost measurement are likely to be included as critical performance measures in any organization's internal business perspective within its balanced scorecard.

Post-sales service processes

This final category relating to the internal business process perspective in warranty and repair activities, treatment of defects and returns and the pro administration of customer payments. Increasing quality, increasin decreasing process time are also objectives that apply to the po addition, excellent community relations is an important str ensuring continuing community support to operate manuf companies where environmental factors are involved. For such environmental measures, such as those relating to the safe d products, should be established.

Kaplan and Norton suggest that companies attempting to expectations for superior post-sales service can measure t some of the time, quality and cost measurements that have been suggested for the operating processes. For example, cycle time from customer request to the ultimate resolution of the problem can measure the speed of response to failures. Activity-cost measurement can be used to measure the cost of the resources used for the post-sale service processes. Also first-pass yields can measure what percentage of customer requests are handled with a single service call, rather than requiring multiple calls to resolve the problem. These time, quality and cost measurements can also be applied to companies with extensive sales on credit. The aim should be to reduce the length of time between project completion and the final cash payment by the customer.

The learning and growth perspective

To ensure that an organization will continue to have satisfied and loyal customers in the future and continue to make excellent use of its resources, the organization and its employees must keep learning and developing. Hence there is a need for an additional perspective that focuses on a group of indicators that capture the company's performance with respect to learning, growth and innovation. Thus, the fourth and final perspective on the balanced scorecard identifies the infrastructure that the business must build to create long-term growth and improvement. This perspective stresses the importance of investing for the future in areas other than investing in assets and new product research and development (which is included in the innovation process of the internal business perspective). Organizations must also invest in their infrastructure (people, systems and organizational procedures) to provide the capabilities that enable the accomplishment of the other three perspectives' objectives. Based upon their experiences of building balanced scorecards across a wide variety of organizations Kaplan and Norton have identified the following three principal categories, or enablers, for the learning and growth objectives:

1. employee capabilities;
2. information system capabilities;
3. motivation, empowerment and alignment.

They point out that although they have found that many companies have made excellent progress on specific measures for their financial, customer, innovation and operating processes virtually no effort has been devoted to measuring the outcomes relating to the above three categories. As companies implement management processes based on the balanced scorecard framework more creative and customized measures relating to the learning and growth perspective are expected to emerge.

ployee capabilities

ton observed that most companies use three common core measurement loyee satisfaction, employee retention and employee productivity. he employee satisfaction objective is generally considered to be the vo measures. Satisfied employees are normally a pre-condition for tisfaction. Many companies periodically measure employee satis- ypically, they are requested to specify on a scale, ranging from isfied, their score for a list of questions that seek to measure example, questions may relate to involvement in decisions and active encouragement to be creative and to use one's initiative. An aggregate index is constructed which can be analysed on a departmental or divisional basis.

Employee retention can be measured by the annual percentage of key staff that leave and many different methods can be used to measure employee productivity. A generic measure of employee productivity that can be applied throughout the organization and compared with different divisions is the sales revenue per employee.

Information system capabilities

For employees to be effective in today's competitive environment they need excellent information on customers, internal processes and the financial consequences of their decisions. Measures of strategic information availability suggested by Kaplan and Norton include percentage of processes with real time quality, cycle time and cost feedback available and the percentage of customer-facing employees having on-line information about customers. These measures seek to provide an indication of the availability of internal process information to front-line employees.

Motivation, empowerment and alignment

The number of suggested improvements per employee is proposed as a measure relating to having motivated and empowered employees. The performance drivers for individual and organizational alignment focus on whether departments and individuals have their goals aligned with the company objectives articulated in the balanced scorecard. A suggested outcome measure is the percentage of employees with personal goals aligned to the balanced scorecard and the percentage of employees who achieve personal goals.

Performance measurement in service organizations

Although Kaplan and Norton illustrate how the balanced scorecard can be applied in both the manufacturing and service sectors much of the performance measurement literature concen- trates on the manufacturing sector. To remed this deficiency this section focuses performance measurement in the service se Based on their research into the manage accounting practices of a range of compa several different service industries Fitzg *al.* (1989) identified four uniq distinguishing service compa turing organizations. First, most services are intangible. Fitzgerald

> *In travelling on a particular airline the customer will be influ of the seat, the meals served, the attitudes and confidence o boarding process and so on. This makes managing and co complex because it is difficult to establish exactly what a buying; is it the journey or the treatment? (Fitzgerald e*

Secondly, service outputs vary from day to day, since services tend to be provided by individuals whose performance is subject to variability that significantly affects the service quality the customer receives. Thirdly, the production and consumption of many services are inseparable such as in taking a rail journey. Fourthly, services are perishable and cannot be stored. Fitzgerald *et al.* illustrate this characteristic with a hotel, which contains a fixed number of rooms. If a room is unoccupied, the sales opportunity is lost for ever and the resource is wasted.

With regard to the control of the intangible aspects, the authors found that companies used the following methods to measure performance:

1 *Measures of satisfaction after the service.* The most common method was the monitoring and analysis of letters of complaint, but some companies interviewed samples of customers or used questionnaires to ascertain the customers' perception of service quality.

2 *Measures during the service.* An approach used by some companies was for management to make unannounced visits, with the aim of observing the quality of service offered. Another mechanism was the use of mystery shoppers', where staff employed by external agencies were sent out to sample the service as customers and formally report back on their findings.

3 *Tangibles as surrogates for intangibles.* The researchers observed that some firms used internal measures of tangible aspects of the service as indicators of how the customers might perceive the service. Some companies measured waiting times and the conditions of the waiting environment as surrogates of customers' satisfaction with the service.

Fitzgerald *et al.* also draw attention to the importance of relating the performance measures to the corporate and marketing strategies of the organizations. For example, if the delivery of high quality service is seen to be a key strategic variable then quality measures should be the dominant performance measures. On the other hand, if a low cost of the service relative to competitors is seen as the key strategic variable then strict adherence to budgets will be a key feature of the control system. There is also a greater danger in service organizations of focusing excessively on financial performance measures, which can be easily quantified, thus placing an undue emphasis on maximizing short-term performance, even if this conflicts with maximizing long-term performance. Consequently, it is more important in service organizations that a range of non-financial performance indicators be developed providing better predictors for the attainment of long-term profitability goals.

In developing an overall framework for a performance measurement system in the service sector Moon and Fitzgerald (1996) draw off the approach advocated by Otley (1987), that is common to all performance measurement systems. Otley suggests that there is a need to answer the following three basic questions when forming the basic uilding blocks of a performance measurement system:

1 What are the *dimensions* of performance that the organization is seeking to encourage?

e appropriate *standards* to be set?

rds and/or penalties are to be associated with the achievement of e targets?

of performance measurement

advocate the measurement of service business performance ey propose that managers of every service organization need to develop their own set of performance measures across the six dimensions to monitor the continued relevance of their competitive strategy. Exhibit 23.5 shows the six dimensions with examples of types of performance measures for each dimension. You should note that the dimensions fall into two conceptually different categories. Competitiveness and financial performance reflect the success of the chosen strategy (i.e. ends or results). The remaining four dimensions (quality, flexibility, resource utilization and innovation) are the drivers or determinants that determine competitive success. Fitzgerald *et al.* conclude that the design of a balanced range of performance measures should be dependent upon the company's service type, competitive environment and chosen strategy.

Moon and Fitzgerald (1996) point out the similarities between the Fitzgerald *et al.* framework and the balanced scorecard. Both frameworks emphasize the need to link performance measures to corporate strategy, include external (customer type) as well as internal measures, include non-financial as well as financial measures and make explicit the trade-offs between the various measures of performance. In addition, both frameworks distinguish between 'results' of actions taken and the 'drivers' or 'determinants' of future performance. The balanced scorecard complements financial measures with operational measures on customer satisfaction, internal processes, and the organization's innovation and improvement activities that are the drivers of future financial performance' (Kaplan and Norton, 1992). The Fitzgerald *et al.* framework specifies that measures of financial performance and competitiveness are the 'results' of actions previously taken and reflect the success of the chosen strategy. The remaining four dimensions (quality, flexibility, resource utilization and innovation) are the factors or drivers that determine competitive success, either now or in the future. The objective of both approaches is to ensure that a balanced set of performance measures is used so that no dimension is overly stressed to the detriment of another.

Setting standards of performance

The second of Otley's questions relates to the setting of appropriate standards once the actual dimensions and performance measures have been established. This involves consideration of who sets the standards, at what levels the standards are set and whether the standards facilitate comparison across business units.

Determining who sets the standards requires a consideration of whether the standards should be imposed on subordinates by their superiors or whether subordinates should be able to fully participate in the setting of standards. The level of achievability influences both the aspiration level and performance. The general conclusion that emerges from th literature is that performance is maximized by setting challenging targets. Finall relative comparisons are only likely to be appropriate where business units face simi environmental and business conditions. For a more detailed discussion of the a issues you should refer back to Chapter 16.

Linking rewards to the achievement of performance measures

The reward structure is concerned with motivating individuals performance measures. Motivation is maximized when indivi the organization is trying to do, what is expected of them, and own contribution to the organization's performance in m

EXHIBIT 23.5
Performance measures for service organizations

	Dimensions of performance	Types of measures
Results	Competitiveness	Relative market share and position
		Sales growth
		Measures of the customer base
	Financial performance	Profitability
		Liquidity
		Capital structure
		Market ratios
	Quality of service	Reliability
		Responsiveness
		Aesthetics/appearance
		Cleanliness/tidiness
Determinants		Comfort
		Friendliness
		Communication
		Courtesy
		Competence
		Access
		Availability
		Security
	Flexibility	Volume flexibility
		Delivery speed flexibility
		Specification flexibility
	Resource utilization	Productivity
		Efficiency
	Innovation	Performance of the innovation process
		Performance of individual innovations

Source: Fitzgerald *et al.*, 1991

appraised. In addition, there is a need to determine the types of rewards and penalties that will apply on achievement or non-achievement of the performance targets. Rewards can take many forms including monetary, promotion, recognition, praise, etc.

mmary

ems relate to the learning objectives listed at the beginning of the chapter.

ferent elements of strategic management accounting.

ty that strategic management accounting has received there is still no
ceptual framework of what strategic management accounting is.
of consensus on what constitutes strategic management accounting
ve been identified in the literature to characterize strategic
have been described. Three elements can be identified: (a) the
management accounting's internal focus to include external

information about competitors; (b) the relationship between the strategic position chosen by a firm and the expected emphasis on management accounting; and (c) gaining competitive advantage by analysing ways to decrease costs and/or enhance the differentiation of a firm's products, through exploiting linkages in the value chain and optimizing cost drivers. Some authors have adopted a broader view of strategic management accounting that encompasses activity-based costing, target costing and the cost management approaches described in the previous chapter.

- **Describe the balanced scorecard.**

  Recent developments in performance evaluation have sought to integrate financial and non-financial measures and assist in clarifying, communicating and managing strategy. The balanced scorecard attempts to meet these requirements. It requires that managers view the business from the following four different perspectives: (a) customer perspective (how do customers see us?); (b) internal business process perspective (what must we excel at?); (c) learning and growth perspective (can we continue to improve and create value?), and (d) financial perspective (how do we look to shareholders?). Organizations should articulate the major goals for each of the four perspectives and then translate these goals into specific performance measures. Each organization must decide what are its critical performance measures. The choice will vary over time and should be linked to the strategy that the organization is following.

- **Explain each of the four perspectives of the balanced scorecard.**

  The financial perspective provides performance measures relating to the financial outcomes of past actions. Thus, it provides feedback on the success of pursuing the objectives identified for the other three perspectives. In the customer perspective managers identify the customer and market segments in which the businesses unit will compete. Performance measures should be developed within this perspective that track a business unit's ability to create satisfied and loyal customers in the targeted segments. They include market share, customer retention, new customer acquisition, customer satisfaction and customer profitability. In the internal business perspective, managers identify the critical internal processes for which the organization must excel in implementing its strategy. The internal business process measures should focus on the internal processes that will have the greatest impact on customer satisfaction and achieving the organization's financial objectives. The principal internal business processes include the innovation processes, operation processes and post-service sales processes. The final perspective on the balanced scorecard identifies the infrastructure that the business must build to create long-term growth and improvement. The following three categories have been identified as falling within this perspective: employee capabilities, information system capabilities and motivation, empowerment and alignment.

- **Provide illustrations of performance measures for each of the four perspectives**

  Within the financial perspective examples include economic value added and resi income. Market share and customer satisfaction are generic measures withi customer perspective. Typical internal business perspective measures i percentage of sales from new products (innovation processes), cycle tim as manufacturing cycle efficiency (operation processes) and percen customers (post-service sales processes). Measures of employee s generic measures within the learning and growth satisfaction.

- **Describe the distinguishing characteristics of service organiz performance measurement.**

  Four unique characteristics distinguishing service compa organizations can be identified. They are (a) most servic outputs vary from day to day, since services tend to be provided by individuals whose performance is subject to variability that significantly affects the service quality the customer receives; (c) the production and consumption of many services are inseparable such as in taking a rail journey; and (d) services are perishable and cannot be stored. For example, a hotel contains a fixed number of rooms. If a room is unoccupied, the sales opportunity is lost forever and the resource is wasted.

Note

1 This illustration has been derived from Shank (1989).

Key terms and concepts

balanced scorecard (p. 1001)
brand value budgeting (p. 998)
brand value monitoring (p. 998)
competitive position monitoring (p. 997)
competitor cost assessment (p. 998)
competitor performance appraisal (p. 997)
cost measures (p. 1012)
customer perspective (p. 1001)
cycle time measures (p. 1011)
financial perspective (p. 1001)
internal business process perspective (p. 1001)
lagging measures (p. 1002)
leading measures (p. 1002)
learning and growth perspective (p. 1001)
learning curve (p. 993)
manufacturing cycle efficiency (MCE) (p. 1011)
quality measures (p. 1012)
strategic costing (p. 998)
strategic management accounting (p. 992)
strategic pricing (p. 997)
target costing (p. 997)
time-based measures (p. 1008)
value-chain analysis (p. 995)
value-chain costing (p. 998)
value propositions (p. 1008)

Recommended reading

For a more detailed discussion of the elements of strategic management accounting you should refer to the articles by Lord (1996) or Roslender (1995, 1996), and Roslender and Hart (2002, 2003). Research relating to a survey of strategic management accounting practices is presented in Guilding *et al.* (2000). Kaplan and Norton designed the balanced scorecard and in their writings they describe its development and the experiences of companies that have implemented it. This chapter has summarised Kaplan and Norton's writings but for a more detailed description of their work you should refer to the books they have written on the balance scorecard – *Translating Strategy into Action: The Balance Scorecard* (1996b) and *The Strategy-Focused Organization (2001a)*. See also Kaplan and Norton (2001b) and Epstein and Manzoni (1998) for shorter articles on the balanced scorecard. You should refer to the writings of Norreklit (2000, 2003) for a critique of the balanced scorecard. For a broader description of performance measurement linked to strategy you should refer to Simons (1998).

Key examination points

Strategic management accounting and the balanced scorecard are relatively new topics so they have not been extensively examined in the past. Consequently fewer past examination questions are included in this chapter. Strategic management accounting can be viewed as incorporating a wide range of topics. In addition, other approaches to performance measurement have been examined that do not adopt a balanced scorecard perspective. Therefore some questions are included that do not relate directly to the chapter content. However, where questions are set on performance measurement you should try and adopt a balanced scorecard approach by emphasizing the need to integrate financial and non-financial measures and link performance measurement to an organization's strategies.

Assessment material

Review questions

The review questions are short questions that enable you to assess your understanding of the main topics included in the chapter. The numbers in parentheses provide you with the page numbers to refer to if you cannot answer a specific question.

Review problems

The review problems are more complex and require you to relate and apply the chapter content to various business problems. Fully worked solutions to the review problems are provided in a separate section at the end of the book. For those questions in the white box the worked solutions are provided in the *Student's Manual* accompanying this book. Further review problems for this chapter are available on the accompanying website www.drury-online.com. The answers to these problems are available for lecturers on the lecturer's password protected section of the website.

Case studies

The website also includes over 30 case study problems. A list of these cases is provided in Part Seven of this book. Several cases are relevant to the content of this chapter. The Baldwin Bicycles, Brunswick Plastics and Sheridan Carpet Company cases include elements of strategic management accounting.

Review questions

23.1 Provide a definition of strategic management accounting. (*p. 992*)

23.2 Describe the three major strands of strategic management accounting that can be identified from the literature. (*pp. 993–95*)

23.3 How do different competitive strategies influence the emphasis that is given to particular management accounting techniques? (*pp. 994–95*)

23.4 What is the purpose of a balanced scorecard? (*p. 1001*)

23.5 Describe the four perspectives of the balanced scorecard. (*pp. 1001–02*)

23.6 Explain the differences between lag measures and lead measures. (*p. 1002*)

23.7 Explain what is meant by cause-and-effect relationships within the balanced scorecard. (*pp. 1001–02*)

23.8 Discuss the benefits and limitations of the balanced scorecard. *(p. 1004)*

23.9 Improving non-financial measures in the balanced scorecard will result in improvements in the financial measures. Therefore there is no need to incorporate the financial perspective within the scorecard. Discuss. *(p. 1006)*

23.10 Identify and describe the core objectives of the customer perspective. *(pp. 1007–08)*

23.11 Describe the three principal internal business processes that can be included within the internal business perspective. *(pp. 1009–13)*

23.12 What is manufacturing cycle efficiency? *(p. 1011)*

23.13 Describe three principal categories within the learning and growth perspective. *(pp. 1013–14)*

23.14 Provide examples of performance measures within each of the four perspectives of the balanced scorecard. *(pp. 1005–14)*

23.15 Describe the four unique characteristics distinguishing service companies from manufacturing organizations. *(pp. 1014–15)*

Review problems

23.16 Advanced: Financial and non-financial performance measures

BS Ltd provides consultancy services to small and medium sized businesses. Three types of consultants are employed offering administrative, data processing and marketing advice respectively. The consultants work partly on the client's premises and partly in BS Ltd premises, where chargeable development work in relation to each client contract will be undertaken. Consultants spend some time negotiating with potential clients attempting to secure contracts from them. BS Ltd has recently implemented a policy change which allows for a number of follow-up (remedial) hours at the client's premises after completion of the contract in order to eliminate any problems which have arisen in the initial stages of operation of the system. Contract negotiation and remedial work hours are not charged directly to each client. BS Ltd carries out consultancy for new systems and also to offer advice on existing systems which a client may have introduced before BS Ltd became involved. BS Ltd has a policy of retaining its consultancy staff at a level of 60 consultants on an ongoing basis.

Additional information for the year ended 30 April is as follows:

(i) BS Ltd invoices clients £75 per chargeable consultant hour.

(ii) Consultant salaries are budgeted at an average per consultant of £30 000 per annum. Actual salaries include a bonus for hours in excess of budget paid for at the budgeted average rate per hour.

(iii) Sundry operating costs (other than consultant salaries) were budgeted at £3 500 000. Actual was £4 100 000.

(iv) BS Ltd capital employed (start year) was £6 500 000.

(v) Table 1 shows an analysis of sundry budgeted and actual quantitative data.

Required:

(a) (i) Prepare an analysis of actual consultancy hours for the year ended 30 April which shows the increase or decrease from the standard/allowed non-chargeable hours. This increase or decrease should be analysed to show the extent to which it may be shown to be attributable to a change from standard in:

1. standard chargeable hours; 2. remedial advice hours; 3. contract negotiation hours; 4. other non-chargeable hours.

(13 marks)

(ii) Calculate the total value of each of 1 to 4 in (a) above in terms of chargeable client income per hour.

(4 marks)

(b) BS Ltd measure business performance in a number of ways. For each of the undernoted measures, comment on the performance of BS Ltd using quantitative data from the question and your answer to (a) to assist in illustrating your answer:

(i) Financial performance

(ii) Competitive performance

(iii) Quality of service

(iv) Flexibility

(v) Resource utilization

(vi) Innovation.

(18 marks)
(Total 35 marks)

Table 1: BS Ltd Sundry statistics for year ended 30 April

	Budget	**Actual**
Number of consultants:		
Administration	30	23
Data processing	12	20
Marketing	18	17
Consultants hours analysis:		
contract negotiation hours	4 800	9 240
remedial advice hours	2 400	7 920
other non-chargeable hours	12 000	22 440
general development work hours (chargeable)	12 000	6 600
customer premises contract hours	88 800	85 800
Gross hours	120 000	132 000
Chargeable hours analysis:		
new systems	70%	60%
existing systems advice	30%	40%
Number of clients enquiries received:		
new systems	450	600
existing systems advice	400	360
Number of client contracts worked on:		
new systems	180	210
existing systems advice	300	288
Number of client complaints	5	20
Contracts requiring remedial advice	48	75

ACCA Paper 9 Information for Control and Decision Making

23.17 Advanced: Financial and non-financial performance measurement in a service organization

The owners of *The Eatwell Restaurant* have diversified business interests and operate in a wide range of commercial areas. Since buying the restaurant in 1997 they have carefully recorded the data below.

Recorded Data for The Eatwell Restaurant (1998–2001)

	1998	1999	2000	2001
Total meals served	3 750	5 100	6 200	6 700
Regular customers attending weekly	5	11	15	26
Number of items on offer per day	4	4	7	9
Reported cases of food poisoning	4	5	7	7
Special theme evenings introduced	0	3	9	13
Annual operating hours with no customers	380	307	187	126
Proposals submitted to cater for special events	10	17	29	38
Contracts won to cater for special events	2	5	15	25
Complimentary letters from satisfied customers	0	4	3	6
Average number of customers at peak times	18	23	37	39
Average service delay at peak time (mins)	32	47	15	35
Maximum seating capacity	25	25	40	40
Weekly opening hours	36	36	40	36
Written complaints received	8	12	14	14
Idle time	570	540	465	187
New meals introduced during the year	16	8	27	11
Financial Data	£	£	£	£
Average customer spend on wine	3	4	4	7
Total Turnover	83 000	124 500	137 000	185 000
Turnover from special events	2 000	13 000	25 000	55 000
Profit	11 600	21 400	43 700	57 200
Value of food wasted in preparation	1 700	1 900	3 600	1 450
Total turnover of all restaurants in locality	895 000	1 234 000	980 000	1 056 000

Required:

(a) Assess the overall performance of the business and submit your comments to the owners. They wish to compare the performance of the restaurant with their other business interests and require your comments to be grouped into the key areas of performance such as those described by Fitzgerald and Moon.

(14 marks)

(b) Identify any additional information that you would consider of assistance in assessing the performance of *The Eatwell Restaurant* in comparison with another restaurant. Give reasons for your selection and explain how they would relate to the key performance area categories used in (a).

(6 marks)
(Total 20 marks)
ACCA Paper 3.3 – Performance Management

23.18 **Advanced**

CM Limited was formed ten years ago to provide business equipment solutions to local businesses. It has separate divisions for research, marketing, product design, technology and communication services, and now manufactures and supplies a wide range of business equipment (copiers, scanners, printers, fax machines and similar items).

To date it has evaluated its performance using monthly financial reports that analyse profitability by type of equipment.

The Managing Director of CM Limited has recently returned from a course on which it had been suggested that the 'Balanced Scorecard' could be a useful way of measuring performance.

Required:

(a) Explain the 'Balanced Scorecard' and how it could be used by CM Limited to measure its performance.

(13 marks)

While on the course, the Managing Director of CM Limited overheard someone mention how the performance of their company had improved after they introduced 'Benchmarking'.

Required:

(b) Explain 'Benchmarking' and how it could be used to improve the performance of CM Limited.

(12 marks)
(Total 25 marks)
CIMA Management Accounting – Performance Management

23.19 **Advanced**

The concept of Generic Strategies was established by Professor Michael Porter during the 1980s. He stated that a company must choose one of these strategies in order to compete and gain sustainable competitive advantage. In addition to assessing the source of competitive advantage. Porter also explained that it was necessary to identify the target for the organization's products or services. This involved distinguishing between whether the target was broad and covered the majority of the overall market, or narrow and concentrated on a small but profitable part of it.

Requirements:

(a) Critically appraise the value of Porter's Generic Strategy model for strategic planning purposes.

(12 marks)

(b) Explain how the theoretical principles of the Experience Curve may be applied to determine a generic strategy for a company.

(8 marks)
(Total 20 marks)
CIMA Stage 4 Strategic Management Accountancy and Marketing

23.20 **Advanced**

The introduction of improved quality into products has been a strategy applied by many organizations to obtain competitive advantage. Some organizations believe it is necessary to improve levels of product quality if competitive advantage is to be preserved or strengthened.

Requirement:

Discuss how a management accountant can assist an organization to achieve competitive advantage by measuring the increase in added value from improvement in its product quality.

(20 marks)

CIMA Stage 4 Strategic Management Accounting and Marketing

23.21 **Advanced: Performance measurement in non-profit organizations**

(a) The absence of the profit measure in Not for Profit (NFP) organizations causes problems for the measurement of their efficiency and effectiveness.

You are required to explain:

(i) why the absence of the profit measure should be a cause of the problems referred to

(9 marks)

(ii) how these problems extend to activities within business entities which have a profit motive. Support your answer with examples.

(4 marks)

(b) A public health clinic is the subject of a scheme to measure its efficiency and effectiveness. Amongst a number of factors, the 'quality of care provided' has been included as an aspect of the clinic's service to be measured. Three features of 'quality of care provided' have been listed:

Clinic's adherence to appointment times
Patients' ability to contact the clinic and make appointments without difficulty
The provision of a comprehensive patient health monitoring programme.

You are required to:

(i) suggest a set of quantitative measures which can be used to identify the effective level of achievement of each of the features listed;

(9 marks)

(ii) indicate how these measures could be combined into a single 'quality of care' measure.

(3 marks)

(Total 25 marks)

CIMA Stage 4 Management Accounting – Control and Audit

Review problems (with answers in the Student's Manual)

23.22 **Advanced**

Thomas Sheridan, writing in *Management Accounting* in February 1989, pointed out that Japanese companies have a different approach to cost information with 'the emphasis – based on physical measures', and 'the use of non-financial indices, particularly at shop floor level'. He argues that their approach is much more relevant to modern conditions than traditional cost and management accounting practices.

You are required

(a) to explain what is meant by 'physical measures' and 'non-financial indices';

(3 marks)

(b) to give *three* examples of non-financial indices that might be prepared, with a brief note of what information each index would provide.

(5 marks)

(c) What existing cost and management accounting practices do you consider inappropriate in modern conditions?

(9 marks)

(Total 17 marks)

CIMA Stage 3 Management Accounting Techniques

23.23 **Advanced**

Discuss the advantages which may be claimed for Kaplan and Norton's balanced scorecard as a basis for performance measurement over traditional management accounting views of performance measurement. Your answer should include specific examples of quantitative measures for each aspect of the balanced scorecard.

(15 marks)

23.24 **Advanced**

'Product costing and pricing strategies will interact in helping to achieve competitive advantage leading to retention or increase of market share and maintenance or improvement of profit levels.'

(a) Discuss this statement in the context of:

(i) Cost leadership;

(ii) Product differentiation.

(7 marks)

(b) Discuss the role of the following in the context of the above statement:

(i) Penetration pricing;

(ii) An activity based approach to pricing.

(8 marks)

(Total 15 marks)

23.25 Advanced: Financial and non-financial performance measures

Compuaid Ltd provides advisory services to home computer customers. Three types of advisor are employed offering advice by telephone, written/e-mail replies and home visits respectively.

Appendix 1.1 shows sundry statistics for the past 12 month period for Compuaid Ltd and also for two competitor companies A and B.

Additional information relating to Compuaid Ltd for the past 12 month period is as follows:

(i) Home visit travel and remedial work hours are not charged directly to customers.

(ii) All service workers incur some 'idle time' which is not charged directly to customers.

(iii) A number of customers pay a fixed annual fee of £100 for the advisory service. This entitles them to 24 hour priority access to the service and a maximum of five hours of advice without further charge.

Appendix 1.1 shows the total hours of advice (both budget and actual) taken up by customers. Assume that no customer requires more than the five hours allowable.

(iv) All other time for the advisory service and home visits is billed to customers at £20 per hour.

(v) The budgeted wage rate per hour for advisory service staff is £8. This was also the actual rate paid.

(vi) Sundry operating expenses (other than advisor wages) were budgeted at £950 000. Actual operating expenses incurred were £1 000 000.

Actual information for the period under review for competitor companies A and B is as follows:

(i) Similar policies to those used by Compuaid Ltd are operated with regard to idle time, home visit travel and remedial hours.

(ii) Fixed annual fee advisory service schemes, similar to that of Compuaid Ltd, are operated. The annual fee charged per customer by company A and company B is £75 and £100 respectively.

(iii) Other revenue and cost information is as follows:

	Company A £	**Company B** £
Total revenue (excluding annual fee income):		
Enquiry advice	756 180	1 266 000
Home visits	87 500	810 000
Total wage costs	720 000	1 099 000
Sundry operating expenses	650 000	1 250 000

Required:

(a) (i) Prepare budgeted and actual profit and loss accounts for the 12 month period under review for Compuaid Ltd and also actual profit and loss accounts for companies A and B.

(8 marks)

The Application of Quantitative Methods to Management Accounting

In this part we examine the application of quantitative methods to various aspects of management accounting. In Chapters 12 and 19 we considered how probability theory and normal distribution theory were applied to decision-making and the investigation of variances; Chapters 24–26 now look at the further applications of quantitative methods to management accounting.

Chapter 24 examines the contribution of mathematical and statistical techniques in determining cost behaviour patterns for cost–volume–profit analysis and the planning and control of costs and revenues. Chapter 25 concentrates on the application of quantitative models to determine the optimum investment in inventories. We also consider in this chapter how the performance evaluation system conflicts with the optimum quantitative decision models. Chapter 26 looks at the application of linear programming to decision-making and planning and control activities.

Rather than delaying the chapters on the application of quantitative techniques to management accounting until Part Six you may prefer to read Chapter 24 immediately after reading Chapter 8 on cost–volume–profit analysis. Chapter 25 is self-contained and may be assigned to follow any of the chapters in Part Four. Chapter 26 should be read only after you have studied Chapter 9.

Cost estimation and cost behaviour

24

Determining how cost will change with output or other measurable factors of activity is of vital importance for decision-making, planning and control. The preparation of budgets, the production of performance reports, the calculation of standard costs and the provision of relevant costs for pricing and other decisions all depend on reliable estimates of costs and distinguishing between fixed and variable costs, at different activity levels.

Unfortunately, costs are not easy to predict, since they behave differently under different circumstances. For example, costs may behave differently when they are tightly controlled compared with a situation where control is relaxed or removed. Direct labour can be classified as a variable cost where a company uses casual labour hired on a daily basis so that the employment of labour can be exactly matched to meet the production requirements. In contrast, direct labour may be classified as a step-fixed cost for activities where a fixed number of people are employed and this number is maintained even when there is a temporary reduction in the quantity of the activity used.

Depreciation is often quoted as a non-variable cost (also known as a fixed cost), but it may well be variable if asset value declines in direct proportion to usage. Therefore we

LEARNING OBJECTIVES

After studying this chapter, you should be able to:

- identify and describe the different methods of estimating costs;
- calculate regression equations using the high–low, scattergraph and least-squares techniques;
- describe multiple regression analysis and indicate the circumstances when it should be used;
- identify and explain the requirements which should be observed when using statistical regression analysis;
- identify and explain the six steps required to estimate cost functions from past data;
- describe the learning curve and compute the average and incremental labour hours for different output levels;
- describe three situations when the learning curve can be applied.

cannot generalize by categorizing direct labour as a variable cost and depreciation as a non-variable cost.

Many costs are fairly easy to classify as purely variable (e.g. direct materials), fixed (e.g. rental of equipment), or step-fixed (e.g. labour costs) but others fall into a mixed-cost category (also known as semi-variable costs). In Chapter 2 it was pointed out that a semi-variable cost is a cost that has both a fixed and variable component. For example, the cost of maintenance is a semi-variable cost consisting of planned maintenance that is undertaken whatever the activity, and a variable element that is directly related to activity. Thus, it is the semi-variable costs that we need to separate into their fixed and variable categories.

Frequently the only information that is available for a semi-variable cost is the cost of the activity and a measure of activity usage. For example, records may only be available for the total cost of the maintenance activity for a given period and the number of maintenance hours used during that period. To separate the total cost into its fixed and variable elements it is necessary to use one of the techniques described in this chapter.

Whether a cost is fixed or variable with respect to a particular activity measure or cost driver is also affected by the length of the time span under consideration. The longer the time span the more likely the cost will be variable. For example, maintenance staff salaries are likely to be fixed in the short run and will thus remain unchanged when the volume of maintenance hours changes. However, in the long run, maintenance salaries are likely to vary with the maintenance time required. If maintenance activity expands, extra staff will be appointed but, if activity contracts, staff will be redeployed or made redundant. It is therefore important to specify the length of the time period under consideration when predicting costs for different activity levels.

The importance of accurately estimating costs and the complexity of cost behaviour means that accountants must use increasingly sophisticated techniques. Advances in information technology have made it possible for more sophisticated techniques to be used for estimating costs, even by small businesses. These development have led to an increasing awareness of the important potential of mathematical and statistical techniques for estimating costs, and it is the aim of this chapter to provide an understanding of these techniques.

Some non-mathematical techniques will also be explained so that you can assess the additional benefits that can be obtained from using the more sophisticated techniques. We shall then examine the effect of experience on cost, which is normally referred to as the learning curve. The emphasis in this chapter will be on manufacturing costs, and we shall consider various techniques for estimating how these costs change with activity; similar techniques, however, can be applied to non-manufacturing costs that change with activity.

A major objective of this chapter is to ascertain the **activity measure** or **cost driver** that exerts the major influence of the cost of a particular activity. A cost driver can be defined as any factor whose change causes a change in the total cost of an activity. Examples of cost drivers include direct labour hours, machine hours, units of output and number of production run set-ups. Throughout this chapter the terms cost-driver' and 'activity measure' will be used synonymously.

General principles applying to estimating cost functions

Before we consider the various methods that are appropriate for estimating costs, we need to look at some of the terms that will be used. A **regression equation** identifies an estimated relationship between a dependent variable (cost) and one or more independent variables (i.e. an activity measure or cost driver) *based on past observations*. When the equation includes only one independent variable, it is referred to as **simple regression** and it is possible in this situation to plot the regression equation on a graph as a regression line. When the equation includes two or more independent variables, it is referred to as **multiple regression**. If there is only one independent variable and the relationship is linear, the regression line can be described by the equation for a straight line:

$$y = a + bx$$

Assuming that we wish to express the relationship between the **dependent variable** (cost) and the **independent variable** (activity), then

y = total cost for the period at an activity level of x

a = total non-variable (fixed) cost for the period

b = average variable cost per unit of activity

x = volume of activity levels or cost driver for the period

If non-variable (fixed) costs for a particular period are £5000, the average unit variable cost is £1, and direct labour hours represent the cost driver, then

$$\text{total cost} = £5000 + [£1 \times \text{direct labour hours } (x)]$$

or

$$y = a + bx$$

so that

$$y = £5000 + £1x$$

The term **cost function** is also used to refer to a regression equation that describes the relationship between a dependent variable and one or more independent variables. Cost functions are normally estimated from past cost data and activity levels. Cost estimation begins with measuring *past* relationships between total costs and the potential drivers of those costs. The objective is to use past cost behaviour patterns as an aid to predicting future costs. Any expected changes of circumstances in the future will require past data to be adjusted in line with future expectations.

There is a danger that cost functions derived from past data may be due to a spurious correlation in the data which can end at any time without warning. High correlation is only likely to continue if the relationship between the variables is economically plausible. Cost functions should not be derived solely on the basis of past observed statistical relationships. The nature of the observed statistical relationship should make sense and be economically plausible. If these conditions do not exist one cannot be confident that the estimated relationship will be repeated when the cost function is used to predict outcomes using a different set of data.

Economic plausibility exists when knowledge of operations or logic implies that a cause-and-effect relationship may exist. For example, the number of component parts is a potential cost driver for material handling costs since the greater the number of parts the higher the material handling costs. Logic suggests that a potential cause-and-effect relationship exists.

Cost estimation methods

The following approaches to cost estimation will be examined:

1 engineering methods;
2 inspection of the accounts method;
3 graphical or scattergraph method;
4 high–low method;
5 least-squares method

These approaches differ in terms of the costs of undertaking the analysis and the accuracy of the estimated cost functions. They are not mutually exclusive and different methods may be used for different cost categories.

Engineering methods

Engineering methods of analysing cost behaviour are based on the use of engineering analyses of technological relationships between inputs and outputs – for example methods study, work sampling and time and motion studies. The approach is appropriate when there is a physical relationship between costs and the cost driver. The procedure when undertaking an engineering study is to make an analysis based on *direct* observations of the underlying physical quantities required for an activity and then to convert the final results into cost estimates. Engineers, who are familiar with the technical requirements, estimate the quantities of materials and the labour and machine hours required for various operations; prices and rates are then applied to the physical measures to obtain the cost estimates. The engineering method is useful for estimating costs of repetitive processes where input–output relationships are clearly defined. For example, this method is usually satisfactory for estimating costs that are usually associated with direct materials, labour and machine time, because these items can be directly observed and measured. However, the engineering method is not a method that can be used for separating semi-variable costs into their fixed and variable elements.

The engineering method is not restricted to manufacturing activities – time and motion studies can also be applied to well-structured administrative and selling activities such as typing, invoicing and purchasing. It is not generally appropriate, however, for estimating costs that are difficult to associate directly with individual units of output, such as many types of overhead costs, since these items cannot easily be directly observed and measured.

One disadvantage of engineering methods is that methods study, work sampling and time and motion study techniques can be expensive to apply in practice. The use of these is most appropriate when direct costs form a large part of the total costs and when input–output relationships are fairly stable over time. Engineering methods may also be applied in situations where there are no historical data to analyse past cost relationships. For an explanation of how engineering methods can be used to derive direct labour and material costs for specific operations you should refer back to Chapter 18 (pages 729–30).

Inspection of the accounts

The **inspection of accounts method** requires that the departmental manager and the accountant inspect each item of expenditure within the accounts for a particular period, and then classify each item of expense as a wholly fixed, wholly variable or a semi-variable cost. A single average *unit* cost figure is selected for the items that are categorized as variable, whereas a single *total* cost for the period is used for the items that are categorized as fixed. For semi-variable items the departmental manager and the accountant agree on a cost function that appears to best describe the cost behaviour. The process is illustrated in Example 24.1.

Note that repairs and maintenance have been classified as a semi-variable cost consisting of a variable element of £0.50 per unit of output plus £5000 non-variable cost. A check on the total cost calculation indicates that the estimate of a unit variable cost of £24.50 will give a total variable cost of £245 000 at an output level of 10 000 units. The non-variable costs of £50 000 are added to this to produce an estimated total cost of £295 000. The cost function is therefore $y = 50\,000 + £24.50x$. This cost function is then used for estimating total cost centre costs at other output levels.

You will see from this example that the analysis of costs into their variable and non-variable elements is very subjective. Also, the latest cost details that are available from the accounts will normally be used, and this may not be typical of either past or future cost behaviour. Whenever possible, cost estimates should be based on a series of observations. Cost estimates based on this method involve individual and often arbitrary judgements, and they may therefore lack the precision necessary when they are to be used in making decisions that involve large sums of money and that are sensitive to measurement errors.

Graphical or scattergraph method

This method involves plotting on a graph the total costs for each activity level. The total cost is represented on the vertical (Y axis) and the activity levels are recorded on the horizontal (X axis). A straight line is fitted to the scatter of plotted points by visual approximation. Figure 24.1 illustrates the procedure using the data presented in Example 24.2.

You will see by referring to Figure 24.1 that the maintenance costs are plotted for each activity level, and a straight line is drawn through the middle of the data points as closely as possible so that the distances of observations above the line are equal to the distances of observations below the line.

The point where the straight line in Figure 24.1 cuts the vertical axis (i.e. £240) represents the non-variable costs, item a in the regression formula $y = a + bx$. The unit variable cost b in the regression formula is found by observing the differences between any two points on the straight line (see the dashed line in Figure 24.1 for observations of 160 and 240 hours) and completing the following calculations:

$$\frac{\text{difference in cost}}{\text{difference in activity}} = \frac{£720 - £560}{240 \text{ hours} - 160 \text{ hours}} = £2 \text{ per hour}$$

This calculation is based on a comparison of the changes in costs that can be observed on the straight line between activity levels of 160 and 240 hours. This gives a regression formula.

$$y = £240 + £2x$$

If x is assigned a value of 100 hours then

$$y = 240 + (2 \times 100) = £440$$

EXAMPLE 24.1

The following cost information has been obtained from the latest monthly accounts for an output level of 10 000 units for a cost centre.

	(£)
Direct materials	100 000
Direct labour	140 000
Indirect labour	30 000
Depreciation	15 000
Repairs and maintenance	10 000
	295 000

The departmental manager and the accountant examine each item of expense and analyse the expenses into their variable and non-variable elements. The analysis might be as follows:

	Unit variable cost (£)	Total non-variable cost (£)
Direct materials	10.00	
Direct labour	14.00	
Indirect labour		30 000
Depreciation		15 000
Repairs and maintenance	0.50	5 000
	24.50	50 000

FIGURE 24.1 *Graph of maintenance costs at different activity levels*

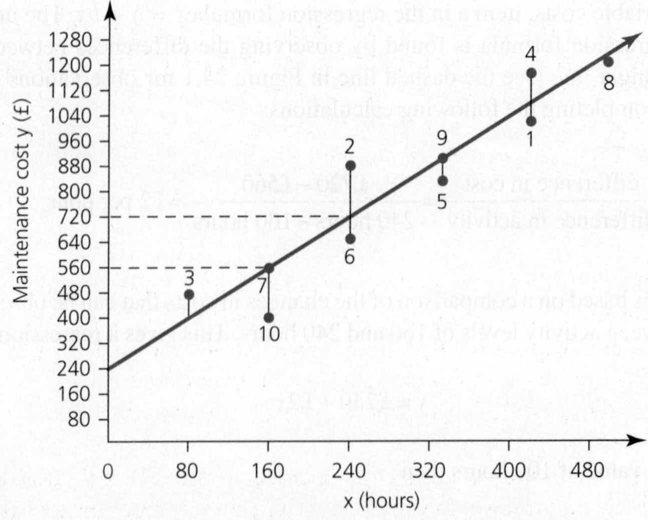

EXAMPLE 24.2

The total maintenance costs and the machine hours for the past ten four-weekly accounting periods were as follows:

Period	Machine hours x	Maintenance cost y
1	400	960
2	240	880
3	80	480
4	400	1200
5	320	800
6	240	640
7	160	560
8	480	1200
9	320	880
10	160	440

You are required to estimate the regression equation using the graphical method.

The graphical method is simple to use, and it provides a useful visual indication of any lack of correlation or erratic behaviour of costs. However, the method suffers from the disadvantage that the determination of exactly where the straight line should fall is subjective, and different people will draw different lines with different slopes, giving different cost estimates. To overcome this difficulty, it is preferable to determine the line of best fit mathematically using the least-squares method.

High–low method

The **high–low method** consists of selecting the periods of highest and lowest activity levels and comparing the changes in costs that result from the two levels. This approach is illustrated in Example 24.3.

The non-variable (fixed) cost can be estimated at any level of activity (assuming a constant unit variable cost) by subtracting the variable cost portion from the total cost. At an activity level of 5000 units the total cost is £22 000 and the total variable cost is £10 000 (5000 units at £2 per unit). The balance of £12 000 is therefore assumed to represent the non-variable cost. The cost function is therefore:

$$y = £12\,000 + £2x$$

The method is illustrated in Figure 24.2, with points A and B representing the lowest and highest output levels, and TC_1 and TC_2 representing the total cost for each of these levels. The other crosses represent past cost observations for other output levels. The straight (blue) line joining the observations for the lowest and highest activity levels represent the costs that would be estimated for each activity level when the high–low method is used.

You will see from this illustration that the method ignores all cost observations other than the observations for the lowest and highest activity levels. Unfortunately, cost observations at the extreme ranges of activity levels are not always typical of normal operating

EXAMPLE 24.3

The monthly recordings for output and maintenance costs for the past 12 months have been examined and the following information has been extracted for the lowest and highest output levels:

	Volume of production (units)	Maintenance costs (£)
Lowest activity	5 000	22 000
Highest activity	10 000	32 000

The variable cost per unit is calculated as follows:

$$\frac{\text{difference in cost}}{\text{difference in activity}} = \frac{£10\,000}{5000} = £2 \text{ variable cost per unit of output}$$

conditions, and therefore may reflect abnormal rather than normal cost relationships. Figure 24.2 indicates how the method can give inaccurate cost estimates when they are obtained by observing only the highest and lowest output levels. It would obviously be more appropriate to incorporate all of the available observations into the cost estimate, rather than to use only two extreme observations.

The lower straight (green) line, using the graphical or scattergraph approach described in the previous section, incorporates all of the observations. It is likely to provide a better estimate of the cost function than a method that relies on only two observations. The high–low method cannot therefore be recommended.

The least-squares method

This method determines mathematically the regression line of best fit. It is based on the principle that the sum of the squares of the vertical deviations from the line that is established using the method is less than the sum of the squares of the vertical deviations from any other line that might be drawn. The regression equation for a straight line that meets this requirement can be found from the following two equations by solving for a and b:

$$\sum y = Na + b\sum x \tag{24.1}$$

$$\sum xy = a\sum x + b\sum x^2 \tag{24.2}$$

where N is the number of observations.

Exhibit 24.1 is used to illustrate the **least-squares method**. It is assumed that past information is available only for total maintenance costs and machine hours used. We can now insert the data derived from Exhibit 24.1 into the above formulae but do note that spreadsheet packages have regression routines that will perform these calculations. Therefore it is unlikely that you will be required to manually perform these calculations. The computations are as follows:

$$19\,800 = 12a + 1260b \tag{24.1}$$

$$2\,394\,000 = 1260a + 163\,800b \tag{24.2}$$

FIGURE 24.2 *High–low method*

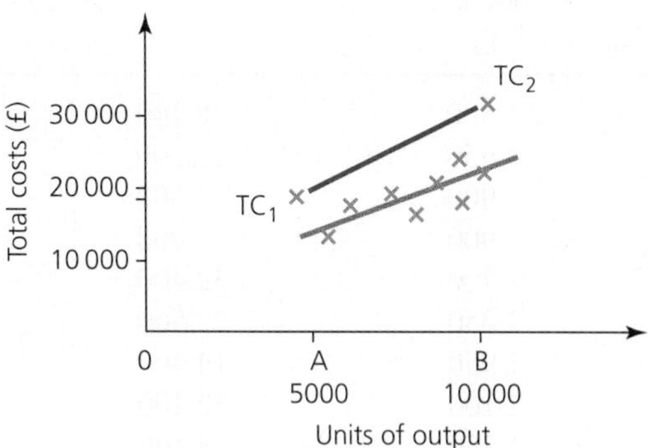

To solve for b multiply equation (24.1) by 105 (1260/12), to give

$$2\,079\,000 = 1260a + 132\,300b \tag{24.3}$$

Subtracting equation (24.3) from equation (24.2), the 'a' terms will cancel out to yield $315\,000 = 31\,500b$, so that

$$b = £10$$

Substituting this value of b into equation (24.1) and solving for a, we have

$$19\,800 = 12a + 1260 \times 10$$

and so

$$a = 600$$

Substituting these values of a and b into the regression equation $y = a + bx$, we find that the regression line (i.e. cost function) can be described by

$$y = £600 + £10x$$

We can now use this formula to predict the cost incurred at different activity levels, including those for which we have no past observations. For example, at an activity level of 100 hours the cost prediction is £600 non-variable cost, plus £1000 variable cost (100 hours × £10). The regression line and the actual observations (represented by the dots) are recorded in Figure 24.3. The closer the vertical distances of the plotted actual observations are to the straight line the more reliable is the estimated cost function in predicting cost behaviour. In other words, the closer the observations are to the line the stronger the relationship between the independent variable (machine hours in our example) and the dependent variable (i.e. total maintenance cost).

In Exhibit 24.1 the cost function was derived using machine hours as the activity measure/cost driver. However, a number of other potential cost drivers exist, such as, direct labour hours, units of output and number of production runs. Various **tests of reliability** can be applied to see how reliable potential cost drivers are in predicting the dependent variable.

EXHIBIT 24.1
Past observations of maintenance costs

Hours x	Maintenance cost y (£)	x^2	xy
90	1 500	8 100	135 000
150	1 950	22 500	292 500
60	900	3 600	54 000
30	900	900	27 000
180	2 700	32 400	486 000
150	2 250	22 500	337 500
120	1 950	14 400	234 000
180	2 100	32 400	378 000
90	1 350	8 100	121 500
30	1 050	900	31 500
120	1 800	14 400	216 000
60	1 350	3 600	81 000
$\sum x = 1260$	$\sum y = 19\,800$	$\sum x^2 = 163\,800$	$\sum xy = 2\,394\,000$

FIGURE 24.3 *Regression line y = 600 + 10x compared with actual observations*

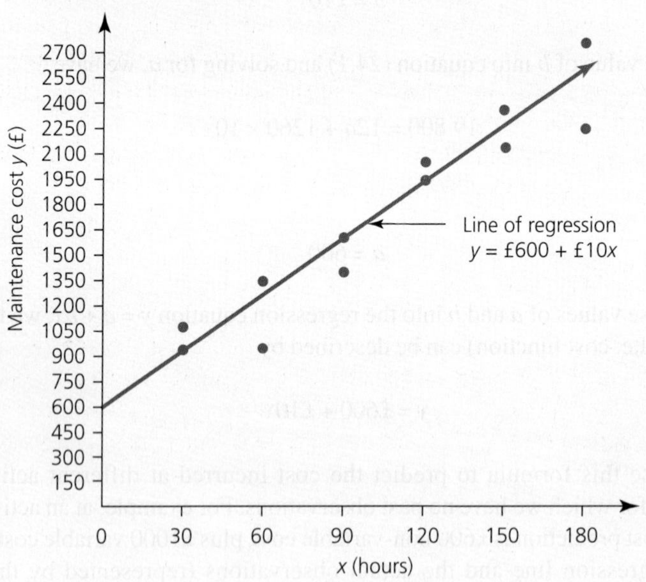

The most simplistic approach is to plot the data for each potential cost driver and examine the distances from a straight line derived either from a visual fit (using the graphical method) or the least-squares method. Alternatively, more sophisticated tests of reliability can be applied. In the appendix to this chapter three methods are described. They are the coefficient of determination, the standard error of the estimate and the standard error of the coefficient. If your curriculum requires an understanding of these methods you should read the appendix after you have completed reading the chapter. You should, however, note at this point that the coefficient of determination calculation (known as r^2) measures the percentage of variation in the dependent variable (i.e. the actual cost observations) that is explained by the independent variable (i.e. maintenance hours in our example). For the data given in Exhibit 24.1 the coefficient of determination is 0.89. This indicates that 89% of the variation in maintenance cost is explained by variations in machine hours and the remaining 11% is explained by random variations and/or the other omitted variables that are not included in the cost function.

The coefficient of determination is a **goodness-of-fit measure**. A goodness-of-fit measure indicates how well the predicted values of the dependent variable (y), based on the chosen cost driver (X), matches the actual cost observations (Y). Generally, an r^2 of 0.30 or higher passes the goodness-of-fit test but remember that the cost diver must also meet the requirement of being economically plausible. Given that a relationship between maintenance hours and maintenance cost is economically plausible, and the high r^2 score of 0.89 we can conclude that maintenance hours would appear to be a suitable cost driver. For a more detailed discussion of tests of reliability you should refer to the appendix to this chapter.

Multiple regression analysis

The least-squares regression equation was based on the assumption that total cost was determined by one activity-based variable only. However, other variables besides activity are likely to influence total cost. A certain cost may vary not only with changes in the hours of operation but also with the weight of the product being made, temperature changes or other factors. With simple least-squares regression, only one factor is taken into consideration; but with multiple regression, several factors are considered in combination. As far as possible, all the factors related to cost behaviour should be brought into the analysis so that costs can be predicted and controlled more effectively.

The equation for simple regression can be expanded to include more than one independent variable. If there are two independent variables and the relationship is assumed to be linear, the regression equation will be

$$y = a + b_1x_1 + b_2x_2$$

Item a represents the non-variable cost item. Item b_1 represents the average change in y resulting from a unit change in x_1, assuming that x_2 and all the unidentified items remain constant. Similarly, b_2 represents the average change in y resulting from a unit change in x_2 assuming that x_1 remains constant. The normal equations for a regression equation with two independent variables are

$$\sum y = aN + b_1\sum x_1 + b_2\sum x_2$$

$$\sum x_1y = a\sum x_1 + b_1\sum x_1^2 + b_2\sum x_1x_2$$

$$\sum x_2y = a\sum x_2 + b_1\sum x_1x_2 + b_2\sum x_2^2$$

The value of y can be determined by solving these equations, but the calculations are very tedious. Fortunately, spreadsheet packages are available that can generate the value of y together with details of standard errors of the individual regression coefficients. We shall therefore now concentrate on the principles and application of multiple regression analysis and ignore the tedious arithmetical calculations.

Consider a plant that generates its own steam and uses this steam for both heating and motive power. A simple least-squares regression based on machine hours is likely to provide a poor estimate of the total cost of steam generation, and will produce a relatively low coefficient of determination. The cost of steam generation is likely to be determined by both temperature and machine hours, and a multiple regression equation is therefore likely to produce a more accurate estimate of the total costs. The equation could take the form

$$y = a + b_1x_1 + b_2x_2$$

where y is the total cost, a the total non-variable cost, x_1 the number of machine hours, b_1 the regression coefficient for machine hours, x_2 the number of days per month in which the temperature is less than 15°C, and b_2 the regression coefficient for temperature. The equations for this formula can be developed by using past monthly observations of the number of machine hours, the days on which the temperature was below 15°C and the total cost. This information is used to develop equations and the result will be an output similar to the following:

$$y = 20 + 4x_1 + 12x_2$$

Estimates of total steam cost can now be developed based on the estimated machine hours and the temperature for future periods. For example, if the number of estimated machine hours for a particular month is 1000, and past experience indicates that the temperature is likely to be below 15°C for the full month of 30 days, the estimated cost will be

$$y = 20 + (4 \times 1000) + (12 \times 30) = £4380$$

The value of the coefficients b_1 and b_2 enables us to determine the marginal cost associated with each of the determining factors. For example, the value of b_1 is £4, which indicates the marginal change in the total cost for each additional machine hour with the effects of temperature remaining constant.

Multicollinearity

Multiple regression analysis is based on the assumption that the independent variables are not correlated with each other. When the independent variables are highly correlated with each other, it is very difficult, and sometimes impossible, to separate the effects of each of these variables on the dependent variable. This occurs when there is a simultaneous movement of two or more independent variables in the same direction and at approximately the same rate. This condition is called **multicollinearity**.

An example of this is where several complementary products are manufactured and the output of each product is treated as an independent variable. If the demand for each of these products is highly correlated, the output of all the products will be similar – all being high in one period and low in another period. In this situation the regression coefficients have no meaning; they cannot estimate the likely changes in cost that will arise from a unit change in given independent variables while the other dependent variables are held constant. This is because there is a lack of independence among the independent variables, which prevents the availability of sufficient information to enable the regression coefficients to be determined. However, multicollinearity does not affect the validity of the predictions of the total cost if the past relationships between the independent variables are maintained.

Multicollinearity can be found in a variety of ways. One way is to measure the correlation between the independent variables. Generally, a coefficient of correlation between independent variables greater than 0.70 indicates multicollinearity. Kaplan (1982) makes the following comment on the effect of multicollinearity and the accounting implications:

> *The collinearity problem is most severe when we are trying to obtain accurate coefficient estimates for product planning, pricing, and a cost–volume–profit analysis. If we are mainly interested in using the regression equation to predict cost behaviour in a period (i.e. as a flexible budget), then we are not concerned with the individual coefficient estimates. The standard error of the regression and of the forecasts from the regression are not affected by collinearity among subsets of the independent variables. Therefore, if the analyst feels that the correlated variables are all necessary for predicting overall costs, they can remain in the regression equation.*

Factors to be considered when using past data to estimate cost functions

Several requirements are necessary to ensure that a sound system is developed for estimating costs. If these requirements are not met, there is a danger that less accurate cost estimates will be produced, and there will be an increased probability that the quality of the information system will be impaired. Let us now consider some of these requirements.

The cost data and activity should be related to the same period

It is not uncommon for some costs to lag behind the associated activity. For example, wages paid in one period may be calculated by reference to the output from a previous period. Let us consider the following situation where a piecework system is in operation and where wages are paid on the basis of £10 per unit produced:

	Activity x (units)	Wages paid y (£)
Week 10	5000	30 000 (output for week 9 was 3000 units)
Week 11	2500	50 000
Week 12	4000	25 000

In this example the firm follows a policy of paying the labour force for the output that was achieved in the previous week. It is clearly incorrect to relate costs to output for each week when calculating the cost estimation equation. It is therefore necessary to correct the bias in the data by relating the cost in period t to the output in period $t - 1$ before the cost equation is calculated.

Number of observations

If acceptable cost estimates are to be produced, a sufficient number of observations must be obtained. If figures are used only from recent periods, there may be insufficient observations.

However, if observations other than those from previous periods are used, some adjustment of the data will be required. If insufficient observations are obtained, the standard error (see the appendix to this chapter for an explanation) is likely to be large, and the confidence intervals or ranges of costs will be quite large for each activity level. Wherever possible, many observations should be obtained over very short time periods. Weekly costs will yield considerably more observations for analysis than will monthly costs.

Accounting policies

The data must be examined to ensure that the accounting policies do not lead to distorted cost functions. For example, if *fixed* maintenance costs are allocated to production departments on the basis of the number of maintenance hours, this accounting allocation may make the fixed costs appear to be variable. There is a danger that the regression analysis will imply that these costs are variable rather than fixed. If the objective is to determine the cost behaviour pattern in a single production department, only those costs incurred within the department should be included. Allocated costs should be excluded from the analysis.

Adjustments for past changes

An analysis of past data will yield estimates of future costs that are based on the cost relationships of previous periods. The appropriateness of using past data depends on the extent to which the future will correspond with the past. Any changes of circumstances in the future will require past data to be adjusted in line with future data. For example, if it is estimated that future costs will increase by 10%, all past data should be adjusted by a price index to future price levels before the cost estimation equation is established.

It is also possible that technological changes in the production process may have taken place (such as changes in the type of equipment used), and past data must then be adjusted to reflect the circumstances which will apply in the future. Conversely, any observations from past periods that represent abnormal situations which are not expected to occur again in the future should be excluded from the analysis. The major problem is one of ensuring that a correct balance is maintained between obtaining sufficient observations to produce a reliable cost estimate, and keeping the time span short enough for the data to be appropriate to the circumstances in the future.

Relevant range and non-linear cost functions

It may be very misleading to use a cost estimation equation (cost function) to estimate the total costs for ranges of activities outside the range of observations that were used to establish the cost function. This is because a cost function is normally only valid within the range of the actual observations that were used to establish the equation.

You will see from Figure 24.4 that in the past the company has operated only between activity levels x_1 and x_2 (this represents the actual observations). A cost equation developed from this information may provide satisfactory cost estimates for activity levels between x_1 and x_2, but it may not do so for activity levels outside this range of observations. For example, the dashed line that meets the vertical axis at A might represent a cost equation that has been developed from these observations; the dashed line will represent a satisfactory estimate of total cost only between activity levels x_1 and x_2. However, any extrapolation of the dashed line outside the range of observations may result in an unsatisfactory estimate of total cost.

You will remember that in Chapter 8 it was stressed that linear cost functions may only apply over the relevant production range (i.e. between activity levels x_1, and x_2 in Figure 24.4),

FIGURE 24.4 *Effect of extrapolation costs*

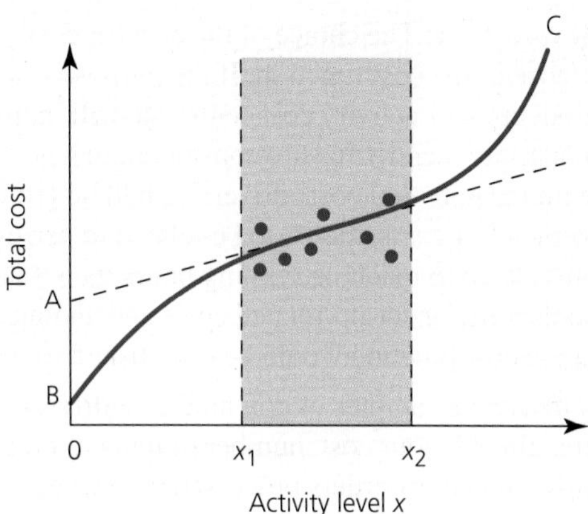

and that over a very wide range of activity a curvilinear (non-linear) relationship may exist, similar to the curved line BC in Figure 24.4. It therefore follows that the extrapolation of the dashed line represents an unsatisfactory estimate outside the relevant range if a curvilinear relationship exists. Also, the non-variable item (i.e. a in the equation $y = a + bx$) is unlikely to represent the total non-variable cost at zero activity. The cost equation in Figure 24.4 gives an estimated non-variable cost of OA compared with an actual non-variable cost of OB. Hence the value of the constant term a in the cost equation is not the amount of cost that would be expected if there were zero output; it should be interpreted only as the amount of cost that does not vary with the activity level in the activity range x_1 to x_2.

In practice, the problem of extrapolation may not occur, since the majority of decisions are normally taken within the relevant operating range over which the firm has had experience of operating in the past. However, if decisions are to be based on cost information that is projected beyond the relevant range, the cost estimates must be used with care.

To determine whether a curvilinear relationship exists, the observations should be plotted on a graph, so that a simple examination of the graph may indicate whether or not such relationships exist. Indeed, it is a good idea always to prepare graphs and look carefully at the plotted data to ensure that some of the important requirements of cost estimation are not violated – blind reliance on mathematical techniques can be very dangerous.

A summary of the steps involved in estimating cost functions

We can now summarize the stages involved in the estimation of a cost function based on the analysis of past data. They are:

1 Select the dependent variable y (the cost variable) to be predicted.

2 Select the potential cost drivers.

3 Collect data on the dependent variable and cost drivers.

4 Plot the observations on a graph.

5 Estimate the cost function.

6 Test the reliability of the cost function.

It may be necessary to undertake each of these stages several times for different potential cost drivers before an acceptable cost function can be identified.

1. *Select the dependent variable y*: The choice of the cost (or costs) to be predicted will depend upon the purpose of the cost function. If the purpose is to estimate the indirect costs of a production or activity cost centre then all indirect costs associated with the production (activity) centre that are considered to have the same cause-and-effect relationship with the potential costs drivers should be grouped together. For example, if some overheads are considered to be related to performing production set-ups and others are related to machine running hours then it may be necessary to establish two cost pools: one for set-up-related costs and another for machine-related costs. A separate cost function would be established for each cost pool.
2. *Select potential cost drivers*: Examples of potential cost drivers include direct labour hours, machine hours, direct labour cost, number of units of output, number of production run set-ups, number of orders processed and weight of materials. A knowledge of operations or activities is necessary to determine the potential cost drivers. This may mean interviewing personnel involved in specific activities to ascertain what causes a particular activity to consume resources and so incur costs. Innes and Mitchell (1992) suggest the following questions might be used to determine potential cost drivers:
   - Why are *X* number of staff needed for this activity?
   - What might cause you to need more/less staff?
   - What determines the amount of time spent on this activity?
   - Why does idle time occur?

   The end result will be a set of potential cost drivers. A potential cost driver should be plausible (i.e. make economic sense) and accurately measurable.
3. *Collect data on the dependent variable and cost drivers*: A sufficient number of past observations must be obtained to derive acceptable cost functions. The data should be adjusted to reflect any changes of circumstance, such as price changes or changes in the type of equipment used. The time period used to measure the dependent variable and the appropriate cost driver should be identical.
4. *Plot the observations on a graph*: A general indication of the relationship between the dependent variable and the cost driver can be observed from the graph. The graph will provide a visual indication as to whether a linear cost function can approximate the cost behaviour and also highlight extreme or abnormal observations. These observations should be investigated to ascertain whether they should be excluded from the analysis.
5. *Estimate the cost function*: The cost function should be estimated using the approaches described in this chapter.
6. *Test the reliability of the cost function*: The reliability of the cost function should be tested using the methods described in the Appendix of this chapter. The cost function should be plausible. A high coefficient of variation r^2 does not necessarily mean a cause-and-effect relationship between the two variables exists. It merely indicates that the two variables move together. The high correlation could be due to a spurious correlation in the data and end at any time without warning. High correlation is only likely to continue if the relationship between the variables is plausible. Cost functions should not be derived solely on the basis of observed past statistical relationships. Instead, they should be used to confirm or reject beliefs that have been developed from a study of the underlying process. The nature of the statistical relationship should be understood and make economic sense.

The intelligent application of regression analysis requires an understanding of the underlying operations. Consider maintenance costs that are scheduled to be undertaken mainly in low-production periods so that production will not be disrupted. In this situation the regression analysis will indicate that the higher the level of production, the lower the maintenance costs, and vice versa. The true underlying relationship, however, is that the higher the level of production, the higher the maintenance costs. It is therefore important that maintenance costs should not be pooled with other costs, since this might result in a failure to isolate the true relationship between maintenance costs and the level of production.

Cost estimation when the learning effect is present

Difficulties occur in estimating costs when technological changes take place in the production process: past data is not then very useful for estimating costs. For example, changes in the efficiency of the labour force may render past information unsuitable for predicting future labour costs. A situation like this may occur when workers become more familiar with the tasks that they perform, so that less labour time is required for the production of each unit. The phenomenon has been observed in a number of manufacturing situations, and is known as the **learning-curve effect**. From the experience of aircraft production during World War II, aircraft manufacturers found that the rate of improvement was so regular that it could be reduced to a formula, and the labour hours required could be predicted with a high degree of accuracy from a **learning curve**. Based on this information, experiments have been undertaken in other industries with learning curves, and these experiments also indicate some regularity in the pattern of a worker's ability to learn a new task.

The first time a new operation is performed, both the workers and the operating procedures are untried. As the operation is repeated, the workers become more familiar with the work, labour efficiency increases and the labour cost per unit declines. This process continues for some time, and a regular rate of decline in cost per unit can be established at the outset. This rate of decline can then be used in predicting future labour costs. The learning process starts from the point when the first unit comes off the production line. From then on, each time cumulative production is doubled, the average time taken to produce each unit of cumulative production will be a certain percentage of the average time per unit of the previous cumulative production.

An application of the 80% learning curve is presented in Exhibit 24.2, which shows the labour hours required on a sequence of six orders where the cumulative number of units is doubled for each order. The first unit was completed on the first order in 2000 hours; for each subsequent order the *cumulative production* was doubled (see column 3), so that the average hours per unit were 80% of the average hours per unit of the previous *cumulative production*. For example, the *cumulative average time* shown in column 4 for each unit of output is calculated as follows:

order number 1 = 2000 hours
2 = 1600 hours (80% × 2000)
3 = 1280 hours (80% × 1600)
4 = 1024 hours (80% × 1280)
5 = 819 hours (80% × 1024)
6 = 655 hours (80% × 819)

EXHIBIT 24.2
Labour hours for 80% learning curve

	Number of units		Cumulative hours		Hours for each order	
(1) Order no.	(2) Per order	(3) Cumulative production	(4) Per unit	(5) Total (3) × (4)	(6) Total	(7) Per unit (6) ÷ (2)
1	1	1	2000	2 000	2000	2000
2	1	2	1600	3 200	1200	1200
3	2	4	1280	5 120	1920	960
4	4	8	1024	8 192	3072	768
5	8	16	819	13 104	4912	614
6	16	32	655	20 960	7856	491

Exhibit 24.2 provides information for specific quantities only. No information is available for other quantities such as 10, 20 or 30 units, although such information could be obtained either graphically or mathematically.

Graphical method

The quantities for the average time per unit of cumulative production (column 4 of Exhibit 24.2) are presented in graphical form in Figure 24.5. The entries in column 4 are plotted on the graph for each level of cumulative production, and a line is drawn through these points. (You should note that more accurate graphs can be constructed if the observations are plotted on log-log graph paper.)

The graph shows that the average time per unit declines rapidly at first and then more slowly, until eventually the decline is so small that it can be ignored. When no further improvement is expected and the regular efficiency level is reached, the situation is referred to as the **steady-state production level**. The cumulative average hours per unit is 953 hours for 10 units and 762 hours for 20 units. To obtain the total number of hours, we merely multiply the average number of hours by the cumulative quantity produced, which gives 9530 total hours for 10 units and 15 240 total hours for 20 units.

Mathematical method

The learning curve can be expressed in equation form as:

$$Y_x = aX^b$$

where Y_x is defined as the cumulative average time required to produce X units, a is the time required to produce the first unit of output and X is the number of units of output under consideration. The exponent b is defined as the ratio of the logarithm of the learning curve improvement rate (e.g. 0.8 for an 80% learning curve) divided by the logarithm of 2. The improvement exponent can take on any value between -1 and zero. For example, for an 80% learning curve

$$b = \frac{\log 0.8}{\log 2} = \frac{-0.2231}{0.6931} = -0.322$$

FIGURE 24.5 *80% learning curve*

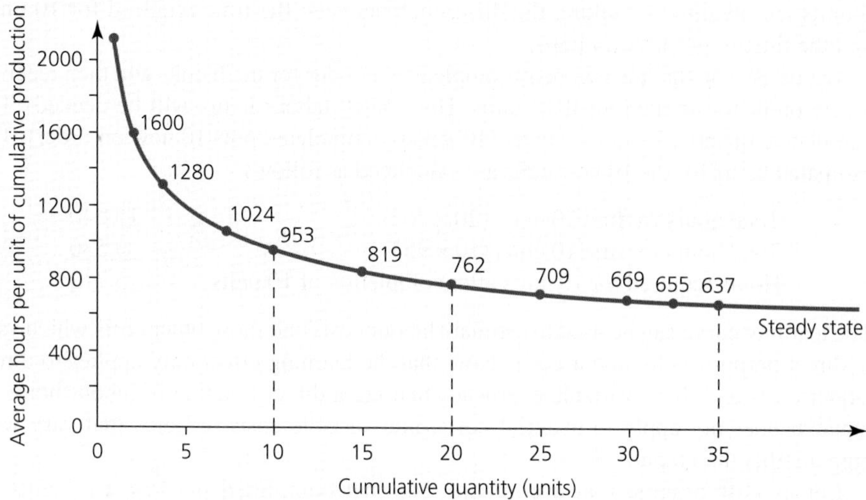

The cumulative average time taken to produce 10 and 20 units can therefore be calculated as follows:

$$Y_{10} = 2000 \times 10^{-0.322}$$
$$= 2000 \times 0.476431$$
$$= \underline{\underline{953}}$$

and

$$Y_{20} = 2000 \times 20^{-0.322}$$
$$= 2000 \times 0.381126$$
$$= \underline{\underline{762}}$$

A computation of the exponent values may be made by using either logarithm tables or a calculator with exponent functions.

Estimating incremented hours and incremental cost

Incremental hours cannot be determined directly from the learning-curve graph or formula, since the results are expressed in terms of cumulative average hours. It is possible, however, to obtain incremental hours by examining the differences between total hours for various combinations of cumulative hours. For example, assume that for Exhibit 24.2 the company has completed orders such that cumulative production is 4 units and that an enquiry has been received for an order of 6 units. We can calculate the incremental hours for these 6 units as follows:

Total hours if an additional 6 units are produced (10 × 953) (cumulative production will be 10 units)	9530
Total hours for the first 4 units (4 × 1280)	5120
Hours required for 6 units after completion of 4 units	= 4410

Note that the total hours are calculated by taking the average hours for cumulative production and multiplying by the cumulative production. The incremental hours for 6 units are obtained by taking the difference between the time required for 10 units and the time required for 4 units.

Let us assume that the company completes the order for the 6 units and then receives a new order for an additional 10 units. How many labour hours will be needed? The cumulative quantity is now 20 units (10 already completed plus 10 now on order). The estimated hours for the 10 new units are calculated as follows:

Total hours for first 20 units (20 × 762)	15 240
Total hours for first 10 units (10 × 953)	9 530
Hours required for 10 units after completion of 10 units	5 710

The learning curve can be used to estimate labour costs and those other costs which vary in direct proportion to labour costs. Note that the learning effect only applies to direct labour costs and those variable overheads that are a direct function of labour hours of input. It does not apply to material costs, non-variable costs or items that vary with output rather than input.

Let us now assume that a company has just completed the first two units of production of a new product that is subject to an 80% learning curve at a labour cost of £10 000. Assuming that the company now receives an enquiry for the production of two further units, what is the estimated labour cost and variable overhead cost if the variable overheads amount to 20% of direct labour cost? As the cumulative production will be doubled if the two units are produced, the incremental labour and variable overhead costs for the two units can be calculated as follows:

(A) Cumulative average labour cost for two first two units was £5000 (£10 000/2)

(B) Cumulative average labour cost for first four units will be £4000 (80% × £5000)

(C) The labour costs for the enquiry for the two units will be calculated as follows:

	(£)
Labour cost for 4 units (£4000 × 4)	16 000
Labour cost for 2 units	10 000
Cost for new order of 2 units	6 000

(D) The estimated labour and variable overhead costs for the 2 additional units are as follows:

	(£)
Direct labour cost	6000
Variable overheads (20% of 6000)	1200

Learning curve applications

The learning curve generally applies to those situations where the labour input for an activity is large and the activity is complex. Learning curves are not theoretical abstractions, but are based on observations of past events. When new products have been made in previous periods, the learning curve principles can be applied from the experience that has been gained. In new situations where there are no historical data the curves for previous products or processes with known improvement factors can be used if management can identify similarities with the new situation. We have considered in this chapter an 80% learning curve, but this percentage may vary, depending on the technology. In the aircraft industry studies indicated that a learning curve of 80% was appropriate, but other industries may suggest that other percentages should be applied to take account of the learning factor. Generally, the figures vary between 70% and 90%.

Unfortunately, the true nature of the learning curve associated with a new product or process will never be known. However, a reasonable assumption of its shape is better than an assumption of no learning curve at all. The learning curve may be applied to the following situations.

1 Pricing decisions

The main impact of the learning curve is likely to be in providing better cost predictions to enable price quotations to be prepared for potential orders. An ability to forecast cost reductions and consequent selling price reductions may make the difference between landing and losing profitable orders. Simmonds (1981) suggests that early experience with a *new* product could confer an unbeatable lead over competitors, and that the leading competitor should be able to reduce its selling price for the product (through the learning curve effect), which would further increase their volume and market share and eventually force some lagging competitors out of the industry.

2 Work scheduling

Learning curves enable firms to predict their required inputs more effectively, and this enables them to produce more accurate delivery schedules. This in turn can lead to improved customer relationships and possibly result in increased future sales.

3 Standard setting

If budgets and standards are set without considering the learning effect, meaningless variances are likely to occur. For example, if the learning effect is ignored, inappropriate labour standards will be set that can be easily attained. If management creates a climate where learning is encouraged and expected then improvements in efficiency are more likely to occur.

Cost estimation techniques used in practice

The survey of Drury *et al.* (1993) reported that statistical techniques are not widely used to separate fixed and variable costs. The following results were reported:

2% used statistical regression techniques;

59% classified costs on a subjective basis based on managerial experience;

28% classified all overheads as fixed costs and direct costs were classified as variable costs;

11% did not separate fixed and variable costs.

With regard to the use of learning curves and multiple regression techniques for cost and sales estimation, the following results were reported:

Extent of usage	Learning curves (%)	Multiple regression techniques (%)
Never	35	64
Rarely	26	23
Sometimes	22	10
Often	14	2
Always	3	1

Summary

The following items relate to the learning objectives listed at the beginning of the chapter.

- **Identify and describe the different methods of estimating costs.**
  The following approaches can be used to estimate costs: (a) engineering methods; (b) inspection of accounts method; (c) graphical or scattergraph method; (d) high-low method; (e) least squares method; and (f) multiple regression analysis. With engineering studies a detailed study of each operation is undertaken under controlled conditions, based on high levels of efficiency, to ascertain the quantities of labour and materials required. Target prices are then applied based on efficient purchasing to ascertain the standard costs. The engineering method is most appropriate for estimating direct costs for repetitive processes where input–output relationships are clearly defined. The inspection of accounts method requires that a subjective estimate is made of the fixed and variable elements for each item of expenditure within the accounts for a particular period. The remaining four methods are described below.

- **Calculate regression equations using high–low, scattergraph and least squares techniques.**
  The high-low method consists of selecting the periods of highest and lowest activity levels and comparing the changes in costs that result from these two levels. The variable cost per unit is derived by dividing the difference in cost between the two levels by the differences in activity. Fixed costs are computed by deducting the derived variable cost from total cost at either the lowest or highest output level (see Example 24.3 for an illustration of the calculations). The scattergraph method involves plotting on a graph the total cost for each observed activity level. A straight line is drawn through the middle of the scatter of points so that the distances of observations below the line are equal to the distances above the line. The variable cost per unit is derived from the straight line by dividing the difference in cost by the difference in activity. The intercept gives the estimated fixed cost (see Example 24.2 and Figure 24.1 for an illustration of the computations). The least squares method determines mathematically the line of best fit. It is based on the principle that the sum of the squares of the vertical deviations from the line that is established using this method is less than the sum of the squares of the vertical deviations from any other line that might be drawn (see Exhibit 24.1 for an illustration of the computations). Because this method uses all of the observations and determines the line of best fit mathematically it is considered superior to the high–low or scattergraph methods.

- **Describe multiple regression analysis and indicate the circumstances when it should be used.**
  The least squares regression method assumes that total costs are determined by one variable only (i.e. activity). Multiple regression can be used when it is considered that

total costs are determined by more than one variable. Thus, if a single activity measure is found to be unreliable, and other variables are considered to significantly influence total costs, multiple regression analysis should be used.

- **Identify and explain the requirements which should be observed when using statistical regression analysis.**

  The following requirements should be considered: (a) the cost data and activity should be related to the same period; (b) a sufficient number of observations must be obtained; (c) the data must be examined to ensure that the accounting policies adopted do not lead to distorted cost functions; and (d) past data must be adjusted to reflect future changes in circumstances (for example past costs must be adjusted to current prices to reflect inflationary price changes).

- **Identify and explain the six steps required to estimate cost functions from past data.**

  The following six steps are required: (a) select the cost (dependent) variable to be predicted; (b) select potential cost drivers (i.e. the causes of costs); (c) collect data on the dependent variable and the selected cost driver; (d) plot the observations on a graph; (e) estimate the cost function; and (f) test the reliability of the cost function.

- **Describe the learning curve and compute the average and incremental labour hours for different output levels.**

  If the labour content per unit is expected to decline, as workers become more familiar with a process, learning curve principles can be applied. Previous experience in some industries has found that the rate of improvement was so regular that it could be reduced to a formula, and that the labour hours required could be predicted with a high degree of accuracy from a learning curve. The learning curve is based on the principle that the learning process starts from the point when the first unit comes off the production line. From then on, each time cumulative production is doubled, the average time taken to produce each unit of cumulative production will be a certain percentage (often assumed to be 80%) of the average time per unit of the previous cumulative production. See Exhibit 24.2 for an illustration of the application of the learning curve.

- **Describe three situations where the learning curve can be applied.**

  The learning curve can be applied for pricing decisions, work scheduling and price setting.

- **Additional learning objective presented in Appendix 24.1**

  The appendix to this chapter includes an additional learning objective: to explain, calculate and interpret the various tests of reliability. Reliability tests are included in the appendix because a knowledge of them is not essential to an understanding of the chapter content. Also, often, they do not form part of a course curriculum. You should therefore check with your course curriculum to ascertain whether you need to study this topic.

Appendix 24.1 Tests of reliability

Various tests of reliability can be applied to see how reliable potential cost drivers are in predicting the dependent variable (i.e. total cost) or the beta coefficient (variable cost). Three such tests will be described. They are:

1. the coefficient of determination;
2. the standard error of the estimate;
3. the standard error of the coefficient.

Throughout this appendix we shall use the data presented in Exhibit 24.1 and Figure 24.3 to illustrate the tests of reliability.

The coefficient of determination

If the regression line (y = £600 + £10x) calculated by the least-squares method for the data given in Exhibit 24.1 were to fit the actual observations perfectly, all of the observed points would lie on the regression line in Figure 24.3. You will see from this diagram that reliability is based on the size of the deviations of the actual observations (y^a) represented by the dots in Figure 24.3 from the estimated values on the regression line (y^e) represented by the straight line in Figure 24.3. The size of these deviations can be ascertained by squaring the difference between the estimated and the actual values. (The sums of the deviations will always add to zero, and it is therefore necessary to square the deviations.) The average of these squared deviations is defined as the residual variation. In statistical terms this represents the variance of the actual observations from the regression line, and is denoted by σ. The calculation of the residual variation for the information represented in Exhibit 24.1 is shown in Exhibit 24A.1.

The residual variation is calculated from the formula:

$$\sigma^2 = \frac{\sum(y_a - y_e)^2}{N} = \frac{405\,000}{12} = 33\,750$$

To determine how reliable the chosen cost driver is in predicting costs, we must determine the total dispersion of the observations and compare this with the dispersion that occurs when machine hours of activity are used in predicting costs. The total dispersion of the cost observations can be found by removing machine hours from the cost equation and working out what the dispersion would then be. Any estimate of cost would then be based on a simple calculation of the average of all the actual cost observations. In Exhibit 24A.1 there are 12 observations of actual cost, which add up to £19 800, the average being £1650 (£19 800/12). Let us now calculate the dispersion of the actual observations around the average. This calculation is shown in Exhibit 24A.2.

The dispersion from the average σ^2, is calculated from the formula

$$\sigma^2 = \frac{\sum(y_a - \bar{y}_a)^2}{N} = \frac{3\,555\,000}{12} = 296\,250$$

The total dispersion is £296 250 but, by introducing hours into the regression equation as a possible way of predicting variations in cost, we have accounted for all but £33 750 of the total variation of £296 250. In percentage terms this means that the activity base used has failed to account for 11.39% (i.e. (33 750/296 250) × 100) of the variation of cost. In other words, 88.61% of the variation in total cost is explained by variations in the activity base (cost driver), and the remaining 11.39% is explained by either entirely random variation or random variation plus the combined effect that other (omitted variables) have on the dependent variable (total cost).

The term used for describing the calculation of 88.61% is the **coefficient of determination, r^2**. This is calculated from the formula

$$r^2 = 1 - \frac{\sum(y_a - y_e)^2/N}{\sum(y_a - \bar{y}_a)^2/N} = 1 - \frac{33\,750}{296\,250} = 0.8861$$

EXHIBIT 24A.1
Calculation of residual variation

Hours x	Actual cost (y_a)	Estimated cost (y_e) ($y = 600 + 10x$)	Deviations ($y_a - y_e$)	Deviations squared $(y_a - y_e)^2$
90	1 500	1500	0	0
150	1 950	2100	−150	22 500
60	900	1200	−300	90 000
30	900	900	0	0
180	2 700	2400	300	90 000
150	2 250	2100	150	22 500
120	1 950	1800	150	22 500
180	2 100	2400	−300	90 000
90	1 350	1500	−150	22 500
30	1 050	900	150	22 500
120	1 800	1800	0	0
60	1 350	1200	150	22 500
	19 800			405 000

EXHIBIT 24A.2
Dispersion of observations around the average

Actual cost (y_a)	Average ($\bar{y}_a$)	Deviation ($y_a - \bar{y}_a$)	Deviation squared $(y_a - \bar{y}_a)^2$
1500	1650	−150	22 500
1950	1650	300	90 000
900	1650	−750	562 500
900	1650	−750	562 500
2700	1650	1050	1 102 500
2250	1650	600	360 000
1950	1650	300	90 000
2100	1650	450	202 500
1350	1650	−300	90 000
1050	1650	−600	360 000
1800	1650	150	22 500
1350	1650	−300	90 000
			3 555 000

The degree of association between two variables such as cost and activity is normally referred to as **correlation**. The **correlation coefficient** r is the square root of the coefficient of determination. If the degree of association between the two variables is very close, it will be almost possible to plot the observations on a straight line, and r and r^2 will be very near to 1. In this situation a high correlation between costs and activity exists, as illustrated in Figure 24A.1.

At the other extreme, costs may be so randomly distributed that there is little or no correlation between costs and the activity base selected. The r^2 calculation will be near to zero. An illustration of the situation where no correlation exists is given in Figure 24A.2

FIGURE 24A.1 *High correlation*

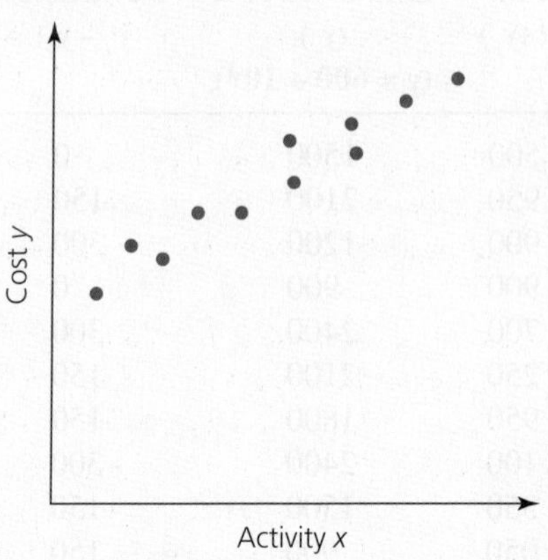

FIGURE 24A.2 *No correlation*

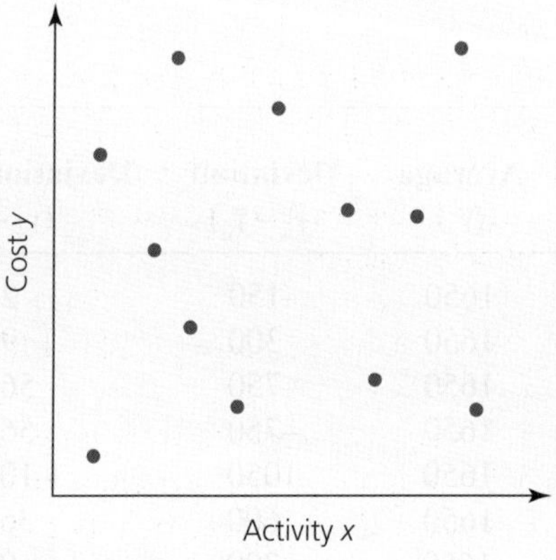

Standard error of the estimate

The coefficient of determination gives us an indication of the reliability of the estimate of *total cost* based on the regression equation but it does not give us an indication of the absolute size of the probable deviations from the line. This information can be obtained by calculating the **standard error of the estimate, Se**, based on the formula

$$\text{Se} = \sqrt{\left[\frac{\sum(y_a - y_e)^2}{N-2}\right]} = \sqrt{\left(\frac{405\,000}{10}\right)} = 201.25$$

The sample size N is reduced by 2 because two variables (a and b) in the regression equation had to be estimated from the sample of observations. Note that $\sum(y_a - y_e)^2$ has been obtained from Exhibit 24A.1.

The calculation of the standard error is necessary because the least-squares line was calculated from sample data. Other samples would probably result in different estimates.

Obtaining the least-squares calculation over all the possible observations that might occur for the maintenance cost would result in a calculation of the true least-squares line. The question is how close does the sample estimate of the least-squares line ($y = 600 + 10x$) come to the true least-squares line. The standard error enables us to establish a range of values of the dependent variable y within which we may have some degree of confidence that the true value lies. Different ranges can be calculated for different degrees of confidence. Thus the standard error of the estimate is quite similar to a standard deviation in normal probability analysis. It is a measure of variability around the regression line.

Statistical theory indicates that for least-squares analysis the points are t-distributed about the regression line and that the distribution becomes normal as the number of observations reaches 30. As our estimate of the regression line was based on twelve observations, we shall assume that the points are t-distributed about the regression line. An important characteristic of this distribution is that there is a 0.90 probability that the true cost lies within ±1.812 standard errors from the estimated cost. (An explanation of this is presented later in this appendix.) If you refer back to Exhibit 24A.1, you will see that the estimated cost for 180 hours of activity is £2400. This means that there is a 0.90 probability that the true cost will fall within the range

$$\pounds 2400 \pm 1.812\,(201.25) = \pounds 2035 \text{ to } \pounds 2765$$

If a narrower range is required, the probability that the true cost will fall within this narrower range will be less than 0.9. For example, the t-distribution (see page 1063) indicates that there is a probability of 0.80 that the true cost will fall within 1.372 standard errors from the estimated cost. This means that there is a 0.80 probability that the true cost will fall within the following range:

$$\pounds 2400 \pm 1.372\,(201.25) = \pounds 2124 \text{ to } \pounds 2676$$

Alternatively, if a greater degree of confidence is required, a probability higher than 0.90 can be obtained, but this will give a wider range within which the true cost lies. The tighter the observations around the regression's line, the lower the value of Se. When observations of costs and output are widely distributed around the regression line, we can expect a high Se, since we need a much larger range to describe our estimate of true costs.

These principles can usefully be applied to flexible budgeting by presenting a flexible budget that portrays a range of possible costs for each level of activity. A flexible budget based on a 0.90 probability for activity levels of 150 and 180 hours is presented in Exhibit 24A.3.

We should expect costs to fall within the given range for 90% of the time. Alternatively, we should expect costs to fall outside the range for 10% of the time when they are from the same population from which the least-squares estimate was derived. Therefore for any actual cost observations that are outside the range there is a high probability that the costs are out of control. We discussed this principle in Chapter 19 when we considered the investigation of variances.

Standard error of the coefficient

We have previously computed the standard error of the estimate to measure the reliability of the estimates of *total cost*. However, we may also be interested in the reliability of the estimate of the regression coefficient b (i.e. the *variable cost*). This is because the analyst

EXHIBIT 24A.3
Flexible budgets

Activity	150 hours			180 hours		
	Lower limit	Mean	Upper limit	Lower limit	Mean	Upper limit
	£1735	£2100	£2465	£2035	£2400	£2765

often focuses on the rate of variability rather than on the absolute level of the prediction. The formula for the **standard error of the *b* coefficient**, Sb can be expressed as

$$\text{Sb} = \frac{Se}{\sqrt{\left[\sum (x - \bar{x})^2\right]}}$$

This can be simplified to

$$\text{Sb} = \frac{Se}{\sqrt{\left(\sum x^2 - \bar{x}\sum x\right)}}$$

If we use the standard error that we have calculated earlier and the data that we used for calculating the regression equation in Exhibit 24.1 (see page 1044), the calculation is as follows:

$$\text{Sb} = \frac{201.25}{\sqrt{[163\,800 - (1260/12)1260]}} = \frac{201.25}{\sqrt{(31\,500)}} = 1.134$$

We can now use the *t*-distribution, again noting that there is a 0.9 probability that the true variable cost lies within ±1.812 standard errors from the estimated cost. Using the regression equation $y = 600 + 10x$, we can state that we are 90% confident that the true variable cost lies within the range.

$$£10 \pm 1.812 \times 1.134 = £7.95 \text{ to } £12.05$$

We can calculate different ranges of variable costs based on different probability levels. For example, the *t*-distribution shown at the end of this appendix indicates that there is a 0.8 probability that the true variable cost lies within 1.372 standard errors from the mean. Therefore we can be 80% confident that the true variable cost lies within the range.

$$£10 \pm 1.372 \text{ Sb}$$

Partial table of *t*-values

The relevant numbers for the probabilities of 0.80 and 0.90 quoted in this chapter are 1.372 and 1.812. These items are obtained from the appropriate columns for the line representing 10 degrees of freedom. The number of degrees of freedom are obtained from the number of observations (namely 12), reduced by the number of variables in the simple regression equation which had to be estimated from the sample observations (i.e. two for regression coefficients *a* and *b* in the equation $y = a + bx$).

FIGURE 24A.3 *A t-distribution*

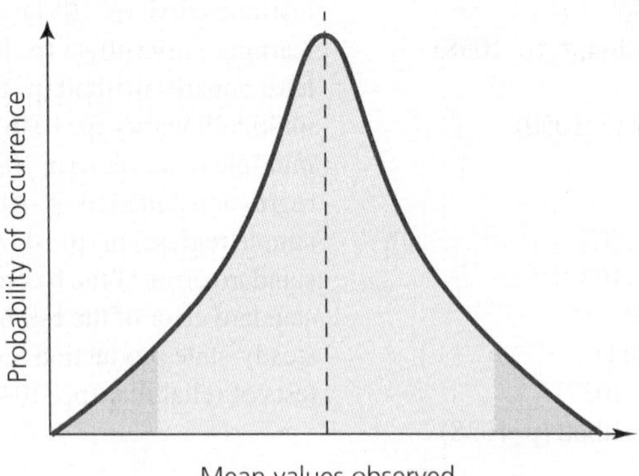

EXHIBIT 24A.4 *Maximum values of t consistent with confidence interval with probability*

Degrees of freedom	Probabilities of occurrence (range 0.80 to 0.99) 0.80	0.90	0.95	0.98	0.99
1	3.078	6.314	12.706	31.821	63.657
2	1.886	2.920	4.303	6.965	9.925
3	1.638	2.353	3.182	4.541	5.841
4	1.533	2.132	2.776	3.747	4.604
5	1.476	2.015	2.571	3.365	4.032
6	1.440	1.943	2.447	3.143	2.707
7	1.415	1.895	2.365	2.998	3.499
8	1.397	1.860	2.306	2.896	3.355
9	1.383	1.833	2.262	2.821	3.250
10	1.372	1.812	2.228	2.764	3.169
11	1.363	1.796	2.201	2.718	3.106
12	1.356	1.782	2.179	2.681	3.055
13	1.350	1.771	2.160	2.650	3.012
14	1.345	1.761	2.145	2.624	2.977
15	1.341	1.753	2.131	2.602	2.947
Infinite	1.282	1.645	1.960	2.326	2.576

Note that the headings of *t*-tables usually identify the probabilities of values falling in one tail of the *t*-distribution. However, to simplify the situation, the normal presentation has been reversed for the sake of greater clarity, and the probabilities of the value falling in the main body of the distribution, and not the tail, are presented. For example, the entries in Exhibit 24A.4 indicate the probability of an observation falling in the orange area of Figure 24A.3.

Assuming that the blue shaded area in each tail of the distribution represents $t = 0.025$, then 0.05 of the area under the curve falls in the tails of the distribution. Consequently, 0.95 of the area under the curve falls in the orange area. Therefore the entries in Exhibit 24A.4 are for 0.95 and not 0.025 which is the normal presentation.

Key terms and concepts

activity measure (p. 1036)
coefficient of determination, r_2 (p. 1058)
correlation (p. 1059)
correlation coefficient, r (p. 1059)
cost driver (p. 1036)
cost function (p. 1037)
dependent variable (p. 1037)
engineering methods (p. 1038)
goodness-of-fit (p. 1045)
high–low method (p. 1041)
independent variable (p. 1037)
inspection of accounts method (p. 1038)
learning curve (p. 1051)
learning-curve effect (p. 1051)
least-squares method (p. 1042)
multicollinearity (p. 1046)
multiple regression (p. 1037)
regression equation (p. 1036)
simple regression (p. 1037)
standard error of the b coefficient, Sb (p. 1062)
standard error of the estimate, Se (p. 1060)
steady-state production level (p. 1052)
tests of reliability (pp. 1043, 1057)

Recommended reading

This chapter has provided an introduction to the various cost estimation techniques. For a more detailed discussion of these techniques you should refer to Chapter 4 of Scapens (1991) and chapters 4 and 5 of Kaplan and Atkinson (1989).

Key examination points

In recent years emphasis has switched from calculation to interpretation. Do make sure you can interpret regression equations and explain the meaning of the various statistical tests of reliability. Different formulae can be used to calculate regression equations, standard errors and r^2 but a formula is likely to be given. The examiner will have set the question assuming you will use the formula. You will probably find that you have insufficient data or excessive calculations are required if you use an alternative formula. Do not worry if you are unfamiliar with the formula. All that is necessary is for you to enter the figures given in the question into it.

Remember with learning curves that only labour costs and variable overheads that vary with labour costs are subject to the learning effect. A common requirement is for you to calculate the incremental hours per order. Make sure that you understand columns 6 and 7 of Exhibit 24.2.

Assessment material

Review questions

The review questions are short questions that enable you to assess your understanding of the main topics included in the chapter. The numbers in parentheses provide you with the page numbers to refer to if you cannot answer a specific question.

Review problems

The review problems are more complex and require you to relate and apply the chapter content to various business problems. The problems are graded by their level of difficulty. The multiple-choice questions are the least demanding and normally take less than 10 minutes to complete. Fully worked solutions to the review problems are provided in a separate section at the end of the book. For those questions in the white box the worked solutions are provided in the *Student's Manual* accompanying this book. Further review problems for this chapter are available on the accompanying website www.drury-online.com. The answers to these problems are available for lecturers on the lecturer's password protected section of the website.

Case studies

The website also includes over 30 case study problems. A list of these cases is provided in Part Seven of this book. The Beta Company is a case study that is relevant to the content of this chapter.

Review questions

24.1 Explain what is meant by the term 'cost function'. (*p. 1037*)

24.2 Under what circumstances can the engineering method be used to estimate costs. (*p. 1038*)

24.3 Describe the high-low method. (*pp. 1041–42*)

24.4 What is the major limitation of the high-low method? (*p. 1042*)

24.5 Describe how the scattergraph method is used to analyse costs into their fixed and variable elements. (*pp. 1039–41*)

24.6 Describe the least squares method. Why is this method better than the high-low and scattergraph methods? (*pp. 1042–43*)

24.7 When is multiple regression required to explain cost behaviour? *(pp. 1045–46)*

24.8 What factors need to be considered when using past costs to estimate cost functions? *(pp. 1047–48)*

24.9 Describe the steps that should be followed in estimating cost functions. *(pp. 1049–50)*

24.10 Why is a scattergraph a useful first step in estimating cost functions? *(p. 1050)*

24.11 Describe what is meant by the learning curve effect. *(pp. 1051–52)*

24.12 Define the steady-state production level. *(p. 1052)*

24.13 Provide illustrations of situations where the learning curve can be applied. *(pp. 1054–55)*

24.14 Describe what is meant by 'goodness of fit'. *(p. 1045)*

24.15 Explain the meaning of coefficient of determination and the standard error of the estimate. *(pp. 1058–61)*

Review problems

24.16 Intermediate

A hospital's records show that the cost of carrying out health checks in the last five accounting periods have been as follows:

Period	Number of patients seen	Total cost $
1	650	17 125
2	940	17 800
3	1260	18 650
4	990	17 980
5	1150	18 360

Using the high-low method and ignoring inflation, the estimated cost of carrying out health checks on 850 patients in period 6 is

A $17 515. B $17 570. C $17 625. D $17 680.

CIMA – Management Accounting Fundamentals

24.17 Advanced

M plc uses time series analysis and regression techniques to estimate future sales demand. Using these techniques, it has derived the following trend equation:

$$y = 10\,000 + 4200x$$

where y is the total sales units; and
x is the time period

Review problems (with answers in the Student's Manual)

24.25 **Advanced: Linear regression analysis with price level adjustments**

Savitt Ltd manufactures a variety of products at its industrial site in Ruratania. One of the products, the LT, is produced in a specially equipped factory in which no other production takes place. For technical reasons the company keeps no stocks of either LTs or the raw material used in their manufacture. The costs of producing LTs in the special factory during the past four years have been as follows:

	1998 (£)	1999 (£)	2000 (£)	(2001) (estimated) (£)
Raw materials	70 000	100 000	130 000	132 000
Skilled labour	40 000	71 000	96 000	115 000
Unskilled labour	132 000	173 000	235 000	230 000
Power	25 000	33 000	47 000	44 000
Factory overheads	168 000	206 000	246 000	265 000
Total production costs	£435 000	£583 000	£754 000	£786 000
Output (units)	160 000	190 000	220 000	180 000

The costs of raw materials and skilled and unskilled labour have increased steadily during the past four years at an annual compound rate of 20%, and the costs of factory overheads have increased at an annual compound rate of 15% during the same period. Power prices increased by 10% on 1 January 1999 and by 25% on the 1 January of each subsequent year. All costs except power are expected to increase by a further 20% during 2002. Power prices are due to rise by 25% on 1 January 2002.

The directors of Savitt Ltd are now formulating the company's production plan for 2002 and wish to estimate the costs of manufacturing the product LT. The finance director has expressed the view that 'the full relevant cost of producing LTs can be determined only if a fair share of general company overheads is allocated to them'. No such allocation is included in the table of costs above.

You are required to:

(a) use linear regression analysis to estimate the relationship of total production costs to volume for the product LT for 2002 (ignore general company overheads and do *not* undertake a separate regression calculation for each item of cost),

(12 marks)

(b) discuss the advantages and limitations of linear regression analysis for the estimation of cost–volume relationships,

(8 marks)

(c) comment on the view expressed by the finance director.

(5 marks)

Ignore taxation.

ICAEW Elements of Financial Decisions

24.26 Advanced: Estimation of costs and incremental hours using the learning curve

BL plc has developed a new product, the Webcam IV, to add to its existing range of computer peripherals. Each unit of the Webcam IV will be sold for £60 in a highly competitive market.

The initial estimated unit costs of a Webcam IV are as follows:

	£
Direct materials	28.00
Variable processing cost:	
18 minutes @ £25/hour	7.50
	35.50

There are also annual product specific fixed costs of £240 000. These are to be incurred at a constant rate throughout the year.

No units of the Webcam IV have yet been made.

BL plc plans to make and sell 1000 units each month during the year commencing 1 April 2002.

The following adjustments are to be made to the initial estimated costs when determining the standard cost of the product:

(i) There is an expected material loss equal to 5% of the material used. This loss has no value and its cost is to be borne by the product.

(ii) A 90% learning curve effect is expected to apply.

Note: The formula for a 90% learning curve is $y = ax^{-0.1520}$

Required:

(a) Calculate the standard variable cost of production of the Webcam IV for April 2002.

(3 marks)

(b) Calculate the standard variable cost of production for September (month 6) given that output in every month will be in accordance with the budgeted output of 1000 units per month and the 90% learning curve effect will continue to apply.

(6 marks)

The actual results for the month of April 2002 were as follows:

Sales	900 units @ £62 each unit
Production	1 000 units
Direct materials used cost	£31 870
Variable processing:	
2425 minutes costing	£1 070
Fixed costs incurred	£24 840

It has now been recognized that an 80% rate of learning should have been used for the original standard cost (instead of the 90% learning curve that was used).

Note: The formula for an 80% learning curve is $y = ax^{-0.320}$

Required:

(c) Prepare a statement for April 2002 using a contribution approach that reconciles the budgeted profit based on the original standard costs (based on the 90% learning curve) with the actual profit. Your statement should clearly identify the revised budgeted profit, the standard profit, and the planning and operating variances in as much detail as possible. Assume that stock is valued at revised standard cost.

(12 marks)

(d) Explain the importance of recognizing the effects of the learning curve when preparing performance reports.

(4 marks)
(Total 25 marks)
CIMA Management Accounting – Performance Management

24.27 **Advanced: Estimation of costs and incremental hours using the learning curve**

(a) Z plc experiences difficulty in its budgeting process because it finds it necessary to quantify the learning effect as new products are introduced. Substantial product changes occur and result in the need for retraining.

An order for 30 units of a new product has been received by Z plc. So far, 14 have been completed; the first unit required 40 direct labour hours and a total of 240 direct labour hours has been recorded for the 14 units. The production manager expects an 80% learning effect for this type of work.

The company uses standard absorption costing. The direct costs attributed to the centre in which the unit is manufactured and its direct material costs are as follows:

Direct material	£30.00 per unit
Direct labour	£6.00 per hour
Variable overhead	£0.50 per direct labour hour
Fixed overhead	£6000 per four-week operating period

There are ten direct employees working a five-day week, eight hours per day. Personal and other downtime allowances account for 25% of the total available time.

The company usually quotes a four-week delivery period for orders.

You are required to

(i) determine whether the assumption of an 80% learning effect is a reasonable one in this case, by using the standard formula $y = ax^b$

where y = the cumulative average direct labour time per unit (productivity)

a = the average labour time per unit for the first batch

x = the cumulative number of batches produced

b = the index of learning

(5 marks)

(ii) calculate the number of direct labour hours likely to be required for an expected second order of 20 units;

(5 marks)

(iii) use the cost data given to produce an estimated product cost for the initial order, examining the problems which may be created for budgeting by the presence of the learning effect.

(10 marks)

(b) It is argued that in many areas of modern technology, the 'learning curve' effect is of diminishing significance. An 'experience curve' effect would still be present and possibly strengthened in importance. However, the experience curve has little to do with short-term standard setting and product costing.

You are required to discuss the validity of the above statement, in particular the assertion that the experience curve has little relevance to costing.

(6 marks)

(Total 26 marks)

CIMA Stage 4 Management Accounting – Control and Audit

Quantitative models for the planning and control of stocks

25

Investment in stocks represents a major asset of most industrial and commercial organizations, and it is essential that stocks be managed efficiently so that such investments do not become unnecessarily large. A firm should determine its optimum level of investment in stocks – and, to do this, two conflicting requirements must be met. First, it must ensure that stocks are sufficient to meet the requirements of production and sales; and, secondly, it must avoid holding surplus stocks that are unnecessary and that increase the risk of obsolescence. The optimal stock level lies somewhere between these two extremes. Our objective in this chapter is to examine the application of quantitative models for determining the optimum investment in stocks, and describe the alternative methods of scheduling material requirements. We shall also consider the economic order quantity and the level at which stocks should be replenished. We shall concentrate here on manufacturing firms, but the same basic analysis can also be applied to merchandising companies and non-profit organizations.

LEARNING OBJECTIVES

After studying this chapter, you should be able to:

- justify which costs are relevant and should be included in the calculation of the economic order quantity (EOQ);
- calculate the EOQ using the formula and tabulation methods;
- determine whether or not a company should purchase larger quantities in order to take advantage of quantity discounts;
- calculate the optimal safety stock when demand is uncertain;
- describe the ABC classification method;
- describe materials requirement planning (MRP) systems;
- explain just-in-time purchasing.

Why do firms hold stocks?

There are three general reasons for holding stocks; the transactions motive, the precautionary motive and the speculative motive. The **transactions motive** occurs whenever there is a need to hold stocks to meet production and sales requirements, and it is not possible to meet these requirements instantaneously. A firm might also decide to hold additional amounts of stocks to cover the possibility that it may have underestimated its future production and sales requirements or the supply of raw materials may be unreliable because of uncertain events affecting the supply of materials. This represents a **precautionary motive**, which applies only when future demand is uncertain.

When it is expected that future input prices may change, a firm might maintain higher or lower stock levels to *speculate* on the expected increase or decrease in future prices. In general, quantitative models do not take into account the **speculative motive**. Nevertheless, management should be aware that optimum stock levels do depend to a certain extent on expected price movements. For example, if prices of input factors are expected to rise significantly, a firm should consider increasing its stocks to take advantage of a lower purchase price. However, this decision should be based on a comparison of future cost savings with the increased costs due to holding additional stocks.

Where a firm is able to predict the demand for its inputs and outputs with perfect certainty and where it knows with certainty that the prices of inputs will remain constant for some reasonable length of time, it will have to consider only the transactions motive for holding stocks. To simplify the introduction to the use of models for determining the optimum investment in stocks, we shall begin by considering some quantitative models which incorporate only the transactions motive for holding stocks.

Relevant costs for quantitative models under conditions of certainty

The relevant costs that should be considered when determining optimal stock levels consist of holding costs and ordering costs. **Holding costs** usually consist of the following:

1 opportunity cost of investment in stocks;
2 incremental insurance costs;
3 incremental warehouse and storage costs;
4 incremental material handling costs;
5 cost of obsolescence and deterioration of stocks.

The relevant holding costs for use in quantitative models should include only those items that will vary with the levels of stocks. Costs that will not be affected by changes in stock levels are not relevant costs. For example, in the case of warehousing and storage only those costs should be included that will vary with changes in the number of units ordered. Salaries of storekeepers, depreciation of equipment and fixed rental of equipment and buildings are often irrelevant because they are unaffected by changes in stock levels. On the other hand, if storage space is owned and can be used for other productive purposes or to obtain rent income then the opportunity cost must be included in the analysis. Insurance costs should be included only when premiums are charged on the fluctuating value of stocks. A fixed annual insurance cost will not vary with different levels of stocks, and is therefore not a relevant holding cost.

To the extent that funds are invested in stocks, there is an opportunity cost of holding them. This opportunity cost is reflected by the required return that is lost from investing in stocks rather than some alternative investment. The opportunity cost should be applied only to those costs that vary with the number of units purchased. The relevant holding costs for other items such as material handling, obsolescence and deterioration are difficult to estimate, but we shall see that these costs are unlikely to be critical to the investment decision. Normally, holding costs are expressed as a percentage rate per pound of average investment.

Ordering costs usually consist of the clerical costs of preparing a purchase order, receiving deliveries and paying invoices. Ordering costs that are common to all stock decisions are not relevant, and only the incremental costs of placing an order are used in formulating the quantitative models. In practice, it is extremely difficult to distinguish between variable and non-variable ordering costs, but this problem can be resolved by developing a cost equation as described in Chapter 24, where the number of orders placed represents the independent variable.

The costs of acquiring stocks through buying or manufacturing are not a relevant cost to be included in the quantitative models, since the acquisition costs remain unchanged, irrespective of the order size or stock levels, unless quantity discounts are available. (We shall discuss the effect of quantity discounts later in this chapter.) For example, it does not matter in terms of acquisition cost whether total annual requirements of 1000 units at £10 each are purchased in one 1000-unit batch, ten 100-unit batches or one hundred 10-unit batches; the acquisition cost of £10 000 will remain unchanged. The acquisition cost is not therefore a relevant cost, but the ordering and holding costs will change in relation to the order size, and these will be relevant for decision-making models.

Determining the economic order quantity

If we assume certainty, the optimum order will be determined by those costs that are affected by either the quantity of stocks held or the number of orders placed. If more units are ordered at one time, fewer orders will be required per year. This will mean a reduction in the ordering costs. However, when fewer orders are placed, larger average stocks must be maintained, which leads to an increase in holding costs. The problem is therefore one of trading off the costs of carrying large stocks against the costs of placing more orders. The optimum order size is the order quantity that will result in the total amount of the ordering and holding costs being minimized. This optimum order size is known as the **economic order quantity (EOQ)**; it can be determined by tabulating the total costs for various order quantities, by a graphical presentation or by using a formula. All three methods are illustrated using the information given in Example 25.1.

Tabulation method

It is apparent from Example 25.1 that a company can choose to purchase small batches (e.g. 100 units) at frequent intervals or large batches (e.g. 10 000 units) at infrequent intervals. The annual relevant costs for various order quantities are set out in Exhibit 25.1.

You will see that the economic order quantity is 400 units. At this point the total annual relevant costs are at a minimum.

Graphical method

The information tabulated in Exhibit 25.1 is presented in graphical form in Figure 25.1 for every order size up to 800 units. The vertical axis represents the relevant annual costs

EXAMPLE 25.1

A company purchases a raw material from an outside supplier at a cost of £9 per unit. The total annual demand for this product is 40 000 units, and the following additional information is available.

	(£)	(£)
Required annual return on investment in stocks (10% × £9)	0.90	
Other holding costs per unit	0.10	
Holding costs per unit		1.00
Cost per purchase order:		
Clerical costs, stationery, postage, telephone etc.		2.00

You are required to determine the optimal order quantity.

EXHIBIT 25.1

Relevant costs for various order quantities

Order quantity	100	200	300	400	500	600	800	10 000
Average stock in units[a]	50	100	150	200	250	300	400	5 000
Number of purchase orders[b]	400	200	133	100	80	67	50	4
Annual holding costs[c]	£50	£100	£150	£200	£250	£300	£400	£5 000
Annual ordering cost	£800	£400	£266	£200	£160	£134	£100	£8
Total relevant cost	£850	£500	£416	£400	£410	£434	£500	£5 008

[a]If there are no stocks when the order is received and the units received are used at a constant rate, the average stock will be one-half of the quantity ordered. Even if a minimum safety stock is held, the average stock relevant to the decision will still be one-half of the quantity order, because the minimum stock will remain unchanged for each alternative order quantity.

[b]The number of purchase orders is ascertained by dividing the total annual demand of 40 000 units by the order quantity.

[c]The annual holding cost is ascertained by multiplying the average stock by the holding cost of £1 per unit.

for the investment in stocks, and the horizontal axis can be used to represent either the various order quantities or the average stock levels; two scales are actually shown on the horizontal axis so that both items can be incorporated. You will see from the graph that as the average stock level or the order quantity increases, the holding cost also increases. Alternatively, the ordering costs decline as stock levels and order quantities are increased. The total cost line represents the summation of both the holding and the ordering costs.

Note that the total cost line is at a minimum for an order quantity of 400 units and occurs at the point where the ordering cost and holding cost curves intersect. That is, the economic order quantity is found at the point where the holding costs equal the ordering costs. It is also interesting to note from the graph (see also Exhibit 25.1) that the total relevant costs are not particularly sensitive to changes in the order quantity. For example, if you refer to Exhibit 25.1 you will see that a 25% change in the order quantity from 400 units to either 300 or 500 units leads to an increase in annual costs from £400 to £410 or £416, an increase of 2.5% or 4%. Alternatively, an increase of 50% in the order quantity from 400 units to 600 units leads to an increase in annual costs from £400 to £434 or 8.5%.

FIGURE 25.1 *Economic order quantity graph*

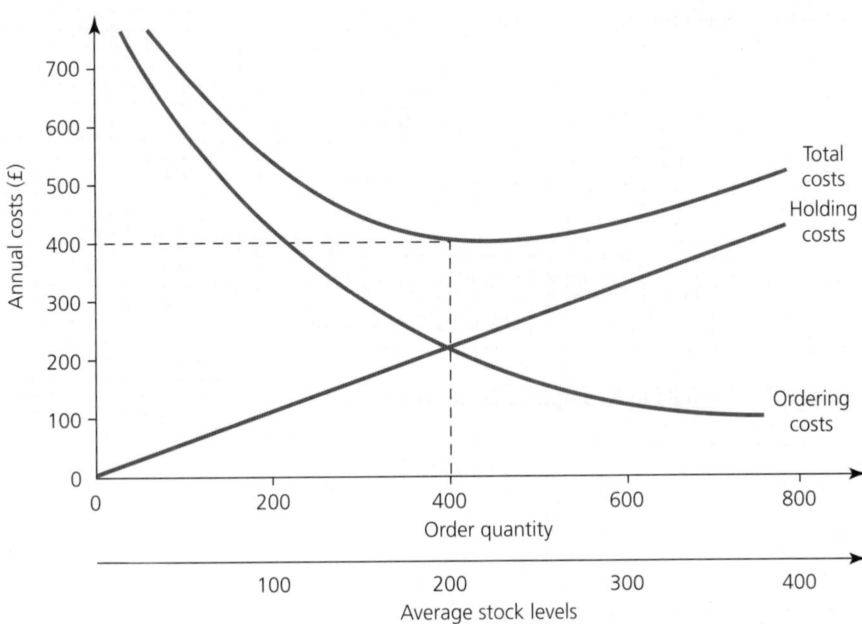

Formula method

The economic order quantity can be found by applying a formula that incorporates the basic relationships between holding and ordering costs and order quantities. These relationships can be stated as follows: the number of orders for a period is the total demand for that item of stock for the period (denoted by *D*) divided by the quantity ordered in units (denoted by *Q*). The total ordering cost is obtained by multiplying the number of orders for a period by the ordering cost per order (denoted by *O*), and is given by the formula

$$\frac{\text{total demand for period}}{\text{quantity ordered}} \times \text{ordering cost per order} = \frac{DO}{Q}$$

Assuming that holding costs are constant per unit, the total holding cost for a period will be equal to the average stock for the period, which is represented by the quantity ordered divided by two ($Q/2$), multiplied by the holding cost per unit (denoted by *H*); it is therefore given by

$$\frac{\text{quantity ordered}}{2} \times \text{holding cost per unit} = \frac{QH}{2}$$

The total relevant cost (TC) for any order quantity can now be expressed as

$$\text{TC} = \frac{DO}{Q} + \frac{QH}{2}$$

We can determine a minimum for this total cost function by differentiating the above formula with respect to Q and setting the derivative equal to zero.[1] We then get the economic order quantity Q:

$$Q = \sqrt{\left(\frac{2\,DO}{H}\right)}$$

or

$$Q = \sqrt{\left(\frac{2 \times \text{total demand for period} \times \text{cost per order}}{\text{holding cost per unit}}\right)}$$

If we apply this formula to Example 25.1, we have

$$Q = \sqrt{\left(\frac{2 \times 40\,000 \times 2}{1}\right)} = 400 \text{ units}$$

Assumptions of the EOQ formula

The calculations obtained by using the EOQ model should be interpreted with care, since the model is based on a number of important assumptions. One of these is that the holding cost per unit will be constant. While this assumption might be correct for items such as the funds invested in stocks, other costs might increase on a step basis as stock levels increase. For example, additional storekeepers might be hired as stock levels reach certain levels. Alternatively, if stocks decline, it may be that casual stores labour may be released once stocks fall to a certain critical level.

Another assumption that we made in calculating the total holding cost is that the average balance in stock was equal to one-half of the order quantity. If a constant amount of stock is not used per day, this assumption will be violated; there is a distinct possibility that seasonal and cyclical factors will produce an uneven usage over time. Despite the fact that much of the data used in the model represents rough approximations, calculation of the EOQ is still likely to be useful. If you examine Figure 25.1, you will see that the total cost curve tends to flatten out, so that total cost may not be significantly affected if some of the underlying assumptions are violated or if there are minor variations in the cost predictions. For example, assume that the cost per order in Example 25.1 was predicted to be £4 instead of the correct cost of, say, £2. The cost of this error would be as follows:

$$\text{revised EOQ} = \sqrt{\left(\frac{2\,DO}{H}\right)} = \sqrt{\left(\frac{2 \times 40\,000 \times 4}{1}\right)} = 565$$

$$\text{TC for revised EOQ but using the correct ordering cost} = \frac{DO}{Q} + \frac{QH}{2}$$

$$= \frac{40\,000 \times 2}{565} + \frac{565 \times 1}{2} = £425$$

TC for original EOQ of 400 units based on actual ordering cost

$$= \frac{40\,000 \times 2}{400} + \frac{400 \times 1}{2} = £400$$

$$\therefore \text{cost of prediction error} = £25$$

The cost of the prediction error of £25 represents an error of 6% from the optimal financial result. Similarly, if the holding cost was predicted to be £2 instead of the correct cost of £1, the calculations set out above could be repeated to show a cost of prediction error of approximately 6%.

Application of the EOQ model in determining the optimum lot size for a production run

The economic order quantity formula can be adapted to determine the optimum length of the production runs when a set-up cost is incurred only once for each batch produced. Set-up costs include incremental labour, material, jigs, machine down-time, and other ancillary costs of setting up facilities for production. The objective is to find the optimum number of units that should be manufactured in each production run, and this involves balancing set-up costs against stock holding costs. To apply the EOQ formula to a production run problem, we merely substitute set-up costs for the production runs in place of the purchase ordering costs.

To illustrate the formula let us assume that the annual sales demand D for a product is 9000 units. Labour and other expenditure in making adjustments in preparation for a production run require a set-up cost S of £90. The holding cost is £2 per unit per year. The EOQ model can be used for determining how many units should be scheduled for each production run to secure the lowest annual cost. The EOQ formula is modified to reflect the circumstances: the symbol O (ordering costs) is replaced by the symbol S (set-up cost). Using the formula

$$Q = \sqrt{\left(\frac{2\,DS}{H}\right)} = \sqrt{\left(\frac{2 \times 9000 \times 90}{2}\right)} = 900$$

With an annual demand of 9000 units and an optimum production run of 900 units, 10 production runs will be required throughout the year. If we assume there are 250 working days throughout the course of the year, this will mean that production runs are undertaken at 25-day intervals. If demand is uniform throughout the year, 36 units will be demanded per working day (i.e. 9000 units annual demand divided by 250 working days). To determine the point when the production run should be started, we need to ascertain the number of days required for a production run. Let us assume it is five. So during this period, 180 units (five days at 36 units per day) will be demanded before any of the production run is available to meet demand. If we assume that no safety stock is required, we can establish that a production run should be started when the stock level reaches 180 units. This situation should occur 25 days after the start of the previous production run. The process is illustrated in Figure 25.2.

FIGURE 25.2 *EOQ model and length of production run*

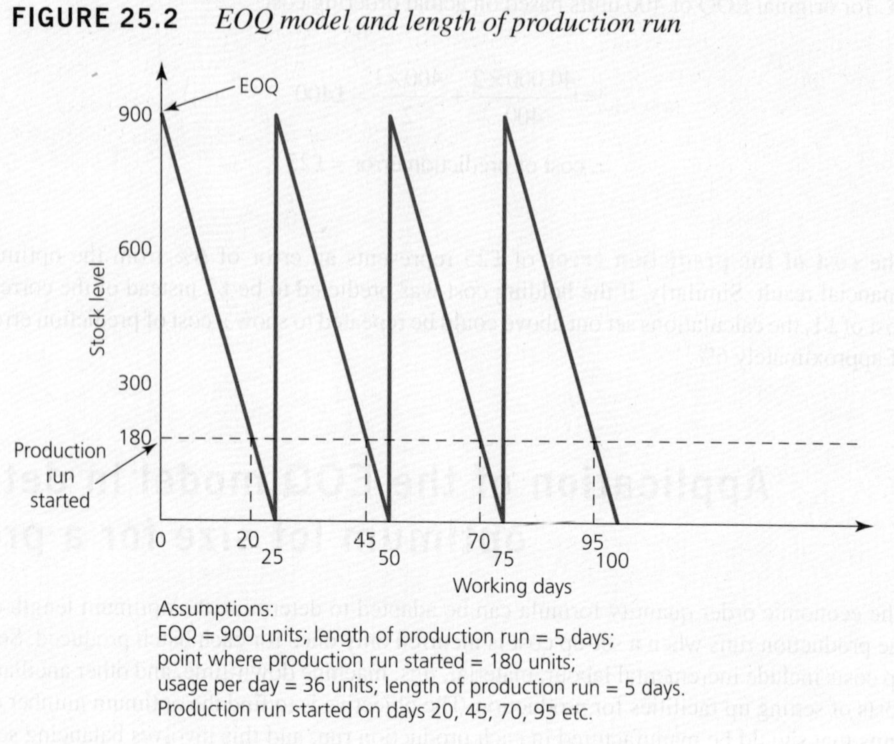

Quantity discounts

Circumstances frequently occur where firms are able to obtain quantity discounts for large purchase orders. Because the price paid per unit will not be the same for different order sizes, this must be taken into account when the economic order quantity is determined. However, the basic EOQ formula can still be used as a starting point for determining the optimum quantity to order. Buying in larger consignments to take advantage of quantity discounts will lead to the following savings:

1. A saving in purchase price, which consists of the total amount of discount for the period.
2. A reduction in the total ordering cost because fewer orders are placed to take advantage of the discounts.

These cost savings must, however, be balanced against the increased holding cost arising from higher stock levels when larger quantities are purchased. To determine whether or not a discount is worthwhile, the benefits must be compared with the additional holding costs. Consider the information presented in Example 25.2.

The starting point is to calculate the economic order quantity and then to decide whether the benefits exceed the costs if the company moves from the EOQ point and purchases larger quantities to obtain the discounts. The procedure is as follows:

$$\text{EOQ} = \sqrt{\left(\frac{2 \times 9000 \times 5}{4}\right)} = 150 \text{ units}$$

EXAMPLE 25.2

A company purchases a raw material from an outside supplier at a cost of £7 per unit. The total annual demand for this product is 9000 units. The holding cost is £4 per unit and the ordering cost is £5 per order. A quantity discount of 3% of the purchase price is available for orders in excess of 1000 units. Should the company order in batches of 1000 units and take advantage of quantity discounts?

The savings available to the firm if it purchases in batches of 1000 units instead of batches of 150 units are as follows:

	(£)
1 Saving in purchase price (3% of annual purchase cost of £63 000)	1890
2 Saving in ordering cost $\frac{DO}{Q_d} - \frac{DO}{Q} = \frac{9000 \times 5}{1000} - \frac{9000 \times 5}{150}$	255
(Q_d represents the quantity order to obtain the discount and Q represents EOQ)	
Total savings	2145

The additional holding cost if the larger quantity is purchased is calculated as

$$\frac{(Q_d - Q)H}{2} = \frac{(1000 - 150) \times £4}{2} = £1700$$

The additional savings of £2145 exceed the additional costs, and the firm should adopt the order quantity of 1000 units. If larger discounts are available, for example by purchasing in batches of 2000 units, a similar analysis should be applied that compares the savings from purchasing in batches of 2000 units against purchasing in batches of 1000 units. The amount of the savings should then be compared with the additional holding costs. Note that the EOQ formula serves as a starting point for balancing the savings against the costs of a change in order size.

Determining when to place the order

To determine the point at which the order should be placed to obtain additional stocks (i.e. the **re-order point**), we must ascertain the time that will elapse between placing the order and the actual delivery of the stocks. This time period is referred to as the **lead time**. In a world of certainty the re-order point will be the number of days/weeks lead time multiplied by the daily/weekly usage during the period. For materials, components and supplies the re-order point is the point in time when the purchase requisition is initiated and the order is sent to the supplier. For the finished goods stock of a manufacturer the re-order point is the level of finished goods stock at which the production order should be issued.

If we assume that an annual usage of a raw material is 6000 units and the weekly usage is constant then if there are 50 working weeks in a year, the weekly usage will be 120 units. If the lead time is two weeks, the order should be placed when stocks fall to 240 units. The economic order quantity can indicate how frequently the stocks should be purchased. For example, if the EOQ is 600 then, with an annual demand of 6000 units, ten orders will be placed every five weeks. However, with a lead time of two weeks, the firm will place an order three weeks after the first delivery when the stock will have fallen to 240 units (600 units EOQ less three weeks usage at 120 units per week). The order will then be repeated at five-weekly intervals. The EOQ model can therefore under certain circumstances be used to indicate when to replenish stocks and the amount to replenish. This process is illustrated in Figure 25.3(a).

Uncertainty and safety stocks

In practice, demand or usage of stocks is not known with certainty. In addition, there is usually a degree of uncertainty associated with the placement of an order and delivery of the stocks. To protect itself from conditions of uncertainty, a firm will maintain a level of **safety stocks** for raw materials, work in progress and finished goods stocks. Thus safety stocks are the amount of stocks that are carried in excess of the expected use during the lead time to provide a cushion against running out of stocks because of fluctuations in demand. For example, a firm that sets its re-order point on the assumption that the average lead time will be two weeks with an average weekly usage of 120 units will re-order when stocks fall to 240 units. However, the firm will run out of stock if actual demand increases to 140 units per week or if the lead time is three weeks. A firm might respond to this possibility by setting a re-order point of 420 units based on a *maximum usage* of 140 units per week and a lead time of three weeks. This will consist of a re-order point based on *expected usage* and lead time of 240 units (two weeks at 120 units) plus the balance of 180 units *safety stocks* to cover the possibility that lead time and expected usage will be greater than expected. Thus when demand and lead time are uncertain the re-order point is computed by adding the safety stock to the average usage during the average lead time.

In this illustration the safety stock was calculated on the basis of maximum demand and delivery time. It may well be that the probability of both these events occurring at the same time is extremely low. Under such circumstances the managers of the company are adopting a very risk-averse approach and taking no chances of running out of stock. Maintaining high safety stocks may not be in the company's best interests if the cost of holding the excessive stocks exceeds the costs that will be incurred if the company runs out of stock. It is therefore desirable to establish a sound quantitative procedure for determining an acceptable level of safety stocks. The level should be set where the cost of a stockout plus the cost of holding the safety stocks are minimized.

Stockout costs are the opportunity cost of running out of stock. In the case of finished goods the opportunity cost will consist of a loss of contribution if customers take their business elsewhere because orders cannot be met when requested. In the case of regular customers who are permanently lost because of a failure to meet delivery, this will be the discounted value of the lost contribution on future sales. When a stockout occurs for raw materials and work in progress stocks, the cost of being out of stock is the stoppage in production and the resulting inefficiencies that occur. This may be reflected by an estimate of the labour costs of idle time assuming that sales are *not* lost because of the stockout. Clearly, stockout costs are very difficult to estimate, and there are strong arguments for applying sensitivity tests to any analysis that uses estimated stockout costs. In practice, the lost contribution resulting from failure to meet demand may provide a reasonable approximation.

Once the stockout costs have been estimated, the costs of holding safety stocks should be compared for various demand levels. However, it is preferable to attach probabilities to

FIGURE 25.3 *Behaviour of stocks under conditions of certainty and uncertainty: (a) demand known with certainty: (b) demand not known with certainty and role of safety stocks*

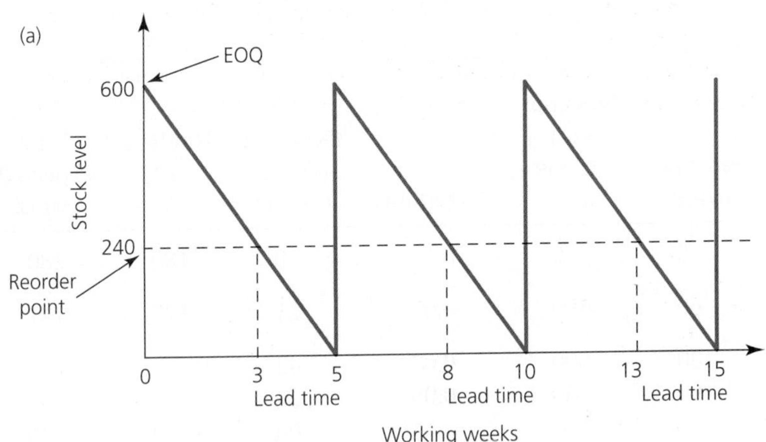

Assumptions:
EOQ = 600 units; lead time = 2 weeks; usage per week = 120 units;
Re-order point 240 units; order placed at end of weeks 3, 8, 13 etc.

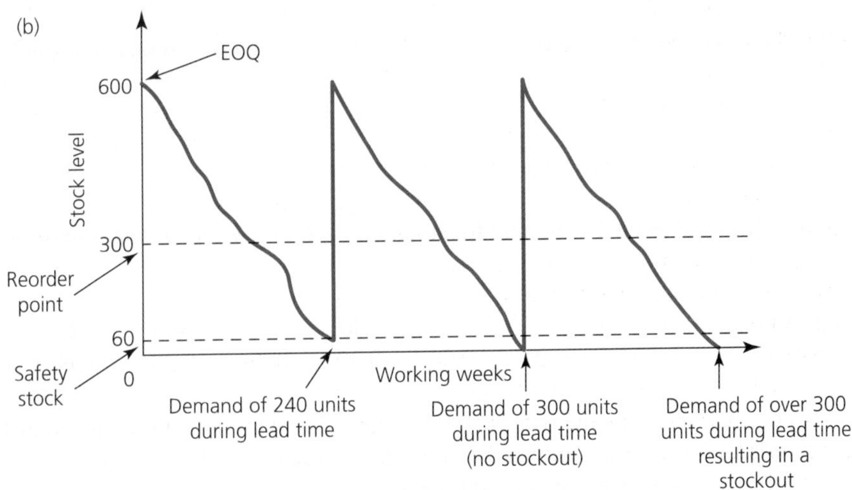

different potential demand levels and to decide on the appropriate quantity of safety stocks by comparing the expected cost values or probability distributions for various levels of safety stocks. Let us now illustrate this process.

The use of probability theory for determining safety stocks

By constructing probability distributions for future demand and lead time, it is possible to calculate the expected values for various safety stock levels. Suppose, for

EXHIBIT 25.2

Expected costs for various safety stocks

Average usage (units)	Safety stock (units)	Re-order point (units)	Stockout (units)	Stockout cost (£5 per unit)	Probability	Expected stockout cost (£)	Holding cost[a] (£)	Total expected cost (£)
240	180	420	0	0	0	0	180	180
240	120	360	60	300	0.07	21	120	141
240	60	300	120	600	0.07	42		
			60	300	0.08	24		
						66	60	126
240	0	240	180	900	0.07	63		
			120	600	0.08	48		
			60	300	0.20	60		
						171	0	171

[a]To simplify the analysis, it is assumed that a safety stock is maintained throughout the period. The average safety stock will therefore be equal to the total of the safety stock.

example, the total usage for an item for stock *over a two-week lead time* is expected to be as follows:

Usage (units)	60	120	180	240	300	360	420
Probability	0.07	0.08	0.20	0.30	0.20	0.08	0.07

The average usage during the two week lead time is 240 units, and it is assumed that the lead time is known with certainty. If the firm carries no safety stock, the re-order point will be set at 240 units (i.e. average usage during the lead time), and there will be no stockouts if actual usage is 240 units or less. However, if usage during the lead time period proves to be 300 units instead of 240 there will be a stockout of 60 units, and the probability of this occurring is 0.20. Alternatively, if usage is 360 or 420 units, there will be stockouts of 120 units and 180 units respectively with associated probabilities of 0.08 and 0.07. By maintaining a safety stock of 180 units, the firm ensures that a stockout will *not* occur.

Assuming we estimate stockout costs of £5 per unit and a holding cost of £1 per unit for the period, we can calculate the expected stockout cost, holding cost and total cost for various levels of safety stock. This information is presented in Exhibit 25.2. Note that if the re-order point is set at 360 units a stockout will only occur if usage is 420 units. Alternatively, if the re-order point is set at 300 units there will be a stockout of 60 units if usage is 360 units (probability = 0.08) and 120 units if usage is 420 units (probability = 0.07).

You will see that a safety stock of 60 units represents the level at which total expected costs are at their lowest. Hence a re-order point of 300 units will be set, consisting of the average usage during the lead time of 240 units plus a safety stock of 60 units.

A re-order point of 300 units with an uncertain demand is illustrated in Figure 25.3(b) for demands of 240, 300 and over 300 units during the lead time period. Note that the declines in stock do not fall on a straight line when demand is uncertain. If the probability distributions for each two-weekly period are expected to remain unchanged throughout the year, this safety stock (60 units) should be maintained.

However, if demand is expected to vary throughout the year, the calculations presented in Exhibit 25.2 must be repeated for the probability distributions for each period in which the probability distribution changes. The safety stock should then be adjusted prior to the commencement of each period.

Because of the difficulty in estimating the cost of a stockout, some firms might prefer not to use quantitative methods to determine the level of safety stocks. Instead, they might specify a maximum probability of running out of stock. If the firm in our illustration does not wish the probability of a stockout to exceed 10%, it will maintain a safety stock of 120 units and a re-order point of 360 units. A stockout will then occur only if demand is in excess of 360 units; the probability of such an occurrence is 7%.

Control of stocks through classification

In large firms it is quite possible for tens of thousands of different items to be stored. It is clearly impossible to apply the techniques outlined in this chapter to all of these. It is therefore essential that stocks be classified into categories of importance so that a firm can apply the most elaborate procedures of controlling stocks only to the most important items. The commonest procedure is known as the **ABC classification method**. This is illustrated in Exhibit 25.3.

The ABC method requires that an estimate be made of the total purchase cost for each item of stock for the period. The sales forecast is the basis used for estimating the quantities of each item of stock to be purchased during the period. Each item is then grouped in decreasing order of annual purchase cost. The top 10% of items in stock in terms of annual purchase cost are categorized as A items, the next 20% as B items and the final 70% as C items. If we assume there are 10 000 stock items then the top 1000 items in terms of annual purchase costs will be classified as A items, and so on. In practice, it will be unnecessary to estimate the value of many of the 7000 C items, since their annual purchase cost will be so small it will be obvious that they will fall into the C category.

You will see from Exhibit 25.3 that 10% of all stock items (i.e. the A items) represents 73% of the total cost; 20% of the items (B items) represent 19% of the total cost; and 70% of the items (C items) represent 8% of the total cost. It follows that the greatest degree of control should be exerted over the A items, which account for the high investment costs, and it is the A category items that are most appropriate for the application of the quantitative techniques discussed in this chapter. For these items an attempt should be made to maintain low safety stocks consistent with avoiding high stockout costs. Larger orders and safety stocks are likely to be a feature of the C-category items. Normally, re-order points for these items will be determined on a subjective basis rather than using quantitative methods, the objective being to minimize the expense in controlling these items. The control of B-category items is likely to be based on quantitative methods, but they are unlikely to be as sophisticated as for the A-category items.

The percentage value of total cost for the A, B and C categories in Exhibit 25.3 is typical of most manufacturing companies. In practice, it is normal for between 10% and 15% of the items in stock to account for between 70% and 80% of the total value of purchases. At the other extreme, between 70% and 80% of the items in stock account for approximately 10% of the total value. The control of stock levels is eased considerably if it is concentrated on that small proportion of stock items that account for most of the total cost.

EXHIBIT 25.3
ABC Classification of stocks

Stage 1. For each item in stock multiply the estimated usage for a period by the estimated unit price to obtain the total purchase cost:

Item	Estimated usage	Unit price (£)	Total purchase cost (£)
1	60 000	1.00	60 000
2	20 000	0.05	1 000
3	1 000	0.10	100
4	10 000	0.02	200
5	100 000	0.01	1 000
6	80 000	2.00	160 000

(This list is continued until all items in stock are included.)

Stage 2. Group all the above items in descending order of purchase price and then divide into class A (top 10%), class B (next 20%) and then class C (bottom 70%). The analysis might be as follows:

	Number of items in stock		Total cost	
	No	%	Amount (£)	%
Class A	1 000	10	730 000	73
Class B	2 000	20	190 000	19
Class C	7 000	70	80 000	8
	10 000	100	1 000 000	100

Other factors influencing the choice of order quantity

Shortage of future supplies

For various reasons, a firm may depart from quantitative models that provide estimates of the economic order quantity and the re-order point. A company may not always be able to rely on future supplies being available if the major suppliers are in danger of experiencing a strike. Alternatively, future supplies may be restricted because of import problems or transportation difficulties. In anticipation of such circumstances a firm may over-order so that stocks on hand will be sufficient to meet production while future supplies are restricted.

Future price increases

When a supplier announces a price increase that will be effective at some future date, it may be in a firm's interest to buy in excess of its immediate requirements before the increase becomes effective. Indeed, in times of rapid inflation firms might have an incentive to maintain larger stocks than would otherwise be necessary.

Obsolescence

Certain types of stocks are subject to obsolescence. For example, a change in technology may make a particular component worthless. Alternatively, a change in fashion may cause a clothes retailer to sell stocks at considerably reduced prices. Where the probability of obsolescence is high or goods are of a perishable nature, frequent purchases of small quantities and the maintenance of low stocks may be appropriate, even when the EOQ formula may suggest purchasing larger quantities and maintaining higher stock levels.

Steps to reduce safety stocks

When demand is uncertain, higher safety stocks are likely to be maintained. However, safety stocks may be reduced if the purchasing department can find new suppliers who will promise quicker and more reliable delivery. Alternatively, pressure may be placed on existing suppliers for faster delivery. The lower the average delivery time, the lower will be the safety stock that a firm needs to hold, and the total investment in stocks will be reduced.

Performance reporting

Formal performance reports may not record all the relevant costs used in the decision models for calculating the economic order quantity or optimum stock levels. In Chapter 16 we noted that a manager is likely to concentrate only on those variables that are measured, and ignore other important variables that are not measured. Indeed, a manager is likely to take action that will improve his or her performance rating, as indicated on the performance report, even if this is not always in the best interest of the company. For example, if annual holding costs are not allocated in a performance report to each manager, a manager may be induced to obtain larger order sizes even though this may not be the correct policy for the company as a whole. This may occur when a production manager engages in longer, but less frequent production runs, since this is likely to reduce the total annual costs that are charged to him or her, although larger stocks (with large holding costs) will be required to meet demand between the production runs.

Thus, it is important that accountants be aware of the adverse motivational implications that are likely to arise when the performance reporting system conflicts with the decision-making model. This type of situation can be avoided by charging holding costs to the appropriate manager. One way of doing this is to charge an imputed interest charge on the stocks for which a manager is responsible. (See the answer to Review problem 25.16 at the end of this chapter for an illustration.)

Materials requirement planning

The discussion so far in this chapter has assumed that the replenishment of stocks and the determination of re-order points and order quantities (i.e. the EOQ) for each item of material occurs independently of other activities. However, in complex manufacturing environments the demand for material purchases is dependent on the volume of the planned output of components and sub-components which include the raw materials that must be purchased. **Materials requirement planning (MRP)** originated in the early 1960s as a computerized approach for coordinating the planning of materials acquisition and production. The major feature of MRP is that it first involves an estimation of the quantity and timing of finished goods demanded and then uses this to determine the requirements for components/sub-components at each of the prior stages of production. This provides the basis for determining the quantity and timing of purchased materials and any bought-in components.

Figure 25.4 provides an overview of the approach. You can see that the top-level items represent three finished goods items (FG1, FG2 and FG3). The MRP system determines

FIGURE 25.4 *An overview of the structure of an MRP system*

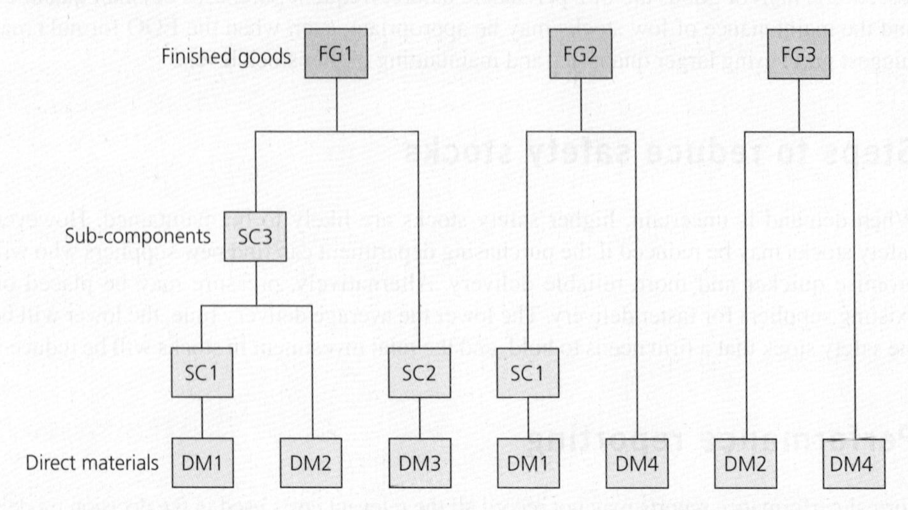

the requirements for each product into its components (or sub-components) and these are further separated into second, third and so on levels of sub-components, until at the lowest level of the hierarchy only purchased items (i.e. direct materials, DM) exist. For both FG1 and FG2 purchased raw materials are used to produce components before production of the end finished product. You should also note that in Figure 25.4 both FG1 and FG2 require the same sub-component (SC1), which in turn require the same direct materials (DM1).

The operation of an MRP system involves the following:

1 A *master production schedule*: This schedule is the starting point for MRP. It specifies both the timing, and quantity demanded of each of the top-level finished goods items.

2 A *bill of materials file*, which specifies the components/sub-components and materials required for each finished product.

3 A *master parts file* containing planned lead times of all items to be purchased and internally produced components.

4 An *inventory file* for each item of material and component/sub-component containing details of the current balance available, scheduled orders and items allocated to production but not yet drawn from stocks.

The aim of MRP is to generate a planned coordinated schedule of materials requirements for a specified time period for each item of material after taking into account scheduled receipts, projected target stock levels and items already allocated to production but not yet drawn from stocks. The EOQ model can be used within MRP systems to determine economic quantity sizes to be purchased provided that the major assumption of the EOQ model of constant demand broadly applies.

Finally, you should note that after its introduction in the 1960s, materials requirement planning was later extended to the management of all manufacturing resources. In particular, it focuses on machine capacity planning and labour scheduling as well as materials requirement planning. This extended system is known as **manufacturing resource planning** or MRP II. The term MRP I is used to describe materials requirement planning.

Just-in-time purchasing arrangements

In Chapter 22 the JIT manufacturing philosophy was described. At this stage you might find it useful to refer back to Chapter 22 and read pages 967–70. You will see that the goals of JIT include eliminating non-value added activities (such as some of the activities related to purchasing), a batch size of one, and zero inventories. To achieve these goals, JIT firms have extended the JIT philosophy to the purchasing function and the management of materials requirements.

JIT purchasing techniques seek to ensure that the delivery of materials immediately precedes their use. By arranging with suppliers for more frequent deliveries, stocks can be cut to a minimum. JIT purchasing also normally requires suppliers to inspect materials before their delivery and guarantee their quality. This can result in considerable savings in material handling expenses. This improved service is obtained by giving more business to fewer suppliers and placing long-term purchase orders. Therefore the supplier has an assurance of long-term sales, and can plan to meet this demand. For JIT purchasing to be successful close cooperation with suppliers, including providing them with planned production schedules, is essential. Thus, a major feature of JIT purchasing is that suppliers are not selected on the basis of price alone. Performance in terms of the quality of the components and materials supplied, the ability to always deliver as needed and a commitment to JIT purchasing are also of vital importance.

Companies that have implemented JIT purchasing techniques claim to have substantially reduced their investment in raw materials and work in progress stocks. Other advantages include significant quantity discounts, savings in time from negotiating with fewer suppliers and a reduction in clerical work from issuing long-term orders to a few suppliers rather than individual purchase orders to many suppliers.

Finally, you should note that the aim of JIT production and purchasing techniques is for production and purchases to immediately precede customer required delivery dates. By seeking to ensure that production and purchases are timed to coincide with demand the determination of economic order quantities and re-order points is no longer required.

Summary

The following items relate to the learning objectives listed at the beginning of the chapter.

- **Justify which costs are relevant and should be included in the calculation of the economic order quantity (EOQ).**

  The relevant costs that should be considered when determining the EOQ consist of holding costs and ordering costs. The relevant holding costs should include only those items that will vary with the levels of stocks. Examples include the opportunity cost in terms of the return that is lost from the capital tied up in stocks and incremental insurance, material handling and warehousing and storage costs. Ordering costs usually consist of the incremental clerical costs of preparing a purchase order, receiving deliveries and paying invoices. The purchase price is not normally a relevant cost since the cost per unit will be the same, irrespective of the order size. Note that special techniques can be applied to incorporate quantity discounts.

- **Calculate the EOQ using the tabulation and formula methods.**

  The tabulation method merely involves listing the ordering and holding costs for each potential order quantity over a selected period. The order costs are computed by multiplying the number of orders by the incremental cost per order. To compute the holding costs the average stock level is multiplied by the holding cost per unit.

Assuming constant usage, average stock levels are derived by dividing the potential order quantities by 2. The computation of the EOQ using both methods was illustrated using Example 25.1.

- **Determine whether or not a company should purchase larger quantities in order to take advantage of quantity discounts.**

  To ascertain whether larger quantities should be purchased the sum of the savings in purchase price arising from the discounts and the reduced ordering costs arising from fewer purchases are compared with the additional holding costs resulting from the increased stock levels associated with the larger order quantity. The computation was illustrated using Example 25.2.

- **Calculate the optimal safety stock when demand is uncertain.**

  Potential alternative levels of safety stock are added to estimated average usage for a particular period to derive potential re-order points. The expected cost, based on probabilities of demand, is determined for each potential re-order point. The optimal safety stock is represented by the safety stock associated with the re-order point that has the lowest expected cost. The analysis should include stockout costs (i.e. the opportunity cost of running out of stock). The computation of the optimal safety stock was illustrated in Exhibit 25.2.

- **Describe the ABC classification method.**

  The ABC method classifies stocks into categories of importance so that the most elaborate procedures of controlling stocks can be applied to the most important items. The ABC classification method requires that an estimate be made of the total purchase cost for each item in stock for a period. Each item is then grouped in decreasing order in terms of their purchase cost for the period. The top 10% of items in stock in terms of the purchase cost for the period are classified as 'A' items. The next 20% as 'B' items and the final 30% as 'C' items. It is generally found that the 'A' items can account for over 70% of the total purchase cost for a period. The most sophisticated procedures for planning and controlling stocks are applied to the 'A' items.

- **Describe materials requirement planning (MRP) systems.**

  The EOQ model assumes that the demand for each item of material occurs independently of other activities. However, in complex manufacturing environments the demand for material purchases is not independent. It is dependent on the volume of the planned output of components and sub-components which include the raw materials that must be purchased. Materials requirement planning (MRP) originated in the early 1960s as a computerized approach for coordinating the planning of materials acquisition and production. The major feature of MRP is that it first involves an estimation of the quantity and timing of finished goods demanded and then uses this to determine the requirements for components/sub-components at each of the prior stages of production. This provides the basis for determining the quantity and timing of purchased materials and any bought-in components. The aim of MRP is to generate a planned coordinated schedule of materials requirements for a specified time period for each item of material.

- **Explain just-in-time purchasing.**

  The JIT philosophy also extends to adopting JIT purchasing techniques, whereby the delivery of materials immediately precedes their use. By arranging with suppliers for more frequent deliveries, stocks can be cut to a minimum. This improved service is obtained by giving more business to fewer suppliers and placing long-term purchase orders. For JIT purchasing to be successful close cooperation with suppliers is essential.

Note

1 The steps are as follows;

$$\text{TC} = \frac{DO}{Q} + \frac{QH}{2}$$

$$\frac{\text{dTC}}{\text{d}Q} = \frac{-DO}{Q^2} + \frac{H}{2}$$

set

$$\frac{\text{dTC}}{\text{d}Q} = 0 : \frac{H}{2} - \frac{DO}{Q^2} = 0$$

$$HQ^2 = 2DO = 0$$

$$Q^2 = \frac{2DO}{H}$$

$$\text{Therefore } Q = \sqrt{\left(\frac{2DO}{H}\right)}$$

Key terms and concepts

ABC classification method (p. 1087)
cost of prediction error (p. 1081)
economic order quantity (EOQ) (p. 1077)
holding costs (p. 1076)
just-in-time purchasing techniques (p. 1091)
lead time (p. 1083)
manufacturing resource planning (p. 1090)
materials requirements planning (MRP) (p. 1089)
ordering costs (p. 1077)
precautionary motive (p. 1076)
re-order point (p. 1083)
safety stocks (p. 1084)
speculative motive (p. 1076)
stockout costs (p. 1084)
transactions motive (p. 1076)

Recommended reading

For a more detailed review of stock control models see Samuels *et al.* (1998) and Wilkes (1989).

Key examination points

A common mistake is to unitize fixed ordering and holding costs and include these costs in the EOQ formula. The EOQ should be calculated using variable unit costs. The EOQ formula does not include the cost of purchasing materials, since it is assumed that the cost per unit is the same for all order quantities. If the question includes quantity discounts, you should adopt the approach illustrated in this chapter.

The EOQ formula should not be used when the purchase cost per unit varies with the quantity ordered. Instead, you should prepare a schedule of the relevant costs for different order quantities. For an illustration of this approach see the answer to Review problem 25.15. You should also ensure that you can cope with problems where future demand is uncertain. Compare your answers with Review problems 25.18 and 25.19.

Assessment material

Review questions

The review questions are short questions that enable you to assess your understanding of the main topics included in the chapter. The numbers in parentheses provide you with the page numbers to refer to if you cannot answer a specific question.

Review problems

The review problems are more complex and require you to relate and apply the chapter content to various business problems. The problems are graded by their level of difficulty. The multiple-choice questions are the least demanding and normally take less than 10 minutes to complete. Fully worked solutions to the review problems are provided in a separate section at the end of the book. For those questions in the white box the worked solutions are provided in the *Student's Manual* accompanying this book. Further review problems for this chapter are available on the accompanying website www.drury-online.com. The answers to these problems are available for lecturers on the lecturer's password protected section of the website.

Case studies

The website also includes over 30 case study problems. A list of these cases is provided in Part Seven of this book.

Review questions

25.1 What are holding costs? Provide some examples. (*p. 1076*)

25.2 What are ordering costs? Provide some examples. (*p. 1077*)

25.3 What determines which holding and ordering costs should be included in the economic order quantity calculation? (*pp. 1076–77*)

25.4 What are the assumptions underlying the economic order quantity? (*p. 1080*)

25.5 Define lead time. (*p. 1083*)

25.6 Explain what is meant by the re-order point. (*p. 1083*)

25.7 What are stockout costs? Provide some examples. (*p. 1084*)

25.8 Explain how safety stocks are used to deal with demand uncertainty. (*pp. 1086–87*)

25.9 Describe the ABC classification method. What purposes does it serve? (*pp. 1087–88*)

25.10 Describe the other factors, besides the economic order quantity, that should be taken into account when choosing an order quantity. (*pp. 1088–89*)

25.11 What are the main features of materials requirements planning? (*pp. 1089–90*)

25.12 What are the essential features of just-in-time purchasing arrangements? (*p. 1091*)

Review problems

25.13 Intermediate

Moura uses the economic order quantity formula (EOQ) to establish its optimal reorder quantity for its single raw material. The following data relates to the stock costs:

Purchase price:	£15 per item
Carriage costs:	£50 *per order*
Ordering costs:	£5 *per order*
Storage costs:	10% of purchase price plus £0.20 per unit per annum

Annual demand is 4000 units.

What is the EOQ to the nearest whole unit?

A 153 units
B 170 units
C 485 units
D 509 units.

ACCA Paper 1.2 – Financial information for Management

25.14 Intermediate

A domestic appliance retailer with multiple outlets stocks a popular toaster known as the Autocrisp 2000, for which the following information is available:

Average sales	75 per day
Maximum sales	95 per day
Minimum sales	50 per day
Lead time	12–18 days
Re-order quantity	1750

(i) Based on the data above, at what level of stocks would a replenishment order be issued?

A 1050. B 1330. C 1710. D 1750.

(ii) Based on the data above, what is the maximum level of stocks possible?

A 1750. B 2860. C 3460. D 5210.

CIMA Stage 1 Cost Accounting

25.15 Intermediate: Calculation of optimum order size

A company is reviewing its stock policy, and has the following alternatives available for the evaluation of stock number 12 789:

(i) Purchase stock twice monthly, 100 units

(ii) Purchase monthly, 200 units

(iii) Purchase every three months, 600 units

(iv) Purchase six monthly, 1200 units

(v) Purchase annually, 2400 units.

It is ascertained that the purchase price per unit is £0.80 for deliveries up to 500 units. A 5% discount is offered by the supplier on the whole order where deliveries are 501 up to 1000, and 10% reduction on the total order for deliveries in excess of 1000.

Each purchase order incurs administration costs of £5.

Storage, interest on capital and other costs are £0.25 per unit of average stock quantity held.

You are required to advise management on the optimum order size.

(9 marks)
AAT

25.16 Intermediate: Relevant costs and cost of prediction error

The annual demand for an item of raw materials is 4000 units and the purchase price is expected to be £90 per unit. The incremental cost of processing an order is £135 and the cost of storage is estimated to be £12 per unit.

(a) What is the optimal order quantity and the total relevant cost of this order quantity?

(b) Suppose that the £135 estimate of the incremental cost of processing an order is incorrect and should have been £80. Assume that all other estimates are correct. What is the cost of this prediction error, assuming that the solution to part (a) is implemented for one year?

(c) Assume at the start of the period that a supplier offers 4000 units at a price of £86. The materials will be delivered immediately and placed in the stores. Assume that the incremental cost of placing this order is zero and the original estimate of £135 for placing an order for the economic batch size is correct. Should the order be accepted?

(d) Present a performance report for the purchasing officer, assuming that the budget was based on the information presented in (a) and the purchasing officer accepted the special order outlined in (c).

25.17 Advanced: Relevant costs and calculation of optimum batch size

Pink Ltd is experiencing some slight problems concerning two stock items sold by the company.

The first of these items is product Exe which is manufactured by Pink. The annual demand for Exe of 4000 units, which is evenly spread throughout the year, is usually met by production taking place four times per year in batches of 1000 units. One of the raw material inputs to product Exe is product Dee which is also manufactured by Pink. Product Dee is the firms major product and is produced in large quantities throughout the year. Production capacity is sufficient to meet in full *all* demands for the production of Dees.

The standard costs of products Exe and Dee are:

Standard costs – per unit

	Product Exe (£)	Product Dee (£)
Raw materials – purchased from external suppliers	13	8
– Dee standard cost	22	—
Labour – unskilled	7	4
– skilled	9	5
Variable overheads	5	3
Fixed overheads	4	2
Standard cost	£60	£22

Included in the fixed overheads for Exe are the set-up costs for each production run. The costs of each set-up, which apply irrespective of the size of the production run, are:

Costs per set-up

	(£)
(i) Labour costs – skilled labour	66
(ii) Machine parts	70
Total	£136

The 'Machine parts' relate to the cost of parts required for modifications carried out to the machine on which Exe is produced. The parts can be used for only one run, irrespective of run length, and are destroyed by replacement on reinstatement of the machine. There are no set-up costs associated with Dee.

The cost of financing stocks of Exe is 15% p.a. Each unit of Exe in stock requires 0.40 square metres of storage space and units *cannot* be stacked on top of each other to reduce costs. Warehouse rent is £20 p.a. per square metre and Pink is only required to pay for storage space actually used.

Pink is not working to full capacity and idle-time payments are being made to all grades of labour except unskilled workers. Unskilled labour is not guaranteed a minimum weekly wage and is paid only for work carried out.

The second stock item causing concern is product Wye. Product Wye is purchased by Pink for resale and the 10 000 unit annual demand is again spread evenly throughout the year. Incremental ordering costs are £100 per order and the normal unit cost is £20. However the suppliers of Wye are now offering quantity discounts for large orders. The details of these are:

Quantity ordered	Unit price (£)
Up to 999	20.00
1000 to 1999	19.80
2000 and over	19.60

The purchasing manager feels that full advantage should be taken of discounts and purchases should be made at £19.60 per unit using orders for 2000 units or more. Holding costs for Wye are calculated at £8.00 per unit per year and this figure will not be altered by any change in the purchase price per unit.

Required:

(a) Show the optimum batch size for the production of Exes. If this differs from the present policy, calculate the annual savings to be made by Pink Ltd from pursuing the optimal policy. Briefly explain the figures incorporated in your calculations. (The time taken to carry out a production run may be ignored.)

(10 marks)

(b) Advise Pink Ltd on the correct size of order for the purchase of Wyes.

(6 marks)

(c) Briefly describe two major limitations, or difficulties inherent in the practical application, of the model used in (a) to determine the optimum batch size.

(4 marks)

(Total 20 marks)

ACCA P2 Management Accounting

25.18 **Advanced: Safety stocks and probability theory**

A company has determined that the EOQ for its only raw material is 2000 units every 30 days. The company knows with certainty that a four-day lead time is required for ordering. The following is the probability distribution of estimated usage of the raw material for the month:

Usage (units)	1800	1900	2000	2100	2200	2300	2400	2500
Probability	0.06	0.14	0.30	0.16	0.13	0.10	0.07	0.04

Stockouts will cost the company £10 per unit, and the average monthly holding cost is £1 per unit.

(a) Determine the optimal safety stock.

(b) What is the probability of being out of stock?

25.19 **Advanced: Safety stocks, uncertain demand and quantity discounts**

Kattalist Ltd is a distributor of an industrial chemical in the north east of England. The chemical is supplied in drums which have to be stored at a controlled temperature.

The company's objective is to maximize profits, and it commenced business on 1 October.

The managing director's view:
The company's managing director wishes to improve stock holding policy by applying the economic order quantity model. Each drum of the chemical costs £50 from a supplier and sells for £60. Annual demand is estimated to be for 10 000 drums, which the managing director assumes to be evenly distributed over 300 working days. The cost of delivery is estimated at £25 per order and the annual variable holding cost per drum at £45 plus 10% of purchase cost. Using these data the managing director calculates the economic order quantity and proposes that this should be the basis for purchasing decisions of the industrial chemical in future periods.

The purchasing manager's view:
Written into the contract of the company's purchasing manager is a clause that he will receive a bonus (rounded to the nearest £1) of 10% of the amount by which total annual inventory holding and order costs before such remuneration are below £10 000. Using the same assumptions as the managing director, the

purchasing manager points out that in making his calculations the managing director has not only ignored his bonus but also the fact that suppliers offer quantity discounts on purchase orders. In fact, if the order size is 200 drums or above, the price per drum for an entire consignment is only £49.90, compared to £50 when an order is between 100 and 199 drums; and £50.10 when an order is between 50 and 99 drums.

The finance director's view.

The company's finance director accepts the need to consider quantity discounts and pay a bonus, but he also feels the managing director's approach is too simplistic. He points out that there is a lead time for an order of three days and that demand has not been entirely even over the past year. Moreover, if the company has no drums in stock, it will lose specific orders as potential customers will go to rival competitors in the region to meet their immediate needs.

To support his argument the finance director summarizes the evidence from salesmen's records over the past year, which show the number of drums demanded during the lead times were as follows:

Drums demanded during 3-day lead time	**Number of times each quantity of drums was demanded**
106	4
104	10
102	16
100	40
98	14
96	14
94	2

In the circumstances, the managing director decides he should seek further advice on what course of action he should take.

Requirements:

(a) Calculate the economic order quantity as originally determined by the company's managing director.

(1 mark)

(b) Calculate the optimum economic order quantity, applying the managing director's assumptions and after allowing for the purchasing manager's bonus and for supplier quantity discounts, but without using an expected value approach.

(3 marks)

(c) Adopting the financial director's assumptions and an expected value approach, and assuming that it is a condition of the supplier's contract that the order quantity is to be constant for all orders in the year, determine the expected level of safety (i.e. buffer) stock the company should maintain. For this purpose, use the figures for the economic order quantity you have derived in answering (b). Show all workings and state any assumptions you make.

(5 marks)

(d) As an outside consultant, write a report to the managing director on the company's stock ordering and stock holding policies, referring where necessary to your answers to (a)–(c). The report should *inter alia* refer to other factors he should consider when taking his final decisions on stock ordering and stock holding policies.

(9 marks)

Note: Ignore taxation.

(Total 18 marks)

ICAEW Management Accounting and Financial Management Part Two

Review problems (with answers in the Student's Manual)

25.20 **Advanced: Calculation of EOQ, discussion of the limitations of EOQ and a discussion of JIT**

The newly-appointed managing director of a division of Bondini plc is concerned about the length of the division's cash operating cycle. Extracts from the latest budget are given below:

Budgeted Profit and Loss Account for the year ending 30 June 2001

	(£000)	(£000)
Sales (43 200 units at £55)		2376
Opening Stock (21 600 units at £30)	648	
Purchases (43 200 units at £30)	1296	
	1944	
Closing Stock (21 600 units at £30)	648	1296
Budgeted Gross Profit		1080

Budgeted Balance Sheet as at 30 June 2001

	(£000)
Current Assets	
Stock	648
Trade debtors	198
Current Liabilities	
Trade creditors	216

The following information has also been gathered for the managing director:

(1) Sales were made evenly during the 12 months to 30 June 2000.

(2) The amount for trade creditors relates only to purchases of stock.

(3) The division is charged interest at the rate of 15% per annum on the average level of net assets held in a year.

(4) The company rents sufficient space in a warehouse to store the necessary stock at an annual cost of £3.25 per unit.

(5) The costs of ordering items of stock are as follows:

Insurance cost per order	£900
Transport cost per order	£750

(6) There will be no change in debtor and creditor payment periods.

In addition, the division maintains a purchasing department at an annual budgeted cost of £72 000.

The managing director has heard about the economic order quantity (EOQ) model and would prefer this basis to be used to calculate the order quantity. He estimates that the buffer stock level should be equal to one month's sales in order to prevent loss of revenue due to stock-outs.

Requirements:

(a) Calculate the EOQ for the division and, assuming that the division uses this as the basis for ordering goods from 1 July 2000, calculate the cash amounts which would be paid to trade creditors in each of the eight months to 28 February 2001.

(12 marks)

(b) Determine the length of the cash operating cycle at 30 June 2000 and calculate the improvement that will have taken place by 30 June 2001.

(4 marks)

(c) Discuss the practical limitations of using the EOQ approach to determining order quantities.

(5 marks)

(d) Describe the advantages and disadvantages of the just-in-time approach (i.e. when minimal stocks are maintained and suppliers deliver as required).

(4 marks)

(Total 25 marks)

ICAEW P2 Financial Management

25.21 Advanced: Calculation of EOQ and safety stocks assuming uncertainty

The retailing division of Josefa plc sells Hofers and its budget for the coming year is given below:

	(£)	(£)
Sales (4200 units at £85 each)		357 000
Cost of goods sold:		
Opening stock (200 units at £65 per unit)	13 000	
Purchases (4200 units at £750 per unit)	294 000	
	307 000	
Closing stock (200 units at £70 per unit)	14 000	293 000
Gross profit		64 000
Purchasing department cost		
Variable (7 orders at £300 per order)	2 100	
Fixed	8 400	
Transportation costs for goods received (7 orders at £750 per order)	5 250	
Stock insurance costs based on average stockholding (500 units at £4 per unit)	2 000	
Fixed warehouse costs	43 000	
		60 750
Budgeted net profit		3 250

The supplier of Hofers is responsible for their transportation and charges Josefa plc accordingly. Recently the supplier has offered to reduce the cost of transportation from £750 per order to £650 per order if Josefa plc will increase the order size from the present 600 units to a minimum of 1000 units.

The management of Josefa plc is concerned about the retailing division's stock ordering policy. At present, a buffer stock of 200 units is maintained and sales occur evenly throughout the year. Josefa plc has contracted to buy 4200 Hofers and, irrespective of the order quantity, will pay for them in equal monthly instalments throughout the year. Transportation costs are to be paid at the beginning of the year. The cost of capital of Josefa plc is 20% p.a.

Requirements:

(a) Determine the quantity of Hofers which Josefa plc should order, assuming the buffer stock level of 200 units is maintained, and calculate the improvement in net profit that will result.

(11 marks)

(b) Calculate what the buffer stock level should be, assuming that:

(i) Josefa plc changes its ordering frequency to one order (of 700 units) every two months;

(ii) stockout costs are £18 per unit;

(iii) the distribution of sales within each two-month period is not even but the following two-monthly sales pattern can occur:

2-monthly sales	Probability
500 units	0.15
600 units	0.20
700 units	0.30
800 units	0.20
900 units	0.15

(7 marks)

(c) Discuss the problems which might be experienced in attempting to maintain a stock control system based upon economic order quantities and buffer stocks.

(7 marks)
(Total 25 marks)

Ignore taxation.

ICAEW P2 Financial Management

25.22 Advanced: Safety stocks and uncertain demand and quantity discounts

Runswick Ltd is a company that purchases toys from abroad for resale to retail stores. The company is concerned about its stock (inventory) management operations. It is considering adopting a stock management system based upon the economic order quantity (EOQ) model.

The company's estimates of its stock management costs are shown below:

Percentage of purchase price of toys per year	
Storage costs	3
Insurance	1
Handling	1
Obsolescence	3
Opportunity costs of funds invested in stock	10

'Fixed' costs associated with placing each order for stock are £311.54

The purchase price of the toys to Runswick Ltd is £4.50 per unit. There is a two week delay between the time that new stock is ordered from suppliers and the time that it arrives.

The toys are sold by Runswick at a unit price of £6.30. The variable cost to Runswick of selling the toys is £0.30 per unit. Demand from Runswick's customers for the toys averages 10 000 units per week, but recently this has varied from 6000 to 14 000 units per week. On the basis of recent evidence the probability of unit sales in any two week period has been estimated as follows:

Sales (units)	Probability
12 000	0.05
16 000	0.20
20 000	0.50
24 000	0.20
28 000	0.05

If adequate stock is not available when demanded by Runswick's customers in any two week period approximately 25% of orders that cannot be satisfied in that period will be lost, and approximately 75% of customers will be willing to wait until new stock arrives.

Required:

(a) Ignoring taxation, calculate the optimum order level of stock over a one year planning period using the economic order quantity model.

(3 marks)

(b) Estimate the level of safety stock that should be carried by Runswick Ltd.

(6 marks)

(c) If Runswick Ltd were to be offered a quantity discount by its suppliers of 1% for orders of 30 000 units or more, evaluate whether it would be beneficial for the company to take advantage of the quantity discount. Assume for this calculation that no safety stock is carried.

(4 marks)

(d) Estimate the expected total annual costs of stock management if the economic order quantity had been (i) 50% higher (ii) 50% lower than its actual level. Comment upon the sensitivity of total annual costs to changes in the economic order quantity. Assume for this calculation that no safety stock is carried.

(4 marks)

(e) Discuss briefly how the effect of seasonal sales variations might be incorporated within the model.

(3 marks)

(f) Assess the practical value of this model in the management of stock.

(5 marks)

(Total 25 marks)

ACCA Level 3 Financial Management

The application of linear programming to management accounting

26

In the previous chapters we have seen that there is an opportunity cost for scarce resources that should be included in the relevant cost calculation for decision-making and variance calculations. Our previous discussions, however, have assumed that output is limited by one scarce resource, but in practice several resources may be scarce. The opportunity costs of these scarce resources can be determined by the use of linear programming techniques. Our objective in this chapter is to examine linear programming techniques and to consider how they can be applied to some specific types of decisions that a firm may have to make.

LEARNING OBJECTIVES

After studying this chapter you should be able to:

- describe the situations when it may be appropriate to use linear programming;
- explain the circumstances when the graphical method can be used;
- use graphical linear programming to find the optimum output levels;
- formulate the initial linear programming model using the simplex method;
- explain the meaning of the term shadow prices.

Single-resource constraints

In Chapter 9 we considered how accounting information should be used to ensure that scarce resources are efficiently allocated. We established that where a scarce resource exists, that has alternative uses, the contribution per unit should be calculated for each of these uses. The available capacity for this resource is then allocated to the alternative uses on the basis of contribution per scarce resource. A typical problem is presented in Exhibit 26.1.

If we follow the procedure suggested in Chapter 9, we can ascertain the contribution per unit of the scarce resource. Product Y yields a contribution of £14 and uses 6 scarce labour hours. Hence the contribution is £2.33 per labour hour. Similarly, the contribution per labour hour for product Z is £2. The company should therefore allocate scarce labour hours to the manufacture of product Y. Sales of product Y, however, are limited to 420 units, which means that 2520 labour hours (420 units at 6 hours per unit) will be used. The remaining 360 hours will then be allocated to product Z. As one unit of product Z requires 8 labour hours, the total output of product Z will be 45 units.

Profits will be maximized when the firm manufactures 420 units of product Y and 45 units of product Z. This will give a total contribution of £6600, which is calculated as follows:

	(£)
420 units of Y at a contribution of £14 per unit	5880
45 units of Z at a contribution of £16 per units	720
	6600

Two-resource constraints

Where more than one scarce resource exists, the optimum production programme cannot easily be established by the process previously outlined. Consider the situation in Exhibit 26.1, where there is an additional scarce resource besides labour. Let us assume that both products Y and Z use a common item of material and that the supply of this material in the next accounting period is restricted to 3440 units. There are now two scarce resources – labour and materials. If we apply the procedure outlined above, the contribution per unit of scarce resource would be as follows:

	Product Y (£)	Product Z (£)
Labour	2.33 (£14/6 hours)	2.00 (£16/8 hours)
Material	1.75 (£14/8 units)	4.00 (£16/4 units)

This analysis shows that product Y yields the largest contribution per labour hour, and product Z yields the largest contribution per unit of scarce materials, but there is no clear indication of how the quantity of scarce resources should be allocated to each product. In such circumstances there is a need to resort to higher-powered mathematical techniques to establish the optimal output programme.

EXHIBIT 26.1

A single-resource constraint problem

The LP company currently produces two products. The standards per unit of product are as follows:

Product Y	(£)	(£)	Product Z	(£)	(£)
Standard selling price		110	Standard selling price		118
Less variable standard costs:			Less variable standard costs:		
Materials (8 units at £4)	32		Materials (4 units at £4)	16	
Labour (6 hours at £10)	60		Labour (8 hours at £10)	80	
Variable overhead			Variable overhead		
(4 machine hours at £1)	4		(6 machine hours at £1)	6	
		96			102
Contribution		14	Contribution		16

During the next accounting period, it is expected that the availability of labour hours will be restricted to 2880 hours. The remaining production inputs are not scarce, but the marketing manager estimates that the maximum sales potential for product Y is 420 units. There is no sales limitation for product Z.

Linear programming

Linear programming is a powerful mathematical technique that can be applied to the problem of rationing limited facilities and resources among [...] alternative uses in such a way that the optimum benefits can be derived from the [...] It seeks to find a feasible combination of output that will maximize or mir[...] [...]ction. The objective function refers to the quantification of an obje[...] [...] of maximizing profits or minimizing costs. Linear progr[...] ships can be assumed to be linear and where an optir[...]

To comply with the linearity assumption, it mu[...] unit for each product and the utilization of resource[...] of output is produced and sold within the outpu[...] assumed that units produced and resources all[...] that an optimal plan that suggests we should [...] will be necessary to interpret the plan as a pr[...]

Let us now apply this technique to the pr[...] labour restriction plus a limitation on the [...] revised problem is presented in Exhibit 2[...]

The procedure that we should follow t[...] algebraically, with Y denoting the numb[...] product Z that are manufactured by t[...] function, which in this example is to [...] input constraints. We can now form[...]

Maximize $C = 14Y + 16Z$ subj[...]
$8Y + 4Z \leqslant 3440$ (material co[...]
$6Y + 8Z \leqslant 2880$ (labour co[...]
$4Y + 6Z \leqslant 2760$ (machine [...]
$0 \leqslant Y \leqslant 420$ (maximum [...]
$Z \geqslant 0$ (minimum sales [...]

EXHIBIT 26.2
Multiple resource constraint problem

The LP company currently makes two products. The standards per unit of product are as follows:

Product Y	(£)	(£)	Product Z	(£)	(£)
Product Y			Product Z		
Standard selling price		110	Standard selling price		118
Less standard costs:			Less standard costs:		
Materials (8 units at £4)	32		Materials (4 units at £4)	16	
Labour (6 hours at £10)	60		Labour (8 hours at £10)	80	
Variable overhead			Variable overhead		
(4 machine hours at £1)	4		(6 machine hours at £1)	6	
		96			102
Contribution		14	Contribution		16

During the next accounting period, the availability of resources are expected to be subject to the following limitations:

Labour	2880 hours
Materials	3440 units
Machine capacity	2760 hours

The marketing manager estimates that the maximum sales potential for product Y is limited to 420 units. There is no sales limitation for product Z. You are asked to advise how these limited facilities and resources can best be used so as to gain the optimum benefit from them.

In this model, 'maximize C' indicates that we wish to maximize contribution with an unknown number of units of Y produced, each yielding a contribution of £14 per unit, and an unknown number of units of Z produced, each yielding a contribution of £16. The labour constraint indicates that 6 hours of labour are required for each unit of product Y that is made, and 8 hours for each unit of product Z. Thus (6 hours × Y) + (8 hours × Z) cannot exceed 2880 hours. Similar reasoning applies to the other inputs.

Because linear programming is nothing more than a mathematical tool for solving constrained optimization problems, nothing in the technique itself ensures that an answer ...ill 'make sense'. For example, in a production problem, for some very unprofitable ...t, the optimal output level may be a negative quantity, which is clearly an impossible ... To prevent such non-sensical results, we must include a non-negativity ...hich is a statement that all variables in the problem must be equal to or ...e must therefore add to the model in our example the constraint that ... than or equal to zero, i.e. $Z \geqslant 0$ and $0 \leqslant Y \leqslant 420$. The latter ... of Y cannot be less than zero or greater than 420 units. The ... or by the Simplex method. When no more than two ...cal method can be used, but this becomes impracti... ...volved, and it is then necessary to resort to the

Graphical method

Taking the first *constraint for the materials* input $8Y + 4Z \leqslant 3440$ means that we can make a maximum of 860 units of product Z when production of product Y is zero. The 860 units is arrived at by dividing the 3440 units of materials by the 4 units of material required for each unit of product Z. Alternatively, a maximum of 430 units or product Y can be made (3440 units divided by 8 units of materials) if no materials are allocated to product Z. We can therefore state that

$$\text{when } Y = 0, Z = 860$$
$$\text{when } Z = 0, Y = 430$$

These items are plotted in Figure 26.1, with a straight line running from $Z = 0$, $Y = 430$ to $Y = 0$, $Z = 860$. Note that the vertical axis represents the number of units of Y produced and the horizontal axis the number of units of Z produced.

The area to the left of line $8Y + 4Z \leqslant 3440$ contains all possible solutions for Y and Z in this particular situation, and any point along the line connecting these two outputs represents the maximum combinations of Y and Z that can be produced with not more than 3440 units of materials. Every point to the right of the line violates the material constraint.

The *labour constraint* $6Y + 8Z \leqslant 2880$ indicates that if production of product Z is zero, then a maximum of 480 units of product Y can be produced (2880/6), and if the output of Y is zero then 360 units of Z (2880/8) can be produced. We can now draw a second line $Y = 480$, $Z = 0$ to $Y = 0$, $Z = 360$, and this is illustrated in Figure 26.2. The area to the left of line $6Y + 8Z \leqslant 2880$ in this figure represents all the possible solutions that will satisfy the labour constraint.

The *machine input constraint* is represented by $Z = 0$, $Y = 690$ and $Y = 0$, $Z = 460$, and the line indicating this constraint is illustrated in Figure 26.3. The area to the left of the line $4Y + 6Z \leqslant 2760$ in this figure represents all the possible solutions that will satisfy the machine capacity constraint.

The final constraint is that the *sales output* of product Y cannot exceed 420 units. This is represented by the line $Y \leqslant 420$ in Figure 26.4, and all the items below this line represent all the possible solutions that will satisfy this sales limitation.

It is clear that any solution that is to fit *all* the constraints must occur in the shaded area ABCDE in Figure 26.5, which represents Figures 26.1–26.4 combined together. The point must now be found within the shaded area ABCDE where the contribution C is the greatest. The maximum will occur at one of the corner points ABCDE. The objective function is $C = 14Y + 16Z$, and a random contribution value is chosen that will result in a line for the objective function falling within the area ABCDE.

If we choose a random total contribution value equal to £2240, this could be obtained from producing 160 units (£2240/£14) of Y at £14 contribution per unit or 140 units of Z (£2240/£16) at a contribution of £16 per unit. We can therefore draw a line $Z = 0$, $Y = 160$ to $Y = 0$, $Z = 140$. This is represented by the dashed line in Figure 26.5. Each point on the dashed line represents all the output combinations of Z and Y that will yield a total contribution of £2240. The dashed line is extended to the right until it touches the last corner of the boundary ABCDE. This is the optimal solution and is at point C, which indicates an output of 400 units of Y (contribution £5600) and 60 units of Z (contribution £960), giving a total contribution of £6560.

The logic in the previous paragraph is illustrated in Figure 26.6. The shaded area represents the feasible production area ABCDE that is outlined in Figure 26.5, and parallel lines represent possible contributions, which take on higher values as we move to the right. If we assume that the firm's objective is to maximize total contribution, it should operate on the

FIGURE 26.1 *Constraint imposed by limitations of materials*

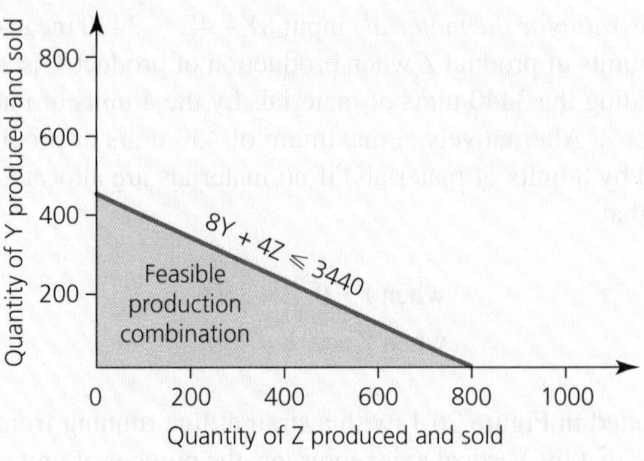

FIGURE 26.2 *Constraint imposed by limitations of labour*

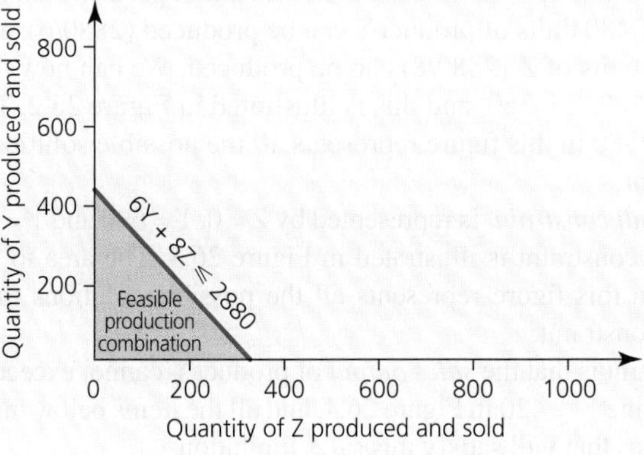

FIGURE 26.3 *Constraint imposed by machine capacity*

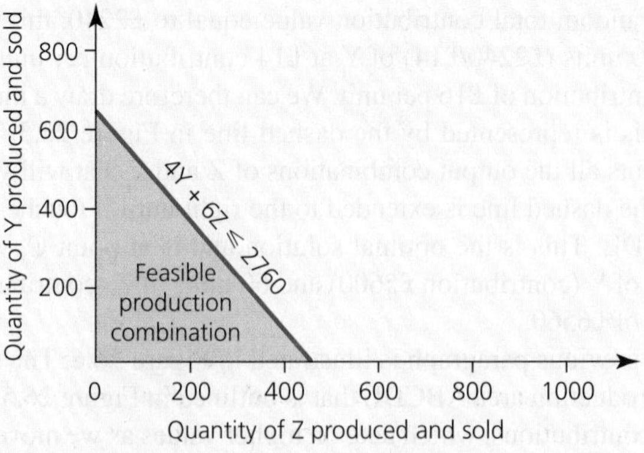

FIGURE 26.4 *Constraint imposed by sales limitation of product Y*

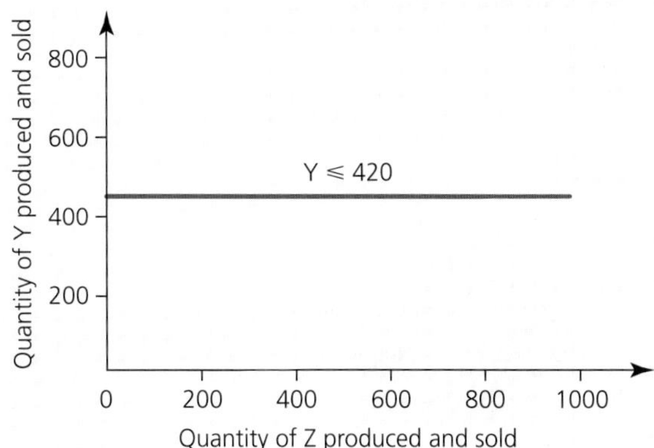

FIGURE 26.5 *Combination of Figures 26.1–26.4*

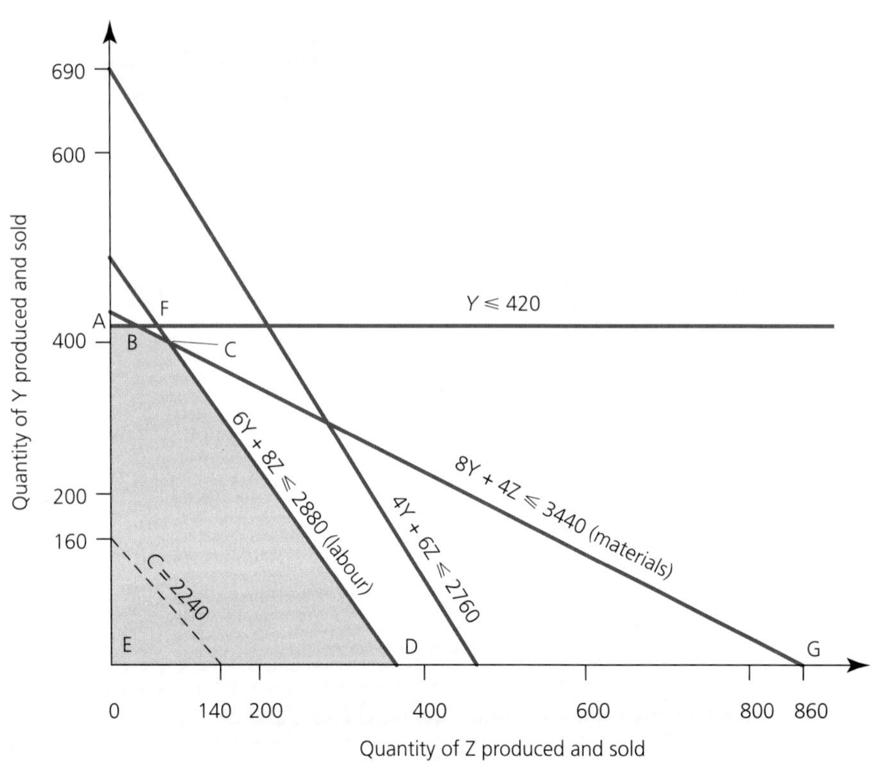

highest contribution curve obtainable. At the same time, it is necessary to satisfy the production constraints, which are indicated by the shaded area in Figure 26.6. You will see that point C indicates the solution to the problem, since no other point within the feasible area touches such a high contribution line.

FIGURE 26.6 *Contribution levels from different potential combinations of products Y and Z*

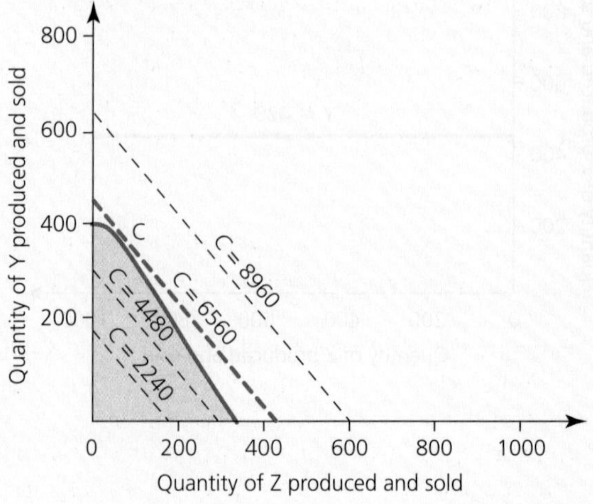

It is difficult to ascertain from Figure 26.5 the exact output of each product at point C. The optimum output can be determined exactly by solving the simultaneous equations for the constraints that intersect at point C:

$$8Y + 4Z = 3440 \quad (26.1)$$

$$6Y + 8Z = 2880 \quad (26.2)$$

We can now multiply equation (26.1) by 2 and equation (26.2) by 1, giving

$$16Y + 8Z = 6880 \quad (26.3)$$

$$6Y + 8Z = 2880 \quad (26.4)$$

Subtracting equation (26.4) from equation (26.3) gives

$$10Y = 4000$$

and so

$$Y = 400$$

We can now substitute this value for Y onto equation (26.3), giving

$$(16 \times 400) + 8Z = 6880$$

and so

$$Z = 60$$

You will see from Figure 26.5 that the constraints that are binding at point C are materials and labour. It might be possible to remove these constraints and acquire additional labour and materials resources by paying a premium over and above the existing acquisition cost. How much should the company be prepared to pay? To answer this question, it is necessary to determine the optimal use from an additional unit of a scarce resource.

We shall now consider how the optimum solution would change if an additional unit of materials were obtained. You can see that if we obtain additional materials, the line $8Y + 4Z \leq 3440$ in Figure 26.5 will shift upwards and the revised optimum point will fall on line CF. If one extra unit of materials is obtained, the constraints $8Y + 4Z \leq 3440$ and $6Y + 8Z \leq 2880$ will still be binding, and the new optimum plan can be determined by solving the following simultaneous equations:

$$8Y + 4Z = 3441 \text{ (revised materials constraint)}$$
$$6Y + 8Z = 2880 \text{ (unchanged labour constraint)}$$

The revised optimal output when the above equations are solved is 400.2 units of Y and 59.85 units of Z. Therefore the planned output of product Y should be increased by 0.2 units, and planned production of Z should be reduced by 0.15 units. This optimal response from an independent marginal increase in a resource is called the **marginal rate of substitution**. The change in contribution arising from obtaining one additional unit of materials is as follows:

	(£)
Increase in contribution from Y (0.2 × £14)	2.80
Decrease in contribution of Z (0.15 × £16)	(2.40)
Increase in contribution	0.40

Therefore the value of an additional unit of materials is £0.40. The value of an independent marginal increase of scarce resource is called the **opportunity cost** or **shadow price**. We shall be considering these terms in more detail later in the chapter. You should note at this stage that for materials purchased in excess of 3440 units the company can pay up to £0.40 over and above the present acquisition cost of materials of £4 and still obtain a contribution towards fixed costs from the additional output.

From a practical point of view, it is not possible to produce 400.2 units of Y and 59.85 units of Z. Output must be expressed in single whole units. Nevertheless, the output from the model can be used to calculate the revised optimal output if additional units of materials are obtained. Assume that 100 additional units of materials can be purchased at £4.20 per unit from an overseas supplier. Because the opportunity cost (£0.40) is in excess of the additional acquisition cost of £0.20 per unit (£4.20 – £4), the company should purchase the extra materials. The marginal rates of substitution can be used to calculate the revised optimum output. The calculation is

Increase Y by 20 units (100 × 0.2 units)
Decrease Z by 15 units (100 × 0.15 units)

Therefore the revised optimal output is 420 outputs (400 + 20) of Y and 35 units (60 – 15) of Z. You will see later in this chapter that the substitution process outlined above is applicable only within a particular range of material usage.

We can apply the same approach to calculate the opportunity cost of labour. If an additional labour hour is obtained, the line $6Y + 8Z \leq 2880$ in Figure 26.5 will shift to the right, and the revised optimal point will fall on line CG. The constraints $8Y + 4Z \leq 3440$ and $6Y + 8Z \leq 2880$ will still be binding, and the new optimum plan can be determined by solving the following simultaneous equations:

$$8Y + 4Z = 3440 \text{ (unchanged materials constraint)}$$
$$6Y + 8Z = 2881 \text{ (revised labour constraint)}$$

The revised optimal output when the above equations are solved is 399.9 units of Y and 60.2 units of Z. Therefore the planned output of product Y should be decreased by 0.1 units and planned production of Z should be increased by 0.2 units. The opportunity cost of a scarce labour hour is

	(£)
Decrease in contribution from Y (0.1 × £14)	(1.40)
Increase in contribution from Z (0.2 × £16)	3.20
Increase in contribution (opportunity cost)	1.80

Simplex method

Where more than two products can be manufactured using the scarce resources available, the optimum solution cannot easily be established from the graphical method. An alternative is a non-graphical solution known as the **Simplex method**. This method also provides additional information on opportunity costs and marginal rates of substitution that is particularly useful for decision-making, and also for planning and control.

The Simplex method involves making many tedious calculations, but there are standard spreadsheet packages that will complete the task within a few minutes. The aim of this chapter is therefore not to delve into these tedious calculations but rather to provide an understanding of their nature and their implications for management accounting. Nevertheless, to provide a basic understanding of the method, the procedure for completing the calculations must be outlined, and we shall do this by applying the procedure to the problem set out in Exhibit 26.2.

To apply the Simplex method, we must first formulate a model that does not include any *inequalities*. This is done by introducing what are called **slack variables** to the model. Slack variables are added to a linear programming problem to account for any constraint that is unused at the point of optimality, and one slack variable is introduced for each constraint. In our example, the company is faced with constraints on materials, labour, machine capacity and maximum sales for product Y. Therefore S_1 is introduced to represent unused material resources, S_2 represents unused labour hours, S_3 represents unused machine capacity and S_4 represents unused potential sales output. We can now express the model for Exhibit 26.2 in terms of equalities rather than inequalities:

$$\text{Maximize } C = 14Y + 16Z$$

subject to

$$8Y + 4Z + S_1 = 3440 \text{ (materials constraint)}$$
$$6Y + 8Z + S_2 = 2880 \text{ (labour constraint)}$$
$$4Y + 6Z + S_3 = 2760 \text{ (machine capacity constraint)}$$
$$1Y + S_4 = 420 \text{ (sales constraint for product } Y\text{)}$$

For labour (6 hours × Y) + (8 hours × Z) plus any unused labour hours (S_2) will equal 2880 hours when the optimum solution is reached. Similar reasoning applies to the other production constraints. The sales limitation indicates that the number of units of Y sold plus any shortfall on maximum demand will equal 420 units.

We shall now express all the above equations in matrix form, with the slack variables on the left-hand side:

First matrix

Quantity	Y	Z	
$S_1 = 3440$	−8	−4	(1) (material constraint)
$S_2 = 2880$	−6	−8	(2) (labour constraint)
$S_3 = 2760$	−4	−6	(3) (machine hours constraint)
$S_4 = 420$	−1	0	(4) (sales constraint)
$C = 0$	+14	+16	(5) contribution

Note that the quantity column in the matrix indicates the resources available or the slack that is not taken up when production is zero. For example, the S_1 row of the matrix indicates that 3440 units of materials are available when production is zero. Column Y indicates that 8 units of materials, 6 labour hours and 4 machine hours are required to produce 1 unit of product Y, and this will reduce the potential sales of Y by 1. You will also see from column Y that the production of 1 unit of Y will yield £14 contribution. Similar reasoning applies to column Z. Note that the entry in the contribution row (i.e. the C row) for the quantity column is zero because this first matrix is based on nil production, which gives a contribution of zero.

Deriving the final matrix

Spreadsheet packages are available that will produce the final matrix. They merely require you to input the initial data (i.e. the objective function and the constraints). Because of this you may wish to omit this section which explains how the final matrix is derived.

To produce the second matrix the starting point is to examine the first matrix to determine which product we should choose. As product Z yields the highest contribution, we should choose this, but our production is limited because of the input constraints. Materials limit us to a maximum production of 860 units (3440 units/4 per unit), labour to a maximum production of 360 units (2880 hours/8 per hour) and machine capacity to a maximum production of 460 units (2760 hours/6 per hour). We are therefore restricted to a maximum production of 360 units of product Z because of a labour constraint. The procedure that we should follow is to *rearrange the equation that results in the constraint (i.e. S_2) in terms of the product we have chosen to make (i.e. product Z)*. Therefore equation (2), which is

$$S_2 = 2880 - 6Y - 8Z$$

becomes

$$8Z = 2880 - 6Y - S_2$$

and so

$$Z = 360 - 3/4Y - 1/8\,S_2$$

We now substitute this value for Z into each of the other equations appearing in the first matrix. The calculations are as follows:

$$\begin{aligned} S_1 &= 3440 - 8Y - 4(360 - \tfrac{3}{4}Y - \tfrac{1}{8}S_2) \\ &= 3440 - 8Y - 1440 + 3Y + \tfrac{1}{2}S_2 \qquad (1) \\ &= 2000 - 5Y + \tfrac{1}{2}S_2 \end{aligned}$$

$$\begin{aligned} S_3 &= 2760 - 4Y - 6(360 - {}^3\!/_4 Y - {}^1\!/_8 S_2) \\ &= 2760 - 4Y - 2160 + 4{}^1\!/_2 Y + {}^3\!/_4 S_2 \qquad (3) \\ &= 600 + {}^1\!/_2 Y + {}^3\!/_4 S_2 \end{aligned}$$

$$\begin{aligned} C &= 0 + 14Y + 16(360 - {}^3\!/_4 Y - {}^1\!/_8 S_2) \\ &= 0 + 14Y + 5760 - 12Y - 2S_2 \qquad (5) \\ &= 5760 + 2Y - 2S_2 \end{aligned}$$

Note that equation (4) in the first matrix remains unchanged because Z is not included. We can now restate the revised five equations in a second matrix:

Second matrix

Quantity	Y	S_2	
$S_1 = 2000$	-5	$+{}^1\!/_2$	(1) (material constraint)
$Z = 360$	$-{}^3\!/_4$	$-{}^1\!/_8$	(2)
$S_3 = 600$	$+{}^1\!/_2$	$+{}^3\!/_4$	(3) (machine hours constraint)
$S_4 = 420$	-1	0	(4) (sales constraint)
$C = 5760$	$+2$	-2	(5)

The substitution process outlined for the second matrix has become more complex, but the logical basis still remains. For example, the *quantity column* of the second matrix indicates that 2000 units of material are unused, 360 units of Z are to be made, 600 machine hours are still unused and sales of product Y can still be increased by another 420 units before the sales limitation is reached. The contribution row indicates that a contribution of £5760 will be obtained from the production and sale of 360 units of product Z. Column Y indicates that production of 1 unit of product Y uses up 5 units of the stock of materials, but, because no labour hours are available, $^3\!/_4$ units of product Z must be released. This will release 3 units of materials ($^3\!/_4 \times 4$), 6 labour hours ($^3\!/_4 \times 8$ hours) and $4^1\!/_2$ machine hours ($^3\!/_4 \times 6$). From this substitution process we now have 8 units of materials (5 units + 3 units), 6 labour hours and $4^1\!/_2$ machine hours.[1]

From the standard cost details in Exhibit 26.2 you can see that one unit of Y requires 8 units of materials, 6 labour hours and 4 machine hours. This substitution process thus provides the necessary resources for producing 1 unit of product Y, as well as providing an additional half an hour of machine capacity. This is because production of 1 unit of product Y requires that production of item Z be reduced by $^3\!/_4$ units, which releases $4^1\!/_2$ machine hours. However, product Y only requires 4 machine hours, so production of 1 unit of Y will increase the available machine capacity by half an hour. This agrees with the entry in column Y of the second matrix for machine capacity. Column Y also indicates that production of 1 unit of Y reduces the potential sales of product Y (S_4) by 1 unit.

The optimum solution is achieved when the contribution row contains only negative or zero values. Because row C contains a positive item, our current solution can be improved by choosing the product with the highest positive contribution. Thus we should choose to manufacture product Y, since this is the only positive item in the contribution row. The second matrix indicates that the contribution can be increased by £2 by substituting 1 unit of Y for $^3\!/_4$ units of Z. We therefore obtain an additional contribution of £14 from Y but lose a £12 contribution from Z ($^3\!/_4 \times 16$) by this substitution process. The overall result is an increased contribution of £2 by adopting this substitution process.

The procedure is then repeated to formulate the third matrix. Column Y of the second matrix indicates that we should use 5 units of materials and release $^3\!/_4$ units of Z to obtain an additional unit of Y, but there are limitations in adopting this plan. The unused materials are 2000 units, and each unit of Y will require 5 units, giving a maximum production of 400 units of Y. We have 360 units of Z allocated to production, and each unit of Y requires us to release $^3/_4$ units of Z. A maximum production of 480 units of Y ($360/^3/_4$) can therefore be obtained from this substitution process. There is no limitation on machine hours, since the second matrix indicates that the substitution process increases machine hours by half an hour for each unit of Y produced. The sales limitation of Y indicates that a maximum of 420 units of Y can be produced. The following is a summary of the limitations in producing product Y:

$$S_1 \text{ (materials)} = 400 \text{ units } (2000/5)$$
$$Z \text{ (substitution of product Z)} = 480 \text{ units } (360/^3/_4)$$
$$S_4 \text{ (maximum sales of Y)} = 420 \text{ units } (420/1)$$

In other words, we merely divide the *negative* items in column Y into the quantity column. The first limitation we reach is 400 units, and this indicates the maximum production of Y because of the impact of the materials constraint.

The procedure that we applied in formulating the second matrix is then repeated; that is, *we rearrange the equation that results in the constraint (S_1) in terms of the product we have chosen to make (i.e. product Y)*. Therefore equation (1), which is

$$S_1 = 2000 - 5Y + {}^1/_2S_2$$

becomes

$$5Y = 2000 - S_1 + {}^1/_2S_2$$

and so

$$Y = 400 - {}^1/_5S_1 + {}^1/_{10}S_2$$

Substituting for Y in each of the other equations in the second matrix, we get the following revised equations:

$$Z = 360 - {}^3/_4(400 - {}^1/_5S_1 + {}^1/_{10}S_2) - {}^1/_8S_2 \qquad (2)$$
$$= 360 - 300 + {}^3/_{20}S_1 + {}^3/_{40}S_2) - {}^1/_8S_2$$
$$= 60 + {}^3/_{20}S_1 - {}^1/_5S_2$$
$$S_3 = 600 + {}^1/_2(400 - {}^1/_5S_1 + {}^1/_{10}S_2) + {}^3/_4S_2 \qquad (3)$$
$$= 600 + 200 - {}^1/_{10}S_1 + {}^1/_{20}S_2 + {}^3/_4S_2$$
$$= 800 - {}^1/_{10}S_1 - {}^4/_5S_2$$
$$S_4 = 420 - 1(400 - {}^1/_5S_1 + {}^1/_{10}S_2) \qquad (4)$$
$$= 20 + {}^1/_5\,S_1 - {}^1/_{10}S_2$$
$$C = 5760 + 2(400 - {}^1/_5S_1 + {}^1/_{10}S_2) = 2S_2 \qquad (5)$$
$$= 5760 + 800 - {}^2/_5S_1 + {}^1/_5S_2 - 2S_2$$
$$= 6560 - {}^2/_5S_1 - 1{}^4/_5S_2$$

We now restate the revised five equations in a third matrix:

Third matrix

Quantity	S_1	S_2	
$Y = 400$	$-{}^1/_5$	$+{}^1/_{10}$	(1)
$Z = 60$	$+{}^3/_{20}$	$-{}^1/_5$	(2)
$S_3 = 800$	$-{}^1/_{10}$	$+{}^4/_5$	(3)
$S_4 = 20$	$+{}^1/_5$	$-{}^1/_{10}$	(4)
$C = 6560$	$-{}^2/_5$	$-1{}^4/_5$	(5)

The contribution row (equation (5)) contains only negative items, which signifies that the optimal solution has been reached. The quantity column for any products listed on the left hand side of the matrix indicates the number of units of the product that should be manufactured when the optimum solution is reached. 400 units of Y and 60 units of Z should therefore be produced, giving a total contribution of £6560. This agrees with the results we obtained using the graphical method. *When an equation appears for a slack variable, this indicates that unused resources exist.* The third matrix therefore indicates that the optimal plan will result in 800 unused machine hours (S_3) and an unused sales potential of 20 units for product Y (S_4). The fact that there is no equation for S_1 and S_2 means that these are the inputs that are fully utilized and that limit further increases in output and profit.

Interpreting the final matrix

The S_1 column (materials) of the third matrix indicates that the materials are fully utilized. (*Whenever resources appear as column headings in the final matrix, this indicates that they are fully utilized.*) So, to obtain a unit of materials, the column for S_1 indicates that we must alter the optimum production programme by increasing production of product Z by $^3/_{20}$ of a unit and decreasing production of product Y by $^1/_5$ of a unit. The effect of removing one scarce unit of material from the production process is summarized in Exhibit 26.3.

Let us focus on the machine capacity column of Exhibit 26.3. If we increase production of product Z by $^3/_{20}$ of a unit then more machine hours will be required, leading to the available capacity being reduced by $^9/_{10}$ of an hour. Each unit of product Z requires 6 machine hours, so $^3/_{20}$ of a unit will require $^9/_{10}$ of an hour ($^3/_{20} \times 6$). Decreasing production of product Y by $^1/_5$ unit will release $^4/_5$ of a machine hour, given that 1 unit of product Y requires 4 machine hours. The overall effect of this process is to reduce the available machine capacity by $^1/_{10}$ of a machine hour. Similar principles apply to the other calculations presented in Exhibit 26.3.

Let us now reconcile the information set out in Exhibit 26.3 with the materials column (S_1) of the third matrix. The S_1 column indicates that to release 1 unit of materials from the optimum production programme we should increase the output of product Z by $^3/_{20}$, and decrease product Y by $^1/_5$ of a unit. This substitution process will lead to the unused machine capacity being reduced by $^1/_{10}$ of a machine hour, an increase in the unfulfilled sales demand of product Y (S_4) by $^1/_5$ of a unit and a reduction in contribution of £$^2/_5$. All this information is obtained from column S_1 of the third matrix, and Exhibit 26.3 provides the proof. Note that Exhibit 26.3 also proves that the substitution process that is required to obtain an additional unit of materials releases exactly 1 unit. In addition, Exhibit 26.3 indicates that the substitution process for labour gives a net effect of zero, and so no entries appear in the S_1 column of the third matrix in respect of the labour row (i.e. S_2).

Opportunity cost

The contribution row of the final matrix contains some vital information for the accountant. The figures in this row represent opportunity costs (also known as shadow prices) for the scarce factors of materials and labour. For example, the reduction in

EXHIBIT 26.3
The effect of removing 1 unit of material from the optimum production programme

	S_3 Machine capacity	S_4 Sales of Y	S_1 Materials	S_2 Labour	Contribution (£)
Increase product Z by $^{3}/_{20}$ of a unit	$-^{9}/_{10}(^{3}/_{20} \times 6)$	–	$-^{3}/_{5}(^{3}/_{20} \times 4)$	$-1^{1}/_{5}(^{3}/_{20} \times 8)$	$+2^{2}/_{5}(^{3}/_{20} \times 16)$
Decrease product Y by $^{1}/_{5}$ of a unit	$+^{4}/_{5}(^{1}/_{5} \times 4)$	$+^{1}/_{5}$	$+1^{3}/_{5}(^{1}/_{5} \times 8)$	$+1^{1}/_{5}(^{1}/_{5} \times 6)$	$-2^{4}/_{5}(^{1}/_{5} \times 14)$
Net effect	$-^{1}/_{10}$	$+^{1}/_{5}$	$+1$	Nil	$-^{2}/_{5}$

contribution from the loss of 1 unit of materials is £$^{2}/_{5}$ (£0.40) and from the loss of one labour hour is £$1^{4}/_{5}$ (£1.80). Our earlier studies have indicated that this information is vital for decision-making, and we shall use this information again shortly to establish the relevant costs of the resources.

The proof of the opportunity costs can be found in Exhibit 26.3. From the contribution column we can see that the loss of one unit of materials leads to a loss of contribution of £0.40.

Substitution process when additional resources are obtained

Management may be able to act to remove a constraint which is imposed by the shortage of a scarce resource. For example, the company might obtain substitute materials or it may purchase the materials from an overseas supplier. A situation may therefore occur where resources additional to those included in the model used to derive the optimum solution are available. In such circumstances the marginal rates of substitution specified in the final matrix can indicate the optimum use of the additional resources. However, when additional resources are available it is necessary to *reverse* the signs in the final matrix. The reason is that the removal of one unit of materials from the optimum production programme requires that product Z be increased by $^{3}/_{20}$ of a unit and product Y decreased by $^{1}/_{5}$ of a unit. If we then decide to return released materials to the optimum production programme, we must reverse this process – that is, increase product Y by $^{1}/_{5}$ of a unit and reduce product Z by $^{3}/_{20}$ of a unit. The important point to remember is that *when considering the response to obtaining additional resources over and above those specified in the initial model, the signs of all the items in the final matrix must be reversed.*

We can now establish how we should best use an additional unit of scarce materials. Inspection of the third matrix indicates that product Y should be increased by $^1/_5$ of a unit and product Z reduced by $^3/_{20}$, giving an additional contribution of £0.40. Note that this is identical with the solution we obtained using the graphical method.

Note that this process will lead to an increase in machine hours of $^1/_{10}$ hour (S_3) and a decrease in potential sales of product Y by $^1/_5$ (S_4). Similarly, if we were to obtain an additional labour hour, we should increase production of Z by $^1/_5$ of a unit and decrease production of product Y by $^1/_{10}$ of a unit, which would yield an additional contribution of £1.80. These are the most efficient uses that can be obtained from additional labour and material resources. From a practical point of view, decisions will not involve the use of fractions; for example, the LP company considered here might be able to obtain 200 additional labour hours; the final matrix indicates that optimal production plan should be altered by increasing production of product Z by 40 units (200 × $^1/_5$ of a unit) and decreasing production of product Y by 20 units. This process will lead to machine capacity being reduced by 160 hours and potential sales of product Y being increased by 20 units.

Note that examination questions often present the final matrix in a different format to the approach illustrated in this chapter. You should refer to the Key examination points section at the end of the chapter for an explanation of how you can reconcile the alternative approaches.

Uses of linear programming

Calculation of relevant costs

The calculation of relevant costs is essential for decision-making. When a resource is scarce, alternative uses exist that provide a contribution. An opportunity cost is therefore incurred whenever the resource is used. The relevant cost for a scarce resource is calculated as

acquisition cost of resource + opportunity cost

When more than one scarce resource exists, the opportunity cost should be established using linear programming techniques. Note that the opportunity costs of materials and labour are derived from the final row (monetary figures expressed in fractions) of the third and final matrix. Let us now calculate the relevant costs for the resources used by the LP company. The costs are as follows:

materials	= £4.40 (£4 acquisition cost plus £0.40 opportunity cost)
labour	= £11.80 (£10 acquisition cost plus £1.80 opportunity cost)
variable overheads	= £1.00 (£1 acquisition cost plus zero opportunity cost)
fixed overheads	= nil

Because variable overheads are assumed to vary in proportion to machine hours, and because machine hours are not scarce, no opportunity costs arise for variable overheads. Fixed overheads have not been included in the model, since they do not vary in the short term with changes in activity. The relevant cost for fixed overheads is therefore zero.

Selling different products

Let us now assume that the company is contemplating selling a modified version of product Y (called product L) in a new market. The market price is £160 and the product requires 10 units input of each resource. Should this product L be manufactured? Conventional accounting information does not provide us with the information necessary to make this decision. Product L can be made only by restricting output of Y and Z, because of the input constraints, and we need to know the opportunity costs of releasing the scarce resources to this new product. Opportunity costs were incorporated in our calculation of the relevant costs for each of the resources, and so the relevant information for the decision is as follows:

	(£)	(£)
Selling price of product L		160
Less relevant costs:		
Materials (10 × 4.40)	44	
Labour (10 × 11.80)	118	
Variable overhead (10 × 1.00)	10	
Contribution		172
		(–12)

Total planned contribution will be reduced by £12 for each unit produced of product L.

Maximum payment for additional scarce resources

Opportunity costs provide important information in situations where a company can obtain additional scarce resources, but only at a premium. How much should the company be prepared to pay? For example, the company may be able to remove the labour constraint by paying overtime. The matrix indicates that the company can pay up to an additional £1.80 over and above the standard wage rate for each hour worked in excess of 2880 hours and still obtain a contribution from the use of this labour hour. The total contribution will therefore be improved by any additional payment below £1.80 per hour. Similarly, LP will improve the total contribution by paying up to £0.40 in excess of the standard material cost for units obtained in excess of 3440 units. Hence the company will increase short-term profits by paying up to £11.80 for each additional labour hour in excess of 2880 hours and up to £4.40 for units of material that are acquired in excess of 3440 units.

Control

Opportunity costs are also important for cost control. In Chapter 19 we noted that standard costing could be improved by incorporating opportunity costs into the variance calculations. For example, material wastage is reflected in an adverse material usage variance. The responsibility centre should therefore be identified not only with the acquisition cost of £4 per unit but also with the opportunity cost of £0.40 from the loss of one scarce unit of materials. This process highlights the true cost of the inefficient usage of scarce resources and encourages responsibility heads to pay special attention to the control of scarce factors of production. This approach is particularly appropriate where a firm has adopted an optimized production technology (OPT) strategy (see Chapter 9) because variance arising from bottleneck operations will be reported in terms of opportunity cost rather than acquisition cost.

Capital budgeting

Linear programming can be used to determine the optimal investment programme when capital rationing exists. This topic is dealt with in the appendix to this chapter.

Sensitivity analysis

Opportunity costs are of vital importance in making management decisions, but production constraints do not exist permanently, and therefore opportunity costs cannot be regarded as permanent. There is a need to ascertain the range over which the opportunity cost applies for each input. This information can be obtained from the final matrix. For materials we merely examine the negative items for column S_1 in the final matrix and divide each item into the quantity column as follows:

$$Y = 400/(-{}^{1}/_{5}) = -2000$$
$$S_3 = 800/(-{}^{1}/_{10}) = -8000$$

The number closest to zero in this calculation (namely –2000) indicates by how much the availability of materials used in the model can be reduced. Given that the model was established using 3440 units of materials, the lower limit of the range is 1440 units (3440 – 2000). The upper limit is determined in a similar way. We divide the positive items in column S_4 into the quantity column as follows:

$$Z = 60/{}^{3}/_{20} = 400$$
$$S_4 = 20/{}^{1}/_{5} = 100$$

The lower number in the calculation (namely 100) indicates by how much the materials can be increased. Adding this to the 3440 units of materials indicates that the upper limit of the range is 3540 units. The opportunity cost and marginal rates of substitution for materials therefore apply over the range of 1440 to 3540 units.

Let us now consider the logic on which these calculations are based. The lower limit is determined by removing materials from the optimum production programme. We have previously established from the final matrix and Exhibit 26.3 that removing one unit of material from the optimum production programme means that product Y will be reduced by ${}^{1}/_{5}$ and machine capacity will be reduced by ${}^{1}/_{10}$ of an hour. Since the final matrix indicates an output of 400 units of product Y, this reduction can only be carried out 2000 times ($400/{}^{1}/_{5}$) before the process must stop. Similarly, 800 hours of machine capacity are still unused, and the reduction process can only be carried out 8000 times ($800/{}^{1}/_{10}$) before the process must stop. Given the two constraints on reducing materials, the first constraint that is reached is the reduction of product Y. The planned usage of materials can therefore be reduced by 2000 units before the substitution process must stop. The same reasoning applies (with the signs reversed) in understanding the principles for establishing the upper limit of the range.

Similar reasoning can be applied to establish that the opportunity cost and marginal rates of substitution apply for labour hours over a range of 2680 to 3880 hours. For any decisions based on scarce inputs outside the ranges specified a revised model must be formulated and a revised final matrix produced. From this matrix revised opportunity costs and marginal rates of substitution can be established.

Summary

The following items relate to the learning objectives listed at the beginning of the chapter.

- **Describe the situations when it may be appropriate to use linear programming.**

  Conventional limiting factor analysis (see Chapter 9) should be used when there is only one scarce factor. Linear programming can be used to determine the production programme that maximizes total contribution when there is more than one scarce input factor.

- **Explain the circumstances when the graphical method can be used.**

  The graphical method can be used with two products. Where more than two products are involved the simplex method should be used.

- **Use graphical linear programming to find the optimum output levels.**

  Production/sales quantities for one of the two products are labelled on the horizontal axis and the vertical axis is used for the other product. Combinations of the maximum output (based on the two products) from fully utilizing each resource, and any sales volume limitations, are plotted on the graph. A series of contribution lines are plotted based on the potential output levels for each product that will achieve a selected total contribution. The optimum output levels are derived at the point where the feasible production region touches the highest contribution line. The process is illustrated in Figure 26.5 using the data presented in Example 26.2.

- **Formulate the initial linear programming model using the simplex method.**

  Assuming that the objective function is to maximize total contribution the objective function should initially be specified expressed in terms of the contributions per unit for each product. Next the constraints should be listed in equation form with slack variables introduced to ensure that model is specified in terms of equalities rather than inequalities. The first tableau is prepared by converting the linear programming model into a matrix format. The process is illustrated using Example 26.2.

- **Explain the meaning of the term shadow prices.**

  The simplex method of linear programming generates shadow prices (also known as opportunity costs) for each of those scarce resources that are fully utilized in the optimum production programme. The shadow prices represent the reduction in total contribution that will occur from the loss of one unit of a scarce resource. Conversely, they represent the increase in total contribution that will occur if an additional unit of the scarce resource can be obtained.

- **Additional learning objective presented in Appendix 26.1**

  The appendix to this chapter includes an additional learning objective: to apply linear programming to determine the optimum capital investment programme when multi-period capital rationing applies. This topic is included in a corporate finance module for some courses whereas in others it is included in a management accounting module. Since the topic is not applicable to all readers it is presented in Appendix 26.1. You should therefore check with your course curriculum to ascertain whether you need to study this topic.

Appendix 26.1 The application of linear programming to capital budgeting

In Chapter 14 we discussed capital rationing and identified this as being a situation where there is a budget ceiling or constraint on the amount of funds that can be invested during a specific period of time. In such a situation we should select the combination of investment proposals that provide the highest net present value, subject to the budget constraint for the period. In Chapter 14 we assumed that investment funds were restricted to one period only, but it was suggested that in practice more than one period constraint must be considered. Where there is multi-period capital rationing, we should use linear programming techniques to maximize the net present value. Let us consider the example set out in Exhibit 26A.1 to illustrate the application of linear programming to capital rationing where there are budget constraints for three periods.[2]

We can formulate the linear programming model by representing each of the projects numbered 1, …, 6 by X_j, (where $j = 1, \ldots, 6$); X_1 represents investment number 1, X_2 represents investment number 2, and so on. Our objective is to maximize the net present value subject to the budget constraints for each of the three periods. The model is as follows:

$$\text{Maximize } 14X_1 + 30X_2 + 17X_3 + 15X_4 + 40X_5 + 6X_6$$

subject to:

$$12X_1 + 54X_2 + 6X_3 + 6X_4 + 30X_5 + 6X_6 + S_1 = 35 \text{ (period 1 constraint)}$$

$$3X_1 + 10X_2 + 6X_3 + 2X_4 + 35X_5 + 10X_6 + S_2 = 20 \text{ (period 2 constraint)}$$

$$5X_1 + 4X_2 + 6X_3 + 5X_4 + 10X_5 + 4X_6 + S_3 = 20 \text{ (period 3 constraint)}$$

$$0 \leqslant X_j \leqslant 1 \ (j = 1, \ldots, 6)$$

The final term in the model indicates that X_j may take any value from 0 to 1. This ensures that a project cannot be undertaken more than once, but allows for a project to be partially accepted. The terms S_1, S_2 and S_3 represent the slack variables (i.e. unused funds) for each of the three periods. *It is assumed that the budgeted capital constraints are absolute and cannot be removed by project generated cash inflows.* The solution to the problem is presented in Exhibit 26A.2.

You can see from these figures that we should fully accept projects 1, 3 and 4, 7% of project 2, 23.5% of project 5 and zero of project 6. Substituting these values into the equations for the objective function gives a net present value of £57.5 million.

The slack variables indicate the opportunity costs of the budget constraints for the various future periods. These variables indicate the estimated present value that can be gained if a budget constraint is relaxed by £1. For example, the slack variable of £0.408 for period 1 indicates that the present value is expected to increase by £0.408 if the budget of funds available for investment in period 1 is increased by £1, while the slack variable of £0.792 indicates that present value can be expected to increase by £0.792 if the budget is increased by £1 million in period 2. If the budget is increased by £1 million in period 1, the present value is expected to increase by £408 000. The slack variables can also indicate how much it is worth paying over and above the market price of funds that are used in the net present value calculation for additional funds in each period. A further use of the opportunity costs is to help in appraising any investment projects that might be suggested as substitutes for projects 1–6. For example, assume that a new project whose cash inflows are all received in year 3 is expected to yield a net present value of £4 million for an investment of £5 million for each of years 1 and 2; this project should be rejected because the opportunity cost of

EXHIBIT 26A.1
Multi-period capital rationing

The Flanders Company is constrained by capital rationing. Details of the projects available during the period where capital rationing applies are as follows:

Investment project	Present value of outlay in period 1 £ million	Present value of outlay in period 2 £ million	Present value of outlay in period 3 £ million	Net present value of investment £ million
1	12	3	5	14
2	54	10	4	30
3	6	6	6	17
4	6	2	5	15
5	30	35	10	40
6	6	10	4	6

The present value of the outlays for the budget constraints for each of periods 1–3 are as follows:

	£ million
Period 1	35
Period 2	20
Period 3	20

You are required to formulate the linear programming model that will maximize net present value.

EXHIBIT 26A.2
Optimum values for multi-period capital rationing problem

$X_1 = 1.0$ $X_2 = 0.07$ $X_3 = 1.0$ $X_4 = 1.0$ $X_5 = 0.235$ $X_6 = 0.0$
$S_1 = 0.408$ $S_2 = 0.792$ $S_3 = 0.0$ Objective function = £57.5 million

the scarce funds will be £6 million (£5 million × £0.408 + £5 million × £0.792), and this is in excess of the net present value.

So far we have assumed that capital constraints are absolute and cannot be removed by project-generated cash inflows. *Let us now assume that project-generated cash inflows are available for investment* and that the cash inflows for period 2 are £5 million, £6 million, £7 million, £8 million, £9 million and £10 million respectively for projects 1–6. The revised constraint for period 2 is

$$3X_1 + 10X_2 + 6X_3 + 2X_4 + 35X_5 + 10X_6 + S_2$$
$$= 20 + 5X_1 + 6X_2 + 7X_3 + 8X_4 + 9X_5 + 10X_6$$

You can see that the cash inflows are entered on the right-hand side of the equation, and this increases the amount of funds available for investment. The same approach should be adopted for cash inflows arising in periods 1 and 3. Note that it is assumed that any unused funds cannot be carried forward and used in future periods. For an illustration of how unused funds can be carried forward to future periods and also how project-generated cash flows are incorporated into the LP model see answer to Question 26.20 in the *Students' Manual*.

Note that in formulating the model we have assumed that the investment projects were divisible in the sense that a partial acceptance of an investment proposal was possible. In the optimal solution both projects 2 and 5 were fractional. However, in practice, investment projects are unlikely to be divisible – acceptance will involve acceptance of the full amount of the investment and rejection will involve zero investment. To overcome this problem, it is possible to use an **integer programming** model by requiring that X_j be an integer – either 0 or 1. This process excludes fractional investments.

The model can also be modified to take account of mutually exclusive projects. For example, if projects 1, 3 and 6 are mutually exclusive, we can simply add the constraint $X_1 + X_3 + X_6 \leq 1$. When this constraint is used with integer programming, we are assured that only one of these projects will appear in the final solution. Also, if project 2 is contingent upon the acceptance of project 1, the constraint $X_2 \leq X_1$ ensures that the contingency is recognized in the final solution of an integer programming model.

The major problem with the application of linear programming to the capital budgeting process is that it is based on the assumption that future investment opportunities are known. However, management may be aware of future investment opportunities for the earliest years only. Budget constraints for later years are likely to be utilized only as new investment proposals are generated, and they are unlikely to be binding. To overcome this problem, the selection process must be revised continually.

Notes

1 The eight units of materials consist of five units from the 2000 unused units plus three units released from the reduction in production of product Z by ¾ unit.

2 This example was adapted from a problem in Salkin, G. and Kornbluth, J. (1973) *Linear Programming in Financial Planning*, Prentice-Hall, p. 59.

Key terms and concepts

capital rationing (p. 1126)
integer programming (p. 1128)
linear programming (p. 1109)
marginal rate of substitution (p. 1115)
objective function (p. 1109)
opportunity cost (p. 1115)
shadow price (p. 1115)
simplex method (p. 1116)
slack variables (p. 1116)

Key examination points

A common error is to state the objective function in terms of profit per unit. This is incorrect, because the fixed cost per unit is not constant. The objective function should be expressed in terms of contribution per unit. You should note that there are several ways of formulating the tableaux for a linear programming model. The approach adopted in this chapter was to formulate the first tableau with positive contribution signs and negative signs for the slack variable equations. The optimal solution occurs when the signs in the contribution row are all negative. Sometimes examination questions are set that adopt the opposite procedure. That is, the signs are the reverse of the approach presented in this chapter. For an illustration of how to cope with this situation you should refer to the answers to Review problems 26.13 and 26.18 (shown in the *Student's Manual*). A more recent approach is to present the output from the model as a computer printout. You should refer to the solution to Review problem 26.14 to make sure you understand this approach.

Most examination questions include the final tableau and require you to interpret the figures. You may also be required to formulate the initial model. It is most unlikely that you will be required to complete the calculations and prepare the final tableau. However, you may be asked to construct a graph and calculate the marginal rates of substitution and opportunity costs.

Assessment material

Review questions

The review questions are short questions that enable you to assess your understanding of the main topics included in the chapter. The numbers in parentheses provide you with the page numbers to refer to if you cannot answer a specific question.

Review problems

The review problems are more complex and require you to relate and apply the chapter content to various business problems. Fully worked solutions to the review problems are provided in a separate section at the end of the book. For those questions in the white box the worked solutions are provided in the *Student's Manual* accompanying this book. Further review problems for this chapter are available on the accompanying website www.drury-online.com. The answers to these problems are available for lecturers on the lecturer's password protected section of the website.

Case studies

The website also includes over 30 case study problems. A list of these cases is provided in Part Seven of this book.

Review questions

26.1 Describe the situations when it may be appropriate to use linear programming. (*pp. 1108–09*)

26.2 Explain what is meant by the term 'objective function'. (*p. 1109*)

26.3 What is the feasible production area? (*pp. 1112–13*)

26.4 What is the marginal rate of substitution? (*p. 1115*)

26.5 Explain what is meant by the term 'shadow price'. (*p. 1115*)

26.6 Explain the circumstances when it is appropriate to use the simplex method. (*p. 1116*)

26.7 What are slack variables? (*p. 1116*)

26.8 Provide illustrations of how the information derived from linear programming can be applied to a variety of management accounting problems. (*pp. 1122–24*)

26.9 Explain how sensitivity analysis can be applied to the output of a linear programming model. (*p. 1124*)

26.10 What is multi-period capital rationing? (*p. 1126*)

26.11 Describe integer programming. (*p. 1128*)

Review problems

26.12 Advanced: Optimal output and calculation of shadow prices using graphical approach

Brass Ltd produces two products, the Masso and the Russo. Budgeted data relating to these products on a unit basis for August are as follows:

	Masso (£)	Russo (£)
Selling price	150	100
Materials	80	30
Salesmen's commission	30	20

Each unit of product incurs costs of machining and assembly. The total capacity available in August is budgeted to be 700 hours of machining and 1000 hours of assembly, the cost of this capacity being fixed at £7000 and £10 000 respectively for the month, whatever the level of usage made of it. The number of hours required in each of these departments to complete one unit of output is as follows:

	Masso	Russo
Machining	1.0	2.0
Assembly	2.5	2.0

Under the terms of special controls recently introduced by the Government in accordance with EEC requirements, selling prices are fixed and the maximum permitted output of either product in August is 400 units (i.e. Brass Ltd may produce a maximum of 800 units of product). At the present controlled selling prices the demand for the products exceeds this considerably.

You are required:

(a) to calculate Brass Ltd's optimal production plan for August, and the profit earned,

(10 marks)

(b) to calculate the value to Brass Ltd of an independent marginal increase in the available capacity for each of machining and assembly, assuming that the capacity of the other department is not altered and the output maxima continue to apply,

(10 marks)

(c) to state the principal assumptions underlying your calculations in (a) above, and to assess their general significance.

(5 marks)

ICAEW Management Accounting

26.13 **Advanced: Optimal output with a single limiting factor and interpretation of a final matrix**

Hint: Reverse the signs in the final matrix.

(a) Corpach Ltd manufactures three products for which the sales maxima, for the forthcoming year, are estimated to be:

Product 1	Product 2	Product 3
£57 500	£96 000	£125 000

Summarized unit cost data are as follows:

	Product 1 (£)	Product 2 (£)	Product 3 (£)
Direct material cost	10.00	9.00	7.00
Variable processing costs	8.00	16.00	10.00
Fixed processing costs	2.50	5.00	4.00
	£20.50	30.00	£21.00

The allocation of fixed processing costs has been derived from last year's production levels and the figures may need revision if current output plans are different.

The established selling prices are:

Product 1	Product 2	Product 3
£23.00	£32.00	£25.00

The products are processed on machinery housed in three buildings:

Building A contains type A machines on which 9800 machine hours are estimated to be available in the forthcoming year. The fixed overheads for this building are £9800 p.a.

Building B1 contains type B machines on which 10 500 machine hours are estimated to be available in the forthcoming year.

Building B2 also contains type B machines and again 10 500 machine hours are estimated to be available in the forthcoming year.

The fixed overheads for the B1 and B2 buildings are, in total, £11 200 p.a.

The times required for one unit of output for each product on each type of machine, are as follows:

	Product 1	Product 2	Product 3
Type A machines	1 hour	2 hours	3 hours
Type B machines	1.5 hours	3 hours	1 hour

Assuming that Corpach Ltd wishes to maximize its profits for the ensuing year, you are required to determine the optimal production plan and the profit that this should produce.

(9 marks)

(b) Assume that, before the plan that you have prepared in part (a) is implemented, Corpach Ltd suffers a major fire which completely destroys building B2. The fire thus reduces the availability of type B machine time to 10 500 hours p.a. and the estimated fixed overhead for such machines, to £8200. In all other respects the conditions set out, in part (a) to this question, continue to apply.

In his efforts to obtain a revised production plan the company's accountant makes use of a linear programming computer package. This package produces the following optimal tableau:

Z	*X1*	*X2*	*X3*	*S1*	*S2*	*S3*	*S4*	*S5*	
0	0	0	0	0.5	1	0	0.143	–0.429	1 150
0	0	1	0	–0.5	0	0	–0.143	0.429	1 850
0	0	0	0	0	0	1	–0.429	0.286	3 800
0	0	0	1	0	0	0	0.429	–0.286	1 200
0	1	0	0	1	0	0	0	0	2 500
1	0	0	0	1.5	0	0	2.429	0.714	35 050

In the above: *Z* is the total contribution,
X1 is the budgeted output of product 1,
X2 is the budgeted output of product 2,
X3 is the budgeted output of product 3,
S1 is the unsatisfied demand for product 1,
S2 is the unsatisfied demand for product 2,
S3 is the unsatisfied demand for product 3,
S4 is the unutilized type A machine time,
S5 is the unutilized type B machine time.
and
The tableau is interpreted as follows:
Optimal plan – Make 2500 units of Product 1,
1850 units of Product 2,
1200 units of Product 3,
Shadow prices – Product 1 £1.50 per unit,
Type A Machine Time £2.429 per hour,
Type B Machine Time £0.714 per hour.

Explain the meaning of the shadow prices and consider how the accountant might make use of them. Calculate the profit anticipated from the revised plan and comment on its variation from the profit that you calculated in your answer to part (a).

(9 marks)

(c) Explain why linear programming was not necessary for the facts as set out in part (a) whereas it was required for part (b).

(4 marks)

(Total 22 marks)

ACCA Level 2 Management Accounting

26.14 Advanced: Interpretation of the linear programming solution

Woodalt plc has two automated machine groups X and Y, through which timber is passed in order to produce two models of an item of sports equipment. The models are called 'Traditional' and 'Hightech'.

The following forecast information is available for the year to 31 December 2001:

	'Traditional'	'Hightech'
(i) Maximum sales potential (units)	6000	10 000
(ii) Equipment unit data:		
Selling price	£100	£90
Machine time: group X (hours)	0.5	0.3
group Y (hours)	0.4	0.45

(iii) Machine groups X and Y have maximum operating hours of 3400 and 3840 respectively. The sports equipment production is the sole use available for the production capacity.

(iv) The maximum quantity of timber available is 34 000 metres. Each product unit requires 4 metres of timber. Timber may be purchased in lengths as required at £5 per metre.

(v) Variable machine overhead cost for machine groups X and Y is estimated at £25 and £30 per machine hour respectively.

(vi) All units are sold in the year in which they are produced.

A linear programme of the situation has been prepared in order to determine the strategy which will maximize the contribution for the year to 31 December 2001 and to provide additional decision making information. Appendix 3.1 shows a print-out of the solution to the LP model.

Required:

(a) Formulate the mathematical model from which the input to the LP programme would be obtained.

(4 marks)

(b) Using the linear programme solution in Appendix 3.1 where appropriate, answer the following in respect of the year to 31 December 2001:

(i) State the maximum contribution and its distribution between the two models;

(3 marks)

(ii) Explain the effect on contribution of the limits placed on the availability of timber and machine time;

(3 marks)

(iii) In addition to the sports equipment models, Woodalt plc has identified additional products which could earn contribution at the rate of £20 and £30 per machine hour for machine groups X and Y respectively. Such additional products would be taken up only to utilize any surplus hours not required for the sports equipment production.

Prepare figures which show the additional contribution which could be obtained in the year to 31 December 2001 from the additional sales outlets for each of machine groups X and Y;

(4 marks)

(iv) Explain the sensitivity of the plan to changes in contribution per unit for each sports equipment product type;

(2 marks)

(v) Woodalt plc expects to be able to overcome the timber availability constraint. All other parameters in the model remain unchanged. *(The additional products suggested in* (iii) *above do not apply).*

Calculate the increase in contribution which this would provide;

(2 marks)

(vi) You are told that the amended contribution maximizing solution arising from (v) will result in the production and sale of the 'Traditional' product being 3600 units.

Determine how many units of the 'Hightech' product will be produced and sold.

(2 marks)

(c) Suggest ways in which Woodalt plc may overcome the capacity constraints which limit the opportunities available to it in the year to 31 December 2001. Indicate the types of cost which may be incurred in overcoming each constraint.

(6 marks)

(d) Explain why Woodalt plc should consider each of the following items before implementing the profit maximizing strategy indicated in Appendix 3.1:

(i) Product specific costs;

(ii) Customer specific costs;

(iii) Life cycle costs.

Your answer should include relevant examples for each of (i) to (iii).

(9 marks)

(Total 35 marks)

Appendix 3.1

Forecast strategy evaluation for the year to 31 December 2001

Target Cell (Max) (£)

Cell	Name	Final Value
C2	Contribution	444 125

Adjustable Cells (Units)

Cell	Name	Final Value
A1	Traditional	4250
B1	Hightech	4250

Adjustable Cells (Units and £)

Cell	Name	Final Value	Reduced Cost	Objective Coefficient	Allowable Increase	Allowable Decrease
A1	Traditional	4250	0	55.50	26.17	6.50
B1	Hightech	4250	0	49.00	6.50	15.70

Constraints (Quantities and £)

Cell	Name	Final Value	Shadow Price	Constraint R.H. Side	Allowable Increase	Allowable Decrease
C3	Timber	34 000	9.8125	34 000	1733.33	6800
C4	Machines X	3 400	32.5	3 400	850	850
C5	Machines Y	3 612.5	0	3 840	IE+30	227.5

ACCA Paper 9 Information for Control and Decision Making

26.15 **Advanced: Multi-period capital rationing**

Alexandra Ltd is a newly established manufacturing company. The company's only asset is £5 million in cash from the amount received on the issue of the ordinary shares. This is available for investment immediately. A call on the shares will be made exactly a year from now. This is expected to raise a further 2.5 million which will be available for investment at that time. The directors do not wish to raise finance from any other source and so next year's (year 1's) investment finance is limited to the cash to be raised from the call plus any cash generated from investments undertaken this year.

Six possible investment projects have been identified. Each of these involves making the necessary initial investment to establish a manufacturing facility for a different product. Information concerning the projects is as follows:

Project Estimated cash flows (including tax cash flows)	A (£m)	B (£m)	C (£m)	D (£m)	E (£m)	F (£m)
Year 0 (immediately)	(2.0)	(0.5)	(2.2)	(4.0)	(1.4)	–
1	0.8	(3.2)	0.5	1.1	(0.8)	(3.0)
2	0.9	2.3	1.2	2.0	1.5	1.0
3	0.6	1.9	1.0	1.8	1.2	2.0
4	0.6	1.1	0.9	1.2	1.0	1.3
5	0.5	–	–	–	–	0.7
Net present value (at 15%)	0.36	0.34	0.31	0.34	0.39	0.56

None of these projects can be brought forward, delayed or repeated. Each project is infinitely divisible.

Any funds not used to finance these projects will be invested in the ordinary shares of a rival listed company, expected to generate a 15% return.

Generally there is no shortage of labour and materials. Both Project A and Project E, however, require the use of a special component which the company will have to obtain from a far eastern supplier. Because of the relatively short notice, the supply of these will be limited during year 1 to 5000 units.

The estimates in the table (above) are based on a usage of the special component during year 1 as follows:

Project A	3000 units
Project E	4000 units

From year 2 onwards the company will be able to obtain as many of the components as it needs.

The finance director proposes using linear programming to reach a decision on which projects to undertake. The company has access to some Simplex linear programming software, but no one in the company knows how to use it and your advice has been sought.

Requirements:

(a) Prepare the objective function and the various constraint statements which can be used to deduce the optimum investment schedule, giving a brief narrative explanation of each statement and stating any assumptions made. The solution to the linear programming problem is not required.

(7 marks)

(b) State the information (not the actual figures) which the linear programming process will produce in respect of Alexandra Ltd's allocation problem and explain how that information can be used.

(4 marks)

(Total 11 marks)

ICAEW Business Finance and Decisions – Part Two

Review problems (with answers in the Student's Manual)

26.16 Optimal output and calculation of shadow prices using graphical approach

MF plc manufactures and sells two types of product to a number of customers. The company is currently preparing its budget for the year ending 31 December 2003 which it divides into 12 equal periods.

The cost and resource details for each of the company's product types are as follows:

	Product type M	Product type F
	£	£
Selling price per unit	200	210
Variable costs per unit		
Direct material P (£2.50 per litre)	20	25
Direct material Q (£4.00 per litre)	40	20
Direct labour (£7.00 per hour)	28	35
Overhead (£4.00 per hour)	16	20
Fixed production cost per unit	40	50
	Units	*Units*
Maximum sales demand in period 1	1000	3000

The fixed production cost per unit is based upon an absorption rate of £10 per direct labour hour and a total annual production activity of 180 000 direct labour hours. One-twelfth of the annual fixed production cost will be incurred in period 1.

In addition to the above costs, non-production overhead costs are expected to be £57 750 in period 1.

During period 1, the availability of material P is expected to be limited to 31 250 litres. Other materials and sufficient direct labour are expected to be available to meet demand.

It is MF plc's policy not to hold stocks of finished goods.

Required:

(a) Calculate the number of units of product types M and F that should be produced and sold in period 1 in order to maximize profit.

(4 marks)

(b) Using your answer to (a) above, prepare a columnar budgeted profit statement for period 1 in a marginal cost format.

(4 marks)

After presenting your statement to the budget management meeting, the production manager has advised you that in period 1 the other resources will also be limited. The maximum resources available will be:

Material P	31 250 litres
Material Q	20 000 litres
Direct labour	17 500 hours

It has been agreed that these factors should be incorporated into a revised plan and that the objective should be to make as much profit as possible from the available resources.

Required:

(c) Use graphical linear programming to determine the revised production plan for period 1. State clearly the number of units of product types M and F that are to be produced.

(10 marks)

(d) Using your answer to part (c) above, calculate the profit that will be earned from the revised plan.

(3 marks)

(e) Calculate and explain the meaning of the shadow price for material Q.

(5 marks)

(f) Discuss the other factors that should be considered by MF plc in relation to the revised production plan.

(4 marks)

(Total 30 marks)

CIMA Management Accounting – Performance Management

26.17 Advanced: Optimal output, shadow prices and decision making using the graphical approach

The instruments department of Max Ltd makes two products: the XL and the YM. Standard revenues and costs per unit for these products are shown below:

	XL		YM	
	(£)	(£)	(£)	(£)
Selling price		200		180
Variable costs:				
Material A (£10 per kg)	(40)		(40)	
Direct labour (£8 per hour)	(32)		(16)	
Plating (£12 per hour)	(12)		(24)	
Other variable costs	(76)		(70)	
		(160)		(150)
Fixed overheads (allocated at £7 per direct labour hour)		(28)		(14)
Standard profit per unit		12		16

Plating is a separate automated operation and the costs of £12 per hour are for plating materials and electricity.

In any week the maximum availability of inputs is limited to the following:

Material A	120 kg
Direct labour	100 hours
Plating time	50 hours

A management meeting recently considered ways of increasing the profit of the instrument department. It was decided that each of the following possible changes to the existing situation should be examined *independently* of each other.

(1) The selling price of product YM could be increased.

(2) Plating time could be sold as a separate service at £16 per hour.

(3) A new product, ZN, could be sold at £240 per unit. Each unit would require the following:

Material A	5 kg
Direct labour	5 hours
Plating time	1 hour
Other variable costs	£90

(4) Overtime could be introduced and would be paid at a premium of 50% above normal rates.

Requirements:

(a) Formulate a linear programme to determine the production policy which maximizes the profits of Max Ltd in the present situation (i.e. ignoring the alternative assumptions in 1 to 4 above), solve, and specify the optimal product mix and weekly profit.

(6 marks)

(b) Determine the maximum selling price of YM at which the product mix calculated for requirement (a) would still remain optimal.

(3 marks)

(c) Show how the linear programme might be modified to accommodate the sale of plating time at £16 per hour (i.e. formulate but do not solve).

(3 marks)

(d) Using shadow prices (dual values), calculate whether product ZN would be a profitable addition to the product range.

(4 marks)

(e) Ignoring the possibility of extending the product range, determine whether overtime working would be worthwhile, and if so state how many overtime hours should be worked.

(3 marks)

(f) Discuss the limitations of the linear programming approach to the problems of Max Ltd.

(6 marks)
(Total 25 marks)
ICAEW P2 Management Accounting

26.18 Advanced: Formulation of an initial tableau and interpretation of final matrix using the Simplex method

Hint: Reverse the signs and ignore the entries of 0 and 1. You are not required to solve the model.

A chemical manufacturer is developing three fertilizer compounds for the agricultural industry. The product codes for the three products are *X*1, *X*2 and *X*3 and the relevant information is summarized below:

Chemical constituents: percentage make-up per tonne

	Nitrate	Phosphate	Potash	Filler
*X*1	10	10	20	60
*X*2	10	20	10	60
*X*3	20	10	10	60

Input prices per tonne

Nitrate	£150
Phosphate	£ 60
Potash	£120
Filler	£ 10

Maximum available input in tonnes per month

Nitrate	1200
Phosphate	2000
Potash	2200
Filler	No limit

The fertilizers will be sold in bulk and managers have proposed the following prices per tonne.

*X*1	£83
*X*2	£81
*X*3	£81

The manufacturing costs of each type of fertilizer, excluding materials, are £11 per tonne.

You are required to:

(a) formulate the above data into a linear programming model so that the company may maximize contribution;

(4 marks)

(b) construct the initial Simplex tableau and state what is meant by 'slack variables' (Define *X*4, *X*5, *X*6 as the slack variables for *X*1, *X*2, and *X*3 respectively);

(2 marks)

(c) indicate, with explanations, which will be the 'entering variable' and 'leaving variable' in the first iteration;

(2 marks)

(d) interpret the final matrix of the simplex solution given below:

Basic Variable	X_1	X_2	X_3	X_4	X_5	X_6	Solution
*X*1	1	0	3	20	–10	0	4 000
*X*2	0	1	–1	–10	10	0	8 000
*X*6	0	0	–0.4	–3	1	1	600
Z	0	0	22	170	40	0	284 000

(8 marks)

(e) use the final matrix above to investigate:

(i) the effect of an increase in nitrate of 100 tonnes per month;

(ii) the effect of a minimum contract from an influential customer for 200 tonnes of *X*3 per month to be supplied.

(4 marks)

(Total 20 marks)

CIMA Stage 3 Management Accounting Techniques

26.19 Advanced: Single- and multi-period capital rationing

The management team of T Ltd, a small venture capital company, is planning its investment activities for the next five years. It has been approached by four start-up companies from the same industry sector which have presented their business plans for consideration. The forecast cash flows and resulting net present value (NPV) for each start-up company are as follows:

Company	Capital Year 0 $000	Operational cash flows Year 1 $000	Year 2 $000	Year 3 $000	Year 4 $000	Year 5 $000	NPV $000
A	(500)	(75)	(40)	50	400	650	60
B	(250)	(30)	(20)	(5)	250	247	0
C	(475)	(100)	(30)	(20)	400	750	77
D	(800)	(150)	(50)	50	900	786	80

The directors of T Ltd use a 12% cost of capital for appraising this type of investment.

You can assume that all investments are divisible and that they are not mutually exclusive. Ignore tax and inflation.

Required:

(a) Advise T Ltd which of the investments, if any, it should invest in.

(3 marks)

(b) If capital for investment now is limited to \$700 000 but T Ltd can raise further capital in one year's time and thereafter at a cost of 12% per annum,

(i) advise T Ltd how it should invest the \$700 000;

(5 marks)

(ii) discuss other factors which may affect the decision.

(4 marks)

(c) T Ltd has now found out that funds will also be restricted in future years and that the constraints are absolute and cannot be removed by project generated incomes. The present values of cash that will be available for future investment are as follows:

	Present value \$000
Year 0	700
Year 1	80
Year 2	35

Required:

Formulate the linear programming model that will maximize net present value and explain the meaning of each variable and the purpose of each constraint you have identified.
(You are not required to attempt a solution.)

(10 marks)

(d) Briefly explain the benefits of using a linear programming format in this situation.

(3 marks)
(Total 25 marks)
CIMA Management Accounting – Decision Making

26.20 **Advanced: Single- and multi-period capital rationing**

Schobert Ltd is a retailing company which operates a small chain of outlets. The company is currently (i.e. December 2000) finalizing its capital budgets for the years to 31 December 2001 and 31 December 2002. Budgets for existing trading operations have already been prepared and these indicate that the company will have cash available of £250 000 on 1 January 2001 and £150 000 on 1 January 2002. This cash will be available for the payment of dividends and/or for the financing of new projects.

Seven new capital projects are currently being considered by Schobert Ltd. Each is divisible but none is repeatable. Relevant data for each of the investments for the periods to 31 December 2003 are provided below:

	Cash Flows Year to 31 December			Net Present Value at 10% per annum	Internal Rate of Return
Project	**2001 (£000)**	**2002 (£000)**	**2003 (£000)**	**(£000)**	
A	(80)	(30)	50	39	36%
B	(70)	20	50	35	38%
C	(55)	40	20	5	20%
D	(60)	30	30	15	28%
E		(140)	55	14	19%
F		(80)	70	32	46%
G		(100)	30	24	29%

The financial director of Schobert Ltd predicts that no new external sources of capital will become available during the period from 1 January 2001 to 31 December 2002, but believes conditions will improve in 2003, when the company would no longer expect capital to be rationed.

The objective of the directors of Schobert Ltd is to maximize the present value of the company's ordinary shares, assuming that the value of ordinary shares is determined by the dividend growth model. The company's cost of capital is 10% per annum, and all cash surpluses can be invested elsewhere to earn 8% per annum. A dividend of at least £100 000 is to be paid to 1 January 2000, and the company's policy is to increase its annual dividend by at least 5% per annum.

Requirements:

(a) Formulate, but do not solve, the company's capital rationing problem as a linear programme.

(8 marks)

(b) Assuming that the results of the linear programme show a dual price of cash in 2001 of £0.25 and 2002 of £0, and a range of cash amounts for which the dual price is relevant of £120 000 to £180 000, explain their significance to the directors of Schobert Ltd.

(7 marks)

(c) Discuss the circumstances under which capital might be rationed, and the problems these present for capital budgeting decisions.

(10 marks)

(Total 25 marks)

Note: Ignore taxation.

ICAEW P2 Financial Management

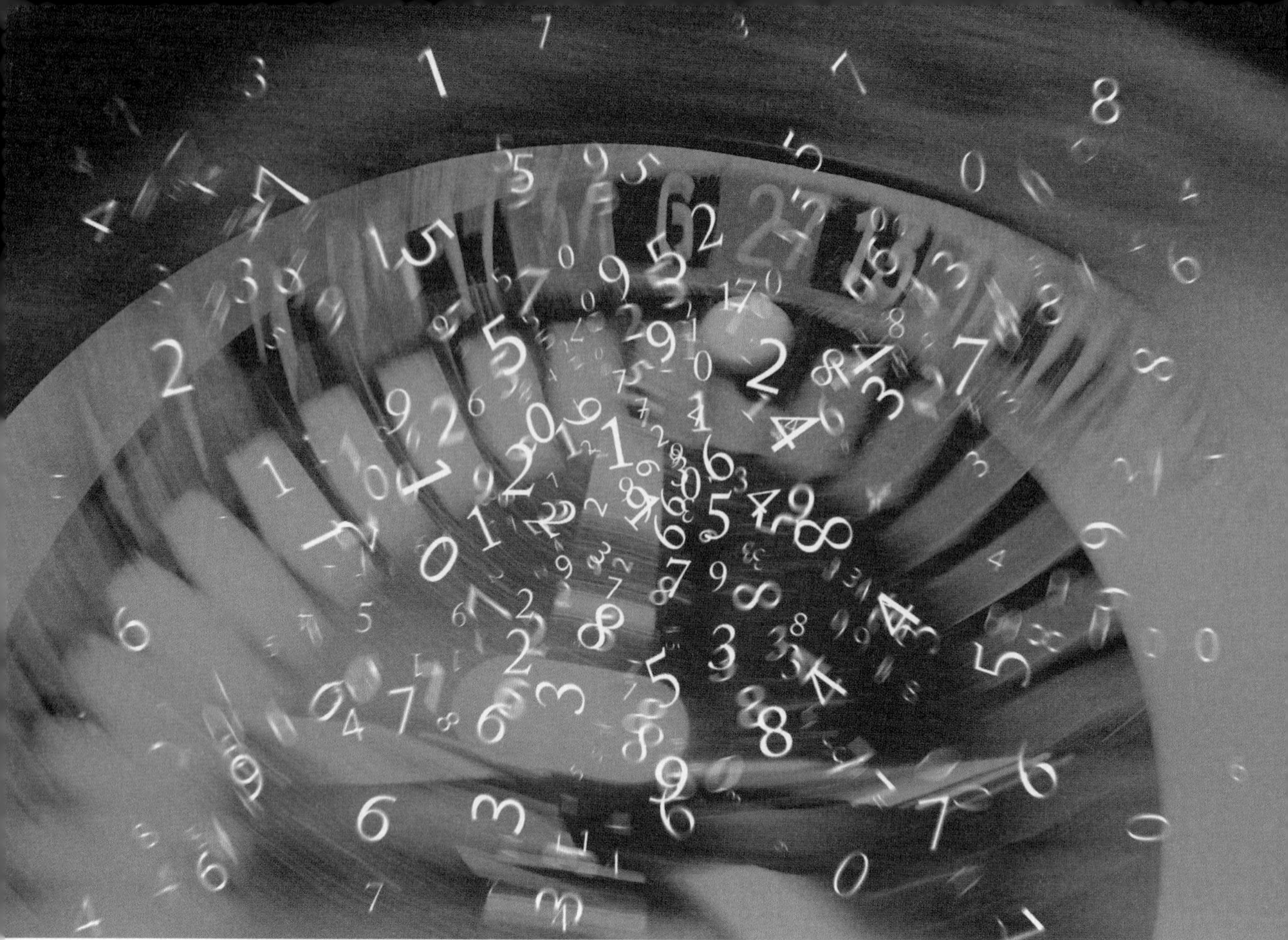

PART 7

Case studies

Case studies available from the website

Eva at Ault Foods Limited

The dedicated website for this book includes over 30 case studies. Both students and lecturers can download these case studies from the open access website. The authors of the cases have provided teaching notes for each case and these can be downloaded only by lecturers from the password protected lecturer's section of the website.

The cases generally cover the content of several chapters and contain questions to which there is no ideal answer. They are intended to encourage independent thought and initiative and to relate and apply the content of this book to more uncertain situations. They are also intended to develop critical thinking and analytical skills.

Details relating to the cases that are available from the website are listed on the following pages. One example case is included at the end of this section. The teaching note for this case is also available on the website.

CASE STUDIES AVAILABLE FROM THE WEBSITE

Airport Complex Peter Nordgaard and Carsten Rhode, Copenhagen Business School
A general case providing material for discussion of several aspects involved in the management control of a service company, which is mainly characterized by mass services.

Anjo Ltd Lin Fitzgerald, Loughborough University Business School
Variance analysis that provides the opportunity to be used as a role playing exercise.

Baldwin Bicycle Company R.N. Anthony and J.S. Reece
Relevant cost analysis and strategic accounting.

Berkshire Threaded Fasteners Company John Shank, The Amos Tuck School of Business Administration Dartmouth College
Cost analysis for dropping a product, for pricing, for product mix and product improvement.

Berkshire Toy Company D. Crawford and E.G. Henry, State University of New York (SUNY) at Oswego
Variance analysis, performance evaluation, responsibility accounting and the balanced scorecard.

Blessed Farm Partnership Rona O'Brien, Sheffield Hallam University
Strategic decision-making, evaluation of alternatives, ethics, sources of information.

Bohemia Industries Colin Drury, Huddersfield University Business School
The implications of variable and absorption costing for internal monthly profit reporting.

Boston Creamery John Shank, The Amos Tuck School of Business Administration Dartmouth College
Management control systems, profit planning, profit variance analysis and flexible budgets.

Brunswick Plastics Anthony Atkinson, University of Waterloo and adapted by John Shank, The Amos Tuck School of Business Administration Dartmouth College
Relevant cost analysis for a new product, short-run versus strategic considerations, pricing considerations.

Company A Mike Tayles, Universtiy of Hull Business School and Paul Walley, Warwick Business School
Evaluation of a product costing system and suggested performance measures to support key success factors.

Company B Mike Tayles, Universtiy of Hull Business School and Paul Walley, Warwick Business School
The impact of a change in manufacturing strategy and method upon product costing and performance measurement systems.

Danfoss Drives Dan Otzen, Copenhagen Business School
The linkage between operational management and management accounting/control of a company including a discussion of the operational implications of JIT for management accounting.

Dumbellow Ltd Stan Brignall, Aston Business School
Marginal costing versus absorption costing, relevant costs and cost–volume–profit analysis.

Electronic Boards plc John Innes, University of Dundee and Falconer Mitchell, University of Edinburgh
A general case that may be used at an introductory stage to illustrate the basics of management accounting and the role it can play within a firm.

Endeavour Twoplise Ltd Jayne Ducker, Antony Head, Brenda McDonnell, Sheffield Hallam University and Susan Richardson, University of Bradford Management Centre
Functional budget and master budget construction, budgetary control and decision-making.

Fleet Ltd Lin Fitzgerald, Loughborough University Business School
Outsourcing decision involving relevant costs and qualitative factors.

Fosters Construction Ltd Deryl Northcott, University of Manchester
Capital investment appraisal, relevant cash flows, taxation, inflation, uncertainty, post-audits.

Global Ltd Susan Richardson, University of Bradford Management Centre
Cash budgeting, links between cash and profit, pricing/bidding, information system design and behavioural aspects of management control.

Gustavsson, AB Colin Drury, Huddersfield University Business School
Alternative choice of cost centres and their implication for overhead assignments for various decisions.

Hardhat Ltd Stan Brignall, Aston Business School
Cost–volume–profit analysis.

High Street Reproduction Furniture Ltd Jayne Ducker, Antony Head, Rona O'Brien, Sheffield Hallam University and Sue Richardson, University of Bradford Management Centre
Relevant costs, strategic decision-making and limiting factors.

Integrated Technology Services (UK) Ltd Mike Johnson, University of Dundee
An examination of the planning and control framework of an information services business which provides outsourced computing support services to large industrial and government organizations.

Kinkead Equipment Ltd John Shank, The Amos Tuck School of Business Administration Dartmouth College
Profit variance analysis that emphasizes how variance analysis should be redirected to consider strategic issues.

Lynch Printers Peter Clarke, University College Dublin
Cost-plus pricing within the context of correctly forecasting activity for a forthcoming period in order to determine the overhead rates. The case illustrates that a company can make a loss even when an anticipated profit margin is added to all jobs.

Majestic Lodge John Shank, The Amos Tuck School of Business Administration Dartmouth College
Relevant costs and cost–volume–profit analysis.

Merrion Products Ltd Peter Clarke, University College Dublin
Cost–volume–profit analysis, relevant costs and limiting factors.

Mestral Robin Roslender, University of Stirling
The different roles and purposes of management accounting relating to aspects covered in Chapter 17.

Moult Hall Jayne Ducker, Antony Head, Brenda McDonnell, Sheffield Hallam University and Susan Richardson, University of Bradford Management Centre
Organizational objectives, strategic decision-making, evaluation of alternatives, relevant costs, debating the profit ethos, break-even analysis.

Oak City R.W. Ingram, W.C. Parsons, University of Alabama and W.A. Robbins, Attorney, Pearson and Sutton
Cost allocation in a government setting to determine the amount of costs that should be charged to business for municipal services. The case also includes ethical considerations.

Quality Shopping Rona O'Brien, Sheffield Hallam University
Departmental budget construction, credit checking, environmental issues, behavioural issues and management control systems.

Rawhide Development Company Bill Doolin, University of Waikato and Deryl Northcott, University of Manchester
Capital investment appraisal involving relevant cash flows, uncertainty, application of spreadsheet tools and social considerations.

Reichard Maschinen, GmbH Professor John Shank, The Amos Tuck School of Business Administration Dartmouth College
Relevant costs and pricing decisions

Rogatec Ltd Jayne Ducker, Antony Head, Brenda McDonnell, Sheffield Hallam University and Susan Richardson, University of Bradford Management Centre
Standard costing and variance analysis, budgets, ethics, sources of information.

Sheridan Carpet Company James S. Reece
Pricing decision, strategic cost analysis.

The Beta Company Peter Clarke, University College Dublin
Cost estimation involving regression analysis and relevant costs.

Traditions Ltd. Jayne Ducker, Antony Head, Brenda McDonnell, Sheffield Hallam University and Susan Richardson, University of Bradford Management Centre
Relevant cost analysis relating to a discontinuation decision and budgeting.

Example Case: EVA at Ault Foods Limited

Richard Ivey School of Business
The University of Western Ontario

Angela Skubovius, Professor Sarah C. Mavrinac, and Henry Fiorillo prepared this case solely to provide material for class discussion. The authors do not intend to illustrate either effective or ineffective handling of a managerial situation. The authors may have disguised certain names and other identifying information to protect confidentiality.

As chief financial officer of Ault Foods Limited, John Hamilton was responsible for enhancing shareholder value through the development and implementation of innovative financial strategies. To accomplish his mission, Hamilton relied heavily on the company's capital budgeting programs, costing systems, and performance measurement tools. One of Hamilton's most valuable tools was the company's EVA (Economic Value Added) system, a system that he had helped install some six months after the company's initial public offering. Hamilton believed that the system had markedly improved his ability to track the company's asset utilization and to evaluate its performance capabilities.

On a crisp October day in the fall of 1996, Hamilton was compiling the data he would need to run a divisional EVA analysis. Graham Freeman, Ault's chief executive officer, had asked him to present this analysis to the company's board of directors at its next meeting. Freeman hoped that when the board members became aware of the divisions' EVA trends, they would finally begin to appreciate the benefits of spinning off some of the company's less profitable divisions. He firmly believed that a spinoff of at least one division would significantly boost the company's growth potential and bolster the confidence of Ault's shareholder base.

Hamilton wondered if pruning one of the company's divisions really was the best strategy for value creation. If it were, he wondered which of the divisions should be divested first. He hoped the EVA analysis would give him the insights he needed.

Company history

Ault Foods Limited (Ault) traced its history to the year 1891 when Jack Ault opened his first small cheese factory in Cass Bridge, Ontario. Run as a small family operation, the company grew modestly over the years until in 1968 it was acquired by John Labatt Limited, one of Canada's largest consumer conglomerates. Between 1968 and the late 1980s, Labatt invested in or acquired an additional 20 dairy operations, ultimately becoming one of the largest milk and dairy producers in Canada.

As Labatt entered the 1990s, its conglomerate structure became unwieldy and shareholders encouraged company management to divest itself of unrelated acquisitions. The dairy businesses were among the first to be spunoff and on May 7, 1993, Ault Foods Limited, a combination of some 14 Labatt dairy acquisitions, emerged as a publicly traded corporation. With the offering, Ault immediately became the largest fully-integrated dairy producer in Canada, with almost 3000 employees, 28 distribution depots and 15 plants in Ontario and Quebec. Ault shares began trading at $15.50 and quickly broke through the $18.00 mark.

The Ault offering was conceived and launched with tremendous optimism on the part of both the company management and its investors on Bay Street. With independence from Labatt came a new strategic vision for the company and the dairy industry at large. Ever since assuming command, Freeman had worked to position the company as the 'dairy that would change the industry as a value-added producer.' His strategic mission was to generate supra-competitive returns by positioning the company as the high technology, premium producer in a commodity business. The premium niche would be realized through investments in research and development (R&D) and through innovative product extensions.

R&D was a priority at Ault and during the early 1990s the company produced a number of new technologies and products. Among its many R&D accomplishments, the company listed the development of: 1) Lactantia PurFiltre, a premium milk boasting a longer shelf life than other milks, 2) Cheestrings™, individually wrapped 'stringable' cheese snacks, 3) Dairylight, an all-natural dairy ingredient providing a low-calorie alternative to butterfat, and 4) Olivina margarine, an olive oil based product that contained the highest level of cholesterol reducing mono-unsaturates of any margarine in the world.

Despite the enthusiasm that defined its offering and despite its R&D capability, the company began to experience serious difficulties after six months of public trading. By the summer of 1996, earnings had fallen from $1.35 per share in 1994 to just under $0.70 per share. (For annual financial data, see **Exhibit 1**.) Over the same period, share price drifted down from a high of $18.87 to a price below $16.00 per share. (See **Exhibit 2** for data on share price movements.) On top of this, Ault faced a continuing price war in the fluid milk market, increasing competitive pressure from a new multinational competitor in the ice cream area, legal battles over its new 'premium' milk product, and an increasingly unhappy shareholder base. Summing up the company's position and prospects, Irene Nattel, a securities analyst at RBC Dominion Securities in Montreal wrote, 'Life is not a lot of fun for Ault right now.'[1]

Despite these difficulties, some of the company's largest investors remained confident. Mike Palmer, an analyst with Equity Research Associates, never faltered in his enthusiasm for the stock. In a 1995 report, for example, he wrote:

> *Fluid milk is a lousy business and Ault's attempt to decommoditize it through the launch of Lactantia PurFiltre, has been a mixed success. Nevertheless, management is committed to improving shareholder returns and there are ample opportunities to do so. ... The stock is cheap and will go higher.*[2]

Other investors, like Keith Graham of the Ontario Teachers' Pension Plan Board (Teachers') were less sanguine. Describing his impression of Ault and its performance over the years, Keith said:

EXHIBIT 1

Financial statements[1]

Consolidated statement of earnings and retained earnings for the years ended April 27, 1996 and April 29, 1995 in thousands of dollars

	1996	1995
Net sales	$1 346 505	$1 292 706
Cost of Sales, selling and administration expenses	1 267 536	1 199 852
Research and development[2]	9 247	8 883
Depreciation and amortization[3]	37 215	33 023
Earnings before the undernoted	$32 507	$50 948
Interest expense, net	11 691	10 233
Unusual items	0	15 800
Earnings before income taxes	$20 816	$24 915
Income taxes		
Current	10 951	12 245
Deferred	(2 576)	(1 939)
Net earnings	$12 441	$14 609
Retained earnings, beginning of year	$19 195	$16 412
Dividends	12 122	11 826
Retained earnings, end of year	$19 514	$19 195
Net earnings per common share	$0.68	$0.80

Consolidated balance sheet as at April 27, 1996 and April 29, 1995 in thousands of dollars

	1996	1995
Assets		
Current assets		
Cash	$2 944	$1 927
Accounts receivable	35 417	74 691
Inventories	173 114	155 152
Prepaid expenses	18 896	30 646
Income and other taxes receivable	5 394	927
Investments and other[4]	$123 696	$121 506
Fixed assets, net	$249 828	$254 405
Total assets	$609 289	$639 254
Liabilities and shareholders' equity		
Current liabilities		
Bank Debt	$13 774	$25 810
Accounts payable and accrued charges	132 382	157 212
Long-term debt due within one year	475	475
Long-term debt	$134 288	$125 031
Deferred income tax	$42 105	$45 231
Shareholders' equity		
Share capital	$266 751	$266 300
Retained earnings	19 514	19 195
Total liabilities and shareholders' equity	$609 289	$639 254

Source: Company Documents

[1]All numbers have been altered slightly from actual.

[2]Ault Foods Limited expensed $7.233, $7.923 and $6.847 million in Research & Development costs during the fiscal years 1994, 1993, and 1992 respectively.

[3]Includes an annual goodwill amortization charge of $2 914 000.

[4]These investment figures include $82 704 and $85 618 in unamortized goodwill for 1996 and 1995, respectively. Accumulated goodwill amortization totalled approximately $15.4 million in 1996 and $12.5 million in 1995.

EXHIBIT 2
Share price movements

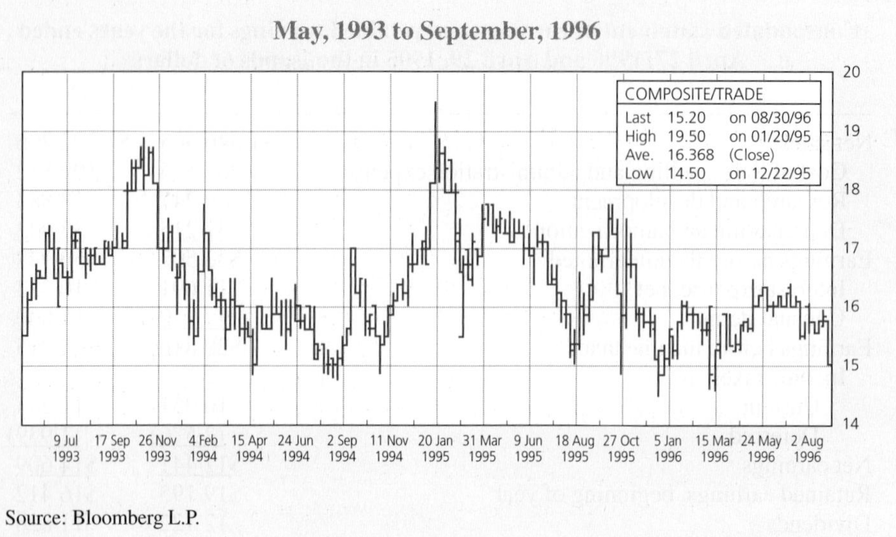

Source: Bloomberg L.P.

We were all very favorably disposed towards Ault when it first went public. One reason why we found the stock so attractive was because we believed the company was undervalued, but Freeman is also a charismatic leader and we were convinced that the company had real earnings power. But sometime in late 1994 or 1995, the company lost its momentum. Its competitive strength was shaken by the entry of Unilever, by Beatrice's restructuring, and by the fluid milk wars. It just lost its strategic position. We had to ask ourselves, 'Will management be able to do what's necessary to repair the damage? Will they do the right thing?' Obviously, we decided 'No'.[3]

In July, 1996, Ault posted another in a series of disappointing earnings announcements. Earnings per share (EPS) for the fourth quarter fiscal year 1996 were 72 per cent below those posted the previous year. Earnings per share for the full year were 50 per cent lower than posted earnings in fiscal year 1995. In the wake of this announcement and the various sell recommendations being launched by industry analysts, Teachers' began unwinding its position.

When word of Teachers' sale reached Ault management, Freeman knew that dramatic action was required not only to boost share price and corporate performance but also to reassure the company's remaining shareholders. He was convinced that divestiture represented Ault's best option. Unfortunately, he also knew the Ault board would resist any effort that reduced the size of the company. When Freeman had entered into tentative discussion with Nestlé over the sale of the Frozen Division, board members had reacted with alarm. Most of the company's directors were sure that divestiture would not only depress earnings in the short term but also seriously impair the company's growth potential over the long term. They made it crystal clear that they would never entertain a downsizing strategy without clear illustration of its value creating potential.

Ault's business line-up

The Ault structure included two main operating groups, the Refrigerated and Frozen Products and the Cheese and Butter Products groups, each of which supported a number of distinct product divisions. When Labatt acquired its various dairy businesses, there had been few apparent synergies between any of them other than that they were dairy-related. In 1996, however, there was one common trait uniting almost all of Ault's operations. Virtually all faced shrinking markets and demand levels. Only a few of the cheese and ice cream operations had consistently posted stable earnings. (See **Exhibit 3** for financial information by segment.)

Refrigerated and Frozen Products Group

The Refrigerated and Frozen Products group included three key product divisions: Fluid Milk, Cultured Products, and Ice Cream and Novelty Products.

Fluid Milk Ault processed and distributed fluid milk throughout the two Canadian provinces of Ontario and Quebec. While most of the company's sales were made through large supermarket chains under the Sealtest brand name, the company also packaged milk under the Royal Oak, Copper Cliff and Dallaire labels. The efficiency, productivity and competitive pricing offered by Ault had allowed the company to realize a 23 per cent market share in Quebec and a full 31 per cent share in Ontario. Competitors in the Ontario market included two long-time producers: Beatrice and Neilson, which boasted market shares of 31 per cent and 21 per cent, respectively, as well as Natrel and Dairyworld, two more recent entrants who were expanding beyond their original market areas. In Quebec the only formidable competitor was Natrel, operating with a 70 per cent share of the market.

While fluid milk products were a staple of the Ault product lineup and had consistently generated at least one third of company revenues, milk margins had suffered throughout the early 1990s, as consumption continued to fall from its peak in the mid-1980s. The period from 1985 to 1995 witnessed a full 10 per cent decrease in milk consumption. While there were a variety of demographic explanations for this demand shift, Graham Freeman believed that the decline in consumption was due at least in part to consumers' switch to lower priced soda.

In addition to these disappointing demand trends, Ault also had to contend with a market that, since 1994, had become increasingly competitive. Natrel and Dairyworld had entered the market from Quebec and British Columbia, respectively; Agropur, a fluid milk processor had begun a national expansion; and Beatrice, in its attempts to divest its fluid milk business, had helped escalate a price war that had reduced margins to rock bottom. Industry analysts speculated that the price war would continue at least until Beatrice had solved its debt problems and finally found a willing buyer for this division. Beatrice had reportedly been looking to divest itself of its milk operations for a number of years but had found little interest.

Late in 1994, in response to the mounting pressure on fluid milk margins and in keeping with its high technology strategy, Ault introduced Lactantia PurFiltre, a new premium milk product that featured a more stringent filtering of bacteria and a fresher taste and longer shelf life. Having invested over $31 million in PurFiltre's development and introduction, Ault management was relying heavily on this value-added product to boost sagging earnings. By the spring of 1995, PurFiltre had realized a retail penetration rate in Quebec of about 85 per cent and management was hoping to recover all its investment costs during the first year of sales. In Ontario, however, Ault had difficulty obtaining shelf space in leading supermarket chains. By June of 1995, retail penetration rates were still less than 50 per cent. Ault was effectively shut out of the Loblaw's grocery chain in large part because of the threat Lactantia posed to the Neilson products which were produced and distributed by Loblaw's owner, Weston's. Compounding the distribution problems were a host of legal problems that were raised as a result of Beatrice's claims of false advertising. By the fall of 1996, the Lactantia PurFiltre product still had not generated the sales forecasted in Ontario and earnings continued to suffer.

While current performance levels were disappointing, there was some suggestion that future performance could be worse still. Trade talks were currently under way which would decide which treaty, the GATT (General Agreement on Tariffs and Trade) agreement or the NAFTA (North American Free Trade Agreement) would most affect the dairy industry. If

EXHIBIT 3

Segment financial data[1]

Estimates of earnings and retained earnings by product segment for the year ended April 27, 1996 in thousands of dollars

		Refrigerated and Frozen Products		Cheese and Butter Products	
	Fluid Milk	Cultured	Ice Cream	Industrial	Intern'l
Net sales	$477 834	$79 639	$166 518	$560 263	$62 251
Cost of Sales, selling and administration[2]	460 434	76 916	152 042	522 379	55 765
Research and Development	4 384	133	1 223	3 398	109
Depreciation and amortization[3]	15 824	2 637	5 514	11 916	1 324
Earnings before the undernoted	($2 808)	($47)	$7 739	$22 570	$5 053
Interest expense, net	3 627	604	1 264	5 576	620
Income taxes Current			1 897	7 832	1 222
Deferred			(447)	(1 842)	(287)
Net earnings	($6 435)	($651)	$5 025	$11 004	$3 498

Identifiable assets and liabilities by product segment as of April 27, 1996 in thousands of dollars

		Refrigerated and Frozen Products		Cheese and Butter Products	
	Fluid Milk	Cultured	Ice Cream	Industrial	Intern'l
Assets					
Current assets					
Cash	$1 045	$174	$364	$1 225	$136
Accounts receivable	12 568	2 095	4 380	14 737	1 637
Inventories	30 988	10 587	52 338	74 198	5 003
Prepaid expenses	4 932	1 822	2 718	6 782	2 642
Income and other taxes receivable	1 267	0	1 236	2 244	647
Investments and other	43 896	7 316	15 297	51 468	5 719
Fixed assets, net	88 656	14 776	30 895	103 950	11 551
Accounts payable and accrued charges	46 977	7 831	16 372	55 084	6 118

Source: Generated by casewriters.

[1]All numbers have been altered slightly from actual.
[2]Includes $17 million in corporate overhead charges allocated on basis of sales.
[3]Includes goodwill amortization charge allocated on basis of net fixed assets.

NAFTA were upheld, import/export restrictions would rapidly be abolished creating an entirely new source of competition for the Canadian producer.

Cultured Products, Juice and Drinks While fluid milk products constituted almost one third of the company's sales, cultured products, juice and drinks accounted for less than 10 per cent. Chief among the product lineup were Sealtest Light 'n Lively yogurts, Florida Squeezed orange juice, Sealtest lemonade, and Sealtest dips and sour creams. Ault had a reasonable position in the yogurt market, holding a 16 per cent market share in Ontario. However, in the sour cream and cottage cheese product markets, Ault was consistently positioned as number one or two in the market. Despite its evident leadership, and while touted in the industry press as a true product innovator, Ault never realized substantial profits from this product line. The intense price competition, oversupply and the rapid entry of private label brands into the market ensured that the cultured, juice, and drinks division never operated above break-even.

Ice Cream and Novelty Products The ice cream and novely products lineup was a major source of Ault's growth and financial profitability. As Canada's only full-line ice cream producer and distributor, Ault enjoyed a national category market share of well over 30 per cent. Underpinning this market position were such brand names as Haagen-Dazs, Eskimo Pie, Drumstick, Oh Henry! and Sealtest Parlour, Canada's best-selling premium brand.

While clearly a dominant force in this market. Ault saw its position severely challenged in 1996 by the entry of Unilever, a multinational competitor with over $46 billion in sales worldwide. Unilever had ensured rapid market dominance by entering through the acquisition of Beatrice's ice cream division rather than through its own start-up. At the time of the acquisition, Unilever had announced publicly that its strategic intent was to expand its ice cream business worldwide to realize a number one position in every national market.

The competitive pricing pressures wrought by Unilever, coupled with the market's natural seasonality and heavy inventory requirements, had damaged Ault's earnings power in this area. Industry analysts speculated that while Ault's ice cream business had generated an estimated $6 million in EBIT (earnings before interest and tax), Ault would achieve little more than break-even returns in 1996 and 1997.

Cheese and Butter Products Group

Ault's Cheese and Butter Products group consisted of two operating divisions: the Industrial and the International Divisions.

Industrial Ault's Industrial Division specialized in the conversion of industrial-grade milk products into whey powders, milk powders, and consumer cheeses and butter. Operating out of seven plants in Ontario and Quebec, the division processed more than 500 million litres of milk each year and had earned the position as the largest butter producer in Canada years before. The division served not only end-use consumers through convenience stores and supermarkets but also a variety of companies in the food service and food processing industries as well. To all of these customers, Ault offered such products as Black Diamond, Lactantia, Balderson, and Plum Hollow cheeses, Lactantia and New Dundee butters, and Olivina and La Croissantiere margarines.

Historically, Ault had performed well in this market and the early 1990s offered no real exception. Lactantia was the largest selling butter brand and Black Diamond was the second-largest cheese brand in Canada. The division was finding still greater success with its new snackfood innovations like Cheestrings™, which were breaking new ground and building record market share. By the spring of 1996, the product had realized a full 72 per cent market share in the cheese snack market. This success was one reason why Ault's Industrial Division was such a consistent contributor to company profits.

In conversation with the casewriters, Graham Freeman commented on the history and potential of this division.

> *You will recall that this division was Ault's first. Our company founder started with the manufacture of cheese products and made a true success of it. The business is still a success, and I believe it has the potential to create real value for shareholders. One reason why the business is so strong is because we focused so much of our R&D talents on it. We really zeroed in on the potential we saw there and we generated very favourable results in both manufacturing and formulation yield applications.*

Despite the evident success of this division with Ault consumers, the market was competitive. Butter consumption was declining drastically, while private label brands were making real inroads into major food retailing outlets. Raw material was also becoming increasingly difficult to obtain. Ault operated under a government-regulated milk supply system that severely regulated the availability of both table and industrial milk. The stated objective of the regulation was to ensure stable revenues for dairy farmers and to maintain balance between supply and demand. The government attempted to achieve these goals by setting the price paid to farmers and limiting the amount of milk that processors were allowed to purchase.

In the mid-1990s, Quebec held 47 per cent of the national industrial milk quota while Ontario held 31 per cent. Recent quota reductions had limited the amounts of raw material available for cheese production and Ault, like its competitors, was beginning to feel the impact. One of Ault's responses to the quota cuts was to acquire the cheese assets of Schneider Corporation in November of 1995. These assets represented a full $80 million in annual sales. With the acquisition of Schneider, the milk quota owned by Ault that had been used for lower-value export butter and skim milk powder, became available for use in higher-margin cheese made under the Schneider label.

International Established in 1992, Ault's International Division was dedicated to marketing Ault's proprietary technologies and product innovations through licensing agreements across the world. A recent licensing coup had been realized when Golden Vale Food Products Inc. of Ireland licensed the Cheestrings™ cheese snacks line for sale in the United Kingdom. The division also provided consulting services to international customers and pursued joint ventures and partnership arrangements with established dairy companies where Ault's technical expertise could add value.

Most of the division's trading activities were conducted through the trading arm of Lovell and Christmas, a trading division acquired by Ault in fiscal year 1995, and focused on the sale of specialty cheeses, pre-blended ice cream mixes, infant formula, milk and whey powder, and other dairy products. During fiscal year 1996, sales were made in more than 35 countries. An increasing penetration of markets in the United States, South America, and Asia was expected in 1997.

EVA at Ault

With such a vast array of businesses operating in such a complex business environment, management often had difficulty understanding the impact of each division's performance on the financial condition of the company overall. In the spring of 1993, recognizing his need for more detailed performance data, Freeman asked his staff to launch an EVA experiment. He had been introduced to the EVA concept several months before and it appeared to be a logical tool for identifying which divisions were creating, and which were destroying, value for Ault's shareholders. The company eventually adopted EVA late in 1993 under the direction of Douglas Shields, John Hamilton's predecessor as chief financial officer.

With the help of Ernst & Young, a management consulting firm, Ault's executives spent the remainder of 1993 examining the EVA performance of a range of different Ault businesses and training divisional managers in the effective use of EVA. In 1994, management expanded the program to encourage the achievement of quarterly EVA goals. These goals were established during management planning meetings and were based on tough negotiations between Freeman and his division leaders. EVA calculations also became a familiar part of capital budgeting and post-investment review processes.

In the summer of 1996, Ault expanded its EVA program yet again. In an attempt to tie management's interests even more closely to shareholders', Ault instituted an EVA-based bonus plan. The plan was to be implemented in two phases. In 1996, it was to run alongside the existing earnings-based bonus plan. After this experimental year, during which the plan was to be further studied and refined, the EVA focused plan was to replace the earnings plan altogether.

EXHIBIT 4

Corporate EVA performance calculations

(All data in 000s)

1. Economic Book Value (EBV) Capital Calculation – Operating Approach

	1996	1995
Assets		
Operating Cash	$2 944	$1 927
Accounts Receivable	35 417	74 691
Inventories	173 114	155 152
Prepaid Expenses	18 896	30 646
Income and Other Taxes Receivable	5 394	927
Total Current Assets	$235 765	$263 343
Less: Accounts Payable	(132 382)	(157 212)
Net Working Capital	$103 383	$106 131
Investments and Other	$123 696	$121 506
Accumulated Amortized Goodwill	15 443	12 529
Net Property, Plant and Equipment	249 828	254 405
Accumulated Research and Development[1], Net	17 205	15 985
EBV Capital	$509 555	$510 556

2. Net Operating Profit After Tax (NOPAT) Calculation – Operating Approach

	1996	1995
Earnings before Unusual Items, Interest and Tax	$32 507	$50 948
Research and Development Add Back	9 247	8 883
Less: Amortization of Acc. R&D Expenses[2]	(8 027)	(7 505)
Goodwill Amortization Add Back	2 914	2 914
Adjusted Net Operating Profit before the Undernoted	$36 641	$55 240
Unusual Items	0	15 800
Adjusted Net Operating Profit before Tax	$36 641	$39 440
Cash Operating Taxes[3]	13 003	14 059
Adjusted Net Operating Profit After Tax (NOPAT)	$23 638	$25 381

3. EVA Calculation

EVA = NOPAT – (EBV Capital × WACC)

1996	1995
EVA = $23 638 – ($509 555 × 0.10)	EVA = $25 381 – ($510 556 × 0.10)
EVA = $23 638 – $50 956	EVA = $25 381 – $51 056
EVA = ($27 318)	EVA = ($25 675)

Source: Generated by casewriters.

[1]Although R&D was recognized as an expense in Ault's financial statements, Ault management recognized R&D expenditures as a legitimate investment in Ault's future product line-up. Consequently, R&D figures were included as an amortizable asset in EVA calculations. In an attempt to generate conservative estimates of R&D value, Hamilton used a straight-line five year amortization schedule.

[2]R&D was amortized at the rate of 20% per annum. For 1996, the amortization figure was $8027, i.e., 20% × ($9247 + $8883 + $7233 + $7923 + $6847).

[3]The corporate income tax rate was approximately 40%. Hamilton estimated cash taxes as equal to EBIT × the tax rate.

It was this last, motivational use that most intrigued John Hamilton. In an interview with the casewriter, he said:

> *Back in 1994 and 1995, our key challenge was to link the income statement and the balance sheet. For too long, we had focused almost exclusively on the income statement. We were earnings driven. Cash and capital were free. Sure, we did some serious capital budgeting and we imposed a twenty per cent hurdle rate on all major projects. But once the project was approved, no one thought about the capital again. By installing the EVA bonus system, we really focused our attention on both the income statement and the balance sheet simultaneously. We really focused on our use of assets and ways to maximize their value.*

Late in the summer of 1996, Hamilton and his team completed their annual EVA analysis for the company as a whole. The results were disappointing: the company had again failed to realize a positive EVA. (See **Exhibit 4** for corporate EVA calculations.) Still more unfortunately, the analysis hadn't made clear either the source of Ault's financial difficulties or its opportunities. Hamilton and Freeman agreed then that more specific divisional analyses would be needed to determine the real drivers of value at Ault.

As soon as Freeman learned of the Teachers' sale, he asked Hamilton to step up the analysis and to present his findings and recommendations to the board at its next meeting a week hence. Hamilton knew that if his presentation were to have any influence, he would have to start from scratch, explaining to the board what EVA was, how it worked, and why it was useful to Ault. Then, he would have to walk through the divisional calculations step by step, making comments about the strengths and weaknesses of each division, before he made any recommendations about sale.

Hamilton also knew that before he could present any of this to the board, he would have to work through all the calculations to be certain in his own mind that it was appropriate to base a divestiture decision on EVA numbers. He pulled out the documents (see **Exhibit 5**) he had compiled years ago to describe the EVA concept and its calculations to Graham Freeman and set to work.

EXHIBIT 5

The principles of EVA[1]

What is EVA?

The term EVA, or Economic Value Added, refers to a specific accounting calculation that has recently been developed as a guide for managers running complex organizations. In simple terms, EVA is a measure of 'economic profit,' calculated as net operating profit after tax less a charge for capital employed. Like accounting profit calculations, economic profit calculations, or EVA calculations, are used to provide a summary of the financial 'success' or 'failure' of the company over some period of time. However, economic profits can be distinguished from accounting profits in that they include this charge for the company's use of capital. That is, a positive EVA is not realized until ***all*** the costs of doing business, like the cost of using capital, have been tallied.

EVA is a particularly useful tool for divisionalized companies which often have a difficult time estimating the profitability of individual businesses. Because it encourages managers to continually assess and maximize the use of divisional assets, EVA can also be a useful vehicle for individual performance measurement and motivation. Any incentive scheme which encourages managers to maximise their EVA will enhance the probability that managers are working in the best interest of shareholders.

Note

[1] Parts of this note are excerpted from the Ivey Business School Note 9A96B043, 'Note on Economic Value Added,' prepared by John Manning and John McCartney under the supervision of Professor James E. Hatch.

The formula for generating the EVA measure is simply:

$$\text{EVA} = \text{Net Operating Profit After Tax} - \text{Required Return on Assets} \qquad (1)$$

where

$$\text{Required Return on Assets} = \text{Assets Employed} \times \text{Cost of Capital} \qquad (2)$$

Note that the manager's goal is to increase EVA. Consequently, moving from a negative EVA to a less negative EVA should be seen as progress.

How does it Increase Shareholder Value?

EVA analyses can be used not only to assess the performance of the organization or individual but also to identify opportunities for performance improvement. There are four general ways to increase EVA performance:

1 increase profitability, e.g., by increasing sales or by minimizing variable costs
2 improve operating efficiency and use of assets
3 rationalize and/or exiting unrewarding businesses, i.e. reduce the asset base, or
4 reduce the cost of capital.

The Uses and Benefits of EVA

One of the great features of EVA is its simplicity. Virtually any employee in the organization can understand the EVA concept and its importance. Consequently, EVA can be used as a powerful motivational and communications tool.

The EVA figure is also a powerful representation of corporate performance. As such, EVA makes irrelevant a number of other corporate measures that simply don't offer as clear and unbiased a signal of performance as this 'residual income' figure. If a manager relies on EVA, he or she does not need to review copious reports or reams of numbers to understand his or her company's financial position. The power of EVA is derived from its focus on shareholder value and its expression of performance as a relative term. Recall that EVA calculations generate positive profits only after deducting a cost for the use of capital. Consequently, performance is measured *relative* to the capital base or set of resources the manager used to measure the profits. EVA links the operating returns to the assets that were used to generate those returns.

The learning which flows from EVA analyses can be extremely insightful and can allow the manager not only to pinpoint areas of weakness in performance but also to easily identify solutions or programs for improvements. EVA's use in multi-businesses stems from the fact that it can help to assess divisional contributors to, or detractors from, overall profitability.

Note that EVA adopters tend to have greater asset dispositions and faster asset turns. The market value to book value measure of EVA adopters also tend to be 60 per cent higher than non-adopters. According to *The Quest for Value*, Stern, Stewart & Co's description of EVA, equity market values tend to be more highly correlated with annual EVA levels than with most other performance measures of return on equity, cash flow growth, EPS growth, or growth in sales or capital.

Shortcomings

Although the EVA tool offers real benefits it also, like any tool, has its limitations and weaknesses. Chief among these weaknesses is EVA's single period focus. EVA is a period measure. Its value can be calculated only for a single period at a time. Consequently, EVA cannot capture all the long-term implications of decision making. Of course, it is possible to run a number of annual EVA forecasts and then reduce the results using discounting techniques, but it is not a simple or perfect process.

Of course, reliance on any single measure can be dangerous. Too strict a reliance on EVA can distract the manager from other pertinent business issues such as customer satisfaction, productivity, or levels of innovation and learning. At times, in an attempt to boost EVA, managers might also divest the company of certain businesses or divisions that are not truly underperforming. As with any other tool used, business sense and prudent judgment must be used.

How does EVA Work?

The three key figures or components of the EVA calculation are: NOPAT, EBV Capital, and the firm's cost of capital. NOPAT is the annual cash flow that is available to cover costs of raising all equity and debt capital on an after-tax basis. EBV (Economic Book Value) Capital is an estimate of total capital utilized by a firm for a period, including debt and equity. The cost of capital is the appropriate risk-adjusted rate applied to the division or entity.

To generate the NOPAT and EBV Capital figures, adjustments must be made to both the traditional capital employed and the operating profit figures. The purpose of these adjustments is to ensure that the numbers accurately reflect the base upon which shareholders expect to earn their returns and the cash flow from the company's activities. According to Stern, Stewart & Co., the developers of the EVA tool, there are over 160 different adjustments that can be made. Which ones are used by any given company will depend on its industry, technology and value-creation process.

Application to Ault

Like other divisionalized businesses. Ault should find substantial value in the EVA performance approach. As suggested above, Ault can find applications for EVA in performance measurement, compensation, business re-engineering, corporate finance, divestiture planning, and resource allocation processes. Ault should also find the EVA tool useful for divisional comparisons.

Now may be an especially appropriate time for Ault to adopt the EVA tool. The EVA calculations generated for the consolidated Ault corporation suggest that the company faces a number of performance challenges. In 1994, Ault earned an EVA of negative $11 million. Indeed, it appears that Ault has returned a negative EVA since 1992. This negative performance trend has clearly impacted share valuation. The current market value of Ault shares is $15.75, only 88 per cent of Ault's equity book value. If Ault continues to generate returns below the cost of capital, there is a strong possibility that the stock will come under additional pressure. Note that the EVA of competitors Ben & Jerry's, Dean Foods, Agropur, and Beatrice was approximately $2 million, $21 million, $0, and negative $6 million.

At this time, we would strongly recommend the adoption of EVA techniques and investment in fuller divisional analysis of EVA trends. To conduct such an analysis, we recommend the use of the following three accounting adjustments:

- use of cash tax v. statutory tax rates,
- add back of goodwill amortization amounts, and
- add back of research and development expenses

Source: Compiled by casewriters.

Notes

1 Nattel, Irene, 'Consumer Products Review: Eat, Drink and Be Merry', RBC Dominion Securities, Montreal, January, 1996

2 Palmer, Michael, 'Ault', Equity Research Associates, Toronto, Ontario, June, 1995

3 Personal Communications

Suggested questions

The questions below are suggested by the author of this book and were not included in the original version of the case study.

1 Assume you are Hamilton. Explain to the board what EVA is, how it works, what its shortcomings are and why it is likely to be useful to Ault.

2 Calculate divisional EVA performance figures for 1996 and explain your calculations to the board.

3 Compare EVA with other alternative measures of divisional performance.

4 Explain how you think cost of capital ought to be derived for computing divisional EVA.

5 Explain how EVA relates to shareholder value.

6 Examine the strengths and weaknesses of each of Ault's divisions. What do you conclude about the performance capabilities and value of Ault's divisions? Is divisional divesture an appropriate course of action? What role do the EVA's that you have calculated play in the decision.

BIBLIOGRAPHY

Abernathy, M.A., Lillis, A.M., Brownell, P. and Carter, P. (2001) Product diversity and costing system design: field study evidence, *Management Accounting Research*, **12**(3), 261–80.

Accounting Standards Committee (1988) Accounting for Stocks and Work in Progress (SSAP 9).

Ackoff, R.L. (1981) *Creating the Corporate Future*, Wiley.

Adelberg, A. (1986) Resolving conflicts in intracompany transfer pricing, *Accountancy*, November, 86–9.

Ahmed, M.N. and Scapens, R.W. (1991) Cost allocation theory and practice: the continuing debate, in *Issues in Management Accounting* (eds D. Ashton, T. Hopper and R.W. Scapens), Prentice-Hall, 39–60.

Ahmed, M.N. and Scapens, R.W. (2000) Cost allocation in Britain: towards an institutional analysis, *The European Accounting Review*, **9**(2), 159–204.

American Accounting Association (1957) *Accounting and Reporting Standards for Corporate Financial Statements and Preceding Statements and Supplements*, 4.

American Accounting Association (1966) *A Statement of Basic Accounting Theory*, American Accounting Association.

Amey, L.R. (1975) Tomkins on residual income, *Journal of Business Finance and Accounting*, **2**(1), Spring, 55; 68.

Ansari, S. (1979) Towards an open system approach to budgeting, *Accounting, Organisations and Society*, **4**(3), 149–61.

Anthony, R.N. and Young, D.W. (1988) *Management Control in Non-Profit Organizations*, R.D. Irwin.

Armitage, H.M. and Nicholson, R. (1993) Activity based costing: a survey of Canadian practice, Issue Paper No. 3, Society of Management Accountants of Canada.

Arnold, G.C. and Hatzopoulos, P.D. (2000) The theory–practice gap in capital budgeting: evidence from the United Kingdom, *Journal of Business Finance and Accounting*, **27**(5) and (6), June/July, 603–26.

Ask, U. and Ax, C. (1992) Trends in the Development of Product Costing Practices and Techniques – A Survey of Swedish Manufacturing Industry, Paper presented at the 15th Annual Congress of the European Accounting Association, Madrid.

Ask, U., Ax, C. and Jonsson, S. (1996) Cost management in Sweden: from modern to post-modern, in Bhimani, A. (ed.) *Management Accounting: European Perspectives*, Oxford, Oxford University Press, 199–217.

Atkinson, M. and Tyrrall, D. (1997) International transfer pricing: the taxman cometh, *Management Accounting (UK)*, December, 32–4.

Ballas, A. and Venieris, G. (1996) A survey of management accounting practices in Greek firms, in Bhimani, A. (ed.) *Management Accounting: European Perspectives*, Oxford, Oxford University Press, 123–39.

Banerjee, J. and Kane, W. (1996) Report on CIMA/JBA survey, *Management Accounting*, October, **30**, 37.

Barbato, M.B., Collini, P. and Quagli, (1996) Management accounting in Italy, in Bhimani, A. (ed.) *Management Accounting: European Perspectives*, Oxford, Oxford University Press, 140–163.

Barrett, M.E. and Fraser, L.B. (1977), Conflicting roles in budget operations, *Harvard Business Review*, July–August, 137–46.

Barton, T.L., Shenkir, W.G. and Hess, J.E. (1995) *CPA Journal*, June, **65**(6), 48–50.

Bastable, C.W. and Bao, B.H.H. (1988) The fiction of sales-mix and sales quantity variances, *Accounting Horizons*, June, 10–17.

Baxter, W.T. and Oxenfeldt, A.R. (1961) Costing and pricing: the cost accountant versus the economist, *Business Horizons*, Winter, 77–90; also in *Studies in Cost Analysis*, 2nd edn (ed. D. Solomons) Sweet and Maxwell (1968), 293–312.

Berliner, C. and Brimson, J.A. (1988) *Cost Management for Today's Advanced Manufacturing*, Harvard Business School Press.

Bierman, H., Fouraker, l.E. and Jaedicke, R.K. (1977) A use of probability and statistics in performance evaluation, in *Contemporary Cost Accounting and Control*, (ed. G.J. Benston) Dickenson Publishing.

Bjornenak T. (1997a) Diffusion and accounting: the case of ABC in Norway, *Management Accounting Research*, **8**(1), 317.

Bjornenak T. (1997b) Conventional wisdom and accounting practices, *Management Accounting Research*, **8**(4), 367–82.

Blayney, P. and Yokoyama, I. (1991), Comparative analysis of Japanese and Australian cost accounting and management practices, Working paper, University of Sydney, Australia.

Boer, G. (1990) Contribution margin analysis: no longer relevant/strategic cost management: the new paradigm, *Journal of Management Accounting Research* (USA), Fall, 24–7.

Boland, R. (1979) Causality and information system requirements, *Accounting, Organisations and Society*, **4**(4), 259–72.

Boons, A., Roozen, R.A. and Weerd, R.J. de (1994), Kosteninformatie in de Nederlandse Industrie, in *Relevantie methoden en ontwikkelingen* (Rotterdam: Coopers and Lybrand).

Borkowski, S.C. (1990) Environmental and organizational factors affecting transfer pricing: a survey, *Journal of Management Accounting Research*, **2**, 78–99.

Bower, J.L. (1970) *Managing the Resource Allocation Process*, Division of Research, Graduate School of Business Administration, Harvard University.

Boyns, T., Edwards, J.R. and Emmanuel, C. (1999) A longitudinal study of the determinants of transfer pricing change, *Management Accounting Research*, **10**(2), 85–108.

Brantjes, M., von Eije, H., Eusman, F. and Prins, W. (1999) Post-completion auditing within Heineken, *Management Accounting (UK)*, April, 20–2.

Brealey, R.A. and Myers, S.C. (2003) *Principles of Corporate Finance*, McGraw-Hill, New York.

Brinkman, S.L. and Appelbaum, M.A. (1994) The quality cost report: It is alive and well at Gilroy Foods, *Management Accounting (USA)*, September, 61–5.

Bromwich, M. (1990) The case for strategic management accounting: the role of accounting information for strategy in competitive markets, *Accounting, Organisations and Society*, **1**, 27–46.

Bromwich, M. and Walker, M. (1998) Residual income past and future, *Management Accounting Research*, **9**(4), 392–419.

Bromwich, M. and Bhimani, A. (1989) *Management Accounting: Evolution not Revolution*, Chartered Institute of Management Accountants.

Bromwich, M. and Bhimani, A. (1994) *Management Accounting: Pathways to Progress*, Chartered Institute of Management Accountants.

Brownell, P. (1981) Participation in budgeting, locus of control and organisational effectiveness, *The Accounting Review*, October, 944–58.

Bruggeman, W., Slagmulder, R. and Waeytens, D. (1996) Management accounting changes; the Belgian experience, in Bhimani, A. (ed.) *Management Accounting: European Perspectives*, Oxford, Oxford University Press, 1–30.

Burchell, S., Clubb, C., Hopwood, A.G., Hughes, J. and Jahapier, J. (1980) The roles of accounting in organizations and society, *Accounting, Organisations and Society*, **1**, 5–27.

Burrows, G.H. (1994) Allocations and common costs in long-run investment and pricing decisions: An historical perspective, *Abacus*, **30**(1), 50–64.

Cats-Baril, W.L. *et al.* (1986) Joint Product Costing, *Management Accounting* (USA), September, 41–5.

Chan, C.W. (1998) Transfer pricing negotiation outcomes and the impact of negotiator mixed-motives and culture: empirical evidence from the US and Australia, *Management Accounting Research*, **9**(2), 139–61.

Chandler, A.D., Jr. (1962) *Strategy and Structure: Chapters in the History of the Industrial Enterprise*, Cambridge, MA: MIT Press.

Charles, I. (1985a) The economics approach to transfer price, *Accountancy*, June, 110–12.

Charles, I. (1985b) Transfer-price solution where market exists, *Accountancy*, July, 96.

Chartered Institute of Management Accountants (2000) *Management Accounting: Official Terminology*, CIMA.

Cheatham, C.B. and Cheatham, L.R. (1996) Redesigning cost systems: Is standard costing obsolete?, *Accounting Horizons*, December, 23–31.

Chenhall, R.H. (2003) Management control system design within its organizational context: findings from contingency-based research and directions for the future, *Accounting, Organizations and Society*, **28**, 127–68.

Chenhall, R.H. and Langfield-Smith, K. (1998a) Adoption and benefits of management accounting practices: an Australian perspective, *Management Accounting Research*, **9**(1), 120.

Chenhall, R.H. and Langfield-Smith, K. (1998b) The relationship between strategic priorities, management techniques and management accounting: An empirical investigation using a systems approach, *Accounting, Organisations and Society*, **23**(3), 243–64.

Chenhall, R.H. and Morris, D. (1985) The impact of structure, environment and interdependence on the perceived usefulness of management accounting systems, *The Accounting Review*, 1, 16–35.

Chow, C., Haddad, K. and Williamson, J. (1997) Applying the Balanced Scorecard to Small Companies, *Management Accounting*, August, 21–7.

Chow, C.W. (1983) The effect of job standards, tightness and compensation schemes on performance: an exploration of linkages, *The Accounting Review*, October, 667–85.

Chua, W.F. (1988) Interpretive sociology and management accounting research: a critical review, *Accounting, Auditing Accountability Journal*, **1**(1), 59–79.

Clarke, P.J. (1992) Management Accounting Practices and Techniques in Irish Manufacturing Firms, The 15th Annual Congress of the European Accounting Association, Madrid, Spain.

Clarke, P. (1995), Management accounting practices and techniques in Irish manufacturing companies, Working paper, Trinity College, Dublin.

Coad, A. (1996) Smart work and hard work: explicating a learning orientation in strategic management accounting, *Management Accounting Research*, **7**(4), 387–408.

Cohen, M.D., March, J.G. and Olsen, J.P. (1972) A garbage can model of organizational change. *Administrative Science Quarterly*, March, 1–25.

Collins, F. (1978) The interaction of budget characteristics and personality variables with budget response attitudes, *The Accounting Review*, April, 324–35.

Cooper, D.J. (1980) Discussion of 'Towards a Political Economy of Accounting', *Accounting, Organisations, and Society*, **5**(1), 161–6.

Cooper, D.J., Hayes, D. and Wolf, F. (1981) Accounting in organised anarchies: understanding and designing accounting systems in ambiguous situations, *Accounting, Organisations and Society*, **6**(3) 175–91.

Cooper, R. (1990a) Cost classifications in unit-based and activity-based manufacturing cost systems, *Journal of Cost Management*, Fall, 4–14.

Cooper, R. (1990b) Explicating the logic of ABC, *Management Accounting*, November, 5860.

Cooper, R. (1996) Costing techniques to support corporate strategy: evidence from Japan, *Management Accounting Research*, **7**, 219–46.

Cooper, R. (1997) Activity-Based Costing: Theory and Practice, in Brinker, B.J. (ed.), *Handbook of Cost Management*, Warren, Gorham and Lamont, B1–B33.

Cooper, R. and Kaplan, R.S. (1987) How cost accounting systematically distorts product costs, in *Accounting and Management: Field Study Perspectives* (eds W.J. Bruns and R.S. Kaplan), Harvard Business School Press, Ch. 8.

Cooper, R. and Kaplan, R.S. (1988) Measure costs right: make the right decisions, *Harvard Business Review*, September/October, 96–103.

Cooper, R. and Kaplan, R.S. (1991) *The Design of Cost Management Systems: Text, Cases and Readings*, Prentice-Hall.

Cooper, R. and Kaplan, R.S. (1992) Activity based systems: measuring the costs of resource usage, *Accounting Horizons*, September, 1–13.

Cornick, M., Cooper, W. and Wilson, S. (1988) How do companies analyse overhead?, *Management Accounting*, June, 41–3.

Coughlan, P. and Darlington, J. (1993) As fast as the slowest operations: the theory of constraints, *Management Accounting (UK)*, June, 14–17.

Covaleski, M. and Dirsmith, M. (1980) Budgeting as a Means for Control and Loose Coupling in Nursing Services (unpublished), Pennsylvania State University.

Cress, W. and Pettijohn, J. (1985) A survey of budget-related planning and control policies and procedures, *Journal of Accounting Education*, **3**, Fall, 61–78.

Currie, W. (1990) Strategic management of advanced manufacturing technology, *Management Accounting*, October, 50–2.

Currie, W. (1991a) Managing technology: a crisis in management accounting, *Management Accounting*, February, 24–7.

Currie, W. (1991b) Managing production technology in Japanese industry, *Management Accounting*, June, 28–9, July/August, 36–8.

Cyert, R.M. and March, J.G. (1969) *A Behavioural Theory of the Firm*, Prentice-Hall.

Dardenne, P. (1998) Capital budgeting practices – Procedures and techniques by large companies in Belgium, paper presented at the 21st Annual Congress of the European Accounting Association, Antwerp, Belgium.

Darlington, J., Innes, J., Mitchell, F. and Woodward, J. (1992) Throughput accounting: the Garrett Automative experience, *Management Accounting (UK)*, April, 32–5, 38.

DeBono, J. (1997) Divisional cost of equity capital, *Management Accounting (UK)*, November, 40–1.

Dekker, H.C. (2003) Value chain analysis in interfirm relationships: a field study, *Management Accounting Research*, **14**(1), 1–23.

Dekker, H. and Smidt, P. (2003) A survey of the adoption and use of target costing in Dutch firms, *International Journal of Production Economics*, **84**(3), 293–306.

Demski, J.S. (1968) Variance analysis using a constrained linear model, in *Studies in Cost Analysis*, 2nd edn (ed. D. Solomons), Sweet and Maxwell.

Demski, J.S. (1977) Analysing the effectiveness of the traditional standard costing variance model, in *Contemporary Cost Accounting and Control* (ed. G.J. Benston), Dickenson Publishing.

Dhavale, D.G. (1989) Product costing in flexible manufacturing systems, *Journal of Management Accounting Research* (USA), Fall, 66–88.

Dirsmith, M.W. and Jablonsky, S.F. (1979) MBO, political rationality and information inductance, *Accounting, Organisations and Society*, **1**, 39–52.

Dittman, D.A. and Ferris, KR. (1978) Profit centre: a satisfaction generating concept, *Accounting and Business Research*, **8**(32), Autumn, 242–5.

Drucker, P.F. (1964) Controls, control and management, in *Management Controls: New Directions in Basic Research* (eds C.P. Bonini, R. Jaedicke and H. Wagner), McGraw-Hill.

Drury, C. (1998) *Costing: An Introduction*, International Thomson Business Press, Ch. 3.

Drury, C. (2003) *Cost and Management Accounting: An introduction*, Thomson Learning.

Drury C. and Tayles M. (1994) Product costing in UK manufacturing organisations, *The European Accounting Review*, **3**(3), 443–69.

Drury C. and Tayles M. (2000), *Cost system design and profitability analysis in UK companies*, Chartered Institute of Management Accountants.

Drury, C., Braund, S., Osborne, P. and Tayles, M. (1993) A survey of management accounting practices in UK manufacturing companies, ACCA Research Paper, Chartered Association of Certified Accountants.

Dugdale, D. (1989) Contract accounting and the SSAP, *Management Accounting*, June, 624.

Dugdale, D. and Jones, T.C. (1998) Throughput accounting: transformation practices?, *British Accounting Review*, **30**(3), 203–20.

Earl, M.J. and Hopwood, A.G. (1981) From management information to information management, in *The Information Systems Environment* (ed. Lucas, H.C. Jr. *et al.*), Amsterdam, Holland.

Egginton, D. (1995) Divisional performance measurement: residual income and the asset base, *Management Accounting Research*, September, 201–22.

Ekholm, B-G. and Wallin, J. (2000) Is the annual budget really dead?, *The European Accounting Review*, **9**(4), 519–39.

Elliott, J. (1998a) International transfer pricing: the consultative document, *Management Accounting (UK)*, March, 34–5.

Elliott, J. (1998b) International transfer pricing: a survey of UK and non-UK groups, *Management Accounting (UK)*, November, 48–50.

Elphick, C. (1983) A new approach to cost allocations, *Management Accounting*, December, 22–5.

El-Shishini, H. and Drury, C. (2001) Divisional performance measurement in UK companies, Paper presented to the Annual Congress of the European Accounting Association, Athens.

Emmanuel, C. and Mehafdi, M. (1994) *Transfer Pricing*, Academic Press.

Emmanuel, C.R. and Otley, D. (1976) The usefulness of residual income, *Journal of Business Finance and Accounting*, **13**(4), Winter, 43–52.

Emmanuel, C., Otley, D. and Merchant, K. (1990) *Accounting for Management Control*, International Thomson Business Press.

Emore, J.R. and Ness, J.A. (1991) The slow pace of meaningful changes in cost systems, *Journal of Cost Management for the Manufacturing Industry*, Winter, 36–45.

Emsley, D. (2000) Variance analysis and performance: two empirical studies, *Accounting, Organisations and Society*, **25**, 1–12.

Emsley, D. (2001) Redesigning variance analysis for problem solving, *Management Accounting Research*, **12**(1), 21–40.

Epstein, M. and Manzoni, J.F. (1998) Implementing corporate strategy: From tableaux de bord to balanced scorecards, *European Management Journal*, **16**(2), 190–203.

Epstein, M. and Roy, M.J. (1997) Environmental management to improve corporate profitability, *Journal of Cost Management*, November–December, 26–34.

Evans, H. and Ashworth, G. (1996) Survey conclusions: wakeup to the competition, *Management Accounting* (UK), May, 16–18.

Ezzamel, M. and Hart, H. (1987) *Advanced Management Accounting: An Organisational Emphasis*. London, Cassell.

Ezzamel, M.A. and Hilton, K. (1980) Divisionalization in British industry: a preliminary study, *Accounting and Business Research*, Summer, 197 214.

Feldman, M.S. and March, J.G. (1981) Information in organizations as signal and symbol, *Administrative Science Quarterly*, **26**(2), 171–86.

Fielden, J. and Robertson, J. (1980) The content of a value for money review of performance audit, *Public Finance and Accounting*, November, 23–5.

Fisher, I. (1930) *The Theory of Interest*, Macmillan.

Fisher, J. (1995) Contingency-based research on management control systems: Categorization by level of complexity, *Journal of Accounting Literature*, **14**, 24–53.

Fitzgerald, L., Johnston, R., Silvestro, R. and Steele, A. (1989) Management control in service industries, *Management Accounting*, April, 44–6.

Fitzgerald, L., Johnston, R., Brignall, T.J., Silvestro, R. and Voss, C. (1991) *Performance Measurement in Service Businesses*, Chartered Institute of Management Accountants.

Fitzgerald, L. and Moon, P. (1996) *Performance Management in Service Industries*, Chartered Institute of Management Accountants.

Flower, J. (1973) *Computer Models for Accountants*, Haymarket, Chs 4, 5.

Foster, G. and Horngren, C.T. (1988) Cost accounting and cost management in a JIT environment, *Journal of Cost Management for the Manufacturing Industry*, Winter, 4–14.

Franklin, L. (1998) Taxation and the capital expenditure decision, *Management Accounting (UK)*, November, 44–6.

Fremgen, J.M. and Liao, S.S. (1981) The Allocation of Corporate Indirect Costs, National Association of Accountants, New York.

Friedman, A.L. and Lynne, S.R. (1995) *Activity-based Techniques: The Real Life Consequences*, Chartered Institute of Management Accountants.

Friedman, A.L. and Lynne, S.R. (1997) Activity-based techniques and the death of the beancounter, *The European Accounting Review*, **6**(1), 19–44.

Friedman, A.L. and Lynne, S.R. (1999) *Success and Failure of Activity-based Techniques: A long-term perspective*, Chartered Institute of Management Accountants.

Galloway, D. and Waldron, D. (1988) Throughput accounting – 1: the need for a new language for manufacturing, *Management Accounting*, November, 34–5.

Gardiner, S.C. (1993) Measures of product attractiveness and the theory of constraints. *International Journal of Retail and Distribution*, **21**(7), 37–40.

Gibson, B. (1990) Determining meaningful sales relational (mix) variances, *Accounting and Business Research*, Winter, 35–40.

Goetz, B. (1949) *Management Planning and Control: A Managerial Approach to Industrial Accounting*, McGraw-Hill, p. 142.

Goldratt, E.M. and Cox, J. (1984) *The Goal*, London, Gower.

Goldratt, E.M. and Cox, J. (1992) *The Goal* (2nd edn), London, Gower.

Gordon, L.A. and Narayanan (1984) Management accounting systems, perceived environmental uncertainty and organizational structure: an empirical investigation, *Accounting, Organizations and Society*, Vol. 9, No. 1, pp 33–47.

Gould, J.R. (1964) Internal pricing on firms when there are costs of using an outside market, *Journal of Business*, **37**(1), January, 61–7.

Govindarajan, V. (1984) Appropriateness of accounting data in performance evaluation: an empirical evaluation of environmental uncertainty as an intervening variable, *Accounting, Organisations and Society*, **9**(2), 125–36.

Govindarajan, V. (1988) A contingency approach to strategy implementation at the business unit level: integrating administrative mechanisms with strategy, *Academy of Management Journal*, **33**, 828–53.

Govindarajan, V. and Gupta, A.K. (1985) Linking control systems to business unit strategy: Impact on performance, *Accounting, Organisations and Society*, **10**(1), 51–66.

Granlund, M. and Lukka, K. (1998) It's a small world of management accounting practices, *Journal of Management Accounting Research*, **10**, 151–79.

Green, F.B. and Amenkhienan, F.E. (1992) Accounting innovations: A cross sectional survey of manufacturing firms, *Journal of Cost Management for the Manufacturing Industry*, Spring 58–64.

Guilding, C., Craven, K.S. and Tayles, M. (2000) An international comparison of strategic management accounting practices, *Management Accounting Research*, **11**(1), 113–35.

Guilding, C., Lamminmaki, D. and Drury, C. (1998) Budgeting and standard costing practices in New Zealand and the United Kingdom, *The International Journal of Accounting*, **33**(5), 41–60.

Gul, F.A. and Chia, Y.M. (1994) The effects of management accounting systems, perceived environmental uncertainty and decentralization on managerial performance: A test of threeway interaction, *Accounting, Organizations and Society*, **19**(4/5), 413–26.

Hansen, D.R. and Mendoza, R. (1999) Costos de Impacto Ambiental: Su Medicion, Asignacion, y Control, *INCAE Revista*, Vol. X, No. 2, 1999.

Hansen, D.R. and Mowen, M. (2000) *Management Accounting*, South Western Publishing, Chapter 12.

Harris, D.G. (1993) The impact of US tax law revision on multinational corporations' capital location and income shifting decisions, *Journal of Accounting Research*, **31** (Supplement), 111–39.

Hedberg, B. and Jonsson, S. (1978) Designing semi-confusing information systems for organizations in changing environments, *Accounting, Organisations and Society*, **1**, 47–64.

Hergert, M. and Morris, D. (1989) Accounting data for value chain analysis, *Strategic Management Journal*, **10**, 175–88.

Hiromoto, T. (1991) Restoring the relevance of management accounting, *Journal of Management Accounting Research*, **3**, 1–15.

Hirshleifer, J. (1956) On the economies of transfer pricing, *Journal of Business*, July, 172–84.

Hirst, M.K. (1981) Accounting information and the evaluation of subordinate performance, *The Accounting Review*, October, 771–84.

Hirst, M.K. (1987) The effects of setting budget goals and task uncertainty on performance: a theoretical analysis, *The Accounting Review*, October, 774–84.

Hofstede, G.H. (1968) *The Game of Budget Control*, Tavistock.

Holton, M. (1998) Implementing ABC in a service driven business – DHL Worldwide Express, in Innes, J. (ed.), *Handbook of Management Accounting*, Gee, Chapter 23.

Holzer, H.P. and Norreklit, H. (1991) Some thoughts on the cost accounting developments in the United States, *Management Accounting Research*, March, 3–13.

Hope, J. and Fraser, R. (2001) Figures of Hate, *Financial Management*, February, 22–5.

Hopper, T.M., Storey, J. and Willmott, H. (1987) Accounting for accounting: towards the development of a dialectical view, *Accounting, Organisations and Society*, **12**(5) 437–56.

Hopper, T., Kirkham, L., Scapens, R.W. and Turley, S. (1992) Does financial accounting dominate management accounting – A research note, *Management Accounting Research*, **3**(4), 307–11.

Hopwood, A.G. (1976) *Accountancy and Human Behaviour*, Prentice-Hall.

Hopwood, A.G. (1978) Towards an organisational perspective for the study of accounting and information systems, *Accounting, Organisations and Society*, **3**(1), 3–14.

Horngren, C.T. (1967) Process costing in perspective: forget FIFO, *Accounting Review*, July.

Horngren, C.T. (1990) Contribution margin analysis: no longer relevant/strategic cost management: the new paradigm, *Journal of Management Accounting Research* (USA), Fall, 21–4.

Horngren, G.T. and Sorter, G.H. (1962) Asset recognition and economic attributes: the relevant costing approach, *The Accounting Review*, **37**, July, 394, also in *Contemporary Cost Accounting and Control*, (ed G.J. Benston), Dickenson (1977), 462–74.

Hornyak, S. (2000) Budgeting made easy, in Reeve, J.M. (ed.), *Readings and Issues in Cost Management*, South Western College Publishing, 341–6.

Imoisili, O.A. (1989) The role of budget data in the evaluation of managerial performance, *Accounting, Organizations and Society*, **14**(4), 325–35.

Innes, J. (1998) Strategic Management Accounting, in Innes, J. (ed.), *Handbook of Management Accounting*, Gee, Ch. 2.

Innes, J. and Mitchell, F. (1991) ABC: A survey of CIMA members, *Management Accounting*, October, 28–30.

Innes, J. and Mitchell, F. (1992) A review of activity based costing practice, in *Handbook in Management Accounting Practice* (ed. C. Drury), Butterworth-Heinemann, Ch. 3.

Innes, J. and Mitchell, F. (1995a) A survey of activity-based costing in the UK's largest companies, *Management Accounting Research*, June, 137–54.

Innes, J. and Mitchell, F. (1995b) Activity-based costing, in *Issues in Management Accounting* (eds D. Ashton, T. Hopper and R.W. Scapens), Prentice-Hall, 115–36.

Innes, J. and Mitchell, F. (1997) The application of activity-based costing in the United Kingdom's largest financial institutions, *The Service Industries Journal*, **17**(1), 190–203.

Innes, J., Mitchell, F. and Sinclear, D. (2000) Activity-based costing in the UK's largest companies: a comparison of 1994 and 1999 survey results, *Management Accounting Research*, **11**(3), 349–62.

Israelsen, P., Anderson, M., Rohde, C. and Sorensen, P.E. (1996) Management accounting in Denmark: theory and practice, in Bhimani, A. (ed.) *Management Accounting: European Perspectives*, Oxford, Oxford University Press, 3153.

Ittner, C.D., Larcker, D.F. and Rajan, M.V. (1997) The choice of performance measures in annual bonus contracts, *The Accounting Review*, **72**(2), 231–55.

Jacob, J. (1996) Taxes and transfer pricing: income shifting and the volume of intrafirm transfers, *Journal of Accounting Research*, **34**(2), 301–15.

Jaedicke R.K. and Robichek, A.A. (1964) Cost–volume–profit analysis under conditions of uncertainty, *The Accounting Review*, **39**(4), October, 917–26; also in *Studies in Cost Analysis* (ed. D. Solomons), Sweet and Maxwell (1968); also in *Cost Accounting, Budgeting and Control* (ed. W.E. Thomas), 192–210, South Western Publishing Company.

Johnson, H.T. (1990) Professors, customers and value: bringing a global perspective to management accounting education, in *Performance Excellence in Manufacturing and Services Organizations* (ed. P. Turney), American Accounting Association.

Johnson, H.T. and Kaplan, R.S. (1987) *Relevance Lost: The Rise and Fall of Management Accounting*, Harvard Business School Press.

Johnson, G. and Scholes, K. (1999) *Exploring Corporate Strategy*, Prentice-Hall.

Johnson, G. and Scholes, K. (2002) *Exploring Corporate Strategy*, Prentice-Hall.

Jones, T.C. and Dugdale, D. (1998) Theory of constraints: transforming ideas?, *British Accounting Review*, **30**(1), 73–92.

Jones, T.C. and Dugdale, D. (2002) The ABC bandwagon and the juggernaut of modernity, *Accounting, Organizations and Society*, **27**, 121–63.

Joseph, N., Turley, S., Burns, J., Lewis, L., Scapens, R.W. and Southworth, A. (1996) External financial reporting and management information: A survey of UK management accountants, *Management Accounting Research* **7**(1), 73–94.

Joshi, P.L. (1998) An explanatory study of activity-based costing practices and benefits in large size manufacturing companies in India, *Accounting and Business Review*, **5**(1), 65–93.

Joye, M.P. and Blayney, P.J. (1990) Cost and management accounting practice in Australian manufacturing companies: survey results, Monograph No. 7, University of Sydney.

Joye, M.P. and Blayney, P.J. (1991) Strategic management accounting survey, Monograph No. 8, University of Sydney.

Kald, M. and Nilsson, F. (2000) Performance measurement at Nordic companies, *European Management Journal*, **1**, 113–27.

Kaplan, R.S. (1975) The significance and investigation of cost variances: survey and extensions, *Journal of Accounting Research*, **13**(2), Autumn, 311–37, also in *Contemporary Issues in Cost and Managerial Accounting* (eds H.R. Anton, P.A. Firmin and H.D. Grove), Houghton Mifflin (1978).

Kaplan, R.S. (1982) *Advanced Management Accounting*, Prentice-Hall.

Kaplan, R.S. (1990) Contribution margin analysis: no longer relevant/strategic cost management: the new paradigm, *Journal of Management Accounting Research* (USA), Fall, 2–15.

Kaplan, R.S. (1994a) Management accounting (1984–1994): development of new practice and theory, *Management Accounting Research*, September and December, 247–60.

Kaplan, R.S. (1994b) Flexible budgeting in an activity-based costing framework, *Accounting Horizons*, June, 104–109.

Kaplan, R.S. and Atkinson, A.A. (1989) *Advanced Management Accounting*, Prentice-Hall.

Kaplan, R.S. and Atkinson, A.A. (1998) *Advanced Management Accounting*, Prentice-Hall, Ch. 3

Kaplan, R.S. and Cooper, R. (1998) *Cost and Effect: Using Integrated Systems to Drive Profitability and Performance*, Harvard Business School Press.

Kaplan, R.S. and Norton, D.P. (1992) The balanced scorecard: measures that drive performance, *Harvard Business Review*, Jan–Feb, 71–9.

Kaplan, R.S. and Norton, D.P. (1993) Putting the balanced scorecard to work, *Harvard Business Review*, September–October, 134–47.

Kaplan, R.S. and Norton, D.P. (1996a) Using the balanced scorecard as a strategic management system, *Harvard Business Review*, Jan–Feb, 75–85.

Kaplan, R.S. and Norton, D.P. (1996b) *The Balanced Scorecard: Translating strategy into action*, Harvard Business School Press.

Kaplan, R.S. and Norton, D.P. (2001a) *The Strategy-focused Organization*, Harvard Business School Press.

Kaplan, R.S. and Norton, D.P. (2001b) Balance without profit, *Financial Management*, January, 23–6.

Kaplan, R.S. and Norton, D.P. (2001c) Transforming the balanced scorecard from performance measurement to strategic management: Part 1, *Accounting Horizons*, March, 87–104.

Kaplan, R.S. and Norton, D.P. (2001d) Transforming the balanced scorecard from performance measurement to strategic management: Part 2, *Accounting Horizons*, June, 147–60.

Kaplan R.S., Weiss, D. and Deseh, E. (1997) Transfer pricing with ABC, *Management Accounting (USA)*, 20–8.

Kato, Y. (1993) Target costing support systems: lessons from leading Japanese companies, *Management Accounting Research*, March, 33–48.

Keef, S. and Roush, M. (2002) Does MVA measure up?, *Financial Management*, January, 20–1.

Kelly, M. and Pratt, M. (1992) Purposes and paradigms of management accounting: beyond economic reductionism, *Accounting Education*, **1**(3), 225–46.

Kenis, I. (1979) The effects of budgetary goal characteristics on managerial attitudes and performance, *The Accounting Review*, October, 707–21.

Kennedy, A. and Dugdale, D. (1999) Getting the most from budgeting, *Management Accounting (UK)*, February, 22–4.

Khandwalla, P.N. (1972) The effects of different types of competition on the use of management controls, *Journal of Accounting Research*, Autumn, 275–85.

Klassan, K., Lang, M. and Wolfson, M. (1993) Geographic income shifting by multinational corporations in response to tax rate changes, *Journal of Accounting Research*, **31**(Supplement), 141–73.

Langfield-Smith, K. (1997) Management control systems and strategy: a critical review, *Accounting, Organizations and Society*, **22**, 207–32.

Lauderman, M. and Schaeberle, F.W. (1983) The cost accounting practices of firms using standard costs, *Cost and Management* (Canada), July/August, 21–5.

Lawrence, P.R. and Lorsch, J.W. (1986) *Organization and Environment*, Harvard Business School Press.

Leauby, B.A. and Wentzel, K. (2002) Know the score: The balanced scorecard approach to strategically assist clients, *Pennsylvania CPA Journal*, Spring, 29–32.

Lee, J.Y. and Jacobs, B.G. (1993) How process and activity-based cost analysis meets the needs of a small manufacturer, *CMA Magazine* (Canada), **67**(3), 15–19.

Lee, T.A. (1996) *Income and Value Measurement*, Thomson Business Press.

Licata, M.P., Strawser, R.H. and Welker, R.B. (1986) A note on participation in budgeting and locus of control, *The Accounting Review*, January, 112–17.

Lindblom, C.E. (1959) The science of 'Muddling Through', *Public Administration Review*, Summer, 79–88.

Lister, R. (1983) Appraising the value of post-audit procedures, *Accountancy Age*, 20 October, 40.

Lord, B.R. (1996), Strategic management accounting: the emperor's new clothes? *Management Accounting Research*, **7**(3), 347–66.

Lovata, L.M. and Costigan, M.L. (2002) Empirical analysis of adopters of economic value added, *Management Accounting Research*, **13**(2), 251–72.

Lucas, M.R. (2003) Pricing decisions and the neoclassical theory of the firm, *Management Accounting Research*, **14**(3), 201–18.

Lukka, K. and Granlund, M. (1996) Cost accounting in Finland: Current practice and trends of development, *The European Accounting Review*, **5**(1), 1–28.

Lukka, K. and Granlund, M. (2002) The fragmented communication structure within the accounting academia: the case of activity-based costing genres, *Accounting, Organizations and Society*, **27**, 165–90.

Macintosh, N.B. (1985) *The Social Software of Accounting and Information Systems*, Wiley.

Macintosh, N.B. (1994) *Management Accounting and Control Systems: An Organisational and Behavioural Approach*, Wiley.

Mak, Y.T. and Roush, M.L. (1994) Flexible budgeting and variance analysis in an activity-based costing environment, *Accounting Horizons*, June, 93–104.

Mak, Y.T. and Roush, M.L. (1996) Managing activity costs with flexible budgets and variance analysis, *Accounting Horizons*, September, 141–6.

Malmi, T. (1997) Balance scorecards in Finnish companies: a research note, *Management Accounting Research*, **12**(2), 207–20.

Malmi, T. (2001) Balanced scorecards in Finnish companies: a research note, *Management Accounting Research*, Vol. 12, No. 2, pp 207–20.

Manes, R.P. (1983) Demand elasticities: supplements to sales budget variance reports, *The Accounting Review*, January, 143–56.

Mauriel, J. and Anthony, R.N. (1986) Mis-evaluation of investment centre performance, *Harvard Business Review*, March/April, 98–105.

McGowan, A.S. and Klammer, T.P. (1997) Satisfaction with activity-based cost management, *Journal of Management Accounting Research*, **9**, 217–38.

McNair, C.J., Polutnik, L. and Silvi. (2001) Cost management and value creation, *European Accounting Review*, **10**(1), 33–50.

Merchant, K.A. (1989) *Rewarding Results: Motivating Profit Center Managers*, Harvard Business School Press.

Merchant, K.A. (1990) How challenging should profit budget targets be? *Management Accounting*, November, 46–8.

Merchant, K.A. (1998) *Modern Management Control Systems: Text and Cases*, Prentice-Hall, New Jersey.

Merchant, K.A. and Shields, M.D. (1993) When and why to measure costs less accurately to improve decision making, *Accounting Horizons*, June, 76–81.

Mia, L. (1989) The impact of participation in budgeting and job difficulty on managerial performance and work motivation: a research note, *Accounting, Organisations and Society*, **14**(4), 347–57.

Milani, K. (1975) The relationship of participation in budget setting to industrial supervisor performance and attitudes: a field study, *The Accounting Review*, April, 274–84.

Miles, R.E. and Snow, C.C. (1978) *Organizational Strategies, Structure and Process*, New York, McGraw-Hill.

Mills, R.W. (1988) Pricing decisions in UK manufacturing and service companies, *Management Accounting*, November, 38–9.

Monden, Y. and Hamada, K. (1991) Target costing and Kaizen costing in Japanese automobile companies, *Journal of Management Accounting Research*, Autumn, 16–34.

Moon, P. and Fitzgerald, L. (1996) *Performance Measurement in Service Industries: Making it Work*, Chartered Institute of Management Accountants, London.

Moore, P.G. and Thomas, H. (1991) *The Anatomy of Decisions*, Penguin.

Narayanan, V.G. and Sarkar, R.G. (2002) The impact of activity-based costing on managerial decisions at Insteel industries: A field study, *Journal of Economics and Management Strategy*, **11**(2), 257–88.

Neale, C.W. and Holmes, D. (1988) Post-completion audits: The costs and benefits, *Management Accounting*, **66**(3), 27–31.

Neale, C.W. and Holmes, D. (1991) *Post-completion Auditing*, Pitman.

Neighbour, J. (2002) Transfer pricing: keeping it at arm's length, *OECD Observer*, January, 29–30.

Nicholls, B. (1992) ABC in the UK – a status report, *Management Accounting*, May, 22–3.

Norreklit, H. (2000) The balance on the balanced scorecard – a critical analysis of some of its assumptions, *Management Accounting Research*, Vol. 11, No. 1, pp 65–88.

Norreklit, H. (2003) The balanced scorecard: what is the score? A rhetorical analysis of the balanced scorecard, *Accounting, Organizations and Society*, **28**, 591–619.

O'Hanlon, J.O. and Peasnell, K. (1998) Wall's Street's contribution to management accounting: the Stern Stewart EVA® financial management system, *Management Accounting Research*, **9**(4), 421–44.

Oliveras, E. and Amat, O. (2002) The balanced scorecard assumptions and the drivers of business growth, Paper presented at the 25th Annual Congress of the European Accounting Association, Copenhagen, Denmark.

Olve, N., Roy, J. and Wetter, M. (2000) *Performance Drivers: A Practical Guide to Using the Balanced Scorecard*, John Wiley & Sons.

Osni, M. (1973) Factor analysis of behavioural variables affecting budgetary stock, *The Accounting Review*, 535–48.

Otley, D.T. (1978) Budget use and managerial performance, *Journal of Accounting Research*, **16**(1), Spring, 122–49.

Otley, D.T. (1980) The contingency theory of management accounting: achievement and prognosis, *Accounting, Organizations and Society*, **5**(4), 413–28.

Otley, D.T. (1987) *Accounting Control and Organizational Behaviour*, Heinemann.

Ouchi, W.G. (1979) A conceptual framework for the design of organizational control mechanisms, *Management Science*, 833–48.

Oyelere, P.B. and Emmanuel (1998) International transfer pricing and income shifting: evidence from the UK, *The European Accounting Review*, **7**(4), 623–35.

Pendlebury, M.E (1994), Management accounting in local government, *Financial Accountability & Management*, May, 117–29.

Pendlebury, M. (1996) Management accounting in local government, in *Handbook of Management Accounting Practice* (ed. C. Drury), Butterworth-Heinemann, London.

Pere, T. (1999) How the execution of strategy is followed in large organisations located in Finland, Masters Thesis (Helsinki School of Economics and Business Administration).

Perera, S., McKinnon, J.L. and Harrison, G.L. (2003) Diffusion of transfer pricing innovation in the context of commercialization – a longitudinal study of government trading enterprises, *Management Accounting Research*, **14**(2),140–64.

Perrin, J. (1987) The costs and joint products of English teaching hospitals, *Financial Accountability and Management*, **3**(2), 209–30.

Pfeffer, J. and Salancik, G.R. (1974) Organisational decision making as a political process: the case of a university budget, *Administrative Science Quarterly*, June, 135–50.

Phyrr, P.A. (1976) Zero-based budgeting – where to use it and how to begin, *S.A.M. Advanced Management Journal*, Summer, 5.

Pike, R.H. (1996) A longitudinal study of capital budgeting practices, *Journal of Business Finance and Accounting*, **23**(1), 79–92.

Pike, R. and Neale, B. (2003) *Corporate Finance and Investment*, Prentice-Hall Europe.

Plunkett, J.J., Dale, B.G. and Tyrrell, R.W. (1985) *Quality Costs*, London, Department of Trade and Industry.

Porter, M. (1980) *Competitive strategy techniques analysing industries and competitors*, New York, Free Press.

Porter, M. (1985) *Competitive Advantage*, New York, Free Press.

Puxty, A.G. (1993) *The Social and Organisational Context of Management Accounting*, Academic Press.

Puxty, A.G. and Lyall, D. (1990) *Cost Control into the 1990s: A Survey of Standard Costing and Budgeting Practices in the UK*, Chartered Institute of Management Accountants; see also *Management Accounting*, February, 1990, 445.

Ramadan, S.S. (1989) The rationale for cost allocation: A study of UK companies, *Accounting and Business Research*, Winter, 31–7.

Ranganathan, J. and Ditz, D. (1996) Environmental accounting: a tool for better management, *Management Accounting*, February, 38–40.

Reece, J.S. and Cool, W.R. (1978) Measuring investment centre performance, *Harvard Business Review*, May/June 29–49.

Roslender, R. (1992) *Sociological Perspectives on Modern Accountancy*, Routledge.

Roslender, R. (1995) Accounting for strategic positioning: Responding to the crisis in management accounting, *British Journal of Management*, **6**, 45–57.

Roslender, R. (1996) Relevance lost and found: Critical perspectives on the promise of management accounting, *Critical Perspectives on Accounting*, **7**(5), 533–61.

Roslender, R. and Hart, S.J. (2002) Integrating management accounting and marketing in the pursuit of competitive advantage: the case for strategic management accounting, *Critical Perspectives on Accounting*, **13**(2), 255–77.

Roslender, R. and Hart, S.J. (2003) In search of strategic management accounting: theoretical and field study perspectives, *Management Accounting Research*, **14**(3), 255–80.

Saez-Torrecilla, A., Fernandez-Fernandez, A., Texeira-Quiros, J. and Vaquera-Mosquero, M. (1996) Management accounting in Spain: trends in thought and practice, in Bhimani, A. (ed.) *Management Accounting: European Perspective 3*, Oxford, Oxford University Press, 180–90.

Salkin, G. and Kornbluth, J. (1973) *Linear Programming in Financial Planning*, Prentice-Hall, Ch. 7.

Samuels, J.M., Wilkes, F.M. and Brayshaw, R.E. (1998) *Management of Company Finance*, Chapman and Hall.

Scapens, R., Jazayeri, M. and Scapens, J. (1998) SAP: Integrated information systems and the implications for management accountants, *Management Accounting (UK)*, September, 46–8.

Scapens, R.W. (1991) *Management Accounting: A Review of Recent Developments*, Macmillan.

Scarborough, P.A., Nanni, A. and Sakurai, M. (1991) Japanese management accounting practices and the effects of assembly and process automation, *Management Accounting Research*, **2**, 27–46.

Scherrer, G. (1996) Management accounting: a German perspective, in Bhimani, A. (ed.), *Management Accounting: European Perspectives*, Oxford, Oxford University Press, 100–22.

Schiff, M. and Lewin, A.Y. (1970) The impact of people on budgets, *The Accounting Review*, April, 259–68.

Schwarzbach, H.R. (1985) The impact of automation on accounting for direct costs, *Management Accounting* (USA), **67**(6), 45–50.

Seal, W., Cullen, J., Dunlop, D., Berry, T., and Ahmed, M. (1999) Enacting a European supply chain: a case study on the role of management accounting, *Management Accounting Research*, **10**(3), 303–22.

Sen, P.K. (1998) Another look at cost variance investigation, *Accounting Horizons*, February, 127–37.

Shank, J.K. (1989) Strategic cost management: new wine or just new bottles?, *Journal of Management Accounting Research* (USA), Fall, 47–65.

Shank, J. and Govindarajan, V. (1992) Strategic cost management: the value chain perspective, *Journal of Management Accounting Research*, **4**, 179–97.

Shields, M.D. (1995) An empirical analysis of firms' implementation experiences with activity-based costing, *Journal of Management Accounting Research*, **7**, Fall, 148–66.

Shim, E. and Stagliano, A. (1997) A survey of US manufacturers on implementation of ABC, *Journal of Cost Management*, March/April, 39–41.

Silk, S. (1998) Automating the balanced scorecard, *Management Accounting*, May, 38–44.

Simmonds, K. (1981) Strategic management accounting, *Management Accounting*, **59**(4), 26–9.

Simmonds, K. (1982) Strategic management accounting for pricing: a case example, *Accounting and Business Research*, **12**(47), 206–14.

Simmonds, K. (1986) The accounting assessment of competitive position, *European Journal of Marketing, Organisations and Society*, **12**(4), 357–74.

Simon, H.A. (1959) Theories of decision making in economics and behavioural science, *The American Economic Review*, June, 233–83.

Simons, R. (1987) Accounting control systems and business strategy, *Accounting, Organizations and Society*, **12**(4), 357–74.

Simons, R. (1998) *Performance Measurement and Control Systems for Implementing Strategy: Text and cases*, Prentice-Hall.

Simons, R. (1999) *Performance Measurement and Control Systems for Implementing Strategy*, Prentice-Hall, New Jersey.

Sizer, J. (1989) *An Insight into Management Accounting*, Penguin, Chs 11, 12.

Sizer, J. and Mottram, G. (1996) Successfully evaluating and controlling investments in advanced manufacturing technology, in *Management Accounting Handbook* (ed. C. Drury), Butterworth-Heinemann.

Skinner, R.C. (1990) The role of profitability in divisional decision making and performance, *Accounting and Business Research*, Spring, 135–41.

Slater, K. and Wootton, C. (1984) *Joint and By-product Costing in the UK*, Institute of Cost and Management Accounting.

Soin, K., Seal, W. and Cullen, J. (2002) ABC and organizational change: an institutional perspective, *Management Accounting Research*, **13**(2), 151–72.

Solomons, D. (1965) *Divisional Performance: Measurement and Control*, R.D. Irwin.

Speckbacher, G., Bischof, J. and Pfeiffer, T. (2003) A Descriptive Analysis on the Implementation of Balanced Scorecards in German-Speaking Countries, *Management Accounting Research*, **14**(4), 361–88.

Stedry, A. and Kay, E. (1966) The effects of goal difficulty on performance: a field experiment, *Behavioural Science*, November, 459–70.

Stewart, G.B. (1991) *The Quest for Value: A Guide for Senior Managers*, Harper Collins, New York.

Stewart, G.B. (1994) EVA(TM): Fact and Fantasy, *Journal of Applied Corporate Finance*, Summer, 71–84.

Stewart, G.B. (1995) EVA(TM) works But not if you make common mistakes, *Fortune*, 1 May, 81–2.

Tang, R. (1992) Canadian transfer pricing in the 1990s, *Management Accounting* (USA), February.

Tani, T., Okano, H., Shimizu, N., Iwabuchi, Y, Fukuda, J. and Cooray, S. (1994) Target cost management in Japanese companies: current state of the art, *Management Accounting Research*, **5**(1), 67–82.

Thompson, J.D. (1967) *Organisations in Action*, McGraw-Hill.

Thompson, J.D. and Tuden, A. (1959) Strategies, structures and processes of organizational decision, in *Comparative Studies in Administration* (eds Thompson, J.D. *et al.*), University of Pittsburg Press.

Thompson, J.L. (2001) *Strategic Management*, Chapman and Hall, London.

Tomkins, C. (1973) *Financial Planning in Divisionalised Companies*, Haymarket, Chs 4 and 8.

Tomkins, C. (1975) Another look at residual income, *Journal of Business Finance and Accounting*, **2**(1), Spring 39–54.

Tomkins, C. and Carr, C. (1996) Editorial in Special Issue of Management Accounting Research: Strategic Management Accounting, *Management Accounting Research*, **7**(2), 165–7.

Tomkins, C. and McAulay, L. (1996) Modelling fair transfer prices where no market guidelines exist, in *Management Accounting Handbook* (ed. C. Drury), Butterworth-Heinemann, Ch. 16.

Trahan, E.A. and Gitman, L.J. (1995) Bridging the theory–practice gap in corporate finance: A survey of chief finance officers, *The Quarterly Review of Economics and Finance*, **35**(1), Spring, 73–87.

Trenchard, P.M. and Dixon, R. (2003) The clinical allocation of joint blood product costs, *Management Accounting Research*, **14**(2), 165–76.

Turney, P. (1993) *Common Cents: The ABC Performance Breakthrough*, Cost Technology, Hillsboro, Oregon, USA.

Umapathy, S. (1987) *Current Budgeting Practices in U.S. Industry: The State of the Art*, New York, Quorum.

Virtanen, K., Malmi, T., Vaivio, J. and Kasanen, E. (1996) Drivers of management accounting in Finland, in Bhimani, A. (ed.) *Management Accounting: European Perspectives*, Oxford, Oxford University Press, 218–41.

Vroom, V.H. (1960) *Some Personality Determinants of the Effects of Participation*, Prentice-Hall.

Ward, K. (1992) Accounting for marketing strategies, in *Management Accounting Handbook* (ed. C. Drury), Butterworth-Heinemann, Ch. 7.

Watson, D.H. and Baumler, J.V. (1975) Transfer pricing: a behavioural context, *Accounting Review*, **50**(3), July, 466–74.

Wetnight, R. B. (1958) Direct costing passes the future benefit test, *NAA Bulletin*, **39**, August, 84.

Weick, K.E. (1969) *The Social Psychology of Organising*, Addison Wesley.

Wildavsky, A. (1974) *The Politics of Budgetary Process*, Little Brown.

Wilkes, F.M. (1989) *Operational Research: Analysis and Applications*, McGraw-Hill.

Wilson, R.M. and Chua W.E. (1993) *Management Accounting: Method and Meaning*, International Thomson Business Press, Ch. 7.

Woodward, J. (1965) *Industrial Organization; Theory and Practice*, Oxford University Press.

Yoshikawa, T., Innes, J., Mitchell, F. and Tanaka, M. (1993) *Contemporary Cost Management*, Chapman and Hall.

Young, P. H. (1985) *Cost Allocation: Methods, Principles, Applications*, Amsterdam: North Holland.

APPENDICES

Appendix A: Present value factors

The table gives the present value of a single payment received *n* years in the future discounted at *x*% per year. For example, with a discount rate of 7% a single payment of £1 in six years' time has a present value of £0.6663 or 66.63p.

Years	1%	2%	3%	4%	5%	6%	7%	8%	9%	10%
1	0.9901	0.9804	0.9709	0.9615	0.9524	0.9434	0.9346	0.9259	0.9174	0.9091
2	0.9803	0.9612	0.9426	0.9426	0.9070	0.8900	0.8734	0.8573	0.8417	0.8264
3	0.9706	0.9423	0.9151	0.8890	0.8638	0.8396	0.8163	0.7938	0.7722	0.7513
4	0.9610	0.9238	0.8885	0.8548	0.8227	0.7921	0.7629	0.7350	0.7084	0.6830
5	0.9515	0.9057	0.8626	0.8219	0.7835	0.7473	0.7130	0.6806	0.6499	0.6209
6	0.9420	0.8880	0.8375	0.7903	0.7462	0.7050	0.6663	0.6302	0.5963	0.5645
7	0.9327	0.8706	0.8131	0.7599	0.7107	0.6651	0.6227	0.5835	0.5470	0.5132
8	0.9235	0.8535	0.7894	0.7307	0.6768	0.6274	0.5820	0.5403	0.5019	0.4665
9	0.9143	0.8368	0.7664	0.7026	0.6446	0.5919	0.5439	0.5002	0.4604	0.4241
10	0.9053	0.8203	0.7441	0.6756	0.6139	0.5584	0.5083	0.4632	0.4224	0.3855
11	0.8963	0.8043	0.7224	0.6496	0.5847	0.5268	0.4751	0.4289	0.3875	0.3505
12	0.8874	0.7885	0.7014	0.6246	0.5568	0.4970	0.4440	0.3971	0.3555	0.3186
13	0.8787	0.7730	0.6810	0.6006	0.5303	0.4688	0.4150	0.3677	0.3262	0.2897
14	0.8700	0.7579	0.6611	0.5775	0.5051	0.4423	0.3878	0.3405	0.2992	0.2633
15	0.8613	0.7430	0.6419	0.5553	0.4810	0.4173	0.3624	0.3152	0.2745	0.2394
16	0.8528	0.7284	0.6232	0.5339	0.4581	0.3936	0.3387	0.2919	0.2519	0.2176
17	0.8444	0.7142	0.6050	0.5134	0.4363	0.3714	0.3166	0.2703	0.2311	0.1978
18	0.8360	0.7002	0.5874	0.4936	0.4155	0.3503	0.2959	0.2502	0.2120	0.1799
19	0.8277	0.6864	0.5703	0.4746	0.3957	0.3305	0.2765	0.2317	0.1945	0.1635
20	0.8195	0.6730	0.5537	0.4564	0.3769	0.3118	0.2584	0.2145	0.1784	0.1486
21	0.8114	0.6598	0.5375	0.4388	0.3589	0.2942	0.2415	0.1987	0.1637	0.1351
22	0.8034	0.6468	0.5219	0.4220	0.3418	0.2775	0.2257	0.1839	0.1502	0.1228
23	0.7954	0.6342	0.5067	0.4057	0.3256	0.2618	0.2109	0.1703	0.1378	0.1117
24	0.7876	0.6217	0.4919	0.3901	0.3101	0.2470	0.1971	0.1577	0.1264	0.1015
25	0.7798	0.6095	0.4776	0.3751	0.2953	0.2330	0.1842	0.1460	0.1160	0.0923
26	0.7720	0.5976	0.4637	0.3607	0.2812	0.2198	0.1722	0.1352	0.1064	0.0839
27	0.7644	0.5859	0.4502	0.3468	0.2678	0.2074	0.1609	0.1252	0.0976	0.0763
28	0.7568	0.5744	0.4371	0.3335	0.2551	0.1956	0.1504	0.1159	0.0895	0.0693
29	0.7493	0.5631	0.4243	0.3207	0.2429	0.1846	0.1406	0.1073	0.0822	0.0630
30	0.7419	0.5521	0.4120	0.3083	0.2314	0.1741	0.1314	0.0094	0.0754	0.0573
35	0.7059	0.5000	0.3554	0.2534	0.1813	0.1301	0.0937	0.0676	0.0490	0.0356
40	0.6717	0.4529	0.3066	0.2083	0.1420	0.0972	0.0668	0.0460	0.0318	0.0221
45	0.6391	0.4102	0.2644	0.1712	0.1113	0.0727	0.0476	0.0313	0.0207	0.0137
50	0.6080	0.3715	0.2281	0.1407	0.0872	0.0543	0.0339	0.0213	0.0134	0.0085

11%	12%	13%	14%	15%	16%	17%	18%	19%	20%	Years
0.9009	0.8929	0.8850	0.8772	0.8696	0.8621	0.8547	0.8475	0.8403	0.8333	1
0.8116	0.7972	0.7831	0.7695	0.7561	0.7432	0.7305	0.7182	0.7062	0.6944	2
0.7312	0.7118	0.6931	0.6750	0.6575	0.6407	0.6244	0.6086	0.5934	0.5787	3
0.6587	0.6355	0.6133	0.5921	0.5718	0.5523	0.5337	0.5158	0.4987	0.4823	4
0.5935	0.5674	0.5428	0.5194	0.4972	0.4761	0.4561	0.4371	0.4190	0.4019	5
0.5346	0.5066	0.4803	0.4556	0.4323	0.4104	0.3898	0.3704	0.3521	0.3349	6
0.4817	0.4523	0.4251	0.3996	0.3759	0.3538	0.3332	0.3139	0.2959	0.2791	7
0.4339	0.4039	0.3762	0.3506	0.3269	0.3050	0.2848	0.2660	0.2487	0.2326	8
0.3909	0.3606	0.3329	0.3075	0.2843	0.2630	0.2434	0.2255	0.2090	0.1938	9
0.3522	0.3220	0.2946	0.2697	0.2472	0.2267	0.2080	0.1911	0.1756	0.1615	10
0.3173	0.2875	0.2607	0.2366	0.2149	0.1954	0.1778	0.1619	0.1476	0.1346	11
0.2858	0.2567	0.2307	0.2076	0.1869	0.1685	0.1520	0.1372	0.1240	0.1122	12
0.2575	0.2292	0.2042	0.1821	0.1625	0.1452	0.1299	0.1163	0.1042	0.0935	13
0.2320	0.2046	0.1807	0.1597	0.1413	0.1252	0.1110	0.0985	0.0876	0.0779	14
0.2090	0.1827	0.1599	0.1401	0.1229	0.1079	0.0949	0.0835	0.0736	0.0649	15
0.1883	0.1631	0.1415	0.1229	0.1069	0.0930	0.0811	0.0708	0.0618	0.0541	16
0.1696	0.1456	0.1252	0.1078	0.0929	0.0802	0.0693	0.0600	0.0520	0.0451	17
0.1528	0.1300	0.1108	0.0946	0.0808	0.0691	0.0592	0.0508	0.0437	0.0376	18
0.1377	0.1161	0.0981	0.0829	0.0703	0.0596	0.0506	0.0431	0.0367	0.0313	19
0.1240	0.1037	0.0868	0.0728	0.0611	0.0514	0.0433	0.0365	0.0308	0.0261	20
0.1117	0.0926	0.0768	0.0638	0.0531	0.0443	0.0370	0.0309	0.0259	0.0217	21
0.1007	0.0826	0.0680	0.0560	0.0462	0.0382	0.0316	0.0262	0.0218	0.0181	22
0.0907	0.0738	0.0601	0.0491	0.0402	0.0329	0.0270	0.0222	0.0183	0.0151	23
0.0817	0.0659	0.0532	0.0431	0.0349	0.0284	0.0231	0.0188	0.0154	0.0126	24
0.0736	0.0588	0.0471	0.0378	0.0304	0.0245	0.0197	0.0160	0.0129	0.0105	25
0.0663	0.0525	0.0417	0.0331	0.0264	0.0211	0.0169	0.0135	0.0109	0.0087	26
0.0597	0.0469	0.0369	0.0291	0.0230	0.0182	0.0144	0.0115	0.0091	0.0073	27
0.0538	0.0419	0.0326	0.0255	0.0200	0.0157	0.0123	0.0097	0.0077	0.0061	28
0.0485	0.0374	0.0289	0.0224	0.0174	0.0135	0.0105	0.0082	0.0064	0.0051	29
0.0437	0.0334	0.0256	0.0196	0.0151	0.0116	0.0090	0.0070	0.0054	0.0042	30
0.0259	0.0189	0.0139	0.0102	0.0075	0.0055	0.0041	0.0030	0.0023	0.0017	35
0.0154	0.0107	0.0075	0.0053	0.0037	0.0026	0.0019	0.0013	0.0010	0.0007	40
0.0091	0.0061	0.0041	0.0027	0.0019	0.0013	0.0009	0.0006	0.0004	0.0003	45
0.0054	0.0035	0.0022	0.0014	0.0009	0.0006	0.0004	0.0003	0.0002	0.0001	50

Years	21%	22%	23%	24%	25%	26%	27%	28%	29%	30%
1	0.8264	0.8197	0.8130	0.8065	0.8000	0.7937	0.7874	0.7813	0.7752	0.7692
2	0.6830	0.6719	0.6610	0.6504	0.6400	0.6299	0.6200	0.6104	0.6009	0.5917
3	0.5645	0.5507	0.5374	0.5245	0.5120	0.4999	0.4882	0.4768	0.4658	0.4552
4	0.4665	0.4514	0.4369	0.4230	0.4096	0.3968	0.3844	0.3725	0.3611	0.3501
5	0.3855	0.3700	0.3552	0.3411	0.3277	0.3149	0.3027	0.2910	0.2799	0.2693
6	0.3186	0.3033	0.2888	0.2751	0.2621	0.2499	0.2383	0.2274	0.2170	0.2072
7	0.2633	0.2486	0.2348	0.2218	0.2097	0.1983	0.1877	0.1776	0.1682	0.1594
8	0.2176	0.2038	0.1909	0.1789	0.1678	0.1574	0.1478	0.1388	0.1304	0.1226
9	0.1799	0.1670	0.1552	0.1443	0.1342	0.1249	0.1164	0.1084	0.1011	0.0943
10	0.1486	0.1369	0.1262	0.1164	0.1074	0.0992	0.0916	0.0847	0.0784	0.0725
11	0.1228	0.1122	0.1026	0.0938	0.0859	0.0787	0.0721	0.0662	0.0607	0.0558
12	0.1015	0.0920	0.0834	0.0757	0.0687	0.0625	0.0568	0.0517	0.0471	0.0429
13	0.0839	0.0754	0.0678	0.0610	0.0550	0.0496	0.0447	0.0404	0.0365	0.0330
14	0.0693	0.0618	0.0551	0.0492	0.0440	0.0393	0.0352	0.0316	0.0283	0.0254
15	0.0573	0.0507	0.0448	0.0397	0.0352	0.0312	0.0277	0.0247	0.0219	0.0195
16	0.0474	0.0415	0.0364	0.0320	0.0281	0.0248	0.0218	0.0193	0.0170	0.0150
17	0.0391	0.0340	0.0296	0.0258	0.0225	0.0197	0.0172	0.0150	0.0132	0.0116
18	0.0323	0.0279	0.0241	0.0208	0.0180	0.0156	0.0135	0.0118	0.0102	0.0089
19	0.0267	0.0229	0.0196	0.0168	0.0144	0.0124	0.0107	0.0092	0.0079	0.0068
20	0.0221	0.0187	0.0159	0.0135	0.0115	0.0098	0.0084	0.0072	0.0061	0.0053
21	0.0183	0.0154	0.0129	0.0109	0.0092	0.0078	0.0066	0.0056	0.0048	0.0040
22	0.0151	0.0126	0.0105	0.0088	0.0074	0.0062	0.0052	0.0044	0.0037	0.0031
23	0.0125	0.0103	0.0086	0.0071	0.0059	0.0049	0.0041	0.0034	0.0029	0.0024
24	0.0103	0.0085	0.0070	0.0057	0.0047	0.0039	0.0032	0.0027	0.0022	0.0018
25	0.0085	0.0069	0.0057	0.0046	0.0038	0.0031	0.0025	0.0021	0.0017	0.0014
26	0.0070	0.0057	0.0046	0.0037	0.0030	0.0025	0.0020	0.0016	0.0013	0.0011
27	0.0058	0.0047	0.0037	0.0030	0.0024	0.0019	0.0016	0.0013	0.0010	0.0008
28	0.0048	0.0038	0.0030	0.0024	0.0019	0.0015	0.0012	0.0010	0.0008	0.0006
29	0.0040	0.0031	0.0025	0.0020	0.0015	0.0012	0.0010	0.0008	0.0006	0.0005
30	0.0033	0.0026	0.0020	0.0016	0.0012	0.0010	0.0008	0.0006	0.0005	0.0004
35	0.0013	0.0009	0.0007	0.0005	0.0004	0.0003	0.0002	0.0002	0.0001	0.0001
40	0.0005	0.0004	0.0003	0.0002	0.0001	0.0001	0.0001	0.0001		
45	0.0002	0.0001	0.0001	0.0001						
50	0.0001									

31%	32%	33%	34%	35%	36%	37%	38%	39%	40%	Years
0.7634	0.7576	0.7519	0.7463	0.7407	0.7353	0.7299	0.7246	0.7194	0.7143	1
0.5827	0.5739	0.5653	0.5569	0.5487	0.5407	0.5328	0.5251	0.5176	0.5102	2
0.4448	0.4348	0.4251	0.4156	0.4064	0.3975	0.3889	0.3805	0.3724	0.3644	3
0.3396	0.3294	0.3196	0.3102	0.3011	0.2923	0.2839	0.2757	0.2679	0.2603	4
0.2592	0.2495	0.2403	0.2315	0.2230	0.2149	0.2072	0.1998	0.1927	0.1859	5
0.1979	0.1890	0.1807	0.1727	0.1652	0.1580	0.1512	0.1448	0.1386	0.1328	6
0.1510	0.1432	0.1358	0.1289	0.1224	0.1162	0.1104	0.1049	0.0997	0.0949	7
0.1153	0.1085	0.1021	0.0962	0.0906	0.0854	0.0806	0.0760	0.0718	0.0678	8
0.0880	0.0822	0.0768	0.0718	0.0671	0.0628	0.0588	0.0551	0.0516	0.0484	9
0.0672	0.0623	0.0577	0.0536	0.0497	0.0462	0.0429	0.0399	0.0371	0.0346	10
0.0513	0.0472	0.0434	0.0400	0.0368	0.0340	0.0313	0.0289	0.0267	0.0247	11
0.0392	0.0357	0.0326	0.0298	0.0273	0.0250	0.0229	0.0210	0.0192	0.0176	12
0.0299	0.0271	0.0245	0.0223	0.0202	0.0184	0.0167	0.0152	0.0138	0.0126	13
0.0228	0.0205	0.0185	0.0166	0.0150	0.0135	0.0122	0.0110	0.0099	0.0090	14
0.0174	0.0155	0.0139	0.0124	0.0111	0.0099	0.0089	0.0080	0.0072	0.0064	15
0.0133	0.0118	0.0104	0.0093	0.0082	0.0073	0.0065	0.0058	0.0051	0.0046	16
0.0101	0.0089	0.0078	0.0069	0.0061	0.0054	0.0047	0.0042	0.0037	0.0033	17
0.0077	0.0068	0.0059	0.0052	0.0045	0.0039	0.0035	0.0030	0.0027	0.0023	18
0.0059	0.0051	0.0044	0.0038	0.0033	0.0029	0.0025	0.0022	0.0019	0.0017	19
0.0045	0.0039	0.0033	0.0029	0.0025	0.0021	0.0018	0.0016	0.0014	0.0012	20
0.0034	0.0029	0.0025	0.0021	0.0018	0.0016	0.0013	0.0012	0.0010	0.0009	21
0.0026	0.0022	0.0019	0.0016	0.0014	0.0012	0.0010	0.0008	0.0007	0.0006	22
0.0020	0.0017	0.0014	0.0012	0.0010	0.0008	0.0007	0.0006	0.0005	0.0004	23
0.0015	0.0013	0.0011	0.0009	0.0007	0.0006	0.0005	0.0004	0.0004	0.0003	24
0.0012	0.0010	0.0008	0.0007	0.0006	0.0005	0.0004	0.0003	0.0003	0.0002	25
0.0009	0.0007	0.0006	0.0005	0.0004	0.0003	0.0003	0.0002	0.0002	0.0002	26
0.0007	0.0006	0.0005	0.0004	0.0003	0.0002	0.0002	0.0002	0.0001	0.0001	27
0.0005	0.0004	0.0003	0.0003	0.0002	0.0002	0.0001	0.0001	0.0001	0.0001	28
0.0004	0.0003	0.0003	0.0002	0.0002	0.0001	0.0001	0.0001	0.0001	0.0001	29
0.0003	0.0002	0.0002	0.0002	0.0001	0.0001	0.0001	0.0001	0.0001		30
0.0001	0.0001									35

Appendix B: Cumulative present value factors

The table gives the present value of n annual payments of £1 received for the next n years with a constant discount of $x\%$ per year.

For example, with a discount rate of £7 and with six annual payments of £1, the present value is £4.767.

Years 0 to:	1%	2%	3%	4%	5%	6%	7%	8%	9%	10%
1	0.990	0.980	0.971	0.962	0.952	0.943	0.935	0.926	0.917	0.909
2	1.970	1.942	1.913	1.886	1.859	1.833	1.808	1.783	1.759	1.736
3	2.941	2.884	2.829	2.775	2.723	2.673	2.624	2.577	2.531	2.487
4	3.902	3.808	3.717	3.630	3.546	3.465	3.387	3.312	3.240	3.170
5	4.853	4.713	4.580	4.452	4.329	4.212	4.100	3.993	3.890	3.791
6	5.795	5.601	5.417	5.242	5.076	4.917	4.767	4.623	4.486	4.355
7	6.728	6.472	6.230	6.002	5.786	5.582	5.389	5.206	5.033	4.868
8	7.652	7.325	7.020	6.733	6.463	6.210	5.971	5.747	5.535	5.335
9	8.566	8.162	7.786	7.435	7.108	6.802	6.515	6.247	5.995	5.759
10	9.471	8.983	8.530	8.111	7.722	7.360	7.024	6.710	6.418	6.145
11	10.368	9.787	9.253	8.760	8.306	7.887	7.499	7.139	6.805	6.495
12	11.255	10.575	9.954	9.385	8.863	8.384	7.943	7.536	7.161	6.814
13	12.134	11.348	10.635	9.086	9.394	8.853	8.358	7.904	7.487	7.103
14	13.004	12.106	11.296	10.563	9.899	9.295	8.745	8.244	7.786	7.367
15	13.865	12.849	11.938	11.118	10.380	9.712	9.108	8.559	8.061	7.606
16	14.718	13.578	12.561	11.652	10.838	10.106	9.447	8.851	8.313	7.824
17	15.562	14.292	13.166	12.166	11.274	10.477	9.763	9.122	8.544	8.022
18	16.398	14.992	13.754	12.659	11.690	10.828	10.059	9.372	8.756	8.201
19	17.226	15.678	14.324	13.134	12.085	11.185	10.336	9.604	8.950	8.365
20	18.046	16.351	14.877	13.590	12.462	11.470	10.594	9.818	9.129	8.514
21	18.857	17.011	15.415	14.029	12.821	11.764	10.836	10.017	9.292	8.649
22	19.660	17.658	15.937	14.451	13.163	12.042	11.061	10.201	9.442	8.772
23	20.456	18.292	16.444	14.857	13.489	12.303	11.272	10.371	9.580	8.883
24	21.243	18.914	16.939	15.247	13.799	12.550	11.469	10.529	9.707	8.985
25	22.023	19.523	17.413	15.622	14.094	12.783	11.654	10.675	9.823	9.077
26	22.795	20.121	17.877	15.983	13.375	13.003	11.826	10.810	9.929	9.161
27	23.560	20.707	18.327	16.330	14.643	13.211	11.987	10.935	10.027	9.237
28	24.316	21.281	18.764	16.663	13.898	13.406	12.137	11.051	10.116	9.307
29	25.066	21.844	19.188	16.984	15.141	13.591	12.278	11.158	10.198	9.370
30	25.808	22.396	19.600	17.292	15.372	13.765	12.409	11.258	10.274	9.427
35	29.409	24.999	21.487	18.665	16.374	14.498	12.948	11.655	10.567	9.644
40	32.835	27.355	23.115	19.793	17.159	15.046	13.332	11.925	10.757	9.779
45	36.095	29.490	24.519	20.720	17.774	15.456	13.606	12.108	10.881	9.863
50	39.196	31.424	25.730	21.482	18.256	15.762	13.801	12.233	10.962	9.915

11%	12%	13%	14%	15%	16%	17%	18%	19%	20%	Years 0 to:
0.901	0.893	0.885	0.877	0.870	0.862	0.855	0.847	0.840	0.833	1
1.713	1.690	1.668	1.647	1.626	1.605	1.585	1.566	1.547	1.528	2
2.444	2.402	2.361	2.322	2.283	2.246	2.210	2.174	2.140	2.106	3
3.102	3.037	2.974	2.914	2.855	2.798	2.743	2.690	2.639	2.589	4
3.696	3.605	3.517	3.433	3.352	3.274	3.199	3.127	3.058	2.991	5
4.231	4.111	3.998	3.889	3.784	3.685	3.589	3.498	3.410	3.326	6
4.712	4.564	4.423	4.288	4.160	4.039	3.922	3.812	3.706	3.605	7
5.146	4.968	4.799	4.639	4.487	4.344	4.207	4.078	3.954	3.837	8
5.537	5.328	5.132	4.946	4.772	4.607	4.451	4.303	4.163	4.031	9
5.889	5.650	5.426	5.216	5.019	4.833	4.659	4.494	4.339	4.192	10
6.207	5.938	5.687	5.453	5.234	5.029	4.836	4.656	4.486	4.327	11
6.492	6.194	5.918	5.660	5.421	5.197	4.988	4.793	4.611	4.439	12
6.750	6.424	6.122	5.842	5.583	5.342	5.118	4.910	4.715	4.533	13
6.982	6.628	6.302	6.002	5.724	5.468	5.229	5.008	4.802	4.611	14
7.191	6.811	6.462	6.142	5.847	5.575	5.324	5.092	4.876	4.675	15
7.379	6.974	6.604	6.265	5.954	5.668	5.405	5.162	4.938	4.730	16
7.549	7.120	6.729	6.373	6.047	5.749	5.475	5.222	4.990	4.775	17
7.702	7.250	6.840	6.467	6.128	5.818	5.534	5.273	5.033	4.812	18
7.839	7.366	6.938	6.550	6.198	5.877	5.584	5.316	5.070	4.843	19
7.963	7.469	7.025	6.623	6.259	5.929	5.628	5.353	5.101	4.870	20
8.075	7.562	7.102	6.687	6.312	5.973	5.665	5.384	5.127	4.891	21
8.176	7.645	7.170	6.743	6.359	6.011	5.696	5.410	5.149	4.909	22
8.266	7.718	7.230	6.792	6.399	6.044	5.723	5.432	5.167	4.925	23
8.348	7.784	7.283	6.835	6.434	6.073	5.746	5.451	5.182	4.937	24
8.422	7.843	7.330	6.873	6.464	6.097	5.766	5.467	5.195	4.948	25
8.488	7.896	7.372	6.906	6.491	6.118	5.783	5.480	5.206	4.956	26
8.548	7.943	7.409	6.935	6.514	6.136	5.798	5.492	5.215	4.964	27
8.602	7.984	7.441	6.961	6.534	6.152	5.810	5.502	5.223	4.970	28
8.650	8.022	7.470	6.983	6.551	6.166	5.820	5.510	5.229	4.975	29
8.694	8.055	7.496	7.003	6.566	6.177	5.829	5.517	5.235	4.979	30
8.855	8.176	7.586	7.070	6.617	6.215	5.858	5.539	5.251	4.992	35
8.951	8.244	7.634	7.105	6.642	6.233	5.871	5.548	5.258	4.997	40
9.008	8.283	7.661	7.123	6.654	6.242	5.877	5.552	5.261	4.999	45
9.042	8.304	7.675	7.133	6.661	6.246	5.880	5.554	5.262	4.999	50

Years 0 to:	21%	22%	23%	24%	25%	26%	27%	28%	29%	30%
1	0.826	0.820	0.813	0.806	0.800	0.794	0.787	0.781	0.775	0.769
2	1.509	1.492	1.474	1.457	1.440	1.424	1.407	1.392	1.376	1.361
3	2.074	2.042	2.011	1.981	1.952	1.923	1.896	1.868	1.842	1.816
4	2.540	2.494	2.448	2.404	2.362	2.320	2.280	2.241	2.203	2.166
5	2.926	2.864	2.803	2.745	2.689	2.635	2.583	2.532	2.483	2.436
6	3.245	3.167	3.092	3.020	2.951	2.885	2.821	2.759	2.700	2.643
7	3.508	3.416	3.327	3.242	3.161	3.083	3.009	2.937	2.868	2.802
8	3.726	3.619	3.518	3.421	3.329	3.241	3.156	3.076	2.999	2.925
9	3.905	3.786	3.673	3.566	3.463	3.366	3.273	3.184	3.100	3.019
10	4.054	3.923	3.799	3.682	3.571	3.465	3.364	3.269	3.178	3.092
11	4.177	4.035	3.902	3.776	3.656	3.543	3.437	3.335	3.239	3.147
12	5.278	4.127	3.985	3.851	3.725	3.606	3.493	3.387	3.286	3.190
13	4.362	4.203	4.053	3.912	3.780	3.656	3.538	3.427	3.322	3.223
14	4.432	4.265	4.108	3.962	3.824	3.695	3.573	3.459	3.351	3.249
15	4.489	4.315	4.153	4.001	3.859	3.726	3.601	3.483	3.373	3.268
16	4.536	4.357	4.189	4.033	3.887	3.751	3.623	3.503	3.390	3.283
17	4.576	4.391	4.219	4.059	3.910	3.771	3.640	3.518	3.403	3.295
18	4.608	4.419	4.243	4.080	3.928	3.786	3.654	3.529	3.413	3.304
19	4.635	4.442	4.263	4.097	3.942	3.799	3.664	3.539	3.421	3.311
20	4.657	4.460	4.279	4.110	3.954	3.808	3.673	3.546	3.427	3.316
21	4.675	4.476	3.292	4.121	3.963	3.816	3.679	3.551	3.432	3.320
22	4.690	4.488	4.302	4.130	3.970	3.822	3.684	3.556	3.436	3.323
23	4.703	4.499	4.311	4.137	3.976	3.827	3.689	3.559	3.438	3.325
24	4.713	4.507	4.318	4.143	3.981	3.831	3.692	3.562	3.441	3.327
25	4.721	4.514	4.323	4.147	3.985	3.834	3.694	3.564	3.442	3.329
26	4.728	4.520	4.328	4.151	3.988	3.837	3.696	3.566	3.444	3.330
27	4.734	4.524	4.332	4.154	3.990	3.839	3.698	3.567	3.445	3.331
28	4.739	4.528	4.335	4.157	3.992	3.840	3.699	3.568	3.446	3.331
29	4.743	4.531	4.337	4.159	3.994	3.841	3.700	3.569	3.446	3.332
30	4.746	4.534	4.339	4.160	3.995	3.842	3.701	3.569	3.447	3.332
35	4.756	4.541	4.345	4.164	3.998	3.845	3.703	3.571	3.448	3.333
40	4.760	4.544	4.347	4.166	3.999	3.846	3.703	3.571	3.488	3.333
45	4.761									
50	4.762	4.545	4.348	4.167	4.000	3.846	3.704	3.571	3.448	3.333

31%	32%	33%	34%	35%	36%	37%	38%	39%	40%	Years 0 to:
0.763	0.758	0.752	0.746	0.741	0.735	0.730	0.725	0.719	0.714	1
1.346	1.331	1.317	1.303	1.289	1.276	1.263	1.250	1.237	1.224	2
1.791	1.766	1.742	1.719	1.696	1.673	1.652	1.630	1.609	1.589	3
2.130	2.096	2.062	2.029	1.997	1.966	1.935	1.906	1.877	1.849	4
2.390	2.345	2.302	2.260	2.220	2.181	2.143	2.106	2.070	2.035	5
2.588	2.534	2.483	2.433	2.385	2.339	2.294	2.251	2.209	2.168	6
2.739	2.677	2.619	2.562	2.508	2.455	2.404	2.355	2.308	2.263	7
2.854	2.786	2.721	2.658	2.598	2.540	2.485	2.432	2.380	2.331	8
2.942	2.868	2.798	2.730	2.665	2.603	2.544	2.487	2.432	2.379	9
3.009	2.930	2.855	2.784	2.715	2.649	2.587	2.527	2.469	2.414	10
3.060	2.978	2.899	2.824	2.752	2.683	2.618	2.555	2.496	2.438	11
3.100	2.013	2.931	2.853	2.779	2.708	2.641	2.576	2.515	2.456	12
3.129	3.040	2.956	2.876	2.799	2.727	2.658	2.592	2.529	2.469	13
3.152	3.061	2.974	2.982	2.814	2.740	2.670	2.603	2.539	2.478	14
3.170	3.076	2.988	2.905	2.825	2.750	2.679	2.611	2.546	2.484	15
3.183	3.088	2.999	2.914	2.834	2.757	2.685	2.616	2.551	2.489	16
3.193	3.097	3.007	2.921	2.840	2.763	2.690	2.621	2.555	2.492	17
3.201	3.104	3.012	2.926	2.844	2.767	2.693	2.624	2.557	2.494	18
3.207	3.109	3.017	2.930	2.848	2.770	2.696	2.626	2.559	2.496	19
3.211	3.113	3.020	2.933	2.850	2.772	2.698	2.627	2.561	2.497	20
3.215	3.116	3.023	2.935	2.852	2.773	2.699	2.629	2.562	2.498	21
3.217	3.118	3.025	2.936	2.853	2.775	2.700	2.629	2.562	2.438	22
3.219	3.120	3.026	2.938	2.854	2.775	2.701	2.630	2.563	2.499	23
3.221	3.121	3.027	2.939	2.855	2.776	2.701	2.630	2.563	2.499	24
3.222	3.122	3.028	2.939	2.856	2.777	2.702	2.631	2.563	2.499	25
3.223	3.123	3.028	2.940	2.856	2.777	2.702	2.631	2.564	2.500	26
3.224	3.123	3.029	2.940	2.856	2.777	2.702	2.631			27
3.224	3.124	3.029	2.940	2.857	2.777	2.702	2.631			28
3.225	3.124	3.030	2.941	2.857	2.777	2.702	2.631			29
3.225	3.124	3.030	2.941	2.857	2.778	2.702	2.631			30
3.226	3.125									35
3.226										40
3.226	3.125	3.030	2.941	2.857	2.778	2.703	2.632	2.564	2.500	45
3.226	3.125	3.030	2.941	2.857	2.778	2.703	2.632	2.564	2.500	50

Appendix C: Areas in tail of the normal distribution

$\frac{x-\mu}{\sigma}$	0.00	0.01	0.02	0.03	0.04	0.05	0.06	0.07	0.08	0.09
0.0	0.5000	0.4960	0.4920	0.4880	0.4840	0.4801	0.4761	0.4721	0.4681	0.4641
0.1	0.4602	0.4562	0.4522	0.4483	0.4443	0.4404	0.4364	0.4325	0.4286	0.4247
0.2	0.4207	0.4168	0.4129	0.4090	0.4052	0.4103	0.3974	0.3936	0.3897	0.3589
0.3	0.3821	0.3783	0.3745	0.3707	0.3669	0.3632	0.3594	0.3557	0.3520	0.3483
0.4	0.3446	0.3409	0.3372	0.3336	0.3300	0.3264	0.3228	0.3192	0.3156	0.3121
0.5	0.3085	0.3050	0.3015	0.2981	0.2946	0.2912	0.2877	0.2843	0.2810	0.2776
0.6	0.2743	0.2709	0.2676	0.2643	0.2611	0.2578	0.2546	0.2514	0.2483	0.2451
0.7	0.2420	0.2389	0.2358	0.2327	0.2296	0.2266	0.2236	0.2206	0.2177	0.2148
0.8	0.2119	0.2090	0.2061	0.2033	0.2005	0.1977	0.1949	0.1922	0.1894	0.1867
0.9	0.1841	0.1814	0.1788	0.1762	0.1736	0.1711	0.1685	0.1660	0.1635	0.1611
1.0	0.1587	0.1562	0.1539	0.1515	0.1492	0.1469	0.1446	0.1423	0.1401	0.1379
1.1	0.1357	0.1335	0.1314	0.1292	0.1271	0.1251	0.1230	0.1210	0.1190	0.1170
1.2	0.1151	0.1131	0.1112	0.1093	0.1075	0.1056	0.1038	0.1020	0.1103	0.0985
1.3	0.0968	0.0951	0.0934	0.0918	0.0901	0.0885	0.0869	0.0853	0.0838	0.0823
1.4	0.0808	0.0793	0.0778	0.0764	0.0749	0.0735	0.0721	0.0708	0.0694	0.0681
1.5	0.0668	0.0655	0.0643	0.0630	0.0618	0.0606	0.0594	0.0582	0.0571	0.0559
1.6	0.0548	0.0537	0.0526	0.0516	0.0505	0.0495	0.0485	0.0475	0.0465	0.0455
1.7	0.0446	0.0436	0.0427	0.0418	0.0409	0.0401	0.0392	0.0384	0.0375	0.0367
1.8	0.0359	0.0351	0.0344	0.0336	0.0329	0.0322	0.0314	0.0307	0.0301	0.0294
1.9	0.0287	0.0281	0.0274	0.0268	0.0262	0.0256	0.0250	0.0244	0.0239	0.0233
2.0	0.02275	0.02222	0.02169	0.02118	0.02068	0.02018	0.01970	0.01923	0.01876	0.01831
2.1	0.01786	0.01743	0.01700	0.01659	0.01618	0.01578	0.01539	0.01500	0.01463	0.01426
2.2	0.01390	0.01355	0.01321	0.01287	0.01255	0.01222	0.01191	0.01160	0.01130	0.01101
2.3	0.01072	0.01044	0.01017	0.00990	0.00964	0.00939	0.00914	0.00889	0.00866	0.00842
2.4	0.00820	0.00798	0.00776	0.00755	0.00734	0.00714	0.00695	0.00676	0.00657	0.00639
2.5	0.00621	0.00604	0.00587	0.00570	0.00554	0.00539	0.00523	0.00508	0.00494	0.00480
2.6	0.00466	0.00453	0.00440	0.00427	0.00415	0.00402	0.00391	0.00379	0.00368	0.00357
2.7	0.00347	0.00336	0.00326	0.00317	0.00307	0.00298	0.00289	0.00280	0.00272	0.00264
2.8	0.00256	0.00248	0.00240	0.00233	0.00226	0.00219	0.00212	0.00205	0.00199	0.00193
2.9	0.00187	0.00181	0.00175	0.00169	0.00164	0.00159	0.00154	0.00149	0.00144	0.00139
3.0	0.00135									
3.1	0.00097									
3.2	0.00069									
3.3	0.00048									
3.4	0.00034									
3.5	0.00023									
3.6	0.00016									
3.7	0.00011									
3.8	0.00007									
3.9	0.00005									
4.0	0.00003									

Appendix D: Capital recovery factors (equal annuity rate)

The table gives the equal annual payment to be made for n years in the future to repay loan principal and interest with interest at x% per year.

For example, to repay £1 borrowed now at 7% in six annual payments, the value of an annual payment is £0.2098 or 20.98p.

Years	1%	2%	3%	4%	5%	6%	7%	8%	9%	10%
1	1.0100	1.0200	1.0300	1.0400	1.0500	1.0600	1.0700	1.0800	1.0900	1.1000
2	0.5075	0.5150	0.5226	0.5302	0.5378	0.5454	0.5531	0.5608	0.5685	0.5762
3	0.3400	0.3468	0.3535	0.3603	0.3672	0.3741	0.3811	0.3880	0.3951	0.4021
4	0.2563	0.2626	0.2690	0.2755	0.2820	0.2886	0.2952	0.3019	0.3087	0.3155
5	0.2060	0.2122	0.2184	0.2246	0.2310	0.2374	0.2439	0.2505	0.2571	0.2638
6	0.1725	0.1785	0.1846	0.1908	0.1970	0.2034	0.2098	0.2163	0.2229	0.2296
7	0.1486	0.1545	0.1605	0.1666	0.1728	0.1791	0.1856	0.1921	0.1987	0.2054
8	0.1307	0.1365	0.1425	0.1485	0.1547	0.1610	0.1675	0.1740	0.1807	0.1874
9	0.1167	0.1225	0.1284	0.1345	0.1407	0.1470	0.1535	0.1601	0.1668	0.1736
10	0.1056	0.1113	0.1172	0.1233	0.1295	0.1359	0.1424	0.1490	0.1558	0.1627

Years	11%	12%	13%	14%	15%	16%	17%	18%	19%	20%
1	1.1100	1.1200	1.1300	1.1400	1.1500	1.1600	1.1700	1.1800	1.1900	1.2000
2	0.5839	0.5917	0.5995	0.6073	0.6151	0.6230	0.6308	0.6387	0.6466	0.6545
3	0.4092	0.4163	0.4235	0.4307	0.4380	0.4453	0.4526	0.4599	0.4673	0.4747
4	0.3223	0.3292	0.3362	0.3432	0.3503	0.3574	0.3645	0.3717	0.3790	0.3863
5	0.2706	0.2774	0.2843	0.2913	0.2983	0.3054	0.3126	0.3198	0.3271	0.3344
6	0.2364	0.2432	0.2502	0.2572	0.2642	0.2714	0.2786	0.2859	0.2933	0.3007
7	0.2122	0.2191	0.2261	0.2332	0.2404	0.2476	0.2549	0.2624	0.2699	0.2774
8	0.1943	0.2013	0.2084	0.2156	0.2229	0.2302	0.2377	0.2452	0.2529	0.2606
9	0.1806	0.1877	0.1949	0.2022	0.2096	0.2171	0.2247	0.2324	0.2402	0.2481
10	0.1698	0.1770	0.1843	0.1917	0.1993	0.2069	0.2146	0.2225	0.2305	0.2385

Appendix E: Future value of £1 at the end of n periods

Period	1%	2%	3%	4%	5%	6%	7%	8%	9%	10%
1	1.0100	1.0200	1.0300	1.0400	1.0500	1.0600	1.0700	1.0800	1.0900	1.1000
2	1.0201	1.0404	1.0609	1.0816	1.1025	1.1236	1.1449	1.1664	1.1881	1.2100
3	1.0303	1.0612	1.0927	1.1249	1.1576	1.1910	1.2250	1.2597	1.2950	1.3310
4	1.0406	1.0824	1.1255	1.1699	1.2155	1.2625	1.3108	1.3605	1.4116	1.4641
5	1.0510	1.1041	1.1593	1.2167	1.2763	1.3382	1.4026	1.4693	1.5386	1.6105
6	1.0615	1.1262	1.1941	1.2653	1.3401	1.4185	1.5007	1.5869	1.6771	1.7716
7	1.0721	1.1487	1.2299	1.3159	1.4071	1.5036	1.6058	1.7138	1.8280	1.9487
8	1.0829	1.1717	1.2668	1.3686	1.4775	1.5938	1.7182	1.8509	1.9926	2.1436
9	1.0937	1.1951	1.3048	1.4233	1.5513	1.6895	1.8385	1.9990	2.1719	2.3579
10	1.1046	1.1290	1.3439	1.4802	1.6289	1.7908	1.9672	2.1589	2.3674	2.5937
11	1.1157	1.2434	1.3842	1.5395	1.7103	1.8983	2.1049	2.3316	2.5804	2.8531
12	1.1268	1.2682	1.4258	1.6010	1.7959	2.0122	2.2522	2.5182	2.8127	3.1384
13	1.1381	1.2936	1.4685	1.6651	1.8856	2.1329	2.4098	2.7196	3.0658	3.4523
14	1.1495	1.3195	1.5126	1.7317	1.9799	2.2609	2.5785	2.9372	3.3417	3.7975
15	1.1610	1.3459	1.5580	1.8009	2.0789	2.3966	2.7590	3.1722	3.6425	4.1772
16	1.1726	1.3728	1.6047	1.8730	2.1829	2.5404	2.9522	3.4259	3.9703	4.5950
17	1.1843	1.4002	1.6528	1.9479	2.2920	2.6928	3.1588	3.7000	4.3276	5.0545
18	1.1961	1.4282	1.7024	2.0268	2.4066	2.8543	3.3799	3.9960	4.7171	5.5599
19	1.2081	1.4568	1.7535	2.1068	2.5270	3.0256	3.6165	4.3157	5.1417	6.1159
20	1.2202	1.4859	1.8061	2.1911	2.6533	3.2071	3.8697	4.6610	5.6044	6.7275
21	1.2324	1.5157	1.8603	2.2788	2.7860	3.3996	4.1406	5.0338	6.1088	7.4002
22	1.2447	1.5460	1.9161	2.3699	2.9253	3.6035	4.4304	5.4365	6.6586	8.1403
23	1.2572	1.5769	1.9736	2.4647	3.0715	3.8197	4.7405	5.8715	7.2579	8.9543
24	1.2697	1.6084	2.0328	2.5633	3.2251	4.0489	5.0724	6.3412	7.9111	9.8497
25	1.2824	1.6406	2.0938	2.6658	3.3864	4.2919	5.4274	6.8485	8.6231	10.834
30	1.3478	1.8114	2.4273	3.2434	4.3219	5.7435	7.6123	10.062	13.267	17.449
40	1.4889	2.2080	3.2620	4.8010	7.0400	10.285	14.974	21.724	31.409	45.259

Period	12%	14%	15%	16%	18%	20%	24%	28%	32%	36%
1	1.1200	1.1400	1.1500	1.1600	1.1800	1.2000	1.2400	1.2800	1.3200	1.3600
2	1.2544	1.2996	1.3225	1.3456	1.3924	1.4400	1.5376	1.6384	1.7424	1.8496
3	1.4049	1.4815	1.5209	1.5609	1.6430	1.7280	1.9066	2.0972	2.3000	2.5155
4	1.5735	1.6890	1.7490	1.8106	1.9388	2.0736	2.3642	2.6844	3.0360	3.4210
5	1.7623	1.9254	2.0114	2.1003	2.2878	2.4883	2.9316	3.4360	4.0075	4.6526
6	1.9738	2.1950	2.3131	2.4364	2.6996	2.9860	3.6352	4.3980	5.2899	6.3275
7	2.2107	2.5023	2.6600	2.8262	3.1855	3.5832	4.5077	5.6295	6.9826	8.6054
8	2.4760	2.8526	3.0590	3.2784	3.7589	4.2998	5.5895	7.2058	9.2170	11.703
9	2.7731	3.2519	3.5179	3.8030	4.4355	5.1598	6.9310	9.2234	12.166	15.916
10	3.1058	3.7072	4.0456	4.4114	5.2338	6.1917	8.5944	11.805	16.059	21.646
11	3.4785	4.2262	4.6524	5.1173	6.1759	7.4301	10.657	15.111	21.198	29.439
12	3.8960	4.8197	5.3502	5.9360	7.2876	8.9161	13.214	19.342	27.982	40.037
13	4.3635	5.4924	6.1528	6.8858	8.5994	10.699	16.386	24.758	36.937	54.451
14	4.8871	6.2613	7.0757	7.9875	10.147	12.839	20.319	31.691	48.756	74.053
15	5.4736	7.1379	8.1371	9.2655	11.973	15.407	25.195	40.564	64.358	100.71
16	6.1304	8.1372	9.3576	10.748	14.129	18.488	31.242	51.923	84.953	136.96
17	6.8660	9.2765	10.761	12.467	16.672	22.186	38.740	66.461	112.13	186.27
18	7.6900	10.575	12.375	14.462	19.673	26.623	48.038	85.070	148.02	253.33
19	8.6128	12.055	14.231	16.776	23.214	31.948	59.567	108.89	195.39	344.53
20	9.6463	13.743	16.366	19.460	27.393	38.337	73.864	139.37	257.91	468.57
21	10.803	15.667	18.821	22.574	32.323	46.005	91.591	178.40	340.44	637.26
22	12.100	17.861	21.644	26.186	38.142	55.206	113.57	228.35	449.39	866.67
23	13.552	20.361	24.891	30.376	45.007	66.247	140.83	292.30	593.19	117.86
24	15.178	23.212	28.625	35.236	53.108	79.496	174.63	374.14	783.02	160.29
25	17.000	26.461	32.918	40.874	62.668	95.396	216.54	478.90	103.25	218.00
30	29.959	50.860	66.211	85.849	143.37	237.37	634.81	1645.5	414.20	101.43
40	93.050	188.88	267.86	378.72	750.37	1469.7	5455.9	1942.6	665.20	219.561

ANSWERS TO REVIEW PROBLEMS

Chapter 2

2.15 (a) SV (or variable if direct labour can be matched exactly to output)
(b) F
(c) F
(d) V
(e) F (Advertising is a discretionary cost. See Chapter 15 'Zero-based budgeting' for an explanation of this cost.)
(f) SV
(g) F
(h) SF
(i) V

2.16 Controllable c, d, f
Non-controllable a, b, e, g, h

2.17 Item (B) will be constant within the relevant range of output.
Item (C) will be constant per unit.
If output declines fixed cost per unit will decrease.
Total variable cost will fall in line with a decline in output and therefore item A is the correct answer.

2.18 Total variable overheads = 17 000 × £3.50 = £59 500
Total variable overhead (£59 500) + Total fixed overhead = Total overhead (£246 500)
Total fixed overhead = £246 500 – £59 500 = £187 000
Answer = C

2.19 Answer = B

2.20 Answer = B

2.21 Answer = B

2.22 Answer = B

2.23 See the description of cost behaviour in Chapter 2 for the answer to these questions. In particular the answer should provide graphs for fixed costs, variable costs, semi-fixed costs and semi-variable costs.

2.24 You will find the answer to this question in Chapter 2. In particular the answer should describe the classification of costs for stock valuation and profit measurement; classification for decision-making and planning; classification for control. In addition the answer should illustrate methods of classification (see Chapter 2 for examples) within the above categories and describe the benefits arising from classifying costs in the manner illustrated.

2.25 See Chapter 2 for the answer to this question.

2.26 (a) See 'Functions of management accounting' in Chapter 1 for the answer to this question. In particular your answer should stress that the cost accountant provides financial information for stock valuation purposes and also presents relevant information to management for decision-making and planning and cost control purposes. For example, the cost accountant provides information on the costs and revenues of alternative courses of action to assist management in selecting the course of action which will maximize future cash flows. By coordinating plans together in the form of budgets and comparing actual performance with plans the accountant can pinpoint those activities which are not proceeding according to plan.
(b) (i) Direct costs are those costs which can be traced to a cost objective. If the cost objective is a sales territory then *fixed* salaries of salesmen will be a direct cost. Therefore the statement is incorrect.
(ii) Whether a cost is controllable depends on the level of authority and time span being considered. For example, a departmental foreman may have no control over the number of supervisors employed in his department but this decision may be made by his superior. In the long term such costs are controllable.
(iii) This statement is correct. See 'Sunk costs' in Chapter 2 for an explanation of why this statement is correct.

2.27 See Chapter 2 for the answer to this question.

2.28 Cost information is required for the following purposes:
(a) costs for stock valuation and profit measurement;
(b) costs for decision-making;
(c) costs for planning and control.
For the alternative measures of cost that might be appropriate for each of the above purposes see Chapter 2.

2.29 (i) See Chapter 2 for a definition of opportunity cost and sunk cost.
(ii) *Opportunity cost:* If scarce resources such as machine hours are required for a special contract then the cost of the contract should include the lost profit that would have been earned on the next best alternative. This should be recovered in the contract price.

Sunk cost: The original cost of equipment used for a contract is a sunk cost and should be ignored. The change in the resale value resulting from the use of the equipment represents the relevant cost of using the equipment.

(iii) The significance of opportunity cost is that relevant costs do not consist only of future cash outflows associated directly with a particular course of action. Imputed costs must also be included.

The significance of sunk costs is that past costs are not relevant for decision-making.

2.30 See Chapter 2 for an explanation of the terms avoidable costs and unavoidable costs and Chapter 3 for an explanation of cost centres. A cost unit is a unit of product or service for which costs are ascertained. In a manufacturing organization a cost unit will be a unit of output produced within a cost centre. In a service organization, such as an educational establishment, a cost unit might be the cost per student.

2.31 See Chapter 2 for the answer to this question.

2.32 (a) (i) Schedule of annual mileage costs

	5000 miles (£)	10 000 miles (£)	15 000 miles (£)	30 000 miles (£)
Variable costs:				
Spares	100	200	300	600
Petrol	380	760	1140	2280
Total variable cost	480	960	1440	2880
Variable cost per mile	0.096	0.096	0.096	0.096
Fixed costs				
Depreciation[a]	2000	2000	2000	2000
Maintenance	120	120	120	120
Vehicle licence	80	80	80	80
Insurance	150	150	150	150
Tyres[b]	—	—	75	150
	2350	2350	2425	2500
Fixed cost per mile	0.47	0.235	0.162	0.083
Total cost	2830	3310	3865	5380
Total cost per mile	0.566	0.331	0.258	0.179

Notes

[a]Annual depreciation $= \dfrac{\text{£5500 (cost)} - \text{£1500 (trade-in price)}}{\text{2 years}} = \text{£2000}$

[b]At 15 000 miles per annum tyres will be replaced once during the two-year period at a cost of £150. The average cost per year is £75. At 30 000 miles per annum tyres will be replaced once each year.

Comments

Tyres are a semi-fixed cost. In the above calculations they have been regarded as a step fixed cost. An alternative approach would be to regard the semi-fixed cost as a variable cost by dividing £150 tyre replacement by 25 000 miles. This results in a variable cost per mile of £0.006.

Depreciation and maintenance cost have been classified as fixed costs. They are likely to be semi-variable costs, but in the absence of any additional information they have been classified as fixed costs.

(ii) See Figure 2.32.

(iii) The respective costs can be obtained from the vertical dashed lines in the graph (Figure 2.32).

(b) The *cost per mile* declines as activity increases. This is because the majority of costs are fixed and do not increase when mileage increases. However, *total cost* will increase with increases in mileage.

FIGURE 2.32 *The step increase in fixed cost is assumed to occur at an annual mileage of 12 500 and 25 000 miles, because tyres are assumed to be replaced at this mileage*

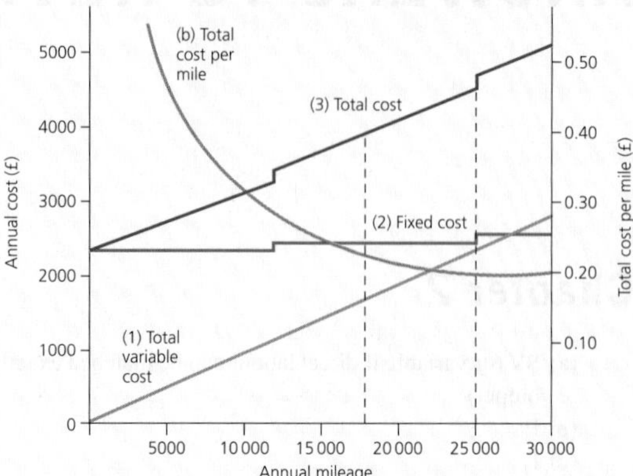

2.33 (a) (i) For an explanation of sunk and opportunity costs see Chapter 2. The down payment of £5000 represents a sunk cost. The lost profit from subletting the shop of £1600 p.a. ((£550 × £12) – £5000) is an example of an opportunity cost. Note that only the £5000 additional rental is included in the opportunity cost calculation. (The £5000 sunk cost is excluded from the calculation.)

(ii) The relevant information for running the shop is:

	(£)
Net sales	100 000
Costs (£87 000 – £5000 sunk cost)	82 000
	18 000
Less opportunity cost from subletting	1 600
Profit	16 400

The above indicates that £16 400 additional profits will be obtained from using the shop for the sale of clothing. It is assumed that Mrs Johnson will not suffer any other loss of income if she devotes half her time to running the shop.

(b) The CIMA terminology defines a notional cost as 'A hypothetical cost taken into account in a particular situation to represent a benefit enjoyed by an entity in respect of which no actual expense is incurred.' Examples of notional cost include:

(i) Interest on capital to represent the notional cost of using an asset rather than investing the capital elsewhere.

(ii) Including rent as a cost for premises owned by the company so as to represent the lost rent income resulting from using the premises for business purposes.

Chapter 3

3.14 Overhead absorbed (£714 000) = Actual hours (119 000) × Pre-determined overhead rate.

Pre-determined overhead rate = £714 000/119 000 = £6.

Budgeted overheads (£720 000) = Budgeted machine hours × Budgeted overhead rate (£6).

Budgeted machine hours = £720 000/£6 = 120 000 hours.

Answer = C

3.15 Budgeted overhead rate = £258 750/11 250 hours = £23 per machine hour
Overheads absorbed = £23 × 10 980 Actual hours = £252 540
Overheads incurred = £254 692
Overheads absorbed = £252 540
Under-absorbed overheads = £2152
Answer = A

3.16 (i) Budgeted overhead rates and not actual overhead rates should be used as indicated in Chapter 3.
Overhead rate = £148 750/8500 hours = £17.50 per hour.
Answer = A
(ii)

	(£)
Actual overheads incurred	146 200
Overheads absorbed (7928 × £17.50)	138 740
Under-absorbed overheads	7 460

Answer = D

3.17 (i) It is assumed that labour cost is to be used as the allocation base.
Total labour cost = £14 500 + £3500 + £24 600 = £42 600
Overhead recovery rate = £126 000/£42 600 = £2.9578 per £1 of labour
Overhead charged to Job CC20 = £24 600 × £2.9578 = £72 761
Answer = C
(ii)

	(£)
Opening WIP	42 790
Direct labour	3 500
Overhead (£3500 × £2.9578)	10 352
	56 642
Selling price (£56 642/0.667)	84 921
or £56 642 divided by 2/3 =	£84 963

Answer = C
(iii) closing WIP = Total cost of AA10 and CC20

	Total (£)	AA10 (£)	CC20 (£)
Opening WIP		26 800	0
Materials in period		17 275	18 500
Labour in period		14 500	24 600
Overheads in period:			
2.9577465 × £14 500		42 887	
2.9577465 × £24 600			72 761
	217 323	101 462	115 861

Answer = D

3.18 Answer = D

3.19 Because production is highly automated it is assumed that overheads will be most closely associated with machine hours. The pre-determined overhead rate will therefore be £18 derived from dividing budgeted overheads (£180 000) by the budgeted machine hours (10 000). Therefore the answer is B.

3.20 Items that contribute to the over-absorption of overheads are if actual production exceeds budgeted production or actual overhead expenditure is less than budgeted expenditure. When both of these items occur overheads will be over-absorbed. Therefore the answer is D.

3.21

Direct materials	10 650
Direct labour	3 260
Prime cost	13 910
Production overhead (140 × \$8.50)	1 190
Non-manufacturing overheads and profit (60% × \$13 910)	8 346
Estimated price	23 446

Answer = C

3.22 Answer = D

3.23 Stores (S) = 6300 + 0.05 Maintenance (M)
M = 8450 + 0.1S
Rearranging the equations:
S = 6300 + 0.05M (1)
–0.1S = 8450 – M (2)
Multiply equation (1) by 20 and (2) by 1
20S = 126 000 + M
–0.1S = 8450 – M
19.9S = 134 450
S = £6756
Substituting for S in equation (1)
6756 = 6300 + 0.05M
0.05M = 456
M = £9126
For production department 1, the total overheads are
= 17 500 + (£6756 × 60%) + (9126 × 75%)
= £28 398
Answer = C

3.24 (a)

	Total (£)	Departments A (£)	B (£)	C (£)	X (£)	Y (£)
Rent and rates[a]	12 800	6 000	3 600	1 200	1200	800
Machine insurance[b]	6 000	3 000	1 250	1 000	500	250
Telephone charges[c]	3 200	1 500	900	300	300	200
Depreciation[b]	18 000	9 000	3 750	3 000	1500	750
Supervisors' salaries[d]	24 000	12 800	7 200	4 000		
Heat and light[a]	6 400	3 000	1 800	600	600	400
	70 400					
Allocated		2 800	1 700	1 200	800	600
		38 100	20 200	11 300	4900	3000
Reapportionment of X		2 450 (50%)	1 225 (25%)	1 225 (25%)	(4900)	
Reapportionment of Y		600 (20%)	900 (30%)	1 500 (50%)		(3000)
		£41 150	£22 325	£14 025		
Budgeted D.L. hours[e]		3 200	1 800	1 000		
Absorption rates		£12.86	£12.40	£14.02		

Notes
[a]Apportioned on the basis of floor area.
[b]Apportioned on the basis of machine value.
[c]Should be apportioned on the basis of the number of telephone points or estimated usage. This information is not given and an alternative arbitrary method of apportionment should be chosen. In the above analysis telephone charges have been apportioned on the basis of floor area.
[d]Apportioned on the basis of direct labour hours.
[e]Machine hours are not given but direct labour hours are. It is assumed that the examiner requires absorption to be on the basis of direct labour hours.

(b)

	Job 123 (£)	Job 124 (£)
Direct material	154.00	108.00
Direct labour:		
Department A	76.00	60.80
Department B	42.00	35.00
Department C	34.00	47.60
Total direct cost	306.00	251.40
Overhead:		
Department A	257.20	205.76
Department B	148.80	124.00
Department C	140.20	196.28
Total cost	852.20	777.44
Profit	284.07	259.15

(c)

Listed selling price	1136.27	1036.59

Note

Let SP represent selling price.

Cost + 0.25SP = SP

Job 123: £852.20 + 0.25SP = 1SP

0.75SP = £852.20

Hence SP = £1136.27

For Job 124: 0.75SP = £777.44

Hence SP = £1036.59

(d) For the answer to this question see sections on materials recording procedure and pricing the issues of materials in Chapter 4.

3.25 (a) (i) Calculation of budgeted overhead absorption rates:

Apportionment of overheads to production departments

	Machine shop (£)	Fitting section (£)	Canteen (£)	Machine maintenance section (£)	Total (£)
Allocated overheads	27 660	19 470	16 600	26 650	90 380
Rent, rates, heat and light[a]	9 000	3 500	2 500	2 000	17 000
Depreciation and insurance of equipment[a]	12 500	6 250	2 500	3 750	25 000
	49 160	29 220	21 600	32 400	132 380
Service department apportionment					
Canteen[b]	10 800	8 400	(21 600)	2 400	—
Machine maintenance section	24 360	10 440	—	(34 800)	—
	84 320	48 060	—	—	132 380

Calculation of absorption bases

		Machine shop		Fitting section	
Product	Budgeted production	Machine hours per product	Total machine hours	Direct labour cost per product (£)	Total direct wages (£)
X	4200 units	6	25 200	12	50 400
Y	6900 units	3	20 700	3	20 700
Z	1700 units	4	6 800	21	35 700
			52 700		106 800

Budgeted overhead absorption rates

Machine shop

$$\frac{\text{budgeted overheads}}{\text{budgeted machine hours}} = \frac{£84\,320}{£52\,700}$$

= £1.60 per machine hour

Fitting section

$$\frac{\text{budgeted overheads}}{\text{budgeted direct wages}} = \frac{48\,060}{106\,800}$$

= 45% of direct wages

Notes

[a]Rents, rates, heat and light are apportioned on the basis of floor area. Depreciation and insurance of equipment are apportioned on the basis of book value.

[b]Canteen costs are reapportioned according to the number of employees. Machine maintenance section costs are reapportioned according to the percentages given in the question.

(ii) The budgeted manufacturing overhead cost for producing one unit of product X is as follows:

	(£)
Machine shop: 6 hours at £1.60 per hour	9.60
Fittings section: 45% of £12	5.40
	15.00

(b) The answer should discuss the limitations of blanket overhead rates and actual overhead rates. See 'Blanket overhead rates' and 'Budgeted overhead rates' in Chapter 3 for the answer to this question.

3.26 (a)

$$\text{Overhead rate} = \frac{\text{Budgeted overhead}}{\text{Budgeted direct wages}} \times 100$$

$$= \frac{£225\,000}{£150\,000} \times 100$$

$$= 150\%$$

(b)

	(£)
Direct materials	190
Direct wages	170
Production overhead (150% × £170)	255
Production cost	615
Gross profit (1/3 × £615)	205
	820

(c) (i) Each department incurs different overhead costs. For example, the overhead costs of department A are considerably higher than those of the other departments. A blanket overhead rate is only appropriate where jobs spend the same proportion of time in each department. See the section on blanket overhead rates in Chapter 4 for an explanation of why departmental overhead rates are preferable.

(ii) *Department A machine-hour overhead rate:*

$$\frac{£120\,000}{40\,000 \text{ machine hours}} = £3 \text{ per machine hour}$$

A machine-hour rate is preferable because machine hours appear to be the dominant activity. Also, most of the overheads incurred are likely to be related to machine hours rather than direct labour hours. Possibly one worker operates four machines since the ratio is 40 000 machine hours to 10 000 direct labour hours. If some jobs do not involve machinery but others do, then two separate cost centres should be established (one related to machinery and the other related to jobs which involve direct labour hours only).

Department B direct labour hour overhead rate:

$$\frac{£30\,000}{50\,000 \text{ direct labour hours}} = £0.60 \text{ per labour hour}$$

Because direct labour hours are five times greater than machine hours a direct labour hour overhead rate is recommended. A comparison of direct labour hours and direct wages for budget, actual and job 657 for department B suggests that wage rate are not equal throughout the department. Therefore the direct wages percentage method is inappropriate.

Department C direct labour hour overhead rate:

$$\frac{£75\,000}{25\,000 \text{ direct labour hours}} = £3 \text{ per direct labour hour}$$

This method is chosen because it is related to time and machine hours are ruled out. A comparison of budgeted direct wages and labour hours for budget, actual and job 657 for department C suggests that wage rates are equal at £1 per hour throughout the department. Therefore direct labour hours or direct wages percentage methods will produce the same results.

(d) Department A (40 machine hours × £3) 120
B (40 labour hours × £0.60) 24
C (10 labour hours × £3) 30
174

(e) (i) *Current rate (actual wages × 150%):*

	Absorbed (£000s)	Actual (£000s)	Over/(under)-absorbed (£000s)
Department A	45	130	(85)
B	120	28	92
C	45	80	(35)
	210	238	(28)

(ii) *Proposed rates:*

	Absorbed (£000s)	Actual (£000s)	Over/(under)-absorbed (£000s)
Department A	135	130	5
B	27	28	(1)
C	90	80	10
	252	238	14

3.27 (a) The calculation of the overhead absorption rates are as follows:

Forming department machine hour rate = £6.15 per machine hour (£602 700/98 000 hours)

Finishing department labour hour rate = £2.25 per labour hour (£346 500/154 000 hours)

The forming department is mechanized, and it is likely that a significant proportion of overheads will be incurred as a consequence of employing and running the machines. Therefore a machine hour rate has been used. In the finishing department several grades of labour are used. Consequently the direct wages percentage method is inappropriate, and the direct labour hour method should be used.

(b) The decision should be based on a comparison of the incremental costs with the purchase price of an outside supplier if spare capacity exists. If no spare capacity exists then the lost contribution on displaced work must be considered. The calculation of incremental costs requires that the variable element of the total overhead absorption rate must be calculated. The calculation is:

Forming department variable machine hour rate = £2.05 (£200 900/98 000 hours)

Finishing department variable direct labour hour rate = £0.75 (£115 500/154 000 hours)

The calculation of the variable costs per unit of each component is:

	A (£)	B (£)	C (£)
Prime cost	24.00	31.00	29.00
Variable overheads: Forming	8.20	6.15	4.10
Finishing	2.25	7.50	1.50
Variable unit manufacturing cost	34.45	44.65	34.60
Purchase price	£30	£65	£60

On the basis of the above information, component A should be purchased and components B and C manufactured. This decision is based on the following assumptions:

(i) Variable overheads vary in proportion to machine hours (forming department) and direct labour hours (finishing department).

(ii) Fixed overheads remain unaffected by any changes in activity.

(iii)Spare capacity exists.

For a discussion of make-or-buy decisions see Chapter 9.

(c) Production overhead absorption rates are calculated in order to ascertain costs per unit of output for stock valuation and profit measurement purposes. Such costs are inappropriate for decision-making and cost control. For an explanation of this see the section in Chapter 3 titled 'Different costs for different purposes'.

3.28 (i) Percentage of direct material cost = $\frac{£250\,000}{£100\,000} \times 100 = 250\%$

Direct labour hour rate = £250 000/50 000 hours = £5 per hour

(ii) Percentage material cost = 250% × £7000 = £17 500
Direct labour cost = 800 × £5 = £4000

(iii) Overhead incurred £350 000
Overhead absorbed £275 000 (55 000 × £5)
Under absorption of overhead £75 000
The under absorption of overhead should be regarded as a period cost and charged to the profit and loss account.

(iv) The answer should stress the limitations of the percentage of direct material cost method and justify why the direct labour hour method is the most frequently used method in non-machine paced environments. See Appendix 3.2 for a more detailed answer to this question.

3.29 (a) (i)

	Machining (£)	Finishing (£)	Assembly (£)	Materials handling (£)	Inspection (£)
Initial cost	400 000	200 000	100 000	100 000	50 000
Reapportion:					
Materials handling	30 000	25 000	35 000	(100 000)	10 000
	430 000	225 000	135 000	—	60 000
Inspection	12 000 (20%)	18 000 (30%)	27 000 (45%)	3 000 (5%)	(60 000)
	442 000	243 000	162 000	3 000	—
Materials handling	900 (30%)	750 (25%)	1 050 (45%)	(3 000)	300 (10%)
	442 900	243 750	163 050	—	300
Inspection	60 (20%)	90 (30%)	135 (45%)	15 (5%)	(300)
	442 960	243 840	163 185	(15)	
	5	4	6		
	442 965	243 844	163 191		

(ii) Let

x = material handling
y = inspection
$x = 100\,000 + 0.05y$
$y = 50\,000 + 0.1x$

Rearranging the above equations:

$x - 0.05y = 100\,000$ (1)
$-0.1x + y = 50\,000$ (2)

Multiply equation (1) by 1 and equation (2) by 10:

$x - 0.05y = 100\,000$
$-x + 10y = 500\,000$

Adding the above equations:

$9.95y = 600\,000$
$y = 60\,301$

Substituting for y in equation (1):

$$x - 0.05 \times 60\,301 = 100\,000$$
$$x = 103\,015$$

Apportioning the values of x and y to the production departments in the agreed percentages:

	Machining (£)	Finishing (£)	Assembly (£)
Initial cost	400 000	200 000	100 000
(x) Materials handling (0.3)	30 905 (0.25)	25 754 (0.35)	36 055
(y) Inspection (0.2)	12 060 (0.3)	18 090 (0.45)	27 136
	442 965	243 844	163 191

(b) Reapportioning production service department costs is necessary to compute product costs for stock valuation purposes in order to meet the financial accounting requirements. However, it is questionable whether arbitrary apportionments of fixed overhead costs provides useful information for decision-making. Such apportionments are made to meet stock valuation requirements, and they are inappropriate for decision-making, cost control and performance reporting.

An alternative treatment would be to adopt a variable costing system and treat fixed overheads as period costs. This would eliminate the need to reapportion service department fixed costs. A more recent suggestion is to trace support/service department costs to products using an activity-based costing system (ABCS). For a description of ABCS you should refer to Chapter 10.

(c) For the answer to this question see 'Under- and over-recovery of overheads'.

Chapter 4

4.13 Answer = B

4.14 Answer = D

4.15 The profits in the financial accounts exceed the profits in the cost accounts by £4958 (£79 252 – £74 294). A stock increase represents a reduction in the cost of sales and thus an increase in profits. Therefore the stock increase in the financial accounts must have been £4958 greater than the increase in the cost accounts. The stock increase in the cost accounts was £13 937 (£24 053 – £10 116) so the increase in the financial accounts was £18 895 (£13 937 + £4958). Thus, the closing stock in the financial accounts was £28 112 (£9217 + £18 895).
Answer = D

4.16 In the financial accounts there is a total stock decrease of £2900 (£1000 materials and £1900 finished goods) and a decrease of £3200 in the costs accounts (£1200 materials and £2000 finished goods). Since a stock decrease represents an increase in cost of goods sold and a decrease in profits the cost accounting profit will be £300 less than the financial accounting profit. In other words, the financial accounting profit will be £300 greater than the cost accounting profit.
Answer = A

4.17

	Cost accounts	Financial accounts	Difference
Stock increase	£33 230	£15 601	£17 629

The stock increase shown in the cost accounts is £17 629 more than the increase shown in the financial accounts. Closing stocks represent expenses to be deferred to future accounting periods. Therefore the profit shown in the cost accounts will be £176 129 (£158 500 + £17 629).
Answer = C

4.18 Where substantial costs have been incurred on a contract and it is nearing completion the following formula is often used to determine the attributable profit to date:

$$2/3 \times \text{Notional profit} \times \frac{\text{cash received}}{\text{value of work certified}}$$

$= 2/3 \times (£1.3\text{m} - £1\text{m}) \times £1.2\text{m}/£1.3\text{m} = £276\,923$
Answer = B

4.19 In Chapter 4 it was pointed out that when prices are rising with the LIFO method the latest and higher prices are assigned to the cost of sales and therefore lower profits will be reported compared with the FIFO method. Also the value of the closing inventory will be valued at the earliest and therefore lower prices. In other words both profits and inventories will be lower with the LIFO method so the answer is A.

4.20 The cost of goods sold will be debited with £100 000 (1000 units at £100). Included within this figure will be £55 000 for conversion costs (1000 units at £55). Conversion costs actually incurred were £60 000. Assuming that an adjustment is made at the end of each month for conversion costs that have not been applied £5000 will be debited in April resulting in the cost of sales account having a debit balance of £105 000 (£100 000 + £5000). Therefore the answer is C.

4.21 (a) (i) *Stores ledger card – FIFO method*

Date	Receipts Qty	Receipts Price (£)	Receipts Value (£)	Issues Qty	Issues Price (£)	Issues Value (£)	Balance Qty	Balance Value (£)
1 April							40	400
4 April	140	11	1540				180	1940
10 April				40	10	400		
				50	11	550		
				90		950	90	990
12 April	60	12	720				150	1710
13 April				90	11	990		
				10	12	120		
				100		1110	50	600
16 April	200	10	2000				250	2600
21 April				50	12	600		
				20	10	200	180	1800
				70		800		
23 April				80	10	800	100	1000
26 April	50	12	600				150	1600
29 April				60	10	600	90	1000

(ii) *Stores ledger card – LIFO method*

Date	Receipts Qty	Receipts Price (£)	Receipts Value (£)	Issues Qty	Issues Price (£)	Issues Value (£)	Balance Qty	Balance Value (£)
1 April							40	400
4 April	140	11	1540				180	1940
10 April				90	11	990	90	950
12 April	60	12	720				150	1670
13 April				60	12	720		
				40	11	440		
				100		1160	50	510
16 April	200	10	2000				250	2510
21 April				70	10	700	180	1810
23 April				80	10	800	100	1010
26 April	50	12	600				150	1610
				50	12	600		
29 April				10	10	100		
				60		700	90	910

(b) Cost of material used in April: LIFO – £4260; FIFO – £4350

(c) The weighted average method determines the issue price by dividing the total value by the number of units in stock. This will tend to smooth out price fluctuations and the closing stock valuation will fall between that resulting from the FIFO and LIFO methods. In times of rising prices the cost of sales figure will be higher than FIFO but lower than LIFO.

4.22 (a)

Date	Receipts Quantity	Receipts Price (£)	Receipts Value (£)	Issues Quantity	Issues Price (£)	Issues Value (£)	Balance Quantity	Balance Price (£)	Balance Value (£)
Day 1							3040	0.765	2325.60
1	1400	0.780	1092.00				4440	0.770	3417.60
2				1700	0.770	1309	2740	0.770	2108.60
3	60	0.770	46.20				2800	0.770	2154.80
4				220	0.780	171.60	2580	0.769	1983.20
4	1630	0.778	1268.14				4210	0.772	3251.34
5				1250	0.772	965	2960	0.772	2286.34

(b) *Material X Account*

	£		£
Opening stock	2325.60	Work-in-progress	1309.00
Cost ledger control	1092.00	Cost ledger control	171.60
Work-in-progress	46.20	Work-in-progress	965.00
Cost ledger control	1268.14	Closing stock	2286.34
	4731.94		4731.94

4.23 The company's cost accounts are not integrated with the financial accounts. For a description of a non-integrated accounting system see 'Interlocking accounts' in Chapter 4. The following accounting entries are necessary:

Cost ledger control account

	(£)		(£)
Sales a/c	410 000	1.5.00 Balance b/f	302 000
Capital under construction a/c	50 150	Stores ledger a/c – Purchases	42 700
Balance c/f	237 500	Wages control a/c	124 000
		Production overhead a/c	152 350
		WIP a/c – Royalty	2 150
		Selling overhead a/c	22 000
		Profit	52 450
	697 650		697 650

Stores ledger control account

	(£)		(£)
1.5.00 Balance b/f	85 400	WIP a/c	63 400
Cost ledger control a/c – Purchases	42 700	Production overhead a/c	1 450
		Capital a/c	7 650
		31.5.X0 Balance c/f	55 600
	£128 100		£128 100

Wages control account

	(£)		(£)
Cost ledger control a/c	124 000	Capital a/c	12 500
		Production	35 750
		WIP a/c	7 550
	£124 000		£124 000

Production overhead control account

	(£)		(£)
Stores ledger a/c	1 450	Capital a/c	30 000
Wages control a/c	35 750	WIP a/c – Absorption (balancing figure)	152 000
Cost ledger control a/c	152 350	Costing P/L a/c (under absorption)	7 550
	£189 550		£189 550

Work in progress control account

	(£)		(£)
1.5.00 Balance b/f	167 350	Finished goods control a/c (balancing figure)	281 300
Stores ledger a/c – Issues	63 400		
Wages control a/c	75 750	31.5.X0 Balance c/f[a]	179 350
Production overhead absorbed	152 000		
Cost ledger control a/c – Royalty	2 150		
	£460 650		£460 650

Finished goods control account

	(£)		(£)
1.5.00 Balance b/f	49 250	Cost sales a/c[b]	328 000
WIP a/c	281 300	31.5.X0 Balance c/f	2 550
	£330 550		£330 550

Capital under construction account

	(£)		(£)
Stores ledger a/c	7 650	Cost ledger control a/c	50 150
Wages control a/c	12 500		
Production overhead absorbed	30 000		
	£50 150		£50 150

Sales account

	(£)		(£)
Costing P/L a/c	£410 000	Cost ledger control a/c	£410 000

Cost of sales account

	(£)		(£)
Finished goods a/c[b]	£328 000	Cost P/L a/c	£328 000

Selling overhead account

	(£)		(£)
Cost ledger control a/c	£22 000	Costing P/L a/c	£22 000

Costing profit and loss account

	(£)		(£)
Selling overhead a/c	22 000	Sales a/c	410 000
Production overhead (under absorbed)	7 550		
Cost of sales a/c	328 000		
Profit – Cost ledger control a/c	52 450		
	£410 000		£410 000

Notes

[a]Closing balance of work in progress = £167 350 (opening balance)
£12 000 (increase per question)
£179 350

[b]Transfer from finished goods stock to cost of sales account: £410 000 sales × (100/125) = £328 000

4.24 (a)

Stores ledger control account

	(£)		(£)
Opening balances b/f	24 175	Materials issued:	
Creditors – materials purchased	76 150	Work in progress control	26 350
		Production overhead control	3 280
		Closing stock c/f	70 695
	£100 325		£100 325

Wages control account

	(£)		(£)
Direct wages:		WIP	15 236
Wages accrued a/c	17 646	Capital equipment a/c	2 670
Employees' contributions a/c	4 364	Factory overhead (idle time)	5 230
Indirect wages:		Factory overhead (indirect wages)	4 232
Wages accrued a/c	3 342		
Employees' contributions a/c	890		
Balances (Wages accrued a/c)	1 126		
	27 368		27 368

Work in progress control account

	(£)		(£)
Opening balance b/f	19 210	Finished goods control – cost of goods transferred	62 130
Stores ledger – materials issued	26 350	Closing stock c/f	24 360
Wages control direct wages	15 236		
Production overhead control: overhead absorbed (15 236 × 150%)	22 854		
Profit and loss a/c: stock gain[a]	2 840		
	£86 490		£86 490

Finished goods control account

	(£)		(£)
Opening balance b/f	34 164	Profit and loss a/c: cost of sales	59 830
Working in progress: cost of goods sold	62 130	Closing stock c/f (difference)	36 464
	£96 294		£92 294

Production overhead control account

	(£)		(£)
Prepayments b/f	2 100	Work in progress: absorbed overheads (15 236 × 150%)	22 854
Stores ledger: materials issued for repairs	3 280	Capital under construction a/c: overheads absorbed (2670 × 150%)	4 005
Wages control: idle time of direct workers	5 230	Profit and loss a/c: underabsorbed overhead balance	183
Wages control: indirect workers' wages (3342 + 890)	4 232		
Cash/creditors: other overheads incurred	12 200		
	£27 042		£27 042

Profit and loss account

	(£)		(£)
Cost of goods sold	59 830	Sales	75 400
Gross profit c/f	15 570		
	£75 400		75 400
Selling and distribution overheads	5 240	Gross profit b/f	15 570
Production overhead control: underabsorbed overhead	183	Stock gain[a]: WIP control	2 840
Net profit c/f	12 987		
	£18 410		£18 410

Note

[a]The stock gain represents a balancing figure. It is assumed that the stock gain arises from the physical count of closing stocks at the end of the period.

Note that value of materials transferred between batches will be recorded in the subsidiary records, but will not affect the control (total) accounts.

(b) (i) Large increase in raw material stocks. Is this due to maintaining uneconomic stock levels or is it due to an anticipated increase in production to meet future demand?

(ii) WIP stock gain.

(iii) Idle time, which is nearly 25% of the total direct wages cost.

(iv) The gross direct wages are £22 010 (£17 646 + £4364), but the allocation amounts to £23 136 (£15 236 + £5230 + £2670).

(c) Stocks are valued at the end of the period because they represent unexpired costs, which should not be matched against sales for the purpose of calculating profits. Stocks represent unexpired costs, which must be valued for inclusion in the balance sheet. Manufacturing expense items such as factory rent are included in the stock valuations because they represent resources incurred in transforming the materials into a more valuable finished product. The UK financial accounting regulations (SSAP 9) states that 'costs of stocks (and WIP) should comprise those costs which have been incurred in bringing the product to its present location and condition, including all related production overheads.'

4.25 (a)

Raw materials stores account

	(£)		(£)
Balance b/d	49 500	Work in progress	104 800
Purchases	108 800	Loss due to flood to P&L a/c	2 400
		Balance c/d	51 100
	£158 300		£158 300
Balance b/d	51 100		

Work in progress control account

	(£)		(£)
Balance b/d	60 100	Finished goods	222 500
Raw materials	104 800	Balance c/d	56 970
Direct wages	40 200		
Production overhead	74 370		
	£279 470		£279 470
Balance b/d	56 970		

Finished goods control account

	(£)		(£)
Balance b/d	115 400	Cost of sales	212 100
Work in progress	222 500	Balance c/d	125 800
	£337 900		£337 900
Balance b/d	125 800		

Production overhead

	(£)		(£)
General ledger control	60 900	Work in progress (185% × £40 200)	74 370
Notional rent (3 × £4000)	12 000		
Overhead over absorbed	1 470		
	£74 370		£74 370

General ledger control account

	(£)		(£)
Sales	440 000	Balance b/d (49 500 + 60 100 + 115 400)	225 000
Balance c/d	233 870	Purchases	108 800
		Direct wages	40 200
		Production overhead	60 900
		Notional rent	12 000
		P & L a/c (profit for period: see (b))	226 970
	673 870		673 870

(b) *Calculation of profit in cost accounts*

	(£)	(£)
Sales		440 000
Cost of sales	212 100	
Loss of stores	2 400	
	214 500	
Less overhead over absorbed	1 470	213 030
Profit		226 970

Reconciliation statement[a]

	(£)	(£)	(£)
Profit as per cost accounts			226 970
Differences in stock values:			
Raw materials opening stock	1500		
Raw materials closing stock	900		
WIP closing stock	1030	3 430	
WIP opening stock	3900		
Finished goods opening stock	4600		
Finished goods closing stock	3900	(12 400)	(8 970)
Add items not included in financial accounts:			
Notional rent			12 000
Profit as per financial accounts			230 000

Note

[a]Stock valuations in the financial accounts may differ from the valuation in the cost accounts. For example, raw materials may be valued on a LIFO basis in the cost accounts, whereas FIFO or weighted average may be used in the financial accounts. WIP and finished stock may be valued on a marginal (variable costing) basis in the cost accounts, but the valuation may be based on an absorption costing basis in the financial accounts. To reconcile the profits, you should start with the profit from the cost accounts and consider what the impact would be on the profit calculation if the financial accounting stock valuations were used. If the opening stock valuation in the financial accounts exceeds the valuation in the cost accounts then adopting the financial accounting stock valuation will reduce the profits. If the closing stock valuation in the financial accounts exceeds the valuation in the cost accounts then adopting the financial accounting stock valuation will increase profits. Note that the notional rent is not included in the financial accounts and should therefore be deducted from the costing profit in the reconciliation statement.

(c) The over recovery of overhead could be apportioned between cost of goods sold for the current period and closing stocks. The justification for this is based on the assumption that the under/over recovery is due to incorrect estimates of activity and overhead expenditure, which leads to incorrect allocations being made to the cost of sales and closing stock accounts. The proposed adjustment is an attempt to rectify this incorrect allocation.

The alternative treatment is for the full amount of the under/over recovery to be written off to the cost accounting profit and loss account in the current period as a period cost. This is the treatment recommended by SSAP 9.

4.26 (a) *HR Construction plc – Contract Accounts*

	A (£000)	B (£000)		A (£000)	B (£000)
Stores	700	150	Stores returns	80	30
Plant	1000	150	Transfers to B	40	—
Transfers from A	—	40	Materials c/fwd	75	15
Plant hire	200	30	Plant c/fwd[a]	880	144
Labour	300	270	Cost of work not certified c/fwd	160	20
Overhead	75	18			
Direct expenses	25	4	Balance – Cost of work certified c/fwd	1065	453
	2300	662		2300	662
Cost of work certified b/fwd	1065	453	Attributable sales revenue[c]	1545	420
Profit recognized this period[b]	480	—	Loss recognized this period[b]		33
	1545	453		1545	453
Cost of work not certified c/fwd	160	20			
Plant b/fwd	880	144			
Materials b/fwd	75	15			

Notes

[a]Value at the start of the year less one year's depreciation for Contract A and 3 months' depreciation for Contract B.

[b]The profits/(losses) recognized for the period are calculated as follows:

	Contract A (£000)	Contract B (£000)
Cost of work certified	1065	453
Cost of work not certified	160	20
Estimated costs to complete	135	110
Estimated cost of the contracts	1360	583
Contract price	2000	550
Estimated profit/(loss)	640	(33)

Profit recognized (Value certified (1500)/Contract price (£2000) x £640 = £480 000 for Contract A.

An alternative more prudent approach would have been to multiply the estimated profit by cash received/contract price.

Applying the prudence concept the full anticipated loss is recognized in the current period.

[c]Profit recognized plus cost of work certified for A

Cost of work certified less loss recognized for B.

(b) *Balance sheet extracts*

	Contract A (£000)	Contract B (£000)
Fixed assets		
Plant at cost	1000	150
Depreciation	120	6
Written down value	880	144
Debtors		
Attributable sales	1545	420
Less cash received	1440	460
	105	(40)
Work-in-progress		
Total costs incurred to date	1225	473
Included in cost of sales	1065	453
	160	20

The loss of 33 000 for Contract A will be shown as a deduction from the total company profits. Alternatively, the loss can be deducted from the total costs incurred to date thus reflecting the fact that £33 000 of the total losses have been recognized during the current period.

(c) See 'job costing systems and process costing systems' in Chapter 2 and 'contract costing' in Chapter 4 for the answer to this question.

Chapter 5

5.13

	Cost (£)	Units completed	Normal loss equiv. units	Abnormal loss equiv. units	Total equiv. units	Cost per unit (£)
Materials	90 000	36 000	3000 (100%)	1000 (100%)	40 000	2.25
Conversion cost	70 200	36 000	2250 (75%)	750 (75%)	39 000	1.80
						4.05

Cost of abnormal loss:

Materials	1000 × £2.25 = £2250
Conversion cost	750 × £1.80 = £1350
	£3600

Answer = A

5.14 Abnormal gain debited to process account and credited to abnormal gain account:

	(£)	(£)
Materials (160 × £9.40)	1504	
Conversion cost (160 × 0.75 × £11.20)	1344	
		2848
Lost sales of scrap (180 × £2)		(360)
Net cost credited to profit and loss account		2528

Answer = C

5.15 Input = Opening WIP (2000 units) + Material input (24 000) = 26 000
Output = Completed units (19 500) + Closing WIP (3000) + Normal Loss (2400) = 24 900
Abnormal Loss = 1100 units (Balance of 26 000 – 24 900)

Equivalent units (FIFO)

	Completed units less Opening WIP equiv. units	Closing WIP equiv. units	Abnormal loss equiv. units	Total equiv. units
Materials	17 500 (19 500 – 2000)	3000 (100%)	1100 (100%)	21 600
Conversion	18 700 (19 500 – 800)	1350 (45%)	1100 (100%)	21 150

It is assumed that losses are detected at the end of the process and that the answer should adopt the short-cut method and ignore the normal loss in the cost per unit calculations.
Answer = C

5.16 Closing stock = Opening stock (Nil) + Input (13 500) – Completed units (11 750) = 1750 units
It is assumed that materials are fully complete (£5.75) and labour and overheads are partly complete (£2.50)
Value of closing stock = (1750 × £5.75) + (1750 × £2.50) = £14 437.50
Answer = B

5.17

Actual input	2500 kg
Normal wastage (10%)	250
Abnormal loss	75
Balance = Good production	2175

Answer = A

5.18 *Equivalent units (FIFO)*

	Completed units less opening WIP equiv. units	Closing WIP equiv. units	Abnormal loss equiv. units[a]	Total equiv. units
Materials	23 000 (24 000 – 1000)	3500	500	27 000
Conversion cost	23 300 (24 000 – 700)	2800 (80%)	300 (60%)	26 400

Note
[a]Total input (30 000 + 1000) – ((30 000 × 10%) + 24 000 + 3500) = 500

It is assumed that the answer should adopt the short-cut method and ignore the normal loss in the cost per unit calculation.
(a) Answer = (iii)
(b) Answer = (i)

5.19 Input = Opening WIP (2400) + Material input (58 000) = 60 400 litres
Output = Completed units (52 500) + Normal loss (5% × 58 000 = 2900) + Closing WIP (3000) = 58 400
Abnormal loss = 60 400 – 58 400 = 2000 litres
It is assumed that the short-cut method described in Appendix 6.1 is adopted whereby the normal loss is not included in the equivalent units calculation. The computation of equivalent units is as follows:

Cost element	Completed units	Abnormal loss equivalent units	Closing WIP equivalent units	Total equivalent units
Materials	52 500	2000	3000	57 500
Conversion cost	52 500	2000	1500	56 000

Answer = D

5.20 (a) The debit side (input) indicates that 4 000 units were input into the process but the output recorded on the credit side is 3850 units thus indicating that the balance must represent an abnormal loss of 150 units. The accounting entries for abnormal losses are to debit the abnormal loss account and credit the process account. Therefore the answer is A.
(b) and (c)
The calculation of the closing WIP value and the cost of finished goods is as follows:

Cost element	Total cost ($)	Completed units	Abnormal loss equivalent units	Closing WIP equivalent units	Total equivalent units	Cost per unit ($)	Closing WIP ($)
Materials[1]	15 300	2750	150	700	3600	4.25	2 975.00
Labour	8 125	2750	150	350	3250	2.50	875.00
Production overhead	3 498	2750	150	280	3180	1.10	308.00
	27 923					7.85	4 158.00
					Finished goods (2750 × $7.85)		21 587.50
					Abnormal loss (150 × $7.85)		1 177.50
							27 923.00

Note
[1]£16 000 materials less £700 scrap value of the normal loss. The above computation is based on the short-cut method described in the Appendix of Chapter 5.

Therefore the answer is B for part both parts (b) and (c).

5.21

Completed units less opening WIP equivalent units	4000 (4100 less 40% × 250 units)
Abnormal loss	275
Closing WIP	45 (150 × 30%)
Equivalent units	4320

It is assumed that the short-cut method (see Appendix 5.1) will be used in respect of normal losses.
Answer = C

5.22

Cost per unit of output

$$= \frac{\text{Input cost } (£52\,500 + £9625 = 62\,125) - \text{less expected loss } (0.25 \times 3500 \times £8 = £7000)}{\text{Expected output } (0.75 \times 3500)}$$

= £21

Value of actual output = 2800 × £21 = £58 800
Answer = C
Note that there is an abnormal gain of 175 units (Actual output of 2800 units less expected output of 2625 units)
The debit side of the process account will consist of:

Input cost (3500 kg)	= £62 125
Abnormal gain (175 kg at £21)	= 3 675
	65 800

The following entries will be made on the credit side:

Normal loss (875 kg at £8)	= £7 000
Value of actual output	= £58 800
	£65 500

5.23

Process 1 account

	(kg)	(£)		(kg)	(£)
Material	3000	750	Normal loss (20%)	600	120
Labour		120	Transfer to process 2	2300	1150
Process plant time		240	Abnormal loss	100	50
General overhead (120/£204 × £357)		210			
	3000	1320		3000	1320

$$\text{cost per unit} = \frac{\text{cost of production less scrap value of normal loss}}{\text{expected output}}$$

$$= \frac{£1320 - £120}{2400 \text{ kg}} = £0.50$$

Process 2 account

	(kg)	(£)		(kg)	(£)
Previous process cost	2300	1150	Normal loss	430	129
Materials	2000	800	Transfer to finished stock	4000	2400
Labour		84			
General overhead (£84/£204 × £357)		147			
Process plant time		270			
		2451			
Abnormal gain (130 kg at £0.60)	130	78			
	4430	2529		4430	2529

$$\text{cost per unit} = \frac{£2451 - £129}{3870 \text{ kg}} = £0.60$$

Finished stock account

	(£)
Process 2	2400

Normal loss account (income due)

	(£)		(£)
Process 1 normal loss	120	Abnormal gain account	39
Process 2 normal loss	129	Balance or cash received	230
Abnormal loss account	20		
	269		269

Abnormal loss account

	(£)		(£)
Process 1	50	Normal loss account (100 × £0.20)	20
		Profit and loss account	30
	50		50

Abnormal gain account

	(£)		(£)
Normal loss account (Loss of income 130 × £0.30)	39	Process 2	78
Profit and loss account	39		
	78		78

5.24 a) *Cleansing agent process account*

	(kg)	(£)		(kg)	(£)
Ingredient A	2 000	1 600	Completed production	8 600	9 460
B	3 000	1 500	WIP c/fwd (1170 + 516)	2 400	1 686
C	6 000	2 400			
Wages		3 764			
Overheads		1 882			
	11 000	11 146		11 000	11 146

Calculation of cost per unit

	Total cost (£)	Completed units	Equivalent WIP(1)	Equivalent WIP(2)	Total equivalent units	Cost per unit (£)
Materials	5 500	8600	600	1800	11 000	0.50
Labour	3 764	8600	360	450	9 410	0.40
Overheads	1 882	8600	360	450	9 410	0.20
	11 146					1.10

		(£)
WIP(1): Materials	600 × £0.50 = 300	
Labour	360 × £0.40 = 144	
Overheads	360 × £0.20 = 72	516
WIP(2): Materials	1800 × £0.50 = 900	
Labour	450 × £0.40 = 180	
Overheads	450 × £0.20 = 90	1 170
Completed units: 8600 × £1.10		9 460
		11 146

Note that 11 000 kg were put into the process and 8600 kg were completed. Therefore the WIP is 2400 kg consisting of two batches – one of 600 units 60% complete and the second of 1800 units 25% complete.

(b) See Chapter 5 for definitions and an explanation of the accounting treatment of abnormal gains and equivalent units. See Chapter 6 for a definition of by-products. Note that income from by-products should be credited to the process account from which the by-product emerges.

5.25 (a) *Production statement*

Input		Output	
Opening stock	3 400	Finished stock	36 000
Input	37 000	WIP	3 200
		Normal loss	1 200
	40 400		40 400

Cost statement

	Opening stock (£)	Current cost (£)	Total cost (£)	Completed units (£)	Normal loss (£)	WIP equivalent units (£)	Total equivalent units	Cost per unit (£)	WIP (£)
Materials	25 500	276 340	301 840	36 000	1200	3200	40 400	7.47	23 904
Conversion cost	30 600	336 000	366 600	36 000	1200	1600	38 800	9.45	15 120
			668 440					16.92	39 024
			Normal loss (1200 × £16.92)				20 304		
			Completed units (36 000 × £16.92)				609 112		629 416
									668 440

The question does not indicate at what stage in the production process the normal loss is detected. It is assumed that the normal loss is detected at the end of the production process, consequently it is not allocated to WIP. Therefore the total cost of production transferred to finished stock is £629 416.

If the short-cut method described in Chapter 5 is adopted and the normal loss equivalent units are excluded from the above unit cost calculations, the closing WIP valuation is £40 240 and the value of completed production is £628 200. This is equivalent to the following calculation, which apportions the normal loss between completed production and WIP on the basis of equivalent production (and not completed units as recommended in Chapter 5):

	Completed production (£)		WIP (£)	
Materials normal loss (1200 × £7.47 = £8964)	8 232	(36 000/39 200)	732	(3200/39 200)
Conversion cost normal loss (1200 × £9.45 = £11 340)	10 857	(36 000/37 600)	483	(1600/37 600)
Normal loss allocation	19 089		1 215	
WIP per cost statement			39 024	
Completed production	609 112			
	628 201		40 239	

(b) The following characteristics distinguish process costing from job costing:

(i) The cost per unit of output with a process costing system is the average cost per unit, whereas job costing traces the actual cost to each individual unit of output.

(ii) Job costing requires that a separate order and job number be used to collect the cost of each individual job.

(iii) With a process costing system, each unit of output is similar, whereas with a job costing system each unit of output is unique and requires different amounts of labour, material and overheads.

(iv) With a job costing system, costs are accumulated for each order and WIP is calculated by ascertaining the costs that have been accumulated within the accounting period. With a process costing system, costs are not accumulated for each order and it is necessary to use the equivalent production concept to value WIP.

(v) With a process costing system, the allocation of costs to cost of goods sold and closing stocks is not as accurate, because each cost unit is not separately identifiable. Consequently WIP is estimated using the equivalent production concept.

5.26 (a)

Cost element	Current period costs (£)	Completed units less opening WIP equiv. units	Closing WIP equiv. units	Current total equiv. units	Cost per unit (£)
Materials	2255	2800	1300	4100	0.55
Conversion costs[a]	3078	3300	975	4275	0.72
	5333				

	(£)	(£)
Completed production:		
Opening WIP (£540 + £355)	895	
Materials (2800 × £0.55)	1540	
Conversion cost (3300 × £0.72)	2376	
		4811
Closing work in progress:		
Materials (1300 × £0.55)	715	
Conversion cost (975 × £0.72)	702	
		1417
		6228

Note

[a]Bonus = Current total equivalent units (4275) – Expected output (4000) = 275 units × £0.80 = £220

Labour cost = 6 men × 37 hours × £5 = £1110 + Bonus (£220) = £1330

Conversion cost = £1748 overhead + £1330 labour = £3078

Process account

	(£)		(£)
Opening WIP	895	Completed output	4811
Materials	2255	Closing WIP	1417
Labour and overhead	3078		
	6228		6228

(b) (i) In most organizations the purchasing function is centralized and all goods are purchased by the purchasing department. To purchase goods, user departments complete a purchase requisition. This is a document requesting the purchasing department to purchase the goods listed on the document.

(ii) See 'Materials recording procedure' in Chapter 4 for the answer to this question.

5.27 (a) *Calculation of input for process 1*

	(litres)	(£)
Opening stock	4 000	10 800
Receipts	20 000	61 000
Less closing stock	(8 000)	(24 200)
Process input	16 000	47 600

Output	(litres)
Completed units	8 000
Closing WIP	5 600
Normal loss (15% of input)	2 400
	16 000

Because input is equal to output, there are no abnormal gains or losses.

Calculation of cost per unit (Process 1)

It is assumed that the loss occurs at the point of inspection. Because WIP has passed the inspection point, the normal loss should be allocated to both completed units and WIP.

(1) Element of cost	(2) (£)	(3) Completed units	(4) Normal loss	(5) Closing WIP	(6) Total equiv. units	(7) Cost per unit	(8) = (5) × (7) WIP
Materials	47 600	8000	2400	5600	16 000	£2.975	£16 660
Conversion cost[a]	21 350	8000	1800	4200	14 000	£1.525	£6 405
	68 950					£4.50	£23 065

Note

[a]Conversion cost = direct labour (£4880) + direct expenses (£4270) + overhead (250% × £4880)

Cost of normal loss	(£)
Materials	2400 × £2.975 = 7140
Conversion cost	1800 × £1.525 = 2745
	9885

The apportionment of normal loss to completed units and WIP is as follows:

	(£)
Completed units	(8000/13 600 × 9885) = 5815
WIP	(5600/13 600 × 9885) = 4070
	9885

The cost of completed units and WIP is as follows:

		(£)	(£)
Completed units:	8000 units × £4.50	36 000	
	Share of normal loss	5 815	41 815
WIP:	Original allocation	23 065	
	Share of normal loss	4 070	27 135
			68 950

For an explanation of the above procedure see Appendix 5.1. *Where the normal loss is apportioned to WIP and completed units, a simple (but less accurate) approach is to use the short-cut approach and not to include the normal loss in the unit cost statement.* The calculation is as follows:

Element of cost	(£)	Completed units	Closing WIP	Total equiv. units	Cost per unit (£)	WIP (£)
Materials	47 600	8000	5600	13 600	3.50	19 600
Conversion cost	21 350	8000	4200	12 200	1.75	7 350
					£5.25	£26 950

Completed units 8000 × £5.25 = £42 000

Process 1 account – May 2000

	(litres)	(£)		(litres)	(£)
Materials	16 000	47 600	Transfers to process 2	8 000	42 000
Labour		4 880	Normal loss	2 400	—
Direct expenses		4 270	Closing stock C/f	5 600	26 950
Overheads absorbed		12 200			
	16 000	68 950		16 000	68 950

With process 2, there is no closing WIP. Therefore it is unnecessary to express output in equivalent units. The cost per unit is calculated as follows:

$$\frac{\text{cost of production less scrap value of normal loss}}{\text{expected output}} = \frac{£54\ 000^{a}}{(90\% \times 8000)} = £7.50$$

Note

[a]Cost of production = transferred in cost from process 1 (42 000) + labour (£6000) + overhead (£6000).

Process 2 account – May 2000

	Litres	(£)		Litres	(£)
Transferred from Process 1	8000	42 000	Finished goods store[b]	7500	56 250
Labour		6 000	Normal loss	800	
Overheads absorbed		6 000	Closing stock	—	—
Abnormal gain[a]	300	2 250			
	8300	56 250		8300	56 250

Finished goods account

	Litres	(£)
Ex Process 2	7500	56 250

Abnormal gain account

	(£)		Litres	(£)
Profit and loss account	2250	Process 2 account	300	2250

Notes

[a]Input = 8000 litres. Normal output = 90% × 8000 litres = 7200 litres. Actual output = 7500 litres. Abnormal gain = 300 litres × £7.50 per litre = £2250.

[b]7500 litres at £7.50 per litre.

(b) If the materials can be replaced then the loss to the company will consist of the replacement cost of materials. If the materials cannot be replaced then the loss will consist of the lost sales revenue less the costs not incurred as a result of not processing and selling 100 litres.

Chapter 6

6.11

	(£)
Joint costs apportioned to P (4500/9750 × £117 000) =	54 000
Further processing costs (4500 × £9) =	40 500
Total cost	94 500
Sales revenues (4050 × £25)	101 250
Profit	6 750

Answer = A

6.12 Answer = D

6.13 Total sales revenue = £1 080 000 (£18 × 10 000 + £25 × 20 000 + £20 × 20 000)

Joint costs to be allocated = £270 000 (277 000 total output cost – £2 × 3500 by-product sales revenue)

Costs allocated to product 3 = 270 000 × (£20 × 20 000)/£1 080 000 = £100 000

Unit cost of product 3 = £5 per unit (£100 000/20 000 units)

Answer = C

6.14 (a) Joint products and by-products arise in situations where the production of one product makes inevitable the production of other products. When a group of individual products is simultaneously produced, and each product has a significant relative sales value, the outputs are usually called joint products. Those products that are part of the simultaneous processes and that have a *minor* sales value when compared to the joint products are called by-products.

Because by-products are of relatively *minor* sales value their net revenues are deducted from the joint processing costs before they are allocated to the joint products.

(b) Costs to apportion to joint products: Joint process costs (£272 926) – Revenues from by-product C (2770 × £0.80) = £270 710.

	(£)
Market value of output:	
Joint product A (16 000 kg × £6.10) =	97 600
Joint product B (53 200 kg × £7.50) =	399 000
	496 600
Apportionment of joint costs:	
Product A (£97 600/£496 600 × £270 710) =	£53 204
Product B (£399 000/£496 600 × £270 710) =	£217 506
	£270 710
Cost per kg:	
Product A = £53 204/16 000 = £3.325	
Product B = £217 506/53 200 = £4.088	

(c) Production costs:

		(£)
Material P:	3220 kg at £5 per kg =	16 100
Material T:	6440 kg at £1.60 per kg =	10 304
	9660	26 404
Conversion costs		23 796
		50 200

	(kg)
Analysis of output:	
Completed production	9130
Normal loss (5% × 9660)	483
Abnormal loss (Balance)	47
Total input	9660

$$\text{Cost per kg} = \frac{\text{Cost of production (£50 200)}}{\text{Expected output (9660 kg} - \text{483 kg)}} = £5.47$$

Process account

	(Units)	(£)		(Units)	(£)
Materials	9660	26 404	Normal loss	483	—
Conversion cost		23 796	Abnormal loss (1)	47	257
			Output (2)	9130	49 943
		50 200			50 200

Notes:
(1) 47 kg × £5.47 = £257
(2) 9130 kg × £5.47 = £49 943

6.15 (a)

	Product X (£)	Material B (£)
Apportionment of joint costs (W1)	35 400	106 200
Further processing costs	18 000	—
	53 400	106 200
Sales (W2)	50 400	180 000
Profit/(loss)	(3 000)	73 800
Profit/(loss) per kg (W3)	(0.33)	2.46

Workings:
(W1) X = (£141 600/40 000 kg) × 10 000 kg
B = (£141 600/40 000 kg) × 30 000 kg
(W2) X = 9000 kg at £5.60, B = 30 000 × £6
(W3) X = £3000/9000 kg, B = £73 800/30 000 kg

(b) The answer should stress that a joint products costs cannot be considered in isolation from those of other joint products. If product X was abandoned the joint costs apportioned to X would still continue and would have to be absorbed by material B. Therefore no action should be taken on product X without also considering the implications for material B. Note that the process as a whole is profitable. The decision to discontinue product X should be based on a comparison of those costs which would be avoidable if X were discontinued with the lost sales revenue from product X. Joint costs apportionments are appropriate for stock valuation purposes but not for decision-making purposes.

(c) An alternative method is to apportion joint costs on the basis of net realizable value at split-off point. The calculations are as follows:

	Sales value	Costs beyond split-off point	Net-realizable value at split-off point	Joint cost apportionment
Product X	50 400	18 000	32 400	21 600 (W1)
Material A	180 000	—	180 000	120 000 (W2)
			212 400	141 600

Workings:
(W1) (£32 400/£212 400) × £141 600
(W2) (£180 000/£212 400) × £141 600

The revised profit calculation for product X is:

		(£)
Sales		50 400
Less Joint costs	21 600	
Processing costs	18 000	39 600
Profit		10 800
Profit per kg		£1.20 (£10 800/9000 kg)

Apportionment methods based on sales value normally ensure that if the process as a whole is profitable, then each of the joint products will be shown to be making a profit. Consequently it is less likely that incorrect decisions will be made.

6.16 (a) See Chapters 5 and 6 for an explanation of the meaning of each of these terms.

(b) No specific apportionment method is asked for in this problem. It is recommended that the joint costs should be apportioned (see Chapter 6) according to the sales value at split-off point:

Product	Sales value (£)	Proportion to total (%)	Joint costs apportioned (£)
A	60 000	20	40 000
B	40 000	13.33	26 660
C	200 000	66.67	133 340
	300 000	100.00	200 000

(c) Assuming all of the output given in the problem can be sold, the initial process is profitable – the sales revenue is £300 000 and the joint costs are £200 000. To determine whether further processing is profitable the additional revenues should be compared with the additional relevant costs:

	A (£)	B (£)	C (£)
Additional relevant revenues	10 (20–10)	4 (8–4)	6 (16–10)
Additional relevant costs	14	2	6
Excess of relevant revenue over costs	(4)	2	–

Product B should be processed further, product A should not be processed further, and if product C is processed further, then profits will remain unchanged.

6.17 (a) Operating statement for October 2000

	(£)	(£)
Sales: Product A (80 000 × £5) =	400 000	
Product B (65 000 × £4) =	260 000	
Product C (75 000 × £9) =	675 000	1 335 000
Operating costs	1 300 000	
Less closing stock[a]	200 000	
		1 100 000
Profit		235 000

Note

[a]Production for the period (kg):

	A	B	C	Total
Sales requirements	80 000	65 000	75 000	
Closing stock	20 000	15 000	5 000	
Production	100 000	80 000	80 000	260 000

$$\text{Cost per kg} = 260\,000 \text{ kg} = \frac{£1\,300\,000}{260\,000} = £5 \text{ per kg}$$

Therefore

Closing stock = 40 000 kg at £5 per kg

(b) Evaluation of refining proposal

	A	B	C	Total (£)
Incremental revenue per kg (£)	12	10	11.50	
Variable cost per kg (£)	4	6	12.00	
Contribution per kg (£)	8	4	(0.50)	
Monthly production (kg)	100 000	80 000	80 000	
Monthly contribution (£)	800 000	320 000	(40 000)	1 080 000
Monthly fixed overheads (specific to B)		360 000		360 000
Contribution to refining general fixed costs (£)	800 000	(40 000)	(40 000)	720 000
Refining general fixed overheads				700 000
Monthly profit				20 000

1. It is more profitable to sell C in its unrefined state and product B is only profitable in its refined state if monthly sales are in excess of 90 000 kg (£360 000 fixed costs/£4 contribution per unit).
2. If both products B and C are sold in their unrefined state then the refining process will yield a profit of £100 000 per month (£800 000 product A contribution less £700 000 fixed costs).
3. The break-even point for the refining process if only product A were produced is 87 500 kg (£700 000 fixed costs/£8 contribution per unit). Consequently if sales of A declined by 12½%, the refining process will yield a loss. Note that 80 000 kg of A were sold in October.

6.18 (a)

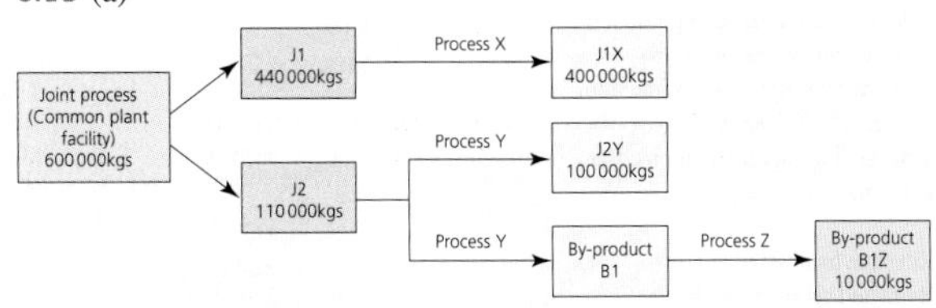

(b) (i) *Physical units allocation basis*

	Product J1X Total (£000)	Cost per unit[b]	Product J2Y Total (£000)	Cost per unit[b]
Joint costs[a]	440	1.100	110	1.100
Further processing costs	410	1.025	135	1.350
By-product net revenues	—	0.000	(5)	(0.050)
Total cost	850	2.125	240	2.400
Sales	970	2.425	450	4.500
Manufacturing profit	120	0.300	210	2.100

Notes

[a]Apportioned 440 000 : 110 000 kg

[b]Divided by 400 000 kg for J1X and 100 000 kg for J2Y

(ii) *Net realizable value allocation basis*

	Product J1X Total (£000)	Cost per unit[a]	Product J2Y Total (£000)	Cost per unit[b]
Joint costs	350	0.875	200	2.000
Further processing costs	410	1.025	135	1.350
By-product net revenues	—	0.000	(5)	(0.050)
Total cost	760	1.900	330	3.300
Sales	970	2.425	450	4.500
Manufacturing profit	210	0.525	120	1.200

Notes

[a]Divided by 400 000 kg for J1X and 100 000 kg for J2Y

[b]Net realizable values are calculated as follows:

Product J1X: Sales (£970 000) – Further processing costs (£410 000) = £560 000.
Product J2Y: Sales (£450 000) + By-product net revenue (£5000) – Further processing costs (£135 000) = £320 000. Joint costs are therefore apportioned in the ratio of £560 000 : £320 000.

For comments on the above two methods of joint cost allocations see 'Methods of allocating joint costs' in Chapter 6.

(c) (i) The answer requires a comparison of the incremental revenues with the incremental costs of further processing. It is assumed that direct materials, direct labour and variable overheads are incremental costs. Note that the order represents 10% of the current volume of J2Y. The extra costs of 10 000 kg of of J2Y are as follows:

10% of common facility variable costs		50 000
10% of finishing process (Y)		13 000
		63 000
Net revenue from J2Y:		
Sales (10 000 kg at £4)	40 000	
Net revenue from sale of 1000 kg of by-product B1Z (£1500 – (10% × £7000))	800	40 800
Shortfall		22 200

It would appear that by itself the order is not justifiable because there is a £22 000 shortfall. By itself a minimum selling price of £6.22 (£4 + £22 200/10 000 kg) is required to break-even. However, production of 10 000 kg of J2Y will result in an extra output of 40 000 kg of J1. To convert J1 into J1X incremental further processing costs of £38 500 (10% of J1X current incremental costs of £338 500) will be incurred. For the offer to be justifiable the extra output of J1X must generate sales revenue in excess of £60 700 (£38 500 incremental costs plus £22 200 shortfall from the order). This represents a minimum selling price of approximately £1.51 per kg (£60 700/40 000 kg) compared with the current market price of £2.425.

(ii) The following should be included in the answer:

(i) Does the company have sufficient capacity to cope with the 10% increase in output? If not the opportunity cost of the lost output should be incorporated in the above analysis.

(ii) Are any of the fixed overheads incremental costs?
(iii) Direct labour is assumed to be an incremental cost. Is this correct or can the existing labour force cope with the extra output from the order?
(iv) What are the long-run implications? At the present selling price the order should be viewed as a one time special short-term order. For a more detailed discussion of the issues involved here you should refer to 'Special pricing decisions' in Chapter 9.

Chapter 7

7.13 Fixed overhead = £2 per unit (£60 000/30 000 units)
Because production exceeded sales by 180 units a sum of £360 (180 × £2) is included in the stock valuation and not charged as an expense of the current period. Fixed overheads of £4640 (£5000 monthly cost – £360) are therefore charged as an expense for the period.

	(£)
Contribution (2220 units sales × £5.50)	12 210
Fixed overheads charged as an expense	4 640
Profit	7 570

Answer = B

7.14 Closing stock = 2500 units (17 500 – 15 000)
With absorption costing fixed overheads of £10 000 (£2500 units × £4) are deferred as a future expense whereas marginal costing treats fixed overheads as a period expense. Therefore absorption costing will be £10 000 greater.
Answer = B

7.15 The profit difference is due to the fixed overheads being incorporated in the stock movements with the absorption costing system.
Profit difference = £15 400 (£76 456 – £61 056)
Fixed overheads in stock movement = £15 400
Physical stock movement = 2800 kg
Fixed overhead rate per kg = £15 400/2800 kg = £5.50 per kg
Answer = B

7.16 Stocks have increased by 2500 units thus resulting in fixed overheads of £20 000 (2500 units at £8) being absorbed in the stock movements with the absorption costing system. Therefore the absorption costing system will record £20 000 less than the fixed overheads incurred for the period. In other words, the marginal costing system will record £20 000 more fixed costs resulting in profit of £22 000 being reported.
Answer = B

7.17 The profit difference is due to the fixed overheads being incorporated in the stock movements with the absorption costing system.
Profit difference = £9750 (£60 150 – £50 400)
Fixed overheads in stock movement = £9750
Physical stock movement = 1500 units
Fixed overhead rate per unit = £9750/1500 units = £6.50
Answer = D

7.18 (a) Budgeted overhead rate = £100 000/8 000 units = £12.50 per unit
Budgeted production exceeded actual production by 1400 units resulting in a favourable volume variance of £17 500 (1400 units × £12.50).
Answer = B

(b) Budgeted break-even point = Fixed costs (£100 000)/ Contribution per unit = 2000 units
Budgeted contribution = £100 000/2000 units = £50 per unit
Given that actual variable cost was £12 less than budget the actual contribution per unit will be £62.

Actual total contribution	= £440 200 (7100 × £62)
Less fixed costs	= 105 000
Actual profit	= 335 200

Answer = A

7.19 Answer = B (unavoidable costs are not relevant for decision-making and the remaining statements are correct).

7.20 (a) *Calculation of unit costs*

Direct material cost	10.00
Direct wages cost	4.00
Variable overhead cost	2.50
Variable manufacturing cost	16.50
Fixed manufacturing overhead (£400 000/320 000 units)	1.25
Total manufacturing cost	17.75

Profit statements

(i) Marginal costing	January–March (£000)		April–June (£000)	
Opening stock	Nil		165	
Production costs: variable	1155	(70 000 × £16.50)	1650	(100 000 × £16.50)
Closing stock	(165)	(10 000 × £16.50)	(330)	(20 000 × £16.50)
	990		1485	
Selling and distribution costs: variable	90		135	
	1080		1620	
Revenue from sales	2700		4050	
Contribution	1620		2430	
Fixed production costs	(100)		(100)	
Fixed selling and distribution costs	(20)		(20)	
Fixed administration costs	(30)		(30)	
Budgeted profit	1470		2280	
(ii) Absorption costing	**(£000)**		**(£000)**	
Opening stock	Nil		177.5	
Total production costs	1242.5	(70 000 × £17.75)	1775.0	(100 000 × £17.75)
	1242.5		1952.5	
Closing stock	(177.5)	(10 000 × £17.75)	(355.0)	(20 000 × £17.75)
	1065.0		1597.5	
Add under absorption of production overhead (10 000 × 1.25)	12.5		—	
Less over absorption of production overhead (20 000 × 1.25)	—		(25.0)	
Total selling and distribution costs	110.0		155.0	
Administration costs	30.0		30.0	
	1217.5		1757.5	
Revenue from sales	2700.0		4050.0	
Budgeted profit	1482.5		2292.5	

(b) The difference in profits of £12 500 is due to the fact that part of the fixed production overheads (10 000 units at £1.25 per unit) are included in the closing stock valuation and not recorded as an expense during the current period. With the marginal costing system all of the fixed manufacturing costs incurred during a period are recorded as an expense of the current period.

(c) It is assumed that the question requires the production overhead account to be written up only in respect of fixed production overhead.

Fixed production overhead control account

	(£)		(£)
Actual expenditure	102 400	WIP a/c (74 000 × £1.25)	92 500
		Under-absorption transferred to P & L a/c	9 900
	102 400		102 400

(d) See 'Some arguments in support of variable costing' in Chapter 7 for the answer to this question.

7.21

	(£)
Calculation of product cost	
Materials	10
Labour	2
Variable production cost	12
Variable distribution cost	1
Total variable cost	13
Fixed overhead (£10 000/1000 units)	10
Total costs	23

The product costs for stock valuation purposes are as follows:
Variable costing £12 (variable production cost)
Absorption costing £22 (variable production cost + fixed manufacturing overhead)

It is assumed that all of the fixed overhead relates to production. Note that the distribution cost is per unit *sold* and not per unit *produced*.

(a) (i) *Variable costing*

	t_1	t_2	t_3
Opening stock	1 200	1 200	1 200
Production	12 000	12 000	12 000
	13 200	13 200	13 200
Closing stock	1 200	1 200	1 200
Cost of sales	12 000	12 000	12 000
Sales at £25 per unit	25 000	25 000	25 000
Gross profit	13 000	13 000	13 000
Distribution costs	1 000	1 000	1 000
Fixed labour costs	5 000	5 000	5 000
Fixed overhead costs	5 000	5 000	5 000
Net profit	£2 000	£2 000	£2 000
Total profit £6000			

Absorption costing

	t_1 (£)	t_2 (£)	t_3 (£)
Opening stock	2 200	2 200	2 200
Production	22 000	22 000	22 000
	24 200	24 200	24 200
Closing stock	2 200	2 200	2 200
Cost of sales	22 000	22 000	22 000
Sales at £25 per unit	25 000	25 000	25 000
Gross profit	3 000	3 000	3 000
Distribution cost	1 000	1 000	1 000
Net profit	£2 000	£2 000	£2 000
Total profit £6000			

(ii) *Variable costing*

	t_1 (£)	t_2 (£)	t_3 (£)
Opening stock	1 200	7 200	4 800
Production	18 000	9 600	8 400
	19 200	16 800	13 200
Closing stock	7 200	4 800	1 200
Cost of sales	12 000	12 000	12 000
Sales at £25 per unit	25 000	25 000	25 000
Gross profit	13 000	13 000	13 000
Distribution costs	1 000	1 000	1 000
Fixed labour costs	5 000	5 000	5 000
Fixed overhead costs	5 000	5 000	5 000
Net profit	£2 000	£2 000	£2 000
Total profit £6000			

Absorption costing

	t_1 (£)	t_2 (£)	t_3 (£)
Opening stock	2 200	13 200	8 800
Production	33 000	17 600	15 400
	35 200	30 800	24 200
Under/(over) recovery	(5 000)	2 000	3 000
	30 200	32 800	27 200
Closing stock	13 200	8 800	2 200
Cost of sales	17 000	24 000	25 000
Sales at £25 per unit	25 000	25 000	25 000
Gross profit	8 000	1 000	—
Distribution cost	1 000	1 000	1 000
Net profit	£7 000	—	£(1 000)
Total profit £6 000			

(iii) *Variable costing*

	t_1 (£)	t_2 (£)	t_3 (£)
Opening stock	1 200	7 200	4 800
Production	12 000	12 000	12 000
	13 200	19 200	16 800
Closing stock	7 200	4 800	1 200
Cost of sales	6 000	14 400	15 600
Sales at £25 per unit	12 500	30 000	32 500
Gross profit	6 500	15 600	16 900
Distribution costs	500	1 200	1 300
Fixed labour costs	5 000	5 000	5 000
Fixed overhead costs	5 000	5 000	5 000
Net profit	£(4 000)	£4 400	£5 600
Total profit £6000			

Absorption costing

	t_1 (£)	t_2 (£)	t_3 (£)
Opening stock	2 200	13 200	8 800
Production	22 000	22 000	22 000
	24 200	35 200	30 800
Closing stock	13 200	8 800	2 200
Cost of sales	11 000	26 400	28 600
Sales at £25 per unit	12 500	30 000	32 500
Gross profit	1 500	3 600	3 900
Distribution cost	500	1 200	1 300
Net profit	£1 000	£2 400	£2 600
Total profit £6000			

(b) For the answer to this question see Chapter 7: Note that profits are identical for both systems in (i), since production equals sales. In (ii) and (iii) profits are higher with absorption costing when production exceeds sales, whereas profits are higher with variable costing when production is less than sales. Taking the three periods as a whole there is no change in the level of opening stock in t_1 compared with the closing stock in t_3, so that the disclosed profit for the three periods is the same under both systems. Also note that the differences in profits disclosed in (a) (ii) and (a) (iii) is accounted for in the fixed overheads included in the stock valuation changes.

Chapter 8

8.12

	Product X	Product Y	Total
Budgeted sales volume (units)	80 000	20 000	
Budgeted contribution per unit	£4	£5	
Budgeted total contribution	£320 000	£100 000	£420 000
Budgeted sales revenue	£960 000	£160 000	£1 120 000

Average contribution per unit = £420 000/100 000 units = £4.20

$$\text{Break-even point} = \frac{\text{Fixed costs (£273 000)}}{\text{Average contribution per unit (£4.20)}} = 65\ 000 \text{ units}$$

Average selling price per unit = £1 120 000/100 000 units = £11.20

Break-even point in sales revenue = 65 000 units × £11.20 = £728 000

Answer = D

8.13

$$\text{Average contribution to sales ratio} = \frac{(40\% \times 1) + (50\% \times 3)}{4} = 47.5\%$$

Break-even point is at the point where 47.5% of the sales equal the fixed costs (i.e. £120 000/0.475 = £252 632).

In other words, the break-even point = $\frac{\text{Fixed costs}}{\text{PV ratio}}$

Answer = C

8.14

	Total cost (1000 units) (£)	Total cost (2000 units) (£)
Production overhead	3500 (£3.50 × 1000)	5000 (£2.50 × 2000)
Selling overhead	1000 (£1 × 1000)	1000 (£0.5 × 2000)

$$\text{Variable cost per unit} = \frac{\text{Change in cost}}{\text{Change in activity}}$$

Production overhead = £1500/1000 units = £1.50
Selling overhead = Fixed cost since total costs remain unchanged.
The unit costs of direct materials are constant at both activity levels and are therefore variable.
Production overheads fixed cost element = Total cost (£3500) – Variable cost (1000 × £1.50) = £2000
Total fixed cost = £2000 + £1000 = £3000
Unit variable cost £4 + £3 + £1.50 = £8.50
Answer = E

8.15 Contribution/sales (%) = (0.33 × 40% Aye) + (0.33 × 50% Bee) + (0.33 × ? Cee) = 48%
Cee = 54% (Balancing figure)
The total contribution/sales ratio for the revised sales mix is:
(0.40 × 40% Aye) + (0.25 × 50% Bee) + (0.35 × 54% Cee) = 47.4%
Answer = C

8.16

Sales	100	110 (100 + 10%)
Variable cost	60	60
Contribution	40	50

Increase = 25%
Answer = D

8.17 Contribution per unit = 40% × £20 = £8

$$\text{Break even point} = \frac{\text{Fixed costs (£60 000)}}{\text{Contribution per units (£8)}} = 7500 \text{ units}$$

Answer = E

8.18 Break-even point in sales value = Fixed costs (£76 800)/Profit–volume ratio (i.e. contribution/sales ratio)
= £76 800/(0.40)
= £192 000

Actual sales = £224 000
Margin of safety = £32 000 (in sales revenues)
Margin of safety in units = £2000 (£32 000/£16)
Answer = A

8.19 (a) Budgeted contribution per unit = \$11.60 – \$3.40 – (5% × \$11.60) = \$7.62
Break-even point (units) = (\$430 500 + 198 150)/\$7.62 = 82 500 units
Break-even point (sales value) = 82 500 × \$11.60 = \$957 000
Budgeted sales = \$1 044 000 (90 000 × \$11.60)
Margin of safety (\$) = \$1 044 000 – \$957 000 = \$87 000
Margin of safety (%) = \$87 000/\$1 044 000 = 8.33%
Answer = B

(b) Budgeted contribution per unit = \$12.25 – \$3.40 – (8% × \$12.25) = \$7.87
Break-even point (units) = (\$430 500 + 198 150)/\$7.87 = 79 879 units

Answer = C

8.20 (a) Answer = A
(b) The increase in fixed costs will result in an increase in the break-even point. The only correct alternative that is listed is item C. This indicates an increase in the break-even point sales value.

8.21 Break-even point (units) = 5220 – (19.575% × 5220) = 4198 units
Fixed costs = Contribution at the break-even point = 4198 × £42 × 40% = £70 526

Answer = B

8.22 Weighted average contribution/sales ratio =

$$\frac{(30\%\times 2)+(20\%\times 5)+(25\%\times 3)}{10}=23.5\%$$

Break-even sales = Fixed costs (£100 000)/contribution to sales ratio (0.235)
= £425 532

Answer = C

8.23 (i) p = total sales revenue
q = total cost (fixed cost + variable cost)
r = total variable cost
s = fixed costs at the specific level of activity
t = total loss at the specific level of activity
u = total profit at that level of activity
v = total contribution at the specific level of activity
w = total contribution at a lower level of activity
x = level of activity of output sales
y = monetary value of cost and revenue function for level of activity

(ii) At event m the selling price per *unit* decreases, but it remains constant. Note that p is a straight line, but with a lower gradient above m compared with below m.

At event n there is an increase in fixed costs equal to the dotted line. This is probably due to an increase in capital expenditure in order to expand output beyond this point. Also note that at this point the variable cost per unit declines as reflected by the gradient of the variable cost line. This might be due to more efficient production methods associated with increased investment in capital equipment.

(iii) Break-even analysis is of limited use in a multi-product company, but the analysis can be a useful aid to the management of a small single product company. The following are some of the main benefits:

(a) Break-even analysis forces management to consider the functional relationship between costs, revenue and activity, and gives an insight into how costs and revenue change with changes in the level of activity.

(b) Break-even analysis forces management to consider the fixed costs at various levels of activity and the selling price that will be required to achieve various levels of output.

You should refer to Chapter 8 for a discussion of more specific issues of break-even analysis. Break-even analysis can be a useful tool, but it is subject to a number of assumptions that restrict its usefulness (see, especially, 'Cost–volume–profit analysis assumptions').

8.24 *Preliminary calculations:*

	Sales (units)	Profit/(loss)
November	30 000	£40 000
December	35 000	£60 000
Increase	5 000	£20 000

An increase in sales of 5000 units increases contribution (profits) by £20 000. Therefore contribution is £4 per unit. Selling price is £10 per unit (given) and variable cost per unit will be £6.

At £30 000 unit sales:

Contribution minus Fixed costs = Profit
£120 000 minus ? = £40 000
∴ Fixed costs = £80 000

The above information can now be plotted on a graph. A break-even chart or a profit–volume graph could be constructed. A profit–volume graph avoids the need to calculate the profits since the information can be read directly from the graph. (See Figure 1 for a break-even chart and Figure 2 for a profit–volume graph.)

(a) (i) Fixed costs = £80 000.

(ii) Variable cost per unit = £6.

(iii) Profit–volume =

$$\frac{\text{Contribution per unit (£4)}}{\text{Selling price per unit (£10)}}\times 100=40\%$$

(iv) Break-even point = 20 000 units.

(v) The margin of safety represents the difference between actual or expected sales volume and the break-even point. Therefore the margin of safety will be different for each month's sales. For example, the margin of safety in November is 10 000 units (30 000 units – 20 000 units). The margin of safety can be read from Figure 2 for various sales levels.

(b) and (c) See the sections on 'The accountants' cost–volume–profit model' and 'Cost–volume–profit analysis assumptions' in Chapter 8 for the answers.

FIGURE 1 *Break-even chart*

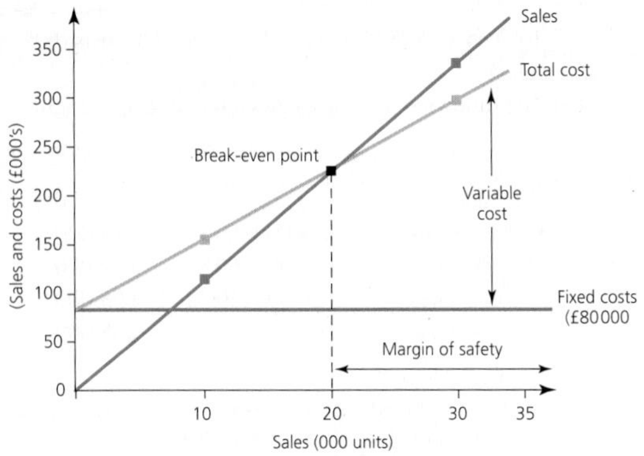

FIGURE 2 *Profit–volume graph*

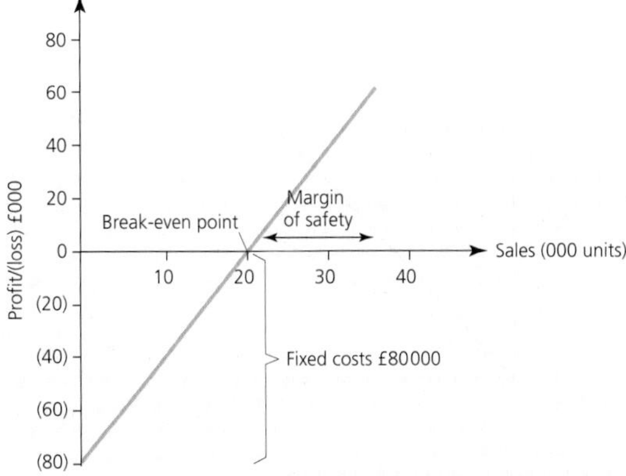

8.25 (a)

	August (£)	September (£)	Change (£)
Sales	80 000	90 000	10 000
Cost of sales	50 000	55 000	5 000
Selling and distribution	8 000	9 000	1 000
Administration	15 000	15 000	Nil

The only activity measure that is given is sales revenue. An increase in sales of £10 000 results in an increase in cost of sales of £5000 and an increase in selling and distribution costs of £1000. It is therefore assumed that the increase is attributable to variable costs and variable cost of sales is 50% of sales and variable selling and distribution costs are 10% of sales.

Fixed costs are derived by deducting variable costs from total costs for either month. The figures for August are used in the calculations below:

	Total cost (£)	Variable cost (£)	Fixed cost (Balance) (£)
Cost of sales	50 000	40 000	10 000
Selling and distribution	8 000	8 000	Nil
Administration	15 000	Nil	15 000
			25 000

Total cost = £25 000 fixed costs + variable costs (60% of sales)

(b) The following items are plotted on the graph (Figure 3):

	Variable cost	Total cost
Zero sales	Nil	£25 000 fixed cost
£80 000 sales	£48 000 (60%)	£73 000
£90 000 sales	£54 000 (60%)	£79 000
£50 000 sales	£30 000 (60%)	£55 000
£100 000 sales	£60 000	£85 000

Break-even point

$$= \frac{\text{Fixed costs (£25 000)}}{\text{Contribution to sales ratio (0.40)}} = \text{£62 500 sales}$$

FIGURE 3 *Contribution break-even graph*

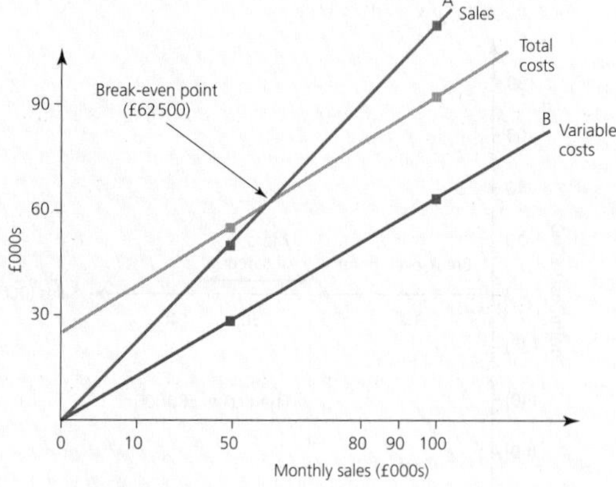

Area of contribution = Area AOB

(c)

		(£)
Actual sales = 1.3 × Break-even sales (£62 500)	=	81 250
Contribution (40% of sales)	=	32 500
Fixed costs	=	25 000
Monthly profit	=	7 500
Annual profit	=	90 000

(d)

		(£)
Annual contribution from single outlet (£32 500 × 12)	=	390 000
Contribution to cover lost sales (10%)	=	39 000
Specific fixed costs	=	100 000
Total contribution required		529 000

Required sales = £529 000/0.4 = £1 322 500

(e) The answer should draw attention to the need for establishing a sound system of budgeting and performance reporting for each of the different outlets working in close conjunction with central office. The budgets should be merged together to establish a master budget for the whole company.

8.26

$$\text{Break-even point} = \frac{\text{Fixed costs}}{\text{Contribution per unit}}$$

Product X	25 000 units (£100 000/£4)
Product Y	25 000 units (£200 000/£8)
Company as a whole	57 692 units (£300 000/£5.20[a])

Note:

[a]Average contribution per unit

$$= \frac{(70\,000 \times £4) + (30\,000 \times £8)}{100\,000 \text{ units}}$$

$$= £5.20$$

The sum of the product break-even points is less than the break-even point for the company as a whole. It is incorrect to add the product break-even points because the sales mix will be different from the planned sales mix. The sum of the product break-even points assumes a sales mix of 50% to X and 50% to Y. The break-even point for the company as a whole assumes a planned sales mix of 70% to X and 30% to Y. CVP analysis will yield correct results only if the planned sales mix is equal to the actual sales mix.

8.27

Workings:	(000)
Sales	1000
Variable costs	600
Contribution	400
Fixed costs	500
Profit/(loss)	(100)

Unit selling price = £20 (£1m/50 000)
Unit variable cost = £12 (£600 000/50 000)
Unit contribution = £8

(a) Sales commission will be £2 per unit, thus reducing the contribution per unit to £6. The break-even point will be 83 333 units (£500 000/£6) or £1 666 666 sales value. This requires an increase of 67% on previous sales and the company must assess whether or not sales can be increased by such a high percentage.

(b) A 10% decrease in selling price will decrease the selling price by £2 per unit and the revised unit contribution will be £6:

	(£)
Revised total contribution (65 000 × £6)	390 000
Less fixed costs	500 000
Profit/(loss)	(110 000)

The estimated loss is worse than last year and the proposal is therefore not recommended.

(c) Wages will increase by 25% – that is, from £200 000 to £250 000 – causing output to increase by 20%.

		(£)
Sales		1 200 000
Direct materials and variable overheads	480 000	
Direct wages	250 000	730 000
Contribution		470 000
Less fixed costs		550 000
Profit/(loss)		(80 000)

This represents an improvement of £20 000 on last year's loss of £100 000.

(d) Revised selling price = £24

Let X = Revised sales volume

∴ sales revenue less (variable costs + fixed costs)	= Profit
24X less (12X + 800 000)	= 0.1 (24X)
∴ 9.6X	= 800 000
∴ X	= 83 333 units

Clearly this proposal is preferable since it is the only proposal to yield a profit. However, the probability of increasing sales volume by approximately 67% plus the risk involved from increasing fixed costs by £300 000 must be considered.

8.28 (a)

$$BEP = \frac{400\ 000\ (\text{fixed costs}) \times £1\ 000\ 000\ (\text{sales})}{£420\ 000\ (\text{contribution})}$$

$= 952\ 380$

(b) (i)

	(£)	(£)
Revised selling price		9.00
Less variable costs:		
Direct materials	1.00	
Direct labour	3.50	
Variable overhead	0.60	
Delivery expenses	0.50	
Sales commission (2% of selling price)	0.18	5.78
Contribution per unit		3.22
Number of units sold	140 000	
Total contribution (140 000 × 3.22)	450 800	
Fixed costs	400 000	
Profit from proposal (i)	50 800	

(ii)

Desired contribution	= 480 000
Contribution per unit for present proposal	= 3.22
Required units to earn large profit	= 149 068

(c) (i) The variable cost of selling to the mail order firm is:

	(£)
Direct material	1.00
Direct labour	3.50
Variable overhead	0.60
Delivery expenses	nil
Sales commission	nil
Additional package cost	0.50
	5.60

To break even, a contribution of £1.20 is required (60 000 fixed cost/50 000 units sold). Therefore selling price to break even is £6.80 (£5.60 + £1.20).

(ii) To earn £50 800 profit, a contribution of £110 800 (£60 000 + £50 800) is required.

That is, a contribution of £2.22 per unit is required. Therefore required selling price is £7.82 (£5.60 + £2.22).

(iii) To earn the target profit of £80 000, a contribution of £140 000 is required. That is, £2.80 per unit. Therefore required selling price = £8.40 (£5.60 + £2.80).

(d) Contribution per unit is £3.22 per (B)

Unit sold	160 000
Total contribution	£515 200
Fixed costs	£430 000
Profit	£85 200

Chapter 9

9.17

	X	Y	Z
Contribution per unit	£41	£54	£50
Kg used (Limiting factor)	2 (£10/5)	1	3
Contribution per kg	£20.5	£54	£16.67
Ranking	2	1	3

Answer = B

9.18 The material is in regular use and if used will have to be replaced at a cost of £1950 (600 × £3.25). The cash flow consequences are £1950.
Answer = D

9.19 The shadow price is the opportunity cost or contribution per unit of a scarce resource.

	Quone	Qutwo
Contribution per unit	£8	£8.50
Kg per unit	3 (£6/£2)	2.50 (£5/£2)
Contribution per kg	£2.67	£3.40

Scarce materials will be used to make Qutwos and will yield a contribution of £3.40 per kg. Therefore the opportunity cost is £3.40 per kg.
Answer = D

9.20 Assuming that fixed costs will remain unchanged whether or not the company makes or buys the components the relevant cost of manufacture will be the variable cost. Under these circumstances the company should only purchase components

if the purchase price is less than the variable cost. Therefore the company should only purchase component T.
Answer = D

9.21 Incremental cost of new employees = £40 000 × 4 = £160 000
Supervision is not an incremental cost.
Incremental costs of retraining
= £15 000 + £100 000 replacement cost = £115 000
Retraining is the cheaper alternative and therefore the relevant cost of the contract is £115 000.
Answer = B

9.22 Answer = B (All of the remaining items are not relevant costs)

9.23 The material is readably available and the use of the materials will necessitate their replacement. The relevant cost is therefore the replacement cost of £4050 (1250 kg at £3.24).
Answer = B

9.24 Specific (avoidable) fixed overheads per division = £262.5 × 60% = £157.5/3 = £52.5
The specific fixed costs are deducted from the divisional contributions to derive the following contributions (£000's) to general fixed costs:
Division A = £17.5
Division B = £157.5
Division C = –£22.5
Only divisions A and B should remain open since they both provide positive contributions to general fixed costs.
Answer = B

9.25 (a) The contribution to sales ratios are:
W = 0.125 (£56 – £49)/£56
X = 0.015 (£67 – £66)/£67
Y = 0.169 (£89 – £74)/£89
Z = 0.115 (£96 – £85)/£96
Answer = C

(b) Budgeted contribution for each batch of 12 units sold = (2 × £7) + (3 × £1) + (£15 × 3) + (£11 × 4) = £106
Break-even point in standard batches = £15 000/£106 = 142 batches
Each standard batch consists of 2 units of W giving 284 units of W (142 × 2)
Answer = D

(c) With throughput accounting labour is assumed to be a fixed cost and contribution consists of sales less variable costs. The contributions per bottleneck minute are:
W = £3.40 (£34/10)
X = £3.60 (£36/10)
Y = £3.40 (£51/15)
Z = £3.33 (£50/15)
Answer = B (X is the highest ranking product)

9.26 With throughput accounting labour is assumed to be a fixed cost and contribution consists of sales less variable costs. The contributions per bottleneck minute are:
J = £13.25 (£1590/120)
K = £13.00 (£1300/100)
L = £17.14 (£1200/70)
M = £12.27 (£1350/110)
The rankings are L, J, K and M.
Answer = D

9.27 (a) Direct wages percentage overhead rate

$$= \frac{£64\,000\ (\text{Variable}) + £96\,000\ (\text{Fixed})}{\text{Direct labour costs}\ (£80\,000)}$$

= 200% of direct wages

Variable overhead rate

$$= \frac{£64\,000\ \text{Variable}}{£80\,000\ \text{Direct labour costs}}$$

= 80% of direct wages

Problem 1:

	(£)	Per unit	2000 units
Additional revenue		16.00	32 000
Additional costs:			
Raw materials	8.00		
Direct labour	4.00		
Variable overhead (80% × £4)	3.20	15.20	30 400
		£0.80	£1 600

The order should be accepted because it provides a contribution to fixed costs and profits. It is assumed that direct labour is a variable cost.

Problem 2:
Relevant manufacturing costs of the component:

	(£)
Raw material	4.00
Direct labour	8.00
Variable overhead (80% × £8)	6.40
	18.40

The additional costs of manufacturing are lower than the costs of purchasing. Therefore the company should manufacture the component. It is assumed that spare capacity exists.

(b) Relevant cost and revenue principles have been followed. See Chapter 9 for an explanation.

9.28 (a)

	V (£)	W (£)	X (£)	Y (£)	Z (£)
Selling price	16	15	18	15	30
Material	3	5	4	7	6
Skilled labour	6	6	9	3	12
Unskilled labour	2.4	2.4	1.2	1.2	4.8
Variable overhead	2	2	2	1	4
Total variable cost	13.4	15.4	16.2	12.2	26.8
Contribution	2.6	(0.4)	1.8	2.8	3.2
Number of skilled hours	1	1	1.5	0.5	2
Contribution per skilled hour	2.6	(0.4)	1.2	5.6	1.6
Ranking	2	Drop	4	1	3
Skilled hours allocated (W1)	3000		5500 (Balance)	3500	18 000

The product mix will be:

	(£)
Y (7000 units × £2.80 contribution)	19 600
V (3000 units × £2.60 contribution)	7 800
Z (9000 units × £3.20 contribution)	28 800
X ($\frac{5500\ \text{hours}}{1.5\ \text{hours}}$ × £1.80 contribution)	6 600
Total contribution	62 800
Less fixed costs	22 800
Maximum profit	40 000

Workings:

(W1) Maximum units demanded X skilled hours per unit.

(b) If the labour hours constraint is removed the output of product X should be increased to the maximum demand of 6000 units. At present the constraint on skilled labour hours results in a lost contribution of £4201 (6000 units less 3666 units allocated in (a) × £1.80 unit contribution). Therefore the company should consider ways of removing this constraint. As long as the costs of removing the constraint are less than £4201, total profit will increase. Product W should be dropped from the range provided it does not affect the sales of other products.

9.29 (a)

	Relevant costs of the project
Material A	(1 750)
Material B	8 000
Direct labour	7 000
Net cost of machinery	4 750
Relevant cost	18 000
Contract price	30 000
Contribution	12 000

Notes:

(1) There is a saving in material costs of £1750 if material A is not used.

(2) The actual cost of material B represents the incremental cost.

(3) The hiring of the labour on the other contract represents the additional cash flows of undertaking this contract.

(4) The net cost of purchasing the machinery represents the additional cash flows associated with the contract.

(5) Supervision and overheads will still continue even if the contract is not accepted and are therefore irrelevant.

(b) The report should indicate that the costs given in the question do not represent incremental cash flows arising from undertaking the contract. As the company is operating at an activity level in excess of break-even point any sales revenue in excess of £18 000 incremental costs will provide an additional contribution which will result in an increase in profits. Assuming that the company has spare capacity, and that a competitor is prepared to accept the order at £30 000, then a tender price slightly below £30 000 would be appropriate.

(c) Before accepting the contract the following non-monetary factors should be considered.

(i) Is there sufficient spare capacity to undertake the project?

(ii) Is the overseas customer credit worthy?

(iii) Has the workforce the necessary skills to undertake the project?

(iv) Is the contract likely to result in repeat business with the customer?

(d) If the company were operating below the break-even point, acceptance of the order would provide a further contribution towards fixed costs and reduce the existing loss. In the short term it is better to accept the order and reduce the total loss but if, in the long run, there are not enough orders to generate sufficient contributions to cover total fixed costs, then the company will not survive.

9.30 (a)

	North East (£)	South coast (£)
Material X from stock (i)	19 440	
Material Y from stock (ii)		49 600
Firm orders of material X (iii)	27 360	
Material X not yet ordered (iv)	60 000	
Material Z not yet ordered (v)		71 200
Labour (vi)	86 000	110 000
Site management (vii)	—	—
Staff accommodation and travel for site management (viii)	6 800	5 600
Plant rental received (ix)	(6000)	—
Penalty clause (x)		28 000
	193 600	264 400
Contract price	288 000	352 000
Net benefit	94 400	87 600

(b) (i) If material X is not used on the North East contract the most beneficial use is to use it as a substitute material thus avoiding future purchases of £19 440 (0.9 × 21 600). Therefore by using the stock quantity of material X the company will have to spend £19 440 on the other materials.

(ii) Material Y is in common use and the company should not dispose of it. Using the materials on the South coast contract will mean that they will have to be replaced at a cost of £49 600 (£24 800 × 2). Therefore the future cash flow impact of taking on the contract is £49 600.

(iii) It is assumed that with firm orders for materials it is not possible to cancel the purchase. Therefore the cost will occur whatever future alternative is selected. The materials will be used as a substitute material if they are not used on the contract and therefore, based on the same reasoning as note (i) above, the relevant cost is the purchase price of the substitute material (0.9 × £30 400).

(iv) The material has not been ordered and the cost will only be incurred if the contract is undertaken. Therefore additional cash flows of £60 000 will be incurred if the company takes on the North East contract.

(v) The same principles apply here as were explained in note (iv) and additional cash flows of £71 200 will be incurred only if the company takes on the South coast contract.

(vi) It is assumed that labour is an incremental cost and therefore relevant.

(vii) The site management function is performed by staff at central headquarters. It is assumed that the total company costs in respect of site management will remain unchanged in the short term whatever contracts are taken on. Site management costs are therefore irrelevant.

(viii) The costs would be undertaken only if the contracts are undertaken. Therefore they are relevant costs.

(ix) If the North East contract is undertaken the company will be able to hire out surplus plant and obtain a £6000 cash inflow.

(x) If the South coast contract is undertaken the company will have to withdraw from the North East contract and incur a penalty cost of £28 000.

(xi) The headquarter costs will continue whichever alternative is selected and they are not relevant costs.

(xii) It is assumed that there will be no differential cash flows relating to notional interest. However, if the interest costs associated with the contract differ then they would be relevant and should be included in the analysis.

(xiii) Depreciation is a sunk cost and irrelevant for decision-making.

9.31 (a) (i)

Product	A (£)	B (£)	C (£)
Selling price	15	12	11
Less variable costs:			
Materials	(5)	(4)	(3)
Labour	(3)	(2)	(1.5)
Variable overhead (1)	(3.50)	(2)	(1.5)
Contribution	3.50	4	5

Note:

(1) Fixed overheads are apportioned to products on the basis of sales volume and the remaining overheads are variable with output.

(ii)

Product	B (£)	C (£)
Selling price	12	9.50
Less variable costs:		
Materials	(4)	(3)
Labour	(2)	(1.80)
Variable overhead	(2)	(1.50)
Contribution	4	3.20

(b) (i)

Product	A	B	C	Total
Total contribution	350 000	480 000	400 000	1 230 000
Less fixed costs:				
Labour				(220 000)
Fixed administration				(900 000)
Profit				110 000

(ii)

Product	B	C	Total
Total contribution[a]	480 000	576 000	1 056 000
Less fixed costs:			
Labour[b]			(160 000)
Fixed administration[c]			(850 000)
Profit			46 000

Notes:

[a]B = 120 000 units × £4 contribution,
C = 18 000 units × £3.20 contribution.

[b](25% × £320 000 for B) plus (25% × £160 000 × 2 for C).

[c]Fixed administration costs will decline by 1/6 of the amount apportioned to Product A (100/300 × £900 000). Therefore fixed overheads will decline from £900 000 to £850 000.

(c) Product A should not be eliminated even though a loss is reported for this product. If Product A is eliminated the majority of fixed costs allocated to it will still continue and will be borne by the remaining products. Product A generates a contribution of £350 000 towards fixed costs but the capacity released can be used to obtain an additional contribution from Product C of £176 000 (£576 000 – £400 000). This will result in a net loss in contribution of £174 000. However, fixed cost savings of £110 000 (£50 000 administration apportioned to Product A plus £100 000 labour for A less an extra £40 000 labour for Product C) can be obtained if Product A is abandoned. Therefore there will be a net loss in contribution of £64 000 (£174 000 – £110 000) and profits will decline from £110 000 to £64 000.

9.32 The following information represents a comparison of alternatives 1 and 2 with the sale of material XY.

Alternative 1: Conversion versus immediate sale	**(£)**	**(£)**	**(£)**
1. Sales revenue (900 units at £400 per unit			360 000
Less Relevant costs:			
2. Material XY opportunity cost		21 000	
3. Material A (600 units at £90)		54 000	
4. Material B (1000 units at £45)		45 000	
5. Direct labour:			
Unskilled (5000 hrs at £6)	30 000		
Semi-skilled	nil		
Highly skilled (5000 hrs at £17)	85 000	115 000	
6. Variable overheads (15 000 hrs at £1)		15 000	
7. Selling and delivery expenses		27 000	
Advertising		18 000	
8. Fixed overheads		–	295 000
Excess of relevant revenues			65 000
Alternative 2: Adaptation versus immediate sale			
9. Saving on purchase of sub-assembly:			
Normal spending (1200 units at £900)		1 080 000	
Revised spending (900 units at £950)		855 000	225 000
Less relevant costs:			
2. Material XY opportunity cost		21 000	
10. Material C (1000 units at £55)		55 000	
5. Direct labour:			
Unskilled (4000 hrs at £6)	24 000		
Semi-skilled	nil		
Skilled (4000 hrs at £16)	64 000	88 000	
6. Variable overheads (9000 hrs at £1)		9 000	
8. Fixed overheads		nil	173 000
Net relevant savings			52 000

Notes

1. There will be additional sales revenue of £360 000 if alternative 1 is chosen.
2. Acceptance of either alternative 1 or 2 will mean a loss of revenue of £21 000 from the sale of the obsolete material XY. This is an opportunity cost, which must be covered whichever alternative is chosen. The original purchase cost of £75 000 for material XY is a sunk cost and is irrelevant.
3. Acceptance of alternative 1 will mean that material A must be replaced at an additional cost of £54 000.
4. Acceptance of alternative 1 will mean that material B will be diverted from the production of product Z. The excess of relevant revenues over relevant cost for product Z is £180 and each unit of product Z uses four units of material. The lost contribution (excluding the cost of material B which is incurred for both alternatives) will therefore be £45 for each unit of material B that is used in converting the raw materials into a specialized product.
5. Unskilled labour can be matched exactly to the company's production requirements. The acceptance of either alternative 1 or 2 will cause the company to incur additional unskilled labour costs of £6 for each hour of unskilled labour that is used. It is assumed that the semi-skilled labour would be retained and that there would be sufficient excess supply for either alternative at no extra cost to the company. In these circumstances semi-skilled labour will not have a relevant cost. Skilled labour is in short supply and can only be obtained by reducing production of product L, resulting in a lost contribution of £24 or £6 per hour of skilled labour. We have already established that the relevant cost for labour that is in short supply is the hourly labour cost plus the lost contribution per hour, so the relevant labour cost here will be £16 per hour. If this point is not clear, refer back now to Example 9.6.
6. It is assumed that for each direct labour hour of input variable overheads will increase by £1. As each alternative uses additional direct labour hours, variable overheads will increase, giving a relevant cost of £1 per direct labour hour.

7. As advertising selling and distribution expenses will be different if alternative 1 is chosen, these costs are clearly relevant to the decision.
8. The company's fixed overheads will remain the same whichever alternative is chosen, and so fixed overheads are not a relevant cost for either alternative.
9. The cost of purchasing the sub-assembly will be reduced by £225 000 if the second alternative is chosen, and so these savings are relevant to the decision.
10. The company will incur additional variable costs of £55 for each unit of material C that is manufactured, so the fixed overheads for material C are not a relevant cost.

When considering a problem such as this one, there are many different ways in which the information may be presented. The way in which we have dealt with the problem here is to compare each of the two stated alternatives with the other possibility of selling off material XY for its scrap value of £21 000. The above answer sets out the relevant information, and shows that of the three possibilities alternative 1 is to be preferred.

An alternative presentation of this information, which you may prefer, is as follows:

	Sale of obsolete materials for scrap	Alternative 1	Alternative 2
Relevant revenues less relevant costs	£21 000	£86 000	£73 000

Difference = £65 000

Difference = £13 000 (£86 000 – £73 000)

We show here *the sale of the obsolete materials as a separate alternative*, and so the opportunity cost of material XY, amounting to £21 000 (see item 2 in the answer) is not included in either alternative 1 or 2, since it is brought into the analysis under the heading 'Sale of obsolete materials for scrap' in the above alternative presentation. Consequently, in both alternatives 1 and 2 the relevant revenues less relevant costs figure is increased by £21 000. The differences between alternative 1 and 2 and the sale of the obsolete materials are still, however, £65 000 and £52 000 respectively, which gives an identical result to that obtained in the above solution.

9.33 (a) *Preliminary calculations*

Variable costs are quoted per acre, but selling prices are quoted per tonne. Therefore, it is necessary to calculate the planned sales revenue per acre. The calculation of the selling price and contribution per acre is as follows:

	Potatoes	Turnips	Parsnips	Carrots
(a) Yield per acre in tonnes	10	8	9	12
(b) Selling price per tonne	£100	£125	£150	£135
(c) Sales revenue per acre, (a) × (b)	£1000	£1000	£1350	£1620
(d) Variable cost per acre	£470	£510	£595	£660
(e) Contribution per acre	£530	£490	£755	£960

(a) (i)

(i) Profit statement for current year

	Potatoes	Turnips	Parsnips	Carrots	Total
(a) Acres	25	20	30	25	
(b) Contribution per acre	£530	£490	£755	£960	
(c) Total contribution (a × b)	£13 250	£9800	£22 650	£24 000	£69 700
				Less fixed costs	£54 000
				Profit	£15 700

(ii) Profit statement for recommended mix

	Area A (45 acres)		Area B (55 acres)		
	Potatoes	Turnips	Parsnips	Carrots	Total
(a) Contribution per acre	£530	£490	£755	£960	
(b) Ranking	1	2	2	1	
(c) Minimum sales requirements in acres[a]		5	4		
(d) Acres allocated[b]	40			51	
(e) Recommended mix (acres)	40	5	4	51	
(f) Total contribution, (a) × (e)	£21 200	£2450	£3020	£48 960	£75 630
				Less fixed costs	£54 000
				Profit	£21 630

Notes

[a]The minimum sales requirement for turnips is 40 tonnes, and this will require the allocation of 5 acres (40 tonnes/8 tonnes yield per acre). The minimum sales requirement for parsnips is 36 tonnes, requiring the allocation of 4 acres (36 tonnes/9 tonnes yield per acre).

[b]Allocation of available acres to products on basis of a ranking that assumes that acres are the key factor.

(b) (i) Production should be concentrated on carrots, which have the highest contribution per acre (£960).

	(£)
(ii) Contribution from 100 acres of carrots (100 × £960)	96 000
Fixed overhead	54 000
Profit from carrots	42 000

(iii) $$\text{Break-even point in acres for carrots} = \frac{\text{fixed costs (£54 000)}}{\text{contribution per acre (£960)}}$$
$$= 56.25 \text{ acres}$$

Contribution in sales value for carrots = £91 125 (56.25 acres at £1620 sales revenue per acre).

9.34 (a) Total hours = 36 750 (120 000 × 0.25) + (45 000 × 0.15)
Fixed overhead rate per hour = £40 (£1 470 000/36 750 hours)

	Product A (£)	Product B (£)
Direct materials	2	40
Variable production overhead	28	4
Fixed production overhead	10 (0.25 × £40)	6 (0.15 × 40)
Total cost	40	50
Selling price	60	70
Profit	20	20

Assuming that the company focuses on profits per unit it will be indifferent between the 2 products.
Total net profit = £3 300 000 (120 000 × £20) + (45 000 × £20)

(b)

	Product A	Product B
Contribution per unit	£30 (60–30)	£26 (70–44)
Bottleneck hours	0.02	0.015
Contribution per bottleneck hour	£1500	£1733

Based on the contribution per bottleneck hour the maximum demand of product B should be produced. The maximum demand of product B requires 810 hours (54 000 × 0.015) leaving 2 265 hours (3075 – 810) to be allocated to product A. This will result in the production of 113 250 units (2265 hours/0.02) of A. The maximum profit is calculated as follows:

	£
Contribution from product A (113 250 × £30)	3 397 500
Contribution from product B (54 000 × £26)	1 404 000
	4 801 500
Less Fixed overhead cost	1 470 000
Net profit	3 331 500

(c) (i) Return per bottleneck hour = (Selling price – material cost)/(Time on bottleneck resource)

Product A = £2900 [(£60 – £2)/0.02 hours]

Product B = £2000 [(£70 – £40)/0.015 hours]

Product A should be sold up to its maximum capacity of utilizing 2880 bottleneck hours (144 000 units × 0.02 hours). This will leave 195 hours for product B thus enabling 13 000 units (195/0.015) to be produced. The maximum profit is calculated as follows:

	£
Throughput return from product A (144 000 × £58)	8 352 000
Contribution from product B (13 000 × £30)	390 000
	8 742 000
Less: variable overheads[a]	3 540 000
fixed overhead cost	1 470 000
Net profit	3 732 000

Note

[a]It is assumed that the variable overheads (e.g. direct labour) are fixed in the short-term. They are derived from part (a) – [(120 000 × £28) + (45 000 × £4)]

(c) (ii) Total overhead cost (£3 540 000 + £1 470 000) = £5 010 000

Overhead cost per bottleneck hour = £1629.27 (£5 010 000/3075 hours)

Throughput return per bottleneck hour = £2000 (see c (i))

Throughput accounting ratio = 1.2275 (£2000/£1 629.27)

(c) (iii) With throughput accounting a product should be sold if the throughput return per bottleneck hour is greater than the production cost (excluding direct materials) per throughput hour. In other words, the throughput accounting ratio should exceed 1.00. Increasing a product's throughput ratio can increase profits. The throughput ratio can be increased by:

1. Increasing the selling price or reducing material costs (note that product B has a very high material cost).
2. Reducing the time required on the bottleneck resource.
3. Creating more capacity of the bottleneck resource and if possible increase the capacity so that the bottleneck can be removed (subject to any additional financial outlays being justified).

Note that product B should be sold because its throughput ratio exceeds 1 but product A has the higher ranking because it has a higher throughput ratio.

(c) (iv) If material costs increase by 20% for product B the revised return per bottleneck hour will be £1467 [(£70 – £48)/0.015] giving a throughput ratio of 0.9 (£1467/£1629.27). Although this is less than 1 production of B can be justified in the short-term, given the special circumstances that apply. Product A is being produced up to its maximum demand and the balance of capacity applied to product B has no incremental cost and is thus fixed in the short-term. Therefore product B will contribute a cash flow of £22 (£70 – £48) per unit.

Chapter 10

10.22

	W (£000)	X (£000)	Y (£000)
Gross margin	1100	1750	1200
Less customer related costs:			
Sales visits at £500 per visit	55	50	85
Order processing at £100 per order placed	100	100	150
Despatch costs at £100 per order placed	100	100	150
Billing and collections at £175 per invoice raised	157	210	262
Profit/(loss)	688	1290	553
Ranking	2	1	3

Answer = C

10.23 Budgeted number of batches per product:

D = 1000 (100 000/100)
R = 2000 (100 000/50)
P = 2000 (50 000/25)
5000

Budgeted machine set-ups:

D = 3 000 (1000 × 3)
R = 8 000 (2000 × 4)
P = 12 000 (2000 × 6)
23 000

Budgeted cost per set-up = £150 000/23 000 = £6.52

Budgeted set-up cost per unit of R = (£6.52 × 4)/50 = £0.52

Answer = A

10.24 The answer to the question should describe the two-stage overhead allocation process and indicate that most cost systems use direct labour hours in the second stage. In today's production environment direct labour costs have fallen to about 10% of total costs for many firms and it is argued that direct labour is no longer a suitable base for assigning overheads to products. Using direct labour encourages managers to focus on reducing direct labour costs when they represent only a small percentage of total costs.

Approaches which are being adopted include:

(i) Changing from a direct labour overhead-recovery rate to recovery methods based on machine time. The justification for this is that overheads are caused by machine time rather than direct labour hours and cost.

(ii) Implementing activity-based costing systems that use many different cost drivers in the second stage of the two-stage overhead allocation procedure.

The answer should then go on to describe the benefits of ABC outlined in Chapter 10. Attention should also be drawn to the widespread use of direct labour hours by Japanese companies. According to Hiromoto[1] Japanese companies allocate overhead costs using the direct labour cost/hours to focus design engineers' attention on identifying opportunities to reduce the products' labour content. They use direct labour to encourage designers to make greater use of technology because this frequently improves long-term competitiveness by increasing quality, speed and flexibility of manufacturing.

Notes

[1]Hiromoto, T. (1988) 'Another hidden edge – Japanese management accounting', *Harvard Business Review*, July/August, pp. 22–6.

10.25 (a) Large-scale service organizations have a number of features that have been identified as being necessary to derive significant benefits from the introduction of ABC:

(i) They operate in a highly competitive environment;
(ii) They incur a large proportion of indirect costs that cannot be directly assigned to specific cost objects;
(iii) Products and customers differ significantly in terms of consuming overhead resources;
(iv) They market many different products and services.

Furthermore, many of the constraints imposed on manufacturing organizations, such as also having to meet financial accounting stock valuation requirements, or a reluctance to change or scrap existing systems, do not apply. Many service organizations have only recently implemented cost systems for the first time. This has occurred at the same time as when the weaknesses of existing systems and the benefits of ABC systems were being widely publicized. These conditions have provided a strong incentive for introducing ABC systems.

(b) The following may create problems for the application of ABC:

(i) Facility sustaining costs (such as property rents etc.) represent a significant proportion of total costs and may only be avoidable if the organization ceases business. It may be impossible to establish appropriate cost drivers;
(ii) It is often difficult to define products where they are of an intangible nature. Cost objects can therefore be difficult to specify;
(iii) Many service organizations have not previously had a costing system and much of the information required to set up an ABC system will be nonexistent. Therefore introducing ABC is likely to be expensive.

(c) The uses for ABC information for service industries are similar to those for manufacturing organizations:

(i) It leads to more accurate product costs as a basis for pricing decisions when cost-plus pricing methods are used;
(ii) It results in more accurate product and customer profitability analysis statements that provide a more appropriate basis for decision-making;
(iii) ABC attaches costs to activities and identifies the cost drivers that cause the costs. Thus ABC provides a better understanding of what causes costs and highlights ways of performing activities more effectively by reducing cost driver transactions. Costs can therefore be managed more effectively in the long term. Activities can also be analysed into value added and non-value added activities and by highlighting the costs of non-value added activities attention is drawn to areas where there is a potential for cost reduction without reducing the products' service potentials to customers.

(d) The following aspects would be of most interest to a regulator:

(i) The costing method used (e.g. Marginal, traditional full cost or ABC). This is of particular importance to verify whether or not reasonable prices are being set and that the organization is not taking advantage of its monopolistic situation. Costing information is also necessary to ascertain whether joint costs are fairly allocated so that cross-subsidization from one service to another does not apply;
(ii) Consistency in costing methods from period to period so that changes in costing methods are not used to distort pricing and profitability analysis;
(iii) In many situations a regulator may be interested in the ROI of the different services in order to ensure that excessive returns are not being obtained. A regulator will therefore be interested in the methods and depreciation policy used to value assets and how the costs of assets that are common to several services (e.g. corporate headquarters) are allocated. The methods used will influence the ROI of the different services.

10.26 (a) Total machine hours = (120 × 4 hrs) + (100 × 3 hrs) + (80 × 2 hrs) + (120 × 3 hrs) = (1300 hrs

$$\text{Machine hour overhead rate} = \frac{£10\,430 + £5250 + £3600 + £2100 + £4620}{1300 \text{ hrs}}$$
$$= £20 \text{ per machine hour}$$

Product	A (£)	B (£)	C (£)	D (£)
Direct material	40	50	30	60
Direct labour	28	21	14	21
Overheads at £20 per machine hour	80	60	40	60
	148	131	84	141
Units of output	120	100	80	120
Total cost	£17 760	£13 100	£6720	£16 920

(b)

Costs	(£)	Cost driver	Cost driver transactions	Cost per unit (£)
Machine department	10 430	Machine hours	1300 hours	8.02
Set-up costs	5 250	Production runs	21	250
Stores receiving	3 600	Requisitions raised	80 (4 × 20)	45
Inspection/quality control	2 100	Production runs	21	100
Materials handling	4 620	Number of orders executed	42	110

Note
Number of production runs = Total output (420 units)/20 units per set-up.
Number of orders executed = Total output (420 units)/10 units per order.
The total costs for each product are computed by multiplying the cost driver rate per unit by the quantity of the cost driver consumed by each product.

	A	B	C	D
Prime costs	8 160 (£68 × 120)	7 100	3520	9 720
Set ups	1 500 (£250 × 6)	1 250 (£250 × 5)	1000	1 500
Stores/receiving	900 (£45 × 20)	900	900	900
Inspection/quality	600 (£100 × 6)	500	400	600
Handling despatch	1 320 (£110 × 12)	1 100 (£110 × 10)	880	1 320
Machine dept cost[a]	3 851	2 407	1284	2 888
Total costs	16 331	13 257	7984	16 928

Note
[a]A = 120 units × 4 hrs × £8.02: B = 100 units × 3 hrs × £8.02

(c) Cost per unit

Costs from (a)	148.00	131.00	84.00	141.00
Costs from (b)	136.09	132.57	99.80	141.07
Difference	(11.91)	1.57	15.80	0.07

Product A is over-costed with the traditional system. Products B and C are under-costed and similar costs are reported with Product D. It is claimed that ABC more accurately measures resources consumed by products. Where cost-plus pricing is used, the transfer to an ABC system will result in different product prices. If activity-based costs are used for stock valuations then stock valuations and reported profits will differ.

10.27 (a) (i) Direct labour overhead rate

$$= \frac{\text{total overheads (£1 848 000)}}{\text{total direct labour hours (88 000)}}$$

= £21 per direct labour hour

Product costs

Product	X (£)	Y (£)	Z (£)
Direct labour	8	12	6
Direct materials	25	20	11
Overhead[a]	28	42	21
Total cost	61	74	38

Note

[a]X = 1⅓ hours × £21
Y = 2 hours × £21
Z = 1 hour × £21

(ii) Materials handling
Overhead rate

$$= \frac{\text{receiving department overheads (£435 000)}}{\text{direct material cost (£1 238 000)}} \times 100$$

= 35.14% of direct material cost

Machine hour overhead rate

$$= \frac{\text{other overheads (£1 413 000)}}{\text{76 000 machine hours}}$$

= £18.59 per machine hour

Product costs

Product	X (£)	Y (£)	Z (£)
Direct labour	8.00	12.00	6.00
Direct materials	25.00	20.00	11.00
Materials handling overhead	8.78 (£25 × 35.14%)	7.03 (£20 × 35.14%)	3.87 (£11 × 35.14%)
Other overheads[a] (machine hour basis)	24.79	18.59	37.18
Total cost	66.57	57.62	58.05

Note

[a]X = 1⅓ × £18.59
Y = 1 × £18.59
Z = 2 × £18.59

(b) The cost per transaction or activity for each of the cost centres is as follows:

Set-up cost
Cost per setup

$$= \frac{\text{setup cost (£30 000)}}{\text{number of production runs (30)}} = £1000$$

Receiving
Cost per receiving order

$$= \frac{\text{receiving cost (£435 000)}}{\text{number of orders (270)}} = £1611$$

Packing
Cost per packing order

$$= \frac{\text{packing cost (£250 000)}}{\text{number of orders (32)}} = £7812$$

Engineering
Cost per production order

$$= \frac{\text{engineering cost (£373 000)}}{\text{number of production orders (50)}} = £7460$$

The total set-up cost for the period was £30 000 and the cost per transaction or activity for the period is £1000 per set-up. Product X required three production runs, and thus £3000 of the set-up cost is traced to the production of product X for the period. Thus the cost per set-up per unit produced for product X is £0.10 (£3000/30 000 units).

Similarly, product Z required 20 set-ups, and so £20 000 is traced to product Z. Hence the cost per set-up for product Z is £2.50 (£20 000/8000 units).

The share of a support department's cost that is traced to each unit of output for each product is therefore calculated as follows:

$$\text{cost per transaction} \times \frac{\text{number of transactions per product}}{\text{number of units produced}}$$

The unit standard costs for products X, Y and Z using an activity-based costing system are

	X	Y	Z
Direct labour	£8.00	£12.00	£6.00
Direct materials	25.00	20.00	11.00
Machine overhead[a]	13.33	10.00	20.00
Set-up costs	0.10	0.35	2.50
Receiving[b]	0.81	2.82	44.30
Packing[c]	2.34	1.17	19.53
Engineering[d]	3.73	3.73	23.31
Total manufacturing cost	53.31	50.07	126.64

Notes

[a]Machine hours × machine overhead rate (£760 000/76 000 hrs)
[b]X = (£1611 × 15)/30 000
Y = (£1611× 35)/20 000
Z = (£1611 × 220)/8000
[c]X = (£7812 × 9)/30 000
Y = (£7812 × 3)/20 000
Z = (£7812 × 20)/8000
[d]X = (£7460 × 15)/30 000
Y = (£7460 × 10)/20 000
Z = (£7460 × 25)/8000

(c) The traditional product costing system assumes that products consume resources in relation to volume measures such as direct labour, direct materials or machine hours. The activity-based system recognizes that some overheads are unrelated to production volume, and uses cost drivers that are independent of production volume. For example, the activity-based system assigns the following percentage of costs to product Z, the low volume product:

Set-up-related costs 66.67% (20 out of 30 set-ups)
Delivery-related costs 62.5% (20 out of 32 deliveries)
Receiving costs 81.5% (220 out of 270 receiving orders)
Engineering-related costs 50% (25 out of 50 production orders)

In contrast, the current costing system assigns the cost of the above activities according to production volume, measured in machine hours. The total machine hours are

Product X 40 000 (30 000 × 1⅓)
Product Y 20 000 (20 000 × 1)
Product Z 16 000 (8 000 × 2)
76 000

Therefore 21% (16 000/76 000) of the non-volume-related costs are assigned to product Z if machine hours are used as the allocation base. Hence the traditional system undercosts the low-volume product, and, on applying the above approach, it can be shown that the high-volume product (product X) is overcosted. For example, 53% of the costs (40 000/76 000) are traced to product X with the current system, whereas the activity-based system assigns a much lower proportion of non-volume-related costs to this product.

10.28 Part one

(a) Single factory direct labour hour overhead rate = £310 000/2000 hours = £155 per direct labour hour

Component	r (£)	s (£)	t (£)
Direct labour costs at £12 per hour	300	5 760	600
Direct materials	1200	2 900	1 800
Overheads (direct labour hours × £155 per hour)	3875	74 400	7 750
Total costs	5375	83 060	10 150
Cost per unit	£9.60	£6.49	£4.23

(b) In Chapter 10 it was pointed out that ABC systems involve the following stages:

(i) identifying the major activities that take place in an organization;
(ii) creating a cost pool/cost centre for each activity;
(iii) determining the cost driver for each activity;
(iv) assigning the cost of activities to cost objects (e.g. products, components, customers, etc.) according to their demand for activities.

The consultants have already identified the most significant activities. They are receiving component consignments from suppliers, setting up equipment for production runs, quality inspections and dispatching orders to customers. The following shows the assignment of the costs to these activities:

	Receiving supplies (£000)	Set-ups (£000)	Quality inspections (£000)	Dispatching (£000)	Total (£000)
Equipment operation expenses[a]	18.75	87.50		18.75	125.00
Maintenance[a]	3.75	17.50		3.75	25.00
Technicians' wages initially allocated to maintenance (30% of £85 = £25.50) and then reallocated to activities on the same basis as maintenance[a]	3.83	17.85		3.82	25.50
Technicians wages allocation (excluding portion allocated to maintenance)[b]		34.00	25.50		59.50
Stores wages[c]	35.00				35.00
Dispatch wages[d]				40.00	40.00
Total	61.33	156.85	25.50	66.32	310.00

Notes
[a]Allocated on the basis 15%, 70% and 15% as specified in the question
[b]Allocated on the basis 30%, 40% and 30% (of £85) as specified in the question
[c]Directly attributable to the receiving component supplies activity
[d]Directly attributable to the dispatching activity

The next stage is to identify cost drivers for each activity and establish cost driver rates by dividing the activity costs by a measure of cost driver usage for the period. The calculations are as follows:

Receiving supplies (£61 330/980) = £62.58 per component consignment received
Performing set-ups (£156 850/1020) = £153.77 per set-up
Quality inspections (£25 500/640) = £39.84 per quality inspection
Dispatching goods (£66 320/420) = £157.93 per goods order dispatched

Finally, the costs are assigned to components based on their cost driver usage. The assignments are as follows:

	r (£)	s (£)	t (£)
Direct labour	300.00	5 760.00	600.00
Direct materials	1 200.00	2 900.00	1 800.00
Receiving supplies	2 628.36	1 501.92	1 752 24
Performing set-ups	2 460.32	2 767.86	1 845.24
Quality inspection	398.40	318.72	717.12
Dispatching goods	3 474.46	13 424.05	7 264.78
Total costs	10 461.54	26 672.55	13 979.38
Number of units produced	560	12 800	2 400
Cost per unit	£18.68	£2.08	£5.82

For component r the overhead costs have been assigned as follows:

Receiving supplies (42 receipts at £62.58)
Performing set-ups (16 production runs at £153.77)
Quality inspection (10 at £39.84)
Dispatching goods (22 at £157.93)

(c) *Cost assigned to component z*

Quarterly charge (for 1000 units)			(£)
Design cost	£40 000 ÷ 8		5 000
Direct labour	80 × £12		960
Direct materials			2 000
Overheads:			
Receiving supplies		£62.58 × 20	1 252
Set-ups		£153.77 × 15	2 307
Quality inspection		£39.84 × 30	1 195
Dispatching goods		£157.93 × 4	632
Total			13 346
25% mark up			3 337
Charge per quarter			16 683

According to the information provided in the question the short-term incremental cost attributable to the order is as follows:

	(£)
Design costs (£40 000/7.02 annuity factor[a])	5 698
Direct labour (80 hours at £12)	960
Direct materials	2 000
Labour related variable overheads[b]	3 720
Inspection related variable overheads[b]	4 359
	16 737

Notes

[a]Represents the present value of £8000 received in 8 quarterly instalments by dividing £40 000 by the annuity factor for 8 periods at 3% (present values are explained in Chapter 13).

[b]The question states that 40% of the overheads are variable in the short-term and 50% of these costs vary with direct labour hours and the remaining 50% vary with the number of quality inspections. Therefore the variable overhead rates are:

Labour related = (310 000 × 0.6 × 0.5)/2000 = £46.50 per direct labour hour
Inspection related = (310 000 × 0.6 × 0.5)/640 = £145.31 per quality inspection
Charge to component Z
Labour related = 80 hours at £46.50 = £3720
Inspection related = 30 inspections at £145.31 = £4359

The method suggested by the sales manager results in a reported product cost that is lower than the short-term incremental costs of the order. This suggests that the proposed costing system does not accurately assign costs to cost objects or that the variable cost analysis implied in the question is incorrect. The discrepancy between the above reported costs should be investigated and the design of the costing system reviewed.

10.28 (Part two)

(a) For the ideas concerning cost behaviour that underpin ABC see 'A comparison of traditional and ABC systems' and activity hierarchies in Chapter 10. You should refer to 'The emergence of ABC systems' in Chapter 10 for an explanation of why ABC may be better attuned to the modern manufacturing environment. For an explanation of why the company might not obtain a more meaningful impression of product costs through the use of ABC see 'Cost versus benefits considerations' and 'Pitfalls in using ABC information' in Chapter 10.

(b) The answer should point out that the current system uses a blanket overhead rate and can be improved by retaining the traditional system and establishing separate departmental or cost centre overhead rates. For a discussion of these issues you should refer to 'Cost-benefit issues and cost system design', 'Blanket overhead rates' and 'Cost centre overhead rates' in Chapter 3.

(c) See 'Pitfalls in using ABC information' in Chapter 10 for the answer to this question.

10.28 (Part three)

(a) See 'Just-in-time systems', 'Cost of quality' and 'Cost management and the value chain' in Chapter 22 for the answer to this question.

(b) Manufacturing in large batches leads to a build up of WIP, increases inventory holding costs and consumes large amounts of space because large batch production normally requires a functional production layout. For a more detailed discussion of the costs associated with large batch sizes you should refer to 'Just-in-time systems' in Chapter 22. However, manufacturing in small batch sizes can also result in additional costs. Examples include the increase in set-up costs (arising from more set-ups associated with producing in small batches) and quality inspection costs where a sample from each batch must be inspected to ensure that the batch meets quality requirements. The statement in the question is referring to the costs associated with different batch sizes.

Traditional volume-based costing systems, such as the one operated by KL's, fail to distinguish between the different costs associated with producing products or components in different batch sizes. To capture the costs associated with producing in different batch sizes requires that non-volume-based cost drivers are used. The use of non-volume-based cost drivers is a distinguishing feature of ABC systems. For a more detailed explanation of how traditional costing systems provide misleading cost information because of their failure to identify and assign batch-related costs you should refer to 'Errors arising from relying on misleading product costs' and 'Batch-level activities' in Chapter 10.

(c) This is a very open ended question and there is no specific answer. Academic research can be viewed as providing a constantly updated stock of concepts and techniques that are available to practitioners and that should be considered alongside existing techniques used in practice. In particular the choice of a particular technique should be based on cost–benefit criteria. If academic research is ignored, or misunderstood, accounting systems would be implemented without an awareness of alternative systems that are available. Consequently, there would be a tendency to perpetuate existing practices rather than selecting a preferable alternative. Also an understanding of research enables practitioners to be aware of the conceptual weaknesses of the techniques that are used in practice and thus seek to avoid the pitfalls when interpreting the information generated by these techniques. Academic research often represents a theoretical ideal and not necessarily a set of techniques that must be implemented. The cost versus benefits criteria must always be considered in determining the extent to which a cost system approximates the theoretical Ideal.

Chapter 11

11.17

Units	Total variable costs (£)	Selling price per unit (£)	Total sales revenue (£)	Total contribution (£)
10	40 000	6 500	65 000	25 000
11	44 400	6 350	69 850	25 450
12	49 200	6 200	74 400	25 200
13	54 400	6 050	78 650	24 250

It is apparent from the cost and revenue functions that contribution declines beyond an output of 11 units so there is no need to compute the contribution for 14 and 20 units. The most profitable output is 11 units.
Answer = B

11.18 (a) Variable cost plus 20% = £30 × 1.20 = £36
Total cost plus 20% = £37 × 1.20 = £44.40

Advantages of variable costs include that it avoids arbitrary allocations, identifies short-term relevant costs, simplicity and mark-up can be increased to provide a contribution to fixed costs and profit. The disadvantages are that it represents only a partial cost, it is short-term oriented and ignores price/demand relationships.

Advantages of total cost include that it attempts to include all costs, reduces the possibility that fixed costs will not be covered and simplicity. The disadvantages are that total cost is likely to involve some arbitrary apportionments and the price/demand relationship is ignored.

(b) See 'Pricing policies' in Chapter 11 for the answer to this question. The answer should point out that price skimming is likely to lead to a higher initial price whereas a pricing penetration policy is likely to lead to a lower initial price.

11.19 (a) The question states that fixed manufacturing costs are absorbed into the unit costs by a charge of 200% of variable cost. Therefore unit variable cost is one third of total unit cost.

Contribution per processing hour

	Product A (£)	Product B (£)	Product C (£)
Selling price	20	31	39
Variable cost	6	8	10
Production contribution	14	23	29
Contribution per processing hour	14	23	14.50
Ranking	3	1	2

Optimal programme

	Output	Hours used	Contribution (£)
Product B	8000	8000	184 000
C	2000	4000	58 000
A	1500	1500	21 000
			263 000

Existing programme

	Output	Hours used	Contribution (£)
Product A	6000	6000	84 000
B	6000	6000	138 000
C	750	1500	21 750
			243 750

Contribution and profits will increase by £19 250 if the optimal production programme is implemented. An additional hour of processing would be used to increase product A by one unit, thus increasing contribution by £14. Therefore the shadow price (or opportunity cost) of one scarce processing hour is £14.

Capacity is limited to 13 500 hours. It is therefore necessary to allocate output on the basis of marginal contribution per hour. Products A and B each require 1 processing hour, whereas product C requires 2 processing hours. To simplify the calculations, hours are allocated in 2000 blocks. Consequently, the allocation of the first 2000 hours will yield a marginal contribution of £37 000 from A, £52 000 from B and £29 500 from C. Note that an output of 2000 units of C will require 4000 processing hours, and will yield a contribution of £59 000. Therefore the contribution from 2000 hours will be £29 500. In other words, the marginal contributions for A and B in the above schedule are expressed in terms of blocks of 2000 hours, whereas the marginal contribution for C is expressed in terms of blocks of 4000 hours. To express the marginal contribution of C in terms of blocks of 2000 hours, it is necessary to divide the final column of the above schedule by 2.

Processing hours are allocated as follows:

	Hours	Marginal contribution (£)
Product B	first 2000	52 000
B	next 2000	48 000
B	2 000	44 000
B	2 000	40 000
A	2 000	37 000
B	2 000	36 000
A	1 500 (balance)	24 250[a]
	13 500	281 250

Note

[a]3500 × (£23.50 – £6) – £37 000 = £24 250

The optimum output is £10 000 units of product B at a selling price of £30 and 3500 units of A at a selling price of £23.50, and contribution will be maximized at £281 250. It is assumed that it is company policy to change selling prices only in steps of £1.

(b)

	Production A			Production B			Production C		
Demand	Price (£)	Total contribution (£000)	Marginal contribution (£000)	Price (£)	Total contribution (£000)	Marginal contribution (£000)	Price (£)	Total contribution (£000)	Marginal contribution (£000)
2 000	24.50	37	37	34	52	52	39.50	59	59
4 000	23.50	70	33	33	100	48	39.00	116	57
6 000	22.50	99	29	32	144	44	38.50	171	55
8 000	21.50	124	25	31	184	40	38.00	224	53
10 000	20.50	145	21	30	220	36	37.50	275	51
12 000	19.50	162	17	29	252	32	37.00	324	49
14 000	18.50	175	13	28	280	28	36.50	371	47

11.20 (a) *New machine not leased*

Marginal cost per unit = materials (£2) + piecework rate (£0.50) + royalties (£0.50) = £3

So total cost function = £50 000 fixed costs + £3x

If the selling price is £5, sales demand will be zero. To increase demand by 1 unit, selling price must be reduced by £0.01/1000 units or £0.00001.

Therefore the maximum selling price attainable for an output of x units is £5 – £0.00001x

Therefore

$$P = 5 - £0.00001x$$
$$TR = x(5 - 0.00001x)$$
$$= 5x - 0.00001x^2$$
$$MR = \frac{dTR}{dx} = 5 - 0.00002x$$
$$\text{Marginal cost} = £3$$

So the optimum output is where MC = MR

i.e. 3 = 5 – 0.00002x

That is,

$$0.00002x = 2$$

Therefore x = 100 000 units (optimum output level)

Selling price at optimum level = 5 – 0.00001 × 100 000 = £4

Maximum profit is TR – TC

$$TR = £400\,000\ (100\,000 \times £4)$$
$$TC = \underline{£350\,000}\ (100\,000 \times £3) + (£50\,000\ FC)$$
$$\text{Profit} = \underline{£50\,000}$$

New machine leased

Revised total cost function = £165 000 + £2x

Note that fixed costs increase by £115 000

Optimal output is where MC = MR

i.e., 2 = 5 – 0.00002x

That is,

$$0.00002x = 3$$

Therefore x = 150 000 units (optimum output level)

Selling price at optimum output level = 5 – 0.00001 × 150 000 = £3.50

Maximum profit is TR – TC

$$TR = £525\,000\ (150\,000 \times £3.50)$$
$$TC = \underline{£465\,000}\ (150\,000 \times £2) + £165\,000$$
$$\text{Profit} = \underline{£60\,000}$$

The new machine should be hired, since profit will increase by £10 000. In order to obtain the maximum profit, a price of £3.50 per unit should be charged, which will produce a demand of 150 000 units.

(b) (i)

$$P = 100 - 2Q$$
$$TR = Q(100 - 2Q)$$
$$= \underline{\underline{100Q - 2Q^2}}$$
$$MR = \frac{dTR}{dQ} = 100 - 4Q$$
$$\text{Total cost function} = Q^2 + 10Q + 500$$
$$MC = \frac{dTC}{dQ} = 2Q = 10$$

The optimal output level is where MC = MR, i.e.

$$2Q + 10 = 100 - 4Q$$

So

$$6Q = 90$$
$$Q = 15$$

Therefore, optimal output level is 15 000 units.

Substituting into the demand function

$$P = 100 - 2Q:$$
$$P = 100 - 2 \times 15$$
$$P = £70 \text{ per unit optimum selling price}$$

$$\text{Profit} = TR - TC$$
$$TR = 1050\ (15 \text{ units} \times £70)$$
$$TC = \underline{875}\ (15^2 + (10 \times 15) + 500))$$
$$\text{Profit} = \underline{175}$$

So the maximum profit = £175 000

(ii) TR = 100Q – 2Q^2

Total revenue will be maximized when MR = 0

MR = 100 – 4Q (see b(i))

So the total revenue is maximized where 100 – 4Q = 0

Q = 25 (i.e. 25 000 units)

Substituting into the demand function:

$$P = 100 - 2Q$$
$$= 100 - 2 \times 25$$
$$= £50 \text{ per unit}$$

Total sales revenue will be £1 250 000 (25 000 units × £50)

$$\text{Loss} = TR - TC$$
$$TR = £1\,250\,000$$
$$TC = \underline{£1\,375\,000}\ (25^2 + (10 \times 25) + 500))$$
$$\text{Loss} = \underline{(£125\,000)}$$

Summary of results

	Output level (units)	Selling price	Total revenue	Total profit (loss)
(i) Profit maximization	15 000	£70	£1 050 000	£175 000
(ii) Sales maximization	25 000	£50	£1 125 000	(£125 000)

11.21 Several factors should be considered in the determination of pricing policy. The most important is price elasticity of demand, but if price is to be set in order to maximize profits then knowledge of cost structures and cost behaviour will also be of great importance. Knowledge of price–demand relationships and costs at different output levels is necessary to determine the optimum price. This is the price that results in marginal revenue being equal to marginal cost. The emphasis should be placed on providing information on the effect of changes in output on total cost rather than providing average unit cost information.

When cost information is presented using absorption costing, the resulting selling price calculation will be a function of the overhead apportionments and recovery methods used and the assumed volume of production. At best, the calculated selling price will only be appropriate for one level of production, and a different selling price would be produced for different output levels. Single cost figures calculated using absorption costing also fail to supply information on the effect of changes in output on total cost.

For other disadvantages that appear when absorption costing is used in the determination of pricing policy see 'Limitations of cost-plus pricing' in Chapter 11.

The advantage claimed from the use of absorption costing in price determination is that all manufacturing costs are included in the cost per unit calculation, so that no major manufacturing cost is overlooked. With variable costing, there is a danger that output will be priced to earn a low contribution that is insufficient to cover total fixed costs. Also, the use of production facilities entails an opportunity cost from the alternative use of capacity forgone. The fixed cost per unit of capacity used can be regarded as an attempt to approximate the opportunity cost from the use of productive capacity. In spite of these claimed advantages, the presentation of relevant costs for pricing decisions (see Chapter 11) is likely to be preferable to information based on absorption cost.

11.22 (a) Short-run profits are maximized at the output level where marginal revenue equals marginal cost. The optimum selling price is that which corresponds to the optimal output level (see Figure 11.3 in Chapter 11). From Figure 11.3 you will see that, with imperfect competition (no pricing decision is necessary with perfect competition), firms are faced with a downward-sloping demand curve. The highest selling price will apply to the first unit sold, but Figure 11.3 indicates that it is unlikely that this will be at the point where marginal revenue equals marginal cost.

(b) The objective is to maximize total contribution not unit contribution. Contribution per unit sold is the difference between marginal revenue and marginal cost. It is unlikely that contribution per unit will remain constant over the entire range of output. In Chapter 8 we noted that variable cost per unit and selling price per unit may change in relation to output. With a downward-sloping demand curve, marginal revenue will decline, thus causing contribution per unit to decline as output is increased. From Figure 11.3 we can see that profit is maximized where MR = MC. This is not at the point where unit contribution (difference between marginal revenue and marginal cost) is the greatest.

(c) Joint costs are allocated on an arbitrary basis, and costs that include arbitrary allocations are inappropriate for product, project or divisional comparisons. Performance should be judged on the basis of comparisons between controllable costs and revenues. With profit centres, measures such as controllable residual income should be used, whereas contribution should be used for comparing products.

(d) This statement presumably refers to the use of cost-plus pricing methods. If prices are set completely on a cost-plus basis then accounting information will determine the selling price. Consequently, the marketing and production people might feel that they have no influence in determining selling prices with pricing dominated by a concern for recovering full costs. If cost-plus pricing is used in a rigid way then marketing and production people may well consider the statement in the question to be correct. Cost information should be used in a flexible manner, and is one of several variables that should be used in determining selling prices. If this approach is adopted then the statement in the question will be incorrect.

(e) Management accounting should not be constrained by the requirements of external reporting. The emphasis should be on assembling financial information so as to help managers make good decisions and to plan and control activities effectively. In Chapter 9 we noted that there are strong arguments for adopting a system of variable costing in preference to absorption costing. If management accounts were consistent with SSAP 9 then the financial information might motivate managers to make wrong decisions.

(f) All costs must be covered in the long run if a firm is to be profitable. Therefore the objective should be to recover R and D expenditure in the long-run. R and D expenditure should be regarded as a pool of fixed costs to which products should generate sufficient contribution. Giant Steps Ltd should not rely on a policy of recovering R and D in relation to expenditure on each individual product. Price/demand relationships for some products might mean that the associated R and D cannot be recovered, while other products might be able to recover more than their fair share. Once a product is launched, only the incremental costs are relevant to the pricing decision. The objective should be to obtain a selling price in excess of relevant short-run costs and to provide a contribution to fixed costs and profit. R and D should be regarded as part of the pool of fixed costs to be recovered.

11.23 (a) See Chapters 9–11 for the answer to this question. In particular, the answer should indicate:

(i) Information presented to the product manager should be *future* costs, not past costs.

(ii) *Incremental* cost and revenue information should be presented, and the excess of incremental revenues over incremental costs compared for different selling price and sales quantity levels. Costs that are common to all alternatives are not relevant for decision-making purposes.

(iii) Decisions involve a choice between alternatives, and this implies that a choice leads to forgoing *opportunities*. Therefore relevant cost information for a pricing decision should include future cash costs and imputed (opportunity) cost.

(iv) *Sunk costs* are past costs and not relevant to the pricing decision.

(v) Pricing decisions should be based on estimates of demand schedules and a comparison of marginal revenues and costs.

(b) See 'Reasons for using cost-based pricing formulae' in Chapter 11 for the answer to this question. Note that overhead allocation is an attempt to provide an estimate of the long-run costs of producing a product.

(c) There is no specific answer to this question. The author's views on this question are expressed in Chapters 10 and 11.

Chapter 12

12.11 The calculation of accurate expected values are dependent on the accuracy of the probability distribution. It also takes no account of risk.

Therefore the answer is D.

12.12 Expected income with advertising = (£200 000 × 0.95) + (£70 000 × 0.05) = £193 500
Expected income without advertising = (£200 000 × 0.7) + (£70 000 × 0.3) = £161 000
The maximum amount the company should pay for advertising is the increase in expected value of £32 500.
Therefore the answer is A.

12.13 (a)

Expected cash flows	Ranking
L = (£500 × 0.2) + (£470 × 0.5) + (£550 × 0.3) = £500	2
M = (£400 × 0.2) + (£550 × 0.5) + (£570 × 0.3) = £526	1
N = (£450 × 0.2) + (£400 × 0.5) + (£475 × 0.3) = £432.5	4
O = (£360 × 0.2) + (£400 × 0.5) + (£420 × 0.3) = £398	5
P = (£600 × 0.2) + (£500 × 0.5) + (£425 × 0.3) = £497.5	3

Answer = B

(b) Without additional information machine M (see part a) will be purchased. If perfect information is obtained the choice will be matched with the level of demand. Therefore if the market condition is predicted to be poor P will be chosen and if the market condition is predicted to be good or excellent M will be chosen. The expected values of these outcomes is:
(£600 × 0.2 for P) + (£550 × 0.5 for M) + (£570 × 0.3 for M) = £566
This represents an increase in £40 000 expected value (£566 – £526)
Answer = D

12.14 (a) There are two possible selling prices and three possible direct material costs for each selling price. The calculation of unit contributions are as follows:

	£15 sales price			£24 sales price		
	No purchasing contract	Contract (40 000 kg)	Contract (60 000 kg)	No purchasing contract	Contract (40 000 kg)	Contract (60 000 kg)
Selling price	15	15	15	24	24	24
Material cost	(8)	(7.50)	(7)	(8)	(7.50)	(7)
Other variable cost	(5)	(5)	(5)	(5)	(5)	(5)
Unit contribution	£2	2.5	3	£11	11.50	12

The realizable value from the sale of excess materials is as follows:

	16 000 kg and over	Less than 16 000 kg
Sales price	2.90	2.40
Less selling, delivery and insurance costs	0.90	0.90
Realizable value per kg	£2.00	£1.50

Statement of outcomes

Sales quantities (000)	Total contribution (£000)	Fixed costs (£000)	Profit/(loss) on sale of materials (£000)	Profit (£000)	Probability	Expected value (£000)
Sales price of £15 (no contract)						
20	40	50	—	–10	0.1	–1
30	60	50	—	10	0.6	6
40	80	50	—	30	0.3	9
						14
Sales price of £15 (40 000 kg contract)						
20	50	50	—	—	0.1	—
30	75	50	—	25	0.6	15
40	100	50	—	50	0.3	15
						30
Sales price of £15 (60 000 kg contract)						
20	60	50	–30[a]	–20	0.1	–2
30	90	50	—	40	0.6	24
40	120	50	—	70	0.3	21
						43
Sales price of £24 (no contract)						
8	88	160	—	–72	0.1	–7.2
16	176	160	—	16	0.3	4.8
20	220	160	—	60	0.3	18.0
24	264	160	—	104	0.3	31.2
						46.8
Sales price of £24 (40 000 kg contract)						
8	92	160	–42[b]	–110	0.1	–11.0
16	184	160	–18[b]	6	0.3	1.8
20	230	160	—	70	0.3	21.0
24	276	160	—	116	0.3	34.8
						46.6
Sales price of £24 (60 000 kg contract)						
8	96	160	–66	–130	0.1	–13
16	192	160	–42	–10	0.3	–3
20	240	160	–30	50	0.3	15
24	288	160	–24	104	0.3	31.2
						30.2

Notes
[a]Sales quantity of 20 000 units results in 40 000 kg being used. Therefore 20 000 kg of the raw material are sold at a realizable value of £2 per kg. The cost of acquiring the raw materials is £3.50 per kg. Consequently 20 000 kg are sold at a loss of £1.50 per kg.
[b]24 000 kg sold at a loss of £1.75 per kg.

(b) (i) The highest expected value of profits occurs when the sales price is £24 with no contract for the supply of raw materials.
(ii) In order to minimize the effect of the worst outcome then the sales price should be £15 and a contract to purchase 40 000 kg entered into.
(iii) Applying Central's own 'Desirability' measure, the best choice is a sales price of £15 combined with entering into a contract of 60 000 kg. The 'Desirability' measure is calculated as follows:

Strategy Price per unit	Contract	Expected monetary value (£000)	Worst outcome (£000)	'Desirability' $L + 3E$
£15	none	14	–10	32
£15	40 000 kg	30	0	90
£15	60 000 kg	43	–20	109
£24	none	46.8	–72	68.4
£24	40 000 kg	46.6	–110	29.8
£24	60 000 kg	30.2	–130	–39.4

(c) (i) Other factors to be considered are:
(A) The reliability of future supplies of raw materials might be subject to uncertainty. In this situation it may be preferable to operate at a lower production volume and sales.

(B) If there is spare production capacity then the labour cost might not be a relevant cost. More information is required regarding the alternative use of the labour if a lower production volume is selected.

(ii) For a discussion of the expected value approach see Chapter 12. The criteria of pessimism in (b) (ii) focuses on the least desirable outcome. The 'desirability' measure is an attempt to formalize the importance of the two relevant measures to a particular decision-maker by attaching a weighting to the expected value and the worst possible outcome. It may be better to compare the probability distributions rather than using summary measures of the distributions.

12.15 (a) Chemical X is added at the rate of 1 kg per 100 kg of waste. Therefore the possible requirements for chemical X are 500 000 kg (50 million of waste at 1 kg per 100 kg of waste), 380 000 and 300 000. The cost of purchasing chemical X is calculated as follows:

Demand (000kg)	Cost per kg (£)	Total cost (£000)
High advance order of 500 000 kg		
500	1.00	500
380	1.00 + 0.25 = 1.25	475
300	1.00 + 0.60 = 1.60	480
Medium advance order of 380 000 kg		
500	1.20 – 0.10 = 1.10	550
380	1.20	456
300	1.20 + 0.25 = 1.45	435
Low advance order of 300 000 kg		
500	1.40 – 0.15 = 1.25	625
380	1.40 – 0.10 = 1.30	494
300	1.40	420

Aluminium is extracted at 15% of waste input thus resulting in the following extraction levels:

	High	Medium	Low
Aluminium extracted (000 kg)	7500	5700	4500
Contribution at 30% of £0.65 per kg (£000)	1462.5	1111.5	877.5

The net contribution is calculated as follows:

Advance order of chemical X	Level of waste	Probability	Contribution (excluding X) (£000)	Chemical X cost (£000)	Net contribution (£000)
High	High	0.30	1462.5	500	962.5
	Medium	0.50	1111.5	475	636.5
	Low	0.20	877.5	480	397.5
Medium	High	0.30	1462.5	550	912.5
	Medium	0.50	1111.5	456	655.5
	Low	0.20	877.5	435	442.5
Low	High	0.30	1462.5	625	837.5
	Medium	0.50	1111.5	494	617.5
	Low	0.20	877.5	420	457.5

(b) The expected value for each advance order is calculated as follows:
High chemical X advance order = (£962.5 × 0.30) + (636.5 × 0.50) + (397.5 × 0.2) = £686 500
Medium chemical X advance order = (£912.5 × 0.30) + (655.5 × 0.50) + (442.5 × 0.2) = £690 000
Low chemical X advance order = (£837.5 × 0.30) + (617.5 × 0.50) + (457.5 × 0.2) = £651 500
Adopting the expected value rule the medium advance order for chemical X should be entered into.

(c) The maximax technique is based on the assumption that the best payoff (i.e. the highest contribution) will occur for each alternative. Based on this criterion the high advance order will be selected because it yields the largest possible net contribution of £962 500. This indicates a risk seeking preference by management. Note also that the high advance order has a 20% probability that the worst possible outcome of £397 500 will occur.

The maximin strategy assumes that the worst possible outcome will occur and that the decision-maker should choose the largest possible payoff under this assumption. The worst possible outcomes are as follows:

High advance order = £397 500
Medium advance order = £442 500
Low advance order = £457 500

Adopting the maximin strategy the low advance order should be selected. This approach indicates a risk averse attitude.

(d) Asssuming perfect information a perfect prediction of the level of demand would be obtained. If the high level of waste is the outcome the high advance order will be made because this gives the highest contribution for the high level of waste. Similarly, if the medium level of waste is the outcome the medium advance order will be made because this gives the highest contribution for the medium level of waste. Finally, if the low level of waste is the outcome the highest contribution will be derived from a low advance order.

When the decision to employ the consultant is made, it is not known which level of waste will be predicted and therefore the best esimates that high, medium and low levels of waste will be predicted are 0.3, 0.5 and 0.2. Therefore the expected value of perfect information will be as follows:

Consultant's advice	Chemical X advance order	Contribution (£000)	Probability	(£000)
High waste	high	962.5	0.30	288.75
Medium waste	medium	655.5	0.50	327.75
Low waste	low	457.5	0.20	91.50
				708.00
Expected value without consultant's advice				690.00
Hence the maximum payable to consultant =				18.00

(e) Imperfect information recognizes that the consultant's information may not give a 100% perfect prediction. Probabilites are attached to the likelihood that the consultant will be correct or incorrect. Revised probabilities of a given waste level based on the combined effect of the original probabilities of waste available for reprocessing and the probability of the actual waste level given the content of a particular report from the consultant are then calculated. These revised probabilities measure the probability of a particular level of waste being available given a high, medium or low forecast. The expected value is then calculated and therefore the maximum sum payable to the consultant for the information. The major problem is that it is necessary to predict in advance the likelihood that the consultant's forecast will be correct or incorrect.

12.16 (a) (i) See the decision tree shown in Figure Q12.16.

(ii) 1. The assumption underlying the maximin technique is that the worst outcome will occur. The decision-maker should select the outcome with the largest possible payoff assuming the worst possible outcome occurs. From the decision tree we can see that the payoffs for the worst possible outcomes are as follows:

	Payoff (£000)
Hire of machine 200	55
Hire of machine 300	45
Hire of machine 600	38.5
Do not franchise	90

The decision is not to franchise using the maximum criterion.

2. The expected values for each alternative (see Figure Q12.16) are as follows:

	(£000)
Hire of machine 200	87.0
Hire of machine 300	101.0
Hire of machine 600	99.0
Do not franchise	90.0

The company will maximize the expected value of the contributions if it hires the 300 batch machine.

3. The probability of a contribution of less than £100 000 for each alternative can be found by adding the joint probabilities from payoffs of less than £100 000. The probabilities are as follows:

Hire of machine 200	= 0.85
Hire of machine 300	= 0.55
Hire of machine 600	= 0.65
Do not franchise	= 1.00

The company should hire the 300 machine adopting this decision criterion.

FIGURE Q12.16

Decision tree

Franchise or do not franchise	Hire of machine	Sales	Outcomes Unit contribution		Payoff (£000)	Joint probabiity	Expected value (£000)
Franchise	Machine 200 (£5000)	600 000 0.5	£0.20 0.1	=	115	0.05	5.75
			£0.15 0.1	=	85	0.05	4.25
			£0.10 0.8	=	55	0.40	22.00
		1 000 000 0.5	£0.20 0.1	=	195	0.05	9.75
			£0.15 0.1	=	145	0.05	7.25
			£0.10 0.8	=	95	0.40	38.00
						1.00	87.00
	Machine 300 (£15 000)	600 000 0.5	£0.20 0.2	=	105	0.10	10.50
			£0.15 0.5	=	75	0.25	18.75
			£0.10 0.3	=	45	0.15	6.75
		1 000 000 0.5	£0.20 0.2	=	185	0.10	18.50
			£0.15 0.5	=	135	0.25	33.75
			£0.10 0.3	=	85	0.15	12.75
						1.00	101.00
	Machine 600 (£21 500)	600 000 0.5	£0.20 0.3	=	98.5	0.15	14.775
			£0.15 0.1	=	68.5	0.05	3.425
			£0.10 0.6	=	38.5	0.30	11.550
		1 000 000 0.5	£0.20 0.5	=	178.5	0.25	44.625
			£0.15 0.2	=	128.5	0.10	12.850
			£0.10 0.3	=	78.5	0.15	11.775
						1.00	99.000
Do not franchise				=	90.0	1.00	90.00

(b) The approaches in part (a) enable uncertainty to be incorporated into the analysis and for decisions to be based on range of outcomes rather than a single outcome. This approach should produce better decisions in the long run. The main problem with this approach is that only a few selected outcomes with related probabilities are chosen as being representative of the entire distribution of possible outcomes. The approach also gives the impression of accuracy, which is not justified. Comments on the specific methods used in (a) are as follows:

Maximin: Enables an approach to be adopted which minimizes risk. The main disadvantage is that such a risk-averse approach will not result in decisions that will maximize long-run profits.

Expected value: For the advantages of this approach see 'Expected value' in Chapter 12. The weaknesses of expected value are as follows:

(i) It ignores risk. Decisions should not be made on expected value alone. It should be used in conjunction with measures of dispersion.

(ii) It is a long-run average payoff. Therefore it is best suited to repetitive decisions.

(iii) Because it is an average, it is unlikely that the expected value will occur.

Probability of earning an annual contribution of less than £100 000: This method enables decision-makers to specify their attitude towards risk and return and choose the alternative that meets the decision-makers risk–return preference. It is unlikely that this approach will be profit-maximizing or result in expected value being maximized.

Chapter 13

13.17 Using the interpolation method the IRR is:

$$15\% + \frac{£3664}{(£3664 + £21\,451)} \times (20\% - 15\%) = 15.7\%$$

Answer = A

13.18 Because the same amount is paid each period the cumulative (annuity) discount tables in Appendix B can be used. For 12 periods at 3% the annuity factor is 9.954. The present value 3 months from now will be £2986 (300 × 9.954). Assuming that the first payment is made at the beginning of month 3 this is the equivalent to the end of month 2 for discounting purposes. Therefore it is necessary to discount the present value back two months (periods) to today (time zero). Using the discount factor from Appendix A for 3% and 2 periods the present value at time zero is £2816 (£2986 × 0.9426). Therefore the answer is A.

13.19 (a) (i) Average capital invested

$$= \frac{£50\,000 + £10\,000}{2} = £30\,000$$

For an explanation of why the project's scrap value is added to the initial cost to calculate the average capital employed, you should refer to note 1 at the end of Chapter 13.

Note that the mid-point of the project's life is two years and the written down value at the end of year 2 is £30 000.

Average annual profit (Project A)

$$= \frac{£25\,000 + £20\,000 + £15\,000 + £10\,000}{4}$$

$= £17\,500$

Average annual profit (Project B)

$$= \frac{£10\,000 + £10\,000 + £14\,000 + £26\,000}{4}$$

$= £15\,000$

Average annual return:

A 58.33% $\left(\frac{£17\,500}{£30\,000} \times 100\right)$

B 50% $\left(\frac{£15\,000}{£30\,000} \times 100\right)$

(ii) Payback period:

Project A 1.5 years $\left(1 + \frac{£15\,000}{£30\,000}\right)$

Project B 2.4 years $\left(2 + \frac{£10\,000}{£24\,000}\right)$

(iii)

Year	Project A Cash inflows (W1) (£)	Project B Cash inflows (W1) (£)	Discount factor	Project A PV (£)	Project B PV (£)
1	35 000	20 000	0.909	31 815	18 180
2	30 000	20 000	0.826	24 780	16 520
3	25 000	24 000	0.751	18 775	18 024
4	20 000	36 000	0.683	13 660	24 588
4	10 000	10 000	0.683	6 830	6 830
				95 860	84 142
		Investment cost		(50 000)	(50 000)
		NPV		45 860	34 142

Workings:
(W1) Cash flows = Profit + depreciation.
Note that the estimated resale value is included as a year 4 cash inflow.

(b) See Chapter 13 for the answer to this section of the problem.

(c) Project A is recommended because it has the highest NPV and also the shortest payback period.

13.20 (a) The IRR is where:

annual cash inflows × discount factor = investment cost
i.e. £4000 × discount factor = £14 000
Therefore discount factor = £14 000 / £4 000
= 3.5

We now work along the five-row table of the cumulative discount tables to find the discount rate with a discount factor closed to 3.5. This is 13%. Therefore the IRR is 13%.

(b) The annual saving necessary to achieve a 12% internal rate of return is where:

annual savings × 12% discount factor = investment cost
i.e. annual savings × 3.605 = £14 000
Therefore annual savings = £14 000 / 3.605
= £3 883

(c) NPV is calculated as follows:

	(£)
£4000 received annually from years 1–5:	
£4000 × 3.791 discount factor	15 164
Less investment cost	14 000
NPV	1 164

13.21 (a) Project A = 3 years + $\frac{350-314}{112}$ = 3.32 years
Project B = 3.0 years
Project C = 2.00 years

(b) Accounting rate of return = average profit/average investment

Project A = 79/175 = 45%
Project B = 84/175 = 48%
Project C = 70/175 = 40%

Note that average profit = (sum of cash flows – investment cost)/project's life.

(c) The report should include:

(i) NPVs of each project (project A = £83 200 (W1), project B = £64 000 (W2), project C = £79 000 (W3). A simple description of NPV should also be provided. For example, the NPV is the amount over and above the cost of the project which could be borrowed, secure in the knowledge that the cash flows from the project will repay the loan.

(ii) The following rankings are based on the different evaluation procedures:

Project	IRR	Payback	ARR	NPV
A	2	3	2	1
B	3	2	1	3
C	1	1	3	2

(iii) A discussion of each of the above evaluation procedures.

(iv) IRR is subject to the following criticisms:
1. Multiple rates of return can occur when a project has unconventional cash flows.
2. It is assumed that the cash flows received from a project are re-invested at the IRR and not the cost of capital.
3. Inability to rank mutually exclusive projects.
4. It cannot deal with different sized projects. For example, it is better to earn a return of 35% on £100 000 than 40% on £10 000.

Note that the above points are explained in detail in Chapter 13.

(v) Payback ignores cash flows outside the payback period, and it also ignores the timing of cash flows within the payback period. For example, the large cash flows for project A are ignored after the payback period. This method may be appropriate for companies experiencing liquidity problems who wish to recover their initial investment quickly.

(vi) Accounting rate of return ignores the timing of cash flows, but it is considered an important measure by those who believe reported profits have a significant impact on share prices.

(vii) NPV is generally believed to be the theoretically correct evaluation procedure. A positive NPV from an investment is supposed to indicate the increase in the market value of the shareholders' funds, but this claim depends upon the belief that the share price is the discounted present value of the future dividend stream. If the market uses some other method of valuing shares then a positive NPV may not represent the increase in market value of shareholders' funds. Note that the cash flows have been discounted at the company's cost of capital. It is only suitable to use the company's cost of capital as the discount rate if projects A, B and C are equivalent to the average risk of all the company's existing projects. If they are not of average risk then project risk-adjusted discount rates should be used.

(viii) The projects have unequal lives. It is assumed that the equipment will not be replaced. If the equipment is to be replaced, it will be necessary to consider the projects over a common time horizon using the techniques described for projects with unequal lives in Chapter 14.

(ix) It is recommended that NPV method is used and project A should be selected.

(d) Stadler prefers project C because it produces the highest accounting profit in year 3. Stadler is assuming that share prices are influenced by short-run reported profits. This is in contrast with theory, which assumes that the share price is the discounted present value of the future dividend stream. Stadler is also assuming that the market only has access to reported historical profits and is not aware of the future benefits arising from the projects. The stock market also obtains company information on future prospects from sources other than reported profits. For example, press releases, chairman's report and signals of future prosperity via increased dividend payments.

Workings

(W1) Project A = (100 × 0.8333) + (110 × 0.6944) + (104 × 0.5787) + (112 × 0.4823) + (138 × 0.4019) + (160 × 0.3349) + (180 × 0.2791) – £350

(W2) Project B = (40 × 0.8333) + (100 × 0.6944) + (210 × 0.5787) + (260 × 0.4823) + (160 × 0.4019) – £350

(W3) Project C = (200 × 0.8333) + (150 × 0.6944) + (240 × 0.5787) + (40 × 0.4823) – £350

13.22 (a)

	Discount factors 10%	20%	Project X NPV at 10% (£000)	NPV at 20% (£000)	Project Y NPV at 10% (£000)	NPV at 20% (£000)
Year 0	1.000	1.000	(200.00)	(200.00)	(200.00)	(200.00)
1	0.9091	0.8333	31.82	29.16	198.19	181.66
2	0.8264	0.6944	66.11	55.55	8.26	6.94
3	0.7513	0.5787	67.62	52.08	7.51	5.79
4	0.683	0.4823	51.22	36.17	2.73	1.93
5	0.6209	0.4019	12.42	8.04	1.87	1.21
			29.19	(19.00)	18.56	(2.47)

Using the interpolation method, the IRRs are:

Project X = 10% + [29.19/(29.19 + 19.00)] × 10% = 16.05%
Project Y = 10% + [18.56/(18.56 + 2.47)] × 10% = 18.83%

(b) The projects are mutually exclusive, and conflicting rankings occur. Where conflicting rankings occur, the NPV method will indicate the correct rankings (see Chapter 13 for an explanation). Therefore project X should be undertaken, since it yields the larger NPV at a discount rate of 10%.

(c) For the answer to this question see 'Comparison of net present value and internal rate of return' in Chapter 13.

(d) The cost of capital at which project Y would be preferred to project X can be ascertained by calculating the IRR on the incremental investment X – Y.

Year	0 (£000)	1 (£000)	2 (£000)	3 (£000)	4 (£000)	5 (£000)
Project X cash flows	–200	35	80	90	75	20
Project Y cash flows	–200	218	10	10	4	3
Project X – Y	0	–183	+70	+80	+71	+17

The IRR on the incremental investment X – Y is 13%. Therefore if the cost of capital were in excess of 13%, the decision in (b) would be reversed (assuming that one of the projects has a positive NPV). For an explanation of this approach see 'Mutually exclusive projects' in Chapter 13. Alternatively, the discount rate can be found by constructing a graph for the NPVs at different discount rates. You can see from the graph shown in Figure Q13.22 that project Y has a higher NPV for discount rates above 13%.

FIGURE Q13.22

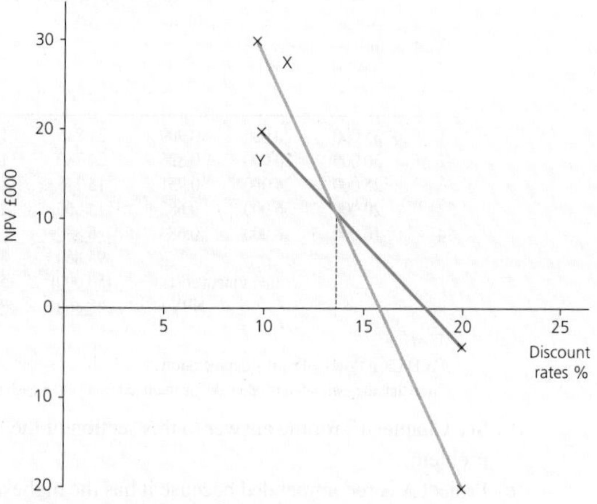

13.23 (a) *NPV calculations*

	Cash flows (£m)	Years	Discount factor	PV (£m)
Initial outlay	(40)	t_0	1.0000	(40.000)
Disposal value	10	t_{10}	0.2472	2.472
Retraining costs[a]	(10)	$t_{0,1}$	1.8696	(18.696)
Annual cost savings	12	t_1–t_{10}	5.0190	60.228
Rental income	2	t_{1-10}	5.0190	10.038
Software	(4)	t_{1-10}	5.0190	(20.076)
Reduction in working capital	5	t_0	1.0000	5.000
NPV				(1.034)

It is assumed that taxation should be ignored.

Note

[a]The question implies that retraining costs do not occur at the end of the year. It is therefore assumed that the cash flows occur at the start of years 1 and 2 (that is, t_0 and t_1).

Calculation of accounting rate of return

	(£m)
Year 1 incremental profits:	
Annual cost savings	12
Retraining costs (20m/10 years)	(2)
Rental income	2
Software	(4)
Depreciation of equipment (40 – 10)/10 years	(3)
Increase in profits	5
Year 1 incremental capital investment:	
Initial outlay	40
Capitalized retraining costs	20
Reduction in working capital	(5)
	55

It is assumed that ROI is calculated based on the opening written-down value:

ROI = 5/55 = 9.1%

The proposed investment fails to meet either of the company's investment criteria and would be rejected.

(b) The answer should include a discussion of the following:

(i) A theoretical explanation of the NPV rule and a justification for its use. In perfect capital markets a positive NPV reflects the increase in the market value of a company arising from acceptance of the project.

(ii) An explanation of the impact of market imperfections on the NPV rule. For NPV to represent the increase in shareholders' value resulting from acceptance of an investment, it is necessary for investors to be aware of the project's existence and also the projected future cash flows. This implies that the efficient market hypothesis applies in its strong form and that changes in short-run reported profits do not affect market prices.

(iii) In imperfect markets shareholders lack information regarding projected future cash flows. Consequently, they may use short-run reported profits and ROI as an indication of potential future cash flows. In such circumstances changes in reported profits will affect share prices. Hence management have reacted to this situation by considering the impact of a project's acceptance on reported ROI.

(iv) Widespread use of ROI and payback in the UK and USA.

(v) Shareholders and financial analysts tend to monitor short-run profits and ROI and use these measures as an input that determines their estimates of future share prices. It is therefore not surprising that companies consider the implications of their investment decisions on reported short-run profits and ROI.

(c) The answer should include a discussion of the specific problems that arise in evaluating investments in advanced manufacturing technologies (AMTs) and an explanation of why the financial appraisal might incorrectly reject such investments. In particular, it is claimed that many of the benefits from investing in AMTs are difficult to quantify and tend not to be included in the analysis (e.g. improved product quality). It is also claimed that inflation is incorrectly dealt with and that excessive discount rates are applied which overcompensate for risk.

A further reason that has been cited why companies underinvest in AMTs is that they fail to properly evaluate the relevant alternatives. There is a danger that the investment will be compared incorrectly against an alternative that assumes a continuation of the current market share, selling prices and costs – in other words, the status quo. However, the status quo is unlikely to apply, since competitors are also likely to invest in the new technology. In this situation the investment should be compared with the alternative of not investing, based on assuming a situation of declining cash flow.

The answer should also stress that taxation has not been incorporated into the analysis. In addition, the project has been discounted at the company's normal cost of capital of 15%. This rate is only justified if the risk of the project is equivalent to the average risk of the firm's existing assets.

Chapter 14

14.16

	Replacement Periods				
	1	2	3	4	5
	(£000)	(£000)	(£000)	(£000)	(£000)
Cash outflows at end of year:					
1	11 (100 – 121)	–110	–110	–110	–110
2		–44 (132 – 88)	–132	–132	–132
3			– 88 (154 – 66)	–154	–154
4				–110 (165 – 55)	–165
5					–151 (176 – 25)
Present value of outflows	9.83	133.30	266.09	383.04	503.64
Purchase cost	220.00	220.00	220.00	220.00	220.00
Present value	210.17	353.30	486.09	603.04	723.64
Annuity factor	0.893	1.690	2.402	3.037	3.605
Equivalent annual cost	235.35	209.05	202.37	198.56	200.73

The lowest equivalent annual cost is £198 560. Therefore the fleet should be replaced at the end of 4 years so the answer is D.

14.17

Expected cash flows	Discount factor	Present value (£)
Year 1 = (£10 000 × 0.2) + (£7000 × 0.5) + (£6400 × 0.3) = £7420	0.909	6 745
Year 2 = (£12 000 × 0.2) + (£8000 × 0.5) + (£7200 × 0.3) = £8560	0.826	7 071
Year 3 = (£9000 × 0.2) + (£7600 × 0.5) + (£6200 × 0.3) = £7420	0.751	5 602
		19 418
Initial outlay		20 000
NPV		–582

Answer = A

14.18 (a) It is assumed that the cost of capital is a nominal rate. The NPV can be calculated by discounting real cash flows at the real discount rate or nominal cash flows at the nominal discount rate. The real discount rate (1 + real discount rate) is (1 + nominal rate)/(1 + anticipated inflation rate) = 0.0485 (1.08/1.03 – 1). The annual cash flows in current prices are £20 000 (£5 × 4000 units).

NPV based on real cash flows and the real discount rate: $(£20\,000)/(1.0485) + (20\,000)/(1.0485)^2 + (20\,000)/(1.0485)^3 – £50\,000 = £4640$

NPV based on discounting nominal cash flows at the nominal discount rate:

$(£20\,000 \times 1.03)/1.08 + (£20\,000 \times 1.03^2)/1.08^2 + (£20\,000 \times 1.03^3)/1.08^3 – £50\,000 = £4640$

Answer = A

(b) NPV will be zero where:

Annual cash flows (£20 000) × Annuity discount factor = Investment outlay (£50 000)

Annuity discount factor = 2.5 (£50 000/20 000)

For a three year life the annuity tables indicate a factor of 2.531 for 9% and 2.487 for 10%. Using interpolation a factor of 2.5 is equivalent to 9.7%. Note that this is a real discount rate (based on using real cash flows). To convert to a nominal (monetary rate):

(1 + nominal rate) = (1 + real discount rate) × (1 + anticipated inflation rate)

= (1 + .097) × (1.04) = 1.141

Nominal rate = 1.141 – 1 = 14.1%

Answer = C

14.19 (a) The NPV calculations can be adjusted in two basic ways to account for inflation. Real cash flows can be discounted at the real discount rate or inflation adjusted cash flows can be discounted at a discount rate which incorporates a premium for inflation. It is only appropriate to leave the cash flows in terms of present-day prices and discount these cash flows at the real cost of capital when all the cash flows are expected to increase at the general level of inflation. The cash flows in the question are subject to different levels of inflation. In particular, capital allowances are based on the original cost and do not change in line with changing prices. Therefore the cash flows should be adjusted for inflation and discounted at a cost of capital which incorporates a premium for inflation. The inflation adjusted revenues, expenses and taxation liabilities are:

Year	1	2	3	4	5
Sales at 5% inflation (W1)	3675	5402	6159	6977	6790
Materials at 10% inflation	(588)	(907)	(1198)	(1537)	(1449)
Labour at 10% inflation	(1177)	(1815)	(2396)	(3075)	(2899)
Overheads at 5% inflation	(52)	(110)	(116)	(122)	(128)
Capital allowances (W2)	(1125)	(844)	(633)	(475)	(1423)
Taxable profits	733	1726	1816	1768	891
Taxation at 35%	256	604	636	619	312

The interest payments are not included because they are taken into account when the cash flows are discounted.

Workings

(W1) Year 1 = £3500 (1.05), year 2 = £4900 $(1.05)^2$, year 3 = £5320 $(1.05)^3$, year 4 = £5740 $(1.05)^4$, year 5 = £5320 $(1.05)^5$. The same approach is used to calculate the inflation adjusted cash flows for the remaining items.

(W2) 25% writing down allowances on £4500 with a balancing allowance in year 5.

The cash flow estimates and NPV calculation are as follows:

Year	0	1	2	3	4	5	6
Inflows							
Sales	—	3675	5402	6159	6977	6790	—
Outflows							
Materials	—	588	907	1198	1537	1449	—
Labour	—	1177	1815	2396	3075	2899	—
Overheads	—	52	110	116	122	128	—
Fixed assets	4500						
Working capital (W1)	300	120	131	144	156	(851)	—
Taxation			256	604	636	619	312
Total outflows	4800	1937	3219	4458	5526	4244	312
Net cash flows	(4800)	1738	2183	1701	1451	2546	(312)
Discount factors at 15%		0.870	0.756	0.658	0.572	0.497	0.432
Present values	(4800)	1512	1650	1119	830	1265	(135)

The NPV is £1 441 000 and it is therefore recommended that the project should be undertaken. Note that the interest cost is already incorporated in the DCF calculation and should not be included in the cash flows when calculating present values.

Workings

(W1) It is assumed that the working capital is released at the end of the project. Year 1 = 400 (1.05) – 300, year 2 = 500 $(1.05)^2$ – 420, and so on.

(b) Calculating the IRR will produce an NPV of zero. NPV is £1 441 000 at a 15% discount rate. In order to use the interpolation method to calculate the IRR, it is necessary to ascertain a negative NPV. At a discount rate of 30% the NPV is

Year	Cash flow (£000)	Discount factor	PV (£000)
0	(4800)	1.0000	(4800)
1	1738	0.7692	1337
2	2183	0.5917	1292
3	1701	0.4552	774
4	1451	0.3501	508
5	2546	0.2693	686
6	(312)	0.2071	(65)
			(268)

Using the interpolation method, the IRR is

$$15\% + \frac{1441}{1441-(-205)} \times 15\% = 28\%$$

(c) See 'Sensitivity analysis' in Chapter 14 for a description and discussion of the weaknesses of sensitivity analysis. Other traditional techniques include the use of probability distributions to calculate expected net present value and standard deviation, simulation and certainty equivalents. More recent techniques include portfolio theory and the capital asset pricing model. Theorists would suggest that risk should be incorporated into the analysis by discounting the expected value of a project's cash flows at a risk-adjusted discount rate using the capital asset pricing model.

14.20 (a) The tax liability calculations are

Standard (£)

Year	1	2	3	4	
Operating cash flows	20 500	22 860	24 210	23 410	
Capital allowance	12 500	9 375	7 031	21 094	(W1)
	8 000	13 485	17 179	2 316	
Taxation (35%)	2 800	4 720	6 013	811	

De-luxe (£)

Year	1	2	3	4	5	6	
Operating cash flows	32 030	26 110	25 380	25 940	38 560	35 100	
Capital allowance	22 000	16 500	12 375	9 281	6 961	20 883	(W1)
	10 030	9 610	13 005	16 659	31 599	14 217	
Taxation (35%)	3 511	3 363	4 552	5 831	11 060	4 976	

The NPV calculations are

Standard (£)

Year	0	1	2	3	4	5
Fixed assets	(50 000)					
Working capital	(10 000)				10 000 (W3)	
Operating cash flows		20 500	22 860	24 210	23 410	
Taxation (W2)	—	—	(2 800)	(4 720)	(6 013)	(811)
	(60 000)	20 500	20 060	19 490	27 397	(811)
Discount factor (12%)		0.893	0.797	0.712	0.636	0.567
Present values	(60 000)	18 307	15 988	13 877	17 424	(460)

Payback period is approximately 3 years
Net present value is £5136

De-luxe (£)

Year	0	1	2	3	4	5	6	7
Fixed assets	(88 000)							
Working capital	(10 000)						10 000 (W3)	
Operating cash flows		32 030	26 110	25 380	25 940	38 560	35 100	
Taxation (W2)	—	—	(3 511)	(3 363)	(4 552)	(5 831)	(11 060)	(4976)
	(98 000)	32 030	22 599	22 017	21 388	32 729	34 040	(4976)
Discount factor (14%)		0.877	0.769	0.675	0.592	0.519	0.456	0.400
Present values	(98 000)	28 090	17 379	14 861	12 662	16 986	15 522	(1990)

Payback period is approximately 4 years
Net present value is £5510

Workings

(W1) Final-year balancing allowance.

(W2) It is assumed that the capital allowance for the purchase of the asset is included in t_1 accounts, which are submitted to the Inland Revenue, and the cash flow effect arises in t_2.

(W3) It is assumed that the working capital is realized immediately the project ends.

The de-luxe model has the largest NPV, but the projects have unequal lives and this factor needs to be taken into account. One method of doing this is to convert the cash flows into an equivalent annual cash flow with NPVs of £5136 for the standard machines and £5510 for the de-luxe machines. The following formula is used to calculate the equivalent annual cash flow:

$$\frac{\text{NPV}}{\text{annuity factor for N years at R\%}}$$

$$\text{Standard} = \frac{5136}{3.605} = £1425$$

$$\text{De-luxe} = \frac{5510}{4.288} = £1285$$

The cash flow effects are for 5 years for the standard machine and 7 years for the de-luxe machine. Therefore the annuity factors are for 5 years at 12% and 7 years at 14% respectively. The equivalent annual cash flow for the standard machine indicates that a sequence of cash flows from this machine is exactly like a sequence of cash flows of £1425 per year. Note that the equivalent annual cash flow method is based on the assumption that reinvestment takes place over a period of 12 years (the common denominator of 4 years and 6 years) or infinity.

As the standard machine has the higher equivalent annual cash flow, it is recommended that this machine be purchased.

(b) Possible reasons for the widespread use of accounting rate of return and payback include:

1. Simple to calculate and widely understood.
2. Appropriate for small projects which do not warrant detailed appraisal.
3. They are often used as initial screening tools and supplementary to a DCF analysis.
4. Return on capital employed (ROCE) is a widely used measure by outsiders to judge company performance and ROCE is also a popular measure for evaluating a divisional manager's performance. Managers might also consider it appropriate to judge individual projects on the same well-known criterion.
5. Payback might be appropriate for companies experiencing liquidity problems who wish to recover their investment quickly.
6. Lack of understanding of more sophisticated techniques.

14.21 (a) *Calculations of expected net present value and profitability indices*

Project A

NPV (£70 000 × 3.605) – £246 000 = £6350

$$\text{Profitability index} = \frac{\text{present value of cash inflows}}{\text{initial outlay}} = \frac{252\,350}{246\,000} = 1.026$$

Project B

NPV (£75 000 × 0.893) + (£87 000 × 0.797) + (£64 000 × 0.712) – £180 000 = £1882

$$\text{Profitability index} = \frac{181\,882}{180\,000} = 1.010$$

Project C

NPV (£48 000 × 1.69) + (£63 000 × 0.712) + (£73 000 × 0.636) – £175 000 = (£2596)

$$\text{Profitability index} = \frac{172\,404}{175\,000} = 0.985$$

Project D
NPV (£62 000 × 3.037) – £180 000 = £8294

$$\text{Profitability index} = \frac{188\ 294}{180\ 000} = 1.046$$

Project E
NPV (£40 000 × 0.893) + (£50 000 × 0.797) + (£60 000 × 0.712) + (£70 000 × 0.636) + (£40 000 × 0.567) – £180 000 = £5490

$$\text{Profitability index} = \frac{185\ 490}{180\ 000} = 1.031$$

Project F
NPV 5 (£35 000 × 0.893) + (£82 000 × 1.509) – £150 000 = £4993

$$\text{Profitability index} = \frac{154\ 993}{150\ 000} = 1.033$$

Project rankings	**NPV**	**PI**
1	D	D
2	A	F
3	E	E
4	F	A
5	B	B
6	C	C

The rankings differ because NPV is an absolute measure whereas the profitability index is a relative measure that takes into account the different investment cost of each project.

(b) The objective is to select a combination of investments that will maximize NPV subject to a total capital outlay of £620 000. Projects A and E are mutually exclusive and project C has a negative NPV. The following are potential combinations of projects:

Projects	Expected NPV (£)	Total expected NPV (£)	Total Outlay (£)
A, B, D	6350 + 1882 + 8294	16 526	606 000
A, B, F	6350 + 1882 + 4993	13 225	576 000
A, D, F	6350 + 8294 + 4993	19 637	576 000
B, D, E	1882 + 8294 + 5490	15 666	540 000
B, D, F	1882 + 8294 + 4993	15 169	510 000
D, E, F	8294 + 5490 + 4993	18 777	510 000

Note that it is not possible to combine four projects within the constraints outlined above and that expected NPV cannot be increased by combining two projects. Accepting projects A, D and F will maximize NPV. This combination will require a total capital outlay of £576 000, and the unused funds will be invested to yield a return of 9%. The risk-adjusted discount rate for the investment will also be 9%. Therefore the NPV of funds invested in the money market will be zero.

(c) Where a company rejects projects with positive NPVs because of capital rationing, the IRR forgone on the most profitable project that has been rejected represents the opportunity cost of capital. For a more detailed explanation of this point see 'Capital rationing' in Chapter 14. Therefore the director is correct in stating that the company's cost of capital might not be appropriate.

(d) *Advantages of mathematical programming:*

(i) Ability to solve complex problems incorporating the effects of complex interactions.
(ii) Speed in solving the problem using computer facilities.
(iii) The output from the model can highlight the key constraints to which attention should be directed.
(iv) Sensitivity analysis can be applied. The effects of changes in the variables can be speedily tested.

Disadvantages of mathematical programming:

(i) Divisibility of projects may not be realistic, and integer programming may have to be used.
(ii) Constraints are unlikely to be completely fixed and precise, as implied in the mathematical models.
(iii) Not all the relevant information can be quantified.
(iv) All the information for the model may not be available. For example, it may not be possible to specify the constraints of future periods.
(v) All the relationships contained within the formulation may not be linear.
(vi) All the potential investment opportunities may not be identified and included in the analysis.
(vii) The linear programming formulation assumes that all the project's cash flows are certain, and therefore it cannot incorporate uncertainty. The solution produced can only be considered optimal given this restrictive assumption.

14.22 (a) *Calculation of expected NPV (£000)*

Year	0	1	2	3	4	5	6
Investment outlay	(1500)						
Sales at £2 per unit		3000	3000	3000	3000	3000	3000
Variable costs at £1.59 per unit[a]		2385	2385	2385	2385	2385	2385
Taxable cash flows		615	615	615	615	615	615
Tax at 35%		215	215	215	215	215	215
Net cash flow[b]	(1500)	400	400	400	400	400	400

NPV at a discount rate of 8%[c] = (£400 × 4.623) – £1500 = £349 200

Notes

[a]Unit variable cost = Purchase cost (£1.50 × 40%) + copyright fee (20% × £3.95) + £0.20 additional variable cost.

[b]Market research is a sunk cost.

[c]See part (b) of the answer for an explanation of why a discount rate of 8% has been used. Note that the financing costs are incorporated in the discount rate and should not be included in the cash flows as this would lead to double counting.

(b) Assuming that the company wishes to maintain its current capital structure the specific cost of financing the project should not be used as a discount rate. The project has been financed by a bank loan but this will result in less borrowing being used in the future as the company re-balances its finance to achieve the target capital structure. To reflect the company's target capital structure the weighted average cost of capital (WACC) should be used.

The money WACC should be used only if the cash flows are expressed in money/nominal terms (i.e. adjusted for inflation). Current cash flows have been used to calculate NPV. Current cash flows are equivalent to real cash flow when all cash flows increase at the general rate of inflation. This situation occurs in this question and therefore the cash flows are equivalent to real cash flows. Thus the real WACC of capital should be used to discount the cash flows.

The WACC represents the discount rate applicable for the company as a whole and reflects the average risk of all of the company's assets. If the project has a different level of risk from the average risk of the assets of the company as a whole, the existing WACC will not represent the appropriate discount rate. In this situation a separate risk adjusted discount rate should be used.

It is also assumed that all of the cash flows increase at the general rate of inflation. If the cash flows are subject to different rates of inflation it will be incorrect to use current prices. If this situation occurs the cash flows should be adjusted by their specific rates of inflation and a nominal discount rate should be used.

(c) (i) *Initial outlay*

The NPV of the project is £349 200. Therefore the investment outlay could increase by £349 200 before NPV becomes negative. This represents a percentage increase of 23.28% (£349.2/£1500 × 100).

Annual contribution

Let x = annual contribution

With a corporate tax rate of 35% the annual contribution at which NPV will be zero can be calculated from the following formula:

$$(1-0.35)\,4.623x - £1500 = 0$$
$$3.005x - 1500 = 0$$
$$x = 1500/3.005 = £499.16$$

Therefore annual contribution can decline from the existing figure of £615 000 to £499 160. A percentage decrease of 18.83% (£115.84/£615 × 100). Note that 4.623 and £1500 in the above formula represents the cumulative discount factor and the investment outlay.

The life of the agreement

Let x = Annuity factor at 8%

NPV will be zero where

$$400x - £1500 = 0$$
$$x = 3.75$$

From the annuity table shown in Appendix B of the text:

PV of annuity for 4 years at 8% = 3.312

PV of annuity for 5 years at 8% = 3.993

Extrapolating, the PV annuity factor is:

$$4 \text{ years} + \frac{3.75-3.312}{3.993-3.312} \times 1 \text{ year} = 4.643 \text{ years}$$

This represents a reduction of 22.61% [(6 – 4.643)/6 years × 100]

Discount rate

Let x = PV of annuity for 6 years

NPV will be zero where:

$$400x = 1500$$
$$x = 3.75$$

From the annuity tables (Appendix B) 15% has a PV annuity factor of 3.784 and 16% is 3.685. Thus the discount rate at which NPV will be zero is approximately 15.5%. This represents an increase of 93.75% [(15.5 – 8)/8 × 100].

The above calculations indicate that the annual contribution is the most sensitive variable.

(ii) See 'Sensitivity Analysis' in Chapter 14 for an outline of the limitations of sensitivity analysis.

(d) Possible additional information includes:

(i) Is the agreement likely to be renewed after 6 years?

(ii) Are competitors likely to enter the market and what impact would this have on the sales volume and price?

(iii) How accurate are the estimated cash flows?

(iv) How reliable is the supplier who supplies microfiche readers? Can the microfiche readers be obtained from any other source or is the company dependent upon the one supplier?

Chapter 15

15.20 Answer = A

15.21

	(£)	(£)
Cash sales		22 000
Credit sales		
April (70% × 0.6 × 0.98 × £70 000)	28 812	
March (27% × 0.6 × £60 000)	9 720	38 532
		60 532

Answer = C

15.22 Total variable costs for year ended March 2002 = £647 080 (£924 400 × 70%)

Analysed by:

	Passengers	Parcels
Variable costs	£388 248 (60%)	258 832 (40%)
Activity for year ending March 2002	1024	24 250 kg
£ per passenger	£379.148	
£ per kg		£10.674
Revised costs based on 3% increase	£390.52	£10.994
Activity for period ending September 2002	209	7200 kg
Budgeted cost (Activity × Revised cost)	£81 619	£79 157

The answer is A for part (a) and C for part (b)

15.23 (a) Raw materials:

(Units)	March	April	May	June
Opening stock	100	110	115	110
Add: Purchases	80	80	85	85
	180	190	200	195
Less: Used in production	70	75	90	90
Closing stock	110	115	110	105
(Units) *Finished production:*				
Opening stock	110	100	91	85
Add: Production	70	75	90	90
	180	175	181	175
Less: Sales	80	84	96	94
Closing stock	100	91	85	81

(b) *Sales:*

					Total
(at £219 per unit)	£17 520	£18 396	£21 024	£20 586	£77 526
Production cost:					
Raw materials (using FIFO)	3 024 (1)	3 321 (2)	4 050	4 050	14 445
Wages and variable costs	4 550	4 875	5 850	5 850	21 125
	£7 574	£8 196	£9 900	£9 900	£35 570

Debtors:

Closing debtors = May + June sales = £41 610

Creditors:

June purchases 85 units × £45 £3825

Notes:

(1) 70 units × £4320/100 units = £3024.

(2) (30 units × £4320/100 units + (45 units × £45) = £3321.

Closing stocks:

Raw materials 105 units × £45 £4725

Finished goods 81 units × £110[1] £8910

Note:

[1] Materials (£45) + Labour and Variable Overhead (£65).

It is assumed that stocks are valued on a variable costing basis.

(c) *Cash budget:*

	March (£)	April (£)	May (£)	June (£)
Balance b/fwd	6 790	4 820	5 545	132 415
Add: Receipts				
Debtors (two months' credit)	7 680	10 400	17 520	18 396
Loan	—	—	120 000	—
(A)	14 470	15 220	143 065	150 811
Payments:				
Creditors (one month's credit)	3 900	3 600 (80 × £45)	3 600	3 825
Wages and variable overheads	4 550	4 875	5 850	5 850
Fixed overheads	1 200	1 200	1 200	1 200
Machinery	—	—	—	112 000
Interim dividend	—	—	—	12 500
(B)	9 650	9 675	10 650	135 375
Balance c/fwd (A) – (B)	4 820	5 545	132 415	£15 436

(d) *Master budget:*

Budgeted trading and profit and loss account for the four months to 30 June

	(£)	(£)
Sales		77 526
Cost of sales: Opening stock finished goods	10 450	
Add: Production cost	35 570	
	46 020	
Less: Closing stock finished goods	8 910	37 110
		40 416
Less: Expenses		
Fixed overheads (4 × £1200)	4 800	
Depreciation		
Machinery and equipment	15 733	
Motor vehicles	3 500	
Loan interest (2/12 × 7½% of £120 000)	1 500	25 533
		14 883
Less: Interim dividends		12 500
		2 383
Add: Profit and loss account balance b/fwd		40 840
		£43 223

Budgeted balance sheet as at 30 June

	Cost (£)	Depreciation to date (£)	Net (£)
Fixed assets			
Land and buildings	500 000	—	500 000
Machinery and equipment	236 000	100 233	135 767
Motor vehicles	42 000	19 900	22 100
	778 000	120 133	657 867
Current assets			
Stock of raw materials		4 725	
Stock of finished goods		8 910	
Debtors		41 610	
Cash and bank balances		15 436	
		70 681	
Less: Current liabilities			
Creditors	3 825		
Loan interest owing	1 500	5 325	65 356
			£723 223

	(£)
Capital employed	
Ordinary share capital £1 shares (fully paid)	500 000
Share premium	60 000
Profit and loss account	43 233
	603 223
Secured loan (7½%)	120 000
	£723 223

(e) See the section of cash budgets in Chapter 15 for possible ways to improve cash management.

15.24

Task 1

Alderley Ltd Budget Statements 13 weeks to 4 April

(a) Production Budget

	Elgar units	Holst units
Budgeted sales volume	845	1235
Add closing stock[a]	78	1266
Less Opening stock	(163)	(361)
Units of production	760	1140

(b) Material Purchases Budget

	Elgar kg	Holst kg	Total kg
Material consumed	5320 (760 × 7)	9120 (1140 × 8)	14 440
Add raw material closing stock[b]			2 888
Less raw material opening stock			(2 328)
Purchases (kg)			15 000

(c) Purchases (£) (1500 × £12) £180 000

(d) Production Labour Budget

	Elgar hours	Holst hours	Total hours
Standard hours produced[c]	6080	5700	11 780
Productivity adjustment (5/95 × 11 780)			620
Total hours employed			12 400
Normal hours employed[d]			11 544
Overtime hours			856

(e) Labour cost

	£
Normal hours (11 544 × £8)	92 352
Overtime (856 × £8 × 125%)	8 560
Total	100 912

Notes:

[a]Number of days per period = 13 weeks × 5 days = 65
Stock: Elgar = (6/65) × 845 = 78, Holst = (14/65) × 1235 = 266
[b](13/65) × (5320 + 9120) = 2888
[c]Elgar 760 × 8 hours = 6080, Holst 1140 × 5 hours = 5700
[d]24 employees × 37 hours × 13 weeks = 11 544

Task 2

(a) Four ways of forecasting future sales volume are:

(i) Where the number of customers is small it is possible to interview them to ascertain what their likely demand will be over the forecasting period.

(ii) Produce estimates based on the opinion of executives and sales personnel. For example, sales personnel may be asked to estimate the sales of each product to their customers, or regional sales managers may estimate the total sales for each of their regions.

(iii) Market research may be necessary where it is intended to develop new products or new markets. This may involve interviews with existing and potential customers in order to estimate potential demand.

(iv) Estimates involving statistical techniques that incorporate general business and market conditions and past growth in sales.

(b) Interviewing customers and basing estimates on the opinions of sales personnel are likely to be more appropriate for existing products and customers involving repeat sales. Market research is appropriate for new products or markets and where the market is large and anticipated revenues are likely to be sufficient to justify the cost of undertaking the research.

Statistical estimates derived from past data are likely to be appropriate where conditions are likely to be stable and past demand patterns are likely to be repeated through time. This method is most suited to existing products or markets where sufficient data is available to establish a trend in demand.

(c) The major limitation of interviewing customers is that they may not be prepared to divulge the information if their future plans are commercially sensitive. There is also no guarantee that the orders will be placed with Alderley Ltd. They may place their orders with competitors.

Where estimates are derived from sales personnel there is a danger that they might produce over-optimistic estimates in order to obtain a favourable performance rating at the budget setting stage. Alternatively, if their future performance is judged by their ability to achieve the budgeted sales they may be motivated to under-estimate sales demand.

Market research is expensive and may produce unreliable estimates if inexperienced researchers are used. Also small samples are often used which may not be indicative of the population and this can result in inaccurate estimates.

Statistical estimates will produce poor demand estimates where insufficient past data is available, demand is unstable over time and the future environment is likely to be significantly different from the past. Statistical estimates are likely to be inappropriate for new products and new markets where past data is unavailable.

15.25 (a) (i) *Cash budget for weeks 1–6*

	Week 1 (£)	Week 2 (£)	Week 3 (£)	Week 4 (£)	Week 5 (£)	Week 6 (£)
Receipts from debtors[a]	24 000	24 000	28 200	25 800	19 800	5 400
Payments:						
To material suppliers[b]	8 000	12 500	6 000	nil	nil	nil
To direct workers[c]	3 200	4 200	2 800	nil	nil	nil
For variable overheads[d]	4 800	3 200	nil	nil	nil	nil
For fixed overhead[e]	8 300	8 300	6 800	6 800	6 800	6 800
Total payments	24 300	28 200	15 600	6 800	6 800	6 800
Net movement	(300)	(4 200)	12 600	19 000	13 000	(1 400)
Opening balance (week 1 given)	1 000	700	(3 500)	9 100	28 100	41 100
Closing balance	700	(3 500)	9 100	28 100	41 100	39 700

Notes

[a]Debtors:

	Week 1	Week 2	Week 3	Week 4	Week 5	Week 6
Units sold*	400	500	400	300	—	—
Sales (£)	24 000	30 000	24 000	18 000	—	—
Cash received (70%)		16 800	21 000	16 800	12 600	
(30%)			7 200	9 000	7 200	5 400
Given	24 000	7 200				
Total receipts (£)	24 000	24 000	28 200	25 800	19 800	5 400

*Sales in week 4 = opening stock (600 units) + production in weeks 1 and 2 (1000 units) less sales in weeks 1–3 (1300 units) = 300 units.

[b]Creditors:

	Week 1 (£)	Week 2 (£)	Week 3 (£)	Week 4	Week 5	Week 6
Materials consumed at £15	9 000	6 000	—	—	—	—
Increase in stocks	3 500	—				
Materials purchased	12 500	6 000				
Payment to suppliers	8 000 (given)	12 500	6000	nil	nil	nil

[c]Wages:

	Week 1 (£)	Week 2 (£)	Week 3 (£)	Week 4	Week 5	Week 6
Wages consumed at £7	4200	2800	nil	nil	nil	nil
Wages paid	3200 (given)	4200	2800	—	—	—

[d]Variable overhead payment = budgeted production × budgeted cost per unit.

[e]Fixed overhead payments for weeks 1–2 = fixed overhead per week (£9000). less weekly depreciation (£700).

Fixed overhead payments for weeks 3–6 = £8300 normal payment less £1500 per week.

(ii) *Comments*

1. Finance will be required to meet the cash deficit in week 2, but a lowering of the budgeted material stocks at the end of week 1 would reduce the amount of cash to be borrowed at the end of week 2.
2. The surplus cash after the end of week 2 should be invested on a short-term basis.
3. After week 6, there will be no cash receipts, but cash outflows will be £6800 per week. The closing balance of £39 700 at the end of week 6 will be sufficient to finance outflows for a further 5 or 6 weeks (£39 700/£6800 per week).

(b) The answer should include a discussion of the matching concept, emphasizing that revenues and expenses may not be attributed to the period when the associated cash inflows and outflows occur. Also, some items of expense do not affect cash outflow (e.g. depreciation).

15.26 (a) Activity based budget for six months ending 30 June 2004

	Product A		Product B		Total
Production	9000 units		15 000 units		
	Per unit (£)	Total (£000)	Per unit (£)	Total (£000)	£000
Product unit-based					
Materials[a]	60.000	540.0	45.000	675.0	1 215.0
Labour, power etc.[b]	16.000	144.0	10.000	150.0	294.0
	76.000	684.0	55.000	825.0	1 509.0
Batch based					
Production scheduling					29.6
WIP movement					36.4
Purchasing and receipt					49.5
Sub-total[c]		63.0		52.5	115.5
Machine set-up[d]		15.0		25.0	40.0
	8.667	78.0	5.167	77.5	155.5
Product sustaining					
Material scheduling[e]		9.0		9.0	18.0
Design/testing[f]		9.6		6.4	16.0
	2.067	18.6	1.027	15.4	34.0
Product line sustaining					
Product line development[g]		20.0		5.0	25.0
Product line maintenance[h]		6.0		3.0	9.0
	2.889	26.0	0.533	8.0	34.0
Factory sustaining					
General factory administration[i]					125.0
General factory occupancy[i]					67.0
	8.000	72.0	8.000	120.0	192.0
Totals	97.623	878.6	69.727	1 045.9	1 924.5

Notes

[a]Output × material cost per unit given in the question.

[b]Machine hours = (9000 × 0.8) + (15 000 × 0.5) = 14 700
Rate per hour = (£294 000/14 700) = £20
Product A = 0.8 hours × £20

[c]Product batches required = (9000/100) + (15 000/200) = 165
Cost per batch = £115 500/165 = £700
Assigned to product A = 90 batches at £700 = £63 000

[d]Cost per set up = £40 000/40 = £1000 per set up
Assigned to product A = 15 set ups × £1000

[e]Components purchased = 180 000 for product A (9000 × 20) and 180 000 for product B (15 000 × 12) resulting in equal costs being allocated to each product.

[f]Design and testing allocated in the ratio 12 : 8 as given in the question.

[g]Allocated 80% and 20% as indicated in the question.

[h]Production line maintenance cost per maintenance hour = £9000/450 = £20
Allocated to product A = 300 hours at £20 per hour = £6000

[i]£768 000 × 25% = £192 000/number of units (24 000) = £8 per unit
Allocated to A = £72 000 (9000 units × £8)

(b) See 'activity hierarchies' and 'designing ABC systems' in Chapter 10 for the answer to this question. Note that cost pools are also known as cost centres. An explanation of cost pools can be found in Chapter 3.

(c) Steps include:
- Ascertaining what activities are being carried out and investigate whether they are necessary.
- Ascertaining how effectively are the activities carried out and investigate ways of performing activities more effectively.
- Identify value-added and non-value-added activities and give priority to reducing non-value-added activities.
- Benchmark (see Chapter 22) activities against best practice.

15.27 (a) See 'Zero-base budgeting' in Chapter 15 for the answer to this question. In particular the answer should stress that the first stage should be to explicitly state the objectives that each part of the organization is trying to achieve. The activities for achieving these objectives should be described in a decision package. A decision package should consist of a base package, which would normally represent a minimum level of activity, plus incremental packages for higher levels of activity and costs. The packages are then evaluated and ranked in order of their decreasing benefits. A cut-off point is determined by the budgeted spending level, and packages are allocated according to their ranking until the budgeted spending level is reached.

(b) For the answer to this question see 'Zero-base budgeting' in Chapter 15.

(c) The problems that might be faced in introducing a zero-base budgeting scheme are:

(i) Implementation of zero-base budgeting might be resisted by staff. Traditional incremental budgeting tends to protect the empire that a manager has built. Zero-base budgeting challenges this empire, and so there is a strong possibility that managers might resist the introduction of such a system.

(ii) There is a need to combat a feeling that current operations are efficient.

(iii) The introduction of zero-base budgeting is time-consuming, and management may lack the necessary expertise.

(iv) Lack of top-management support.

(d) Beneficial results are likely to be obtained from a company with the following features:

(i) A large proportion of the expenditure is of a discretionary nature.

(ii) Management and employees of the company are unlikely to be resistant to change.

(iii) Suitable output measures can be developed.

(iv) A senior manager is employed who has some experience from another organization of implementing zero-base budgeting.

15.28 (a) (i) A three-level budget involves preparing budgets based on the following assumptions about uncertain future events:

1. The most likely outcome occurs.
2. The optimistic outcome occurs.
3. The pessimistic outcome occurs.

In its simplest form, a three-level budget might be prepared for sales volume only, but three-level budgets can also be prepared for uncertain cost items such as changes in wage rates or material prices.

(ii) Probabilistic budgets can be prepared using joint probabilities ascertained from decision tree analysis. When more than one variable is uncertain and the value of one variable is dependent on the value of other variables, a decision tree is a useful analytical tool for clarifying the range of alternative courses of action and their possible outcomes. For an illustration of the process see 'Decision tree analysis' and 'A more complex problem' in Chapter 12. In the budgeting process a decision tree is a useful tool for calculating the expected values of sales revenues and costs when interdependencies exist. A decision tree is also a useful tool for assisting in constructing probability distributions. Such probability distributions can be used to aid decision-making at the planning stage and assessing the significance of actual deviations from the budget. For example, a probability distribution might indicate that the probability of spending in excess of £100 000 of the expected value is 0.05. If a difference of £100 000 actually occurs then the probability distribution provides a useful indication of the significance of the variance.

(iii) For a description of how the simulation approach can be applied to the budgeting process see 'Simulation' in Chapter 14.

(b) (i) The three-level budget approach recognizes that more than one outcome is possible, and indicates the range of possible outcomes. Such an approach enables managers to quantify their predictions, and provides more useful information than a single value estimate.

(ii) The probability approach using the decision tree technique is an improvement on method (i) because it enables uncertainty of the range of possible outcomes to be quantified in the form of an expected value calculation. This is preferable to a three-level budget, which merely identifies uncertainty but does not quantify it. When probability distributions are constructed, the budget indicates the probabilities of possible outcomes occurring. It was noted in (a) (ii) that this approach is useful for selecting alternative courses of action at the planning stage and enabling actual outcomes to be interpreted more meaningfully.

Hence, from a decision-making and control point of view, the probability approach is superior to adopting a three-level budget.

(iii) Simulation enables complex inter-relationships to be expressed in terms of probability distributions and expected values. For a description of the advantages of simulation over the decision tree approach see

'Simulation' in Chapter 14. In addition, simulation enables one to test the sensitivity of the outcomes by asking 'What if?' questions for a wide range of eventualities and environmental changes.

15.29 (a) See 'The budgeting process in non-profit organizations' in Chapter 15 for the answer to this question. In particular, the answer should cover the following points:

(i) Insufficient strategic thinking and long-term planning. The annual budgeting process based on short-term plans was frequently used for policy planning. Allocation of resources should be based on a long-term planning process and not the annual budgeting process.

(ii) Traditional approaches failed to identify the costs of activities and the programmes to be implemented.

(iii) Traditional approaches tend to be based on incremental budgeting rather than considering alternative ways of achieving objectives.

(iv) Emphasis tended to be on separate planning for each department rather than focusing on activities or functions necessary to achieve organizational objectives.

(b) See 'Planning, programming budgeting systems' in Chapter 15 for an illustration of PPBS.

(c) Problems that have made PPBS difficult to introduce include:

(i) PPBS cuts across departmental activities and focuses on programmes rather than departments. Consequently, the system does not focus on traditional lines of authority and there is a tendency for heads of departments to be resistant to such changes.

(ii) Difficulty in matching programme structure to the organization's structure for the purpose of cost control (see 'Planning, programming budgeting systems' in Chapter 15 for an explanation of this).

(iii) Difficulty in defining objectives and stating objectives in quantitative terms. It is extremely difficult to measure the output of *services* and compare actual accomplishments with planned accomplishments.

Chapter 16

16.22 (a) A fixed budget refers to a budget which is designed to remain unchanged irrespective of the level of activity, whereas a flexible budget is a budget which adjusts the expense items for different levels of activity. See 'Flexible budgets' in Chapter 16 for an explanation of the objectives of flexible budgeting.

(b) (i)

Direct labour	£180 000	£202 500	£225 000
Direct labour hours	48 000	54 000	60 000
Flexible budget (overhead expenditure):			
Activity levels	80%	90%	100%
Direct labour hours	48 000	54 000	60 000

Variable costs	(£)	(£)	(£)
Indirect labour at £0.75 per direct labour hour	36 000	40 500	45 000
Consumable supplies at £0.375 per direct labour hour	18 000	20 250	22 500
Canteen and other welfare services at 6% of direct plus indirect wages	12 960	14 580	16 200
Semi-variable: variable (W1)	9 600	10 800	12 000
	76 560	86 130	95 700
Semi-variable: fixed (W1)	8 000	8 000	8 000
Fixed costs:			
Depreciation	18 000	18 000	18 000
Maintenance	10 000	10 000	10 000
Insurance	4 000	4 000	4 000
Rates	15 000	15 000	15 000
Management salaries	25 000	25 000	25 000
	156 560	166 130	175 700

Workings:

(W1) Obtained by using High and Low points method:

			(£)
High	64 000	Direct labour hours	20 800
Low	40 000	Direct labour hours	16 000
	24 000		4 800

$\frac{£4\ 800}{24\ 000} = £0.20$ per direct labour hour

64 000 × £0.20 = £12 800 variable costs

Total costs £20 800

∴ Fixed costs £8 000

(ii) Variable cost

(57 000/60 000 × £95 700)	90 915
Fixed costs	80 000
Budgeted cost allowance	170 915

16.23 (a) (i) Activity varies from month to month, but quarterly budgets are set by dividing total annual expenditure by 4.

(ii) The budget ought to be analysed by shorter intervals (e.g. monthly) and costs estimated in relation to monthly activity.

(iii) For control purposes monthly comparisons and cumulative monthly comparisons of planned and actual expenditure to date should be made.

(iv) The budget holder does not participate in the setting of budgets.

(v) An incremental budget approach is adopted. A zero-based approach would be more appropriate.

(vi) The budget should distinguish between controllable and uncontrollable expenditure.

(b) The information that should flow from a comparison of the actual and budgeted expenditure would consist of the variances for the month and year to date analysed into the following categories:

(i) controllable and uncontrollable items;

(ii) price and quantity variances with price variance analysed by inflationary and non-inflationary effects.

(c) (i) Flexible budgets should be prepared on a monthly basis. Possible measures of activity are number of patient days or expected laundry weight.

(ii) The laundry manager should participate in the budgetary process.

(iii) Costs should be classified into controllable and non-controllable items.

(iv) Variances should be reported and analysed by price and quantity on a monthly and cumulative basis.

(v) Comments should be added explaining possible reasons for the variances.

16.24

Task 1:

Performance Statement – Month to 31 October

Number of guest days = Original budget			9 600
Flexed budget			11 160
	Flexed budget (£)	Actual (£)	Variance (£)
Controllable expenses			
Food (1)	23 436	20 500	2936F
Cleaning materials (2)	2 232	2 232	0
Heat, light and power (3)	2 790	2 050	740F
Catering staff wages (4)	8 370	8 400	30A
	36 828	33 182	3646F
Non-controllable expenses			
Rent, rates, insurance and depreciation (5)	1 860	1 860	0

Notes:
(1) £20 160/9600 × 11 160.
(2) £1920/9600 × 11 160.
(3) £2400/9600 × 11 160.
(4) £11 160/40 x £30.
(5) Original fixed budget based on 30 days but October is a 31-day month (£1800/30 × 31).

Task 2:

(a) See the sections on the multiple functions of budgets (motivation) in Chapter 15, and 'Setting financial performance targets' in Chapter 16 for the answers to this question.

(b) Motivating managers ought to result in improved performance. However, besides motivation, improved performance is also dependent on managerial ability, training, education and the existence of a favourable environment. Therefore motivating managers is not guaranteed to lead to improved performance.

(c) The use of a fixed budget is unlikely to encourage managers to become more efficient where budgeted expenses are variable with activity. In the original performance report actual expenditure for 11.160 guest days is compared with budgeted expenditure for 9600 days. It is misleading to compare actual costs at one level of activity with budgeted costs at another level of activity. Where the actual level of activity is above the budgeted level adverse variances are likely to be reported for variable cost items. Managers will therefore be motivated to reduce activity so that favourable variances will be reported. Therefore it is not surprising that Susan Green has expressed concern that the performance statement does not reflect a valid reflection of her performance. In contrast, most of Brian Hilton's expenses are fixed and costs will not increase when volume increases. A failure to flex the budget will therefore not distort his performance.

To motivate, challenging budgets should be set and small adverse variances should normally be regarded as a healthy sign and not something to be avoided. If budgets are always achieved with no adverse variances this may indicate that undemanding budgets may have been set which are unlikely to motivate best possible performance. This situation could apply to Brian Hilton who always appears to report favourable variances.

16.25 (a) Recommendations are as follows:

(i) For cost control and managerial performance evaluation, expenses should be separated into their controllable and non-controllable categories. Two separate profit calculations should be presented: controllable profit, which is appropriate for measuring managerial performance, and a 'bottom-line' net profit, which measures the economic performance of each store rather than the manager.

(ii) The report should be based on an ex-post basis. In other words, if the environment is different from that when the original budget was set, actual performance should be compared with a budget that reflects any changed conditions. For example, the budget should be adjusted to reflect the effect of the roadworks.

(iii) Actual expenses should be compared with flexed budgets and not the original budget.

(iv) Each store consists of three departments. The report should therefore analyse gross profits by departments. Selling prices and the cost of goods sold are beyond the control of the stores' managers, but each departmental manager can influence sales volume. An analysis of gross profits by departments and a comparison with previous periods should provide useful feedback on sales performance and help in deciding how much space should be allocated to each activity.

(v) Stock losses should be minimized. Such losses are controllable by departmental managers. The cost of stock losses should therefore be monitored and separately reported.

(vi) The budget should include cumulative figures to give an indication of trends, performance to date and the potential annual bonus.

(vii) Any imputed interest charges should be based on economic values of assets and not historic costs.

(b) The report should include a discussion of the following:

(i) *Review of delegation policies:* Head office purchases the goods for sale, fixes selling prices, appoints permanent staff and sets pay levels. Stores managers are responsible for stores' running expenses, employment of temporary staff and control of stocks.

Purchasing is centralized, thus enabling the benefits of specialized buying and bulk purchasing to be obtained. Purchasing policies are coordinated with expected sales by consultation between head office buyers and stores and departmental managers. It is wise to make stores managers responsible for controlling stocks because they are in the best position to assess current and future demand.

Managers are responsible for sales volume but they cannot fix selling prices. There are strong arguments for allowing stores to set selling prices, and offer special discounts on certain goods. Central management may wish to retain some overall control by requiring proposed price changes beyond certain limits referred to them for approval. There are also strong arguments for allowing the stores' managers to appoint permanent staff. The stores' managers are likely to be in a better position to be able to assess the abilities necessary to be a successful member of their own team.

(ii) *Strengths of the management control system:*

1. Sales targets are set after consultation between head office and the departmental managers.
2. The budgets are prepared well in advance of the start of the budget year, thus giving adequate time for consultation.
3. Performance reports are available one week after the end of the period.
4. Budgets are adjusted for seasonal factors.
5. Significant variations in performance are investigated and appropriate action is taken.

(iii) *Weaknesses of the management control system:*

1. There is no consultation in the setting of expense budgets.
2. Actual costs are compared with a fixed budget and not a flexible budget.
3. Costs are not separated into controllable and non-controllable categories.
4. Budgets are set on an incremental basis with budgets set by taking last year's base and adjusting for inflation.
5. Budgets are not revised for control purposes. Targets set for the original budget before the start of the year may be inappropriate for comparison with actual expenses incurred towards the end of the budget year.
6. Using a budget that does not include ex-post results and that is not linked to controllable profit is likely to be demotivating, and results in managers having little confidence in the budget system.

(iv) *Recommendations:*

1. Compare actual costs with a flexed budget.
2. The performance report should separate costs into controllable and uncontrollable categories, and controllable profit should be highlighted. Any bonus payments should be related to controllable profit and not 'bottom-line' profits.
3. Introduce monthly or quarterly rolling budgets.
4. Ensure that the stores managers participate in setting the budget and accept the target against which they will be judged.
5. Set targets using a zero-base approach.
6. Consider extending the bonus scheme to departmental managers.

16.26 (a) See 'Performance measurement in service organizations' in Chapter 23 for the answer to this question.

(b) Products are often difficult to specify in service organizations. For example, in banks or building societies savers invest funds in savings accounts and these funds are used to provide mortgage loans to customers. Profits can be computed for a combination of both products but to compute profit for each product a transfer price must be established. This transfer price represents revenue for the savings account products and a cost for the mortgage products.

Further problems arise if costs are assigned to the different types of products within each product group. For example, most of the costs incurred in operating savings or mortgage products are joint to all products within each product group. Direct costs at the individual product level within a product group are virtually non-existent.

In service organizations only a very small proportion of total costs are variable. In contrast, variable costs consisting mainly of direct materials, represent a significant proportion of total costs in manufacturing organizations. Thus, marginal/variable costing principles may have little to offer in service organizations.

A further feature relating to service organizations is that they generally do not hold stocks. Thus product costs are not required for stock valuation and service organizations do not therefore have the conflict of producing separate product costs for decision-making and inventory valuation.

(c) In manufacturing organizations quality can be monitored at various stages of the production process and the finished product can be inspected prior to customer delivery. In many service organizations no tangible product is provided and quality can only be measured after the service has been delivered. In contrast, in manufacturing organizations the quality of the product can be judged prior to use.

Fitzgerald *et al.* (see Bibliography in the main text) suggest 12 areas of quality in service organizations. They are reliability, responsiveness, aesthetics, cleanliness, comfort, friendliness, communication, courtesy, competence, access, availability and security. For more detailed illustrations of measures of service quality you should refer to the three areas listed in the section in Chapter 23 on performance measurement in service organizations.

16.27 (a) The desirable attributes of a suitable measure of activity for flexing the budget are as follows:

(i) The selected measure should exert a major influence on the cost of the activity. The objective is to flex the budget to ascertain the costs that should be incurred for the actual level of activity. Therefore the costs of the activity and the measure selected should be highly correlated.

(ii) The measure selected should not be affected by factors other than volume. For example, if direct labour cost is selected as the activity measure then an increase in wage rates will cause labour cost to increase even when activity remains constant.

(iii) The measure should be easily understood. Complicated indexes are unlikely to be satisfactory.

(iv) The measure should be easily obtainable without too much cost.

(v) The measure should be based on output rather than input in order to ensure that managers do not obtain larger budget allowances for being inefficient.

(b) Because the activities of a service or overhead department tend not to be repetitive, it is unlikely that a system of standard costing can be justified. Output will be fairly diverse, and it may not be possible to find a single output measure that is highly correlated with costs. It might be necessary to flex the budget on inputs rather than outputs. Also, several variables are likely to cause changes in cost rather than a single measure of output, and an accurate flexible budget may require the use of multiple regression techniques. However, because multiple regression measures might not be easily obtainable and understood, a single input measure may be preferable.

It may be necessary to use several measures of activity within a cost centre for the different costs. For example, machine maintenance costs might be flexed according to machine hours, and lighting and heating costs might be flexed according to labour hours of input.

(c) Suitable measures include the following:

(i) *Standard hours of output:* This measure is suitable when output is sufficiently standardized to enable standard labour times to be established for each activity. It is unsatisfactory where labour efficiency is unlikely to be constant or output is too diverse to enable standard time to be established.

(ii) *Direct labour hours of input:* This measure is suitable where costs are highly correlated with labour hours of input, output cannot be measured in standard hours and labour efficiency is fairly constant. It is unsatisfactory if these conditions do not hold, because labour hours will be an unsatisfactory guide to output.

(iii) *Direct labour costs:* This measure is suitable where the same conditions apply as those specified in (ii) and the wage rates are not consistently changing. If these conditions do not apply then it will be unsatisfactory.

16.28 (a) The cybernetic system referred to in the question is illustrated in Fig. 16.1 in Chapter 16. The main limitations are:

(i) The human dimension is ignored. Individual behaviour varies and they do not react to deviations from objectives in a single prescribed manner as predicted by the model.

(ii) The time dimension is not incorporated into the model. If feedback response and action is too rapid then this may be counterproductive, whereas inefficiencies will be allowed to continue if feedback is too slow.

(iii) The model is based on feedback controls whereas it is more appropriate for organizations to focus on feedforward controls.

(iv) The model assumes that control operates only on the inputs to the system, whereas control may entail changing the goals, expected outputs or the measurement system.

(b) (i) The main pre-requisites are:

1. A single clearly specified objective (or multiple objectives if they are all consistent).
2. A clear input–output relation so that the impact that changing the inputs has on outputs can be predicted.
3. Outputs can be easily and accurately measured.
4. Clearly specified control responses where actual outcomes differ from predicted outcomes.

If the above conditions exist then it is likely that the system will work in a similar manner to that predicted by the mechanical control system.

(ii) The answer should draw attention to the fact that there is no single unifying objective such as profit. Instead, they are likely to have several objectives some of which may conflict. Consequently, it is difficult to specify clear aims for the system. Furthermore, management perceptives of what are the major objectives may differ. This is likely to result in conflict and raise political issues.

Because of the multiple objectives and the absence of an over-riding profit motive it is difficult to measure the outputs. Hence, there is a greater emphasis on subjective rather than objective measurement. Control is therefore difficult to implement because it is difficult to predict the impact that changes in inputs will have on outputs. As a result, there tends to be an overemphasis on measuring inputs rather than outputs.

16.29 (a) See 'Setting financial performance targets' in Chapter 16 for the answer to this question.

(b) See 'Participation in the budgeting and target setting process' in Chapter 16 for the answer to this question.

(c) Management by exception is based on the principle that accounting reports should highlight those activities that do not conform to plans, so that managers can devote their scarce time to focusing on these items. Effective control requires that corrective action be taken so that actual outcomes conform to planned outcomes. These principles are based on the following assumptions:

(i) Valid targets and budgets can be set.

(ii) Suitable performance measures exist that enable divergencies from plans to be correctly measured.

(iii) Plans and divergencies from plan are communicated to the individuals who are responsible for implementing the plan.

(iv) Performance reports correctly distinguish those items that are controllable by a manager from those that are non-controllable.

(v) Feedback information is translated into corrective action.

(vi) Management intervention is not required where no adverse variances exist.

(vii) Divergencies from plan can only be remedied by corrective action.

Management by exception as an effective system of routine reporting will depend on the extent to which the above conditions hold. The system will have to be supplemented by informal controls to the extent that the above conditions do not hold. Management by exception can only be a very effective means of control if behavioural factors are taken into account when interpreting the divergencies from plan. Otherwise there is a danger that other systems of control will have a greater influence on future performance.

(d) The answer should include the following:

(i) An explanation of why it is considered necessary to distinguish between controllable and uncontrollable costs at the responsibility level.

(ii) Difficulty in assigning variances to responsibility centres when dual responsibilities apply or interdependencies exist.

(iii) Possible dysfunctional consequences that might occur when a manager's performance is measured by his or her success in controlling only those items that have been designated as controllable by him or her.

(iv) Arguments for including those uncontrollable items that a manager might be able to influence in a separate section of the performance report.

The above items are discussed in 'The controllability principle' in Chapter 16.

(e) Budget statements should not be expressed only in monetary terms. This is because all aspects of performance relating to a firm's goals cannot be expressed in monetary terms. Therefore budgetary statements should be supplemented by non-monetary measures. Monetary gains can be made at the expense of items that cannot easily be measured in monetary terms but that may be critical to an organization's long-term profitability. For example, monetary gains can be made by hierarchical pressure to cut costs, but such gains might be at the expense of adverse motivational changes, increased labour turnover and reduced product quality. The long-term costs of these items might be far in excess of the cost-cutting benefits.

A range of non-monetary measures is presented in the the balanced scorecard (see Chapter 23). Some qualitative variables (e.g. measurement of attitudes) are difficult to measure, but judgements based on interviews can be made. The inclusion of behavioural and qualitative factors in budget statements more accurately reflects the complexity of managerial performance in relation to a number of objectives rather than a single monetary objective. The difficulty with incorporating qualitative variables into budget statements is not sufficient grounds for expressing budget statements only in monetary terms.

16.30 (i) Budgets are used for a variety of purposes, one of which is to evaluate the performance of budgetees. When budgets form the basis for future performance evaluation, there is a possibility that budgetees will introduce bias into the process for personal gain and self-protection. Factors that are likely to cause managers to submit budget estimates that do not represent their best estimates include:

1. *The reward system:* If managers believe that rewards depend upon budget attainment then they might be encouraged to underestimate sales budgets and overestimate cost budgets.
2. *Past performance:* If recent performance has been poor, managers may submit favourable plans so as to obtain approval from their supervisors. Such an approach represents a trade-off advantage of short-run security and approval against the risk of not being able to meet the more optimistic plans.
3. *Incremental budgeting:* Incremental budgeting involves adding increments to past budgets to reflect expected future changes. Consequently, the current budget will include bias that has been built into previous budgets.
4. *External influences:* If managers believe that their performance is subject to random external influences then, from a self-protection point of view, they might submit budgets that can easily be attained.
5. *Style of performance evaluation:* A budget-constrained style of evaluation might encourage the budgetee to meet the budget at all costs. Consequently, budgetees will be motivated to bias their budget estimates.

(ii) The following procedures should be introduced to minimize the likelihood of biased estimates:

1. Encourage managers to adopt a profit-conscious style of evaluation.
2. Adopt a system of zero-base budgeting.
3. Key figures in the budget process (e.g. sales estimates) should be checked by using information from different sources.
4. Planning and operating variances (see 'Ex-post variance analysis' in Chapter 19 for a discussion of planning and operating variances) should be segregated. Managers might be motivated to submit more genuine estimates if they are aware that an ex-post budget will be used as a basis for performance appraisal.
5. Participation by the budgetees in the budget process should be encouraged so as to secure a greater commitment to the budget process and improve communication between budgetees, their superior and the budget accountants.

16.31 (a) (i) Managers can improve short-term performance at the expense of long-term in many different ways. For example, they can reduce discretionary expenses such as training, advertising and research and development. Reduced expenses on these items are likely to have little impact in the short-term but they will have adverse long-term impacts.

(ii) The answer to this question should describe the content of Figure 16.2. See 'harmful side-effects of controls' for a possible answer to this question.

(iii) Over-simplification of specific measures relates to a narrow focus on specific measures possibly as a result of an over-emphasis on financial measures. For example, a purchasing officer might be judged on his/her ability to achieve the budgeted purchase cost. However, this might encourage the manager to purchase inferior quality materials in large quantities to obtain maximum discounts. This may be reflected in an improved performance measure for the purchasing officer but the additional stockholding costs and extra costs and lost sales arising from poor quality may outweigh the reduced purchase cost. Thus the actions taken by the purchasing officer may be detrimental to the organization as a whole. Rather than relying on a single simplistic financial measure it may be preferable to judge performance on the basis of financial and non-financial measures.

(iv) Deliberate distortion arises from manipulating data to improve performance. Managers may also choose to underperform in order to obtain an easier target next period.

(b) See 'addressing the dysfunctional consequences of short-term financial performance measures' in Chapter 20 for a possible answer to this question. In addition, the answer should stress the need to adopt a more profit-conscious style of evaluation and incorporate a combination of financial and non-financial measures for performance evaluation.

Chapter 17

17.11 (a) Contingency theory has been criticized on the grounds that organizational responses to environmental changes will be influenced by organizational culture, managerial styles and the impact of individuals within the organization. Established working practices and the set of values, beliefs and social norms which tend to be shared by organizational members can have a dramatic impact on organizational strategies and policies. It is claimed that organizational culture is one of the key determinants of the control system but it does not feature prominently in contingency theory studies. Indeed, it does not feature in the contingent factors listed in Exhibit 17.1 in the main text.

A possible reason for this is that areas of culture, power and interpersonal relationships are difficult to measure whereas the typical factors identified in the literature, summarized in Exhibit 17.1, can be more easily measured and observed. The contingency theory literature is criticized because it fails to take into account important factors influencing the control system, such as employee reward and incentive schemes, selection and training of employees and culture and power relationships.

(b) The answer to this question should briefly discuss the different broad categories of control described in Chapter 16 and stress that greater emphasis can be placed on personnel and cultural or social controls when a policy is adopted of promoting from internal staff. In addition, greater emphasis can be given to focusing on judging managerial performance over a longer term time horizon since managers are likely to remain in employment with the company for a longer time period.

17.12 The answer requires a discussion of:

(i) The assumptions underpinning conventional approaches (such as, the decision-maker having all necessary information for all possible alternatives, having the mental capacity to evaluate all alternatives and that he or she will act rationally and seek to maximize utility).

(ii) The theoretical criticisms of the above assumptions. Examples include:
- Cooper *et al.* (1981) relating to limited rationality, anarchic nature of organizational processes and experimentation and confusion rather than planned action;
- Simon (1959) relating to satisficing rather than maximizing behaviour;
- Lindblom (1959) relating to 'muddling through';
- Cohen, March and Olsen's (1972) 'garbage can' model of decision-making.

(iii) The empirical work:
- Mintzberg (1973) and Bruns and McKinnon (1993) concerning discontinuity, disorder and brevity of managerial decision-making, the role of informal information and the time allocated to the informational role by managers.
- Cooper *et al.* (1981) relating to accounting information being used for symbolic and political/bargaining purposes.
- Burchell *et al.* (1980) comparing actual and ideal uses of accounting information.
- Ouchi (1979) relating to the circumstances when formal financial control systems are inappropriate

References

Bruns, W.J. Jr. and McKinnon, S.M. (1993), Information and managers: a field study, *Journal of Management Accounting Research*, Fall, 84; 108.

Mintzberg, H. (1973), *The Nature of Managerial Work*, Harper and Row.

See Bibliography of the main text for the remaining references.

17.13 The answer could include a discussion of the following points:

(i) The difficulty in specifying objectives in clear and unambiguous terms.

(ii) The difficulty in measuring outputs.

(iii) Problems arising from the use of conventional accounting controls in public and not-for-profit organizations. For example, the emphasis on short-run performance measures, the subjectivity of accounting information not being recognized and the assumption of unitary goals.

(iv) The appropriateness of different types of controls when goals range from clear and unambiguous to ambiguous drawing off the work of Macintosh relating to scorekeeping and uncertainty described in Chapter 17.

(v) The ideal and actual uses of accounting information based on various states of uncertainty relating to objectives and cause and effect relationships that determine the consequences of actions. Here the answer could draw off the work of Burchell *et al.* described in Chapter 17.

(vi) The different purposes for which management accounting information is likely to be used with an emphasis on relating the comments to public sector and not-for-profit organizations.

(vii) How the writings of Macintosh and Burchell *et al.* described above apply to public sector organizations and point towards the use of accounting information for judgmental and political purposes. In such circumstances simplistic cybernetic control mechanisms underpinning accounting controls are likely to be inappropriate.

17.14–17.18

The answers to these questions require a repetition of much of the content of Chapter 17. Outline answers are therefore not provided for these questions.

Chapter 18

18.16 A favourable labour efficiency variance indicates that actual hours used were less than the standard hours produced. The favourable variance was £7800. Therefore the standard hours produced were 18 700 (17 500 + £7800/£6.50).

Answer = D

18.17 Materials price variance = (Standard price – Actual price) × Actual quantity
= (Actual quantity × Standard price) – Actual cost
= (8200 × £0.80) – £6888
= £328 Adverse
Material usage variance = (Standard quantity – Actual quantity) × Standard price
= (870 × 8 kg = 6960 – 7150) × £0.80
= £152 Adverse
Answer = D

18.18 Fixed overhead variance = Budgeted cost (not flexed) – Actual cost
= £10 000 per month – £9800
= £200 Favourable
Answer = B

18.19 $\text{Standard fixed overhead rate} = \frac{\text{Budgeted cost (£48 000)}}{\text{Budgeted output (4800 units)}} = £10$

Overheads incurred = Budgeted cost + Expenditure variance (£2000) = £50 000
Overheads absorbed = £50 000 – Under-absorption (£8000) = £42 000
Actual number of units produced = £42 000/£10 = 4200
Answer = C

18.20 Volume variance
= (Actual production – Budgeted production) × Fixed overhead rate
= (19 500 – 20 000) × (£100 000/20 000)
= £2500A
Answer = B

18.21 Sales volume variance = (Actual sales volume – Budgeted sales volume) × Standard contribution margin
= (4500 – 5000) £4.40
= £2200 Adverse
Answer = B

18.22 Budgeted fixed overhead hour rate = £135 000/9000 = £15
Capacity variance = [Actual hours (9750) – Budgeted hours (9000)] × £15 = £11 250F
Answer = B

18.23 (a) Budgeted fixed overhead hour rate = £45 000/10 000 = £4.50
Capacity variance = [Actual hours (11 135) – Budgeted hours (10 000)] × £4.50 = £5107.50F
Answer = D
(b) Volume efficiency variance = [Standard hours (10 960) – Actual hours (11 135)] × £4.50 = £787.50A
Answer = D

18.24 1. *Preliminary calculations*
The standard product cost and selling price are calculated as follows:

	(£)
Direct materials	
X (10 kg at £1)	10
Y (5 kg at £5)	25
Direct wages (5 hours × £3)	15
Fixed overhead (5 hours × 200% of £3)	30
Standard cost	80
Profit (20/(100 – 20)) × £80	20
Selling price	100

The actual profit for the period is calculated as follows:

	(£)	(£)
Sales (9500 at £110)		1 045 000
Direct materials: X	115 200	
Y	225 600	
Direct wages (46 000 × £3.20)	147 200	
Fixed overhead	290 000	778 000
Actual profit		267 000

It is assumed that the term 'using a fixed budget' refers to the requirement to reconcile the budget with the original fixed budget.

	(£)	(£)
Material price variance:		
(standard price – actual price)		
× actual quantity		
X: (£1 – £1.20) × 96 000	19 200 A	
Y: (£5 – £4.70) × 48 000	14 440 F	4800 A
Material usage variance:		
(standard quantity – actual quantity)		
× standard price		
X: (9500 × 10 = 95 000 – 96 000) × £1	1 000 A	
Y: (9500 × 5 = 47 500 – 48 000) × £5	2 500 A	3500 A

The actual materials used are in standard proportions. Therefore there is no mix variance.

Wage rate variance:		
(standard rate – actual rate) × actual hours		
(£3 – £3.20) × 46 000	9 200 A	
Labour efficiency variance:		
(standard hours – actual hours) × standard rate		
(9500 × 5 = 47 500 – 46 000) × £3	4 500 F	4 700 A
Fixed overhead expenditure:		
budgeted fixed overheads – actual fixed overheads		
(10 000 × £30 = £300 000 – £290 000)		10 000 F
Volume efficiency variance:		
(standard hours – actual hours) × fixed		
overhead rate (47 500 – 46 000) × £6	9 000 F	
Volume capacity variance:		
(actual hours – budgeted hours) × fixed		
overhead rate (46 000 – 50 000) × £6	24 000 A	15 000 A
Sales margin price variance:		
(actual margin – standard margin) × actual		
sales volume (£30 – £20) × 9500	95 000 F	
Sales margin volume variance:		
(actual sales volume – budgeted sales volume)		
× Standard margin		
(9500 – 10 000) × £20	10 000 A	85 000 F
Total variance		67 000 F

	(£)
Budgeted profit (10 000 units at £20)	200 000
Add favourable variances (see above)	67 000
Actual profit	267 000

18.25 (a) *Standard product cost for one unit of product XY*

	(£)
Direct materials (8 kg (W2) at £1.50 (W1) per kg)	12.00
Direct wages (2 hours (W4) at £4 (W3) per hour)	8.00
Variable overhead (2 hours (W4) at £1 (W5) per hour)	2.00
	22.00

Workings

(W1) Actual quantity of materials purchased at standard price is £225 000 (actual cost plus favourable material price variance).
Therefore standard price = £1.50 (£225 000/150 000 kg).

(W2) Material usage variance = 6000 kg (£9000/£1.50 standard price).
Therefore standard quantity for actual production = 144 000 kg (150 000 – 6000 kg).
Therefore standard quantity per unit = 8 kg (144 000 kg/18 000 units).

(W3) Actual hours worked at standard rate = £128 000 (£136 000 – £8000).
Therefore standard rate per hour = £4 (£128 000/32 000 hours).

(W4) Labour efficiency variance = 4000 hours (£16 000/£4).
Therefore standard hours for actual production = 36 000 hours (32 000 + 4000).
Therefore standard hours per unit = 2 hours (36 000 hours/18 000 units).

(W5) Actual hours worked at the standard variable overhead rate is £32 000 (£38 000 actual variable overheads less £6000 favourable expenditure variance).
Therefore, standard variable overhead rate = £1 (£32 000/32 000 hours).

(b) See 'Types of cost standards' in Chapter 18 for the answer to this question.

18.26 (a) (i) A fixed overhead volume variance only occurs with an absorption costing system. The question indicates that a volume variance has been reported. Therefore the company must operate an absorption costing system and report the sales volume variance in terms of profit margins, rather than contribution margins.

Budgeted profit margin = Budgeted profit (£4250)/Budgeted volume (1500 units) = £2.83

Adverse sales volume variance in units = £850/£2.83 = 300 units

Therefore actual sales volume was 300 units below budgeted sales volume

Actual sales volume = 1200 units (1500 units – 300 units)

(ii) Standard quantity of material used per units of output:
Budgeted usage (750 kg)/Budgeted production (1500 units) = 0.5 kg
Standard price = Budgeted material cost (£4500)/Budgeted usage (750 kg) = £6
Material usage variance = (Standard quantity – Actual Quantity) Standard price
£150A = (1550 × 0.5 kg = 775 kg – AQ) £6
– £150 = 4650 – 6AQ
6AQ = 4800
Actual quantity used = 800 kg

(iii) Material price variance = (Standard price – Actual price) × Actual purchases
£1000F = (£6 – Actual price) × 1000 kg
£1000F = £6000 – 1000AP
1000AP = £5000
AP = £5 per kg
Actual material cost = 1000 kg × £5 = £5000

(iv) Standard hours per unit of output = $\frac{\text{Budgeted hours (1125)}}{\text{Budgeted output (1500 units)}}$
= 0.75 hours
Standard wage rate = Budgeted labour cost (£4500)/Budgeted hours (1125)
= £4
Labour efficiency variance = (Standard hours – Actual hours) × Standard rate
£150A = (1550 × 0.75 = 1162.5 – Actual hours) × £4
– £150 = £4650 – 4AH
4AH = £4800
Actual hours = 1200

(v) Total labour variance = Standard cost – Actual cost
(£200A + £150A)= (1550 × 0.75 hrs × £4) – Actual cost
£350A = £4650 – Actual cost
Actual cost = £5000

(vi) Standard variable overhead cost per unit
= $\frac{\text{Budgeted variable overheads (2250)}}{\text{Budgeted output (1500 units)}}$
= £1.50 hours
Total variable overhead variance = Standard cost – Actual cost
(£600A + £75A) = (1550 × £1.50 = £2325) – Actual cost
£675A = £2325 – Actual cost
Actual cost = £3000

(vii) Fixed overhead expenditure variance = Budgeted cost – Actual cost
£2500F = £4500 – Actual cost
Actual cost = £2000

(b) See Chapter 18 for an explanation of the causes of the direct material usage, direct labour rate and sales volume variances

18.27 (a) The following variances can be calculated.

		(£)
(i)	Wage rate: (standard wage rate – actual wage rate) × actual hours [£2 – (£14 000/6500)] × 6500	= 1 000A
(ii)	Labour efficiency: (standard hours – actual hours) × standard rate [(500 × 14 = 7000) – 6500] × £2	= 1 000F
(iii)	Price variance: (standard price – actual price) × actual quantity (Output of Dept A) [£9 – (£21 000/1400)] × 1400	= 8 400A
(iv)	Usage variance: (standard quantity – actual quantity) × standard rate (Output of Dept A) [(500 × 3 = 1500) – 1400] × £9	= 900F
(v)	Price variance: (standard price – actual price) × actual quantity (Material X) [£5 – (£11 500/1900)] × 1900	= 2 000A
(vi)	Usage variance: (standard quantity – actual quantity) × standard rate (Material X) [(500 × 4 = 2000) – 1900] × £5	= 500F
(vii)	Variable overhead: (flexed budget – actual variable overheads) Expenditure (6500 × £1 = £6500) – £8000	= 1 500A
(viii)	Variable overhead: (standard hours – actual hours) × variable overhead rate Efficiency (7000 – 6500) × £1	= 500F
(ix)	Fixed overhead expenditure: (budgeted fixed overheads × actual fixed overheads)	
	Department B (400 × £3 = £1200) – £1600	= 400A
	Allocated (400 × £8 = £3200) – £2900	= 300F
(x)	Volume variance: (actual production – budgeted production) × fixed overhead rate	
	Department B (500 – 400) × £3	= 300F
	Allocated (500 – 400) × £8	= 800F
	Departmental standard cost for actual production (500 × £100)	= 50 000
	Actual cost	= 59 000
	Total departmental variance	9 000A

Variances (i)–(x) add to £9000 adverse. However, not all of the variances are within the control of department B. From the information given in the question, it is not possible to specify which variances are controllable and non-controllable by department B. The following are assumed to be non-controllable:

Wage rate: Assumed wage rates are set by the personnel department and that the correct grade of labour has been used.

Material price: Assumed that a central purchasing department exists and that the purchasing officer is responsible for the price variance of material X. The manager of department A is responsible for the price variance for the output of department A.

Allocated fixed overhead expenditure variance: This expenditure is controllable at the point where it is incurred. The actual spending on allocated fixed overheads is not determined by department B.

The following variances might be controllable by the manager of department B:

Labour efficiency
Material usage
Variable overhead efficiency
Fixed overhead volume
Fixed overhead expenditure

Fixed overhead volume might be due to a failure to achieve budgeted sales, or machine breakdowns may have occurred that are beyond the control of department B. Any meaningful analysis of the overhead expenditure variance requires a comparison of actual and budgeted expenditure for each individual item. Only by comparing individual items of expenditure and ascertaining the reasons for the variance can one determine whether the variances are controllable or non-controllable. The foregoing analysis assumes the volume variance and overhead expenditure variances to be controllable by the manager of department B. The performance report should analyse variances into their controllable and non-controllable elements:

Department B performance report: Month 7

	(£)	(£)	(£)
Standard cost for actual production			50 000
Controllable variances			
Labour efficiency		1 000F	
Material usage: Department A	900F		
Material X	500F	1 400F	
Overhead expenditure: Fixed	400A		
Variable	1500A	1 900A	
Variable overhead efficiency		500F	
Volume variance: Department B	300F		
Allocated	800F	1 100F	2 100F
Non-controllable variances			
Wage rate		1 000A	
Material price: Department A	8400A		
Material X	2000A	10 400A	
Fixed overhead expenditure (allocated)		300F	11 100A
Actual cost			59 000

(b) The standard costing system is not being operated effectively at present. The variances attributed to department B are not analysed into their controllable and non-controllable elements. In addition, the production manager appears to be using the system in an incorrect manner. He or she appears to be using the system in a punitive manner that might lead to some of the behavioural problems discussed in Chapter 16. Performance reports should be used to help managers control their activities and not as a recriminatory device.

18.28 (a)

	Favourable (£)	Adverse (£)	(£)
Standard cost for actual production (*W1*)			31 638
Material variances:			
Price (*W2*)	85		
Usage (*W3*)	196		
Labour variances:			
Rate (*W4*)		154	
Overtime (*W4*)		100	
Efficiency (*W5*)		250	
Variable overhead efficiency (*W6*)		30	
Overhead expenditure variance (*W7*)	—	288	
	281	822	541A
Actual cost			32 179

Workings

(*W1*) Variable cost per unit:

	(£)
Direct materials	49
Direct labour	25
Variable overhead	3
	77

Standard cost for actual production:

Variable cost	22 638	(294 × £77)
Fixed cost	9 000	
	31 638	

Note that the above calculation is based on a variable costing basis, with fixed costs treated as a period cost.

(*W2*) Material price variance: [£7 – (£14 125/2030)] × 2030 = £85F
(*W3*) Material usage variance: [(294 × 7 = 2058) – 2030] × £7 = £196F
(*W4*) Wage rate variance: [£5 – (£7854/1520)] × 1520 = £254A
£100 of the variance is due to overtime (40 hrs at £2.50)
(*W5*) Labour efficiency: [(294 × 5 = 1470) – 1520] × £5 = £250A
(*W6*) Variable overhead efficiency: [(294 × 5 = 1470) – 1520] × £0.60 = £30A
(*W7*) Overhead expenditure: [£9000 + (1520 × £0.60)] – £10 200 = £288A

(b) A variable costing approach has been adopted in (a). Therefore the fixed overheads are not unitized and included in the product costs. Consequently, a fixed overhead volume variance does not arise. With a variable costing system, the fixed overhead volume variance is not considered to be of economic significance, since fixed overheads are a sunk cost. The fixed overhead expenditure variance should be calculated, because actual expenditure may be different from budget, and is therefore of economic significance. It is not possible to separate the expenditure variance into the fixed and variable elements from the information given in the question. In practice, the variances should be separated, since this will provide more useful control information. Note that the variable overhead efficiency variance is included with the labour variances, since this is due to labour efficiency.

An alternative presentation would have been to calculate the variances based on an absorption costing system. This approach would result in the following additional variances:

Volume capacity [1520 – (300(*W1*) × 5)] × £6	= £120 F
Volume efficiency [(294 × 5 = 1470) – 1520] × £6	= £300 A
Volume variance	180 A

The revised report is as follows:

			(£)
Standard cost for actual production (294 × £107)			31 458
	Favourable	Adverse	
Variances calculated in (a)		541	
Volume capacity	120		
Volume efficiency		300	
Actual cost	120	841	721A
			32 179

Note that fixed overheads are now unitized and charged to production at £30 per unit. This approach is necessary for external reporting, but is questionable for cost control. The amounts attached to the volume capacity and efficiency variances have no economic significance because the fixed overheads are a sunk cost.

Working

(*W1*) Budgeted fixed overheads are £9000 and the budgeted rate per unit is £30. Therefore budgeted production is 300 units (9000/30).

(c) For a description of the approaches see 'Establishing cost standards' in Chapter 18 and 'Engineering methods' Chapter 24. Note that the approaches outlined in Chapter 18 also refer to engineering methods. If the product has been produced in the past the standard quantity can be estimated from historical records. The limitation of this approach is that standard quantities might be set that incorporate existing inefficiencies. Any adjustments from the historical standard are likely to be resisted unless inducements are offered. The advantage of using historical records is that it avoids the intensive and expensive studies of operations (e.g. time and motion studies) which are associated with engineering methods. Operatives may also be hostile to a standard costing system if time and motion studies are employed to set standard times.

The advantage of engineering methods is that the most efficient methods of operating are established and rigorous scientific methods are used to set standards. This might result in tight standards that are not internalized by the budgetees. It is therefore important that production staff participate in setting the standards.

It is normally possible to set reliable quantity standards, but this is unlikely to be the case with price standards. Price changes are normally due to external factors that are beyond the control of the purchasing officer (for materials) or the personnel officer (for wages rates). It is likely that price variances are due to incorrect forecasts rather than purchasing performance. Nevertheless, feedback information should be produced indicating the ability of the purchasing officer to predict future prices. This feedback might help to improve the accuracy of future forecasts of material prices.

A major problem in setting standards is that future changes might occur that were not envisaged when the standard was set. It is therefore important that standards be reviewed frequently and changes made. Wherever possible, variances should be split into planning and operational variances.

18.29 (a) See 'purposes of standard costing' in Chapter 18 for the answer to this question.

(b) See 'Types of cost standards' in Chapter 18 for the answer. Currently attainable standards are generally considered to be appropriate for meeting all of the purposes specified in (a).

(c) Standard costing is best suited to manufacturing organizations but it can be applied to activities within service organizations where output can be measured and there are clearly defined input/output relationships. For a discussion of how standard costing might be affected by modern initiatives see 'criticisms of standard costing' and 'future role of standard costing' in Chapter 19.

(d) The answer to this question could discuss the problem of the joint price/usage variance (see Chapter 18) and the limitations of fixed overhead variances for cost control purposes (see also Chapter 18). In addition, the answer could question the linking of direct labour hours to overhead variances since overheads may be caused by cost drivers other than direct labour.

Chapter 19

19.15 (a)

Material	Actual mix (litres)	Standard mix (litres)	Difference	Standard price (£)	Variance (£)
X	984	885.6 (40%)	98.4A	2.50	246.0A
Y	1230	1328.4 (60%)	98.4F	3.00	295.2F
	2214	2214.0			49.2F

Answer = B

(b) Expected output = 73.8 units (2314/30)
Actual output = 72 units
Standard cost per unit of output = £84
Yield variance = 1.8 units × £84 = £151.20A
Answer = D

19.16 Budgeted average price = [(£100 × 100) + (£50 × 150) + (£35 × 250)]/500 = £52.50

The market share variance is calculated as follows:
(Actual market share – budgeted market share) × (Actual industry volume × budgeted average selling price)
(494/2650 – 500/2500) × (2650 × £52.50) = £1890A

Sales mix variance calculation:

Product	Actual sales (units)	Actual sales in budgeted mix	Difference	Budgeted price (£)	Variance (£)
R	108	98.8 (20%)	9.2F	100	920F
S	165	148.2 (30%)	16.8F	50	840F
T	221	247.0 (50%)	26.0A	35	910A
	494	494.0			850F

Answer = E

19.17 (a) Market size variance = (Budgeted market share percentage) × (Actual industry sales – budgeted industry sales) × budgeted contribution
= (15 000/75 000) × (10% × 75 000) × £80 = £120 000A
Answer = C

(b) The market share variance is calculated as follows:
(Actual market share – budgeted market share) × (Actual industry volume × budgeted average contribution)
[(13 000/67 500) – 0.20] (67 500 × £80) = £40 000A
Answer = A

19.18 (a) Planning variance = (Original standard price) – (Market price during the period) × Quantity purchased
The difference between the original standard and the market price is £0.40A. Multiplying this by the actual purchases of

7700 kg gives £3080A. This is not listed in the possible answers. It is therefore assumed that it is the examiner's intention is to define quantity purchased as the standard quantity for actual production (7 kg × 1000 = 7000 kg). Using this figure the planning variance is £2800A.
Answer = B

(b) The standard quantity is 7000 kg (1000 × 7 kg) and the actual quantity is 7700 kg giving an adverse variance of 700 kg. Multiplying this by the *ex-post* standard (market) price of £4.50 gives a usage variance of £3150A.
Answer = C

19.19 (a) Material price:
(standard price – actual price) × actual quantity
(£3 – £4) × 22 000 = £22 000 A
Material usage:
(standard quantity – actual quantity) × standard price ((1400 × 15 = 21 000) – 22 000) × £3 = 3000 A
Wage rate:
(standard rate – actual rate) × actual hours
(£4 – £5) × 6800 = £6800 A
Labour efficiency:
((1400 × 5 = 7000) – 6800) × £4 = £800 F
Fixed overhead expenditure:
(budgeted fixed overheads – actual fixed overheads) (1000 × £5 = £5000 – £6000) = £1000 A
Volume efficiency:
(standard hrs – actual hrs) × FOAR
(1400 × 5 = 7000 – 6800) × £1 = 200 F
Volume capacity:
(actual hrs – budgeted hrs) × FOAR
(6800 – 5000) × £1 = £1800 F
Variable overhead efficiency:
(standard hrs – actual hrs) × VOAR
(7000 – 6800) × £2 = £400 F
Variable overhead expenditure:
(flexed budgeted variable overheads – actual variable overheads) (6800 × £2 – £11 000) = £2600 F
Sales margin price:
(actual margin – standard margin) × actual sales volume
(£102 – £80 = £22 – £20) × 1200 = £2400 F
Sales margin volume:
(actual sales – budgeted sales) × standard margin (1200 – 1000) × £20 = 4000 F

Reconciliation of budgeted and actual profit

	Adverse (£)	Favourable (£)	(£)
Budgeted profit			20 000
Sales margin price		2 400	
Sales margin volume		4 000	
Material price	22 000		
Material usage	3 000		
Wage rate	6 800		
Labour efficiency		800	
Fixed overhead expenditure	1 000		
Fixed overhead efficiency		200	
Fixed overhead capacity		1 800	
Variable overhead expenditure		2 600	
Variable overhead efficiency		400	
	32 800	12 200	
Net adverse variance			20 600
Actual profit/(loss)			(600)

(b)

Stores ledger control account

Creditors	66 000	WIP	63 000
		Material usage variance	3 000
	66 000		66 000

Variance accounts

Creditors	22 000	Wages control (labour efficiency)	800
Stores ledger (material usage)	3 000	Fixed overhead (volume)	2 000
Wages control (wage rate)	6 800	Variable overhead (expenditure)	2 600
Fixed overhead (expenditure)	1 000	Variable overhead (efficiency)	400
		Costing P + L a/c (balance)	27 000
	32 800		32 800

Costing P + L account

Cost of sales	96 000	Sales	122 400
Variance account (net variances)	27 000	Loss for period	600
	123 000		123 000

WIP control account

Stores ledger	63 000	Finished goods stock	112 000
Wages control	28 000		
Fixed factory overhead	7 000		
Variable factory overhead	14 000		
	112 000		112 000

Wages control account

Wages accrued account	34 000	WIP	28 000
Labour efficiency variance	800	Wage rate variance	6 800
	34 800		34 800

Fixed factory overhead account

Expense creditors	6 000	WIP	7 000
Volume variance	2 000	Expenditure variance	1 000
	8 000		8 000

Variable factory overhead account

Expense creditors	11 000	WIP	14 000
Expenditure variance	2 600		
Efficiency variance	400		
	14 000		14 000

Finished goods stock

WIP	112 000	Cost of sales	96 000
		Closing stock c/fwd	16 000
	112 000		112 000

Cost of sales account

Finished goods stock	96 000	Cost P + L a/c	96 000

19.20 (a)

	(£)	(£)
(i) *Actual quantity at actual prices (given)*		17 328
(ii) *Actual quantity in actual mix at standard prices*		
F 1680 × £4	6720	
G 1650 × £3	4950	
H 870 × £6	5220	16 890
(iii) *Actual quantity in standard mix at standard prices*		
F (4200 × 15/35 = 1800) × £4	7200	
G (4200 × 12/35 = 1440) × £3	4320	
H (4200 × 8/35 = 960) × £6	5760	17 280

Material price variance
= (Standard price – Actual price) Actual quantity
= (Actual quantity × Standard price) – Actual cost
= (ii) – (i) 438A
Mix variance = (iii) – (ii) 390F
Yield variance = (Actual yield – Standard yield for actual input) × standard cost per unit of output

= (3648 – (4200/35 × 32 = 3840)) × £4.50 (i.e. £144/32) 864A

Material usage variance = Mix variance (£390F) + Yield variance (£864A) 474A

or Standard cost for actual output (3648 × £4.50 = £16 416) – Actual quantity at standard prices (£16 890) = £474A

(b) *Mix variances*

	Total	F	G	H
Standard mix		1800	1440	960
Actual usage		1680	1650	870
Difference		120	210	90
Standard price		£4	£3	£6
Variance	390F	£480F	£630A	£540F
Price variances				
Standard price (£)		4.00	3.00	6.00
Actual price (£)		4.25	2.80	6.40
Actual quantity used		1680	1650	870
Variance	438A	420A	330F	348A

(c) *Labour cost variance*

(Standard cost for actual production) – (Actual cost)

Department P (120 batches × £40 = £4800 – £6360) £1560A

Department Q (120 × £12 = £1440 – £1512) £72A

Labour efficiency variance

(Standard hours for actual production – Actual hours) × Standard rate

Department P (120 batches × 4 hours = 480 hours – 600 hours) × £10 £1200A

Department Q (120 × 2 hours = 240 hours – 270 hours) × £6 £180A

Labour rate variance

(Standard rate – Actual rate) × Actual hours

Department P (£10 – £10.60) × 600 £360A

Department Q (£6 – £5.60) × 270 £108F

(d) *Total sales margin variance*

(Actual margin) – (Budgeted margin)

(3648 kg at (£16.75 – £6.125[a])) – (4096 kg at (£16 – £6.125)) £1688A

Sales volume variance

(Actual sales volume – Budgeted sales volume) × Standard margin

(3648 – 4096) at (£16 – £6.125) £4424A

Sales margin price variance

(Actual margin – Standard margin) × Actual sales volume

((£16.75 – £6.125) – (£16 – £6.125)) × 3648 £2736F

Note

[a]the standard cost per kg sold is £196/32 kg = £6.125

(e) The answer should indicate that a different mix of the materials from the standard mix was used. Less of materials F and H and more of the lower cost material G were used compared with the standard mix. This may explain the adverse yield variance. Also the purchase price for material G was less than standard which may indicate the purchase of poorer quality materials which may have had an adverse impact on the yield.

19.21 (a)

	Superb	Excellent	Good	Total
1. Budget sales (units)	30 000	50 000	20 000	100 000
2. Actual sales (units) in std. proportions	28 800	48 000	19 200	96 000
3. Actual sales (units)	36 000	42 000	18 000	96 000
Standard unit valuations:				
4. Selling price (£)	100	80	70	
5. Contribution (£)	60	55	48	
6. Profit (£)	35	30	23	
Sales volume variance:				
On turnover basis				
(3–1) × 4 (£)	600 000(F)	640 000(A)	140 000(A)	180 000(A)
On contribution basis				
(3–1) × 5 (£)	360 000(F)	440 000(A)	96 000(A)	176 000(A)
On profit basis				
(3–1) × 6 (£)	210 000(F)	240 000(A)	46 000(A)	76 000(A)

Note: Fixed cost per unit = £2 500 000/100 000 units = £25

(b) The answer should:

(i) Explain the limitations of using sales revenues to value the sales variances (see 'Sales variances' in Chapter 18).

(ii) Point out the limitations of using a net profit margin derived from unitizing fixed costs. Fixed costs remain unchanged in the short term with variations in sales volumes. Therefore total profits will change by the sales volumes multiplied by the contribution per unit sold and not the net profit per unit sold.

(iii) Argue in favour of using contribution margins based on the point made in (ii) above. Contribution most closely represents the changes in cash flows. Also contribution does not involve arbitrary apportionments of fixed overheads and thus avoids the reporting of misleading sales variances.

(c) *Sales mix variance*

	Actual sales volume	Actual sales volume in budgeted proportions	Difference	Standard contribution margin (£)	Sales margin mix variance (£)
Superb	36 000	28 800 (30%)	–7200	60	+ 432 000
Excellent	42 000	48 000 (50%)	+6000	55	–330 000
Good	18 000	19 200 (20%)	+1200	48	–57 600
					+44 400F

Sales quantity variance

	Actual sales volume in budgeted proportions	Budgeted sales quantity	Difference	Standard contribution margin (£)	Sales margin quantity variance (£)
Superb	28 800 (30%)	30 000	–1200	60	–72 000
Excellent	48 000 (50%)	50 000	–2000	55	–110 000
Good	19 200 (20%)	20 000	–800	48	–38 400
					–220 000A

(d) See 'Criticisms of sales margin variances' in Chapter 19 for the answer to this question.

(e) (i)

	Original standard (£)	Revised standard (£)	Actual (£)
Selling price	100	94.00	90
Variable cost	40	38.80	38
Unit contribution	60	55.20	52

Reconciliation of actual with original budget (Ex-post variance analysis)

		£
Original budget (30 000 × £60)		1 800 000
Planning variances:		
Sales price (30 000 × £6)	180 000A	
Variable cost (30 000 × £1.20)	36 000F	144 000A
Revised ex-post budgeted contribution		1 656 000
Operational variances		
Sales volume (6000 × £55.20)	331 200F	
Sales price (36 000 × £4)	144 000A	
Variable cost (36 000 × £0.80)	28 800F	216 000F
Actual contribution (36 000 × £52)		1 872 000

(e) (ii) For the answer to this question see '*Expost* variance analysis' in Chapter 19.

19.22 (a) The traditional variance analysis is as follows:

		(£)
Sales margin volume variance:		nil
(actual sales volume = budgeted sales volume)		
Sales margin price variance:		
(actual unit margin – standard unit margin)		
× actual sales volume		
(£84 – £26) × 1000		58 000F
		58 000F
	(£)	
Material price:		
(standard price – actual price) × actual quantity		
(£5 – £9) × 10 800	43 200A	
Material usage:		
(standard quantity – actual quantity) × standard price		
(10 000 –10 800) × £5	4 000A	47 200A
Wage rate:		
(standard rate – actual rate) × actual hours		
[£4 – (£34 800/5800)] × 5800	11 600A	
Labour efficiency:		
(standard hours – actual hours) × standard rate		
[(1000 × 6 = 6000) – 5800] × £4	800F	10 800A
Total variances		nil
Reconciliation:		
Budgeted contribution (1000 × £26)	26 000	
Add adverse cost variances	58 000	
Less favourable sales variances	(58 000)	
Actual contribution	26 000	

(b)

(A) Original plan (£)	(B) Revised ex-post plan (£)	(C) Actual results (£)
Sales (1000 × £100) = 100 000	(1000 × £165) = 165 000	(1000 × £158) = 158 000
Labour (6000 × £4) = 24 000	(6000 × £6.25) = 37 500	(5800 × £6) = 34 800
Materials:		
Aye (10 000 × £5) = 50 000	(10 000 × £8.50) = 85 000	(10 800 × £9) = 97 200
Bee	(10 000 × £7) = 70 000	

	(£)	
Uncontrollable planning variances (A – B)		
Sales price	65 000F	
Wage rate	13 500A	
Material price[a] (50 000 – 70 000)	20 000A	
Substitution of materials variance[a] (85 000 – 70 000)	15 000A	16 500F
Operational variances		
Sales price (B – C)	7 000A	
Wage rate (5800 × £0.25)	1 450F	
Labour efficiency (200 hrs at £6.25)	1 250F	
Material price (10 800 × £0.50)	5 400A	
Material usage (800 × £8.50)	6 800A	16 500A
Total variances		nil

Note

[a]If the purchasing officer is committed to buying Aye and it is not possible to change to Bee in the short term then the £15 000 substitution variances is an uncontrollable price variance, and the total planning variance will be £35 000 for materials. However, if the purchasing officer can respond to changes in the relative prices then the £15 000 should be added to the operational price variance.

Comment on operational variances

The operational variances are calculated on the basis of the revised *ex-post* plan. The *ex post* plan represents what the target would have been, given the benefit of hindsight. This represents a more realistic target than the original plan. For example, given the conditions for the period, the target sales should have been £165 000. Actual sales were £158 000. Therefore the operational sales variance is £7000 adverse. An explanation of planning and operational variances is presented in '*Ex post* variance analysis' in Chapter 19.

(c) *Advantages*

(i) The traditional price variance includes unavoidable/uncontrollable elements due to change in environment of £20 000 or £35 000. The revised analysis is more indicative of current purchasing efficiency.

(ii) Traditional approach incorrectly values deviations from budgeted efficiency in calculating usage or efficiency variances. A better indication is provided by attributing the current standard cost per unit to the deviations (a variance of £6800 is a better indication of the excess usage of the materials than the £4000 under the traditional method).

Disadvantages

(i) Classification into planning (uncontrollable) and avoidable may be difficult (e.g. substitution variance) and arbitrary.

(ii) Any error in producing *ex post* standards will cause a corresponding error in the classification of the variances (for example, we could have used a £9 *ex post* standard for materials, thus affecting both the planning and operational variance).

(iii) Excessive costs compared with benefits derived.

(iv) Who sets the *ex post* standard? If the purchasing officer sets the standard then there is a danger that the standard may be biased to avoid unfavourable operational variances.

19.23 (a) Standard cost of materials per kg of output (0.65 kg × £4) + (0.3 kg × £6) + (0.2 kg × £2.50) = £4.90

Standard overhead rate = £12 000/Budgeted standard quantity of ingredient F (4000 × 0.65) = £4.6154 per kg of ingredient F

Standard overhead rate per kg of output of FDN = 0.65 kg × £4.6154 = £3

	(£)
Standard cost of actual output:	
Materials (4200 × £4.90)	20 580
Overheads (4200 × £3)	12 600
	34 180
Actual cost of output	
Materials	20 380
Overheads (£7800 + £4800)	12 600
	32 980

Variance calculations

Material price variance = (Standard price – Actual price)Actual quantity = (Standard price × Actual quantity) – Actual cost = (£4 × 2840) + (£6 × 1210) + (£2.50 × 860) = £20 770 – £20 380	390A
Material yield variance = (Actual yield – Standard yield) × Standard material cost per unit of output = (4200 – 4910 materials used/1.15) × £4.90	341A

Material mix variance

(Actual quantity in actual mix at standard prices) – (Actual quantity in standard mix at standard prices)

	(£)	
F (4910 × 0.65/1.15 = 2775 – 2840) × £4	260A	
D (4910 × 0.30/1.15 = 1281 – 1210) × £6	426F	
N (4910 × 0.20/1.15 = 854 – 860) × 2.50	15A	151F

Overhead efficiency variance = (Standard quantity of ingredient F – Actual quantity) × standard overhead rate per kg of ingredient F
= (4200 × 0.65 = 2730 – 2840) × £4.6154 508A
Overhead capacity variance = (Budgeted input of ingredient F – Actual input) × standard overhead rate per kg of ingredient F
= (4000 × 0.65 = 2600 – 2840) × £4.6154 1108A
Overhead expenditure = Budgeted cost (£12 000) – Actual cost (£12 600) 600A

Reconciliation of standard cost and actual cost of output

	(£)	(£)
Standard cost of actual production		33 180
Material variances		
Material price variance	390F	
Material yield variance	341A	
Material mix variance	151F	200F
Overhead variances:		
Overhead efficiency	508A	
Overhead capacity	1108A	
Overhead expenditure	600A	Nil
Actual cost		32 980

(b)

Standard number of deliveries (4000 × 1.15 kg)/460 kg	10
Standard cost per supplier delivery (£4000/10)	£400
Standard number of despatches to customers (4000/100)	40
Standard cost per customer despatch (£8000/40)	£200

Actual output exceeds budgeted output by 5% (4200/4000)

Activity-based costing reconciliation statement

		(£)
Standard cost for actual output:		
Deliveries (1.05 × 10 deliveries = 10.5 × £400 per delivery)	4200	
Despatches (1.05 × 40 despatches = 42 × £200 per despatch)	8400	12 600
Activity usage variance		
Deliveries (10.5 – 12) × £400	600A	
Despatches (42 – 38) × £200	800F	200F
Activity expenditure variances		
Deliveries (12 × £400 = £4800 – £4800)	Nil	
Despatches (38 × £200 = £7600 – £7800)	200A	200A
Actual overheads		12 600

Note that the expenditure variance has been flexed. An alternative presentation would be to work in whole numbers only since 10.5 deliveries is not feasible.

(c) See 'Designing ABC systems' in Chapter 10 for the answer to this question. In particular, the answer should stress the need to interview the employees engaged on the activities to ascertain what causes the activities.

19.24 (a) (i) *Decision tree if an investigation is carried out*

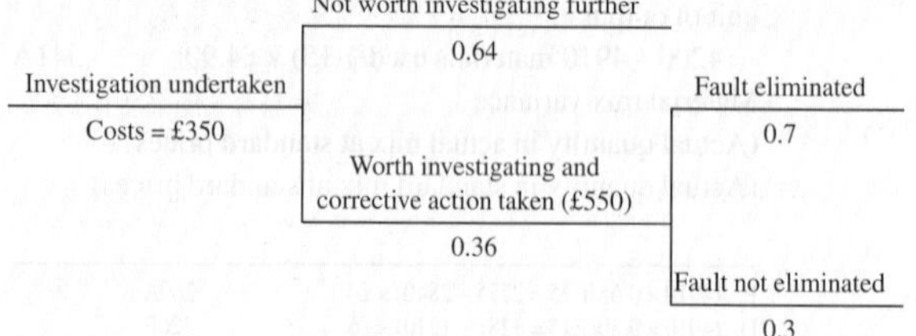

It is assumed that the £550 correction cost applies to all variances that the initial investigation indicates are worthy of further investigation. The expected cost if the investigation is carried out is:

$$£350 + 0.36 \times £550 \text{ (corrective action)} + 0.36 \times 0.3 \times £2476^{a} \text{ (continuing variance)} = \underline{£815}$$

Note

[a]£2476 represents the PV of £525 for 5 months at 2% (£525 × 4.7135) for variances that are not eliminated.

(ii) *Decision tree if an investigation is not carried out*

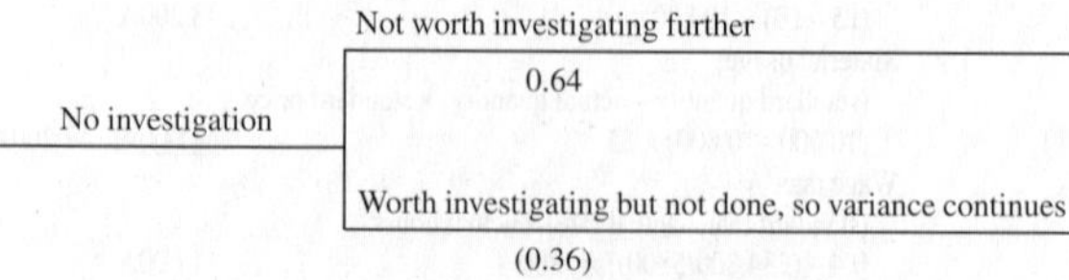

The expected cost if no investigation is undertaken is:

$$0.36 \times £525 \times 4.7135 = £891$$

(b) Applying the expected value decision rule, the company should follow a policy of investigating variances as a matter of routine. The expected cost of investigation is £815, compared with an expected cost if no investigation is undertaken of £891. On average, the benefits from investigation are £75 per variance.

(c) Examples of category 1 variances include:
(i) The variance is due to random uncontrollable factors and is under control. (See 'Random uncontrollable factors' in Chapter 19 for an explanation.)
(ii) Where the cause is obvious (e.g. a machine fault) and future action has been taken to remedy the situation.

Examples of category 2 variances include:
(i) Excessive usage of materials and labour due possibly to wrong working practices on a repetitive operation which is likely to continue if not corrected.
(ii) Where the variance is significant and exceeds a specified percentage of standard usage.

(d) The above analysis assumes that the average variance is £525 and additional costs of £525 in excess of standard continue for five months. Presumably, working practices are changed every five months. Costs of investigation and corrective action are £350 and £550 irrespective of the amount of the variance. It would therefore be appropriate to determine the value of variances which justify investigation. Let x = savings per month. The expected cost of investigation is equal to the expected cost of no investigation where:

$$£350 + (0.36 \times £550) + (0.36 \times 0.3 \times 4.7135x) = 0.36 \times 4.7135x$$
$$x = £461$$

Only variances in excess of £461 should be investigated.

19.25 (a) See 'Criticisms of standard costing' and 'The future role of standard costing' in Chapter 19 for the answer to this question.

(b) The creation of budget centres at the lowest defined management level would enable managers to participate in the budget setting process. Lower level managers would therefore be involved in the budget negotiation process, and this should improve communication with their superiors and create a greater awareness of the need for the activities of the budget centres to be in congruence with the goals of the organization. By participating in the process, it is claimed that managers will be more committed and strive to achieve their budgets. The creation of budget centres should also improve a manager's attitude towards the budget system. In particular, the potential for improved communication and the acceptance of budgets as relevant standards to achieve should lead to improved motivation.

Creating budget centres at lower levels will place greater administrative demands on operating the system and lengthen the budget preparation period.

In addition, the cost of reporting will be increased. Whether or not the additional benefits exceed the additional costs is likely to depend on the circumstances of the company. For example, in an environment where an organization faces considerable uncertainty or where an organization undertakes a diverse range of activities, decentralization and the creation of budget centres at lower levels might be preferable. However, where the activities of an organization can be programmed in detail and close coordination and swift reaction is necessary it might be preferable not to create budget centres at lower levels. In particular, if the activities of budget centres are heavily dependent on the activities of other centres, there is a greater likelihood that the benefits from increased motivation will not outweigh the administrative and coordination difficulties.

19.26 For the answer to these questions see 'Criticisms of standard costing' and 'The future role of standard costing'. In part (c) the answer should also include a discussion of the role of non-financial measures. See the section on operation processes in Chapter 23 for a discussion of non-financial measures in non-manufacturing organizations. The answer could also include a discussion of activity-based management. This topic is covered in Chapter 22.

19.27 (a) For the answer to this question see 'Investigation of variances' in Chapter 19. In particular the answer should explain that variances may be due to several causes, and not all are worthy of investigation. In addition the answer should stress the possible approaches to investigating variances:

(i) *Use of rule of thumb percentages:* For example, all variances in excess of 10% of standard cost might be investigated. This approach ignores the costs and benefits of investigation.

(ii) *Use of statistical quality control charts:* Control limits are set using an analysis of historical results to indicate suitable confidence intervals. This method utilizes a statistical probability approach of not investigating a variance unless there is a high probability that the process is out of control.

(iii) *Use of a statistical decision theory approach:* This approach is described in Chapter 19.

It is unlikely that statistical decision theory can be applied in practice, because of the difficulty in estimating costs and benefits of investigation. Nevertheless, the approach provides a suitable model that gives a manager an insight into the important factors that should be considered when deciding whether or not to investigate a variance. Experience and an understanding of the model is likely to be the best way of establishing whether or not investigation is worthwhile.

(b) See Chapter 16 for the answer to this question.

(i) The level of budget difficulty is likely to have a motivational influence on a manager's actions to eliminate variances. If a manager believes a target to be unattainable, he or she is unlikely to strive to eliminate variances. (See 'The effect of budget difficulty on motivation and performance' in Chapter 16.)

(ii) Managers may manipulate information in order to avoid adverse variances. This is most likely to occur if a budget-constrained style of performance evaluation is used. Genuine performance improvements are most likely to occur if a profit-conscious style of evaluation is used. For a detailed discussion of styles of evaluation see 'Side effects from using accounting information in performance evaluation' in Chapter 16.

(iii) Managers are most likely to strive to eliminate variances if they accept the budget and this becomes a motivational target. Budget acceptance is more likely to be achieved by participation and not by imposed budgets. See 'Participation in the budgeting and target setting process' in Chapter 16 for a more detailed discussion of the influence of participation on acceptance of budgets.

(iv) The extent to which performance appraisal, future promotion and cash bonuses are tied to meeting the budget will provide a major motivation stimulus to meeting the budget. However, if too much stress is placed on meeting the budget, there is a danger that over-generous budgets will be sought or information will be distorted so as to avoid adverse variances.

(v) Performance reports comparing actual with budget should be provided soon after the end of the budget period (weekly or monthly). A manager is more likely to be motivated to eliminate variances if feedback reports are timely and understandable. A climate of failure and punishment should be avoided, and the emphasis should be on *helping* managers to eliminate adverse variances.

Chapter 20

20.15 Divisional managers do not control the cash function. Therefore controllable net assets should exclude the cash overdraft so controllable net assets are £125 000 (£101 000 + £24 000).

Controllable residual income	=	£69 000 (Profit before interest and tax)
Less cost of capital	=	12 500 (10% × 125 000)
Residual income	=	56 500

Answer = B

20.16 Working backwards to derive the divisional contribution:

	£
Cost of capital charge	150 000 (£1.25m × 12%)
Residual income	47 200
Profit	197 200
Depreciation	247 500
Fixed costs	487 000
Total contribution	931 700

Contribution per unit = £31.06 (£931 700/30 000 units)
Answer = D

20.17 *Assumptions*
It is assumed in this question that additional capital is introduced to finance the capital expenditure in transaction A. (All calculations are in £000.)

(a) *Alpha basis*

(i) $\dfrac{\text{profit for the year}}{\text{capital employed } (1000+250)} = 18\%$

(ii) $\dfrac{\text{profit } (225+(35-20))}{\text{capital employed } (1250+120)}$

(iii) It is assumed that depreciation (50) and contribution to profit (30) from the equipment are already included in the profit for the year of £225. If the profit is adjusted by writing back these items, the equipment will have a book value of £50, and a loss on sale of £30 will arise:

$\dfrac{\text{profit } 225+(50 \text{ depn} - 30 \text{ loss on sales} - 30 \text{ profit contrib.})}{\text{capital employed } (1250-200+20)}$

Therefore ROCE = 20.1%

(iv) $\dfrac{\text{profit } (225+4)}{\text{capital employed } (1250)} = 18.3\%$

The overdraft will increase and creditors will fall. Therefore net current assets will remain unchanged.

(v) $\dfrac{\text{profit } (225-6)}{\text{capital employed } (1250)} = 17.5\%$

It is assumed that net current assets remain unchanged, with stock declining by 25 and cash increasing by 25. The additional contribution is assumed to be paid out as dividends and not to increase capital employed.

(b) *Theta basis*

(i) $\dfrac{225}{525+250} = 29\%$

(ii) $\dfrac{225+(35-20)}{775+(120-20)} = 27.4\%$

(iii) $\dfrac{215 \text{ (as Alpha basis)}}{775+20} = 27.0\%$

The WDV of the fixed assets of £525 will exclude the equipment, since it has a WDV of zero at the end of the year.

(iv) $\dfrac{225+4}{775} = 29.5\%$

(v) $\dfrac{225-6}{775} = 28.2\%$

(c) (i) The correct approach is to evaluate transaction A on the basis of the NPV rule. The NPV calculation is as follows:

	(£)
Cash flow savings (35 000 × 3.8887)	136 105
Less investment cost	120 000
NPV	16 105

The correct decision is to purchase the equipment, but a manager will be motivated to reject the purchase using both the Alpha and Beta basis of performance evaluation. Therefore there will be a lack of goal congruence. This is because the equipment yields a lower accounting rate of return in 2000 than the present return. Consequently ROCE will decline if the project is accepted. With the Theta basis, the manager's performance will be improved in the long run as the asset base of £120 000 will decline (through depreciation) but profit will remain unchanged. Therefore the ROCE of the equipment will increase over time, and it is likely that the overall return will also increase in later years.

ROCE is a weak method of measuring performance because it focuses on a percentage return rather than the magnitude of earnings. For a discussion of the weaknesses of ROCE and a comparison with the residual income method see 'Return on investment' and 'Residual Income' in Chapter 20.

(ii) Transaction B involves a proposal to sell a machine for £20 000 that produces a cash flow of £30 000. This will result in a negative present value. The proposal can only be justified if the £20 000 received can be invested to yield a cash inflow in excess of £30 000. This is most unlikely.

The Theta measure shows a decline in ROCE, whereas the Alpha measure shows an increase in ROCE. Therefore it is likely that a manager evaluated on the Theta measure will reject the proposal, whereas a manager evaluated on the Alpha measure will accept the proposal. Consequently, the Theta measure will encourage goal congruence whereas the Alpha measure will not.

20.18 *Division A*
Both items represent discretionary expenditure. Management can choose to determine whatever is deemed necessary to spend on these activities but the amount of expenditure should seek to maximize long-term profitability. The proposed actions are likely to harm long-term profitability but they will have a beneficial short-term effect on the divisional performance measure. There are no financial accounting issues involved and, although the published accounts are likely to be slightly misleading, there would not be any problem in getting the accounts externally audited. Divisional management are, however, manipulating the budget for their own benefit at the expense of the long-term success of the organization. They are therefore engaging in unethical behaviour.

Division B
This action is an attempt to defer expenditure. The cost of consultancy services received to date should, however, be accrued and provided for in the current year's accounts for the division. This would prevent the divisional management

from enhancing the profit for the current period and thus affect the bonuses. A failure to make a provision would be in breach of financial accounting regulations. If management does not make the provision it will be acting in an unethical manner and if the accountant becomes aware of the circumstances it is his, or her, professional duty to insist that the provision is made. Failure to do so would be classed as unethical behaviour. If no provision is made next year's budgeted expenses should be increased to reflect the deferred expenditure. As with division A the divisional managers are motivated to manipulate the results to achieve the budget.

Division C

Financial accounting regulations require that revenues are recognized at the point of delivery. Therefore the action does not contravene financial accounting regulations and there should be no problems with the audit of the accounts. However, future profitability may be impaired because stocks will be very low at the end of the year. This may result in a loss in future profits arising from lost sales from a failure to meet demand and also a loss of customer goodwill. The behaviour is therefore unethical and also requires that some existing customers become involved in the collusion. The motivational desire to obtain the bonus is causing the dysfunctional behaviour.

Comment on whether group management action is necessary

None of the actions are illegal but it is questionable whether managers should be able to earn bonuses arising from the actions. On the other hand divisions have been created to enhance managerial autonomy and any interference by corporate top management will undermine divisional autonomy. Some dysfunctional behaviour is likely to apply with all performance measurement systems and, as long as major dysfunctional consequences do not arise, it could be argued that the actions should be tolerated as part of the costs of decentralization. Non-interference also ensures that the motivational benefits arising from divisional autonomy are not eroded. If major dysfunctional consequences do arise from the current system then it will be necessary for central management to take appropriate action to reduce the harmful side effects. For a discussion of potential actions see 'Addressing the dysfunctional consequences of short-term financial measures' in Chapter 20.

20.19 (a) The annual ROI and residual income calculations for each plant are as follows:

	2001	2002	2003	2004	Total
Aromatic					
(1) Net cash flow (£m)	2.4	2.4	2.4	2.4	9.6
(2) Depreciation	1.6	1.6	1.6	1.6	
(3) Profit	0.8	0.8	0.8	0.8	3.2
(4) Cost of capital (16% of 6)	(1.02)	(0.77)	(0.51)	(0.26)	
(5) Residual income	(0.22)	0.03	0.29	0.54	
(6) Opening WDV of asset	6.4	4.8	3.2	1.6	
(7) ROI (Row 3/Row 6)	12.5%	16.67%	25%	50%	
Zoman					
(1) Net cash flow	2.6	2.2	1.5	1.0	7.3
(2) Depreciation	1.3	1.3	1.3	1.3	
(3) Profit	1.3	0.9	0.2	(0.3)	2.1
(4) Cost of capital (16%)	(0.83)	(0.62)	(0.42)	(0.21)	
(5) Residual income	0.47	0.28	(0.22)	(0.51)	
(6) Opening WDV of asset	5.2	3.9	2.6	1.3	
(7) ROI	25%	23%	7.7%	(23%)	

The answer should indicate:

(i) Over the whole life of the project both ROI and residual income (RI) favour the Aromatic plant. The average ROI and RI figures are 25% and £0.16m (£0.64m/4) for the Aromatic plant and 20% and £0.005m (£0.02m/4) for the Zoman plant. The ROI calculations are based on expressing the average profits as a percentage of the average investment (defined as one half of the initial capital investment).

(ii) An explanation that Mr Elton will favour the Zoman plant because it yields a higher ROI and RI over the first two years. Mr Elton will probably focus on a two-year time horizon because of his personal circumstances, since choosing the Aromatic plant is likely to result in him losing his bonus. Therefore he will choose the plant with the lower NPV and there will be a lack of goal congruence.

(iii) Suggestions as to how alternative accounting techniques can assist in reconciling the conflict between accounting performance measures and DCF techniques:

1. Avoiding short-term evaluations and evaluating performance at the end of the project's life. Thus bonuses would be awarded with hindsight;
2. Use alternative asset valuations other than historic cost (e.g. replacement cost);
3. Choose alternative depreciation methods that are most consistent with NPV calculations (e.g. annuity depreciation);
4. Incorporate a range of variables (both financial and non-financial when evaluating managerial performance) that give a better indication of future results that can be expected from current actions.

(b) Managers may use pre-tax profits to evaluate divisional performance because it is assumed that taxation is non-controllable. Taxation payable is based on total group profits and present and past capital expenditure rather than individual divisional profitability. After tax cash flows are used to appraise capital investments because the focus is on decision-making and accepting those projects that earn a return in excess of the investors' opportunity cost of capital. To do this IRRs and NPVs should be based on after-tax cash flows.

The following potential problems can arise:

(i) Managers may ignore the taxation impact at the decision-making stage because it is not considered when evaluating their performance;

(ii) Confusion and demotivation can occur when different criteria are used for decision-making and performance evaluation.

Possible solutions include evaluating divisional profitability after taxes or evaluating performance based on a comparison of budgeted and actual cash flows. Adopting the latter approach is an attempt to ensure that the same criteria is used for decision-making and performance evaluation.

(c) Steps that can be taken to avoid dysfunctional behaviour include:

(i) Not placing too much emphasis on short-term performance measures and placing greater emphasis on the long term by adopting a profit-conscious style of evaluation.

(ii) Focusing on controllable residual income or economic value added combined with asset valuations derived from depreciation models that are consistent with NPV calculations (see Appendix to Chapter 20). Alternatively, performance evaluation might be based on a comparison of budgeted and actual cash flows. The budgeted cash flows should be based on cash flows that are used to appraise capital investments.

(iii) Supplementing financial performance measures with non-financial measures when evaluating performance (see 'Addressing the dysfunctional consequences of short-term financial measures' in Chapter 20).

20.20 (a) *Summary statement 1 (Straight-line depreciation)*

Year	1 (£000)	2 (£000)	3 (£000)	4 (£000)	5 (£000)
Investment at start of year	600	480	360	240	120
Net cash flow (40% of sales)	200	200	200	200	200
Less: depreciation	120	120	120	120	120
Net profit	80	80	80	80	80
Less: interest on capital[a]	96	76.8	57.6	38.4	19.2
Residue income	(16)	3.2	22.4	41.6	60.8
ROCE[b]	13.3%	16.7%	22.2%	33.3%	66.7%

Notes

[a]16% of investment at the start of the year.

[b]Net profit expressed as a percentage of the investment at the start of the year.

Calculation of annuity depreciation

Year	(1) Annual repayment (£000)	(2) 16% interest on capital outstanding (£000)	(3) = (1) – (2) Capital repayment (£000)	(4) = (4) – (3) Capital outstanding (£000)
0				600.0
1	183.24	96.0	87.24	512.76
2	183.24	82.04	101.20	411.56
3	183.24	65.85	117.39	294.17
4	183.24	47.07	136.17	158.00
5	183.24	25.28	158.00	—

For an explanation of the calculations see 'Annuity depreciation' in Appendix 20.1. Note that the annual repayment is determined by referring to the capital recovery table in Appendix D of the text for 5 years at 16%. The capital recovery factor is 0.3054 and this is multiplied by the capital outlay to give an annual repayment of £183 240. Alternatively, the annual repayment could have been calculated by dividing the investment of £600 000 by the cumulative discount factor for 5 years at 16% (3.274 shown in Appendix B).

Summary statement 2 (Annuity depreciation)

Year	1 (£000)	2 (£000)	3 (£000)	4 (£000)	5 (£000)
Investment at start of year	600	512.76	411.56	294.17	158.00
Net cash flow	200	200	200	200	200
Depreciation	87.24	101.20	117.39	136.17	158.00
Net profit	112.76	98.80	82.61	63.83	42.0
Imputed interest	96.00	82.04	65.85	47.07	25.28
Residual income	16.76	16.76	16.76	16.76	16.72
ROCE	18.8%	19.3%	20.1%	21.7%	26.6%

(b) (i) Management are motivated to focus only on the outcomes of the first year for any new project because of the criterion used for performance measurement and investment decisions. When straight-line depreciation is used residual income is negative and the ROCE of 13.3% is less than the target return of 20%. Therefore if the focus is only on the performance measures for the first year the project will be rejected even though residual income and ROCE rise steadily throughout the five-year period.

When annuity depreciation is used residual income is positive and constant for each year of the project's life and therefore the proposal would be accepted if the residual income method is used. ROCE is 18.8% and this is less than the target return of 20% and the project would be rejected using this method. However, ROCE ranges from 18.8% to 26.6% when annuity depreciation is used, compared with 13.3% to 66.7% with straight-line depreciation. Therefore, when compared with straight-line depreciation annuity depreciation does not distort ROCE to the same extent.

(ii) NPV = £200 000 × cumulative discount factor for 5 years at 16% (3.274) – Investment outlay (£600 000) = £54 800

The project has a positive NPV and should be accepted. Residual income is the long-run counterpart of NPV. The present value of residual income of £16 760 per year for 5 years discounted at 16% is approximately £54 800. When cash flows are constant and the annuity method of depreciation is used residual income will also be constant. For a more detailed discussion of the relationship between residual income and NPV see the Appendix to Chapter 20.

(c) (i)

	Year 1 (straight-line depreciation) (£000)	Year 1 (annuity depreciation) (£000)
Investment at beginning of year	600	600
Net cash flow (40% × £700 000)	280	280
Less:		
Depreciation (see part (a))	(120)	(87.3)
Profit	160	192.7
Less:		
Interest on capital	(96)	(96)
Residual income	64	96.7
ROCE	26.7%	32.1%

(ii) *Discounted cash flow approach:*

Year	Physical (£000)	Discount factor at 16%	DCF (£000)
0	(600)	1.000	(600)
1	280	0.862	241.36
2	200	0.743	148.60
3	200	0.641	128.20
4	120	0.552	66.24
5	80	0.476	38.08
		NPV	22.48

(iii) Adopting the criteria used by management both projects yield a positive residual income and a ROCE in excess of the target return in the first year using either straight-line or annuity methods of depreciation. The project therefore will be accepted. The project also has a positive NPV and, in this situation, the criteria used by management will be consistent with the NPV decision model. The decline in NPV reflects the fact that sales revenue has declined over the five-year period.

20.21 (a) The answer to this question should include much of the content included in the section entitled 'Economic value added' in Chapter 20. In addition, the answer should include the following points:

(i) Some of the revenue expenditure, such as research and development and advertising, provide future benefits over several years but financial accounting requirements often require such expenditure to be written off in the year in which they are incurred. This understates the value added during a particular period.

(ii) The profits computed to meet financial accounting requirements do not take into account the cost of equity finance provided by the shareholders. The only cost of capital that is taken into account is interest on borrowed funds (i.e. the cost of debt finance). Profits should reflect the cost of both debt and equity finance.

(iii) A better measure of the managers' ability to create value is to adjust the traditional financial statements for those expenses that are likely to provide benefits in future periods. The economic value added measure attempts to meet this requirement.

The following comments relate to the treatment of specific adjustments:

Research and development

The expenditure of £2.1 million is added back because it represents an investment that will yield future benefits. Therefore it should be capitalized and allocated to the future periods based on the benefits received in the particular period. The expenditure of £17.4m is added back based on the assumption that the company is continuing to benefit from such expenditures that have previously been written off against profits. There should be an element of this expenditure written off as depreciation based on the value that has been eroded during the period.

Advertising

Advertising expenditure adds value by supporting future sales arising from increasing customer awareness and brand loyalty. Based on the same justification as research and development expenditure, advertising should be capitalized for the EVA calculation and added back to profits. The £10.5m added back in the balance sheet reflects the costs incurred in building up future income. Some of this cost should be depreciated based on the value of future benefits eroded during the period.

Interest and borrowings

The aim is to ascertain whether value is being added for the shareholders in the sense of whether the funds invested in the business generate a return in excess of the opportunity cost of capital (see Chapter 14). To do this a profit figure is calculated that initially does not include any charges for the cost of capital. Interest on borrowings is therefore added back to avoid the situation where the cost of capital on debt finance is included in the traditional profit calculation whereas the cost of equity capital is not. To ascertain the total source of funds invested in the business borrowings are added back to the capital base in the balance sheet. The required return (i.e. the opportunity cost of capital) of £17.5m on the resulting capital base is calculated and compared with the adjusted profit of £16.1m generated from the funds. This comparison captures the cost of both debt and equity and indicates that value added is a negative figure.

Goodwill

Goodwill refers to the price paid for the business in excess of the current cost of net assets. Goodwill payments should therefore add value to the company. Hence the amount written off is added back to profits since it represents part of the intangible asset value of the business. The cumulative write off of £40.7m is added back in order to provide a more realistic value of the capital base from which a return should be generated. This is because it represents an element of the value of the business. The value of goodwill should be regularly reviewed and the amount eroded written off against profits.

(b) *Revised divisional profit statements*

	Division A (£m)	Division B (£m)	Division C (£m)	Head office (£m)	Total (£m)
Profit before interest and tax	5.7	5.6	5.8	(1.9)	15.2
Add back:					
Advertising	2.3				2.3
Research and development		2.1			2.1
Goodwill[a]		0.3	1.0		1.3
Allocation of head office expenses[b]	(0.4)	(0.3)	(1.2)	1.9	
Less tax paid[c]	(2.0)	(1.6)	(1.2)		(4.8)
Revised profit	5.6	6.1	4.4		16.1

Revised balance sheet

	Division A (£m)	Division B (£m)	Division C (£m)	Head office (£m)	Total (£m)
Total assets less current liabilities	27.1	23.9	23.2	3.2	77.4
Add back:					
Advertising	10.5				10.5
Research and development		17.4			17.4
Goodwill		10.3	30.4		40.7
Head office net assets[d]	0.7	0.5	2.0	(3.2)	
Revised capital base	38.3	52.1	55.6		146.0
Cost of capital at 12% of revised capital base	4.6	6.2	6.7		17.5
Revised profit	5.6	6.1	4.4		16.1
Value added	1.0	(0.1)	(2.3)		(1.4)

Notes

[a]Allocated on the same basis as previous goodwill write-offs (10.3/40.7 to Division B and 30.4/40.7 to Division C

[b]Apportioned on the basis of divisional turnover. Ideally head office costs should be allocated to divisions on the basis of the benefits received by the divisions.

[c]Allocated on the basis of profits before interest and tax less head office allocated costs plus interest received less interest paid. The outcome of this calculation is £5.7m for Division A, £4.6m for Division B and £3.7m for Division C and tax is allocated pro-rata to these figures.

[d]Arbitrary allocation on the basis of sales revenue adopting the same allocation base as that used for head office expenses.

The above analysis suggests that value is being 'destroyed' in Division C and to a minor extent in Division B. Division A is adding value. This is not apparent from the initial presentation which indicates a ROCE of 25% (£5.6m/£23.2m) for Division C. The limitations of the analysis include:

(i) The use of arbitrary apportionments to allocate head office expenses, the tax liability and head office net assets to the business.

(ii) The assumption that the same cost of capital is applicable to all divisions.
(iii) The use of historical asset values rather than economic values.
(iv) The failure to distinguish between managerial and economic divisional performance. The analysis focuses on the economic performance of the divisions.

(c) See 'Return on investment' and the discussion of the survey evidence within the section entitled 'Residual income' in Chapter 20 for the answer to this question. For a discussion of how the problems of short-termism might be overcome see 'Addressing the dysfunctional consequences of short-term financial measures' in Chapter 20.

20.22 (a) If divisional budgets are set by a central planning department and imposed on divisional managers then it is true that divisional independence is pseudo-independence. However, if budget guidelines and goals are set by the central planning department and divisional managers are given a large degree of freedom in the setting of budgets and conduct of operations then it is incorrect to claim that pseudo-independence exists.

One of the reasons for creating a divisionalized organization structure is to improve motivation by the delegation of responsibility to divisional managers, thus giving them greater freedom over the control of their activities. Nevertheless, complete independence cannot be granted, since this would destroy the very idea that divisions are an integral part of a single business. The granting of freedom to divisions in conducting their operations can be allowed only if certain limits are applied within which that freedom can be exercised. This normally takes the form of the presentation of budgets by divisions to corporate management for approval. By adopting this approach, divisions pay a modest price for the extensive powers of decentralized decision-making.

As long as budgets are not imposed by the central planning department, and divisions are allowed to determine their own budgets within the guidelines set, then divisional managers will have greater independence than the managers of centralized organizations.

(b) The answer should consist of a discussion of divisional profit, return on capital employed and residual income. A discussion of each of these items is presented in Chapter 20.

20.23 (a) Examples of the types of decisions that should be transferred to the new divisional managers include:
(i) Product decisions such as product mix, promotion and pricing.
(ii) Employment decisions, except perhaps for the appointment of senior managers.
(iii) Short-term operating decisions of all kinds. Examples include production scheduling, subcontracting and direction of marketing effort.
(iv) Capital expenditure and disinvestment decisions (with some constraints).
(v) Short-term financing decisions (with some constraints).

(b) The following decisions might be retained at company head office:
(i) Strategic investment decisions that are critical to the survival of the company as a whole.
(ii) Certain financing decisions that require that an overall view be taken. For example, borrowing commitments and the level of financial gearing should be determined for the group as a whole.
(iii) Appointment of top management.
(iv) Sourcing decisions such as bulk buying of raw materials if corporate interests are best served by centralized buying.
(v) Capital expenditure decisions above certain limits.
(vi) Common services that are required by all profit centres. Corporate interests might best be served by operating centralized service departments such as an industrial relations department. Possible benefits include reduced costs and the extra benefits of specialization.
(vii) Arbitration decisions on transfer pricing disputes.
(viii) Decisions on items which benefit the company rather than an individual division, e.g. taxation and computer applications.

(c) The answer to this question should focus on the importance of designing performance reports which encourage goal congruence. For a discussion of this topic see Chapter 20.

20.24 (a) For the answer to this question see 'Return on investment' and 'Residual income' and 'The effect of performance measurement on capital investment decisions' in Chapter 20. Note that discounted future earnings are the equivalent to discounted future profits.

(b) The existing ROCE is 20% and the estimated ROCE on the additional investment is 15% (£9000/£60 000). The divisional manager will therefore reject the additional investment, since adding this to the existing investments will result in a decline in the existing ROCE of 20%.

The residual income on the additional investment is £600 (£9000 average profit for the year less an imputed interest charge of 14% × £6000 = £8400). The manager will accept the additional investment, since it results in an increase in residual income.

If the discounted future earnings method is used, the investment would be accepted, since it will yield a positive figure for the year (that is, £9000 × 3.889 discount factor).

Note that the annual future cash flows are £19 000 (£9000 net profit plus £10 000 depreciation provision). The project has a 6-year life. The annual cash inflow must be in excess of £15 428 (£60 000/3.889 annuity factor – 6 years at 14%) if the investment is to yield a positive NPV. If annual cash flows are £19 000 each year for the next 6 years, the project should be accepted.

The residual income and discounted future earnings methods of evaluation will induce the manager to accept the investment. These methods are consistent with the correct economic evaluation using the NPV method. If ROCE is used to evaluate performance, the manager will incorrectly reject the investment. This is because the manager will only accept projects that yield a return in excess of the current ROCE of 20%.

Note that the above analysis assumes that the cash flows/profits are constant from year to year.

Chapter 21

21.15 The loss of contribution (profits) in Division A from lost internal sales of 2500 units at £18 (£40 – £22) is £45 000.

The impact on the whole company is that the external purchase cost is £87 500 (2500 × £35) compared with the incremental cost of manufacture of £55 000 (2500 × £22). Therefore the company will be worse off by £32 500.
Answer = D

21.16 The dual market price in respect of Division A will be the market price of £25. The two-part tariff transfer price per unit is the marginal cost of £15.
Answer = B

21.17 (i) The proposed transfer price of £15 is based on cost plus 25% implying that the total cost is £12. This comprises of £9 variable cost (75%) and £3 fixed cost. The general transfer pricing guideline described in Chapter 21 can be applied to this question. That is the transfer price that should be set at marginal cost plus opportunity. It is assumed in the first situation that transferring internally will result in Helpco having a lost contribution of £9 (£15 external market price less £9 variable cost for the external market). The marginal cost of the transfer is £7.50 (£9 external variable cost less £1.50 packaging costs not required for internal sales). Adding the opportunity cost of £6 gives a transfer price of £13.50 per kg. This is equivalent to applying the market price rule where the transfer price is set at the external market price (£15) less selling costs avoided (£1.50) by transferring internally.

(ii) For the 3000 kg where no external market is available the opportunity cost will not apply and transfers should be at the variable cost of £7.50. The remaining output should be transferred at £13.50 as described above.

(iii) The lost contribution for the 2000 kg is £3 per kg (£6000/2000 kg) giving a transfer price of £10.50 (£7.50 variable cost plus £3 opportunity cost). The remaining 1000 kg for which there is no external market should be transferred at £7.50 variable cost and the balance for which there is an external market transferred at £13.50.

21.18 (a) The effects on each division and the company as a whole of selling the motor unit at each possible selling price are presented in the following schedules:

(i) *EM division*

Output level (units)	Total revenues (£)	Variable costs (£)	Total contribution (£)
1000	16 000	6 000	10 000
2000	32 000	12 000	20 000
3000	48 000	18 000	30 000
4000	64 000	24 000	40 000
6000	96 000	36 000	60 000
8000	128 000	48 000	**80 000**

(ii) *IP division*

Output level (units)	Total revenues (£)	Variable costs (£)	Total cost of transfers (£)	Total contribution (£)
1000	50 000	4 000	16 000	30 000
2000	80 000	8 000	32 000	40 000
3000	105 000	12 000	48 000	**45 000**
4000	120 000	16 000	64 000	40 000
6000	150 000	24 000	96 000	30 000
8000	160 000	32 000	128 000	nil

(iii) *Enormous Engineering plc*

Output level (units)	Total revenues (£)	Variable costs (EMD) (£)	Variable costs (IPD) (£)	Total contribution (£)
1000	50 000	6 000	4 000	40 000
2000	80 000	12 000	8 000	60 000
3000	105 000	18 000	12 000	75 000
4000	120 000	24 000	16 000	80 000
6000	150 000	36 000	24 000	**90 000**
8000	160 000	48 000	32 000	80 000

The above schedules indicate that EM division maximizes profits at an output of 8000 units, whereas IP division maximizes profits at an output level of 3000 units. Profits are maximized for the company as a whole at an output level of 6000 units.

(b) (i) Based on the tabulation in (a), IPD should select a selling price of £35 per unit. This selling price produces a maximum divisional contribution of £45 000.

(ii) The company as a whole should select a selling price of £25 per unit. This selling price produces a maximum company contribution of £90 000.

(iii) If IPD selected a selling price of £25 per unit instead of £35 per unit, its overall marginal revenue would increase by £45 000 but its marginal cost would increase by £60 000. Consequently it is not in IPD's interest to lower the price from £35 to £25 when the transfer price of the intermediate product is set at £16.

(c) (i) Presumably profit centres have been established so as to provide a profit incentive for each division and to enable divisional managers to exercise a high degree of divisional autonomy. The maintenance of divisional autonomy and the profitability incentive can lead to sub-optimal decisions. The costs of sub-optimization may be acceptable to a certain extent in order to preserve the motivational advantages which arise with divisional autonomy.

Within the EE group, EMD has decision-making autonomy with respect to the setting of transfer prices. EMD sets transfer prices on a full cost-plus basis in order to earn a target profit. The resulting transfer price causes IPD to restrict output to 3000 units, which is less than the group optimum. The cost of this sub-optimal decision is £15 000 (£90 000 – £75 000). A solution to the problem is to set the transfer price at the variable cost per unit of the supplying division. This transfer price will result in IPD selecting the optimum output level, but will destroy the profit incentive for the EM division. Note that fixed costs will not be covered and there is no external market for the intermediate product.

Possible solutions to achieving the motivational and optimality objectives include:

1. operating a dual transfer pricing system;
2. lump sum payments.

See 'Proposals for resolving transfer pricing conflicts' in Chapter 21 for an explanation of the above items.

(ii) Where there is no market for the intermediate product and the supplying division has no capacity constraints, the correct transfer price is the marginal cost of the supplying division for that output at which marginal cost equals the receiving division's net marginal revenue from converting the intermediate product. When unit variable cost is constant and fixed costs remain unchanged, this rule will result in a transfer price which is equal to the supplying division's unit variable cost. Therefore the transfer price will be set at £6 per unit when the variable cost transfer pricing rule is applied. IPD will then be faced with the following marginal cost and net marginal revenue schedule:

Output level (units)	**Marginal cost of transfers (£)**	**Net marginal revenue of IPD (£)**
1000		
2000	6 000	26 000
3000	6 000	21 000
4000	6 000	11 000
6000	12 000	22 000
8000	12 000	2 000

IPD will select an output level of 6000 units and will not go beyond this because NMR < marginal cost. This is the optimal output for the group, but the profits from the sale of the motor unit will accrue entirely to the IP division, and the EM division will make a loss equal to the fixed costs.

21.19 (a) The variable costs per unit of output for sales *outside* the company are £11 for the intermediate product and £49 [£10(A) + £39(B)] for the final product. Note that selling and packing expenses are not incurred by the supplying division for the transfer of the intermediate product. It is assumed that the company has sufficient capacity to meet demand at the various selling prices.

Optimal output of intermediate product for sale on external market

Selling price (£)	20	30	40
Unit contribution (£)	9	19	29
Demand (units)	15 000	10 000	5 000
Total contribution (£)	135 000	190 000	145 000

Optimal output is 10 000 units at a selling price of £30.

Optimal output for final product

Selling price (£)	80	90	100
Unit contribution (£)	31	41	51
Demand (units)	7 200	5 000	2 800
Total contribution (£)	223 200	205 000	142 800

Optimal output is 7200 units at a selling price of £80.

Optimal output of Division B based on a transfer price of £29

Division B will regard the transfer price as a variable cost. Therefore total variable cost per unit will be £68 (£29 + £39), and Division B will calculate the following contributions:

Selling price (£)	80	90	100
Unit contribution (£)	12	22	32
Demand (units)	7 200	5 000	2 800
Total contribution (£)	86 400	110 000	89 600

The manager of Division B will choose an output level of 5000 units at a selling price of £90. This is sub-optimal for the company as a whole. Profits for the *company as a whole* from the sale of the final product are reduced from £223 200 (7200 units) to £205 000 (5000 units). The £205 000 profits would be allocated as follows:

Division A £95 000 [5000 units at (£29 – £10)]
Division B £110 000

(b) At a transfer price of £12, the variable cost per unit produced in Division B will be £51 (£12 + £39). Division B will calculate the following contributions:

Selling price (£)	80	90	100
Unit contribution (£)	29	39	49
Demand (units)	7 200	5 000	2 800
Total contribution (£)	208 800	195 000	137 200

The manager of Division B will choose an output level of 7200 units and a selling price of £80. This is the optimum output level for the company as a whole. Division A would obtain a contribution of £14 400 [7200 × (£12 – £10)] from internal transfers of the intermediate product, whereas Division B would obtain a contribution of £208 800 from converting the intermediate product and selling as a final product. Total contribution for the company as a whole would be £223 200. Note that Division A would also earn a contribution of £190 000 from the sale of the intermediate product to the external market.

21.20 (a) *Preliminary comments*

The answer to this question requires that we compare the relevant costs for each of the three alternatives. Relevant costs will include incremental costs plus any lost contribution where a division has no spare capacity. Only RR is working at full capacity. Therefore the relevant costs are as follows:

Work undertaken by RP, RS and RT: Relevant cost equals incremental cost for the group as a whole.
Work undertaken by RR: Relevant cost equals incremental cost plus lost contribution from the displaced work. (This is equivalent to the lost sales revenue.)

Relevant cost of company A quote	£33 000
	(£)
Relevant cost of company B quote	
Cost of quote	35 000
Less benefits to group of subcontract work[a]	2 420
Relevant cost	32 580

Note

[a]It is assumed that the £13 000 RS charge to Company B includes 25% on the cost of its own work but no additional margin is added to the £7500 market price for the parts purchased from RR. Therefore the price of £13 000 by RS to Company B is assumed to include

£7500 in respect of RR work plus the balance of £5500 for RS work. The total cost of RS work is £4400 (the question indicates that RS expects to earn a profit of 25% on its *own* work). Therefore the group contribution from subcontract work is as follows:

	(£)	(£)
Selling price of special unit		13 000
Less incremental cost to group of RR's own work (70% x £4400)	3080	
Relevant cost of RR's work (market price)	7500	10 580
Contribution to group		2 420

Relevant cost of RS quote

The following diagram illustrates the inter-group transfers:

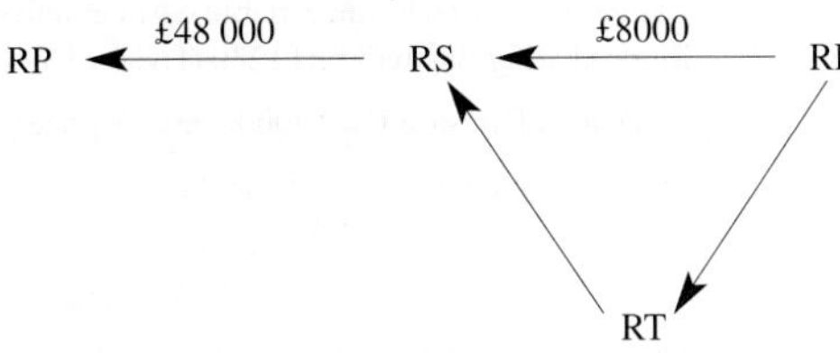

From the above information, it is necessary to ascertain the relevant cost of the *group* from producing the electronic control system. The relevant cost of RR work is the market price of £19 000 (£11 000 + £8000). The relevant cost of RS and RT work is the variable cost (excluding the cost of transfers within the group). The calculations are as follows:

	(£)
RS conversion cost:	
RS total cost	42 000
Less costs transferred from other members of the group (£30 000 + £8000)	38 000
Cost of RS conversion work	4 000
Variable cost of RS conversion work (70% of £4000)	2 800

	(£)
RT conversion cost:	
Price charged by RT to RS	30 000
Less profit margin (20% on total cost)	5 000
Total cost of RS work (including transfer from RR)	25 000
Less transfer price of parts purchased from RR	11 000
Total cost of work added by RT	14 000
Variable cost of work added by RT (65% x £14 000)	9 100

Therefore the relevant cost to the group is as follows:

	(£)
Work undertaken by RR	19 000
Variable costs of conversion work by RT	9 100
Variable costs of conversion work by RS	2 800
Relevant cost	30 900

The order should be awarded to RS because this is the lowest relevant cost alternative.

(b) The following assumptions have been made in part (a):

(i) Incremental costs are represented by variable costs, and no additional fixed costs will be incurred for each alternative.

(ii) Variable costs are linear with respect to output changes.

(iii) RS and RT have sufficient spare capacity to accept the work. Hence no orders will be turned away and opportunity costs are assumed to be zero.

(iv) RP is not free to select its own source of supply. If RP has complete independence then it is likely to accept the quote that will minimize its costs (i.e. the Company A quote).

21.21 (a) The answer to this question can be found in the section headed 'A perfect market for the intermediate product with different buying and selling prices' in Appendix 20.1 to Chapter 20.

(b) *Schedule 1: Calculation of marginal cost, marginal revenue and net marginal revenue*

Output of Alpha (units)	Alpha marginal cost (£000)	Alpha marginal revenues[a,b] (£000)	Beta net marginal revenue[a] (£000)
0–10	<28 [c]	65 (1)	57(3) [d]
10–20	<28 [c]	60 (2)	55 (4/5) [d]
20–30	<28 [c]	55 (4/5)	53 (6) [d]
30–40	<28 [c]	50 (8)	51(7) [d]
40–50	<28 [c]	45 (11/12)	49 (9) [d]
50–60	<28 [c]	40	47 (10)
60–70	28	35	45 (11/12)
70–80	30	30	43 (13)
80–90	33	25	40
90–100	35	20	36
100–110	37	15	33
110–120	40	10	30
120–130	44	5	25

Notes

[a]The numbers in parentheses represent the descending order of ranking of marginal revenue/net marginal revenue for Alpha and Beta.

[b]The question indicates that the marginal revenue function for Alpha decreases in increments of £5000 for each 10 units increase in sales value of Alpha for output levels from 60 to 130 units. This implies that the total revenue and marginal revenue function of Alpha can be computed from this information on the basis of a £5000 decline in marginal revenue for each 10 units of output.

[c]The marginal cost per 10 units of Alpha increases as output expands. This implies that the marginal cost per 10 units of Alpha is less than £28 000 for output of less than 60 units.

[d]The NMR of Beta declines as output rises, thus suggesting an imperfect final product market. The implication of this is that NMR is in excess of £47 000 for increments of 10 units sales of Beta at less than 50 units. The NMR for the first 50 units sales of Beta has been estimated based on the information given in the question. We shall see that the accuracy of the estimates for output levels below 60 units is not critical for calculating the optimum transfer price and activity level.

The output of Alpha is allocated between the sale of the intermediate product on the external market and the transfer of the intermediate product for sale as a final product on the basis of the ranking indicated in Schedule 1. The allocation is presented in the following schedule:

Schedule 2: Allocation of output of Alpha

(1) Output of Alpha (units)	(2) Alpha marginal cost (£000)	(3) Allocation per ranking in Schedule 1[a]	(4) Marginal revenue or NMR[b]
0–10	<28	Alpha	65
10–20	<28	Alpha	60
20–30	<28	Beta	57
30–40	<28	Beta	55
40–50	<28	Alpha	55
50–60	<28	Beta	53
60–70	28	Beta	51
70–80	30	Alpha	50
80–90	33	Beta	49
90–100	35	Beta	47
100–110	37	Beta	45
110–120	40	Alpha	45
120–130	44	no allocation (MR/NMR < MC)	43

Notes

[a]Alpha refers to sale of Alpha as an intermediate product. Beta refers to the transfer of Alpha internally for conversion to Beta and sale in the final product market.

[b]Appropriate MR/NMR per ranking in Schedule 1.

Conclusions

The optimal output level is 120 units. Below this output level MR > MC, but beyond 120 units MC > MR. To induce the output of 120 units, the transfer price should be set at £44 so as to prevent the receiving division from requesting a further 10 units, which will yield an NMR of £43. Examination of Schedule 2 indicates that 70 units should be transferred internally for sale as a final product and 50 units of the intermediate product sold externally. A transfer price of £44 will result in both divisions arriving at this production plan independently. Therefore, the optimal transfer price is the marginal cost of the supplying division for that output at which marginal cost equals the sum of the receiving division's net marginal revenue from using the intermediate product and the marginal revenue from the sale of the intermediate product – in other words, where column 2 equals column 4 in Schedule 2.

21.22 (a) The starting point to answering this question is to ascertain whether the capacity of the supplying division is sufficient to meet the demand from both the external market and the receiving division. To increase demand by one unit of Aye the selling price must be reduced by £0.04 (£1/25 units). Thus the maximum selling price for an output of x units is:

SP = £1000 – £0.04x

Total revenue for an output of x units = £1000x – £0.0x^2

Marginal revenue = dTR/dx = £1000 – £0.08x

Marginal cost = variable cost = £280

At the optimum output level where MR = MC:

£1000 – 0.08x = £280

x = 9000 units

The highest selling price at which the optimum output can be sold is: SP = £1000 – £0.04 (9000) = £640. This leaves 21 000 units spare capacity for Division A. Therefore Division A can meet the maximum output for Bee of 18 000 units without restricting sales and a forgone contribution from Aye. The maximum selling price for Bee for output of x units is:

SP = £4000 – £0.10x

Total revenue for an output of x units = £4000x – £0.10x^2

Marginal revenue = dTR/dx = £4000 – £0.20x

Marginal costs = £280 + £590 = £870

At the optimum output level where MR = MC:

£4000 – £0.20x = £870

x = 15 650 units

The highest selling price at which the optimum output can be sold is: SP = £4000 – 0.10 (15 650) = £2435. The contributions at the optimal selling prices are:

Division A	= £ 3 240 000 [9000 × (£640 – £280)]
Division B	= <u>£24 492 250</u> [15 650 × (£2435 – £870)]
Group	= <u>£27 732 250</u>

(b) If Division A sets the transfer price at the optimum selling price of £640 the variable cost per unit of output for producing Bee will be £1230 (£640 + £590).

MR of Division B = £4000 – £0.20x (See part (a))

The optimum output level is where:

£4000 – £0.20x = £1230

x = 13 850 units

The optimum selling price is: £4000 – £0.10 (13 850) = £2615

(c) The revised contributions if the transfer price is set at £640 will be as follows:

	(£)
Division A: External sales [9000 × (£640 – £280)]	3 240 000
Internal transfers [13 850 × (£640 – £280)]	4 986 000
Division B: External sales [13 850 × (£2615 – £1230)]	<u>19 182 250</u>
Total contribution	<u>27 408 250</u>

Setting the transfer price at the market price results in an increase in total contribution of Division A and a decline in the total contribution of Division B. The contribution for the group as a whole declines by £324 000.

As a result of the increase in the transfer price Division B's marginal cost increases and it will therefore restrict output and set a higher selling price. Where the market for the intermediate product is imperfect, the optimal transfer price is the marginal cost of producing the intermediate product at the optimum output level for the group as a whole. Since marginal cost per unit is constant and equal to variable cost, the optimum transfer price is variable cost. If the transfer price is set at variable cost the receiving division will have a cost function identical to that specified in (a) and will set the selling price at the optimum output for the group as a whole.

21.23 (a) See 'International transfer pricing' in Chapter 21 for the answer to this question. Besides the ethical issues and legal considerations other criticisms relate to the distortions in the divisional profit reporting system. Also divisional autonomy will be undermined if the transfer prices are imposed on the divisional managers.

(b) The ethical limitations relate to multinational companies using the transfer pricing system to reduce the amount paid in custom duties, taxation and the manipulation of dividends remitted. Furthermore, using the transfer prices for these purposes is likely to be illegal, although there is still likely to be some scope for manipulation that is within the law. It is important that multinational companies are seen to be acting in a socially responsible manner. Any bad publicity relating to using the transfer pricing system purely to avoid taxes and custom duties will be very harmful to the image of the organization. Nevertheless tax management and the ability to minimize corporate taxes is an important task for management if it is to maximize shareholder value. Thus it is important that management distinguish between tax avoidance and tax evasion. Adopting illegal practices is not acceptable and management must ensure that their transfer pricing policies do not contravene the regulations and laws of the host counties in which they operate.

Chapter 22

22.16 (a) (i)

	Units
Components worked on in the process	6120
Less: planned defective units	612
replacements to customers (2% × 5400)	108
Components invoiced to customers	5400

Therefore actual results agree with planned results.

(ii) Planned component cost = (3 × £18 for material A) + (2 × £9 for material B) + £15 variable cost = £87
Comparing with the data in the appendix:
Materials = £440 640/6120 = £72
Variable overhead = £91 800/6120 = £15
This indicates that prices were at the planned levels.

(b) Internal failure costs = £53 244 (612 units × £87)
External failure costs = £9396 (108 units × £87)

(c) (i)

	Period 2 (units)	Period 3 (units)
Components invoiced to customers	5500	5450
Planned replacement (2%)	110	109
Unplanned replacements	60 (170 – 110)	–69 (40 – 109)
Components delivered to customers	5670	5490
Planned process defects (10% of worked on in the process)	620	578
Unplanned defects (difference to agree with final row)	–90	–288
Components worked on in the process	6200	5780

(ii)

	Period 2 (£)	Period 3 (£)
Internal failure costs	46 110 (620 – 90) × £87	25 230 (578 – 288) × £87
External failure costs	14 790 (110 + 60) × £87	3 480 (109 – 69) × £87
Appraisal costs	10 000	15 000
Prevention costs	5 000	8 000

(iii) The following points should be included in the report:

1. Insufficient detail is provided in the statistics shown in the appendix thus resulting in the need to for an improvement in reporting .
2. The information presented in (c) (i) indicates that free replacements to customers were 60 greater than planned in period 2 but approximately 70 less than planned in period 3. In contrast, the in process defects were 90 less than planned (approximately 15%) in period 2 and 288 less than plan (approximately 50%) in period 3.
3. Internal failures costs show a downward trend from periods 1–3 with a substantial decline in period 3. External failure costs increased in period 2 but declined significantly in period 3.
4. The cost savings arising in periods 2 and 3 are as follows:

	Period 2 (£)	Period 3 (£)
Increase/decrease from previous period:		
Internal failure costs	–7134 (£53 244 – £46 110)	–20 880 (£46 110 – £25 230)
External failure costs	+5394 (£9396 – £14 790)	–11 310 (£14 790 – £3480)
Total decrease	–1740	–32 190

The above savings should be compared against the investment of £10 000 appraisal costs and £5000 prevention costs for period 2 and £15 000 and £8000 respectively in period 3. It can be seen that the costs exceed the savings in period 2 but the savings exceeded the costs in period 3. There has also been an increase in the external failure costs from period 1 to period 2. Investigations should be made relating to the likely time lag from incurring prevention/appraisal costs and their subsequent benefits.

5. The impact on customer goodwill from the reduction in replacements should also be examined.

22.17 (a) The annual cost savings are as follows:

	£000
Direct labour 0.2 (£1120 + £1292 + £1980) × 75 000	+65 880
Variable set-ups (30% × £13 000) × 3500	–13 650
Variable materials handling (30% × 4000 × 14 600)	–17 520
Variable inspection (30% × £18 000 × 3500)	–18 900
Variable machining (15% × £40 × 4 560 000)	–27 360
Variable distribution and warehousing (£3000 × 14 600)	–43 800
Fixed costs [30% (£42 660 + £52 890 + £59 880) + (15% × £144 540) + £42 900]	–111 210
Total savings	166 560

(b) The total variable overhead costs allocated to each product is as follows:

	C1 (£000)	C2 (£000)	C3 (£000)
Set-up costs at £9100 per production run	9 100	9 100	13 650
Materials handling at £2800 per order	11 200	14 000	15 680
Inspection at £12 600 per production run	12 600	12 600	18 900
Machining at £34 per machine hour	36 720	61 200	57 120
	69 620	96 900	105 350
Total output (000's)	75	75	75
Variable overhead per car (£)	928.26	1 292.00	1 404.67
Direct materials	2 520.00	2 924.00	3 960.00
Direct labour	1 344.00	1 550.40	2 376.00
Total variable cost per car	4 792.26	5 766.40	7 740.67

The above variable costs per car are now used to derive the following contributions for various price/demand levels:

Selling price (£)	Demand	Unit contribution (£)	Total contribution (£000)
C1 Car			
5000	75 000	207.74	15 581
5750	65 000	957.74	62 253
6000	50 000	1207.74	60 387
6500	35 000	1707.74	59 771
C2 Car			
5750	75 000	–16.40	–1 230
6250	60 000	483.60	29 016
6500	45 000	733.60	33 012
7500	35 000	1733.60	60 676
C3 Car			
6500	75 000	–1240.67	–93 050
6750	60 000	–990.67	–59 440
7750	45 000	9.33	420
8000	30 000	259.33	7 780

The profit maximizing price and output levels are £5750 and 65 000 demand for C1, £7500 and 35 000 for C2 and £8000 and 30 000 for C3.

(c)

	C1 (£000)	C2 (£000)	C3 (£000)
Total contribution	62 253	60 676	7 780
Avoidable fixed costs	9 266	11 583	18 533
Contribution to general fixed costs and profit	52 987	49 093	−10 753

The above analysis suggests (ignoring any qualitative factors) that C3 should be discontinued and that C1 and C2 are produced.

(d) The report should include the following points:

1 The need for smooth and uniform production rates and the need to avoid fluctuations in production rates since this will lead to excess work in progress.
2 A description of the pull/ kanban system.
3 The need to ensure a cell production layout and that workers have multiple skills.
4 Focus on eliminating non-value added activities.
5 Focus on routine and preventative maintenance to avoid machine downtime.
6 Focus on reducing set-up times to a minimum.
7 Establishment of JIT purchasing arrangements accompanied by establishing close relationships with suppliers.

22.18 (a) (i) *Performance report for period ending 30 November (Traditional analysis)*

Expenses

	Budget (£)	Actual (£)	Variance (£)
Salaries	600 000	667 800	67 800A
Supplies	60 000	53 000	7 000F
Travel cost	120 000	127 200	7 200A
Technology cost	100 000	74 200	25 800F
Occupancy cost	120 000	137 800	17 800A
Total	1 000 000	1 060 000	60 000A

Performance report for period ending 30 November (Activity-based analysis)

Activities

	(£)	(£)	(£)
Routing/scheduling – new products	200 000	169 600	30 400F
Routing/scheduling – existing products	400 000	360 400	39 600F
Remedial re-routing/scheduling	50 000	127 200	77 200A
Special studies – specific orders	100 000	84 800	15 200F
Training	100 000	159 000	59 000A
Management and administration	150 000	159 000	9 000A
Total	1 000 000	1 060 000	60 000A

(ii) See 'Activity-based budgeting' in Chapter 15 for the answer to this question. In particular, the answer should stress:

(i) The enhanced visibility of activity-based budgeting (ABB) by focusing on outcomes (activities) rather than a listing by expense categories.
(ii) The cost of activities are highlighted thus identifying high cost non-value added activities that need to be investigated.
(iii) ABB identifies resource requirements to meet the demand for activities whereas traditional budgeting adopts an incremental approach.
(iv) Excess resources are identified that can be eliminated or redeployed.
(v) ABB enables more realistic budgets to be set.
(vi) ABB avoids arbitrary cuts in specific budget areas in order to meet overall financial targets.
(vii) It is claimed that ABB leads to increased management commitment to the budget process because it enables management to focus on the objectives of each activity and compare the outcomes with the costs that are allocated to the activity.

(iii) The ABB statement shows a comparison of actual with budget by activities. All of the primary value-adding activities (i.e. the first, second and fourth activities in the budget statement) have favourable variances. Remedial rerouting is a non-value added activity and has the highest adverse variance. Given the high cost, top priority should be given to investigating the activity with a view to eliminating it, or to substantially reducing the cost by adopting alternative working practices. Training and management and administration are secondary activities which support the primary activities. Actual training expenditure exceeds budget by 50% and the reason for the over-spending should be investigated.

For each activity it would be helpful if the costs were analysed by expense items (such as salaries, supplies, etc.) to pinpoint the cost build up of the activities and to provide clues indicating why an overspending on some activities has occurred.

Cost driver usage details should also be presented in a manner similar to that illustrated in Exhibit 15.1 in Chapter 15. Many organizations that have adopted ABC have found it useful to report budgeted and actual cost driver rates. The trend in cost driver rates is monitored and compared with similar activities undertaken within other divisions where a divisionalized structure applies. As indicated in Chapter 15, care must be taken when interpreting cost driver rates.

For additional points to be included in the answer see 'Activity-based management' in Chapter 22.

(b) The cost driver rates are as follows:

Product design = £250 per design hour (£2m/8000 hours)
Purchasing = £50 per purchase order (£200 000/4000 orders)
Production (excluding depreciation) = £100 per machine hour ((£1 500 000 – £300 000)/12 000 hours)
Packing = £20 per cubic metre (£400 000/20 000)
Distribution = £5 per kg (£600 000/120 000)

The activity-based overhead cost per unit is as follows:

		(£)
Product design	(400 design hours at £250 per hour = £100 000 divided by life-cycle output of 5000 units)	20.00
Purchasing	(5 purchase orders at 50 units per order costing a total of £250 for an output of 250 units)	1.00
Production	(0.75 machine hours at £100 per machine hour)	75.00
Depreciation	(Asset cost over life cycle of 4 years = 16 quarters' depreciation at £8000 per quarter divided by life-cycle output of 5000 units)	25.60
Packing	(0.4 cubic metres at £20)	8.00
Distribution	(3 kg at £5)	15.00
Total cost		144.60

22.19 See 'Cost of quality', 'Just-in-time systems' and 'Activity-based management' in Chapter 22 for the answer to this question. You should also refer to 'Activity-based budgeting' in Chapter 15. All of the approaches seek to eliminate waste and therefore when the principles are applied to budget preparation there should be a move away from incremental budgeting to the resources that are required to meet budgeted demand. For an explanation of this point see 'Activity-based budgeting' in Chapter 15. Within the budgeting process a total quality ethos would result in a move towards a zero-defects policy when the budgets are prepared. There would be reduced budget allocations for internal and external failure costs and an increase in the allocation for prevention and appraisal costs. The just-in-time philosophy would result in a substantial budgeted reduction in stocks and establishing physical targets that support JIT systems, such as manufacturing cycle efficiency and set-up times. See 'Operation processes' and 'Cycle time measures' in Chapter 23 for an explanation of some of the performance targets that are appropriate for JIT systems. The activity-based focus should result in the implementation of activity-based budgeting (see Chapter 15).

22.20 Benchmarking is a continuous process that involves comparing business processes and activities in an organization with those in other companies that represent world-class best practices in order to see how processes and activities can be improved. The comparison involves both financial and non-financial indicators.

Two different approaches are adopted in most organizations. Cost-driven bench-marking involves applying the principles of benchmarking from a distance and comparing some aspects of performance with those of competitors, usually using intermediaries such as consultants. The outcome of the exercise is cost reduction. The second approach involves process-driven benchmarking. It is a process involving the philosophy of continuous improvement. The focus is not necessarily on competitors but on a benchmarking partner. The aim is to obtain a better understanding of the processes and questions the reason why things take place, how they take place and how often they take place. The outcome should be superior performance through the strengthening of processes and business behaviour.

Inter-firm comparisons place much greater emphasis on the use of financial data and mostly involve comparisons at the company or strategic business unit level rather than at the business process or activity level. Inter-firm comparisons tend to compare data derived from published financial accounts whereas benchmarking also makes use of both internal and external data.

Benchmarking contributes to cost reduction by highlighting those areas where performance is inferior to competitors and where opportunities for cost reduction exist (e.g. elimination of non-value added activities or more efficient ways of carrying out activities).

Activity-based budgeting (ABB) is an extension of ABC applied to the preparation of budgets. It focuses on the costs of activities necessary to produce and sell products and services by assigning costs to separate activity cost pools. The cause and effect criterion based on cost drivers is used to establish budgets for each cost pool.

ABB involves the following stages:

1. Determining the budgeted cost (i.e. the cost driver rate) of performing each unit of activity for all major activities.
2. Determining the required resources for each individual activity to meet sales and production requirements.
3. Computing the budgeted cost for each activity.

Note that ABB focuses on budgets for the cost of activities rather than functional departments.

Zero-base budgeting tends to be used more as a one-off cost reduction programme. The emphasis is on functional responsibility areas, rather than individual activities, with the aim of justifying all costs from a zero base.

Activity analysis is required prior to implementing ABB. This process can help to identify non-value added activities that may be candidates for elimination or performing the activities in different ways with less resources. Activity performance measures can be established that enable the cost per unit of activity to be monitored and used as a basis for benchmarking. This information should highlight those activities where there is a potential for performing more efficiently by reducing resource consumption and future spending.

See 'Target costing' in Chapter 22 for an explanation of the objectives and workings of target costing.

Continuous cost improvement is a process whereby a firm gradually reduces costs without attempting to achieve a specific target. Target costing is emphasized more at a product's design and development stage whereas continuous cost improvement occurs throughout a product's life. The principles of target costing can also be applied to cost reduction exercises for existing products. Where this approach is applied there is little difference between the two methods. Both approaches clearly focus on reducing costs throughout a product's life cycle but target costing emphasizes cost reduction at the design and development stage. At this stage there is a greater potential for reducing costs throughout the product life cycle.

22.21 (a) The factors influencing the preferred costing system are different for every firm. The benefits from implementing ABC are likely to be influenced by the level of competition, the number of products sold, the diversity of the product range and the proportion of overheads and direct costs in the cost structure. Companies operating in a more competitive environment have a greater need for more accurate cost information, since competitors are more likely to take advantage of any errors arising from the use of distorted cost information generated by a traditional costing system. Where a company markets a small number of products special studies can be undertaken using the decision-relevant approach. Problems do not arise in determining which product or product combinations should be selected for undertaking special studies. Increased product diversity arising from the manufacture and sale of low-volume and high-volume products favours the use of ABC systems. As the level of diversity increases so does the level of distortion reported by traditional costing systems. Finally, organizations with a large proportion of overheads and a low proportion of direct costs are likely to benefit from

ABC, because traditional costing systems can be relied upon only to report accurately direct product costs. Distorted product costs are likely to be reported where a large proportion of overheads are related to product variety rather than volume.

(b) For a more detailed answer to this question you should refer to 'Activity-based management' in Chapter 22. In particular, the answer should draw attention to the fact that ABM attaches costs to activities and identifies the cost drivers that cause the costs. Thus ABM provides a better understanding of what causes costs, and highlights ways of performing activities more efficiently by reducing cost driver transactions.

Costs can therefore be managed more effectively in the long run. Activities can be analysed into value added and non-value added activities and by highlighting the costs of non-value added activities attention is drawn to areas where there is an opportunity for cost reduction, without reducing the products' service potentials to customers.

Finally, the cost of unused activity capacity is reported for each activity, thus drawing attention to where capacity can be reduced or utilized more effectively to expand future profitability.

(c) See 'Target Costing' in Chapter 22 for the answer to this question.

22.22 (a) Total quality management (TQM) is a term that is used to describe a situation where all business functions are involved in a process of continuous quality improvement. The critical success factors for the implementation of TQM are:

(i) The focus should be on customer needs. This should not just represent the final customer. All sections within a company should be seen as a potential customer of a supplying section and a potential supplier of services to other sections.

(ii) Everyone within the organization should be involved in TQM. Senior management should provide the commitment that creates the culture needed to support TQM.

(iii) The focus should be on continuous improvement. Continuous improvement seeks to eliminate non-value activities, produce products and provide services with zero defects and simplify business processes. All employees, rather than just management, should be involved in the process since employees involved in the processes are often the source of the best ideas.

(iv) The aim should be to design quality into the product and the production process. This requires a close working relationship between sales, production, distribution and research.

(v) Senior management should promote the required culture change by promoting a climate for continuous improvement rather than imposing blame for a failure to achieve static targets.

(vi) An effective performance measurement system that measures continuous improvement from the customer's perspective should be introduced. Simple non-financial measures involving real time reporting should be seen as a vital component of the performance measurement system.

(vii) Existing rewards and performance measurements should be reviewed to ensure that they encourage, rather than discourage, quality improvements.

(viii) Appropriate training and education should be given so that everyone is aware of the aims of TQM.

(b) For the answer to this question you should refer to 'Cost of quality' in Chapter 22. In particular the answer should describe the different categories of cost that are included in a Cost of Quality Report and indicate how the report can be used to draw management's attention to the possibility of reducing total quality costs by a wiser allocation of costs between the different categories.

22.23 (a) For the answer to this section you should refer to 'Activity-based management' in Chapter 22. In this section it was pointed out that some organizations have opted for behaviourally oriented overhead allocations that aim to induce desired behavioural responses instead of seeking to accurately assign overheads to cost objects. For example, some Japanese companies have allocated overheads using direct labour as the allocation base even though there was no cause-and-effect relationship between direct labour and overheads. Their aim was, through overhead allocations, to make direct labour expensive and to encourage managers to replace labour with machinery. For a discussion of how the choice of overhead allocation bases can also be used to influence product design decisions you should refer to Chapter 22.

(b) The answer to this question should explain how absorption costing systems can encourage managers to over-produce in order to defer the allocation of fixed overheads to future accounting periods. For an explanation of this point you should refer to 'Variable costing and absorption costing: a comparison of their impact on profit' in Chapter 7. This problem can be reduced by:

1 using residual income whereby managers bear a cost of capital charge on the investment in stocks;
2 implementing a just-in-time production system;
3 reporting stock levels and monitoring their trends over time.

22.24 (a) The answer to this question should point out that production will be organized based on a batch production functional layout (see Chapter 22) and materials scheduled using a material resources planning system (see Chapter 25). There will be a need for a detailed product costing system that tracks work in progress movements throughout the factory and ensures that it can be valued at various stages at frequent intervals. Standard costing is likely to be extensively used to control costs.

(b) The answer to this question should describe a just-in-time production system and just-in-time purchasing (see Chapter 22).

(c) For the answer to this question you should refer to 'JIT and management accounting' (Chapter 22), 'The future role of standard costing' (Chapter 19) and 'Backflush costing' (Chapter 4). In addition, the answer should stress the need to place greater emphasis on non-financial measures (see balanced scorecard internal business perspective in Chapter 23), activity-based cost management and various other approaches to cost management described in Chapter 22.

Chapter 23

23.16 (a)

	Original budget based on 120 000 gross hours	Standard hours based on actual gross hours	Actual hours	Variance (hours)	Variance (£) at £75 per hour
Gross hours	120 000	132 000	132 000		
Contract negotiation	4 800 (4%)	5 280 (4%)	9 240 (7%)	3 960A	297 000A
Remedial advice	2 400 (2%)	2 640 (2%)	7 920 (6%)	5 280A	396 000A
Other non-chargeable	12 000 (10%)	13 200 (10%)	22 440 (17%)	9 240A	693 000A
Chargeable hours	100 800 (84%)	110 880 (84%)	92 400 (70%)	18 480A	1 386 000A

There was a capacity gain over budget of 10 080 (110 880 – 100 800) hours at a client value of £756 000 (10 080 hours at £75) but because all of this was not converted into actual chargeable hours there was a net fall in chargeable hours compared with the original budget of 8400 (100 800 – 92 400) hours at a client value of £630 000.

(b) *Financial performance*

Profit statement and financial ratios for year ending 30 April

	Budget (£000)	Actual (£000)
Revenue from client contracts		
(chargeable hours × £75)	7560	6930
Costs:		
Consultant salaries	1800	1980
Sundry operating costs	3500	4100
	5300	6080
Net profit	2260	850
Capital employed	6500	6500
Financial ratios:		
Net profit: Turnover	29.9%	12.3%
Turnover: Capital employed	1.16 times	1.07 times
Net profit: Capital employed	34.8%	13.1%

The above figures indicate a poor financial performance for the year. The statement in (a) indicates an increase in gross hours from 120 000 to 132 000 hours providing the potential for 110 880 chargeable hours compared with the budget of 100 800 hours. This should have increased fee income by £756 000 (10 080 × £75). However, of the potential 110 880 hours there were only 92 400 chargeable hours resulting in a shortfall of 18 480 hours at a lost fee income of £1 386 000. The difference between these two monetary figures of £630 000 represents the difference between budgeted and actual revenues.

Competitiveness

Competitiveness should be measured in terms of market share and sales growth. Sales are less than budget but the offer of free remedial advice to clients presumably represents the allocation of staff time to improve longer term competitiveness even though this has had an adverse impact on short-term profit.

Competitiveness may also be measured in terms of the relative success/failure in obtaining business from clients. The data shows that the budgeted uptake from clients is 40% for new systems and 75% for existing systems compared with actuals of 35% and 80% respectively. For new systems worked on there is a 16.7% increase compared with the budget whereas for existing systems advice actual is 4% less than budget.

Quality

The data indicate that client complaints were four times the budgeted level and that the number of clients requiring remedial advice was 75 compared with a budgeted level of 48. These items should be investigated.

Flexibility

Flexibility relates to the responsiveness to customer enquiries. For BS Ltd this relates to its ability to cope with changes in volume, delivery speed and the employment of staff who are able to meet changing customer demands. The company has retained 60 consultants in order to increase its flexibility in meeting demand. The data given show a change in the mix of consultancy specialists that may reflect an attempt to respond to changes in the marketing mix. The ratio of new systems to existing systems advice has changed and this may indicate a flexible response to market demands.

Resource utilization

The budget was based on chargeable hours of 84% of gross hours but the actual percentage was 70% (see part (a)). There was an increased level of remedial advice (6% of gross hours compared with 2% in the budget) and this may represent an investment with the aim of stimulating future demand.

Innovation

Innovation relates to the ability of the organization to provide new and better quality services. The company has established an innovative feature by allowing free remedial advice after completion of a contract. In the short term this is adversely affecting financial performance but it may have a beneficial long-term impact. The answer to part (a) indicates that remedial advice exceeded the adjusted budget by 5280 hours. This should be investigated to establish whether or not this was a deliberate policy decision.

Other points

Only budgeted data were given in the question. Ideally, external benchmarks ought to be established and the trend monitored over several periods rather than focusing only on a single period.

23.17 (a) The key areas of performance referred to in the question are listed in Exhibit 23.5 – financial, competitiveness, quality of service, flexibility, resource utilization and innovation.

Financial

- There has been a continuous growth in sales turnover during the period – increasing by 50% in 1999, 10% in 2000 and 35% in 2001.
- Profits have increased at a higher rate than sales turnover – 84% in 1999, 104% in 2000 and 31% in 2001.
- Profit margins (profit/sales) have increased from 14% in 1998 to 31% in 2001.

Competitiveness

Market share (total turnover/total turnover of all restaurants) has increased from 9.2% in 1998 to 17.5% in 2001.The proposals submitted to cater for special events has increased from 2 in 1998 to 38 in 2002. This has also been accompanied by an increase in the percentage of contracts won which has increased over the years (20% in 1998, 29% in 1999, 52% in 2000 and 66% in 2001).

Although all of the above measures suggest good performance in terms of this dimension the average service delay at peak times increased significantly in 2001. This area requires investigating.

Quality of service

The increasing number of regular customers attending weekly suggests that they are satisfied with the quality of service. Other factors pointing to a high level quality of service are the increase in complementary letters from satisfied customers. Conversely the number of letters of complaints and reported cases of food poisoning have not diminished over the years. Therefore the performance measures do not enable a definitive assessment to be made on the level of quality of service.

Innovation/flexibility

Each year the restaurant has attempted to introduce a significant number of new meals. There has also an increase each year in the number of special theme evenings introduced and the turnover from special events has increased significantly over the years. These measures suggest that the restaurant has been fairly successful in terms of this dimension.

Resource utilization

The total meals served have increased each year. Idle time and annual operating hours with no customers have also decreased significantly each year. There has also been an increase in the average number of customers at peak times. The value of food wasted has varied over the years but was at the lowest level in 2001. All of the measures suggest that the restaurant has been particularly successful in terms of this dimension.

(b) *Financial*

Details of the value of business assets are required to measure profitability (e.g. return on investment). This is important because the seating capacity has been increased. This may have resulted in an additional investment in assets and there is a need to ascertain whether an adequate return has been generated. Analysis of expenditure by different categories (e.g. food, drinks, wages, etc.) is required to compare the trend in financial ratios (e.g. expense categories as a percentage of sales) and with other restaurants.

Competitiveness

Comparison with other restaurants should be made in respect of the measures described in (a) such as percentage of seats occupied and average service delay at peak times.

Quality of service

Consider using mystery shoppers (i.e. employment of outsiders) to visit this and competitor restaurants to assess the quality of service relative to competitors and to also identify areas for improvement.

Innovation/flexibility

Information relating to the expertise of the staff and their ability to perform multi-skill activities is required to assess the ability of the restaurant to cope with future demands.

Resource utilization

Data on the number of employees per customer served, percentage of tables occupied at peak and non-peak times would draw attention to areas where there may be a need to improve resource utilization.

23.18 (a) See 'The balanced scorecard' in Chapter 23 for the answer to this question. In particular, the answer should describe the four different perspectives of the balanced scorecard, the assumed cause-and-effect relationships and also provide illustrations of performance measures applicable to CM Ltd.

(b) See 'Benchmarking' in Chapter 22 for the answer to this question. The answer should stress the need to identify important activities or processes that may be common to other organizations (e.g. dispatching, invoicing or ordering activities) and to compare these activities with an organization that is considered to be a world leader in undertaking these activities.

23.19 (a) For an explanation of the generic strategies identified by Porter you should refer to the section on identifying potential strategies in Chapter 15. The value of Porter's work could be criticized on the grounds that it is too general. For example, being the lowest cost producer and selling at the lowest prices in the industry does not guarantee success. There are many other factors besides selling prices and a low cost structure that can have an affect on the success of an organization. Differentiation can take many different forms. Also the tastes of customers and the availability of alternative products are factors that will influence the level of sales. In addition, the pricing policy will influence the extent of competitive advantage.

(b) For an explanation of how the experience curve can affect a firm's cost structure you should refer to 'Cost estimation when the learning effect is present' in Chapter 24. The experience curve can be used as a means of obtaining strategic advantage by forecasting cost reductions and consequently selling price reductions of competitors. Early experience with a new product can provide a means of conferring an unbeatable lead over competitors. Through the experience curve the leading competitor should be able to reduce its selling price for the product which should further increase its volume and market share and eventually force some lagging competitors out of the industry. Exploiting the principles of the experience curve can ensure that a firm has the lowest costs in the industry and therefore adopt a strategy of cost leadership in terms of Porter's generic strategy model.

23.20 See 'Cost of quality' in Chapter 22 and 'Quality measures' in the section relating to the balanced scorecard in Chapter 23 for the answer to this question. The answer could also draw off some of the content relating to performance measurement in service organizations described in Chapter 23 (note in particular the determinants of quality of service in Exhibit 23.5). The answer should also stress the need to monitor quality internally and externally. Internal controls and performance measures should be implemented as described in Chapters 22 and 23 so as to ensure that only products that meet customer quality requirements are despatched. To monitor quality externally customer feedback should be obtained and comparisons made with competitors. With service organizations the quality of the service can be assessed by using methods such as mystery shoppers. You should refer to Chapter 23 for a more detailed description of how quality can be monitored in service organizations.

23.21 (a) (i) Efficiency measures focus on the relationship between outputs and inputs. Optimum efficiency levels are achieved by maximizing the output from a given input or minimizing the resources used in order to achieve a particular output. Measures of effectiveness attempt to measure the extent to which the outputs of an organization achieve the latter's goals. An organization can be efficient but not effective. For example, it can use resources efficiently but fail to achieve its goals.

In organizations with a profit motive, effectiveness can be measured by return on investment. Inputs and outputs can be measured. Outputs represent the quality and amount of service offered. In profit-orientated organizations output can be measured in terms of sales revenues. This provides a useful proxy measure of the quality and amount of services offered. In non-profit-making organizations outputs cannot be easily measured in monetary terms. Consequently, it is difficult to state the objectives in quantitative terms and thus measure the extent to which objectives are being achieved.

If it is not possible to produce a statement of a particular objective in measurable terms, the objectives should be stated with sufficient clarity that there is some way of judging whether or not they have been achieved. However, the focus will tend to be on subjective judgements rather than quantitative measures of effectiveness. Because of the difficulty in measuring outputs, efficiency measures tend to focus entirely on input measures such as the amount of spending on services or the cost per unit of input.

(ii) Similar problems to those of measuring effectiveness and efficiency in nonprofit-making organizations arise in measuring the performance of non-manufacturing activities in profit-orientated organizations. This is because it is extremely difficult to measure the output of non-manufacturing activities. For a discussion of the problems that arise when measuring the performance of non-manufacturing activities see 'Effectiveness tests' and 'Efficiency tests' in Chapter 17.

(b) (i) *Adherence to appointment times*

1. Percentage meeting appointment times.
2. Percentage within 15 minutes of appointment time.
3. Percentage more than 15 minutes late.
4. Average delay in meeting appointments.

Ability to contact and make appointments

It is not possible to obtain data on all those patients who have had difficulty in contacting the clinic to make appointments. However, an indication of the difficulties can be obtained by asking a sample of patients at periodic intervals to indicate on a scale (from no difficulty to considerable difficulty) the difficulty they experienced when making appointments. The number of complaints received and the average time taken to establish telephone contact with the clinic could also provide an indication of the difficulty patients experience when making appointments.

Monitoring programme

1. Comparisons with programmes of other clinics located in different regions.
2. Questionnaires asking respondents to indicate the extent to which they are aware of monitoring facilities currently offered.
3. Responses on level of satisfaction from patients registered on the programme.
4. Percentage of population undertaking the programme.

(ii) Combining the measures into a 'quality of care' measure requires that weights be attached to each selected performance measure. The sum of the performance measures multiplied by the weights would represent an overall performance measure. The problems with this approach are that the weights are set subjectively, and there is a danger that staff will focus on those performance measures with the higher weighting and pay little attention to those with the lower weighting.

Chapter 24

24.16

Low	650 patients	\$17 125
High	1260 patients	18 650
Difference	610 patients	1 525

Variable cost per patient = \$1525/610 = \$2.50
Total fixed cost using 650 patients = Total cost (\$17 125) – variable cost (650 × \$2.50) = \$15 500
Estimated cost for 850 patients = Variable costs (850 × \$2.50) + \$15 500 = \$17 625
Answer = C

24.17 Trend value = 10 000 + (4200 × 33) = 148 600
Seasonal variation index value = 120
Forecasted unit sales = 148 600 × 120% = 178 320
Answer = D

24.18 Total cost for 1525 machine hours = £14 000 + 0.0025(1525^2) = £19 814
Inflation adjusted figure = £19 814 × 1.06 = £21 003
Variance = £4580F (£21 003 – £16 423)
Answer = D

24.19 Machine hours = [100 000 + (30 × 240)] × 1.08 = 115 776
Overhead cost = Overhead cost = £10 000 + (0.25 × 115 776) = £38 944
Answer = C

24.20 Applying the formula $Y_x = aX^b$ described in Chapter 24 where Y^x is the cumulative average time to produce x units, a is the time required to produce the first unit (22 minutes), the exponent b is –0.322 for an 80% learning curve (see text) and X is the number of units of output under consideration the cumulative average times are:

3 units = 22 × $3^{-.322}$ = 22 × .7020 = 15.45 minutes
4 units = 22 × $4^{-.322}$ = 22 × .6399 = 14.08 minutes

Total time to produce 3 units = 46.35 minutes (3 × 15.45)
Total time to produce 4 units = 56.32 minutes (4 × 14.08)
Time required to produce the fourth unit = 9.97 minutes
Answer = B

24.21 The experience curve states that the cost of production will decrease as greater experience is gained with a product or process. Although cost reduction will be a function of the learning curve the experience curve covers a greater number of areas such as product innovation and management skills. The experience curve can be used as a means of obtaining strategic advantage by forecasting cost reductions and consequently the selling price reductions of competitors. Early experience with a new product can provide a means of conferring an unbeatable lead over competitors. Through the experience curve the leading competitor should be able to reduce its selling price for the product which should further increase its volume and market share and eventually force some lagging competitors out of the industry. Exploiting the principles of the experience curve can ensure that a firm has the lowest costs in the industry. It is therefore important that managers are aware of their organization's position on the experience curve at the strategic planning stage.

By exploiting the cost reductions of the experience curve a firm can lower its selling prices and thus extend a product's life cycle by stimulating demand from existing customers and/or enticing new customers by price reductions. Furthermore, a knowledge of an organization's experience curve relative to that of its competitors will allow it to maximize market share and prolong the life cycle of its products or services.

A favourable position on the experience curve via product innovation and management skills will enable a firm to take appropriate steps to ensure that its products are competitive and prolong their profitable lives. In particular, it will enable managers to modify existing products and introduce new products that ensures that the organization is at the forefront of product development. This will help to delay the decline in demand for its products and prolong their life cycles. Also the experience of managers will enable them to react to environmental and technological changes so that the organization remains competitive. It will thus be able to respond effectively to changes in demand for its products and take steps to prolong their life cycles.

24.22 (a) (i) *High- and low-point method*

	Machine hours 000s	Fuel oil expenses (£000's)
High point (June 2000)	48	680
Low point (January 2000)	26	500
Difference	22	180

Variable cost per machine hour £8.182 (£180/22)

Substituting for January 2000

	(£000's)
Variable cost (26 × £8.182) =	212.73
Fixed Cost (difference)	287.27
Total cost	500.00

The total cost equation is $y = 287.27 + 8.182x$

(ii) *Least-squares regression method*

	Hours x	Fuel oil y	x^2	xy
July	34	640	1 156	21 760
August	30	620	900	18 600
September	34	620	1 156	21 080
October	39	590	1 521	23 010
November	42	500	1 764	21 000
December	32	530	1 024	16 960
January	26	500	676	13 000
February	26	500	676	13 000
March	31	530	961	16 430
April	35	550	1 225	19 250
May	43	580	1 849	24 940
June	48	680	2 304	32 640
	$\Sigma x = 420$ $\bar{x} = 35$	$\Sigma x = 6840$ $\bar{y} = 570$	$\Sigma x^2 = 15\,212$	$\Sigma xy = 241\,670$

$$\Sigma y = Na + b x \quad (1)$$
$$\Sigma xy = \Sigma xa + b\Sigma x^2 \quad (2)$$

Substituting from the above table:

$$6840 = 12a + 420b \quad (1)$$
$$241\,670 = 420a + 15\,212b \quad (2)$$

Multiply equation (1) by 35 (= 420/12):

$$239\,400 = 420a + 14\,700 \quad (3)$$

Subtract equation (3) from equation (2):

$$2270 = 512b, \text{ and so } b = 2270/512 = 4.4336$$

Substitute in equation (1), giving

$$6840 = 12a + 420 \times 4.4336, \text{ so } a = \frac{6840 - 1862.112}{12}$$
$$= 414.824$$
$$y = 414.82 + 4.43x$$

(b) For the answer to this question see Chapter 24.

(c) An r^2 calculation of 0.25 means that 75% of the total variation of y from its mean is not caused by variations in x (machine hours). This means that a large proportion of changes in fuel oil expenses do not result from changes in machine hours. The cost must depend on factors other than machine hours. Other measures of activity might be examined in order to test whether they are closely related to changes in costs. If other measures do not yield a close approximation then this might indicate that cost is dependent on several variables. In these circumstances multiple regression techniques should be used.

24.23 (a/b) See 'Cost estimation when the learning effect is present' in Chapter 24 for the answer to this question.

(c) See 'Learning-curve applications' in Chapter 24 for the answer to this question.

(d)

Cumulative production	Hours per unit of cumulative production
1	1000
2	800
4	640
8	512

The average unit costs are as follows:

4 machines	(£)	8 machines	(£)
Labour (640 × £3)	1920	Labour (512 × £3)	1536
Direct materials	1800	Direct materials	1800
Fixed costs (£8000/4)	2000	Fixed costs (£8000/8)	1000
	5720		4336

24.24 (a)

Cumulative production (boats)	Completion time (days)	Cumulative time (days)	Average time (days)
1	10.0	10.0	10.0
2	8.1	18.1	9.05 (18.1/2)
3	7.4	25.5	8.50 (25.5/3)
4	7.1	32.6	8.15 (32.6/4)

As production doubles from one to two boats, average time falls to 90.5% of the time for producing the first boat. As production doubles from two to four boats, average time falls to 90.06% (8.15/9.05) of the previous average. The objective is to calculate the *average* learning rate. You should now refer to Exhibit 24.2 in Chapter 24. You can see that the average time for producing four units is 0.64 of the time for producing the first unit (1280/2000). The average learning rate is $\sqrt{(0.64)}$ = 0.8 or 80%. The average time for producing eight units is 0.512 of the time for producing the first unit (1024/2000). The average learning rate is $^3\sqrt{(0.512)}$ = 0.8. Similarly, the average time for producing 16 units is 0.4095 of the time for producing the first unit (819/2000). The average learning rate is $^4\sqrt{(0.4095)}$ = 0.80. In Exhibit 24.2 the learning rate remained constant at 80% throughout, and it was therefore unnecessary to calculate the average learning rate.

Applying the approach outlined above, the average time for four boats is 0.815 of the time for the first boat, thus indicating an average learning rate of $\sqrt{(0.815)}$ = 0.903 or 90.3%.

An alternative approach is to use the learning curve equation:

$$y_x = ax^b$$

where y_x is defined as the cumulative average time required to produce x units, a is the time required to produce the first unit of output and x is the number of units of output under consideration. The exponent b is defined as the ratio of the logarithm of the learning curve improvement rate to the logarithm of 2. Therefore:

$$y^4 = 10 \times 4^b$$
$$8.15 = 10 \times 4^b$$
$$4^b = 0.815$$

Our objective is to calculate the exponent function that, when multiplied by 4, equals 0.815. A trial-and-error approach is now adopted:

exponent function for 80% learning curve = –0.322 (see Chapter 24)
exponent function for 90% learning curve = –0.152 (log 0.9/log 2)
exponent function for 91% learning curve = –0.136 (log 0.91/log 2)

$$4^{-0.322} = 0.64$$
$$4^{-0.152} = 0.810$$
$$4^{-0.136} = 0.828$$

The average learning rate is between 90% and 91%.

(b) The following points should be discussed:

(i) Only four observations have been used, and this might be insufficient to establish an average learning rate for the production of 15 boats.

(ii) It is assumed that working methods, equipment and staff will remain constant. Improvements in working procedures, staff changes or absenteeism might affect the learning rate.

(iii) Uncertainty as to when the learning process will stop. If the learning process stops before the steady-state phase is reached then the assumption that the learning rate will continue might result in inaccurate estimates.

(iv) The learning rate may not be constant throughout the process, and the use of an average learning rate might result in inaccurate estimates for different output levels.

(c) Materials, other direct expenses and overheads will remain unchanged irrespective of whether the boats are completed in normal time (possibly involving penalties) or working weekends. Overheads appear to be fixed since they are allocated on the basis of *normal* working days. The total times required, assuming a 90% learning rate, are as follows:

Average time for 15 boats = $y_{15} = 10 \times 15^{-0.152}$	= 6.6257 days
Total time for 15 boats = 15×6.6257	= 99.4 days
Total time for 14 boats = $14 \times 10 \times 14^{-0.152}$	= 93.7 days
Total time for 13 boats = $13 \times 10 \times 13^{-0.152}$	= 88.0 days

The contract is for 4 months (therefore 92 working days are available without overtime or 120 days with overtime) and penalties are charged at £10 000 per boat late. Thirteen boats can be delivered within the contract period. To complete 15 boats within the contract period, it will be necessary to work 7.4 days (99.4 days – 92 days) overtime. If overtime is not worked, two boats will incur a penalty. Without overtime, the total labour cost plus penalties will be:

(99.4 days × £2500 = £248 500) + (2 × £10 000) = £268 500

With overtime, the total labour cost will be:

(92 days × £2500 = £230 000) + (7.4 days × 5000) = £267 000

It is assumed that payments can be made for part days only. It is slightly cheaper to work overtime and avoid the penalty cost. Another possibility is to complete 14 boats using overtime and deliver 1 boat late:

Cost for 14 boats = (92 days × £2500) + (1.7 days × £5000)	= £238 500
Cost for 15th boat = (5.7 days × £2500) + (1 × £10 000)	= £ 24 250
	£262 750

The most profitable alternative is to deliver one boat late. Other factors to be considered include:

(i) the four factors outlined in part (b);
(ii) the possibility of bad weather affecting production times;
(iii) the effect on customer goodwill and the possibility of not obtaining future orders if the contract is not completed on time;
(iv) the promise of overtime work might induce the workforce to slow down in order to obtain overtime work.

Chapter 25

25.13 $EOQ = \sqrt{(2DO)/H} = \sqrt{\dfrac{[2\times(50+5)\times4000}{(15\times0\cdot1)+0\cdot2]}}$

$= 509$ units

Answer = D

25.14 (i) Re-order level = Maximum usage × Maximum lead time
= 95 × 18 = 1710

Answer = C

(ii) Maximum stock = Re-order level + Re-order quantity – Minimum usage during minimum lead time
= 1710 + 1750 – (50 × 12)
= 2860

Answer = B

25.15 The purchase cost is not constant per unit. It is therefore not possible to use the EOQ formula. Instead the following schedule of costs should be prepared:

Evaluation of optimum order size

Size of order	No. of orders	Annual purchase cost (WI) (£)	Storage cost (£)	Admin. cost (£)	Total cost (£)
2400	1	1728 (£0.72)	300	5	2033
1200	2	1728 (£0.72)	150	10	1888
600	4	1824 (£0.76)	75	20	1919
200	12	1920 (£0.80)	25	60	2005
100	24	1920 (£0.80)	12.50	120	2052.50

It is recommended that two orders be placed per year for 1200 units.

		(£)
Calculation of cost 2(1200 × £0.80 – 10%)	=	£1728
Add: Storage, average quantity held 600 × £0.25	=	150
Add two orders placed per annum × £5	=	10
		£1888

Workings (W1) Annual demand of 2400 units × unit purchase cost

25.16 (a)

$$EOQ = \sqrt{\left(\frac{2DO}{H}\right)} = \sqrt{\frac{2\times4000\times135}{12}} = 300$$

The relevant cost is

$$\text{holding cost} + \text{ordering cost} = \frac{300\times12}{2} + \frac{4000\times135}{300} = 3600$$

(b)

$$\text{Revised EOQ} = \sqrt{\left(\frac{2\times4000\times80}{12}\right)} = 231$$

The relevant cost is

$$\text{holding cost} + \text{ordering cost} = \frac{231\times12}{2} + \frac{4000\times80}{231} = 2772$$

The relevant cost using the original EOQ of 300 units but with an incremental ordering cost of £80 is

$$\frac{300\times12}{2} + \frac{4000\times80}{300} = 2867$$

Cost of prediction error = £95 (£2867 – £2772)

(c) The annual costs of purchasing, ordering and holding the materials consist of:

Special offer at £86:

holding cost + ordering cost + purchase cost

$$\frac{4000\times12}{2} + 0 = 4000\times86 = £368\,000$$

Normal price of £90:

$$\frac{300\times12}{2} + \frac{4000\times135}{300} + 4000\times90 = £363\,600$$

Additional cost of specific offer £4 400

Therefore the purchase of 4000 units at £86 is not recommended.

(d)

	Budget (£)	Actual (£)	Variance (£)
Material cost	360 000 (4000 × £90)	344 000 (4000 × £86)	16 000F
Ordering cost $\left(\frac{D}{Q}\times O\right)$	1800	0	1 800F
			17 800F

It can be seen that favourable variances would appear on the performance report, and goal congruence would not exist. The performance evaluation system conflicts with the EOQ decision model. This is because the purchasing officer is not charged for the use of capital but the EOQ model includes a charge for the use of capital. Therefore if an imputed capital charge is not included in the performance report, there is a danger that goal congruence will not exist. The revised performance report including a capital charge is shown below:

	Budget (£)	Actual (£)	Variance (£)
Material cost	360 000	344 000	16 000F
Ordering cost	1 800	0	1 800F
Holding cost	1 800	24 000	22 200A
			4 400A

25.17 (a) The question requires the calculation of the optimum number of units to be manufactured in each production run in order to secure the lowest annual cost. In Chapter 25 we noted that the formula for the optimum number of units to be manufactured (Q) is as follows:

$$Q = \sqrt{\left(\frac{2DS}{H}\right)}$$

where D = total demand for period, S = set-up costs, H = holding cost per unit. The set-up costs and holding cost per unit to be used in the formula are relevant or incremental costs. Those costs that will not change as a result of changes in the number of units manufactured in each batch should not be included in the analysis. These costs include:

(i) Skilled labour costs. (Skilled labour is being paid idle time. Its total cost will not alter as a result of the current decision.)

(ii) Fixed overheads. (These costs are independent of the batch size.)

Therefore the relevant cost of producing product Exe is as follows:

			(£)
Raw materials – external suppliers			13
– Dee standard cost:	Raw materials	8	
	Unskilled labour	4	
	Variable overheads	3	15
Unskilled labour			7
Variable overheads			5
Incremental cost of production			40

The relevant decision variables for the formula are as follows:

Annual demand of Exe (D) = 4000 units
Set-up costs (S) = £70 (skilled labour of £66 is not an incremental cost)
Annual holding costs = £14 [cost of storage (£8) plus cost of capital tied up in stocks (£6)]
Storage cost per unit (0.40 m² × £20) = £8
Incremental interest tied up in each unit of Exe stock (15% × £40 incremental cost of Exe) = £6
Applying the above figures to the formula, we have:

$$Q = \sqrt{\left(\frac{2 \times 4000 \times £70}{£14}\right)}$$
$$= 200 \text{ units}$$

	(£)
Cost of current policy	
Set-up costs (4 production runs at £70)	280
Holding costs (average stocks × unit holding cost)	
$\frac{1000}{2} \times £14$	7000
Total cost	7280
Cost of optimum policy	
Set-up costs [(4000/200) production runs at £70]	1400
Holding costs (average stocks × unit holding cost)	
$\frac{200}{2} \times £14$	1400
Total cost	2800
Annual savings (£7280 – £2800)	£4480

(b)
$$Q = \sqrt{\left(\frac{DO}{H}\right)}$$

where D = annual demand, O = incremental ordering cost per order, H = holding cost per unit. For producing Wye:

$$Q = \sqrt{\left(\frac{2 \times 10\,000 \times £100}{£8}\right)} = 500 \text{ units}$$

Buying in larger quantities in order to take advantage of bulk discounts results in the following savings:

(i) a saving in purchase price for the period consisting of the total amount of the discount for the period;

(ii) a reduction in total ordering cost because of fewer orders being placed to take advantage of bulk discounts.

The above cost savings must be compared with the increased holding costs resulting from higher stock levels.

We now compare the cost savings with the increased holding costs from increasing the quantity purchased from the EOQ of 500 units to the lowest purchase quantity at which Wye can be purchased at £19.80 per unit (i.e. 1000 units):

	(£)
Savings in purchase price (10 000 annual purchases at £0.20)	2000
Saving in ordering cost[a]	
$\frac{DO}{Q_d} - \frac{DO}{Q} = \frac{10\,000 \times 100}{1000} - \frac{10\,000 \times 100}{500}$	1000
Total savings	3000

Note
[a] Q_d represents quantity ordered to obtain discount and Q represents EOQ.

The additional holding cost if the larger quantity is purchased is calculated as follows:

$$\frac{(Q_d - Q)H}{2} = \frac{(1000 - 500) \times £8}{2} = £2000$$

Therefore a saving of £1000 is made if the firm purchases in quantities of 1000 units at a price of £19.80 per unit.

We now follow the same procedure in order to determine whether it would be better to purchase in quantities of 2000 units:

	(£)
Savings in purchase price (10 000 annual purchases at £0.40)	4000
Saving in ordering cost	
$\frac{DO}{Q_d} - \frac{DO}{Q} = \frac{10\,000 \times 100}{2000} - \frac{10\,000 \times 100}{500}$	1500
Total savings	5500

The additional holding cost if we purchase in 2000-unit quantities instead of 500-unit quantities is as follows:

$$\frac{(Q_d - Q)H}{[2]} = \frac{(2000 - 500) \times £8}{2} = £6000$$

Therefore an additional £500 will be incurred if the firm purchases in 2000-unit batches compared with purchasing in 500-unit batches.

The above analysis indicates that Pink should purchase in batches of 1000 units at a price of £19.80 per unit.

(c) Limitations include the following:

(i) It is very difficult to obtain relevant data. Incremental holding, ordering and set-up costs are very difficult to estimate in practice. In addition, many of the fixed costs that were excluded in the analysis may not be fixed over the whole range of output. Some fixed costs may increase in steps as the quantity purchased is increased.

(ii) Model assumes certainty. A more sophisticated approach is required where the demand and the cost structure are uncertain.

(iii) Model assumes that demand is constant throughout the year. In practice, there may be seasonal variations in demand throughout the year.

25.18 (a)

Safety stock	Stockout	Stockout cost at £10 (£)	Probability	Expected cost (£)	Total (£)
500	0	0	0	0	0
400	100	1000	0.04	40	40
300	200	2000	0.04	80	
	100	1000	0.07	70	150
200	300	3000	0.04	120	
	200	2000	0.07	140	
	100	1000	0.10	100	360
100	400	4000	0.04	160	
	300	3000	0.07	210	
	200	2000	0.10	200	
	100	1000	0.13	130	700
0	500	5000	0.04	200	
	400	4000	0.07	280	
	300	3000	0.10	300	
	200	2000	0.13	260	
	100	1000	0.16	160	1200

Safety stock	Stockout cost (£)	Holding cost (£)	Total cost (£)
0	1200	0	1200
100	700	100	800
200	360	200	560
300	150	300	450
400	40	400	440
500	0	500	500

The optimal safety stock is 400 units.

(b) The probability of being out of stock at an optimal safety stock of 400 units is 0.04.

25.19 (a)

$$\text{EOQ} = \sqrt{\frac{2DO}{H}} = \sqrt{\frac{2 \times 10\,000 \times 25}{(45+5)}} = 100 \text{ units}$$

(b) Without any discount prices the EOQ =

$$\sqrt{\frac{2 \times 10\,000 \times 25}{(45+5.01)}} = 99.99 \text{ units}$$

Thus it is preferable to purchase 100 units at £50 rather than pay £50.10 for purchasing 99 units. To ascertain whether it is worthwhile increasing the purchase quantity from 100 to 200 units we must compare the total costs at each of these quantities:

	(£)
Total costs with a reorder quantity of 100 units	
Annual holding cost (100/2 × £50)	2 500
Annual ordering costs (10 000/100 × £25)	2 500
	5 000
Purchasing manager's bonus (10% × £5000)	500
Annual purchase cost (10 000 × £50)	500 000
Total annual costs	505 500
Total costs with a reorder quantity of 200 units	
Annual holding costs (200/2 × £49.99)	4 999
Annual ordering costs (10 000/200 × £25)	1 250
	6 249
Purchasing manager's bonus (10% × (£10 000 – £6249))	375
Annual purchase cost (10 000 × £49.90)	499 000
Total annual costs	505 624

The optimal order quantity is still 100 units.

(c) The probability distribution of demand over the three day lead time is as follows:

Demand lead time	Frequency	Probability	Expected value
106	4	0.04	4.24
104	10	0.10	10.40
102	16	0.16	16.32
100	40	0.40	40.00
98	14	0.14	13.72
96	14	0.14	13.44
94	2	0.02	1.88
	100	1.00	100.00

It is assumed that the reorder point will be set at 100 units (expected value). The expected costs for various levels of safety stock are as follows:

Safety stock (units)	Reorder point (units)	Stockout per order (units)	Stockout per year[a] (units)	Probability of stockout	Expected stockout cost[b] (£)	Holding cost[c] (£)	Total expected cost[d] (£)
6	106	0	0	0	0	270	270
4	104	2	200	0.04	80	180	260
2	102	2	200	0.10	200		
		4	400	0.04	160	90	450
0	100	2	200	0.16	320		
		4	400	0.10	400		
		6	600	0.04	240	0	960

Notes

[a]During the year 100 orders will be made (10 000 units annual demand/EOQ of 100 units). Stockout per year in units is calculated by multiplying the stockouts per order by 100 orders;

[b]Expected stockout costs = Annual stockout in units × probability of stockout × £10 lost contribution

[c]Holding cost = Safety stock × (Holding cost of £50 – saving of 10% on purchasing manager's bonus)

[d]It is assumed that stockout costs are equal to the lost contribution on the lost sales.

Conclusion

Costs are minimized if a safety stock of 4 units is maintained.

(d) The following items should be included in the report:

(i) The disadvantages of ordering from only one supplier (e.g. vulnerability of disruption of supplies due to strikes/production difficulties or bankruptcy);

(ii) Failure to seek out cheap or alternative sources of supply;

(iii) It is assumed no large price increases are anticipated that will justify holding additional stocks or that the stocks are not subject to deterioration or obsolescence;

(iv) It is assumed that lead time will remain unchanged. However, investigations should be made as to whether this, or other suppliers, can guarantee a shorter lead time;

(v) The need to ascertain the impact on customer goodwill if a stockout occurs. The answer to (c) assumes that the company will merely lose the contribution on the sales and long-term sales will not be affected if a stockout occurs.

Chapter 26

26.12 (a) Let M = number of units of Masso produced and sold.
Let R = number of units of Russo produced and sold.
The linear programming model is as follows:

Maximize Z = $40M + 50R$ (production contributions)

subject to
$M + 2R \leq 700$ (machining capacity)
$2.5M + 2R \leq 1000$ (assembly capacity)
$M \leq 400$ (maximum output of Masso constraint)
$R \leq 400$ (maximum output of Russo constraint)
$M \geq 0$
$R \geq 0$

The constraints are plotted on the graph as follows:
Machining constraint: line from ($M = 700$, $R = 0$) to ($R = 350$, $M = 0$)
Assembly constraint: line from ($M = 400$, $R = 0$) to ($R = 500$, $M = 0$)
Output of Masso constraint: line from $M = 400$
Output of Russo constraint: line from $R = 400$

At the optimum point (B in the graph) the output mix is as follows:

	(£)
200 units of Masso at a contribution of £40 per unit =	8 000
250 units of Russo at a contribution of £50 per unit =	12 500
Total contribution	20 500
Less fixed costs (£7000 + £10 000)	17 000
Profit	3 500

The optimum output can be determined exactly by solving the simultaneous equations for the constraints that intersect at point B:

$$2.5M + 2R = 1000 \quad (1)$$
$$M + 2R = 700 \quad (2)$$

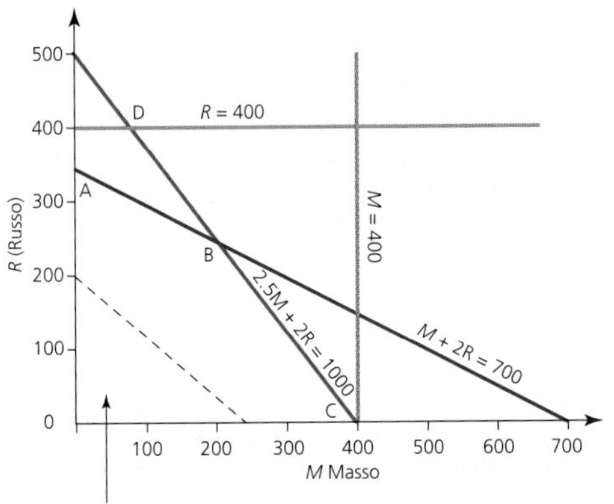

Objective function line Z = 10 000 (arbitrarily chosen contribution figure)
Feasible region = OABC

Subtract equation (2) from equation (1):

$$1.5M = 300$$
$$M = 200$$

Substituting in equation (1):

$$2.5 \times 200 + 2R = 1000$$
$$R = 250$$

(b) *Machining capacity*
If we obtain additional machine hours, the line $M + 2R = 700$ will shift upward. Therefore the revised optimum point will fall on the line BD. If one extra machine hour is obtained, the constraints $M + 2R = 700$ and $2.5M + 2R$ will still be binding and the new optimal plan can be determined by solving the following equations:

$$M + 2R = 701 \text{ (revised machining constraint)}$$
$$2.5M + 2R = 1000 \text{ (unchanged assembly constraint)}$$

The values for M and R when the above equations are solved are $M = 199.33$ and $R = 250.83$.

Therefore Russo is increased by 0.83 units and Masso is reduced by 0.67 units and the change in contribution will be as follows:

		(£)
Increase in contribution from Russo (0.83 × £50)	=	41.50
Decrease in contribution from Masso (0.67 × 40)	=	(26.80)
Increase in contribution		14.70

Hence the value of an independent marginal increase in machine capacity is £14.70 per hour.

Assembly capacity
With an additional hour of assembly capacity, the new optimal plan will be given by the solution of the following equations:

$$M + 2R = 700 \text{ (unchanged machining constraint)}$$
$$2.5M + 2R = 1001 \text{ (revised assembly constraint)}$$

The values for M and R when the above equations are solved are $M = 200.67$ and $R = 249.67$. Therefore Masso is increased by 0.67 units and Russo is decreased by 0.33 units, and the change in contribution will be as follows:

		(£)
Increase in contribution from Masso (0.67 × £40)	=	26.80
Decrease in contribution from Russo (0.33 × £50)		(16.50)
Increase in contribution		10.30

Hence the value of an independent marginal increase in assembly capacity is £10.30 per hour.

(c) The assumptions underlying the above calculations are:
(i) linearity over the whole output range for costs, revenues and quantity of resources used;
(ii) divisibility of products (it is assumed that products can be produced in fractions of units);
(iii) divisibility of resources (supplies of resources may only be available in specified multiples);
(iv) the objectives of the firm (it is assumed that the single objective of a firm is to maximize short-term contribution);
(v) all of the available opportunities for the use of the resources have been included in the linear programming model.

26.13 (a)

	Product 1	Product 2	Product 3	Total
Maximum sales value (£)	57 500	96 000	125 000	
Unit selling price (£)	23	32	25	
Maximum demand (units)	2 500	3 000	5 000	
Hours required on type A machine	2 500 (2500 × 1)	6 000 (3000 × 2)	15 000 (5000 × 3)	23 500
Hours required on type B machine	3 750 (2500 × 1½)	9 000 (3000 × 3)	5 000 (5000 × 1)	17 750

We now compare the machine capacity available with the machine hours required to meet the maximum sales so as to determine whether or not production is a limiting factor.

	Machine type A	Machine type B
Hours required (see above)	23 500	17 750
Hours available	9 800	21 000

Because hours required are in excess of hours available for machine type A, but not for machine type B, it follows that machine type A is the limiting factor. Following the approach illustrated in Example 9.2 in Chapter 9, we calculate the contribution per limiting factor. The calculations are as follows:

	Product 1	Product 2	Product 3
Unit contribution (£)	5	7	8
Contribution per hour of type A machine time (£)	5 (5/1)	3.50 (7/2)	2.67 (8/3)
Ranking	1	2	3

The optimal allocation of type A machine hours based on the above ranking is as follows:

Production	Machine hours used	Balance of machine hours available
2500 units of product 1	2500	7300 (9800–2500)
3000 units of product 2	6000	1300 (7300–6000)
433 units of product 3	1300	—

The 433 units of product 3 are obtained by dividing the 1300 unused machine hours by the 3 machine hours required for each unit of product 3. The proposed production programme results in the following calculation of total profit:

	(£)
2500 units of product 1 at £5 per unit contribution	12 500
3000 units of product 2 at £7 per unit contribution	21 000
433 units of product 3 at £8 per unit contribution	3 464
Total contribution	36 964
Less fixed overheads	21 000
Profit	15 964

(b) There are several ways of formulating the tableau for a linear programming model. The tableau from the computer package can be reproduced as follows:

	Quantity	S1	S4	S5
S2	1 150	–0.5	–0.143	0.429
X2	1 850	0.5	0.143	–0.429
S3	3 800		0.429	–0.286
X3	1 200		–0.429	0.286
X1	2 500	–1	0	0
C	35 050	–1.5	–2.429	–0.714

In Chapter 26 the approach adopted was to formulate the first tableau with positive contribution signs and negative signs for the slack variable equations. The optimal solution occurs when the signs in the contribution row are all negative. The opposite procedure has been applied with the tableau presented in the question. Therefore the signs have been reversed in the above tableau to ensure that it is in the same format as that presented in Chapter 26. Note that an entry of 1 in the tableau presented in the question signifies the product or slack variable that is to be entered in each row of the above tableau.

The total contribution is £35 050, consisting of:

2500 units of product 1 at a contribution of £5 per unit
1850 units of product 2 at a contribution of £7 per unit
1200 units of product 3 at a contribution of £8 per unit

The revised fixed overheads are £18 000, resulting in a total profit of £17 050. This is higher than the profit before the fire (£15 964) because the fixed overheads saved by the fire exceed the lost contribution.

The shadow prices (or opportunity costs) for *S*4 indicate that if an additional type A machine hour can be acquired then profits will increase by £2.429 by increasing production of product 3 by 0.429 units and reducing production of product 2 by 0.143 units. Similarly, if an additional Type B machine hour can be acquired, then profits will increase by £0.714 by increasing production of product 2 by 0.429 units and reducing production of product 3 by 0.286 units. An extra unit of demand for product 1 will yield a contribution of £5, but, in order to obtain the resources, it is necessary to sacrifice half a unit of product 2. This will result in a loss of contribution of £3.50 (½ × £7). Therefore the net gain is £1.50.

The shadow prices indicate the premium over and above the present acquisition costs that the company should be willing to pay in order to obtain extra hours of machine time. The shadow price for product 1 indicates the upper limit to advertising or promotional expenses that should be incurred in order to stimulate demand by one further unit.

(c) In part A there was only one limiting factor. In Chapter 26 we noted that the optimal solution can be derived by using the contribution per key factor approach whenever there is only one production constraint. Where more than one limiting factor exists then it is necessary to use linear programming to determine the optimal production programme.

26.14 (a) Traditional (T) contribution per unit = £55.50 (£100 – (0.5 × £25 + 0.4 × £30 overheads + £20 timber))
Hightech (H) contribution per unit = £49

The linear programming model is as follows:
Maximize 55.5T + 49H (contribution)
Where
0·5T + 0·3H = 3400 (capacity X)
0·4T + 0·45H = 3840 (capacity Y)
4T + 4H = 34 000 (timber available)
subject to $0 \leq T \leq 6000$ and $0 \leq H \leq 10\,000$

(b) (i) The maximum contribution is shown as £444 125 and is derived as follows:
Traditional = 4250 units × £55·50 = £235 875
Hightech = 4250 units × £49·00 = £208 250

(ii) The shadow prices indicate the extra contribution that can be obtained for each extra metre of timber (£9·8125) or additional machine group X hour (£32·50). Machine group Y has a zero shadow price because there is still some available capacity (slack) which has not been utilized (3840 hours available – 3612.5 hours allocated = 227·5 unused hours).

(iii) There is no surplus capacity for machine group X and 227.5 hours surplus capacity for machine group Y giving an additional contribution of £6825 (227·5 hours × £30 = £6825).

(iv) The adjustable cells table show the sensitivity of the plan to changes in the contribution per unit of each product. For the 'Traditional' product the contribution would have to be greater than £81·67 (i.e. an increase of £26·17) or less than £49 (i.e. a decrease of £6·50) for a change in the planned sales mix to occur. For the 'Hightech' product the contribution would have to exceed £55·50 (i.e. an increase of £6·50) or be less than £33·30 (i.e. a decrease of £15·70) for a change in the planned sales mix to occur.

(v) For each additional metre an extra contribution of £9.8125 can be obtained but the parameters of the existing model indicate that this applies only for an extra 1733.33 metres of timber. The additional contribution from an extra 1733.33 metres of timber is £17 008 (1733·33 × £9·8125).

(vi) A total of 35 733.33 metres (34 000 + 1733.33) will be allocated to production. The timber requirements for producing 'Hightech' are 14 400 metres resulting in 21 333.33 metres (35 733.33 – 14 400) being available for 'Traditional'. This will result in the production of 5333.33 units of 'Traditional'.

(c) The following should be considered as a means of overcoming the capacity constraints:

- Investigate alternative sources of supply for the timber. Such supplies may only be obtainable at additional costs (e.g. purchasing from overseas suppliers).
- Increase the operating hours of the machinery. This may result in additional overtime payments to operators or require the appointment of extra staff.
- Increase the output per machine hour. This may result in additional labour payments and an increase in maintenance costs.
- Acquire additional machinery. To ascertain whether this is worthwhile, a capital investment appraisal should be undertaken that incorporates the cash flow consequences over the whole life of the machinery.
- Sub-contract some of the production to outside companies. This is likely to be more expensive than the internal incremental production costs and may also create quality control problems.

(d) Only variable costs are included in the model. Therefore product specific (avoidable) fixed costs are not taken into account. Such costs may be relevant if they are avoidable or involve step functions. Examples include staff dedicated to a single product such as marketing costs attributable to only one of the products.

Customer specific costs may differ between customers. For example distribution costs may vary according to the location of customers or some customers may rely on many small volume frequent orders whereas others may rely on large volume infrequent orders. The costs of servicing the latter category of customers are likely to be less than the former.

Life cycle costs represent the costs incurred over a product's life cycle from the introduction, growth, maturity and decline stages. Costs may vary at the different stages. If one of the products is at the introductory stage it may incur additional marketing costs in order to promote it. Thus costs may differ between the two products if they are subject to different stages within their life cycles.

26.15 (a) Let a = proportion of project A undertaken
b = proportion of project B undertaken
c = proportion of project C undertaken
d = proportion of project D undertaken
e = proportion of project E undertaken
f = proportion of project F undertaken
s_0 = Amount invested in rival company at time 0
s_1 = Amount invested in rival company at time 1

The linear programming model is as follows:

Maximize $0.36a + 0.34b + 0.31c + 0.34d + 0.39e + 0.56f$
Subject to $2a + 0.5b + 2.2c + 4d + 1.4e + s_0 \leqslant 5$ (Time 0 cash constraint)
$3.2b + 0.8c + 3f + s_1 \leqslant 2.5 + 1.15s_0 + 0.8a + 0.5c + 1.1d$ (Time 1 cash constraint)
$3000a + 4000e \leqslant 5000$ (Special component constraint)
$a, b, c, d, e, f \leqslant 1$ (Maximum investment constraint)
$a, b, c, d, e, f, s_0, s_1 \geqslant 0$ (Non-negativity constraint)

Note that the NPV from a cash investment in a rival company can be ignored since the cost of capital is equal to the return on investment. Thus cash investments will yield a zero NPV.

(b) The linear programming process will provide information on:

(i) The project mix that will maximize NPV subject to the constraints.
(ii) Which constraints are limiting and which are not limiting.
(iii) The opportunity costs of scarce funds.

For an explanation of how the information can be used see the appendix to Chapter 26.

INDEX